Nuevo
DICCIONARIO
REVISADO
Appleton-Cuyás
ESPAÑOL-INGLÉS
INGLÉS-ESPAÑOL

The New REVISED
Appleton-Cuyás
SPANISH-ENGLISH
ENGLISH-SPANISH
DICTIONARY

Prentice Hall
New York • London • Toronto
Sydney • Tokyo • Singapore

Second Edition

Prentice Hall General Reference
15 Columbus Circle
New York, NY 10023

A Prentice Hall Book

PRENTICE HALL is a registered trademark
of Prentice-Hall, Inc.
Colophon is a trademark of Prentice-Hall, Inc.

Library of Congress Cataloging-in-Publication Data

Cuyás, Arturo
    The new revised Appleton-Cuyás dictionary.
    ISBN 0-13-615559-6
        1. Spanish language—Dictionaries—English.
2. English language—Dictionaries—Spanish.   I. Title.
PC4640.C8   1982   463'.21   81-15816
                                AACR2

Manufactured in the United States of America

16   17   18   19

CONTENTS

PART I
SPANISH-ENGLISH

PARTE II
INGLÉS-ESPAÑOL

PREFACE

Few prefatory remarks are necessary in presenting *The New Appleton-Cuyás Dictionary*. It is an offspring of *Appleton's Spanish-English English-Spanish Dictionary* by Arturo Cuyás, a work whose reputation is solidly established in both the English- and Spanish-speaking worlds. It is based on the Fourth Edition of that work, as revised and enlarged by Dr. Lewis E. Brett and Miss Helen S. Eaton. The same exacting scientific standards that characterized the work of Don Arturo Cuyás and Dr. Brett and Miss Eaton have been followed in the long, detailed and careful compilation of the present dictionary.

The New Appleton-Cuyás Dictionary is intended for those general students of Spanish or English whose needs do not warrant the acquisition of as exhaustive a dictionary as the large Cuyás. It is also designed for college students, translators, businessmen, travelers, social workers, and others who, although they may already own the parent Cuyás, also require a smaller book that can be carried around for ready consultation on the spot. The main objective in the preparation of this portable dictionary has been to offer, concisely and effectively, as much matter from the parent dictionary as is compatible with the aims and size of the new work. Within its scope, this dictionary answers the basic expressional needs in every capital field of human endeavor and covers all levels of accepted usage in both tongues. We believe that because of efficient condensation of definitions and thrifty use of space, *The New Appleton-Cuyás* offers a greater number of principal and subsidiary terms than any other dictionary of similar size.

In the selection of lexical matter judicious use has been made of all frequency counts and lists of words and idioms available in both languages. Terms and expressions of high oral and written incidence that appear in the parent work have been included in the present dictionary. New, up-to-date words and phrases have been added. The criterion for selection of entries has been the standard, educated use in both languages. For standard usage of Spanish on the American continents, the dictionaries of Santamaría and Malaret were duly consulted, among other sources of reference. In the Spanish vocabulary, the western hemisphere currency of word and idiom has been properly indicated, thus: (Am.) for general continental usage, and (Mex.), (Arg.), etc., for those of only regional validity.

We call the attention of the reader to the following special, useful features, seldom encountered together in portable dictionaries: lists of cardinal, ordinal, and fractional numbers; complete tables of irregular verbs; clear and simple keys to speech sounds; tables of weights and measures; thermometer equivalences; abbreviations in common usage; and lists of proper and geographical names.

We were indeed fortunate to have as direct collaborators in this endeavor Professor Alberto Andino, formerly of the University of Las Villas, Cuba, Dr. Fernando Figueredo, formerly a distinguished member of the Cuban Bar Association, and Mr. Bernard Witlieb, a lexicographer who holds an A.M. degree from New York University; and none the less fortunate in having at all moments the wise and experienced counsel in editorial matters of Miss Catherine B. Avery, of the staff of Appleton-Century-Crofts.

E.G.D.

New York University
New York

ADVICE TO THE USER

1. *Arrangement.* In order to save space and make our dictionary richer in entries, we have grouped together families of words closely related in origin and meaning or in spelling, whenever this arrangement did not interfere with alphabetical order. For further saving of space, the common parts of words of the same family have been omitted. The omitted part is always referred to the head entry of the group. All main entries are in boldface type. Idioms and expressions within entries are italicized and alphabetized by the first word. In definitions, semicolons are used to separate different areas of meaning; commas for synonyms within areas. The user must be aware that the Spanish alphabet is different from its English counterpart: ch, ll, and ñ are independent letters; therefore, all words or syllables beginning with ch, ll, or ñ come after c, l, and n, respectively—thus, **fecha** follows **fecundo, ella** follows **eludir** and **añadido** follows **anzuelo.**

2. *Gender of Nouns.* In the Spanish-English section the gender of Spanish nouns is indicated as follows: *m.* for nouns that are exclusively masculine (ex., **hombre, banco, buey, sofá, amor**), *f.* for nouns that are only feminine (ex., **mujer, casa, fe, libertad, costumbre**), *mf.* for those which have a masculine and a feminine meaning without change in form (ex., **artista, amante, testigo**), and *n.* for those which have a masculine form ending in *o* and a corresponding feminine form ending in *a* (ex., **obrero, abogado**), in which case only the masculine form is entered. Nouns having a gender inflexion different from the above are listed separately for the masculine and feminine (ex., **actor, actriz**).

3. *Diminutives.* Diminutives are entered only when they have special meanings or when they have become nouns in their own right (ex., **ahorita, cucharilla, ventanilla, portezuela**).

4. *Verbs.* All irregular verbs are identified by the abbreviations *vti., vii., vri.,* and *vai.* The numbers and letters in brackets next to the abbreviations refer to the *Table of Irregular Verbs* on page iii.

5. *Adverbs.* All Spanish adverbs of manner are formed by adding *-mente* to the feminine singular form of the corresponding adjective (ex., **rápido: rápida, rápidamente**). Only those Spanish adverbs not conforming to the above or whose meaning does not correspond to their English cognates are entered.

6. *Abbreviations.* All abbreviations used to indicate limitations of range, geographic or otherwise (ex., *Mex.*, Mexico; *aer.*, aeronautics; *med.*, medicine), are fully identified in the list of *Abbreviations used in Part II* on page xxxi.

7. *Pronunciation.* Spanish being a quasi-phonetic language, the transcription of each individual word has been considered unnecessary. A clear, simple explanation of approximate English equivalents of Spanish phonemes is given on page v.

8. *Accentuation.* Words ending in a vowel, *n,* or *s* are stressed in the next to the last syllable (ex., **casa, comen, puertas.**) Words ending in a consonant other than *n* or *s* are stressed in the last syllable (ex., **comprar, atroz, paste!**). Stresses that do not follow these two rules are indicated by a written acute accent (ex., **árbol, acción, rápido.**)

SPANISH PRONUNCIATION

I. VOWELS

Approximate English Equivalents

a About midway between the *a* in father and the *a* in cat.

e About midway between the *a* in hate and the *e* in bet.

i Very like the *i* in machine or the *ee* in teeth.

o Somewhat similar to the *o* in note or the *o* in or.

Approximate English Equivalents

u Very close to the *oo* in moon or the *u* in rule. It is always silent after *q* and also after *g*, unless marked with dieresis (ex., vergüenza).

y It is a vowel when standing alone or at the end of a word, and as such it is pronounced as *i* above.

II. CONSONANTS

b As in English but slightly softer at the beginning of a word or when preceded by *m* or *n*. Between vowels or preceded by a vowel and followed by *l* or *r* it is pronounced without the lips coming into complete contact.

c Before *e* or *i* it has the sound of the *th* of think in the Castilian speech of Spain. In the popular speech of many parts of Spain and in all Spanish America it is pronounced like the English *s* in say. Before *a*, *o* and *u* and at the end of a syllable or a word it is always like the English *k* in key.

ch It is considered a single letter and always pronounced like the *ch* in church.

d Similar to English *d* in dance. Between vowels or at the end of a word it has the sound of the English *th* in mother.

f As English *f*.

g Before *a*, *o* and *u* or preceding a consonant it is like the *g* in go. Before *e* and *i* it sounds like the *ch* in the Scottish word loch.

h Always silent.

j Like *g* above before *e* or *i*.

l As English *l*.

ll Treated like a single letter. Sounds very close to the *lli* in million or in brilliant in the Castilian speech of Spain. In many parts of Spain and in most of Spanish America it is pronounced like the *y* in yet.

m As English *m*.

n As English *n* but before *b* or *v* it is sounded like an *m*.

ñ It sounds very similar to the *ny* in canyon or the *ni* in onion.

p As in English but somewhat softer.

q Occurs only in the combinations que, qui in which the *u* is silent. It has the sound of the English *k* in key.

r At the beginning of a word or preceded by *l*, *n*, or *s* it is strongly rolled. Otherwise it is pronounced with a single touch of the tongue.

rr It is treated as a single letter, and it is strongly trilled.

s Like the English *s* in see.

t Similar to the English *t* but less explosive.

v Same as *b* above.

x Sounds like *ks* or *gs* when placed between vowels. When followed by a consonant it is pronounced as the English *s* in same.

y (See Vowels above.) Preceding a vowel it is similar to the English *y* in year.

z In Castile it is pronounced like the *th* of thick. In many parts of Spain and in all Spanish America it sounds like the English *s* in case.

SYNOPSIS OF SPANISH GRAMMAR

I. GENERAL REMARKS

The Spanish alphabet consists of 28 separate symbols, compared to the 26 letters of the English alphabet. Ch, ll, and ñ are distinct symbols and occupy separate places in the alphabet, following c, l and n respectively. The w of the English alphabet is not a part of the Spanish alphabet. Rr, though considered a separate symbol, does not occupy a separate place in the Spanish alphabet. The double consonants in Spanish are cc and nn. Each letter or symbol has a fixed pronunciation that is, under clearly defined rules, invariable. There is no gliding or blending of sounds, as in English, nor do changes occur in the pronunciations of the same letters when they appear in different words, as is so often the case in English. (See pp. v-xvi SPANISH PRONUNCIATION, for a description of the pronunciation of individual Spanish letters and combinations of letters.) The differences between the Spanish of Spain and that of other Spanish-speaking countries consist in minor variations of pronunciation and in additions to the vocabulary that arise from geographical location and ethnic background.

A written accent over a vowel indicates that the syllable containing the vowel is accented, as: lápiz (*pencil*), biología (*biology*), automóvil (*automobile*), termómetro (*thermometer*), condición (*condition*). When a syllable is added to a word that has no written accent, as in forming certain plurals, a written accent may be added to show retention of the original stress, as: germen, gérmenes; virgen, vírgenes. Words without a written accent and ending in a vowel, -n or -s, have the accent on the next to the last syllable. Accordingly, certain words that add a syllable in the plural or in forming the feminine, drop the written accent, as: condición, condiciones; japonés, japonesa. All other words are accented on the last syllable.

There are three genders in Spanish: masculine, feminine and neuter.

Capital letters are used in Spanish as in English, with the following exceptions:

a) the subject pronouns yo, usted and ustedes are not capitalized except at the beginning of a sentence, or when usted and ustedes are abbreviated, as they usually are. Vd. and Vds. are commonly used abbreviations for usted and ustedes respectively.

b) names of months and days of the week are masculine and are not capitalized;

| El sábado, 17 de julio | Saturday, July 17 |

Only sábado (*Saturday*) and domingo (*Sunday*) of the days of the week have plural forms;

c) adjectives formed from proper nouns are not capitalized, even when used as nouns, as: los españoles (*the Spaniards*);

d) titles spelled out (señor, señora, señorita, don, doña) are not capitalized except when they begin a sentence. When these titles are abbreviated, they are capitalized (Sr., Sra., Srta., D., Da.);

e) book and film titles are not capitalized except for the first word and proper names;

La verdad sospechosa
El capitán veneno

Punctuation in Spanish is much the same as in English, except that the Spanish add an inverted question mark and an inverted exclamation point before a question and an exclamation respectively.

| ¿Qué cosa quiere? | What does he want? |
| ¡Fuego! | Fire! |

II. PARTS OF SPEECH

A. Articles

1. The indefinite articles in Spanish are un, una, unos and unas. They agree in gender and number with the nouns and are generally repeated before each noun.

un libro (masculine)	a book
un ojo (masculine)	an eye
una pluma (feminine)	a pen
una manzana (feminine)	an apple
unos muchachos (masculine)	some boys
unas pinturas (feminine)	some paintings
Tengo un coche, una casa y una televisión	I have a car, house and television

It is not necessary to use the indefinite article in the following cases:

a) when denoting a quantity, as: otro (*another*), medio (*half*), cien, ciento (*a, one hundred*), and mil (*a, one thousand*);

| Hay cien soldados aquí | There are a hundred soldiers here |
| Necesito otro lápiz | I need another pencil |

b) when a predicate noun is unmodified;

| Juan es médico | John is a doctor |

c) when the meaning of *one* is obvious;

| Lleva abrigo | He is wearing a coat |

2. The definite articles in Spanish are el, los, la, las and the neuter form lo. Every Spanish noun has its corresponding article. The article appears in conjunction with the noun in most cases and agrees with it in gender and number.

el libro (masculine)	the book
la pluma (feminine)	the pen
los muchachos (masculine)	the boys
las pinturas (feminine)	the paintings
lo útil (neuter)	the useful
Los libros, los lápices y la pluma están en la mesa	The books, pencils and pen are on the desk
El señor Martínez está enfermo	Mr. Martin is ill
Vende los huevos a veinte centavos la docena	He sells eggs at twenty cents a dozen
Va a la iglesia los domingos	He goes to church on Sundays
El año que viene	Next year
Es la una	It is one o'clock

The definite article is not generally used with **mediodía** (*noon*) and **media-noche** (*midnight*).

Es medianoche   *It is midnight*

The definite article **el** replaces **la** before feminine nouns beginning with stressed **a** or **ha**.

El agua está fría   *The water is cold*

El following the preposition **a** contracts to **al**.

Juan va al taller   *John is going to the shop*

El following the preposition **de** contracts to **del**.

Él lleva el abrigo del padre   *He is wearing his father's coat*

The neuter form **lo** is used with an adjective to form a noun.

Lo importante es estudiar mucho *The important thing is to study a great deal*

The definite article is not used:
a) with **don** and **doña**;

Doña María está aquí   *Madam Mary is here*

b) when speaking directly to a person;

¿Cómo está Vd., señor Martínez? *How are you, Mr. Martin?*

c) when the noun is preceded by a possessive or demonstrative pronoun or adjective;

Este libro es negro   *This book is black*

d) before a numeral in a title.

Carlos Quinto   *Charles the Fifth*

B. Nouns

1. Spanish nouns are masculine or feminine or have one form for both genders; there are no neuter nouns. Nouns ending in -o are usually masculine. Nouns ending in -dad, -ción and -sión are feminine. Nouns ending in -a, -ie, -ud and -umbre are usually feminine. The gender is indicated in the vocabulary of this dictionary.

2. The plural of Spanish nouns is generally formed by adding -s to the singular of those that end in an unaccented vowel, and -es to those that end in an accented vowel or a consonant. Those ending in -z change the -z to -c and add -es. Some nouns (generally those ending in -s in the singular) have the same form for both the singular and the plural.

SINGULAR		PLURAL	
la casa	*house*	las casas	*houses*
la decisión	*decision*	las decisiones	*decisions*
la dificultad	*difficulty*	las dificultades	*difficulties*
el libro	*book*	los libros	*books*
la raíz	*root*	las raíces	*roots*
el lápiz	*pencil*	los lápices	*pencils*
el paraguas	*umbrella*	los paraguas	*umbrellas*

The masculine plural is used to indicate both masculine and feminine when both genders are included collectively.

Mis primos   *My cousins*
Mis hermanos   *My brothers and sisters*

C. Adjectives

1. Adjectives agree in gender and number with the nouns they modify and generally, but not necessarily, follow the noun. Those that end in -o are generally masculine; those that end in -a are generally feminine. An adjective ending in -o changes -o to -a to form the feminine and adds an -s to form the plural.

la casa roja	*the red house*
el libro rojo	*the red book*
las casas rojas	*the red houses*
los libros rojos	*the red books*

Some adjectives have only one ending and are both masculine and feminine.

una situación artificial	*an artificial situation*
un satélite artificial	*an artificial satellite*
un pintor modernista	*a modernistic painter*
las tendencias modernistas	*modernistic tendencies*

Some adjectives lose their masculine singular ending when preceding the noun they modify.

el buen hombre	*the good man*
el primer piso	*the first floor*
un mal paso	*a false step*

2. *Comparison of adjectives.* The comparative and superlative degrees of adjectives in Spanish are formed by placing más (*more*) or menos (*less*), for the comparative degree, and el más (*most*) or el menos (*least*), for the superlative degree, before the positive form of the adjective.

POSITIVE		COMPARATIVE		SUPERLATIVE	
bonito	*pretty*	más bonito	*prettier*	el más bonito	*prettiest*
feliz	*happy*	más feliz	*happier*	el más feliz	*happiest*
listo	*clever*	menos listo	*less clever*	el menos listo	*least clever*

Comparisons employing que (*than*) as a conjunction are expressed by más (or menos) . . . que.

Hablo más despacio que él	*I speak slower than he*
Este libro es menos interesante que ése	*This book is less interesting than that one*

Comparisons employing tan (*as*) are expressed by tan . . . como.

Mi casa es tan grande como la tuya	*My house is as big as yours*

In Spanish there is an absolute superlative which is formed by placing muy (*very*) before the adjective, or by adding the endings -ísimo or -érrimo to the positive degree of the adjective. These endings are not equivalent to the -est of English superlatives. They have an intensive force and are translated by *very* or *extremely* followed by the adjective.

POSITIVE		COMPARATIVE	
hermoso	*beautiful*	más hermoso	*more beautiful*
difícil	*difficult*	más difícil	*more difficult*
célebre	*famous*	más célebre	*more famous*

SUPERLATIVE		ABSOLUTE SUPERLATIVE	
el más hermoso	*most beautiful*	muy hermoso	*very beautiful*
		hermosísimo	*extremely beautiful*
el más difícil	*most difficult*	muy difícil	*very difficult*
		dificilísimo	*extremely difficult*
el más célebre	*most famous*	celebérrimo	*extremely famous*

The comparison of some adjectives is irregular.

POSITIVE		COMPARATIVE		SUPERLATIVE	
bueno	good	mejor	better	el mejor	best
grande	big, great	más grande	bigger, greater	el más grande	biggest, greatest
		mayor	greater, older	el mayor	greatest, oldest
malo	bad	peor	worse	el peor	worst
pequeño	small	más pequeño	smaller	el más pequeño	smallest
		menor	smaller, younger	el menor	smallest, youngest

3. *Possessive adjectives.* Like all adjectives in Spanish, the possessive adjectives agree in number and gender with the nouns they modify. The Spanish possessive adjectives are:

SINGULAR		PLURAL
mi	my	mis
tu	your	tus
su	his, her, your, its	sus
nuestro	our	nuestros
vuestro	your	vuestros
su	their, your	sus

D. Adverbs. As in English, Spanish adverbs modify a verb, an adjective or another adverb. Many adverbs are formed by adding -mente to the feminine singular form of the adjective.

ADJECTIVE		ADVERB	
clara	clear	claramente	clearly
rápida	rapid	rápidamente	rapidly

The comparative and superlative degrees of adverbs are formed in the same manner as the comparative and superlative degrees of adjectives, but the superlative degree of adverbs is seldom used.

POSITIVE		COMPARATIVE		SUPERLATIVE	
claramente	clearly	más claramente	more clearly	el más claramente	most clearly
rápidamente	rapidly	más rápidamente	more rapidly	el más rápidamente	most rapidly

The comparison of some adverbs is irregular.

POSITIVE		COMPARATIVE		SUPERLATIVE	
bien	well	mejor	better	mejor	best
mal	bad	peor	worse	peor	worst
mucho	much	más	more	más	most
poco	little	menos	less	menos	least

E. Pronouns

1. *Personal pronouns.* Personal pronouns serve as subjects, direct objects of a verb, indirect objects of a verb, and possessives. In Spanish, the verb ending indicates the subject. It is therefore unnecessary to use a subject pronoun with the verb, unless clarity or emphasis is desired. *It,* when used as a subject, is never translated. The third person, usted, Vd. and ustedes, Vds. (*you*), is generally used when addressing persons. The second person singular or plural (the *you* of English) is the familiar form in Spanish and is limited in use. The following table lists personal pronouns used as the subject and as the direct object of a verb.

SINGULAR

SUBJECT			DIRECT OBJECT	
1st person	yo	*I*	me	*me*
2nd person	tú	*you*	te	*you*
3rd person	él	*he*	lo	*him*
	ella	*she*	la	*her*
	usted, Vd.	*you*	lo, la	*him, her*
	ello	*it* (seldom used)	lo	*it*

PLURAL

1st person	nosotros	*we*	nos	*us*
2nd person	vosotros	*you*	os	*you*
3rd person	ellos	*they*	los	*them*
	ellas	*they*	las	*them*
	ustedes, Vds.	*you*	los, las	*them*

Direct object pronouns follow, and are attached to, an infinitive, a present participle, or a verb in the affirmative command.

Él quiere traerlo después	*He wants to bring it later*
Estoy buscándola	*I am looking for her*
Hágalo ahora	*Do it now*

In other cases, they are placed before the verb.

Nos llamaron ayer	*They called us yesterday*

Indirect object pronouns are placed in the same order in a sentence as direct object pronouns. The indirect object pronouns are:

	SINGULAR			PLURAL	
1st person	me	*to me*		nos	*to us*
2nd person	te	*to you*		os, vos	*to you*
3rd person	le, se	*to him, her, you*		les	*to them, you*

Se as a 3rd person indirect object pronoun should not be confused with the reflexive se. Since le and se mean *to him, to her* or *to you*, it may be necessary in a sentence to add a clarifying phrase, a él, a ella, or a Vd. Possessive pronouns agree in gender and number with the object possessed. They are as follows:

SINGULAR		PLURAL	
el mío	*mine*	los míos	
la mía	*mine*	las mías	
el tuyo	*yours*	los tuyos	
la tuya	*yours*	las tuyas	
el suyo	*his*	los suyos	
la suya	*hers*	las suyas	
el nuestro	*ours*	los nuestros	
la nuestra	*ours*	las nuestras	
el vuestro	*yours*	los vuestros	
la vuestra	*yours*	las vuestras	
el suyo	*theirs*	los suyos	
la suya	*theirs*	las suyas	

Éste es mi libro y ése es el suyo *This is my book and that one is yours*
(de Vd.)

2. *Relative pronouns.* Relative pronouns refer to nouns or pronouns that are antecedents in a sentence, and may be the subject or the object of a verb. The most common relative pronouns are:

que	*which, that, who, whom, when*
cual	*which, as, such as*
quien	*who, whom, whoever, whomever, which, whichever*
cuyo	*whose, of which, of whom, whereof*

Que and cual are used without distinction as to gender. Que refers to persons or things and may be the subject or the object of a verb; it has no plural.

El hombre que vino a comer — *The man who came to dinner*

El hombre que vimos es mi hermano — *The man whom we saw is my brother*

The prepositons a, de and en are used with que when referring to things.

El cine delante del que . . . — *The movie in front of which . . .*

Lo que and lo cual are used when referring to a clause or an idea.

No comió esta mañana, lo que me sorprendió — *He didn't eat this morning, which surprised me*

The following are interchangeable forms; the article indicates gender.

el que	*who, whom, which*	el cual
la que		la cual
los que		los cuales
las que		las cuales

Quien is both masculine and feminine. In both its singular (quien) and plural (quienes) forms, it may serve as the object of a preposition.

La muchacha con quien fue al cine está aquí — *The girl with whom he went to the movies is here*

Quien is sometimes used in the singular with a plural antecedent. Cuyo has masculine (cuyo), feminine (cuya) and plural (cuyos, cuyas) forms, and agrees in gender and number with its antecedent.

3. *Demonstrative pronouns.* Demonstrative pronouns specify particular persons or objects and indicate their relative distance from the speaker or from the person addressed. Demonstrative pronouns become demonstrative adjectives when preceding a noun and are written without an accent.

DEMONSTRATIVE PRONOUNS			DEMONSTRATIVE ADJECTIVES	
SINGULAR	PLURAL		SINGULAR	PLURAL
éste (*m.*)	éstos	*this, these,* near speaker	este	estos
ésta (*f.*)	éstas		esta	estas
esto (*neut.*)				
ése (*m.*)	ésos	*that, those,*	ese	esos
ésa (*f.*)	ésas	near person	esa	esas
eso (*neut.*)		addressed		
aquél (*m.*)	aquéllos	*that, those,* away	aquel	aquellos
aquélla (*f.*)	aquéllas	from speaker	aquella	aquellas
aquello (*neut.*)		and addressee		

The neuter forms, esto, eso and aquello carry no accent and are used to refer to some general idea or to an object not yet identified.

| tal | tales | *such, such a one, such things* |
| tanto | tantos | *that* |

Tal and tanto are adjectives as well as pronouns and carry no accent as either.

4. *Indefinite Pronouns.* Indefinite pronouns have the same function in Spanish as in English. They are:

alguien	*somebody, someone*
nadie	*nobody, no one, none*
cualquiera	*any one*
quienquiera	*whoever*
algo	*some*
nada	*nothing*

Alguien, nadie, algo and **nada** have the same form for the masculine and feminine. They have no plural forms. Other parts of speech may also act as indefinite pronouns, among these are the interrogatives **cuál** (*which*) and **quién** (*who*), the demonstrative pronoun **tal** (*such a*), and the adjectives **alguno** (*some*), **ninguno** (*none*), **todo** (*all*), **mucho** (*many*), **demasiado** (*too much, too many*), **bastante** (*sufficient, enough*), **harto** (*sufficient*), and **poco** (*few*).

F. Interrogatives. Interrogatives in Spanish always carry an accent. Some common interrogatives are.

¿qué?	*what? which?*	¿cuándo?	*when?*
¿quién?	*who? whom?*	¿cómo?	*how?*
¿de quién?	*whose?*	¿dónde?	*where?*
¿cuál	*which one?*	¿adónde?	*to where?*
¿cuánto?	*how much?*	¿por qué?	*why?*

Quién, cuál and **cuánto** have the plural forms **quiénes, cuáles** and **cuántos,** and are used as pronouns. The other interrogatives have no plural form. **Qué** may be used as an adjective or a pronoun and may refer to either persons or things.

G. Verbs. Verbs in Spanish are regular, radical-changing, orthographic-changing, and irregular in their conjugations. The following remarks describe some of the more important characteristics of verbs and their conjugations. A table of model conjugations of regular, radical-changing, orthographic-changing and irregular verbs at the end of this section.

1. Many verbs require a preposition before an infinitive. Some of the most common are:

a) those that require the preposition **a**;

acertar	*to manage, succeed*	enviar	*to send*
acostumbrarse	*to accustom oneself, get used to*	invitar	*to invite*
acudir	*to come to, resort to*	ir	*to go*
aprender	*to learn*	llegar	*to arrive*
apresurarse	*to hasten*	negarse	*to refuse*
atreverse	*to dare*	obligar	*to compel*
ayudar	*to help*	pasar	*to pass, go by*
bajar	*to come down*	persuadir	*to persuade*
comenzar	*to begin*	ponerse	*to start*
correr	*to run*	proceder	*to proceed*
disponerse	*to prepare*	subir	*to go up*
echar(se	*to start*	tornar	*to return, turn*
empezar	*to begin*	venir	*to come*
enseñar	*to teach*	volar	*to fly*
entrar	*to enter*	volver	*to return, do again*

b) those that require the preposition **de**;

acabar	*to finish, conclude*	dejar	*to discontinue, leave*
acordarse	*to remember*	encargarse	*to undertake, take on oneself*
alegrarse	*to be glad*	extrañarse	*to be surprised*
avergonzarse	*to be ashamed*	gozar	*to enjoy*
cesar	*to cease*	olvidarse	*to forget*
concluir	*to conclude, finish*	tratar	*to try*

Acabar de is also used to mean *to have just.*

Acabo de llegar a Nueva York   *I have just come to New York*

c) those that require the preposition **en**;

acordar	*to agree*	pensar	*to think*
complacerse	*to take pleasure*	persistir	*to persist*
consentir	*to consent*	quedar	*to agree, decide*
empeñarse	*to persist, insist*	tardar	*to be slow, delay*
insistir	*to insist*	vacilar	*to hesitate*

d) those that require the preposition con.

contar	to count on, rely
soñar	to dream

2. The infinitive of the verb is sometimes used as a noun, and often takes el in this case.

El estudiar es difícil	Studying is difficult

The infinitive follows most common verbs (poder, saber, desear, esperar, etc.) without a preposition, but some verbs require a preposition before the infinitive, see above.

3. The present participle (gerund) is formed by adding -ando to the stem of verbs whose infinitives end in -ar, and -iendo to the stem of verbs whose infinitives end in -er and -ir.

INFINITIVE		PRESENT PARTICIPLE
hablar	to speak	hablando
comer	to eat	comiendo
vivir	to live	viviendo

Some verbs having an irregular form of the present participle are:

INFINITIVE	PRESENT PARTICIPLE	INFINITIVE	PRESENT PARTICIPLE
caer	cayendo	oír	oyendo
corregir	corrigiendo	pedir	pidiendo
creer	creyendo	poder	pudiendo
decir	diciendo	seguir	siguiendo
divertirse	divirtiéndose	sentir	sintiendo
dormir	durmiendo	servir	sirviendo
ir	yendo	traer	trayendo
leer	leyendo	venir	viniendo

The present participle is used with some tense of estar to form a progressive tense.

Estoy hablando	I am speaking

4. The past participle is formed by adding -ado to the stem of verbs whose infinitives end in -ar, and -ido to the stem of verbs whose infinitives end in -er and -ir.

INFINITIVE	PAST PARTICIPLE
hablar	hablado
comer	comido
vivir	vivido

Some verbs having an irregular form of the past participle are:

INFINITIVE	PAST PARTICIPLE	INFINITIVE	PAST PARTICIPLE
abrir	abierto	poner	puesto
cubrir	cubierto	proveer	provisto
decir	dicho	pudrir	podrido
escribir	escrito	romper	roto
freír	frito	soltar	suelto
hacer	hecho	ver	visto
imprimir	impreso	volver	vuelto
morir	muerto		

The past participles of compounds of the above verbs, as entreabrir, descubrir, describir, etc., are also irregular.

5. There are three regular conjugations in Spanish.

a) The first conjugation includes the verbs ending in -ar in the infinitive.

INFINITIVE		PRESENT PARTICIPLE	PAST PARTICIPLE
hablar	to speak	hablando	hablado
estudiar	to study	estudiando	estudiado
caminar	to walk	caminando	caminado

b) The second conjugation includes the verbs ending in **-er** in the infinitive

INFINITIVE		PRESENT PARTICIPLE	PAST PARTICIPLE
comer	*to eat*	comiendo	comido
entender	*to understand*	entendiendo	entendido
beber	*to drink*	bebiendo	bebido

c) The third conjugation includes the verbs ending in **-ir** in the infinitive.

INFINITIVE		PRESENT PARTICIPLE	PAST PARTICIPLE
vivir	*to live*	viviendo	vivido
partir	*to depart*	partiendo	partido
subir	*to go up*	subiendo	subido

6. *Tenses of the indicative mood.*

a) *Present Tense.* The present tense is used to express action in the present, habitual or customary action, or a general truth.

Juan trabaja en el jardín   *John works in the garden*

It is formed by dropping the infinitive endings and adding personal endings. Verbs of the first regular conjugation add -o, -as, -a, -amos, -áis, -an; verbs of the second regular conjugation add -o, -es, -e, -emos, -éis, -en; verbs of the third regular conjugation add -o, -es, -e, -imos, -ís, -en.

b) *Imperfect Tense.* The imperfect tense is used to describe the past, a continuing action in the past, or what was habitual or customary in the past.

La ventana estaba abierta	*The window was open*
Caminaba por la calle	*I was walking down the street*
Jugábamos cuando estábamos de vacaciones	*We played when we were on vacation*

It is formed by dropping the infinitive endings and adding personal endings. Verbs of the first regular conjugation add -aba, -abas, -aba, -ábamos, -abais, -aban; verbs of the second and third regular conjugations add -ía, -ías, -ía, -íamos, -íais, -ían. Ir, ser and ver (and its compounds) are irregularly conjugated in the imperfect tense, see the Verb Table.

c) *Preterit (Past) Tense.* The preterit tense is used to express an action completed in the past and to form the passive voice in the past.

Concha cerró la puerta	*Concha closed the door*
América fue descubierta por Colón	*America was discovered by Columbus*

It is formed by dropping the infinitive endings and adding personal endings. Verbs of the first regular conjugation add -é, -aste, -ó, -amos, -asteis, -aron; verbs of the second and third regular conjugations add -í, -iste, -ió, -imos, -isteis, -ieron.

d) *Future Tense.* The future tense is used as in English. In addition, it expresses probability or conjecture in the present; its use corresponds exactly to that of the conditional in the past.

Él trabajará mañana	*He will work tomorrow*
¿Qué hora será?	*I wonder what time it is*
Serán las tres	*It is probably three o'clock*

It is formed by dropping the infinitive endings and adding the same personal endings in all three conjugations, -é, -ás, -á, -emos, -éis, -án. The future endings are the same for all verbs, whether regular or irregular.

7. *Conditional Mood.* The conditional mood is used as in English. It also expresses probability in the past. Its use corresponds exactly to that of the future tense.

Si fuera Vd. lo compraría	*If I were you, I would buy it*
Serían las siete	*It was probably seven o'clock*

It is formed by adding the personal endings of the imperfect tense of the second and third conjugations to the infinitive, -ía, -ías, -ía, -íamos, -íais, -ían.

8. *Subjunctive mood and tenses.* The subjunctive mood expresses wish, obligation, or a condition improbable or contrary to fact.

a) The tense of the subjunctive in a subordinate clause is determined by the tense of the verb in the main clause. When the verb in the main clause is in the present or in the future tense, the verb in the subordinate clause will be in the present subjunctive. When the verb in the main clause is in the preterit, imperfect or conditional, the verb in the subordinate clause will be in the imperfect subjunctive.

b) When futurity is implied, the subjunctive is required following such adverbs, or adverbial locutions, of time as:

cuando	*when*
después que	*after*
hasta que	*until*
luego que	*as soon as*
mientras que	*while*
antes (de) que	*before* (always followed by the subjunctive)
Lo veré cuando él venga	*I shall see him when he comes*

c) The subjunctive is required following such conjunctive locutions as:

a menos que	*unless*
antes (de) que	*before*
para que	*in order that*
como si	*as if, as though*
con tal que	*provided that, as long as*
sin que	*without*
Me habló como si fuera mi padre	*He spoke to me as though he were my father*
Lo haré con tal que me ayude	*I shall do it provided you help me*

d) The subjunctive is used in noun clauses introduced by que (*that*) when the following conditions exist at the same time:

1. the sentence contains two clauses;
2. the subject in the subordinate clause differs from the subject of the main clause;
3. when a verb of emotion or feeling, command, request, permission, prohibition, approval, advice, necessity, cause, denial, doubt, or an impersonal locution in the main clause, affects the subject and/or the verb of the subordinate clause.

Me alegro de que ellos se vayan	*I am glad that they are going*
Ellos temían que no llegásemos a tiempo	*They feared that we would not arrive on time*
Dígale a Pedro que me ayude	*Tell Peter to help me*
No creo que él diga la verdad	*I don't believe he is telling the truth*
Es posible que le escribamos	*It is possible that we will write to him*

e) *Present Subjunctive.* In addition to its uses in subordinate clauses, the present subjunctive expresses a command.

No sea Vd. tonto	*Don't you be silly*
Escriban Vds. la lección	*Write the lesson*

It is formed by dropping the infinitive endings and adding personal endings. Verbs of the first regular conjugation add -e, -es, -e, -emos, -éis, -en; verbs of the second and third regular conjugations add -a, -as, -a, -amos, -áis, -an.

f) *Imperfect Subjunctive.* The imperfect subjunctive is formed by dropping the ending -ron of the third person plural of the preterit and adding personal endings. There are two sets of endings that are usually interchangeable, but the form in -ra is the more commonly used in modern Spanish. The two sets of endings are the same for all three conjugations. They are: -ra, -ras, -ra, -ramos, -rais, -ran and -se, -ses, -se, -semos, -seis, -sen. The imperfect subjunctive is rarely used by itself, but it may appear in such simple sentences as:

Quisiera verlo	*I should like to see him*
Debiera Vd. ir	*You should go*
¿Pudiera Vd. decírmelo?	*Would you be able to tell it to me?*

g) *Future Subjunctive.* The future subjunctive is formed by dropping the infinitive endings and adding personal endings. Verbs of the first regular conjugation add -are, -ares, -are, -áremos, -areis, -aren; verbs of the second and third conjugations add -iere, -ieres, -iere, -iéremos, -iereis, -ieren.

9. *Imperative Mood.* The imperative mood expresses a command. There is one tense only, the present. The forms of the imperative mood are the second person singular and plural (familiar form) and they are formed by dropping the infinitive ending and adding -a and -ad respectively in the first conjugation, -e and -ed in the second conjugation, and -e and -id in the third conjugation.

10. *Compound Tenses.* The compound tenses express a completed action. There is a corresponding compound tense for each of the simple tenses. They are formed with the auxiliary verb haber (regularly conjugated) and the uninflected past participle of the verb.

PERFECT INDICATIVE

	SINGULAR	PLURAL
1st person	he amado	hemos amado
2nd person	has amado	habéis amado
3rd person	he amado	han amando

PLUPERFECT INDICATIVE

1st person	había amado
2nd person	habías amado
	etc.

PRETERIT ANTERIOR INDICATIVE

1st person	hube amado
2nd person	hubiste amado
	etc.

FUTURE PERFECT INDICATIVE

1st person	habré amado
2nd person	habrás amado
	etc.

CONDITIONAL PERFECT

1st person	habría amado
2nd person	habrías amado
	etc.

PERFECT SUBJUNCTIVE

1st person	haya amado
2nd person	hayas amado
	etc.

PLUPERFECT SUBJUNCTIVE

1st person	hubiera amado
2nd person	hubieras amado
	etc.

FUTURE PERFECT SUBJUNCTIVE

1st person	hubiere amado
2nd person	hubieres amado
	etc.

11. *The Passive Voice.* The passive voice is formed with the auxiliary verb ser (*to be*) and an inflected past participle; it is seldom used in Spanish. It should be noted that not all constructions employing ser and a past participle are passive, for some past participles have an active meaning in certain constructions. The same can be said of the verb ser when used with the past participle of an intransitive verb.

Los libros fueron escritos por Cervantes *The books were written by Cervantes*

La niña está acompañada por su madre *The girl is accompanied by her mother*

12. *Radical-changing Verbs.* In these verbs a change occurs in the radical when the tonic accent (voice stress) falls on the radical vowel -e or -o. Radical-changing verbs are divided into three classes.

a) To the first class belong those verbs ending in -ar and -er whose radical vowels -e or -o change to -ie and -ue respectively when the radical receives the stress. The changes occur in all of the singular and in the third person plural of the present indicative, in the present subjunctive, and in the imperative singular. See acertar and volver in the Verb Table.

b) To the second class belong those verbs ending in -ir whose radical vowels -e or -o change to -ie and -ue respectively when the radical receives the stress. The changes occur as in the verbs of the first class. They also change -e to -i and -o to -u in the first and second persons plural of the present subjunctive, in the third person singular and plural of the preterit, in all of the imperfect subjunctive, and in the present participle. See sentir and dormir in the Verb Table.

c) To the third class also belong those verbs ending in -ir whose radical vowel -e changes to -i when the radical receives the stress. The change occurs in all of the singular and in the third person plural of the present indicative, in all of the present subjunctive, in the third person singular and plural of the preterit, in all of the imperfect subjunctive, in the imperative singular, and in the present participle. See pedir in the Verb Table. Other verbs of this class are those ending in -eir. See reír in the Verb Table.

Note. Most common verbs that have -e or -o in the radical are radical-changing verbs.

13. *Orthographic-changing Verbs.* Orthographic-changing verbs are those which undergo a change in spelling in order to maintain the sound of the final consonant before the infinitive ending.

a) Verbs ending in -car change to -c to -qu before an -e. See embarcar in the Verb Table.

b) Verbs ending in -gar change the -g to -gu before an -e. See amargar in the Verb Table.

c) Verbs ending in -zar change the -z to -c before an -e. See alcanzar in the Verb Table.

d) Verbs ending in -guar change the -gu to -gü before an -e. See averiguar in the Verb Table.

e) Verbs ending in -cer or -cir preceded by a consonant change the -c to -z before -a and -o. See mecer and zurcir in the Verb Table.

f) Verbs ending in -cer or -cir preceded by a vowel change the -c to -zc before -a and -o. See agradecer and conducir in the Verb Table. Some notable exceptions to this rule are: cocer and its compounds, and mecer, in which the -c changes to -z, and hacer and decir, which are highly irregular. See the Verb Table.

g) Verbs ending in -ger or -gir change the -g to -j before -a and -o. See recoger in the Verb Table.

h) Verbs ending in -guir change the -gu to -g before -a and -o. See distinguir in the Verb Table.

i) Verbs ending in -quir change the -qu to -c before -a and -o. See delinquir in the Verb Table.

j) Verbs ending in -eer change the -i of the ending to -y. See leer in the Verb Table.

k) Verbs ending in -uir (except those ending in -guir and -quir) insert -y before -a, -e and -o, and replace an unstressed -i between vowels with -y. See construir in the Verb Table.

14. *Reflexive Verbs.* Reflexive verbs are used more frequently in Spanish than in English. Verbs that are intransitive in English are often reflexive in Spanish. Some Spanish verbs are always reflexive. Others may be reflexive or not, depending on the use. Reflexive verbs always occur in conjunction with a reflexive pronoun.

PRESENT INDICATIVE

SINGULAR		PLURAL
1st person	yo me lavo	nosotros nos lavamos
2nd person	tú te lavas	vosotros os (vos) laváis
3rd person	él se lava	ellos se lavan

Lavar is an example of a verb that may be reflexive or not. In the sample conjugation above, it is reflexive, in the sense of *to wash oneself*. It can also be used transitively and without the reflexive pronoun.

When the subject of a reflexive verb is two or more persons or things, and the action of the verb falls upon the plural subject, the verb is used with a reciprocal meaning.

Las muchachas se visitan	*The girls visit each other*
José, Pedro y Juan se escriben	*Joseph, Peter and John write each other*

15. *Impersonal Verbs.* These verbs are used only in the infinitive and in the third person singular. They are generally used in a causative sense, their subject being implied but not stated. The verbs haber and hacer, when used impersonally, mean *there is* or *there are*. Some impersonal verbs are used transitively but only in a metaphorical sense. The pronoun se and the active form of the verb is also used to form some impersonal constructions.

Llueve hoy	*It is raining today*
Nieva	*It is snowing*
Hay polvo	*It is dusty*
Se prohibe fumar	*It is forbidden to smoke*

Some typical impersonal verbs are.

alborear	*to dawn*	helar	*to freeze*
amanecer	*to dawn*	llover	*to rain*
anochecer	*to grow dark*	lloviznar	*to drizzle*
diluviar	*to rain heavily*	nevar	*to snow*
escarchar	*to frost*	relampaguear	*to lighten*
granizar	*to hail*	tronar	*to thunder*

16. *Defective Verbs.* These are verbs that lack some tenses and persons. They must not be confused with some verbs that, while not being truly defective, are seldom used in some of their persons. Defective verbs are sometimes used in a metaphorical sense. Some typical defective verbs are:

abolir	*to abolish*
agredir	*to assault*
aguerrir	*to accustom to war*
arrecirse	*to become stiff with cold*
atañer	*to concern*
aterirse	*to become stiff with cold*
balbucir	*to stammer*
concernir	*to concern*
despavorir	*to be aghast*
embaír	*to deceive*
empedernir	*to harden*
garantir	*to guarantee*
manir	*to keep meat until it becomes gamey*
soler	*to be in the habit of*
transgredir	*to transgress*
usucapir	*to usucapt*

17. *Ser and Estar.* Each of these verbs means *to be,* but they are not interchangeable. Ser denotes a permanent state or condition.

La casa es blanca   *The house is white*

Estar denotes a temporary state or condition.

La puerta está abierta   *The door is open*

18. *Negation.* In Spanish, the negative no always precedes the verb.

No quiero ir   *I don't want to go*
No la veo   *I don't see her*

H. Prepositions. Some common prepositions are:

a	*at, to, for*	hacia	*towards*
antes, ante	*before*	hasta	*until*
con	*with*	para	*for, to*
contra	*against*	por	*by, for, through*
de	*of, from*	según	*according*
desde	*from*	sin	*without*
en	*in, on, at*	sobre	*on, upon*
entre	*between, among*	tras, detrás	*behind*

I. Conjunctions. Some common conjunctions are:

que	*that*	porque, que	*because*
también	*also*	pues, pues que	*since*
además	*moreover*	por	*by, for*
y, e	*and*	por tanto	*therefore*
ni	*neither, nor*	por cuanto	*whereas*
o, u, ya	*or, either, whether*	para que	*that*
sea que	*whether*	a fin de	*in order that*
tampoco	*neither*	si	*if*
mas, pero	*but*	sino	*but*
aun, cuando, aun cuando	*even*	con tal que	*provided*
aunque	*although, though*		
a menos de, a menos que	*unless*	como, así como	*as*
pues, puesto que	*since*	así	*so*

E is used instead of **y** when the following word begins with **i** or **hi. U** is employed instead of **o** when the word immediately following begins with **o** or **ho.**

IRREGULAR VERBS

KEY FOR THE IDENTIFICATION OF TENSES AND PARTS OF SPANISH VERBS

A	Present Indicative.	F	Conditional.
B	Present Subjunctive.	G	Imperfect Subjunctive.
C	Imperfect Indicative.	H	Imperative.*
D	Preterite Indicative.	I	Past Participle.
E	Future Indicative.	J	Gerund.

* For all positive and negative imperative forms with *usted*, *ustedes*, and *nosotros* and for the negative forms with *tú* and *vosotros* the present subjunctive is used.

Reflexive and reciprocal verbs attach the object pronouns (**me, te, se, nos, os, se**) at the end of the infinitive (*peinarse; amarse*), the positive imperative (*péinate, péinese; amaos*), and the gerund (*peinándose; amándose*). In all the tenses of the indicative and the subjunctive these pronouns are detached and placed before the verb (**me** *peino*, **te** *peinas*, **se** *peina*, **nos** *peinamos*, **os** *peináis*, **se** *peinan*; **nos** *amamos*, **os** *amáis*, **se** *aman*, etc.).

SPANISH IRREGULAR AND ORTHOGRAPHIC CHANGING VERBS

1) A number placed next to the entry indicates that the irregular verb follows the pattern of conjugation of the model given under that number in Part I below. (Example: **pensar** [1], behaves like the model **acertar** —changes e to ie—in the same tenses A, B, H.)
2) A letter placed next to the entry indicates that the orthographic changing verb follows the spelling irregularities of the model verb given under that letter in Part II below. (Example: **aplazar** [a], behaves like the model **alcanzar**.)
3) A number and a letter placed next to the entry indicate that the verb belongs to both of the above categories. (Example: **almorzar** [12-a] behaves like both **contar** *and* **alcanzar**.)
Only the irregular forms are given.

I. IRREGULAR VERBS

No.	Verb	Irregular Tenses (See Key)	
1	acertar	A	acierto, aciertas, acierta; aciertan.
		B	acierte, aciertes, acierte; acierten.
		H	acierta, acierte; acierten.
2	adquirir	A	adquiero, adquieres, adquiere; adquieren.
		B	adquiera, adquieras, adquiera; adquieran.
		H	adquiere, adquiera; adquieran.
3	agradecer	A	agradezco.
		B	agradezca, agradezcas, agradezca; agradezcamos, agradezcáis, agradezcan.
		H	agradezca; agradezcamos, agradezcan.
4	andar	D	anduve, anduviste, anduvo; anduvimos, anduvisteis, anduvieron.
		G	anduviera or anduviese, anduvieras or anduvieses, anduviera or anduviese; anduviéramos or anduviésemos, anduvierais or anduvieseis, anduvieran or anduviesen.
5	asir	A	asgo.
		B	asga, asgas, asga; asgamos, asgáis, asgan.
6	bendecir	A	bendigo, bendices, bendice; bendicen.
		B	bendiga, bendigas, bendiga; bendigamos, bendigáis, bendigan.
		D	bendije, bendijiste, bendijo; bendijimos, bendijisteis, bendijeron.

No.	Verb	Irregular Tenses (See Key)	
		G	bendijera or bendijese, bendijeras or bendijeses, bendijera or bendijese; bendijéramos or bendijésemos, bendijerais or bendijeseis, bendijeran or bendijesen.
		H	bendice, bendiga; bendigamos, bendigan.
		I	bendito (also the regular: bendecido).
		J	bendiciendo.
7	caber	A	quepo.
		B	quepa, quepas, quepa; quepamos, quepáis, quepan.
		D	cupe, cupiste, cupo; cupimos, cupisteis, cupieron.
		E	cabré, cabrás, cabrá; cabremos, cabréis, cabrán.
		F	cabría, cabrías, cabría; cabríamos, cabríais, cabrían.
		G	cupiera or cupiese, cupieras or cupieses, cupiera or cupiese; cupiéramos or cupiésemos, cupierais or cupieseis, cupieran or cupiesen.
		H	quepa, quepamos, quepan.
8	caer	A	caigo.
		B	caiga, caigas, caiga; caigamos, caigáis, caigan.
		H	caiga; caigamos, caigan.
9	ceñir	A	ciño, ciñes, ciñe; ciñen.
		B	ciña, ciñas, ciña; ciñamos, ciñáis, ciñan.
		D	ciñó; ciñeron.
		G	ciñera or ciñese, ciñeras or ciñeses, ciñera or ciñese; ciñéramos or ciñésemos, ciñerais or ciñeseis, ciñeran or ciñesen.
		H	ciñe, ciña; ciñamos, ciñan.
		J	ciñendo.
10	cerner, cernir	A	cierno, ciernes, cierne; cernimos, cernís, ciernen.
		B	cierna, ciernas, cierna; ciernan.
		E	cerniré, cernirás, cernirá; cerniremos, cerniréis, cernirán.
		F	cerniría, cernirías, cerniría; cerniríamos, cerniríais, cernirían.
		H	cierne, cierna; ciernan.
11	conducir	A	conduzco.
		B	conduzca, conduzcas, conduzca; conduzcamos, conduzcáis, conduzcan.
		D	conduje, condujiste, condujo; condujimos, condujisteis, condujeron.
		G	condujera or condujese, condujeras or condujeses, condujera or condujese; condujéramos or condujésemos, condujerais or condujeseis, condujeran or condujesen.
		H	conduzca; conduzcamos, conduzcan.
12	contar	A	cuento, cuentas, cuenta; cuentan.
		B	cuente, cuentes, cuente; cuenten.
		H	cuenta, cuente; cuenten.
13	dar	A	doy.
		D	di, diste, dio; dimos, disteis, dieron.
		G	diera or diese, dieras or dieses, diera or diese; diéramos or diésemos, dierais or dieseis, dieran or diesen.

No.	Verb	Irregular Tenses (See Key)	
14	decir	A	digo, dices, dice; dicen.
		B	diga, digas, diga; digamos, digáis, digan.
		D	dije, dijiste, dijo; dijimos, dijisteis, dijeron.
		E	diré, dirás, dirá; diremos, diréis, dirán.
		F	diría, dirías, diría; diríamos, diríais, dirían.
		G	dijera or dijese, dijeras or dijeses, dijera or dijese; dijéramos or dijésemos, dijerais or dijeseis, dijeran or dijesen.
		H	di, diga; digamos, digan.
		I	dicho.
		J	diciendo.
15	desosar	A	deshueso, deshuesas, deshuesa; deshuesan.
		B	deshuese, deshueses, deshuese; deshuesen.
		H	deshuesa, deshuese; deshuesen.
16	discernir	A	discierno, disciernes, discierne; disciernen.
		B	discierna, disciernas, discierna; disciernan.
		H	discierne, discierna; disciernan.
17	dormir	A	duermo, duermes, duermo; duermen.
		B	duerma, duermas, duerma; durmamos, durmáis, duerman.
		D	durmió; durmieron.
		G	durmiera or durmiese, durmieras or durmieses, durmiera or durmiese; durmiéramos or durmiésemos, durmierais or durmieseis, durmieran or durmiesen.
		H	duerme, duerma; durmamos, duerman.
		J	durmiendo.
18	entender	A	entiendo, entiendes, entiende; entienden.
		B	entienda, entiendas, entienda; entiendan.
		H	entiende, entienda; entiendan.
19	erguir	A	yergo, yergues, yergue; yerguen.
		B	yerga, yergas, yerga; irgamos, irgáis, yergan.
		D	irguió; irguieron.
		G	irguiera or irguiese, irguieras or irguieses, irguiera or irguiese; irguiéramos or irguiésemos, irguierais or irguieseis, irguieran or irguiesen.
		H	yergue, yerga; irgamos, yergan.
		J	irguiendo.
20	estar	A	estoy, estás, está; están.
		B	esté, estés, esté; estén.
		D	estuve, estuviste, estuvo; estuvimos, estuvisteis, estuvieron.
		G	estuviera or estuviese, estuvieras or estuvieses, estuviera or estuviese; estuviéramos or estuviésemos, estuvierais or estuvieseis, estuvieran or estuviesen.
		H	está, esté; estén.
21	haber	A	he, has, ha or hay (impersonal form); hemos or habemos, han.
		B	haya, hayas, haya; hayamos, hayáis, hayan.
		D	hube, hubiste, hubo; hubimos, hubisteis, hubieron.
		E	habré, habrás, habrá; habremos, habréis, habrán.
		F	habría, habrías, habría; habríamos, habríais, habrían.
		G	hubiera or hubiese, hubieras or hubieses, hubiera or hubiese; hubiéramos or hubiésemos, hubierais or hubieseis, hubieran or hubiesen.
		H	he, haya; hayamos, hayan.

No.	Verb	Irregular Tenses (See Key)	
22	hacer	A	hago.
		B	haga, hagas, haga; hagamos, hagáis, hagan.
		D	hice, hiciste, hizo; hicimos, hicisteis, hicieron.
		E	haré, harás, hará; haremos, haréis, harán.
		F	haría, harías, haría; haríamos, haríais, harían.
		G	hiciera or hiciese, hicieras or hicieses, hiciera or hiciese; hiciéramos or hiciésemos, hicierais or hicieseis, hicieran or hiciesen.
		H	haz, haga; hagamos, hagan.
		I	hecho.
23	huir	A	huyo, huyes, huye; huyen.
		B	huya, huyas, huya; huyamos, huyáis, huyan.
		H	huye, huya; huyamos, huyan.
24	ir	A	voy, vas, va; vamos, vais, van.
		B	vaya, vayas, vaya; vayamos, vayáis, vayan.
		C	iba, ibas, iba; íbamos, ibais, iban.
		D	fui, fuiste, fue; fuimos, fuisteis, fueron.
		G	fuera or fuese, fueras or fueses, fuera or fuese; fuéramos or fuésemos, fuerais or fueseis, fueran or fuesen.
		J	yendo.
25	jugar	A	juego, juegas, juega; juegan.
		B	juegue, juegues, juegue; jueguen.
		H	juega, juegue; jueguen.
26	mover	A	muevo, mueves, mueve; mueven.
		B	mueva, muevas, mueva; muevan.
		H	mueve, mueva; muevan.
27	mullir	D	mulló; mulleron.
		G	mullera or mullese, mulleras or mulleses, mullera or mullese; mulléramos or mullésemos, mullerais or mulleseis, mulleran or mullesen.
		J	mullendo.
28	oir	A	oigo, oyes, oye; oyen.
		B	oiga, oigas, oiga; oigamos, oigáis, oigan.
		H	oye, oiga; oigamos, oigan.
28'	oler	A-B-H	It is conjugated in the same way that No. 26 (mover) but with an "h" before diphthong "ue": huelo, hueles, etc.
29	pedir	A	pido, pides, pide; piden.
		B	pida, pidas, pida; pidamos, pidáis, pidan.
		D	pidió; pidieron.
		G	pidiera or pidiese, pidieras or pidieses, pidiera or pidiese; pidiéramos or pidiésemos, pidierais or pidieseis, pidieran or pidiesen.
		H	pide, pida; pidamos, pidan.
		J	pidiendo.
30	placer	A	plazco.
		B	plazca, plazcas, plazca (or plegue or plega); placamos, placáis, plazcan.
		D	plugo (or plació); pluguieron (or placieron).
		G	pluguiera or pluguiese (or placiera or placiese).
		H	plazca; plazcamos, plazcan.

No.	Verb	Irregular Tenses (See Key)	
31	poder	A	puedo, puedes, puede; pueden.
		B	pueda, puedas, pueda; puedan.
		D	pude, pudiste, pudo; pudimos, pudisteis, pudieron.
		E	podré, podrás, podrá; podremos, podréis, podrán.
		F	podría, podrías, podría, podríamos, podríais, podrían.
		G	pudiera or pudiese, pudieras or pudieses, pudiera or pudiese; pudiéramos or pudiésemos, pudierais or pudieseis, pudieran or pudiesen.
		H	puede, pueda; puedan.
		J	pudiendo.
32	poner	A	pongo.
		B	ponga, pongas, ponga; pongamos, pongáis, pongan.
		D	puse, pusiste, puso; pusimos, pusisteis, pusieron.
		E	pondré, pondrás, pondrá; pondremos, pondréis, pondrán.
		F	pondría, pondrías, pondría; pondríamos, pondríais, pondrían.
		G	pusiera or pusiese, pusieras or pusieses, pusiera or pusiese; pusiéramos or pusiésemos, pusieseis, pusieran or pusiesen.
		H	pon, ponga; pongamos, pongan.
		I	puesto.
33	pudrir or podrir	I	podrido. (When the infinitive used is "podrir," the verb is conjugated as "pudrir," which only is irregular in its p.p.)
34	querer	A	quiero, quieres, quiere; quieren.
		B	quiera, quieras, quiera; quieran.
		D	quise, quisiste, quiso; quisimos, quisisteis, quisieron.
		E	querré, querrás, querrá; querremos, querréis, querrán.
		F	querría, querrías, querría; querríamos, querríais, querrían.
		G	quisiera or quisiese, quisieras or quisieses, quisiera or quisiese; quisiéramos or quisiésemos, quisierais or quisieseis, quisieran or quisiesen.
		H	quiere, quiera; quieran.
35	reir	A	río, ríes, ríe; ríen.
		B	ría, rías, ría; riamos, riáis, rían.
		D	rió; rieron.
		G	riera or riese, rieras or rieses, riera or riese; riéramos or riésemos, rierais or rieseis, rieran or riesen.
		H	ríe, ría; riamos, rían.
		J	riendo.
36	roer	A	It is a regular form but it can be conjugated "roigo" and "royo" in the first person singular.
		B	It is a regular form too but it can be conjugated "roiga" and "roya," etc.
37	saber	A	sé.
		B	sepa, sepas, sepa; sepamos, sepáis, sepan.
		D	supe, supiste, supo; supimos, supisteis, supieron.
		E	sabré, sabrás, sabrá; sabremos, sabréis, sabrán.
		F	sabría, sabrías, sabría; sabríamos, sabríais, sabrían.
		–	

No.	Verb	Irregular Tenses (See Key)	
		G	supiera or supiese, supieras or supieses, supiera or supiese; supiéramos or supiésemos, supierais or supieseis, supieran or supiesen.
		H	sepa; sepamos, sepan.
38	salir	A	salgo.
		B	salga, salgas, salga; salgamos, salgáis, salgan.
		E	saldré, saldrás, saldrá; saldremos, saldréis, saldrán.
		F	saldría, saldrías, saldría; saldríamos, saldríais, saldrían.
		G	sal, salga; salgamos, salgan.
39	sentir	A	siento, sientes, siente; sienten.
		B	sienta, sientas, sienta; sintamos, sintáis, sientan.
		D	sintió; sintieron.
		G	sintiera or sintiese, sintieras or sintieses, sintiera or sintiese; sintiéramos or sintiésemos, sintierais or sintieseis, sintieran or sintiesen.
		H	siente, sienta; sintamos, sientan.
		J	sintiendo.
40	ser	A	soy, eres, es; somos, sois, son.
		B	sea, seas, sea; seamos, seáis, sean.
		C	era, eras, era; éramos, erais, eran.
		D	fui, fuiste, fue; fuimos, fuisteis, fueron.
		G	fuera or fuese, fueras or fueses, fuera or fuese; fuéramos or fuésemos, fuerais or fueseis, fueran or fuesen.
		H	sea; seamos, sean.
41	tañer	D	tañó; tañeron.
		G	tañera or tañese, tañeras or tañeses, tañera or tañese; tañéramos or tañésemos, tañerais or tañeseis, tañeran or tañesen.
		J	tañendo.
42	tener	A	tengo, tienes, tiene; tienen.
		B	tenga, tengas, tenga; tengamos, tengáis, tengan.
		D	tuve, tuviste, tuvo; tuvimos, tuvisteis, tuvieron.
		E	tendré, tendrás, tendrá; tendremos, tendréis, tendrán.
		F	tendría, tendrías, tendría; tendríamos, tendríais, tendrían.
		G	tuviera or tuviese, tuvieras or tuvieses, tuviera or tuviese; tuviéramos or tuviésemos, tuvierais or tuvieseis, tuvieran or tuviesen.
		H	ten, tenga; tengamos, tengan.
43	traer	A	traigo.
		B	traiga, traigas, traiga; traigamos, traigáis, traigan.
		D	traje, trajiste, trajo; trajimos, trajisteis, trajeron.
		G	trajera or trajese, trajeras or trajeses, trajera or trajese; trajéramos or trajésemos, trajerais or trajeseis, trajeran or trajesen.
		H	traiga; traigamos, traigan.
44	valer	A	valgo.
		B	valga, valgas, valga; valgamos, valgáis, valgan.
		E	valdré, valdrás, valdrá; valdremos, valdréis, valdrán.
		F	valdría, valdrías, valdría; valdríamos, valdríais, valdrían.
		H	val(e), valga; valgamos, valgan.

No.	Verb	Irregular Tenses (See Key)	
45	venir	A	vengo, vienes, viene; vienen.
		B	venga, vengas, venga; vengamos, vengáis, vengan.
		D	vine, viniste, vino; vinimos, vinisteis, vinieron.
		E	vendré, vendrás, vendrá; vendremos, vendréis, vendrán.
		F	vendría, vendrías, vendría; vendríamos, vendríais, vendrían.
		G	viniera or viniese, vinieras or vinieses, viniera or viniese; viniéramos or viniésemos, vinierais or vinieseis, vinieran or viniesen.
		H	ven, venga; vengamos, vengan.
		J	viniendo.
46	ver	A	veo.
		B	vea, veas, vea; veamos, veáis, vean.
		C	veía, veías, veía; veíamos, veíais, veían.
		H	vea; veamos, vean.
		I	visto.
47	volver	A	vuelvo, vuelves, vuelve; vuelven.
		B	vuelva, vuelvas, vuelva; vuelvan.
		H	vuelve, vuelva; vuelvan.
		I	vuelto.
48	yacer	A	yazco (or yazgo or yago).
		B	yazca (yazga, yaga), yazcas (yazgas, yagas), yazca (yazga, yaga); yazcamos (yazgamos, yagamos), yazcáis (yazgáis, yagáis), yazcan (yazgan, yagan).
		H	yace (or yaz), yazca (yazga, yaga); yazcamos (yazgamos, yagamos), yazcan (yazgan, yagan).

No. 49 — Verbs with Irregular Participles

Verbs	Regular Participle	Irregular Participle
abrir	—	abierto
absolver	—	absuelto
absorber	absorbido	absorto
abstraer	abstraído	abstracto
adscribir	—	adscrito
afligir	afligido	aflicto
circunscribir	—	circunscrito
cubrir	—	cubierto
descubrir	—	descubierto
despertar	despertado	despierto
devolver	—	devuelto
disponer	—	dispuesto
elegir	elegido	electo
encubrir	—	encubierto
enjugar	enjugado	enjuto
entreabrir	—	entreabierto
entrever	—	entrevisto
escribir	—	escrito
excluir	excluido	excluso
eximir	eximido	exento
expresar	expresado	expreso
extender	extendido	extenso
extinguir	extinguido	extinto
freír	freído	frito
fijar	fijado	fijo
hartar	hartado	harto
imponer	—	impuesto
imprimir	imprimido	impreso
incluir	incluido	incluso
inscribir	—	inscrito

Verbs with Irregular Participles

Verbs	Regular Participle	Irregular Participle
insertar	insertado	inserto
interponer	—	interpuesto
invertir	invertido	inverso
maldecir	maldecido	maldito
matar	matado	muerto
morir	—	muerto
nacer	nacido	nato
poner	—	puesto
posponer	—	pospuesto
predecir	—	predicho
predisponer	—	predispuesto
prender	prendido	preso
prescribir	—	prescrito
presumir	presumido	presunto
presuponer	—	presupuesto
pretender	pretendido	pretenso
prever	—	previsto
propender	propendido	propenso
proponer	—	propuesto
proscribir	—	proscrito
prostituir	prostituído	prostituto
proveer	proveído	provisto
reabrir	—	reabierto
reelegir	reelegido	reelecto
rehacer	—	rehecho
reimprimir	—	reimpreso
reponer	—	repuesto
resolver	—	resuelto
romper	—	roto
sobreponer	—	sobrepuesto
sofreír	sofreído	sofrito
sujetar	sujetado	sujeto
superponer	—	superpuesto
suponer	—	supuesto
surgir	surgido	surto
suscribir	—	suscrito
suspender	suspendido	suspenso
sustituir	sustituído	sustituto
transcribir	—	transcripto
tra(n)sponer	—	tra(n)spuesto
truncar	truncado	trunco
yuxtaponer	—	yuxtapuesto

No. 50 Defective Verbs or Verbs Which Have Some Especial Characteristics

Verbs	
abolir	Only tenses having endings with "i" are used; abolió, abolía, aboliré, etc.
acaecer	Used only in the infinitive and in the third person of all tenses.
acontecer	See *Acaecer.*
agredir	See *Abolir.*
atañer	Used only in the third person of all tenses, especially "atañe," "atañen."
aterirse	See *Abolir.*
balbucir	Persons of this verb which do not have the ending "i" are conjugated in the same way as the regular verb "balbucear."
concernir	Only the gerund (concerniendo) and the third person of all tenses are used, especially: concierne, conciernes; concernía, concernían; concierna, conciernan.
granizar	See *Acaecer.*
preterir	See *Abolir.*
soler	Used only in the present and imperfect indicative. The participle "solido" is used only in the present perfect tense.
transgredir	See *Abolir.*

II. ORTHOGRAPHIC CHANGING VERBS

Verbs marked with letter		
a	"z" changes to "c" before "e" and "i," and "c" changes to "z" before "a," "o," "u."	alcanzar; alcance, alcancemos, etc. mecer: mezo, mezas, etc. zurcir: zurza, zurzo, etc.

b	1) Verbs ending -gar: "g" changes to "gu" before "e," "i."	1) amargar: amargue, amarguen, etc.
	2) Verbs ending -guar: "gu" changes to "gü" before "e," "i."	2) averiguar: averigüe, averigüemos, etc.
	3) The group "gu" changes to "g" before "a," "o."	3) distinguir: distingo, distingamos, etc.
c	"g" changes to "j" before "a," "o."	recoger: recojo; recojas, etc.
d	"qu" changes to "c" before "a," "o."	delinquir: delinco; delinca, etc.
	"c" changes to "qu" before "e," "i."	embarcar: embarque, embarquemos, etc.
e	verbs ending -aer, -eer, -uir: tonic "i" of verb ending changes to "y" in the gerund and in the third person of tenses "D" and "G."	caer: cayó; cayera or cayese; cayendo. construir: construyó; construyera or construyese; construyendo. leer: leyó; leyera or leyese; leyendo.

ABBREVIATIONS USED IN PART I

a.	adjective.
abbr.	abbreviation.
adv.	adverb.
(aer.)	aeronautics.
(agr.)	agriculture.
(alg.)	algebra.
(Am.)	Spanish America(n).
(anat.)	anatomy.
(app.)	applied.
(arch.)	architecture.
(Arg.)	Argentina.
(arith.)	arithmetic.
art.	article.
(artil.)	artillery.
(astr.)	astronomy; astrology.
aug.	augmentative.
(bib.)	Biblical.
(biol.)	biology.
(bot.)	botany.
(carp.)	carpentry.
(chem.)	chemistry.
(coll.)	colloquial.
(collect.)	collectively.
(com.)	commerce.
comp.	comparative.
conj.	conjunction.
(contempt.)	contemptuous.
contr.	contraction.
(cook.)	cooking.
defect.	defective.
dim.	diminutive.
(eccl.)	ecclesiastic.
(econ.)	economics.
(elec.)	electricity.
(eng.)	engineering.
(esp.)	especially.
f.	feminine; feminine noun.
(fam.)	familiar.
(fig.)	figurative(ly).
(fort.)	fortifications.
fut.	future.
(gen.)	generally.
(geog.)	geography.
(geol.)	geology.
(geom.)	geometry.
ger.	gerund.
(gram.)	grammar.
(herald.)	heraldry.
(hist.)	history.
(hort.)	horticulture.
(humor.)	humorous.
(hydraul.)	hydraulics.
(ichth.)	ichthyology.
imp.	imperfect.
imper.	imperative.
impers.	impersonal.
ind.	indicative.
inf.	infinitive.
interj.	interjection.
interrog.	interrogative.
(jewel.)	jewelry.
(lit.)	literally.
m.	masculine; masculine noun.
(mason.)	masonry.
(math.)	mathematics.
(mech.)	mechanics.
(med.)	medicine.
(metal.)	metallurgy.
(Mex.)	Mexico.
mf.	noun (not inflected to show gender).
(mil.)	military.
(min.)	mining, mineralogy.
(mus.)	music.
n.	noun (inflected, usually -o to -a, to show gender).
(naut.)	nautical.
(neol.)	neologism.
neut.	neuter.
nom.	nominative case.
(opt.)	optics.
(ornith.)	ornithology.
(pej.)	pejorative.
pers.	person; personal.
(pert.)	pertaining (to).
(pharm.)	pharmaceutical.
(philos.)	philosophy.
(phot.)	photography.
(phys.)	physics.
(physiol.)	physiology.
pl.	plural.
(poet.)	poetry.
(pol.)	politics.
poss.	possessive.
pp.	past participle.
prep.	preposition.
pret.	preterit.
(print.)	printing.
pron.	pronoun.
(ref.)	referring (to).
refl.	reflexive.
rel.	relative (pronoun).
(rhet.)	rhetoric.
(RR.)	railroad.
(S.A.)	South America(n).
(sew.)	sewing.
sing.	singular.
(Sp.)	Spain, Spanish.
subj.	subject; subjunctive.
super.	superlative.
(surg.)	surgery.
(tech.)	technology.
(tel.)	telegraph(y); telephone.
(theat.)	theater.
V.	see.
va.	auxiliary verb.
vai.	irregular auxiliary verb.
vi.	intransitive verb.
vii.	irregular intransitive verb.
vr.	reflexive verb.
vri.	irregular reflexive verb.
vt.	transitive verb.
vti.	irregular transitive verb.
(vulg.)	vulgar, low.
(zool.)	zoology.

TABLES OF WEIGHTS
AND MEASURES

Metric Weights
(Unidades Métricas de Peso)
1 gramo (g.) = .03527 ounces (oz.)
1 kilogramo (kg.) = 1.000 gramos = 2.2046 pounds (lb.)
1 quintal métrico = 100 kg. = 220.55 pounds
1 tonelada métrica = 10 quintales = 2,205 pounds

Old Weights Still Encountered
(Unidades antiguas todavía en uso)
1 libra = 16 onzas = 0,460 kg. = 1.014 lb.
1 arroba = 25 libras = 11,51 kg. = 25.-36 lb.
1 quintal = 4 arrobas = 46,09 kg. = 101.43 lb.
1 tonelada = 20 quintales = 922 kg. = 2,028 lb.

Metric Liquid and Dry Measures
(Unidades métricas de capacidad)
1 litro (l.) = 1 decímetro cúbico (dm.) = .908 qt. U.S. dry measure = 1.0567 qt. U.S. liquid measure
1 decálitro (dl.) = 10 litros = 9.08 U.S. qt. dry measure = 2.64 gal. U.S. liquid measure = 2.837 bushels
1 hectólitro (hl.) = 100 l. = 26.417 gal.
1 kilólitro (kl.) = 1.000 l. = 28.337 bushels = 264.17 gal.

Old Measures Still Encountered
(Unidades antiguas todavía en uso)
1 cuartillo = 0,005 l. = 1.05 qt.
1 celemín = 4 cuartillos

Metric Linear Measures
(Unidades métricas de longitud)
1 milímetro (mm.) = .039 inches (in.)
1 centímetro (cm.) = 10 mm. = .393 inches
1 decímetro (dm.) = 10 cm. = 3.94 inches
1 metro (m.) = 10 dm. = 3.28 feet (ft.)
1 kilómetro (km.) = 1,000 m. = 3,280 feet, approx. 5/8 of a mile

Old Measures Still Encountered
(Unidades antiguas todavía en uso)
1 pulgada = 2,3 cm. = .92 inches
1 pie = 12 pulgadas
1 vara = 3 pies
1 legua = 6,666 varas = 5,572 km.

Metric Square Measures   (Unidades métricas de superficie)
1 centiárea = 1 metro cuadrado (m.²) = 1.196 square yards (sq. yd.)
1 área = 100 metros cuadrados = 119.6 square yards
1 hectárea = 1.000 metros cuadrados = 2.471 acres

THERMOMETER

0 centigrade (freezing point) = 32 Fahrenheit
100 centigrade (boiling point) = 212 Fahrenheit

To reduce degrees centigrade to degrees Fahrenheit multiply by 9/5 and add 32.

A

a, *prep.* to; in; at; according to; by; for; of; on; toward.—*a beneficio de,* for the benefit of.—*a caballo,* on horseback.—*a la derecha,* at the right.—*a máquina,* by machine. —*a mi gusto,* according to my taste. —*a oscuras,* in the dark.—*a tiempo,* on time.—*al anochecer,* toward the evening.—*di el libro a Pedro,* I gave the book to Peter.

abacería, *f.* grocery.—**abacero,** *n* grocer.

abad, *m.* abbot.—**abadía,** *f.* abbey.

abajo, *adv.* under, underneath, below, down.—*a. de,* beneath.—*boca a.,* face down.—*de arriba a a.,* from top to bottom.—*venirse a.,* to fall.

abalanzar, *vti.* [a] to balance; to hurl, impel.—*vri.* to rush on or upon; to venture on.

abalorio, *m.* glass bead; bead work.

abandonado, *a.* negligent; slovenly.— **abandonar,** *vt.* to abandon, desert; to give up.—*vi.* to despair; to give oneself up to; to be neglectful.— **abandono,** *m.* abandon; neglect; despondency.

abanicar, *vti.* [d] to fan.—**abanico,** *m.* fan.

abaratar, *vt.* to cheapen; to abate.— *vr.* to fall in price.

abarcar, [d] *vti.* to clasp, embrace, contain; to comprise.

abarrotar, *vt.* to stow; to overstock. —**abarrotero,** *n.* (Am.) retail grocer.—**abarrotes,** *m. pl.* (Am.) groceries; goods; foodstuffs.

abastecedor, *n.* caterer, provider, purveyor, supplier.—**abastecer,** *vti.* [3] to purvey; to supply.—**abastecimiento,** *m.* providing; supply; provisions, supplies.—**abasto,** *m.* supply of provisions; (fig.) abundance.—*dar a.,* to be sufficient (for); to provide, furnish.

abatido, *a.* dejected, crestfallen; abject; lowered.—**abatimiento,** *m.* depression, low spirits.—**abatir,** *vt.* to throw down; to knock (bring, shoot) down; to humble, abase; to discourage; to lower, strike (a flag). —*vr.* to become disheartened; to swoop down.

abdicación, *f.* abdication.—**abdicar,** *vti.* [d] to abdicate.

abdomen, *m.* abdomen.—**abdominal,** *a.* abdominal.

abducción, *f.* (logic & anat.) abduction.

abecé, *m.* a-b-c, alphabet; rudiments.—**abecedario,** *m.* alphabet; primer; rudiments.

abedul, *m.* birch.

abeja, *f.* bee.—**abejón,** *m.* drone.— **abejorro,** *m.* bumblebee.

aberración, *f.* aberration; error; mania.

abertura, *f.* aperture, opening; cleft, crevice, slit; gap.

abeto, *m.* spruce; fir; hemlock.

abierto, *pp.* of ABRIR.—*a.* open, clear; frank, sincere; full-blown.

abigarrado, *a.* variegated, motley.

abismado, *a.* dejected; overwhelmed; absorbed in meditation.—**abismal,** *a.* abysmal.—**abismar,** *vt.* to depress; to overwhelm.—*vr.* to be immersed (in thought, grief, etc.).— **abismo,** *m.* abyss; chasm; precipice.

abjuración, *f.* abjuration.—**abjurar,** *vt.* to abjure, forswear, retract under oath.

ablandamiento, *m.* softening, mollification.—**ablandar,** *vt.* & *vi.* to soften; to loosen; to mitigate.—*vr.* to soften, relent, mellow.

abobado, *a.* silly, stultified; openmouthed.

abochornar, *vt.* to overheat; to shame; to embarrass.—*vr.* to blush; to become embarrassed.

abofetear, *vt.* to slap.

abogacía, *f.* law, legal profession.— **abogado,** *n.* lawyer, advocate; mediator.—**abogar,** *vii.* [b] to advocate, plead (as a lawyer); to intercede.

abolengo, *m.* ancestry, lineage; inheritance.

abolición, *f.* abolition, extinction.— **abolir,** *vti.* [50] to abolish; to revoke, repeal.

abolladura, *f.* denting; embossing; bump; bulge.—**abollar,** *vt.* to emboss; to dent; to batter; to crumple.

abominable, *a.* abominable, detestable.—**abominación,** *f.* abomination, execration.—**abominar,** *vt.* to abominate, abhor.

abonado, *n.* subscriber; commuter.— *a.* reliable, apt, inclined; (agr.) rich (soil).—**abonar,** *vt.* (com.) to credit with; to pay; to guarantee, indorse, answer for; (agr.) to manure.— *vr.* to subscribe; to buy a season or commutation ticket.—**abono,** *m.* surety; assurance; payment; subscription; indorsement; fertilizer; installment.

abordaje, *m.* the act of boarding a ship.—**abordar,** *vt.* (naut.) to ram, collide with, board (a ship); to broach (a subject), enter upon (a matter); to accost, approach (a person).

aborrecer, vti. [3] to hate, abhor.—
aborrecible, a. hateful; abhorrent.
—**aborrecimiento,** m. abhorrence,
hatred.

abortar, vi. to miscarry, abort; to
fail; (med.) to have a miscarriage;
to have an abortion.—**abortivo,** a.
abortive, producing abortion.—
aborto, m. miscarriage, abortion;
monstrosity.

abotagarse, abotargarse, vri. [b] to
swell; to bloat.

abotonar, vt. to button.—vi. to bud.
—vr. to button up.

abrasador, a. burning, extremely hot.
—**abrasar,** vt. to burn; to parch,
scorch; to dry up.—vr. (en or de)
to burn (with); to boil (with) (any
violent passion); to burn up, down.

abrasivo, m. & a. abrasive.

abrazadera, f. clasp, clamp, cleat.—
abrazar, vti. [a] to embrace, hug;
to clamp, cleat; to contain; to
adopt (a religion, etc.).—**abrazo,** m.
hug, embrace.

abrelatas, m. sing. can opener.

abreviación, f. abbreviation; abridgment; shortening; hastening.—**abreviar,** vt. to hasten; to abridge, abbreviate.—**abreviatura,** f. abbreviation (of word); contraction.—en a.,
in abbreviation.

abridor, m. opener; nectarine.—a. de
latas, can opener.

abrigar, vti. [b] to shelter, shield; to
cover; to keep warm; to cherish.—
vri. to take shelter; to cover oneself; to put on a wrap.—**abrigo,** m.
overcoat; shelter, protection; wrap;
aid, support; cover.—al a. de,
sheltered from, shielded by.

abril, m. April.

abrillantar, vt. to polish, shine; to
brighten; to add splendor.

abrir, vti. [49] to open, unlock, unfasten, uncover; to cut open; to
dig.—a. paso, to make way, to clear
the way.—vii. to open; to clear (of
weather).—vri. to open, expand; to
crack.

abrochar, vt. to clasp, button, fasten.

abrojo, m. (bot.) thistle, thorn,
prickle.—pl. hidden reefs.

abrumador, a. overwhelming, crushing; wearisome.—**abrumar,** vt. to
crush, overwhelm, oppress; to annoy.—vr. to become foggy.

abrupto, a. abrupt; craggy; rugged.

absceso, m. abscess.

absolución, f. absolution; pardon,
acquittal.

absolutismo, m. despotism, absolut-
ism.—**absoluto,** a. absolute, unconditional; despotic.—en a., unquali-
fiedly; absolutely; (in negative

sentences) at all.—lo a., the absolute.

absolutorio, a. absolutory, absolving.
—**absolver,** vti. [47-49] to absolve;
to acquit.

absorber, vti. [49] to absorb; to
imbibe.—**absorción,** f. absorption.—
absorto, pp. i. of ABSORBER.—a.
amazed; absorbed in thought.

abstemio, a. abstemious.—n. teetotaler.

abstenerse, vri. [42] to abstain, forbear.—**abstinencia,** f. abstinence,
temperance; fasting.

abstracción, f. abstraction; concentration.—**abstracto,** pp. i. de ABS-
TRAER.—a. & m. abstract.—**abstraer,**
vti. [43-49] to abstract.—**abstraído,**
a. retired; absent-minded.

absuelto, pp. of ABSOLVER.—a. acquit-
ted, absolved.

absurdo, a. absurd, nonsensical.—m.
absurdity, nonsense.

abuchear, vt. to boo, hoot.—**abucheo,**
m. booing, hooting.

abuela, f. grandmother.—**abuelo,** m.
grandfather; elderly man; ancestor.

abultar, vt. to bulge.—vi. to be bulky
or large.

abundamiento, m. abundance.—a
mayor a., furthermore; with greater
reason.—**abundancia,** f. abundance,
plenty.—**abundante,** a. abundant,
plentiful, teeming.—**abundar,** vi. to
abound.

aburrido, a. bored; tiresome, boresome.—**aburrimiento,** m. weariness,
annoyance.—**aburrir,** vt. to vex; to
tire, bore.—vr. to grow tired; to be
bored.

abusar, vi. to exceed, go too far; to
take undue advantage.—a. de, to
abuse, use wrongly; to betray (a
confidence); to take undue advantage of; to impose upon.—**abusivo,**
a. abusive.—**abuso,** m. misuse,
abuse.

abyección, f. abjection, abjectness;
degradation.—**abyecto,** a. abject,
servile, slavish.

acá, adv. here; hither.—¿de cuándo
a.? since when?—por a., here, here-
abouts; this way.

acabado, a. perfect, faultless; wasted;
dilapidated.—m. (art) finish.— **aca-
bamiento,** m. completion, end;
physical decline.—**acabar,** vt. & vi.
to finish; to complete; to end.—
a. con, to finish, destroy.—a. de
(foll. by inf.), to have just (foll. by
pp.).—a. por, to end by, to . . .
finally.—vr. to be finished; to end,
be over; to grow feeble or wasted;
acabársele a uno (el dinero, la

paciencia, etc.) to run out of (money, patience, etc.).

academia, *f.* academy; literary, scientific or artistic society; university. —**académico,** *a. & n.* academic; academician.

acaecer, *vii.* [3-50] to happen, come to pass.—**acaecimiento,** *m.* event.

acalorado, *a.* heated, excited, angry. —*n.* (fig.) hothead.—**acaloramiento,** *m.* ardor, heat, excitement.—**acalorar,** *vt.* to heat, inflame, excite. —*vr.* to grow warm; to get overheated; to get excited.

acallar, *vt.* to quiet, hush; to mitigate.

acampar, *vt., vi. & vr.* to encamp.

acanalado, *a.* striated, fluted, corrugated, grooved.—**acanalar,** *vt.* to make a channel in; to flute, corrugate, groove.

acantilado, *m.* cliff; escarpment. *a.* steep, sheer.

acantonar, *vt.* to quarter (troops).

acaparador, *n.* monopolizer.—**acaparar,** *vt.* to monopolize; to corner, control (the market); to buy up, hoard.

acariciar, *vt.* to fondle, caress; to cherish.

acarrear, *vt.* to carry, cart, transport.—*vr.* to bring upon oneself.—**acarreo,** *m.* carrying, transportation; cartage.

acaso, *m.* chance, accident.—*adv.* perhaps; by chance, by accident.—*por si a.,* just in case.

acatamiento, *m.* obeisance, respect, homage.—**acatar,** *vt.* to obey; to accept; to respect.

acatarrarse, *vr.* to catch cold

acaudalado, *a.* rich, opulent.

acaudillar, *vt.* to command, lead.

acceder, *vi.* to accede, agree, consent. —**accesible,** *a.* accessible, approachable; attainable.—**acceso,** *m.* access; entrance; admittance; (med.) access, fit, attack.—**accesorio,** *a.* accessory; secondary.—*pl.* spare parts; accessories.

accidentado, *a.* seized with a fit; rugged, uneven (ground).—**accidentarse,** *vr.* to have a fit or stroke. —**accidente,** *m.* accident; chance; sudden fit; (gram.) inflection.—*por a.,* accidentally, by chance.

acción, *f.* action; feat; lawsuit; battle; (lit.) plot; (com.) stock, share. —*a. de gracias,* thanksgiving.—**accionar,** *vi.* to gesticulate.—*vt.* (mech.) to operate, move.—**accionista,** *mf.* stockholder, shareholder.

acechanza, *f.* waylaying; snare, trap. —**acechar,** *vt.* to lie in ambush for; to spy on.—**acecho,** *m.* waylaying, lying in ambush.—*al a.* or *en a.,* in wait, in ambush.

acedía, *f.* acidity, heartburn, sourness; roughness; asperity of address.

aceitar, *vt.* to oil; to rub with oil. —**aceite,** *m.* oil; essential oil.—*a. de ricino,* castor oil.—**aceitera,** *f.* oil cruet; oil can.—**aceitoso,** *a.* oily. —**aceituna,** *f.* olive.—**aceitunado,** *a.* olive-colored.

aceleración, *f.* acceleration; haste. —**acelerador,** *a.* accelerating.—*m.* accelerator.—**acelerar,** *vt.* to accelerate; to hasten, hurry, rush. —*vr.* to move fast; to make haste.

acémila, *f.* pack animal.

acendrado, *a.* purified, refined; unspotted, stainless.—**acendrar,** *vt.* to purify or refine; to free from stain or blemish.

acento, *m.* accent, stress; way of speaking; written accent.—**acentuación,** *f.* accentuation.—**acentuar,** *vt.* to accentuate; to emphasize; to write accents.

aceptable, *a.* acceptable, admissible. —**aceptación,** *f.* acceptation; acceptance, approval, applause.—**aceptar,** *vt.* to accept, admit; (com.) to honor.

acera, *f.* sidewalk; row of houses on either side of a street.

acerado, *a.* steely; strong; hard; sharp.

acerbo, *a.* tart; harsh, cruel; poignant.

acerca de, *prep.* about, with regard to.—**acercamiento,** *m.* approximation, approach, rapprochement. —**acercar,** *vti.* [d] to bring or place near or nearer.—*vri.* to draw near, come, approach.

acerico, *m.* pincushion.

acero, *m.* steel; sword; courage.

acérrimo, *a. super.* very strong (taste, odor); very harsh; very vigorous; very stanch or stalwart.

acertado, *a.* fit, proper; wise.—**acertar,** *vti.* [1] to hit the mark; to do the right thing; to guess, be right. —*vii.* to guess right.—*a. con,* to find, come upon.—**acertijo,** *m.* riddle.

aciago, *a.* unfortunate, sad; fateful.

acíbar, *m.* aloes; bitterness; displeasure.

acicalar, *vt.* to embellish.—*vr.* to dress in style; (coll.) to doll up.

acicate, *m.* inducement; goad.

acidez, *f.* acidity, tartness.—**ácido,** *m.* acid.—*a.* acid; sour; harsh.

acierto, *m.* good judgment; accuracy; rightness; skill; good aim; good guess.

aclamación, *f.* acclamation.—**aclamar,** *vt.* to shout, applaud, acclaim.

aclaración, *f.* explanation.—**aclarar,** *vt.* to make clear; to explain; to thin; to rinse.—*vi.* to clear up; to recover brightness.

aclimatar, *vt.* to acclimatize.—*vr.* to get acclimatized.

acobardar, *vt.* to intimidate, frighten. —*vr.* to become frightened, intimidated.

acogedor, *a.* welcoming, kindly.— **acoger,** *vti.* [c] to receive; (fig.) to harbor, shelter.—*vri.* to take refuge. —**acogida,** *f.*, **acogimiento,** *m.* reception; place of meeting; refuge; shelter.—*tener buena (mala) a.,* to be well (unfavorably) received.

acogotar, *vt.* to grab by the neck; to strangle.

acojinar, *vt.* to quilt; (mech.) to cushion.

acolchado, *a.* quilted.—*m.* (hydraul. eng.) mattress.—**acolchar, acolchonar,** *vt.* to quilt.

acólito, *m.* altar boy, acolyte; assistant.

acometedor, *n.* aggressor; enterprising person.—*a.* aggressive; enterprising.—**acometer,** *vt.* to attack, rush on, (coll.) go for; to undertake. —**acometida,** *f.,* **acometimiento,** *m.* attack, assault; branch or outlet (in a sewer).

acomodado, *a.* convenient, fit; wealthy; fond of comfort; reasonable.—**acomodador,** *n.* usher (*f.* usherette) in a theater.—**acomodar,** *vt.* to arrange; to accommodate; to set to rights; to place; to reconcile; to furnish, supply; to take in, lodge.—*vi.* to fit; to suit.—*vr.* to condescend; to adapt oneself; to put up with; to settle.—**acomodaticio,** *a.* compliant, accommodating.—**acomodo,** *m.* employment, situation; arrangement; lodgings.

acompañamiento, *m.* accompaniment; retinue; attendance.—**acompañante,** *mf.* chaperon; companion; (mus.) accompanist.—*a.* accompanying.— **acompañar,** *vt.* to accompany; to attend, escort; to enclose (in letters).

acompasado, *a.* measured; rhythmical; slow.

acondicionado, *a.* of a (good, bad) disposition; in (good, bad) condition; of (good, bad) qualit·.—*aire a.,* air-conditioned.—**acondicionar.** *vt.* to condition; to prepare, arrange.

acongojar, *vt.* to afflict, grieve.—*vr.* to become anguished; to grieve.

aconsejable, *a.* advisable.—**aconsejar,** *vt.* to advise, counsel.—*vr.* **(con) to** consult (with).

acontecer, *vii.* [3-50] to happen, come about.—**acontecimiento,** *m.* event, happening.

acopio, *m.* gathering; storing; assortment; collection; supply; stock.

acoplamiento, *m.* coupling; joint; scarfing.—**acoplar,** *vt.* to couple, join, connect; to hitch, yoke; to scarf (timber); to reconcile; to pair; to mate (animals).—*vr.* to settle a difference, come to an agreement; to mate (of animals).

acoquinar, *vt.* to cow, intimidate. —*vr.* to be cowed.

acorazado, *m.* armored ship, ironclad. —*a.* ironclad; (elec.) shell.—**acorazar,** *vti.* [a] to armor.

acordar, *vti.* [12] to resolve; to agree upon; to remind; to tune, harmonize.—*vii.* to agree.—*vri.* (de) to remember, recollect.—*si mal no me acuerdo,* if I remember rightly. —**acorde,** *a.* agreed; in tune; in accord.—*m.* chord; harmony of sounds and colors.—**acordeón,** *m.* accordion.

acordonar, *vt.* to lace; to mill (a coin); to cord; to cordon or rope off.

acorralar, *vt.* to corral; to surround; to corner.

acortar, *vt.* to shorten, lessen, reduce; to obstruct.—*a. la marcha,* to slow down.—*vr.* to shrivel, contract; to be bashful; to fall back.

acosamiento, **acoso,** *m.* relentless persecution.—**acosar,** *vt.* to pursue relentlessly; to vex, harass.

acostado, *a.* reclining, lying down; in bed.—**acostar,** *vti.* [12] to lay down; to put to bed.—*vri.* to lie down; to go to bed.

acostumbrado, *a.* habitual, customary; used to, accustomed.—**acostumbrar,** *vt.* to accustom, train.— *vi.* to be accustomed, to be in the habit of.—*vr.* to get used to, become accustomed to.

acotación, *f.* stage direction (in a play); marginal note; elevation marked on a map.—**acotamiento,** *m.* enclosure, reservation; boundary mark.—**acotar,** *vt.* to set boundary marks on; to mark out; to annotate; to select.

acre, *a.* sour; acrimonious; tart; mordant.—*m.* acre (square measure).

acrecentamiento, *m.* increase.—**acrecentar,** *vti.* [1] to increase; to improve.

acreditado, *a.* reputable.—**acreditar,** *vt.* to assure, affirm; to verify, prove; (com.) to recommend, an-

swer for, guarantee; to accredit, authorize.—*vr.* to establish one's reputation.

acreedor, *a.* meritorious, deserving. —*n.* creditor.—*a. hipotecario,* mortgagee.

acribillar, *vt.* to perforate; to riddle; to cover with wounds.

acrisolado, *a.* honest, virtuous, upright.

acrobacia, *f.* stunt.—**acróbata,** *mf.* acrobat.

acta, *f.* document; minutes; certificate.—*levantar a.,* to draw up the minutes; to note, set down.

actitud, *f.* attitude; position, posture.

activar, *vt.* to make active; to expedite, hasten.—**actividad,** *f.* activity, energy.—*en a.,* in operation. —**activo,** *a.* active.—*m.* (com.) assets.

acto, *m.* act, action, deed; public function.—*a. seguido,* immediately after.—*en el a.,* at once.—**actor,** *m.* player, actor.—*parte actora,* plaintiff.—**actriz,** *f.* actress.—**actuación,** *f.* actuation; action; part played. —*pl.* (law) proceedings.

actual, *a.* present, of the present time.—**actualidad,** *f.* present time. —*en la a.,* nowadays.—*pl.* current affairs; newsreel.

actuar, *vi.* to act; to perform judicial acts.—*vt.* to put in action, actuate.

actuario, *n.* actuary.

acuarela, *f.* water color (painting).

acuario, *m.* aquarium.

acuartelamiento, *m.* quartering or billeting (of troops); quarters.— **acuartelar,** *vt.* to quarter, billet.

acuático, *a.* aquatic.—**acuatizar,** *vii.* [a] (aer.) to alight on the water.

acuchillar, *vt.* to cut, hack; to slash, cut open; to knife.

acudir, *vi.* to go; to come; to attend; to respond (to a call); to go or come to the rescue; to resort; to have recourse.

acueducto, *m.* aqueduct; water-supply line.

acuerdo, *m.* resolution; determination; opinion; report; advice; remembrance; accord; agreement. convention, pact; harmony.—*de a.,* in agreement; of the same opinion; in accordance.

acumulación, *f.* accumulation; gathering.—**acumulador,** *n.* accumulator. —*m.* battery.—**acumular,** *vt.* to accumulate, gather, pile up.—**acumulativo,** *a.* cumulative; joint.

acuñación, *f.* coining, minting; wedging.—**acuñar,** *vt.* to coin, mint; to wedge.

acuoso, *a.* watery.

acurrucarse, *vri.* [d] to huddle up.

acusación, *f.* accusation.—**acusado,** *n. & a.* defendant, accused.—**acusador,** *n.* acuser; prosecutor.—**acusar,** *vt.* to accuse; to prosecute; to indict; to acknowledge (receipt).—*vr.* (de) to confess (to).—**acuse,** *m.* acknowledgment (of receipt).

acústica, *f.* acoustics.

achacar, *vti.* [d] to impute.—**achacoso,** *a.* sickly, ailing.—**achaque,** *m.* indisposition; minor chronic ailment; excuse, pretext; motive; subject, matter.

achatar, *vt.* to flatten, squash.

achicar, *vti.* [d] to diminish, lessen; to shorten; to humble, belittle; to bail, drain.—*vri.* to humble oneself; to be cowed.

achicharrar, *vt. & vr.* to burn to a crisp.

adagio, *m.* adagio; proverb, maxim.

adán, *m.* (fig.) slovenly man.

adaptabilidad, *f.* versatility.—**adaptable,** *a.* adaptable; versatile.—**adaptación,** *f.* adaptation.—**adaptar,** *vt.* to adapt, fit.—*vr.* to adapt oneself.

adecuación, *f.* fitness; adequateness. —**adecuado,** *a.* adequate, suitable, proper.—**adecuar,** *vt.* to fit; to adapt.

adefesio, *m.* (coll.) nonsense, absurdity; blunder; queer person; ridiculous attire.

adelantado, *a.* anticipated; advanced; far ahead; proficient; precocious; bold, forward; (of a clock) fast; early (fruits, plants).—*por a.,* in advance.—**adelantamiento,** *m.* advance; progress; improvement; increase; anticipation; promotion.— **adelantar,** *vt. & vi.* to progress, advance; to grow; to keep on; to anticipate; to pay beforehand; to improve; to go fast; (of a clock) to gain.—*vr.* to take the lead; to come forward.—*a. a,* to surpass, outdo.—**adelante,** *adv.* ahead; farther on; forward.—*de a.,* ahead, in the front; forward, head (as a.).—*de aquí en a., de hoy en a.,* or *en a.,* henceforth, from now on, in the future.—*llevar a.,* to go ahead with, carry on.—*más a.,* farther on. —*salir a.,* to come through, come out well or ahead.—*interj.* forward! go on!—**adelanto,** *m.* advance, progress; improvement; (com.) advance payment.

adelfa, *f.* rosebay.

adelgazamiento, *m.* slimming; thinness.—**adelgazar,** *vti.* [a] to make slender; to thin out; to lessen.—*vri.* to become thin or slim.

ademán, *m.* gesture; attitude.—*pl.* manners.

además, *adv.* moreover, furthermore, besides.—*a. de,* besides.

adentro, *adv.* within, inside.—*mar a.,* out to sea.—*tierra a.,* inland.—*interj.* come in! let's go in!—*m. pl.* innermost thoughts.

adepto, *a.* adept; initiated.—*n.* follower, partisan.

aderezamiento, *m.* embellishment; dressing.—**aderezar,** *vti.* [a] to dress, embellish, adorn; to prepare; to cook, season; to size (cloth).—**aderezo,** *m.* dressing; adorning; arrangements, preparation; finery; set of jewelry; trappings.

adeudado, *a.* indebted; in debt.—**adeudar,** *vt.* to owe; (com.) to be subject to duty; to charge, debit.—*vr.* to run into debt.

adherencia, *f.* adhesion; adherence.—**adherir,** *vti.* [39] & *vri.* to adhere; to stick.—**adhesión,** *f.* adhesion; attachment; following.—**adhesivo,** *a.* adhesive.

adición, *f.* addition; remark or note added to a text.—**adicional,** *a.* additional.—**adicionar,** *vt.* to add to; to extend.

adicto, *n.* & *a.* follower; addict; addicted, devoted.

adiestramiento, *m.* training; practice; drill.—**adiestrar,** *vt.* to instruct, train.—*vr.* to practice, train.

adinerado, *a.* rich, wealthy.

¡adiós!, *interj.* good-bye!—*m.* good-bye, farewell.

aditamento, *m.* addition, adjunct.

adivinación, *f.* divination, foretelling.—**adivinanza,** *f.* riddle.—**adivinar,** *vt.* to guess; to divine; to solve (a riddle).—**adivino,** *n.* diviner; fortuneteller; soothsayer.

adjetivo, *n.* & *a.* adjective.

adjuntar, *vt.* to enclose, send enclosed or with something else.—**adjunto,** *a.* adjoined; enclosed, attached; adjunct.—*n.* assistant.

administración, *f.* administration, management; board (of directors); central office.—*a. de correos,* post-office station.—**administrador,** *n.* administrator; manager; director; trustee.—*a. de aduanas,* collector of customs.—*a. de correos,* postmaster.—**administrar,** *vt.* to administer, govern.—**administrativo,** *a.* administrative.

admirable, *a.* admirable, excellent.—**admiración,** *f.* admiration; wonder.—*punto de a.,* exclamation point (!).—**admirador,** *n.* admirer.—**admirar,** *vt.* to admire.—*vr.* (de) to be surprised, amazed at.

admisible, *a.* admissible.—**admisión,** *f.* admission, acceptance.—**admitir,** *vt.* to receive; to admit; to let in; to accept.

adobar, *vt.* to dress, prepare or cook (food); to pickle (meat, fish); to tan (hides).

adobo, *m.* dressing for seasoning or pickling (meat, fish); mending, repairing.

adocenado, *a.* common, ordinary, vulgar.

adoctrinar, *vt.* to instruct, indoctrinate.

adolecer, *vii.* [3] (de) (fig.) to suffer from.

adolescencia, *f.* adolescence; teen-age.—**adolescente,** *mf.* & *a.* adolescent; teen-age(r).

adonde, *adv.* (interr. **¿adónde?**) where; (where to?).—**adondequiera,** *adv.* wherever.

adopción, *f.* adoption.—**adoptar,** *vt.* to adopt; to embrace (an opinion).—**adoptivo,** *a.* adoptive, adopted.

adoquín, *m.* cobblestone; (coll.) blockhead.—**adoquinado,** *m.* & *a.* pavement; paved.—**adoquinar,** *vt.* to pave.

adorable, *a.* adorable.—**adoración,** *f.* adoration, worship.—**adorar,** *vt.* to adore, worship.

adormecedor, *a.* soporific.—**adormecer,** *vti.* [3] to cause drowsiness or sleep; to lull to sleep; to calm.—*vri.* to fall asleep; to grow numb.—**adormecimiento,** *m.* drowsiness; sleepiness; numbness.—**adormilado,** *a.* drowsy.

adornar, *vt.* to adorn, embellish, ornament; to furnish, garnish.—**adorno,** *m.* adornment, ornament; trimming.

adquirir, *vti.* [2] to acquire, obtain, get.—**adquisición,** *f.* acquisition; purchase.—**adquisitivo,** *a.*—*poder a.,* purchasing power.

adrede, *adv.* purposely, intentionally.

adrenalina, *f.* adrenaline.

adscribir, *vti.* [49] to inscribe; to add as an employee.—**adscrito,** *pp.* of ADSCRIBIR.—*a.* written after.

aduana, *f.* custom house.—**aduanero,** *n.* custom house officer; revenue officer.—*a.* custom house, customs.

adueñarse, *vr.* to take possession.

adulación, *f.* flattery, adulation.—**adulador,** *n.* flatterer, adulator.—**adular,** *vt.* & *vi.* to flatter, adulate.—**adulón,** *n.* & *a.* toady, cringer; cringing.

adulteración, *f.* adulteration.—**adulterar,** *vt.* to adulterate; to corrupt; to sophisticate; to tamper with.

—**adulterio**, *m.* adultery.—**adúltero**, *n.* adulterer, adulteress.

adulto, *n.* & *a.* adult.

adusto, *a.* austere, stern; sullen.

advenedizo, *n.* newcomer; outsider; upstart.—*a.* strange; extraneous; newly arrived.—**advenimiento**, *m.* advent, coming.

adventicio, *a.* accidental.

adverbial, *a.* adverbial.—**adverbio**, *m.* adverb.

adversario, *n.* opponent, adversary; enemy.—**adversidad**, *f.* adversity, misfortune.—**adverso**, *a.* adverse; unfavorable; untoward.

advertencia, *f.* advice; warning; notice; foreword.—**advertido**, *a.* forewarned; wise.—**advertir**, *vti.* [39] to take notice of; to advise; to give notice or warning; to point out.

adyacente, *a.* adjacent.

aéreo, *a.* aerial; airy; aeronautical; air.—*por correo a.*, by air mail.—*fuerza a.*, air force.—**aerodinámica**, *f.* aerodynamics.—*a.* streamline(d). —**aeródromo**, *m.* military airport.—**aeromoza**, *f.* (airplane) stewardess. —**aeronauta**, *mf.* aeronaut.—**aeronáutica**, *f.* aeronautics.—**aeronave**, *f.* airship, dirigible.—**aeroplano**, *m.* airplane, aircraft.—**aeropuerto**, *m.* airport.

afabilidad, *f.* affability, friendliness.—**afable**, *a.* affable, kind, friendly.

afamado, *a.* celebrated, noted, famous.

afán, *m.* anxiety, solicitude, eagerness. —**afanarse**, *vr.* to act or work eagerly or anxiously; to toil.—**afanoso**, *a.* solicitous; laborious, painstaking; hard, difficult.

afear, *vt.* to deform, deface; to make ugly or faulty; to impair; to decry, censure.

afectación, *f.* sophistication; affectation.—**afectado**, *a.* affected; moved; sophisticated; stuffy.—**afectar**, *vt.* to affect, concern; to move; to affect, feign, put on.—**afectividad**, *f.* affection.—**afectivo**, *a.* affective; easily moved.—**afecto**, *m.* affection, love, fondness.—*a.* affectionate; (a) fond (of), inclined (to).—**afectuoso**, *a.* affectionate.

afeitado, *m.* shave, shaving.—**afeitar**, *vt.* to shave.—*vr.* to shave (oneself).—**afeite**, *m.* rouge, cosmetic, paint; make-up.

afelpado, *a.* velvety.

afeminado, *a.* & *m.* effeminate (man). —**afeminamiento**, *m.*, **afeminación**, *f.* effeminacy.

aferrado, *a.* headstrong, obstinate.—**aferramiento**, *m.* grasping, seizing;

attachment; obstinacy.—**aferrar**, *vt.* to grasp, grip, seize; to moor, anchor.—*vr.* to persist obstinately, to cling.

afianzamiento, *m.* bail; support; fastening, securing.—**afianzar**, *vti.* [a] to prop up; to fasten, secure.—*vri.* to steady oneself, make oneself firm.

afición, *f.* fondness; taste, inclination; affection.—*tomar a. a*, to become fond of.—**aficionado**, *n.* & *a.* amateur; (sports) fan.—*a. a*, fond of. —**aficionar**, *vt.* to inspire affection, fondness or liking.—*vr.* **(a) to** fancy; to become fond of.

afijo, *a.* affixal.—*m.* affix.

afilado, *a.* sharp, keen.—**afilador**, *m.* sharpener.—**afilar**, *vt.* to sharpen, whet, grind.

afiliar, *vt.* (a) to affiliate (with).—*vr.* (a) to join, affiliate oneself (with).

afín, *a.* akin, kindred; related.

afinación, *f.* finishing touch, refining; tuning.—**afinador**, *n.* finisher; piano tuner; tuning key.—**afinamiento**, *m.* refinement.—**afinar**, *vt.* to perfect; to refine; to tune.—*vr.* to become polished.

afinidad, *f.* affinity; resemblance; analogy.

afirmación, *f.* affirmation.—**afirmar**, *vt.* to affirm, assert; to make fast, secure, fasten.—*vr.* to hold fast; to steady oneself or make oneself firm; to maintain firmly.—**afirmativo**, *a.* affirmative.

aflicción, *f.* affliction, sorrow, grief.—**aflictivo**, *a.* afflictive, distressing.—**afligir**, *vt.* [49-c] to afflict, grieve. —*vri.* to grieve, languish, become despondent.

aflojamiento, *m.* relaxation; loosening, slackening.—**aflojar**, *vt.* to loosen, slacken, relax, let loose.—*vi.* to grow weak; to abate.—*vr.* to weaken; to grow cool in fervor or zeal; to lose courage.

afluencia, *f.* flowing; influx.—**afluente**, *m.* affluent, tributary.—**afluir**, *vii.* [23-e] **(a)** to congregate, assemble (in); to flow (into).

afonía, *f.* laryngitis.

afortunado, *a.* lucky, fortunate.

afrenta, *f.* affront, outrage; disgrace. —**afrentar**, *vt.* to affront; to insult. —*vr.* to be ashamed; to blush.—**afrentoso**, *a.* ignominious.

africano, *n.* & *a.* African.

afrontar, *vt.* to confront; to face.

afta, *f.* (med.) thrush.

afuera, *adv.* out; outside; in public. —*interj.* out! clear the way! one side!—*f. pl.* suburbs, outskirts.

agachar, *vt.* to lower, bow down.— *vr.* to stoop, squat, cower.—*a. las orejas*, (coll.) to humble oneself; to bend the knee.

agalla, *f.* gill; tonsil.—*pl.* (coll.) courage.—*tener a.* (coll.) to have guts; (Am.) to be greedy; to be shrewd.

agarrada, *f.* tussle.—**agarradero**, *n.* holder, handle.—**agarrado**, *a.* (coll.) stingy, close-fisted.—**agarrar**, *vt.* to grasp, seize; (coll.) to obtain; to catch; to come upon.—*vr.* to clinch, grapple, hold on to.

agarrotar, *vt.* to tie firmly; to execute; to strangle.

agasajar, *vt.* to receive and treat kindly; to regale; to entertain.— **agasajo**, *m.* friendly treatment, consideration, regard.

agazaparse, *vr.* to hide by crouching or squatting; to huddle up.

agencia, *f.* agency; commission; agent's bureau, office.—**agenciar**, *vt.* to solicit, promote, negotiate.— **agente**, *m.* agent; broker; promoter; policeman.

ágil, *a.* nimble, fast, light.—**agilidad**, *f.* agility, nimbleness.

agitación, *f.* agitation; excitement.— **agitador**, *n.* agitator, rouser.—*a.* agitating, stirring.—**agitar**, *vt.* to agitate; to stir, shake up; to ruffle. —*vr.* to flutter; to become excited.

agobiar, *vt.* to weigh down; to overwhelm; to oppress.—*vr.* to bow; to crouch.—**agobio**, *m.* bending down; oppression, burden.

agonía, *f.* agony; death struggle; violent pain; anxious desire.—**agonizante**, *a. & mf.* dying; dying person.—**agonizar**, *vii.* [a] to be dying, in the throes of death.

agostar, *vt.* to scorch, wither.—*vr.* to become parched; to dry up, wilt.— **agosto**, *m.* August.—*hacer su a.*, to take the opportunity to feather one's nest.

agotamiento, *m.* draining; exhaustion. —**agotar**, *vt.* to drain; to exhaust, use up.—*vr.* to become exhausted; to give out; to wear oneself out; to be out of print.

agraciado, *a.* graceful, gracious.—*n.* grantee.—**agraciar**, *vt.* to adorn, embellish; to favor; to grace; to grant.

agradable, *a.* agreeable; pleasing, pleasant.—**agradar**, *vi.* to be pleasing; to please.

agradecer, *vti.* [3] to thank for; to be grateful for.—**agradecido**, *a.* thankful.—**agradecimiento**, *m.* gratefulness, gratitude.

agrado, *m.* affability, agreeableness;

pleasure; liking.—*ser del a. de uno*, to like someone.

agrandamiento, *m.* enlargement.— **agrandar**, *vt.* to enlarge; to increase; to let out (dress).

agrario, *a.* agrarian.

agravar, *vt.* to aggravate; to make worse, more serious.—*vr.* to get worse, more serious.

agraviar, *vt.* to wrong, offend, insult. *vr.* to take offense.—**agravio**, *m.* offense, insult, affront.

agraz, *a.* unripe.—*m.* unripe grape; (coll.) displeasure.

agredir, *vti.* [50] to attack, assault.

agregado, *m.* aggregate; assistant; attaché.—**agregar**, *vti.* [b] to add, join; to collect, gather; to aggregate.

agresión, *f.* aggression.—**agresivo**, *a.* aggressive, offensive.—**agresor**, *n.* aggressor, assaulter.

agreste, *a.* rustic, wild; rude, uncouth.

agriar, *vt.* to make sour or tart; to irritate, exasperate.—*vr.* to sour, turn acid.

agrícola, *a.* agricultural.—**agricultor**, *n.* farmer, agriculturist.—**agricultura**, *f.* agriculture, farming.

agridulce, *a.* bittersweet.

agrietarse, *vr.* to crack; to chap (skin).

agrimensor, *m.* land surveyor.— **agrimensura**, *f.* land surveying.

agrio, *a.* sour, acrid; rude.

agrupación, *f.* cluster; crowd; group; gathering.—**agrupar**, *vt.* to group; to cluster.—*vr.* to crowd together; to form groups.

agua, *f.* water; liquid; rain; slope of a roof.—*pl.* luster of diamonds; clouds (in silk, etc.); gloss (in feathers, stones).—*a. abajo*, downstream.—*a. arriba*, upstream.—*a. bendita*, holy water.—*a. dulce*, fresh water.—*a. nieve*, sleet.—*estar con el a. hasta el cuello*, to be in a fix, in difficulties.—*estar entre dos aguas*, to be undecided, be on the fence.— *hacer aguas*, to urinate.—*¡hombre al a.!* man overboard!—**aguacate**, *m.* avocado, alligator pear.—**aguacero**, *m.* heavy rain.—**aguachirle**, *m.* inferior wine.—**aguada**, *f.* watering station; drinking water source.— **aguado**, *a.* watery, watered.—**aguafuerte**, *m.* etching.—**aguafiestas**, *mf.* spoilsport.—**aguamarina**, *f.* aquamarine.

aguantar, *vt.* to bear, endure; to resist; to maintain; to hold.—*vr.* to forbear.—**aguante**, *m.* strength, resistance; patience, endurance.

aguar, *vt.* [b] to dilute with water; to mar (pleasure).—*vr.* to be spoiled,

ruined; to become thin (appl. to liquids), get watery; (Am.) to back down, be intimidated.

aguardar, *vt.* to wait for, await; to expect.

aguardentoso, *a.* mixed with hard liquor; harsh (voice).—**aguardiente,** *m.* brandy, firewater.

aguarrás, *m.* turpentine.

aguazal, *m.* marsh, fen.

agudeza, *f.* sharpness; fineness; wit, witticism; repartee.—**agudo,** *a.* sharp, acute; keen-edged; shrill, screechy; witty, clever, sparkling.

agüero, *m.* omen.

aguerrido, *a.* battle-tested, veteran.

aguijón, *m.* sting (of insect); prick; spur, goad.—**aguijonazo,** *m.* thrust with a goad.—**aguijonear,** *vt.* to prick, goad; to push, urge.

águila, *f.* eagle.—**aguileño,** *a.* aquiline. —**aguilucho,** *m.* eaglet.

aguinaldo, *m.* Christmas bonus or gratuity.

aguja, *f.* needle; hatpin; spire, steeple; bodkin; obelisk; hornfish; needle shell; hand (of a clock); magnetic compass; (RR.) switch rail; spindle.—**agujerear,** *vt.* to pierce, perforate.—**agujero,** *m.* hole; dugout.—**agujeta,** *f.* little needle.— *pl.* charley horse, pain from over-exercise.

agusanarse, *vr.* to become worm-eaten, putrid.

aguzador, *n.* sharpener.—*a.* sharpening.—**aguzar,** *vti.* [a] to whet, sharpen; to urge, excite.—*a. las orejas,* to prick up one's ears.

aherrojar, *vt.* to chain, put in irons.

ahí, *adv.* there; yonder.—*de a.,* hence. —*por a.,* somewhere around here; that way; over there; more or less.

ahijado, *n.* godchild; protegé.

ahinco, *m.* earnestness, eagerness, ardor.

ahito, *a.* gorged, sated; stuffed; full; replete; disgusted, bored.—*m.* indigestion; satiety.

ahogado, *a.* drowned; close, unventilated; suffocated.—*estar* or *verse a.,* to be overwhelmed or swamped.—*n.* suffocated or drowned person.—**ahogar,** *vti.* [b] to drown; to choke, throttle, smother; to oppress; to quench, extinguish.—*vri.* to drown; to be suffocated.—**ahogo,** *m.* oppression, tightness (of the chest, etc.); suffocation; pain.

ahondar, *vt.* to deepen; to dig; to go deep into.—*vi.* to go deep, penetrate; to progress in knowledge.

ahora, *adv.* now.—*a. bien,* now, now then.—*a. mismo,* right now, just now; at once.—*hasta a.,* so far;

hitherto, until now.—*por a.,* for the present.

ahorcado, *n. & a.* hanged (person). —**ahorcar,** *vti.* [d] to hang (execute by hanging).—*vri.* to hang, be hanged; to hang oneself.

ahorita, *adv.* (Am.) just now.—*a. mismo,* this very minute, just now; at once.

ahormar, *vt.* to fit, shape, adjust; to last, break in (shoes); to bring to reason.

ahorrar, *vt.* to save, economize; to spare; to avoid.—**ahorrativo,** *a.* thrifty, frugal.—**ahorro,** *m.* economy.—*pl.* savings.—*caja de ahorros,* savings bank.

ahuecar, *vti.* [d] to make hollow, scoop out; to loosen.—*a. la voz,* to speak in a deep, solemn tone.—*vri.* to become hollow; to swell, put on airs.

ahumado, *a.* smoky; smoked.—**ahumar,** *vt.* to smoke; to cure in smoke. —*vi.* to fume; to emit smoke.—*vr.* to be blackened by smoke.

ahuyentar, *vt.* to put to flight; to drive away.

aindiado, *a.* half-breed, mestizo-looking.

airado, *a.* angry, wrathful.

aire, *m.* air; atmosphere; wind; air, appearance; carriage, gait; tune.—*al a. libre,* outdoors.—*de buen,* or *mal a.,* in a good, or a bad humor.—*en el a.,* in suspense, in the air.—*tomar el a.,* to take a walk.—**airear,** *vt.* to air; to ventilate; to aerate.—*vr.* to take the air; to cool oneself.—**airoso,** *a.* airy, windy; graceful, gracious; successful.

aislado, *a.* isolated; insulated.—**aislador,** *m.* isolator; insulator.—*a.* isolating; insulating.—**aislamiento,** *m.* isolation; insulation; insulating material.—**aislar,** *vt.* to isolate; to insulate.—*vr.* to become isolated; to seclude oneself.

ajar, *vt. & vr.* to crumple; to wilt, wither.

ajedrecista, *n.* chess player.—**ajedrez,** *m.* chess.

ajeno, *a.* another's; alien, foreign; unaware, ignorant; oblivious.

ajetrearse, *vr.* to tire oneself out; to bustle about.—**ajetreo,** *m.* bustle; fatigue; agitation.

ají, *m.* (Am.) green pepper.

ajo, *m.* garlic; swear word.—*echar ajos (y cebollas),* to swear, curse.

ajuar, *m.* trousseau; household furniture.

ajustado, *a.* agreed upon; tight; fitted.—**ajustar,** *vt.* to adjust; to adapt, fit; to regulate; to agree

about, concert; to tighten; to engage, hire.—*vr.* to settle; to conform; to be engaged or hired.—
ajuste, *m.* adjustment; fitting; agreement; engagement; settlement. —*pl.* couplings.

ajusticiar, *vt.* to execute, put to death.

al, (*contr.* of **a** & **el**) to the; on, at; about.—*le dí la carta al criado*, I gave the letter to the servant.—*al llegar*, on arrival.—*al amanecer*, at daybreak.—*estoy al partir*, I am about to leave.

ala, *f.* wing; row; wing (of a building); brim (of a hat); leaf (of a door, table).—*cortar las alas a uno*, to clip one's wings.—*dar alas*, to embolden, encourage.

alabanza, *f.* praise.—**alabar**, *vt.* to praise, commend.—*vr.* to boast.

alabastro, *m.* alabaster.

alabear, *vt.* & *vr.* to warp.

alacena, *f.* cupboard; closet; cabinet.

alacrán, *m.* scorpion.

alado, *a.* winged.

alambicado, *a.* pedantic, affected; rarified.—**alambicamiento**, *m.* distillation; pedantry, affectation.—**alambicar**, *vti.* [d] to distill; to use affected language.—**alambique**, *m.* still.

alambrada, *f.* wire fence; wire defenses.—**alambrado**, *m.* wire cover; electric wiring.—**alambrar**, *vt.* to fence with wire.—**alambre**, *m.* wire. —*a. de puas*, barbed wire.—**alambrera**, *f.* wire netting; wire screen.

alameda, *f.* alameda, public walk shaded with trees; poplar grove.—**álamo**, *m.* poplar.

alarde, *m.* ostentation, boasting, bluff. —*hacer a.*, to boast; to show off.—**alardear**, *m.* to boast.

alargar, *vti.* [b] to lengthen; to extend; to stretch out; to protract, prolong.—*vri.* to be prolonged; to drag; to become longer; to enlarge.

alarido, *m.* howl, outcry, shout, scream, screech.

alarma, *f.* alarm.—**alarmante**, *a.* alarming.—**alarmar**, *vt.* to alarm.—*vr.* to become alarmed.—**alarmista**, *n.* alarmist.

alazán, *a.* sorrel-colored (of horses). —*m.* a horse of that color.

alba, *f.* dawn; alb.—*al a.*, or *al rayar el a.*, at daybreak.

albacea, *mf.* (law) executor, executrix.

albanés, *n.* & *a.* Albanian.

albañil, *m.* mason, bricklayer.—**albañilería**, *f.* masonry (occupation or work).

albarda, *f.* packsaddle.

albaricoque, *m.* apricot.

albayalde, *m.* white lead.

albedrío, *m.* will; free will; impulsiveness.

alberca, *f.* pond, reservoir; (Am.) swimming pool.

albergar, *vti.* [b] to lodge, shelter, harbor; to take in (lodgers).—*vr* to lodge; to find shelter or lodging.—**albergue**, *m.* lodging; shelter; (animal) den.

albóndiga, *f.* meat ball.

albor, *m.* dawn; whiteness; beginning. —**alborear**, *vi.* to dawn.

albornoz, *m.* hooded cloak; bathrobe.

alborotador, *n.* agitator, rioter.—*a.* rowdy.—**alborotar**, *vt.* to disturb, agitate.—*vi.* to create an uproar; to act noisily.—*vr.* to become excited; to fuss; to riot.—**alboroto**, *m.* excitement; disturbance; tumult; hubbub, fuss.

alborozar, *vti.* [a] to gladden, exhilarate.—*vri.* to rejoice.—**alborozo**, *m.* merriment, gaiety, joy.

albur, *m.* risk, chance.—*correr un a.*, to venture, chance, risk.

alcachofa, *f.* artichoke.

alcahueta, *f.* bawd, procuress, go-between.—**alcahuete**, *m.* procurer; abettor; gossip.—**alcahuetear**, *vt.* & *vi.* to aid, abet; to pander.

alcaide, *m.* warden; jailer.

alcalde, *m.* mayor.—**alcaldesa**, *f.* mayoress; wife of the mayor.—**alcaldía**, *f.* mayor's office; city hall.

álcali, *m.* alkali.—**alcalino**, *a.* alkaline.

alcance, *m.* reach; overtaking; pursuit; arm's length; range (of fire arms, etc.); deficit; scope.—*pl.* mental powers; ability.—*al a. de*, within reach of.—*a largo a.*, long term.—*dar a.*, to catch up with.

alcancía, *f.* piggy bank; money box.

alcanfor, *m.* camphor.—**alcanforado**, *a.* camphoric.

alcantarilla, *f.* sewer; drain.—**alcantarillado**, *m.* sewerage system.—*a.* provided with sewers.—**alcantarillar**, *vt.* to make or install sewers.

alcanzado, *a.* needy; in debt.—**alcanzar**, *vti.* [a] to reach; to overtake, come up to; to obtain, attain.—*a. a uno algo*, to hand, pass something to someone.

alcaparra, *f.* caper.

alcatraz, *m.* pelican.

alcayata, *f.* spike; wall hook.

alcázar, *m.* castle, fortress.

alce, *m.* elk; moose.

alcoba, *f.* alcove; bedroom.

alcohol, *m.* alcohol.—**alcohólico**, *a.* alcoholic.

alcornoque, *m.* cork tree; (coll.) blockhead.

alcurnia, *f.* lineage.

aldaba, *f.* knocker (of a door); latch; handle (door, furniture).—*tener buena a.,* or *buenas aldabas,* to have powerful friends.—**aldabonazo,** *m.* knocking.

aldea, *f.* village, hamlet.—**aldeano,** *n.* villager, peasant.—*a.* rustic, unpolished.

aleación, *f.* alloy; alloying.

alebrestarse, *vr.* (Am.) to cut capers; to become frightened or excited.

aleccionador, *a.* instructive.—**aleccionamiento,** *m.* instruction, coaching.—**aleccionar,** *vt.* to teach, instruct, coach.

aledaño, *a.* bounding, bordering.—*m.* boundary, border.

alegación, *f.* allegation, argument.—**alegar,** *vti.* [b] to allege, affirm; to quote; to adduce; to argue.—**alegato,** *m.* allegation; (law) summing-up.

alegrar, *vt.* to make merry, exhilarate; to enliven; to brighten.—*vr.* (de) to rejoice (at); to be glad (of or to); to be happy; to get tipsy.—**alegre,** *a.* merry, joyful; lively; cheerful; funny; gay; bright (of (colors)); optimistic; tipsy.—*a. de cascos,* featherbrained.—**alegría,** *f.* mirth, merriment; gaiety; rejoicing, joy.—**alegrón,** *m.* (coll.) sudden, unexpected joy; a flash.

alejamiento, *m.* removal to a distance; receding; retiring; withdrawal.—**alejar,** *vt.* to remove to a distance; to move away; to separate; to estrange.—*vr.* to recede; to withdraw or move away.

alelarse, *vr.* to become stupefied.

alelí, *m.* = ALHELÍ.

alemán, *n. & a.* German.

alentador, *a.* encouraging, cheering.—**alentar,** *vii.* [1] to breathe.—*vti.* to encourage, cheer; to inspire.

alergia, *f.* allergy.—**alérgico,** *a.* allergic.

alero, *m.* eaves, overhang; splashboard of a carriage.

alerta, *m.* alarm, alert.—*a.* watchful, vigilant, alert.—*interj.* look out! watch out!—**alertar,** *vt.* to render vigilant; to put on guard.

aleta, *f.* fin; (mech.) leaf of a hinge; blade (of a propeller); fender (of a car).

aletargar, *vti.* [b] to cause drowsiness.—*vri.* to become drowsy, sluggish.

aletazo, *m.* blow with the wing; flapping.—**aletear,** *vi.* to flutter (wings or fins).—**aleteo,** *m.* fluttering (of wings or fins).

alevosía, *f.* perfidy, treachery.—**alevoso,** *a.* treacherous.

alfabético, *a.* alphabetical.—**alfabeto,** *m.* alphabet.

alfarería, *f.* pottery; potter's art.—**alfarero,** *n.* potter.

alféizar, *m.* window sill or embrasure.

alfeñique, *m.* sugar paste; weakling.

alférez, *m.* ensign; second lieutenant.

alfil, *m.* bishop (in chess).

alfiler, *m.* pin; scarfpin; brooch.—*a. de seguridad,* safety pin.—*pegar* or *prender con alfileres,* to do in a slipshod way.—**alfilerazo,** *m.* pinprick.—**alfiletero,** *m.* pincase, needle case; pincushion.

alfombra, *f.* carpet.—**alfombrar,** *vt.* to carpet.

alforja, *f.* saddlebag.

alforza, *f.* pleat, tuck; (coll.) scar.

alga, *f.* seaweed.

algarabía, *f.* jargon; din, hubbub.

algarroba, *f.* carob.—**algarrobo,** *m.* locust tree; carob tree.

algazara, *f.* din, clamor.

álgebra, *f.* algebra.—**algebraico,** *a.* algebraic.

algo, *pron.* something.—*adv.* somewhat, a little.—*a. es a.,* every little bit counts.

algodón, *m.* cotton; cotton plant.—*a. en rama,* raw cotton.—**algodonal,** *m.* cotton plantation.—**algodonero,** *a.* pertaining to cotton.—*m.* cotton plant; cotton dealer.

alguacil, *m.* constable; bailiff; mayor; sheriff.

alguien, *pron.* somebody, someone.

algún, alguno, *a.* some, any.—*alguna que otra vez,* sometimes, once in a while.—**alguno,** *pron.* somebody, someone.—*a. que otro,* a few, some.—*pl.* some, some people.

alhaja, *f.* jewel, gem; valuable object.

alharaca, *f.* clamor, fuss, ado.

alhelí, *m.* (bot.) wallflower.

alhucema, *f.* lavender.

aliado, *n. & a.* ally, allied.—**alianza,** *f.* alliance; agreement; wedding ring.—**aliarse,** *vr.* to become allied; to form an alliance.

alicaído, *a.* drooping, weak; dejected, crestfallen.

alicates, *m. pl.* pliers.

aliciente, *m.* attraction, inducement.

alienado, *a.* insane.—**alienista,** *mf.* alienist.

aliento, *m.* breath, wind; breathing; encouragement; bravery.—*dar a.,* to encourage.

aligeramiento, *m.* alleviation, lightening.—**aligerar,** *vt.* to lighten; to alleviate; to hasten; to shorten.

alimaña, *f.* destructive animal.

alimentación, *m.* feeding; food, nourishment.—**alimentar,** *vt.* to feed, nourish; to nurture; to encourage;

to foster. —**alimenticio,** *a.* nourishing; nutritious.—**alimento,** *m.* food, nourishment.—*pl.* allowance; alimony; board.

alineación, *f.* alignment.—**alinear,** *vt.* to align; to line up; to put into line.—*vr.* to fall in line; to form a line.

aliñar, *vt.* to dress or season (food); to adorn.—**aliño,** *m.* dressing or seasoning; ornament, decoration; cleanliness.

alisar, *vt.* to plane, smooth; to polish, burnish.

alisios, *m. pl.* trade winds.

alistamiento, *m.* enrollment; conscription, levy.—**alistar,** *vt. & vr.* to enlist, enroll; to get or make ready.

aliviar, *vt.* to alleviate, relieve, soothe; to lighten; to reprieve.—**alivio,** *m.* alleviation, easement, mitigation, relief; reprieve.

aljibe, *m.* cistern; reservoir, pool; water tank.

alma, *f.* soul; human being; inhabitant; essence, core; bore of a gun. —*a. de cántaro,* fool.—*a. de Dios,* kind-hearted person; harmless creature.—*a. en pena,* ghost.—*a. mía, mi a.,* my dearest; my love.

almacén, *m.* store, shop; warehouse, repository; storage house, depot; grocery store; dockyard.—*pl.* department store.—**almacenaje,** *m.* storage.—**almacenar,** *vt.* to store; to lay up, hoard; to put in storage. —**almacenista,** *m.* wholesaler; department store or warehouse owner.

almanaque, *m.* almanac, calendar.

almeja, *f.* clam.

almena, *f.* battlement.

almendra, *f.* almond.—**almendrado,** *a.* almond-shaped.—*m.* macaroon.—**almendro,** *m.* almond tree.

almíbar, *m.* syrup.—**almibarado,** *a.* syrupy, sugary; flattering.

almidón, *m.* starch.—**almidonado,** *a.* starched; stiff; straightlaced, stuffy. —**almidonar,** *vt.* to starch.

almirantazgo, *m.* admiralty.—**almirante,** *m.* admiral.

almirez, *m.* brass mortar.

almizcle, *m.* musk.—**almizclero,** *a.* musk.

almohada, *f.* pillow; bolster.—*consultar con la a.,* to sleep on the matter. —**almohadilla,** *f.* pincushion; pad; small pillow.—**almohadón,** *m.* cushion.

almorranas, *f. pl.* hemorrhoids, piles.

almorzar, *vii.* [12-a] to lunch.—*vti.* to have for lunch.—**almuerzo,** *m.* lunch.

alocado, *a.* half-witted; wild; reckless.

alojamiento, *m.* lodging; quartering of soldiers.—**alojar,** *vt.* to lodge; to quarter (troops).—*vr.* to take lodgings; to lodge; to room, put up at.

alondra, *f.* lark.

alpargata, *f.* hemp sandal.

alpinismo, *m.* mountain climbing.—**alpinista,** *mf.* mountain climber.

alpiste, *m.* birdseed.

alquilar, *vt.* to let, rent; to hire; to fee.—*vr.* to serve for wages; to hire out.—**alquiler,** *m.* wages; rent, rental; the act of hiring or letting.

alquitrán, *m.* tar, pitch; (naut.) stuff made of pitch, grease, etc.—**alquitranado,** *a.* tarry.

alrededor, *adv.* around.—*a. de,* about, around, (coll.) approximately.—**alrededores,** *m. pl.* environs, outskirts.

alta, *f.* (med.) discharge (from hospital); (mil.) certificate of enlistment. —*darse de a.,* to be admitted (in a profession, social club), to become a member.

altanería, *f.* haughtiness, insolence.—**altanero,** *a.* haughty, arrogant, insolent.

altar, *m.* altar.

altavoz, *m.* loudspeaker.

altea, *f.* marshmallow.

alterable, *a.* alterable, changeable.—**alteración,** *f.* alteration; strong emotion; tumult; commotion.—**alterado,** *a.* disturbed, agitated.—**alterar,** *vt.* to alter, change, transform; to disturb, stir up.—*vr.* to become altered, disturbed, agitated; to become angry.

altercado, *m.* altercation, quarrel, wrangle.—**altercar,** *vti.* [d] to dispute, altercate; to quarrel, wrangle.

alternador, *m.* (elec.) alternator.—**alternar,** *vt., vi. & vr.* to alternate.—**alternativa,** *f.* alternative, choice; service by turn.—**alternativo, alterno,** *a.* alternate, alternating.—*corriente alterna,* alternating current.

alteza, *f.* Highness (title); loftiness.

altibajos, *m. pl.* unevenness of ground; ups and downs, vicissitudes.

altiplanicie, *f.,* **altiplano,** *m.* plateau, tableland.

altisonante, *a.* high-sounding, pompous.

altitud, *f.* height; altitude.

altivez, *f.* haughtiness, arrogance, insolence; pride.—**altivo,** *a.* haughty, proud; overbearing, arrogant.

alto, *a.* high; elevated; tall; eminent; lofty; loud.—*altas horas,* the small hours.—*altos hornos,* blast furnaces.

—*de lo a.*, from above.—*m.* height, elevation; hill; top; story, floor; summit, mountain top, crest; top floor; heap, pile; (mil.) halt; place or time of rest.—*hacer a.*, to halt. —*pasar por a.*, to overlook, forget.— *adv.* high, high up; loud, loudly; (voice) high.—*interj.* (mil. command) halt!—**altoparlante**, *m.* v. ALTAVOZ.—**altozano**, *m.* hillock, knoll; height.—**altura**, *f.* height, altitude; tallness, stature; summit, top; (naut.) the latitude; altitude; level, standard.—*estar a la a. de*, to be equal to.—*pl.* the heavens, Heaven. —*a estas alturas*, at this moment.

alucinación, *f.* hallucination.—**alucinar**, *vt.* & *vr.* to dazzle, fascinate, delude.

alud, *m.* avalanche.

aludido, *a.* referred, aforementioned. —**aludir**, *vi.* to allude, refer.

alumbrado, *m.* illumination, lighting. —*a.* lit, lighted; tipsy.—**alumbramiento**, *m.* childbirth; lighting.— **alumbrar**, *vt.* to light; to illuminate, light up; to enlighten.—*vi.* to give, or shed light; to give birth.— *vr.* to get tipsy.

aluminio, *m.* aluminum.

alumno, *n.* pupil, student.

alusión, *f.* allusion, reference, hint.— **alusivo**, *a.* allusive, hinting.

alza, *f.* rise (in price).—**alzada**, *f.* height (of horse); (law) appeal.— **alzado**, *a.* & *n.* (of) a lump sum; revolted, insurgent.—**alzamiento**, *m.* lifting, raising; insurrection.—**alzar** *vti.* [a] to raise; to lift; to pick up; (eccl.) to elevate the host.—*a. cabeza*, to recover from a calamity or a disease.—*a. velas*, to sail away; to move.—*vri.* to revolt; to rise; (law) to appeal.—*alzarse con*, to run off with something, steal something.

allá, *adv.* there; thither, over there. —*a. en mi niñez*, in the old times of my childhood.—*a. por el año de 1900*, about 1900.—*a. veremos*, we shall see.—*a. voy*, I am coming.—*el más a.*, the beyond.—*más a.*, farther. —*muy a.*, much beyond, far beyond.

allanamiento, *m.* leveling; smoothing; acceptance of a judicial finding; breaking into, trespassing.— **allanar**, *vt.* to level, smooth; to flatten; to remove or overcome (difficulties); to pacify, subdue; to break into (a house).—*vr.* to abide (by), acquiesce.

allegado, *a.* near, related.—*n.* relative; ally.—**allegar**, *vti.* [b] to reap; to collect; to solicit, procure.—*vri.* to come near, approach; to adhere to.

allende, *adv.* beyond, over, on the other side.—*a. el mar*, overseas.

allí, *adv.* there, in that place; thereto. —*por a.*, that way; through there, thereabouts.

ama, *f.* mistress of the house; landlady; (woman) owner.—*a. de llaves*, housekeeper.

amabilidad, *f.* amiability, affability; kindness.—**amable**, *a.* amiable, affable; kind.

amaestrar, *vt.* to instruct, train, coach.

amagar, *vti.* [b] to threaten; to hint. —*vii.* to threaten; to be impending; to feign.—**amago**, *m.* threat; hint; indication, sign.

amalgama, *f.* amalgam.—**amalgamar**, *vt.* to amalgamate.

amamantar, *vt.* to nurse, suckle.

amanecer, *vii.* [3] to dawn.—*m.* dawn, daybreak.—*al a.*, at dawn, at daybreak.

amanerado, *a.* full of mannerisms.— **amanerarse**, *vr.* to adopt mannerisms; to become affected.

amansamiento, *m.* taming; breaking (horses).—**amansar**, *vt.* to tame, domesticate; to break (a horse); to pacify, soothe.—*vr.* to calm down; to become subdued.

amante, *mf.* & *a.* lover; mistress; loving.

amanuense, *m.* clerk; scribe.

amañar, *vt.* to do cleverly.—*vr.* to be handy; to manage things cleverly.

amapola, *f.* poppy.

amar, *vt.* to love.

amarar, *vi.* to set down on water.

amargar, *vti.* [b] to make bitter.— *vri.* to become bitter.—**amargo**, *a.* bitter.—*m.* bitterness; bitters; (Am.) maté tea.—**amargor**, *m.*, **amargura**, *f.* bitterness.

amarillear, *vi.* to show a yellow tinge. —**amarillento**, *a.* yellowish.—**amarillez**, *f.* yellowness.—**amarillo**, *a.* & *n.* yellow.

amarra, *f.* cable; rope.—**amarradero**, *m.* hitching post; tying or fastening place; moor'ng berth.—**amarrar**, *vt.* to tie, fasten; to lash, moor.— **amarre**, *m.* tying; mooring; mooring line or cable.

amartillar, *vt.* to hammer; to cock (a gun).

amasar, *vt.* to knead; to mash; to amass, accumulate.—**amasijo**, *m.* dough; (act of) kneading; paste, mixture; medley, hodgepodge.

amatista, *f.* amethyst.

amatorio, *a.* amatory.

amazona, *f.* Amazon; horsewoman.— **amazónico**, *a.* Amazonian.

ambages, *m. pl.* circumlocutions;

maze; beating around the bush.— *sin a.*, in plain language.

ámbar, *m.* amber.—**ambarino,** *a.* amberlike.

ambición, *f.* ambition; aspiration.— **ambicionar,** *vt.* to seek eagerly; to aspire to; to covet.—**ambicioso,** *a.* ambitious, aspiring; covetous, greedy.

ambiente, *m.* atmosphere, air; environment.

ambigüedad, *f.* ambiguity.—**ambiguo,** *a.* ambiguous, uncertain, doubtful.

ámbito, *m.* bounds, area; scope.

ambos, *a.* both.

ambulancia, *f.* ambulance; field hospital.—**ambulante,** *a.* walking; shifting; roving, wandering; moving.

amedrentar, *vt.* to scare, frighten, intimidate.

amén, *m.* amen, so be it.—*a. de,* besides; aside from.

amenaza, *f.* threat, menace.— **amenazador,** *a.* threatening, menacing.— **amenazar,** *vti.* [a] to threaten, menace; to be impending.

amenguar, *vti.* [b] to diminish; to defame.

amenidad, *f.* amenity.—**amenizar,** *vti.* [a] to render pleasant or agreeable. —**ameno,** *a.* pleasant, agreeable; readable.

americano, *a. & n.* American.

ametralladora, *f.* machine gun, tommy gun.—**ametrallar,** *vt.* to shell; to machine-gun.

amianto, *m.* asbestos.

amiga, *f.* female friend; mistress.— **amigable,** *a.* friendly; fit, affable.

amígdala, *f.* tonsil.—**amigdalitis,** *f.* tonsilitis.

amigo, *m.* friend.—*ser a. de,* to be a friend of; to have a taste for.— **amigote,** *m.* pal, chum.

amilanamiento, *m.* abject fear; terror.—**amilanar,** *vt.* to frighten; to cow.—*vr.* to become terrified; to cower, quail; to flag.

aminorar, *vt.* to lessen; to enfeeble.

amistad, *f.* friendship, friendliness.— *pl.* friends.—*hacer a.,* or *amistades,* to become acquainted; to make friends.—*hacer las amistades,* to make up, become reconciled.—**amistoso,** *a.* friendly, amicable.

amnistía, *f.* amnesty.—**amnistiar,** *vt.* to pardon, grant amnesty.

amo, *m.* master; owner; boss.

amodorrado, *a.* drowsy, sleepy.—**amodorrarse,** *vr.* to become drowsy.

amohinarse, *vr.* to sulk.

amolador, *n. & a.* grinder, sharpener, whetter; grinding, sharpening, whetting.—**amoladura,** *f.* whetting,

grinding.—**amolar,** *vti.* [12] to grind, sharpen, hone.

amoldar, *vt.* to mold, shape; to adjust; to adapt.—*vr.* to conform, adapt oneself.

amonestación, *f.* admonition, warning.—*pl.* banns.—*correr las amonestaciones,* to publish the banns.— **amonestar,** *vt.* to admonish, warn, advise; to publish the banns.

amoníaco, *m.* ammonia.

amontonamiento, *m.* heaping; piling; crowding.—**amontonar,** *vt. & vr.* to heap up, pile up; to crowd.

amor, *m.* love; the object of love.— *pl.* love affairs.—*a. propio,* self-respect, self-esteem.—*con* or *de mil amores,* with all one's heart, with the greatest pleasure.

amoratado, *a.* livid, bluish.—**amoratarse,** *vr.* to grow or become purplish.

amordazar, *vti.* [a] to gag, muzzle.

amorío, *m.* love affair; love making. —**amoroso,** *a.* affectionate, loving; tender.

amortajar, *vt.* to shroud (a corpse).

amortiguación, *f.,* **amortiguamiento,** *m.* softening, mitigation, lessening. —**amortiguador,** *m.* shock absorber; muffler.—**amortiguar,** *vti.* [b] to lessen; to muffle; to deafen (a sound); to soften; to absorb (shocks).

amortización, *f.* amortization.—**amortizar,** *vti.* [a] to amortize; to pay on account; to redeem (debt, etc.).

amoscarse, *vri.* [d] to get peeved, annoyed.

amotinado, *a.* mutinous, riotous.—*n.* mutineer.—**amotinamiento,** *m.* mutiny.—**amotinar,** *vt. & vr.* to excite to rebellion or riot; to mutiny, rebel.

amovible, *a.* removable.

amparar, *vt.* to shelter; to protect, help.—*vr.* to enjoy protection; to defend oneself; to seek shelter.— **amparo,** *m.* aid; protection; shelter.

amperaje, *m.* amperage.—**amperímetro,** *m.* amperimeter.—**amperio,** *m.* ampere.

ampliación, *f.* enlargement.—**ampliador,** *n.* amplifier.—*a.* amplifying.— **ampliar,** *vt.* to amplify; to enlarge; to magnify.—**amplificador,** *a.* amplifying.—*n.* amplifier, loudspeaker. —**amplificar,** *vti.* [d] = AMPLIAR.— **amplio,** *a.* ample, roomy, extensive, large.—**amplitud,** *f.* largeness, fullness; amplitude; extent.

ampolla, *f.* blister; decanter; water bubble; bulb.—**ampollar,** *vt.* to blister; to make hollow.—*vr.* to

bubble up.—**ampolleta,** *f.* small vial; sandglass.

ampulosidad, *f.* verbosity.—**ampuloso,** *a.* pompous, bombastic.

amputación, *f.* amputation.—**amputar,** *vt.* to amputate.

amueblar, *vt.* to furnish (a room, a house, etc.).

anacrónico, *a.* anachronistic.—**anacronismo,** *m.* anachronism.

ánade, *n.* duck; goose.

analfabetismo, *m.* illiteracy.—**analfabeto,** *a.* & *n.* illiterate (person).

análisis, *mf.* analysis.—**analista,** *mf.* analyst.—**analítico,** *a.* analytical.—**analizador,** *m.* analyzer.—**analizar,** *vti.* [a] to analyze.

analogía, *f.* analogy; resemblance:—**analógico, análogo,** *a.* analogous, similar.

anaquel, *m.* shelf.—**anaquelería,** *f.* shelving, case of shelves.

anaranjado, *a.* orange-colored.—*n.* orange (color).

anarquía, *f.* anarchy.—**anárquico,** *a.* anarchical.—**anarquismo,** *m.* anarchism.—**anarquista,** *n.* & *a.* anarchist(ic).

anatema, *m.* anathema, excommunication.—**anatematizar,** *vti.* [a] to anathematize.

anatomía, *f.* anatomy; dissection.—**anatómico,** *a.* anatomical.

anca, *f.* haunch, croup (animals); rump; hip.

ancestral, *a.* ancestral.

ancianidad, *f.* old age.—**anciano,** *n.* & *a.* aged; old (man, woman).

ancla, áncora, *f.* anchor.—**echar anclas,** to anchor.—**levar anclas,** to weigh anchor.—**anclar,** *vi.* to anchor.

ancho, *a.* broad, wide—*m.* width, breadth.—*a sus anchas,* with absolute freedom.

anchoa, ancheva, *f.* anchovy.

anchura, *f.* width, breadth.—**anchuroso,** *a.* vast, spacious, extensive.

andada, *f.* walk, track, trail.—*pl.* footprints.—*volver a las andadas,* to go back to one's old tricks.—**andadura,** *f.* gait; amble (of horses).

andaluz, *n.* & *a.* Andalusian.

andamiada, *f.,* **andamiaje,** *m.* scaffolding.—**andamio,** *m.* scaffold.

andanada, *f.* broadside; grandstand for spectators; reproof; tirade.

andante, *a.* walking.—**andanza,** *f.* occurrence, event.—*pl.* rambles, wanderings.—**andar,** *vii.* [4] to walk, go; (watch, machine, etc.) to run, work, move, go; to act, behave; to elapse, pass; to be; to get along, be going.—*¡anda!* move on! get up! go ahead!—*a. en,* to be attending to,

or engaged in; to be going on, be near; to ride in (a carriage, automobile, etc.).—*andarse con rodeos,* or *por las ramas,* to beat around the bush.—*a todo a.,* at full speed.—**andariego,** *a.* restless, roving; fast walker, runner.—**andarín,** *m.* professional walker, runner.

andas, *f. pl.* stretcher; litter; bier.

andén, *m.* sidewalk by a road, wharf or bridge; platform (of a RR. station).

andino, *a.* & *n.* Andean, of the Andes.

andrajo, *m.* rag, tatter; despicable person.—**andrajoso,** *a.* ragged, in tatters.

andurriales, *m. pl.* byroads, lonely places.

anécdota, *f.* anecdote.—**anecdótico,** *a.* anecdotal.

anegado, *a.* overflowed; wet, soaked.—**anegar,** *vt.* to inundate, flood; to submerge; to flush; to drown, sink.—*vr.* to become wet or soaked; to be flooded.

anejo, *a.* = ANEXÓ.

anemia, *f.* anemia.—**anémico,** *a.* anemic.

anestesia, *f.* anesthesia.—**anestesiar,** *vt.* to anesthetize.—**anestésico,** *m.* & *a.* anesthetic.

anexar, *vt.* to annex.—**anexión,** *f.* annexation.—**anexo,** *a.* annexed, joined.

anfibio, *n.* amphibian.—*a.* amphibious.

anfiteatro, *m.* amphitheater; balcony of a theater.

anfitrión, *m.* host (at a banquet).

angarillas, *f. pl.* handbarrow; panniers; cruet stands.

ángel, *m.* angel.—**angélico,** *a.* angelic(al).

angina, *f.* angina.

angostar, *vt.* & *vr.* to narrow; to become narrow, contract.—**angosto,** *a.* narrow.—**angostura,** *f.* narrowness; narrows (in a river, etc.).

anguila, *f.* eel.

angular, *a.* angular.—*piedra a.,* cornerstone.—**ángulo,** *m.* angle.

angustia, *f.* anguish, grief, sorrow.—**angustiar,** *vt.* to cause anguish, distress.—**angustioso,** *a.* full of, or causing, anguish.

anhelante, *a.* eager, yearning, longing.—**anhelar,** *vi.* to desire anxiously, long for, covet.—**anhelo,** *m.* strong desire; longing; panting.—**anheloso,** *a.* anxious, panting.

anidar, *vi.* to nest; to nestle; to dwell; to shelter.—*vr.* to nest; to settle (in a place).

anilina, *f.* aniline.

anilla, *f.* ring; curtain ring; hoop.—**anillado,** *a.* in the form of a ring.

annulated.—**anillo,** *m.* finger ring; small hoop.

ánima, *f.* soul; bore of a gun.—**animación,** *f.* animation, liveliness.—**animado,** *a.* lively, animated.—**animador,** *n.* one who animates or enlivens, master of ceremonies.—**animadversión,** *f.* animadversion; enmity.

animal, *m.* animal; dunce, blockhead. —*a.* animal; stupid, brutish.

animar, *vt.* to animate, give life; to encourage.—*vr.* to become lively; to cheer up.—**ánimo,** *m.* spirit, soul; courage.—**animosidad,** *f.* animosity; courage.—**animoso,** *a.* brave, spirited.

aniñado, *a.* childish.—**aniñarse,** *vr.* to become childish.

aniquilamiento, *m.* destruction, annihilation.—**aniquilar,** *vt.* to annihilate, wipe out.

anís, *m.* anise, anisette; licorice.

aniversario, *m.* anniversary.—*a.* annual, yearly.

ano, *m.* anus.

anoche, *adv.* last night.—**anochecer,** *vii.* [3] to grow dark (at the approach of night).—*m.* nightfall, dusk.—**anochecida,** *f.* nightfall.

anodino, *n.* & *a.* anodyne; insignificant.

anonadamiento, *m.* annihilation; crushing.—**anonadar,** *vt.* to annihilate; to crush, overwhelm.

anónimo, *a.* anonymous, nameless.—*m.* anonymous letter.

anormal, *a.* abnormal.—**anormalidad,** *f.* abnormality.

anotación, *f.* annotation; note; entry. —**anotar,** *vt.* to write down; to annotate; to enter (in register).

ansia, *f.* anxiety; eagerness; anguish. —*pl.* pangs.—**ansiar,** *vt.* to desire anxiously.—**ansiedad,** *f.* anxiety; worry.—**ansioso,** *a.* anxious; eager.

antagónico, *a.* antagonistic.—**antagonismo,** *m.* antagonism.—**antagonista,** *mf.* antagonist; opponent.

antaño, *adv.* yesteryear; yore.

antártico, *a.* antarctic.

ante, *prep.* before; in the presence of.—*a. todo,* above all.—*m.* elk; buffalo; buffalo skin.

anteanoche, *adv.* night before last.

anteayer, *adv.* day before yesterday.

antebrazo, *m.* forearm.

antecámara, *f* antechamber; lobby.

antecedente, *a.* & *m.* antecedent.—**antecesor,** *n.* predecessor, forefather.

antedatar, *vt.* to antedate.

antedicho, *a.* aforesaid.

antelación, *f.* precedence in order of time.

antemano, *a.* beforehand.—*de a.,* beforehand.

antena, *f.* antenna; aerial (of radio); feeler.

antenoche, *adv.* = ANTEANOCHE.

anteojo, *m.* spyglass; small telescope. —*pl.* eyeglasses, spectacles; binoculars; opera glasses.

antepasado, *a.* (of time) passed.—*año a.,* year before last.—*n.* ancestor.

antepecho, *m.* railing; window sill.

anteponer, *vti.* [32] to prefer; to place before.

anterior, *a.* previous; earlier; former; above, preceding.—**anterioridad,** *f.* priority.—*con a.* beforehand.

antes, *adv.* before; formerly; first; rather.—*a. bien,* on the contrary; rather.

antesala, *f.* anteroom, waiting room. —*hacer a.,* to be kept waiting.

antiaéreo, *a.* antiaircraft.

antibiótico, *m.* & *a.* antibiotic.

anticipación, *f.* anticipation; foretaste.—**anticipado,** *a.* early, ahead of time.—*por a.,* in advance.—**anticipar,** *vt.* to anticipate (in the sense of "to do, cause to happen," etc., before the regular time); to advance (money, payment); to lend. —*vr.* to anticipate, act first; to happen earlier than the expected time.—**anticipo,** *m.* advance; advance payment; (law) retainer.

anticomunista, *mf.* & *a.* anticommunist.

anticongelante, *m.* & *a.* antifreeze.

anticuado, *a.* antiquated, obsolete.—**anticuario,** *n.* & *a.* antiquarian.

anticuerpo, *m.* antibody.

antideslizante, *m.* & *a.* antiskid.

antidetonante, *m.* & *a.* antiknock.

antídoto, *m.* antidote.

antier, *adv.* (Am.) v. ANTEAYER.

antifaz, *m.* veil that covers the face; mask.

antigualla, *f.* object of remote antiquity; outmoded custom or object.—**antigüedad,** *f.* antiquity; ancient times; antique.—**antiguo,** *a.* antique; ancient, old.—*a la a.,* after the manner of the ancients, in an old-fashioned manner.—*de a.,* since old times.—*los antiguos,* the ancients.

antihigiénico, *a.* unsanitary.

antílope, *m.* antelope.

antillano, *n.* & *a.* West Indian.

antimonio, *m.* antimony.

antinomía, *f.* antinomy; contradiction; paradox.

antipatía, *f.* antipathy; dislike, aversion.—**antipático,** *a.* uncongenial, disagreeable.

antipatriótico, *a.* unpatriotic.

antípoda, *a.* antipodal.—*m. pl.* antipodes.

antisemita, *mf. & a.* anti-Semite.

antiséptico, *n. & a.* antiseptic.

antojadizo, antojado, *a.* capricious, whimsical, fanciful.—**antojarse,** *vr.* to arouse a fancy; to cause a capricious desire.—*se me antojó,* I took a fancy to.—**antojo,** *m.* whim, fancy; birth mark.—*a su a.,* as one pleases; arbitrarily.

antología, *f.* anthology.

antorcha, *f.* torch.

antracita, *f.* anthracite.

antropología, *f.* anthropology.

anual, *a.* annual, yearly.—**anuario,** *m.* yearbook; trade or professional directory.

anudar, *vt.* to knot; to tie, unite.

anuencia, *f.* compliance, consent.

anulación, *f.* annulment, voiding, nullification; abatement.—**anular,** *vt.* to annul, make void; to cancel, quash.—*a.* ring-shaped.—*dedo a.,* ring finger.

anunciador, *n. & a.* announcer, announcing; advertiser, advertising.—**anunciante,** *n.* announcer; advertiser.—**anunciar,** *vt.* to announce; to advertise; to foretell.—**anuncio,** *m.* announcement; notice; advertisement.

anzuelo, *m.* fishhook; lure.

añadido, *m.* hair switch.—*a.* annexed.—**añadidura,** *f* addition, increase, extra, over—*por a.,* in addition, to make matters worse.—**añadir,** *vt.* to add, join.

añagaza, *f* allurement, enticement, trick.

añejo, *a.* óld, of old vintage, stale

añicos, *m. pl.* shreds, fragments.—*hacer a.,* to shatter.

añil, *m* indigo; indigo blue—**añilar,** *vt.* to blue (clothes)

año, *m.* year.—*al a.,* by the year, after a year.—*a. bisiesto,* leap year *a económico,* or *fiscal,* fiscal year *—a. escolar,* school year —*a. nuevo,* New Year.—*tener 10 años,* to be 10 years old.—**añoso,** *a.* old, aged

añoranza, *f.* longing; yearning.—**añorar,** *vi.* to long for, to yearn for, be homesick; to reminisce

apabullar, *vt.* to flatten, crush.

apacentar, *vti.* [1] to graze, pasture, (fig.) to nourish

apacible, *a.* gentle, placid, calm.

apaciguamiento, *m.* pacification, appeasement.—**apaciguar,** *vti.* [b] to appease, pacify.

apachurrar, *vt.* to crush, flatten.

apadrinar, *vt.* to sponsor; to favor; to protect; to be godfather at a christening; to be best man at a wedding; to act as a second in a duel.

apagar, *vti.* [b] to put out, extinguish; to turn off; to soften; to deaden.—*vri.* to become extinguished, die out; to go out.—**apagón,** *m.* blackout.

apaisado, *a.* more wide than high.

apalabrar, *vt.* to make an arrangement; to come to an agreement; to speak about, discuss; to engage.

apalancar, *vti.* [d] to lever.

apalear, *vt.* to beat up, thrash; to cane; to horsewhip.

apañar, *vt.* to grasp, seize; to carry away; to pilfer; to patch, mend; to contrive, manage.

aparador, *m.* sideboard, cupboard; show window.

aparato, *m.* apparatus; appliance; pomp, show; system.—**aparatoso,** *a.* pompous, showy.

aparcería, *f.* (agricultural) partnership.—**aparcero,** *n.* (agricultural) partner.

aparear, *vt.* to match, mate; to pair.

aparecer, *vii. & vri.* [3] to appear, show up, turn up.—**aparecido,** *n.* ghost, specter.

aparejado, *a.* fit; ready; equipped.—**aparejar,** *vt.* to prepare; to saddle or harness; to rig; to equip.—*vr.* to get ready; to equip oneself.—**aparejo,** *m.* preparation; harness, gear; packsaddle, tackle; rigging.—*pl.* equipment, trappings.

aparentar, *vt.* to feign, pretend.—**aparente,** *a.* apparent

aparición, *f* apparition, appearance (coming in sight); ghost.

apariencia, *f* appearance, aspect; probability; semblance.

apartadero, *m.* (RR.) siding.

apartado, *a.* distant; aloof; remote; different.—*m.* compartment; P.O. letter box; paragraph, section.—**apartamento,** *m.* apartment.

apartamiento, *m.* separation; retirement; aloofness; secluded place; (Am.) apartment.—**apartar,** *vt.* to set apart; to separate, divide; to dissuade; to remove; to sort.—*vr.* to withdraw; to hold off; to desist; to retire; to separate.—**aparte,** *m.* paragraph; (theat.) aside.—*adv.* separately; aside.

apasionado, *a.* passionate; impassioned; partial.—*n.* admirer.—**apasionamiento,** *m.* passion; partiality.—**apasionar,** *vt.* to rouse, excite, thrill; to fill with passion.—*vr.* to become impassioned, passionately fond; to fall passionately in love.

apatía, *f.* apathy, indolence.—**apático,** *a.* apathetic, indolent.

apeadero, *m.* (RR.) secondary station; landing.—**apear,** *vt.* to dismount, cause to alight; to bring down; to dissuade.—*vr.* to alight, get off.

apechugar, *vti.* [b] to push with the chest.—*a. con,* to put up with something courageously; to accept.

apedrear, *vt.* to stone.

apegarse, *vri.* [b] to become attached to; to become fond of.—**apego,** *m.* attachment, fondness.

apelable, *a.* appealable.—**apelación,** *f.* appeal; remedy, help.—**apelar,** *vt.* & *vi.* to appeal; to have recourse to.—**apelativo,** *m.* appellation.

apelotonar, *vt.* & *vr.* to form into balls; to pile up.

apellidado, *a.* named (last name), by the name of.—**apellidar,** *vt.* to call by name (last name).—*vr.* to be called (have the last name of).—**apellido,** *m.* family name, last name.

apenar, *vt.* & *vr.* to cause pain, sorrow; to grieve; (Am.) to cause embarrassment, shame.

apenas, *adv.* scarcely, hardly; no sooner than; as soon as.

apéndice, *m.* appendix.—**apendicitis,** *f.* appendicitis.

apercibimiento, *m.* readiness; warning; summons.—**apercibir,** *vt.* to provide; to prepare; to warn, advise; to summon.—*vr* **(a)** to get ready (to).—*a. de,* to notice

apergaminado, *a.* like parchment; dried up

aperitivo, *m.* aperitif; appetizer

apero, *m.* farm implement; tool —*pl* equipment (for an activity)

apertura, *f* (act of) opening or beginning.

apesadumbrar. *vt* & *vi.* to grieve; to make (become) sad, griefstricken.

apestado, *a.* & *n.* pestered, annoyed; satiated.—**apestar,** *vt.* to infect with the plague; to corrupt, turn putrid; to annoy, bother; to sicken, nauseate.—*vi.* to stink.—**apestoso,** *a.* stinking, sickening; offensive; boring.

apetecer, *vti.* [3] to hunger for; to like; to desire.—*vii.* to be desirable, appetizing.—**apetecible,** *a.* desirable; appetizing.—**apetencia,** *f* appetite, hunger; desire.—**apetito,** *m.* appetite; appetence.—**apetitoso,** *a.* appetizing, inviting, palatable.

apiadarse, *vr* **(de)** to pity, take pity (on).

ápice, *m.* apex, summit, top, pinnacle.

apilar, *vt.* to heap, pile up.

apiñado, *a.* crowded, close together.—**apiñamiento,** *m.* pressing together; crowding, congestion.—**apiñar,** *vt.* & *vr.* to press together, crowd.

apio, *m.* celery.

apisonamiento, *m.* tamping.—**apisonar,** *vt.* to tamp; to roll.

aplacar, *vti.* [d] to appease, pacify, placate.

aplanamiento, *m.* leveling, flattening; dejection.—**aplanar,** *vt.* to make level, even; to flatten; to terrify or astonish.—*vr.* to tumble down; to dismay; to get depressed.

aplastante, *a.* crushing, overpowering.—**aplastar,** *vt.* to smash, crush, squash; to confound.—*vr.* to flatten; to collapse.

aplaudir, *vt.* to applaud, clap, to approve; to praise.—**aplause,** *m.* applause; clapping; approbation.

aplazamiento, *m.* postponement; adjournment.—**aplazar,** *vti.* [a] to postpone; to adjourn; to procrastinate.

aplicable, *a.* applicable, suitable, fitting.—**aplicación,** *f.* studiousness; diligence.—**aplicado,** *a.* applied, studious; industrious.—**aplicar,** *vti.* [d] to apply; to put on; to clap; to attribute or impute; to adjudge.—*vri.* to apply oneself; to devote oneself diligently.

aplomado, *a.* calm, grave; serious; plumbed, vertical.—**aplomar,** *vt* to make straight or vertical, to plumb.—*vi.* to plumb, be vertical.—**aplomo,** *m* self-assurance, aplomb; verticalness.

apocado, *a.* pusillanimous, timid, irresolute —**apocar,** *vti.* [d] to lessen; to belittle.—*vri.* to humble, belittle oneself

apodar, *vt.* to nickname.

apoderado, *n.* proxy; attorney —**apoderar,** *vt.* to empower; to grant power of attorney to.—*apoderarse de,* to take possession of, seize.

apodo, *m.* nickname.

apogeo, *m* apogee; height (of fame, etc.).

apolillarse, *vr* to be moth-eaten, worm-eaten.

apolítico, *a.* non-political.

apología, *f* apologia, defense, praise.

apoltronarse, *vr* to grow lazy; to loiter.

aporreado, *a.* cudgeled; miserable, dragged out.—**aporrear,** *vt.* to beat, cudgel, maul; to pester.—*vr.* to overwork, to become overtired.—**aporreo,** *m.* beating, cudgeling; pestering

aportación, *f.,* **aporte,** *m.* contribution.—**aportar,** *vi.* to contribute; to make port; to arrive.

aposentar, *vt.* to lodge.—*vr.* to take lodgings.—**aposento,** *m.* room or apartment.

aposta, *adv.* on purpose.

apostar, *vti.* [12] to bet; to post, station.—*a. a que,* to bet that.—*apostárselas a,* or *con,* to compete with.

apostasía, *f.* apostasy.—**apóstata,** *mf.* & *a.* apostate.

apóstol, *m.* apostle.—**apostolado,** *m.* apostleship.—**apostólico,** *a.* apostolic.

apostrofar, *vt.* to apostrophize.—**apóstrofe,** *f.* apostrophe.—**apóstrofo,** *m.* apostrophe (').

apostura, *f.* natural elegance, graceful bearing.

apoyar, *vt.* to rest, lean, support; to back, defend; to aid; to abet.—*vi.* (en or sobre) to rest (on).—*vr.* (en) to rest (on); to lean (on or against); to be supported (by); to be based (on).—**apoyo,** *m.* prop, stay; support; protection, aid; backing.

apreciable, *a.* appreciable, noticeable; worthy of esteem; nice, fine; valuable.—**apreciación,** *f.* estimation, valuation; appreciation.—**apreciar,** *vt.* to appreciate, price, value; to esteem.—**aprecio,** *m.* esteem, high regard; appraisement, valuation.

aprehender, *vt.* to apprehend, arrest, seize.—**aprehensión,** *f* seizure, capture; apprehension; fear.—**aprehensor,** *n* captor.

apremiante, *a.* urgent, pressing. **apremiar,** *vt.* to press, urge; to compel, oblige.—**apremio,** *m.* pressure, constraint; judicial compulsion.

aprender, *vt.* & *vi.* to learn.—**aprendiz,** *n.* apprentice.—**aprendizaje,** *m.* apprenticeship

aprensión, *f.* apprehension; scruple, fear; distrust, suspicion.—**aprensivo,** *a.* apprehensive, fearing.

apresar, *vt.* to seize, grasp; to capture; to imprison.

aprestar, *vt.* to prepare, make ready; to size.—*vr* to get ready.

apresurado, *a.* hasty, quick.—**apresuramiento,** *m.* hastiness, quickness.—**apresurar,** *vt* to hurry, hasten.—*vr.* to make haste, hurry up.

apretar, *vti.* [1] to tighten, to press down, compress; to clench (teeth, fist), to grip (hand in greeting), to squeeze; to urge.—*vii.* to pinch (of shoes, etc.); to be tight (of clothes).—**apretón,** *m.* sudden pressure, struggle conflict, squeeze;

short run, spurt.—*a. de manos,* handshake.—**apretujar,** *vt.* (coll.) to squeeze tightly.—**aprieto,** *m.* jam, crush; stringency, difficulty, quandary; cramp; tight spot.

aprisa, *adv.* quickly, hurriedly, promptly; fast.

aprisionar, *vt.* to imprison; to tie, handcuff.

aprobación, *f.* approval, approbation; consent.—**aprobar,** *vti.* [12] to approve; to pass (in an examination).

aprontar, *vt.* to prepare quickly; to make ready; to expedite.

apropiación, *f.* appropriation; giving or taking possession; confiscation; adaptation.—**apropiado,** *a.* appropriate, proper, fitting.—**apropiar,** *vt.* to adapt; to fit.—*apropiarse de,* to take illegal possession of.

aprovechable, *a.* available, fit to be used.—**aprovechado,** *a.* saving, thrifty, studious.—*n.* go-getter.—**aprovechamiento,** *m.* utilization, use; exploitation; profit, benefit; progress, diligence.—**aprovechar,** *vt.* to utilize, make good use of; to profit.—*vi.* to be useful, profitable or beneficial; to avail; to progress, get ahead.—*aprovecharse de,* to take advantage of, make the most of.

aprovisionar, *vt.* to supply.

aproximación, *f.* approximation, approach.—**aproximado,** *a.* approximate; nearly correct.—**aproximar,** *vt.* to place or bring near; to approximate.—*vr.* to get near, approach

aptitud, *f.* aptitude, natural ability. *pl.* qualifications.—**apto,** *a.* apt, capable, competent.

apuesta, *f.* bet, wager

apuesto, *a.* elegant, stylish, spruce.

apuntación, *f.* note; memorandum; musical notation.—**apuntador,** *n.* one who takes or keeps notes; (theat.) prompter

apuntalar, *vt.* to prop; to shore up.

apuntar, *vt.* to aim, level; to point out, mark; to note, make a note of; to hint; to sketch; (theat.) to prompt.—*vi.* to begin to appear.

apunte, *m.* annotation, memorandum; rough sketch.

apuñalar, *vt* to stab

apurado, *a.* worried; needy; exhausted, difficult; in haste.—**apurar,** *vt.* to drain to the last drop; to exhaust (a subject); to press, hurry; to worry, annoy.—*vr.* to hurry up; to get worried.—**apuro,** *m.* need, want; worry; plight, predicament, quandary, rush, hurry

aquejar, *vt* to grieve afflict ail

aquel (*fem.* **aquella**), *a.* that (over there).—*pl.* those (yonder).—**aquél** (*fem.* **aquélla**), *pron.* that one; the former; those.—**aquello**, *pron. neut.* that, that thing, that matter.

aquí, *adv.* here; hither.—*de a. en adelante*, from now on, hereafter.—*hasta a.*, up till now.—*por a.*, this way, through here.

aquiescencia, *f.* (law) acquiescence, consent.

aquietar, *vt.* to quiet; to pacify.—*vr.* to become calm; to quiet down.

aquilatar, *vt.* to examine closely; to assay.

ara, *f.* altar.

árabe, *mf.* Arab.—*a.* Arabian; Arabic.—**arábigo**, *a.* Arabian, Arabic.

arado, *m.* plow; (Am.) piece of cultivated land.

aragonés, *n. & a.* Aragonese.

arancel, *m.* tariff.—*a. de aduanas*, customs, duty.—**arancelario**, *a.* pertaining to tariff.

arandela, *f.* (mech.) washer; pan of a candlestick; sconce.

araña, *f.* spider; chandelier.

arañar, *vt.* to scratch.—**arañazo**, *m.* scratch.

arar, *vt.* to plow.

arbitraje, *m.* arbitration.—**arbitrar**, *vt.* to arbitrate; to umpire; to act unhampered; to contrive.—**arbitrariedad**, *f.* arbitrariness; arbitrary act.—**arbitrario**, *a.* arbitrary; arbitral.—**arbitrio**, *m.* free will; means; arbitration; bond; compromise; discretion, judgment.—**árbitro**, *m.* arbitrator, arbiter, umpire, referee.

árbol, *m.* tree; mast; upright post; axle or shaft; arbor; spindle; drill. —*a. genealógico*, family tree.—**arbolado**, *a.* wooded; masted.—*m.* woodland.—**arboleda**, *f.* grove.—**arbusto**, *m.* shrub.

arca, *f.* ark; chest, coffer.

arcada, *f.* arcade; row of arches. *pl.* retching.

arcángel, *m.* archangel.

arcano, *a.* occult.—*m.* deep secret.

arce, *m.* maple, maple tree.

arcilla, *f.* clay.

arco, *m.* arc; arch, bow.—*a. iris*, rainbow.

arcón, *m.* large chest, bin, bunker

archimillonario, *a. & n.* multimillionaire.

archipiélago, *m.* archipelago

archivar, *vt.* to file; to deposit in archives.—**archivero**, *n.* archivist; file-case, file-drawers.—**archivo**, *m.* archives; file; public records.

arder, *vi.* to burn; to rage (of war, etc.); to be consumed.—*a. en rescoldo*, to smolder

ardid, *m.* trick, scheme, stratagem.

ardiente, *a.* ardent, burning; passionate, fervent.

ardilla, *f.* squirrel.

ardor, *m.* ardor; hotness, heat; dash, valor.—**ardoroso**, *a.* ardent; fiery, vigorous.

arduo, *a.* arduous.

área, *f.* area; square decameter (See Table).

arena, *f.* sand, grit; arena.—**arenal**, *m.* sandy ground; desert.—**arenero**, *m.* sand dealer; sandbox.

arenga, *f.* harangue, speech.—**arengar**, *vii.* [b] to harangue, deliver a speech.

arenque, *m.* herring.

arete, *m.* eardrop, earring.

argamasa, *f.* mortar.

argelino, *a. & n.* Algerian.

argentado, *a.* silvered, silver-plated.**argentar**, *vt.* to plate or adorn with silver; to polish like silver.—**argentino**, *a. & n.* Argentinian.—*a.* silvery.

argolla, *f.* ring; staple; hoop.

argucia, *f.* trick, scheme; cunning.

argüir, *vii. & vti.* [23-e] to argue. —**argumentación**, *f.* argumentation; reasoning.—**argumentar**, *vi.* to argue, dispute.—**argumento**, *m.* argument; summary; plot (of a play, etc.).

aridez, *f.* drought; barrenness, aridity.—**árido**, *a.* arid, dry, barren.—*pl* dry articles, esp grains and vegetables.

ariete, *m.* battering ram.

ario, *n. & a.* Aryan.

arisco, *a.* churlish, cross, unsociable, shy

arista, *f* sharp edge or angle.

aristocracia, *f.* aristocracy —**aristócrata**, *mf. & a.* aristocrat.

aritmética, *f.* arithmetic.—**aritmético**, *a.* arithmetical.—*m.* arithmetician.

arma, *f.* weapon, arm; technical division of military forces; means, power, reason.—*pl.* armed forces, military profession.—**armada**, *f* navy; fleet; squadron.—**armador**, *n.* outfitter, ship owner; adjuster, fitter, assembler, jacket.—**armadura**, *f.* armor; framework, shell of a building; setting, fitting; truss; framing, mounting, trestle; reinforcement (of concrete); armature (of a dynamo etc.).—**armamento**, *m.* armament, accoutrements.—**armar**, *vt.* to arm, to man; to bind; to assemble, mount; to adjust, set, frame; to reinforce (concrete); to form, prepare, to start, cause; (naut) to equip, fit out, put in

commission.—*vr.* to prepare oneself; to arm oneself.

armario, *m.* wardrobe; clothes closet; cabinet; bookcase.

armatoste, *m.* hulk; unwieldy machine; cumbersome piece of furniture; fat, clumsy fellow.

armazón, *f.* framework, skeleton, frame; hulk (of a ship).

armería, *f.* armory, arsenal; gunsmith trade or shop.—**armero,** *m.* armorer, gunsmith; keeper of arms.

armiño, *m.* ermine.

armisticio, *f.* armistice.

armonía, *f.* harmony.—**armónico,** *a.* harmonious.—**armonio,** *m.* harmonium, reed organ.—**armonioso,** *a.* harmonious.—**armonización,** *f.* harmonization.—**armonizar,** *vti.* & *vii.* [a] to harmonize.

arnés, *m.* harness; coat of mail.

aro, *m.* hoop, rim; staple; earring; wedding band; arum.—*entrar por el a.,* to be forced to yield.

aroma, *m.* aroma; perfume, fragrance. —**aromático,** *a.* aromatic, fragrant. —**aromatizar,** *vti.* [a] to perfume.

arpa, *f.* harp.

arpía, *f.* shrew, harpy; fiend.

arpillera, *f.* sackcloth, burlap.

arpón, *m.* harpoon.—**arponear,** *vt.* to harpoon.—**arponero,** *n.* harpooner.

arquear, *vt.* to arch; to beat (wool); to gauge (ships).—*vr.* to arch, become arched.—**arqueo,** *m.* arching; bending; checking of effects in a safe; balance (in accounting); (naut.) tonnage.

arquería, *f.* series of arches; arcade; archery.—**arquero,** *n.* treasurer, cashier; archer; bowmaker.

arquetipo, *m.* archetype.

arquitecto, *m.* architect.—**arquitectónico,** *a.* architectural.—**arquitectura,** *f.* architecture.

arrabal, *m.* outlying district.—*pl.* outskirts, slums.—**arrabalero,** *a.* ill-bred.

arracimarse, *vr.* to cluster.

arraigado, *a.* inveterate, fixed.—**arraigar,** *vii.* [b] to take root.—*vri.* to settle, establish oneself; to take root.—**arraigo,** *m.* settling in a place; the act of taking root.

arrancada, *f.* sudden departure; violent sally.—**arrancado,** *a.* (Am.) broke, poor, penniless.—**arrancar,** *vti.* [d] to root out, extirpate; to pull out, tear off.—*vii.* to start.—**arranque,** *m.* extirpation; impulse (of passion, charity, love, etc.); sudden start, sudden impulse; starter.

arrasar, *vt.* to level, raze, demolish. —*vi.* to clear up (of sky).

arrastrado, *a.* miserable, wretched; dragging out (of life, etc.); knavish; contemptible.—*n.* downcast one.— **arrastrar,** *vt.* to drag; to drag down, degrade; to pull along; to haul; to attract; to influence, persuade.—*vi.* to drag, touch the floor or ground; to play a trump (in cards). —*vr.* to crawl, creep, drag along.— **arrastre,** *m.* dragging; haulage.

¡arre! *interj.* gee, get up!—**arrear,** *vt.* to drive (horses, etc.).

arrebatado, *a.* rash, impetuous; sudden, violent.—**arrebatador,** *a.* ravishing.—**arrebatar,** *vt.* to carry off; to snatch; to attract, hold (the attention, etc.); to enrapture, captivate.—*vr.* to be carried away by passion.—**arrebatiña,** *f.* struggle, scuffle, free-for-all.—**arrebato,** *m.* sudden attack; rapture; surprise.

arrebol, *m.* redness; rouge; red sky or clouds.—**arrebolar,** *vr.* to redden.

arrebujar, *vt.* to jumble together; to huddle, bundle.—*vr.* to wrap oneself up.

arreciar, *vt.* & *vi.* to increase in strength or intensity.

arrecife, *m.* reef.

arrechucho, *m.* fit of anger; sudden and passing indisposition.

arredrar, *vt.* to scare, intimidate.— *vr.* to be or become afraid; to be intimidated.

arreglar, *vt.* to arrange; to adjust, settle; to regulate.—*vr.* to tidy oneself up; to turn out right; to settle differences, come to an agreement; to compromise.—**arreglo,** *m.* disposition, arrangement; adjustment; repair; (com.) agreement; compromise, settlement.—*con a. a,* according to; in accordance with.

arrellanarse, *vr.* to sit at ease, make oneself comfortable.

arremangar, *vti.* [b] to tuck up, turn up, roll up (the sleeves, etc.).—*vri.* to roll up one's sleeves.

arremeter, *vt.* to assail, attack.—**arremetida,** *f.* attack, assault.

arremolinarse, *vr.* to whirl; to crowd together; to mill around.

arrendador, *n.* hirer; tenant.— **arrendar,** *vti.* [1] to rent, let, lease, hire.—**arrendatario,** *n.* lessee, tenant.

arreo, *m.* ornament, decoration.—*pl.* harness, trappings, accessories.—*adv.* successively, uninterruptedly.

arrepentido, *a.* remorseful, repentant. —**arrepentimiento,** *m.* repentance. —**arrepentirse,** *vri.* [39] to repent, regret.

arrestado, *a.* bold, audacious.—**arrestar,** *vt.* to arrest, imprison.—*vr.* (Am.) to dare.—**arresto,** *m.* imprisonment, arrest; spirit, enterprise.

arriar, *vt.* to lower, strike (a flag, etc.).

arriba, *adv.* up, above, high; upstairs; upwards; overhead.—*a. de,* above; higher up.—*cuesta a.,* uphill. —*de a. a abajo,* from top to bottom; up and down.—*para a.,* upwards.—*por a.,* at, or from, the top. —*por a. de,* above, over.—*interj.* up!—**arribada,** *f.* arrival (of a ship).—**arribar,** *vi.* to put into port; to reach; to recover; to prosper by dubious means.—**arribo,** *m.* = ARRIBADA.

arriendo, *m.* renting; lease; rent.

arriero, *m.* muleteer.

arriesgar, *vti.* [b] to risk, hazard, jeopardize.—*vri.* to venture; to dare; to run a risk.

arrimar, *vt.* to place near; to stow; to put beside or against; to put by; to give up.—*vr.* to go near (to); to seek the protection (of); to join.—**arrimo,** *m.* putting near, beside or against; support, protection.

arrinconar, *vt.* to corner; to put away, lay aside; to pigeonhole; to neglect, forsake.—*vr.* to live secluded; to retire.

arriscado, *a.* bold, rash; brisk, spirited; craggy.

arroba, *f.* weight of twenty-five pounds.

arrobador, *a.* enchanting, entrancing. —**arrobamiento, arrobo,** *m.* rapture, bliss; ravishment; trance.—**arrobarse,** *vr.* to be enraptured, entranced.

arrocero, *m.* rice planter or dealer.— *a.* pertaining to rice.

arrodillar, *vt.* to make kneel down.— *vr.* to kneel down.

arrogancia, *f.* arrogance; stately carriage.—**arrogante,** *a.* arrogant; spirited.

arrogar, *vti.* [b] to arrogate; to adopt.—*vri.* to usurp; to assume (power or rights).

arrojado, *a.* rash, dashing, fearless.— **arrojar,** *vt.* to throw, fling; to cast out; to vomit; to emit; to bring forth; to dismiss, drive out.—*vr.* to launch, throw oneself forward; to venture.—**arrojo,** *m.* fearlessness, dash, boldness.

arrollador, *a.* rolling; violent, sweeping.—**arrollar,** *vt.* to roll up; to carry off, sweep away; to trample, run over; to defeat, destroy

arropar, *vt.* to cover, wrap.—*vr.* to wrap oneself, bundle up.

arrostrar, *vt.* to defy, face.

arroyo, *m.* small stream, brook; gutter.—**arroyuelo,** *m.* rivulet, rill.

arroz, *m.* rice.—**arrozal,** *m.* rice field.

arruga, *f.* wrinkle, crease.—**arrugar,** *vti.* [b] to wrinkle; to crease, crumple.—*vri.* to become wrinkled, creased or crumpled; (Am.) to become intimidated.

arruinar, *vt.* to demolish, ruin, destroy.—*vr.* to become ruined.

arrullador, *a.* lulling, soothing.— **arrullar,** *vt.* to lull; to bill and coo.—**arrullo,** *m.* billing and cooing; lullaby.

arrumaco, *m.* caress, fondling.

arrumbar, *vt.* to put away as useless; to silence; to remove from a trust; (naut.) to determine the direction.—*vi.* to take bearings.

arsenal, *m.* shipyard, navy yard; arsenal.

arsenical, *a.* (chem.) arsenical.

arte, *m.* art; skill, craft; trade, profession; artifice, device; intrigue.— *bellas artes,* fine arts.—**artefacto,** *m.* manufacture, handiwork, contrivance, appliance, device.

arteria, *f.* artery; trunk or main line; main highway.

artería, *f.* cunning, trick, artfulness. —**artero,** *a.* cunning, artful.

artesa, *f.* trough.

artesanía, *f.* workmanship, artisanship.—**artesano,** *n.* artisan; craftsman; mechanic.

artesiano, *a.* artesian.

artesonado, *a.* paneled (ceiling).

ártico, *a.* arctic.

articulación, *m.* articulation, joint.— **articulado,** *a.* jointed; articulate.— **articular,** *vt.* to unite, join; to articulate.—*a.* articular.—**artículo,** *m.* article.—*a. de fondo,* leading article (newspaper).

artífice, *mf.* artisan, craftsman.—**artificial,** *a.* artificial; sophisticated.— **artificio,** *m.* workmanship, craft; artifice; cunning; trick, ruse; contrivance, device.—**artificioso,** *a.* skillful, ingenious; artful, cunning.

artillar, *vt.* to mount (cannon).— **artillería,** *f.* artillery, gunnery.— **artillero,** *m.* artilleryman, gunner.

artimaña, *f.* trap, snare, stratagem.

artista, *a.* & *mf.* artist.—**artístico,** *a.* artistic.

arveja, *f.* (Am.) green pea.

arzobispado, *m.* archbishopric.—**arzobispo,** *m.* archbishop.

as, *m.* ace.

asa, *f* handle

asado, *m.* & *a.* roast.—**asador,** *m.* spit (rod); roaster.—**asadura,** *f.* entrails.

asalariado, *a.* working for a salary or wages; serving for hire.—*n.* salaried person, wage earner; hireling.—**asalariar,** *vt.* to fix a salary for; to hire.

asaltante, *mf.* assailant, assaulter; highwayman.—**asaltar,** *vt.* to assault, storm, assail; to surprise.—**asalto,** *m.* assault; attack.

asamblea, *f.* assembly; legislature; meeting.—**asambleísta,** *mf.* assemblyman.

asar, *vt.* to roast.—*vr.* to be roasting; to be very hot.

asaz, *adv.* enough; greatly, very.

asbesto, *m.* asbestos.

ascendencia, *f.* lineage.—**ascendente,** *a.* ascendant, ascending.—**ascender,** *vii.* [18] to ascend, climb; to be promoted.—*vti.* to promote.—**ascendiente,** *mf.* ancestor.—*m.* influence.—**ascensión,** *f.* ascension.—**ascenso,** *m.* promotion; ascent.—**ascensor,** *m.* elevator.

asceta, *m.* ascetic, hermit.—**asceticismo, ascetismo,** *m.* asceticism.

asco, *m.* nausea, disgust, loathing; despicable thing.—*darle a uno a.,* to make one sick.—*estar hecho un a.,* to be very dirty.—*hacer ascos,* to turn up one's nose.

ascua, *f.* red-hot coal, ember.—*estar en ascuas,* to be on tenterhooks.

aseado, *a.* clean, neat.—**asear,** *vt.* to clean; to adorn, embellish.—*vr.* to clean oneself up.—**aseo,** *m.* cleanliness, neatness, tidiness.

asechanza, asechar, asecho, = ACECHANZA, ACECHAR, ACECHO.

asediar, *vt.* to besiege, blockade.—**asedio,** *m.* siege, blockade.

asegurado, *n.* & *a.* insured (person).—**asegurador,** *n.* & *a.* insurer; insuring.—**asegurar,** *vt.* to assure; to secure, fasten; to affirm; to insure.—*vr.* to make sure; to hold fast; to be insured, take out insurance.

asemejar, *vt.* to liken, compare.—*vr.* **(a)** to look like, resemble.

asentaderas, *f. pl.* buttocks.—**asentador,** *m.* razor strop.—**asentar,** *vti.* [1] to place, seat; to adjust; to arrange, settle; to enter (an account, etc.); to hone.—*vii.* to fit, settle.—*vri.* to establish oneself, settle.

asentimiento, *m.* assent.—**asentir,** *vii.* [39] to agree, to assent.

aseo, *m.* cleanliness, cleanness, tidiness.

asepsia, *f.* asepsis.—**aséptico,** *a.* aseptic.

asequible, *a.* attainable, obtainable, available.

aserción, *f.* assertion, affirmation.

aserradero, *m.* sawmill; sawpit; sawhorse.—**aserrar,** *vti.* [1] to saw.—**aserrín,** *m.* sawdust.

asesinar, *vt.* to murder; to assassinate.—**asesinato,** *m.* murder, assassination.—**asesino,** *n.* & *a.* murderer(ess), assassin.

asesor, *n.* consultant, adviser.—**asesorar,** *vt.* to give legal advice.—*vr.* to take advice.—**asesoría,** *f.* office, pay and fees of a consultant.

aserto, *m.* assertion, affirmation.

asestar, *vt.* to point, aim; to level.—*a. un golpe,* to deal a blow.

aseveración, *f.* asseveration, assertion.—**aseverar,** *vt.* to asseverate, affirm, assert.

asfaltar, *vt.* to asphalt.—**asfalto,** *m.* asphalt.

asfixia, *f.* asphyxia.—**asfixiante,** *a.* asphyxiating.—**asfixiar,** *vt.* to asphyxiate, suffocate.—*vr.* to be asphyxiated.

así, *adv.* so, thus, in this manner, like this; therefore.—*a. a.,* so-so, middling.—*a. como,* as soon as, just as.—*a. como a.,* just like that, without rhyme or reason.—*a. no más,* so so, just so.—*a. que,* so that.—*a. y todo,* and yet; just the same.

asiático, *n.* & *a.* Asian, Asiatic.

asidero, *m.* hold; handle; occasion, pretext.

asiduidad, *f.* assiduity, perseverance.—**asiduo,** *a.* assiduous, persevering.

asiento, *m.* seat; site; solidity; settling; bottom; sediment; treaty, contract; entry; registry; stability, permanence; list, roll.

asignación, *f.* assignment; allocation of money.—**asignar,** *vt.* to assign; to appoint; to ascribe.—**asignatura,** *f.* subject (in school curriculum).

asilar, *vt.* to shelter; to place in an asylum.—**asilo,** *m.* asylum; refuge; shelter; private hospital, nursing home.

asimilable, *a.* assimilable.—**asimilación,** *f.* assimilation.—**asimilar,** *vt.* to assimilate.

asimismo, *adv.* likewise, in like manner.

asir, *vti.* [5] & *vii.* to grasp or seize; to hold; to take root.—*vri.* **(de)** to take hold (of); to avail oneself of.

asistencia, *f.* attendance, presence; assistance, aid.—**asistente,** *mf.* assistant, helper; military orderly.—**asistir,** *vi.* to attend, be present (at).—*vt* to tend; to attend; to

take care of; to assist, help, serve; to accompany.

asma, f. asthma.—**asmático,** a. asthmatic.

asno, m. donkey, ass.

asociación, f. association; fellowship, union.—**asociado,** n. & a. associate(d).—**asociar,** vt. to associate. —vr. to associate; to form a partnership; to join.

asolar, vti. [12] to raze, devastate, lay waste.

asolear, vt. to sun.—vr. to be sunburned; to bask in the sun.

asomar, vi. to begin to appear.—vt. to show, put out (as, one's head out the window).—vr. to show oneself at (window, etc.).

asombradizo, a. timid, shy.—**asombrar,** vt. to astonish, amaze; to frighten.—vr. (de) to wonder, be astonished (at).—**asombro,** m. amazement or astonishment; dread, fear.—**asombroso,** a. astonishing, marvelous.

asomo, m. indication, sign; conjecture, suspicion.—ni por a., not even remotely.

asonada, f. attack of a mob, mobbing; riotous crowd.

aspa, f. vane of a windmill; reel; cross stud.—**aspaviento,** m. exaggerated wonder or fear; fuss.

aspecto, m. aspect, look, appearance.

aspereza, f. asperity; roughness; severity; harshness, rough place.— **áspero,** a. rough; harsh; uneven; gruff.—**asperón,** m. scourer.

aspillera, f. loophole; embrasure.

aspiración, f. aspiration; ambition; breathing in.—**aspirador,** m. vacuum cleaner.—**aspirante,** mf. candidate, applicant.—bomba a., suction pump. —**aspirar,** vt. to inhale; to aspire; to covet; to aspirate; to suck.—vi. to aspire; to draw, breathe in, inhale.

aspirina, f. aspirin.

asquear, vt. to disgust, nauseate, sicken.—**asquerosidad,** f. filthiness, baseness.—**asqueroso,** a. filthy, loathsome, squalid; vile, revolting.

asta, f. horn; antler; mast, pole, flagstaff; lance.

asterisco, m. asterisk.

astilla, f. chip, splinter.—**astillar,** vt. to splinter.—vr. to break into splinters.—**astillero,** m. shipyard, dockyard.

astro, m. star; planet; heavenly body.—**astrología,** f. astrology.— **astrólogo,** n. astrologer.—**astronauta,** mf. astronaut.—**astronomía,** f. astronomy.—**astronómico,** a. as-

tronomic.—**astrónomo,** n. astronomer.

astucia, f. astuteness, cunning, slyness.

astur, asturiano, n. & a. Asturian.

astuto, a. astute, cunning, sly, crafty, sneaky.

asueto, m. recess, vacation, holiday; leisure.

asumir, vt. to assume, take upon oneself (command, responsibilities, etc.); to raise, elevate.

asunto, m. topic, theme, subject, matter; affair, business.

asustadizo, a. scary, easily frightened —**asustar,** vt. to frighten, scare.— vr. to be frightened.

atacar, vti. [d] to attack; to button; to fit; to ram (gun); to corner.

atadijo, m. ill-shaped parcel.—**atado,** m. bundle, parcel.—a. faint-hearted, good-for-nothing; fastened, tied.— **atadura,** f. fastening, binding; knot.

atajar, vt. to intercept; to interrupt; to take a short cut.—**atajo,** m. short cut; interception.

atalaya, f. watchtower; height.—m. guard; lookout.

atañer, vii. [50] to relate, affect; to belong, pertain, concern.

ataque, m. attack; offensive works; fit, seizure; wrangle.

atar, vt. to tie, fasten, bind; to lace; to deprive of motion.

atarantado, a. astonished; dizzy.— **atarantar,** vt. to astound, dumbfound.—vr. to be or become dumbfounded.

atardecer, m. late afternoon.—vii. [3] to draw towards evening.

atareado, a. busy, overworked.— **atarear,** vt. to overwork, load with. —vr. to be exceedingly busy.

atascadero, m. muddy place; obstruction.—**atascar,** vti. [d] to stop up; to jam, obstruct.—vri. to get stuck; to stick; to jam, become obstructed; to stall.

ataúd, m. coffin, casket.

ataviar, vt. to adorn; to deck out, trim.—vr. to dress up.—**atavío,** m. dress; finery, gear.

ateísmo, m. atheism.

atemorizar, vti. [a] to scare, frighten.

atemperar, vt. to temper, soften; to accommodate.

atención, f. attention; civility; kindness.—pl. affairs, business.—**atender,** vii. [18] to attend, be attentive; to pay attention.—vti. to take care of; to show courtesy to; to wait on.

atenerse (a), vri. [42] to follow, adhere to; to abide (by), stick (to).

atentado, m. offense, violation, trans-

gression; crime.—**atentar**, *vt.* to attempt, try.

atento, *a.* attentive; polite, courteous.

ateo, *n.* & *a.* atheist(ic).

aterciopelado, *a.* velvety.

aterido, *a.* stiff with cold.—**aterirse**. *vri.* [50] to become stiff with cold.

aterrador, *a.* frightful, terrifying, dreadful.—**aterrar**, *vt.* to terrify; to awe; to appall.—*vr.* to be filled with terror, to be awed or appalled.

aterrizaje, *m.* landing.—**aterrizar**, *vii.* [a] to land.

aterrorizar, *vti.* [a] to frighten, terrify, terrorize.—*vri.* to be terrified.

atesorar, *vt.* to treasure; to hoard, accumulate.

atestación, *f.* testimonial.—**atestado**, *m.* attestation.—**atestar**, *vt.* to attest, witness; to cram, stuff.

atestiguar, *vti.* [b] to depose, witness, attest; to give evidence.

atiborrar, *vt.* to stuff.—*vr.* to stuff oneself.

ático, *a.* Attic; elegant.

atildamiento, *m.* meticulousness in dress or style.—**atildarse**, *vr.* to dress up.

atinar, *vi.* to hit the mark; to guess right; to say or do the right thing. —*a. con*, to find, hit upon.

atisbar, *vt.* to watch, pry; to scrutinize.—**atisbo**, *m.* sign, indication; glimpse, peek.

atizador, *m.* poker.—**atizar**, *vti.* [a] to poke (the fire); to snuff or trim (a candle, etc.); to rouse, stir.—*a. un golpe*, to deliver a blow.

atizonarse, *vr.* (of plants) to become mildewed.

atlántico, *n.* & *a.* Atlantic.

atlas, *m.* atlas.

atleta, *mf.* athlete.—**atlético**, *a.* athletic.—**atletismo**, *m.* athletics.

atmósfera, *f.* atmosphere.—**atmosférico**, *a.* atmospheric.

atol(e), *m.* (Am.) non-alcoholic cornflour drink.

atolondrado, *a.* hare-brained, thoughtless, giddy, careless.—**atolondramiento**, *m.* thoughtlessness, bewilderment.—**atolondrar**, *vt.* to confound, stun.—*vr.* to become confused, stunned.

atolladero, *m.* morass, quagmire, bog. —**atollarse**, *vr.* to be bogged, to stick in the mud; to be in a quandary.

atómico, *a.* atomic.—**átomo**, *m.* atom.

atónito, *a.* astonished, amazed, aghast.

atontado, *a.* foolish, stupid.—**atontamiento**, *m.* stupefaction, stunning. —**atontar**, *vt.* to stun, stupefy; to confound, confuse.—*vr.* to become stupid, dull, stunned.

atorar, *vt.* (Am.) to obstruct; to jam, choke, clog.—*vr.* to stick in the mire; to fit the bore closely; to choke; to stuff oneself.

atormentador, *n.* torturer, tormentor. —**atormentar**, *nt.* to torment, torture; to afflict.

atornillar, *vt.* to screw; to turn a screw.

atosigar, *vti.* [b] to harass, press.

atrabancar, *vti.* [d] to huddle; to perform in a hurry.

atrabiliario, *a.* ill-tempered; unpredictable.

atracar, *vti.* [d] to dock, moor; to come alongside; to cram; to hold up, rob.—*vri.* to overeat, stuff oneself with food.—**atraco**, *m.* holdup, robbery.—**atracón**, *m.* overeating.— *darse un a.*, to gorge, stuff oneself.

atracción, *f.* attraction.—**atractivo**, *a.* attractive.—**atraer**, *vti.* [43] to attract; to allure.

atragantarse, *vr.* to choke; to gobble up food.

atrancar, *vti.* [d] to bar, bolt (a door); to obstruct.—*vri.* to lock oneself in; to become crammed, obstructed.

atrapar, *vt.* to catch, grab; to trap; to overtake; to deceive.

atrás, *adv.* back; aback; backward, behind; past; ago.—**atrasado**, *a.* late; behind time; backward.— **atrasar**, *vt.* to retard, delay; to set, put back (timepiece).—*vi.* (of timepiece) to lose or be slow.—*vr.* to remain, be left or fall behind; to lose time; to be late.—**atraso**, *m.* lateness; tardiness; delay; backwardness.—*pl.* arrears.

atravesar, *vti.* [1] to place across; to go through; to cross; to pierce.— *vr.* to lie across, be in the way; to break in, interrupt, intrude (in); to meddle; to have an encounter or fight (with).

atrayente, *a.* attractive.

atreverse, *vr.* to dare; to venture.— *a. con*, to be insolent to.—**atrevido**, *a.* bold, fearless; forward, insolent. —**atrevimiento**, *m.* boldness, audacity, insolence.

atribución, *f.* attribution; attribute; power, authority.—**atribuir**, *vti.* [23-e] to attribute, ascribe, impute. —*vri.* to take to or on oneself.

atribular, *vt.* to grieve, afflict, distress.—*vr.* to be or become grieved or distressed.

atributo, *m.* attribute, quality.

atrición, *f.* contrition; attrition.

atril, *m.* music stand; lectern; book stand.

atrincheramiento, *m.* entrenchment; trenches.—**atrincherar,** *vt.* & *vr.* to entrench; to mound.

atrio, *m.* court; portico; entrance hall.

atrocidad, *f.* atrocity.

atronador, *a.* thundering, stunning.—**atronar,** *vti.* [12] to deafen, stun; to stupefy, bewilder.

atropellamiento, *m.* confusion.—**atropellar,** *vt.* to trample under foot; to knock down; to run over, hit, injure; to push through; to outrage.—*vr.* to move or act hastily or recklessly; to rush.—**atropello,** *m.* trampling, running over; injuring, abuse, outrage.

atroz, *a.* atrocious; huge, vast, enormous.

atuendo, *m.* dress, garb, attire.

atún, *m.* tunny fish; stupid person.

aturdido, *a.* hare-brained, giddy.—**aturdimiento,** *m.* bewilderment; confusion.—**aturdir,** *vt.* to bewilder, daze; to rattle; to stun.—*vr.* to become bewildered.

aturrullar, *vt.* to confound, bewilder.

atusar, *vt.* to trim; to comb and smooth (the hair).—*vr.* to smooth one's hair, mustache, beard.

audacia, *f.* audacity, boldness.—**audaz,** *a.* bold, fearless, audacious.

audiencia, *f.* audience, hearing; provincial court.—**auditivo,** *a.* auditory. —**auditor,** *n.* judge.—**auditorio,** *m.* audience, assembly of listeners.

auge, *m.* apogee; culmination; summit.—*ir en a.,* to be on the increase.

aula, *f.* classroom; lecture room.

aullar, *vi.* to howl; to yell, cry.—**aullido, aúllo,** *m.* howl.

aumentar, *vt.* & *vr.* to augment, increase, enlarge, magnify.—**aumentativo,** *a.* increasing; (gram.) augmentative.—**aumento,** *m.* increase, augmentation, etc.

aún (aun), *adv.* & *conj.* even.—*adv.* yet, still; as yet.—*a. cuando,* even though.

aunar, *vt.* to unite, join; to combine; to unify.—*vr.* to be united or confederated.

aunque, *conj.* (al)though, notwithstanding, even if.

¡aúpa!, *interj.* up!

aura, *f.* gentle breeze; applause, acclamation; (Am.) buzzard.

aureola, *f.* aureola, halo.

aureomicina, *f.* aureomycin.

auricular, *a.* auricular.—*m.* telephone receiver; earphone.

auscultar, *vt.* to sound (with stethoscope).

ausencia, *f.* absence.—**ausentarse,** *vr.*

to absent oneself.—**ausente,** *a.* absent.

auspiciar, *vt.* to sponsor; to promote. —*auspiciado por,* under the auspices of, sponsored by.—**auspicios,** *m. pl.* auspices, sponsorship; presage; omens.

austeridad, *f.* austerity.—**austero,** *a.* austere.

australiano, *n.* & *a.* Australian.

austríaco, *n.* & *a.* Austrian.

autenticar, *vti.* [d] to authenticate; to attest.—**autenticidad,** *f.* authenticity.—**auténtico,** *a.* authentic, genuine.

auto, *m.* automobile; judicial decree or sentence; edict.—*pl.* (law) records of a case.

autobús, *m.* bus.—**autocamión,** *m.* truck.

autocracia, *f.* autocracy.—**autócrata,** *mf.* autocrat.

autóctono, *a.* aboriginal, native.

autógrafo, *m.* autograph.

autómata, *m.* robot, automaton.—**automático,** *a.* automatic.

automóvil, *m.* automobile.—**automovilismo,** *m.* motoring.—**automovilista,** *n.* devotee of motoring.—*a.* automotive.

autonomía, *f.* autonomy; home rule; self-determination.

autopsia, *f.* autopsy.

autor, *m.* author.—**autora,** *f.* authoress.—**autoridad,** *f.* authority.—**autoritario,** *a.* authoritarian; authoritative; overbearing.—**autorización,** *f.* authorization.—**autorizar,** *vti.* [a] to authorize, empower; to legalize; to prove by quotation; to approve, exalt.

aval, *m.* guarantee; indorsement.

auxiliar, *vt.* to aid, help, assist; to attend.—*a.* auxiliary, assisting.—*mf.* helper, assistant.—**auxilio,** *m.* aid, assistance, help.

avalar, *vt.* to vouch for.

avalorar, *vt.* to estimate, value, appraise.

avaluar, *vt.* to estimate, assess, appraise.—**avalúo,** *m.* valuation, appraisal.

avance, *m.* advance; improvement; attack.—**avanzada, avanzadilla,** *f.* (mil.) outpost; advance guard.—**avanzar,** *vii.* [a] to advance, progress; to improve.—*vti.* to advance, push forward.

avaricia, *f.* avarice.—**avaricioso, avariento,** *a.* avaricious, miserly.—**avaro,** *n.* miser.—*a.* avaricious, miserly.

avasallador, *a.* overwhelming, dominating.—**avasallar,** *vt.* to subject, dominate, enslave, subdue.

ave, *f.* fowl; bird.—*a. de corral,* poultry.

avecindarse, *vr.* to settle, become a resident; to establish oneself.

avejentar, *vt. & vr.* to age.

avellana, *f.* hazelnut.—**avellanado,** *a.* nutbrown; wrinkled.—**avellano,** *m.* hazelnut tree.

avemaría, *f.* Hail Mary; rosary bead. —¡Ave María!, *interj.* Good Heavens!

avena, *f.* oats.

avenencia, *f.* agreement.

avenida, *f.* avenue; way of access; flood.—**avenido,** *a.*—*bien* or *mal avenidos,* on good or bad terms.— **avenirse,** *vri.* [45] to settle differences; to agree; to compromise.

aventajar, *vt.* to advance, improve; to surpass; to prefer.—*vr.* to excel, exceed; to advance, rise.

aventar, *vti.* [1] to fan, blow; to winnow.—*vii.* to breathe hard.—*vri.* to be inflated or puffed up; to escape, run away.

aventura, *f.* adventure; contingency, chance, event, risk.—**aventurar,** *vi.* to venture, hazard, risk.—*vr.* (a) to run the risk of.—**aventurero,** *n.* adventurer.—*a.* adventurous; undisciplined.

avergonzar, *vti.* [12-a-b] to shame. —*vr.* to be ashamed.

averiguación, *f.* investigation.—**averiguar,** *vti.* [b] to inquire, investigate, ascertain, find out.

avería, *f.* damage; mischief; misfortune.—**averiar,** *vt.* to damage.— *vr.* to be damaged; to spoil (foods).

aversión, *f.* aversion, dislike.

avestruz, *f.* ostrich.

avezado, *a.* accustomed; trained; practiced.

aviación, *f.* aviation.—**aviador,** *n.* aviator.—*f.* aviatrix.

aviar, *vt.* to equip; to lend, advance money to; to supply; to prepare; to go, get on the way.

avidez, *f.* covetousness, avidity.— **ávido,** *a.* (de) avid, eager, anxious.

aviejarse, *vr.* to age, grow old.

avieso, *a.* perverse; mischievous; crooked, irregular.

avinagrado, *a.* sour, acrimonious.— **avinagrar,** *vt.* to sour, acidulate.— *vr.* to become sour.

avío, *m.* preparation, provision; money advanced.—*pl.* gear, utensils; paraphernalia.

avión, *m.* airplane.—*a. de caza,* pursuit plane.—*a. de chorro,* jet plane.

avisado, *a.* cautious, sagacious, clearsighted.—**avisar,** *vt.* to inform, announce, give notice of; to warn, advise.—**aviso,** *m.* information, notice; advertisement; advice, warning.

avispa, *f.* wasp.—**avispado,** *a.* lively, brisk, clever.—**avisparse,** *vr.* to be on the alert; to fret.—**avispero,** *m.* nest of wasps; carbuncle.

avistar, *vt.* to sight at a distance. —*vr.* to have an interview, meet.

avituallar, *vt.* to provide food.

avivar, *vt.* to quicken, enliven; to encourage; to revive.—*vr.* to revive; to cheer up.

avizor, *a.* alert, watchful.—**avizorar,** *vt.* to watch; to keep a sharp lookout.

axila, *f.* armpit.

axioma, *m.* axiom; maxim.

ay, *m.* moan, lament.—*interj.* ouch!; alas!

aya, *f.* governess, instructress.—**ayo,** *m.* tutor or guardian; teacher.

ayer, *adv.* yesterday.

ayuda, *f.* help, aid.—**ayudante,** *mf.* assistant; helper; adjutant.—**ayudar,** *vt.* to aid, help, assist.

ayunar, *vi.* to fast.—**ayuno,** *m.* fast, abstinence.—*a.* (de) uninformed (of); ignorant (of); unaware (of). —*estar en ayunas,* to fast; to be uninformed.—*quedarse en ayunas,* not to catch on; to miss the point.

ayuntamiento, *m.* municipal government; town hall; sexual intercourse.

azabache, *m.* jet (stone).

azada, *f.* hoe.—**azadón,** *m.* hoe, spud.

azafata, *f.* stewardess, air hostess.

azafrán, *m.* saffron.

azahar, *m.* orange or lemon blossom.

azar, *m.* hazard, chance; disaster; accident.—*al a.,* at random.—*correr* (*ese* or *el*) *a.,* to take (that) chance, run the risk.—**azaroso,** *a.* unlucky; hazardous.

ázoe, *m.* nitrogen.

azogar, *vti.* [b] to silver with mercury.—**azogue,** *m.* mercury, quicksilver.

azoramiento, *m.* embarrassment, uneasiness.—**azorar,** *vt.* to disturb, startle; to confound, embarrass; to bewilder.—*vr.* to become embarrassed, uneasy, or startled.

azotaina, *f.* drubbing, flogging, spanking.—**azotar,** *vt.* to whip, lash; to thrash.—**azotazo,** *m.* lash.—**azote,** *m.* whip; scourge; stroke, blow.

azotea, *f.* flat roof.

azteca, *mf. & a.* Aztec.

azúcar, *m.* sugar.—**azucarado,** *a.* sugary; affectedly sweet or affable.— **azucarar,** *vt.* to sugar; to sweeten; to coat or ice with sugar.—**azucarera,** *f.* sugar bowl.—**azucarero,** *m.* sugar master; sugar bowl; sugar producer or dealer.—*a.* sugar.

azucena, *f.* white lily.

azufre, *m.* sulfur; brimstone.

azul, *a.* & *m.* blue.—*a. celeste,* sky blue.—*a. marino,* navy blue.—**azulado,** *a.* bluish.

azulejado, *a.* tiled.—**azulejo,** *m.* glazed tile; little bluebird.

azur, *a.* azure.

azuzar, *vti.* [a] to urge, set (dogs) on; to incite, goad.

B

baba, *f.* drivel, spittle, saliva; slime.—**babear,** *vi.* to drivel; to slaver.—**babero,** *m.* bib, feeder.

Babia, *f.*—*estar en B.,* to be woolgathering.—**babieca,** *m.* ignorant, stupid fellow.

babor, *m.* (naut.) port, portside.—*de b. a estribor,* athwart ship.

babosa, *f.* (zool.) slug.—**babosear,** *vi.* = BABEAR.—**baboso,** *a.* driveling, slavering; silly; overaffectionate.

babucha, *f.* slipper.

bacalao, *m.* cod.

bacía, *f.* metal basin; shaving dish.

bacilo, *m.* bacillus.

bacín, *m.* high chamber pot; stupid man.

bacteria, *f.* bacterium.—**bacteriano,** *a.* bacterial.—**bacteriología,** *f.* bacteriology.—**bacteriológico,** *a.* bacteriological.—**bacteriólogo,** *n.* bacteriologist.

báculo, *m.* walking stick, staff; support, aid.—*b. pastoral,* bishop's crosier.

bache, *m.* deep hole, pothole, rut (in the road).

bachiller, *n.* bachelor (degree); babbler, prater.—**bachillerato,** *m.* baccalaureate, B.A. degree.

badajo, *m.* clapper of a bell.

badana, *f.* dressed sheepskin.

badulaque, *a.* foolish; good-for-nothing.—*m.* fool.

bagaje, *m.* beast of burden; baggage of an army.—*pl.* equipment of an army on the march.

bagatela, *f.* trifle.

bahía, *f.* bay, harbor.

bailable, *a.* (of music) composed for dancing.—*m.* ballet.—**bailador,** *n.* dancer.—**bailar,** *vi.* to dance, spin.—*b. al son que le toquen,* to adapt oneself to circumstances.—*b. como un trompo,* to dance well.—**bailarín,** *n.* dancer; ballet dancer.—**baile,** *m.* dance, ballet; ball.—*b. de etiqueta,* formal dance.—*b. de máscaras,* masquerade.—*b. de trajes,* fancy-dress ball.—**bailotear,** *vi.* (coll.) to dance clumsily, frequently.—**bailoteo,** *m.* awkward dancing.

baja, *f.* fall in price; (mil.) casualty; vacancy.—*dar de b.,* to drop (a person from a list, etc.).—*darse de b.,* to drop out, resign from.—**bajada,** *f.* descent; slope.—**bajamar,** *f.* low water, low tide.—**bajar,** *vi.* to descend; to fall; to come or go down; to drop, lessen, diminish.—*vt.* to lower, reduce; to bring or take down, let down.—*vr.* to bend over, stoop; to crouch, grovel; to alight; to get out (of a vehicle); to get down; to bow down.

bajeza, *f.* meanness; vile act or remark; low action.

bajío, *m.* shoal, sand bank; (Am.) low land.

bajo, *a.* low, shallow; short; abject; base; common; (of color) dull; (of sound) deep, low; coarse, vulgar; downcast.—*por lo b.,* on the sly; in an undertone.—*adv.* softly, in a low voice.—*prep.* under.—*m.* bass (voice, singer, instrument); ground floor; sand bank.—*pl.* underskirts; trousers' cuffs.

bala, *f.* bullet, shot, ball; bale.—*b. perdida,* stray bullet; (fig.) a good-for-nothing.

balada, *f.* ballad.

baladí, *a.* trivial, frivolous; trashy.

baladronada, *f.* boast, bravado.

balance, *m.* oscillation, rolling, rocking, swinging; balance; balance sheet; (Cuba) rocking chair; (aer.) rolling.—**balancear,** *vt.* to balance; to put into equilibrium.—*vi.* & *vr.* to roll, rock, swing; to waver.—**balanceo,** *m.* rocking, rolling; wobbling.—**balancín,** *m.* splinter bar, swing bar; (mec.) walking beam; oscillating beam.

balandro, *n.* sloop.

balanza, *f.* scales; balance.

balar, *vi.* to bleat.

balastar, *vt.* to ballast.—**balasto,** *m.* (RR.) ballast.

balazo, *m.* shot, bullet wound.

balbucear, *vi.,* **balbucir,** *vii.* [11] to hesitate in speech, stammer.—**balbuceo,** *m.* stammer, babble.—**balbuciente,** *a.* stammering, stuttering.

balcón, *m.* balcony; porch.

baldar, *vt.* to cripple.

balde, *m.* bucket, pail.—*de b.,* gratis; free.—*en b.,* in vain, with no result.—**baldear,** *vt.* to wash (floors, decks).—**baldeo,** *m.* washing (floors, decks).

baldío, *a.* untilled, uncultivated; barren.—*m.* wasteland.

baldón, *m.* affront, insult.

baldosa, *f.* paving tile; slab; flat paving stone.—**baldosado,** *m.* tile pavement.

balear, *a.* & *mf.* Balearic; person

of or from the Balearic Islands.—
vt. (Am.) to shoot (wound or kill).

balido, *m.* bleating, bleat.

balín, *m.* small bullet.—*pl.* buckshot.

baliza, *f.* buoy.—**balizar,** *vti.* [a] to
mark with buoys.

balneario, *a.* pertaining to baths.—*m.*
bathing resort; watering place.

balompié, *m.* football.—**balón,** *m.*
football; (auto) balloon tire.—*b. de
gas,* gas bag.—**baloncesto,** *m.* basketball. Also BASKETBOL.

balsa, *f.* raft; pool, pond.

bálsamo, *m.* balsam, balm; (fig.)
balm.—**balsámico,** *a.* balsamic,
balmy.

baluarte, *m.* bastion; bulwark; defense.

balumba, *f.* bulk, heap; jumble.

ballena, *f.* whale; whalebone.—**balle-
nato,** *m.* young whale.—**ballenera,**
f. whaleboat.—**ballenero,** *a.* whal-
ing, whale.—*n.* whaler, whale fisherman.

ballesta, *f.* crossbow.

bambalina, *f.* fly (in theatrical
scenery).

bambolear, *vi. & vr.* to swing, sway.
—**bamboleo,** *m.* swinging, swaying.

bambolla, *f.* (coll.) boast, sham.—
bambollero, *n. & a.* boaster; boasting.

banana, *f.,* **banano,** *m.* banana.

banca, *f.* bench; stand; (com.) banking.—**bancario,** *a.* banking; financial.—**bancarrota,** *f.* bankruptcy;
failure.

bancaza, *f.* bedplate.

banco, *m.* bench; settee; pew;
(mech.) bed, table; pedestal;
school of fish, shoal; (com.) bank.—
b. de ahorros, savings bank.—*b.,* or
cámara de compensaciones, clearing
house.

banda, *f.* band; ribbon; sash; scarf;
band, gang; covey; edge; side of
a ship; cushion (of a billiard table).
—**bandada,** *f.* covey; flock of birds.
—**bandazo,** *m.* (of ship) violent roll
to side.—**bandear,** *vi.* to band.—*vr.*
to conduct for oneself.

bandeja, *f.* tray; salver.

bandera, *f.* flag, banner; colors.—*b.
de popa,* ensign.—**bandería,** *f.* band,
faction.—**banderilla,** *f.* baiting dart
(bullfight).—*poner a uno una b.,*
to taunt or provoke one.—**banderín,**
m. camp colors; flag; railway signal; recruiting post.—**banderola,** *f.*
streamer; pennant; signal flag.

bandidaje, *m.* banditry; gang.—**bandido,** *m.* bandit, robber.

bando, *m.* proclamation, edict; faction, party.

bandolera, *f.* woman bandit; bando-

leer, shoulder belt.—**bandolerismo,**
m. banditry.—**bandolero,** *m.* highwayman, robber.

bandullo, *m.* (coll.) belly; guts.

banquero, *n.* banker.

banqueta, *f.* backless bench; stool;
footstool; (Mex.) sidewalk.

banquete, *m.* banquet.—**banquetear,**
vt., vi. & vr. to banquet, feast.

banquillo, *m.* little stool.—*b. de los
acusados,* defendant's seat.—**ban-
quito,** *m.* stool, footstool.

bañadera, *f.* (Am.) bathtub.—**bañar,**
vt. to bathe, wash, lave; to wet,
water; to dip; to coat, apply a
coating or layer to, plate.—*vr.* to
take a bath.—**bañera,** *f.* bathtub.—
bañista, *mf.* bather.—**baño,** *m.*
bath; bathing; bathtub; bath-
room; coat, coating (of paint, etc.);
(chem.) bath.—*b. María,* double
boiler.—*pl.* bathhouse; spa.

baqueano, *n. & a.* = BAQUIANO.

baqueta, *f.* ramrod.—*pl.* drumsticks.—
a la b., harshly, despotically.

baquiano, *n.* (Am.) guide.—*a.* skillful,
expert.

bar, *m.* bar (for drinks); saloon,
tavern.

baraja, *f.* pack of cards; game of
cards.—**barajar,** *vt.* to shuffle (the
cards); to jumble together.

baranda, *f.* railing; banister.—**barandilla,** *f.* balustrade, railing.

barata, *f.* (fam.) barter, exchange;
(Am.) bargain sale.—**baratear,** *vt.*
to sell cheap; to haggle.—**baratijas,**
f. pl. trifles, trinkets.—**baratillero,**
n. peddler; seller of secondhand
goods or articles.—**baratillo,** *m.*
secondhand shop; remnant sale;
bargain counter.—**barato,** *a.* cheap;
low (priced), reasonable.—*adv.*
cheaply.—*m.* bargain sale, bargain
counter.—*cobrar el b.,* to sell protection by compulsion.—**baratura,**
f. cheapness.

baraúnda, *f.* noise, hurly-burly, confusion.

barba, *f.* chin; beard; whiskers;
wattle.—*pl.* beard, whiskers; fibers;
rough edges of paper.—*b. corrida* or
cerrada, thick beard.—*b. de ballena,*
whalebone.—*en sus barbas,* to his
face.—*tener pocas barbas,* to be
young or inexperienced.

barbacoa, *f.* (Am.) barbecue; barbecued meat.

barbaridad, *f.* barbarity; atrocity;
cruelty; rudeness; (Am.) excess (in
anything); nonsense; blunder.—
barbarie, *f.* fierceness; cruelty; barbarity; lack of culture.—**barbarismo,**
m. barbarism; barbarousness.—**bar-
barizar,** *vti.* [a] to barbarize.—*vii.*

to make wild statements.—**bárbaro,**
a. barbarous, uncivilized; barbarian; rude, unpolished.—*n.* barbarian.

barbechar, *vt.* to plow for seeding;
to fallow.—**barbecho,** *m.* fallow.

barbería, *f.* barber's shop.—**barbero,**
m. barber.—**barbilla,** *f.* point of
the chin.—**barboquejo,** *m.* chin
strap; hat guard.

barbotar, *vt. & vi.* to mumble.

barbudo, *a.* having a long or thick
beard.

barca, *f.* boat, barge, bark.—*b. chata,*
ferryboat.—**barcaza,** *f.* (naut.)
barge.

barco, *m.* boat, vessel, ship.

bardo, *m.* bard, poet.

barítono, *m.* baritone.

barloventear, *vi.* to ply to windward;
to beat about.—**barlovento,** *m.*
windward.

barniz, *m.* varnish.—**barnizar,** *vti.*
[a] to varnish.

barométrico, *a.* barometric.—**barómetro,** *m.* barometer.

barquero, *m.* bargeman, boatman,
ferryman.—**barquichuelo,** *m.* small
barge or boat.—**barquilla,** *f.* little
boat; car, basket (of a dirigible).

barquillo, *m.* thin rolled wafer.

barra, *f.* (mech., eng.) bar, beam,
rod, crowbar; stripe; sand bar;
stick (cosmetics); shaft of a carriage; (Arg.) gang (of boys);
(naut.) spar; thill; railing in a
court room; (Am.) fans (at a
game); (theat.) claque.

barrabasada, *f.* serious mischief;
reckless, harmful action.

barraca, *f.* barrack, cabin, hut.—
barracón, *m.* big cabin.

barranca, *f.,* **barrancal, barranco,** *m.*
deep hollow; cliff; gorge, ravine;
precipice; great difficulty, obstacle.

barredura, *f.* sweeping.—*pl.* sweepings, chaff.

barreminas, *m.* minesweeper (ship).

barrena, *f.* drill; auger; gimlet;
(aer.) spin; spinning dive.—*b. de
gusano,* wimble; rock drill.—*b.
grande,* borer, auger.—**barrenado,** *a.*
bored, drilled.—*m.* boring, drilling.
—**barrenador,** *m.* auger or borer.—
barrenar, *vt.* to drill, bore; to foil;
to infringe (a law).—*b. una roca,*
or *mina,* to blast a rock or a mine.

barrendero, *n.* sweeper, dustman
(woman).

barrenillo, *m.* insect that bores into
trees; (Am. coll.) worries.—**barreno,**
m. large borer, drill or auger; bored
hole, blast hole.

barreña, *f.,* **barreño,** *m.* earthenware
basin.

barrer, *vt.* to sweep; (naut.) to rake.
—*al b.,* (com.) on an average.

barrera, *f.* barricade, barrier, parapet; turnpike, tollgate; clay pit.

barriada, *f.* district, quarter, neighborhood.

barrica, *f.* cask, keg.

barricada, *f.* barricade.

barrido, *m.* sweeping.

barriga, *f.* belly; pregnancy.—**barrigón, barrigudo,** *a.* big-bellied,
paunchy.

barril, *m.* barrel; keg.

barrio, *m.* district, ward, quarter;
suburb.—*barrios bajos,* slums.—*el
otro b.,* the other world; eternity.

barro, *m.* mud; clay; earthenware.—
pl. pimples on the face.

barrote, *m.* short and thick iron bar;
round rung (of a ladder).

barruntar, *vt.* to conjecture, guess.—
barrunto, *m.* conjecture; presentiment; guess; hint; indication, sign.

bártulos, *m. pl.* household goods;
tools.

barullo, *m.* confusion, disorder.

basamento, *m.* (arch.) base and
pedestal.—**basar,** *vt.* to support,
give a base to; to base; (surv.) to
refer (operation, etc.) to a base
line.—*vr.* (en) to base one's opinion
(on).

basca, *f.* nausea; squeamishness.

base, *f.* base, basis; (mil., chem.,
alg., geom.) base.—**básico,** *a.* basic.

basílica, *f.* basilica, privileged church.

basilisco, *m.* basilisk (animal, cannon).—*estar hecho un b.,* to be
furious.

basketbol, basquetbol, *m.* basketball.—
basketbolista, *mf.* basketball player.

¡**basta!,** stop! that will do!

bastante, *a.* sufficient, enough.—*adv.*
enough; rather, fairly, pretty.

bastar, *vi.* to suffice; to be enough.

bastardilla, *f.* italics (type).—*a.*
italic.—**bastardo,** *n.* illegitimate son,
bastard.—*a.* degenerate; false.

bastidor, *m.* frame; easel; embroidery
frame; stretcher for canvas; wing
of stage scenery; window sash.—
entre bastidores, behind the scenes.

bastilla, *f.* hem.

bastión, *m.* bulwark, bastion.

basto, *m.* packsaddle; pack; (cards)
ace of clubs.—*pl.* clubs (cards).—*a.*
coarse, rude; homespun.

bastón, *m.* cane, walking stick; gad;
baton.—**bastonazo,** *m.* blow with a
walking stick.

basura, *f.* sweepings, litter, rubbish;
garbage, refuse.—**basurero,** *m.* dunghill, garbage dump; garbage man;
street cleaner; scavenger.

bata, *f.* house coat; smock; wrap; dressing gown; lounging robe.

batacazo, *m.* violent, noisy fall; thud.

batahola, *f.* bustle, hubbub, uproar.

batalla, *f.* battle, struggle.—*b. campal,* pitched battle.—**batallador,** *n.* & *a.* battler; battling; fighter; fighting.—**batallar,** *vi.* to battle, fight, struggle.—**batallón,** *m.* battalion.

batán, *m.* fulling mill.—**batanear,** *vt.* (coll.) to beat, strike.

batata, *f.* sweet potato.

bate, *m.* (Am.) baseball bat.

batea, *f.* tray; foot tub; flat-bottomed boat.

bateador, *n.* (Am.) batter.—**batear,** *vt.* & *vi.* to bat.

batería, *f.* battery; (mus.) percussion instruments; (Am. baseball) battery.—*b. de cocina,* kitchen utensils.

batey, *m.* (Cuba) center square in a sugar mill.

batiburrillo, *m.* = BATURRILLO.

batida, *f.* hunting party.—**batido,** *a.* beaten, trodden (as roads).—*m.* batter of flour, eggs, etc.—**batidor,** *m.* beater; scout; ranger; leather beater; stirring rod.—**batiente,** *m.* jamb (of a door); leaf (of a door).

batintín, *m.* (Am.) gong.

batir, *vt.* to beat, pound; to defeat; to strike; to demolish; to flap; to stir; to reconnoiter.—*b. el record,* to beat, or break the record.—*b. palmas,* to clap the hands.—*vr.* to fight; to duel.

baturrillo, *m.* hodgepodge; confusion.

batuta, *f.* conductor's wand; baton.—*llevar la b.,* to lead; to preside.

baúl, *m.* trunk, chest.

bautismal, *a.* baptismal.—**bautismo,** *m.* baptism, christening.—**bautista,** *mf.* baptizer; Baptist.—**bautizar,** *vti.* [a] to baptize, christen; to nickname.—**bautizo,** *m.* baptism; christening party.

baya, *f.* berry, any small globular fruit.

bayeta, *f.* baize, thick flannel.

bayo, *a.* bay, cream-colored.—*m.* bay horse.

bayoneta, *f.* bayonet.—**bayonetazo,** *m.* bayonet thrust or wound.

baza, *f.* trick (at cards).—*meter b.,* to meddle, intrude, butt in.—*no dejar meter b.,* not to let one put in a single word.

bazar, *m.* bazaar, market place; department store; fair.

bazo, *m.* spleen; milt.

bazofia, *f.* scraps; garbage; waste meat; refuse.

beatería, *f.* affected piety, sanctimoniousness; bigotry.—**beatitud,** *f.* beatitude, blessedness, holiness.—**beato,** *a.* blessed; beatified; devout; sanctimonious, overpious.—*n.* pious person; overpious, prudish person.

bebé, *m.* baby; doll.

bebedero, *m.* drinking place or trough; spout.—**bebedor,** *n.* tippler, toper.—**beber,** *vt.* & *vi.* to drink; to swallow; to pledge, toast.—*b. como una esponja,* to drink like a fish.—**bebida,** *f.* drink, beverage; potion.—**bebido,** *a.* drunk; intoxicated.

beca, *f.* scholarship; fellowship; academic sash.—**becario,** *n.* scholarship or fellowship holder.

becerro, *m.* yearling calf; calfskin.

becuadro, *m.* (mus.) natural (tone).

bedel, *m.* beadle, warden; usher (at school, etc.).

beduíno, *n.* & *a.* Bedouin; uncivil.

befa, *f.* jeer, scoffing.

befo, *a.* = BELFO.

beisbol, *m.* baseball (game).—**beisbolero,** *n.* **beisbolista,** *mf.* baseball player.

bejuco, *m.* rattan.

beldad, *f.* beauty.

belén, *m.* Christmas creche; confusion; bedlam.

belfo, *a.* having a thick lower lip.—*m.* lip of an animal.

belga, *mf.* & *a.* Belgian.

bélico, *a.* warlike.—**belicoso,** *a.* warlike, bellicose; quarrelsome.

beligerancia, *f.* belligerency.—**beligerante,** *mf.* & *a.* belligerent.

bellaco, *a.* artful, sly, cunning, roguish.—*m.* rogue, villain, knave.—**bellaquear,** *vi.* to cheat, swindle; to play knavish, roguish tricks.—**bellaquería,** *f.* knavery, roguery, cunning; vile act or expression.

belleza, *f.* beauty.—**bello,** *a.* beautiful, fair.

bellota, *f.* acorn.

bembo, *n.* & *a.* thick-lipped.—*n.* thick lip, esp. Negro's lip.—**bembón,** *a.* (of persons) thick-lipped.

bemol, *m.* (mus.) flat.—*tener bemoles,* (coll.) to be very difficult, a tough job.

bencina, *f.* benzine.

bendecir, *vti.* [6] to bless.—**bendición,** *f.* blessing, benediction.—**bendito,** *pp. i.* of BENDECIR.—*a.* blessed, sainted; simple-minded.

benefactor, *n.* benefactor.

beneficencia, *f.* beneficence, charity; department of public welfare.—**beneficiar,** *vt.* to benefit; to cultivate, develop, exploit; to purchase.—*vr.* to profit.—**beneficiario,** *n.* beneficiary.—**beneficio,** *m.* benefit; profits; favor, benefaction.—*b. bruto,* gross profit.—*b. neto,* clear

profit.—**beneficioso, a.** beneficial, profitable.—**benéfico, a.** beneficent, charitable.

benemérito, a. meritorious, worthy.

beneplácito, m. approval, consent.

benevolencia, f. benevolence, kindness.—**benévolo, a.** benevolent, kind.

benignidad, f. benignity, kindness; mildness.—**benigno, a.** benign, kind; mild.

beodo, a. drunk.—**n.** drunkard.

berbiquí, m. drill brace; wimble.

berenjena, f. eggplant.—**berenjenal, m.** bed of eggplants.—*meterse en un b.*, to get into a mess.

bergante, m. brazen-faced villain, rascal.

bermejizo, a. crimson, reddish.—**bermejo, a.** bright reddish.

bermellón, bermillón, m. vermilion.

berrear, vi. to cry like a goat, bellow.—**berrido, m.** bellowing.

berrinche, m. tantrum; rage, temper.

berro, m. watercress.

berza, f. cabbage.

besar, vt. to kiss.—**beso, m.** kiss.

bestia, f. beast, quadruped; (fig.) dunce, idiot; ill-bred fellow.—*b. de carga,* beast of burden.—**bestial, a.** bestial, brutal.—**bestialidad, f.** brutality; stupid notion.

besugo, m. sea bream; red gilthead.

besuquear, vt. & vi. to kiss repeatedly; to spoon.—**besuqueo, m.** (coll.) spooning.

betabel, f. (Mex.) beet.

betún, m. bitumen, pitch; shoeblacking; coarse wax.—**betunar, vt.** to pitch, tar.

biberón, m. nursing bottle.

Biblia, f. Bible.—**bíblico, a.** Biblical.—**biblioteca, f.** library.—**bibliotecario, n.** librarian.

bicarbonato, m. bicarbonate.

bicicleta, f. bicycle.

bichero, m. boat hook.

bicho, m. bug, insect; grub; any animal (gen. small); ridiculous fellow; (Cuba) clever fellow.

bidé, bidel, m. bidet.

biela, f. connecting rod; crank.

bien, m. good, supreme goodness; benefit; righteousness; object of love.—*en b. de,* for the sake, good, or benefit of.—*pl.* property; possessions; estate.—*bienes de fortuna,* worldly possessions.—*bienes gananciales,* matrimonial common property.—*bienes inmuebles,* real estate.—*bienes muebles,* goods and chattels.—*hombre de b.,* honest man.—*adv.* well; all right; right; very; happily; perfectly.—*b. que,* although.—*encontrar,* or *hallar b.,* approve.—*más b.,* rather.—*o b.,* or

else; otherwise.—*si b.,* while, though, —*y b.,* well, now then.

bienaventurado, a. blessed; fortunate. —**bienaventuranza, f.** beatitude; bliss; well-being.—*pl.* beatitudes.—

bienestar, m. comfort; well-being. —**bienhechor, n.** benefactor.—**bienvenida, f.** welcome; safe arrival.—**bienvenido, a.** welcome.

biftec, m. beefsteak.

bifurcación, f. a forking or branching out.—**bifurcarse, vri.** [d] to branch off, fork; to divide into two branches.

bigamia, f. bigamy.—**bígamo, a. & n.** bigamous; bigamist.

bigornia, f. anvil.

bigote, m. mustache.—**bigotudo, a.** having a heavy mustache.

bilingüe, a. bilingual.

bilioso, a. bilious.—**bilis, f.** bile.

billar, m. billiards.—**billarista, mf.** billiard player.

billete, m. bill, bank note; note, brief letter; ticket.—*b. de ida y vuelta,* round-trip ticket.—**billetera, f.** wallet.

billón, m. billion.

bimensual, a. occurring twice a month. —**bimestral, bimestre, a.** bimonthly. —**bimestre, m.** a period of two months.

binóculos, m. pl. opera glasses; binoculars.

biografía, f. biography.—**biográfico, a.** biographical.—**biógrafo, n.** biographer.

biología, f. biology.—**biólogo, n.** biologist.

biombo, m. folding screen.

bioquímica, f. biochemistry.—**bioquímico, a.** biochemical.—**n.** biochemist.

birlar, vt. to snatch away; to rob, pilfer; to kill or knock down at one blow.

birlibirloque, m.—*por arte de b.,* by magic.

birmano, n. & a. Burmese.

birreta, f., birrete, m. biretta; academic cap.

bisabuela, f. great-grandmother.—**bisabuelo, m.** great-grandfather.

bisagra, f. hinge.

bisbisar, vi. to mutter.—**bisbiseo, m.** muttering.

bisel, m. bevel, bevel edge.—**biselado, m.** beveling.—**biselar, vt.** to bevel.

bisiesto, a.—*año b.,* leap year.

bisnieta, bisnieto = BIZNIETA, BIZNIETO.

bisojo, a. cross-eyed.

bisoño, n. & a. novice; inexperienced.

bisturí, m. surgical knife.

bizarría, *f.* bravery; magnanimity.—**bizarro**, *a.* brave; gallant; generous.

bizco, *a.* cross-eyed.

bizcocho, *m.* biscuit; sponge cake.

biznieta, *f.* great-granddaughter.—**biznieto**, *m.* great-grandson.

blanco, *a.* white.—*n.* white person.—*m.* white (color); aim, goal.—*dar en el b.*, to hit the mark.—*de punta en b.*, cap-a-pie; in full regalia.—*quedarse en b.*, to be frustrated, disappointed.—**blancura**, *f.* whiteness.—**blancuzco**, *a.* whitish.

blandir, *vt.* to brandish, flourish, swing.

blandengue, *a.* bland, exceedingly kind.—**blando**, *a.* soft, pliant; smooth; bland; pusillanimous; gentle, kind.—**blanducho, blandujo**, *a.* flabby.—**blandura**, *f.* softness; delicacy; gentleness.

blanqueador, *m.* blancher, whitewasher; bleacher.—**blanqueadura**, *f.*, **blanqueamiento, blanqueo**, *m.* whitening, bleaching, whitewashing.—**blanquear**, *vt.* to whiten; to whitewash; to bleach.—*vi.* to show white; to begin to turn white.—**blanquecino**, *a.* whitish.—**blanquillo**, *m.* (Mex.) egg.

blasfemar, *vi.* to blaspheme.—**blasfemia**, *f.* blasphemy.—**blasfemo**, *n. & a.* blasphemer; blasphemous.

blasón, *m.* coat of arms; honor, glory.—**blasonar**, *vi.* to boast, brag.

bledo, *m.* wild amaranth.—*no me importa un b.*, I don't care a straw.

blindado, *n. & a.* iron-clad.—**blindaje**, *m.* blindage; armor.—**blindar**, *vt.* to armor; to protect with blindage.

bloque, *m.* block; coalition.—**bloqueador**, *n. & a.* blockader; blocking.—**bloquear**, *vt.* to blockade; to block, freeze (funds).—**bloqueo**, *m.* blockade.

blusa, *f.* blouse.

boardilla, *f.* = BUHARDILLA.

boato, *m.* ostentation, pomp.

bobina, *f.* bobbin; coil.

bobada, bobería, *f.* foolish speech or action.—**bobalicón**, *n.* blockhead, simpleton.—**bobear**, *vi.* to act or talk foolishly; fritter away (time).—**bobo**, *a.* foolish, simple.—*n.* fool, booby.

boca, *f.* mouth; entrance; opening.—*a b. de jarro*, at close range.—*andar de b. en b.*, to be the talk of the town.—*b. abajo*, prone, face downwards.—*b. arriba*, supine, on one's back.—*b. de agua*, hydrant.—*b. del estómago*, pit of the stomach.—*b. de riego*, hydrant.—*no decir esta b.*

es mía, to be mum.—**bocacalle**, *f.* opening of a street or street intersection.—**bocadillo**, *m.* mid-morning luncheon or small luncheon; sandwich, roll.—**bocado**, *m.* mouthful, morsel, bite; bit (of a bridle).—**bocamanga**, *f.* part of a sleeve near the wrist.—**bocanada**, *f.* mouthful (of liquor); puff (of smoke).

boceto, *m.* sketch.

bocina, *f.* horn; trumpet; speaking tube; megaphone.

bocio, *m.* goiter.

bocón, *n.* braggart; wide-mouthed person.

bocha, *f.* bowl, ball for playing at bowls or bowling.

bochinche, *m.* tumult, hubbub.

bochorno, *m.* embarrassment; sultry weather.—**bochornoso**, *a.* embarrassing; shameful; sultry; humiliating.

boda, *f.* wedding, nuptials.

bodega, *f.* wine vault or cellar; winery; retail grocery; storeroom, warehouse; hold (of ship).—**bodegón**, *m.* tavern; still life.—**bodeguero**, *m.* keeper of a wine vault; liquor dealer; grocer.

bodoque, *m.* pellet; wad; lump; dunce, idiot.

bofe, *m.* lung; (Am. coll.) snap, easy job.—*echar los bofes*, to toil; to pant, be out of breath.

bofetada, *f.* **bofetón**, *m.* slap in the face, buffet.

boga, *f.* rowing.—*en b.*, vogue, popularity.—**bogar**, *vii.* [b] to row.

bogavante, *m.* large lobster; stroke oar.

bohardilla, *f.* = BUHARDILLA.

bohemio, *n. & a.* Bohemian; Czech; gypsy; bohemian (life or person).

bohío, *m.* Indian hut, hovel, cabin.

boicot, *m.* boycott.—**boicoteador**, *n. & a.* boycotter; boycotting.—**boicotear**, *vt. & vi.* to boycott.—**boicoteo**, *m.* boycott(ing).

boina, *f.* beret.

boj, *m.* box tree, boxwood.

bola, *f.* ball; marble; globe; falsehood, fib; (Mex.) shoe blacking; (Mex.) tumult, riot.—**bolazo**, *m.* blow with a ball; fib, lie.—**boleada**, *f.* (Mex.) shoeshine.—**boleador**, *m.* bowler; (Mex.) bootblack.—**bolear**, *vi.* to bowl; to boast; to lie, fib.—**boleo**, *m.* bowling.—**bolera**, *f.* bowling alley.—**bolero**, *m.* bolero; (Mex.) bootblack.

boleta, *f.* ballot; pass; pay order; certificate; lodging billet.—**boletería**, *f.* box, or ticket, office.—**boletín**, *m.* bulletin; ticket.—**boleto**, *m.* ticket.

boliche, *m.* bowl, bowling alley; saloon; gambling joint; small stove.

bolígrafo, *m.* ball-point pen.
boliviano, *n.* & *a.* Bolivian.
bolo, *m.* (bowling) a ninepin; dunce. —*pl.* bowls, bowling.
bolsa, *f.* purse; pouch, bag, satchel; stock exchange; exchange center.— **bolsillo,** *m.* pocket; purse.—*rascarse el b.,* to spend much money.— **bolsista,** *m.* stockbroker; speculator. —**bolso,** *m.* moneybag; purse.
bollo, *m.* small loaf or roll, muffin, bun; lump; tuft; dent; swelling; fritter.
bomba, *f.* pump; bomb; fire engine; skyrocket; high hat.—*a prueba de b.,* bomb proof, indestructible.—*b. neumática,* air pump.—*fruta b.,* papaya.—**bombardear,** *vt.* to bombard; to bomb.—**bombardeo,** *m.* bombardment.—**bombardero,** *m.* bomber (airplane); bombardier.— **bombazo,** *m.* explosion; bomb hit; bad news.—**bombear,** *vt.* to pump. —**bombeo,** *m.* pumping; curving, bulging.—**bombero,** *m.* fireman.— **bombilla,** *f.* small tube for drinking maté; electric light bulb.
bombo, *m.* large drum; bass drum; pomp, ostentation.—*dar b.* to flatter, praise excessively.—*a.* dazed, stunned; stupid; lukewarm; slightly rotten.
bombón, *m.* chocolate, bonbon, sweet. —**bombonera,** *f.* box for bonbons.
bonachón, *a.* good-natured, kind; innocent.
bonanza, *f.* fair weather; prosperity.
bondad, *f.* goodness; kindness.—*tener la b. (de),* please.—**bondadoso,** *a.* kind, kind-hearted.
bonete, *m.* bonnet, college cap; skullcap; secular clergyman; bonnet of a fortress; preserve jar; second stomach of ruminants.
bonhomía, *f.* honesty, kindliness.
boniato, *m.* sweet potato.
bonificación, *f.* discount; allowance; bonus.—**bonificar,** *vti.* [d] to discount (the price of something).
bonitamente, *adv.* brazenly; craftily; neatly.—**bonito,** *a.* pretty.—*m.* bonito, striped tunny.
boñiga, *f.* cow dung; castings.
boqueada, *f.* gasp, gasping.—**boquear,** *vi.* to gape, gasp; to breathe one's last; to end.—**boquera,** *f.* crack in the corner of the mouth.—**boquete,** *m.* gap, narrow entrance.—**boquiabierto,** *a.* astonished; openmouthed.—**boquilla,** *f.* cigar or cigarette holder; mouthpiece of a wind instrument; small mouth.
borbotar, *vi.* to gush out; to boil or bubble fiercely; to spurt.—**borbollón, borbotón,** *m.* bubbling, gush-

ing up of water.—*a borbotones,* impetuously.
borceguí, *m.* high laced shoe; halfboot.
bordado, *m.* embroidery; embroidering.—*a.* embroidered.—**bordador,** *n.* embroiderer.—**bordadura,** *f.* embroidery.—**bordar,** *vt.* to embroider.
borde, *m.* border, edge, rim, brim; flange.—*al b. de,* on the verge of.— **bordear,** *vt.* to skirt, go along the edge of; to approach, get near.
bordo, *m.* board, the side of a ship.— *a b.,* on board, aboard.
bordón, *m.* walking staff; bass-string of guitar.
borinqueño, *n.* & *a.* Porto Rican.
borla, *f.* tassel, tuft; powder puff; doctorate.—*tomar la b.,* to graduate.
borra, *f.* sediment, waste; yearling ewe; coarse wool.
borrachera, *f.* drunkenness; madness, great folly.—**borrachín, borrachón,** *m.* drunkard; sot.—**borracho,** *n.* drunkard.—*a.* drunk.
borrador, *m.* eraser; rough draft.— **borradura,** *f.* erasure, striking out, deletion.—**borrar,** *vt.* to erase, rub out, cross out, blot out; to obliterate.
borrasca, *f.* storm; hazard, danger. —**borrascoso,** *a.* stormy.
borrego, *n.* yearling sheep; simpleton, blockhead.
borricada, *f.* drove of donkeys; stupid word or action.—**borrico,** *m.* donkey; blockhead.
borrón, *m.* blot; blur; rough draft; stigma.—**borroso,** *a.* full of dregs; blurred, indistinct.
boscaje, *m.* cluster of trees; thicket.
bosque, *m.* woods, forest.
bosquejar, *vt.* to sketch, outline; to plan; to make a rough model of.— **bosquejo,** *m.* sketch; rough outline.
bostezar, *vii.* [a] to yawn, gape.— **bostezo,** *m.* yawn, yawning.
bota, *f.* boot; small leather wine bag. —*ponerse las botas,* to hit the jackpot.
botadura, *f.* launching (of a ship).
botánica, *f.* botany.—**botánico,** *a.* botanical.—*n.* botanist.
botar, *vt.* to cast, pitch, throw; to throw out (of a job), fire; to launch; to misspend; to throw away.—*vi.* & *vr.* (of unbroken horse) to jump and kick, caper; to bound; to rebound.—**botarate,** *m.* spendthrift; madcap, thoughtless person.
botavara, *f.* (mar.) gaff; boat hook.
bote, *m.* leap, bound, bounce; rearing of a horse; can or jar; rowing

boat.—*de b. en b.,* crowded, crammed.

botella, *f.* bottle.—botellón, *m.* demijohn.

botica, *f.* drug store.—boticario, *n.* apothecary, druggist.

botija, *f.* earthen round, short-necked jug; fat person.

botillería, *f.* ice-cream parlor.—botillero, *n.* one who prepares or sells ice cream and refreshments.

botín, *m.* booty, spoils of war; spats; bootee.—botina, *f.* woman's boot.—botinería, *f.* shoe shop or factory.

botiquín, *m.* medicine chest; first-aid kit; (Am.) wine shop.

botón, *m.* button; knob; sprout, bud, blossom.—botonadura, *f.* set of buttons.—botones, *m. sing.* bellboy.

bóveda, *f.* arch; vault; vault for the dead.

boxeador, *n.* boxer, pugilist.—boxear, *vi.* to box.—boxeo, *m.* boxing.

boya, *f.* buoy.

boyada, *f.* herd of oxen.

boyante, *a.* buoyant, floating; prosperous.—boyar, *vi.* to buoy; to float.

boyero, *m.* ox driver.

bozal, *m.* muzzle (for dogs, etc.).—*a.* of pure breed, unmixed; newly immigrating; inexperienced; simple, half-witted; coarse; wild.

bozo, *m.* down (on face); mustache; area around the lips.

braceada, *f.* violent stretching out of the arms.—bracear, *vi.* to move or swing the arms.—braceo, *m.* repeated swinging of the arms.—bracero, *m.* day laborer.—*de b.,* or *de bracete,* arm in arm.

bragas, *f. sing. & pl.* breeches; child's diaper; hoisting rope.—braguero, *m.* truss, bandage for a rupture.—bragueta, *f.* fly of trousers.

bramante, *a.* roaring.—*m.* twine, packthread.—bramar, *vi.* to roar, groan, bellow.—bramido, *m.* roar, bellow.

brasa, *f.* ember; red-hot coal or wood.—*estar en brasas,* to be on tenterhooks.—brasero, *m.* brazier; fire pan.

brasileño, brasilero, *n. & a.* Brazilian.

bravata, *f.* bravado, boast; bluster, threat.—braveza, bravura, *f.* bravery; courage; anger.—bravío, *a.* ferocious, wild.—bravo, *a.* brave; angry; wild, fierce.—bravucón, *m. & a.* bully; boaster; boasting.

braza, *f.* fathom (measure).—brazada, *f.* stroke (swimming, rowing); uplifting of the arms; armful.—brazado, *m.* armful.—brazal, *m.* armband; bracer; armlet.—brazalete,

m. bracelet.—brazo, *m.* arm (of the body, a chair, etc.); branch, bough; strength, power.—*pl.* workmen, hands.—*a b. partido,* hand to hand, with all one's strength.—*del b.,* by the arm; arm in arm.

brea, *f.* pitch, tar.

brebaje, *m.* beverage, potion.

brécol, *m.* broccoli.—brecolera, *f.* flowering broccoli.

brecha, *f.* breach, opening, gap.

brega, *f.* struggle; fight.—*andar a,* or *en, la b.,* to work hard.—bregar, *vii.* [b] to contend, struggle; to overwork.

breña, *f.,* breñal, breñar, *m.* craggy and brambled ground.—breñoso, *a.* craggy and brambled.

brete, *m.* fetter, shackle; difficulty.—*en un b.,* in a difficult situation, hard pressed to do it.

bretón, *n. & a.* Breton.

breva, *f.* early fruit of a fig tree; choice cigar; advantage, profit.

breve, *a.* brief, short.—*en b.* shortly, in a little while.—brevedad, *f.* brevity, briefness.—breviario, *m.* breviary; epitome.

brezal, *m.* moor, heath.—brezo, *m.* (bot.) heath, heather.

bribón, *n.* vagrant, rogue.—bribonada, *f.* knavery, petty villainy.—bribonear, *vi.* to loiter about, idle.—bribonería, *f.* rascality; vagrancy.

brida, *f.* bridle, rein.

brigada, *f.* brigade; group of people doing a task together; sub-lieutenant.—brigadier, *m.* brigadier general.

brillante, *a.* brilliant, bright; shining, sparkling.—*m.* brilliant, diamond.—brillantez, *f.* dazzle, brilliance.—brillo, *m.* shine, brightness, luster, sparkle.—brillar, *vi.* to shine, sparkle, glitter; excel.

brincar, *vii.* [d] to leap, jump, caper, skip.—brinco, *m.* leap, jump, hop, caper.

brindar, *vt.* to toast, drink the health; to offer.—brindis, *m.* drinking the health of another; toast.

brío, *m.* vigor, enterprise, courage.—brioso, *a.* vigorous, courageous, spirited.

brisa, *f.* breeze.

británico, *a. & n.* British; Britisher.

britano, *n. & a.* Briton; British.

brizna, *f.* fragment; splinter or chip• string (of beans, etc.); shred.

broca, *f.* reel, bobbin; drill bit.

brocado, *m.* (gold or silver) brocade.

brocal, *m.* curbstone of a well.

bróculi, *m.* broccoli.

brocha, *f.* painter's or shaving brush.—*de b. gorda,* crude, badly done.—

brochada, *f.,* **brochazo,** *m.* stroke of the brush.

broche, *m.* clasp; hook and eye; fastener; brooch.

broma, *f.* joke, jest; gaiety, fun; prank.—**bromear,** *vi.* to joke, jest, make fun.—**bromista,** *mf.* joker; wag.—*a.* joking, waggish, prankish.

bronca, *f.* quarrel, wrangle; dispute.

bronce, *m.* bronze.—**bronceado,** *a.* bronzed; bronze-colored.—*m.* bronzing.—**broncear,** *vt.* to bronze; to adorn with brass.

bronco, *a.* rough, unpolished; morose; rude; hard; abrupt; hoarse; wild (of horse).

bronconeumonía, *f.* bronchopneumonia.—**broncopulmonía,** *f.* bronchial pneumonia.

bronquedad, *f.* harshness; brittleness.

bronquial, *a.* bronchial.—**bronquio,** *m.* bronchus.—**bronquitis,** *f.* bronchitis.

broquel, *m.* shield, buckler; support, protection.

brotar, *vi.* to bud, germinate, shoot forth; to gush, rush out; to break out; to issue, appear.—**brote,** *m.* germination of vines; bud of trees; shoot; outbreak (of a disease).

broza, *f.* rotted branches, leaves, etc. on the ground; rubbish, chaff; undergrowth, brushwood.

bruces, *n. pl.*—*caer de b.,* to fall flat on one's face.—*de b.,* forward; face downward; on one's stomach.

bruja, *f.* witch.—**brujería,** *f.* witchcraft, sorcery.—**brujo,** *m.* sorcerer, conjurer, wizard.

brújula, *f.* magnetic needle; compass.

bruma, *f.* mist, fog.—**brumoso,** *a.* foggy, misty.

bruno, *m.* & *a.* dark brown, blackish.

bruñir, *vti* [27] to polish, burnish.

brusco, *a.* blunt, rude, brusk; abrupt, sudden.

brusquedad, *f.* bluntness, rudeness; bruskness; abruptness.

brutal, *a.* brutal, brutish.—*m.* animal (quadruped).—**brutalidad,** *f.* brutality; brutishness, unkindness; brutal or stupid action.—**bruto,** *a.* brutish; crude (of oil, etc.); gross (profits, etc.); unpolished.—*en b.,* in a rough state, in the rough.—*m.* beast, brute; blockhead.

bruza, *f.* horse brush; stove brush; scrubbing brush; printer's brush.

bu, *m.* bugaboo.—*hacer el b.,* to scare, frighten.

bubón, *m.* bubo.—**bubónico,** *a.* bubonic.

búcaro, *m.* flower vase.

bucear, *vi.* to dive, plunge.—**buceo,** *m.* diving; searching under water.

bucle, *m.* ringlet, curl, lock of hair.

buchada, *f.* mouthful.—**buche,** *m.* belly; (coll.) bosom; mouthful (of liquids); double chin; (Am.) goiter.

budismo, *m.* Buddhism.—**budista,** *mf.* & *a.* Buddhist.

buen(o), *a.* good; kind; suited, fit; appropriate; well, in good health; in good condition.—*buenos días,* good morning, good day.—*buenas noches,* good evening.—*buenas tardes,* good afternoon.—*de buenas a primeras,* unexpectedly.—*adv.* all right; that is enough.—**buenamente,** *adv.* freely, spontaneously.—**buenaventura,** *f.* good luck; fortune (as told by a fortune teller).

buey, *m.* ox, bullock.

bufanda, *f.* scarf, muffler.

bufar, *vi.* to puff and blow with anger; to snort.

bufete, *m.* desk or writing table; lawyer's office or clientele.

bufido, *m.* snort, bellow, roar.

bufo, *a.* & *n.* comic; farcical, clownish; crude.

bufón, *m.* buffoon; jester.—*a.* funny, comical.—**bufonada,** *f.* buffoonery; jest.

buhardilla, *f.* garret; skylight.

buho, *m.* owl.

buhonero, *m.* peddler, hawker.

buitre, *m.* vulture.

bujía, *f.* spark plug; candlestick; candle; candle power.

bula, *f.* papal bull; (eccl.) dispensation.

bulbo, *m.* bulb (plants).

búlgaro, *n.* & *a.* Bulgarian.

bulto, *m.* bulk, volume, size; bundle; package; lump, swelling; indistinct shape or form.—*escurrir, huir,* or *sacar el b.,* to sneak out; to dodge.

bulla, *f.* chatter, noise, shouting; noisy crowd.—**bullanga,** *f.* noise, tumult.—**bullanguero,** *a.* fond of noisy merriment.—**bullicio,** *m.* noise, bustle.—**bullicioso,** *a.* boisterous riotous; merry and noisy.

bullir, *vii.* [27] to boil, bubble up; to swarm, teem; to bustle; to stir, move about.

buñuelo, *m.* fritter, bun; anything poorly done or spoiled; failure.

buque, *m.* vessel, ship; steamer.

burbuja, *f.* bubble.—**burbujear,** *vi.* to bubble.—**burbujeo,** *m.* bubbling.

burdel, *m.* brothel.

burdo, *a.* coarse, rough; ordinary, common.

buril, *m.* chisel; graver.—**burilar,** *vt.* to engrave.

burla, *f.* scoffing, mockery, taunt, gibe; jest, fun; trick, deception.—**burlador,** *n.* seducer; jester.—**burlar,** *vt.* to ridicule, mock, scoff;

to abuse; to deceive; to evade.—*vr.* (de) to mock, laugh (at), make fun (of).—**burlesco**, *a.* burlesque, ludicrous.—**burlón**, *a.* bantering, waggish, mocking.—*n.* scoffer; joker, teaser.

buró, *m.* bureau; writing desk.— **burocracia**, *f.* bureaucracy.—**burocrático**, *a.* bureaucratic.—**burocratismo**, *m.* red tape.

burrada, *f.* stupid action or saying.— **burro**, *n.* ass, donkey; windlass. —*a.* stupid.

bursátil, *a.* relating to the stock exchange.

busca, *f.* search; pursuit.—**buscapleitos**, *mf.* trouble maker.—**buscar**, *vti.* [d] to seek, search for.—*vri.* to bring upon oneself.—**buscavidas**, *mf.* busybody; hustler; thrifty person.

busilis, *m.* (coll.) difficulty, difficult point, snag.

búsqueda, *f.* search.

buste, *m.* bust, bosom.

butaca, *f.* armchair; easy-chair; (theater) orchestra seat.

butifarra, *f.* sausage.

buzo, *m.* diver.

buzón, *m.* letter drop; letter box.

C

cabal, *a.* just, complete; perfect, thorough; full; faultless.—*estar en sus cabales*, to be in one's right mind.

cábala, *f.* premonition; cabal, intrigue.

cabalgadura, *f.* riding horse or mule. —**cabalgar**, *vii.* [b] to ride on horseback.

caballa, *f.* horse mackerel.

caballeresco, *a.* knightly, chivalrous; gentlemanly.—**caballería**, *f.* riding animal; cavalry; horsemanship; mount; horse; knighthood; chivalry; (Am.) land measure (about 33½ acres).—**caballeriza**, *f.* stable. —**caballerizo**, *m.* head groom of a stable.—**caballero**, *m.* knight; cavalier; gentleman.—*a.* riding, mounted; gentlemanly.—*c. de industria*, defrauder, swindler.—**caballerosidad**, *f.* chivalry, quality of a gentleman; nobleness.—**caballeroso**, *a.* noble, generous; gentlemanly.—**caballete**, *m.* ridge of a roof; sawhorse; trestle; easel; gallows of a printing press.—**caballista**, *m.* horseman; expert in horses.—**caballo**, *m.* horse; (cards) the queen; (chess) the knight.—*a mata c.*, at breakneck speed.—*c. de batalla*, favorite idea.

cabaña, *f.* cabin, hut; hovel.

cabaret, *f.* cabaret, nightclub.

cabecear, *vi.* to nod; to raise or lower the head (pert. to horses); to incline to one side; (naut., aer.) to pitch, tilt.—**cabeceo**, *m.* nodding, nod of the head; (naut., aer.) pitching.

cabecera, *f.* head-board of a bed; seat of honor; chief city of a district.

cabecilla, *f.* small head.—*m.* ringleader.

cabellera, *f.* head of hair; wig.— **cabello**, *m.* a hair; hair of the head.—*asirse de un c.*, to catch at trifles.—*traer por los cabellos*, to drag in irrelevantly.—**cabelludo**, *a.* hairy.—*cuero c.*, scalp.

caber, *vii.* [7] to fit into, go into; to be contained; to have enough room for.—*c. la posibilidad*, to be within possibility.—*no cabe duda*, there is no doubt.—*no c. en sí*, to be filled with conceit.

cabestrillo, *m.* sling (for injured arm). —**cabestro**, *m.* halter; bullock; rope, cord.

cabeza, *f.* head; leader; upper part; intelligence.—*c. de chorlito*, harebrained.—*de c.*, headfirst, headlong. —*de pies a c.*, all over.—*levantar c.*, to be restored in health or fortune.—*ni pies ni c.*, neither rhyme nor reason.—**cabezada**, *f.* butt (with the head); nod; headshake; headgear (of a harness); headstall of a bridge; (naut.) pitching.—**cabezazo**, *m.* blow with the head.—**cabezón**, **cabezota**, **cabezudo**, *a.* & *n.* largeheaded (one); headstrong (one).

cabida, *f.* content, capacity; space, room.—*tener c.*, to be appropiate, to fit.

cabildo, *m.* chapter of a cathedral or collegiate church; municipal council; city hall.

cabilla, *f.* (naut.) dowel, pin; (mason.) reinforcement pin; iron rod.

cabina, *f.* (mar.) cabin.

cabizbajo, *a.* crestfallen; thoughtful; melancholy.

cable, *m.* cable.—**cablegrafiar**, *vt.* to cable.—**cablegrama**, *m.* cablegram.

cabo, *m.* extreme; tip; bit; cape, headland; handle; piece of rope; corporal; end.—*al c.*, at last.—*al c. de*, at the end of.—*dar c. a*, to finish.—*de c. a rabo*, from head to tail, from the beginning to the end. —*llevar a c.*, to carry out; to accomplish.

cabotaje, *m.* coasting trade; pilotage.

cabra, *f.* goat.—**cabria**, *f.* crane, winch.—**cabrío**, *m.* herd of goats. —*a.* goatish.—**cabriola**, *f.* caper,

hop, somersault.—**cabritilla**, f. kid, dressed kidskin.—**cabritillo, cabrito,** m. kid.—**cabrón,** m. buck, he-goat; (fig.) acquiescing cuckold.

cabuya, f. (Am.) sisal or hemp cord.

cacahual, m. cacao plantation.

cacahuate, cacahué, cacahuete, m. peanut.

cacao, m. cacao; cacao tree; chocolate.

cacarear, vi. to cackle; (coll.) to brag, boast.—**cacareo,** m. cackling; boast, brag.

cacatúa, f. cockatoo.

cacería, f. hunt, hunting.

cacerola, f. casserole; saucepan.

cacique, m. Indian chief; (coll.) political boss.—**caciquismo,** m. caciquism; political bossism.

caco, m. pickpocket; thief.

cacumen, m. acumen, keen insight.

cacha, f. each of the two leaves of a knife or gun (handle).

cachalote, m. sperm whale.

cacharrería, f. crockery store; collection or stock of earthen pots.—**cacharro,** m. coarse earthen pot; (Am.) cheap trinket; (Cuba) jalopy.

cachaza, f. first froth on cane juice when boiled; slowness, tardiness.—**cachazudo,** a. slow, calm, phlegmatic.

cachemir, m. cashmere.

cacheo, m. search for hidden arms.

cachetada, f. slap on the face.—**cachete,** m. cheek; punch in the face or head.—**cachetudo,** a. plump-cheeked, fleshy.

cachimba, f. smoking pipe.

cachiporra, f. cudgel.

cachivache, m. piece of junk; (Am.) trinket.

cacho, m. slice, piece; (Chile) unsold goods.

cachorro, n. cub; puppy; small pistol.

cachucha, f. small rowboat; slap.

cada, a. every, each.—**c. cual, c. uno,** each; every one.—**c. vez que,** every time; whenever.

cadalso, m. gallows; scaffold for capital punishment.

cadáver, m. corpse, cadaver.—**cadavérico,** a. cadaverous.

cadena, f. chain; range (of mountains).—**c. perpetua,** imprisonment for life.—**c. radial,** broadcasting system.

cadencia, f. cadence; rhythm; flow of verses or periods; (mus.) cadenza.—**cadencioso,** a. rhythmical.

cadeneta, f. lace or needlework worked in form of chain.

cadera, f. hip.

cadete, m. cadet.

caducar, vii. [d] to dote; to be worn out by service; to fall into disuse; to become obsolete or extinct; to prescribe; (law) to lapse; to expire.—**caducidad,** f. (law) lapse, expiration.—**caduco,** a. senile; decrepit; perishable.

caer, vii. [8-e] to fall, drop; to fall off; to hang down, droop; to fall due; to befall.—**c. bien,** to create a good impression; to fit; to be becoming.—**c. de la noche,** nightfall.—**c. en cama,** or **enfermo,** to be taken ill.—**c. en gracia,** to please.—**c. en la cuenta,** to understand the situation; to realize.—**c. redondo,** to drop unconscious.—**dejar c.,** to drop; to let fall.—**vri.** to fall down or off; to tumble; to become downcast.—**c. de su peso,** to be self-evident, to be obvious; to fall by itself.—**caérsele a uno la cara de vergüenza,** to be deeply ashamed.

café, m. coffee (tree, berry, beverage); coffee house; café.—**c. retinto,** black coffee.—**cafeína,** f. caffein.—**cafetal,** m. coffee plantation.—**cafetera,** f. coffeepot.—**cafetería,** f. retail coffee shop; cafeteria.—**cafetero,** m. coffee merchant.—**cafetín,** m. small café.—**cafeto,** m. coffee tree.

caída, f. fall; falling; tumble; drop; droop; descent.—**a la c. del sol,** at sunset.—**la c. de la tarde,** at the close of the afternoon.—**caído,** a. languid; downfallen.

caimán, m. cayman; alligator.

caimito, m. star apple.

caja, f. box; case; cash box or safe; (com.) cash, funds; cashier's office; printer's case; shell, block (of a pulley).—**c. contadora, c. registradora,** cash register.—**c. de ahorros,** savings bank.—**c. de caudales, c. fuerte** (Am.), safe, strongbox.—**c. de seguridad,** safe-deposit box.—**con cajas destempladas,** roughly, without ceremony.—**en c.,** cash, cash kept in the safe.—**cajero,** n. cashier; box maker.—**cajetilla,** f. package (of cigarettes).—**cajista,** mf. compositor (in printing).—**cajón,** m. large box, case; drawer; locker; mold for casting.—**c. de sastre,** odds and ends.—**cajuela,** f. small box; (Am.) automobile trunk.

cal, f. lime.—**c. viva,** quicklime.

cala, f. cove, small bay; creek; fishing ground; sample slice (of a fruit).

calabacín, m. calabash.

calabaza, f. pumpkin; (fig.) nincompoop.—**dar calabazas,** to jilt (a suitor); to flunk (a student).

calabozo, *m.* dungeon; prison cell; calaboose.

calado, *m.* open work in metal, stone, wood, or linen; draught of a vessel; lace trimmings.

calafate, calafateador, *m.* calker.— **calafatear,** *vt.* to calk.—**calafateo,** *m.* calking.

calamar, *m.* squid.

calambre, *m.* cramp (of muscles), spasm.

calamidad, *f.* calamity.—**calamitoso,** *a.* calamitous; unfortunate.

calandria, *f.* lark, skylark.

calar, *vt.* to penetrate, soak through, drench; to go through; to make open work in (metal, wood, linen or paper); to fix (the bayonet); to see through (a person); to take or cut out a sample of.—*vi.* (of ships) to draw.—*vr.* to become drenched.

calavera, *f.* skull; madcap; rake, profligate; (Mex.) tail light.—**calaverada,** *f.* foolishness, rash action.

calaña, *f.* sort, kind, quality; (fig.) evil moral character.

calcar, *vti.* [d] to trace; to imitate.

calceta, *f.* hose, stocking.—*hacer c.,* to knit.—**calcetín,** *m.* sock.

calcio, *m.* calcium.

calco, *m.* tracing, transfer; copy, imitation; near image.

calculador, *n.* calculator, computer.— **calcular,** *vt.* to calculate, compute; to estimate.—**calculista,** *mf.* calculator; designer, schemer.—**cálculo,** *m.* calculation; conjecture; calculus (differential, integral, etc.); (med.) calculus, (kidney, etc.) stone.

caldear, *vt.* to heat; to weld.—*vr.* to become warm; to become overheated; to become overexcited.

caldera, *f.* caldron; kettle; boiler.— **calderero,** *m.* coppersmith; boiler maker.—**calderilla,** *f.* any copper coin.—**caldero,** *m.* semispherical caldron or boiler; caldronful.

caldo, *m.* broth; gravy; bouillon.

calefacción, *f.* heating system; heating, warming.

calendario, *m.* calendar, almanac.

caléndula, *f.* marigold.

calentador, *m.* heater.—**calentar,** *vti.* [1] to heat, warm; (fig.) to give a beating.—*vr.* to become hot; to become excited or angry; to be in heat.—**calentura,** *f.* fever.—**calenturiento,** *a.* feverish.

caletre, *m.* (coll.) judgment, acumen.

calibrador, *m.* gauge (instrument); calipers.—**calibrar,** *vt.* to calibrate (a firearm); to gauge.—**calibre,** *m.* caliber; bore (of a cylinder); gauge; diameter (of a wire).

calicanto, *m.* stone masonry.

calidad, *f.* quality; grade; rank; importance.—*pl.* conditions; personal qualifications; parts.

cálido, *a.* warm; hot.

calidoscopio, *m.* kaleidoscope.

caliente, *a.* warm, hot; (Am.) angry. —*en c.* at once.

calificación, *f.* qualification; judgment; mark (in an examination).— **calificar,** *vti.* [d] to qualify; to rate, class; to judge.—**calificativo,** *a.* qualifying; descriptive.

caligrafía, *f.* calligraphy.

calina, *f.* haze, mist, fog.

cáliz, *m.* chalice; communion cup; (bot.) calyx.

calma, *f.* calm; calmness, tranquility; lull, quiet.—*c. chicha,* dead calm.— *con c.,* calmly, quietly.—*en c.,* (of the sea) calm, smooth.—**calmado,** *a.* quiet, calm, still.—**calmante,** *a.* mitigating; quieting; soothing.—*m. & a.* sedative; narcotic.—**calmar,** *vt.* to calm, quiet, pacify; to mitigate, soothe.—*vi.* to abate; to be becalmed.—*vr.* to quiet down; to calm oneself, be pacified.—**calmoso,** *a.* calm; slow; phlegmatic.

calor, *m.* heat; warmth, ardor.—*c. de una batalla,* brunt of a battle. —*tener c.,* to be, feel warm.— **caloría,** *f.* calorie.—**calórico,** *m.* caloric.—**calorífero,** *m.* heater, radiator.—**caluroso,** *a.* warm, hot; cordial, enthusiastic.

calumnia, *f.* calumny, slander.— **calumniador,** *n. & a.* slander(ing). —**calumniar,** *vt.* to slander.

calva, *f.* baldhead; clearing.

calvario, *m.* Calvary; tribulation.

calvicie, *f.* baldness.—**calvo,** *a.* bald; barren.—*m.* baldhead.

calza, *f.* wedge, shoehorn.—*pl.* tights. —**calzada,** *f.* paved road; highway. —**calzado,** *m.* footwear.—**calzador,** *m.* shoehorn.—**calzar,** *vti.* [a] to put on (shoes, etc.); to make steady by wedging.—**calzo,** *m.* wedge.

calzón, *m.,* **calzones,** *m. pl.* breeches; trousers.—*calzón corto,* knee breeches; shorts.—*tener los calzones bién puestos,* to have the heart in the right place.—**calzoncillos,** *m. pl.* drawers, men's shorts.

callandito, *adv.* quietly, stealthily, softly.—**callar,** *vi. & vt.* to be silent, keep silent; to stop, cease (talking, singing, etc.); to shut up. —*vt. & vr.* to hush, conceal; to suppress, keep secret.—*vt.* to silence; to gag.—*dar la callada por respuesta,* to answer by silence.

calle, *f.* street; passage; lane.—*abrir c.,* to clear the way.—*c. abajo,* down

the street.—*dejar en la c.*, to leave penniless.—*echar a la c.*, to put out of the house.—*llevarse de c.*, to sweep away.—**callejear,** *vi.* to saunter, loiter about the streets.—**callejero,** *n.* loiterer; loafer.—**callejón,** *m.* alley.—*c. sin salida*, blind alley; dead end.—**callejuela,** *f.* lane; passage; dingy street.

callista, *mf.* chiropodist.—**callo,** *m.* corn, callus (on foot); callus, hard skin.—*pl.* tripe (food).—**callosidad,** *f.* callousness.—**calloso,** *a.* callous; hard-skinned.

cama, *f.* bed; couch; cot.—*guardar*, or *hacer c.*, to be confined to bed. —**camada,** *f.* brood, litter; gang.

camafeo, *m.* cameo.

camaleón, *m.* chameleon.

cámara, *f.* chamber; parlor; bedroom; camera.—*c. alta*, senate; House of Lords.—*c. baja*, chamber of deputies; House of Commons.— *c. frigorífica*, icebox; refrigerator.

camarada, *n.* comrade; pal, chum.— **camaradería,** *f.* comradeship; companionship.

camarera, *f.* chambermaid; waitress. —**camarero,** *m.* waiter; valet.

camarilla, *f.* small room; coterie; clique.

camarón, *m.* shrimp, prawn.

camarote, *m.* cabin, berth, stateroom.

cambalache, *m.* (coll.) barter, swap.— **cambalachear,** *vt.* to barter, to swap.—**cambalachero,** *n.* barterer.

cambiante, *a.* bartering, exchanging; changing.—*m. pl.* iridescent sheen or colors.—**cambiar,** *vt.* to change; to barter; to exchange; to alter.— *vi.* to change, shift.—*c. de marcha*, to shift gear.—*c. de opinión*, to change one's mind.—**cambio,** *m.* change; barter; exchange; rate of exchange (of money); alteration.— *en c.* in return; on the other hand. —*en c. de*, in lieu of, instead of.— **cambista,** *mf.* banker, money broker.

camelar, *vt.* to flirt; to court, woo; to seduce.

camelia, *f.* camellia.

camello, *m.* camel.—**camellón,** *m.* ridge turned up by plow.

camilla, *f.* stretcher; litter; couch; cot.—**camillero,** *m.* stretcher-bearer.

caminante, *m.* traveler, walker.— **caminar,** *vi.* to journey, walk, travel, go, move along.—*c. con pies de plomo*, to act cautiously.— **caminata,** *f.* long walk; hike; jaunt. —**camino,** *m.* road; highway; course; passage; way; journey.—*c. de hierro*, railroad.—*de c., en c.*, on the way.—*ponerse en c.*, to set out, start.

camión, *m.* truck; (Mex.) bus.— **camionero,** *m.* truck driver.—**camioneta,** *f.* small or delivery truck; (Am.) bus.

camisa, *f.* shirt, chemise.—*c. de fuerza*, strait jacket.—*c. de vapor*, steam jacket.—**camisería,** *f.* haberdashery.—**camisero,** *n.* shirt maker.

camiseta, *f.* undershirt.—**camisón,** *m.* nightshirt; nightgown; chemise.

camorra, *f.* quarrel.—**camorrista,** *mf.* noisy, quarrelsome person.

camote, *m.* (Am.) sweet potato.

campamento, *m.* encampment; camp.

campana, *f.* bell.—*c. de buzo*, diving bell.—*c. de rebato*, alarm bell.— **campanada,** *f.* stroke of a bell, clang.—**campanario,** *m.* belfry.— **campanear,** *vi.* to ring the bells frequently.—*vt.* to divulge; to noise about.—**campanero,** *m.* bellman; bell founder.—**campanilla,** *f.* small bell; hand bell; uvula; (bot.) bellflower.—**campanillazo,** *m.* violent ringing of a bell.—**campanilleo,** *m.* ringing, tinkling of small bells.

campante, *a.* cheerful; self-satisfied.

campanudo, *a.* high-flown, bombastic.

campar, *vi.* to excel; to encamp.—*c. por sus respetos*, to act as one pleases, be subject to no control.

campaña, *f.* campaign; countryside, fields, open country.

campear, *vi.* to be in the field; to frisk about; to be prominent.

campechano, *a.* frank; cheerful; hearty; open.

campeón, *m.* champion; defender.— **campeonato,** *m.* championship.

campesino, *a.* rural, rustic.—*n.* countryman (-woman); peasant; farmer. —**campestre,** *a.* rural, bucolic.— **campiña,** *f.* field; country.—**campo,** *m.* country; countryside; field; space, camp; flat land.—*a c. raso*, in the open air.—*a c. traviesa*, across country.—*c. de golf*, golf course.—*c. santo*, or *camposanto*, cemetery.

camuesa, *f.* pippin (apple).

camuflaje, *m.* camouflage.—**camuflar,** *vt.* to camouflage.

cana, *f.* gray hair.—*echar una c. al aire*, to go on a lark.

canadiense, *mf.* & *a.* Canadian.

canal, *m.* channel; canal; strait; groove.—*abrir en c.*, to cut from top to bottom.—*f.* slot in metal work; drinking trough.

canalete, *m.* bladed paddle for canoeing.

canalizar, *vti.* [a] to construct channels or canals in or for; to channel.

canalla, *f.* rabble, riffraff; mob.—*m.* mean fellow, cur.—**canallada,** *f.*

base, despicable act.—**canallesco,** a. base, churlish.

canana, f. cartridge belt.

canapé, m. couch; lounge; settee.

canario, m. canary.—n. & a. (native) of the Canary Islands.

canasta, f. basket; crate.—**canasto,** m. large basket, crate.—¡canastos! interj. gracious! confound it!

cáncamo, m. (Am.) ringbolt.

cancela, f. front door grating or screen.

cancelación, f. cancellation.—**cancelar,** vt. to cancel.

cáncer, m. cancer.—**canceroso,** a. cancerous.

canciller, m. chancellor.—**cancillería,** f. chancellery.

canción, f. song; love poem.—**cancionero,** m. song book; song writer.—**cancionista,** mf. composer or singer of songs, songster.

cancha, f. (tennis, handball, etc.) court; (bowling) alley; game grounds; (Am.) roasted corn or beans.

candado, m. padlock.

candela, f. candle; fire; light.—**candelabro,** m. candelabrum; bracket.—**candelero,** m. candlestick.

candente, a. incandescent, red-hot.

candidato, n. candidate.—**candidatura,** f. candidacy.

candidez, f. ingenuousness; naiveté; candor.—**cándido,** a. candid; simple, innocent; white; unsuspecting.

candil, m. oil lamp; hand lamp.—**candileja,** f. oil receptacle of a lamp.—pl. footlights of a theater.

candor, m. pure whiteness; candor; innocence.—**candoroso,** a. sincere; innocent; pure-minded.

canela, f. cinnamon.

cangrejo, m. crab.

canguro, m. kangaroo.

caníbal, m. cannibal, man-eater.

canica, f. marble; little ball.

canilla, f. tibia; shinbone; (Am.) faucet; spool (for thread).—**canillera,** f. (baseball) shin guard.

canino, a. canine.—tener un hambre canina, to be ravenous.

canje, m. exchange; interchange.—**canjear,** vt. to exchange, interchange.

cano, a. gray-haired.

canoa, f. canoe.

canon, m. canon; rule, precept; catalogue.—**canónigo,** m. (eccl.) canon.—**canonización,** f. canonization.—**canonizar,** vti. [a] to canonize; to consecrate.

canoso, a. gray-haired.

cansado, a. tired; tiring; tiresome; boring.—**cansancio,** m. weariness,

fatigue.—**cansar,** vt. to weary, tire, fatigue; to bore.—vr. to become tired or weary.—vi. to be tiring or tiresome.

cantante, mf. singer, songster, vocalist.—**cantar,** m. song; epic poem.—ese es otro c., that is a horse of another color.—vt. to sing.—cantarlas claras, not to mince words.—vi. to sing; to speak out; (coll.) to squeal.—c. de plano, to make a full confession.

cántaro, m. pitcher; jug.—llover a cántaros, to rain cats and dogs.

cantera, f. (stone) quarry.—**cantero,** m. stone mason.

cántico, m. canticle.

cantidad, f. quantity; amount; large portion; sum of money.

cantimplora, f. canteen; carafe; wine flask.

cantina, f. canteen; bar room, saloon; lunch room; railroad station restaurant; lunch-box.—**cantinero,** n. bartender.

canto, m. singing; song; canto; chant or canticle; end, edge, border; back of a knife; front edge of a book; stone; pebble; quarry stone, block.—de c., on edge.

cantón, m. canton; corner.

cantor, n. singer, songster; minstrel.—a. that sings.

caña, f. cane; reed; reed spear; stem, stalk; walking stick; sugar cane brandy.—c. brava, bamboo.

cañada, f. dell, ravine; cattle path.

cáñamo, m. hemp; cloth made of hemp.—**cañamón,** m. hemp seed; birdseed.

cañaveral, m. cane or reed field.

cañería, f. conduit; pipe line.—**caño,** m. tube, pipe; spout; (Am.) branch of a river, stream.

cañón, m. cannon, gun; barrel of a gun; canyon; flue of a chimney; quill; beard's stubble.—**cañonazo,** m. cannon shot.—**cañonear,** vt. to cannonade, bombard.—vr. to cannonade each other.—**cañoneo,** m. bombardment; cannonade.—**cañonero,** m. cañonera, f. gunboat.

caoba, f. mahogany.

caos, m. chaos.—**caótico,** a. chaotic.

capa, f. cloak, mantle, cape; layer; coat, coating; cover; coat of paint; disguise; pretense.—andar de c. caída, to go downhill.

capacidad, f. capacity; contents; ability.—**capacitación,** f. training.—**capacitar,** vt. & vr. to enable, qualify, prepare; to empower.

capar, vt. (coll.) to castrate.

caparazón, m. shell of crustaceans; caparison.

capataz, *m.* foreman; overseer.

capaz, *a.* capable, able, competent; roomy, large.

capcioso, *a.* captious; insidious; artful.

capellán, *m.* chaplain; clergyman, priest.

caperuza, *f.* pointed hood.

capilar, *a.* capillary.

capilla, *f.* chapel; hood.

capirote, *m.* hood.—*tonto de c.,* dunce.

capital, *m.* capital, funds.—*f.* capital (city).—*a.* capital; main; leading; great.—*pena c.,* death sentence.—**capitalismo,** *m.* capitalism.—**capitalista,** *mf.* & *a.* capitalist(ic).—**capitalización,** *f.* capitalisation.—**capitalizar,** *vti.* [a] to capitalize.

capitán, *m.* captain; commander.—*c. de corbeta,* lieutenant commander. —*c. de fragata,* navy commander. —*c. de navío,* navy captain.—*c. general del ejército,* field marshal.—**capitanear,** *vt.* to command; to lead.—**capitanía,** *f.* captainship; captaincy.

capitel, *m.* spire over the dome of a church; capital of a column or pilaster.

capitolio, *m.* capitol.

capítulo, *m.* (book or organization) chapter.

caporal, *m.* ringleader; (Mex.) foreman of a ranch.

capota, *f.* top of convertible vehicles.

capote, *m.* cloak with sleeves; bullfighter's cape.—*dar c.,* to deceive.—*decir para su c.,* to say to oneself.

capricho, *m.* caprice, whim, fancy; (mus.) capriccio.—**caprichoso, caprichudo,** *a.* capricious, whimsical; stubborn.

cápsula, *f.* cartridge shell; capsule.

captar, *vt.* to captivate, attract, win over; to tune in (radio station).—**captura,** *f.* capture, seizure.—**capturar,** *vt.* to arrest; to apprehend.

capucha, *f.* hood.

capullo, *m.* cocoon; flower bud; acorn cup.

caqui, *m.* & *a.* khaki.

cara, *f.* face; countenance; front; facing; surface.—*buena c.,* good appearance.—*c. de pocos amigos,* churlish look.—*c. o cruz,* heads or tails.—*de c.,* facing.—*echar en c.,* to reproach, blame.—*sacar la c. por alguien,* to defend another person.

carabina, *f.* carbine.—*la c. de Ambrosio,* a worthless thing.—**carabinero,** *m.* customs armed guard.

caracol, *m.* snail.—*escalera de c.,* winding staircase.—**caracola,** *f.* shell of sea snails.—**caracolear,** *vi.* (of horses) to caracole, to prance.—

caracoleo, *m.* caracoling, prancing about.—**¡caracoles!** *interj.* good gracious!

carácter, *m.* character; temper; energy.—*caracteres de imprenta,* printing types.—**característica,** *f.* characteristic; feature.—**característico,** *a.* characteristic, distinctive.—*n.* character actor or actress.—**caracterizar,** *vti.* [a] to characterize; (theat.) to act a part.—*vti.* & *vri.* (theat.) to make up, dress up for a part.

¡caramba!, *interj.* (coll.) gracious! great guns!

carámbano, *m.* icicle.

carambola, *f.* carom in billiards.—*por c.,* (coll.) indirectly; by chance.

caramelo, *m.* caramel.

caramillo, *m.* small flute; (mus.) recorder; confused heap of things.

carapacho, *m.* shell (of crabs, lobsters, etc.).

carátula, *f.* title page of a book; mask; (Am.) dial of a watch.

¡caray!, *interj.* good gracious!

carbón, *m.* coal; carbon.—*c. de leña,* charcoal.—**carbonera,** *f.* coal cellar, coal bin.—**carbonería,** *f.* coal yard. —**carbonero,** *a.* pert. to coal or charcoal.—*n.* coal or charcoal seller. —**carbonilla,** *f.* coal dust, cinder.—**carbonizar,** *vti.* [a] & *vri.* to carbonize; to char.—**carbono,** *m.* carbon.

carbunclo, carbunco, *m.* carbuncle; anthrax.

carburador, *m.* carburetor.—**carburante,** *m.* fuel oil.—**carburar,** *vt.* to carburize.—**carburo,** *m.* carbide.

carcaj, *m.* quiver (for arrows).

carcajada, *f.* outburst, or peal, of laughter; guffaw.

cárcel, *f.* jail; prison.—**carcelero,** *n.* jailer, warden.

carcoma, *f.* wood borer.—**carcomido,** *a.* worm-eaten; consumed; decayed.

cardador, *n.* carder, comber.—**cardar,** *vt.* to card or comb wool.

cardenal, *m.* cardinal; cardinal bird; welt, bruise.

cardenillo, *m.* verdigris.—**cárdeno,** *a.* livid; dark purple.

cardíaco, *a.* cardiac.

cardinal, *a.* cardinal (point); main, fundamental.

cardo, *m.* thistle.

carear, *vt.* to confront (criminals).—*vr.* to meet face to face.

carecer, *vii.* [3] (de) to lack, to be wanting in.—**carencia,** *f.* lack; scarcity; deficiency.—**carente,** *a.* lacking, wanting.

carero, *a.* overcharging; profiteering.

—*m.* profiteer.—**carestía,** *f.* scarcity, dearth; famine; high price.

careta, *f.* mask.

carey, *m.* hawksbill; tortoise; hawksbill or tortoise shell.

carga, *f.* charge (all meanings); load; burden; freight; cargo; loading; impost, duty, tax; obligation.—*volver a la c.,* to insist; to harp on a subject.—**cargado,** *a.* full; loaded; fraught; strong, thick.—*c. de espaldas,* stoop-shouldered.—**cargador,** *m.* shipper; carrier; stevedore; porter; ramrod.—**cargamento,** *m.* cargo; shipment.—**cargar,** *vti.* & *vii.* to load; to burden; to carry (a load); to charge (all meanings); to ship; to bore; to be burdensome.—*vii.* to incline, lean towards; to be supported by; (con) to assume responsibility; to bear the blame.—*vri.* (of sky) to become overcast; to be full of; to load oneself (with).—**cargazón,** *f.* cargo; abundance.—*c. de cabeza,* heaviness of the head.—*c. del tiempo,* cloudy, thick weather.—**cargo,** *m.* post, position; duty, responsibility; (com.) debit; charge, custody; accusation.—*c. de conciencia,* remorse, sense of guilt.—*hacerse c. de,* to take charge of; to take into consideration; to realise.—**carguero,** *a.* freight-carrying.—*n.* beast of burden.

cariacontecido, *a.* sad, mournful, downcast.

caribe, *mf.* Carib; savage.

caricatura, *f.* caricature; cartoon.—**caricaturista,** *mf.* caricaturist; cartoonist.—**caricaturizar,** *vti.* [a] to caricature, mock.

caricia, *f.* caress; petting.

caridad, *f.* charity, charitableness.—**caritativo,** *a.* charitable.

caries, *f.* bone decay, tooth decay.

cariño, *m.* love, fondness, affection.—**cariñoso,** *a.* affectionate, loving.

cariz, *m.* aspect.

carlinga, *f.* (aer.) cockpit.

carmelita, *n.* & *a.* Carmelite.—*m.* & *a.* (Cuba, Chile) brown.

carmesí, carmín, *m.* & *a.* crimson, bright red.

carnada, *f.* bait.

carnal, *a.* carnal, sensual.—*primo c.,* first cousin.

carnaval, *m.* carnival; Mardi gras.—**carnavalesco,** *a.* pertaining to a carnival or Mardi gras.

carnaza, *f.* bait.

carne, *f.* flesh; meat; pulp (of fruit).—*c. de cañón,* cannon fodder.—*c. de gallina,* (fig.) goose flesh.—*c. de res,* (Am.) beef.—*c. fiambre,* cold meat.—*c. viva,* quick or raw flesh in a wound.—*c. y hueso,* flesh and blood.—*ni c. ni pescado,* neither fish nor fowl; insipid.—*ser uña y c.,* to be hand and glove, to be one.—**carnero,** *m.* sheep, mutton, ram.—**carnicería,** *f.* meat market, butcher's shop; slaughter.—**carnicero,** *a.* carnivorous; sanguinary, cruel.—*n.* butcher.—**carnívoro,** *n.* carnivore.—*a.* carnivorous.—**carnosidad,** *f.* fleshiness; proud flesh.—**carnoso,** *a.* fleshy; meaty; fat.

caro, *a.* dear, expensive, costly; dear, beloved.—*cara mitad,* better half.—*adv.* dearly, at a high price or cost.

carozo, *m.* core of an apple, pear, etc.; corn cob.

carpa, *f.* (ichth.) carp; canvas tent; circus tent.

carpeta, *f.* table cover; portfolio; desk pad; folder.—**carpetazo,** *m.*—*dar c.,* to lay aside; to pigeonhole.

carpintería, *f.* carpentry; carpenter's shop.—**carpintero,** *m.* carpenter.—*pájaro c.,* woodpecker.

carraspear, *vi.* to clear one's throat; to be hoarse.—**carraspera,** *f.* (coll.) hoarseness; sore throat.

carrera, *f.* run, running race; course; race track; profession, career.—*a la c., de c.,* hastily, hurriedly.

carreta, *f.* wagon, cart.—**carretada,** *f.* cartful.—*pl.* great quantities.—*a carretadas,* (coll.) copiously, in abundance.—**carrete,** *m.* spool, bobbin, reel; coil.—**carretel,** *m.* fishing reel.—**carretera,** *f.* highway; drive.—**carretero,** *m.* cart driver; cartwright.—**carretilla,** *f.* wheelbarrow, handcart; (RR.) gocart.—*de c.,* mechanically; by rote.—**carretón,** *m.* wagon, cart.

carril, *m.* rut; furrow; (RR.) rail.—**carrilera,** *f.* rut (in road).

carrillo, *m.* cheek; small cart.

carro, *m.* car, cart; (Am.) automobile; carriage (of typewriter); cartload.—*c. de combate,* (mil.) tank.—*untar el c.,* (fig.) to grease the palm, to bribe.—**carrocería,** *f.* (auto) body.—**carromato,** *m.* low, strong cart, covered wagon.

carroña, *f.* carrion, putrid carcass.

carroza, *f.* carriage for state occasions.—*c. morturria,* hearse.—**carruaje,** *m.* vehicle; carriage; car.

carta, *f.* letter; map, chart; playing card; charter.—*c. blanca,* carte blanche, full powers.—*c. certificada,* registered letter.—*c. de marear, c. náutica,* sea chart.—*c. de pago,* acquittance, receipt.—*tomar cartas,* to take part; to take sides.

cartabón, *m.* carpenter's square; drawing triangle.

cartapacio, *m.* memorandum book; student's notebook; dossier.

cartear, *vr.* to write to each other, correspond.

cartel, *m.* poster, handbill; placard; cartel.—**cartelera,** *f.* billboard.—**cartelón,** *m.* show bill.

cartera, *f.* brief case; pocketbook; handbag; wallet; portfolio; office and position of a cabinet minister.—**carterista,** *m.* pickpocket.—**cartero,** *m.* letter carrier, postman.

cartílago, *m.* cartilage; parchment.

cartilla, *f.* primer; identity card; passbook.

cartografía, *f.* cartography.—**cartógrafo,** *m.* cartographer.

cartón, *m.* pasteboard; cardboard; cartoon.—*c. piedra,* papier-maché.—**cartulina,** *f.* bristol board, thin cardboard.

cartuchera, *f.* cartridge box or belt; gun holster.—**cartucho,** *m.* paper cone or bag; cartridge.

casa, *f.* house; home; household; firm, concern.—*c. consistorial,* city hall.—*c. de beneficencia,* asylum, poorhouse.—*c. de empeños,* pawnshop.—*c. de huéspedes,* boarding house.—*c. de moneda,* mint.—*c. de socorro,* emergency hospital.—*c. de vecindad,* tenement house.—*c. pública,* brothel.

casaca, *f.* dresscoat.

casado, *a. & n.* married (person).—**casamentero,** *n.* matchmaker.—**casamiento,** *m.* marriage; wedding.—**casar,** *vi. & vr.* to marry, get married.—*vt.* to marry off; to couple.

cascabel, *m.* jingle bell; snake's rattle; rattlesnake.—*poner el c. al gato,* to bell the cat.—**cascabelero,** *a.* light-witted.

cascada, *f.* cascade, waterfall.

cascado, *a.* broken, burst; decayed.

cascajo, *m.* gravel, fragments; rubbish.

cascanueces, *m.* nutcracker.—**cascar,** *vti.* [d] to crack, break into pieces; to crunch; (coll.) to beat, strike.—*vi.* (coll.) to talk too much.—*vri.* to break open.

cáscara, *f.* peel, shell, rind, hull, husk; bark (of trees).—*pl. interj.* by Jove!—**cascarilla,** *f.* powdered eggshell for cosmetic.—**cascarón,** *m.* eggshell.

cascarrabias, *mf.* crab, irritable person.

cascarudo, *a.* having a thick shell, hull, etc.

casco, *m.* skull; broken fragment of glassware; hull (of a ship); helmet; hoof.—*calentarse los cascos,* to bother one's brain.—*ligero de cascos,* featherbrained.

casera, *f.* housekeeper; landlady; caretaker.—**caserío,** *m.* village, settlement; group of houses.—**casero,** *m.* landlord; caretaker; tenant farmer.—*a.* domestic; home-bred; home-made; homely, homey, informal; household (of articles).—**caseta,** *f.* small house; cabin; booth.

casi, *adv.* almost, nearly.—*c. c.,* very nearly.

casilla, *f.* ticket office; post office box; hut; stall; booth; pigeonhole; square of chessboard.—*sacar a uno de sus casillas,* (coll.) to vex beyond one's patience.—**casillero,** *m.* desk or board with pigeonholes.

casimir, *m.* cashmere.

caso, *m.* case; occurrence, event; matter, question, point.—*c. que,* in case.—*dado el c. que,* supposing that.—*el c. es que,* the fact is that.—*en tal c.,* in such a case.—*en todo c.,* at all events, anyway.—*hacer c.,* to mind, obey, pay attention.—*no venir al c.,* to have nothing to do with the case.—*poner por c.,* to assume, suppose.—*vamos al c.,* let us come to the point.—*verse en el c. de,* to be obliged to, have to.

casorio, *m.* (coll.) wedding.

caspa, *f.* dandruff.

casquillo, *m.* empty cartridge; cap; socket.

casta, *f.* breed, lineage, caste; pedigree; quality.

castaña, *f.* chestnut; (fig.) chignon.

castañetear, *vt.* to rattle the castanets.—*vi.* to chatter (the teeth); to creak (the knees).—**castañeteo,** *m.* sound of castanets; chattering of the teeth.

castaño, *m.* chestnut tree and wood.—*a.* hazel, brown, auburn.

castañuela, *f.* castanet.

castellano, *m.* Spanish language.—*n.* native of Castile.—*a.* Castilian; Spanish (lang., gram., etc.).

castidad, *f.* chastity.

castigar, *vti.* [b] to chastise, punish, castigate.—**castigo,** *m.* chastisement, punishment; penalty.

castillo, *m.* castle.

castizo, *a.* pure, correct (language), of good breed.

casto, *a.* chaste.

castor, *m.* beaver; castor.

castrar, *vt.* to castrate, geld.

castrense, *a.* military.

casual, *a.* accidental, occasional, chance.—**casualidad,** *f.* chance

event; accident; coincidence.—*por c.*, by chance.

casucha, *f.* hut, shack, hovel.

cataclismo, *m.* upheaval; catastrophe.

catacumbas, *f.* catacombs.

catador, *m.* taster, sampler.—**catadura,** *f.* act of tasting; (coll.) aspect, looks.—**catar,** *vt.* to sample, try by tasting.

catalán, *n.* & *a.* Catalan, Catalonian.

catalejo, *m.* telescope.

catalogar, *vti.* [b] to catalogue, list. —**catálogo,** *m.* catalogue, list.

cataplasma, *f.* poultice; (fig.) nuisance, vexer.

catarata, *f.* cataract, cascade, waterfall; cataract of the eye.

catarro, *m.* catarrh; cold, snuffles.

catastro, *m.* census of real property of a county or state.

catástrofe, *f.* catastrophe.

catecismo, *m.* catechism.

cátedra, *f.* subject taught by a professor; professorship; seat or chair of a professor.—**catedrático,** *n.* full professor.

catedral, *f.* cathedral.

categoría, *f* category; class, condition; rank.—*de c.*, of high rank, prominent.—**categórico,** *a.* categorical; positive.

catequizar, *vti.* [a] to catechize; to proselytize by religious instruction; to persuade, induce.

caterva, *f.* multitude; crowd, throng; herd.

catire, *a.* & *n.* (Am) blond, blonde.

católico, *a.* catholic, universal.—*n.* & *a.* (Roman) Catholic.—*no estar muy c*, to feel under the weather. —**catolicismo,** *m.* Catholicism.

catre, *m.* small bedstead; cot.—*c de tijera,* folding cot.

caucásico, *n.* & *a.* Caucasian

cauce, *m* bed of a river, river course.

caución, *f.* caution, precaution, surety, guarantee; bail.

caucho, *m.* rubber (material and tree).

caudal, *m.* volume (of water); abundance, fortune, wealth —**caudaloso,** *a.* carrying much water; copious, abundant; wealthy.

caudillaje, caudillismo, *m* leadership; bossism; tyranny.—**caudillo,** *m.* leader, chief; political boss

causa, *f* cause; motive, reason; lawsuit, case, trial (at law).—*a or por c. de,* on account of, because of, due to—**causante,** *mf.* originator; (law) the person from whom a right is derived; constituent, principal.—**causar,** *vt* to cause

cáustico, *a.* caustic, burning.—*m.* caustic.

cautela, *f* caution, prudence, cunning.

—**cauteloso,** *a.* cautious, prudent, wary.

cauterizar, *vti.* [a] to cauterize; to blame.

cautivador, cautivante, *a.* captivating, charming.—**cautivar,** *vt.* to captivate, charm; to take prisoner. —**cautiverio,** *m.*, **cautividad,** *f.* captivity.—**cautivo,** *n.* captive.

cauto, *a.* cautious, prudent, wary.

cavar, *vt.* to dig, excavate.—*vi.* to dig; to get to the bottom (of a subject, etc.).

caverna, *f.* cave, cavern.—**cavernoso,** *a.* cavernous; hollow.—*voz cavernosa,* deep-throated voice.

cavidad, *f.* cavity.

cayo, *m.* key, cay, island reef.

cayuco, *m.* (Am.) dugout canoe.

caza, *f.* hunt(ing); wild game.—*dar c.*, to pursue.—**cazador,** *a.* hunting. —*n.* hunter.—**cazar,** *vti.* [a] to chase, hunt; to catch; to pursue.— **cazatorpedero,** *m.* destroyer.

cazo, *m.* dipper; pan; pot.

cazón, *m.* small shark.

cazuela, *f.* cooking pan; stewing pan; stew; crock; (theat.) top gallery.

cazuz, *m.* ivy.

cebada, *f.* barley.—**cebar,** *vt.* & *vi.* to fatten (animals); to stuff; to feed (a fire, lamp); to prime (a firearm); to excite and cherish (a passion); to bait (a fishhook).—*vr.* to gloat over (a victim).—**cebo,** *m.* bait; incentive; fodder.

cebolla, *f.* onion; onion bulb.— **cebolleta,** *f.* spring onion; scallion.

cebra, *f.* zebra.

cebú, *m.* zebu.

cecear, *vi.* to lisp.—**ceceo,** *m.* lisping, lisp.

cecina, *f.* corned, dried beef.

cedazo, *m.* sieve.

ceder, *vt.* to transfer, cede, yield.— *vi.* to yield, submit; to fail; to slacken, to abate.

cedro, *m* cedar.

cédula, *f.* scrip, bill; charter; order, decree, warrant; share.—*c. de identidad,* or *c personal,* official identity document.

céfiro, *m* zephyr, west wind, breeze.

cegar, *vn* [1-b] to grow or go blind. —*vti.* to blind, to confuse; to close up, stop up, block up, fill up.—*vri.* to become or be blinded (by passion, etc).—**cegato,** *a.* (coll) short-sighted.—**ceguedad, ceguera,** *f.* blindness; ignorance

ceja, *f* eyebrow —*quemarse las cejas,* to burn the midnight oil.—*tener entre c y c.*, to dislike; to think constantly about

cejar, vi. to give up; to give in, yield; to cede; to relax, slacken.

cejijunto, a. frowning, scowling; with knitted eyebrows.

celada, f. ambush; artful trick; trap; helmet.—celador, n. watchman (-woman); caretaker.—celar, vt. to watch over zealously or jealously; to watch, keep under guard; to protect; to conceal.

celda, f. cell (in a convent, prison, etc.).—celdilla, f. cell in beehives; (bot.) cell.

celebración, f. celebration; praise; applause.—celebrar, vt. to celebrate; to praise, applaud; to revere; to rejoice at; to say (mass); to hold (formal meeting).—célebre, a. famous, renowned.—celebridad, f. celebrity; renown, fame.

celeridad, f. celerity, quickness.

celeste, a. celestial, heavenly.—azul c., sky-blue.—celestial, a. celestial, heavenly.

celestina, f. procuress, go-between

celibato, m. celibacy.—célibe, a. & mf. unmarried (person); bachelor.

celo, m. zeal; devotion, mating, heat (of animals) —pl. jealousy.—dar celos, to inspire jealousy.

celofán, m. cellophane

celosía, f. lattice work; venetian blind.

celoso, a. jealous, zealous, eager; suspicious

celta, n & a Celt(ic).—céltico, a. Celtic

célula, f. (biol.) cell.—celular, a. cellular

celuloide, m. celluloid

celulosa, f. cellulose.

cementar, vt. to cement

cementerio, m. cemetery, graveyard.

cemento, m. cement, concrete —c armado, reinforced concrete

cena, f. late dinner, supper

cenagal, m. quagmire, slough, arduous, unpleasant affair.

cenagoso, a. muddy, miry, marshy.

cenar, vi. to sup.—vt to take supper

cencerrada, f., cencerreo, m. serenade with cowbells, pots and pans, etc.—cencerro, m cowbell.

cendal, m. gauze, crepe.

cenefa, f border; fringe; valance.

cenicero, m. ashtray; ash pan.—cenicienta, f thing or person illtreated.—la C., Cinderella.—ceniciento, a. ash-colored, ashen.

cenit, m zenith.

ceniza, f ash(es), cinder(s) —cenizo, a. ash-colored.

censo, m. census.

censor, m, censor, critic.—censura, f censorship; censure blame, re

proach.—censurable, a. reprehensible, blameworthy.—censurar, vt. to review, criticize; to censure, blame.

centavo, m. cent.

centella, f. lightning; thunderbolt.—centell(e)ante, a. sparkling, flashing.—centellar, centellear, vi. to twinkle, sparkle.—centelleo, m. sparkling; twinkling.

centena, f. a hundred.

centeno, m. rye.

centesimal, a. (of a number) between one and one hundred.—centésimo, n. & a. (a) hundredth.

centígrado, a. centigrade.—centigramo, m centigram.—centilitro, m. centiliter.—centímetro, m. centimeter. (See Table of Measures.)

céntimo, m. penny.

centinela, m. sentry, sentinel.

central, a. central.—f. main office of a public service; (Am.) sugar mill.—c. eléctrica, powerhouse.—centralización, f. centralization.—centralizar, vti. [a] to centralize.—centrar, vt. to center —céntrico, a. central.

centrífugo, a. centrifugal.

centrípeto, a. centripetal.

centro, m center; middle; midst.—c. de mesa, centerpiece (for table).—estar en su c., to be in one's element.—centroamericano, n. & a. Central American.

centuria, f. century (period of time); division of Roman army.

ceñir, vti [9] to gird; to surround, girdle; to fit tight; to hem in.—vri. to confine or limit oneself.

ceño, m frown, scowl.—fruncir el c., to frown; to scowl —ceñudo, a. frowning, scowling.

cepa, f. stump, stub; vinestock, stock of a family.—de buena c., ón good authority; of good stock.

cepillar, vt. to brush; to plane; to polish.—cepillo, m. brush; (carp.) plane, charity box.

cepo, m. stocks, pillory; stock (of an anchor); trap, snare, clamp.

cera, f. wax, beeswax, wax tapers.—pl. honeycombs.

cerámica, f. ceramic art, ceramics.

cerbatana, f. pea shooter, blowgun; ear trumpet for the deaf

cerca, f. fence; hedge, enclosure adv near, close by, nigh.—c. de, closely, close at hand —cercanía, f. nearness; surroundings, neighborhood.—cercano, a. near, close; neighboring.—cercar, vti. [d] to fence in; to circle, gird; to surround; to besiege.

cercenar, vt. to clip, trim, pare; to sever, mutilate to reduce, curtail

cerciorar, *vt.* to assure, affirm.—*vr.* (de) to ascertain, make sure of.

cerco, *m.* fence; ring; circle; rim, border; blockade, siege.—*levantar el c.*, to raise a blockade.—*poner c. a*, to lay siege to, to blockade.

cerda, *f.* bristle; horse's hair.

cerdo, *m.* hog, pig; pork.

cerdoso, *a.* bristly; hairy.

cereal, *m.* cereal.

cerebro, *m.* brain.

ceremonia, *f.* ceremony; formality.— *guardar c.*, to comply with the formalities.—**ceremonial**, *a. & m.* ceremonial.—**ceremonioso**, *a.* ceremonious, formal.

cereza, *f.* cherry.—**cerezo**, *m.* cherry tree, cherry wood.

cerilla, *f.* wax match; wax taper; ear wax.—**cerillo**, *m.* (Am.) wax match.

cerner, cernir, *vti.* [10] to sift.—*vii.* to drizzle.—*vri.* to soar

cero, *m.* zero, naught.

cerquillo, *m.* hair bangs.

cerquita, *adv.* very near; at a short distance.

cerrado, *a.* incomprehensible, obscure, close; closed; obstinate; inflexible; cloudy; overcast; stupid.—*a puerta cerrada*, closed (meeting, etc.).— **cerradura**, *f.* lock; closure.—**cerrajería**, *f.* locksmith's shop or forge.— **cerrajero**, *m.* locksmith.—**cerrar**, *vti.* [1] & *vii.* to close, shut, fasten, lock; to fold and seal (a letter).— *vri.* to close; to remain firm in one's opinion; to become cloudy and overcast; to get close to each other. —*cerrársele a uno todas las puertas*, to find all avenues closed.— **cerrazón**, *f.* dark and cloudy weather preceding a storm

cerrero, *a.* untamed; wild; unbroken (horse).

cerro, *m.* hill.

cerrojo, *m.* bolt, latch.

certamen, *m.* contest; competition.

certero, *a.* well-aimed, accurate, sure; skillful; unfailing.

certeza, *f.* certainty, assurance.— **certidumbre**, *f* certainty, conviction.

certificación, *f.* certificate, affidavit.— **certificado**, *m.* certificate, attestation; testimonial; piece of registered mail.—**certificar**, *vti.* [d] to certify, attest; to register (a letter); to prove by a public instrument.

cervato, *m.* fawn.

cervecería, *f.* brewery; alehouse, beer tavern.—**cervecero**, *a.* beer.—*n.* brewer; beer seller.—**cerveza**, *f.* beer, ale

cerviz, *f.* cervix, nape of the neck.— *doblar la c.*, to humble oneself.

cesación, *f.* cessation, discontinuance, stop, pause.—**cesante**, *a.* ceasing.— *mf.* dismissed civil servant —**cesantía**, *f.* dismissal from a post.— cesar, *vi.* to cease, stop; to desist; to retire; to leave a post or employment.—**cese**, *m.* cease; cessation of payment (pension, salary).

cesión, *f.* cession, transfer, conveyance; concession.—**cesionario**, *n.* grantee, assignee, transferee.— **cesionista**, *mf.* transferrer, assigner, grantor.

césped, *m* lawn; turf; grass; grass plot.

cesta, *f.* basket, pannier; basketful. —**cesto**, *m.* large basket; hutch; hamper

cetrino, *a.* sallow; jaundiced.

cetro, *m.* scepter, reign.

cibelina, *f.* sable.

cicatería, *f.* niggardliness, stinginess. —**cicatero**, *a.* niggardly, stingy

cicatriz, *f.* scar.—**cicatrización**, *f.* healing —**cicatrizar**, *vii.* [a] to heal.

ciclismo, *m* bicycling.—**ciclista**, *mf.* cyclist.

ciclo, *m* cycle, period of time.

ciclón, *m* cyclone; hurricane.

ciclotrón, *m.* cyclotron.

cicuta, *f.* hemlock.

ciego, *a* blind; blinded.—*n.* blind person; (anat.) blind gut —*a ciegas*, blindly, in the dark.

cielo, *m.* sky, firmament, heaven(s); ceiling, glory, paradise; roof *llovido del c.*, godsend.—*ver el c abierto*, to find an unforeseen opportunity.

ciempiés, *m.* centipede

ciénaga, *f.* marsh, moor

ciencia, *f.* science; knowledge, certainty —*a c. cierta*, with certainty.

cieno, *m* mud, mire, slime, slough.

científico, *a.* scientific.—*n.* scientist.

cierre, *m* act and mode of closing, shutting, locking; fastener; clasp; plug of a valve

cierto, *a.* sure, positive; certain; true, a certain.—*de c.*, certainly, surely.—*lo c. es que*, the fact is that.—*no por c.*, certainly not.— *por c. que*, indeed; by the way.

cierva, *f* hind, doe.—**ciervo**, *m.* deer, stag.

cierzo, *m* cold northerly wind.

cifra, *f* figure, number; cipher; symbol —**cifrar**, *vt.* to write in cipher, to abridge.—*c las esperanzas*, to place one's hopes.

cigarra, *f.* locust.

cigarrera, *f.* cigar cabinet; pocket cigar or cigarette case, woman ciga-

rette maker or dealer.—**cigarrero,** *m.* cigarette maker or dealer.—**cigarrillo,** *m.* cigarette.—**cigarro,** *m.* cigar; cigarette.

cigüeña, *f.* stork; crane; bell-crank; crank.—**cigüeñal,** *m.* crankshaft.

cilíndrico, *a.* cylindrical.—**cilindro,** *m.* cylinder; roller; press roll; chamber.

cima, *f.* summit, peak; top, tiptop.—*dar c.,* to conclude successfully, crown.

címbalo, *m.* cymbal.

cimbrar, *vt.* = CIMBREAR.—**cimbreante,** *a.* willowy.—**cimbrear,** *vt.* to brandish; to shake; to sway; to arch. —*vr.* to bend; to vibrate; to shake. —**cimbreño,** *a.* pliant, flexible.—**cimbreo,** *m.* act of bending, brandishing, swaying, vibrating.

cimentación, *f.* foundation; laying of a foundation.—**cimentar,** *vti.* [1] to lay the foundations of; to found; to ground.—**cimiento,** *m.* foundation; groundwork, bed; base; root.

cinc, *m.* zinc.

cincel, *m.* chisel; engraver.—**cincelar,** *vt.* to chisel, engrave, carve.

cincuentón, *a.* fifty-year old.—*n.* fifty-year-old person.

cincha, *f.* girth, cinch.—**cinchar,** *vt.* to girth, cinch up.

cine, cinema, *m.* moving picture, "movie"; movie theater.—**cinematografía,** *f.* cinematography.—**cinematógrafo,** *m.* cinematograph; moving-picture.

cínico, *a.* cynical; impudent; barefaced.—*n.* cynic.—**cinismo,** *m.* cynicism.

cinta, *f.* ribbon; tape, band, strip, sash; (moving-picture) film, reel.—**cintarazo,** *m.* slap with a belt.—**cintillo,** *m.* hatband; coronet; headline.—**cinto,** *m.* belt, girdle.—**cintura,** *f.* waist, waistline.—*meter en c.,* to control, to discipline.—**cinturón,** *m.* belt; (fig.) girdle.

ciprés, *m.* cypress.—**cipresal,** *m.* cypress grove.

circo, *m.* circus.

circuito, *m.* circuit.

circulación, *f.* circulation, currency; traffic.—**circulante,** *a.* circulatory, circulating.—*biblioteca c.,* lending library.—**circular,** *vi.* to circulate, move.—*vt.* to circulate, pass round. —*a.* circular; circulatory; circling. —*f.* circular letter, notice.—**circulatorio,** *a.* circulatory.—**círculo,** *m.* circle; circumference; ring; social circle, club, association.

circuncidar, *vt.* to circumcise.—**circuncisión,** *f* circumcision.

circundar, *vt* to surround, encircle

circunferencia, *f.* circumference.

circunscribir, *vti.* [49] to circumscribe.

circunspección, *f.* circumspection, prudence.—**circunspecto,** *a.* circumspect, cautious.

circunstancia, *f.* circumstance.—**circunstancial,** *a.* circumstantial.

circunstante, *a.* surrounding; present, attending.—*m. pl.* bystanders; audience.

cirio, *m.* wax taper.

ciruela, *f.* plum.—*c. pasa,* prune.—**ciruelo,** *m.* plum tree.

cirugía, *f.* surgery.—**cirujano,** *n.* surgeon.

cisco, *m.* coal dust; (coll.) bedlam.

cisma, *m.* schism; discord.—**cismático,** *n.* & *a.* schismatic.

cisne, *m.* swan.

cisterna, *f.* cistern; reservoir; underground water tank.

cisura, *f.* incision.

cita, *f.* appointment, engagement, date; quotation.—**citación,** *f.* citation, quotation; summons, judicial notice.—**citar,** *vt.* to make an appointment with; to convoke; to quote; to summon; to give judicial notice.

ciudad, *f.* city.—**ciudadanía,** citizenship.—**ciudadano,** *a.* pertaining to a city.—*n.* citizen.—**ciudadela,** *f* citadel; tenement house.

cívico, *a.* civic.

civil, *a.* polite.—**civilización,** *f.* civilization.—**civilizador,** *a.* & *n.* civilizing; civilizer.—**civilizar,** *vti.* [a] to civilize.—**civismo,** *m.* good citizenship.

cizaña, *f* darnel; weed; discord. **cizañar,** *vi.* to sow discord.—**cizañero,** *n.* troublemaker.

clamar, *vi.* to whine; to clamor, vociferate.—*c. por,* to demand, cry out for.—**clamor,** *m.* clamor, outcry; whine; toll of bells, knell.—**clamorear,** *vi.* to clamor; to toll, knell.—**clamoreo,** *m.* repeated or prolonged clamor; knell.—**clamoroso,** *a.* clamorous, loud, noisy

clan, *m.* clan; (fam.) clique.

clara, *f.* glair, white of an egg:—*a las claras,* clearly, openly

claraboya, *f* skylight; transom, bull's-eye.

clarear, *vt.* to give light to.—*vi.* to dawn; to clear up.—*vr* to be transparent, translucent.

clarete, *m.* claret.

claridad, *f.* brightness, splendor, light; clearness.—*pl.* plain language, plain truths.—**clarificar,** *vti.* [d] to brighten; to clarify; to purify

clarín, *m* bugle, clarion bugler·

clarinada, *f.* tart remark.—**clarinete,** *m.* clarinet; clarinet player.

clarividencia, *f.* clairvoyance; clear-sightedness.—**clarividente,** *a.* clairvoyant; clear-sighted.—**claro,** *a.* clear, distinct; bright, cloudless; light (color); transparent; thin; spaced out; frank; outspoken; obvious, evident; open.—*m.* clearing; light spot; clear spot in the sky.—*adv.* clearly.—*¡c. (está)!* of course, naturally.—*pasar la noche en c.,* not to sleep a wink.—*poner en c.,* to make plain.—*sacar en c.,* to conclude, to arrive at a conclusion.

clase, *f.* class, kind, sort; class in school; classroom.—*de c.,* of distinction, of high standing.

clásico, *a.* classic(al).—*n.* classicist.

clasificación, *f.* classification.—**clasificar,** *vti.* [d] to classify; to class.

claudicar, *vii.* [d] to halt, limp; to bungle; to yield.

claustro, *m.* cloister; faculty of a university; monastic state.

cláusula, *f.* period; sentence; clause; article.

clausura, *f.* cloister; inner recess of a convent; closing; clausure, confinement. **clausurar,** *vti.* to close; conclude, adjourn.

clavar, *vt.* to nail; to fix, fasten; to stick, pin, prick; to pierce; (coll.) to cheat, deceive.—*c. la vista,* or *los ojos,* to stare.

clave, *f.* key of a code; (mus.) key; clef; keystone.

clavel, *m.,* **clavellina,** *f.* pink, carnation.

clavetear, *vt.* to nail; to decorate or stud with nails.

clavícula, *f.* clavicle, collar bone.

clavija, *f.* pin, peg; peg of a string instrument.—*apretar las clavijas,* to put on the thumb screws; to dress down.

clavo, *m.* nail; spike; clove.—*dar en el c.,* to hit the nail on the head.—*un c. saca otro c.,* one grief cures another.

clemencia, *f.* clemency, mercy.—**clemente,** *a.* merciful.

cleptómano, *n. & a.* kleptomaniac.

clerical, *a.* clerical, pert. to the clergy.—**clérigo,** *m.* clergyman.—**clero,** *m.* clergy.

cliente, *mf.* client; customer.—**clientela,** *f.* following, clientele; customers; practice (of lawyers, doctors).

clima, *m.* climate, clime.

clímax, *m.* climax.

clínica, *f.* clinic; private hospital; doctor's or dentist's office; nursing home.

clisé, *m* cliché; stereotype plate; (phot.) negative.

cloaca, *f.* sewer; cesspool.

eloquear, *vi.* to cluck, cackle.

cloro, *m.* chlorine.—**clorofila,** *f.* chlorophyll.—**cloroformar,** *vt.,* **cloroformizar,** *vti.* [a] to chloroform.—**cloroformo,** *m.* chloroform.

club, *m.* private club.

clueca, *f.* brooding hen.—**clueco,** *a.* broody; (coll.) decrepit.

coacción, *f.* force; coercion.—**coactivo,** *a.* forcible; coercive.

coagular, *vt.* to coagulate; to curdle.—*vr.* to coagulate, clot; to curdle.

coalición, *f.* coalition.

coartada, *f.* alibi.—**coartar,** *vt.* to limit, restrain.

coba, *f.* (coll.) fawning, adulation.—*dar c.,* to flatter.

cobarde, *mf.* coward; poltroon.—*a.* cowardly.—**cobardía,** *f.* cowardice.

cobertizo, *m.* shed, hut; penthouse.—**cobertor,** *m.* bedcover.—**cobertura,** *f.* cover, wrapper, covering, coverlet.

cobija, *f.* cover; (Am.) blanket.—**cobijar,** *vt.* to cover; to shelter; to lodge.—*vr.* to take shelter.

cobrador *m.* collector; receiving teller.—**cobranza,** *f.* receipt, collection (of money).—**cobrar,** *vt.* to collect (bills, debts); to receive (what is due); to retrieve (shot game); to gain; to charge (price, fee); to cash (check).—*c. ánimo,* to take courage.—*c. fuerzas,* to gather strength.

cobre, *m.* copper; brass kitchen utensils; brass instruments of an orchestra.—*batir el c.,* to hustle.—**cobrizo,** *a.* coppery; copper-colored.

cobro, *m.* receipt, collection (of money); cashing.—*poner en c.,* to put in a safe place.—*ponerse en c.,* to seek a safe place; to withdraw to safety.

coca, *f.* coca; coca leaves.—**cocaína,** *f.* cocaine.

cocal, *m.* coconut plantation.

cocción, *f.* cooking.

cocear, *vt. & vi.* to kick.

cocer, *vti.* [26-a] to boil; to bake; to cook; to calcine (brick, etc.).—*vii.* to boil, cook.—**cocido,** *a.* boiled, baked, cooked.—*m.* a Spanish stew.

cociente, *m.* quotient.

cocimiento, *m.* boiling, concoction.

cocina, *f.* kitchen; cuisine, cookery.—**cocinar,** *vt. & vi.* to cook.—**cocinero,** *n.* cook; chef.

coco, *m.* coconut (tree, shell, fruit); bogey.

cocodrilo, *m.* crocodile.

cocotero, *m.* coconut tree.

coctel, *m.* cocktail.—coctelera, *f.* cocktail shaker.

cocuyo, *m.* firefly.

cochambre, *m.* (coll.) greasy, dirty thing.—cochambroso, *a.* filthy, smelly.

coche, *m.* carriage; coach; car.—*c. cama,* Pullman, sleeping car.—*c. salón,* parlor car.—cochero, *m.* coachman.

cochinada, *f.* (coll.) hoggishness; dirty action, dirty trick.—cochinilla, *f.* cochineal.—cochinillo, *n.* suckling pig.—*c. de Indias,* guinea pig.—cochino, *n.* hog (sow), pig.—*a. & n.* dirty, vile (person).—cochiquera, *f.* (coll.) hog sty, pigpen.

codazo, *m.* blow with the elbow.—codear, *vi.* to elbow.—*vt.* to nudge. —*vr.* to rub shoulders, be on intimate terms.—codeo, *m.* elbowing; familiarity.

codeína, *f.* codeine.

codiciar, *vt.* & *vi.* to covet.—codicioso, *a.* covetous, greedy; ambitious.

codificar, *vti.* [d] to codify.—código, *m.* code (of laws).

codo, *m.* elbow; bend.—*alzar el empinar el c.,* to drink too much.—*hablar por los codos,* to talk too much.

codorniz, *f.* quail.

coeducación, *f.* coeducation.

coeficiente, *m.* coefficient.

coerción, *f.* coercion.

coetáneo, *a.* contemporary.

coexistencia, *f.* coexistence.—coexistir, *vi.* to coexist.

cofia, *f.* coif; hair net.

cofrade, *mf.* member (of a confraternity, brotherhood, etc.).—cofradía, *f.* brotherhood, sisterhood; guild.

cofre, *m.* coffer; trunk; chest.—cofrecito, *m.* casket, jewel box.

coger, *vti.* [c] to catch; to seize, grasp; to gather up, collect; to take, receive, hold.—*cogerse una cosa,* to steal something.—cogida, *f.* toss or goring by bull; a catch of the ball by a baseball player.

cogollo, *m.* heart of garden plants; shoot of a plant; sugar cane top, used as forage.

cogote, *m.* back of the neck, nape.

cohechar, *vt.* to bribe.—cohecho, *m.* bribery.

coherencia, *f.* coherence; connection. —coherente, *a.* coherent.—cohesión, *f.* cohesion.—cohesivo, *a.* cohesive.

cohete, *m.* skyrocket; rocket

cohibición, *f.* reserve, shyness, restraint.—cohibido, *a.* inhibited; embarrassed, uneasy—cohibir, *vt* to restrain, inhibit.

coincidencia, *f* coincidence.—coincidente, *a.* coincident.—coincidir, *vi.* to coincide.

coito, *m.* copulation.

cojear, *vi.* to limp.—*c. del mismo pie,* to have the same weakness.—cojera, *f.* limp, lameness.

cojín, *m.* cushion; pad.—cojinete, *m.* bearing; pillow block; small cushion.

cojo, *a.* lame, crippled; one-legged; (of table, etc.) unsteady, tilting.—*n.* cripple.

cok, *m.* coke.

col, *f.* cabbage.

cola, *f.* tail; line of people; hind portion of anything; glue.—*estar a la c.,* to be in the last place.—*hacer c.,* to stand in line.—*tener* or *traer c.,* to have serious consequences.

colaboración, *f.* collaboration; contribution (to a periodical, etc.).—colaborador, *m.* collaborator; contributor (to a periodical, etc.).—colaborar, *vi.* to collaborate.

colación, *f.* collation.—*traer a c,* to bring up for discussion.

coladera, *f.* strainer, sieve.—colador, *m.* colander.—colar, *vti.* & *vii.* [12] to strain, drain, pass through, percolate.—*vri.* to slip in or out, sneak in.

colapso, *m.* collapse.

colateral, *a.* collateral.

colcha, *f.* coverlet, quilt, bedspread; saddle and trappings.

colchón, *m.* mattress.

colear, *vi.* to wag (the tail).—*vt* to pull down (cattle) by the tail.

colección, *f.* collection.—coleccionador, coleccionista, *n.* collector (of stamps, etc.).—coleccionar, *vt.* to form a collection of, collect.—colecta, *f.* collection of voluntary contributions, tax assessment.—colectar, *vt.* to collect.—colectividad, *f.* collectivity; mass of people; community.—colectivo, *a.* collective.—colector, *m.* collector, gatherer.

colega, *mf.* colleague; fellow worker

colegial, *a.* collegiate.—*n.* first or secondary school student; (coll.) inexperienced person, greenhorn.—colegiatura, *f.* membership in a professional association (bar, medical, engineering, etc.).—colegio, *m* body of professional men; school, academy; elementary or secondary school.

colegir, *vti.* [29-c] to deduce, infer, conclude.

cólera, *f.* anger, rage, fury.—*m.* cholera.—colérico, *a.* angry, irascible; choleric.

coleta, *f* pigtail.—*cortarse la c.,* to

retire, quit the profession (esp. bull-fighters).—**coletilla,** *f.* postscript; small queue (hair).

coleto, *m.* leather jacket; inner self. —*decir para su c.,* to say to oneself. —*echarse al c.,* to drink down; to devour.

colgado, *a.* suspended, hanging; disappointed.—**colgadura,** *f.* tapestry; bunting.—**colgajo,** *m.* tatter or rag hanging from (clothes, etc.).—**colgante,** *m.* drop; pendant; hanger; king post.—*a.* hanging.—**colgar,** *vti.* [12-b] to hang up; to impute, charge with; to kill by hanging; to flunk a student.—*vii.* to be suspended; to dangle; to flag, droop. —*vri.* to hang oneself.

colibrí, *m.* hummingbird.

cólico, *m.* colic.

coliflor, *f.* cauliflower.

coligarse, *vri.* [b] to band together, become allies.

colilla, *f.* cigar stub; cigarette butt.

colina, *f.* hill.

colindante, *a.* contiguous, adjacent, abutting.—**colindar,** *vi.* (con) to be contiguous, or adjacent (to); to abut (on).

coliseo, *m.* theater, opera house; coliseum.

colisión, *f.* collision, clash.

colmado, *a.* (de) abundant; full (of), filled (with).—*m.* specialty eating house (gen. for sea food); grocery store, supermarket.—**colmar,** *vt.* (de) to heap up, fill to the brim (with); to fulfill, make up; to bestow liberally.

colmena, *f.* beehive, (Am.) bee.— **colmenar,** *m.* apiary.

colmillo, *m.* eyetooth; fang; tusk.

colmo, *m.* fill; overflowing; overmeasure; limit; climax, extreme, acme. —*a. c.,* abundantly.—*llegar al c., ser el c.,* to be the limit.

colocación, *f.* situation, position; employment, job; placing, setting, arrangement.—**colocar,** *vti.* [d] to arrange, put in due place or order; to place, provide with employment, take on (in a job).—*vri.* to take (a job); to place oneself.

colombiano, *n.* & *a.* Colombian.

colombino, *a.* pertaining to Columbus; pertaining to pigeons or doves.

colonia, *f.* settlement, colony; plantation; cologne water.—**colonial,** *a.* colonial.—**colonización,** *f.* settlement, colonization.—**colonizador,** *n.* & *a.* colonizer; colonizing.—**colonizar,** *vti.* [a] to colonize, settle.— **colono,** *m.* colonist, settler; tenant farmer.

coloquio, *m.* conversation, dialogue.

color, *m.* color; paint; rouge; coloring tint; pretext.—*sacarle los colores a uno,* to shame, make one blush. —**coloración,** *f.* coloration, coloring, painting.—**colorado,** *a.* red; ruddy; colored.—*ponerse c.,* to blush.— **colorante,** *m.* color, paint; coloring tint.—*a.* coloring.—**colorar, colorear,** *vt.* to color, paint, dye, stain; to make plausible; to palliate.— **coloreado,** *a.* colored.—**colorete,** *m.* rouge.—**colorido,** *m.* coloring or color; pretext, pretense.

colosal, *a.* colossal, huge.

columbrar, *vt.* to perceive faintly, discern at a distance; to conjecture.

columna, *f.* column, pillar.—*c. vertebral,* or *dorsal,* spine.

columpiar, *vt.* & *vr.* to swing.—**columpio,** *m.* swing; seesaw.

collado, *m.* height, hill.

collar, *m.* necklace; collar, collet.— **collarín,** *m.* collar of a coat; (mech.) tube, sleeve; ruff.—**collera,** *f.* horse collar.

coma, *f.* comma (,).—*m.* coma, unconsciousness.

comadre, *f.* mother and godmother with respect to each other; midwife; gossip; go-between.—**comadrear,** *vi.* to gossip, tattle.—**comadreja,** *f.* weasel.—**comadreo,** *m.* gossiping.—**comadrón,** *m.* male midwife, accoucheur.—**comadrona,** *f.* midwife.

comandancia, *f.* command; office of a commander; province or district of a commander.—**comandante,** *m.* commander, commandant.—**comandar,** *vt.* to command.

comandita, *f.* (com.) silent partnership.—**comanditario,** *a.* (com.) pertaining to a silent partnership.

comando, *m.* military command.

comarca, *f.* territory, region.

comba, *f* curvature, warp, bend.— **combadura,** *f.* bending, bend.— **combar,** to bend, curve.—*vr.* to warp, bulge; to sag.

combate, *m.* combat, fight, battle; struggle.—**combatiente,** *mf.* & *a.* combatant, fighter; fighting.—**combatir,** *vt.* & *vi.* to combat, fight; to attack, oppose; to struggle.

combinación, *f.* combination; connection; compound; plan; slip (underwear).—**combinar,** *vt.* & *vr.* to combine, unite.

combustible, *m.* fuel.—*a.* combustible. —**combustión,** *f.* combustion.

comedero, *m.* feeding-trough; (coll.) eating place.—*a.* edible, eatable.

comedia, *f.* comedy; farce; play.— **comediante,** *mf.* actor, actress,

comedian; hypocrite.—*a.* (coll.) hypocritical.

comedido, *a.* courteous, polite; prudent, moderate.—comedimiento, *m.* moderation; politeness.—comedirse, *vri.* [29] to govern oneself; to be moderate, polite.

comedor, *m.* dining room.—*n.* & *a.* eater; eating.

comején, *m.* termite.

comensal, *n.* table guest; companion at meals.

comentar, *vt.* to comment; to annotate, expound.—comentario, *m.* commentary.—comentarista, *mf.* commentator.

comenzar, *vti.* [1-a] & *vii.* to commence, begin.

comer, *vt.* to eat; to take (in chess, checkers, etc.).—*vi.* to eat; to lunch, dine.—*vr.* to eat up; to omit, skip. —*dar de c.*, to feed.—*ganar para c.*, to make a living.

comercial, *a.* commercial.—comerciante, *mf.* trader.—comerciar, *vi.* to trade, engage in commerce.—comercio, *m.* commerce, trade,—*c. sexual*, sexual intercourse.

comestible, *a.* eatable, edible.—*m. pl.* food, provisions, groceries.

cometa, *m.* comet.—*f.* kite.

cometer, *vt.* to commit, perpetrate.—cometido, *m.* commission; charge; task, duty.

comezón, *f.* itch(ing); longing, desire.

comicios, *m. pl.* elections, primaries; district assemblies.

cómico, *m.* player, actor, comedian. —*a.* comic; comical, funny.

comida, *f.* eating; food; luncheon, dinner, supper.

comienzo, *m.* start, beginning.—*dar c.*, to begin, start.

comilón, *m.* great eater, glutton.

comillas, *f. pl.* quotation marks (" ").

comino, *m.* cumin (plant, seed).—*no valer un c.*, not to be worth a bean.

comisaría, *f.* police station; office of the commissary.—comisario, *m.* commissary; police inspector; purser.

comisión, *f.* commission; committee; assignment; perpetration.—comisionado, *m.* commissioner.—*a.* commissional or commissionary; commissioned.—comisionar, *vt.* to commission; to appoint.—comisionista, *mf.* commission merchant; commission agent; commissioner.

comité, *m.* committee; commission.

comitiva, *f.* retinue; group of attendants or followers.

como, *adv.* & *conj.* how; in what manner; to what degree; as; since; like; as if; about, approximately; if; such as; inasmuch as; as.—*c. quiera que*, although; since.—cómo, *interrog.* what? how? why?—*¿a cómo?* how much?—*¿a cómo estamos?* what is the date?—*¿cómo?* what is it? what did you say?—*¿cómo así?* how? how so?—*¿cómo no?* why not? of course.—*interj* why! is it possible!

cómoda, *f.* chest of drawers, bureau.

comodidad, *f.* comfort, convenience; commodity.—comodín, *m.* something or someone of general utility; joker (at card).—cómodo, *a.* comfortable; cozy; convenient.

comodoro, *m.* commodore.

compacto, *a.* compact.

compadecer, *vti.* [3] to pity, be sorry for.—*vri.* (de) to pity; (con) to conform, agree, tally.

compadraje, compadrazgo, *m.* alliance for mutual protection and advancement (used in a bad sense); clique.—compadre, *m.* godfather and father of a child with respect to each other; friend, pal.

compaginar, *vt.* to arrange in proper order; to unite, join.

compañerismo, *m.* good fellowship, comradeship.—compañero, *m.* companion, pal; fellow member; partner; one of a pair, mate.—compañía, *f.* company; partnership; co-partnership.

comparación, *f.* comparison.—comparar, *vt.* to compare; to confront.—comparativo, *a.* comparative.

comparecencia, *f.* appearance.—comparecer, *vii.* [3] to appear (before a judge, etc.).

comparsa, *f.* (theat.) retinue of persons.—*mf.* (theat.) extra, supernumerary actor.

compartimiento, *m.* division of a whole into parts; compartment; department.—compartir, *vt.* to divide into equal parts; to share.

compás, *m.* compass; measure; beat. —*llevar el c.*, to beat time.

compasión, *f.* compassion, pity.—compasivo, *a.* compassionate, merciful.

compatibilidad, *f.* compatibility.—compatible, *a.* compatible, suitable.

compatriota, *mf.* compatriot, fellow-countryman.

compeler, *vt.* to compel, force.

compendiar, *vt.* to abridge, condense —compendio, *m.* compendium, abridgment.

compenetración, *f.* intermixture.—compenetrarse, *vr.* to pervade, intermix; to be in full agreement.

compensación, *f.* compensation; recompense, reward.—**compensar,** *vt.* & *vi.* to compensate, recompense; to counterbalance; to balance, equilibrate; to indemnify.

competencia, *f.* competition, rivalry; competence, aptitude; jurisdiction; dispute.—**competente,** *a.* competent, apt; applicable (to); adequate.—**competición,** *f.* competition.—**competidor,** *n.* opponent, competitor.—*a.* competing.—**competir,** *vii.* [29] to compete, vie, rival.

compilación, *f.* compilation.—**compilador,** *n.* & *a.* compiler, compiling.—**compilar,** *vt.* to compile.

compinche, *m.* bosom friend, pal.

complacencia, *f.* pleasure, satisfaction; complacency.—**complacer,** *vti.* [3] to please, accommodate.—*vri.* (en) to be pleased (with or to); to delight (in); to take pleasure (in).—**complaciente,** *a.* pleasing, kind, agreeable.

complejidad, *f.* complexity.—**complejo,** *a.* complex; intricate, arduous.—*m.* complex.

complementario, *a.* complementary.—**complemento,** *m.* complement.

completar, *vt.* to complete, perfect, finish.—**completo,** *a.* complete, unabridged; completed; unqualified.—*por c.,* completely.

complexión, *f.* constitution; temperament, nature.

complicación, *f.* complication, complexity.—**complicar,** *vti.* [d] to complicate; to jumble together.—*vri.* to become difficult, confused.

cómplice, *mf.* accomplice.—**complicidad,** *f.* complicity.

complot, *m.* plot, conspiracy.

componenda, *f.* adjustment, compromise.—**componente,** *mf.* & *a.* component.—**componer,** *vti.* [32] to compose; to compound; to prepare; to repair; to heal, restore; to brace up; to trim, fit up; to reconcile.—*vri.* to prink, (coll.) doll up; to calm oneself.

comportamiento, *m.* behavior.—**comportar,** *vr.* to behave.

composición, *f.* composition; repair.—**compositor,** *n.* composer (of music).—**compostura,** *f.* composure; repair, repairing; cleanliness, neatness of dress.

compota, *f.* compote, stewed fruits; preserves.

compra, *f.* purchase; buying; shopping.—*hacer compras,* to shop.—*ir* or *salir de compras,* to go shopping.—**comprador,** *m.* buyer; purchaser; user.—**comprar,** *vt.* to buy, purchase; to shop.

comprender, *vt.* to understand, comprehend; to comprise, include, cover.—**comprensible,** *a.* comprehensible, understandable.—**comprensión,** *f.* comprehension, understanding, comprehensiveness; act of comprising or containing.—**comprensivo,** *a.* comprehensive; capable of understanding; containing.

compresa, *f.* compress.

compresión, *f.* compression.—**comprimir,** *vt.* to compress.—*vr.* to become compact.

comprobación, *f.* verification, checking; proof, substantiation.—**comprobante,** *m.* proof, evidence; voucher.—**comprobar,** *vti.* [12] to verify, confirm, check.

comprometer, *vt.* to compromise; to endanger; to arbitrate; to engage; to risk; to expose, jeopardize.—*vr.* to commit oneself; to undertake; to expose oneself; to become engaged; to become involved; to expose oneself to risk.—**compromiso,** *m.* compromise; obligation; embarrassment; engagement, appointment.

compuerta, *f.* hatch or half-door; lock, floodgate.

compuesto, *pp.* of COMPONER.—*m.* compound, preparation, mixture.—*a.* compound; composed; repaired; arranged; made up.

compungirse, *vri.* [c] to feel compunction or remorse.

computar, *vt.* to compute, calculate.—**cómputo,** *m.* computation, calculation.

comulgar, *vii.* [b] to take communion; to commune.

común, *a.* common, public; usual, customary; current; vulgar.—*por lo c.,* usually.

comunicación, *f.* communication; communiqué, official statement.—*pl.* means of communication.—**comunicado,** *m.* letter to a paper; communiqué.—**comunicar,** *vti.* [d] to communicate; to notify.—*vri.* to communicate; to connect; to be in touch.—**comunicativo,** *a.* communicative, talkative.

comunidad, *f.* the common people; community; corporation; religious group.—**comunión,** *f.* communion; political party.—**comunismo,** *m.* communism.—**comunista,** *mf.* & *a.* communist(ic).

con, *prep.* with; (when followed by infinitive) by; although.—*c. que,* and so, then, so then.—*c. tal que,* provided that.—*c. todo,* nevertheless, notwithstanding.

conato, *m.* endeavor; effort, exertion; attempt, attempted crime.

concavidad, *f.* hollowness, concavity. **—cóncavo,** *a.* hollow, concave.—*m.* concavity.

concebible, *a.* conceivable.—**concebir,** *vti.* [29] & *vii.* to conceive, become pregnant; to imagine; to comprehend.

conceder, *vt.* to concede, admit; to give, grant.

concejal, *m.* councilman.—**concejo,** *m.* municipal council; civic body of a small town; board of aldermen.

concentración, *f.* concentration.—**concentrar,** *vt.* to concentrate.—*vr.* to concentrate (mentally); to come together.—**concéntrico,** *a.* concentric.

concepción, *f.* conception; idea.—**concepto,** *m.* concept, thought; judgment, opinion.—**conceptuar,** *vt.* to judge, think, form an opinion of.—**conceptuoso,** *a.* witty; overelaborate.

concerniente, *a.* (a) concerning, relating (to).—*en lo c. a,* with regard to, as for.—**concernir,** *vii.* [50] to concern, relate to.

concertar, *vti.* [1] to concert, arrange by agreement, adjust, settle.—*vii.* to agree, accord.—*vri.* to come to an agreement; to go hand in hand.

concesión, *f.* concession, grant.—**concesionario,** *m.* concessionary.

conciencia, *f.* conscience; conscientiousness; consciousness.—**concienzudo,** *a.* conscientious.

concierto, *m.* concert; agreement; good order and arrangement.

conciliábulo, *m.* unlawful meeting, or agreement.—**conciliar,** *vt.* to conciliate; to reconcile.—*c. el sueño,* to get to sleep.—**concilio,** *m.* (eccl.) council.

concisión, *f.* conciseness, succinctness.—**conciso,** *a.* concise, succinct.

concitar, *vt.* to excite, stir up, agitate.

conciudadano, *n.* fellow citizen, countryman.

concomitancia, *f.* concomitance.

concubina, *f.* concubine, mistress.—**concubinato,** *m.* concubinage.

concha, *f.* shell; shell-fish; tortoiseshell, conch.

concluir, *vti.* [23-e] to conclude, bring to an end; to decide finally, determine; to infer, deduce.—*vii.* & *vri.* to come to an end, finish.—**conclusión,** *f.* conclusion (all senses).—**concluyente,** *a.* concluding, conclusive.

concordancia, *f.* concordance; harmony; concord, agreement.—**concordar,** *vti.* [12] to reconcile; to make agree; to harmonize.—*vii.* to be in accord; to agree.—**concordia,**

f. concord, harmony; agreement; peace, good will.

concretar, *vt.* to summarize, sum up; to combine, unite.—*vr.* to limit or confine oneself (to a subject).—**concreto,** *a.* concrete (not abstract).—*en c.,* concretely; in brief, in a few words.—*m.* concrete (building material).

conculcar, *vti.* [d] to trample underfoot; to violate, infringe.

concupiscencia, *f.* lust.—**concupiscente,** *a.* sensual.

concurrencia, *f.* attendance; concurrence; audience, gathering, assembly.—**concurrido,** *a.* frequented; (of a meeting, etc.) well-attended.—**concurrir,** *vri.* to concur, agree; to meet in one point, time or place; to attend.

concurso, *m.* competitive contest or examination; concourse; aid, assistance; call for bids (on a piece of work, a service, etc.); gathering.

condado, *m.* earldom; county; dignity of a count.—**conde,** *m.* count, earl.

condecoración, *f.* medal; badge; decoration.—**condecorar,** *vt.* to bestow a medal or insignia on; to decorate.

condena, *f.* penalty; sentence, term of imprisonment.—**condenable,** *a.* condemnable.—**condenación,** *f.* condemnation; punishment; damnation.—**condenado,** *n.* & *a.* damned (in hell); convict; condemned; convicted.—**condenar,** *vt.* to condemn; to damn; to declare guilty; to censure, disapprove; to nail or wall up (a door, etc.); to annoy.—*vr.* to be damned (to hell).

condensación, *f.* condensation.—**condensador,** *a.* condensing.—*m.* (steam, elec., etc.) condenser.—**condensar,** *vt.* to condense, thicken.—*vr.* to be condensed.

condesa, *f.* countess.

condescendencia, *f.* condescension; compliance.—**condescender,** *vii.* [18] to condescend; to yield, comply.

condición, *f.* condition, state; temper; constitution; rank; stipulation.—**condicionado,** *a.* conditioned; conditional.—**condicional,** *a.* conditional.—**condicionar,** *vi.* to impose conditions; to agree, accord.

condimentar, *vt.* to season or dress (foods).—**condimento,** *m.* seasoning, condiment.

condiscípulo, *n.* schoolmate, fellow student.

condolencia, *f.* condolence, expression of sympathy.—**condolerse,** *vri.* [26] (de) to condole (with), be sorry (for), sympathize (with).

condominio, *m.* joint ownership.

cóndor, *m.* condor.

conducción, *f.* conveyance; carriage; transportation; leading, guiding; conducting; driving; conduit.—**conducente,** *a.* conducive, conducent.—**conducir,** *vti.* [11] & *vii.* to convey; carry; to take, accompany; to direct, lead; to manage, conduct; to drive.—*vii.* (a) to conduce, contribute (to); to be suitable (for); to lead, tend (to).—*vri.* to behave, act, conduct oneself.—**conducta,** *f.* conduct, behavior.—**conducto,** *m.* duct, conduit, pipe.—**conductor,** *n.* (Am.) conductor (RR., bus, etc.); leader; driver.—*a.* conducting, conductive (of heat, electricity, etc.).

conectar, *vt.* to connect.

conejo, *m.* rabbit.—*conejillo de Indias,* guinea pig.

conexión, *f.* connection; joint; coherence.

confección, *f.* any handwork; workmanship; fancy work, ready-made article.—**confeccionar,** *vt.* to make, prepare; to compound.

confederación, *f.* confederacy, confederation.—**confederado,** *m.* & *a.* confederate.—**confederar,** *vt.* & *vr.* to confederate, join, form a confederacy.

conferencia, *f.* conference, meeting, interview; lecture.—**conferenciante,** **conferencista,** *mf.* lecturer.—**conferenciar,** *vi.* to consult together, hold a conference; to lecture.

conferir, *vti.* [39] to confer; to give, bestow.

confesar, *vti.* [1] to confess, hear confession.—*vri.* to confess or make confessions.—**confesión,** *f.* confession.—**confesionario,** *m.* confessional.—**confesor,** *m.* father confessor.

confiable, *a.* trusty, reliable.—**confiado,** *a.* unsuspecting, trusting; confident.—**confianza,** *f.* confidence; familiarity, informality.—**confianzudo,** *a.* (coll.) fresh, over-friendly.—**confiar,** *vii.* (en) to rely (on), to trust (in).—*vt.* to confide; to commit to the care of another.—**confidencia,** *f.* trust, confidence; confidential information.—**confidencial,** *a.* confidential.—**confidente,** *mf.* confidant; police spy.—*m.* love seat.—*a.* faithful, trusty.

confín, *m.* limit, boundary, border.—*a.* bordering; limiting.—**confinamiento,** *m.* confinement.—**confinar,** *vt.* & *vr.* to confine; to banish to a definite place; to border on.

confirmación, *f.* confirmation; corroboration.—**confirmar,** *vt.* to confirm.

confiscación, *f.* confiscation.—**confiscar,** *vti.* [d] to confiscate.

confitar, *vt.* to candy; to preserve (fruit); to sweeten.—**confite,** *m.* candy, bonbon; sweets.—**confitería,** *f.* confectionery; confectioner's shop.—**confitura,** *f.* confection.

conflagración, *f.* conflagration.

conflicto, *m.* conflict.

confluencia, *f.* confluence.—**confluente,** *a.* confluent.—**confluir,** *vii.* [23-e] to join (rivers and sea currents); to assemble in one place.

conformación, *f.* conformation; shape.—**conformar,** *vt.* to conform, adjust, fit.—*vi.* to suit, fit, conform.—*vr.* to comply; to submit; to resign oneself.—**conforme,** *a.* alike, similar; correct, acceptable; compliant; resigned.—*adv.* in due proportion; agreeably, accordingly.—**conformidad,** *f.* likeness; conformity; agreement; resignation, submission.

confortar, *vt.* to comfort; to console; to strengthen.

confrontar, *vt.* to confront; to collate; to compare, check.

confundir, *vt.* to confound; to perplex, confuse; to mystify.—*vr.* to be bewildered, perplexed; to become ashamed and humbled.—**confusión,** *f.* confusion, disorder; perplexity; embarrassment.—**confuso,** *a.* confused, confounded; unintelligible; perplexed.

congelar, *vt.* & *vr.* to congeal, freeze.

congénere, *a.* kindred, of like kind.

congeniar, *vi.* to be congenial; to get along well (with).

congestión, *f.* congestion.—**congestionar,** *vt.* to congest.—*vr.* to get congested.

congoja, *f.* anguish, sorrow, grief.

congraciarse, *vr.* (con) to ingratiate oneself, to win favor.

congratulación, *f.* congratulation.—**congratular,** *vt.* to congratulate.—*vr.* to congratulate oneself, rejoice.

congregación, *f.* congregation; meeting, assembly; religious fraternity, brotherhood.—**congregar,** *vti.* [b] & *vri. to* assemble, congregate.—**congresista,** *mf.* congressman, congresswoman.—**congreso,** *m.* congress; convention, assembly.—*C. de los Diputados,* House of Representatives.

congruencia, *f.* congruence; convenience; fitness.—**congruente,** *a.* congruent, corresponding.

congruencia, *f.* congruence; convenience; fitness.—**congruente,** *a.* congruent, corresponding.

cónico, *a.* conical, conic.

conjetura, *f.* conjecture.—**conjeturar,** *vt.* to conjecture.

conjugación, *f.* conjugation.—**conjugar,** *vti.* [b] to conjugate.

conjunción, *f.* conjunction, union; act of coupling or joining together.

conjunto, *a.* united.—*m.* whole, aggregate.—*en c.,* altogether, as a whole.

conjura, **conjuración,** *f.* conspiracy, conjuration, plot.—**conjurado,** *m.* conspirator.—**conjurar,** *vi.* to conspire.—*vt.* to exorcise, conjure; to entreat, implore; to avert, ward off.—**conjuro,** *m.* conjuration; exorcism; entreaty.

conllevar, *vt.* to aid; to bear with patience.

conmemoración, *f.* remembrance; commemoration; anniversary.—**conmemorar,** *vt.* to commemorate.

conmensurable, *a.* commensurable.

conmigo, *pron.* with me, with myself.

conmiseración, *f.* commiseration, pity.

conmoción, *f.* commotion, excitement.—**conmovedor,** *a.* touching; sad, pathetic; exciting, thrilling.—**conmover,** *vti.* [26] to touch, move; to appeal to; to disturb, shock; to excite, stir.

conmutación, *f.* commutation, exchange.—**conmutador,** *m.* electric switch; telegraph key.—**conmutar,** *vt.* to exchange, barter.

connivencia, *f.* connivance; plotting.

cono, *m.* cone.

conocedor, *a.* **(de)** familiar (with), expert (in).—*n.* expert, connoisseur.—**conocer,** *vti.* [3] to know; to meet; to experience, comprehend.—*vii.* to know, be competent.—*vri.* to know oneself.—**conocido,** *a.* prominent, well-known.—*n.* acquaintance.—**conocimiento,** *m.* knowledge; skill, ability; acquaintance; bill of lading.—*poner en c. de,* to inform, notify.

conque, *conj.* so then; now then; and so; well then; therefore.

conquista, *f.* conquest, subjugation; conquered territory, thing or person.—**conquistador,** *m. & a.* conqueror, conquering; (fig.) Don Juan.—**conquistar,** *vt.* to conquer; to win, acquire; to win over, persuade.

consabido, *a.* well-known; in question; before-mentioned, aforesaid.

consagración, *f.* consecration.—**consagrar,** *vt.* to consecrate; to deify; to devote, dedicate.—*vr.* to devote or give oneself to (study, work, etc.)

consanguíneo, *a.* related by blood.—**consanguinidad,** *f.* blood relationship.

consciencia, *f.* consciousness.—**consciente,** *a.* conscious.

consecución, *f.* attainment, obtaining, acquisition.—**consecuencia,** *f.* consequence; consistency; result.—*a c. de,* because of.—*en* or *por c.,* consequently, therefore.—**consecuente,** *m.* effect, issue, consequence.—*a.* consequent, following; logical, consistent.—**consecutivo,** *a.* consecutive, successive.

conseguir, *vti.* [29-b] to attain, get, obtain; to succeed in.

conseja, *f.* story, fairy tale, fable, old wives' tale.

consejero, *m.* counsellor, member of a council; adviser.—**consejo,** *m.* counsel, advice; council, consulting body.—*c. de guerra,* court martial; council of war.—*c. de ministros,* cabinet.—*presidente del c.,* prime minister.

consenso, *m.* general assent; consensus; verdict.

consentido, *a. & n.* spoiled (child); cuckold.—**consentidor,** *m.* complier, conniver; coddler.—**consentimiento,** *m.* consent; coddling; acquiescence.—**consentir,** *vti.* [40] to consent, permit; to acquiesce in; to accept, admit; to pamper, spoil.

conserje, *n.* doorman, janitor, porter.

conserva, *f.* canned food, preserve, jam; pickle.—**conservación,** *f.* conservation; preservation; maintenance, upkeep.—**conservador,** *m.* conservator, preserver; curator.—*m. & a.* conservative.—**conservar,** *vt.* to conserve, maintain, preserve; to guard; to preserve or pickle (fruit); to can.—*vr.* to keep young, be well preserved; to last, keep well.—**conservatorio,** *m.* (music) conservatory.

considerable, *a.* considerable, important.—**consideración,** *f.* consideration; importance; respect.—**considerado,** *a.* prudent; considerate; thoughtful; esteemed, distinguished.—**considerar,** *vt.* to consider; to treat with consideration.

consigna, *f.* watchword, password; slogan; (RR.) checkroom.—**consignación,** *f* consignment, shipment.—**consignar,** *vt.* to consign, assign; to deliver; to check (baggage); to set apart.

consigo, *pron.* with oneself (himself, herself, itself, themselves, yourself, yourselves).

consiguiente, *m.* (log.) consequence, result, effect.—*a.* consequent.—*por c.,* therefore.

consistencia, *f.* consistence, consistency.—**consistente,** *a.* consistent, firm, solid.—**consistir,** *vi.* to con-

sist; to be comprised, contained.—
c. en, to consist in, to be a matter
of.

consistorio, m. consistory; municipal
council, board of aldermen.

consocio, n. partner.

consola, f. console; bracket shelf.

consolación, f. consolation.—consolador, a. consoling.—consolar, vti.
[12] to console, comfort.

consolidación, f. consolidation.—
consolidar, vt. to consolidate; to
harden, strengthen; to fund (debts).
—vr. to consolidate, grow firm; to
unite.

consonante, m. rhyming word; (mus.)
consonant or corresponding sound.—
f. & a. (letter) consonant; harmonious.

consorcio, m. syndicate, partnership.

consorte, n. consort, mate.

conspicuo, a. conspicuous; prominent.

conspiración, f. conspiracy, plot.—
conspirador, n. conspirator.—a.
conspiring.—conspirar, vi. to conspire, plot.

constancia, f. written evidence; constancy, perseverance.—constante, a.
constant; uninterrupted; firm.

constar, vi. to be clear, evident, certain; to be recorded, registered;
(de) to be composed (of), consist
(of).

constatar, vt. to verify, confirm.

constelación, f. constellation.

consternación, f. consternation.—
consternar, vt. to dismay; to
amaze; to distress, grieve.

constipado, m. head cold.—a. suffering
from a cold.—constipar, vr. to catch
cold.—vt. to cause a cold.

constitución, f. constitution.—constitucional, a. constitutional.—cons-
titucionalidad, f. constitutionality.—
constituir, vti. [23-e] to constitute.
—vri. (en), to set oneself up as.—
constituyente, mf. & a. constituent.

constreñir, vti. [9] to constrain, compel, force; to contract.

construcción, f. construction; act and
art of constructing; structure;
building.—constructor, m. builder;
maker.—construir, vti. [23-e] to
construct, build, form.

consuelo, m. consolation, relief, solace; joy.

consuetudinario, a. customary, generally practiced.

cónsul, mf. consul.—consulado, m.
consulate.

consulta, f. consultation, conference;
office hours (of a doctor).—consultante, mf. consulter.—a. consulting.
—consultar, vt. to consult.—consul-

tor, n. consulter.—a. consulting.—
consultorio, m. clinic, doctor's office.

consumación, f. consummation; extinction.—consumar, vt. to consummate, finish, perfect; to commit (a crime).

consumidor, n. & a. consumer, user;
consuming.—consumir, vt. to consume; to waste away.—vr. to be
consumed, exhausted; to run out;
to languish.—consumo, m. consumption (of provision, fuel, merchandise).

consunción, f. consumption, wasting
away.

consustancial, a. consubstantial.

contabilidad, f. bookkeeping, accounting.—contable, a. countable.—mf.
bookkeeper, accountant.

contacto, m. contact.

contado, a. scarce, rare.—al c., cash.
—por de c., of course, as a matter
of course.—contador, m. accountant; auditor; paymaster; purser;
counter; meter (for gas, water,
etc.).—caja contadora, or contadora,
cash register.—contaduría, f. office
of a cashier, paymaster or treasurer; box office (in a theater, etc.);
accountant's or auditor's office.

contagiar, vt. to infect, contaminate;
to corrupt, pervert.—vr. (de) to become infected (with).—contagio, m.
contagion; corruption of morals.—
contagioso, a. contagious; perverting.

contaminación, f. contamination, pollution; defilement.—contaminado, a.
corrupted, contaminated.—contaminar, vt. to contaminate; to pervert;
to infect by contagion.

contante, a. (money) ready.—m.
cash.—dinero c., or dinero c. y
sonante, cash.—contar, vti. [12] to
count; to relate, tell.—vti. to compute, figure.—c. con, to depend on,
rely on; to reckon with, take into
account; to possess, have at one's
disposal.

contemplación, f. contemplation,
meditation; complaisance.—contemplar, vt. to contemplate; to meditate; to be lenient or complaisant
with; to humor.—contemplativo, a.
contemplative; studious; lenient.—
n. contemplator.

contemporáneo, n. & a. contemporary.—contemporización, f. tempo-
rizing, compliance.—contemporizar,
vii. [a] to temporize; to comply;
to adapt oneself.

contender, vii. [18] to fight, combat;
to contend, debate.—contendiente,
mf. fighter, disputant; opponent.—a.
fighting.

contener, *vti*. [42] to contain; to include; to curb, stop.—*vri*. to control oneself, to refrain.—**contenido**, *a*. moderate, restrained.—*n*. content(s).

contentar, *vt*. to content, satisfy, make happy.—*vr*. to be contented, satisfied; to become reconciled, make up.—**contento**, *a*. content, contented; satisfied; happy.—*m*. contentment, satisfaction.

contera, *f*. metal tip (of umbrella, cane, etc.).

conterráneo, *n*. = COTERRANEO.

contestación, *f*. answer, reply.—**contestar**, *vt*. to answer, reply.

contexto, *m*. context.—**contextura**, *f*. texture.

contienda, *f*. struggle, fight; debate, dispute.

contigo, *pron*. with you [thee]; with yourself [thyself].

contigüidad, *f*. contiguity, closeness.—**contiguo**, *a*. contiguous, next, adjacent.

continencia, *f*. continence, self-control; abstinence; moderation; chastity.

continente, *m*. continent; container; countenance.—*a*. abstemious, continent; chaste; moderate.

contingencia, *f*. contingency, risk, possibility.—**contingente**, *m*. quota, contingent, share.—*a*. contingent, accidental.

continuación, *f*. continuation, continuance; stay.—*a c.*, immediately, right after; as follows.—**continuar**, *vt. & vi*. to continue; to go on; to pursue; to endure, last, remain; to prolong.—**continuidad**, *f*. continuity.—**continuo**, *a*. continuous, uninterrupted; connected; steady, constant.

contonearse, *vr*. to walk with a waddle; to strut.—**contoneo**, *m*. strut, waddle.

contorn(e)ar, *vt*. to trace the contour or outline of.—**contorno**, *m*. outline, contour; neighborhood; environs of a place.

contorsión, *f*. contortion, twist; grotesque gesture.

contra, *prep*. against, in opposition to, contrary to, opposite to, versus.—*m*. opposite sense; opposite opinion.—*f*. difficulty, obstacle.—*c. viento y marea*, against all odds.—*el pro y el c.*, the pros and cons.—*en c. (de)*, against, in opposition to.—*hacer* or *llevar la c.*, to oppose; to contradict.

contraalmirante, *m*. rear admiral.

contraataque, *m*. counterattack.

contrabajo, *m* bass fiddle

contrabandear, *vi*. to smuggle.—**contrabandista**, *mf*. smuggler, contrabandist.—**contrabando**, *m*. smuggling, running.

contracción, *f*. contraction, shrinking; corrugation; abbreviation.

contrachap(e)ado, *a*.—*madera c.*, plywood.

contradecir, *vti*. [14] to contradict.—**contradicción**, *f*. contradiction.—**contradicho**, *pp*. of CONTRADECIR.—**contradictorio**, *a*. contradictory.

contraer, *vti*. [43] & *vii*. to contract; to catch; to reduce.—*vri*. to contract, diminish; to shrink.

contrafuerte, *m*. buttress; spur (of a mountain).

contragolpe, *m*. back or reverse stroke.

contrahacer, *vti*. [22] to counterfeit, forge; to copy, imitate.—**contrahecho**, *pp*. of CONTRAHACER.—*a*. deformed; counterfeit, forged.

contralor, *m*. (Am.) controller, comptroller.

contraluz, *f*. view (of thing) seen against the light.

contramaestre, *m*. overseer, foreman; boatswain.

contramarcha, *f*. countermarch.

contraorden, *f*. countermand.

contraparte, *f*. counterpart.

contrapartida, *f*. emendatory or corrective entry.

contrapelo, *m*.—*a c.*, against the grain.

contrapesar, *vt* to counterbalance; to counteract, offset.—**contrapeso**, *m*. counterweight, counterbalance; balancing weight.

contraproducente, *a*. self-defeating, producing the opposite of the desired effect.

contrapuesto, *a*. compared, contrasted (with); opposed (to).

contrapunto, *m*. counterpoint, harmony.

contrariar, *vt*. to contradict, oppose; to disappoint.—**contrariedad**, *f*. disappointment; impediment; setback.—**contrario**, *a*. contrary; adverse.—*m*. opponent.—*al c.*, or *por lo c.*, on the contrary.—*de lo c.*, otherwise.

contrarrestar, *vt*. to oppose, resist; to check, arrest; to counteract.

contrarrevolución, *f*. counterrevolution.

contrasentido, *m*. contradiction in terms; conclusion contrary to premises.

contraseña, *f* countersign, password; watchword; check for hat, baggage, etc.—*c. de salida*, check to readmit one who went out from theater, etc.

contrastar, *vt*. to contrast; to test (scales, etc.), to assay (metals)

contraste, *m.* contrast, opposition; inspector (of weights); assayer; assayer's office.

contrata, *f.* contract, agreement.—**contratación,** *f.* contractual transaction.—**contratar,** *vt.* to contract for; to engage, hire; to trade.

contratiempo, *m.* disappointment, setback.

contratista, *mf.* contractor.—**contrato,** *m.* contract.

contraveneno, *m.* antidote.

contravenir, *vti.* [45] to contravene.

contraventana, *f.* window shutter.

contraventor, *n.* transgressor.

contrayente, *mf.* contracting party (to a marriage).—*a.* engaged (to be married).

contribución, *f.* contribution; tax, scot.—**contribuir,** *vii.* [23-e] to contribute.—**contribuyente,** *a.* contributing; contributory.—*mf.* taxpayer.

contrición, *f.* contrition, compunction.

contrincante, *mf.* opponent, competitor, rival.

contrito, *a.* contrite, penitent.

control, *m.* control.—**controlar,** *vt.* to control.

controversia, *f.* controversy, debate.—**controvertible,** *a.* controvertible, disputable.

contubernio, *m.* cohabitation; infamous alliance.

contumacia, *f.* obstinacy; contumacy; persistence in error; (law) contempt of court.—**contumaz,** *a.* obstinate; contumacious.

contundente, *a.* producing contusion; forceful; conclusive, decisive; trenchant.

conturbar, *vt.* to perturb, disturb.—*vr.* to become uneasy, agitated, anxious.

contusión, *f.* contusion, bruise.—**contuso,** *a.* bruised.

conuco, *m.* (Am.) patch of cultivated ground (maize field, etc.).

convalecencia, *f.* convalescence.—**convalecer,** *vii.* [3] to be convalescing.—**convaleciente,** *mf.* & *a.* convalescent.

convalidar, *vt.* to confirm, ratify.

convecino, *m.* neighbor.—*a.* neighboring, near.

convencer, *vti.* [a] to convince.—*vri.* to become convinced.—**convencimiento,** *m.* belief, conviction.

convención, *f.* convention; assembly; pact, agreement.—**convencional,** *a.* conventional.—**convencionalismo,** *m.* conventionalism, conventionality.

convenido, *a.* agreed.—**conveniencia,** *f.* convenience; utility; self-interest; agreement.—**conveniente,** *a.* useful; advantageous; suitable, befitting.—**convenio,** *m.* convention, agreement.—**convenir,** *vii.* [45] to befit; to agree; to convene, gather; to coincide; to be a good thing to.—*vri.* to agree, make a deal; to suit one's interests.

convento, *m.* convent.

conversación, *f.* conversation, talk.—**conversador,** *n.* talker.—*a.* conversational.—**conversar,** *vi.* to talk, converse; chat.

conversión, *f.* conversion; change.—**convertir,** *vti.* [39] to convert; to change.—*vri.* to become converted; to turn into, become.

convexidad, *f.* convexity.—**convexo,** *a.* convex.

convicción, *f.* conviction.—**convicto,** *a.* convicted, guilty.

convidada, *f.* invitation to drink, treat.—**convidado,** *n.* & *a.* invited (guest).—**convidar,** *vt.* to invite.

convincente, *a.* convincing.

convite, *m.* invitation; treat; banquet.

convocación, *f.* convocation, calling.—**convocar,** *vti.* [d] to convoke, convene, call together.—**convocatoria,** *f.* call, notice of a meeting.

convoy, *m.* convoy.—*c. de mesa,* cruet stand.—**convoyar,** *vt.,* to convoy, escort.

convulsión, *f.* convulsion.—**convulsivo,** *a.* convulsive.—**convulso,** *a.* convulsed; agitated.

conyugal, *a.* conjugal, wedded.—**cónyuge,** *mf.* spouse, consort.—*m. pl.* husband and wife.

coñac, *m.* brandy, cognac.

cooperación, *f.* cooperation.—**cooperador,** *n.* & *a.* cooperator, cooperating, cooperative.—**cooperar,** *vi.* to cooperate.—**cooperativa,** *f.* cooperative (society).—**cooperativo,** *a.* cooperating.

coordinación, *f.* coordination.—**coordinar,** *vt.* to coordinate.

copa, *f.* goblet, wineglass; drink (of liquor); treetop; crown of a hat; (in cards) a card of heart suit.

copar, *vt.* to cut off and capture; to cover (the whole bet); to sweep (all posts in an election); to corner.

copartícipe, *mf.* participant, copartner.

copete, *m.* tuft, bun (hair); forelock; crest; summit.—*de alto c.,* of high rank, aristocratic.—**copetudo,** *a.* tufted, crested; haughty.

copia, *f.* copy, imitation; abundance.—**copiar,** *vt.* to copy.

copiloto, *m.* copilot.

copiosidad, *f.* copiousness, abundance.—**copioso,** *a.* copious, abundant.

copista, *mf.* copyist, transcriber.

copla, *f.* short popular folk song; certain kind of stanza (poetry).

copo, *m.* small bundle of cotton, flax, etc.; snowflake.

cópula, *f.* joining, coupling two things together; connection; copulation.—**copular,** *vi.* to mate (of animals).

coqueluche, *f.* whooping cough.

coqueta, *f.* flirtatious girl.—**coquetear,** *vi.* to flirt.—**coqueteo,** *m.* flirtation.—**coquetería,** *f.* flirtation; affectation.—**coquetón,** *a.* kittenish.—*m.* lady-killer.

coraje, *m.* courage, bravery; anger.

coral, *m.* coral; a white-and-red poisonous snake.—*a.* choral.

coraza, *f.* armor plating; carapace; armor (of a vessel, cable, etc.).

corazón, *m.* heart; core, center; (fig.) courage; love; charity.—*anunciar,* or *decir el c. algo,* to have a presentiment.—*arrancársele a uno el c.,* to be heartbroken.—*de c.,* heartily.—**corazonada,** *f.* premonition, hunch.

corbata, *f.* necktie, cravat.

corbeta, *f.* corvette.—*capitán de c.,* lieutenant commander.

corcel, *m.* war-horse, charger, steed.

corcova, *f.* hump, hunch.—**corcovado,** *a.* & *n.* humpback(ed), hunch-back(ed).

corchete, *m.* clasp, hook, hook and eye; snaplock; bracket.

corcho, *m.* cork; cork stopper.

cordaje, *m.* cordage; rigging.

cordal, *m.* wisdom tooth.

cordel, *m.* cord; thin rope; land measure.—*a c.,* in a straight line.—*dar c.,* to banter.

cordero, *m.* lamb; lambskin.

cordial, *a.* hearty, cordial.—*m.* cordial, tonic.—**cordialidad,** *f.* cordiality.

cordillera, *f.* mountain range.

cordobán, *m.* cordovan, goatskin.—**cordobés,** *n.* & *a.* Cordovan; of Córdoba.

cordón, *m.* cord, braid, string; cordon (of soldiers); chord.—**cordoncillo,** *m.* milling on edge of a coin; twisted or small cord; lacing; braid.

cordura, *f.* prudence, practical wisdom, sanity.

coreano, *a.* & *n.* Korean.

corear, *vt.* to chorus, accompany with a chorus; to answer in chorus.—*vi.* to chorus.—**coreografía,** *f.* choreography.—**coreográfico,** *a.* choreographic.—**coreógrafo,** *n.* choreographer.—**corista,** *n.* chorister; member of a chorus.—*f* chorus girl.

coriza, *f.* head cold.

cornada, *f.* thrust with the horns,

goring.—**cornamenta,** *f.* horns, antlers.—**cornear,** *vt.* to butt; to gore.

corneta, *f.* cornet, bugle.—*m.* bugler.—**cornetín,** *m.* cornet; cornetist.

cornisa, *f.* cornice.

cornudo, *a.* horned.—*m.* (fig.) cuckold.

coro, *m.* choir; chorus.

corola, *f.* corolla.—**corolario,** *m.* corollary.

corona, *f.* crown; wreath; tonsure.—**coronación,** *f.* coronation; crowning.—**coronar,** *vt.* to crown; to top; to complete.

coronel, *m.* colonel.

coronilla, *f.* top of the head.—*estar hasta la c.,* to be fed up.

corpiño, *m.* bodice.

corporación, *f.* corporation; institution.

corporal, *a.* corporal, pertaining to the body.

corporativo, *a.* corporate, pertaining to a corporation.

corpóreo, *a.* corporeal, bodily.

corpúsculo, *m.* corpuscle.

corral, *m.* corral; yard; poultry yard.

correa, *f.* leather strap; leash; belt.—*tener c.,* to be able to endure a lot.—**correaje,** *m.* a set of straps.—**correazo,** *m.* a blow with a strap.

corrección, *f.* correction; correctness.—**correccional,** *a.* corrective.—*m.* reformatory.—**correcto,** *a.* polite, well-bred; proper; correct.—**corrector,** *m.* corrector, amender; proofreader.

corredizo, *a.* running; sliding.—**corredor,** *m.* runner; gallery; corridor; covert way; broker.—*a.* running.

corregir, *vt.* [29-c] to correct; to adjust (an instrument); to remedy; to rebuke, reprove; to punish.—*c. pruebas* (print.) to read proofs.—*vri.* to mend, reform.

correlación, *f.* correlation.—**correlativo,** *a.* correlative.

correntón, *m.* gadder; man about town.

correo, *m.* post, mail; correspondence; courier; letter carrier; post office.—*c. aéreo,* airmail.—*c. certificado,* registered mail.—*echar al c.,* to mail, post.

correr, *vi.* to run; to race; to flow; to extend, expand; to pass, elapse; to go on, continue; to be said, be common talk.—*c. a cargo de,* to be the concern of.—*c. con,* to charge oneself with a matter, take care of.—*c. la voz,* to be said or rumored.—*c. por cuenta de uno,* to be one's affair.—*vt.* to run or move swiftly; to race (a horse, car, etc.); to slide; to pursue, chase; to throw out.—*vr.* to file right or left; to

slide, go through easily; to become embarrassed; to run away, to flee.—**correría,** f. incursion, foray, raid; excursion.—*pl.* youthful escapades.

correspondencia, f. correspondence, relation; interchange; mail, correspondence.—**corresponder,** vi. (a) to reciprocate (a favor, etc.); to match, correspond; to respond (to); to fit, suit; to pertain (to); to concern; to agree.—vr. to correspond, keep in contact by mail.—**correspondiente,** a. corresponding, respective.—mf. correspondent.—**corresponsal,** mf. correspondent; newspaper correspondent.

corretaje, m. brokerage.—**corretear,** vi. to walk the streets, ramble; to romp.—**correvedile, correveidile,** mf. tablebearer; gossip.

corrida, f. course, run, running, race; career.—c de toros, bullfight.

corrido, a. experienced, wise; embarrassed, ashamed; continuous, flowing, unbroken.—m. Mexican folk ballad.

corriente, a. current; running, fluent, flowing; present, current (month or year); plain, easy; generally received, admitted; ordinary, common; regular, standard.—f. current (river, electricity, etc.); tendency; course; trend.—llevar la c., to humor.

corrillo, m. group of talkers, clique. —**corro,** m. group of gossipers or spectators; circular space.

corroboración, f corroboration —**corroborar,** vt to corroborate.

corroer, vt. to corrode.—vr. to corrode, decay.

corromper, vt to corrupt, to vitiate; to debauch.—vr to rot, putrefy; to become corrupt(ed)

corrosivo, a. corrosive.

corrugado, a. corrugated

corrupción, f. corruption, putrefaction; depravity, immorality.—**corruptela,** f corrupt practice.—**corrupto,** a. corrupt, rotten.

corsé, m. corset.

cortada, f. (Am.) cut, slash, gash.

cortador, m. (tailoring, bootmaking, etc.) cutter.—**cortadura,** f cut; cutting, incision.—**cortante,** a. cutting, sharp, trenchant.—**cortapisa,** f. obstacle, restriction.—**cortaplumas,** m. pocketknife; penknife.— —**cortar,** vt to cut, cut down, cut off, cut out, cut open; to disjoin, separate; to interrupt, stop.—vr. to be ashamed, confused.—**corte,** m. cutting edge, cutting; cut; material necessary for a garment, style (clothing); sectional view.—f royal court; (Am.) court of justice.— **cortedad,** f. smallness; pusillanimity; timidity.

cortejar, vt. to woo, court; to curry favor.—**cortejo,** m. courtship; cortege, retinue; procession.

cortés, a. polite, courteous; urbane.— **cortesano,** a. courtly.—m. courtier.— f. prostitute.—**cortesía,** f. courtesy.

corteza, f. bark of a tree; peel, rind, skin; crust of bread, pies, etc.; outward appearance.

cortina, f. curtain.—**cortinaje,** m. curtains, hangings.

cortisona, f. cortisone.

corto, a. short; brief; scanty; timid, bashful.—c. de alcances, stupid.— a la corta o a la larga, sooner or later.—**cortocircuito,** m. short circuit.

corva, f. back of the knee.—**corvadura,** f. curvature.

corvejón, m. hock joint of a quadruped.

corveta, f. curvet, leap, buck or bound of a horse.

corvo, a. bent; arched.

corzo, n. roe deer, fallow deer.

cosa, f. thing, matter, affair.—como si tal c., as if nothing had happened.—c. de, about, approximately. —no es c., it is not worth anything. —otra c., something else.—poca c., matter of slight importance; weak or timid person.

coscorrón, m. blow on the head.

cosecha, f. harvest, crop, yield; results.—**cosechar,** vt & vi. to reap, gather in; to harvest.—**cosechero,** m. owner or reaper of a crop, harvester „ grower.

coser, vt to sew (up, on); to stitch.

cosmético, m. & a. cosmetic.

cósmico, a. cosmic.

cosmopolita, a. & mf. cosmopolitan.

coso, m. arena, ring.

cosquillas, f. tickling.—buscarle a uno las c, to tease.—hacer c., to tickle. —con'squillear, vt to tickle.—**cosquilleo,** m. tickling sensation.— **cosquilloso,** a. ticklish; touchy.

costa, f. coast, shore; cost, price. a c. de, at the expense of.

costado, m. side, flank.

costal, m. sack or large bag.—**costalada,** f. (a) falling flat on the ground.

costar, vii. [12] to cost.—c. trabajo, to be difficult

costarricence, mf. & a. Costa Rican.

coste, m. cost, price, expense.

costear, vt. to pay the cost.—vi. to pay, be profitable; to sail along the coast.

costeño, costero, a coastal

costilla, *f.* rib; chop; cutlet; (fig.) wife.—*medirle a uno las costillas,* to cudgel one.—**costillaje, costillar,** *m.* the ribs, or rib system; frame of a ship.

costo, *m.* cost, price; expense.—**costoso,** *a.* expensive.

costra, *f.* crust; deposit; scab.—**costroso,** *a.* crusty, scabby.

costumbre, *f.* custom; habit.

costura, *f.* sewing; seam; stitching; needlework; suture.—**costurera,** *f.* seamstress, dressmaker.—**costurero,** *m.* sewing box, table or room.—**costurón,** *m.* large, coarse seam; big scar.

cota, *f.* = CUOTA; coat of mail; coat of arms; number indicating elevation above sea level, etc.—*c. de malla,* coat of mail.

cotarro, *m.*—*alborotar el c.,* to cause disturbance; to produce riot.

cotejar, *vt.* to compare. collate; to confront.—**cotejo,** *m.* comparison, collation.

coterráneo, *a.* fellow citizen.

cotidiano, *a.* daily; quotidian.

cotización, *f.* quotation of prices; current price.—**cotizar,** *vti.* [a] to quote prices; to call out current prices in the stock exchange; to pay (one's share).

coto, *m.* enclosed pasture; preserve; landmark, boundary.—*poner c. a,* to put a stop to.

cotorra, *f.* parrot; (fig.) chatterbox.—**cotorrear,** *vi.* to chatter; to gossip.—**cotorreo,** *m.* chattering; gossiping.

covacha, *f.* small cave or hollow underground; grotto; (fig.) den.

coxis, *m.* coccyx.

coyunda, *f.* strap for yoking oxen; dominion; matrimonial union.

coyuntura, *f.* joint; occasion; nick of time.

coz, *f.* kick; drawback; unprovoked bruskness.

cráneo, *m.* cranium, skull.

cráter, *m.* crater.

creación, *f.* creation.—**creador,** *n.* & *a.* creator, creating, creative.—**crear,** *vt.* to create, establish, found.

crecer, *vii.* [3] to grow; to bud forth; to increase.—*vr.* to swell with pride, authority, etc.—**creces,** *f.* *pl.* augmentation, excess.—*con c.,* amply.—**crecida,** *f.* swelling of rivers.—**crecido,** *a.* grown, increased.—**creciente,** *a.* growing, increasing; waxing (moon); crescent (moon).—*f.* flood of rivers; crescent (of the moon).—**crecimiento,** *m.* growth; growing; increase.

credencial, *f* letter or document of appointment to a post.—*pl.* credentials.

crédito, *m.* credit; reputation; credence, belief.—*dar c.,* to believe.

credo, *m.* creed, articles of faith, tenet.—**credulidad,** *f.* credulity.—**crédulo,** *a.* credulous.—**creencia,** *f.* belief; creed; religion.—**creer,** *vti.* [e] to believe; to credit; to think; to assume.—¡*ya lo creo!,* of course.

crema, *f.* cream of milk; custard; select society; cold cream; dieresis.

cremación, *f.* cremation, incineration.

cremallera, *f.* ratchet, rack; toothed bar; zipper fastener.

crematorio, *m.* crematory; incinerator.

crencha, *f.* parting of the hair into two parts; each of these parts.

crepuscular, *a.* crepuscular.—**crepúsculo,** *m.* crepuscule, twilight; dawn; dusk.

crespo, *a.* curly; crispy.—*m.* curl.

crespón, *m.* crepe.

cresta, *f.* comb (of a bird); cockscomb; crest of a helmet; wave crest; top; crest or summit of a mountain.

cretona, *f.* cretonne.

creyente, *mf.* & *a.* believer, believing.

creyón, *m.* crayon; charcoal pencil.

cría, *f.* act of nursing; breeding; bringing up; rearing; brood; litter of animals; suckling; nursing; infant.—**criada,** *f.* female servant, maid.—**criadero,** *m.* breeding place; tree nursery; hatchery.—**criado,** *a.* bred.—*m.* male servant.—**crianza,** *f.* nursing, suckling; secretion of milk; breeding; manners, education, upbringing.—**criar,** *vt.* to breed; to bring up; to nurse; to foster.—**criatura,** *f.* creature; baby; infant; child; tool; puppet.

criba, *f.* sieve, screen. **cribar,** *vt.* to sift, sieve.

cricquet, *m.* = CRIQUET.

crimen, *m.* crime; murder.—**criminal,** *mf.* & *a.* criminal; murderer.—**criminalidad,** *f.* criminality.—**criminalista,** *m.* criminologist, penologist.

crin, *f.* mane, horsehair.

crío, *m.* (coll.) nursing baby.

criollo, *m.* Spanish-American native; Creole.—*a.* national, traditional (in Spanish America).

cripta, *f.* crypt.

criquet, *m.* (sport) cricket.

crisálida, *f.* pupa, chrysalis.

crisantemo, *m.* chrysanthemum.

crisis, *f.* crisis.

crisma, *m.* chrism.—*f.* (coll.) head.—*romperse la c.,* to break one's neck.

crisol, *m.* crucible, melting pot; hearth of a furnace.

crispar, *vt.* to contract (muscles); to clench (fists).—*vi.* to twitch.

cristal, *m.* crystal; glass; lens; (window) pane.—**cristalería,** *f.* glassware; glass store.—**cristalino,** *a.* crystalline, clear.—*m.* crystalline of the eye.—**cristalización,** *f.* crystallization.—**cristalizar,** *vii.* [a] & *vri.* to crystalize.

cristiandad, *f.* Christendom; Christianity.—**cristianismo,** *m.* Christianity; the body of Christians.—**cristiano,** *a.* & *n.* Christian (person).

criterio, *m.* criterion; judgment, discernment.

crítica, *f.* criticism; critique; censure. —**criticar,** *vti.* [d] to criticize; to judge.—**crítico,** *a.* critical; decisive. —*m.* critic, reviewer.—**criticón,** *m.* & *a.* faultfinder; faultfinding.

croar, *vi.* to croak.

crónica, *f.* chronicle.—**crónico,** *a.* chronic.—**cronista,** *mf.* chronicler, annalist, historian.

cronología, *f.* chronology.—**cronológico,** *a.* chronological, chronologic. —**cronométrico,** *a.* chronometric.— **cronómetro,** *m.* chronometer, timepiece.

croqueta, *f.* croquette, fritter.

croquis, *m.* sketch, rough draft.

cruce, *m.* crossing; crossroads; crossbreeding.—**crucero,** *m.* transept; crossroads; railroad crossing; crosspiece; cruiser, cruise, cruising.— **crucificar,** *vti.* [d] to crucify, torture; to sacrifice, to ruin.—**crucifijo,** *m.* crucifix.—**crucigrama,** *m.* crossword puzzle.

cruda, *f.* (Am.) hangover.—**crudeza,** *f.* crudity, crudeness; rawness.— **crudo,** *a.* raw; crude, uncooked; harsh.

cruel, *a.* cruel, remorseless.—**crueldad,** *f.* cruelty.

crujido, *m.* crack, creak, crackling, creaking; rustle; crunch.—**crujir,** *vi.* to crackle, creak; to rustle.

cruz, *f.* cross; (fig.) affliction; tails (of coin).—*echar a cara o c.,* to toss up.—**cruzada,** *f* crusade; holy war; campaign.—**cruzamiento,** *m.* crossing.—**cruzar,** *vti.* [a] to cross; to go across, pass; to cruise, to interbreed.

cuadernillo, *m.* quire of paper.— **cuaderno,** *m.* writing book, memorandum book; note or exercises book; booklet.

cuadra, *f.* stable; city block, block of houses; hospital or prison ward.

cuadrado, *a.* square; perfect.—*m.* square; quadrate; (print.) quad, quadrat.—**cuadrante,** *m.* quadrant; sundial.—**cuadrar,** *vt* & *vi.* to square; to form into or reduce to a square; to please, suit; to fit in; to correspond.—*vr.* to stand at attention.—**cuadricular,** *vt.* to divide or design into squares.—**cuadriga,** *f.* chariot.—**cuadrilla,** *f.* gang; party; crew; band of armed men; team of bullfighters.—**cuadriplicado,** *a.* quadrupled.—**cuadro,** *m.* square; picture, painting; frame; scene; impressive spectacle; vivid description; (Am.) blackboard.—**cuadrúpedo,** *m.* & *a.* quadruped.—**cuádruple, cuádruplo,** *a.* quadruple, fourfold.

cuajada, *f.* curd.—**cuajar,** *vt.* to coagulate; to curd, curdle; to yell; to overdecorate.—*vi.* to succeed, materialize.—*vr.* to coagulate; to curdle; to fill, become full.—**cuajarón,** *m.* clot.—**cuajo,** *m.* rennet; curd; thickening (of a liquid).— *de c.,* radically; by the roots.

cual (*pl.* **cuales**), *rel. pron.* which, such as, as.—*cada c.,* each one.— *c. más c. menos,* some people more, others less.—*el c., la c., los cuales, las cuales,* which, who.—*lo c.* which. —*adv.* as, like.—*c. si,* as if.—¿**cuál?** *pron. interr.* which one? what?

cualidad, *f.* quality; trait.

cualquier(a), (*pl.* **cualesquier, cualesquiera**), *a.* any.—*pron.* any(one), anybody; someone, somebody; whichsoever, whoever.—*un cualquiera,* a nobody, a person of no account.

cuando (*interr.* ¿**cuándo?**), *adv.* when, at, or during the time of, in case that, if; though, although, even; sometimes.—*c. más,* at most. —*c. menos,* at the least.—*de c. en c.,* from time to time.

cuantía, *f* amount, quantity; rank, importance, degree.—**cuantioso,** *a.* numerous, abundant.—**cuanto,** *a.* as much as, all the, whatever.—*pl.* as many as, all the, whatever.—*pron.* all that, everything that.—*pl.* all those, who or which.—**cuánto, cuánta,** *a.* & *pron. interr.* how much.—*pl.* how many.—*adv.* as, the more.—*c. antes* as soon as possible. —*c. más que,* all the more so.— *en c.,* as soon as.—*en c. a,* as for, as regards.—*por c.,* therefore, inasmuch.

cuarentena, *f* forty days; quarantine.—**cuarentón,** *n.* & *a.* (man or woman) in the forties.

cuaresma, *f.* Lent.

cuarta, *f.* fourth; fourth part; span of the hand; short whip.—**cuartazo,** *m.* blow with a whip.—**cuartear,** *vt* to quarter, divide into four

parts; to whip.—*vr.* to split, crack, rive.

cuartel, *m.* quarter, fourth part; barracks; mercy; district, ward.— *no dar c.,* to give no quarter.— **cuartelada,** *f.,* **cuartelazo,** *m.* military coup d'état.

cuarteta, *f.* quatrain.—**cuarteto,** *m.* (mus.) quartet.

cuartilla, *f.* sheet of paper; (print.) sheet of copy; fourth part of an *arroba* (about 6 lbs.).—**cuartillo,** *m.* pint. (See Table of Measures).

cuarto, *m.* & *a.* fourth, fourth part, quarter.— *m.* room, chamber.—*pl.* cash, money.—*no tener un c.,* not to be worth a cent.

cuarzo, *m.* quartz.

cuate, *m.* (Mex.) twin.—*eso no tiene c.,* that has no match.

cuatrero, *m.* horse thief, cattle thief.

cuba, *f.* cask; big-bellied person; drunkard.

cubano, *n.* & *a.* Cuban.

cubeta, *f.* small barrel or cask.

cubicación, *f.* measurement; volume, capacity; cubing of a number.

cúbico, *a.* cubic.

cubierta, *f.* cover, covering; lid; deck of ship; book wrapper.

cubierto, *pp.* of CUBRIR.—*m.* covert; place for one at the table.

cubil, *m.* lair, den.

cubilete, *m.* dicebox.

cúbito, *m.* ulna, larger bone of forearm.

cubo, *m.* cue; pail, bucket; hub of a wheel; shaft case; millpond; bastion of a castle.

cubrecama, *f.* coverlet, bedspread.— **cubremesa,** *f.* table cover.

cubrir, *vti.* [49] to cover; to coat; to hide; to roof; to meet (a bill or check).—*vri.* to cover oneself; to protect oneself; to hedge; to put on one's hat.

cucaña, *f.* greased pole to climb for a prize; the sport itself.

cucaracha, *f.* cockroach.

cuclillas.—*en c.,* in a crouching or squatting position.

cuclillo, cuco, *a.* cunning; prim.—*m.* cuckoo; (Am.) peach, peach tree.

cucurucho, *m.* wrapping in the form of a cone; paper or cardboard cone.

cuchara, *f.* spoon; ladle; scoop.— *meter la c.,* or *su c.,* to meddle, intrude.—**cucharada,** *f.* spoonful.— **cucharadita,** *f.* teaspoonful.—**cucharilla,** *f.* teaspoon, coffee spoon.— **cucharón,** *m.* ladle; large spoon; scoop.

cuchichear, *vi.* to whisper.—**cuchicheo,** *m.* whisper, whispering.

cuchilla, *f.* cleaver; blade of a knife;

any cutting blade; razor blade; penknife.—**cuchillada,** *f.* a cut with a knife; stab; slash; gash.—**cuchillería,** *f.* cutlery, cutler's shop. —**cuchillo,** *m.* knife; gusset.

cuchitril, *m.* narrow hole or corner; very small room; hut; den.

cuchufleta, *f.* joke, jest, fun.

cuelga, *f.* cluster of grapes; string (of garlic, onion, etc.); (Am.) (coll.) birthday present.

cuello, *m.* neck; collar.

cuenca, *f.* wooden bowl; socket of the eye; river basin; deep valley.— **cuenco,** *m.* earthen or wooden bowl.

cuenta, *f.* computation, calculation; account; bill, (coll.) tab; note; bead (of a rosary, etc.).—*a fin de cuentas,* in the end.—*caer en la c.,* (coll.) to catch on, get the point.— *correr de la c. de uno,* to be one's responsibility.—*darse c.,* to realize.— *en resumidas cuentas,* in short.—*no tenerle a uno c.,* to be of no profit to one.—*rendir c.,* to inform, report. —*tener* or *tomar en c.,* to take into account.—*tomar una cosa por su c.,* to take upon oneself.

cuento *m.* tale; story; short story; piece of gossip.—*dejarse de cuentos,* to come to the point.—*sin c.,* numberless.—*traer a c.,* to bring to bear upon the subject; to drag into the subject.—*venir a c.,* to be pertinent.

cuerda, *f.* cord, rope, string; chord; watch spring.—*bajo c.,* or *por debajo de c.,* underhandedly, deceitfully.—*dar c. a,* to wind up (a watch, etc.).

cuerdo, *a.* sane; prudent, wise.

cuerno, *m.* horn; antenna, feeler. *mandar al c.,* to send to the devil —*poner cuernos,* to be unfaithful (to a husband).

cuero, *m.* rawhide, skin; leather; wineskin.—*en cueros,* or *en cueros vivos,* or *en el puro c.,* naked.

cuerpo, *m.* body; bulk; corps.—*a. c. descubierto,* without cover or shelter.—*c. a c.,* hand to hand; in single combat.—*en c. y alma,* wholly, sincerely, with pleasure.—*estar de c. presente,* to lie in state.—*tomar c.,* to increase, to grow, to thicken.

cuervo, *m.* crow; raven; (Am.) buzzard.

cuesco, *m.* kernel; stone (of a fruit); the breaking of wind.

cuesta, *f.* hill, slope, grade.—*c. abajo,* downhill.—*c. arriba,* uphill.—*a cuestas,* on one's back.

cuestación, *f.* petition; solicitation or collection for a charitable purpose.

cuestión, *f.* question, dispute, contro

versy; matter, problem, affair.—**cuestionario,** *m.* questionnaire.

cueva, *f.* cave, grotto, cavern; cellar.

cuidado, *m.* care, attention; custody; carefulness, caution; worry, anxiety.—*no hay c. (de que),* there is no danger that.—*¡no pase c.!* or *¡pierda c.!* don't worry!—*tener c.,* to be careful; to be worried.—*interj.* look out! beware!—**cuidadoso,** *a.* careful.—**cuidar,** *vt.* to care for, tend, mind, keep; to execute with care.—*c. de,* to take care of.—*vr.* to take care of oneself.—*cuidarse de,* to look out for, to guard against; to avoid.

cuita, *f.* care, grief, affliction, trouble.—**cuitado,** *a.* unfortunate, wretched.

cuje, *m.* withe; pole supported by two vertical ones for hanging tobacco.—*pl.* hop poles.

culata, *f.* butt, stock (of a firearm); (Am.) rear (of car, house).—**culatazo,** *m.* blow with the butt; recoil of a firearm.

culebra, *f.* snake; coil.—**culebrear,** *vi.* to twist, wriggle (as a snake).

culero, *m.* baby's diaper.

culinario, *a.* culinary.

culminación, *f.* culmination.—**culminar,** *vi.* to culminate.

culo, *m.* buttocks; bottom; anus; bottom of anything.

culpa, *f.* fault; guilt; blame.—*echar la c. a,* to blame.—*tener la c. de,* to be to blame, or responsible for.—**culpabilidad,** *f.* culpability, guilt.—**culpable,** *a.* guilty.—**culpar,** *vt.* to blame, accuse; to condemn.

cultivar, *vt.* to cultivate; to farm, till, grow.—**cultivo,** *m.* cultivation; farming.—**culto,** *a.* cultivated; cultured.—*m.* cult, worship.—**cultura,** *f.* culture; cultivation.

cumbre, *f.* top, tiptop, summit, crest.

cumpleaños, *m.* birthday.

cumplido, *a.* fulfilled, expired; polite; faultless; large, ample.—*m.* compliment; courtesy.—**cumplimentar,** *vt.* to compliment; to show courtesy; to congratulate.—**cumplimiento,** *m.* fulfillment, completion, performance; expiration; courtesy, compliment.—**cumplir,** *vt.* to fulfill, carry out; to reach (age).—*vi.* to fall due, expire; to do one's duty.—*c. años,* to have a birthday.—*vr.* to be realized, come to an end.

cúmulo, *m.* heap, pile; large quantity or number; cumulus (clouds).

cuna, *f.* cradle; place of birth; lineage, origin.

cundir, *vi.* to spread, propagate; to yield abundantly; to grow, expand.

cuneta, *f.* road drain; side ditch; gutter.

cuña, *f.* wedge; splinter.

cuñada, *f.* sister-in-law.—**cuñado,** *m.* brother-in-law.

cuño, *m.* die (for coining money); impression made by die; (fig.) stamp.

cuota, *f.* quota, share; dues, fee.

cuotidiano, *a.* = COTIDIANO.

cupo, *m.* quota; tax rate; contents, capacity.

cupón, *m.* coupon.

cúpula, *f.* dome, cupola.

cura, *m.* curate, priest.—*f.,* or **curación,** *f.* healing; cure.—**curador,** *m.* caretaker.—**curandero,** *n.* quack, charlatan.—**curar,** *vt. & vi.* to treat, heal, cure; to season, dry (meats, woods, etc.).—*vr.* to recover from sickness; to heal.—**curativo,** *a.* curative, healing.

curiosear, *vi.* to pry, snoop, spy, peek, peer.—**curiosidad,** *f.* curiosity; curious thing; rare object or person.—**curioso,** *a.* curious, prying; careful, diligent, skillful; rare; neat, clean.

cursar, *vt.* to study; to attend a course of study; to transmit, expedite.—**curso,** *m.* course, direction, career; course of study; scholastic year.

cursi, *a.* ridiculously pretentious in appearance, behavior or taste.

curtido, *m.* tanning; tanned leather.—**curtidor,** *m.* tanner.—**curtir,** *vt.* to tan; to bronze the skin; to harden; to inure.—*vr.* to become tanned, sunburned, weather-beaten; to become hardened or experienced.

curva, *f.* curve; curvature; bend.—**curvatura,** *f.* curvature; curving.—**curvo,** *a.* curved; bent; arched.

cúspide, *f.* cusp, apex, top, peak, summit.

custodia, *f.* custody, safe-keeping; guardian; (eccl.) monstrance.—**custodiar,** *vt.* to guard; to convoy; to take care of.—**custodio,** *m.* guard, custodian; watchman.

cutícula, *f.* cuticle.

cutis, *m.* skin, complexion.

cuyo, cuya (pl. **cuyos, cuyas**), *pron. poss.* of which, of whom, whose, whereof.

CH

chabacanería, *f.* coarseness; bad taste; vulgar expression or action.—**chabacano,** *a.* coarse, crude, vulgar.—*m.* (Am.) apricot.

chabola, *f.* hut; dugout.

chacal, *m.* jackal.

chacota, *f.* mockery; ridicule.—*hacer ch. de,* to mock at.—**chacotear,** *vi.* to make merry; to joke boisterously.

chacra, *f.* (Am.) small piece of farm land.

cháchara, *f.* chitchat, idle talk.—**chacharear,** *vi.* to chatter.

chafar, *vt.* to flatten, crush; to cut short.

chaflán, *m.* bevel (in buildings).

chal, *m.* shawl.

chalado, *a.* lightwitted, crazy.

chalán, *m.* cattle trader; horsedealer; huckster.

chaleco, *m.* vest.

chalina, *f.* cravat; scarf.

chalupa, *f.* sloop; long boat; small canoe.

chamaco, *m.* (Am.) youngster.

chamarra, *f.* windbreaker; wool jacket; leather jacket.—**chamarreta,** *f.* a short, loose jacket.

chambón, *a.* clumsy, bungling; lucky. —*n.* bungler.

champaña, *m.* champagne.

champú, *m.* shampoo.

chamuscar, *vti.* [d] to singe or scorch. —**chamusquina,** *f.* scorching.

chancear, *vi. & vr.* to jest, joke, fool. —**chancero,** *a.* merry, jolly.

chancla, *f.* old shoe with worn-down heel.—**chancleta,** *f.* slipper.—**chancleteo,** *m.* clatter of slippers.—**chanclo,** *m.* overshoe.

chancho, *n.* (Am.) pig; dirty person. —*a.* dirty, unclean.

chanchullero, *n.* trickster; smuggler. —**chanchullo,** *m.* unlawful conduct; vile trick; (coll.) racket.

changador, *m.* (Am.) carrier, porter; handy man.

chantaje, *m.* blackmail.—**chantajista,** *mf.* blackmailer.

chanza, *f.* joke, jest, fun.

chapa, *f.* veneer; plate, sheet (of metal); rosy spot on the cheek.—**chapado,** *a.* veneered; having red cheeks.—*ch. a la antigua,* old fashioned.

chapapote, *m.* mineral tar, asphalt.

chaparrear, *vi.* to shower; to pour.

chaparreras, *f. pl.* chaps.

chaparro, *a. & n.* short, stocky (person).

chaparrón, *m.* violent shower, downpour.

chapotear, *vi.* to paddle in the water, dabble.—**chapoteo,** *m.* splash, splatter.

chapucear, *vt.* to botch, bungle.—**chapucería,** *f.* bungle; clumsy fib.—**chapucero,** *a.* rough, unpolished, slapdash; clumsy; rude.

chapurrar, chapurrear, *vt.* to jabber (a language); to speak brokenly; to mix drinks.

chapuzar, *vti.* [a] to duck.—*vii. & vri.* to dive, duck.

chaqueta, *f.* jacket; sack coat; (mech.) casing, jacket.—**chaquetear,** *vi.* to run away in fright.

charanga, *f.* military brass band; fanfare.

charca, *f.* pool, basin, pond.—**charco,** *m.* pool, puddle.

charla, *f.* prattle, chat; informal address.—**charlador,** *n.* prater, talker. —*a.* prating, talking.—**charlar,** *vi.* to chat, prattle, prate.—**charlatán,** *n.* prater, babbler, windbag; charlatan, humbug.—**charlatanería,** *f.* garrulity, verbosity; charlatanism, humbug.—**charlatanismo,** *m.* quackery; verbosity.

charnela, *f.* hinge.

charol, *m.* patent leather.—**charola,** *f.* (Am.) tray.—**charolar,** *vt.* to varnish.

charro, *n.* churl; coarse, ill-bred person; (Mex.) cowboy.—*a.* showy, flashy.

chascarrillo, *m.* joke, spicy anecdote.

chasco, *m.* failure, disappointment; trick, prank.

chasquear, *vt.* to crack or snap (a whip).—*vi.* to crack, snap.—*vt.* to fool; to play a trick on; to disappoint, fail; to cheat.—**chasquido,** *m.* crack of a whip or lash; crack.

chata, *f.* bedpan; barge; (RR.) flatcar.—**chato,** *a.* flat; flat-nosed.

chayote, *m.* vegetable pear; silly fool, dunce.

checo, checo(e)slovaco, *n. & a.* Czechoslovak, Czechoslovakian.

chelín, *m.* shilling.

cheque, *m.* check.—**chequear,** *vt.* (Am.) to check, verify; to check (mark).

chico, *a.* little, small.—*n.* (*f.* chica) child; boy; youngster; fellow; chap.

chicotazo, *m.* blow with a whip; lash.—**chicote,** *m.* whip; cigar; cigar butt.

chicha, *f.* (Am.) a popular fermented beverage (made from maize, pineapple, etc.).

chícharo, *m.* pea.

chicharra, *f.* locust; horse fly; (fig.) talkative woman.

chicharrón, *m.* crackling, fried scrap; overroasted meat.

chichón, *m.* bump; bruise.

chiflado, *a.* flighty, crazy.—**chifladura,** *f.* eccentricity; mania, craziness.—**chiflar,** *vi.* to hiss, whistle.—*vr.* to become mentally unbalanced; to lose one's head.—*vt.* (a) to show

noisy disapproval to someone (artist, etc.).—**chiflido**, *m.* shrill whistling sound.

chile, *f.* red pepper.

chileno, *n. & a.* Chilean.

chillar, *vi.* to screech, scream; to crackle, creak.—**chillido**, *m.* screech, scream; bawling of a woman or child.—**chillón**, *n.* screamer, bawler; whiner.—*a.* whining; screechy; showy; loud (of colors).

chimenea, *f.* chimney; fireplace.

chimpancé, *m.* chimpanzee.

china, *f.* pebble; Chinese woman; porcelain, chinaware; (Mex.) girl, sweetheart; (Am.) orange.

chinche, *f.* bedbug; thumbtack; tedious, pestering person.

chinchín, *m.* (Am.) drizzle.

chinchorro, *m.* small dragnet; small fishing boat.

chinela, *f.* slipper.

chino, *n. & a.* Chinese.—*m.* Chinese language.

chiquero, *m.* pigpen; hut for goats; bullpen.

chiquillada, *f.* childish speech or action.—**chiquillería**, *f.* swarm of children.—**chiquillo**, *n.* child.—**chiquitín**, *n.* baby boy; baby girl; very little child.—**chiquito**, *a.* small, little; very small.—*n.* little boy (girl), little one.

chiribitil, *m.* garret; small room.

chirigota, *f.* jest, joke, fun.

chiripa, *f.* stroke of good luck; chance or unexpected event.—*de ch.*, by chance.

chirivía, *f.* parsnip.

chirle, *a.* insipid, tasteless.—**chirlo**, *m.* wound or scar on the head.

chirona, *f.* (coll.) prison, jail.

chirriar, *vi.* to squeak, creak; to sizzle.—**chirrido**, *m.* squeak; screech.

chisguete, *m.* squirt.

chisme, *m.* gossip, piece of gossip; gadget.—**chismear**, **chismorrear**, *vi. & vt.* to gossip, to blab; to tattle.—**chismorreo**, *m.* gossiping, blabber.—**chismoso**, *n.* talebearer, telltale, gossip.—*a.* gossiping.

chispa, *f.* spark; very small diamond; little bit; cleverness, wit; state of drunkenness.—*coger una ch.*, to get drunk.—*echar chispas*, to show anger, to be furious.—**chispeante**, *a.* sparkling, sparking.—**chispear**, *vi.* to spark; to sparkle.—**chisporrotear**, *vi.* to sputter sparks.—**chisporroteo**, *m.* sputtering of sparks.

chistar, *vi.* to mumble, mutter; to open one's lips.

chiste, *m.* joke, jest; witty saying.—**chistoso**, *a.* witty.

chistera, *f.* top hat; fish basket.

¡**chitón**!, *interj.* hush! not a word!

chiva, *f.* she-goat; (Am.) goatee.—**chivato**, *n.* informer, talebearer.—**chivo**, *m.* he-goat.

chocante, *a.* disagreeable; strange, surprising.—**chocar**, *vii.* [d] to strike; to collide; to meet, fight; to happen upon; to irritate; to surprise.

chocarrería, *f.* raillery; coarse jest.—**chocarrero**, *a.* vulgar, scurrilous.

chocolate, *m.* chocolate.

chocha, *f.* (orn.) grouse.

chochear, *vi.* to drivel, act senile; to dote.—**chochera**, **chochez**, *f.* senility; dotage.—**chocho**, *a.* doting, senile.

chofer, **chófer**, *mf.* chauffeur.

cholo, *n.* (Am.) mestizo, half-breed.—*a.* coarse; uncouth; dark-skinned.

chopo, *m.* black poplar.

choque, *m.* impact; collision; clash; dispute, clash.

chorizo, *m.* red pork sausage.

chorlito, *m.* curlew.—*cabeza de c.*, harebrained.

chorrear, *vi.* to spout; to drip; to be dripping wet.—**chorro**, *m.* spurt, jet, gush; stream, flow.—*a chorros*, abundantly.

chotacabras, *f.* (ornith.) nighthawk.

chotear, *vt.* to banter, gibe; to make fun of.—**choteo**, *m.* joking; jeering.

choza, *f.* hut, hovel.

chubasco, *m.* squall, shower.

chuchería, *f.* trifle, trinket.

chucho, *m.* dog; whip; railway switch; electric switch.

chueco, *a.* crooked, bent; (Am.) left-handed.

chuleta, *f.* chop; cutlet; slap.

chulo, *a.* (Am.) pretty, nice, attractive.—*n.* lower-class native of Madrid.—*m.* pimp; bully.

chunga, *f.* jest, joke.

chupar, *vt.* to suck; to absorb; to sip; to sponge on.—**chupete**, *m.* pacifier (for children); teething ring.—**chupón**, *a.* sucking.—*n.* sponger.

churrasco, *m.* piece of broiled meat.—**churrasquear**, *vi.* to barbecue, roast over coals; to prepare (meat) for barbecuing; to eat barbecued meat.

churre, *mf.* filth.—**churriento**, *a.* dirty, greasy.

chuscada, *f.* pleasantry, joke.—**chusco**, *a.* merry, funny.

chusma, *f.* rabble, mob.

chuzo, *m.* (mil.) pike.

D

dable, *a.* possible, practicable; grantable.

dactilógrafo, *n.* typist.
dádiva, *f.* gift, gratification.—**dadivoso,** *a.* bountiful, liberal.
dado, *m.* die; block.—*pl.* dice.
dador, *n.* giver, donor; bearer (of letter).
daga, *f.* dagger.
daltonismo, *m.* color blindness.
dama, *f.* lady; gentlewoman; mistress; (theat.) leading lady.—*juego de damas,* checkers.—**damisela,** *f.* young woman, damsel.
damnificar, *vti.* [d] to hurt, damage, injure.
dandi, *m.* dandy, fop, coxcomb.
danés, *a.* Danish.—*n.* Dane.
danza, *f.* dance.—**danzante,** *mf.* dancer; (coll.) busybody.—**danzar,** *vii.* [a] to dance; to whirl.—**danzarín,** *n.* dancer.
dañado, *a.* spoiled, tinted; dammed.
dañar, *vt.* to hurt, damage; to harm; to spoil; to weaken.—*vr.* to spoil; to be damaged; to hurt oneself.—**dañino,** *a.* destructive, harmful; vicious.—**daño,** *m.* damage, hurt, loss, spoilage; nuisance.—**dañoso,** *a.* injurious.
dar, *vti.* [13] to give; to hand; to grant; to emit; to hit, strike; to yield.—*d. a conocer,* to make known.—*d. a entender,* to insinuate, to suggest.—*d. a luz,* to give birth to.—*d. comienzo,* to begin.—*d. con,* to find, come upon.—*d. cuerda a,* to wind up (clock, watch, etc.).—*d. de baja,* to dismiss.—*d. de comer,* to feed animals.—*d. de sí,* to give, stretch.—*d. fin a,* to complete, finish.—*d. (frente) a,* to face, look out on.—*d. golpes a,* to beat, thrash.—*d. gritos,* to shout.—*d. la razón a,* to say (a person) is right, agree with.—*d. largas a,* to postpone.—*d. las espaldas,* to turn one's back.—*darle a uno por,* to take to.—*d. lugar a,* to give rise to.—*d. parte (de),* to report (about), communicate.—*d. pasos,* to take steps.—*d. prestado,* to lend.—*d. que decir,* to give occasion for censure or criticism.—*d. que hacer,* to give trouble.—*d. que pensar,* to give food for thought.—*d. satisfacciones,* to apologize.—*no d. pie con bola,* not to do a thing right, to make a mess of it.—*vri.* to yield, surrender; to devote oneself.—*darse cuenta de,* to realize.—*darse por,* to consider oneself as.—*darse por vencido,* to give up.—*darse prisa,* to hurry.—*darse tono,* to put on airs.
dardo, *m.* dart, arrow.
dársena, *f.* dock; yacht basin, marina.
data, *f.* date; item in an account.—

datar, *vt.* to date; (com.) to credit on account.—*vi.* to take origin, date from.
dátil, *m.* date.—**datilera,** *f.* date palm.
dato, *m.* datum.—*pl.* data.
de, *prep.* of; from; for; by; than; in.
deán, *m.* (ecl.) dean.
debajo, *adv.* beneath, underneath.—*d. de,* under, beneath.—*por d.,* from below; underneath.—*por d. de,* under; below.
debate, *m.* debate; altercation.—**debatir,** *vt.* to argue, discuss, debate.—*vr.* to struggle.
debe, *m.* debit.—**deber,** *vt.* to owe; to have to, be obliged to, must, ought, should.—*d. de,* must have, must be.—*m.* duty, obligation.—**debido,** *a.* fitting, right, just.—*d. a,* owing to, on account of; due to.
débil, *a.* weak, feeble, sickly.—**debilidad,** *f.* weakness, feebleness.—**debilitación,** *f.,* **debilitamiento,** *m.* weakening.—**debilitar,** *vt.* to weaken.—*vr.* to grow weaker.
débito, *m.* debt; debit.
debut, *m.* debut.—**debutar,** *vi.* to make one's debut.
década, *f.* decade; series of ten.
decadencia, *f.* decadence, decay, decline.—**decadente,** *a.* decaying, decadent, declining.—**decaer,** *vii.* [8-e] to decay, fail; to fall off.—**decaimiento,** *m.* decay; weakness.
decano, *n.* dean (of a University); senior member of a group or organization.
decapitación, *f.* beheading.—**decapitar,** *vt.* to behead, decapitate.
decena, *f.* series of ten.—**decenio,** *m.* decade; decennial.
decencia, *f.* decency; modesty; honesty.—**decente,** *a.* decent; honest; modest.
decepción, *f.* disappointment; disillusionment.—**decepcionar,** *vt.* to disappoint.
decidir, *vt.* to decide, determine, resolve.—*vr.* to decide, make up one's mind; to be determined.
decimal, *a. & m.* decimal.
decir, *vti.* [14] & *vii.* to say, tell; to speak; to name.—*como quien dice,* as if meaning.—*d. bien,* to be right.—*d. mal,* to be wrong.—*d. para sí or para su capote,* to say oneself.—*d. por d.,* to talk for the sake of talking.—*es d.,* that is to say, that is.—*querer d.,* to mean, signify.—*por decirlo así,* so to speak.—*m.* saying, proverb.—*al d. de,* according to.

decisión, *f.* decision, determination, resolution, issue.—**decisivo,** *a.* decisive, final.

declamación, *f.* declamation, speech; reading, recitation.—**declamador,** *n.* orator; reciter.—**declamar,** *vi.* to declaim; to recite.

declaración, *f.* declaration; statement; manifestation; (law) deposition.—**declarado,** *a.* declared.—**declarante,** *a.* declaring, expounding.—*mf.* declarer; witness.—**declarar,** *vt.* to declare, make known; (law) to testify.—*vr.* to declare one's opinion; (coll.) to make a declaration of love.—**declarativo,** *a.* declarative.

declinación, *f.* declination, fall, decline; (gram.) declension, inflection.—**declinar,** *vi.* to decline; to decay; to diminish.—*vt.* (gram.) to decline.

declive, *m.* declivity; slope, fall; (RR.) grade.—*en d.,* slanting, sloping.

decomisar, *vt.* to confiscate.—**decomiso,** *m.* confiscation.

decoración, *f.* decoration; ornament; (theat.) setting.—**decorado,** *m.* decoration, ornamentation.—**decorador,** *n.* & *a.* decorator; decorating.—**decorar,** *vt.* to decorate; to adorn, embellish.—**decorativo,** *a.* decorative.

decoro, *m.* decency, decorum; honor; propriety.—**decoroso,** *a.* decorous, decent.

decrecer, *vii.* [3] to decrease, diminish.—**decreciente,** *a.* diminishing, decreasing.

decrépito, *a.* decrepit.—**decrepitud,** *f.* decrepitude.

decretar, *vt.* to decree, resolve; to decide.—**decreto,** *m.* decree; decision.

dechado, *m.* model; sample, pattern.

dedal, *m.* thimble.

dedicación, *f.* dedication; consecration.—**dedicar,** *vti.* [d] to dedicate, devote; to autograph (a literary work).—*vri.* (a) to devote oneself (to); to make a specialty (of).—**dedicatoria,** *f.* dedication; dedicatory inscription.

dedillo, *m.—saber al d.,* to know perfectly.—**dedo,** *m.* finger; toe; finger's breadth; small bit.—*d. auricular* or *meñique,* little finger.—*d. gordo* or *pulgar,* thumb.

deducción, *f.* deduction, inference, conclusion.—**deducir,** *vti.* [11] to deduce, infer; to draw; to offer as a plea; to deduct.

defecto, *m.* defect, imperfection.—**defectuoso,** *a.* defective, imperfect, unsound.

defender, *vti.* [18] to defend.—

defensa, *f.* defense; protection; shelter; bumper; (football) back.—**defensiva,** *f.* defensive.—**defensivo,** *a.* defensive.—*m.* defense.—**defensor,** *n.* defender; supporter; (law) counsel for the defense, defender.

deferencia, *f.* deference.—**deferir,** *vii.* [2] to yield, submit.—*vti.* to communicate; to delegate.

deficiencia, *f.* deficiency.—**deficiente,** *a.* deficient, faulty.

definición, *f.* definition.—**definible,** *a.* definable.—**definido,** *a.* definite.—**definir,** *vt.* to define; to establish, determine.—**definitivo,** *a.* definitive. —*en definitiva,* in conclusion; in short.

deflación, *f.* deflation.

deformación, *f.* deformation, distortion; deformity.—**deformar,** *vt.* to deform, disfigure.—*vr.* to become deformed, change shape.—**deforme,** *a.* deformed, disfigured; hideous.—**deformidad,** *f.* deformity; ugliness.

defraudación, *f.* defrauding; fraud, deceit.—**defraudador,** *n.* defrauder; defaulter.—**defraudar,** *vt.* to defraud; to rob of.

defunción, *f.* death, demise.

degeneración, *f.* degeneration, degeneracy.—**degenerado,** *n.* & *a.* degenerate.—**degenerar,** *vi.* to degenerate.

deglución, *f.* swallowing.—**deglutir,** *vt.* to swallow.

degollación, *f.* beheading.—**degollar,** *vti.* [12] to behead, decapitate.—**degollina,** *f.* slaughter; butchery.

degradación, *f.* degradation, humiliation, debasement; depravity, degeneracy.—**degradante,** *a.* degrading.—**degradar,** *vt.* to degrade, debase; humiliate, revile.—*vr.* to degrade or lower oneself.

degüello, *m.* beheading, throat-cutting.

dehesa, *f.* pasture ground.

deidad, *f.* deity; goddess.—**deificar,** *vti.* [d] to deify.

dejación, *f.* abandonment, relinquishment.—*d. de bienes,* (law) assignment.—**dejadez,** *f.* slovenliness, neglect.—**dejado,** *pp.* of DEJAR.—*a.* slovenly; indolent, negligent.—**dejar,** *vt.* to leave; to let; to let go, relinquish; to permit, allow; to abandon, quit; to forsake; to yield; to omit.—*d. atrás,* to outdistance.—*d. caer,* to drop.—*d. de,* to stop; to fail to.—*vr.* to be slovenly; to abandon oneself.—**dejo,** *m.* aftertaste; trace; slight accent.

del, *contraction* of DE *and* EL; of the.

delación, *f.* accusation, information.

delantal, *m.* apron.

delante, *adv.* before, ahead, in front. —**d. de** *prep.* before, in front of, in the presence of.—**delantera**, *f.* front, fore end; front seats in theaters, etc.; lead, advantage.— **delantero**, *a.* foremost, first; front. —*m.* front part; (sport) forward.

delatar, *vt.* to accuse, denounce.— **delator**, *n.* informer, accuser, denouncer.

delegación, *f.* delegation; proxy; office of a delegate.—**delegado**, *n.* delegate, proxy.—**delegar**, *vti.* [b] to delegate.

deleitable, *a.* delectable, delightful.— **deleitación**, *f.* delectation, pleasure, delight.—**deleitar**, *vt.* to delight, please.—*vr.* to delight or please.— **deleite**, *m.* pleasure, delight; lust.— **deleitoso**, *a.* delightful, pleasing.

deletrear, *vt.* to spell.—**deletreo**, *m.* spelling.

deleznable, *a.* ephemeral; worthless; negligible; contemptible.

delfín, *m.* porpoise; dolphin.

delgadez, *f.* thinness; slenderness; leanness.—**delgado**, *a.* thin; lean; slender, slim.—**delgaducho**, *a.* thinnish, lanky.

deliberación, *f.* deliberation.—**deliberar**, *vi.* to deliberate, ponder; to consult or take counsel together.

delicadeza, *f.* delicacy, refinement; softness; tenderness.—**delicado**, *a.* delicate; gentle; tender; sickly, frail; dainty; exquisite.

delicia, *f.* delight, pleasure.—**delicioso**, *a.* delicious; delightful.

delincuencia, *f.* delinquency.—**delincuente**, *mf.* delinquent, offender.—*a.* delinquent, guilty.

delineación, *f.* delineation, draft, sketch.—**delineante**, *mf.* draftsman, designer.—**delinear**, *vt.* to delineate, sketch.

delirante, *a.* delirious.—**delirar**, *vi.* to be delirious; to talk nonsense; to rave.—**delirio**, *m.* delirium; frenzied rapture; nonsense.

delito, *m.* crime; transgression of the law.

demacrado, *a.* emaciated.—**demacrarse**, *vr.* to waste away.

demagogia, *f.* demagogy.

demanda, *f.* (law) claim, complaint; petition; question, inquiry; (com.) demand.—*la oferta y la d.*, supply and demand.—**demandado**, *n.* defendant.—**demandante**, *mf.* plaintiff, complainant.—**demandar**, *vt.* to demand, ask, solicit; to desire; (law) to sue.

demás, *a.* other.—*estar d.*, to be useless; to be unwelcome, not wanted. —*lo d.*, the rest.—*los d.*, *las d.*,

the rest; the others.—*por lo d.*, aside from this; furthermore.—*todo lo d.*, everything else.—*y d.*, and other things, or persons; and so forth.—*adv.* besides, moreover.— **demasía**, *f.* excess, surplus; insolence, outrage.—*en d.*, excessively.— **demasiado**, *a.* excessive; too much. —*pl.* too many.—*adv.* too, excessively; too much.

demencia, *f.* madness, insanity.— **demente**, *a.* insane, mad.—*mf.* lunatic.

demérito, *m.* demerit.

democracia, *f.* democracy.—**demócrata**, *mf.* democrat.—**democrático**, *a.* democratic.

demoledor, *n.* & *a.* demolisher; demolishing.—**demoler**, *vti.* [26] to demolish, destroy, raze.—**demolición**, *f.* demolition.

demonio, *m.* demon; devil.

demora, *f.* delay.—**demorar**, *vt.* to delay.—*vi.* to delay, tarry.—*vr.* to linger, tarry; to be delayed.

demostración, *f.* demonstration; proof.—**demostrar**, *vti.* [12] to demonstrate, show; to prove.

demudado, *a.* wan, pale (from illness, fright, etc.).—**demudarse**, *vr.* to lose one's calm; to turn pale.

denegación, *f.* denial, refusal.—**denegar**, *vti.* [1-b] to deny, refuse.

dengoso, *a.* fastidious; coy.—**dengue**, *m.* fastidiousness; coyness; (med.) dengue.—*hacer dengues*, to act coy.

denodado, *a.* daring, intrepid.

denominación, *f.* denomination.— **denominador**, *m.* denominator.— **denominar**, *vt.* & *vr.* to call, give a name to.

denostar, *vti.* [12] to insult; to revile.

denotar, *vt.* to denote, express.

densidad, *f.* density.—**denso**, *a.* dense, thick; close, compact.

dentado, *a.* toothed, serrated.—**dentadura**, *f.* set of teeth.—*d. postiza*, false teeth, denture.—**dental**, *a.* dental.—**dentellada**, *f.* bite; tooth marks.—**dentera**, *f.* teeth on edge; (coll.) envy.—**dentición**, *f.* teething. —**dentífrico**, *m.* toothpaste or toothpowder.—**dentista**, *mf.* dentist.

dentro, *adv.* inside, within.—*de d.*, from inside.—*d. de*, within; inside. —*d. del año*, in the course of the year.—*d. de poco*, shortly, soon.— *hacia d.*, inwards.—*por d.*, inside; inwardly.

denuedo, *m.* boldness, bravery, courage.

denuesto, *m.* affront, insult.

denuncia, *f.* accusation, arraignment; denunciation; (min.) claim.—**denun-**

ciante, *mf.* denouncer; accuser.—*a.* denouncing; accusing.—**denunciar,** *vt.* to denounce; to advise, give notice; to squeal; (min.) to claim.

deparar, *vt.* to offer, afford, furnish, present.

departamento, *m.* department; compartment, section; apartment.

departir, *vi.* to chat, converse.

dependencia, *f.* dependence, dependency; subordination; branch office; outbuildings.—**depender,** *vi.* (de) to depend, rely (on).—**dependiente,** *a.* dependent, subordinate.—*mf.* clerk, salesman (-woman); retainer.

deplorable, *a.* deplorable.—**deplorar,** *vt.* to deplore, regret.

deponer, *vti.* [32] to depose; to declare; to attest; to lay down.

deportación, *f.* deportation.—**deportar,** *vt.* to deport.

deporte, *m.* sport.—**deportista,** *mf.* sportsman (-woman).—**deportivo,** *a.* athletic, sportive.

deposición, *f.* assertion, affirmation; testimony; removal from office; bowel movement.

depositar, *vt.* to deposit; to entrust; to lay aside.—*vr.* (chem.) to settle. —**depositario,** *n.* depositary, trustee. —**depósito,** *m.* deposit, trust; depot, repository, warehouse; storage; sediment.—*d. de agua,* reservoir.

depravación, *f.* depravity, viciousness. —**depravar,** *vt.* to deprave, corrupt.

depreciación, *f.* depreciation.—**depreciar,** *vt.* & *vr.* to depreciate.

depresión, *f.* depression.—**depresivo, deprimente,** *a.* depressive, depressing.—**deprimir,** *vt.* to depress; to belittle.—*vr.* to become depressed or compressed.

depuesto, *pp.* of DEPONER.

depuración, *f.* purifying; purge.—**depurar,** *vt.* to purify; to purge.

derecha, *f.* right hand; right side; (pol.) right wing.—*a derechas,* right; rightly.—**derechista,** *mf.* rightist.—**derecho,** *a.* straight; right (opposite to left); right-handed; vertical; upright.—*adv.* straight ahead, straightaway.—*m.* right; (D.) the Law.—*pl.* fees, dues, duties.—*derechos de autor,* copyright; royalties. —**derechura,** *f.* straightness.

deriva, *f.* ship's course; deviation, drift.—**derivación,** *f.* derivation.—**derivar,** *vi.* & *vr.* to derive.—*vi.* to drift.—*vt.* to derive, trace to its origin.

derogación, *f.* derogation, repeal.—**derogar,** *vti.* [b] to derogate; to annul, revoke, repeal.

derramamiento, *m.* pouring out; spilling, shedding; overflow; scat-

tering.—*d. de sangre.* bloodshed.—**derramar,** *vt.* to pour out; to spill; to shed; to scatter; to spread.—*vr.* to overflow, run over; to be scattered or spread.—**derrame,** *m.* overflow; scattering; shedding; leakage; (med.) discharge.

derredor, *m.* circuit.—*al d.,* or *en d.,* round about.—*al d. de,* or *en d. de,* about, around.

derrengado, *a.* crooked; lame, crippled; swaybacked.—**derrengar,** *vti.* [1-b] to injure the back; to cripple; to make crooked.

derretir, *vti.* [29] to melt, fuse.—*vr.* to melt, fuse; to be deeply in love.

derribar, *vt.* to demolish, knock down; to overthrow.—**derribo,** *m.* wrecking, demolition; debris.

derrocamiento, *m.* throwing down, overthrow.—**derrocar,** *vti.* [12-d] to pull down; to oust; to overthrow.

derrochador, *n.* spendthrift, squanderer.—*a.* extravagant, prodigal.—**derrochar,** *vt.* to waste, squander. —**derroche,** *m.* waste, squandering, wastefulness.

derrota, *f.* defeat; (naut.) ship's course.—**derrotar,** *vt.* to defeat; (naut.) to cause to drift.—**derrotero,** *m.* (naut.) collection of seacharts; ship's course; course of action, way.—**derrotista,** *mf.* defeatist.

derruir, *vti.* [23-e] to demolish, tear down.

derrumbamiento, *m.* landslide; collapse; downfall.—**derrumbar,** *vt.* to throw down headlong.—*vr.* to tumble down; to crumble away; to cave in.—**derrumbe,** *m.* tumbling down, collapse; landslide.

desabonarse, *vr.* to cancel a subscription.

desabotonar, *vt.* to unbutton.

desabrido, *a.* harsh, sour; ill-humored; tasteless.—**desabrimiento,** *m.* ill humor; tastelessness.

desabrigar, *vti.* [b] to uncover; to strip.—*vri.* to take off outer clothing, expose oneself to cold.

desabrochar, *vt.* to unclasp, unfasten. —*vr.* to unclasp, or unfasten oneself; to become unclasped or unfastened.

desacatar, *vt.* to treat disrespectfully. —**desacato,** *m.* disrespect; lack of reverence.

desacertado, *a.* unwise, mistaken.—**desacierto,** *m.* error, mistake, blunder.

desacostumbrado, *a.* unusual; unaccustomed.

desacreditar, *vt.* to discredit.

desacuerdo, *m.* discordance, disagreement.

desafiar, *vt.* to challenge; to defy; to compete with.

desafinación, *f.* discordance, being out of tune.—**desafinar,** *vi.* to be discordant, out of tune.—*vr.* to get out of tune.

desafío, *m.* challenge; duel; struggle, contest, competition.

desaforado, *a.* disorderly; lawless; outrageous.

desafortunado, *a.* unfortunate, unlucky.

desafuero, *m.* excess, outrage.

desagradable, *a.* disagreeable, unpleasant, unattractive.—**desagradar,** *vt.* to displease, offend, miff.

desagradecido, *a.* ungrateful.

desagrado, *m.* discontent, displeasure.

desagraviar, *vt.* to apologize; to make amends for.—**desagravio,** *m.* apology, satisfaction; reparation.

desaguar, *vti.* [b] to drain.—*vii.* to empty (rivers); to urinate.—**desagüe,** *m.* drainage; drain, outlet; waste.

desaguisado, *m.* outrage, wrong.

desahuciado, *a.* despaired of, hopeless; given over; evicted.—**desahuciar,** *vt.* to give over; to evict.—**desahucio,** *m.* eviction.

desahogado, *a.* free, unencumbered; comfortable; well-off; impudent, brazen-faced.—**desahogar,** *vti.* [b] to ease, relieve.—*vri.* to unbosom oneself; to give a piece of one's mind; to relieve oneself.—**desahogo,** *m.* ease, relief; unburdening; relaxation; comfort.

desairar, *vt.* to disregard; to slight; to scorn; to rebuff.—**desaire,** *m.* slight, rebuff, disdain.

desajustar, *vt.* to disarrange, disorder. —*vr.* to get out of order or adjustment.—**desajuste,** *m.* disarrangement, lack of adjustment.

desalentador, *a.* dispiriting, discouraging.—**desalentar,** *vti.* [1] to discourage; to dismay.—*vri.* to jade, become exhausted.—**desaliento,** *m.* dismay, depression of spirits, discouragement; faintness.

desaliñado, *a.* slipshod.—**desaliñar,** *vt.* & *vr.* to disarrange, disorder, ruffle; to make slovenly.—**desaliño,** *m.* slovenliness, negligence of dress; disarray; neglect.

desalmado, *a.* soulless, merciless, inhuman; impious.

desalojamiento, desalojo, *m.* dislodging; displacement.—**desalojar,** *vt.* to dislodge, oust; to displace.

desalquilado, *a.* unrented, vacant.—vacant.—**desalquilarse,** *vr.* to become vacant.

desamarrar, *vt.* to untie; (naut.) to unmoor; to unbend (a rope).—*vr.* to untie oneself; to get loose.

desamparado, *a.* forsaken; helpless; unsheltered.—**desamparar,** *vt.* to forsake, abandon.—**desamparo,** *m.* abandonment; helplessness.

desamueblado, *a.* unfurnished.—**desamueblar,** *vt.* to strip of furniture.

desandar, *vti.* [4] to retrace one's steps.

desangramiento, *m.* bleeding to excess.—**desangrar,** *vt.* to bleed; to drain.—*vr.* to bleed to death.

desanimación, *f.* lack of enthusiasm; dullness.—**desanimado,** *a.* dull, flat; discouraged.—**desanimar,** *vt.* to discourage, dishearten.—*vr.* to get discouraged; to jade.

desapacible, *a.* disagreeable, unpleasant.

desaparecer, *vii.* [3] & *vri.* to disappear, vanish; to get out of sight.—**desaparición,** *f.* disappearance, vanishing.

desapercibido, *a.* unaware; unprepared, unguarded; unnoticed.

desaplicado, *a.* indolent, careless, neglectful.

desaprensivo, *a.* unscrupulous.

desapretar, *vti.* [1] to slacken, loosen, loose.

desaprobación, *f.* disapproval.—**desaprobar,** *vti.* [12] to disapprove of; to condemn.

desarmado, *a.* unarmed.—**desarmar,** *vt.* to disarm; to dismount; to disassemble.—**desarme,** *m.* disarmament.

desarraigar, *vti.* [b] to eradicate, root out.

desarrapado, *a.* ragged.

desarreglado, *a.* slovenly, disorderly; disarranged; immoderate.—**desarreglar,** *vt.* to disarrange, disorder.—**desarreglo,** *m.* disarrangement, disorder.

desarrollar, *vt.* to develop, unfold; to expound.—*vr.* to develop; to evolve; to unfold.—**desarrollo,** *m.* development; unfolding; expounding.

desarzonar, *vt.* to unseat (from a saddle).

desaseado, *a.* untidy, slovenly.—**desaseo,** *m.* untidiness, slovenliness.

desasir, *vti.* [5] to loosen.—*vri.* (de) to get loose (from); to extricate oneself (from).

desasosiego, *m.* restlessness, uneasiness.

desastrado, *a.* shabby, ragged.—**desastre,** *m.* disaster.—**desastroso,** *a.* disastrous.

desatar, *vt.* to untie, unfasten, loosen. —*vr.* to loosen; to break loose, break out (as a storm).—**d. en,**

to break out into, to pour out (insults, etc.).

desatascar, *vti*. [d] to pull or draw out of the mud.

desatención, *f.* inattention; discourtesy.—**desatender**, *vti*. [18] to pay no attention to; to disregard, slight, neglect.—**desatento**, *a.* inattentive, careless, discourteous.

desatinado, *a.* nonsensical; foolish.—**desatinar**, *vt.* to rattle, bewilder.—*vi.* to get rattled or bewildered; to talk nonsense.—**desatino**, *m.* foolish act or expression; nonsense.

desatracar, *vti*. [d] to sheer off; to bear away; to unmoor.

desautorizado, *a.* unauthorized.—**desautorizar**, *vti*. [a] to disauthorize.

desavenencia, *f.* discord, disagreement.—**desavenido**, *a.* discordant, disagreeing.

desayunarse, *vr.* to have breakfast.—**desayuno**, *m.* breakfast.

desazón, *f.* displeasure; uneasiness; insipidity.—**desazonar**, *vt.* to displease, annoy.—*vr.* to become indisposed; to become uneasy.

desbancar, *vti*. [d] to break the bank; to supplant, oust.

desbandada, *f.* disbanding.—*a la d.*, in disorder.—**desbandarse**, *vr.* to disband, disperse, scatter.

desbarajuste, *m.* disorder, confusion.

desbaratar, *vt.* to break to pieces, smash.—*vr.* to fall to pieces.

desbarrar, *vi.* to act foolishly; to talk nonsense.

desbastar, *vt.* to hew, pare, trim.

desbocado, *a.* runaway (horse); foul-mouthed, indecent.—**desbocar**, *vti*. [d] & *vri*. to run away.—*vr.* to use abusive language, unloosen one's tongue.

desbordamiento, *m.* overflowing, flooding.—**desbordar**, *vi.* & *vr.* to overflow; to lose one's self-control.

descabalgar, *vii*. [b] to dismount (from a horse).

descabezar, *vti*. [a] to behead; to cut the upper parts or points of.—*d. el sueño*, to take a nap, grab forty winks.

descabellado, *a.* illogical, absurd.

descalabradura, *f.* wound on the head.—**descalabrar**, *vt.* to wound on the head; to injure; to defeat.—*vr.* to injure one's skull.—**descalabro**, *m.* calamity; misfortune.

descalificar, *vti*. [d] to disqualify.

descalzar, *vti*. [a] to unshoe, to pull off the shoes.—*vr.* to take off one's shoes.—**descalzo**, *a.* barefoot, shoeless.

descaminado, *a.* misguided, ill-advised, mistaken.

descamisado, *a.* shirtless, ragged.—*m.* (coll.) ragamuffin.

descampado, *a.* disengaged, open, clear.—*en d.*, in the open air.

descansar, *vi.* to rest, lean upon; to depend.—*vt.* to place or set down on a support or base.—**descanso**, *m.* rest; relief; landing of stairs; (mech.) support.

descarado, *a.* impudent, barefaced.

descarga, *f.* unloading, unburdening; (mil.) volley; (elec.) discharge.—**descargar**, *vti*. [b] to unload, unburden; to ease, lighten; to empty; (mil.) to fire; to discharge or unload firearms; (elec.) to discharge; to acquit.—*vii.* to strike with violence (as a storm).—**descargo**, *m.* (com.) acquittance, receipt; (law) plea or answer to an impeachment.

descarnar, *vt.* to remove flesh from; to eat away.—*vr.* to lose flesh, become emaciated.

descaro, *m.* impudence, barefacedness; effrontery.

descarriar, *vt.* to lead astray, misguide, mislead; to separate (cattle).—*vr.* to be separated; to go astray.

descarrilamiento, *m.* derailment.—**descarrilar**, *vt.* to derail.—*vi.* & *vr.* to run off the track, be derailed.

descartar, *vt.* to discard; to lay aside.—*vr.* to discard (at cards).

descascar, **descascarar**, *vt.* to peel, shell.—*vr.* to peel off, shell off.

descendencia, *f.* descent, origin; descendants.—**descendente**, *a.* descending.—**descender**, *vii.* [18] to descend; to get, come or go down; to drop (of temperature); to derive, come from.—**descendiente**, *a.* descending.—*mf.* descendant, offspring.—**descendimiento**, *m.* descent, lowering.—**descenso**, *m.* descent; lowering; fall.

descifrar, *vt.* to decipher, make out.

descocado, *a.* bold, forward.—**descoco**, *m.* impudence, sauciness.

descolgar, *vti*. [12-b] to unhang; to take down; to lower.—*vri.* to climb down (a rope, etc.); to turn up unexpectedly.

descolorar, *vt.* & *vr.* to discolor; to lose color, fade.—**descolorido**, *a.* pale, faded.

descollar, *vii.* [12] & *vti.* to tower, excel, surpass.

descomedido, *a.* excessive, disproportionate; rude, impolite.—**descomedimiento**, *m.* rudeness, incivility.

descompasado, *a.* excessive, disproportionate; out of tune or time.

descomponer, *vti*. [32] to disarrange, upset; to put out of order; (chem.) to decompose.—*vri.* to decompose,

rot; to get out of order; to lose one's temper.—**descomposición,** *f.* disarrangement; disorder; decomposition, decay.—**descompuesto,** *pp.* of DESCOMPONER.—*a.* insolent; out of temper; immodest; out of order.

descomulgar, *vti.* [b] to excommunicate.

descomunal, *a.* extraordinary; monstrous, enormous.

desconcertante, *a.* disconcerting, baffling.—**desconcertar,** *vti.* [1] to disarrange, disturb, confuse; to disconcert, baffle, mystify; to disjoint. —*vri.* to become perplexed, confused.—**desconcierto,** *m.* discord, disagreement; disorder, confusion.

desconectar, *vt.* to disconnect.

desconfiado, *a.* distrustful; mistrustful.—**desconfianza,** *f.* diffidence; distrust.—**desconfiar,** *vi.* (de) to mistrust; to have no confidence (in); to suspect, doubt.

desconforme, *a.* = DISCONFORME.—**desconformidad,** *f.* = DISCONFORMIDAD.

descongelar, *vt.* to defrost.

desconocer, *vti.* [3] to fail to recognize; to disregard, ignore; to not know; to disown.—**desconocido,** *a.* unknown.—*n.* unknown person, stranger.—**desconocimiento,** *m.* ignorance; disregard.

desconsideración, *f.* inconsiderateness —**desconsiderado,** *a.* inconsiderate, thoughtless.

desconsolado, *a.* disconsolate, grief stricken, downhearted —**desconsolador,** *a.* discouraging; lamentable —**desconsolar,** *vti.* [12] to afflict.—*vri.* to despair, be disconsolate.—**desconsuelo,** *m* affliction, disconsolateness.

descontar, *vti.* [12] to discount, deduct; to take for granted.—*vri.* to miscount.

descontentadizo, *a.* hard to please — **descontentar,** *vt.* to displease.— **descontento,** *a.* discontent, displeased.—*m.* discontent, displeasure.

descontinuar, *vt.* to discontinue, leave off.

descorazonar, *vt.* to dishearten, discourage.

descorchar, *vt* to uncork, to break open.

descortés, *a.* impolite, discourteous.— **descortesía,** *f.* discourtesy.

descortezar, *vti.* [a] to strip bark, to take off the crust of.

descoser, *vt.* to rip, unstitch, unseam. —*vr.* to rip.

descoyuntar, *vt* to dislocate or dis joint.—*vr* to become disjointed.

d. de risa, to split one's sides with laughter

descrédito, *m.* discredit.

descreer, *vti.* [e] to disbelieve; to deny due credit to.—**descreído,** *n.* & *a.* unbeliever; infidel; unbelieving.

describir, *vti.* [49] to describe, depict. —**descripción,** *f.* description; sketch. —**descriptivo,** *a.* descriptive.—**descrito,** *pp.* of DESCRIBIR.—*a.* described.

descuartizamiento, *m.* quartering; breaking or cutting in pieces; carving.—**descuartizar,** *vti.* [a] to quarter; to carve; to cut into pieces.

descubierto, *pp.* of DESCUBRIR.—*a.* discovered; uncovered; unveiled; bareheaded; manifest; exposed.—*m.* deficit; overdraft.—*al d.,* openly; in the open.—*en d.,* overdrawn.— **descubridor,** *n.* discoverer.—**descubrimiento,** *m.* discovery; invention; find.—**descubrir,** *vti.* [49] to discover; to disclose; to uncover; to reveal.—*vri.* to take off one's hat.

descuento, *m.* discount; deduction, allowance.

descuidado, *a.* careless, negligent, slapdash; slovenly; unthinking.— **descuidar,** *vt* to neglect.—*¡descuide!* don't worry —*vi.* to lack attention or diligence; to be careless. —*vr.* to be careless, negligent.— **descuido,** *m.* carelessness; oversight, slip; lack of attention.—*al d.,* unobserved, on the sly; carelessly

desde, *prep* since, from.—*d. ahora,* from now on.—*d entonces,* since then, ever since —*d luego,* of course. —*d que,* since, ever since.

desdecir, *vri.* [14] to be unworthy (of); to detract (from).—*vri.* to retract, recant.

desdén, *m.* disdain, slight, scorn.

desdentado, *a.* toothless.

desdeñable, *a.* contemptible, despicable.—**desdeñar,** *vt.* to disdain scorn.—**desdeñoso,** *a.* disdainful, contemptuous.

desdicha, *f* misfortune, ill luck. **desdichado;** *a.* unfortunate; unlucky; wretched.—*n.* wretch; poor devil.

desdoblar, *vt.* to unfold, spread open.

desdoro, *m* dishonor, blemish, stigma.

deseable, *a.* desirable —**desear,** *vt.* to desire, wish

desecar, *vti.* [d] to drain, to dry.

desechar, *vt* to reject; to exclude; to put or lay aside; to throw away; to cast off.—**desecho,** *m.* surplus, remainder; junk.—*de d.,* cast off, discarded, scrap (iron, etc.).

desembalar, *vt.* to unpack, open.

desembarazar, *vti.* [a] to free, ease. —*vri.* to rid oneself of difficulties.

desembarcar, *vti* [d] to unload; to

put ashore.—*vii.* to land, disembark, go ashore.

desembocadura, *f.* outlet; mouth (of a river, canal, etc.).—**desembocar,** *vii.* [d] (en) to flow (into); to end (at), lead (to).

desembolsar, *vt.* to pay out, disburse. —**desembolso,** *m.* disbursement, expenditure.

desembragar, *vti.* [b] to disengage the clutch.

desembrollar, *vt.* to unravel, clear, disentangle.

desembuchar, *vt.* to disgorge; to turn out of the maw; (coll.) to tell all.

desempacar, *vti.* [d] to unpack.

desempatar, *vt.* to decide a tie vote; to run, play, or shoot off a tie.

desempedrado, *a.* unpaved.

desempeñar, *vt.* to redeem (from pawn).—*d. un cargo,* to fill a post. —*d. un papel,* to play a part.—*vr.* to extricate oneself from debt.— **desempeño,** *m.* redemption (of a pledge); discharge (of an obligation).

desempleado, *n.* & *a.* unemployed.— **desempleo,** *m.* unemployment.

desempolvar, *vt.* to dust, remove dust or powder from.

desencadenar, *vt.* to unchain; to free, liberate.—*vr.* to break loose, free oneself from chains; to break out with fury (as a storm); to come down in torrents (the rain).

desencajado, *a.* disjointed; ill-looking, emaciated.

desenfado, *m.* freedom, ease, naturalness.

desenfrenado, *a.* ungoverned, unchecked, wanton; riotous.—**desenfreno,** *m.* rashness, wantonness, licentiousness.

desenganchar, *vt.* to unhook, unfasten; to unhitch, unharness.

desengañar, *vt.* to undeceive, set right; to disillusion.—*vr.* to become disillusioned.—**desengaño,** *m.* disillusionment, disappointment.

desengrasar, *vt.* to remove the grease from.

desenlace, *m.* conclusion, end, ending. —**desenlazar,** *vti.* [a] to unlace, untie, loose; to unravel.

desenmarañar, *vt.* to disentangle, to unravel, make clear.

desenmascarar, *vt.* to unmask.

desenredar, *vt.* to untangle, unravel.— *vr.* to extricate oneself.

desenroscar, *vti.* [d] to untwist; to unscrew.

desensillar, *vt.* to unsaddle.

desentenderse, *vri.* [18] (de) to have nothing to do with; to ignore; to pay no attention (to).—*hacerse el*

desentendido, to pretend not to see, notice or understand.

desenterrar, *vti.* [1] to dig up, unearth.

desentonación, *f.* dissonance.—**desentonado,** *a.* out of tune; discordant. —**desentonar,** *vi.* to be off key, out of tune; to clash (in colors); to be out of keeping with.

desentrañar, *vt.* to penetrate or dive into; to bring out, reveal, dig out.

desenvoltura, *f.* sprightliness, ease; impudence.—**desenvolver,** *vti.* [47] to unfold, unwrap, unroll; to unravel; to develop.—*vri.* to behave with self-assurance; to unfold, unroll.—**desenvolvimiento,** *m.* unfolding, development.—**desenvuelto,** *pp.* of DESENVOLVER.—*a.* forward; free, easy.

deseo, *m.* desire, wish.—**deseoso,** *a.* desirous, eager.

desequilibrado, *a.* unbalanced; deranged.—**desequilibrar,** *vt.* to put out of balance.—*vr.* to become deranged.—**desequilibrio,** *m.* lack of balance; derangement.

deserción, *f.* desertion.—**desertar,** *vt.* to desert; to abandon.—*vi.* (de) to desert (from).—**desertor,** *n.* deserter.

desesperación, *f.* despair, desperation; anger.—**desesperado,** *a.* desperate, despairing; hopeless.—**desesperante,** *a.* causing despair; maddening.

desesperanza, *f* despair.—**desesperanzado,** *a.* discouraged; hopeless, in despair.

desesperar, *vi.* to lose hope, despair. —*vt.* to make one despair; to discourage hope; (coll.) to drive crazy. —*vr.* to despair, despond; to fret. **desespero,** *m.* despair; vexation.

desestimar, *vt.* to undervalue; to reject, deny.

desfachatado, *a.* impudent, saucy.— **desfachatez,** *f.* effrontery, impudence.

desfalcar, *vti.* [d] to embezzle. **desfalco,** *m.* embezzlement.

desfallecer, *vii.* [3] to pine; to weaken; to faint.—**desfalleciente,** *a.* pining, languishing.—**desfallecimiento,** *m.* languor; dejection; swoon.

desfavorable, *a.* unfavorable; untoward.

desfigurar, *vt.* to disfigure, deform; to deface; to disguise (as the voice); to distort.

desfiladero, *m.* defile, gorge; road at the side of a precipice.—**desfilar,** *vi.* to file past; to march in review, parade.—**desfile,** *m.* parade, procession.

desflorar, *vt.* to tarnish; to deflower; to violate.

desfogar, *vri.* [b] to vent one's anger. —*vti.* to vent.

desfondar, *vt.* to break or take off the bottom of.

desgaire, *m.* carelessness, indifference. —*al* d., in an affectedly careless manner; disdainfully.

desgajar, *vt.* to tear, break off (branches).—*vr.* to be torn off; to fall off.

desgañifarse, desgañitarse, *vr.* to shriek, scream at the top of one's voice.

desgarbado, *a.* ungraceful, uncouth, gawky.

desgarrador, *a.* tearing; heartbreaking, heart-rending.—**desgarradura,** *f.* laceration, tear, break.—**desgarrar,** *vt.* to rend, tear; to claw; to expectorate.—*vr.* to tear.—**desgarrón,** *m.* large rent or tear (in clothing, etc.).

desgastar, *vt.* to wear away, consume, waste by degrees.—*vr.* to lose strength and vigor; to wear down or away.—**desgaste,** *m.* slow waste; abrasion; wear and tear; erosion.

desgobierno, *m.* mismanagement; misrule.

desgracia, *f.* misfortune, wretchedness; affliction; disgrace.—**desgraciado,** *a. & n.* unfortunate (person), wretched (person).—**desgraciar,** *vt.* to ruin; to maim; to spoil.—*vr.* to disgrace; to lose favor; to become a cripple.

desgranar, *vt.* to remove the grain from; to thrash, thresh (corn, etc.); to shell (peas, etc.).—*vr.* to shed the grains; to scatter about (as beads).

desgreñar, *vt.* to dishevel.

desguarnecer, *vti.* [3] to disarm (an opponent); to unharness; to strip of trimmings and ornaments.

deshabitado, *a.* uninhabited, untenanted, deserted.

deshacer, *vti.* [22] to undo; to destroy; to untie.—*vri.* to be consumed, destroyed; to wear oneself out; to grieve, mourn; to outdo oneself.—*deshacerse de,* to get rid of.

desharrapado, *a.* shabby, ragged, tattered.

deshecho, *pp.* of DESHACER.—*a.* ruined, destroyed, in pieces; undone; worn-out.

deshelar, *vti.* [1] & *vri.* to thaw; to melt.

desherbar, *vti.* [1] to weed.

desheredar, *vt.* to disinherit.

deshermanar, *vt.* to unmatch, spoil a pair

deshielo, *m.* thaw, thawing.

deshilachar, *vt.* to ravel.—*vr.* to fuzz; to ravel.

deshilar, *vt.* to ravel; to scrape (lint). —*vr.* to fuzz; to grow thin.

deshilvanado, *a.* disconnected, incoherent (of speech).

deshinchar, *vt.* to reduce the swelling of; to deflate.—*vr.* to become deflated; to go down (of anything swollen).

deshojar, *vt.* to strip off the leaves.— *vr.* to shed leaves.

deshollejar, *vt.* to husk, hull; to peel.

deshollinador, *m.* chimney-sweeper.

deshonestidad, *f.* dishonesty; indecency.—**deshonesto,** *a.* dishonest, dishonorable; lewd.

deshonor, *m.* dishonor, disgrace; insult, affront.—**deshonra,** *f.* dishonor; seduction or violation (of a woman).—**deshonrar,** *vt.* to affront, insult, defame; to dishonor, disgrace; to seduce or ruin (a woman). —**deshonroso,** *a.* dishonorable.

deshora, *f.* inconvenient time.—*a* d., or *a deshoras,* untimely, extemporarily.

deshuesar, *vt.* to bone (an animal); to take the pits out of (fruits).

desidia, *f.* laziness, indolence.—**desidioso,** *a.* lazy, indolent.

desierto, *m.* desert.—*a.* uninhabited, deserted, lonely.

designación, *f.* designation.—**designar,** *vt.* to appoint, designate.—**designio,** *m.* design, purpose, intention.

desigual, *a.* unequal, unlike; uneven, rough; changeable.—**desigualdad,** *f.* inequality, difference; roughness, unevenness.

desilusión, *f.* disappointment, disillusionment.—**desilusionar,** *vt.* to dispillusion.—*vr.* to become disillusioned.

desinfección, *f.* disinfection; disinfecting.—**desinfectante,** *m. & a.* disinfectant; disinfecting.—**desinfectar,** *vt.* to disinfect; to sterilize.

desenrollar, *vt.* to unroll, uncoil.

desinflamar, *vt. & vr.* to remove the inflammation of.

desinflar, *vt. & vr.* to deflate.

desintegración, *f.* disintegration.— **desintegrar,** *vt., vi. & vr.* to disintegrate.

desistir, *vi.* (de) to desist (from).

desleal, *a.* disloyal; perfidious.— **deslealtad,** *f.* disloyalty, treachery, unfaithfulness.

desleir, *vti.* [35-e] to dilute; to dissolve.—*vri.* to become diluted.

deslenguado, *a.* impudent; foulmouthed.

desligar, *vti.* [b] to loosen, untie.— *vri* to get loose; to give way

deslindar, *vt.* to mark the boundaries of; to clear up, define.—**deslinde,** *m.* demarcation, determination of boundaries.

desliz, *m.* slip, slide; false step.—**deslizamiento,** *m.* slip, slipping; glide; skidding, sliding.—**deslizante,** *a.* gliding, sliding.—**deslizar,** *vii.* [a] & *vri.* to slip; to slide; to skid; to glide; to act or speak carelessly.—*vri.* to shirk, evade.

deslucido, *a.* dull, shabby, shopworn; unsuccessful.—**deslucir,** *vti.* [3] to tarnish, dull; to discredit.—*vri.* to fail, be a failure.

deslumbrador, *a.* dazzling, glaring.—**deslumbramiento,** *m.* glare, dazzling; confusion of sight or mind.—**deslumbrante,** *a.* dazzling.—**deslumbrar,** *vt.* to dazzle.

deslustrar, *vt.* to tarnish; to obscure, dim; to remove the glaze from; to stain (reputation, etc.).

desmadejamiento, *m.* languishment, weakness.—**desmadejar,** *vt.* to enervate.—*vr.* to languish.

desmán, *m.* misbehavior; excess.

desmandar, *vr.* to be impudent; to lose moderation or self-control.

desmantelamiento, *m.* dismantling; dilapidation.—**desmantelar,** *vt.* to dismantle; to abandon.

desmañado, *a.* clumsy, awkward.

desmayar, *vi.* to falter, lose heart.—*vr.* to faint.—**desmayo,** *m.* swoon, faint; discouragement.

desmejorar, *vt.* to debase; to make worse.—*vi.* & *vr.* to decline, become worse; to deteriorate.

desmelenado, *a.* disheveled.

desmemoriado, *a.* forgetful.

desmentir, *vti.* [39] to give the lie to; to contradict.—*vri.* to recant, retract.

desmenuzar, *vti.* [a] to crumble; to shred; to tear into bits; to examine minutely.—*vri.* to crumble, fall into small pieces.

desmerecer, *vti.* [3] to become unworthy of.—*vii.* to deteriorate; to compare unfavorably.—**desmerecimiento,** *m.* demerit, unworthiness.

desmesurado, *a.* disproportionate, excessive.

desmigajar, *vt.* & *vr.* to crumb; to crumble.

desmochar, *vt.* to lop or cut off the top of (a tree, etc.).—**desmoche,** *m.* cutting off.

desmontar, *vt.* to clear (a wood); to uncock (firearms); to take apart (machines).—*vi.* to dismount; to alight (from a horse, mule, etc.).

desmoralización, *f.* demoralization.—**desmoralizar,** *vti.* [a] to demoral-ize, corrupt.—*vri.* to become demoralized.

desmoronamiento, *m.* crumbling.—**desmoronar,** *vt.* to demolish gradually; to destroy.—*vr.* to fall, crumble.

desmovilizar, *vti.* [a] to demobilize.

desnivel, *m.* unevenness, drop.—**desnivelado,** *a.* unlevel.—**desnivelar,** *vt.* to make uneven.—*vr.* to lose its level.

desnucar, *vti.* [d] to break the neck of.—*vri.* to break one's neck.

desnudar, *vt.* & *vr.* to strip, undress, unclothe.—**desnudez,** *f.* nudity, nakedness.—**desnudismo,** *m.* nudism.—**desnudista,** *mf.* nudist.—**desnudo,** *a.* nude, naked; bare, evident.

desnutrición, *f.* malnutrition.

desobedecer, *vti.* [3] & *vii.* to disobey.—**desobediencia,** *f.* disobedience.—**desobediente,** *a.* disobedient.

desocupación, *f.* leisure; unemployment.—**desocupado,** *a.* idle, without occupation; vacant, unoccupied.—*n.* unemployed person; idler.—**desocupar,** *vt.* to vacate; to evacuate; to empty.—*vr.* to retire (from a business or occupation).

desodorante, *m.* & *a.* deodorant.

desoír, *vti.* [28-e] to pretend not to hear; not to heed.

desolación, *f.* desolation; destruction; affliction.—**desolado,** *a.* desolate; disconsolate.—**desolar,** *vti.* [12] to lay waste.—*vri.* to grieve.

desollar, *vti.* [12] to flay, skin.

desorden, *m.* disorder, confusion; lawlessness; disturbance, riot.—**desordenar,** *vt.* to disorder, disturb, disarrange.

desorientación, *f.* disorientation, loss of bearings; perplexity.—**desorientar,** *vt.* to mislead, confuse.—*vr.* to lose one's bearings.

desosar, *vti.* [15] = DESHUESAR.

desovar, *vii.* [15] to spawn.

despabilado, *a.* vigilant; wakeful; lively, smart.—**despabilar,** *vt.* to trim or snuff (a candle); to rouse; to enliven.—*vr.* to wake up.

despacio, *adv.* slowly; deliberately.—**despacioso,** *a.* slow.—**despacito,** *adv.* very slowly, gently, softly.

despachar, *vt.* to dispatch; to expedite; to attend to; to wait on (as in a shop); to dismiss, discharge.—*vr.* to make haste.—**despacho,** *m.* dispatch; study; office; salesroom; telegram; communiqué; shipment.

despachurrar, *vt.* to squash, smash, crush.

desparpajo, *m.* self-confidence, pertness, cockiness.

desparramar, *vt.* & *vr.* to scatter, disseminate, spread.

despatarrarse, *vr.* (coll.) to sprawl, go sprawling.

despavorido, *a.* terrified.

despectivo, *a.* contemptuous.

despechar, *vt.* to spite.—*vr.* to be spited.—**despecho**, *m.* spite.—*a despecho de*, in spite (of), despite.

despedazar, *vti.* [a] to tear to pieces, cut up.—*vri.* to break or fall to pieces.

despedida, *f.* leave-taking, farewell; send-off; dismissal.—**despedir**, *vti.* [29] to dismiss; to emit; to see a person off (at a station, airport, etc.).—*vri.* to take leave (of), say goodbye (to); to leave (a post).

despegado, *a.* unglued; unaffectionate, unfeeling.—**despegar**, *vti.* [b] to unglue, disjoin.—*vii.* to rise, take off (of a plane).—*vri.* to come off; to become indifferent.—**despego**, *m.* coolness, indifference; aversion.—**despegue**, *m.* take-off (of a plane).

despeinado, *a.* uncombed.—**despeinar**, *vt.* & *vr.* to disarrange the hair.

despejado, *a.* smart; clear, cloudless; unobstructed.—**despejar**, *vt.* to remove impediments from, clear; (math.) to find the value of.—*vr.* to become bright and smart; to clear up.

despellejar, *vt.* to flay, skin; to speak ill of.

despensa, *f.* pantry; storeroom (for food); food, provisions.—**despensero**, *n.* butler; (naut.) steward.

despeñadero, *m.* precipice, crag.—**despeñar**, *vt.* to precipitate, to hurl down.—*vr.* to throw oneself headlong.

desperdiciar, *vt.* to squander, waste, misspend.—**desperdicio**, *m.* waste, spoilage; profusion.—*pl.* garbage.

desperdigar, *vti.* [b] to separate, disjoin; to scatter.

desperezarse, *vri.* [a] to stretch one's limbs.

desperfecto, *m.* deterioration; slight injury or damage, imperfection.

despertador, *m.* alarm clock.—**despertar**, *vti.* [1-49] to wake up; to arouse, to stir up.—*vii.* & *vri.* to wake up.

despiadado, *a.* unmerciful, pitiless.

despido, *m.* discharge, dismissal, lay-off.

despierte, *a.* awake; watchful; diligent; smart.

despilfarrar, *vt.* to waste, squander. —**despilfarro**, *m.* extravagance, squandering; waste.

despintar, *vt.* to take the paint off. —*vr.* to lose color, fade.

despistar, *vt.* to throw off the scent.

desplazamiento, *m.* displacement.—**desplazar**, *vti.* [a] to displace.

desplegar, *vti.* [1-b] to unfold, unfurl; to display.—*vri.* to deploy (as troops).—**despliegue**, *m.* unfurling, unfolding; deployment.

desplomar, *vr.* to tumble down, collapse.—**desplome**, *m.* tumbling down, downfall, collapse.

desplumar, *vt.* & *vr.* to pluck (a bird); to fleece, skin; to strip of property.

despoblación, *f.* depopulation.—**despoblado**, *m.* uninhabited place, wilderness.—*a.* uninhabited, desolate.—**despoblar**, *vti.* [12] to depopulate; to despoil or desolate.—*vri.* to become depopulated.

despojar, *vt.* to despoil, strip of property; to deprive of; to cut off from.—*vr.* (de) to take off (as a coat).—**despojo**, *m.* spoliation; spoils.—*pl.* leavings, scraps from the table; giblets of fowl; remains.

desposado, *n.* betrothed; bride; bridegroom.—**desposar**, *vt.* to marry (to perform the marriage ceremony for).—*vr.* to be betrothed, or married.

desposeer, *vti.* [e] to dispossess, oust.

déspota, *m.* despot.—**despótico**, *a.* despotic.—**despotismo**, *m.* despotism, tyranny.

despreciable, *a.* contemptible, despicable, insignificant.—**despreciar**, *vt.* to despise, scorn.—**desprecio**, *m.* scorn, contempt.

desprender, *vt.* to unfasten; to separate.—*vr.* to give way; to issue (from), come out (of); to follow, be a consequence (of).—**desprendimiento**, *m.* detachment, landslide; disinterestedness.

despreocupación, *f.* freedom from bias; unconventionality.—**despreocupado**, *a.* unprejudiced; unconventional; carefree.—**despreocuparse**, *vr.* to become unbiased, lose prejudice; (de) to ignore; to pay no attention (to).

desprestigiar, *vt.* to discredit.—*vr.* to lose reputation or prestige.—**desprestigio**, *m.* loss of reputation or prestige.

desprevenido, *a.* unprovided; unprepared.

despropósito, *m.* absurdity, nonsense.

desprovisto, *a.* (de) unprovided (with), lacking (in).

después, *adv.* after, afterward; next, then, later.—*d. de*, after; next to. —*d. de que*, or *d. que*, after.

despuntar, *vt.* to blunt; to crop.—

vi. to sprout or bud; to be outstanding; to excel.

desquiciar, *vt.* to unhinge; to unsettle.—*vr.* to become unhinged; to fall down.

desquitarse, *vr.* **(de)** to win one's money back, recoup; to get even.—**desquite,** *m.* compensation; recovery of a loss; revenge; return game or bout.

destacamento, *m.* (mil.) detachment.—**destacar,** *vti.* [d] to bring out, make conspicuous; (mil.) to detach.—*vri.* to stand out, be conspicuous; to be outstanding.

destajo, *m.* piece work, task.—*a d.,* by the job, piece work.

destapar, *vt.* to uncover, uncork, take off (cover, lid, cap).—*vr.* to become uncovered.

destartalado, *a.* handled, jumbled; ramshackle, scantily and poorly furnished.

destellar, *vi.* to flash, twinkle, gleam.—**destello,** *m.* flash, sparkle, gleam.

destemplado, *a.* inharmonious; out of tune; out of tone; intemperate; without its temper (of metal).—**destemplanza,** *f.* indisposition.

desteñir, *vti.* [9] & *vri.* to discolor, fade.

desternillarse (de risa), *vr.* to split one's sides with laughter.

desterrar, *vti.* [1] to banish, exile.—**desterrado,** *n.* exile, outcast.

destetar, *vt.* to wean.—**destete,** *m.* weaning.

destiempo, *adv.*—*a d.,* unseasonably, untimely, inopportunely.

destierro, *m.* exile.

destilar, *vt.* to distill; to filter.—*vi.* to distill, to drip, drop; to ooze.—**destilería,** *f.* distillery.

destinar, *vt.* to destine; to appoint; to assign.—**destinatario,** *n.* addressee; consignee.—**destino,** *m.* destiny; destination; employment.—*con d. a,* bound for, going to.

destitución, *f.* dismissal from employment, office or charge.—**destituir,** *vti.* [23-e] to dismiss from office.

destornillador, *m.* screwdriver.—**destornillar,** *vt.* to unscrew.

destrabar, *vt.* to loosen, to unfetter.

destreza, *f.* skill, dexterity, ability; nimbleness.

destripar, *vt.* to disembowel, gut; to smash, crush.

destrozar, *vti.* [a] to break into pieces, smash up.—**destrozo,** *m.* destruction; havoc.

destrucción, *f.* destruction.—**destructivo,** *a.* destructive.—**destructor,** *m.* destroyer.—*a.* destroying.—**destruir,**

vti. [23-e] to destroy; to ruin: to demolish, raze.

desunir, *vt.* to separate, take apart. —*vr.* to become separated.

desusado, *a.* unusual; obsolete, out of date.—**desuso,** *m.* disuse, obsoleteness.

desvalido, *a.* helpless, unprotected, unsheltered.

desvalijar, *vt.* to rob.

desván, *m.* attic; loft; garret.

desvanecer, *vti.* [3] to dispel; to fade; to cause to vanish.—*vri.* to vanish, disappear; to faint.

desvariar, *vi.* to rave, be delirious.—**desvarío,** *m.* delirium, raving; madness; absurdity.

desvelar, *vt.* to keep awake.—*vr.* to go without sleep; to pass a sleepless night; to be watchful or vigilant.—**desvelo,** *m.* insomnia, lack of sleep; watchfulness; anxiety, uneasiness.

desvencijado, *a.* ramshackle, rickety, loose-jointed.

desventaja, *f.* disadvantage.—**desventajoso,** *a.* disadvantageous.

desventura, *f.* misfortune, mishap.—**desventurado,** *a.* unfortunate, unlucky, faint-hearted.

desvergonzado, *a.* impudent; shameless.—**desvergüenza,** *f.* impudence; shamelessness.

desvestir, *vti.* [29] & *vri.* to undress.

desviación, *f.* deviation.—**desviadero,** *m.* (RR.) siding.—**desviar,** *vt.* to deflect; to sway; to dissuade; (fencing) to ward off; (RR.) to switch.—*vr.* to turn aside; to deviate; to swerve; to drift (away from).—**desvío,** *m.* deviation, turning away; coldness, indifference; (RR.) siding, side track.

desvirtuar, *vt.* to impair; to lessen the merit of; to detract from the value of.

desvivirse, *vr.* **(por)** to have excessive fondness (for); to do one's utmost (in behalf of); to be dying (for, to).

detallar, *vt.* to detail, relate minutely; to specify; to retail.—**detalle,** *m.* detail, particular; (com.) retail.—**detallista,** *mf.* (com.) retailer; one addicted to details (painter, etc.).

detective, *mf.* detective.—**detector,** *m.* (elec., radio) detector.

detención, *f.* delay, stop; arrest.—**detener,** *vti.* [42] to stop, detain; to arrest; to retain, reserve.—*vri.* to tarry, stay; to stop, halt; to pause.—**detenimiento,** *m.* care, thoroughness.

detergente, *a.* & *m.* detergent.

deteriorar, *vt. & vr.* to deteriorate, spoil, wear out.—**deterioro**, *m.* deterioration, damage, wear and tear.

determinación, *f.* determination; resolution; firmness.—**determinado**, *a.* determined, decided; resolute, purposeful; settled, definite.—**determinar**, *vt.* to determine, fix; to limit; to specify; to distinguish, discern; to assign (as time and place); to resolve, decide.—*vr.* to determine, resolve; to make up one's mind.

detestable, *a.* detestable, hateful.—**detestar**, *vt.* to detest.

detonación, *f.* detonation.—**detonante**, *a.* detonating.—**detonar**, *vi.* to detonate, explode.

detracción, *f.* detraction, defamation.—**detractor**, *n. & a.* detractor, slanderer.—*a.* detracting.

detrás, *adv.* behind; back, in the rear.—*d. de,* behind, in back of.—*por d.,* from the rear, from behind; behind one's back.

detrimento, *m.* detriment, damage.

deuda, *f.* debt; indebtedness.—**deudo**, *m.* relative, kinsman.—**deudor**, *n. & a.* debtor; indebted.

devanar, *vt.* to reel, wind.—*devanarse los sesos,* to rack one's brain.

devaneo, *m.* delirium, giddiness; frenzy; dissipation; love affair.

devastación, *f.* devastation, destruction.—**devastador**, *n. & a.* devastator; devastating.—**devastar**, *vt.* to devastate, ruin, lay waste.

devengar, *vti.* [b] to earn, draw (as salary, interest, etc.)

devenir, *vii.* [45] to become; to happen; to befall.

devoción, *f.* devotion, piety; faithful attachment.—**devocionario**, *m.* prayer book.

devolución, *f.* return, restitution; devolution.—**devolver**, *vti.* [47-49] to return, give back; to restore; to pay back.

devorador, *n.* devourer.—*a.* devouring, ravenous.—**devorar**, *vt.* to devour, swallow up, gobble, wolf.

devoto, *a.* devout, pious; devoted.

devuelto, *pp.* of **DEVOLVER.**

día, *m.* day.—*al d.,* up to date; by the day.—*a los pocos días,* a few days later.—*al otro d.,* on the following day.—*de d.,* by day.—*d. de fiesta* or *festivo,* holiday.—*el d. menos pensado,* when least expected. —*el mejor d.,* some fine day.—*en su d.,* at the proper time.—*hoy (en) d.,* nowadays.—*un d. sí y otro no,* every other day.

diablo, *m.* devil.—**diablura**, *f.* devil-

try, mischief, wild prank.—**diabólico**, *a.* diabolical, devilish.

diácono, *m.* deacon.

diafragma, *m.* diaphragm.

diagnosticar, *vti.* [d] to diagnose.—**diagnóstico**, *m.* diagnosis.—*a.* diagnostic.

diagonal, *a.* diagonal; oblique.—*f.* (geom.) diagonal.

diagrama, *m.* diagram.

dialecto, *m.* dialect.

dialogar, *vii.* [b] to dialogize; to chat, converse.—**diálogo**, *m.* dialogue.

diamante, *m.* diamond.

diámetro, *m.* diameter.

diana, *f.* target, bull's eye; reveille.

diapasón, *m.* tuning fork.

diapositiva, *f.* lantern slide; (phot.) plate.

diario, *a.* daily.—*m.* journal, diary; daily newspaper; daily expense.—*a d.,* daily, every day.

diarrea, *f.* diarrhea.

dibujante, *mf.* designer, draftsman.—**dibujar**, *vt.* to draw, sketch; to depict.—**dibujo**, *m.* drawing; sketch; delineation.

dicción, *f.* diction.—**diccionario**, *m.* dictionary.

diciembre, *m.* December.

dictado, *m.* dictation.—*pl.* dictates, promptings.—**dictador**, *n.* dictator.—**dictadura**, *f.* dictatorship.—**dictamen**, *m.* judgment, opinion.—**dictaminar**, *vi.* to express an opinion, pass judgment.—**dictar**, *vt.* to dictate.

dicterio, *m.* taunt; insult.

dicha, *f.* happiness; good luck.

dicharachero, *a.* witty; wisecracking.—**dicharacho**, *m.* smart remark; wisecrack.—**dicho**, *pp.* of DECIR.—*a.* (the) said, mentioned; this.—*m.* saying, proverb.

dichoso, *a.* lucky, fortunate; happy.

diente, *m.* tooth; tusk.—*decir* or *hablar entre dientes,* to mumble, to mutter.—*de dientes afuera,* without sincerity, as mere lip service.

diestra, *f.* right hand.—**diestro**, *m.* bullfighter.—*a.* skillful, able; right.

dieta, *f.* diet; traveling allowance.

diezmar, *vt.* to decimate.—**diezmo**, *m.* tithe.

diferencia, *f.* difference; disagreement.—**diferenciación**, *f.* differentiation.—**diferenciar**, *vt.* to differentiate, distinguish between.—*vi.* to differ, disagree.—*vr.* to be different. —**diferente**, *a.* different.

diferir, *vti.* [39] to defer, postpone; to procrastinate.—*vii.* to differ.

difícil, *a.* difficult, hard.—**dificultad**, *f.* difficulty.—**dificultar**, *vt.* to make

difficult; to impede.—**dificultoso**, *a.* difficult, hard.

difteria, *f.* diphtheria.

difundir, *vt. & vr.* to diffuse, spread out; to spread (as news); to divulge, publish; to broadcast.

difunto, *a.* defunct, dead.—*n.* corpse.

difusión, *f.* diffusion; diffusiveness, dispersion; broadcasting.—**difuso**, *a.* diffuse; wordy; widespread.

digerir, *vti.* [39] to digest.—**digestión**, *f.* digestion.

dignarse, *vr.* to condescend.—**dignatario**, *n.* dignitary.—**dignidad**, *f.* dignity; high rank; stateliness.—**digno**, *a.* meritorious, worthy; fitting, appropriate.

digresión, *f.* digression.

dije, *m.* trinket; locket; charm.

dilación, *f.* delay.

dilapidación, *f.* dilapidation; squandering.—**dilapidar**, *vt.* to dilapidate; to squander.

dilatación, *f.* dilatation, expansion; enlargement.—**dilatado**, *a.* vast, extensive; drawn out.—**dilatar**, *vt. & vr.* to dilate; to prolong; to retard, delay.

dilema, *m.* dilemma.

diligencia, *f.* diligence; activity; stagecoach; errand; judicial proceeding.—*hacer d.*, or *la d.*, to try.—**diligente**, *a.* diligent; prompt, swift.

diluir, *vti. & vri.* [23-e] to dilute.

diluvio, *m.* flood; deluge.

dimanar, *vi.* (de) to spring or flow (from); to originate (in).

dimensión, *f.* dimension; extent, size.

diminución, *f.* diminution.—**diminutivo**, *a.* diminishing; diminutive.—*m.* (gram.) diminutive.—**diminuto**, *a.* tiny.

dimisión, *f.* resignation (from post).—**dimitir**, *vt.* to resign, give up (post).

dinamarqués, *n. & a.* Dane, Danish.

dinámico, *a.* dynamic, energetic.

dinamita, *f.* dynamite.

dinamo, dínamo, *f.* (gen. *m.* in Am.) dynamo.

dinastía, *f.* dynasty.

dineral, *m.* a lot of money.—**dinero**, *m.* money; currency; wealth.—*d. contante y sonante*, ready money, cash.—*d. suelto*, small change.

dintel, *m.* lintel, doorhead.

diócesis, *f.* diocese.

dios, *m.* god; (D.) God.—*D. mediante*, God willing.—¡*D. mío!* my God!—**diosa**, *f.* goddess.

diploma, *m.* diploma; bull, patent, license; title.—**diplomacia**, *f.* diplomacy.—**diplomático**, *a.* diplomatic.—*n.* diplomat.

diptongo, *m.* diphthong.

diputado, *n.* deputy, representative, delegate; assignee.

dique, *m.* dike; dry dock; check, restraint.

dirección, *f.* direction, course; management; postal address; office of a director.—**directivo**, *a.* directive, managing.—*f.* governing board, board of directors, management.—*n.* member of a board of directors; officer of a society, club, etc.—**directo**, *a.* direct; straight.—**director**, *n. & a.* director; directing.—*n.* director, manager; chief; editor (of a newspaper); principal (of a school); conductor (of an orchestra).—**directorio**, *a.* directive, directorial.—*m.* directory; directorate.—**dirigente**, *a.* directing, leading, ruling.—*mf.* leader.—**dirigir**, *vti.* [c] to direct; to address (a letter, etc.); to command; to govern, manage.—*vri.* (a) to address, speak (to); to apply, resort (to); to go (to or toward).

dirimir, *vt.* to solve (a difficulty); to settle (a controversy).

discar, *vti.* [d] (tel.) to dial.

discernimiento, *m.* discernment, judgment.—**discernir**, *vii.* [16] to discern, discriminate.

disciplina, *f.* discipline, training; obedience; rule of conduct; any art or science.—*pl.* whip, scourge.—**disciplinar**, *vt.* to discipline, educate; to drill.

discípulo, *n.* disciple, follower; pupil.

disco, *m.* disk; phonograph record; dial of telephone.

díscolo, *a.* ungovernable; undisciplined.

disconforme, *a.* discordant, disagreeing.—**disconformidad**, *f.* non-conformity; disparity; disagreement.

discontinuo, *a.* discontinuous.

discordancia, *f.* disagreement, discord; maladjustment.—**discordante**, *a.* discordant, dissonant.—**discordar**, *vii.* [12] to be in discord, disagree.—**discorde**, *a.* discordant; dissonant.—**discordia**, *f.* discord, disagreement.

discreción, *f.* discretion; prudence; liberty of action and decision.—*a d.*, at will, unconditionally.

discrepancia, *f.* discrepancy.—**discrepante**, *a.* disagreeing, differing.—**discrepar**, *vi.* to differ, disagree.

discreto, *a.* discreet, prudent, unobtrusive; fairly good.

discriminar, *vt.* to discriminate.

disculpa, *f.* apology, excuse.—**disculpable**, *a.* excusable; pardonable.—**disculpar**, *vt. & vr.* to exculpate

(oneself); to excuse (oneself); to apologize.

discurrir, *vi.* to roam, ramble about; to flow (as a river); to reflect, think; to discourse.—*vt.* to invent; to infer.

discurso, *m.* speech; dissertation; space of time; discourse.

discusión, *f.* discussion.—**discutible,** *a.* controvertible, disputable.—**discutidor,** *n.* & *a.* arguer; arguing.—**discutir,** *vt.* & *vi.* to discuss; to argue.

disecación, *f.* = DISECCION.—**disecar,** *vti.* [d] to dissect; to stuff (dead animals).—**disección,** *f.* dissection; anatomy.

diseminación, *f.* scattering, spreading.—**diseminar,** *vt.* to spread, scatter.

disensión, *f.* dissent; contest, strife.

disentería, *f.* dysentery.

disentir, *vii.* [39] to dissent, disagree, differ.

diseñador, *n.* designer, delineator.—**diseñar,** *vt.* to draw; to sketch, outline.—**diseño,** *m.* design, sketch, outline; description.

disertación, *f.* dissertation.—**disertar,** *vi.* (**sobre** or **acerca de**) to discourse (on), treat (of), discuss.

disforme, *a.* deformed; hideous; out of proportion.

disfraz, *m.* disguise, mask; costume; dissimulation.—**disfrazar,** *vti.* [a] to disguise; to misrepresent.—*vri.* to disguise oneself; to masquerade.

disfrutar, *vt.* to benefit by; to have the benefit of; to enjoy (good health, etc.).—*vi.* (**de**) to enjoy; to have.—**disfrute,** *m.* use, benefit.

disgregación, *f.* separation; dissociation.—**disgregar,** *vti.* [b] to separate, disperse.

disgustar, *vt.* to displease; to annoy; to offend.—*vr.* to be, or become displeased, hurt or annoyed; to fall out (with each other).—**disgusto,** *m.* disgust; affliction; displeasure; unpleasantness; quarrel; annoyance; grief.

disimular, *vt.* to dissimulate; to tolerate, overlook; to misrepresent.—**disimulo,** *m.* dissimulation; tolerance.

disipación, *f.* dissipation; waste.—**disipar,** *vt.* & *vr.* to dissipate; to vanish.—*vt.* to squander.

dislocación, *f.* dislocation; sprain.—**dislocar,** *vti.* [d] & *vri.* to dislocate, disjoint; to sprain.

disminución, *f.* diminution; retrenchment.—**disminuir,** *vti.* [23-e] to diminish, lessen; to detract from.—*vii.* to diminish, decrease.

disociación, *f.* separation, dissociation.—**disociar,** *vt.* to dissociate, separate.

disolución, *f.* dissolution; solution.—**disoluto,** *a.* dissolute.—**disolvente,** *m.* solvent.—**disolver,** *vti.* [47] to dissolve; to break up (as a meeting); to separate.—*vri.* to dissolve; to break up.

disonancia, *f.* harsh sound; discord; dissonance.—**disonante,** *a.* dissonant; discordant.

dispar, *a.* unlike; unequal; unmatched.

disparador, *m.* shooter; trigger; ratchet wheel.—**disparar,** *vt.* & *vi.* to shoot, discharge, fire; to throw, hurl.—*vr.* to dart off; to run away (as a horse); to go off (as a gun).

disparatar, *vi.* to talk nonsense; to blunder.—**disparate,** *m.* blunder; absurdity, nonsense.—**disparatero,** *n.* bungler.

disparejo, *a.* uneven.

disparidad, *f.* disparity, inequality.

disparo, *m.* shooting, discharge; shot; sudden dash.

dispendio, *m.* extravagance, prodigality.—**dispendioso,** *a.* costly; extravagant.

dispensa, *f.* exemption, dispensation.—**dispensar,** *vt.* to dispense; to excuse, pardon.—**dispensario,** *m.* dispensary; clinic.

dispersar, *vt.* to disperse, scatter, put to flight.—*vr.* to disperse, disband.—**disperso,** *a.* dispersed; scattered.

displicencia, *f.* disagreeableness; indifference.—**displicente,** *a.* disagreeable, unpleasant; peevish.

disponer, *vti.* [32-49] & *vii.* to dispose; to arrange; to resolve, direct, order.—*d. de,* to have at one's disposal.—*vri.* (**para** or **a**) to prepare oneself; to get ready (to); to make one's will.—**disponible,** *a.* available, disposable.—**disposición,** *f.* disposition, arrangement; disposal; aptitude; temper; proportion, order; specification.—**dispositivo,** *m.* device; mechanism; appliance.—**dispuesto,** *pp.* de DISPONER.—*a.* ready, disposed; fit; smart, clever; skillful.

disputa, *f.* dispute, controversy; debate.—**disputar,** *vt.* & *vi.* to dispute, debate, argue; to quarrel.

distancia, *f.* distance; interval; range.—*a d.,* from afar.—**distante,** *a.* distant, far.—**distar,** *vi.* to be distant; to be different.

distender, *vti.* [18] & *vri.* to distend, to expand.—**distensión,** *f.* distention, expansion.

distinción, *f.* distinction; honor, award.—**distinguir,** *vti.* [b] to distinguish, tell apart; to see clearly at a distance, make out, spot; to esteem.—*vri.* to distinguish oneself, to excel; **(de)** to differ, be distinguished.—**distintivo,** *a.* distinctive.—*m.* distinctive mark; badge, insignia.—**distinto,** *a.* distinct; clear; different.

distracción, *f.* absent-mindedness; lack of attention; pastime; oversight.—**distraer,** *vti.* [43] to distract; to amuse; to entertain; to lead astray.—*vri.* to be absentminded; to be inattentive; to amuse oneself.—**distraído,** *a.* inattentive; absent-minded.

distribución, *f.* distribution.—**distribuidor,** *n.* & *a.* distributor; distributing.—**distribuir,** *vti.* [23-e] to distribute, deal out; to sort (as mail).

distrito, *m.* district.

disturbio, *m.* disturbance.

disuelto, *pp.* of DISOLVER.—*a.* dissolved, melted.

disyuntiva, *f.* dilemma; alternative.

diurno, *a.* daily.

divagación, *f.* wandering, digression.—**divagar,** *vii.* [b] to roam, ramble; to digress.

diván, *m.* couch, divan.

divergencia, *f.* divergence, divergency.—**divergente,** *a.* divergent; dissenting.—**divergir,** *vii.* [c] to diverge; to dissent.

diversidad, *f.* diversity, variety.—**diversificar,** *vti.* [d] to diversify, vary.

diversión, *f.* entertainment, amusement.—**divertido,** *a.* amusing.—**divertir,** *vti.* [39] to amuse, entertain.—*vri.* to amuse oneself; to have a good time.

diverso, *a.* diverse, different; various.

dividendo, *m.* dividend.—**dividir,** *vt.* & *vi.* to divide.—*vr.* to divide; to split; to be divided; to separate (from), part company (with).

divinidad, *f.* divinity.—**divinizar,** *vti.* [a] to deify.—**divino,** *a.* divine.

divisa, *f.* badge, emblem.—*pl.* foreign currency.

divisar, *vt.* to sight, make out, perceive.

división, *f.* division; distribution; section; disunity.—**diviso,** *a.* divided, disunited.—**divisor,** *n.* divider.—*a.* dividing.

divorciar, *vt.* to divorce; to separate.—*vr.* to get divorced.—**divorcio,** *m.* divorce; breach.

divulgación, *f.* disclosure, divulgation; publication.—**divulgar,** *vti.*

[b] to divulge; to disclose; to publish; to popularize.—*vri.* to become widespread.

dobladillo, *m.* (sewing) hem, border; trousers cuff.—**doblar,** *vt.* to double; to fold; to crease; to bend; to subdue.—*d. la esquina,* to turn the corner.—*vi.* to toll the knell.—*vr.* to bend; to bow, stoop; to submit.—**doble,** *a.* double, twofold, duplicate; thick, heavy; thick-set, strong.—**doblegar,** *vti.* [b] to sway, dominate, force to yield; to fold, bend.—*vr.* to yield, give in; to fold, bend.—**doblez,** *m.* crease, fold.—*f.* double-dealing; hypocrisy.

docena, *f.* dozen.

docente, *a.* educational; teaching.

dócil, *a.* docile; obedient; pliable, malleable.—**docilidad,** *f.* docility, tameness.

docto, *a.* learned, well-informed.—**doctor,** *n.* (academic) doctor.—**doctorado,** *m.* doctorate.—**doctorar,** *vt.* to confer (*vr.* to obtain) the degree of doctor.

doctrina, *f.* doctrine.

documentación, *f.* documentation; documents.—**documentado,** *a.* documented; well-informed; having the necessary documents or vouchers.—**documental,** *a.* documentary.—**documento,** *m.* document.

dogal, *m.* halter; hangman's noose.

dogma, *m.* dogma, tenet.—**dogmático,** *a.* dogmatical or dogmatic.

dolencia, *f.* aching; disease, ailment.—**doler,** *vii.* [26] to pain, ache; to hurt, grieve.—*vri.* to repent; to regret; to be moved, take pity; to complain.—**doliente,** *a.* aching, suffering; sorrowful; sick.—*mf.* mourner; sick person.—**dolor,** *m.* pain, aching, ache; sorrow, affliction.—**dolorido,** *a.* doleful, afflicted; painful.—**doloroso,** *a.* painful; pitiful.

doma, *f.* breaking in (of a horse).—**domador,** *n.* horsebreaker, tamer.—**domar,** *vt.* to tame; to break in; to subdue.—**domeñar,** *vt.* to tame, subdue; to dominate.—**domesticar,** *vti.* [d] to domesticate.—*vri.* to become tame.—**doméstico,** *a.* domestic.—*n.* household servant.

domiciliar, *vt.* to lodge.—*vr.* to take up residence; to dwell, reside.—**domiciliario,** *a.* domiciliary.—**domicilio,** *m.* domicile; home; residence.

dominación, *f.* dominion, domination; rule; power.—**dominante,** *a.* domineering; prevailing; dominant.—**dominar,** *vt.* to dominate; to stand out above (as a hill); to master (a subject, language, etc.); to sub-

due, repress.—*vr.* to control oneself.

dominio, *m.* domain; dominion; power, authority.

domingo, *m.* Sunday.—**dominguero,** *a.* done on Sunday; pertaining to Sunday.—**dominical,** *a.* pertaining or relative to Sunday.—**dominicano,** *n.* & *a.* Dominican.

don, *m.* gift, present; natural gift, knack; Don (title for a gentleman, equivalent to Mr. or Esq. in English, used only when the given name is mentioned).

donación, *f.* donation; contribution.

donaire, *m.* gracefulness, gentility.—**donairoso,** *a.* graceful, elegant; witty.

donante, *mf.* & *a.* giver; giving.—**donar,** *vt.* to donate, bestow.—**donativo,** *m.* donation, gift.

doncella, *f.* maidservant; maiden.—*a.* virginal.—**doncellez,** *f.* maidenhood.

donde (*interr.* dónde), *adv.* where; wherein; in which; wherever.—*a d.,* where, whereto.—*¿de dónde?* where from, whence?—*¿en dónde?* where?.—*¿por dónde?* whereabout? by what way or road?—**dondequiera,** *adv.* anywhere; wherever.—*por d.,* everywhere, in every place.

Doña, *f.* title given to a lady, equivalent to the English Mrs. or Miss, used only when the given name is mentioned.

dorado, *a.* gilt, golden.—*m.* gilding.—**dorar,** *vt.* to gild; to palliate.

dormilón, *n.* (coll.) sleepy head.—**dormir,** [17] *vii.* to sleep.—*vri.* to go to sleep, fall asleep.—**dormitar,** *vi.* to doze, nap.—**dormitorio,** *m.* bedroom; dormitory.

dorsal, *a.* dorsal.—**dorso,** *m.* spine; back.

dosel, *m.* canopy; portiere.—**doselera,** *f.* valance.

dosificación, *f.* proportioning; dosage.—**dosificar,** *vti.* [d] to measure out the doses of.—**dosis** *f.* dose; quantity.

dotación, *f.* endowment, foundation; equipment; crew of warship; personnel (of office, etc.).—**dotado,** *a.* endowed with, gifted with.—**dotar,** *vt.* to bestow; to endow; to give a dowry to.—**dote,** *m.* & *f.* dowry.—*f. pl.* gifts, natural talents.

draga, *f.* dredge.—**dragado,** *m.* dredging.—**dragar,** *vti.* [b] to dredge.

drama, *m.* drama; play.—**dramático,** *a.* dramatic.—**dramatizar,** *vti.* [a] & *vii.* to dramatize.—**dramaturgo,** *n.* dramatist; playwright.

drenaje, *m.* drainage.—**drenar,** *vt.* to drain.

dril, *m.* drill, strong cloth.

droga, *f.* drug; medicine; trick.—**droguería,** *f.* drug store; drug trade.—**droguero,** *n.,* **droguista,** *mf.* druggist; impostor.

dúctil, *a.* ductile, malleable.

ducha, *f.* douche, shower bath.

ducho, *a.* skillful, expert.

duda, *f.* doubt.—**dudar,** *vi.* & *vt.* to doubt; to hesitate.—**dudoso,** *a.* doubtful, dubious; hazardous.

duelo, *m.* duel; sorrow, affliction; mourning; mourners; condolence.

duende, *m.* elf, hobgoblin.—**duendecillo,** *m.* pixie, little elf.

dueño, *n.* owner.

dueto, *m.* duet.

dulce, *a.* sweet; fresh (of water); pleasing; ductile (of metals).—*m.* confection, sweetmeat, candy.—**dulcería,** *f.* confectionery shop.—**dulcero,** *n.* confectioner.—**dulcificar,** *vti.* [d] to sweeten.

dulzaina, *f.* (mus.) recorder.

dulzón, *a.* saccharine.—**dulzura,** *f.* sweetness; kindliness.

duna, *f.* dune.

duplicación, *f.* duplication, doubling.—**duplicado,** *m.* copy, duplicate; counterpart.—*por d.,* in duplicate.—**duplicar,** *vti.* [d] to double, duplicate; to repeat.—**duplo,** *m.* double, twice as much.

duque, *m.* duke.—**duquesa,** *f.* duchess.

durabilidad, *f.* durability, permanence.—**durable,** *a.* durable, lasting.—**duración,** *f.* duration.—*ser de d.,* to wear well, last.—**duradero,** *a.* lasting, durable.—**durante,** *prep.* during.—**durar,** *vi.* to last; to endure; to wear well (of clothes).

durazno, *m.* peach; peach tree.

dureza, *f.* hardness, solidity; cruelty, unkindness.—**duro,** *a.* hard, steely; solid, firm; rigorous; rude.—*a duras penas,* with difficulty; scarcely.

durmiente, *a.* sleeping.—*mf.* sleeper.—*f.* (RR.) tie.

E

e, *conj.* and (used only before words that begin with *i* or *hi* not followed by *e*).

ebanista, *mf.* cabinetmaker.—**ebanistería,** *f.* cabinetwork.—**ébano,** *m.* ebony.

ebrio, *a.* intoxicated, drunk.

ebullición, *f.* boiling.

eclesiástico, *a.* ecclesiastical.—*m.* clergyman, priest.

eclipsar, *vt.* to eclipse; to outshine.—*vr.* to be eclipsed.—**eclipse,** *m.* eclipse.

eco, *m.* echo.—*hacer e.,* to become important or famous.

economía, *f.* economy.—*e. política,* economics.—*pl.* savings.—**económico,** *a.* economic(al); saving, thrifty.— **economista,** *mf.* economist.—**economizar,** *vti.* [a] to economize; to save.

ecuación, *f.* equation.

ecuador, *m.* equator.

ecuánime, *a.* equable, calm, serene.— **ecuanimidad,** *f.* equanimity.

ecuatoriano, *n.* & *a.* Ecuadorian.

echar, *vt.* to throw, cast; to expel; to dismiss, fire; to pour (as wine); to put (in, into); to turn (as a key); to give off, emit, eject; to bear (shoots, fruit); to play one's turn (in games).—*e. a,* to start, begin to.—*e. abajo,* to overthrow; to tear down, demolish.—*e. a perder,* to spoil, ruin.—*e. a pique,* to sink a ship.—*e. de menos,* to miss.—*e. de ver,* to notice.—*e. el bofe,* to work very hard.—*e. la cuenta,* to balance the account.—*e. mano,* to seize, grab.—*e. mano de,* to resort to.— *e. suertes,* to draw lots.—*vr.* to lie down; to throw oneself down.— *e. a perder,* to spoil; to become ruined.—*echárselas de,* to fancy oneself as.

edad, *f.* age.—*e. madura,* middle age. —*mayor de e.,* of (legal) age.— *menor de e.,* under age, minor.

edición, *f.* edition, issue; publication.

edicto, *m.* edict, proclamation.

edificación, *f.* edification; construction.—**edificante,** *a.* edifying; erecting.—**edificar,** *vti.* [d] & *vii.* to edify; to build, construct.—**edificio,** *m.* edifice, building, structure.

editar, *vt.* to publish.—**editor,** *n.* & *a.* publisher; publishing.—**editorial,** *mf.* & *a.* editorial.—*f.* publishing house.—*a.* publishing.

edredón, *m.* comforter, quilted blanket.

educación, *f.* education, upbringing; good breeding, politeness.—*e. física,* physical culture.—**educador,** *n.* & *a.* educator; educating.—**educar,** *vti.* [d] to educate, instruct, raise, train. —**educativo,** *a.* educational.

efectivo, *a.* effective; real, actual.— *hacer e.,* to cash (a check, etc.).— *m.* cash, specie.—*en e.,* in cash, in coin.—**efecto,** *m.* effect; impression; end, purpose.—*pl.* assets; goods; drafts.—*efectos públicos,* public securities.—*en e.,* as a matter of fact, actually.—*tener e.,* to become effective.—**efectuar,** *vt.* to effect, carry out, do, make.

eficacia, *f.* efficacy, efficiency.—**eficaz,** *a.* efficacious, effective, telling.— **eficiencia,** *f.* efficiency, effectiveness. —**eficiente,** *a.* efficient, effective.

efigie, *f.* effigy, image.

efusión, *f.* effusion, shedding; warmth of manner.—*e. de sangre,* bloodshed. —**efusivo,** *a.* effusive.

egipcio, *n.* & *a.* Egyptian.

egoísmo, *m.* selfishness.—**egoísta,** *a.* selfish.—*mf.* egoist.—**ególatra,** *mf.* = EGOTISTA.—**egolatría,** *f.* = EGOTISMO.—**egotismo,** *m.* egotism.— **egotista,** *mf.* & *a.* egostist; egotistic.

eje, *m.* axis; axle; (fig.) main point.

ejecución, *f.* execution; carrying out. —**ejecutar,** *vt.* to execute; to perform, carry out; (law) to levy, seize property.—**ejecutivo,** *a.* executive; executory.—*m.* executive (power or person).—**ejecutor,** *n.* executor; executer.—*e. de la justicia,* executioner. —**ejecutoria,** *f.* sentence, judgment; pedigree.

ejemplar, *a.* exemplary.—*m.* specimen, sample; copy.—**ejemplificar,** *vti.* [d] to be an example, typify.— **ejemplo,** *m.* example, instance.— *dar e.,* to set an example.

ejercer, *vti.* [a] to practice (a profession); to perform; to exert.— **ejercicio,** *m.* exercise; practice.— *e. fiscal,* fiscal year.—*hacer e.,* to exercise; (mil.) to drill.—**ejercitar,** *vt.* to exercise, to put into practice; to drill (troops); to train.—*vr.* to practice.—**ejército,** *m.* army.

ejido, *m.* common, public land.

ejote, *m.* (Mex.) stringbean.

el, *art. m. sing.* (*pl.* **los**) the.—**él,** *pron. m. sing.* (*pl.* **ellos**) he.

elaboración, *f.* elaboration, manufacture.—**elaborar,** *vt.* to elaborate; to manufacture.

elasticidad, *f.* elasticity.—**elástico,** *a.* elastic, springy.—*pl.* suspenders.

elección, *f.* election; choice.—**electivo,** *a.* elective.—**electo,** *ppi.* of ELEGIR.— *a.* elect, chosen.—**elector,** *n.* & *a.* elector; electing.—*m.* elector, voter. —**electorado,** *m.* electorate.—**electoral,** *a.* electoral.

electricidad, *f.* electricity.—**electricista,** *mf.* electrician.—**eléctrico,** *a.* electric(al).—**electrificación,** *f.* electrification.—**electrificar,** *vti.* [d] to electrify.—**electrización,** *f.* electrification.—**electrizar,** *vti.* [a] to electrify.—*vri.* to become electrified.— **electrocutar,** *vt.* to electrocute.— **electrón,** *m.* electron.—**electrónica,** *f.* electronics.—**electrotecnia,** *f.* electrical engineering.

elefante, *n.* elephant.

elegancia, *f.* elegance, gracefulness;

neatness.—**elegante**, a. elegant, stylish, graceful.

elegible, a. eligible.—**elegir**, vti. [29-49-c] to elect; to choose.

elemental, a. elemental, elementary; fundamental.—**elemento**, m. element. —pl. elements, rudiments.

elenco, m. (theat.) cast; catalogue.

elevación, f. elevation; altitude; rise; rapture.—**elevador**, m. (Am.) elevator, hoist.—**elevar**, vt. to raise, heave; to exalt.—vr. to rise, soar.

eliminación, f. elimination.—**eliminar**, vt. to eliminate.

elocución, f. elocution; effective diction, style.—**elocuencia**, f. eloquence. —**elocuente**, a. eloquent.

elogiar, vt. to praise, extol.—**elogio**, m. praise, eulogy.

elote, m. (Mex., C.A.) ear of green corn; corn on the cob.

eludir, vt. to elude, avoid.

ella, pron. f. sing. (pl. **ellas**) she.— **ello**, pron. neut. sing. it.—e. dirá, the event will tell.—e. es que, the fact is that.—**ellos**, pron. m. pl.; **ellas**, pron. f. pl. they.

emancipación, f. emancipation.— **emancipar**, vt. to emancipate.—vr. to free oneself; to become free or independent.

embadurnar, vt. to smear.

embajada, f. embassy; errand, mission.—**embajador**, n. ambassador.

embalador, n. packer.—**embalaje**, m. packing, baling.—**embalar**, vt. to bale, pack.

embaldosado, m. tile floor.—**embaldosar**, vt. to pave with tiles or flagstones.

embalsamamiento, m. embalming.— **embalsamar**, vt. to embalm; to perfume.

embalse, m. dam.

embarazada, a. pregnant.—**embarazar**, vti. [a] to embarrass, hinder; to make pregnant.—**embarazo**, m. impediment; embarrassment, confusion; perplexity; pregnancy.—**embarazoso**, a. embarrassing; entangled, cumbersome.

embarcación, f. boat, ship; embarkation.—**embarcadero**, m. wharf, pier. —**embarcador**, n. shipper.—**embarcar**, vti. [d] to ship; to embark.— vri. to embark; to board (ship or train).

embargar, vti. [b] to restrain, suspend; (law) to embargo, to seize.— **embargo**, m. embargo, seizure.— sin e., notwithstanding, however, nevertheless.

embarque, m. shipment (of goods).

embarrancar, vii. [d] & vri. to run aground.

embarrar, vt. to smear; to daub; to vilify.—vr. to be covered with mud; to lose one's self-respect.

embate, m. dashing of the waves; sudden impetuous attack.—embates de la fortuna, sudden reverses of fortune.

embaucador, n. impostor.—**embaucar**, vti. [d] to deceive, trick, fool.

embebecimiento, m. amazement; rapture; absorption.—**embeber**, vt. to imbibe, absorb; to soak.—vi. to shrink.—vr. to be enraptured; to be absorbed.

embelesamiento, m. rapture, ecstasy. —**embelesar**, vt. to charm, delight.— vr. to be charmed, or delighted.— **embeleso**, m. rapture, delight; charm.

embellecer, vti. [3] to beautify, embellish.—**embellecimiento**, m. embellishment, beautifying.

emberrenchinarse, **emberrincharse**, vr. (coll.) to throw a tantrum.

embestida, f. assault, violent attack, onset.—**embestir**, vti. [29] to assail, attack; to make a drive on.—vii. to attack, rush.

embetunar, vt. to blacken; to polish (shoes).

emblema, m. emblem, symbol.

embobar, vt. to enchant, fascinate.— vr. to be struck with astonishment.

embocadura, f. entrance by a narrow passage; mouthpiece of a wind instrument; mouth of a river.—**embocar**, vti. [d] to enter through a narrow passage.

emborrachar, vt. to intoxicate.—vr. to become intoxicated, get drunk.

émbolo, m. piston; (med.) embolus.

embolsar, vt. to put into a purse.— vr. to pocket, put into one's pocket.

emborronar, vt. to blot.—vt. & vi. to scribble.

emboscada, f. ambush, ambuscade.— **emboscar**, vti. [d] to place in ambush.—vri. to lie in ambush.

embotado, a. blunt, dull.—**embotamiento**, m. blunting; bluntness, dullness.—**embotar**, vt. to blunt, to dull (an edge or point); to enervate, debilitate; to dull.—vr. to become dull.

embotellar, vt. to bottle; to bottle up.

embozado, a. muffled, with face covered (with a cloak).—**embozar**, vti. [a] to muffle; to cloak; to muzzle.— vr. to muffle oneself up.

embragar, vti. [b] to throw in the clutch.—**embrague**, m. clutch; coupling.

embreado, a. tarry.—**embrear**, vt. to tar.

embriagador, *a.* spirituous, intoxicating; ravishing.—**embriagar,** *vti.* [b] to intoxicate; to enrapture.—*vri.* to get drunk.—**embriaguez,** *f.* intoxication, drunkenness; rapture.

embrión, *m.* embryo.

embrollar, *vt.* to entangle, mess up; to ensnare, embroil.—**embrollo,** *m.* tangle; trickery, deception; embroilment.

embromar, *vt.* to banter, tease; to vex, annoy; (Am.) to harm.—*vr.* to be annoyed, disgusted.

embrujar, *vt.* to bewitch.—**embrujo,** *m.* bewitchment.

embrutecer, *vti.* [3] to brutalize; to stupefy, stultify.—*vri.* to become brutalized; to grow stupid.

embudo, *m.* funnel.

embullar, *vt.* (Am.) to incite to revelry.—*vi.* (Am.) to make noise.—*vr.* (Am.) to revel, make merry.—**embullo,** *m.* (Am.) gaiety, revelry.

embuste, *m.* lie; trick, fraud.—**embustero,** *n.* liar; trickster, cheat.

embutido, *m.* sausage; inlaid work.—**embutir,** *vt.* to inlay, emboss; to insert; to stuff; (coll.) to cram; to eat much.

emergencia, *f.* emergence, emergency.—**emergente,** *a.* emergent, issuing.—**emerger,** *vii.* [c] to emerge, arise.

emigración, *f.* emigration.—**emigrado,** *n.* emigrant; emigré.—**emigrante,** *mf.* & *a.* emigrant.—**emigrar,** *vi.* to emigrate.

eminencia, *f.* eminence; height; outstanding person.—**eminente,** *a.* eminent; high, lofty.

emisario, *m.* emissary.—**emisión,** *f.* emission; issue (of paper money, bonds, etc.); radiation.—*emisiones radiofónicas,* broadcasting.—**emisor,** *a.* emitting; broadcasting.—*m.* radio transmitter.—*f.* broadcasting station.—**emitir,** *vt.* to emit, send forth; to issue (as bonds, etc.); to broadcast.

emoción, *f.* emotion.—**emocional,** *a.* emotional.—**emocionante,** *a.* moving, impressive, thrilling.—**emocionar,** *vt.* to touch, move, shock.—*vr.* to be moved, touched.—**emotivo,** *a.* moving, emotive.

empacador, *n.* packer.—**empacar,** *vti.* [d] to pack; to bale.—*vri.* (Am.) (coll.) to put on airs.

empachar, *vt.* to embarrass; to cram; to cause indigestion.—*vr.* to be embarrassed; to suffer indigestion.—**empacho,** *m.* bashfulness; embarrassment; indigestion.—*sin e.,* without ceremony; unconcernedly.

empadronar, *vt.* to register, take the census of.

empalagar, *vti.* [b] to pall, cloy; to bother.—**empalagoso,** *a.* cloying, too rich or sweet; wearisome, boresome.

empalizada, *f.* palisade, stockade.

empalmar, *vt.* to couple, join; to splice.—*vi.* (RR.) to branch; to join.—**empalme,** *m.* joint, connection; (RR.) junction.

empanada, *f.* meat pie.—**empanadilla,** *f.* small meat pie.—**empanar,** *vt.,* **empanizar,** *vti.* [a] to bread.

empañar, *vt.* to dim, blur, mist; to soil (reputation).

empapar, *vt.* to imbibe; to soak, drench.—*vr.* (en) to imbibe; to be soaked (in); to steep oneself (in).

empapelador, *n.* paperhanger.—**empapelar,** *vt.* to paper; to wrap up in paper.

empaque, *m.* packing; appearance, air; (Am.) boldness, impudence.—**empaquetador,** *n.* packer.—**empaquetadura,** *f.* packing; gasket.—**empaquetar,** *vt.* to pack; to stuff.—*vr.* to dress up.

emparedado, *a.* & *n.* recluse.—*m.* sandwich.—**emparedar,** *vt.* to wall, shut up.

emparejar, *vt.* & *vi.* to level, smooth; to match.

emparentar, *vii.* [1] to become related by marriage.

emparrado, *m.* vine arbor.

empastar, *vt.* to fill a tooth; to paste; to bind books.—**empaste,** *m.* filling (of a tooth); binding.

empatar, *vt.* to equal; to tie (in voting or games); (Am.) to join, tie.—**empate,** *m.* tie (in voting or games); joint.

empecinado, *a.* stubborn.—**empecinarse,** *vr.* (en) to persist (in), be stubborn (about).

empedernido, *a.* hard-hearted; hardened.

empedrado, *m.* stone pavement.—**empedrar,** *vti.* [1] to pave with stones.

empeine, *m.* instep.

empellón, *m.* jostle, shove.—*a empellones,* pushing, by pushing rudely.

empeñado, *a.* determined, persistent.—**empeñar,** *vt.* to pawn; to pledge; to engage.—*vr.* (en) to persist (in); to insist; to begin (a battle); to go into debt.—**empeño,** *m.* pledge, pawn; engagement; earnest desire; persistence; determination.—*casa de empeños,* pawnshop.—*con e.,* eagerly.

empeoramiento, *m.* deterioration.—**empeorar,** *vt.* to impair; to make worse.—*vi.* & *vr.* to grow worse.

empequeñecer, *vti.* [3] to make smaller, diminish; to belittle.

emperador, *m.* emperor.—**emperatriz,** *f.* empress.

emperchar, *vt.* to hang on a perch.—*vr.* (coll.) to dress up.

emperejilar, emperifollar, *vt.* & *vr.* to dress elaborately, to doll up.

emperramiento, *m.* obstinacy.—**emperrarse,** *vr.* (en) (coll.) to be obstinate or stubborn (about).

empezar, *vti.* [1-a] & *vii.* to begin.

empicotar, *vt.* to pillory; to picket.

empinado, *a.* steep; high, lofty.—**empinar,** *vt.* to raise; to tip, incline.—*e. el codo,* to drink heavily.—*vr.* to stand on tiptoe; to tower, rise high; (aer.) to zoom.

emplasto, *m.* plaster, poultice.

emplazamiento, *m.* (law) summons.—**emplazar,** *vti.* [a] to summon.

empleado, *n.* employee.—**emplear,** *vt.* to employ; to engage, hire.—*vr.* to be employed.—**empleo,** *m.* employ, employment, job; use.

emplomar, *vt.* to lead; to put lead seals on.

emplumar, *vt.* to feather; to tar and feather.

empobrecer, *vti.* [3] to impoverish.—*vri.* to become poor.—**empobrecimiento,** *m.* impoverishment.

empolvar, *vt.* & *vr.* to cover with dust; to powder.

empollar, *vt.* to hatch, brood.

emponzoñamiento, *m.* poisoning.—**emponzoñar,** *vt.* to poison; to corrupt.

empotrar, *vt.* to embed; to fix in a wall; to splice.

emprendedor, *n.* & *a.* enterpriser; enterprising.—**emprender,** *vt.* to undertake, engage in.—*e. a,* or *con,* to address, accost.

empreñar, *vt.* to make pregnant.

empresa, *f.* enterprise, undertaking; company, firm; management of a theater.—**empresario,** *n.* promoter; contractor; theatrical manager; impresario.

empréstito, *m.* loan.—*e. público,* government loan.

empujar, *vt.* to push, impel, shove.—**empuje,** *m.* push, shove; energy; (eng.) thrust.—**empujón,** *m.* push, violent shove.—*a empujones,* pushing, jostling.

empuñadura, *f.* hilt (of a sword); handle, grip.—**empuñar,** *vt.* to clinch, grip.

emulsión, *f.* emulsion.—**emulsionar,** *vt.* to emulsify.

en, *prep.* in; at; on, upon; to; into.

enagua(s), *f.* petticoat, slip.

enajenación, *f.,* **enajenamiento,** *m.* alienation (of property); absence of mind; rapture.—*e. mental,* mental derangement.—**enajenar,** *vt.* to alienate; to transfer (property); to transport, enrapture.—*vr.* to be enraptured.

enaltecer, *vti.* [3] to extol, exalt.

enamoradizo, *a.* inclined to fall in love.—**enamorado,** *a.* fond of lovemaking; in love, enamored.—*n.* lover; sweetheart.—**enamoramiento,** *m.* love, being in love; courting, love-making.—**enamorar,** *vt.* to inspire love in; to make love to, woo.—*vr.* to fall in love.—**enamoriscarse,** *vri.* [d] (coll.) to become infatuated.

enano, *a.* dwarfish, small.—*n.* dwarf.

enarbolar, *vt.* to hoist, raise high, hang out (a flag, etc.).

enardecer, *vti.* [3] to fire with passion, excite, inflame.—*vri.* to be kindled, get excited, inflamed (with passion).—**enardecimiento,** *m.* ardor; passion; inflaming; excitement.

encabezamiento, *m.* headline, heading, title; tax roll.—**encabezar,** *vti.* [a] to draw up (a tax roll); to put a heading or title to; to head, lead.

encabritarse, *vr.* to rear, rise up on the hind legs.

encadenamiento, *m.* chaining; linking.—**encadenar,** *vt.* to chain; to enslave; to link together (as thoughts).

encajar, *vt.* to fit in, insert, adjust; to join.—*vi.* to fit snugly; to fit, suit, be appropriate.—*vr.* to intrude; to squeeze oneself in.—**encaje,** *m.* lace, inlaid work; adjusting, fitting or joining together; socket.

encajonar, *vt.* to box; to case; to narrow.

encallar, *vi.* to run aground.

encallecer, *vti.* [3] & *vii.* to get corns or calluses.—*vri.* to become hardened or callous.

encaminar, *vt.* to guide; to direct.—*vr.* (a) to take the road (to); to be on the way (to).

encandilar, *vt.* to dazzle; to daze, bewilder; (coll.) to stir (the fire).

encanecer, *vii.* [3] to grow grayhaired; to grow old.

encanijamiento, *m.* frailty, lack of development.—**encanijar,** *vt.* to weaken (a baby) by poor nursing.—*vr.* to pine; to become emaciated.

encantado, *a.* enchanted, delighted, charmed; haunted.—**encantador,** *n.* charmer; enchanter.—*a.* charming; delightful.—**encantamiento,** *m.* enchantment.—**encantar,** *vt.* to enchant, charm; to delight; to bewitch.—**encanto,** *m.* enchantment, charm; delight.

encañonar, *vt.* to level a gun at.

encapotamiento, *m.* cloudiness.—**encapotarse,** *vr.* to become cloudy.

encapricharse, *vr.* to indulge in whims; to be stubborn.

encaramar, *vt.* & *vr.* to raise; to elevate; to extol; to climb; to perch upon.

encarar, *vi.* to face.—*vt.* to aim.—*vr.* (con) to face, be face to face.

encarcelación, *f.,* **encarcelamiento,** *m.* imprisonment.—**encarcelar,** *vt.* to imprison.

encarecer, *vti.,* [3] *vii.* & *vri.* to raise the price; to extol; to enhance.—**encarecidamente,** *adv.* eagerly, earnestly.—**encarecimiento,** *m.* enhancement.

encargado, *a.* in charge.—*n.* person in charge; agent; foreman; (E.U.) superintendent.—**encargar,** *vti.* [b] to entrust, put under the care (of a person); to order (goods, etc.).—*vri.* to take charge.—**encargo,** *m.* charge, commission; errand; assignment; (com.) order.

encariñamiento, *m.* fondness, attachment.—**encariñarse,** *vr.* (con) to become fond (of).

encarnación, *f.* incarnation; personification.—**encarnado,** *a.* incarnate; flesh-colored; red.—**encarnar,** *vi.* to become incarnate.—*vt.* to incarnate; to embody; to bait (a fishhook).

encarnizado, *a.* bloody; fierce, hard-fought.—**encarnizarse,** *vri.* [a] to become enraged; to fight with fury.—*e. con* or *en,* to be merciless to; to treat inhumanely.

encarrilar, *vt.* to put on the right track; to set right.

encasillar, *vt.* to pigeonhole; to include in a list of (candidates).

encasquetar, *vt.* & *vr.* to pull down (one's hat) tight.

encasquillar, *vr.* to stick, get stuck (a bullet in a gun).

encastillado, *a.* lofty, haughty.—**encastillarse,** *vr.* to shut oneself up in a castle; to be unyielding or headstrong.

encausar, *vt.* to prosecute, indict.

encauzar, *vti.* [a] to channel; to conduct through channels; to guide, direct.

encenagarse, *vri.* [b] to wallow in dirt, mire, or vice.

encendedor, *m.* (cigarette, etc.) lighter.—**encender,** *vti.* [18] to light, kindle.—*vri.* to take fire; to light up.—**encendido,** *a.* inflamed; red.—*m.* (engine) ignition.

encerado, *a.* waxed; wax-colored.—*m.* oilcloth; tarpaulin; blackboard.—**encerar,** *vt.* to wax.

encerrar, *vti.* [1] to lock or shut up; to confine; to contain, involve.—*vri.* to live in seclusion; to be locked up.—**encerrona,** *f.* allurement.

encía, *f.* gum (of the mouth).

enciclopedia, *f.* encyclopedia.

encierro, *m.* confinement; act of closing or locking up; retreat; prison; fold (of cattle).

encima, *adv.* above; at the top; overhead; over and above, besides; in addition, to boot.—*e. de,* on, upon.—*por e.,* superficially, hastily.—*por e. de,* over, above; regardless of.

encina, *f.* evergreen oak, live oak.

encinta, *a.* pregnant.

encintado, *m.* sidewalk curb.

enclenque, *a.* weak, feeble, sickly.

encoger, *vti.* [c] to contract, shorten, shrink.—*vri.* to shrink; to shrivel.—*encogerse de hombros,* to shrug the shoulders.—**encogimiento,** *m.* contraction, shrinkage; bashfulness.

encolado, *m.,* **encoladura,** *f.* gluing; priming, sizing.—**encolar,** *vt.* to glue; to stick.

encolerizar, *vti.* [a] to anger.—*vri.* to become angry.

encomendar, *vti.* [1] to entrust, commend.—*vri.* to entrust oneself; to pray.

encomiar, *vt.* to praise, eulogize.—**encomio,** *m.* praise, testimonial, eulogy.

encomienda, *f.* commission, charge.—*e. postal,* (Am.) parcel post.

enconar, *vt.* to inflame; to infect.—*vr.* to rankle; to fester, become infected.—**encono,** *m.* rancor, ill-will; soreness; sore spot.

encontrado, *a.* opposite; in front; opposed.—**encontrar,** *vti.* [12] to find; to meet.—*vii.* to meet; to collide.—*vri.* to meet; to collide; to be, find oneself; to feel (app. to health); to be opposed to each other; to conflict; to find; (con) to meet, come across or upon.—**encontronazo,** *m.* collision; bump.

encopetado, *a.* presumptuous; of high social standing.

encordar, *vti.* [12] to string (instruments); to lash or bind with ropes.

encorvar, *vt.* & *vr.* to bend, curve.

encrespamiento, *m.* curling; fury, roughness (of the sea, etc.).—**encrespar,** *vt.* to curl; to set (the hair) on end; to ruffle (the feathers).—*vr.* to become rough (the sea, the waves).

encrucijada, *f.* crossroads, ambush.

encuadernación, *f.* binding (books); bindery.—**encuadernador,** *n.* book-

binder.—**encuadernar**, *vt.* to bind (books).

encubierto, *ppi.* of ENCUBRIR.—**encubridor**, *n. & a.* concealer; concealing; accomplice.—**encubrimiento**, *m.* concealment.—**encubrir**, *vti.* [49] to conceal, hide, cloak.

encuentro, *m.* encounter, meeting; collision, clash; find, finding; (mil.) encounter, fight.—*salir al e. de*, to go to meet; to encounter.

encumbrado, *a.* high, elevated; lofty. **encumbramiento**, *m.* elevation, exaltation; height, eminence.—**encumbrar**, *vt.* to raise, elevate.—*vi.* to ascend.—*vr.* to rise; to be proud, rate oneself high.

encurtido, *m.* pickle.—**encurtir**, *vt.* to pickle.

enchapado, *m.* veneer; plates or sheets forming a cover or lining.—**enchapar**, *vt.* to veneer; to cover with metal plates or sheets.

encharcarse, *vri.* [d] to form puddles.

enchilada, *f.* (Mex.) pancake of maize with chili.

enchufar, *vt. & vr.* to plug in; to fit (a tube) into another; to telescope.—**enchufe**, *m.* socket joint; sliding of one thing into another; (elec.) plug; socket; outlet.

endeble, *a.* feeble, weak; flimsy.

endemoniado, *a.* devilish, fiendish, perverse.—**endemoniar**, *vt. & vr.* (coll.) to irritate.

endentado, *a.* serrated.—**endentar**, *vti.* [1] & *vii.* to gear, engage.

enderezamiento, *m.* straightening; setting right.—**enderezar**, *vti.* [a] to straighten; to right, set right.—*vri.* to straighten up.

endeudarse, *vr.* to contract debts.

endiablado, *a.* devilish, diabolical; perverse, wicked.

endilgar, *vti.* [b] to spring something on (a person).

endiosar, *vt.* to deify.—*vr.* to be elated with pride.

endosar, *vt.* to indorse (a draft, etc.).—**endosatario**, *n.* indorsee.—**endose**, **endoso**, *m.* indorsement.

endulzar, *vti.* [a] to sweeten; to soften.

endurecer, *vti.* [3] & *vri.* to harden; to inure.—**endurecido**, *a.* hard, hardy; inured.—**endurecimiento**, *m.* hardness; hardening; hard-heartedness.

enema, *m.* enema.

enemigo, *a.* hostile; inimical.—*n.* enemy, foe —*m.* (mil) enemy.—*el e. malo*, the devil.—**enemistad**, *f.* enmity, hatred.—**enemistar**, *vt.* to make enemies of.—*vr.* (con) to become an enemy (of); to fall out (with).

energía, *f.* energy; power.—**enérgico**, *a.* energetic, lively.

energúmeno, *n.* violent, impulsive person; person possessed with a devil.

enero, *m.* January.

enervar, *vt.* to enervate, weaken.—*vr.* to become weak.

enfadar, *vt.* to vex, anger.—*vr.* to become angry.—**enfado**, *m.* vexation, anger; trouble, drudgery.—**enfadoso**, *a.* annoying, troublesome.

enfangar, *vti.* [b] & *vri.* to soil with mud; (coll.) to soil one's reputation.—*vr.* to sink (into vice, etc.).

enfardar, *vt.* to pack, bale.

énfasis, *m.* emphasis.—**enfático**, *a.* emphatic; bombastic.

enfermar, *vi.* (Am. *vr.*) to fall ill, be taken ill.—*vt.* to make ill.—**enfermedad**, *f.* illness, sickness.—**enfermera**, *f.* nurse.—**enfermería**, *f.* infirmary, sanitarium.—**enfermero**, *m.* male nurse.—**enfermizo**, *a.* sickly; unhealthful.—**enfermo**, *a.* ill, sick.—*n.* patient.

enfiestarse, *vr.* (Am.) to have a good time; to go on a spree.

enfilar, *vt.* to place in a row or line.

enflaquecer, *vti.* [3] to make thin or lean.—*vii. & vri.* to become thin, lose weight; to weaken.—**enflaquecimiento**, *m.* loss of flesh; thinness.

enfocar, *vti.* [d] to focus, focus on.—**enfoque**, *m.* focusing; approach (to a problem, etc.).

enfrascarse, *vri.* [d] to be entangled or involved; to be absorbed, engrossed (in work, affairs, etc.).

enfrentar, *vt.* to confront, put face to face; to face.—*vr.* to confront, face, meet face to face.—*e. con*, to face; to oppose.—**enfrente**, *adv.* opposite, in front.—*de e.*, opposite, across (the street, etc.).

enfriamiento, *m.* refrigeration; cooling; cold, chill (illness).—**enfriar**, *vt.* to cool.—*vr.* to cool; to cool off or down; to become chilled.

enfundar, *vt.* to case, put into a case (as a pillow); to fill up, stuff.

enfurecer, *vti.* [3] to enrage, make furious.—*vri.* to rage; to become furious or stormy.

enfurruñarse, *vr.* (coll.) to become angry; to grumble.

engalanar, *vt.* to adorn, deck; (naut.) to dress.—*vr.* to dress up, doll up.

engallado, *a.* erect, upright; haughty.—**engallarse**, *vr.* to draw oneself up arrogantly.

enganchar, *vt.* to hook, hitch; to ensnare; to press into military service.

—*vr.* to engage; to enlist in the army.—**enganche,** *m.* hooking; enlistment in the army.

engañador, *n. & a.* deceiver; deceiving.—**engañar,** *vt.* to deceive; to cheat; to fool, hoax; to while away (time).—*vr.* to deceive oneself; to make a mistake, be mistaken.—**engaño,** *m.* deceit, fraud; hoax; mistake, misunderstanding.—**engañoso,** *a.* deceitful, artful, misleading.

engarce, *m.* linking; setting (of precious stone).

engarzar, *vti.* [a] to link; to set (precious stone).

engarrotarse, *vr.* to become numb with cold; (fig.) to be very cold, frozen.

engastar, *vt.* to set (jewels).—**engaste,** *m.* setting (of stones).

engatusar, *vt.* (coll.) to inveigle, wheedle, cajole.

engendrar, *vt.* to father, sire, engender, generate, procreate; to bear.—**engendro,** *m.* shapeless embryo; badly-made thing.

englobar, *vt.* to inclose, embody.

engolfarse, *vr.* to become engrossed, absorbed into.

engomar, *vt.* to gum, to size; to glue.

engordar, *vt.* to fatten.—*vi. &* (Am.) *vr.* to become fat.

engorro, *m.* embarrassment, nuisance.—**engorroso,** *a.* troublesome, annoying.

engranaje, *m.* gear, gearing.—**engranar,** *vi.* to gear; to interlock.

engrandecer, *vti.* [8] to aggrandize; to enlarge; to exalt, extol; to magnify.—**engrandecimiento,** *m.* increase, enlargement; exaltation.

engrasador, *m.* oiler, lubricator.—**engrasar,** *vt.* to grease, oil, lubricate.—**engrase,** *m.* lubrication, oiling, greasing.

engreído, *a.* conceited.—**engreimiento,** *m.* conceit, presumption, vanity.—**engreír,** *vti.* [35] to encourage the conceit of, to make vain; to elate.—*vri.* to become vain or conceited.

engrifar, *vt. & vr.* to curl, crisp.

engrosar, *vti.* [12] to enlarge; to increase; to thicken, broaden.—*vii. &* (Am.) *vri.* to become fat; to increase, swell.

engrudo, *m.* paste, glue.

engullir, *vti.* [27] to gobble, gorge, wolf.

enhebrar, *vt.* to thread; to string.

enhiesto, *a.* erect, upright.

enhorabuena, *f.* congratulation, felicitation.

enigma, *m.* enigma, riddle.—**enigmático,** *a.* enigmatic.

enjabonadura, *f.* soaping.—**enjabonar,** *vt.* to soap; to wash with soap; (coll.) to soft-soap.

enjaezar, *vti.* [a] to harness.

enjambre, *m.* swarm of bees; crowd, agglomeration.

enjaular, *vt.* to cage; to confine.

enjuagar, *vti.* [b] & *vri.* to rinse, rinse the mouth.—**enjuagatorio,** *m.* rinsing; mouth wash; finger bowl.—**enjuague,** *m.* rinse, rinsing; mouthwash; plot, scheme.

enjugar, *vti.* [b-49] to dry; to wipe.—*vri.* to dry oneself.

enjuiciamiento, *m.* (law) indictment.—**enjuiciar,** *vt.* to indict; to carry on (a case); to pass judgment on.

enjundia, *f.* grease or fat of fowl; substance.

enjuto, *ppi.* of ENJUGAR.—*a.* dried; lean, skinny.

enladrillar, *vt.* to pave with bricks.

enlace, *m.* connection; tie; link; marriage; (mil.) scout.

enlatar, *vt.* to can.

enlazar, *vti.* [a] to lace, bind; to rope, lasso.—*vri.* to interlock, join; to marry.

enlodar, *vt.* to soil with mud.—*vr.* to get muddy.

enloquecer, *vti.* [3] to madden, drive insane.—*vii. & vri.* to become insane.—**enloquecimiento,** *m.* madness.

enlosado, *m.* flagstone pavement.—**enlosar,** *vt.* to pave with tiles or slabs.

enlutar, *vt.* to put in mourning; to darken, sadden.—*vr.* to go into mourning.

enmarañamiento, *m.* entanglement.—**enmarañar,** *vt.* to tangle (as hair, etc.); to entangle, involve in difficulties; to embroil.

enmascarar, *vt.* to mask.—*vr.* to masquerade, put on a mask.

enmasillar, *vt.* to putty, cement.

enmendar, *vti.* [1] to amend, correct; to repair; to reform.—*vri.* to mend, reform.—**enmienda,** *f.* emendation, correction, amendment.

enmohecer, *vti.* [3] & *vri.* to rust; to mold.—**enmohecimiento,** *m.* rusting; molding.

enmudecer, *vti.* [3] hush, silence.—*vii.* to become dumb; to be silent.

ennegrecer, *vti.* [3] to blacken; to darken, obscure.—**ennegrecimiento,** *m.* blackening.

ennoblecer, *vti.* [3] to ennoble; to impart dignity to.

enojadizo, *a.* fretful, peevish, ill-tempered.—**enojado,** *a.* angry, cross.—**enojar,** *vt.* to make angry, irri-

tate; to annoy.—**enojo**, *m.* anger; annoyance.—**enojoso**, *a.* troublesome; annoying.

enorgullecer, *vti.* [3] to make proud. —*vri.* to be proud; to swell with pride.—**enorgullecimiento**, *m.* pride; haughtiness.

enorme, *a.* enormous.—**enormidad**, *f.* enormousness, great quantity or size; enormity, atrocity.

enraizar, *vii.* [a] & *vri.* to take root.

enramada, *f.* bower, arbor; grove.

enrarecer, *vti.* [3] to thin, rarefy.— *vri.* to become thin or rarefied.— **enrarecimiento**, *m.* rarefaction, rarity.

enredadera, *f.* (bot.) climber; vine.— **enredador**, *n.* entangler; tattler.— **enredar**, *vt.* to entangle, snarl; to puzzle; to mess up, involve in difficulties; to lay, set (snares, nets).— *vr.* to get entangled, snarled; to get involved.—**enredo**, *m.* tangle, entanglement; puzzle; mischievous lie; plot.

enrejado, *m.* railing, grating; lattice. —**enrejar**, *vt.* to fence with railings; to put a trellis or lattice on.

enrevesado, *a.* frisky; difficult.

enriquecer, *vti.* [3] to enrich.—*vri.* to become rich.

enrojecer, *vti.* [3] to redden; to make red-hot.—*vri.* to blush; to turn red.

enrolar, *vt.* to sign on (a crew); to enroll; to enlist.—*vr.* to become a crew member.

enrollar, *vt.* to roll, wind, wrap up.

enronquecer, *vti.* [3] to make hoarse. —*vii.* & *vri.* to get hoarse.—**enronquecimiento**, *m.* hoarseness.

enroscar, *vti.* [d] to twine, to twist. —*vri.* to curl up, roll up.

ensalada, *f.* salad; hodgepodge, medley.—**ensaladera**, *f.* salad dish or bowl.

ensalmo, *m* enchantment, spell, charm.—*como por e.*, or *por e.*, as if miraculously, suddenly and unexpectedly.

ensalzar, *vti.* [a] to extol, exalt, praise.

ensambladura, *f.*, **ensamble**, *m.* joinery; joint.—**ensamblar**, *vt.* to join, couple, connect.

ensanchamiento, *m.* widening, enlargement, expansion.—**ensanchar**, *vt.* to widen, enlarge.—*e. el corazón*, to cheer up.—*vr.* to expand, enlarge.—**ensanche**, *m.* enlargement, widening, expansion.

ensangrentar, *vti.* [1] & *vri.* to stain with blood.—*vri.* to cover oneself with blood.

ensañamiento, *m* ferocity, cruelty

ensañarse, *vr.* to vent one's fury; to be merciless.

ensartar, *vt.* to string (as beads); to thread; to link.

ensayar, *vt.* to practice, try, rehearse; to test; to assay.—*vr.* to train oneself, practice.—**ensayista**, *mf.* essay writer.—**ensayo**, *m.* test; essay; trial, experiment; rehearsal; preparatory practice.

ensenada, *f.* creek; cove.

enseña, *f.* standard, colors, ensign.

enseñado, *a.* accustomed; trained.— **enseñanza**, *f.* teaching; education. —**enseñar**, *vt.* to teach; to train; to show, point out.

enseñorear, *vt.* to lord, to domineer. —*vr.* to take possession (of a thing).

enseres, *m. pl.* chattels; fixtures, accessories; implements; household goods.

enseriarse, *vr.* (Am.) to become serious; to become angry.

ensillar, *vt.* to saddle.

ensimismarse, *vr.* to become absorbed in thought.

ensoberbecer, *vti.* [3] to make proud. —*vri.* to become proud and haughty.

ensopar, *vt.* to steep, soak; to drench.

ensordecedor, *a.* deafening.—**ensordecer**, *vti.* [3] to deafen.—*vii.* & *vri.* to become deaf.—**ensordecimiento**, *m.* deafness.

ensortijar, *vt.* & *vr.* to curl, form ringlets.

ensuciar, *vt* to stain, soil, dirty.— *vr.* to soil one's bed, clothes, etc.; to get dirty; (coll.) to be dishonest.

ensueño, *m.* dream; illusion, fantasy.

entablar, *vt* to cover with boards; to plank; to initiate, start (as a negotiation, etc.); to bring (a suit or action).—**entablillar**, *vt.* (surg.) to splint.

entallar, *vt.* to notch.—*vi.* to fit well or closely (a dress).

entarimado, *m.* parquet floor.—**entarimar**, *vt.* to floor with boards, parquet.

ente, *m.* entity, being; (coll.) guy.

enteco, *a.* sickly; thin, skinny.

entenada, *f.* (Am.) stepdaughter. **entenado**, *m.* (Am.) stepson.

entendederas, *f. pl.* understanding, brains.—**entender**, *vti.* [18] & *vii.* to understand.—*dar a e.*, to insinuate, hint.—*e. de*, to be an expert in, know.—*vri.* to understand one another; to be understood; to be meant.—*entenderse con*, to have to do with; to deal with.—*m.* understanding, opinion.—*a mi e.*, *según mi e.*, in my opinion, according to my understanding.—**entendido**, *a.*

expert; able; posted.—*tener e.*, to understand.—**entendimiento**, *m.* intellect, mind; understanding; comprehension.

enterado, *a.* posted, informed.—*no darse por e.*, to ignore; to pretend not to understand.—**enterar**, *vt.* to inform, acquaint, advise.—*enterarse de*, to learn, become informed about or familiar with, find out about.

entereza, *f.* entirety; integrity; fortitude, firmness; presence of mind.

enterizo, *a.* of, or in, one piece; whole.

enternecedor, *a.* moving, touching.—**enternecer**, *vti.* [3] to soften; to touch, move to pity.—*vri.* to be moved to pity; to be affected.—**enternecimiento**, *m.* compassion, pity, softening.

entero, *a.* entire, whole; perfect; honest, upright; unqualified, complete; pure; strong, vigorous; uncastrated (animal).—*por e.*, entirely, fully.—*m.* (arith.) integer.

enterrador, *m.* gravedigger.—**enterramiento**, *m.* burial, funeral.—**enterrar**, *vti.* [1] to bury, inter.

entibiar, *vt.* to make lukewarm; to temper.—*vr.* to cool down.

entidad, *f.* entity; value, importance.

entierro, *m.* burial; funeral.

entintar, *vt.* to ink, ink in (a drawing); to tint or dye.

entoldar, *vt.* to cover with an awning; to adorn with hangings.—*vr.* to swell with pride.

entonación, *f.* modulation; intonation.—**entonado**, *a.* haughty, snobbish; (fig.) starchy.—**entonar**, *vt.* to modulate, intone; to sing in tune; to harmonize colors.—*vr.* to put on grand airs.—**entono**, *m.* harmony; snobbishness.

entonces, *adv.* then, at that time; in that case.—*interrog.* then what? and then?—*desde e.*, from then on. *hasta e.*, up to that time.—*por e.*, at the time.

entornar, *vt.* to half-close; to set ajar.

entorpecer, *vti.* [3] to make numb; to stupefy; to obstruct.—**entorpecimiento**, *m.* torpor, numbness, stupefaction; dullness, stupidity

entrada, *f.* entrance; gate; admission; admittance; entry; arrival; beginning (of a season); familiar access; entrée (course at dinner); (com.) entry (in a book).—*pl.* receding hair at temples; (com.) income.

entrambos, *a. & pron.* both.

entrampar, *vt.* to ensnare; to trick, deceive; to entangle; to encumber with debts.—*vr.* (coll.) to get into debt; to get into difficulties.

entrante, *a.* entering; coming.—*mes e.*, next month.

entraña, *f.* entrail.—*pl.* entrails; humaneness; (fig.) heart; affection; the inmost recess of anything.—*hijo de mis entrañas*, child of my heart.—*sin entrañas*, heartless.—**entrañable**, *a.* most affectionate; deep (affection).

entrar, *vi.* **(a, en, por)** to go (in), come (in), enter; to go (into); to flow (into); to be admitted or have free entrance (to); to join; to begin; to fit (of shoes, garment). —*vt.* to introduce, put in.

entre, *prep.* between, among, amongst, amidst; within, in.—*e. manos*, in hand.—*e. tanto*, in the meantime, meanwhile.

entreabierto, *ppi.* of ENTREABRIR.—*a.* half-opened, ajar.—**entreabrir**, *vti.* [49] to half-open, to set ajar.

entreacto, *m.* intermission.

entrecano, *a.* grayish (hair or beard).

entrecejo, *m.* space between inclosures; scowl.

entrecortado, *a.* confused, hesitating; breathless.—**entrecortar**, *vt.* to cut without severing; to interrupt at intervals.

entrecruzar, *vti.* [a] to intercross; to interlace, interweave.

entredicho, *m.* interdiction.

entrega, *f.* delivery, conveyance; installment of a publication; surrender.—**entregar**, *vti.* [b] to deliver; to give up, surrender; to hand (over); (com.) to transfer; to pay. —*a e.*, (com.) to be supplied.—*vri.* to deliver oneself up, surrender, give in.—*entregarse a*, to abandon oneself to or devote oneself to.

entrelazar, *vti.* [a] to interlace, entwine.—**entremés**, *m.* (theat.) oneact farce; side dish.

entremeter, *vt.* to place between. *vr.* to intrude; to meddle.—**entremetido**, *a.* meddlesome.—*n.* meddler; intruder; busybody.—**entremetimiento**, *m.* intrusion; meddlesomeness.

entremezclar, *vt.* to intermingle, intermix.

entrenador, *n.* trainer, coach.—**entrenamiento**, *m.* training, coaching. **entrenar**, *vt.*, *vi. & vr.* to train.

entrepaño, *m.* panel; shelf.—**entrepiernas**, *f.* crutch, fork of legs.—**entresacar**, *vti.* [d] to pick out or choose; to select; to sift; to thin out.—**entresuelo**, *m.* mezzanine.—**entretanto**, *adv. & m.* meanwhile. —**entretejer**, *vt.* to intertwine, inter-

weave.—**entretela**, *f.* (sewing) interlining.

entretener, *vti.* [42] to amuse, entertain; to allay (pain); to delay. —*vri.* to amuse oneself; to tarry. —**entretenido**, *a.* entertaining, pleasant, amusing; readable.—**entretenimiento**, *m.* amusement, entertainment, pastime.

entretiempo, *m.* spring or fall (autumn).

entrever, *vti.* [46-49] to glimpse; to see vaguely.

entreverado, *a.* streaky; intermixed. —**entreverar**, *vt.* to intermix, intermingle.

entrevista, *f.* interview, meeting.— **entrevistar**, *vt.* to interview.—**entrevisto**, *ppi.* of ENTREVER.

entristecer, *vti.* [3] to sadden, afflict. —*vri.* to become sad.—**entristecimiento**, *m.* sadness; fretting.

entremeter, *vt. & vr.* = ENTREMETER. —**entremetido**, *a. & n.* = ENTREMETIDO. —**entremetimiento**, *m.* = ENTREMETIMIENTO.

entroncar, *vii.* [d] (RR.) to form a junction.—**entronque**, *m.* connection; (RR.) junction.

entronizar, *vti.* [a] to enthrone; to exalt.

entubar, *vt.* to provide with casing (oil well, etc.).

entumecer, *vti.* [3] to make numb.— *vri.* to become numb (the limbs), go to sleep.—**entumecimiento**, *m.* torpor; deadness; numbness; swelling.—**entumirse**, *vr.* to become numb.

enturbiar, *vt.* to muddle; to make muddy; to dim, confuse.—*vr.* to get muddy.

entusiasmado, *a.* enthusiastic.—**entusiasmar**, *vt.* to make enthusiastic; to enrapture.—*vr.* to become enthusiastic.—**entusiasmo**, *m.* enthusiasm.—**entusiasta**, *mf.* enthusiast.—*a.* enthusiastic.

enumeración, *f.* enumeration.—**enumerar**, *vt.* to enumerate.

enunciación, *f.*, **enunciado**, *m.* statement.—**enunciar**, *vt.* to state.

envainar, *vt.* to sheathe.

envalentonar, *vt.* to encourage; to make bold.—*vr.* to become bold; to brag.

envanecer, *vti.* [3] to make vain.— *vri.* to become vain.—**envanecimiento**, *m.* conceit.

envasador, *n.* filler, packer; funnel. —**envasar**, *vt.* to put into a container; to pack; to can; to sack (grain).—**envase**, *m.* container; filling, bottling; packing.

envejecer, *vti.* [3] to make old; to

make look old.—*vii. & vri.* to grow old; to look older.—**envejecimiento**, *m.* oldness, age; aging.

envenenador, *n. & a.* poisoner; poisoning.—**envenenamiento**, *m.* poisoning.—**envenenar**, *vt.* to poison.

envergadura, *f.* breadth of the sails; wingspread of birds; (aer.) span; forcefulness.

envés, *m.* back or wrong side; back; shoulders.

enviado, *n.* envoy; messenger.— **enviar**, *vt.* to send; to ship.

enviciar, *vt.* to corrupt; to vitiate.— *vr.* (en) to acquire bad habits; to take (to) (drinking, etc.).

envidia, *f.* envy.—**envidiar**, *vt.* to envy.—**envidioso**, *a.* envious.

envilecer, *vti.* [3] to vilify, debase.— *vri.* to degrade oneself.—**envilecimiento**, *m.* vilification, debasement.

envío, *m.* remittance; consignment of goods, shipment.

envite, *m.* stake at cards; invitation; push.—*al primer e.*, at once; at the start.

enviudado, *a.* widowed.—**enviudar**, *vi.* to become a widower or widow.

envoltorio, *m.* bundle.—**envoltura**, *f.* cover, wrapper.—**envolver**, *vti.* [47] to wrap; to swaddle; to imply; to contain, carry with it; (mil.) to surround.—*vri.* to be implicated, involved.—**envuelto**, *pp.* of ENVOLVER.

enyesado, *m.* plasterwork; plaster, plastering.—**enyesadura**, *f.* plastering.—**enyesar**, *vt.* to plaster; to chalk; to whitewash.

épica, *f.* epic poetry.—**épico**, *a.* epic.

epidemia, *f.* epidemic.

epifanía, *f.* Epiphany; Twelfth Night.

epigrama, *m.* epigram; witticism.— **epigramático**, *a.* epigrammatic.

epiléptico, *n. & a.* epileptic.

epílogo, *m.* epilogue; summing up.

episcopal, *a.* episcopal; Episcopal.

episodio, *m.* episode; incident.

epístola, *f.* epistle, letter.

epitafio, *m.* epitaph.

epitalamio, *m.* nuptial song.

epíteto, *m.* epithet.

epítome, *m.* epitome.

época, *f.* epoch, era.—*hacer e.*, to be a turning point.

epopeya, *f.* epic poem.

equidad, *f.* equity; justice.

equilibrar, *vt.* to equilibrate; to counterpoise, counterbalance.—**equilibrio**, *m.* equilibrium, balance, counterbalance.—**equilibrista**, *mf.* juggler; acrobat.

equipaje, *m.* baggage; luggage.— **equipar**, *vt.* to fit out, equip, furnish.—**equipo**, *m.* equipment; team; work crew.

equiparación, *f.* comparison, collation. —**equiparar,** *vt.* to compare, collate; to equate.

equitación, *f.* horsemanship; riding.

equitativo, *a.* equitable, fair, just.

equivalencia, *f.* equivalence.—**equivalente,** *a.* equivalent, tantamount.—**equivaler,** *vii.* [44] to be equivalent.

equivocación, *f.* mistake, error; equivocation.—**equivocar,** *vti.* [d] to mistake; to confuse; to equivocate. —*vri.* to be mistaken; to make a mistake.—**equívoco,** *m.* equivocation; quibble; pun.—*a.* equivocal, ambiguous.

era, *f.* era, age; threshing floor.

erario, *m.* public treasury.

erección, *f.* erection; erectness, elevation.

erguir, *vti.* [19] to erect; to set up straight.—*vri.* to straighten up; to stand or sit erect; to swell with pride.

erial, *m.* unimproved land.—*a.* uncultivated.

erigir, *vti.* [c] to erect, raise; to build; to found, establish.—*erigirse en,* to set oneself up as.

erizado, *a.* covered with bristles, spiky.—*e. de,* beset with; covered with; bristling with.—**erizar,** *vti.* [a] to set on end; to bristle.—*vri.* to bristle; to stand on end (of the hair).—**erizo,** *m.* hedgehog; prickly husk.

ermita, *f.* hermitage.—**ermitaño,** *n.* hermit.

erogación, *f.* expense.

erosión, *f.* erosion, wearing away.

erótico, *a.* erotic(al).—**erotismo,** *m.* eroticism.

errado, *a.* mistaken; erroneous.—**errante,** *a.* wandering, nomadic; errant.—**errar,** *vti.* [1-e] to miss (the target, blow, etc.); to fail in (one's duty to).—*vii.* to wander.—*vii. & vri.* to be mistaken; to commit an error.—**errata,** *f.* misprint.—**erróneo,** *a.* erroneous, mistaken; unsound.—**error,** *m.* mistake.—*e. craso,* gross error.

eructar, *vi.* to belch.—**eructo,** *m.* belching.

erupción, *f.* eruption; bursting forth; rash.

esa, V. **ese.**

esbelto, *a.* slender, svelte, willowy.

esbirro, *m.* bailiff; henchman.

esbozar, *vti.* [a] to sketch.—**esbozo,** *m.* sketch, outline; rough draft.

escabechar, *vt.* to pickle; to stab and kill.—**escabeche,** *m.* pickle; pickled fish.

escabel, *m.* footstool.

escabrosidad, *f.* unevenness, ruggedness; harshness; wildness.—**escabroso,** *a.* uneven; craggy; rude; off-color.

escabullirse, *vii.* [27] to slip away; to scamper, sneak away.

escafandra, *f.* diver's helmet.

escala, *f.* ladder, stepladder; graduated rule or instrument; port of call; stopover; (mus.) scale.—*hacer e. en,* to touch, or stop at (a place). —**escalafón,** *m.* official personnel roster, or register.—**escalamiento,** *m.* scaling.—**escalar,** *vt.* to scale.

escaldar, *vt.* to burn, scald; to make red-hot.—*vr.* to get scalded.

escalera, *f.* staircase; stairs; stairway; ladder.—*e. de caracol,* winding stair.—*e. de mano,* ladder, stepladder.

escalinata, *f.* flight of stairs (outside of a building).

escalfar, *vt.* to poach (eggs).

escalofrío, *m.* chill.

escalón, *m.* step of a stairway; rung; rank; social position; (mil.) echelon.—**escalonar,** *vt.* (mil.) to form in echelon; to stagger, spread out; to terrace.

escalpelo, *m.* scalpel, dissecting knife.

escama, *f.* fish or reptile scale; suspicion.—**escamar,** *vt.* to scale (fish); to cause suspicion.—**escamoso,** *a.* scaly.

escamoteador, *n.* juggler, prestidigitator; swindler.—**escamotear,** *vt.* (in juggling) to palm; to rob by artful means.

escampar, *vi.* to stop raining.

escandalizar, *vti.* [a] to scandalize, shock.—*vri.* to be shocked, scandalized.—*vii.* to create commotion, to behave noisily.—**escándalo,** *m.* scandal; licentiousness; tumult, commotion.—**escandaloso,** *a.* scandalous, shocking; turbulent.

escandinavo, *n. & a.* Scandinavian.

escaño, *m.* bench (with back).

escapada, *f.* escape, flight, escapade.—*en una e.,* in a minute, in a jiffy.—**escapar,** *vi. & vr.* to escape; to run away.—**escapatoria,** *f.* escape, fleeing; excuse, subterfuge; way out (of difficulty, etc.).—**escape,** *m.* escape, flight; subterfuge; exhaust (of steam, etc.).—*a e.,* or *a todo e.,* at full speed, in great haste.

escapulario, *m.* (eccl., med.) scapular.

escarabajo, *m.* black beetle.

escaramuza, *f.* skirmish; dispute.

escarapela, *f.* badge, rosette in lapel; quarrel ending in blows.

escarbar, *vt.* to scrape or scratch (as fowl); to dig; to poke (the fire); to dig into, investigate.

escarcha, *f.* frost; rime; icing.—

escarchar, *vi.* to freeze.—*vt.* to ice, frost (cakes, etc.).

escardillo, *n.* gardener's hoe.

escariar, *vt.* to ream.

escarlata, *f.* & *a.* scarlet, red.—**escarlatina,** *f.* scarlet fever.

escarmentar, *vii.* [1] to learn by experience; to take warning.—*vti.* to inflict an exemplary punishment on. —**escarmiento,** *m.* warning, lesson, punishment.

escarnecer, *vti.* [3] to scoff, mock.— **escarnio,** *m.* scoffing, gibe, mockery.

escarola, *f.* endive; ruff, frill.

escarpa, *f.* slope, bluff; (mil.) scarp. —**escarpado,** *a.* steep, craggy, rugged.

escarpín, *m.* thin-soled shoe; dancing pump; woolen socks.

escasear, *vi.* to be scarce; to diminish. —**escasez,** *f.* scarcity, shortage; niggardliness; want; scantiness.— **escaso,** *a.* small, limited; little; scarce; niggardly.

escatimar, *vt.* to curtail, lessen.

escayola, *f.* stucco, plasterwork.

escena, *f.* stage; scenery; scene; sight, view.—**escenario,** *m.* (theat.) stage.

escepticismo, *m.* skepticism.—**escéptico,** *n.* & *a.* skeptic.

escindir, *vt.* & *vr.* to split (an atom, etc.)

escisión, *f.* division; schism; fission.

esclarecer, *vti.* [3] to lighten, illuminate; to enlighten, elucidate; to ennoble.—**esclarecido,** *a.* illustrious, prominent.—**esclarecimiento,** *m.* enlightening; elucidation; ennoblement.

esclavina, *f.* short cape.

esclavitud, *f.* slavery.—**esclavizar,** *vti.* [a] to enslave, overwork.—**esclavo,** *n.* slave.

esclusa, *f.* lock; sluice, floodgate.

escoba, *f.* broom.—**escobazo,** *m.* blow with a broom.—**escobilla,** *f.* whisk broom; (elec.) brush of a dynamo.

escocer, *vii.* [26-a] to sting, burn; to smart.

escocés, *n.* & *a.* Scotchman; Scottish.

escofina, *f.* rasp, file.—**escofinar,** *vt.* to rasp.

escoger, *vti.* [c] to choose, select; to elect.

escolar, *mf.* pupil, student.—*a.* scholastic.

escolta, *f.* escort, guard.—**escoltar,** *vt.* to escort, guard.

escollo, *m.* reef; difficulty, danger.

escombrar, *vt.* to clear of rubbish.— **escombro,** *m.* rubbish.

esconder, *vt.* to hide, conceal; to include, contain.—*vr.* to hide; to skulk.—**escondidas, escondidillas,** *f.*

pl.—*a e.,* on the sly, secretly.— **escondite, escondrijo,** *m.* lurking place; hiding place.

escopeta, *f.* shotgun, fowling piece.— **escopetazo,** *m.* gunshot; gunshot wound.

escoplo, *m.* chisel.

escorar, *vt.* (naut.) to prop; to shore up.

escorbuto, *m.* scurvy.

escoria, *f.* dross, slag, scum.

escorpión, *m.* scorpion.

escotar, *vt.* to cut a dress low in the neck.—**escote,** *m.* low neck, décolletage; tucker; scot, share, quota. —**escotilla,** *f.* (naut.) hatchway.— **escotillón,** *m.* scuttle, trapdoor; stage trap.

escozor, *m.* burning, smarting.

escriba, *m.* scribe.—**escribano,** *m.* actuary; court clerk.—**escribiente,** *mf.* clerk.—**escribir,** *vti.* [49] to write.—*e. a máquina,* to type.—*vri.* to carry on correspondence with each other.—**escrito,** *ppi.* of ESCRIBIR. —*m.* writing; manuscript; literary composition.—*por e.,* in writing.— **escritor,** *n.* writer, author.—**escritorio,** *m.* writing desk; countinghouse; office.—**escritura,** *f.* writing, handwriting; deed, instrument; (E.) Scripture.

escrófula, *f.* scrofula.

escrúpulo, *m.* scruple, hesitation; squeamishness.—**escrupulosidad,** *f.* scrupulousness; exactness, thoroughness.—**escrupuloso,** *a.* scrupulous, thorough, particular; squeamish.

escrutar, *vt.* to count ballots; to scrutinize.—**escrutinio,** *m.* scrutiny; inquiry.

escuadra, *f.* carpenter's square; drawing triangle; angle iron; knee, angle brace; (mil.) squad; (naut.) squadron, fleet.—**escuadrón,** *m.* (mil.) squadron.

escuálido, *a.* weak; squalid; emaciated.

escuchar, *vt.* to listen to; to mind, heed.—*vi.* to listen.

escudar, *vt.* to shield, protect.— **escudero,** *m.* shield-bearer, squire. —**escudo,** *m.* shield; escutcheon; protection; coin of different values. —*e. de armas,* coat of arms.

escudriñar, *vt.* to scrutinize, search, pry into.

escuela, *f.* school; schoolhouse; (art) school, style.

esculpir, *vt.* & *vi.* to sculpture; to engrave.—**escultor,** *n.* sculptor, (*f.*) sculptress.—**escultórico, escultural,** *a.* sculptural.—**escultura,** *f.* sculpture; carved work.

escupidera, *f.* spittoon.—**escupir,** *vt.*

& vi. to spit.—**escupitajo,** *m.* spit, spittle, phlegm.

escurridizo, *a.* slippery.—**escurridor,** *m.* colander; dish-draining rack.—**escurriduras,** *f. pl.* rinsings, dregs.—**escurrir,** *vt.* to drain off; to strain off; to wring (as clothes).—*e. el bulto,* to sneak away.—*vr.* to drop, drip; to slip, slide; to escape, sneak away.

ese, *m.* **esa,** *f.* (*pl.* **esos, esas**), *a. dem.* that.—*pl.* those; ése, ésa (*pl.* **ésos, ésas**), *pron. dem.* that (one); (*pl.* those); the former.—**eso,** *pron. dem. neut.* that.—*e. es,* that's it.—*e. mismo,* that's right, precisely.—*ni por ésas,* in no way.—*por eso,* so, therefore.

esencia, *f.* essence.—**esencial,** *a.* essential.

eses, *s. pl.,* reeling of a drunken man.—*hacer e.,* to reel.

esfera, *f.* sphere; clock dial.—**esférico,** *a.* spherical.

esfinge, *f.* sphinx.

esforzar, *vti.* [12-a] to strengthen; to encourage.—*vri.* to exert oneself, make efforts, try hard.—**esfuerzo,** *m.* courage, spirit; effort, strong endeavor.

esfumar, *vt.* (art) to shade.—*vr.* to vanish, disappear.

esgrima, *f.* fencing.—**esgrimir,** *vt.* to fence; to wield, brandish (a weapon).

eslabón, *m.* link of a chain; steel for striking fire with a flint.—**eslabonamiento,** *m.* linking, uniting; connection, sequence.—**eslabonar,** *vt.* to link; to join.

eslavo, *n. & a.* Slav.

eslovaco, *n. & a.* Slovak.

esmaltar, *vt.* to enamel; to embellish.—**esmalte,** *m.* enamel; enamel work.

esmerado, *a.* careful; carefully done; painstaking.

esmeralda, *f.* emerald.

esmerarse, *vr.* to do one's best, to take pains (with).

esmeril, *m.* emery.—**esmerilar,** *vt.* to polish with emery.

esmero, *m.* careful attention, nicety.

esnob, *mf.* (neol.) snob.—**esnobismo,** *m.* (neol.) snobbery.

eso, V. **ESE.**

espaciar, *vt.* to space; (printing) to lead.—**espacio,** *m.* space; capacity; interval; blank, empty space.—**espaciosidad,** *f.* spaciousness, capacity.—**espacioso,** *a.* spacious, ample.

espada, *f.* sword; swordsman; (cards) spade; swordfish; matador.—**espadachín,** *m.* dexterous swordsman; bully.

espadaña, *f.* (bot.) gladiolus.

espalda, *f.* (anat.) back.—*pl.* back or back part.—*a espaldas,* treacherously.—*de espaldas,* backwards; from behind.—**espaldar,** *m.* back of a seat.

espantada, *f.* stampede, running away.—**espantadizo,** *a.* timid, skittish.—**espantajo,** *m.* scarecrow; fright.—**espantar,** *vt.* to scare; to chase or drive away.—*vr.* to be astonished.—**espanto,** *m.* fright; horror; threat.—**espantoso,** *a.* frightful; fearful.

español, *n. & a.* Spanish.—*n.* Spaniard (*f.*) Spanish woman.

esparadrapo, *m.* adhesive tape, court plaster.

esparcimiento, *m.* scattering; amusement, relaxation.—**esparcir,** *vti.* [a] to scatter, spread; to divulge.

espárrago, *m.* asparagus.

espasmo, *m.* spasm.—**espasmódico,** *a.* spasmodic, convulsive.

espátula, *f.* spatula; (art) palette knife; putty knife.

especia, *f.* spice.—*pl.* medicinal drugs.

especial, *a.* special.—*en e.,* specially, in particular.—**especialidad,** *f.* specialty; course, subject (of study).—**especialista,** *mf.* specialist.—**especialización,** *f.* specialization; specializing.—**especializar,** *vti.* [a] to specialize.—*vri.* (en) to specialize (in).

especie, *f.* species; kind, sort; piece of news; statement.—*en e.,* in kind.—**especificar,** *vti.* [d] to specify.—**específico,** *a.* specific.—*m.* (med.) specific.—**espécimen,** *m.* specimen, sample.

espectacular, *a.* spectacular.—**espectáculo,** *m.* spectacle, show.—**espectador,** *n.* spectator.—*pl.* audience.

espectro, *m.* specter; spectrum.

especulación, *f.* speculation.—**especulador,** *n. & a.* speculator; speculating.—**especular,** *vt. & vi.* to speculate.—**especulativo,** *a.* speculative.

espejismo, *m.* mirage; illusion.—**espejo,** *m.* mirror.—**espejuelos,** *m. pl.* (Am.) eyeglasses.

espeluznante, *a.* hair-raising.

espera, *f.* waiting; stay, pause.—*en e. de,* waiting for.—*sala de e.,* waiting room.—**esperanza,** *f.* hope; (often *pl.*) prospects.—*dar esperanza(s),* to promise.—**esperanzar,** *vti.* [a] to give hope to.—**esperar,** *vt.* to wait for; to hope.—*vi.* to wait; to hope.—*vr.* to wait, stay.

esperma, *f.* sperm; tallow.

esperpento, *m.* hideous thing or person; absurdity, nonsense.

espesar, *vt.* to thicken, curdle.—*vr.* to thicken; to condense.—**espeso,** *a.*

thick, dense; dull, heavy.—**espesor**, *m.* thickness.—**espesura**, *f.* thicket, close wood; thickness, density.

espetar, *vt.* to skewer, spit; to spring (something) on (one).—**espetera**, *f.* kitchen rack.

espía, *mf.* spy.—**espiar**, *vt.* to spy on; (coll.) to tail.

espiga, *f.* tassel, ear (as of corn, wheat); pin; dowel; spigot.—**espigado**, *a.* tall, grown; (agr.) eared, ripe.—**espigar**, *vii.* [b] to glean; to tenon; to tassel (as corn).—*vri.* to grow tall; to go to seed.

espina, *f.* thorn; fishbone; spine; splinter; suspicion.—*dar mala e.*, to cause suspicion or anxiety.—**espinaca**, *f.* spinach.—**espinazo**, *m.* spine, backbone.—**espinilla**, *f.* shinbone; blackhead.—**espino**, *m.* hawthorn.—**espinoso**, *a.* thorny; arduous; dangerous.

espionaje, *m.* espionage, spying.

espiral, *a.* spiral, winding.

espirar, *vt. & vi.* to breathe, exhale; to emit.

espíritu, *m.* spirit; soul; genius; essence; courage.—*pl.* spirits.—**espiritual**, *a.* spiritual; soulful; ghostly.—**espirituoso**, *a.* spirituous; ardent; spirited.

espita, *f.* faucet, spigot; tap; drunkard.

esplendidez, *f.* splendor; abundance; liberality.—**espléndido**, *a.* splendid, generous; resplendent.—**esplendor**, *m.* splendor; nobleness.—**esplendoroso**, *a.* splendid, radiant.

espliego, *m.* lavender.

espolazo, *m.* violent prick with a spur.—**espolear**, *vt.* to spur; to incite.—**espoleta**, *f.* fuse (of a bomb).—**espolón**, *m.* cock's spur; (naut.) ram; breakwater; buttress.

espolvorear, *vt.* to sprinkle with powder.

esponja, *f.* sponge.—**esponjar**, *vt.* to sponge.—*vr.* to swell.—**esponjoso**, *a.* spongy, porous; springy.

esponsales, *m. pl.* betrothal, engagement.

esposa, *f.* spouse, wife.—*pl.* manacles, handcuffs.—**esposar**, *vt.* to shackle.—**esposo**, *m.* spouse, husband.

espuela, *f.* spur; incitement.

espuerta, *f.* two-handled fruit basket.—*a espuertas*, abundantly.

espulgar, *vti.* [b] to clean lice or fleas from; to examine closely.

espuma, *f.* foam; lather; suds; froth; scum.—**espumadera**, *f.* skimmer, colander.—**espumar**, *vt.* to skim, to scum.—*vi.* to froth, foam.—**espumarajo**, *m.* foam or froth

from the mouth.—**espumoso**, *a.* foamy, frothy; sparkling (wine).

esputar, *vt. & vi.* to expectorate, spit.—**esputo**, *m.* spittle, saliva; sputum.

esquela, *f.* billet, note.

esquelético, *a.* thin; skeletal.—**esqueleto**, *m.* skeleton; very thin person.

esquema, *m.* scheme, plan; outline.—**esquemático**, *a.* schematic.—**esquematizar**, *vti.* [a] to sketch, outline.

esquí, *m.* ski.—**esquiador**, *n.* skier.—**esquiar**, *vi.* to ski.

esquife, *m.* skiff, small boat.

esquila, *f.* small bell; cattle bell; sheep shearing.—**esquilador**, *n.* shearer.—**esquilar**, *vt.* to shear, crop, clip.

esquilmar, *vt.* to impoverish; to exploit.

esquilón, *m.* cattle bell.

esquimal, *n. & a.* Eskimo.

esquina, *f.* corner, angle (outside).—**esquinazo**, *m.* corner.—*dar e.*, to evade.

esquirla, *f.* splinter of a bone.

esquivar, *vt.* to elude, avoid; to shun.—*vr.* to disdain, withdraw.—**esquivez**, *f.* disdain; aloofness; coldness.—**esquivo**, *a.* elusive, evasive; cold.

estabilidad, *f.* stability.—**estable**, *a.* stable, steady.

establecer, *vti.* [3] to establish, found; to decree.—*vri.* to establish or settle oneself.—**establecimiento**, *m.* establishment; institution.

establo, *m.* stable; cattle barn.

estaca, *f.* stake, pole; stick, cudgel.—**estacada**, *f.* palisade; paling, fence work.—*dejar (a uno) en la e.*, to leave (one) in the lurch.

estación, *f.* season (of the year); moment, time; (RR., radio, tel., police, etc.) station.—**estacionamiento**, *m.* (auto) parking; stationing, settling.—**estacionar**, *vt.* to park (a car, etc.).—*vr.* to park; to remain stationary; to stagnate.—**estacionario**, *a.* stationary, motionless.

estada, **estadía**, *f.* stay, sojourn, detention; demurrage; cost of such stay.—**estadio**, *m.* stadium.

estadista, *m.* statesman.

estadística, *f.* statistics.—**estadístico**, *a.* statistical.

estado, *m.* state, condition (of persons or things); estate, class, rank; status; state, commonwealth; state, government; statement, account, report.—*estar en e.*, to be pregnant.—*e. mayor*, (mil.) staff.—*hombre de e.*, statesman.

estadounidense, estadunidense, *mf.* & *a.* of the U.S., North American.

estafa, *f.* swindle.—**estafador,** *n.* swindler, sharper.—**estafar,** *vt.* to swindle.

estafermo, *m.* idle fellow.

estafeta, *f.* post office.

estallar, *vi.* to explode, burst; (of fire, etc.) to break out.—**estallido,** *m.* outburst.

estambre, *m.* worsted, woolen yarn; stamen.

estameña, *f.* serge.

estampa, *f.* print, stamp; image; picture; engraving.—**estampado,** *m.* cotton print, calico; stamping; cloth printing.—**estampar,** *vt.* to print, stamp.

estampida, *f.* stampede.—**estampido,** *m.* report of a gun; outburst.

estampilla, *f.* rubber stamp; seal; (Am.) postage stamp.

estancamiento, *m.* stagnation.—**estancar,** *vti.* [d] to stanch, check, stem.—*vri.* to stagnate, become stagnant.

estancia, *f.* stay; dwelling, habitation; ranch.—**estanciero,** *n.* (Am.) ranch owner, cattle raiser.

estanco, *a.* watertight.—*m.* monopoly; store for monopolized goods; cigar store.

estandarte, *m.* standard, banner, colors.

estanque, *m.* pool, reservoir, pond.—**estanquillo,** *m.* cigar store; small shop.

estante, *m.* shelf; bookcase.—**estantería,** *f.* shelving, shelves.

estaño, *m.* tin.

estar, *vii.* [20] to be.—*¿a cómo estamos? ¿a cuánto estamos?* what day is it? what is the date?—*¿estamos?* is it agreed? do you understand?—*e. bien,* to be well.—*e. con,* to live in company with; to have a (disease), to be ill with; to be in a state of (hurry, anger, etc.).—*e. de más,* to be out of place, in the way.—*e. para,* to be about to; to be in a mood or in condition to or for.—*e. por,* to be in favor of; to feel like.—*e. por ver,* to remain to be seen.—*e. sobre sí,* to be on one's guard.—*vri.* to be, to keep; to stay, to remain.

estarcido, *m.* stencil.—**estarcir,** *vti.* [a] to stencil.

estatal, *a.* pertaining to the state.

estática, *f.* statics.—**estático,** *a.* static, statical.

estatua, *f.* statue.

estatuir, *vti.* [23-e] to establish, ordain, enact.

estatura, *f.* stature, height of a person.

estatuto, *m.* statute, ordinance.

este, *m.* east, orient.

este, *dem. a.* (*f.* esta; *pl.* estos, estas) this (*pl.* these).—**éste,** *dem. pron.* (*f.* ésta; *pl.* éstos, éstas; *neut.* esto) this, this one; the latter (*pl.* these; the latter).—*a todo esto,* meanwhile.—*en esto,* at this juncture, point; herein (to).—*esto es,* that is; that is to say.—*por esto,* for this reason; on this account.

estela, *f.* wake of a ship.

estenografía, *f.* stenography.—**estenógrafo,** *n.* stenographer.

estera, *f.* mat, matting.

estercolero, *m.* dung heap.

estereoscópico, *a.* stereoscopic.—**estereoscopio,** *m.* stereoscope.

estereotipar, *vt.* to stereotype; to print from stereotypes.

estéril, *a.* sterile, barren; unfruitful.—**esterilidad,** *f.* sterility, barrenness, unfruitfulness.—**esterilizar,** *vti.* [a] to sterilize.

esterlina, *a.* sterling.

esternón, *m.* breastbone.

estero, *m.* inlet, estuary.

estertor, *m.* death rattle.

estética, *f.* esthetics.—**estético,** *a.* esthetic.

estetoscopio, *m.* stethoscope.

estiba, *f.* stowage.—**estibador,** *n.* stevedore, longshoreman.—**estibar,** *vt.* to stow.

estiércol, *m.* dung, manure.

estigma, *m.* birthmark; stigma, mark of infamy; (bot.) stigma.—**estigmatizar,** *vti.* [a] to stigmatize.

estilar, *vi.* & *vr.* to be customary.

estilete, *m.* stiletto (dagger); small chisel; (surg.) flexible probe.

estilista, *mf.* stylist.—**estilo,** *m.* style.—*al e. de,* in the style of.—*por el e.,* or *por ese e.,* of that kind, like that.—**estilográfica,** *f.* fountain pen.

estima, *f.* esteem.—**estimable,** *a.* estimable, worthy.—**estimación,** *f.* esteem, regard; estimate.—**estimar,** *vt.* to estimate, value; to esteem; to judge, to think.

estimulante, *a.* stimulating.—*m.* stimulant.—**estimular,** *vt.* to stimulate; to goad, incite, encourage.—**estímulo,** *m.* stimulus; inducement; incitement; stimulation.

estío, *m.* summer.

estipendio, *m.* stipend, fee.

estipulación, *f.* stipulation.—**estipular,** *vt.* to stipulate, specify.

estirpe, *f.* lineage, pedigree.

estirado, *a.* affected, pompous, stuffy; haughty; (fig.) starchy.—**estiramiento,** *m.* stretching.—**estirar,** *vt.*

to stretch, lengthen.—**estirón**, *m.* pull(ing); haul(ing); rapid growth.

estival, *a.* summer.

esto, V. ESTE.

estocada, *f.* stab, sword thrust.

estofa, *f.* quality, class, sort; stuff, cloth.—**estofado**, *m.* stew.—**estofar**, *vt.* to stew; to quilt.

estoicismo, *m.* stoicism.—**estoico**, *n.* & *a.* stoic(al).

estolidez, *f.* stupidity.—**estólido**, *a.* stupid, imbecile.

estómago, *m.* stomach.

estopa, *f.* tow; burlap; oakum.

estoque, *m.* rapier; matador's sword.

estorbar, *vt.* to hinder; to obstruct; to impede.—**estorbo**, *m.* hindrance, obstruction, nuisance.

estornino, *m.* starling.

estornudar, *vi.* to sneeze.—**estornudo**, *m.* sneeze.

estrado, *m.* dais; lecturing platform.

estrafalario, *a.* odd, eccentric.

estragar, *vti.* [b] to deprave, spoil. —**estrago**, *m.* ravage, ruin, havoc; wickedness.

estrambótico, *a.* odd, eccentric.

estrangulación, *f.* strangling; strangulation; throttling.—**estrangular**, *vt.* to strangle, choke, throttle.

estratagema, *f.* stratagem; trick.

estrategia, *f.* strategy.—**estratégico**, *a.* strategic.

estratificar, *vti.* [d] & *vri.* to stratify. —**estrato**, *m.* stratum; layer.

estratosfera, *f.* stratosphere.

estrechar, *vt.* to tighten; to narrow; to take in (a coat, etc.); to constrain.—*s. la mano*, to shake hands; to greet.—*vr.* to narrow; to bind oneself strictly.—**estrechez**, *f.* narrowness; tightness; poverty.—**estrecho**, *a.* narrow, tight.—*m.* strait, channel.

estregar, *vti.* [1-b] to rub; to scour. —**estregón**, *m.* rough rubbing.

estrella, *f.* star.—**estrellar**, *vt.* to dash to pieces, smash up.—*vr.* to fail; to smash; (contra) to crash or dash (against), be shattered (by).

estremecer, *vti.* [3] & *vri.* to shake, tremble, shudder.—**estremecimiento**, *m.* trembling; shaking; shudder(ing).

estrenar, *vt.* to use or to do for the first time.—*vr.* to begin to act in some capacity; to make one's debut; (of a play) to open.—**estreno**, *m.* inauguration; first performance; debut.

estreñimiento, *m.* constipation.—**estreñir**, *vti.* [9] to constipate.

estrépito, *m.* noise, din; crash.—**estrepitoso**, *a.* noisy, deafening; boisterous.

estriar, *vt.* to flute; to gutter.—*vr.* to become grooved, striated.

estribación, *f.* spur of a mountain.— **estribar**, *vi.* (en) to rest (on); to be based (on); to lie (in).

estribillo, *m.* refrain of a song.

estribo, *m.* stirrup; runningboard, step or footboard of a coach; (anat.) stirrup bone; abutment; support.—*perder los estribos*, to talk nonsense; to lose one's head.

estribor, *m.* (naut.) starboard.

estricto, *a.* strict.

estridente, *a.* strident.

estrobo, *m.* loop; oarlock.

estrofa, *f.* (poet.) stanza.

estropajo, *m.* swap; esparto scrubbing pad; worthless thing.

estropear, *vt.* to maim, cripple; to damage, spoil.—*vr.* to get out of order, damaged.—**estropicio**, *m.* breakage, crash.

estructura, *f.* structure.—**estructural**, *a.* structural.

estruendo, *m.* din, clatter; uproar.— **estruendoso**, *a.* obstreperous, noisy.

estrujamiento, *m.* crushing, squeezing.—**estrujar**, *vt.* to squeeze, crush. —**estrujón**, *m.* crush, squeeze.

estuario, *m.* estuary, inlet.

estuco, *m.* stucco; plaster.

estuche, *m.* fancy box or case (as for jewelry, etc.).

estudiante, *mf.* student.—**estudiantil**, *a.* student, pertaining to students.— **estudiar**, *vt.* to study.—**estudio**, *m.* study; reading room; studio.—**estudioso**, *a.* studious.

estufa, *f.* stove; heater; hothouse; drying chamber; small brazier.

estupefacción, *f.* stupefaction, numbness.—**estupefaciente**, *a.* & *m.* narcotic.—**estupefacto**, *a.* motionless; stupefied.

estupidez, *f.* stupidity.—**estúpido**, *a.* & *n.* stupid (person).

estupor, *m.* stupor; amazement.

estupro, *m.* ravishment, rape.

etapa, *f.* stage; station, stop.

éter, *m.* ether.—**etéreo**, *a.* ethereal.

eternidad, *f.* eternity.—**eternizar**, *vti.* [a] to prolong indefinitely.—*vri.* to be everlasting; to be exceedingly slow; to stay forever.—**eterno**, *a.* eternal, everlasting, timeless.

ética, f. ethics.—**ético**, *a.* ethical.

etimología, *f.* etymology.—**etimológico**, *a.* etymological.

etíope, *mf.* Ethiopian.—**etiópico**, *a.* Ethiopic, Ethiopian.

etiqueta, *f.* etiquette, formality; formal dress; label.—*de e.*, ceremonious; formal.

étnico, *a.* ethnic.—**etnología**, *f.* ethnology.

eucalipto, *m.* eucalyptus.

eurasiático, eurasio, *n.* & *a.* Eurasian. —**europeo,** *n.* & *a.* European.

eutanasia, *f.* mercy killing.

evacuación, *f.* evacuation; exhaustion. —**evacuar,** *vt.* to evacuate, empty; to quit, leave, vacate.

evadir, *vt.* to evade, elude, avoid.— *vr.* to escape; to sneak away.

evaluación, *m.* appraisal, valuation.— **evaluar,** *vt.* to rate, value, appraise; to price.

evangélico, *a.* evangelical.—**evangelio,** *m.* gospel.—**evangelizar,** *vti.* [a] to evangelize.

evaporación, *f.* evaporation.—**evaporar,** *vt.* & *vr.* to evaporate, vaporize.

evasión, *f.,* **evasiva,** *f.* evasion, dodge, escape.—**evasivo,** *a.* evasive, elusive.

evento, *m.* event, contingency.—**eventual,** *a.* contingent; fortuitous.— **eventualidad,** *f.* contingency.

evidencia, *f.* evidence, proof; obviousness.—**evidenciar,** *vt.* to prove, make evident.—**evidente,** *a.* evident.

evitable, *a.* avoidable.—**evitar,** *vt.* to avoid; to shun; to prevent.

evocación, *f.* evocation, evoking.— **evocar,** *vti.* [d] to evoke.

evolución, *f.* evolution; change.— **evolucionar,** *vi.* to evolve; to change; to develop; to perform evolutions or maneuverings.

exacerbación, *f.* exasperation; exacerbation.—**exacerbar,** *vt.* to irritate, exasperate; to aggravate (disease, etc.).

exactitud, *f.* exactness; punctuality; accuracy.—**exacto,** *a.* exact; accurate; precise; punctual.

exageración, *f.* exaggeration.—**exagerar,** *vt.* to exaggerate, overstate.

exaltación, *f.* exaltation.—**exaltado,** *a.* hot-headed; ultra-radical.—**exaltar,** *vt.* to exalt; to praise.—*vr.* to become excited, upset.

examen, *m.* examination; inquiry.— **examinar,** *vt.* to examine; investigate.—*vr.* to take an examination.

exánime, *a.* spiritless, lifeless.

exasperación, *f.* exasperation.—**exasperar,** *vt.* to exasperate.—*vr.* to become exasperated.

excavación, *f.* excavation.—**excavar,** *vt.* to excavate.

excedente, *a.* exceeding.—*m.* surplus. —**exceder,** *vt.* to exceed, surpass; to overstep.—*vr.* to go too far; to overstep one's authority.

excelencia, *f.* excellence; excellency (title).—**excelente,** *a.* excellent, first-rate, tiptop.—*interj.* good! fine!

excelso, *a.* elevated, sublime, lofty.

excentricidad, *f.* eccentricity.—**excéntrico,** *a.* eccentric(al); odd.

excepción, *f.* exception.—**excepcional,** *a.* exceptional, unusual.—**excepto,** *adv.* excepting, except, with the exception of.—**exceptuar,** *vt.* to except.

excesivo, *a.* excessive.—**exceso,** *m.* excess; atrocity; surplus.

excitable, *a.* excitable.—**excitación,** *f.* excitation, exciting; excitement.— **excitante,** *a.* exciting, stimulating. —**excitar,** *vt.* to excite.—*vr.* to become excited.

exclamación, *f.* exclamation.—**exclamar,** *vi.* to exclaim.

excluir, *vti.* [23-e] to exclude; to bar.—**exclusión,** *f.* exclusion, shutting out, debarring.—**exclusiva,** *f.* refusal; rejection, exclusion; sole right or agency.—**exclusivo,** *a.* exclusive.

excomulgar, *vti.* [b] to excommunicate.—**excomunión,** *f.* excommunication.

excremento, *m.* excrement.

exculpar, *vt.* & *vr.* to exonerate.

excursión, *f.* excursion, trip, tour.— **excursionista,** *mf.* excursionist.

excusa, *f.* excuse.—**excusado,** *a.* unnecessary; reserved, private.—*m.* toilet.—**excusar,** *vt.* to excuse.—*vr.* to excuse oneself; to apologize.

exención, *f.* exemption.—**exento,** *ppi.* of EXIMIR.—*a.* exempt; free.

exequias, *f. pl.* obsequies.

exhalación, *f.* exhalation; bolt of lightning; shooting star; fume, vapor, emanation.—**exhalar,** *vt.* to exhale, breathe forth, emit.

exhausto, *a.* exhausted.

exhibición, *f.* exhibition, exposition. —**exhibir,** *vt.* to exhibit, expose; to show.

exigencia, *f.* demand; requirement; unreasonable request.—**exigente,** *a.* demanding; exacting.—**exigir,** *vti.* [c] to require; to exact, demand.

eximio, *a.* famous, most excellent.

eximir, *vti.* [49] to exempt, excuse, except.

existencia, *f.* existence.—*pl.* (com.) stock in hand.—*en e.,* in stock.— **existente,** *a.* existent, existing; in stock.—**existir,** *vi.* to exist, to be.

éxito, *m.* success; issue, result.

éxodo, *m.* exodus, emigration; **(E.),** Exodus.

exoneración, *f.* exoneration.—**exonerar,** *vt.* to exonerate.

exorbitancia, *f.* exorbitance.—**exorbitante,** *a.* exorbitant, excessive.

exótico, *a.* exotic, foreign.

expansión, *f.* expansion, extension;

recreation.—**expansivo,** *a.* expansive; communicative, sociable.

expatriación, *f.* expatriation.—**expatriar,** *vt.* to expatriate.—*vr.* to emigrate, leave one's country.

expectación, *f.* expectation, expectancy.—**expectante,** *a.* expectant. —**expectativa,** *f.* expectation, expectancy, hope.

expectoración, *f.* expectoration; sputum.—**expectorar,** *vt.* & *vi.* to expectorate.

expedición, *f.* expedition; dispatch; journey.—**expedicionario,** *a.* expeditionary.—**expediente,** *m.* file of papers bearing on a case; dispatch; (law) action, proceeding; means; pretext.—*cubrir el e.,* to keep up appearances.—**expedienteo,** *m.* (coll.) red tape.—**expedir,** *vti.* [29] to expedite; to issue; to draw out; to ship, send.—**expeditivo,** *a.* expeditious, speedy.

expeler, *vt.* to expel, eject.

expender, *vt.* to spend; to sell.—**expensas,** *f. pl.* expenses, charges, costs.—*a e. de uno,* at one's expense.

experiencia, *f.* experience; experiment.—*e. de la vida,* sophistication. —**experimental,** *a.* experimental.—**experimentar,** *vt.* to experience; to experiment, test.—**experimento,** *m.* experiment, test.—**experto,** *n.* & *a.* expert.

expiación, *f.* expiation.—**expiar,** *vt.* to expiate, atone for.

expiración, *f.* expiration.—**expirar,** *vi.* to expire; to die.

explanada, *f.* lawn; esplanade.

explayar, *vt.* to extend.—*vr.* to expatriate; to have a good time; to confide (in a person).

explicable, *a.* explainable.—**explicación,** *f.* explanation.—**explicar,** *vti.* [d] to explain.—*vri.* to explain oneself; to understand (the reason, cause, etc.).—**explícito,** *a.* explicit, clear.

exploración, *f.* exploration.—**explorador,** *n.* & *a.* explorer; exploring; scout.—**explorar,** *vt.* to explore; to scout.

explosión, *f* explosion.—*hacer e.,* to explode.—**explosivo,** *m.* & *a.* explosive.—**explotación,** *f.* exploitation; development, working (of a mine, etc.); plant, works; operation, running (of a factory, RR., etc.).—**explotador,** *n.* & *a.* exploiter; exploiting.—**explotar,** *vt.* to exploit; to work (a mine, etc.); to operate, run (a business, RR., etc.); to exploit (to one's own advantage); (Am.) to explode, detonate.—*vi.* to explode.—*hacer e.,* to explode.

expoliación, *f.* spoliation.—**expoliar,** *vt.* to plunder, despoil.

exponente, *m.* & *a.* exponent.—**exponer,** *vti.* [32-49] to expose; to show; to jeopardize.—*vri.* to run a risk, lay oneself open to.

exportación, *f.* exportation, export.—**exportar,** *vt.* to export.

exposición, *f.* exposition, statement; risk, jeopardy; exposure; exhibition.

expresar, *vti.* [49] to express.—*vri.* to express oneself; to speak.—**expresión,** *f.* expression; wording; statement; form; phrase, utterance.—**expreso,** *ppi.* of EXPRESAR.—*a.* expressed; express, clear; fast (train, etc.).—*m.* express (train, etc.).

exprimir, *vt.* to squeeze, press out.

expropiar, *vt.* to expropriate.

expuesto, *ppi.* of EXPONER.—*a.* on display; exposed, liable; dangerous; in danger.

expulsar, *vt.* to expel, eject.—**expulsión,** *f.* expulsion, ejection.

exquisito, *a.* exquisite, delicious.

extasiar, *vt.* & *vr.* to enrapture, delight.—**éxtasis,** *m.* ecstasy.—**extático,** *a.* ecstatic.

extemporáneo, *a.* untimely, inopportune.

extender, *vti.* [18-49] to extend; to unfold; to spread out; to stretch out; to draw up or issue (a document).—*vri.* to extend, last; to spread, become popular.—**extensión,** *f.* extension; extent, length; expanse, spaciousness; stretch; duration.—**extensivo,** *a.* extensive; ample.—**extenso,** *ppi.* of EXTENDER.—*a.* extended, extensive; spacious.

extenuación, *f.* attenuation; exhaustion.—**extenuar,** *vt.* to exhaust, weaken.—*vr.* to languish, waste away.

exterior, *a.* exterior; external, outer; foreign.—*m.* outside; personal appearance; foreign countries.—**exteriorizar,** *vti.* [a] to externalize, make manifest.—*vri.* to unbosom oneself.

exterminador, *n.* & *a.* exterminator; exterminating.—**exterminar,** *vt.* to exterminate; to raze.—**exterminio,** *m.* extermination, ruin.

externo, *a.* external, outward; exterior.—*n.* day pupil.

extinción, *f.* extinction; extinguishing. —**extinguir,** *vti.* [49-b] & *vri.* to quench, extinguish; to suppress, destroy.—**extinto,** *ppi.* of EXTINGUIR.—*a.* extinct.—**extintor,** *m.* fire-extinguisher.

extirpar, *vt*. to extirpate, root out; eradicate.

extorsión, *f*. extortion.

extracción, *f*. extraction.—**extractar**, *vt*. to epitomize, abstract.—**extracto**, *m*. summary, abstract; extract.

extradición, *f*. extradition.

extraer, *vti*. [43] to extract, draw out, remove.

extralimitarse, *vr*. to overstep one's authority; to take advantage of another's kindness.

extranjero, *a*. foreign, alien.—*n*. foreigner.—*en el e.*, abroad.

extrañar, *vt*. to banish; to estrange; to wonder at, find strange; to miss.—**extrañeza**, *f*. oddity; surprise; estrangement.—**extraño**, *a*. strange; foreign; extraneous; unaccountable.—*n*. stranger, foreigner, outsider.

extraoficial, *a*. unofficial.

extraordinario, *a*. extraordinary.—*m*. extra.—*horas extraordinarias*, overtime.

extravagancia, *f*. oddness; folly; eccentricity.—**extravagante**, *a*. eccentric; unusual, odd.

extraviar, *vt*. to mislead, misguide; to misplace, mislay; to embezzle.—*vr*. to go astray; to lose one's way; to miscarry (as a letter); to deviate; to err.—**extravío**, *m*. deviation; aberration; misconduct; misplacement.

extremar, *vt*. to carry to an extreme.—*vr*. to exert oneself to the utmost, take special pains.—**extremidad**, *f*. extremity; end; edge, border; extreme or remotest part.—**extremo**, *a*. extreme, last; furthest; greatest, utmost.—*m*. extreme, highest degree; apex; furthest end, extremity; greatest care.—*con* or *en e.*, extremely.—*hacer extremos*, to express one's feelings with vehemence, to gush.—**extremoso**, *a*. extreme, vehement.

exudar, *vi*. & *vt*. to exude; to ooze out.

eyaculación, *f*. ejection; ejaculation.—**eyacular**, *vt*. to eject; to ejaculate.

F

fábrica, *f*. fabrication; structure; factory; mill.—**fabricación**, *f*. manufacturing; manufacture.—**fabricante**, *mf*. & *a*. maker, manufacturer; making, manufacturing.—**fabricar**, *vti*. [d] to manufacture, make; to build, construct.—**fabril**, *a*. manufacturing.

fábula, *f*. fable, tale, fiction.—**fabuloso**, *a*. fabulous; marvelous; mythical.

facción, *f*. faction, turbulent political party.—*pl*. features, lineaments.—**faccioso**, *a*. factious.—*n*. rebel.

faceta, *f*. oblique side; facet.

facial, *a*. facial.

fácil, *a*. easy; docile, handy; yielding; likely.—**facilidad**, *f*. ease; facility.—*dar facilidades*, to facilitate.—**facilitar**, *vt*. to facilitate, make easy; to provide.

facineroso, *a*. wicked, villainous.

factible, *a*. feasible, practicable.

factor, *m*. factor, element, cause; (com.) agent, commissioner.—**factoría**, *f*. agency; trading post.

factótum, *m*. handyman; busybody.

factura, *f*. invoice, bill; workmanship.—**facturar**, *vt*. (com.) to invoice; to bill; (RR.) to check (baggage).

facultad, *f*. faculty; power; branch, school.—**facultar**, *vt*. to empower, authorize.—**facultativo**, *a*. facultative; optional; pertaining to a faculty.—*m*. physician.

facundia, *f*. eloquence.—**facundo**, *a*. eloquent, fluent.

facha, *f*. (coll.) appearance, look, aspect.—**fachada**, *f*. (arch.) façade; (coll.) outward appearance.

fachenda, *f*. vanity, boastfulness.—**fachendoso**, *a*. vain, boastful.

faena, *f*. work, labor, task.

faisán, *m*. pheasant.

faja, *f*. band; sash; girdle; (geog.) zone; belt.—**fajar**, *vt*. to band, belt, girdle.—*vr*. (Am.) (coll.) to fight.—**fajo**, *m*. sheaf; bundle.

falacia, *f*. fallacy, fraud, deceit.—**falaz**, *a*. deceitful, false, fallacious.

falange, *f*. phalanx.

falda, *f*. skirt, flap; the lap; slope; loin (of beef).—*pl*. (fig.) women.—**faldeta**, *f*. small skirt; covering cloth or canvas, flap.—**faldón**, *m*. coattail, shirttail; flap.

falsario, *n*. forger; liar.—**falsear**, *vt*. to forge; to misrepresent.—*vi*. to slacken.—**falsedad**, *f*. falsehood, lie; deceit.—**falsete**, *m*. (mus.) falsetto.—**falsificación**, *f*. falsification, counterfeit, forgery.—**falsificador**, *n*. counterfeiter, falsifier, forger.—**falsificar**, *vti*. [d] to counterfeit, falsify, forge; to sophisticate.—**falso**, *a*. false, untrue; incorrect; deceitful, untruthful; forged; counterfeit; sham, imitation (as jewels); unsound.

falta, *f*. lack, want, dearth; fault, mistake; defect; offense, misdemeanor; (law) default; (sport) fault.—*a f. de*, for lack of.—*hacer*

f., to be necessary.—*sin f.*, without fail.—**faltar**, *vi.* to be wanting, lacking; to be needed; to fall short; to fail in; to commit a fault; to offend; to be absent or missing.—*falta un cuarto para las dos*, it is quarter to two.—*f. a la verdad*, to lie.—*f. al respeto*, to treat disrespectfully.—*¡no faltaba más!* (coll.) of course! that would be the limit! —**falto**, *a.* short; deficient.

faltriquera, *f.* pocket.

falla, *f.* fault, defect; failure; (geol.) fault, slide.—**fallar**, *vt.* to pass sentence, render a verdict on.—*vi.* to fail, be deficient or wanting; to miss, fail to hit; to give way.

falleba, *f.* shutter bolt.

fallecer, *vii.* [3] to die.—**fallecimiento**, *m.* decease, death.

fallido, *a.* disappointed, frustrated.

fallo, *m.* verdict, judgment, decision.

fama, *f.* fame; reputation.

famélico, *a.* hungry, ravenous.

familia, *f.* family.—**familiar**, *a.* familiar; domestic; common, frequent; well-known; homelike; colloquial.—*mf.* relative.—**familiaridad**, *f.* familiarity.—**familiarizar**, *vti.* [a] to acquaint, accustom, familiarize.—*vri.* to accustom, habituate oneself; to become familiar.

famoso, *a.* famous; (coll.) great, excellent.

fanal, *m.* lighthouse; lantern; headlight; bell glass.

fanático, *n. & a.* fanatic; (sports) fan.—**fanatismo**, *m.* fanaticism.

fanega, *f.* Spanish grain measure (roughly equivalent to a bushel); land measure.

fanfarrón, *n.* blusterer, swaggerer; boaster.—**fanfarronada**, *f.* boast, bluff, swagger.—**fanfarronear**, *vi.* to brag, swagger.—**fanfarronería**, *f.* bragging.

fangal, *m.* marsh, slough, quagmire.—**fango**, *m.* mire, mud.—**fangoso**, *a.* muddy, miry.

fantasear, *vi.* to fancy; to imagine. —**fantasía**, *f.* fantasy, fancy, whim, imagination.

fantasma, *m.* phantom, ghost.—**fantasmagórico**, *a.* phantasmagoric.—**fantasmón**, *m.* an inflated, presumptuous person.

fantástico, *a.* fantastic; whimsical.

fantoche, *m.* vain and insignificant person; puppet.

farallón, *m.* headland; cliff.

farándula, *f.* strolling troop of players.—**farandulero**, *n.* comedian, player.

fardo, *m.* bale, bundle; load.

farfullar, *vi.* (coll.) to gabble, jabber

faringe, *f.* pharynx.

farmacéutico, *a.* pharmaceutical.—*n.* pharmacist, druggist.—**farmacia**, *f.* pharmacy; drugstore.

faro, *m.* lighthouse; beacon; (auto) light, headlight.—**farol**, *m.* lantern, light; street lamp; bluff.—*echar un f.*, to bluff.—**farola**, *f.* street lamp; lighthouse.—**farolear**, *vi.* (coll.) to boast, brag.

farra, *f.* spree.

farsa, *f.* farce; company of players; sham, humbug.—**farsante**, *mf. & a.* humbug; fake.

fascinación, *f.* fascination, enchantment.—**fascinador**, *n. & a.* fascinator, charmer; fascinating, charming.—**fascinante**, *a.* fascinating, charming.—**fascinar**, *vt.* to fascinate, bewitch, charm.

fase, *f.* phase, aspect.

fastidiar, *vt.* to annoy, bore.—*vr.* to weary; to become vexed, bored or displeased.—**fastidio**, *m.* dislike; weariness; nuisance, annoyance.—**fastidioso**, *a.* annoying; tiresome; displeased, bothersome.

fastuoso, *a.* magnificent, lavish; pompous, ostentatious.

fatal, *a.* fatal; mortal; disastrous; fated.—**fatalidad**, *f.* fatality; fate, destiny; calamity.

fatiga, *f.* fatigue, weariness; hardship; anxiety; hard breathing.—**fatigar**, *vti.* [b] to fatigue, tire.—*vri.* to tire, get tired.—**fatigoso**, *a.* tiring; tiresome, boring; tired, fatigued.

fatuo, *a.* foolish, conceited.—*fuego f.*, will-o'-the-wisp.

fauces, *f. pl.* gullet.

favor, *m.* favor; help, aid; grace; compliment.—*a f. de*, in behalf of; in favor of.—*f. de, hágame el f.* or *por f.*, please.—**favorable**, *a.* favorable.—**favorecer**, *vti.* [3] to favor; to help, befriend; to abet; (of colors, clothes, etc.) to be becoming.—**favoritismo**, *m.* favoritism. —**favorito**, *n. & a.* favorite.

faz, *f.* face; outside.

fe, *f.* faith, faithfulness; testimony. —*dar f.*, to attest, certify; to witness.—*f. de bautismo* or *de nacimiento*, baptism or birth certificate.

fealdad, *f.* ugliness, homeliness.

febrero, *m.* February

febril, *a.* feverish.

fécula, *f.* starch.—**feculento**, *a.* starchy

fecundación, *f.* fecundation, fertilization.—**fecundar**, *vt.* to fertilize, fecundate.—**fecundidad**, *f.* fecundity, fertility, fruitfulness.—**fecundo**, *a.* fecund, fertile; abundant copious.

fecha, *f.* date; standing.—**fechar,** *vt.* to date.

fechoría, *f.* misdeed, villainy.

federación, *f.* federation, confederation.—**federal,** *a.* federal.

felicidad, *f.* happiness, felicity.—*¡felicidades!* congratulations!—**felicitación,** *f.* congratulation, felicitation.—**felicitar,** *vt.* to congratulate, felicitate.

feligrés, *n.* parishioner.

feliz, *a.* happy, fortunate.

felonía, *f.* felony, treachery.

felpa, *f.* plush.—**felpilla,** *f.* chenille.—**felpudo,** *a.* plushy.—*m.* doormat.

femenino, *a.* feminine.—**feminidad,** *f.* femininity.

fenecer, *vii.* [3] to die; to end.

fenomenal, *a.* phenomenal, extraordinary.—**fenómeno,** *m.* phenomenon; (coll.) freak.

feo, *a.* ugly, homely; improper; offensive.—*m.* slight, affront.—*hacerle un f. a alguien,* to slight someone.

feraz, *a.* fertile, fruitful; abundant, plentiful.

féretro, *m.* bier, coffin.

feria, *f.* fair, market, bazaar.—**feriado,** *a.—día f.,* holiday.

fermentación, *f.* fermentation.—**fermentar,** *vi. & vt.* to ferment.—**fermento,** *m.* ferment, leavening; (chem.) enzyme.

ferocidad, *f.* ferocity.—**feroz,** *a.* ferocious, fierce.

férreo, *a.* of or containing iron; harsh, severe.—*vía férrea,* railroad.—**ferretería,** *f.* hardware; hardware shop.—**ferretero,** *n.* hardware dealer.

ferrocarril, *m.* railroad, railway.—*f. de cremallera,* rack railroad.—**ferrocarrilero, ferroviario,** *a.* pertaining to a railroad.—*n.* railroad employee.

fértil, *a.* fertile; plentiful.—**fertilidad,** *f.* fertility; abundance.—**fertilizante,** *m. & a.* fertilizer; fertilizing.—**fertilizar,** *vti.* [a] to fertilize, make fruitful.

ferviente, fervoroso, *a.* fervent; zealous; devout.—**fervor,** *m.* zeal, fervor.

festejar, *vt.* to entertain; to feast; to woo; to celebrate.—**festejo,** *m.* feast, entertainment; courtship.

festín, *m.* banquet, feast.

festival, *m.* festival.—**festividad,** *f.* festivity; gaiety; holiday.—**festivo,** *a.* festive, gay; humorous, witty; festival.—*día f.,* holiday.

fétido, *a.* fetid, stinking.

feto, *m.* fetus.

fiado, *m.—al f.,* on credit, on trust.—**fiador,** *n.* bondsman, guarantor, surety.—*salir f.,* to go surety.

fiambre, *m.* cold food, cold meats; (coll.) old or late news.—**fiambrera,** *f.* lunch basket; dinner pail.

fianza, *f.* surety, bail; caution; security.—*bajo f.,* on bail.—**fiar,** *vt.* to trust; to bail; to sell on trust, give credit for; to entrust, confide.—*vi.* to confide; to sell on trust, give credit.—*ser de f.,* to be trustworthy.—*vr.* (de) to have confidence (in), depend (on), trust.

fibra, *f.* fiber, filament; energy, stamina, vigor; (min.) vein of ore.—**fibroso,** *a.* fibrous.

ficción, *f.* fiction; tale, story.—**ficticio,** *a.* fictitious.

ficha, *f.* chip or man (in games); token; personal record; (fig.) rascal, bad person.—**fichar,** *vt.* to file a card of personal record (police, etc.); (coll.) to blacklist.—**fichero,** *m.* card index, catalogue.

fidedigno, *a.* trustworthy; creditable.

fidelidad, *f.* fidelity, faithfulness; accuracy.

fideos, *m. pl.* vermicelli; spaghetti; noodles.

fiebre, *f.* fever; intense excitement.—*f. palúdica,* malaria.

fiel, *a.* faithful, devoted; true, accurate; (pol.) stalwart.—*m.* pointer of a balance or steelyard.—*al f.,* equal weight, even balance.

fieltro, *m.* felt; felt hat.

fiera, *f.* wild beast; vicious animal or person.—**fierabrás,** *m.* (coll.) spitfire, bully; wayward child.—**fiereza,** *f.* fierceness, ferocity.—**fiero,** *a.* fierce, cruel; ferocious; huge; wild, savage.

fierro, *m.* V. HIERRO.

fiesta, *f.* feast, entertainment, party; festivity, holiday.—*aguar la f.,* to mar one's pleasure.—*hacer fiestas,* to caress; to wheedle, to fawn on.—**fiestero,** *a.* gay, jolly.—*n.* jolly person.

figura, *f.* figure; shape; build; image; face card.—**figurado,** *a.* figurative, metaphorical.—**figurar,** *vt.* to shape, fashion; to represent.—*vi.* to figure.—*vr.* to fancy, imagine to occur, come to mind; to seem.—**figurín,** *m.* fashion plate; well-dressed man.

fijador, *n. & a.* fixer; fastener; fixing; fastening;—*m.* hair tonic.—**fijar,** *vti.* [49] to fix, fasten; to determine, establish; to post (bills); to set (a date).—*vri.* (en) to settle (in); to fix one's attention (on); to stare at; to take notice (of), pay close attention (to).—**fijeza,** *f.* firmness, stability; steadfastness.—**fijo,** *ppi.* of FIJAR.—*a.* fixed; settled; per-

manent; (mech.) stationary.—*a punto f.*, exactly; with certitude.—*de f.*, certainly.—*hora fija*, time agreed on.

fila, *f.* row, tier, line; (mil.) rank; hatred.—*en f.*, in a row

filamento, *m.* filament.

filantropía, *f.* philanthropy.—**filántropo**, *n.* philanthropist.

filarmónico, *a.* philharmonic.

filete, *m.* (arch.) fillet; (sewing) narrow hem; edge, rim; (print.) ornamental line; tenderloin.

filfa, *f.* (coll.) fib, hoax, fake.

filiación, *f.* filiation; personal description.—**filial**, *a.* filial.

filibustero, *m.* filibuster; buccaneer.

filigrana, *f.* filigree; watermark in paper; fanciful thing.

filipino, *n. & a.* Filipino.

filmar, *vt.* (neol.) to film (a moving picture).

filo, *m.* cutting edge.

filón, *m.* (geog.) vein, lode.

filoso, *a.* (Am.) sharp.

filosofía, *f.* philosophy.—**filosófico**, *a.* philosophic(al).—**filósofo**, *n.* philosopher.

filtración, *f.* filtration, leak(age).—**filtrar**, *vt. & vi.* to filter.—*vi.* to percolate, filter.—*vr.* to leak out; to disappear; to filter through.—**filtro**, *m.* filter.

fin, *m.* end, conclusion; object, purpose.—*a f. de*, in order to, so as to.—*a f. de que*, so that, to the end that.—*al f.*, at last.—*al f. y al cabo*, at last; lastly; after all.—*en f.*, finally, lastly; in short; well.—*poner f.*, to put an end to, stop, get rid of.—*por f.*, at last, finally.—*sin f.*, endless.—**final**, *a.* final; conclusive.—*m.* end, conclusion.—*pl.* (sports) finals.—**finalidad**, *f.* finality; intention.—**finalista**, *mf.* (sports) finalist.—**finalizar**, *vti.* [a] to finish, conclude; (law) to execute (a contract, deed).—*vii.* to end, to be finished or concluded.

financiamiento, *m.* financing.—**financiar**, *vt.* (Am.) to finance.—**financiero**, *a.* financial.—*n.* financier.—**financista**, *mf.* (Am.) financier.—**finanzas**, *f. pl.* public finances.

finca, *f.* real estate, land; country estate, farm, ranch.

finés, *a.* Finnish.—*n.* Finn.

fineza, *f.* fineness; kindness, courtesy; gift, favor.

fingimiento, *m.* simulation, pretense, sham.—**fingir**, [c] *vti. & vri.* to feign, dissemble; to affect; to imagine.

finiquitar, *vt.* to settle and close (an account).

finlandés, *a.* Finnish.—*n.* Finn.

fino, *a.* fine; thin, slender; subtle; delicate, nice; affectionate; sharp (as a point); polite, urbane.—**finura**, *f.* fineness; politeness; courtesy.

firma, *f.* signature; hand (as hand and seal); act of signing; (com.) firm, house; firm name.

firmamento, *m.* firmament, sky.

firmante, *mf.* signer, subscriber.—**firmar**, *vt.* to sign; to subscribe, set one's hand.

firme, *a.* firm, stable; hard; unyielding; resolute.—*m.* groundwork, bed; roadbed.—*en f.*, definitive, final, in final form.—*adv.* firmly, strongly.—**firmeza**, *f.* firmness; hardness.

fiscal, *a.* fiscal.—*m.* attorney general; district attorney, public prosecutor.—**fiscalización**, *f.* discharge of a FISCAL's duties; control.—**fiscalizar**, *vti.* [a] to prosecute; to criticize, censure; to control.

fisgar, *vii.* [b] to snoop; to peep; to pry.—**fisgón**, *n.* snooper; busybody.—*a.* snooping.—**fisgonear**, *vi.* to pry; to snoop.

física, *f.* physics.—**físico**, *a.* physical.—*n.* physicist.—*m.* (coll.) physical appearance, physique.

fisiología, *f.* physiology.—**fisiológico**, *a.* physiological.

fisonomía, *f.* features; face.

fisura, *f.* (geol.) fissure, cleft; (surg.) fissure of bone.

flaco, *a.* thin, lean; feeble; frail.—*m.* weak point, weakness.—**flacura**, *f.* thinness.

flagrante, *a.* flagrant.—*en f.*, in the act.

flama, *f.* V. LLAMA.—**flamante**, *a.* flaming, bright; brand-new.—**flamear**, *vi.* to flame, blaze; to flutter (banners, sails, etc.).

flamenco, *a. & n.* Flemish.—*n.* flamingo.—*cante f.*, Andalusian gypsy singing.

flan, *m.* rich custard.

flanco, *m.* side; flank.

flanera, *f.* pudding pan.

flanquear, *vt.* to flank.

flaquear, *vi.* to flag, weaken; to slacken.—**flaqueza**, *f.* leanness, thinness; weakness; frailty.

flatulencia, *f.* belch, wind.

flauta, *f.* flute.—**flautín**, *m.* piccolo.—**flautista**, *mf.* flute player.

fleco, *m.* fringe, purl, flounce.

flecha, *f.* arrow.—**flechar**, *vt.* to shoot an arrow; (fig.) to inspire sudden love.—**flechazo**, *m.* arrow wound; love at first sight.

fleje, *m.* iron hoop or strap.

flema, *f.* phlegm.—**flemático,** *a.* phlegmatic.

flemón, *m.* gumboil.

fletar, *vt.* to charter (a ship); to freight; to hire.—*salir fletado,* to escape fast; to leave on the run.—**flete,** *m.* freight, freightage; hire price (for transporting freight, cargo).

flexibilidad, *f.* flexibility.—**flexible,** *a.* flexible; docile.—**flexión,** *f.* flection, flexure.

flirtear, *vi.* (neol.) to flirt.

flojear, *vi.* to slacken; to grow weak. —**flojedad, flojera,** *f.* weakness, feebleness; laxity, negligence.—**flojo,** *a.* loose, lax; weak; flaccid; lazy; cowardly.

flor, *f.* flower; blossom; prime; compliment.—*decir,* or *echar flores,* to pay compliments, to flatter.—*f. y nata,* flower, elite.—**floreado,** *a.* flowered, figured (goods); made of the finest flour.—**florear,** *vt.* to flower; to bolt (flour); to flourish; to pay compliments to.—**florecer,** *vii.* [3] to flower, bloom; to prosper. —**floreciente,** *a.* flourishing, thriving. —**florecimiento,** *m.* flowering; flourishing.—**floreo,** *m.* idle talk; compliment; (fencing, mus.) flourish. —**florero,** *n.* (Am.) flower vendor. —*m.* flowerpot; flower vase; flower stand.—**floresta,** *f.* wooded field.— **florete,** *m.* fencing foil.—**florido,** *a.* flowery; full of flowers, in bloom; choice, select.—**florista,** *mf.* florist.

flota, *f.* fleet.—**flotación,** *f.* flotation, floating.—*linea de f.,* waterline.— **flotador,** *n.* & *a.* floater; floating.—*m.* float.—**flotante,** *a.* floating.—**flotar,** *vi.* to float; to waft.

fluctuación, *f.* fluctuation; wavering. —**fluctuar,** *vi.* to fluctuate; waver.

fluente, *a.* fluent, flowing.—**fluidez,** *f.* fluidity; fluency.—**fluido,** *a.* fluid; fluent.—*m.* fluid.—**fluir,** [23-e] *vii.* to flow.—**flujo,** *m.* flux, flow.

fluorescencia, *f.* fluorescence.—**fluorescente,** *a.* fluorescent.

foca, *f.* (zool.) seal.

foco, *m.* focus; center, source; electric-light bulb.

fofo, *a.* spongy, soft.

fogarada, fogata, *f.* bonfire, blaze.— **fogón,** *m.* fireside; cooking place, cooking stove, kitchen range; touchhole of a gun; firebox (of a boiler, locomotive, etc.).—**fogonazo,** *m.* powder flash.—**fogonero,** *n.* fireman, stoker.—**fogosidad,** *f.* fieriness, heat, vehemence.—**fogoso,** *a.* fiery; ardent; impetuous; spirited.

foliar, *vt.* to paginate, number the pages of a book, etc.—**folio,** *m.* folio.

follaje, *m.* foliage; leafage.

folletín, *m.* newspaper serial.—**folleto,** *m.* pamphlet, booklet, brochure.

fomentar, *vt.* to foment; to warm; to promote, encourage.—**fomento,** *m.* fomentation; promotion; development.

fonda, *f.* inn; eating house; second-rate hotel.

fondeadero, *m.* anchoring ground; haven.—**fondear,** *vt.* (naut.) to sound; to search (a ship).—*vi.* to cast anchor.—**fondeo,** *m.* (naut.) search; casting anchor.

fondillo, *m.* seat of trousers; (coll.) bottom, posterior.

fondista, *mf.* innkeeper.

fondo, *m.* bottom; depth; background; nature (of a person); principal or essential part of a thing; fund, capital.—*pl.* funds, resources. —*a f.,* thoroughly.—*andar mal de fondos,* to be short of money.— *en f.,* abreast.

fonética, *f.* phonetics.—**fonético,** *a.* phonetic.—**fónico,** *a.* phonic, acoustic.

fonógrafo, *m.* phonograph.

fontana, *f.* fountain, spring, water jet.—**fontanar,** *m.* water spring.

football, *m.* football.

forajido, *n.* outlaw, fugitive; bandit.

forastero, *a.* foreign.—*n.* stranger; outsider.

forcejar, forcejear, *vi.* to struggle, strive; to contest, contend; to resist; to tussle.

forestal, *a.* pertaining to a forest.— *ingeniería f.,* forestry.

forja, *f.* smelting furnace; smithy; forge; forging.—**forjador,** *n.* blacksmith, forger.—**forjar,** *vt.* to forge; to frame, form.

forma, *f.* form, shape; manner; method, order; pattern, mold; format; block (for hats, etc.).—*pl.* (of persons) figure.—*de f. que,* so as, so that.—*en f.,* in due form; in a thorough and proper manner.— *tomar f.,* to develop, to materialize. —**formación,** *f.* formation, forming. —**formal,** *a.* formal, regular, methodical; proper; serious; truthful, reliable; well-behaved.—**formalidad,** *f.* formality; exactness, punctuality; seriousness, solemnity; requisite; established practice.—**formalismo,** *m.* formalism.—**formalista,** *mf.* formalist.—**formalizar,** *vti.* [a] to put in final form; to legalize.—*vri.* to become serious or earnest.—**formar,** *vt.* to form; to shape.—*f. parte de,* to be a member of.—*vr.* to develop; to take form.—**formativo,** *a.* forma-

tive.—formato, *m.* format (of a book).

fórmula, *f.* formula; recipe, prescription.—**formular,** *vt.* to formulate.—**formulismo,** *m.* formulism; red tape.

fornido, *a.* robust, husky, stout, stalwart.

foro, *m.* forum; court of justice; bar, the legal profession; back (in stage scenery).

forraje, *m.* forage, fodder; foraging.

forrar, *vt.* to line (as clothes); to cover (as a book, umbrella, etc.); (anat.) to sheathe.—**forro,** *m.* lining, doubling; cover.

fortalecedor, *n. & a.* fortifier; fortifying.—**fortalecer,** *vti.* [3] to fortify, strengthen, corroborate.—**fortalecimiento,** *m.* fortifying; fortification, defenses.—**fortaleza,** *f.* fortitude; strength, vigor; fortress, fort.—**fortificación,** fortification; fort; military architecture.—**fortificar,** *vti.* [d] to strengthen; (mil.) to fortify.—**fortín,** *m.* small fort.

fortuna, *f.* fortune; good luck; wealth.—*por f.,* fortunately.

forúnculo, *m.* = FURUNCULO.

forzar, *vti.* [12-a] to force, break in (as a door); to compel; to subdue by force; to ravish.—**forzoso,** *a.* obligatory, compulsory; unavoidable.—**forzudo,** *a.* strong, vigorous.

fosa, *f.* grave.

fosco, *a.* frowning; cross.

fosfato, *m.* phosphate.

fosforescencia, *f.* phosphorescence.—**fosforecer,** *vii.* [3] to phosphoresce.—**fósforo,** *m.* phosphorous; friction match.

foso, *m.* pit; stage pit; moat.

foto, *f.* photo (photograph).—**fotocopia,** *f.* photostat.—**fotoeléctrico,** *a.* photoelectric.—**fotogénico,** *a.* photogenic.—**fotograbado,** *m.* photoengraving, photogravure.—**fotografía,** *f.* photography; photograph.—**fotografiar,** *vt.* to photograph.—**fotógrafo,** *n.* photographer.

frac, *m.* tail coat.

fracasar, *vi.* to fail.—**fracaso,** *m.* downfall; failure.

fracción, *f.* fragment; fraction.—**fraccionamiento,** *m.* division into fractions.—**fraccionario,** *a.* fractional.

fractura, *f.* fracture; breaking, crack.—**fracturar,** *vt. & vi.* to fracture, break.

fragancia, *f.* fragrance, scent.—**fragante,** *a.* fragrant.

frágil, *a.* brittle, breakable, fragile.—**fragilidad,** *f.* fragility; frailty.

fragmentario, *a.* fragmentary.—**fragmento,** *m.* fragment.

fragor, *m.* clamorous noise; blare.

fragosidad, *f.* roughness; impenetrability, thickness, wildness (of a forest); craggedness.—**fragoso,** *a.* craggy, rough; full of brambles and briers; roaring.

fragua, *f.* forge; smithy.—**fraguar,** *vt.* to forge; to hammer out; to plan, plot.—*vi.* (of concrete, etc.) to set.

fraile, *m.* friar, monk.

frambuesa, *f.* (bot.) raspberry.

francachela, *f.* (coll.) lark, spree; gala meal.

francés, *a.* French.—*m.* French language.—*n.* Frenchman (-woman.)

franco, *a.* frank, open; franc; free, clear, disengaged; exempt.—*f. a bordo,* free on board.—*m.* franc.

francotirador, sniper.

franela, *f.* flannel.

franja, *f.* fringe, trimming, band; stripe; strip (of land).

franquear, *vt.* to exempt; to grant immunity to; to enfranchise; to prepay (postage); to open, clear.—*vr.* to unbosom oneself.—**franqueo,** *m.* postage.—**franqueza,** *f.* frankness.—*con f.,* frankly.—**franquicia,** *f.* exemption from taxes; franchise, grant.

frasco, *m.* flask, vial.

frase, *f.* phrase.—**fraseología,** *f.* phraseology; verbosity; wording.

fraternal, *a.* brotherly, fraternal.—**fraternidad,** *f.* fraternity, brotherhood.—**fraternizar,** *vii.* [a] to fraternize.

fraude, *m.,* **fraudulencia,** *f.* fraud.—**fraudulento,** *a.* fraudulent.

frazada, *f.* blanket.

frecuencia, *f.* frequency.—*con f.,* frequently.—**frecuentar,** *vt.* to frequent.—**frecuente,** *a.* frequent.

fregadero, *m.* kitchen sink.—**fregar,** *vti.* [1-b] to rub; to wash; to scrub, scour; (Am.) to annoy, bother.—**fregona,** *f.* kitchenmaid; dishwasher.

freír, *vti.* [35-49] to fry; to pester, irritate.

frenar, *vt.* to brake, apply the brake to; to restrain; to bridle.

frenesí, *m.* frenzy, fury, madness; folly.—**frenético,** *a.* mad, frantic, frenzied.

freno, *m.* brake; bridle or bit of the bridle; curb, restraint, control.

frente, *f.* forehead; countenance.—*m.* front, fore part, façade.—*al f.,* opposite; carried forward.—*al f. de,* in front of; in charge of.—*de f.,* from the front; front; facing;

abreast.—*f. a,* opposite, facing.—*f. a f.,* face to face.—*f. por f.,* directly opposite.—*hacer f.,* to face (a problem, etc.); to meet (a demand, etc.).

fresa, *f.* strawberry; (mech.) drill, bit, milling tool.

fresca, *f.* cool air, fresh air; fresh remark.—fresco, *a.* fresh; (of weather, etc.) cool; just made, finished, or gathered.—*m.* cool or fresh air; (art) fresco.—*hacer f.,* to be cool.—*tomar el f.,* to get or go out for some fresh air.—frescor, *m.* cool; freshness.—frescura, *f.* freshness; impudence; unconcern.

fresno, *m.* ash tree; ash wood.

frialdad, *f.* coldness; unconcern, coolness.

fricasé, *m.* fricassee.

fricción, *f.* friction, rubbing.—friccionar, *vt.* to rub.

friega, *f.* friction, rubbing.

frigidez, *f.* frigidity.—frígido, *a.* frigid.—frigorífico, *a.* refrigerating. —*m.* refrigerator, storage house or room.

frijol, *m.* bean.

frío, *a.* cold; frigid; indifferent, unemotional; dull.—*m.* cold, coldness. —*hacer f.,* to be cold.—*tener f.,* to feel cold.—friolento, *a.* chilly; very sensitive to cold.

friolera, *f.* trifle, bauble.

frisar, *vi.* (en) to approach; to be near (to)

frita, *f.* (Am.) hamburger.—fritada, *f.* fry; dish of anything fried.— frito, *ppi.* of FREÍR.—*estar f,* to be lost; to be annoyed.—*m.* fry.— fritura, *f.* fry, fritter.

frivolidad, *f.* frivolity.—frívolo, *a.* frivolous, trifling.

fronda, *f.* leaf; frond.—*pl.* foliage, verdure.—frondosidad, *f.* frondage, leafy foliage.—frondoso, *a.* leafy, luxuriant.

frontal, *a.* frontal, pertaining to the forehead.—*m.* (eccl.) frontal; (anat.) frontal bone.

frontera, *f.* frontier, border —fronterizo, *a.* frontier; facing, opposite.— frontero, *a.* opposite, facing.

frontis, *m.* frontispiece, façade.— frontispicio, *m.* frontispiece.

frontón, *m.* main wall of a handball court; Jai-Alai court.

frotación, *f.* rubbing.—frotamiento, *m.* rubbing.—frotar, *vt.* to rub.

fructífero, *a.* fruit-bearing; fruitful. —fructificación, *f.* fructification.— fructificar, *vii.* [d] to bear fruit, to yield profit.

frugal, *a.* frugal.—frugalidad, *f.* frugality, thrift.

fruición, *f.* fruition, enjoyment.

fruncimiento, *m.* wrinkling; shirring. —fruncir, *vti.* [a] to wrinkle; to gather in pleats; to shrivel.—*f. el ceño,* or *f. las cejas,* to frown.—*f. los labios,* to curl or pucker the lips.

fruslería, *f.* trifle, bauble, tidbit.

frustración, *f.* frustration.—frustrar, *vt.* to frustrate.—*vr.* to fail.

fruta, *f.* fruit.—frutal, *a.* fruit-bearing; fruit.—*m.* fruit tree.—frutería, *f.* fruit store.—frutero, *n.* fruit seller; fruit basket, fruit dish.— fruto, *m.* fruit; fruits, result; benefice, profit.

fuego, *m.* fire; (Am.) skin eruption; firing of firearms; passion.—*f. fatuo,* will-o'-the-wisp.—*fuegos artificiales,* fireworks.—*hacer f.,* to fire, shoot. —*romper f.,* to start shooting.

fuelle, *m.* bellows; blower; puckers in clothes.

fuente, *f.* water spring; fountain; source; serving dish, platter.—*beber en buenas fuentes,* to be well-informed.

fuera, *adv.* out, outside.—*de f.,* from the outside.—*f. de,* besides, in addition.—*f. de sí,* beside oneself; aghast.—*hacia f.,* outward.—*por f.,* on the outside.—*interj.* out! away! put him out! get out!

fuero, *m.* statute, law; jurisdiction; privilege or exemption; compilation of laws.

fuerte, *a.* strong; powerful; intense; firm, compact; hard, not malleable. —*m.* fort, fortress; strong point; (mus.) forte.—*adv.* strongly, hard, copiously.—fuerza, *f.* force; power; strength; stress; violence; firmness; (mil.) force(s).—*a f. de,* by dint of, by force of.—*a la f.,* a viva f.,* by main force, forcibly.—*f. mayor,* superior force.

fuetazo, *m.* (Am.) blow with a whip. —fuete, *m.* horsewhip, riding whip.

fuga, *f.* flight; escape; runaway; elopement; leak, leakage; fugue.— fugacidad, *f.* brevity.—fugarse, *vri.* [b] to flee, run away; to escape, leak out.—fugaz, *a.* brief.—fugitivo, *n. & a.* fugitive, runaway.—*a.* brief, perishable, unstable.

fulano, *n.* (Mr.) so-and-so.

fulgor, *m.* brilliancy —fulgurar, *vi.* to flash, shine with brilliancy.

fullero, *a.* (coll) shady, dishonest.— *n.* cheat, sharper; card sharp.

fumada, *f.* puff, whiff, (of smoke).— fumadero, *m* smoking room.— fumador, *n.* smoker.—*a.* addicted to smoking.—fumar, *vt. & vi.* to smoke (cigars, etc.).

fumigación, *f.* fumigation.—**fumigar,** *vti.* [b] to fumigate.

función, *f.* function; duty; functioning; religious ceremony; (theat.) performance, play.—**funcional,** *a.* functional.—**funcionamiento,** *m.* functioning, working, operation, performance.—**funcionar,** *vi.* to function; to work, run.—**funcionario,** *n.* functionary, public official.

funda, *f.* case, sheath, cover, envelope, slip.—*f. de almohada,* pillowcase.

fundación, *f.* foundation; founding; beginning, origin.—**fundador,** *n.* founder.—**fundamental,** *a.* fundamental, basal.—**fundamentar,** *vt.* to establish on a basis; to base; to set firm.—**fundamento,** *m.* basis; reason, fundamental principle; root; good behavior, orderliness.—**fundar,** *vt.* to found; to raise; to establish, institute; to base, ground.—*vr.* (en) to base one's opinion (on).

fundición, *f.* smelting; foundry.—**fundir,** *vt.* to fuse or melt; to merge, blend; to be ruined.

fúnebre, *a.* funereal, mournful; funeral; dark, lugubrious.—**funeral(es),** *m.* funeral.—**funeraria,** *f.* funeral parlor.—**funerario, funeral,** *a.* funeral.—**funesto,** *a.* ill-fated; fatal; mournful; regrettable.

fungir, *vii.* [c] to act in some capacity.

fungosidad, *f.* fungus, fungous growth; spongy morbid growth.

furgón, *m.* wagon; boxcar.

furia, *f.* fury, rage; ill-tempered person.—**furibundo, furioso,** *a.* furious; frantic.—**furor,** *m.* furor, fury, anger; enthusiasm; exaltation of fancy.—*hacer f.,* to be the rage.

furtivo, *a.* furtive, clandestine.

furúnculo, *m.* (med.) boil.

fuselaje, *m.* fuselage.

fusible, *a.* fusible.—*m.* (elec.) fuse.

fusil, *m.* rifle, gun.—**fusilamiento,** *m.* execution by shooting.—**fusilar,** *vt.* to shoot, execute by shooting.—**fusilazo,** *m.* rifle shot.—**fusilería,** *f.* (mil.) guns, rifles.—**fusilero,** *m.* rifleman.

fusión, *f.* fusion, melting; union; merger.—**fusionar,** *vt.* to unite, merge—*vr.* to merge, form a merger.

fusta, *f.* whiplash.—**fustigar,** *vti.* [b] to lash.

fútbol, *m.* soccer.

futesa, *f.* trifle, bagatelle.—**fútil,** *a.* trifling, trivial.

futuro, *a.* future.—*n.* betrothed, future husband (wife); future.—*en lo f.,* in the future, hereafter.

G

gabacho, *a.* (coll.) Frenchlike.—*m.* (coll.) Frenchman.

gabán, *m.* overcoat.

gabardina, *f.* gabardine.

gabinete, *m.* cabinet (of a government); sitting room; private parlor; studio, study; dentist's or doctor's office.

gacela, *f.* gazelle.

gaceta, *f.* official gazette.—**gacetilla,** *f.* personal-news column; gossip; newspaper squib.—**gacetillero,** *n.* gacetista, *mf.* newsmonger, gossip.

gacho, *a.* bent; drooping; turned down.—*a gachas,* (coll.) on all fours.—*con las orejas gachas,* (coll.) crestfallen.

gafas, *f. pl.* spectacles.

gago, *n.* stammerer, stutterer.—**gaguear,** *vi.* to stutter.—**gaguera,** *f.* stuttering.

gaita, *f.* hurdy-gurdy.—*asomar la g.,* to stick out one's neck.—*g. gallega,* bagpipe.—**gaitero,** *n.* piper, bagpipe player.

gaje, *m.*—*pl.* fees.—*gajes del oficio,* fisherman's luck.

gajo, *m.* torn off branch (of a tree); bunch of fruit; segment of fruit.

gala, *f.* full dress; array; gala.—*pl.* trappings.—*galas de novia,* bridal trousseau.—*hacer g. de,* to be proud of, glory in, boast of.

galán, *m.* gallant; lover, wooer; (theat.) leading man.—**galante,** *a.* gallant, polished, attentive to ladies.—**galantear,** *vt.* to court, woo.—**galanteo,** *m.* gallantry, courtship, wooing.—**galantería,** *f.* gallantry, courtesy, politeness; compliment to a lady.

galápago, *m.* fresh-water tortoise.

galardón, *m.* reward, prize.

galeno, *m.* (coll.) physician.

galeote, *m.* galley slave.

galera, *f.* (naut., print.) galley; wagon, van; prison.—**galerada,** *f.* (print.) galley; galley proof.

galería, *f.* gallery, lobby, corridor; (theat.) gallery; art museum; collection of paintings.

galerna, *f.* (naut.) stormy northwest wind.

galés, *n. & a.* Welshman; Welsh.

galgo, *n.* greyhound.

galillo, *m.* uvula, soft palate.

galocha, *f.* galosh, clog.

galón, *m.* gallon; braid, tape, binding lace; stripe, chevron (on uniforms).—**galonear,** *vt.* (sewing) to bind; to trim with braid.

galopar, *vi.* to gallop.—**galope,** *m.* gallop; haste, speed—*a g. hur-*

riedly, speedily.—**galopín**, *m.* ragamuffin; rascal; shrewd fellow.

galpón, *m.* (Am.) shed.

galvanizar, *vti.* [a] to galvanize; to electroplate.

gallardete, *m.* pennant, streamer.

gallardía, *f.* gracefulness; bravery; nobleness.—**gallardo**, *a.* graceful, elegant; lively; brave.

gallear, *vi.* to raise the voice in anger; to crow; to bully.

gallegada, *f.* a Galician dance and its tune.—**gallego**, *n.* & *a.* Galician; (Am.) (nickname) Spanish; Spaniard.

galleta, *f.* cracker, biscuit, hardtack; cookie; slap.—**galletica**, *f.* small or fine cracker or biscuit.

gallina, *f.* hen.—*g. de Guinea* or *guineo*, guinea hen.—*mf.* coward.—*g. ciega*, blindman's buff.—**gallinero**, *m.* poultry yard, hen coop or house; (coll., theat.) top gallery.—**gallito**, *m.* small cock; cock of the walk, bully.—**gallo**, *m.* cock, rooster; false note in singing; bully.—*g. de pelea*, or *inglés*, gamecock.—*patas de g.*, wrinkles in the corner of the eye.

gamo, *m.* buck of the fallow deer.

gamuza, *f.* chamois; chamois skin.

gana, *f.* appetite, hunger; desire; mind.—*dar g.*, or *ganas de*, to arouse desire to.—*de buena g.*, willingly.—*de mala g.*, unwillingly.—*no me da la g.*, I don't want to, I won't.—*tener g.*, or *ganas de*, to desire; to wish to.

ganadería, *f.* cattle raising; cattle ranch; cattle brand.—**ganadero**, *n.* cattleman; cattle dealer; stock farmer.—*a.* pertaining to cattle.—**ganado**, *m.* cattle; herd.—*g. caballar*, horses.—*g. de cerda*, swine, hogs.—*g. lanar*, sheep.—*g. vacuno*, cattle.

ganador, *n.* & *a.* winner; winning.—**ganancia**, *f.* gain, profit.—**ganancioso**, *a.* lucrative, profitable; gaining.—**ganapán**, *m.* drudge; common laborer; coarse man.—**ganar**, *vt.* to win; to gain; to earn.—*g. el pan, la vida*, or *el sustento*, to make a living.

gancho, *m.* hook; crook; crotch.—*echar el g.*, (fig.) to catch; to hook.—*g. del pelo*, hairpin.—*tener g.*, (coll.) to be attractive.

gandul, *n.* (coll.) idler, loafer, tramp.—**gandulería**, *f.* idleness, laziness.

ganga, *f.* bargain; windfall.

gangoso, *a.* twangy.

gangrena, *f.* gangrene.—**gangrenarse**, *vr.* to become gangrenous.

ganguear, *vi* to snuffle; to speak nasally.—**gangueo**, *m.* snuffle; nasal speech.

gansada, *f.* (coll.) stupidity.—**ganso**, *n.* goose, gander; silly person, ninny.

ganzúa, *f.* picklock, skeleton key; burglar.

gañán, *m.* farm hand; rustic; (fig.) uncouth, brutal person.

gañote, *m.* (coll.) throat.

garabateo, *m.* scribbling, scrawling.—**garabato**, *m.* scrawl, scribble; hook.

garaje, *m.* garage.

garantía, *f.* guarantee; (com. and law) warranty, guaranty, security.—**garantizar**, *vti.* [a] to guarantee, vouch for.

garañón, *m.* stallion.

garapiñado, *a.* candied, sugarcoated.

garbanzo, *m.* chickpea.

garbo, *m.* grace, gracefulness, elegant carriage.—**garboso**, *a.* graceful, sprightly.

garete, *m.*—*al g.*, (naut.) adrift.

garfio, *m.* hook; gaff.

garganta, *f.* throat; gullet; gorge.—**gargantilla**, *f.* necklace.

gárgara, *f.*, **gargarismo**, *m.* gargle, gargling.—*hacer gárgaras*, to gargle.—**gargarizar**, *vii.* [a] to gargle.

garita, *f.* sentry box; lodge, hut.

garito, *m.* gambling house or den.

garlopa, *f.* (carp.) jack plane, long plane.

garra, *f.* claw, paw, talon; hook.—*echarle g.*, (coll.) to arrest, grasp.—*sacar de las garras de*, to free from.

garrafa, *f.* carafe, decanter.—**garrafal**, *a.* great, huge.—**garrafón**, *m.* large carafe.

garrapata, *f.* (entom.) tick.—**garrapatear**, *vi* to scribble, scrawl.

garrocha, *f.* (sports) pole; goad stick.

garrotazo, *m.* blow with club or cudgel.—**garrote**, *m.* club, cudgel; garrote (for capital punishment).—*dar g.*, to garrote.—**garrotero**, *n.* beater; (coll.) usurer.

garrucha, *f.* pulley.

garza, *f.* heron.

garzo, *a.* blue-eyed.

gas, *m.* gas; vapor; (coll.) gaslight.

gasa, *f.* gauze.

gaseosa, *f.* soda water.—**gaseoso**, *a.* gaseous.—**gasificar**, *vti.* [d] to gasify.—**gasolina**, *f.* gasoline, gas.

gastable, *a.* expendable.—**gastado**, *a.* worn-out; shabby; blasé.—**gastador**, *a.* lavish, prodigal.—*n.* spender, spendthrift.—**gastar**, *vt.* to spend, expend; to waste, wear out; to use.—*vr* to become old or useless; to waste away, wear out; to fray.

gasto, *m.* expenditure, outlay, expense; consumption; spending, con

suming.—*gastos de explotación*, operating or working expenses.—*gastos de representación*, incidental expenses.

gatas, *f. pl.—andar a g.*, on all fours. —**gatazo**, *m.* large cat; (coll.) artful trick, cheat.—**gatear**, *vi.* (of children) to creep; to climb up; to go upon all fours.

gatillo, *m.* trigger.

gato, *n.* cat.—*m.* (mech.) jack; (coll.) shrewd fellow.—*cuatro gatos*, (contempt.) just a few people.—*dar or meter g. por liebre*, (coll.) to cheat, to give chalk for cheese.—*aquí hay g. encerrado*, (coll.) there is something fishy here.

gauchada, *f.* artifice; act of a Gaucho.—*hacer una g.*, (Arg.) to do a favor.—**gauchaje**, *m.* (Am.) Gaucho folk, group of Gauchos.—**gaucho**, *n.* Gaucho, pampas cowboy (-girl).

gaveta, *f.* drawer.

gavilán, *m.* sparrow hawk.

gavilla, *f.* bundle or sheaf of grain; gang of thugs.

gaviota, *f.* sea gull, gull.

gaza, *f.* loop of a bow.

gazapo, *m.* young rabbit; (coll.) blunder, mistake.

gazmoñería, *f.* prudery.—**gazmoño**, *a.* prudish, priggish.

gaznápiro, *n.* churl; simpleton.

gaznate, *m.* throttle; windpipe.— **gaznatón**, *m.* (Am.) slap in the face.

gazofia, *f.* = BAZOFIA.

gelatina, *f.* gelatine; jelly.—**gelatinoso**, *a.* gelatinous.

gema, *f.* jewel, gem, precious stone; bud.

gemelo, *n.* twin.—*m.* cufflink.—*pl.* binoculars; opera, field or marine glasses.

gemido, *m.* moan; whine; whimper.— **gemir**, *vii.* [29] to moan; to whine; to whimper.

gendarme, *mf.* (Am.) gendarme, policeman (-woman).

generación, *f.* generation.—**generador**, *n. & a.* generator; generating.—*m.* (mech., elec.) generator.

general, *a.* general; usual.—*por lo g.*, in general, generally.—*m.* (mil.) general.—**generalidad**, *f.* generality. —**generalizar**, *vti.* [a] to generalize. —*vri.* to become general, usual, or popular.

genérico, *a.* generic.—**género**, *m.* genus; class; kind; sort; material, cloth; (gram.) gender.—*pl.* dry goods; (com.) merchandise—*g. humano*, mankind.

generosidad, *f.* generosity.—**generoso**, *a.* generous.

genial, *a.* genial; pleasant.—**genio**, *m.*

genius; temperament, disposition, temper; character; spirit.—*mal g.*, ill temper.

genital, *a.* genital.—*m.* testicle.

gente, *f.* people, folk, crowd; race, nation; (coll.) folks, family.—*g. baja*, lower classes; mob.—*g. bien*, upper class.—*g. de bien* honest people.—*g. de paz*, friends.—*g. menuda*, children, small fry.

gentil, *a.* graceful, genteel; polite.— *mf.* gentile; pagan.—**gentileza**, *f.* gentility, gracefulness; courtesy.

gentío, *m.* crowd, multitude.—**gentuza**, *f.* rabble, riffraff; mob.

genuino, *a.* genuine; unadulterated.

geografía, *f.* geography.—**geográfico**, *a.* geographical.—**geógrafo**, *n.* geographer.—**geología**, *f.* geology.— **geólogo**, *n.* geologist.—**geometría**, *f.* geometry.—**geométrico**, *a.* geometrical.

geranio, *m.* geranium.

gerencia, *f.* (com.) management, administration.—**gerente**, *mf.* (com.) manager.

germen, *m.* germ; source.—**germinación**, *f.* (bot.) germination.—**germinar**, *vi.* to germinate.

gerundio, *m.* gerund.

gestación, *f.* gestation, pregnancy.

gestión, *f.* management, negotiation; effort.—**gestionar**, *vt.* to manage; to negotiate; to undertake.

gesto, *m.* facial expression; grimace; gesture.—*hacer gestos*, to make faces.

giba, *f.* hump, hunch.—**giboso**, *a.* humpbacked.

gigante, *mf.* giant; giantess.—*a.* gigantic.—**gigantesco**, *a.* gigantic.

gimnasia, *f.* calisthenics.—**gimnasio**, *m.* gymnasium.—**gimnasta**, *mf.* gymnast.—**gimnástica**, *f.* gymnastics.

gimotear, *vi.* (coll.) to whine.—**gimoteo**, *m.* whining.

ginebra, *f.* gin (liquor).

ginecología, *f.* gynecology.

girador, *n.* (com.) drawer of draft.— **girar**, *vi.* to whirl, revolve, rotate; to turn; (com.) to draw (checks, drafts).—*g. contra or a cargo de*, to draw on.—**girasol**, *m.* sunflower. —**giratorio**, *a.* revolving, rotary.— **giro**, *m.* turn; rotation; bend; trend, bias; turn of phrase; (com.) draft; line of business.—*g. postal*, money order.—*tomar otro g.* to take another course.

gitano, *a.* gypsy; gypsylike; honeymouthed.—*n.* gypsy.

glacial, *a.* glacial.—**glaciar**, *m.* glacier.

gladiolo, *m.* gladiolus.

glándula, *f.* gland.—**glandular**, *a.* glandular.

global, *a.* global, overall.—**globo**, *m.* globe, sphere; balloon.—*en g.*, as a whole; in bulk.—*g. terráqueo* or *terrestre*, (the) globe, (the) earth. —**globular**, *a.* globular.—**glóbulo**, *m.* globule.

gloria, *f.* glory, fame; heavenly state, bliss; splendor.—*saber a g.*, to taste delicious.—**gloriarse**, *vr.* (de or en) to boast (of), to take delight (in).— **glorieta**, *f.* circle or square at intersection of streets; bower, arbor. —**glorificación**, *f.* glorification; praise.—**glorificar**, *vti.* [d] to glorify; to exalt; to praise.—*vri.* = GLORIARSE.—**glorioso**, *a.* glorious.

glosa, *f.* gloss; (mus.) variation of a theme.—**glosar**, *vt.* to gloss, comment; (mus.) to vary (a theme).— **glosario**, *m.* glossary.

glotón, *n.* & *a.* glutton; gluttonous. —**glotonería**, *f.* gluttony.

gluglú, *m.* gurgle, gurgling sound.

gobernación, *f.* government.—**gobernador**, *n.* governor; ruler.—**gobernante**, *mf.* ruler.—*a.* ruling.—**gobernar**, *vti.* [1] & *vii.* to govern, rule. —*vri.* to manage (one's affairs), carry on.—**gobierno**, *m.* government; management, direction; control (of a business, an automobile, an airplane); helm, rudder.—*para su g.*, for your guidance.

goce, *m.* enjoyment; joy; fruition.

godo, *n.* & *a.* Goth(ic); (Colombia, pol.) conservative, Spaniard.

gol, *m.* (sports) goal scored.

gola, *f.* ruff; gullet, throat.

goleta, *f.* (naut.) schooner.

golfo, *m.* gulf; sea; bum; ragamuffin.

golondrina, *f.* (ornith.) swallow.

golosear, golosinear, *vi.* to nibble on sweets.—**golosina**, *f.* dainty, delicacy, sweet morsel, tidbit; daintiness; trifle.—**goloso**, *a.* fond of tidbits or sweets.

golpe, *m.* blow; stroke, hit, knock, beat; shock, clash; attack, spell; action.—*de g.*, suddenly.—*g. de vista*, glance; sight.—**golpear**, *vt.* to strike, hit, hammer.—*vi.* to beat; to knock, pound (as a piston).— **golpetear**, *vt.* & *vi.* to strike or pound continually; to rattle.—**golpeteo**, *m.* knocking, pounding, rattling.

gollería, *f.* dainty; delicious morsel; superfluity, excess.

gollete, *m.* throttle, gullet; neck of a bottle.

goma, *f.* gum; rubber; glue; tire; rubber band; rubber eraser; overshoes, rubbers; (Am.) hangover.— *g. de borrar*, rubber eraser.—*g. de*

mascar, chewing gum.—**gomoso**, *a.* gummy; gum-producing.

gonce, *m.* hinge.

góndola, *f.* gondola.—**gondolero**, *n.* gondolier.

gong, *m.* gong.

gonorrea, *f.* gonorrhea.

gordinflón, *a.* (coll.) chubby, flabby, fat.—**gordo**, *a.* fat.—*hacer la vista gorda*, to pretend not to see, wink at.—*m.* fat, suet.—**gordura**, *f.* grease, fat; fatness.

gorgojo, *m.* grub, weevil; (coll.) dwarfish person.

gorgotear, *vi.* to gurgle.—**gorgoteo**, *m.* gurgle, gurgling sound.

gorguera, *f.* ruff.

gorila, *m.* gorilla.

gorjear, *vi.* to warble, trill.—*vr.* to gabble (as a child).—**gorjeo**, *m.* warble, trilling; gabble of a child.

gorra, *f.* cap; (coll.) intrusion at feast without invitation.—*de g.*, at other people's expense.—*ir, comer, andar, etc., de g.*, (coll.) to sponge.

gorrión, *m.* sparrow.

gorrista, *mf.* (coll.) sponger.—**gorro**, *m.* cap, coif.—**gorrón**, *n.* sponger, parasite.

gota, *f.* drop of liquid; gout.—*sudar la g. gorda*, (coll.) to sweat blood.— **gotear**, *vi.* to drop, drip, dribble, leak; to sprinkle, begin to rain.— **gotera**, *f.* leak, leakage; drip, dripping.

gótico, *a.* Gothic.

gotoso, *a.* gouty.

gozar, *vti.* [a] to enjoy; to have possession or result of.—*vii.* (de) to enjoy, have possession (of).—*vri.* to rejoice.

gozne, *m.* hinge.

gozo, *m.* joy, pleasure, gladness.— *saltar de g.*, to be in high spirits, to be very happy.—**gozoso**, *a.* joyful, cheerful, merry.

grabado, *a.* engraved, carved, cut.— *m.* engraving; art of engraving; cut, picture, illustration.—*g. al agua fuerte*, etching.—*g. en madera*, wood engraving, wood carving.—**grabador**, *n.* engraver, carver; cutter, sinker.— **grabar**, *vt.* to engrave; to cut, carve; to impress upon the mind.

gracejo, *m.* graceful, winsome way. —**gracia**, *f.* grace; gracefulness; benefaction; graciousness; pardon, mercy; remission of a debt; witticism, wit; joke, jest; name of a person.—*pl.* thanks; accomplishments.—*caer en g.*, to please, to be liked.—*hacer g.*, to please; to amuse, strike as funny.—*tener g.*, to be witty; to be funny.—**grácil**, *a.*

slender.—**gracioso,** a. graceful, pleasing; witty, funny; gracious.

grada, f. step of a wide staircase; harrow.—pl. stands, seats of bullring or amphitheater.—**gradación,** f. (mus.) gradation; graded series of things or events.—**gradería,** f. series of steps or seats at bullring or stadium stands.

grado, m. degree; step of a staircase; (mil.) rank; grade, class.—de g., or de buen g., willingly, with pleasure.—**graduación,** f. graduation; (mil.) rank.—**gradual,** a. gradual.—**graduar,** vt. to graduate, give a degree or a military rank; to grade; to gauge; to adjust.—vr. (en) to graduate (from); to take a degree.

gráfico, a. graphic(al); clear, vivid.—n. graph, diagram.

grafito, m. graphite.

grajo, m. jackdaw.

grama, f. grama grass; lawn.

gramática, f. grammar.—**gramatical,** a. grammatical.—**gramático,** a. grammatical.—n. grammarian.

gramo, m. gram (weight). See Table.

gran, a. contr. of GRANDE.

grana, f. scarlet color; scarlet cloth.

granada, f. pomegranate; (mil.) grenade.—**granado,** a. remarkable, illustrious; mature; select, choice.—m. pomegranate tree.—**granar,** vi. to bloom, mature, come to fruition.—**granate,** m. garnet.

grande, a. large, big; great; grand.—en g., on a large scale.—mf. grandee.—**grandeza,** f. greatness; grandeur; grandeeship; bigness; size, magnitude.—**grandiosidad,** f. greatness; grandeur; abundance.—**grandioso,** a. grandiose, grand, magnificent.—**grandullón,** a. overgrown.

granear, vt. to sow (grain); to stipple; to grain (lithographic stone).—**granel,** m. heap of grain.—a g., in a heap; (com.) in bulk.—**granero,** m. granary, barn; grange; cornloft.

granito, m. granite; small grain; pimple; granule.

granizada, f. hailstorm; shower of objects, facts, etc.; water ice.—**granizar,** vii. [a-50] to hail.—**granizo,** m. hail.

granja, f. grange, farm, farmhouse.—**granjear,** vt. to gain, earn, profit.—vt. & vr. to get, win (as the good will of another).—**granjería,** f. gain, profit, advantage.—**granjero,** n. farmer.

grano, m. grain; cereal; each single seed; pimple.—pl. (com.) cereals, corn, breadstuffs.—ir al g., to come to the point.

granuja, mf. rogue; waif, urchin.

granulación, f. granulation.—**granular,** vt. to granulate.—vr. to become covered with granules or pimples.—a. granular.—**granuloso,** a. granulous, granular.

grapa, f. staple; paper clip; clamp, clasp.—**grapón,** m. brace, hook.

grasa, f. grease; fat; suet; oil.—**grasiento,** a. greasy; filthy.—**graso,** a. fat, unctuous.—**grasoso,** a. greasy.

gratificación, f. reward; gratuity, tip; fee; gratification.—**gratificar,** vti. [d] to reward, recompense; to tip, fee; to gratify, please.—**gratis,** adv. gratis, free.—**gratitud,** f. gratitude, gratefulness.—**grato,** a. pleasing, pleasant; grateful.—**gratuito,** a. gratis; gratuitous, uncalled-for; unfounded.

grava, f. gravel.

gravamen, m. tax, scot; charge, obligation; nuisance; (law) mortgage, lien.—**gravar,** vt. to burden; to tax; (law) to encumber.

grave, a. weighty, heavy; grave, serious; (mus.) grave; deep (voice).—**gravedad,** f. gravity, graveness; seriousness.

gravitación, f. gravitation.—**gravitar,** vi. to gravitate; to rest, press (on).

gravoso, a. costly; onerous; vexatious.

graznar, vi. to croak, caw, cackle.—**graznido,** m. croak, caw, cackle; croaking.

greda, f. clay, chalk, marl, potter's clay.

gremio, m. guild; society, brotherhood; trade union.

greña, f. entangled or matted mop of hair.—andar a la g., (of women) to pull each other's hair; to argue excitedly.—**greñudo,** a. with long, disheveled hair; shy (horse).—m. shy horse.

gresca, f. wrangle, brawl, row.

griego, n. & a. Greek, Grecian.—m. the Greek language; unintelligible language.

grieta, f. crevice, crack; chink, fissure; scratch in the skin.

grifo, a. (print.) script; bristling (hair, fur); kinky, tangled (of hair).—m. griffin or griffon; (Am.) child of a negro and an Indian; faucet, spigot, cock.—pl. frizzled hair.

grillete, m. fetter, shackle.—**grillo,** m. (entom.) cricket.—pl. fetters.

grima, f. fright, horror.—dar g., to set the teeth on edge.—**grimoso,** a. horrible; repulsive.

gringo, n. (Am.) foreigner (esp. English or American).

gripe, f. grippe.

gris, *a.* gray.—*m.* gray color.—**grisáceo**, *a.* grayish.

grita, *f.* clamor, outcry; screaming; hooting.—**gritar**, *vi.* to shout, cry out, scream; to hoot.—**gritería**, *f.* outcry, uproar, shouting.—**grito**, *m.* cry, scream; hoot, whoop.—*a gritos, a g. pelado, a todo g.,* at the top of one's voice.—*estar en un g.,* to be in continual pain.—*poner el g. en el cielo,* to complain loudly.

grosella, *f.* currant; gooseberry.

grosería, *f.* rudeness, ill-breeding. discourtesy; clumsiness; vulgarity.—**grosero**, *a.* coarse, rough; rude, discourteous; vulgar, uncouth.

grosor, *m.* thickness.

grúa, *f.* crane, derrick.

gruesa, *f.* gross (12 dozen).

grueso, *a.* thick; bulky, corpulent; fleshy.—*m.* thickness; bulk, corpulence; main part; main body of an army.

grulla, *f.* (ornith.) crane.

grumete, *m.* apprentice sailor.

grumo, *m.* clot.—**grumoso**, *a.* full of clots, clotted.

gruñido, *m.* grunt.—**gruñir**, *vii.* [27] to grunt.—**gruñón**, *n.* & *a.* crank, irritable.

grupa, *f.* croup, rump of a horse.

grupo, *m.* group; set; clump, cluster.

gruta, *f.* cavern, grotto.

guacamayo, *m.* (ornith.) macaw.

guaco, *m.* (Am.) grouse.

guacho, *a.* & *n.* (Am.) orphan, foundling; solitary, forlorn; odd (only one of a pair).

guadaña, *f.* scythe.—**guadañar**, *vt.* to mow.

guagua, *f.* (Am.) insect that destroys fruit; trivial thing; omnibus; baby.—*de g.,* free, gratis.—**guagüero**, *n.* (Am.) bus driver; sponger.

guajalote, *m.* (Am.) turkey.

guajiro, *n.* & *a.* Cuban peasant.

guanaco, *m.* (Am.) a kind of llama; boor, rustic; (coll.) simpleton, idiot.

guanajo, *n.* (Am.) turkey.—*a.* & *n.* (coll.) fool.

guano, *m.* guano; palm leaves; (coll., Cuba) money.

guante, *m.* glove.—*echarle (a uno) el g.,* (coll.) to seize, grasp; to imprison.—**guantelete**, *m.* gauntlet.

guapear, *vi.* (coll.) to boast of courage.—**guapetón**, *a.* daring, bold. —**guapo**, *a.* (coll.) brave, daring; good-looking or handsome; spruce, neat; ostentatious; gay, sprightly. —*m.* gallant, beau; brawler, quarrelsome person.—*ponerse g.,* (Am.) to get angry.

guaraní, *a.* & *mf.* Guarani.—*m.* Guarani language.

guarapo, *m.* juice of the sugar cane.

guarda, *mf.* guard; keeper.—*f.* custody; trust, wardship, safe-keeping; observance of a law; outside rib or guard (of a fan, etc.); ward of a lock or of a key.—**guardabarrera**, *m.* (RR.) gatekeeper.—**guardabarro**, *m.* fender, splashboard.—**guardabosque**, *m.* forester; game warden.—**guardacantón**, *m.* protective stone at corner of buildings.—**guardacostas**, *m.* Coast Guard; (naut.) revenue cutter.—**guardafango**, *m.* = GUARDABARRO.—**guardafrenos**, *m.* (RR.) brakeman. —**guardamonte**, *m.* guard of a gunlock; forester, keeper of a forest. —**guardamuebles**, *m.* warehouse.—**guardar**, *vt.* to keep; to guard, protect, watch over; to store, save, reserve.—*vr.* (de) to guard (against), avoid, beware (of), take care not (to).—**guardarropa**, *m.* wardroom; wardrobe; cloakroom.—**guardarropía**, *f.* (theat.) wardrobe, properties. —**guardia**, *f.* guard; defense, protection.—*m.* uniformed policeman.—**guardiamarina**, *m.* midshipman.—**guardián**, *n.* keeper, watchman.

guarecer, *vti.* [3] to shelter, protect. —*vri.* to take refuge or shelter.—**guarida**, *f.* den, cave; lair of a wild beast; shelter; lurking place, cover, haunt.

guarnecer, *vti.* [3] to garnish, adorn, decorate; (sew.) to trim, bind, line; (jewelry) to set in gold, silver, etc.; (mason.) to plaster; (mil.) to garrison.—**guarnición**, *f.* trimming, etc.; setting; (mech.) packing; guard of a sword; garrison; adornment.—*pl.* harness; fittings; accessories.

guasa, *f.* joking, jesting; joke, jest.

guaso, *m.* lasso; Chilean cowboy.

guasón, *a.* (coll.) jocose, witty.—*n.* joker, wag.

guatemalteco, *n.* & *a.* Guatemalan.

guayaba, *f.* guava.—**guayabo**, *m.* guava tree.

gubernamental, *a.* governmental.—**gubernativo**, *a.* administrative, governmental, gubernatorial.

gubia, *f.* (carp.) gouge, centering chisel.

guedeja, *f.* long lock of hair; forelock; lion's mane.

guerra, *f.* war, warfare.—*dar g.,* to cause annoyance or trouble.—**guerrear**, *vi.* to war, wage war, fight.—**guerrera**, *f.* (mil.) tunic.—**guerrero**, *a.* martial, warlike.—*m.* warrior, fighter.—**guerrilla**, *f.* guerrilla.—**guerrillero**, *m.* guerrilla fighter.

guía, *mf.* guide; leader.—*f.* guide-

book; (mech.) guide, rule, guide pin, guide screw, etc.—**guiar**, *vt.* to guide, lead; to drive (auto, etc.).—*vr.* (**por**) to go or be governed (by); to follow.

guija, *f.* pebble; gravel.—*pl.* (coll.) force, vigor.—**guijarro,** *m.* pebble, cobble.—**guijo,** *m.* gravel.

guiñada, *f.* wink; (naut.) yaw; lurch.

guiñapo, *m.* tatter, rag; ragamuffin.

guiñar, *vt.* to wink; (naut.) to yaw; to lurch.—**guiño,** *m.* wink.

guión, *m.* hyphen; dash; (theat., radio, T.V.) script; explanatory text or reference table; cross (carried before a prelate in a procession); leader (among birds and animals); leader in a dance.

guirnalda, *f.* garland, wreath.

güiro, *m.* (Am.) fruit of the calabash tree; bottle gourd; gourd used as a musical instrument.

guisa, *f.* manner, fashion.—*a g. de,* like, in the manner of.

guisante, *m.* pea.—*g. de olor,* sweet pea.

guisar, *vt.* to cook or dress (food); to arrange, prepare.—**guiso,** *m.* cooked dish; seasoning, condiment.

guitarra, *f.* guitar.—**guitarrista,** *mf.* guitarist.

gula, *f.* gluttony, inordinate appetite.

gusano, *m.* worm, grub, caterpillar; meek, dejected person.

gustar, *vt.* to taste, try.—*vi.* to be pleasing; to cause pleasure.—*gustarle a uno una cosa,* to like something.—**gusto,** *m.* taste; tasting; pleasure; liking; choice; discernment.—*a g.,* to one's taste or judgment;—*dar g.,* to please.—**gustoso,** *a.* savory; tasty; cheerful; pleasing; willing.

H

haba, *f.* broad bean; lima bean.

habano, *m.* Havana cigar.

haber, *vti.* [21] to have (used as *aux.*). —*hay (había, hubo, etc.),* there is, there are (there was, there were).—*hay que,* one must, it is necessary.—*no hay de que,* don't mention it.—*m.* (bookkeeping) credit. —*pl.* property, assets; estate.

habichuela, *f.* kidney bean.—*h. verde,* string bean.

hábil, *a.* capable, skillful.—*día h.,* work day.—**habilidad,** *f.* ability, skill.—*pl.* accomplishments.

habilitación, *f.* habilitation; outfit, equipment.—**habilitar,** *vt.* to qualify, enable; to fit out, equip.

habitable, *a.* habitable.—**habitación,** *f.* room, chamber, suite of rooms,

apartment; lodging; (law) caretaking.—**habitante,** *a.* inhabiting.—*mf.* inhabitant.—**habitar,** *vt.* to inhabit, live, reside.

hábito, *m.* habit, custom; dress of ecclesiastics.—*tomar el h.,* to become a nun or a monk.—**habitual,** *a.* habitual, usual, customary.—**habituar,** *vt.* to accustom, habituate.—*vr.* to become accustomed, accustom oneself, get used to.

habla, *f.* speech; language; talk.—*ponerse al h.,* to communicate, get in touch, speak.—**hablador,** *a.* talkative.—*n.* talker, gabber.—**habladuría,** *f.* gossip, empty talk.—**hablar,** *vi.* to speak; to talk.—*h. a tontas y a locas,* to speak recklessly.—*h. claro,* or *en plata,* to speak in plain language, to call a spade a spade.—*h. por h.,* to talk for the sake of talking.—*h. por los codos,* to talk incessantly; to chatter.—*vt.* to speak.—*vr.* to speak to each other; to be on speaking terms.—**hablilla,** *f.* rumor, gossip.

hacedero, *a.* feasible, practicable.—**hacedor,** *m.* maker.—*el Supremo H.,* the Maker, the Creator.

hacendado, *n.* landholder, farmer, rancher.—**hacendoso,** *a.* industrious.

hacer, *vti.* [22] to make; to produce; to do; to gain, earn; to suppose, think; to cause.—*h. alarde,* to boast. —*h. caso,* to mind, pay attention.—*h. daño,* to hurt, harm.—*h. de,* to act as.—*h. juego,* to match.—*h. la vista gorda,* to wink at, to connive at.—*h. una pregunta,* to ask a question.—*no le hace,* never mind, let it go.—*v. impers.—¿cuánto (tiempo) hace?* how long ago?—*¿cuánto (tiempo) hace que?* since when?—*hace años,* many years ago. —*hace calor,* it is warm.—*hace tiempo,* a long time ago.—*hace un año,* a year ago, or, it is now one year.—*hace viento,* it is windy.—*vri.* to become, grow; to pretend to be. —*h. a,* to become accustomed.

hacia, *prep.* toward; near, about.—*h. abajo,* downward.—*h. arriba,* upward.—*h. atrás,* backward.

hacienda, *f.* landed property; plantation; ranch; estate, fortune; finance.—*h. pública,* public treasury; public finances.

hacina, *f.* stack; pile.—**hacinamiento,** *m.* accumulation; heaping or stacking.—**hacinar,** *vt.* to stack; to pile; to accumulate.

hacha, *f.* ax; hatchet; torch.—**hachazo,** *m.* blow or stroke with an ax.—**hachuela,** *f.* hatchet.

hada, *f.* fairy.—**hado,** *m.* fate, destiny, doom.

haitiano, *n.* & *a.* Haitian.

halagador, *a.* flattering; coaxing.—*n.* flatterer, cajoler, coaxer.—**halagar,** *vti.* [b] to cajole; to flatter; to coax, allure; to fondle.—**halago,** *m.* cajolery, allurement, flattery; caress.—**halagüeño,** *a.* flattering; alluring; attractive, promising.

halar, *vt.* to haul, pull, tow.—*vi.* to pull ahead.

halcón, *m.* falcon.

hálito, *m.* breath; vapor.

halo, *m.* halo.

hallar, *vt.* to find; to find out; to discover.—*vr.* to be (in a place or condition); to feel (as to health); to fare.—**hallazgo,** *m.* find, thing found; discovery.

hamaca, *f.* hammock.

hambre, *f.* hunger; appetite; famine.—*h. canina,* inordinate hunger.—*tener h.,* to be hungry.—**hambrear,** *vt.* to starve, famish.—*vi.* to be hungry.—**hambriento,** *a.* hungry; starved; greedy, covetous; longing.

hamburgués, *a.* from or pertaining to Hamburg.—**hamburguesa,** *f.* (Am.) hamburger.

hampa, *m.* underworld.—**hampón,** *m.* gangster, bully, rowdy.

hangar, *m.* (neol.) hangar.

haragán, *n.* idler, loiterer, loafer; lazy person.—*a.* lazy, indolent, idle.—**haraganear,** *vi.* to be lazy; to lounge, idle, loiter.—**haraganería,** *f.* idleness, laziness, sloth.

harapiento, *a.* ragged, tattered.—**harapo,** *m.* tatter, rag.

harina, *f.* flour, meal.—*h. de otro costal,* another matter, a horse of a different color.—**harinoso,** *a.* mealy.

hartar, *vti.* [49] & *vri.* to glut, gorge; to sate, satiate; to satisfy; to fill to excess.—**hartazgo,** *m.* satiety, fill.—**harto,** *ppi.* of HARTAR.—*a.* sufficient, full, complete.—*adv.* enough or sufficiently; very much, abundantly.—**hartura,** *f.* satiety, fill; superabundance.

hasta, *prep.* till, until; up to, down to; as far as; even (emphatic).—*h. después,* or *h. luego,* good-by, so long.—*h. la vista,* (in parting) so long, see you later.—*h. mañana,* (in parting) see you tomorrow.—*conj.* even.—*h. que,* until.

hastiar, *vt.* to disgust; to cloy, sate.—**hastío,** *m.* disgust; boredom.

hatillo, *m.* small bundle; a few clothes.—*coger el h.,* (coll.) to quit, to pack and go.

hato, *m.* herd of cattle; flock of sheep; (Am.) farm or cattle ranch; shepherd's lodge; lot; gang, crowd.

hawaiano, *a.* & *n.* Hawaiian.

hay, *impers. irreg.* of HABER; there is, there are.

haya, *f.* beech tree.

haz, *m.* fagot, bundle, bunch; (agr.) sheaf.

hazaña, *f.* feat, heroic deed.

hazmerreír, *m.* laughing stock.

hebilla, *f.* buckle, clasp.

hebra, *f.* thread fiber; string; strand.

hebreo, *n.* & *a.* Hebrew.—*m.* Hebrew language.

hechicería, *f.* witchcraft, enchantment; charm; sorcery, wizardry.—**hechicero,** *n.* witch, wizard; sorcerer; charmer, enchanter.—*a.* charming, bewitching.—**hechizar,** *vti.* [a] to bewitch, enchant; to charm.—**hechizo,** *m.* charm (used to bewitch), enchantment.

hecho, *ppi.* of HACER.—*a.* made; done; ready-made; finished; ripe or developed.—*h. y derecho,* real; complete.—*m.* fact; act, action, deed.—*de h.,* in fact, as a matter of fact.—**hechura,** *f.* making, make; workmanship; form; build (of a person); creature, creation.

heder, *vi.* [18] to stink.—**hediondez,** *f.* stench, stink.—**hediondo,** *a.* stinking, fetid.—**hedor,** *m.* stench, stink.

helada, *f.* frost; nip.—**heladera, heladora,** *f.* refrigerator; ice-cream dish.—**helado,** *a.* icy; freezing, frosty; cold.—*m.* ice cream.—**helar,** *vti.* [1] & *vii.* to freeze; to amaze.—*vri.* to freeze, be frozen.

helecho, *m.* fern.

hélice, *f.* propeller; helix.

helicóptero, *m.* helicopter.

helio, *m.* helium.

hembra, *f.* female; (mech.) nut of a screw.

hemisférico, *a.* hemispherical.—**hemisferio,** *m.* hemisphere.

hemorragia, *f.* hemorrhage.—**hemorrágico,** *a.* hemorrhagic.

hemorroides, *f. pl.* piles, hemorrhoids.

henchir, *vti.* [29] to fill, stuff.—*vri.* to fill or stuff oneself.

hender, *vti.* [19] to crack, split; to cut (as the water).—**hendidura,** *f.* fissure, crack, cut.

heno, *m.* hay.

heráldica, *f.* heraldry.—**heraldo,** *m.* herald; harbinger.

herbazal, *m.* grassy place; pasture ground.

heredad, *f.* improved piece of ground; country estate, farm.—**heredar,** *vt.* to inherit; to deed to another.—**heredero,** *n.* heir; heiress; inheritor; successor.—*h. forzoso,* general

or legal heir.—**hereditario,** a. hereditary.

hereje, mf. heretic.—**herejía,** f. heresy; injurious expression.

herencia, f. inheritance, heritage; heredity.

herético, a. heretical.

herida, f. injury, wound.—**herido,** a. & n. wounded (person).—mal h., dangerously wounded.—**herir,** vti. [39] to wound; to hurt, harm; to strike; to offend (the senses).

hermanar, vt. to mate, match, pair; to suit.—vi. to fraternize; to match.

hermanastro, n. stepbrother; f. stepsister.—**hermandad,** f. fraternity, brotherhood.—**hermano,** n. brother; (f. sister); twin (app. to objects).—h. de leche, foster brother. —h. político, brother-in-law.

hermético, a. hermetic, air-proof, airtight; close-mouthed.—**hermetismo,** m. secrecy, complete silence.

hermosear, vt. to beautify, embellish. —**hermoso,** a. beautiful, handsome. —**hermosura,** f. beauty; belle.

hernia, f. hernia.

héroe, m. hero.—**heroicidad,** f. heroism; heroic deed.—**heroico,** a. heroic.—**heroína,** f. heroine.—**heroísmo,** m. heroism.

herradura, f. horseshoe.—**herraje,** m. ironwork; iron or metal fittings or accessories, hardware (gen. pl.).— **herramienta,** f. tool; implement; set of tools.—**herrar,** vti. [1] to shoe (horses); to brand (cattle); to garnish or trim with iron.—**herrería,** f. smithy; forge; ironworks.—**herrero,** n. blacksmith.

herrumbre, f. rust; iron taste.—**herrumbroso,** a. rusty, rusted.

hervidero, m. boiling; small spring whence water bubbles out; multitude, crowd.—**hervir,** vti. [39] & vii. to boil; to seethe.—vii. to become choppy (the sea); to bubble.— **hervor,** m. boiling; fervor, heat.— h. de sangre, rash.

heterodoxo, a. unorthodox.

heterogéneo, a. heterogenous.

hez, f. sediment, dregs of liquor; scum.—pl. dregs; excrement.

híbrido, n. & a. hybrid.

hidráulica, f. hydraulics.—**hidráulico,** a. hydraulic.—**hidroavión,** m. seaplane.—**hidrógeno,** m. hydrogen.— **hidroplano,** m. seaplane.

hiedra, f. ivy.

hiel, f. gall, bile; bitterness.

hielo, m. ice; frost; coolness, indifference.

hiena, f. hyena.

hierba, f. grass; weed; herb; herbage; (Am.) maté.—mala h., weed;

bad character; marijuana.—**hierbabuena,** f. mint.

hierro, m. iron; brand stamped with a hot iron.—pl. fetters, shackles, handcuffs.—h. colado or fundido, cast iron.—h. forjado, wrought iron.

hígado, m. liver.—pl. courage, bravery.—echar el h. or los hígados, to work very hard.

higiene, f. hygiene; sanitation.— **higiénico,** a. hygienic, sanitary.— **higienizar,** vti. [a] to make sanitary.

higo, m. fig.—**higuera,** f. fig tree.

hija, f. daughter, child.—h. política, daughter-in-law.—**hijastro,** n. stepchild.—**hijo,** m. son, child; (bot.) shoot; fruit, result.—pl. children, offspring.—h. natural, illegitimate child.—h. político, son-in-law.

hila, f. line.—a la h., in a row, single file.—pl. (surg.) lint.—**hilacha,** f., **hilacho,** m. fraying, shred, filament or thread raveled out of cloth.— pl. lint.—**hilada,** f. row or line; (mason.) course.—**hilado,** m. spinning; yarn.—**hilandera,** f. woman spinner.—**hilandería,** f. spinning mill.—**hilandero,** n. & a. spinner; spinning.—m. spinning room, spinnery.—**hilar,** vt. & vi. to spin.

hilaza, f. yarn; fiber; uneven thread. —pl. lint.

hilera, f. row, line, file.

hilo, m. thread; yarn; filament, fiber; linen; wire.—al h., along the thread, with the grain.

hilván, m. (sew.) tacking, basting.— **hilvanar,** vt. to tack, baste; to plan.

himen, m. hymen.—**himeneo,** m. hymen, nuptials.

himno, m. hymn.

hincapié, m. stamping the foot.— hacer h., to emphasize, stress.— **hincar,** vti. [d] to thrust, drive; to plant.—h. el diente, to bite; to slander.—h. la rodilla, or hincarse de rodillas, to kneel down.

hinchar, vt. to swell; to inflate.—vr. to swell; to become arrogant, conceited or puffed up.—**hinchazón,** m. swelling; ostentation, vanity, airs; inflation.

hinojo, m. fennel; knee.—de hinojos, kneeling.

hipar, vi. to hiccough; to pant.

hipertensión, f. high blood pressure.

hípico, a. equine, pertaining to horses.

hipo, m. hiccough.

hipocresía, f. hypocrisy.—**hipócrita,** mf. & a. hypocrite; hypocritical.

hipódromo, m. race track.

hipoteca, f. mortgage.—**hipotecar,** vti. [d] to mortgage.

hipótesis, *f.* hypothesis.

hiriente, *a.* hurting, cutting, offensive.

hirsuto, *a.* hairy, bristly.

hirviente, *a.* boiling.

hispánico, *a.* Hispanic.—**hispano**, *a.* Hispanic, Spanish.—*n.* Spaniard.—**hispanoamericano**, *n.* & *a.* Spanish-American.

histérico, *a.* & *n.* histeric(al); hysterics.—**histerismo**, *m.*, **histeria**, *f.* hysteria.

historia, *f.* history; tale, story.—*dejarse de historias*, to come to the point.—**historiador**, *n.* historian.—**histórico**, *a.* historic(al).—**historieta**, *f.* short story; comics, comic strip.

histrión, *n.* actor, player; buffoon, juggler.

hito, *m.* landmark; guidepost; milestone.—*mirar de h. en h.*, to stare at.

hocicar, *vti.* [d] to root (as hogs).—*vii.* to fall on one's face; to muzzle.—**hocico**, *m.* snout, muzzle, nose (of animal).—*de hocicos*, face downwards.—*meter el h.*, to meddle.

hogar, *m.* home; hearth, fireplace.

hogaza, *f.* large loaf of bread.

hoguera, *f.* bonfire; blaze; pyre.

hoja, *f.* leaf; petal; sheet of paper or metal; blade.—*doblemos la h.*, no more of that.—*h. de lata*, tin plate.—*h. de servicios*, record.—**hojalata**, *f.* tin plate.—**hojalatería**, *f.* tinware; tin shop.—**hojalatero**, *n.* tinsmith.

hojarasca, *f.* dead leaves; excessive foliage; trash, rubbish.

hojear, *vt.* to turn the leaves of; to glance at (a book), look over hastily.

hojuela, *f.* small leaf; flake; thin pancake.

¡hola! *interj.* hello! hi!

holandés, *n.* & *a.* Dutch.—*m.* Dutch language.

holgado, *a.* loose, wide; large, spacious; at leisure; well-off.—**holganza**, *f.* leisure; idleness.—**holgar**, *vii.* [12-b] to rest; to quit work; to be idle; to be needless or useless.—*vri.* to be glad; to idle; to relax, amuse oneself.—**holgazán**, *a.* idle, lazy.—*n.* idler, loiterer, lounger.—**holgazanear**, *vi.* to idle; to loiter; to lounge.—**holgazanería**, *f.* idleness, laziness.—**holgorio**, *m.* frolic, spree.—**holgura**, *f.* ease, comfort; roominess; (mech.) play.

hollar, *vti.* [12] to tread upon, trample under foot.

hollejo, *m.* skin, peel, pod, husk.

hollín, *m.* soot, lampblack.

hombrada, *f.* manly action; impulse.—**hombre**, *m.* man.

hombrera, *f.* shoulder pad; shoulder armor.

hombría, *f.* manliness.—*h. de bien*, probity, integrity, honesty.

hombro, *m.* shoulder.—*arrimar el h.*, to lend a hand.—*encogerse de hombros*, to shrug one's shoulders.

hombruno, *a.* mannish.

homenaje, *m.* homage, honor.

homicida, *a.* homicidal.—*mf.* murderer, homicide (person).—**homicidio**, *m.* homicide (act).

homogeneidad, *f.* homogeneity.—**homogéneo**, *a.* homogeneous.

homosexual, *a.* & *mf.* homosexual.

honda, *f.* slingshot.

hondo, *a.* deep, profound.—*m.* depth.—**hondón**, *m.* bottom; depths.—**hondonada**, *f.* dale, glen; gully, ravine.—**hondura**, *f.* depth; profundity.—*meterse en honduras*, (fig.) to go beyond one's depth.—**hondureño**, *a.* & *n.* Honduran.

honestidad, *f.* decency, decorum; honesty; chastity; modesty.—**honesto**, *a.* honest; decent, decorous; chaste.

hongo, *m.* mushroom; fungus; derby hat.

honor, *m.* honor; dignity; reputation. *pl.* rank, position, honors.—**honorable**, *a.* honorable; illustrious; reputable.—**honorario**, *a.* honorary.—*m. pl.* professional fees.—**honorífico**, *a.* honorary; honorable.

honra, *f.* honor; reputation; chastity.—*pl.* obsequies.—**honradez**, *f.* honesty, probity, integrity.—**honrado**, *a.* honest, honorable, reputable.—**honrar**, *vt.* to honor, do honor to; to respect; to be an honor for.—*vi.* to honor; to be honored.—**honrilla**, *f.* keen sense of honor or duty; punctiliousness.—**honroso**, *a.* honorable; decorous; honoring, honorgiving.

hora, *f.* hour; time.—*altas horas*, small hours.—*dar la h.*, to strike the hour; to tell the time.—*h. de*, time to, or for.—*horas extraordinarias*, overtime.

horadar, *vt.* to perforate, bore; to burrow.

horario, *m.* timetable, schedule; hour hand of a clock or watch.

horca, *f.* gallows; pitchfork; forked prop; rope or string of onions or garlic.

horcajadas, *f. pl.—a h.*, astride or astraddle.

horcón, *m.* forked pole, forked prop; post; (Am.) roof.

horda, *f.* horde.

horizontal, *a.* & *f.* horizontal.—**hori-**

zontalidad, *f.* horizontality.—**horizonte,** *m.* horizon.

horma, *f.* mold; shoemaker's last; hatter's block; (mason.) dry wall.

hormiga, *f.* ant.—**hormigón,** *m.* (eng.) concrete.—*h. armado,* reinforced concrete.—**hormigonera,** *f.* concrete mixer.—**hormiguear,** *vi.* to itch; to swarm, teem.—**hormigueo,** *m.* itching.—**hormiguero,** *m.* ant hill or hillock; ant hole or nest; swarm of people or little animals.—*oso hormiguero,* anteater.

hormona, *f.* hormone.

hornada, *f.* batch of bread, baking; melt (of a blast furnace).—**hornilla,** *f.* burner; grate (of a stove).—**hornillo,** *m.* portable furnace or stove.—**horno,** *m.* oven; kiln; furnace.

horquilla, *f.* forked pole, bar, pipe, etc.; pitchfork; hairpin; double-pointed tack.

horrendo, *a.* hideous, awful.—**horrible,** *a.* horrid, horrible; hideous, heinous.—**hórrido,** *a.* horrible, hideous.—**horripilante,** *a.* horrifying, harrowing.—**horripilar,** *vt. & vi.* to cause or feel horror.—*vr.* to be horrified.—**horrísono,** *a.* of a terrifying noise.—**horror,** *m.* horror; enormity, frightfulness.—**horrorizar,** *vti.* [a] to horrify, terrify.—*vri.* to be terrified.—**horroroso,** *a.* horrible; hideous, frightful.

hortaliza, *f.* garden produce, vegetables.

hosco, *a.* sullen, gloomy.

hospedaje, *m.* lodging, board.—**hospedar,** *vt.* to lodge, harbor.—*vi. & vr.* (en) to lodge or take lodging (at); to live (in).

hospicio, *m.* hospice; orphan asylum.

hospital, *m.* hospital.—*h. de sangre,* (mil.) field hospital.—**hospitalario,** *a.* hospitable.—**hospitalidad,** *f.* hospitality.

hosquedad, *f.* sullenness.

hostia, *f.* (eccl.) Host.

hostigamiento, *m.* chastisement; vexation.—**hostigar,** *vti.* [b] to lash, scourge, chastise; to vex, trouble; to gall.

hostil, *a.* hostile.—**hostilidad,** *f.* hostility.—**hostilizar,** *vti.* [a] to commit hostilities against, be hostile to, antagonize.

hotel, *m.* hotel.—**hotelero,** *n.* hotel manager.

hoy, *adv.* today; at the present time. —*de h. a mañana,* before tomorrow; when you least expect it.—*de h. en adelante,* hence forward, in the future.—*h. día,* or *h. en día,* nowadays. —*h. mismo,* this very day.—*h.* *por h.,* at the present time; this very day.

hoya, *f.* hole, pit; grave; valley, dale, glen; basin (of a river).—**hoyo,** *m.* hole, excavation; dent, hollow; pockmark; grave.

hoz, *f.* sickle; narrow pass.

hozar, *vti.* [a] to root (as hogs).

huacal, *m.* (Am.) crate.

huarache, *m.* (Am.) Mexican leather sandal.

huaso, *m.* (Am.) Chilean cowboy; peasant; halfbreed; lasso.—*a.* rustic, uncouth.

hucha, *f.* money box, bank; savings.

huchear, *vi.* to hoot, shout, cry out, call.

hueco, *a.* hollow; empty; vain, empty-headed; resonant.—*m.* hole; hollow, gap; interval of time or space.

huelga, *f.* labor strike, walkout; rest, repose.—*declararse en h.,* to strike.—**huelguista,** *mf.* striker.

huella, *f.* track, footprint; trace, sign; trail.

húerfano, *n. & a.* orphan(ed).

huero, *a.* vain, empty; (Am.) blonde.

huerta, *f.* orchard; vegetable garden; irrigated land.—**huerto,** *m.* small orchard; garden patch.

hueso, *m.* bone; stone, pit; core, center.—*estar en los huesos,* to be very thin.—*la sin h.,* the tongue.—**huesoso,** *a.* = HUESUDO.

huésped, *n.* guest, roomer, lodger; host.—*casa de huéspedes,* boarding house.

hueste, *f.* host, army.

huesudo, *a.* bony, having large bones; rawboned.

hueva, *f.* spawn of fishes, roe.—**huevo,** *m.* egg.—*h. duro,* hard-boiled egg. —*huevos escalfados,* poached eggs. —*huevos fritos,* fried eggs.—*huevos pasados por agua,* soft-boiled eggs. —*huevos revueltos,* scrambled eggs.

huida, *f.* flight, escape.—**huidizo,** *a.* elusive; fugitive, fleeing.—**huir,** *vii.* [23-e] *& vri.* to flee; to escape; to run away; to slip away; (de) to keep away (from), shun, avoid.—*h. la cara de,* to avoid, keep away from.

hule, *m.* oilcloth, oilskin; (Am.) India rubber.

hulla, *f.* mineral coal.—*h. blanca,* white coal (water power).

humanidad, *f.* humanity; mankind; humaneness; (coll.) corpulence, fleshiness.—*pl.* humanities.—**humanitario,** *a.* humanitarian.—**humano,** *a.* human; humane.—*m.* man, human being.

humarada, *f.* great deal of smoke.—

humazo, *m.* dense and abundant smoke.—**humeante,** *a.* smoking, steaming, fuming.—**humear,** *vi.* to smoke; emit smoke, fumes, or vapors.

humedad, *f.* humidity, moisture, dampness.—**humedecer,** *vti.* [3] to moisten, dampen.—**húmedo,** *a.* wet, humid, moist, damp.

humildad, *f.* humility, humbleness; meekness.—**humilde,** *a.* humble; meek; lowly.

humillación, *f.* humiliation; humbling.—**humillar,** *vt.* to humiliate; to humble; to subdue.—*vr.* to humble oneself; to lower oneself.

humo, *m.* smoke; fume.—*pl.* airs, conceit.

humor, *m.* humor, wit; disposition, temper, mood.—**humorada,** *f.* pleasant joke, humorous saying.—**humorismo,** *m.* humor; humorism.—**humorístico,** *a.* humorous; amusing; facetious.

hundimiento, *m.* sinking; cave-in; downfall, collapse.—**hundir,** *vt.* to submerge, sink; to stave in, crush; to destroy, ruin.—*vr.* to sink; to cave in, fall down.

húngaro, *n.* & *a.* Hungarian.

huracán, *m.* hurricane.

huraño, *a.* unsociable, shy.

hurgar, *vti.* [b] to stir; to poke; to stir up, excite.

¡hurra!, *interj* hurrah!

hurtadillas.—*a h.,* by stealth, on the sly.—**hurtar,** *vt.* to steal, rob of; to cheat in weight or measure.—*h el cuerpo,* to flee, to dodge, shy away; to hide.—**hurto,** *m.* theft, robbery, stealing.

husmear, *vt* to scent, smell; (coll.) to pry, peep.

huso, *m.* spindle; bobbin.

I

ibérico, *a.*, **ibero,** *n.* & *a.* Iberian.—**iberoamericano,** *n.* & *a.* Ibero-American.

ictericia, *f.* jaundice.

ida, *f.* departure; going.—*i. y vuelta,* round trip.

idea, *f.* idea.—**ideal,** *a.* & *m.* ideal.—**idealismo,** *m.* idealism.—**idealista,** *mf.* & *a.* idealist; idealistic.—**idealizar,** *vti.* [a] to idealize.—**idear,** *vt.* to conceive the idea of; to devise.

ídem, *a.* & *pron.* ditto, the same.

idéntico, *a.* **(a)** identical (with).—**identidad,** *f.* identity.—*de i.,* identification (as *a.*).—**identificación,** *f.* identification.—**identificar,** *vti.* [d]

to identify.—*vri.* to identify oneself.

ideología, *f.* ideology.—**ideológico,** *a.* ideological.

idioma, *m.* language, tongue.—**idiomático,** *a.* idiomatic.

idiota, *mf.* & *a.* idiot; idiotic.—**idiotez,** *f.* idiocy.—**idiotismo,** *m.* expression, idiom; idiotic action.

ido, *ppi.* of IR.

idólatra, *a.* idolatrous; heathen.—*mf.* idolater; (coll.) ardent lover.—**idolatrar,** *vt.* to idolize, worship.—**idolatría,** *f.* idolatry; idolization.—**ídolo,** *m.* idol.

idóneo, *a.* fit, able, suitable.

iglesia, *f.* church.

ignición, *f.* ignition.

ignorancia, *f.* ignorance.—**ignorante,** *a.* ignorant.—**ignorar,** *vt.* to be ignorant of, not to know.

igual, *a.* equal; even, flat; unvarying.—*(me) es i.,* it is all the same (to me).—*m.* equal.—*al i.,* equally.—*sin i.,* unrivaled, matchless; without parallel.—**iguala,** *f.* stipend on agreement.—**igualar,** *vt.* to equalize; to match; to level, smooth; to adjust.—*vi.* to be equal; (sports) to be tied (in score).—*vr.* (a, con) to put oneself on the same plane (as).—**igualdad,** *f.* equality.

ijada, *f.,* **ijar,** *m.* flank (of an animal).—*dolor de i.,* pain in the side.

ilación, *f.* inference; connection.

ilegal, *a.* illegal, unlawful.—**ilegalidad,** *f.* illegality, unlawfulness.

ilegible, *a.* illegible.

ilegitimidad, *f.* illegitimacy.—**ilegítimo,** *a.* illegal, unlawful; illegitimate.

ileso, *a.* unhurt; uninjured.

ilícito, *a.* illicit; unlawful.

ilimitado, *a.* unlimited.

ilógico, *a.* illogical; irrational.

iluminación, *f.* illumination, lighting; (art) painting in distemper.—**iluminar,** *vt.* to illuminate, to light; to enlighten.

ilusión, *f.* illusion; delusion; eagerness.—*hacerse ilusiones,* to delude oneself.—**ilusionar,** *vt.* to cause illusion; to delude.—*vr.* (con) to have illusions; to get up hopes (of); to bank on.—**iluso,** *a.* deluded, deceived.—*m.* dreamer.

ilustración, *f.* illustration; elucidation, explanation.—**ilustrar,** *vt.* to illustrate.—*vr.* to acquire knowledge, learn.—**ilustrativo,** *a.* illustrative.—**ilustre,** *a.* illustrious, distinguished.

imagen, *f.* image.—**imaginable,** *a.* imaginable.—**imaginación,** *f.* imagination; imagining.—**imaginar,** *vt.*

& vr. to imagine; to suspect.—
imaginaria, f. (mil.) reserve guard;
(math.) imaginary.—**imaginario,** a.
imaginary, imagined; mythical.—
imaginativa, f. imagination.—**imaginativo,** a. imaginative.

imán, m. magnet; magnetism, charm.
imanar, imantar, vt. to magnetize.
imantación, f. magnetization.

imbécil, mf. & a. imbecile.—**imbecilidad,** f. imbecility.

imborrable, a. indelible; unforgettable.

imitable, a. imitable.—**imitación,** f.
imitation.—**imitador,** n. & a. imitator; imitating.—**imitar,** vt. to imitate.

impaciencia, f. impatience.—**impa-
cientar,** vt. to vex, irritate, make
(one) lose patience.—vr. to become
impatient.—**impaciente,** a. impat-
tient.

impacto, m. impact.

impar, a. odd.

imparcial, a. impartial.—**imparcialidad,** f. impartiality.

impartir, vt. to impart.

impasibilidad, f. impassiveness.—**impasible,** a. impassive, unmoved.

impávido, a. impassive, stolid; fearless; impudent.

impecable, a. impeccable.

impedido, a. disabled, crippled.—**impedimento,** m. impediment; obstacle, hindrance.—**impedir,** vti. [29]
to impede, hinder, prevent.—i. el
paso, to block (the way)

impeler, vt. to impel; to spur, stimulate.

impenetrable, a. impenetrable, impervious.

impenitente, a. impenitent, unrepentant.

impensado, a. unforeseen, unexpected

imperante, a. commanding, reigning.
—**imperar,** vi. to command; to prevail.—**imperativo,** a. imperative,
urgent; domineering, bossy.—m.
(gram.) imperative.

imperceptible, a. imperceptible.

imperdible, a. that cannot be lost.—
m. safety pin.

imperdonable, a. unpardonable, unforgivable.

imperfecto, a. imperfect, defective.

imperial, a. imperial.—**imperialismo,**
m. imperialism.—**imperialista,** mf. &
a. imperialist; imperialistic.

impericia, f. unskillfulness, inexpertness.

imperio, m. empire; rule; influence;
pride.—**imperioso,** a. imperious,
overbearing; pressing, urgent.

impermeable, a. waterproof; watertight; impervious.—m. raincoat.

impersonal, a. impersonal.

impertérrito, a. serene; stolid.

impertinencia, f. impertinence, folly,
nonsense.—**impertinente,** a. not
pertinent; impertinent, meddlesome.
—m. pl. lorgnette.

imperturbable, a. imperturbable, undisturbed, unruffled.

ímpetu, m. impetus, impulse.—**impetuoso,** a. impetuous, violent.

impiedad, f. impiety; irreligion, infidelity.—**impío,** a. impious; god-
less.—n. impious person; enemy of
religion.

implacable, a. implacable.

implicar, vti. [d] to implicate, involve; to imply.

implícito, a. implicit.

implorar, vt. to implore, beg, entreat.

imponente, a. imposing.—**imponer,**
vti. [32-49] to impose; to command
(respect, fear).—vri. to assert oneself, impose one's authority; to
command respect.

impopular, a. unpopular.—**impopularidad,** f. unpopularity.

importación, f. (com.) importation,
imports.—**importador,** n. & a. im-
porter; importing.

importancia, f. importance.—**importante,** a. important.—**importar,** vi.
to be important; to concern.—eso
no importa, that doesn't matter.—
eso no le importa a Ud., that is
none of your business.—no importa,
never mind —no me importa, I
don't care; that makes no difference to me.—¿qué importa? what
does it matter? what difference
does it make?—vt. to import; to
amount to; to be worth; to imply.
—**importe,** m. amount, price, value.

importunar, vt. to importune, pester.
—**importuno,** a. inopportune; persistent, annoying.

imposibilidad, f. impossibility.—**imposibilitado,** a. helpless, without
means; disabled, unfit for service.—
imposibilitar, vt to disable, make
unfit for service.—**imposible,** a. impossible.

imposición, f. imposition (of a duty,
etc.); tax, burden.

impostor, n. impostor.—**impostura,** f.
imposture.

impotencia, f. impotence.—**impotente,**
a. impotent, powerless.

impracticable, a. impracticable.

impregnación, f. impregnation.—**impregnar,** vt. to impregnate; to
saturate.—vr. to become impreg-
nated.

imprenta, f. printing; printing office
or house; press.

imprescindible, *a.* indispensable, essential.

impresión, *f.* impression; print, printing; stamping; footprint.—*i. digital,* fingerprint.—**impresionable,** *a.* impressionable, emotional.—**impresionar,** *vt.* to impress; to affect. —*vr.* to be moved.—**impreso,** *ppi.* of IMPRIMIR.—*a.* printed; stamped.— *m.* publication; printed matter, print; blank.—**impresor,** *n.* printer.

imprevisión, *f.* lack of foresight; improvidence.—**imprevisto,** *a.* unforeseen, unexpected.—*m. pl.* incidental or unforeseen expenses.

imprimir, *vti.* [49] to print, stamp, imprint.

improbable, *a.* improbable, unlikely.

ímprobo, *a.* laborious, painful, arduous.

improcedente, *a.* contrary to law.

improperio, *m.* insult, indignity.

impropio, *a.* inappropriate, unfitting; improper, unbecoming.

improvisación, *f.* improvisation.—**improvisado,** *a.* makeshift, improvised. —**improvisar,** *vt.* to improvise.— **improviso,** *a.* unexpected, unforeseen.—*de i.,* suddenly.

imprudencia, *f.* imprudence, indiscretion.—**imprudente,** *a.* imprudent, indiscreet.

impudicia, *f.* immodesty.—**impúdico,** *a.* immodest; impudent; revealing (of a dress).

impuesto, *ppi.* of IMPONER.—*a.* imposed; informed.—*estar,* or *quedar i. de,* to be informed about.—*m.* tax, duty.

impulsar, *vt.* to impel, move; (mech.) to drive, force.—**impulsión,** *f.* impulsion, impulse, impetus.—**impulsivo,** *a.* impulsive.—**impulso,** *m.* impulsion; impulse.

impureza, *f* impurity; unchastity.— **impuro,** *a.* impure; defiled.

inacabable, *a.* everlasting, endless.— **inacabado,** *a.* unfinished.

inaccesible, *a.* inaccessible, unapproachable.

inacción, *f.* inaction, inactivity.

inactividad, *f.* inactivity.—**inactivo,** *a.* inactive.

inadecuado, *a.* inadequate.

inadaptable, *a.* unadaptable.—**inadaptación,** *f.* maladjustment.

inadmisible, *a.* inadmissible.

inadvertencia, *f.* inadvertence, oversight.—**inadvertido,** *a.* careless; unseen, unnoticed.

inaguantable, *a.* unbearable.

inalámbrico, *a.* wireless.

inalienable, *a.* inalienable.

inamovible, *a.* immovable.

inanición, *f* starvation

inanimado, *a.* inanimate, lifeless.

inapelable, *a.* irrevocable.

inapetencia, *f.* lack of appetite.

inaplazable, *a.* that cannot be deferred.

inaplicable, *a.* irrelevant.

inapreciable, *a.* invaluable; imperceptible.

inasequible, *a.* unattainable, unobtainable, unavailable.

inaudito, *a.* unheard of, most extraordinary.

inauguración, *f.* inauguration.—**inaugurar,** *vt.* to inaugurate; to open (exhibition, etc.); to unveil (statue, monument, etc.).

inca, *mf.* & *a.* Inca.—**incaico,** *a.* Inca.

incalculable, *a.* incalculable; innumerable.

incalificable, *a.* extremely bad, most reprehensible.

incandescencia, *f.* incandescence.— **incandescente,** *a.* incandescent.

incansable, *a.* indefatigable, tireless.

incapacidad, *f.* incapacity; incompetence.—**incapacitar,** *vt.* to incapacitate, disable.—**incapaz,** *a.* incapable; unable; incompetent.

incauto, *a.* unwary; gullible.

incendiar, *vt.* to set on fire.—*vr.* to catch fire.—**incendiario,** *n.* & *a.* arsonist; incendiary.—**incendio,** *m.* fire, conflagration.

incensar, *vti.* [1] (eccl.) to incense; to bestow excessive praise or adulation.

incentivo, *m.* incentive, inducement; encouragement.

incertidumbre, *f* uncertainty; quandary.

incesante, *a.* unceasing, incessant.

incidencia, *f.* incident; incidence. **incidental,** *u.* incidental.—**incidente,** *a.* incidental.—*m.* incident.—**incidir,** *vi.* (en) to fall (into) (as an error).

incienso, *m.* incense.

incierto, *a.* uncertain; untrue; unknown.

incinerar, *vt.* to incinerate, cremate.

incisión, *f.* incision, cut.—**incisivo,** *a.* incisive; keen, sharp.

incitante, *a.* inciting, exciting.—**incitar,** *vt.* to incite, spur, instigate.— **incitativo,** *a.* inciting.—*m.* incitement.

incivil, *a.* uncivil; rude.

inclasificable, *a.* unclassifiable, nondescript.

inclinación, *f.* inclination; tendency, proclivity, bent; pitch; slope; (RR.) grade.—**inclinado,** *a.* inclined; sloping; disposed.—**inclinar,** *vt.* to incline; to bow; to influence.

—*vr.* to incline, slope; to lean; to stoop, bow.

incluir, *vti.* [23-49-e] to include; to enclose.—**inclusión,** *f.* inclusion.—**inclusive,** *adv.* inclusively.—**inclusivo,** *a.* inclusive.—**incluso,** *ppi.* of INCLUIR.—*a.* enclosed; including, included.

incobrable, *a.* (com.) uncollectable.

incógnito, *a.* unknown.—*de i.,* incognito.—*f.* (math.) unknown (quantity).

incoherencia, *f.* incoherence.—**incoherente,** *a.* incoherent.

incoloro, *a.* colorless.

incólume, *a.* sound, safe, unharmed.

incombustible, *a.* fireproof.

incomodar, *vt.* to disturb, inconvenience, trouble.—*vr.* to become vexed or angry.—**incomodidad,** *f.* inconvenience; discomfort; nuisance, annoyance.—**incómodo,** *a.* inconvenient; uncomfortable.

incomparable, *a.* incomparable.

incompetencia, *f.* incompetence.—**incompetente,** *a.* incompetent, unqualified.

incompleto, *a.* incomplete.

incomprensible, *a.* incomprehensible.—**incompresión,** *f.* misunderstanding; lack of understanding.

incomunicado, *a.* isolated; in solitary confinement.—**incomunicar,** *vti.* [d] to isolate, put in solitary confinement.

incondicional, *a.* unconditional; unqualified.

inconexo, *a.* unconnected, not pertinent; incoherent.

inconfundible, *a.* unmistakable.

incongruente, *a.* incongruous, out of place.

inconmensurable, *a.* immeasurable; vast.

inconmovible, *a.* unrelenting, unshakable.

inconsciencia, *f.* unconsciousness; (the) unconscious; unawareness; (coll.) irresponsibility.—**inconsciente,** *a.* unconscious; unaware; (coll.) irresponsible.

inconsecuencia, *f.* inconsistency.—**inconsecuente,** *a.* inconsistent.

inconsistente, *a.* unsubstantial, unstable.

inconstancia, *f.* inconstancy, fickleness, mutability.—**inconstante,** *a.* inconstant, fickle, mutable.

incontable, *a.* countless, innumerable.

incontestable, *a.* unanswerable.

incontrovertible, *a.* unanswerable.

inconveniencia, *f.* inconvenience; discomfort.—**inconveniente,** *a.* inconvenient, uncomfortable.—*m.* difficulty, obstacle.

incorporar, *vt.* to incorporate, embody; to make (someone) sit up.—*vr.* to incorporate; to join (as a mil. unit); to form a corporation; to sit up.

incorpóreo, *a.* bodiless, ethereal, immaterial.

incorrección, *f.* incorrectness: impropriety.—**incorrecto,** *a.* incorrect; improper.

incredulidad, *f.* incredulity.—**incrédulo,** *a.* incredulous.—*n.* unbeliever.—**increíble,** *a.* incredible, unbelievable.

incrementar, *vt.* (neol.) to increase, make bigger.—*vi.* to be increased.—**incremento,** *m.* increment, increase.

increpar, *vt.* to rebuke.

incriminar, *vt.* to incriminate.

incrustar, *vt.* to incrust; to encase; to inlay.

incubación, *f.* incubation; hatching.—**incubadora,** *f.* incubator (apparatus); hatchery.—**incubar,** *vt.* to incubate; to hatch.

inculpar, *vt.* to accuse, blame.

inculto, *a.* uncultured, untutored; uncultivated.—**incultura,** *f.* lack of culture.

incumbencia, *f.* incumbency; concern.—**incumbir,** *vt.* to concern, pertain.

incumplimiento, *m.* nonfulfillment.

incurable, *a.* incurable.

incurrir, *vi.* (en) to incur, become liable (to); to commit (error or crime).

incursión, *f.* (mil.) incursion, raid.

indagación, *f.* investigation, search, inquiry.—**indagar,** *vti.* [b] to investigate, inquire into or about.

indebidamente, *adv.* unduly; improperly; illegally.—**indebido,** *a.* improper; illegal.

indecencia, *f.* indecency; obscenity.—**indecente,** *a.* indecent, obscene.

indecible, *a.* inexpressible, untold.

indecisión, *f.* indecision, irresolution.—**indeciso,** *a.* hesitant, irresolute; undecided.

indecoroso, *a.* indecorous, unbecoming; undignified.

indefectible, *a.* unfailing.

indefendible, *a.* indefensible.—**indefenso,** *a.* defenseless.

indefinible, *a.* undefinable.—**indefinido,** *a.* indefinite; undefined.

indeleble, *a.* indelible.

indemne, *a.* undamaged, unhurt.—**indemnización,** *f.* compensation; indemnity.—**indemnizar,** *vti.* [a] to indemnify, compensate; to recoup.

independencia, *f.* independence.—**independiente,** *a.* independent.—**independizar,** *vti.* [a] to free, emanci-

pate.—*vri.* to become independent, win freedom.
indescifrable, *a.* undecipherable.
indescriptible, *a.* indescribable.
indeseable, *a.* undesirable, unwelcome.
indeterminado, *a.* indeterminate, undetermined.
indiada, *f.* (Am.) crowd or multitude of Indians.— **indiano,** *m.* a Spaniard who returns rich from America.
indicación, *f.* indication; hint.— **indicar,** *vti.* [d] to indicate, suggest, show.—**indicativo,** *a.* indicative, pointing.—*m.* (gram.) indicative.
índice, *m.* index; catalog; pointer; forefinger.—**indicio,** *m.* indication, clue, sign.
indiferencia, *f.* indifference.—**indiferente,** *a.* indifferent.
indígena, *a.* native, indigenous; (Am.) Indian.—*mf.* native; (Am.) Indian.
indigestarse, *vr.* to cause indigestion; to suffer from indigestion; to be unbearable.—**indigestión,** *f.* indigestion.—**indigesto,** *a.* indigestible.
indignación, *f.* indignation.—**indignar,** *vt.* to irritate, anger.—*vr.* to become indignant.—**indignidad,** *f.* indignity; unworthy act.—**indigno,** *a.* unworthy, undeserving; unbecoming, contemptible; low.
índigo, *m.* indigo.
indio, *n.* & *a.* Indian; Hindu.
indirecta, *f.* innuendo, hint.—*echar indirectas,* to make insinuations.— **indirecto,** *a.* indirect.
indisciplina, *f.* lack of discipline.— **indisciplinado,** *a.* undisciplined; untrained.
indiscreción, *f.* indiscretion.—**indiscreto,** *a.* indiscreet.
indiscutible, *a.* unquestionable, indisputable.
indispensable, *a.* indispensable, vital.
indisponer, *vti.* [32-49] to indispose; to make ill; (con) to prejudice (against).—*vri.* to become ill; to fall out (with a person).—**indisposición,** *f.* indisposition, slight ailment; dislike.—**indispuesto,** *ppi.* of INDISPONER.—*a.* indisposed; ill.
indistinto, *a.* indistinct, vague.
individual, *a.* individual.—**individualidad,** *f.* individuality.—**individuo,** *n.* individual, person; fellow.
indivisible, *a.* indivisible.
indócil, *a.* headstrong, unruly.
indocto, *a.* ignorant, untaught, untutored.
indochino, *a.* & *n.* Indo-Chinese.
índole, *f.* class, kind; disposition, nature.
indolencia, *f.* indolence.—**indolente,** *a.* indolent.

indomable, *a.* untamable, indomitable; unmanageable.—**indómito,** *a.* untamed; unruly.
indostánico, *a.* Hindu.
inducción, *f.* inducement, persuasion; (elec., log.) induction.—**inducir,** *vti.* [11] to induce; to persuade.—**inductor,** *a.* (elec.) inducive.—*m.* magnetic field.
indulgencia, *f.* indulgence; forbearance; forgiveness.—**indulgente,** *a.* indulgent, forbearing.
indultar, *vt.* to pardon.—**indulto,** *m.* pardon, amnesty.
indumentaria, *f.* garb, apparel, garments.
industria, *f.* industry.—*caballero de i.,* swindler; confidence man.—**industrial,** *a.* industrial.—*mf.* industrialist.—**industrializar,** *vti.* [a] to industrialize.—**industrioso,** *a.* industrious.
inédito, *a.* unpublished.
ineficacia, *f.* inefficacy.—**ineficaz,** *a.* ineffectual, ineffective.
inelegible, *a.* ineligible.
ineludible, *a.* inevitable, unavoidable.
inenarrable *a.* inexplicable; inexpressible, ineffable.
ineptitud, *f.* ineptitude, incompetency. —**inepto,** *a.* inept, incompetent, unqualified.
inequívoco, *a.* unmistakable.
inercia, *f.* inertia; inertness, inactivity.—**inerte,** *a.* inert; slow, sluggish.
inescrutable, *a.* inscrutable; unconfirmable.
inesperado, *a.* unexpected.
inestabilidad, *f.* instability.—**inestable,** *a.* unstable, unsteady.
inestimable, *a.* inestimable, invaluable.
inevitable, *a.* inevitable, unavoidable.
inexactitud, *f.* inexactness; inaccuracy; unfaithfulness.—**inexacto,** *a.* inexact, inaccurate.
inexistente, *a.* nonexistent.
inexorable, *a.* inexorable, relentless.
inexperiencia, *f.* inexperience.—**inexperto,** *a.* inexperienced, unskillful; unpractical.
inexplicable, *a.* inexplicable, unexplainable, unaccountable.
inexplotado, *a.* undeveloped.
inexpresivo, *a.* inexpressive, wooden.
infalible, *a.* infallible, unerring.
infame, *a.* & *mf.* infamous (person). —**infamia,** *f.* infamy; baseness; dishonor; opprobrium.
infancia, *f.* infancy; childhood.— **infante,** *n.* infante, prince; (*f.* infanta, princess).—**infantería,** *f.* infantry.—**infantil,** *a.* infantile, childlike.

infatigable, *a.* untiring, tireless.

infausto, *a.* unlucky; unhappy.

infección, *f.* infection.—**infeccioso,** *a.* infectious.—**infectar,** *vt.* to infect; to corrupt.—*vr.* to become infected.

infecundo, *a.* barren, sterile.

infelicidad, *f.* unhappiness, infelicity. —**infeliz,** *a.* unhappy, unfortunate.— *mf.* poor devil.

inferencia, *f.* inference.

inferior, *a.* inferior; lower; under (part).—*mf.* subordinate.—**inferioridad,** *f.* inferiority.

inferir, *vti.* [39] to infer; to imply; to inflict (as a wound).

infernal, *a.* infernal, hellish.

infestar, *vt.* to infest, plague; to infect.

inficionar, *vt.* to infect; to corrupt.

infidelidad, *f.* infidelity; unfaithfulness.—**infiel,** *a.* unfaithful, faithless; infidel, pagan; inaccurate.— *mf.* infidel.

infiernillo, *m.* spirit lamp.—**infierno,** *m.* hell, inferno.

infiltración, *f.* infiltration.—**infiltrar,** *vt. & vr.* to infiltrate, filter through.

ínfimo, *a.* lowest; least.

infinidad, *f.* infinity; infinite number, a lot.—**infinitivo,** *m. & a.* infinitive. —**infinito,** *a.* infinite.—*adv.* infinitely, immensely.—*m.* infinity.

inflación, *f.* inflation; conceit, airs.

inflamable, *a.* inflammable.—**inflamación,** *f.* inflammation.—**inflamar,** *vt.* to inflame; to set on fire.—*vr.* to catch fire; to become fiery; (med.) to become inflamed.

inflar, *vt.* to inflate; to exaggerate.— *vr.* to swell; to puff up (with pride, etc.).

inflexibilidad, *f.* inflexibility; stiffness, rigidity.—**inflexible,** *a.* inflexible, rigid, steely; unbending, unyielding.—**inflexión,** *f.* inflection; accent, modulation.

infligir, *vti.* [c] to impose (a penalty), condemn to.

influencia, *f.* influence.—**influenza,** *f.* influenza, grippe.—**influir,** *vti.* [23-e] to influence; to act on.—*vii.* (en) to have influence (on); to contribute (to).—**influjo,** *m.* influence. —**influyente,** *a.* influential.

infolio, *m.* folio.

información, *f.* information; report; inquiry; (law) brief.—**informal,** *a.* informal; unreliable; unconventional.—**informalidad,** *f.* informality; breach of etiquette; unreliability.—**informar,** *vt.* to inform, report to.—*vi.* (law) to plead.—*vr.* (de) to acquaint oneself (with), to inquire (into); to find out (about).

—**informativo,** *a.* instructive, informative.—**informe,** *a.* shapeless.— *m.* information; report; news; account; (law) pleading.

infortunado, *a.* unfortunate, unlucky. —**infortunio,** *m.* misfortune, ill luck; mishap; misery.

infracción, *f.* infraction, infringement, transgression.

infranqueable, *a.* insurmountable.

infrascrito, *a.* undersigned; hereinafter mentioned.

infrecuente, *a.* unusual, infrequent.

infringir, *vti.* [c] to infringe, violate, break.

infructuoso, *a.* fruitless; unsuccessful, unavailing.

ínfulas, *f. pl.* conceit, airs.—*darse í.,* to put on airs.

infundado, *a.* groundless, baseless.

infundio, *m.* (coll.) fib, story.

ingeniería, *f.* engineering.—**ingeniero,** *n.* engineer.—**ingenio,** *m.* talent; wit; cleverness, ingenuity; (Am.) sugar mill; device.—**ingeniosidad,** *f.* ingeniousness, ingenuity.—**ingenioso,** *a.* ingenious; witty, sparkling; resourceful.

ingénito, *a.* inborn, innate.

ingenuidad, *f.* ingenuousness, candor. —**ingenuo,** *a.* ingenuous, candid, unsophisticated.

ingerencia, *f.* interference, meddling. —**ingerir,** *vti.* [39] to insert, introduce.—*vri.* to interfere.

ingle, *f.* groin.

inglés, *a.* English.—*n.* Englishman (-woman).—*m.* English language.

ingratitud, *f.* ingratitude, ungratefulness.—**ingrato,** *a.* ungrateful; thankless; disagreeable.

ingrediente, *m.* ingredient.

ingresar, *vt.* (en) to enter; to deposit (money); to join (a party, group). —**ingreso,** *m.* entrance; entering; joining; (com.) entry, money received.—*pl.* receipts; earnings.

inhábil, *a.* unable; incompetent; unfit, unskillful.—**inhabilitación,** *f.* disabling or disqualifying; disqualification; disability.—**inhabilitar,** *vt.* to disqualify; to disable, render unfit.—*vr.* to lose a right; to become disabled.

inhabitable, *a.* uninhabitable.

inhalación, *f.* inhalation.—**inhalar,** *vt.* to inhale.

inherente, *a.* inherent.

inhibición, *f.* inhibition; prohibition. —**inhibir,** *vt.* to inhibit.—**inhibitorio,** *a.* inhibitory.

inhospitalario, *a.* inhospitable; unsheltering.—**inhóspito,** *a.* inhospitable.

inhumano, *a.* inhuman, cruel.

iniciación, *f.* initiation, introduction.
—**inicial,** *mf.* & *a.* initial.—**iniciar,**
vt. to initiate; to begin, start.—*vr.*
to be initiated.—**iniciativa,** *f.* initiative; resourcefulness.

inicuo, *a.* iniquitous, wicked.

inimaginable, *a.* unimaginable, incon-
ceivable, unthinkable.

inimitable, *a.* inimitable.

ininteligible, *a.* unintelligible.

injerir, *vti.* & [39] *vri.* = INGERIR.

injertar, *vt.* to graft.

injuria, *f.* offense, insult, affront.—**injuriar,** *vt.* to insult, offend.—**injurioso,** *a.* injurious; insulting, offensive.

injusticia, *f.* injustice.—**injustificable,**
a. unjustifiable.—**injustificado,** *a.*
unjustified, unjustifiable.—**injusto,** *a.*
unjust, unfair.

inmaculado, *a.* immaculate.

inmanente, *a.* inherent.

inmaterial, *a.* immaterial.

inmaturo, *a.* immature.

inmediación, *f.* contiguity.—*pl.* suburbs; neighborhood.—**inmediato,** *a.*
close, adjoining, immediate.

inmejorable, *a.* most excellent.

inmensidad, *f.* immensity, vastness;
infinity; great multitude or number.
—**inmenso,** *a.* immense; infinite;
countless.

inmerecido, *a.* unmerited, undeserved.

inmersión, *f.* immersion.

inmigración, *f.* immigration.—**inmigrante,** *mf.* immigrant.—**inmigrar,**
vi. to immigrate.—**inmigratorio,** *a.*
immigration.

inminencia, *f.* imminence, nearness.—
inminente, *a.* imminent, near.

inmiscuir, *vti.* [23-e] (fig.) to discuss
elements alien to the question.—*vri.*
to interfere; to meddle.

inmodestia, *f.* immodesty.—**inmodesto,** *a.* immodest.

inmoral, *a.* immoral.—**inmoralidad,** *f.*
immorality.

inmortal, *a.* immortal.—**inmortalidad,**
f. immortality.—**inmortalizar,** *vti.*
[a] to immortalize.—*vri.* to become
immortal.

inmovible, *a.* immovable.—**inmóvil,** *a.*
a. motionless; fixed; unshaken.—**inmovilidad,** *f.* immovability, fixed-
ness.—**inmovilizar,** *vti.* [a] to immobilize, fix.

inmueble, *a.* (law) immovable, real
(property).—*m.* (law) immovables.

inmundicia, *f.* filth, dirt; garbage;
filthiness; uncleanliness; impurity.—
inmundo, *a.* unclean, filthy.

inmune, *a.* immune; exempt.—**inmunidad,** *f.* immunity; exemption.—
inmunizar, *vti.* [a] to immunize.

innato, *a.* innate; inborn.

innecesario, *a.* unnecessary.

innegable, *a.* undeniable.

innoble, *a.* ignoble.

innovación, *f.* innovation.—**innova-
dor,** *n.* & *a.* innovator; innovating.
innovar, *vt.* to innovate.

innumerable, *a.* innumerable, numberless.

inocencia, *f.* innocence.—**inocente,** *a.*
innocent.—**inocentón,** *n.* simpleton.

inoculación, *f.* inoculation.—**inocular,**
vt. to inoculate; to contaminate.

inodoro, *a.* odorless.—*m.* water closet.

inofensivo, *a.* inoffensive, harmless.

inolvidable, *a.* unforgettable.

inopinado, *a.* unexpected, unforeseen.

inoportuno, *a.* inopportune, untimely.

inorgánico, *a.* inorganic.

inoxidable, *a.* nonrusting.

inquebrantable, *a.* unbreakable; unshakable; inflexible.

inquietante, *a.* disquieting, disturbing.
—**inquietar,** *vt.* to disquiet, trouble,
worry; to vex, harass; to stir up
or excite.—*vr.* to become uneasy or
restless; to fret, worry.—**inquieto,**
a. restless; uneasy, worried.—**inquietud,** *f.* restlessness, uneasiness,
anxiety.

inquilinato, *m.* occupancy; lease,
leasing.—**inquilino,** *n.* tenant, lodger,
renter, lessee.

inquina, *f.* (coll.) aversion, hatred,
grudge.

inquirir, *vti.* [2] to inquire, search,
investigate.

inquisición, *f.* inquest, examination,
inquiry; Inquisition, Holy Office.

insalubre, *a.* unhealthful, unsanitary.
—**insalubridad,** *f.* unhealthfulness.

insania, *f.* insanity.—**insano,** *a.* insane, crazy.

inscribir, *vti.* [49] to inscribe, register, record, book.—*vri.* to register;
to enroll.—**inscripción,** *f.* inscription; record, register, entry; registration; government bond.—**ins-
crito,** *ppi.* of INSCRIBIR.

insecticida, *m.* & *a.* insecticide; in-
secticidal.—**insecto,** *m.* insect.

inseguridad, *f.* insecurity; uncertainty.—**inseguro,** *a.* insecure, unsafe; uncertain.

insensatez, *f.* stupidity, folly.—**insensato,** *a.* stupid; mad.

insensibilidad, *f.* insensibility, unconsciousness; hard-heartedness.—
insensibilizar, *vti.* [a] to make
insensible or insensitive.—**insensible,**
a. insensible, thick-skinned; imperceptible; unfeeling.

inseparable, *a.* inseparable; unde-
tachable.

inserción, *f.* insertion; grafting.—
insertar, *vti.* [49] to insert.—**in-
serto,** *ppi.* of INSERTAR.

inservible, *a.* unserviceable, useless.

insidia, *f.* ambush, snare.—**insidioso,** *a.* insidious, sly, guileful.

insigne, *a.* noted, famous, renowned.

insignia, *f.* decoration, medal, badge, standard; (naut.) pennant.—*pl.* insignia.

insignificancia, *f.* insignificance; trifle.—**insignificante,** *a.* insignificant.

insinuación, *f.* insinuation; hint, suggestion.—**insinuar,** *vt.* to insinuate, hint, suggest.—*vr.* to ingratiate oneself; to creep in.

insípido, *a.* insipid, tasteless; unsavory; spiritless, flat; unseasoned.

insistencia, *f.* persistence, insistence, obstinacy.—**insistir,** *vi.* **(en)** to insist (on), persist (in); to dwell (upon), emphasize.

insolación, *f.* sunstroke.

insolencia, *f.* insolence.—**insolentar,** *vt.* to make bold.—*vr.* to become insolent.—**insolente,** *a.* insolent.

insólito, *a.* unusual, unaccustomed.

insomnio, *m.* insomnia, sleeplessness.

insondable, *a.* unfathomable, fathomless; inscrutable.

insoportable, *a.* unbearable, intolerable.

insostenible, *a.* indefensible.

inspección, *f.* inspection; inspector's office.—**inspeccionar,** *vt.* to inspect. —**inspector,** *n.* inspector; supervisor, overseer.

inspiración, *f.* inspiration; inhalation.—**inspirar,** *vt.* to inspire; to inhale.

instalación, *f.* installation.—**instalar,** *vt.* to install.—*vr.* to establish oneself, settle.

instancia, *f.* instance; petition; request.

instantáneo, *a.* instantaneous.—*f.* snapshot.—**instante,** *m.* instant, moment, trice.—**al i.,** immediately.

instar, *vt.* to press, urge.—*vi.* to be urgent.

instaurar, *vt.* to establish; to renovate.

instigador, *n.* instigator, abettor.— **instigar,** *vti.* [b] to instigate, incite.

instintivo, *a.* instinctive.—**instinto,** *m.* instinct.

institución, *f.* institution, establishment.—**instituir,** *vti.* [23-e] to institute, establish, found.—**instituto,** *m.* institute.—**institutriz,** *f.* governess.

instrucción, *f.* instruction; education, learning; tutoring; (law) court proceedings.—*pl.* instructions, orders.— **instructivo,** *a.* instructive.—**instruir,** *vti.* [23-e] to instruct, teach, train; to inform; to put in legal form.

instrumentación, *f.* (mus.) instrumentation, orchestration.—**instrumental,** *a.* (mus.) instrumental; (law) pertaining to legal instruments.—*m.* set of instruments.— **instrumento,** *m.* instrument, implement, apparatus; agent or means.

insubordinación, *f.* insubordination.— **insubordinar,** *vt.* to incite to insubordination.—*vr.* to rebel, mutiny.

insuficiencia, *f.* insufficiency.—**insuficiente,** *a.* insufficient.

insula, *f.* isle, island.—**insular,** *a.* insular.

insulso, *a.* insipid; dull, heavy.

insultar, *vt.* to insult.—**insulto,** *m.* insult, affront.

insuperable, *a.* insuperable, impassable.

insurgente, *mf. & a.* insurgent.

insurrección, *f.* insurrection, rebellion. —**insurreccionar,** *vt.* to cause to rebel.—*vr.* to rebel.—**insurrecto,** *n. & a.* insurgent, rebel.

insustancial, *a.* unsubstantial.

intacto, *a.* untouched, intact, whole, undisturbed.

intachable, *a.* unexceptionable, irreproachable.

intangible, *a.* intangible, untouchable.

integración, *f.* integration.—**integral,** *a.* integral; whole.—**integrar,** *vt.* to integrate; to compose, make up; (com.) to reimburse.—**integridad,** *f.* wholeness; integrity, honesty; virginity.—**íntegro,** *a.* entire, complete, whole; upright, honest; unabridged.

intelecto, *m.* intellect.—**intelectual,** *a. & mf.* intellectual.—**inteligencia,** *f.* intelligence; understanding (between persons).—**inteligente,** *a.* intelligent; smart, clever.

intemperancia, *f.* intemperance, excess.—**intemperante,** *a.* intemperate. —**intemperie,** *f.* rough or bad weather.—**a la i.,** in the open air, outdoors, unsheltered.

intempestivo, *a.* unseasonable, inopportune.

intención, *f.* intention. purpose.—*de primera i.,* provisionally, tentatively.

intendencia, *f.* intendancy; administration; office or district of an intendant.—**intendente,** *n.* intendant; administrator; (mil.) quartermaster.

intensidad, *f.* intensity; vehemence.— **intensivo, intenso,** *a.* intense, intensive, vehement.

intentar, *vt.* to try, attempt, endeavor; to intend; (law) to enter (an action), commence (a lawsuit).— **intento,** *m.* intent, purpose.—*de i.,* purposely, knowingly.—**intentona,** *f.* (coll.) rash attempt.

intercalar, *vt.* to interpolate, place between.

intercambio, *m.* interchange, intercourse.

interceder, *vi.* to intercede.

interceptar, *vt.* to intercept, cut off.

intercesión, *f.* intercession, mediation.

interdicción, *f.* interdiction, prohibition.

interés, *m.* interest.—*pl.* interests.—*intereses creados*, vested interests.—**interesado**, *a.* interested; mercenary, selfish.—*n.* associate; person interested; (law) party in interest.—**interesante**, *a.* interesting.—**interesar**, *vi.* & *vr.* **(en, por, con)** to be concerned (with) or interested (in); to take an interest.—*vt.* to invest; to give an interest; to interest, attract.

interfecto, *n.* (law) murdered person, victim.

interferencia, *f.* interference.—**interferir**, *vi.* to interfere; to meddle.

ínterin, *adv.* meanwhile, interim.—**interino**, *a.* provisional, temporary, acting, interim.

interior, *a.* interior, inner, inside; domestic (as commerce, etc.).—*m.* interior; inside; inner part; mind, soul.—*pl.* entrails, intestines, (coll.) insides.—**interioridades**, *f. pl.* family secrets; inwardness.

interjección, *f.* interjection.

interludio, *m.* (mus.) interlude.

intermediario, *a.* intermediary.—*n.* intermediary; mediator; middleman.—**intermedio**, *a.* intermediate, interposed.—*m.* interval, interim; (theat.) interlude, intermission.

interminable, *a.* interminable, endless.

intermisión, *f.* intermission, interruption.

intermitente, *a.* intermittent.

internacional, *a.* international.

internado, *m.* boarding school; boarding.—**internar**, *vt.* to intern, confine; to place in an institution.—*vi.* to enter.—*vr.* **(en)** to go into the interior (of); to go deeply (into).—**interno**, *a.* interior, internal, inward; boarding.—*n.* boarding student; interne.

interpelar, *vt.* to interrogate, question.

interponer, *vti.* [32-49] to interpose, place between; to appoint as a mediator; (law) to present (a petition) to a court.—*vri.* to go between, to interpose.—**interposición**, *f.* mediation; interjection; interposal; intervention.

interpretación, *f.* interpretation; rendering.—**interpretar**, *vt.* to interpret.—**intérprete**, *mf.* interpreter.

interpuesto, *ppi.* of INTERPONER.—*a.* interposed.

interrogación, *f.* interrogation, question; question mark.—**interrogante**, *a.* interrogative; interrogating.—*mf.* interrogator, questioner.—*m.* question mark.—**interrogar**, *vti.* [b] to question, interrogate.—**interrogatorio**, *m.* interrogatory; (law) cross-examination.

interrumpir, *vt.* to interrupt.—**interrupción**, *f.* interruption.—**interruptor**, *n.* interrupter.—*m.* (elec.) switch; circuit-breaker.

intersección, *f.* intersection.

intervalo, *m.* interval; interlude.

intervención, *f.* intervention; mediation, auditing of accounts; (surg.) operation.—**intervenir**, *vii.* [45] to intervene, mediate, intermediate; to interfere.—*vt.* to supervise; to audit; to control.—**interventor**, *n.* comptroller; supervisor; auditor.

intestino, *a.* intestine, internal; civil, domestic.—*m.* intestine.

intimación, *f.* intimation, hint.—**intimar**, *vt.* to intimate, indicate.—*vr.* to pierce, penetrate.—**intimidad**, *f.* intimacy.

íntimo, *a.* internal, innermost; intimate.

intocable, *a.* untouchable.

intolerable, *a.* intolerable, unbearable.—**intolerancia**, *f.* intolerance.—**intolerante**, *a.* intolerant.

intoxicación, *f.* poisoning.—**intoxicar**, *vti.* [d] to poison.—*vri.* to get poisoned.

intraducible, *a.* untranslatable.

intranquilidad, *f.* restlessness, uneasiness.—**intranquilizar**, *vti.* [a] to worry, make uneasy.—*vri.* to become disquieted, to worry.—**intranquilo**, *a.* uneasy, restless.

intransferible, *a.* not transferable.

intransitable, *a.* impassable; impracticable.

intransitivo, *a.* (gram.) intransitive.

intrepidez, *f.* intrepidity, bravery.—**intrépido**, *a.* intrepid, daring.

intriga, *f.* intrigue.—**intrigante**, *mf.* & *a.* intriguer; intriguing, scheming.—**intrigar**, *vti.* [b] to arouse (one's) interest or curiosity; to mystify.—*vii.* to intrigue.—*vri.* to be interested (in) or curious (about).

intrincado, *a.* intricate, involved.

introducción, *f.* introduction.—**introducir**, *vti.* [11] to introduce; to usher in, put in, insert; to present (a person).—*vri.* **(en)** to gain access (to); to get in; to ingratiate oneself (with); to interfere (in).

intromisión, *f.* influx; interference, meddling.

intrusión, f. intrusion, obtrusion.—
intruso, a. intrusive, intruding.—n.
intruder, outsider.
intuición, f. intuition.—intuir, vti.
[23-e] to know or perceive by intuition.—intuitivo, a. intuitive.
inundación, f. inundation, flood.—
inundar, vt. to inundate, flood.
inusitado, a. unusual, rare.
inútil, a. useless; fruitless, unavailing; needless.—inutilidad, f. uselessness;   needlessness.—inutilización, f. spoilage.—inutilizar, vti.
[a] to render useless; to disable;
to spoil, ruin.—vri. to become useless.
invadir, vt. to invade; to encroach
upon.
invalidar, vt. to invalidate, nullify;
to quash.—inválido, a. invalid;
crippled; feeble; null, void.—n.
invalid.
invariable, a. invariable, constant.
invasión, f. invasion.—invasor, n. &
a. invader; invading.
invectiva, f. invective.
invencible, a. invincible, unconquerable.
invención, f. invention.
invendible, a. unsalable.
inventar, vt. to invent; to fib.
inventariar, vt. to inventory, take
inventory of.—inventario, m. inventory.
inventiva, f. inventiveness, ingenuity,
resourcefulness.—invento, m. invention.—inventor, n. inventor.
invernadero, m. winter quarters;
hothouse.—invernal, a. winter,
wintry.—invernar, vii. [1] to
winter, pass the winter.
inverosímil, a. unlikely, improbable.
inversión, f. inversion; (com.) investment.—inversionista, mf. (neol.)
investor.—inverso, ppi. of INVERTIR.
—a. inverse, inverted.—invertido, a.
& n. homosexual.—a. inverted.—
invertir, vti. [39-49] to invert; to
reverse; to spend (time); (com.) to
invest.
investidura, f. ceremonial investment.
investigación, f. investigation, research; inquest.—investigador, n. &
a. investigator; investigating.—investigar, vti. [b] to investigate,
ascertain, inquire into; to do research work.
investir, vti. [29] to invest; to confer
upon.
inveterado, a. inveterate, ingrained.
invicto, a. invincible, unconquered.
invierno, m. winter.
invisible, a. invisible.
invitación, f. invitation.—invitado, n.

guest.—invitar, vt. to invite; to
entice; to treat.
invocación, f. invocation.—invocar,
vti. [d] to invoke, implore.
involucrar, vt. to involve.
involuntario, a. involuntary, unintentional.
inyección, f. injection.—poner una i.,
to give an injection.—inyectado, a.
bloodshot, inflamed.—inyectar, vt.
to inject.
iodo, m. = YODO.
ir, vii. [24] to go; to walk; to be becoming; to fit, suit.—¿cómo le va?
how are you?—i. a, to go to; to be
going to, to purpose or intend to.—
i. a buscar, to get, fetch.—i. a
caballo, to ride, to be riding on
horseback.—i. a medias, to go
halves.—i. a pie, to walk.—i. pasando, to be so-so, to be as usual,
to be getting along.—no me va ni
me viene, it does not affect me in
the least.—¡qué va! nonsense!—
¡vámonos! let's go!—¡vamos a ver!
let's see!—vri. to go, go away.—i.
abajo, to topple down.—i. a pique,
to founder, go to the bottom.
ira, f. ire, anger.—iracundo, a.
wrathful;   angry,   enraged.—irascible, a. irascible, irritable, short-
tempered.
iridiscente, a. iridescent.
iris, m. (anat.) iris.—arco i., rainbow.
—irisado, a. rainbow-hued.
irlandés, a. Irish.—m. Irishman; Irish
language.—f. Irishwoman.
ironía, f. irony.—irónico, a. ironical,
sarcastic.
irracional, a. irrational, unreasoning.
irradiación, f. radiation.—irradiar,
vt. to radiate.
irrazonable, a. unreasonable, impracticable.
irreal, a. unreal.—irrealidad, f. un-
reality.—irrealizable, a. unrealizable.
irrebatible, a. indisputable.
irreflexión, f. rashness, thoughtlessness.—irreflexivo, a. thoughtless,
impulsive, unthinking.
irregular, a. irregular.—irregularidad,
f. irregularity.
irreligioso, a. irreligious.
irrespetuoso, a. disrespectful.
irrespirable, a. not fit to be breathed.
irresponsable, a. irresponsible.
irreverencia, f. irreverence.—irreverente, a. irreverent.
irrevocable, a. irrevocable.
irrigación, m. irrigation.—irrigar, vti.
[b] to irrigate, water.
irrisión, f. derision, ridicule.—irrisorio, a. derisive.
irritable, a. irritable.—irritación, f.

irritation.—**irritante**, *a.* irritating; irritant.—**irritar**, *vt.* to irritate.

irrogar, *vti.* [b] to cause (harm or damage).

irrupción, *m.* raid, incursion.

isla, *f.* island.—**islandés, islándico**, *a. & n.* Icelandic.—**isleño**, *n. & a.* islander; (Cuba) native of the Canary Islands.—**islote**, *m.* small barren island, key.

israelita, *mf. & a.* Israelite; Israeli.

istmo, *m.* isthmus.

italiano, *n. & a.* Italian.—*m.* Italian language.—**itálico**, *a.* Italic; italic.

ítem, *m.* section, clause, article; addition.—**í.**, or **í. más**, also, likewise, furthermore.

itinerario, *a.* itinerary.—*m.* itinerary; railroad guide, timetable, schedule.

izar, *vti.* [a] to hoist, heave, haul up.

izquierda, *f.* left hand; (pol.) left wing.—*a la i.*, to the left.—**izquierdista**, *mf. & a.* (pol.) leftist, radical.—**izquierdo**, *a.* left-handed; left, left-hand side.

J

jaba, *f.* (Am.) basket; crate.

jabalí, *m.* wild boar.—**jabalina**, *f.* sow of a wild boar; javelin.

jabón, *m.* soap; a piece of soap.—*j. de olor*, toilet soap.—**jabonadura**, *f.* washing.—*pl.* suds or soap suds; lather.—**jabonera**, *f.* soap dish.—**jabonería**, *f.* soap factory or shop.

jaca, *f.* pony, cob; gelding.

jacal, *m.* (Mex.) Indian hut.

jacarandoso, *a.* blithe, merry, gay.

jacinto, *m.* hyacinth.

jaco, *m.* sorry nag, jade.

jactancia, *f.* boasting.—**jactancioso**, *a.* boastful, vainglorious.—**jactarse**, *vr.* to boast, vaunt.

jaculatoria, *f.* short prayer.

jade, *m.* (jewel.) jade.

jadeante, *a.* panting, out of breath.—**jadear**, *vi.* to pant.—**jadeo**, *m.* pant, palpitation.

jaez, *m.* harness; trappings; (fig.) manner, kind, quality.—*pl.* trappings.

jaiba, *f.* (Am.) (ichth.) a kind of crab; a cunning, crafty or sneaky person.

jalar, *vt.* = HALAR.—*vr.* (Am.) to get drunk.

jalea, *f.* jelly.

jalear, *vt.* to animate dancers by clapping hands.—**jaleo**, *m.* (coll.) carousal; clapping of hands to encourage dancers.

jaletina, *f.* (Am.) calf's foot jelly; gelatine.

jalón, *m.* landmark, stake; (Am.)

pull, jerk.—**jalonar**, *vt.* to stake out, mark.—**jalonear**, *vt.* (Am.) to pull, jerk.

jamaiquino, *n. & a.* Jamaican.

jamás, *adv.* never.—*nunca j.*, never, nevermore.—*por siempre j.*, forever and ever.

jamelgo, *m.* swaybacked nag.

jamón, *m.* ham.—**jamona**, *f.* (coll.) middle-aged woman; (Am.) spinster.

japonés, *n. & a.* Japanese; Japanese language.

jaque, *m.* (chess) check; bully.—*j. mate*, checkmate.

jaqueca, *f.* migraine; headache.

jáquima, *f.* part of a halter which encloses the head.—**jaquimazo**, *m.* (coll.) blow; displeasure; disappointment.

jarabe, *m.* syrup; any sweet mixed drink; (Am.) a Mexican folk dance.—*j. de pico*, empty talk, prattling.

jarana, *f.* (coll.) carousal, revelry.—**jaranear**, *vi.* (coll.) to carouse.—**jaranero**, *a.* jolly.

jarcia, *f.* (naut.) rigging and cordage; shrouds.

jardín, *m.* flower garden.—**jardinería**, *f.* gardening.—**jardinero**, *n.* gardener.—*f.* flowerstand.

jaretón, *m.* (sewing) hem.

jarra, *f.* jar; pitcher.—*en j.*, or *de jarras*, akimbo.

jarrete, *m.* hock (of an animal).

jarro, *m.* pitcher, jug, pot.—**jarrón**, *m.* flower vase; large jar.

jaspe, *m.* (min.) jasper.—**jaspeado**, *a.* mottled, variegated.

jaula, *f.* cage; (Am.) cattle or freight car; cell (in a prison).

jauría, *f.* pack of hounds.

javanés, *a. & n.* Javanese.

jazmín, *m.* jasmine.

jefatura, *f.* position or headquarters of a chief.—**jefe**, *n.* chief, head, leader; (fam.) boss; (mil.) commanding officer.

jején, *m.* (Cuba) gnat.

jengibre, *m.* ginger.

jerarquía, *f.* hierarchy.

jerez, *m.* sherry wine.

jerga, *f.* jargon; gibberish; slang.

jergón, *m.* straw bed; mattress, pallet; zircon.

jerigonza, *f.* (coll.) jargon; gibberish; slang.

jeringa, *f.* syringe.—**jeringar**, *vti.* [b] to inject with a syringe; to bother, vex.—**jeringazo**, *m.* injection; squirt.—**jeringuilla**, *f.* syringe.

jeroglífico, *m.* hieroglyph.—*a.* hieroglyphic.

jersey, *m.* sweater, pullover.

jesuita, *m.* Jesuit.

jeta, f. hog's snout; (coll.) person's face.

jíbaro, a. (Am.) wild, rustic.—n. countryman(-woman).

jibia, f. cuttlefish.

jícara, f. (Am.) small chocolate or coffee cup; bowl made out of a gourd.

jiga, f. jig (dance and tune).

jigote, m. hash, minced meat.

jilguero, m. linnet.

jinete, m. trooper; cavalryman; horseman, rider, equestrian.—**jinetear,** vt. (Am.) to break in (a horse).—vi. to ride around on horseback, mainly for show.

jipijapa, f. Panama hat.

jira, f. picnic, outing; tour.

jirafa, f. giraffe.

jirón, m. shred, tear; rag; small part (of anything).

jitomate, m. (Am.) tomato.

jocoso, a. jocose, humorous, facetious.

jofaina, f. washbasin, washbowl.

jolgorio, m. = HOLGORIO; boisterous frolic.

jornada, f. one-day march; working day; stage, journey, travel, trip; (mil.) expedition; act of a play.—**jornal,** m. salary; day's wages.—a j., by the day.—**jornalero,** n. day laborer.

joroba, f. hump; (coll.) importunity, annoyance, nuisance.—**jorobado,** a. crooked, humpbacked.—n. hunchback.—**jorobar,** vt. (coll.) to importune, bother, annoy.

jota, f. name of the letter j; jot, tittle, bit; iota; an Aragonese dance and tune.

joven, a. young.—mf. youth; young man; young woman; young person.

jovial, a. jovial, gay, cheerful.—**jovialidad,** f. joviality, gaiety.

joya, f. jewel, gem; piece of jewelery.—**joyería,** f. jeweler's shop.—**joyero,** n. jeweler.—m. jewel case.

juanete, m. bunion.

jubilación, f. retirement; pension.—**jubilar,** vt. to retire; to pension off.—vr. to become a pensioner; to be retired.—**jubileo,** m. jubilee.—**júbilo,** m. glee, merriment, rejoicing.—**jubiloso,** a. joyful, merry, gay.

judaico, a. Judaical, Jewish.—**judaismo,** m. Judaism.—**judía,** f. Jewess; bean, string bean.

judicatura, f. judicature; judgeship.—**judicial,** a. judicial, juridical.

judío, n. Jew (f. Jewess).—a. Jewish.

juego, m. play, sport, game; gambling; set of cards; movement, work, working (of a mechanism); set; (mech.) play, free space.—hacer j., to match, to fit; to bet (in games of chance).—j. de manos, legerdemain.—j. de palabras, pun.

juerga, f. spree, carousal.

jueves, m. Thursday.

juez, m. judge, justice; umpire.

jugada, f. play, act of playing; a throw, move, stroke; ill turn.—**jugador,** n. player; gambler.—**jugar,** vti. [25-b] & vii. to play; to sport; to gamble; to stake; to move in a game; to take active part in an affair; to intervene; to make game of.—j. a cara o cruz, to bet on the toss of a coin.—j. a la bolsa, to dabble in stocks.—vri. to gamble, to risk (one's salary, one's life).—jugarse el todo por el todo, to stake all, to shoot the works.—**jugarreta,** f. (coll.) bad play; bad turn, nasty trick.

juglar, m. juggler; minstrel.

jugo, m. juice, sap; marrow, pith, substance.—**jugosidad,** f. succulence, juiciness.—**jugoso,** a. juicy, succulent, full of sap.

juguete, m. toy.—**juguetear,** vi. to play, frolic; trifle, toy.—**juguetería,** f. toyshop, toy trade.—**juguetón,** a. playful, frolicsome, rollicking, waggish.

juicio, m. judgment; decision; prudence, wisdom; thinking; good behavior; (law) trial.—estar fuera de su j., to be crazy.—perder el j., to become insane.—tener j., to be wise; to be cautious; to be well-behaved.—**juicioso,** a. judicious, wise; well-behaved.

julio, m. July.

juma, f. (coll.) spree.

jumento, m. donkey; stupid person.

junco, m. (bot.) reed, rush; Chinese junk.

jungla, f. (Am.) jungle.

junio, m. June.

junquillo, m. (bot.) jonquil; reed, rattan.

junta, f. board, council; meeting, conference; session; joint; coupling.—**juntar,** vt. to join, connect, unite; to assemble, congregate; to amass, collect; to pool (resources).—vr. to join, meet, assemble; to be closely united; to copulate; (con) to associate (with).—**junto,** adv. near, close at hand, near at hand; at the same time.—j. a, next to, by, beside.—j. con, together with.—a. united, joined; together.—**juntura,** f. juncture, joining.

jurado, m. jury; juryman.—**juramentar,** vt. to swear in.—vr. to be sworn in, take an oath.—**juramento,** m. oath; act of swearing; curse, imprecation.—**jurar,** vt. & vi. to

swear; to take an oath.—*j. en falso*, to commit perjury.—*jurársela(s) a uno*, to threaten one with revenge.
—**jurídico**, *a.* legal, juridical.—**jurisconsulto**, *n.* jurist; lawyer.—**jurisdicción**, *f.* jurisdiction; territory.—**jurisprudencia**, *f.* jurisprudence; laws, legislation.—**jurista**, *mf.* jurist; lawyer.

justa, *f.* joust, tournament; contest.

justicia, *f.* justice, rightness.—**justiciero**, *a.* just and strict.—**justificable**, *a.* justifiable.—**justificación**, *f.* justification, defense; production of evidence.—**justificar**, *vti.* [d] to justify; to vindicate.—**justipreciar**, *vt.* to appraise.—**justo**, *a.* just; pious; correct, exact, strict; fit; tight, close.—*m.* just and pious man. —*adv.* tightly.

juvenil, *a.* juvenile, youthful.—**juventud**, *f.* youthfulness, youth; young people.

juzgado, *m.* court of justice.—**juzgar**, *vti.* [b] & *vii.* to judge; to pass or render judgment (on).

K

kaki, *m.* khaki.

kerosén, *m.*, **keroseno**, *m.*, **kerosina**, *f.* kerosene.

kilo, *m.* kilo, kilogram.—**kilogramo**, *m.* kilogram.—**kilolitro**, *m.* kiloliter. —**kilométrico**, *a.* kilometric; mileage (ticket); (coll.) very long, interminably long.—**kilómetro**, *m.* kilometer.—**kilovatio**, *m.* kilowatt.

kiosco, *m.* kiosk, small pavilion; newsstand.

L

la, *art. f. sing.* the.—*pron. pers. f. sing.* her, it.—*m.* (mus.) la, A.

laberinto, *m.* labyrinth, maze.

labia, *f.* (coll.) gift of gab, palaver, fluency.—**labial**, *a.* labial; lip.—**labio**, *m.* lip.

labor, *f.* labor, task; work; (sew.) needlework; trimming.—**laborable**, *a.* workable; tillable.—*día l.*, working day.—**laborar**, *vt.* & *vi.* to work; to till.

laboratorio, *m.* laboratory.

laboriosidad, *f.* laboriousness; industry.—**laborioso**, *a.* laborious; industrious.

labrado, *a.* cultivated, tilled; wrought; figured, hewn.—*m.* cultivated land.—**labrador**, *n.* farmer, peasant, tiller.—**labranza**, *f.* cultivation, tillage; farming.—**labrar**, *vt.* to till, cultivate; to carve (stone); to work (metals).—**labriego**, *n.* farmer, peasant; rustic.

laca, *f.* lacquer; shellac.

lacayo, *m.* lackey, footman.

lacio, *a.* straight (as hair); flaccid, languid.

lacónico, *a.* laconic.

lacra, *f.* mark left by illness; fault, defect.

lacrar, *vt.* to seal with sealing wax.—**lacre**, *m.* sealing wax.

lacrimoso, *a.* tearful.

lactancia, *f.* weaning period; nursing (of a baby).—**lactar**, *vt.* to nurse; to feed with milk.—*vi.* to suckle; to feed on milk.—**lácteo**, *a.* milky.—*Vía Láctea*, Milky Way.

ladear, *vt.* & *vr.* to tilt, tip, incline to one side.—*vi.* to skirt; to deviate. —*vr.* to lean; to tilt, incline to one side.—**ladeo**, *m.* inclination or motion to one side; tilt.

ladera, *f.* slope, hillside.

ladino, *a.* cunning, crafty.

lado, *m.* side, edge.—*al l.*, just by; near at hand; next door.—*a un l.*, aside.—*hacerse a un l.*, to get out of the way, to move aside.—*l. a l.*, side by side.—*por otro l.*, on the other hand.

ladrador, *n.* & *a.* barker (dog); barking.—**ladrar**, *vi.* to bark.—**ladrido**, *m.* barking, bark.

ladrillazo, *m.* blow with a brick.—**ladrillo**, *m.* brick, tile.

ladrón, *n.* thief; robber.—**ladronzuelo**, *n.* petty thief.

lagaña, *f.* bleariness.—**lagañoso**, *a.* blear-eyed.

lagartija, *f.*, **lagartijo**, *m.* small lizard.—**lagarto**, *m.* lizard; (Am.) alligator; (coll.) sly, artful person.

lago, *m.* lake.

lágrima, *f.* tear.—**lagrimal**, *m.* tear-duct.—**lagrimar**, **lagrimear**, *vi.* to shed tears.—**lagrimeo**, *m.* shedding tears.—**lagrimoso**, *a.* tearful; (of eyes) watery.

laguna, *f.* lagoon; gap.

laico, *a.* lay, laic.

laja, *f.* flagstone; slab.

lamedura, *f.* lick, act of licking.

lamentable, *a.* lamentable, deplorable. —**lamentación**, *f.* lamentation, wail. —**lamentar**, *vt.* to lament, mourn.—*vi.* & *vr.* to lament, grieve, wail; to complain; to moan.—**lamento**, *m.* lament, moan.

lamer, *vt.* to lick; to lap.

lámina, *f.* plate, sheet; print, illustration.—**laminado**, *a.* laminated; (of metals) rolled.—**laminar**, *vt.* to roll or beat (metal) into sheets.

lámpara, *f.* lamp.—**lamparón**, *m.* large grease spot; (med.) scrofula.

lampazo, *m.* mop, swab.

lampiño, *a.* beardless.

lana, *f.* wool.—**lanar,** *a.* wool, woolen.

lance, *m.* cast, throw; incident, episode; event; quarrel; move or turn in a game.—*l. de honor,* duel.

lancear, *vt.* to wound with a lance.—**lancero,** *m.* lancer.—**lanceta,** *f.* (surg.) lancet.

lancha, *f.* boat; launch; flagstone, slab.—*l. cañonera,* gunboat.—**lanchón,** *m.* (naut.) barge, scow.

langaruto, *a.* (coll.) tall and skinny; thin.

langosta, *f.* lobster; locust.—**langostino,** *m.* crayfish.

languidecer, *vii.* [3] to languish.—**languidez,** *f.* languor, pining.—**lánguido,** *a.* languid, faint.

lanilla, *f.* nap (of cloth), down; fine flannel.—**lanudo,** *a.* woolly, fleecy; (Am.) crude; ill-bred; dull.

lanza, *f.* lance, spear.—**lanzada,** *f.* thrust or blow with a lance.

lanzadera, *f.* shuttle.

lanzador, *n.* thrower, ejecter; (baseball) pitcher.—**lanzamiento,** *m.* launching, casting, or throwing; (law) dispossessing, eviction.—**lanzaminas,** *m.* mine layer; mine-laying boat.—**lanzar,** *vti.* [a] to throw, fling; to launch; to throw (a ball) up; (law) to evict, dispossess; (baseball) to pitch.—*vr.* to rush or dart; to launch forth; to engage or embark (in).—**lanzatorpedos,** *m.* torpedo boat; torpedo tube.

lanzazo, *m.* thrust or blow with a lance.

lapa, *f.* barnacle.

lapicero, *m.* mechanical pencil.

lápida, *f.* tombstone, gravestone; memorial tablet.

lápiz, *m.* pencil; crayon.—*l. de los labios,* lipstick.

lapón, *n.* Laplander.—*a.* pertaining to Lapland or Laplanders.

lapso, *m.* lapse, slip.

lardo, *m.* lard.

larga, *f.* (gen. in the *pl.*) delay, procrastination.—*a la corta o a la l.,* sooner or later.—*a. la l.,* in the end, in the long run.—*dar largas,* to delay, put off.

largar, *vti.* [b] to loosen; to let go, set free; to expel; to give (as a slap); to heave (as a sigh).—*vri.* (coll.) to get out, quit, leave.—**largo,** *a.* long; generous; shrewd, cunning.—*a lo l.,* lengthwise; at full length.—*traje l.,* evening dress.—*m.* length.—*de l.,* in length, long.—*pasar de l.,* to pass by without stopping.—*adv.* largely, profusely.—*interj.* ¡*l.!* or ¡*l. de ahí!* get out!—**largor,**

m. length.—**larguero,** *m.* jamb post; stringer.—**largueza,** *f.* liberality, generosity.—**larguirucho,** *a.* (coll.) long and thin.—**largura,** *f.* length.

laringe, *f.* larynx.

larva, *f.* larva.

las, *art. pl.* of LA, the.—*pron. f.* them.

lasca, *f.* slice; chip from a stone.

lascivia, *f.* lasciviousness.—**lascivo,** *a.* lascivious.

lasitud, *f.* lassitude, weariness, faintness.

lástima, *f.* pity; compassion; pitiful object.—*dar l.,* to arouse pity or regret.—*es l.,* it's a pity.—**lastimadura,** *f.* sore, hurt.—**lastimar,** *vt.* to hurt; to injure, damage.—*vr.* to hurt oneself; to get hurt.—**lastimero, lastimoso,** *a.* pitiful, sad, doleful.

lastrar, *vt.* to ballast.—**lastre,** *m.* ballast.

lata, *f.* tin plate or tinned iron plate; tin can; annoyance, nuisance.—*dar (la) l.,* (coll.) to pester.

latente, *a.* latent.

lateral, *a.* lateral, side.

latido, *m.* beat, beating, throb.

latifundio, *m.* large entailed estate.

latigazo, *m.* lash, whipping; crack of a whip.—**látigo,** *m.* whip.

latín, *m.* Latin (language).—**latino,** *a.* Latin.

latir, *vi.* to palpitate, throb, beat.

latitud, *f.* latitude; breadth.

latón, *m.* brass.—**latoso,** *a.* boring, annoying.

latrocinio, *m.* robbery, larceny.

laúd, *m.* (mus.) lute.

laudable, *a.* laudable, praiseworthy.—**laudatorio,** *a.* laudatory, full of praise.—**laudo,** *m.* (law) award; finding (of an arbitrator).

laureado, *a.* laureate.—**laurear,** *vt.* to honor, reward; to crown with laurel.—**laurel,** *m.* laurel; honor.—**lauro,** *m.* glory, honor; laurel.

lava, *f.* lava.

lavabo, *m.* lavatory; washstand; washroom.—**lavadero,** *m.* washing place; laundry.—**lavado,** *m.* wash, washing; laundry work.—**lavadora,** *f.* washing machine.—**lavamanos,** *m.* lavatory; washstand.

lavanda, *f.* lavender.

lavandera, *f.* laundress, washerwoman.—**lavandería,** *f.* laundry.—**lavandero,** *m.* launderer, laundryman.—**lavaplatos,** *mf.* dishwasher.—**lavar,** *vt.* to wash; to launder; (mason.) to whitewash.—**lavativa,** *f.* enema; syringe; nuisance.—**lavatorio,** *m.* washing; lavatory; washstand.

laxante, *m.* & *a.* laxative.

lazada, *f.* bowknot; (sew.) bow.—**lazar,** *vti.* [a] to lasso, capture with a lasso.

lazareto, *m.* leper hospital.

lazarillo, *m.* blind person's guide.

lazarino, *a.* leprous.—*n.* leper.

lazo, *m.* bow, loop; trap or snare (for persons); lasso, lariat; slipknot; tie, bond.

le, *pron.* him; you; to him; to her; to you.

leal, *a.* loyal; (pol.) stalwart.—**lealtad,** *f.* loyalty.

lebrel, *n.* greyhound.

lección, *f.* lesson; lecture; reading.—*dar una l.,* to say or recite a lesson; to give a lesson.—**lector,** *n.* reader; lecturer.—**lectura,** *f.* reading.

lechada, *f.* mixture of water and plaster; whitewash.

leche, *f.* milk.—**lechera,** *a.* milch (app. to animals).—*f.* milkmaid, dairymaid; milk jug.—**lechería,** *f.* dairy.—**lechero,** *a.* milky.—*m.* milkman.

lecho, *m.* bed; bed of a river.

lechón, *n.* pig; suckling pig.

lechoso, *a.* milky.—*f.* (Am.) papaya.

lechuga, *f.* (bot.) lettuce.—**lechuguino,** *m.* (coll.) dandy, dude.

lechuza, *f.* barn owl.

leer, *vti.* [e] to read.

legación, *f.* legation.—**legado,** *m.* (law) legacy; legate.

legajo, *m.* docket, file, bundle of papers.

legal, *a.* legal, lawful; faithful.—**legalidad,** *f.* legality, lawfulness.—**legalización,** *f.* legalization.—**legalizar,** *vti.* [a] to legalize.

legaña, *f.* = LAGAÑA.—**legañoso,** *a.* = LAGAÑOSO.

legar, *vti.* [b] to send as a legate; (law) to bequeath.—**legatario,** *n.* (law) legatee.

legendario, *a.* legendary.

legible, *a.* legible, readable.

legión, *f.* legion.—**legionario,** *n. & a.* legionary.

legislación, *f.* legislation.—**legislador,** *n. & a.* legislator; legislating, legislative.—**legislar,** *vt.* to legislate.—**legislativo,** *a.* legislative.—**legislatura,** *f.* legislature; term of a legislature.

legitimidad, *f.* legitimacy, legality.—**legítimo,** *a.* legitimate, lawful, rightful; genuine.

lego, *a.* lay, laic; ignorant.—*m.* layman.

legua, *f.* league (measure of length).—*a la l., de cien leguas,* or *desde media l.,* very far, at a great distance.

leguleyo, *m.* petty lawyer; shyster.

legumbre, *f.* vegetable, garden stuff.

leído, *a.* well-read, well-informed.—*l. y escribido,* (coll. & contempt.) affecting learning.

lejanía, *f.* distance, remoteness; remote place.—**lejano,** *a.* distant, far.

lejía, *f.* lye; (coll.) severe reprimand.

lejos, *adv.* far away, far off, afar.—*a lo l.,* in the distance.—*m.* perspective, background.

lelo, *a.* stupid, dull.

lema, *m.* theme; motto; slogan.

lencería, *f.* linen goods; linen-draper's shop; linen room.

lengua, *f.* (anat.) tongue; language.—*irsele, a uno la l.,* to give oneself away.—*morderse la l.,* to hold one's tongue.

lenguado, *m.* (ichth.) sole, flounder.

lenguaje, *m.* language; speech; style.—**lenguaraz,** *a.* loquacious.—**lengüeta,** *f.* tongue (of a shoe); (mus.) languette; (mec.) feather, wedge; (coll.) bill, tab.—**lengüetada,** *f.* act of licking.—**lengüilargo,** *a.* (coll.) garrulous; scurrilous.

lenidad, *f.* leniency, mildness.

lente, *m.* lens.—*pl.* glasses, spectacles.

lenteja, *f.* lentil.—**lentejuela,** *f.* spangle, sequin.

lentitud, *f.* slowness, tardiness.—**lento,** *a.* slow.

leña, *f.* firewood, kindling wood; (coll.) beating.—*echar l. al fuego,* to add fuel to the fire.—**leñador,** *n.* woodman(-woman), woodcutter.—**leñazo,** *m.* cudgeling.—**leño,** *m.* log; timber.

león, *m.* lion; brave man.—**leona,** *f.* lioness; undaunted woman.—**leonera,** *f.* cage or den of lions; (coll.) disorderly room.—**leonino,** *a.* leonine; (law) one-sided, unfair.

leontina, *f.* watch chain.

leopardo, *m.* leopard.

lépero, *n.* (Am.) one of the rabble.

lepra, *f.* leprosy.—**leproso,** *a.* leprous.—*n.* leper.

lerdo, *a.* slow, heavy; dull, obtuse.

les, *pers. pron.* them; to them; you; to you.

lesión, *f.* lesion, wound, injury; damage.—**lesionar,** *vt.* to injure, wound; to damage, impair.—**lesivo,** *a.* prejudicial, injurious.

lesna, *f.* = LEZNA.

letal, *a.* mortal, deadly, lethal.

letanía, *f.* (eccl.) litany.

letargo, *m.* lethargy, drowsiness.

letra, *f.* letter; handwriting; (print.) type; motto, inscription; literal meaning; lyrics.—*pl.* letters, learning.—*l. de cambio,* (com.) draft, bill of exchange.—*l. de molde,* print, printed letter.—**letrado,** *a.* learned,

erudite.—*n.* lawyer.—**letrero,** *m.* sign, notice; label; legend.

letrina, *f.* privy, latrine.

leucemia, *f.* leukemia.

leva, *f.* (naut.) act of weighing anchor; (mil.) levy, press; (mech.) cam.—**levadura,** *f.* leaven, yeast.—**levantamiento,** *m.* elevation, raising; insurrection, uprising.—**levantar,** *vt.* to raise; to lift, pick up; to erect, build; to rouse; to impute; to stand up.—*vr.* to rise, get up (from bed, chair, etc.); to rise up.—**levante,** *m.* Levant, east coast of Spain.—**levantino,** *a.* & *n.* Levantine.—**levantisco,** *a.* turbulent, restless.—**levar,** *vt.* (naut.) to weigh (anchor).—*vr.* to set sail.

leve, *a.* light, of little weight; trifling; slight.

levita, *f.* frock coat; Levite.

léxico, *m.* lexicon.—**lexicografía,** *f.* lexicography.

ley, *f.* law; rule of action; loyalty.—*de buena l.,* sterling.—*de mala l.,* vicious; crooked; low, base.—*l. del embudo,* oppressive law.—**leyenda,** *f.* reading; legend, inscription; motto.

lezna, *f.* awl.

liar, *vt.* to tie, bind, do up; (coll.) to embroil, draw into an entanglement.—*vr.* to bind oneself; to get tangled up.

libar, *vt.* to suck; to taste.

libelo, *m.* libel.

libélula, *f.* dragon fly.

liberación, *f.* liberation; (law) quittance.—**liberal,** *a.* & *mf.* liberal.—**liberalidad,** *f.* liberality, generosity.—**liberalismo,** *m.* Liberalism.—**libertad,** *f.* liberty, freedom; familiarity; unconventionality; ransom.—**libertador,** *n.* & *a.* liberator, rescuer; liberating.—**libertar,** *vt.* to free, liberate; to exempt; to acquit; to rid, clear.—**libertinaje,** *m.* licentiousness.—**libertino,** *n.* & *a.* libertine, (fam.) wolf; dissolute.

líbico, *a.* & *n.* Libyan.

libidinoso, *a.* lustful.

libio, *a.* & *n.* Libyan.

libra, *f.* pound (weight, coin).

librador, *n.* deliverer; (com.) drawer of a check or draft.—**libramiento,** *m.* delivery, delivering; warrant, order of payment.—**libranza,** *f.* (com.) draft, bill of exchange.—**librar,** *vt.* to free, deliver; to exempt; to pass (sentence); to issue (a decree); (com.) to draw.—*l. batalla* or *combate,* to engage in battle.—*vr.* (de) to escape, avoid, be free (from), get rid (of).—**libre,** *a.* free; unencumbered; independent; vacant; disengaged; clear, open; exempt; single, unmarried.

librea, *f.* livery, uniform.

librería, *f.* bookstore.—**librero,** *n.* bookseller.—*m.* bookcase.—**libreta,** *f.* notebook, copybook.—**libretista,** *mf.* librettist.—**libreto,** *m.* libretto.—**libro,** *m.* book.

licencia, *f.* permission, license; licentiousness, wantonness; (mil.) furlough; degree of licentiate.—**licenciado,** *n.* licentiate; (Am.) lawyer.—**licenciamiento,** *m.* graduation as a licentiate; (mil.) discharge.—**licenciar,** *vt.* to license; to confer a degree on; (mil.) to discharge.—*vr.* to get a master's degree.—**licenciatura,** *f.* degree of licentiate; graduation as a licentiate.—**licencioso,** *a.* licentious, dissolute.

licitar, *vt.* & *vi.* to bid (on, for) at auction or on public works.—**lícito,** *a.* licit, lawful; just.

licor, *m.* liquor; liqueur.

lid, *f.* contest, fight.

líder, *mf.* leader.

lidia, *f.* battle, fight; bullfight.—**lidiar,** *vi.* to fight; to struggle.—*vt.* to run or fight (bulls).

liebre, *f.* hare; coward.

liendre, *f.* nit, egg of a louse.

lienzo, *m.* linen cloth; (art) canvas.

liga, *f.* garter; birdlime; league, alliance; alloy; rubber band.—**ligadura,** *f.* ligature; subjection.—**ligamento,** *m.* bond, tie; ligament.—**ligar,** *vti.* [b] to tie, bind, fasten; to alloy; to join.—*vii.* to combine cards of the same suit.—*vri.* to league, join together; to bind oneself.

ligereza, *f.* lightness; swiftness; inconstancy, fickleness.—**ligero,** *a.* light; fast, nimble; (of cloth) thin; gay; unsteady, giddy; unimportant, trifling; easily disturbed (as sleep).—*a la ligera,* superficially.—*adv.* fast, rapidly.

lija, *f.* sandpaper.—**lijar,** *vt.* to sandpaper.

lila, *f.* lilac tree; lilac flower; lilac color.

liliputiense, *mf.* & *a.* midget; Lilliputian.

lima, *f.* sweet lime; (mech.) file; finish, polishing.—**limar,** *vt.* to file; to polish; to touch up.

limaza, *f.* slug.

limitación, *f.* limitation, limit.—**limitar,** *vt.* to limit; to bound; to restrict; to reduce (expense).—*vr.* to confine oneself to.—**límite,** *m.* limit; boundary.—**limítrofe,** *a.* bounding.

limo, *m.* slime, mud.

137 LIM—LOG

limosna, *f.* alms.—**limosnero,** *a.* charitable.—*n.* (Am.) beggar.
limón, *m.* lemon.—**limonada,** *f.* lemonade.—**limonero,** *m.* lemon tree.
limpia, *f.* cleaning; dredging.—**limpiabotas,** *mf.* bootblack.—**limpiador,** *n.* & *a.* cleaner, scourer; cleaning.—**limpiar,** *vt.* to clean, cleanse; (coll.) to steal; (coll.) to clean out.—**límpido,** *a.* limpid, crystal-clear.—**limpieza,** *f.* cleanness, cleanliness; neatness, tidiness; purity; honesty.—**limpio,** *a.* clean; clear; neat; (coll.) broke.—*poner en l.,* to make a clear copy.—*sacar en l.,* to conclude, infer; to make out, understand.
linaje, *m.* lineage, descent, ancestry.
linaza, *f.* linseed.
lince, *m.* lynx; very keen person.—*a.* keen-sighted, observing.
linchamiento, *m.* lynching.—**linchar,** *vt.* to lynch.
lindar, *vi.* to be contiguous, to border.—**linde,** *m.* landmark; boundary.—**lindero,** *a.* limit, boundary.
lindeza, *f.* neatness, elegance, prettiness.—*pl.* pretty things; (ironic) improprieties, insults.—**lindo,** *a.* pretty.—*de lo l.,* very much; wonderfully; greatly.—**lindura,** *f.* beauty; beautiful thing.
línea, *f.* line; (of persons) lines, figure; boundary, limit; progeny; (mil.) file.—**lineal,** *a.* lineal, linear.—**lineamiento,** *m.* lineament, feature.
lingote, *m.* (foundry) ingot; slug.
lingüista, *mf.* linguist.—**lingüística,** *f.* linguistics.—**lingüístico,** *a.* linguistic.
lino, *m.* flax; linen.
linóleo, *m.* linoleum.
linotipia, *f.* linotype.—**linotipista,** *mf.* linotypist.—**linotipo,** *m.* linotype.
linterna, *f.* lantern; flashlight.
lío, *m.* bundle; (coll.) mess, confusion, scrape.—*armar un l.,* to tangle, mess up, make difficulties.
liquidación, *f.* liquidation, settlement; bargain sale.—**liquidar,** *vt.* to liquefy; (com.) to liquidate, sell out; to settle, pay up; to squander; (coll.) to wipe out; to murder.—*vr.* to liquefy.—**líquido,** *a.* liquid; (econ.) liquid; (com.) net.—*m.* liquid; (com.) balance, net profit.
lira, *f.* (mus.) lyre; lira.—**lírico,** *a.* lyric(al).—*f.* lyric poetry.
lirio, *m.* lily.
lirón, *m.* dormouse; (coll.) sleepy head.
lirondo, *a.* pure, clean, neat.
lis, *f.* (heraldry) lily; iris.
lisiar, *vt.* to cripple.—*vr.* to become crippled.

liso, *a.* smooth, even, flat; plain, unadorned; straight (hair); plain-dealing.—*l. y llano,* clear, evident.
lisonja, *f.* flattery.—**lisonjear,** *vt.* to flatter.—**lisonjero,** *n.* flatterer.—*a.* flattering; complimentary.
lista, *f.* list; strip; stripe.—*l. de correos,* Post Office general delivery.—*pasar l.,* to call the roll.—**listado,** *a.* striped, streaky.
listo, *a.* ready; quick, prompt; clever, resourceful.—*estar l.,* to be ready.
listón, *m.* ribbon; tape; (carp.) strip.
lisura, *f.* smoothness, evenness; sincerity, candor.
litera, *f.* litter, stretcher; berth.
literal, *a.* literal.—**literario,** *a.* literary.—**literato,** *n.* writer.—**literatura,** *f.* literature.
litigar, *vti.* [b] & *vii.* to litigate.—**litigio,** *m.* litigation, lawsuit.
litografía, *f.* lithography.
litoral, *a.* coastal.—*m.* coast, shore.
litro, *m.* liter. (See Table.)
liviandad, *f.* lightness; levity, frivolity; lewdness.—**liviano,** *a.* light (not heavy); inconstant, fickle; frivolous; slight; lewd.
lividez, *f.* lividness.—**lívido,** *a.* livid.
lo, *art. neut.* the.—*pron.* him; you; it; so; that.—*lo de,* that of; that matter of, what.—*lo de siempre,* the same old story.—*lo que,* what, that which.—*sé lo hermosa que es,* I know how beautiful she is.
loable, *a.* laudable, praiseworthy.—**loar,** *vt.* to praise.
lobanillo, *m.* wen, tumor.
lobato, lobezno, *m.* wolf cub.—**lobo,** *n.* wolf.
lóbrego, *a.* murky, obscure; sad, somber.—**lobreguez,** *f.* obscurity, darkness.
local, *a.* local.—*m.* place, site, premises.—**localidad,** *f.* locality, location; (theat., etc.) seat.—**localización,** *f.* localization.—**localizar,** *vti.* [a] to localize; to find out where.
loción, *f.* lotion.
loco, *a.* insane, crazy; excessive.—*n.* insane person, lunatic.
locomoción, *f.* locomotion.—**locomotora,** *f.,* **locomotriz,** *a.* locomotive.
locuacidad, *f.* loquacity, talkativeness, volubility.—**locuaz,** *a.* loquacious, talkative.—**locución,** *f.* diction; phrase, locution.
locura, *f.* madness, insanity; folly.
locutor, *n.* radio announcer or speaker.
lodazal, *m.* bog, mire.—**lodo,** *m.* mud, mire.—**lodoso,** *a.* muddy, miry.
lógica, *f.* logic.—**lógico,** *a.* logical.
lograr, *vt.* to get, obtain; to attain.—*vr.* to succeed, be successful.—

logro, *m.* gain, profit, benefit; success, accomplishment; attainment; usury.

loma, *f.* little hill.

lombarda, *f.* red cabbage.

lombriz, *f.* earthworm.—*l. solitaria,* tapeworm.

lomo, *m.* loin; back of an animal; chine of pork; back of a book or cutting tool.

lona, *f.* canvas.

longaniza, *f.* pork sausage.

longevidad, *f.* longevity.

longitud, *f.* length; longitude.—**longitudinal,** *a.* longitudinal.

loncha, *f.* thin slice.

lonja, *f.* (com.) exchange; grocer's shop; warehouse; slice (of meat); strip; leather strap.

lontananza, *f.*—*en l.,* far away, in the distance.

loquero, *n.* attendant in an insane asylum; (Am.) insane asylum.

loro, *m.* parrot.

los, *art. m. pl.* the.—*pron. m. pl.* them.—*l. que,* those who, those which; which.

losa, *f.* slab, flagstone; gravestone; grave.—**loseta,** *f.* tile.

lote, *m.* lot; share, part.

lotería, *f.* lottery; raffle; lotto.

loza, *f.* chinaware; porcelain; crockery.

lozanía, *f.* luxuriance; freshness; vigor, lustiness.—**lozano,** *a.* luxuriant; fresh; brisk, spirited.

lubricación, *f.* lubrication.—**lubricante,** *m. & a.* lubricator; lubricating.—**lubricar,** *vti.* [d] to lubricate.

lucero, *m.* bright star; light hole; star on the forehead of horses; brightness, splendor.

lucidez, *f.* brilliancy; brightness; success.—**lucido,** *a.* magnificent, splendid, brilliant; most successful.—**lúcido,** clear, lucid; brilliant, shining.—**luciente,** *a.* shining, luminous, bright.—**luciérnaga,** *f.* glowworm, firefly.—**lucimiento,** *m* brilliance; success.—**lucir,** *vii.* [3] to shine, glitter, glow; to outshine, exceed; to look, appear.—*vti.* to light, illuminate; to show off, display, exhibit. —*vri.* to shine, be brilliant; to dress to advantage; to be very successful; to do splendidly.

lucrar, *vt. & vr.* to profit.—**lucrativo,** *a.* lucrative, profitable.—**lucro,** *m.* gain, profit.

luctuoso, *a.* sad mournful.

lucha, *f.* struggle, strife; wrestling, wrestle; dispute, argument.—**luchador,** *n.* wrestler; fighter.—**luchar,** *vi.* to fight, struggle; to wrestle.

luego, *adv.* presently, immediately; afterwards; next; later.—*desde l.,* of course, naturally.—*hasta l.,* so long, see you later.—*l. que,* after, as soon as.—*conj.* therefore.

lugar, *m.* place, spot, site; town, village; room, space; seat; employment; time, opportunity; cause, reason.—*dar l. a,* to cause, give occasion for.—*en l. de,* instead of.—*hacer l.,* to make room.—*tener l.,* to take place, happen.—**lugarteniente,** *mf.* second in command, deputy, substitute.

lúgubre, *a.* sad, gloomy, dismal.

lujo, *m.* luxury.—**lujoso,** *a.* showy, luxurious; lavish.

lujuria, *f.* lewdness, lechery, lust; excess.—**lujuriante,** *a.* lusting; luxuriant, exuberant.—**lujurioso,** *a.* lustful, lecherous, lewd.

lumbre, *f.* fire (in stove, fireplace, etc.); light (from a match, etc.); splendor.—**lumbrera,** *f.* luminary.

luna, *f.* moon; mirror plate; plate glass.—**lunar,** *a.* lunar.—*m.* mole; beauty spot.—**lunático,** *a. & n.* lunatic.

lunes, *m.* Monday.

luneta, *f.* lens; orchestra chair in a theater.

lupa, *f.* magnifying glass.

lupanar, *m.* brothel.

lúpulo, *m.* hops.

lustrar, *vt.* to polish.—**lustre,** *m.* polish, glaze, sheen; splendor, glory. —**lustroso,** *a.* lustrous, glossy, shining.

luterano, *n. & a.* Lutheran, Protestant.

luto, *m.* mourning; grief.—*pl.* mourning draperies.—*de l.,* in mourning.

luz, *f.* light.—*pl.* culture, enlightenment.—*a todas luces,* evidently.—*dar a l.,* to give birth to; to publish.—*entre dos luces,* by twilight.

LL

llaga, *f.* ulcer, sore.—**llagar,** *vti.* [b] & *vri.* to ulcerate.

llama, *f.* flame, blaze; (zool.) llama.

llamada, *f.* call; beckoning; (print.) reference mark to a note.—**llamamiento,** *m.* calling, call; appeal; convocation.—**llamar,** *vt.* to call, summon; to beckon; to invoke; to name.—*ll. la atención,* to attract attention; to call to task.—*ll. por teléfono,* to telephone.—*vi.* to ring; to knock (at the door).—*ll. a capítulo,* to call to account.—*vr.* to be called or named.—*¿cómo se llama Ud.?* what is your name?

llamarada, *f.* sudden blaze; flash; sudden flush.

llamativo, *a.* showy, gaudy, flashy; causing thirst.

llameante, *a.* blazing, flaming.—**llamear**, *vi.* to blaze; to flame.

llanero, *n.* plainsman (-woman).—**llaneza**, *f.* plainness, simplicity; familiarity.—**llano**, *a.* even, level, smooth; plain, unadorned; open, frank.—*de ll.*, openly; clearly.—*m.* plain.

llanta, *f.* rim (of vehicle wheel); (auto) tire.

llanto, *m.* crying, weeping; tears.

llanura, *f.* plain, prairie; flatness.

llave, *f.* key; faucet, spout; (print.) brace; clock winder; key, explanation of anything difficult; switch; (mus.) clef, key.—*bajo ll.*, under lock and key.—*echar ll.*, to lock.—*ll. inglesa*, monkey wrench.—*ll. maestra*, master key, passkey.—**llavero**, *m.* key ring.—**llavín**, *m.* latch key; key.

llegada, *f.* arrival, coming.—**llegar**, *vii.* [b] to arrive; to come; to reach, go as far as; to amount.—*ll. a las manos*, to come to blows.—*ll. a saber*, to find out, get to know.—*ll. a ser*, to become, get to be.—*no ll. a*, not to amount to; not to come up, or be equal, to.—*vri.* (a) to approach; to go up to.

llenar, *vt.* to fill, stuff, pack; to pervade; to satisfy, content.—*vr.* to fill, fill up; (de) to become full (of), or covered (with); (coll.) to lose patience; to get crowded, packed; (of the moon) to be full. —**lleno**, *a.* full, filled, replete; complete; teeming.—*de ll.*, fully, totally —*m.* fill, fullness; (theat.) full house.

llevadero, *a.* tolerable, bearable.—**llevar**, *vt.* to carry; to bear; to take; to bring; to take off, carry away; to lead (a life); to wear (clothing, etc.); to spend (time); to keep (books).—*ll. a cabo*, to accomplish, carry out.—*ll. a cuestas*, to carry on one's back; to support. —*ll. el compás*, to beat or keep time.—*ll. la contra*, to oppose, antagonize.—*ll. la delantera*, to be ahead.—*lleva un año aquí*, he has been here one year.—*me lleva cinco años*, he is five years older than I. —*vr.* to take or carry away; to get along.—*ll. bien* (or *mal*), to be on good (or bad) terms.—*ll. chasco*, to be disappointed.

llorar, *vi.* to cry, weep.—*vt.* to weep over, bewail, mourn.—**lloriquear**, *vi.* to whimper, whine, snivel, sniffle.—**lloriqueo**, *m.* whining; whimper.—**lloro**, *m.* weeping, crying.—**llorón**, *a.* given to weeping.—*n.* weeper, crybaby.—**lloroso**, *a.* mournful, sorrowful, tearful.

llover, *vii.* [26] to rain; to shower.—**llovizna**, *f.* drizzle, sprinkling.—**lloviznar**, *vi.* to drizzle, sprinkle.—**lluvia**, *f.* rain.—**lluvioso**, *a.* rainy.

M

macabro, *a.* macabre; ugly, hideous.

macaco, *m.* monkey.

macana, *f.* (Am.) club, cudgel; (Am.) blunder; fib, joke.

macarela, *f.* (Am.) mackerel.

macarrones, *m. pl.* macaroni.

maceración, *f.*, **maceramiento**, *m.* maceration, steeping.—**macerar**, *vt.* to macerate, steep.

macero, *m.* mace bearer; sergeant-at-arms.

maceta, *f.* flowerpot; mallet; stonecutter's hammer; (Am.) slow person.—**macetero**, *m.* flowerpot stand.

macilento, *a.* pale; emaciated; haggard.

macizo, *a.* solid; massive; firm.—*m.* massiveness; massif; flower bed.

machacar, *vti.* [d] to pound; to crush.—*vii.* to importune; to harp on a subject.—**machacón**, *a.* monotonous; tenacious.

machetazo, *m.* blow with a machete. —**machete**, *m.* machete.—**machetero**, *n.* (Am.) sugar cane cutter.

machihembrar, *vt.* (carp.) to dovetail.

macho, *a.* male; masculine, robust.—*m.* male; he-man; he-mule; hook (of hook and eye); bolt (of a lock); sledge hammer; ignorant fellow; (arch.) buttress; spigot.—*m. cabrío*, he-goat, buck.

machucar, *vti.* [d] to pound; to bruise; to crush.

machuno, *a.* mannish, masculine.

madeja, *f.* hank, skein; lock of hair.

madera, *f.* wood; timber, lumber.—**maderaje**, **maderamen**, *m.* timber; timber work; woodwork.—**madero**, *m.* beam; timber, piece of lumber; log; blockhead.

madrastra, *f.* stepmother.—**madre**, *f.* mother; origin, source; womb; bed (of a river); dregs.—*m. política*, mother-in-law.—*salirse de m.*, to overflow.—**madreperla**, *f.* mother-of-pearl.—**madreselva**, *f.* (bot.) honeysuckle.

madriguera, *f.* burrow; den, lair, nest.

madrileño, *a. & n.* Madrilenian, native of Madrid

madrina, *f.* godmother; bridesmaid; protectress, patroness.

madrugada, *f.* dawn; early morning; early rising.—*de m.,* at daybreak. —**madrugador,** *a.* early rising.—*n.* early riser.—**madrugar,** *vii.* [b] to rise early; to anticipate, to be beforehand.—**madrugón,** *m.* (coll.) very early rising.

madurar, *vt. & vi.* to ripen; to mature.—**madurez,** *f.* maturity; ripeness; wisdom.—**maduro,** *a.* ripe; mature; wise, judicious; middle-aged.

maestra, *f.* teacher, schoolmistress; (mason.) guide line.—**maestría,** *f.* mastery; great skill.—**maestro,** *a.* masterly; master.—*obra m.,* masterpiece.—*m.* master, teacher; expert; skilled artisan.—*m. de obras,* builder.

magia, *f.* magic, wizardry.—**mágico,** *a.* magic(al).

magín, *m.* (coll.) imagination.

magisterio, *m.* mastery; mastership; teaching profession.—**magistrado,** *m.* judge, magistrate.—**magistral,** *a.* magisterial, masterly, masterful.—**magistratura,** *f.* judges (as a body).

magnánimo, *a.* magnanimous, generous.

magnate, *m.* magnate; (coll.) tycoon.

magnético, *a.* magnetic.—**magnetismo,** *m.* magnetism.—**magnetizar,** *vti.* [a] to magnetize; to hypnotize.

magnificencia, *f.* magnificence, grandeur, splendor.—**magnífico,** *a* magnificent; excellent.

magnitud, *f.* magnitude; quantity.— **magno,** *a.* great.

mago, *n.* magician, wizard.—*pl.* magi. —*los Reyes Magos,* The Three Wise Men.

magra, *f.* slice of ham.—**magro,** *a.* meager, lean.

magulladura, *f.* bruise.—**magullar,** *vt.* to bruise; to mangle.

mahometano, *n. & a.* Mohammedan, Mahometan.

maíz, *m.* corn, maize.—**maizal,** *m.* cornfield.

majada, *f.* sheepfold; dung.

majadería, *f.* foolish act, foolishness —**majadero,** *a.* silly, foolish.—*n.* bore, fool; pestle.—**majar,** *vt.* to pound, bruise, mash; (coll.) to importune, vex, annoy.

majestad, *f.* majesty; stateliness.— **majestuosidad,** *f.* majesty, dignity. —**majestuoso,** *a.* majestic, grand.

majo, *a.* gay, gaudy, handsome, pretty.—*n.* low class dandy or belle.

mal, *a. contr.* of MALO.—*m.* evil; harm; disease, illness.—*adv.* badly; wrongly; deficiently.

malabarista, *mf.* juggler

malagradecido, *a.* ungrateful.

malandanza, *f.* misfortune, misery.

malanga, *f.* (Am.) (bot.) arum.

malaria, *f.* malaria.

malayo, *n. & a.* Malayan.

malbaratador, *n.* spendthrift, squanderer.—**malbaratar,** *vt.* to squander; to undersell.

malcriado, *a.* ill-bred, rude; spoiled. —**malcriar,** *vt.* to spoil (a child).

maldad, *f.* wickedness, iniquity; badness.

maldecir, *vti.* [14-49] to damn, curse, accurse.—**maldición,** *f.* curse, malediction; damnation.—**maldito,** *ppi.* of MALDECIR.—*a.* damned, accursed; perverse, wicked.—*¡m. lo que me importa!* little do I care!

maleable, *a.* malleable.

maleante, *mf. & a.* rogue; roguish.— **malear,** *vt.* to pervert, corrupt.

malecón, *m.* dike, mole; quay, jetty.

maledicencia, *f.* slander, calumny.

maleficio, *m.* spell; witchcraft, charm. —**maléfico,** *a.* evil-doing; harmful.

malentendido, *m.* misunderstanding.

malestar, *m.* indisposition, slight illness; discomfort.

maleta, *f.* valise, suitcase; (fam.) bungler; (Am.) hump.—*hacer la m.,* to pack.—**maletero,** *m.* porter, (coll.) red cap.—**maletín,** *m.* small valise or case, overnight bag, satchel.

malévolo, *a.* malevolent, malignant, wicked.

maleza, *f.* weeds; underbrush, shrubbery; thicket.

malgastar, *vt.* to waste, squander.

malhablado, *a.* foul-mouthed.

malhadado, *a.* wretched, unfortunate.

malhechor, *n.* evildoer, criminal.

malherir, *vti.* [39] to wound badly.

malhumorado, *a.* ill-humored, peevish.

malicia, *f.* malice, malignity; suspicion; shrewdness.—**maliciar,** *vt.* to suspect —**malicioso,** *a.* malicious; wicked, knavish; suspicious.

malignidad, *f.* malignity; viciousness. —**maligno,** *a.* malignant; vicious; harmful; baleful.

malintencionado, *a* ill-intentioned.

malo, *a.* bad, evil, wicked; ill, sick; difficult, hard.—*estar de malas,* to be unlucky; to be ill-disposed.—*por buenas o por malas,* willy-nilly.

malograr, *vt.* to waste, lose.—*vr.* **to** fail, miscarry.

malparir, *vi.* to miscarry.

malquerencia, *f.* ill-will, hatred.

malquistar, *vt* to estrange; to create prejudice against.—*m. a uno con,* to set one against.—*vi.* to incur dislike, make oneself unpopular.

malsano, *a.* unhealthy, sickly; noxious.

malta, *f.* malt.

maltratar, *vt.* to ill-treat, abuse; to use roughly, maul.—**maltrato**, *m.* ill-treatment; rough usage.—**maltrecho**, *a.* ill-treated; in bad condition, damaged; badly off, battered.

malvado, *a.* wicked, fiendish.—*n.* wicked man (woman).

malversación, *f.* misuse of funds, embezzlement.—**malversador**, *n.* one who misapplies funds, embezzler.— **malversar**, *vt.* to misapply (funds); to embezzle.

malla, *f.* mesh (of a net); (naut.) network.—*pl.* tights.

mamá, *f.* mamma (mother).—**mama**, *f.* breast.

mamada, *f.* (coll.) act of sucking, suckling.—**mamadera**, *f.* (Am.) nursing bottle.—**mamar**, *vt. & vi.* to suck, suckle.—*vr.* (Am.) to get drunk.

mamarracho, *m.* daub; grotesque figure or ornament.

mameluco, *m.* (Am.) child's nightdress; (Am.) overalls; (coll.) dolt.

mamífero, *n.* mammal.—*a.* mammalian.

mamón, *a. & n.* suckling.

mamotreto, *m.* bulky book or bundle of papers.

mampara, *f.* screen.

mampostería, *f.* masonry, rubble work.

mamut, *m.* mammoth.

manada, *f.* herd; flock; drove.

manantial, *m.* spring, source; origin. —**manar**, *vi.* to issue, flow out; to ooze; to abound.

manatí, *m.* manatee.

manceba, *f.* mistress.

mancilla, *f.* stain, blemish, smirch.— **mancillar**, *vt.* to stain, smirch, sully.

manco, *n.* armless; handless; one-handed or one-armed person.—*a.* handless; armless; one-handed; one-armed; maimed; faulty.

mancha, *f.* stain, spot, blot; patch of ground or vegetation.—**manchado**, *a.* spotted, speckled.—**manchar**, *vt.* to stain, soil; to tarnish.

mandadero, *n.* messenger, porter; errand boy or girl.—**mandado**, *m.* mandate, order; errand.—**mandamiento**, *m.* order, command; commandment; (law) writ.—**mandar**, *vt. & vi.* to command, order; to send.

mandarina, *f.* tangerine.

mandarria, *f.* iron maul, sledge hammer.

mandatario, *n.* proxy; representative; (law) attorney.—**mandato**, *m.* mandate; command, injunction, order, behest.

mandíbula, *f.* jaw; jawbone.

mando, *m.* command, power; control. —**mandón**, *a.* imperious, domineering.—*n.* imperious, haughty person; (Am.) (min.) boss or foreman.

mandril, *m.* baboon; (mech.) collet.

manducar, *vti.* [d] (coll.) to chew; to eat.

manear, *vt.* to hobble (a horse).

manecilla, *f.* small hand; (print.) fist (𝕴𝕾); hand of a clock or watch.

manejable, *a.* manageable, tractable. —**manejar**, *vt.* to manage, handle; (Am.) to drive (a vehicle, a horse, etc.); to run (an engine, a business). —*vr.* to behave; to get along, manage.—**manejo**, *m.* handling; management, conduct.

manera, *f.* manner, way, mode; fly of trousers; side placket of skirt.— *pl.* ways, customs; manners.—*de mala m.*, blunderingly; roughly; reluctantly.—*de m. que*, so that, so as to.—*de ninguna m.*, in no way; by no means, not at all.—*de otra m.*, otherwise.—*de tal m.*, in such a way; so much.—*de todas maneras*, at any rate.—*sobre m.*, exceedingly.

manga, *f.* sleeve; (water) hose; straining bag; fish trap.—*m. de viento*, whirlwind.—*tener m. ancha*, to be broadminded.

mangana, *f.* lasso, lariat.

manganeso, *m.* manganese.

manglar, *m.* grove of mangrove trees. —**mangle**, *m.* mangrove.

mango, *m.* handle, haft; tiller; (bot.) mango.

mangonear, *vi.* (coll.) to meddle for power, to interfere in order to dominate.—**mangoneo**, *m.* (coll.) domination.

manguera, *f.* (watering) hose; waterspout.

manguito, *m.* muff; wristlet, half-sleeve; oversleeve; (mech.) muff.

maní, *m.* (Am.) peanut.

manía, *f.* mania; whim, fancy.

maniatar, *vt.* to handcuff; to manacle.

maniático, *a. & n.* crank; queer, mad (person).—**manicomio**, *m.* insane asylum, madhouse.

manicura, *f.* manicurist; manicure.

manido, *a.* commonplace, trite.

manifestación, *m.* manifestation, statement; (public) demonstration. —**manifestante**, *mf.* (public) demonstrator.—**manifestar**, *vti.* [1-49] to state, declare; to manifest, reveal; to tell, let know —*vri.* to make

a demonstration.—**manifiesto,** *ppi.* of MANIFESTAR.—*a.* manifest, plain. —*m.* manifesto, public declaration; (com.) custom-house manifest.— *poner de m.,* to make evident; to show plainly; to make public.

manigua, *f.* (Am.) thicket, jungle.

manija, *f.* handle, haft; crank; (mech.) brace, clamp.

manilla, *f.* small hand; bracelet; manacle, handcuff.

maniobra, *f.* maneuver; operation, procedure.—**maniobrar,** *vt. & vi.* to maneuver.

manipulación, *f.* manipulation.—**manipular,** *vt.* to manipulate, handle.

maniquí, *m.* manikin; tailor's dummy; puppet.—*f.* model.

manirroto, *n.* squanderer.—*a.* lavish, prodigal, wasteful.

manivela, *f.* (mech.) crank; crank-shaft.

manjar, *m.* food, dish; delicacy, morsel.

mano, *f.* hand; forefoot; hand of a clock or watch; first hand at cards; round of any game; power or means of making or attaining something; coat (of paint, varnish, etc.).—*a la m.,* near, at hand.— *a m.,* by hand; at hand, near by. —*a manos llenas,* liberally, abundantly.—*de la m.,* by the hand; hand in hand.—*de manos a boca,* suddenly, unexpectedly.—*entre manos,* in hand.—*a m.,* in friendly cooperation, together; on equal terms.—*¡manos a la obra!* lend a hand! to work!—*m. sobre m.,* idle, doing nothing.—**manojo,** *m.* bunch; handful; bundle.—**manopla,** *f.* gauntlet.—**manosear,** *vt.* to fumble; to touch, feel of.—**manoseo,** *m.* handling, fingering.—**manotazo,** *m.* slap, blow with the hand.— **manotear,** *vi.* to gesticulate.—**manoteo,** *m.* gesturing with the hands.

mansalva, *adv.*—*a m.,* without risk or danger; in a cowardly manner.

mansedumbre, *f.* meekness; tameness.

mansión, *f.* stay, sojourn; mansion, abode; residence.

manso, *a.* tame; gentle, mild; calm; soft, quiet; meek.—*m.* bellwether.

manta, *f.* blanket; (Am.) poncho.— *m. de algodón,* wadding.

manteca, *f.* lard; fat.—**mantecado,** *m.* butter cake; (Am.) ice cream.— **mantecoso,** *a.* greasy, buttery.

mantel, *m.* tablecloth; altar cloth.— **mantelería,** *f.* table linen.—**manteleta,** *f.* lady's shawl.

mantener, *vti.* [42] to support; to maintain; to defend or sustain (an opinion); to keep up (conversation,

correspondence).—*vri.* to support oneself; to remain, continue (in one place).—**mantenimiento,** *m.* maintenance, support; living.

mantequilla, *f.* butter.—**mantequillera,** *f.* butter dish.

mantilla, *f.* mantilla; saddlecloth.— **manto,** *m.* cloak, mantle; robe; (min.) layer, stratum.—**mantón,** *m.* large shawl; (Am.) mantilla.—*m. de Manila,* embroidered silk shawl, Spanish shawl.

manuable, *a.* easy to handle, handy. —**manual,** *a.* manual; handy.—*m.* manual, handbook.

manubrio, *m.* handle; crank.

manufactura, *f.* manufacture.—**manufacturar,** *vt. & vi.* to manufacture. —**manufacturero,** *a.* manufacturing. —*n.* manufacturer.

manuscrito, *m. & a.* manuscript.

manutención, *f.* maintaining; maintenance, support.

manzana, *f.* apple; block (of houses), square.—**manzanilla,** *f.* (bot.) common camomile; dry white sherry wine.—**manzano,** *m.* apple tree.

maña, *f.* skill, cleverness, knack; cunning; evil habit or custom.— *darse m.,* to contrive, manage.

mañana, *f.* morning.—*m.* [the] future. —*de m.,* in the morning; very early. —*por la m.,* in the morning.—*adv.* tomorrow; in the future.—*hasta m.,* until tomorrow, see you tomorrow. —*m. mismo,* tomorrow without fail. —*m. por la m.,* tomorrow morning. —*pasado m.,* day after tomorrow.— **mañanero,** *a.* early rising.

mañoso, *a.* skillful, handy, clever; cunning, shifty, careful; (Am.) lazy.

mapa, *m.* map. chart.

mapache, *m.* raccoon.

mapamundi, *m.* map of the world.

maquillaje, *m.* (neol.) make-up (face).—**maquillar,** *vt. & vr.* (neol.) to make-up, paint.

máquina, *f.* machine, engine.—*a toda m.,* at full speed.—*m. de escribir,* typewriter.—**maquinación,** *f.* machination, plotting; plot.—**maquinal,** *a.* mechanical; unconscious, automatic. —**maquinar,** *vt. & vi.* to machinate, scheme, plot.—**maquinaria,** *f.* machinery.—**maquinista,** *mf.* engineer; machinist.

mar, *m. & f.* sea.—*alta m.,* high seas. —*hacerse a la m.,* to put out to sea.—*la m.,* (coll.) a great deal, a lot, lots.—*m. de fondo,* (sea) swell.

maraña, *f.* tangle, snare; puzzle; intrigue, plot; undergrowth.

maravilla, *f.* wonder, marvel; (bot.) marigold.—*a las mil maravillas,* wonderfully well.—**maravillar,** *vt*

to surprise, astonish.—vr. (de) to wonder (at), marvel.—**maravilloso**, a. wonderful, marvelous.

marbete, m. label, tag; index card; baggage check.

marca, f. mark, stamp; sign; make, brand.—*de m.*, excellent, reputed.—*m. de fábrica*, trademark.—**marcador**, m. marker; (sports) score board; scorer.—**marcar**, vti. [d] to mark, stamp, impress, brand; (sports) to score; to dial (telephone); to note.—*m. el compás*, to beat time, keep time.

marcial, a. martial, warlike, soldierly.

marco, m. frame; mark (German coin).

marcha, f. march; progress; turn, course, run; departure; (naut.) speed; movement of a watch.—*apresurar la m.*, to hurry, speed up.—*¡en marcha!* forward march! go on! let's go!—*poner en m.*, to start, put in motion.—*sobre la m.*, at once, right away.

marchamo, m. custom-house mark on goods.

marchante, mf. dealer; (Am.) customer, buyer.

marchar, vi. to march, parade; to progress, go ahead; to work, run, go (as a machine, engine, clock, etc.).—vr. to go; to go away, leave.

marchitar, vt. to wither, fade.—vr. to wither, fade, decay.—**marchito**, a. faded, withered.

marea, f. tide.—*contra viento y m.*, against all odds; come what may.—**mareado**, a. seasick; dizzy.—**marear**, vt. to navigate; (coll.) to vex, annoy, bother.—vr. to get dizzy, seasick, carsick.—**marejada**, f. swell, surf; tidal wave; commotion, disturbance.—**maremágnum**, m. (coll.) confusion, bedlam.—**mareo**, m. dizziness, seasickness, carsickness; nausea; (coll.) vexation.

marfil, m. ivory.

margarina, f. margarine.

margarita, f. common daisy.

margen, mf. margin; border, edge; bank (of a river).—*dar m.*, to give an opportunity or an occasion.—**marginal**, a. marginal.—**marginar**, vt. to leave a margin on; to make marginal notes.

marica, m. effeminate man, sissy, (coll.) pansy.

marido, m. husband.

marimacho, m. (coll.) shrew, mannish woman.

marina, f. shore, sea coast; seascape; seamanship; navy, fleet, marine.—**marinería**, f. seamanship; body of seamen; ship's crew.—**marinero**, a.

seaworthy.—m. sailor, seaman.—**marino**, a. marine, sea.—m. seaman, mariner.

mariposa, f. butterfly; moth.—**mariposear**, vi. to flutter about.

mariscal, m. (mil.) marshal.

marisco, m. shellfish.

marisma, f. marsh, swamp.

marital, a. marital.

marítimo, a. maritime, marine, sea.

marmita, f. kettle, pot, boiler.

mármol, m. marble (stone).—**marmóreo**, a. marbled, marble.

marmota, f. (zool.) marmot; (coll.) sleepy head.

maroma, f. rope, cable; (Am.) acrobat's performance.—**maromero**, n. (Am.) tight-rope dancer, acrobat.

marqués, m. marquis.—**marquesa**, f. marchioness, marquise.—**marquesina**, f. marquee, awning.

marquetería, f. marquetry.

marrana, f. sow, female pig; (coll.) dirty woman.—**marranada**, f. (coll.) hoggish action; nastiness.—**marrano**, m. hog; (coll.) dirty man.

marrón, a. maroon; brown.

marroquí, mf. & a. Moroccan.

marrullería, f. wheedling, cajolery.—**marrullero**, n. wheedler, coaxer, cajoler.

marsopa, f. porpoise.

marta, f. sable.

martes, m. Tuesday.

martillar, vt. to hammer.—**martillazo**, m. blow with a hammer.—**martilleo**, m. hammering; clatter.—**martillo**, m. hammer.

martinete, m. drop hammer; pile driver; hammer of a piano.

mártir, mf. martyr.—**martirio**, m. martyrdom; torture, grief.—**martirizar**, vti. [a] to martyr; to torture; to torment.

marzo, m. March.

mas, conj. but, yet.—**más**, a. & adv. more; most; (math.) plus.—*a lo m.*, at the most.—*a m.*, besides.—*a m. tardar*, at the latest.—*m. bien*, rather.—*no m. que*, only.—*por m. que*, however much.—*sin m. ni m.*, without more ado.

masa, f. dough, mash; (mason.) mortar; (phys.) mass; volume; crowd of people.

masacre, m. (neol.) massacre.

masaje, m. massage.—**masajista**, mf. massagist; masseur, masseuse.

mascada, f. chewing; (Am.) chew of tobacco; (Mex.) silk handkerchief.—**mascar**, vti. [d] to chew; (coll.) to mumble.

máscara, f. mask.—pl. masquerade.—mf. mask, masquerader.—**masca-**

rada, *f.* masquerade.—**mascarilla,** *f.* death mask; half mask.

mascota, *f.* mascot; (baseball) catcher's mitt.

masculino, *a.* masculine; male.

mascullar, *vt.* to mumble; to munch.

masilla, *f.* putty.

masón, *m.* freemason.—**masonería,** *f.* freemasonry, masonry.

masticación, *f.* chewing.—**masticar,** *vti.* [d] to chew.

mástil, *m.* mast, post; tent-pole.

mastín, *n.* mastiff.

mastuerzo, *m.* dolt, simpleton; (bot.) common cress.

mata, *f.* (bot.) plant; sprig, blade; grove, orchard.—*m. de pelo,* head of hair.

matadero, *m.* slaughterhouse; drudgery.—**matador,** *n.* & *a.* killer; killing.—*m.* matador.—**matadura,** *f.* sore, gall.—**matanza,** *f.* slaughter, butchery.—**matar,** *vt.* to kill.—*a mata caballo,* in a great hurry.—*m. de hambre,* to starve.—*vr.* to kill oneself; to get killed; to commit suicide.—**matarife,** *m.* slaughterer.—**matasanos,** *m.* (coll.) quack, charlatan, quack doctor.—**matasellos,** *m.* postmark.

mate, *a.* dull, lusterless, mat.—*m.* (chess) checkmate; (bot.) Brazilian holly; maté, Paraguay tea.—*dar m.,* to checkmate.

matemática(s), *f.* (*pl.*) mathematics.—**matemático,** *a.* mathematical.—*n.* mathematician.

materia, *f.* matter; material, stuff; subject, topic; (med.) matter, pus.—*entrar en m.,* to come to the point.—*m. prima,* raw material.—**material,** *a.* material.—*m.* material, stuff; ingredient; (elec. and RR.) equipment.—**materialismo,** *m.* materialism.—**materialista,** *mf.* & *a.* materialist(ic).—**materializar,** *vti.* [a] to materialize.—*vri.* to become (morally) materialistic.

maternal, *a.* maternal.—**maternidad,** *f.* maternity.—**materno,** *a.* maternal, motherly; mother.

matinal, *a.* of the morning; morning.—**matiné,** *m.* matinée.

matiz, *m.* tint, hue, shade.—**matizado,** *a.* many-hued.—**matizar,** *vti.* [a] to blend (colors); to tint, shade.

matojo, *m.* bush; (bot.) glasswort.

matón, *m.* (coll.) bully.

matorral, *m.* thicket; bush.

matraca, *f.* wooden rattle.—*dar m.,* to banter.

matrero, *a.* cunning, shrewd; (Am.) suspicious.—*n.* trickster, swindler; (Am.) cattle thief.

matrícula, *f.* register, list; matricula-tion; license; car license plate.—**matricular,** *vt.* & *vr.* to matriculate, register, enroll.

matrimonial, *a.* matrimonial.—**matrimonio,** *m.* marriage, wedlock, matrimony; married couple.

matriz, *a.* first, principal, main.—*f.* womb; mold, form, matrix; screw nut.

matrona, *f.* matron.

matutino, *a.* morning.—*m.* (Am.) morning newspaper.

maula, *f.* rubbish, trash, junk; cunning, craft; deceitful trick.—*mf.* (coll.) malingerer, sluggard; cheat, tricky person.

maullar, *vi.* to mew.—**maullido,** *m.* mew(ing).

máxima, *f.* maxim, proverb; rule.—**máxime,** *adv.* especially, principally.—**máximo,** *m.* & *a.* maximum.

maya, *mf.* Maya (people and language).—*a.* Mayan.—*f.* daisy.

mayar, *vi.* to mew.

mayo, *m.* May.

mayonesa, *f.* mayonnaise.

mayor, *a.* greater; greatest; larger; largest; older, elder; oldest, eldest; senior; main, principal; major.—*altar m.,* high altar.—*m.* superior; (mil.) major.—*pl.* ancestors, forefathers; superiors; elders.—*al por m.,* (by) wholesale.—*m. de edad,* of age.

mayoral, *m.* foreman, overseer; head shepherd; coach driver.

mayordomo, *m.* butler, steward; major-domo.

mayoría, *f.* majority (in age or number); superiority.

mayorista, *mf.* wholesale merchant or dealer.

mayúscula, *a.* & *f.* capital (letter).—**mayúsculo,** *a.* large, good-sized; important, prominent.

maza, *f.* mace; drop hammer; war club; roller of a sugar-cane mill.

mazacote, *m.* concrete; dry, tough mass.

mazmorra, *f.* dungeon.

mazo, *m.* mallet, maul, wooden hammer; bundle, bunch.

mazorca, *f.* ear of corn.

me, *pron.* me; to me; for me; myself.

mecanografía, *f.* typewriting.—**mecanógrafo,** *n.* typist, stenographer.

mecate, *m.* (Mex.) maguey rope or cord.

mecedora, *f.* rocking chair.—**mecer,** *vti.* [a] to rock; to swing; to move (a child) gently; to shake.—*vri.* to rock, swing, sway.

mecha, *f.* wick; fuse (of explosive); slice of bacon (for larding); (Am.)

lock of hair.—**mechar**, *vt.* to lard (meat, etc.).—**mechero**, *m.* lamp burner; gas burner; cigarette lighter.—**mechón**, *m.* large lock of hair.

medalla, *f.* medal.—**medallón**, *m.* locket; medallion.

médano, *m.* sand bank; dune.

media, *f.* stocking; hose; (Am.) sock; (math.) mean.—**mediación**, *f.* mediation; intercession.—**mediado**, *a.* half-filled, half-full.—*a mediados de*, (of period of time) about the middle of.—**mediador**, *n.* mediator; intercessor.—**medianamente**, *adv.* middling, so-so, fairly.—**medianería**, *f.* partition wall.—**medianero**, *a.* mediating, interceding; intermediate. —*n.* mediator; adjacent owner.— **medianía**, *f.* halfway; average; mediocrity; moderate means.—**mediano**, *a.* moderate, middling, medium; middle sized; mediocre, tolerable.—**medianoche**, *f.* midnight. —**mediante**, *a.* interceding, intervening.—*adv.* by means of, through.— **mediar**, *vi.* to be at the middle; to intercede, mediate; to intervene.

medicación, *f.* medication.—**medicamento**, *m.* medicine, medicament.— **medicastro**, *m.* quack doctor.— **medicina**, *f.* medicine; remedy.— **medicinal**, *a.* medicinal.—**medicinar**, *vt.* to prescribe or give medicines (to a patient).

medición, *f.* measurement, measuring.

médico, *a.* medical.—*n.* physician.— *m. forense*, coroner.

medida, *measure*; (shoe, etc.) size, number; gauge; measuring, measurement; rule; moderation, prudence.—*a la m.*, to order, custommade.—*a m. del deseo*, according to one's wishes.—*a m. que*, as, according as, while.—*sin m.*, to excess.— *tomar medidas*, to take measures or steps.—**medidor**, *n.* measurer.

medieval, *a.* medieval.

medio, *a.* half; medium; middle; mean, intermediate.—*media naranja*, (fam.) better half, wife.—*media vuelta*, right about face.—*m.* middle, center; (often *pl.*) means, resources; expedient, measure; environment.— *por m. de*, by means of.—*adv.* half; partially.—*de m. a m.*, completely, entirely.—*de por m.*, between.

mediocre, *a.* mediocre.—**mediocridad**, *f.* mediocrity.

mediodía, *m.* noon, midday; south.

medioeval, *a.* = MEDIEVAL.

medir, *vti.* [29] to measure; to scan (verses).—*vri.* to be moderate; to act with prudence.

meditabundo, *a.* pensive, musing.—

meditación, *f.* meditation.—**meditar**, *vt.* & *vi.* to meditate, muse.— **meditativo**, *a.* meditative.

mediterráneo, *a.* Mediterranean.

medrar, *vi.* to thrive, prosper.

medroso, *a.* timorous, faint-hearted, cowardly; dreadful, scary.

médula, *f.* marrow; pith; substance, essence.—*m. espinal*, spinal cord.

medusa, *f.* jellyfish.

megáfono, *m.* megaphone.

mejicano, *n.* & *a.* Mexican.

mejilla, *f.* cheek.

mejillón, *m.* mussel.

mejor, *a.* better, best.—*el m. día*, some fine day.—*lo mejor*, the best thing.—*m. postor*, highest bidder. —*adv.* better; rather.—*a lo m.*, perhaps, maybe.—*m. que*, rather than, instead of.—**mejora**, *f.* improvement, betterment; higher bid.— **mejoramiento**, *m.* improvement.

mejorana, *f.* marjoram.

mejorar, *vt.* to improve, better, enhance; to outbid.—*vi.* & *vr.* to recover from a disease; to improve; to reform.—**mejoría**, *f.* improvement; betterment; advantage; improvement in health.

mejunje, *m.* concoction.

melado, *m.* cane-juice syrup.

melancolía, *f.* melancholia, gloom, blues.—**melancólico**, *a.* melancholy, gloomy.

melaza, *f.* molasses.—**melcocha**, *f.* (Am.) molasses candy, taffy.

melena, *f.* long hair; mane.—**melenudo**, *a.* bushy-haired.

melifluo, *a.* honeyed (of speech and voice).

melindre, *m.* a sort of fritter; fastidiousness; prudery.—**melindroso**, *a.* prudish, finicky.

melocotón, *m.* peach.—**melocotonero**, *m.* peach tree.

melodía, *f.* melody, tune.—**melodioso**, *a.* melodious.

melón, *m.* melon; muskmelon; cantaloupe.—*m. de agua*, (Am.) watermelon.—**melosidad**, *f.* sweetness; mildness.—**meloso**, *a.* honeyed, sweet, syrupy; soft-voiced; gentle.

mella, *f.* notch, nick, dent; jag in edged tools; gap.—*hacer m.*, to make an impression on the mind; to strike home.—**mellado**, *a.* gaptoothed.—**mellar**, *vt.* to jag, notch; to injure (as honor, credit).

mellizo, *n.* & *a.* twin (brother, sister).

membrana, *f.* membrane.

membrete, *m.* letterhead; heading.

membrillo, *m.* quince; quince tree.

membrudo, *a.* strong, robust, muscular.

memo, *a.* silly, foolish.

memorable, *a.* memorable.—**memorándum,** *m.* memorandum.—**memoria,** *f.* memory; remembrance, recollection; memoir; report, statement.—*pl.* memoirs; regards, compliments.—*de m.,* by heart.—*hacer m.,* to remember.—**memorial,** *m.* memorial; petition, application; (law) brief.

mención, *f.* mention.—**mencionar,** *vt.* to mention.

mendicidad, *f.* beggary.—**mendigar,** *vti.* [b] & *vii.* to beg; to entreat.—**mendigo,** *n.* beggar.

mendrugo, *m.* crumb of bread.

menear, *vt.* to stir; to shake; to wag, waggle.—*vr.* (coll.) to hustle, be active, get a move on; to waggle.—**meneo,** *m.* shake, shaking; wagging, wriggling; (coll.) drubbing, beating.

menester, *m.* need, want; employment, occupation, office.—*pl.* natural or bodily necessities.—*ser. m.,* to be necessary.—**menesteroso,** *a.* & *n.* needy, indigent (person).

mengano, *n.* (Mr. or Mrs.) so-and-so.

mengua, *f.* diminution, waning, decrease.—**menguar,** *vii.* [b] to diminish, decrease, wane.

menor, *a.* smaller, lesser, younger; smallest, least, youngest; minor.—*mf.* minor.—*m. de edad,* minor, underage.—*por m.,* by retail.—*m.* (mus.) minor.—**menoría,** *f.* inferiority, subordination; underage (person).

menos, *a.* less; least.—*adv.* less; least; except, save.—*al m.* or *a lo m.,* at least.—*a m. que,* unless.—*de m.,* less; wanting, missing.—*echar de m.,* to miss.—*m. mal,* it could be worse, not so bad.—*poco más o m.,* more or less, about.—*por lo m.,* at least.—*venir a m.,* to decline; to become poor.—*prep.* minus, less.—*las ocho m. veinte,* twenty minutes to eight.—**menoscabar,** *vt.* to lessen, diminish; to impair, damage; to discredit.—**menoscabo,** *m.* impairment, damage, detriment.—**menospreciar,** *vt.* to underrate, undervalue; to despise, scorn.—**menosprecio,** *m.* undervaluation; contempt; scorn.

mensaje, *m.* message; errand.—**mensajero,** *n.* messenger; errand boy or girl.

menstruación, *f.* menstruation, period.—**menstruar,** *vi.* to menstruate.—**menstruo,** *m.* menstruation.

mensual, *a.* monthly.—**mensualidad,** *f.* monthly salary or allowance; monthly installment.

ménsula, *f.* bracket; rest for the elbows.

mensurable, *a.* mensurable, measurable.

menta, *f.* mint; peppermint.

mental, *a.* mental.—**mentalidad,** *f.* mentality.

mentar, *vti.* [1] to mention, name.

mente, *f.* mind; intelligence.

mentecatería, mentecatez, *f.* foolishness, silliness.—**mentecato,** *a.* silly, foolish, stupid.—*n.* fool.

mentir, *vti.* [39] & *vii.* to lie.—**mentira,** *f.* lie, falsehood; fib.—*de mentiras,* in jest.—**mentiroso,** *a.* lying, untruthful.

mentón, *m.* chin.

menú, *m.* menu, bill of fare.

menudear, *vt.* to repeat; to do over and over again.—*vi.* to occur frequently; to go into details; to sell by retail.—**menudencia,** *f.* trifle; minuteness.—*pl.* small matters.—**menudeo,** *m.* (com.) retail.—*al m.,* by retail.—**menudo,** *a.* small, little; minute; insignificant.—*m.* small coins, change.—*pl.* entrails of an animal.—*a m.,* often, frequently.

meñique, *a.* little (finger).—*m.* little finger.

meollo, *m.* brain; marrow; judgment; substance.

meple, *m.* (Am.) maple.

mequetrefe, *m.* coxcomb, busybody.

mercachifle, *m.* peddler, hawker, huckster; cheap fellow.—**mercader,** *m.* merchant, dealer.—**mercadería,** *f.* commodity, merchandise; trade.—*pl.* goods, wares, merchandise.—**mercado,** *m.* market; marketplace.—*m. de valores,* stock market.—**mercancía,** *f.* merchandise, goods, wares.—**mercante, mercantil,** *a.* merchant, mercantile, commercial.—**mercar,** *vti.* [d] to buy, purchase.

merced, *f.* favor, grace; mercy.—*estar a m. de,* to be or to live at the mercy of.—*m. a,* thanks to.

mercenario, *a.* mercenary.—*n.* mercenary soldier.

mercería, *f.* small wares, haberdashery, notions.

mercurial, *a.* mercurial.—**mercurio,** *m.* mercury, quicksilver.

merecedor, *a.* deserving, worthy.—**merecer,** *vti.* [3] to deserve, merit.—**merecido,** *m.* fitting punishment.—*a.* deserved.—**merecimiento,** *m.* merit.

merendar, *vti.* [1] to snack on.—*vii.* to have a snack.—**merendero,** *m.* lunchroom; picnic grounds.

merengue, *m.* meringue, sugarplum.

meretriz, *f.* prostitute.

meridiano, *a.* meridian; meridional

(section, cut).—*m.* meridian.—**meridional**, *a.* southern, southerly.—*mf.* southerner.

merienda, *f.* (afternoon) snack; packed meal; picnic.

mérito, *m.* merit; excellence, value.—*hacer méritos*, to make oneself deserving.—**meritorio**, *a.* meritorious, deserving.—*n.* apprentice, unpaid probationer.

merluza, *f.* hake; (coll.) drunkenness.

merma, *f.* decrease; shrinkage.—**mermar**, *vi.* to decrease, wear away. —*vt.* to lessen, reduce, decrease.

mermelada, *f.* marmalade; jam.

merodeador, *n.* marauder.—**merodear**, *vi. to* maraud.—**merodeo**, *m.* marauding.

mes, *m.* month; monthly salary; menstruation.

mesa, *f.* table; desk; executive board; plateau.—*m. de noche*, bedside table.—*poner la m.*, to set the table.

mesada, *f.* monthly wages or allowance.

meseta, *f.* plateau; landing of a staircase.

mesón, *m.* inn, hostel.—**mesonero**, *n.* innkeeper.

mestizaje, *m.* crossing of races.—**mestizo**, *a.* hybrid.—*n. & a.* half-breed, mestizo.

mesura, *f.* civility, politeness; moderation.—**mesurar**, *vr.* to control oneself.

meta, *f.* goal, aim; boundary; finish line.

metáfora, *f.* metaphor.

metal, *m.* metal; (mus.) brass.—*m. de voz*, tone or timbre of the voice. —**metálico**, *a.* metallic.—*m.* cash.—**metalizar**, *vti.* [a] to metallize. —*vri.* to become mercenary.—**metalurgia**, *f.* metallurgy.

metamorfosear, *vt. & vr.* to metamorphose, transform.—**metamorfosis**, *f.* metamorphosis, transformation.

meteórico, *a.* meteoric.—**meteoro**, *m.* meteor.—**meteorología**, *f.* meteorology.—**meteorológico**, *a.* meteorological.—*parte m.*, weather report.

meter, *vt.* to put in(to), insert, introduce; to make (as a noise); to cause (as fear); to induce, get (one into business, etc.).—*vr.* to meddle, intrude; to plunge into.—*m. a*, to undertake to; to turn to; to set oneself up as, pretend to be.—*m. con*, to pick a quarrel with.—*m. en*, (coll.) to meddle with, poke one's nose into.

meticuloso, *a.* meticulous, scrupulous.

metódico, *a.* methodical.—**método**, *m.* method; technique.

metralla, *f.* grapeshot; shrapnel.

métrico, *a.* metric(al).—**metro**, *m.* meter; subway.

metrónomo, *m.* metronome.

metrópoli, *f.* metropolis.—**metropolitano**, *a.* metropolitan.—*m.* subway.

mexicano, *n. & a.* V. MEJICANO.

mezcal, *m.* Mexican alcoholic beverage.

mezcla, *f.* mixture; medley; mortar; mixed cloth.—**mezclar**, *vt.* to mix, mingle; blend.—*vr.* to mix; to intermarry; to intermeddle.

mezclilla, *f.* pepper and salt cloth.

mezcolanza, *f.* (coll.) mix-up, hodgepodge.

mezquindad, *f.* niggardliness, stinginess.—**mezquino**, *a.* niggardly, stingy; petty, puny.

mezquita, *f.* mosque.

mi, *pron.* me.—*a.* my.

miaja, *f* = MIGAJA.

mico, *n.* monkey.

microbio, *m.* microbe.—**micrófono**, *m.* microphone.—**microscopio**, *m.* microscope.

miedo, *m.* fear.—*tener m.*, to be afraid.—**miedoso**, *a.* fearful, afraid.

miel, *f.* honey; molasses.—*m. de abejas*, bee's honey.

miembro, *m.* member; limb; penis.

mientes, *f.* thoughts, ideas.—*parar m. en*, or *poner m. en*, to consider, reflect on.—*traer a las m.*, to remind.

mientras, *adv. & conj.* while; whereas. —*m. más*, the more.—*m. que*, while, as long as, so long as.—*m. tanto*, meanwhile, in the meantime.

miércoles, *m.* Wednesday.

mies, *f.* ripe grain; harvest time.—*pl.* grain fields.

mero, *a.* mere, pure, simple; (Am.) real, true; (Am.) very, very same.—*m.* (ichth.) halibut.

miga, *f.* crumb, soft part of bread; fragment, bit; (coll.) marrow, substance, pith.—*hacer buenas (malas) migas*, (coll.) to get on well (badly) with.—**migaja**, *f.* crumb or bit of bread; fragment, chip or bit; (coll.) little or nothing.—*pl.* leavings; bits of foods.

migración, *f.* migration.

migraña, *f.* migraine, headache.

migratorio, *a.* migrating, migratory.

milagro, *m.* miracle.—**milagroso**, *a.* miraculous.

milicia, *f.* militia; science of war; military profession.—**miliciano**, *n.* militiaman.

militar, *vi.* to serve in the army; to militate.—*m. contra*, to be against.

—*a.* military, soldierly.—*m.* soldier, military man.

milla, *f.* mile.

millar, *m.* thousand.—*pl.* (fig.) a great number.—**millón**, *m.* million; (fig.) a great deal.—*pl.* (fig.) a multitude, a great number.—**millonario**, *n.* & *a.* millionaire.

mimar, *vt.* to pet, fondle; to pamper, spoil (a child); to coax.

mimbre, *m.* osier; willow; wicker.—**mimbrera**, *f.* willow.

mímica, *f.* pantomime, sign language.—**mímico**, *a.* mimic; imitative.

mimo, *m.* caress, petting; pampering; coaxing.—**mimoso**, *a.* soft, spoiled; delicate; fastidious, finicky.

mina, *f.* mine; lead of pencil; (fig.) a gold mine.—**minar**, *vt.* to mine, excavate; to undermine; to consume; to ruin.—**mineral**, *a.* mineral; rich mine.—**mineralogía**, *f.* mineralogy.—**minería**, *f.* mining; force of miners.—**minero**, *a.* pertaining to mines.—*m.* miner; mine operator; source, origin.

mingo, *s.* (billiards) object ball.

miniatura, *f.* miniature.

mínimo, *a.* least, smallest.—*m.* minimum.

ministerio, *m.* ministry; office and term of a cabinet minister; government department and building.—**ministro**, *m.* cabinet minister; minister; judge or justice.

minoría, *f.* minority (in age or in number).—**minoridad**, *f.* minority (in age).

minucia, *f.* minuteness, smallness; mite.—*pl.* minutiae.—**minuciosidad**, *f.* minuteness, thoroughness; trifle; small detail.—**minucioso**, *a.* minutely precise, thorough.

minúsculo, *a.* very small, tiny; of little importance.—*f.* small letter, lower-case letter.

minuta, *f.* first draft; lawyer's bill; memorandum; list.—*pl.* minutes (of a meeting).

minutero, *m.* minute hand.—**minuto**, *m.* minute (in time and geom.).—*al m.*, at once, right away.

mío, **mía**.—*pl.* **míos**, **mías**, *pron.* mine.—*a.* my, of mine.

miope, *a.* near-sighted, myopic; shortsighted.—*mf.* near-sighted person.—**miopía**, *f.* myopia, near-sightedness.

mira, *f.* sight (firearms and instruments); vigilance; design, purpose, intention, view.—*estar a la m.*, to be on the lookout, to be on the watch.—**mirada**, *f.* glance, gaze, look.—*echar una m.*, to glance, cast a glance.—**mirado**, *a.* considerate;

circumspect, prudent; considered, reputed.—*bien m.*, carefully considered; looking well into the matter; in fact.—**mirador**, *m.* veranda; bay window, vantage-point.—**miramiento**, *m.* consideration, reflection; circumspection, prudence; attention, courtesy.—*pl.* fuss, bother, worry.—**mirar**, *vt.* to look, look at; to gaze, gaze upon; to view, survey; to see, regard; to consider, think; to have regard for, esteem; to watch, be careful; to watch, spy; to notice; to concern.—*m. de hito en hito*, to stare at.—*m. de reojo*, to look askance.—*m. por encima*, to examine slightly, glance at.—*vi.* to look.—*m. a*, to face, front on.—*m. por*, to take care of; look after.—*vr.* to look at oneself; to look at each other, one another.

miríada, *f.* myriad, large quantity or number.

mirilla, *f.* peephole; sight (firearms, etc.).

mirlo, *m.* blackbird.

mirón, *n.* spectator, onlooker; kibitzer; busybody, gazer.—*a.* inquisitive, curious.

mirra, *f.* myrrh.

mirto, *m.* myrtle.

misa, *f.* (eccl.) Mass.—*m. mayor*, high Mass.—*no saber de la m. la media*, to know nothing.

miscelánea, *f.* miscellany.—**misceláneo**, *a.* miscellaneous.

miserable, *a.* miserable, wretched, unhappy.—*mf.* wretch, cur, cad.—**miseria**, *f.* misery, wretchedness; need, squalor, poverty; stinginess; trifle, pittance.—**misericordia**, *f.* mercy, mercifulness, pity.—**misericordioso**, *a.* merciful.—**mísero**, *a.* = MISERABLE.

misión, *f.* mission; errand.—**misionero**, *n.* missionary.—**misiva**, *f.* missive, letter.

mismo, *a.* same; similar, like; equal, selfsame.—*ahora m.*, right now.—*el hombre m.*, the man himself.—*el m. hombre*, the same man.—*este m. mes*, this very month.—*lo m.*, the same thing.—*lo m. da*, it is all the same.—*yo m.*, I myself.

misógino, *m.* woman hater.

misterio, *m.* mystery.—**misterioso**, *a.* mysterious.

místico, *n.* & *a.* mystic(al).

mistificador, *n.* = MIXTIFICADOR.—**mistificar**, *vti.* [d] = MIXTIFICAR.

mitad, *f.* half; middle, center.—*cara m.*, better half, spouse.—*por la m.*, in two.

mítico, *a.* mythical.

mitigar, *vti.* [b] to mitigate, alleviate, soothe.

mitin, *m.* political meeting; rally.

mito, *m.* myth.—**mitología,** *f.* mythology.—**mitológico,** *a.* mythological.

mitón, *m.* mitt, mitten.

mitra, *f.* miter; bishopric.

mixtificador, *n.* cheat, deceiver.—**mixtificar,** *vti.* [d] to cheat, deceive.

mixto, *a.* mixed, mingled; composite; halfbreed; assorted.—**mixtura,** *f.* mixture, compound.

mobiliario, moblaje, *m.* household furniture.

mocasín, *m.* moccasin (shoe and snake).—**mocasina,** *f.* moccasin (shoe).

mocedad, *f.* youth; youthfulness.—**mocetón,** *n.* strapping youth; lad.

moción, *f.* motion.

moco, *m.* mucus, snivel, snot.—*llorar a m. tendido,* (coll.) to cry like a child.—**mocoso,** *a.* given to sniveling.—*n.* child; inexperienced youth.

mochar, *vt.* to cut, lop off.

mochila, *f.* knapsack; haversack.

mocho, *a.* cropped, shorn, cut-off; maimed, mutilated.—*m.* butt end.

mochuelo, *m.* red owl.

moda, *f.* fashion, mode, style.—*pasado de m.,* out of style.

modales, *m. pl.* manners.

modelado, *m.* modeling.—**modelar,** *vt.* to model.—**modelo,** *m.* model, pattern, copy.—*mf.* life model.

moderación, *f.* moderation.—**moderador,** *n. & a.* moderator, moderating.—**moderar,** *vt.* to moderate, regulate, curb.—*vr.* to calm down, moderate, refrain from excesses.

modernizar, *vti.* [a] & *vri.* to modernize.—**moderno,** *a.* modern.

modestia, *f.* modesty.—**modesto,** *a.* modest, unpretentious; unobtrusive; unassuming.

módico, *a.* reasonable, economical.

modificación, *f.* modification.—**modificar,** *vti.* [d] to modify.

modismo, *m.* idiom, idiomatic expression.

modista, *f.* dressmaker, modiste.—*m. de sombreros,* milliner.—**modisto,** *m.* couturier, fashion designer.

modo, *m.* mode, way, manner, (gram.) mood.—*a m. de,* like, by way of.—*de buen (mal) m.,* politely (impolitely).—*de m. que,* so that; and so.—*de ningún m.,* by no means, under no circumstances.—*de otro m.,* otherwise.—*de todos modos,* at any rate, anyway.

modorra, *f.* drowsiness.

modoso, *a.* temperate, well-behaved.

modulación, *f.* modulation.—**modular,** *vt. & vi.* to modulate.

mofa, *f.* mockery, jeering, ridicule.—**mofar,** *vi. & vr.* to jeer, scoff, mock.—*mofarse de,* to mock, sneer at, make fun of.

mofeta, *f.* skunk.

moflete, *m.* fat cheek.—**mofletudo,** *a.* fat-cheeked.

mogol, *a. & n.* Mogul, Mongol.

mohín, *m.* grimace, gesture.—**mohino,** *a.* gloomy, sulky; sad, mournful; (of horses, etc.) black.

moho, *m.* mold, mildew; rust.—**mohoso,** *a.* rusty; moldy, musty, mildewed.

mojadura, *f.* drenching, moistening, wetting.—**mojar,** *vt.* to wet, drench; to moisten, dampen; (coll.) to stab.—*vr.* to get wet.

mojicón, *m.* bun; punch, blow.

mojigatería, mojigatez, *f.* hypocrisy, sanctimoniousness; bigotry; prudery.—**mojigato,** *n.* prude, hypocrite; bigot, fanatic.—*a.* hypocritical, sanctimonious; prudish; bigoted.

mojón, *m.* landmark; milestone; heap, pile; (Am.) solid excrement.

molar, *a.* molar.

molde, *m.* mold, cast; pattern; (eng.) form; (print.) form ready for printing.—**moldear,** *vt.* to mold.—**moldura,** *f.* molding.

mole, *f.* huge mass or bulk.—*m.* (Mex.) chilli gravy.

molécula, *f.* molecule.—**molecular,** *a.* molecular.

moler, *vti.* [26] to grind, mill; to overtire; to vex, bore; to waste, consume.—*m. a palos,* to give a sound beating.

molestar, *vt.* to disturb; to trouble; to annoy, vex; to tease.—*vr.* **(en)** to bother, put oneself out.—**molestia,** *f.* annoyance, bother; inconvenience, trouble; discomfort; hardship; grievance.—**molesto,** *a.* annoying, vexatious, bothersome; troublesome; uncomfortable.

molicie, *f.* softness; effeminacy.

molienda, *f.* milling, grinding; season for grinding (sugar cane, etc.).—**molimiento,** *m.* grinding, pounding; fatigue, weariness.—**molinero,** *n.* miller, grinder.—**molinete,** *m.* little mill; pinwheel; ventilating wheel; friction roller.—**molinillo,** *m.* hand mill; coffee grinder.—**molino,** *m.* mill.

molusco, *m.* mollusk.

molleja, *f.* gizzard.

mollera, *f.* crown of head; (fig.) intelligence.—*ser duro de m.,* to be dull or obstinate.

momentáneo, *a.* momentary; prompt. —**momento**, *m.* moment, trice; opportunity.—*a cada m.*, continually, every minute.—*al m.*, in a moment, immediately.

momia, *f.* mummy.

mona, *f.* female monkey; (coll.) ludicrous imitator; (coll.) drunkenness. —*dormir la m.*, to sleep off a drunk. —**monada**, *f.* grimace; fawning, flattery; a pretty person or thing.

monaguillo, *m.* (eccl.) acolyte, altar boy.

monarca, *m.* monarch.—**monarquía**, *f.* monarchy; kingdom.—**monárquico**, *a.* monarchical.

monasterio, *m.* monastery.—**monástico**, *a.* monastic.

mondadientes, *m.* toothpick.—**mondadura**, *f.* cleaning, cleansing.—*pl.* paring, peelings.—**mondar**, *vt.* to clean, cleanse; to trim, prune; to hull, peel.—**mondo**, *a.* neat, pure, unmixed.—*m. y lirondo*, (coll.) pure, without adornment.

mondongo, *m.* tripe; intestines.

moneda, *f.* coin; money; specie; coinage.—*m. corriente*, currency.—*m. suelta*, small change.—**monedero**, *n.* coiner.—*m.* purse.

monería, *f.* grimace, mimicry, monkeyshine; cunning action.

monetario, *a.* monetary.

mongol, *n.* Mongol.—**mongólico**, *a.* Mongolian, Mongolic.

monigote, *m.* puppet.

monja, *f.* nun.—**monje**, *m.* monk.

mono, *n.* monkey.—*m.* overalls.—*a.* (coll.) dainty; (coll.) cute.

monograma, *m.* monogram.

monologar, *vii.* [b] to soliloquize.—**monólogo**, *m.* monologue, soliloquy.

monopolio, *m.* monopoly.—**monopolizar**, *vti.* [a] to monopolize.

monosilábico, *a.* monosyllabic.—**monosílabo**, *m. & a.* monosyllable; monosyllabic.

monotonía, *f.* monotony.—**monótono**, *a.* monotonous.

monserga, *f.* (coll.) gabble, gibberish, annoyance.

monstruo, *m.* monster, freak.—**monstruosidad**, *f.* monstrosity; monstrousness.—**monstruoso**, *a.* monstrous; huge; hideous; hateful; shocking.

monta, *f.* act of mounting, amount, sum total.—*poca m.*, little value; little importance.—**montacargas**, *m.* hoist, winch, freight elevator. —**montador**, *n.* mounter; installer (electrician, etc.).—**montaje**, *m.* setting up, installing; assembling.—**montante** *m* (carp & mech.)

upright, standard, post, strut, jamb; (arch.) transom; (com.) amount.

montaña, *f.* mountain.—**montañés**, *a.* mountain, of or from the mountains or highlands.—*n.* mountaineer, highlander; native of Santander, Spain. —**montañoso**, *a.* mountainous.

montar, *vi.* to mount, get on top; to ride horseback; to amount; to be of importance.—*m. en cólera*, to fly into a rage.—*vt.* to ride, straddle; to amount (to); to cover (as a horse, etc.); (mech.) to mount, set up; to establish; to assemble; (jewelry) to set; to cock (as a gun); (mil.) to mount (guard).—*vr.* (en) to get into, board (vehicles); to mount (saddle animals).

montaraz, *a.* wild, untamed; uncouth, boorish.—**monte**, *m.* mountain, mount; woods, forest, woodland.—*m. de piedad*, pawnshop.—**montés**, *a.* wild, undomesticated, uncultivated.—**montículo**, *m.* mound.

monto, *m.* sum (of money); amount; sum total.—**montón**, *m.* heap, pile; great number; mass; mound.—*a montones*, abundantly, in heaps.—*del m.*, mediocre, run of the mill.

montuno, *a.* pertaining to the highlands; rustic, boorish.—**montuoso**, *a.* mountainous, hilly.

montura, *f.* riding horse, mount; saddle trappings; (jewelry) frame, setting.

monumental, *a.* monumental.—**monumento**, *m.* monument.

moña, *f.* (Am.) dressmaker's mannequin; doll; (coll.) drunkenness; rosette, ribbon head ornament; elaborate badge on bull's neck when in the arena.

moño, *m.* (of hair) chignon, bun; crest, tuft.

moquear, *vi.* to sniffle, snivel; to run from the nose.—**moquita**, *f.* sniffle, snivel; running from the nose.

mora, *f.* blackberry; mulberry; Moorish woman.

morada, *f.* habitation, residence; stay.—**morado**, *a.* purple.—**morador**, *n.* resident, inhabitant.

moral, *a.* moral.—*f.* morals, morality; morale; mulberry tree.—**moraleja**, *f.* moral, maxim, lesson.—**moralidad**, *f.* morality; morals.—**moralizar**, *vti.* [a] & *vii.* to moralize.

morar, *vi.* to inhabit, dwell, reside.

morbidez, *f.* softness, mellowness.—**mórbido**, *a.* morbid; soft, mellow, delicate.—**morbo**, *m.* disease, infirmity.—**morboso**, *a.* diseased, morbid.

morcilla, *f.* blood sausage; (theat., coll.) gag, ad-libbing.

mordacidad, *f.* pungency, sharpness, sarcasm.—**mordaz,** *a.* corrosive, biting; sarcastic, trenchant.

mordaza, *f.* gag; muzzle.

mordedor, *n. & a.* biter; biting.—**mordedura,** *f.* bite; sting.—**morder,** *vti.* [26] to bite; to eat away; to backbite; to nip.—**mordiscar,** *vti.* [d] to nibble.—**mordisco, mordiscón,** *m.* bite; biting; bit, piece bitten off.

moreno, *a.* brown; dark, swarthy; brunette.—*n.* dark-haired person; (Am.) colored person.

morfina, *f.* morphine.—**morfinómano,** *n.* drug addict.

morigeración, *f.* temperance, moderation.

morillos, *m. pl.* andirons.

morir, *vii.* [17-49] & *vri.* to die; to die out (as fire).—*m. por,* to crave for.

moro, *a.* Moorish.—*n.* Moor.

morosidad, *f.* slowness, tardiness.—**moroso,** *a.* slow, tardy; sluggish.

morral, *m.* nose bag; game bag; knapsack.

morralla, *f.* small fry (fish); rubbish; rabble.

morriña, *f.* (coll.) homesickness; sadness, blues.

morro, *m.* muzzle; snout; promontory; thick lip.

morsa, *f.* walrus.

mortaja, *f.* shroud, winding sheet.—**mortal,** *a.* mortal, fatal, deadly.—*mf.* mortal.—**mortalidad,** *f.* mortality; death rate.—**mortandad,** *f.* mortality; slaughter; butchery.—**mortecino,** *a.* dying away or extinguishing; pale, subdued (color).

mortero, *m.* mortar.

mortífero, *a.* death-dealing, fatal.—**mortificación,** *f.* mortification; humiliation.—**mortificar,** *vti.* [d] & *vri.* to mortify; to subdue (passions); to vex; to bother; to humiliate.—**mortuorio,** *a.* mortuary.—*m.* burial, funeral.

moruno, *a.* Moorish.

mosaico, *a.* Mosaic.—*m* mosaic (work), concrete tile.

mosca, *f.* fly; (coll.) dough, money; nuisance, pest.—*aflojar la m.,* to give or spend money.—*m. muerta,* one who feigns meekness.—*papar moscas,* to gape with astonishment.—**moscardón, moscón,** *m* bumblebee; (coll.) bore, pest.—**mosquearse,** *vr.* to show resentment.

mosquitero, *m.* mosquito bar or net.—**mosquito,** *m.* gnat; mosquito.

mostacho, *m.* bushy mustache.

mostaza, *f.* mustard.

mosto, *m.* must, grape juice.

mostrador, *m.* counter (in a shop); stand.—**mostrar,** *vti.* [12] to show; to point out.—*vri.* to appear; to show oneself, prove to be.

mostrenco, *a.* (coll.) homeless; unclaimed, unowned; masterless; stray; dull, stupid.

mota, *f.* small knot (in cloth); mote, speck.

mote, *m.* nickname; motto.

motear, *vt.* to speckle, mottle.

motejar, *vt.* to chaff, call offensive names; to censure.—*m. de,* to brand as.

motín, *m.* mutiny, riot.

motivar, *vt.* to give a reason or motive for; to cause; to motivate.—**motivo,** *m.* motive, cause, reason, occasion; (mus.) motif, theme.—*con m. de,* owing to, by reason of; on the occasion of.

moto, motocicleta, *f.* motorcycle.—**motociclista,** *mf.* motorcyclist.—**motor,** *n. & a.* mover; moving.—*m.* motor; engine.—**motorista,** *mf.* motorman (-woman); motorist, driver.—**motorización,** *f.* mechanization.—**motorizar,** *vti.* [a] to mechanize.—**motriz,** *a.* moving.

movedizo, *a.* movable; shaky, unsteady; inconstant, shifting.—**mover,** *vti.* [26] to move; to make move; to drive, propel; to persuade, induce; to prompt; to incite, promote; to stir.—*vri.* to move, stir.—**movible,** *a.* movable; mobile; changeable, fickle.—**móvil,** *a.* movable; mobile; unsteady, portable.—*m.* motive, incentive, inducement; mover, motor; moving body.—**movilidad,** *f.* mobility; movableness; fickleness; unsteadiness.—**movilización,** *f.* mobilization.—**movilizar,** *vti.* [a] & *vri.* to mobilize.—**movimiento,** *m.* movement, move, activity; stir, agitation; life, liveliness; animation; motion; (art) distribution of lines, etc., technique; (mus.) tempo, time.

mozalbete, *m.* teenager, youth.—**mozo,** *a.* young, youthful; single, unmarried.—*m.* lad; manservant; waiter; porter.—*f* lass, maid.—*buen m.,* good-looking.

mu, *m.* lowing of cattle, moo.

mucamo, *n.* (Am.) servant

mucosidad, *f* mucosity, mucousness.—**mucoso,** *a.* mucous; slimy, viscous.—*f.* mucous membrane.

muchacha, *f.* girl; maid (servant).—**muchachada,** *f.* boyish act; prank.—**muchachería,** *f.* boyish trick; crowd of boys.—**muchacho,** *m.* boy, lad

muchedumbre, *f.* multitude; crowd; populace, rabble.

mucho, *a.* much, a great deal of; (of time) long.—*pl.* many.—*adv.* much, very much; a great deal; in a great measure; often; (of time) long; very.—*ni con m.,* not by far; far from it.—*ni m. menos,* nor anything like it.—*no es m.,* it is no wonder. —*no ha m., no hace m.,* not long since.—*por m. que,* no matter how much.

muda, *f.* change, alteration; change of underwear; molt, molting; change of voice in boys; roost of birds of prey.—**mudable,** *a.* changeable; fickle; shifty.—**mudanza,** *f.* change; mutation; removal, moving (residence); inconstancy; fickleness. —**mudar,** *vt.* to change; to remove; to vary, alter; to molt.—*vi.* **(de)** to change (opinion, mind, etc.).—*vr.* to reform, mend, change; to change one's clothes; to move, change one's place of residence.

mudez, *f.* dumbness.—**mudo,** *a.* & *n.* dumb; silent; mute.

mueblaje, *m.* = MOBILIARIO.—**mueble,** *a.* movable.—*m.* piece of furniture. —*pl.* chattels, furniture, household goods.

mueca, *f.* grimace, wry face, grin.

muela, *f.* molar tooth; millstone, grindstone.—*m. del juicio,* wisdom tooth.

muelle, *m.* (naut.) pier, wharf; (RR.) freight platform; metal spring.—*a.* delicate, soft, voluptuous.

muérdago, *m.* mistletoe.

muerte, *f.* death; murder.—*a la m.,* at the point of death —*de mala m ,* miserable, of no account —*de m.,* implacably.—**muerto,** *ppi* of MORIR. —*a.* dead, deceased, killed; languid; slaked.—*estar m. por,* (coll.) to be crazy about.—*m. de,* (fig.) dying with.—*n.* dead person, corpse.— *echarle a uno el m.,* (coll.) to put the blame on one.—*tocar a m.,* to toll.

muesca, *f* notch, groove, indentation.

muestra, *f.* sample, specimen; shop sign; placard, bill; model, pattern, copy; sign, indication.—**muestrario,** *m.* collection of samples; specimen or sample book.

mugido, *m.* lowing of cattle, moo.— **mugir,** *vii.* [c] to low, bellow.

mugre, *f* grease, grime, filth; squalor. —**mugriento,** *a.* greasy, grimy, filthy.

mujer, *f* woman; wife, mate.—**mujeriego,** *a.* fond of women.—*m.* (coll.) wolf.—**mujeril,** *a.* womanish, womanly, feminine.—**mujerío,** *m* gather

ing of women.—**mujerzuela,** *f.* woman of no account.

muladar, *m.* dungheap; rubbish heap.

mulato, *n.* & *a.* mulatto.

muleta, *f.* crutch.—**muletilla,** *f.* pet word or phrase often repeated in talking.

mulo, *n.* mule.

multa, *f.* (money) fine.—**multar,** *vt.* to fine.

multicolor, *a.* many-colored, variegated, motley.—**múltiple,** *a.* multiple, complex; (int. combust. eng.) manifold.—**multiplicación,** *f.* multiplication.—**multiplicar,** *vti.* [d] & *vri.* to multiply.—**múltiplo,** *m.* & *a.* multiple.

multitud, *f.* multitude; crowd; the masses.

mullir, *vti.* [27] to fluff, make soft, mollify.

mundanal, *a.* mundane, worldly.— **mundanidad,** *f.* worldliness, sophistication.—**mundano,** *a.* = MUNDANAL. —**mundial,** *a.* world, world-wide.— **mundo,** *m.* world; (coll.) great multitude, great quantity; social life, circle; experience.—*gran m.,* high society.—*medio m.,* many people.— *ser hombre de m.,* to be a man of experience.—*todo el m.,* everybody.

munición, *f.* ammunition; small shot; birdshot; charge of firearms.

municipal, *a.* municipal.—**municipalidad,** *f* municipality; town hall; municipal government.—**municipio,** *m.* municipality

munificencia, *f* munificence, liberality.

muñeca, *f* wrist; doll; (mech.) puppet, polishing bag.—**muñeco,** *m.* puppet, manikin; boy doll; soft fellow.

muñón, *m.* stump (of mutilated limb).

mural, *a.* mural.—*m.* mural painting. —**muralla,** *f.* rampart; wall (of a city).—**murar,** *vt.* to wall.

murciélago, *m.* (zool) bat.

murmullo, *m.* whisper, whispering; murmuring, murmur; muttering.

murmuración, *f.* backbiting, gossip.— **murmurar,** *vi.* to purl, ripple; to whisper, murmur; to gossip, backbite.

muro, *m.* wall, (fort.) rampart.

murria, *f* (coll) blues; surliness, sullenness.

musa, *f* Muse, poetic inspiration. *pl.* (The) Muses.

musaraña, *f* shrew-mouse; any small animal, insect or vermin.—*mirar a,* or *pensar en las musarañas,* to be absent-minded.

muscular, *a* muscular —**músculo,** *m.*

muscle.—**musculoso,** *a.* muscular; brawny.

muselina, *f.* muslin.

museo, *m.* museum.

musgo, *m.* moss.—**musgoso,** *a.* mossy; moss-covered.

música, *f.* music; band; musical composition; sheet music.—**musical,** *a.* musical.—**músico,** *a.* musical.—*n.* musician.

musitar, *vi.* to mumble, mutter, whisper.

muslo, *m.* thigh.

mustio, *a.* withered; sad, languid.

musulmán, *n.* & *a.* Moslem.

mutabilidad, *f.* mutability; fickleness. —**mutación,** *f.* mutation, change; (theat.) change of scene.

mutilación, *f.* mutilation.—**mutilar,** *vt.* to mutilate.

mutis, *m.* (theat.) exit.

mutismo, *m.* muteness, silence.

mutualismo, *m.* system of organized mutual aid.—**mutuo,** *a.* mutual, reciprocal.

muy, *adv.* very; greatly, most.

N

nabo, *m.* turnip (plant and root).

nácar, *m.* mother-of-pearl; pearl color.

nacer, *vii.* [3-49] to be born; to sprout, grow (as branches, plants); to rise (as the sun); to originate, start; to spring (as a stream, a river).—*n. de pies,* to be born lucky. —**naciente,** *a.* rising (sun).—*m.* Orient, East.—**nacimiento,** *m.* birth; beginning; origin; source of a river or spring; model scene of the Nativity at Yuletide.

nación, *f.* nation.—**nacional,** *a.* national.—**nacionalidad,** *f.* nationality; citizenship.—**nacionalización,** *f.* nationalization; naturalization.—**nacionalizar,** *vti.* [a] to nationalize; to naturalize.

nada, *f.* nothing, naught; nothingness.—*indef. pron.* nothing, not anything.—*de n.,* insignificant, good-for-nothing; (after thanks) you are welcome! don't mention it!—*n. de eso,* none of that; not so.—*por n.,* for nothing; under no circumstances; (Am.) you are welcome!—*adv.* not at all, by no means.

nadador, *n.* & *a.* swimmer; swimming. —**nadar,** *vi.* to swim; to float.

nadería, *f* (coll.) insignificant thing, trifle.

nadie, *indef. pron.* nobody, no one, none; (after negative) anybody, anyone

nafta, *f.* naphtha.—**naftalina,** *f.* naphthalene.

naipe, *m.* (playing) card.—*pl.* cards; pack or deck of cards.

nalga, *f.* buttock, rump.—**nalgada,** *f.* spanking.—*dar una n.,* to spank.

nana, *f.* (coll.) child's nurse; lullaby.

naranja, *f.* orange.—*media n.,* (coll.) better half (spouse).—**naranjada,** *f.* orangeade.—**naranjal,** *m.* orange grove.—**naranjo,** *m.* orange tree.

narciso, *m.* narcissus; daffodil; coxcomb.

narcótico, *a.* & *m.* narcotic, dope.— **narcotizar,** *vti.* [a] to drug, dope.

nardo, *m.* spikenard.

nariz, *f.* nose; nostril; sense of smell. —*meter la n. en todas partes,* to nose about.

narración, *f.* narration, account.— **narrador,** *n.* narrator; storyteller. —**narrar,** *vt.* to narrate, relate, tell. —**narrativa,** *f.* narrative.—**narrativo,** *a.* narrative.

nata, *f.* cream; prime or choice part; elite.—*pl.* whipped cream with sugar.

natación, *f.* swimming.

natal, *a.* natal, native.—*m.* birthday, birth.—**natalicio,** *m.* birthday.— **natalidad,** *f.* birth rate.

natatorio, *a.* swimming.

natilla, *f.* custard.

natividad, *f.* nativity; Christmas, Yuletide.—**nativo,** *a.* native.

natural, *a.* natural; native; inherent; common, usual; unaffected; plain. —*mf.* native.—*m.* temper, disposition, nature.—*al n.,* without art or affectation.—*del n.,* (art) from life, from nature.—**naturaleza,** *f.* nature; constitution; sort, character, kind; nationality; temperament or disposition.—*n. muerta,* still life.—**naturalidad,** *f* naturalness; birthright, nationality.—**naturalista,** *mf.* & *a.* naturalist(ic).—**naturalización,** *f.* naturalization.—**naturalizar,** *vti.* [a] to naturalize; to acclimatize.—*vri.* to become naturalized; to get accustomed to.

naufragar, *vii.* [b] to be ship wrecked; to fail.—**naufragio,** *m.* shipwreck; failure.—**náufrago,** *a.* & *n.* shipwrecked (person).

náusea, *f.* nausea, disgust, squeamishness.—**nauseabundo,** *a.* nauseous, sickening, loathsome.

náutica, *f.* navigation.—**náutico,** *a.* nautical.

navaja, *f* claspknife; jack knife, penknife.—*n. de afeitar,* razor.—**navajazo,** *m.* thrust or gash with a claspknife or razor; stab wound.

naval, *a.* naval.—**nave,** *f.* ship, vessel; (arch) nave; aisle **navegable,** *a.*

navigable.—**navegación**, *f.* navigation; sea voyage.—*n. aérea*, aviation. —**navegante**, *m.* & *a.* navigator; navigating.—**navegar**, *vii.* [b] to navigate, sail, steer.

navidad, *f.* Nativity; Christmas.—*pl.* Christmas season.

naviero, *a.* shipping, ship.—*n.* ship owner.—**navío**, *m.* ship, vessel.

neblina, *f.* fog, mist.—**nebulosa**, *f.* nebula.—**nebulosidad**, *f.* cloudiness; mistiness; nebulousness.—**nebuloso**, *a.* nebulous, hazy, misty.

necedad, *f.* stupidity, foolishness; nonsense; (coll.) tripe.

necesario, *a.* necessary.—**neceser**, *m.* dressing case, toilet case.—*n. de costura*, sewing case.—**necesidad**, *f.* necessity; need, want.—*por n.*, from necessity; necessarily.—**necesitado**, *a.* & *n.* indigent, needy (person).—**necesitar**, *vt.* to need; to necessitate.—*vi.* (de) to be in need (of).

necio, *a* stupid, idiotic, foolish.—*n.* fool.

necrópolis, *f.* cemetery.

nefando, *a.* nefarious, heinous.—**nefasto**, *a.* sad, ominous, unlucky.

negación, *f.* negation; denial; want or total privation; (gram.) negative particle.—**negar**, *vti.* [1-b] to deny; to refuse, withhold; to prohibit; to disown.—*n. el saludo*, to give the cold shoulder to.—*vri.* to decline, refuse.—**negativa**, *f.* negative, refusal.—**negativo**, *a.* negative.—*n.* (photog.) negative.

negligencia, *f.* negligence, neglect, carelessness.—**negligente**, *a.* negligent, careless, neglectful.

negociable, *a.* negotiable.—**negociación**, *f.* negotiation; business transaction, deal.—**negociado**, *m.* bureau, division or section in official departments.—**negociante**, *a.* negotiating, trading.—*mf.* dealer, merchant, trader.—**negociar**, *vi.* to trade; to negotiate.—**negocio**, *m.* business; transaction.—*pl.* business, commercial affairs.—*n. redondo*, good bargain.

negrear, *vi.* to become black; to appear black.—**negro**, *a.* black; gloomy, dark; sad, unfortunate.—*n.* Negro; (Am.) (coll.) dearest, darling, honey.—*m.* black (color).—*n. de humo*, lampblack.—**negrura**, *f.* blackness.—**negruzco**, *a.* blackish, dark brown.

nena, *f.* baby girl; babe.—**nene**, *m.* (coll.) infant, baby boy; dear, darling.

neolatino, *a.* & *m.* Neo-Latin.—*a.* Romance.

neologismo, *m* neologism

neozelandés, *n.* New Zealander.—*a.* of or from New Zealand.

nervio, *m.* nerve; energy, stamina, vigor.—**nerviosidad**, *f.*, **nerviosismo**, *m.* nervousness; strength, vigor.—**nervioso**, *a.* nervous.—**nervudo**, *a.* strong, sinewy, vigorous.

neto, *a.* neat, pure; (com.) net (profit, etc.).

neumático, *m.* tire.—*a.* pneumatic.

neumonía, *f.* (med.) pneumonia.—**neumónico**, *a.* pneumonic; pulmonary.

neurastenia, *f.* neurasthenia.—**neurasténico**, *n.* & *a.* neurasthenic.—**neurosis**, *f.* neurosis.—**neurótico**, *n.* & *a.* neurotic.

neutral, *a.* neutral, neuter.—**neutralidad**, *f.* neutrality.—**neutralizar**, *vti.* [a] to counteract; to neutralize.—**neutro**, *a.* (gram.) neuter; neutral.

nevada, *f.* snowfall.—**nevado**, *a.* white as snow.—*m.* snow-covered peak.—**nevar**, *vii.* [1] to snow.—*vti.* to make white as snow.—**nevera**, *f.* icebox, refrigerator.—**nevisca**, *f.* gentle fall of snow.

nexo, *m.* bond, tie, union.

ni, *conj.* neither, nor; not even.—*ni con mucho*, not by a good deal.—*ni siquiera*, not even.

nicaragüense, *mf.* & *a.* Nicaraguan.

nicotina, *f.* nicotine.

nicho, *m.* niche; alcove.

nidada, *f.* nestful of eggs, nest; brood, covey; sitting.—**nidal**, *m.* nest; nest egg; basis, motive; haunt.—**nido**, *m.* nest; haunt; den.

niebla, *f.* fog, mist, haze.

nieto, *n.* grandson (*f.* granddaughter).

nieve, *f.* snow.

nimbo, *m.* halo.

nimiedad, *f.* superfluity, prolixity; excess.—**nimio**, *a.* prolix.

ninfa, *f.* nymph.

ningún, (contr. of) **ninguno**, *a.* no, not one, not any.—*de ningún modo, de ninguna manera*, by no means.—*ninguna cosa*, nothing.—**ninguno**, *pron.* nobody, none, no one, not one.—*n. de los dos*, neither of the two.

niñada, *f.* puerility, childishness.—**niñera**, *f.* nurse, nursery-maid.—**niñería**, *f.* puerility, childish action; child's play; plaything; trifle.—**niñez**, *f.* childhood, infancy.—**niño**, *a.* childish, childlike; young; inexperienced.—*n.* child.—*desde n.*, from childhood.—*niña del ojo*, pupil of the eye.—*niñas de los ojos*, (coll.) apple of one's eye; treasure.

nipón, *n.* & *a.* Nipponese, Japanese.

níquel, *m.* nickel.—**niquelar**, *vt* to plate with nickel

nitidez, *f.* neatness; brightness, clarity.—**nitido,** *a.* neat; bright, clear.

nitrato, *m.* nitrate.—**nítrico,** *a.* nitric.—**nitro,** *m.* niter, saltpeter.—**nitrógeno,** *m.* nitrogen.

nivel. *m.* level; levelness; watermark.—*a n.,* level, true; on the same level.—*n. de aire* or *de burbuja,* spirit level.—*n. de la vida,* standard of living.—**nivelación,** *f.* leveling; grading.—**nivelar,** *vt.* to level; to grade; to make even.—*vr.* to level off.

no, *adv.* no, not, nay.—*interrog.* isn't it? isn't that so? do you see?—*n. bien,* no sooner.—*n. más,* only; no more.—*n. obstante,* notwithstanding.—*n. sea que,* lest; or else.—*n. tal,* no such thing.—*por sí o por n.,* just in case, anyway.

noble, *a.* noble.—*mf.* nobleman (-woman).—**nobleza,** *f.* nobleness; nobility; noblesse.

noción, *f.* notion, idea; element, rudiment.

nocivo, *a.* noxious, harmful, injurious.

nocturno, *a.* nocturnal, night.—*m.* (mus., lit.) nocturne.

noche, *f.* night; evening (after sunset); (fig.) obscurity, ignorance.—*ayer n.,* last night.—*buenas noches,* good evening; goodnight.—**Nochebuena,** *f.* Christmas eve.

nodo, *m.* (med., astr.) node.

nodriza, *f.* wet nurse.

nódulo, *m.* small node.

nogal, *m.* walnut.

nómada, *mf. & a.* nomad; nomadic.

nombradía, *f.* renown, fame, reputation.—**nombramiento,** *m.* nomination, naming; appointment.—**nombrar,** *vt.* to name; to nominate; to appoint.—**nombre,** *m.* name; fame, reputation; (gram.) noun; watchword.—*n. de pila* or *de bautismo,* Christian name.—*n. y apellidos,* full name.

nómina, *f.* payroll; roster, roll, register.—**nominal,** *a.* nominal.—**nominar,** *vt.* to name.—**nominativo,** *a. & m.* (gram.) nominative.

non, *a.* odd, uneven.—*m.* odd number.—*pl.* refusal.—*estar de n.,* to be unpaired.—*dar* or *echar nones,* to say no.

nonada, *f.* trifle, nothing.

nordeste, *m.* northeast.—**nórdico,** *n. & a.* Nordic.

norma, *f.* standard, norm, rule.—**normal,** *a.* normal; standard.—*f.* normal school; (geom.) normal.—**normalidad,** *f.* normality.—**normalizar,** *vti.* [a] to normalize; to standardize.—*vri.* to become normal, return to normal

noroeste, *m.* northwest.—**norte,** *m.* north; northwind; rule, guide, clue, direction.—**norteamericano,** *n. & a.* North American, American, from the U. S.—**norteño,** *n. & a.* Northerner; northern.

noruego, *n. & a.* Norwegian.

noruéste, *m.* = NOROESTE.

nos, *pron.* us, to us; ourselves.—**nosotros,** *pron.* we; ourselves; us (after preposition).

nostalgia, *f.* nostalgia, longing, homesickness.—**nostálgico,** *a.* nostalgic, homesick.

nota, *f.* note; mark (in exam); annotation; memorandum; (com.) account, bill, check; fame.—**notabilidad,** *f.* notability; a notable (person).—**notable,** *a.* notable, remarkable, telling; distinguished, prominent.—**notación,** *f.* note; notation.—**notar,** *vt.* to note, observe; to notice, take notice of.—**notaría,** *f.* notary's office.—**notario,** *m.* notary public.

noticia, *f.* news item; news; notice, information.—**noticiero,** *m.* newsman, reporter; news sheet or column or bulletin; newsreel (also **noticiario**).—**noticioso,** *a.* news-giving.—**notificación,** *f.* notification; notice.—**notificar,** *vti.* [d] to notify.

notoriedad, *f.* quality of being well-known; notoriety.—**notorio,** *a.* well-known; evident.

novatada, *f.* hazing (in colleges).—**novato,** *n.* novice, beginner.

novedad, *f.* novelty; newness; surprise, recent occurrence; fad; change.—**novel,** *a.* new, inexperienced.

novela, *f.* novel; story, fiction.—**novelero,** *a.* fond of novels, fads, and novelties; newfangled; fickle.—*n.* newsmonger, gossip.—**novelesco,** *a.* novelistic, fictional; fantastic.—**novelista,** *mf.* novelist.

novia, *f.* bride; fiancée; sweetheart, girl friend.—**noviazgo,** *m.* engagement, betrothal; courtship.

noviciado, *m.* (eccl.) novitiate; apprenticeship; probation.—**novicio,** *a.* new, inexperienced.—*n.* novice, probationer; freshman.

noviembre, *m.* November.

novilla, *f.* young cow, heifer.—**novillada,** *f.* fight with young bulls; drove of young cattle.—**novillero,** *m.* novice fighter; (coll.) truant, idler.—**novillo,** *m.* young bull.—*hacer novillos,* (coll.) to play truant or hooky.

novio, *m.* bridegroom; fiancé; sweetheart, boyfriend.

nubarrón, *m.* large threatening cloud.

—**nube,** f. cloud; film on the eye; shade in precious stones; crowd, multitude.—**nublado,** a. cloudy.—m. thundercloud; (fig.) threat of danger.—**nublar,** vt. to cloud, obscure.—vr. to become cloudy.

nuca, f. nape or scruff of the neck.

nuclear, a. nuclear.—**núcleo,** m. nucleus; center.

nudillo, m. knuckle; small knot.

nudismo, m. nudism.—**nudista,** mf. nudist.

nudo, m. knot; tangle; (bot.) node; joint; knotty point, intricacy; crisis of a drama.—**nudoso,** a. knotty, knotted.

nuera, f. daughter-in-law.

nuestro, a. our, ours.—pron. ours.

nueva, f. news, tidings.—**nuevo,** a. new.—de n., again, once more.—¿qué hay de n.? what's the news? what's new?

nuez, f. walnut; nut; Adam's apple.

nulidad, f. nullity; inability, incompetency; incompetent person, a nobody.—**nulo,** a. null, void; of no account.

numeración, f. numeration; numbering.—**numeral,** a. & m. numeral.—**numerar,** vt. to number; to enumerate.—**numerario,** a. numerary.—m. cash, coin, specie.—**numérico,** a. numerical.—**número,** m. number; numeral; size (shirt, etc.); number, issue (magazine, etc.).—**numeroso,** a. numerous.

nunca, adv. never.—n. jamás, never, never more.

nupcial, a. nuptial.—**nupcias,** f. pl. nuptials, wedding.

nutria, f. otter.

nutrición, f. nutrition, nourishing.—**nutrido,** a. full, abundant, numerous, dense.—**nutrir,** vt. to nourish, feed.—**nutritivo,** a. nutritive, nourishing.

Ñ

ñandú, m. (Am.) ostrich.

ñapa, f. (Am.) something over or extra.—de ñ., to boot, into the bargain.

ñato, a. (Am.) pug-nosed.

ñongo, n. (coll), (Cuba), peasant.—a. (Chile) lazy, good-for-nothing; (Colomb.) (of dice) loaded.—f. (Chile) laziness.

ñoñería, ñoñez, f. dotage, senility, drivel; shyness; silliness.—**ñoño,** a. (coll.) timid, shy; stupid; soft, feeble; flimsy.

O

o, conj. or, either.—o sea, that is.

oasis, m. oasis.

obedecer, vti. [3] to obey.—**obediencia,** f. obedience.—**obediente,** a. obedient.

obelisco, m. obelisk.

obertura, f. (mus.) overture.

obesidad, f. obesity, fatness.—**obeso,** a. obese, fat.

óbice, m. obstacle, hindrance.

obispado, m. bishopric; episcopate.—**obispo,** m. bishop.

obituario, m. obituary.

objeción, f. objection.—**objetar,** vt. to object to, oppose.

objetivo, a. objective.—m. (opt.) objective, eyepiece.—**objeto,** m. object; subject matter; thing; purpose; aim.

oblea, f. wafer.

oblicuo, a. oblique, slanting.

obligación, f. obligation, duty; bond, security.—pl. engagements; (com.) liabilities.—**obligar,** vti. [b] to obligate, compel, bind; to oblige.—vri. to obligate or bind oneself.—**obligatorio,** a. obligatory, compulsory.

óbolo, m. donation, alms, contribution; mite.

obra, f. work, creation; literary work; manufacture; structure, building; repairs in a house; toil, labor.—o. maestra, masterpiece.—o. muerta, (naut.) gunwale.—**obrar,** vt. to work; to act; to operate; to perform, execute.—vi. to act; to ease nature.—**obrero,** n. worker, workman (-woman), laborer.

obscenidad, f. obscenity.—**obsceno,** a. obscene.

obscurecer, = OSCURECER.—**obscuridad,** f. = OSCURIDAD.—**obscuro,** a. = OSCURO.

obsequiar, vt. to treat, entertain; to make presents to; to present, make a gift of.—**obsequio,** m. courtesy, attention shown; gift, present.—en o. de, for the sake of, out of respect to.—**obsequioso,** a. obsequious; compliant; attentive, obliging.

observación, f. observation, remark, note.—en o., under observation.—**observador,** n. & a. observer; observing.—**observancia,** f. observance, fulfillment.—**observar,** vt. to observe; to notice, remark, spot; to watch; to conform to (a rule, etc.).—**observatorio,** m. observatory.

obstaculizar, vti. [a] to impede, obstruct.—**obstáculo,** m. obstacle; stumbling block.

obstar, vi. to oppose, obstruct, hinder

—*no obstante*, notwithstanding; nevertheless, however.

obstinación, *f.* obstinacy, stubbornness.—**obstinado,** *a.* obstinate, stubborn, headstrong.—**obstinarse,** *vr.* **(en)** to be obstinate (about), to persist (in); to insist (on).

obstrucción, *f.* obstruction, stoppage.—**obstruccionismo,** *m.* obstructionism.—**obstruccionista,** *mf.* & *a.* obstructionist(ic).—**obstruir,** *vti.* [23-e] to obstruct, block, stop up.—*vri.* to become obstructed, clogged up.

obtención, *f.* obtainment, attainment.—**obtener,** *vti.* [42] to obtain, get, procure; to attain.

obturador, *m.* (photog.) shutter; throttle; plug, stopper.

obtuso, *a.* obtuse; blunt, dull.

obús, *m.* howitzer, mortar.

obviar, *vt.* to obviate, remove, prevent.—*vi.* to hinder.—**obvio,** *a.* obvious, evident.

ocasión, *f.* occasion; opportunity; cause, motive.—*de o.*, second-hand; at a bargain.—*en ocasiones*, at times.—**ocasional,** *a.* occasional, accidental, casual.—**ocasionar,** *vt.* to cause, occasion.

ocaso, *m.* sunset; setting of any heavenly body; decadence, decline; west.

occidental, *a.* occidental, western.—**occidente,** *m.* occident, west.

oceánico, *a.* oceanic.—**océano,** *m.* ocean.

ocio, *m.* leisure, idleness, pastime, diversion.—*ratos de o.*, spare time.—**ociosidad,** *f.* idleness, leisure.—**ocioso,** *a.* idle; fruitless; useless.

oclusión, *f.* occlusion.

octava, *f* (mus.) octave.

octubre, *m.* October.

ocular, *a* ocular.—*testigo o.*, eye witness.—*m.* eyepiece.—**oculista,** *mf* oculist.

ocultar, *vt* to hide, conceal.—**oculto,** *a.* hidden, concealed; occult.

ocupación, *f* occupation; employment, trade, business.—**ocupado,** *a.* occupied, busy, engaged.—**ocupante,** *mf.* occupant.—**ocupar,** *vt* to occupy; to take possession of, to hold (a job); to employ; to engage the attention.—*vr* **(en** or **de)** to busy oneself (with), to be engaged (in), devote oneself (to); to pay attention (to).

ocurrencia, *f* occurrence, incident; notion; witticism.—**ocurrente,** *a.* occurring, humorous, witty.—**ocurrir,** *vi.* to occur, happen.—*vr.* to occur (to one); to strike one (as an idea)

oda, *f.* ode.

odiar, *vt.* to hate.—**odio,** *m.* hatred.—**odioso,** *a.* odious, hateful, revolting.

odisea, *f.* odyssey.

odre, *m.* wine skin; (coll.) drunkard.

oeste, *m.* west; west wind.

ofender, *vt.* to offend; to make angry.—*vr.* to become angry; to take offense.—**ofensa,** *f.* offense.—**ofensivo,** *a.* offensive; attacking.—*f.* offensive.—**ofensor,** *n.* & *a.* offender; offending.

oferta, *f.* offer; offering.—*o. y demanda*, supply and demand.

oficial, *a.* official.—*mf.* officer, official; skilled worker; clerk.—**oficialidad,** *f.* (mil.) body of officers.—**oficiar,** *vi.* (eccl.) to officiate, minister; to notify officially.—*o. de*, to act as.—**oficina,** *f.* office; bureau; workshop.—**oficinesco,** *a.* departmental, office.—**oficinista,** *mf.* clerk, employee; office worker.—**oficio,** *m.* employ, work or occupation, vocation; function; official letter; trade or business.—*pl.* (eccl.) office, service.—*de o.*, officially; by trade, by occupation or profession.—**oficioso,** *a.* diligent; officious, meddlesome; useful, fruitful; semi-official, unofficial.

ofrecer, *vti.* [3] to offer; to promise; to show.—*vri.* to offer, occur, present itself; to offer oneself.—*¿se le ofrece algo?* what do you want? may I help you?—**ofrecimiento,** *m.* offer, offering.—**ofrenda,** *f.* offering, gift—**ofrendar,** *vt* to present offerings.

oftamólogo, *n.* oculist.

ogro, *m.* ogre, fabulous monster.

oído, *m.* sense of hearing; ear.—*al o.*, whispering, confidentially.—*dar oídos*, to lend an ear.—*de o.*, by ear.—*de oídas*, by hearsay.—**oír,** *vti.* [28] to hear, to listen; to attend (as lectures).—*o. decir*, to hear (it said) —*o. hablar de*, to hear of.

ojal, *m.* buttonhole; loop.

¡ojalá! *interj.* God grant! would to God! I wish.

ojeada, *f* glance, glimpse.—**ojear,** *vt.* to eye, look at, stare at; to startle, frighten.—**ojera,** *f.* circle under the eye.—**ojeriza,** *f* spite, grudge, ill-will.—**ojeroso,** *a.* haggard, with circles under the eyes.—**ojete,** *m.* (sew.) eyelet.—**ojo,** *m.* eye; eye of a needle; hole; arch of a bridge.—*a los ojos de*, in the presence of.—*a ojos cerrados*, blindly, without reflection.—*costar un o.*, to cost a fortune.—*en un abrir y cerrar de ojos*, in the twinkling of an eye.—*o. avizor*, sharp lookout.—*o de agua*,

spring (of water).—*o. de la cerradura,* keyhole.—*interj.* take notice!
look out!

ola, *f.* wave, billow.—**oleada,** *f.* big
wave; surge, swell of the sea; surg-
ing of a crowd.

oleaginoso, *a.* oily; unctuous.

oleaje, *m.* continuous movement of
waves.

óleo, *m.* oil; extreme unction; holy oil.
—*al ó.,* in oil colors.—**oleoso,** *a.* oily.

oler, *vti.* [28] to smell, scent.—*vii.* to
smell; to smack of.—**olfatear,** *vt.* &
vi. to smell, scent, sniff.—**olfato,** *m.*
sense of smell.—**oliente,** *a.* smelling.
—*mal o.,* (coll.) smelly.

olimpíada, *f.* Olympic games.—**olímpico,** *a.* Olympic.

oliva, *f.* olive; olive tree.—**olivar,** *m.*
olive grove, yard.—**olivo,** *m.* olive
tree.

olmo, *m.* elm tree.

olor, *m.* smell, fragrance; odor; suspicion, smack.—**oloroso,** *a.* fragrant;
(coll.) smelly.

olvidadizo, *a.* forgetful, short of
memory.—**olvidar,** *vt.* to forget.—
vr. to be forgotten, to forget.—
olvido, *m.* forgetfulness; oversight;
oblivion.—*echar al o.* or *en o.,* to
forget; to cast into oblivion.

olla, *f.* pot, kettle.—*o. de grillos,*
great confusion, pandemonium.—*o.
exprés,* pressure cooker.

ombligo, *m.* navel.

ominoso, *a.* ominous, foreboding

omisión, *f* omission; carelessness,
neglect.—**omiso,** *ppi* of OMITIR.—*a.*
neglectful, remiss—**omitir,** *vti* [49]
to omit.

ómnibus, *m* omnibus, stagecoach

omnipotencia, *f* omnipotence.—**omnipotente,** *a.* omnipotent.

onda, *f* wave; ripple—**ondear,** *vi.*
to wave, ripple, undulate; to flicker.
—**ondulación,** *f.* wave, or wavy
motion.—**ondulado,** *a.* undulated,
rippled; scalloped, wavy; corrugated.—**ondulante,** *a* waving, undu
lating; rolling.—**ondular,** *vt.* to
undulate, to ripple

oneroso, *a.* burdensome onerous.

onomástico, *a* onomastic, nominal
m. saint's day, name day.

onza, *f* ounce See Table.

opaco, *a.* opaque, dark; dull

ópalo, *m* opal

opción, *f* option, choice; right.
opcional, *a.* optional

ópera, *f.* opera.

operación, *f* operation; process.—
operar, *vt.* to operate; (surg.) to
operate on.—*vi.* to operate, act,
work.—**operario,** *n.* workman
(-woman); operator.

opereta, *f.* operetta, light opera.

opinar, *vi.* to be of the opinion.—
opinión, *f.* opinion.

opio, *m.* opium.

opíparo, *a.* sumptuous (of a meal).

oponente, *mf.* & *a.* opponent.—**oponer,**
vti. [32-49] to oppose, place against
—*vri.* to oppose, resist; to act
against; to be opposed to; to compete.

oporto, *m.* port wine.

oportunidad, *f.* opportunity; timeli-
ness.—**oportunismo,** *m.* (pol.) op-
portunism.—**oportunista,** *mf.* & *a.*
(pol.) opportunist; opportunistic.—
oportuno, *a.* opportune, timely.

oposición, *f.* opposition, clash; competition for official position.—**oposicio-
nista,** *mf.* & *a.* (pol.) oppositionist.
—**opositor,** *n.* opponent; competitor
(for a position).

opresión, *f.* oppression.—**opresivo,** *a.*
oppressive.—**opresor,** *n.* oppressor.—
oprimir, *vt* to oppress.

optar, *vi.* (**por**) to choose, select.—
optativo, *a.* optional.

óptica, *f.* optics.—**óptico,** *a.* optic(al).
—*n.* optician.

optimismo, *m.* optimism.—**optimista,**
mf. & *a.* optimist; optimistic.

óptimo, *a.* very best.

opuesto, *ppi.* of OPONER.—*a.* opposite.

opulencia, *f.* opulence.—**opulento,** *a.*
opulent, wealthy.

oquedad, *f.* hollow, cavity.

ora, *conj* whether; either; or.

oración, *f.* (gram.) sentence; speech;
prayer, dusk

oráculo, *m.* oracle

orador, *n.* orator, speaker.—**oral,** *a.*
oral, vocal.—**orar,** *vi.* to pray

orangután, *m* orang-utan

orate, *mf.* lunatic, crazy person.

oratoria, *f.* oratory, eloquent speak
ing.—**oratorio,** *a.* oratorical.—*m*
oratory, chapel; (mus.) oratorio.

orbe, *m* orb, sphere; the earth.

órbita, *f.* orbit; eye socket.

orden, *m* order, orderliness, tidiness;
class, group; proportion, relation.
—*f.* order, command; (com) order;
religious or honorary order.—*pl*
orders, instructions.—**ordenación,** *f*
arrangement; disposition; array;
ordination.—**ordenamiento,** *m.* or-
daining, regulating.—**ordenanza,** *f.*
method, order; statute, ordinance,
military regulation; ordination.—*m.*
(mil.) orderly—**ordenar,** *vt* to arrange, put in order; to order, command, to ordain—*vr* (eccl.) to be
ordained.

ordeñar, *vt* to milk.

ordinal, *m.* & *a.* ordinal;

ordinariez, *f.* rough manners, ordinariness.—**ordinario,** *a.* ordinary, usual; coarse, unrefined.—*n.* unrefined person.—*de o.,* usually, ordinarily, regularly.

orear, *vt.* to air, expose to the air.—*vr.* to take an airing.

oreja, *f.* ear (external); flap of a shoe; small flap; flange.—*aguzar las orejas,* to prick up one's ears.—*bajar las orejas,* to come down from one's high horse.—**orejera,** *f.* ear muff, earcap.—**orejudo,** *a.* flap-eared, long-eared.

oreo, *m.* airing; ventilation.

orfanato, *m.* orphan asylum, orphanage.—**orfandad,** *f.* orphanage (the state of being an orphan).

orfebre, *mf.* goldsmith, silversmith.—**orfebrería,** *f.* gold or silver work.

orfeón, *m.* glee club; choral society.

orgánico, *a.* organic.—**organillo,** *m.* hand organ, barrel organ.—**organismo,** *m.* organism; organization, association.—**organista,** *mf.* (mus.) organist.—**organización,** *f.* organization; arrangement.—**organizar,** *vti.* [a] to organize, set up; to arrange. —**órgano,** *m.* (physiol., & mus.) organ; instrument, agency.

orgasmo, *m.* orgasm.

orgía, *f.* orgy.

orgullo, *m.* pride; haughtiness.—**orgulloso,** *a.* proud; haughty; conceited.

orientación, *f.* orientation; bearings.—**oriental,** *a.* oriental, eastern.—*mf.* Oriental.—**orientar,** *vt.* to orientate, orient.—*vr.* to find one's way about, get one's bearings.—**oriente,** *m.* east, orient; luster (in pearls)

orificación, *f.* (dent.) gold filling.

orificio, *m.* orifice, small hole, opening.

origen, *m.* origin; source; beginning. —**original,** *a.* original, new; quaint, odd.—*m.* original, first copy; (print.) manuscript.—**originalidad,** *f* originality.—**originar,** *vt* to originate, create; to start—*vr.* to originate, arise, spring.—**originario,** *a.* originating; native; derived.

orilla, *f.* border, margin; edge; bank (of a river); shore; sidewalk.

orín, *m.* rust.—*pl.* urine.—**orina,** *f* urine.—**orinal,** *m* urinal; chamber pot.—**orinar,** *vt.* & *vi.* to urinate

oriundo, *a.* native, coming (from).

orla, *f.* fringe, trimming; matting; ornamental border.—**orlar,** *vt.* to border with an edging.

ornamentación, *f.* ornamentation.—**ornamentar,** *vt* to adorn, decorate. —**ornamento,** *m.* ornament; decoration, accomplishment.—**ornar,** *vt* to adorn, embellish, garnish.—**ornato,** *m.* ornament, decoration, embellishment.

ornitología, *f.* ornithology.

oro, *m.* gold; gold color.—*pl.* diamonds (in Spanish cards).

orondo, *a.* pompous, showy; hollow.

oropel, *m.* tinsel; brass foil; glitter.

oropéndola, *f.* golden oriole.

orquesta, *f.* orchestra.—**orquestación,** *f.* orchestration.—**orquestar,** *vt.* to orchestrate.

orquídea, *f.* orchid.

ortiga, *f.* nettle.

ortodoxia, *f.* orthodoxy.—**ortodoxo,** *a.* orthodox.

ortografía, *f.* orthography, spelling.—**ortográfico,** *a.* orthographical.

oruga, *f.* (entom.) caterpillar; (bot.) rocket.

orzuelo, *m.* (med.) sty.

os, *pron.* you; to you; yourselves.

osadía, *f.* audacity, daring.—**osado,** *a.* daring, bold, audacious.—**osar,** *vi.* to dare, venture; to outdare.

oscilación, *f.* oscillation.—**oscilar,** *vi.* to oscillate.—**oscilatorio,** *a.* oscillatory.

oscuras.—*a o.,* in the dark.—**oscurecer,** *vti.* [3] to obscure, darken; to dim; to tarnish; (art) to shade.—*vii.* to grow dark.—*vri.* to become dark; to cloud over.—**oscurecimiento,** *m.* darkening; blackout.—**oscuridad,** *f.* obscurity; darkness; gloominess.—**oscuro,** *a.* obscure; dark; gloomy; dim

óseo, *a.* bone, bony

osezno *m.* whelp or cub of a bear

oso, *m.* (zool.) bear.—*o. blanco,* polar bear.—*o. gris,* grizzly bear. *o. hormiguero,* anteater.—*o. marino,* fur seal, seal.

ostensible, *a.* ostensible, apparent.

ostentación, *f.* ostentation.—**ostentar,** *vt.* to make a show of, exhibit. —*vi.* to boast, brag; to show off.—**ostentoso,** *a.* sumptuous, magnificent.

ostión, *m.* large oyster.—**ostra,** *f* oyster.—**ostracismo,** *m.* ostracism.

otear, *vt.* to observe, examine, pry into.—**otero,** *m.* hill, knoll.

otoñal, *a.* autumnal.—**otoño,** *m* autumn, fall.

otorgamiento, *m.* grant, granting; (law) executing an instrument.—**otorgar,** *vti.* [b] to consent, agree to; (law) to grant

otro, *a.* another, other.—*pron.* other one, another one.

ovación, *f.* ovation.—**ovacionar,** *vt.* to give an ovation to; to acclaim.

oval, ovalado, *a.* oval.—**óvalo,** *m.* oval

ovario, *m.* ovary.

ovas, *f. pl.* roe.

oveja, *f.* sheep.—**ovejuno,** *a.* pertaining to sheep.

overol, *m.,* **overoles,** *m. pl.* (Am.) overalls.

ovillar, *vt.* to wind (thread) in a ball or skein.—*vr.* to curl up.—**ovillo,** *m.* skein, ball of yarn.

oxiacanta, *f.* hawthorn.

oxidar, *vt. & vr.* to oxidize; to rust.—**óxido,** *m.* oxide; rust.

oxígeno, *m.* oxygen.

oyente, *mf.* hearer.—*pl.* audience.

ozono, *m.* ozone.

P

pabilo, *m.* wick (of candle); burnt end of wick.

pábulo, *m.* encouragement; nourishment, food.—*dar p.,* to give basis for (gossip); to stimulate (gossip).

paca, *f.* bale of goods.

pacana, *f.* pecan nut; pecan tree.

pacer, *vii.* [3] to pasture; to graze.

paciencia, *f.* patience.—**paciente,** *a.* patient.—*mf.* patient, sick person.—**pacienzudo,** *a.* long-suffering.

pacificador, *n.* pacifier, peacemaker.—**pacificar,** *vti.* [d] to pacify, appease.—*vri.* to become calm.—**pacífico,** *a.* peaceful, pacific.—**pacifismo,** *m.* pacifism.—**pacifista,** *mf. & a.* pacifist; pacifistic.

paco, *m.* alpaca; sniper.

pacotilla, *f.* (com.) venture.—*de p.,* of poor or inferior quality.

pactar, *vt.* to make an agreement, contract; to stipulate.—**pacto,** *m.* agreement, pact; treaty.

pachorra, *f.* sluggishness, slowness.

padecer, *vti.* [3] to suffer.—*vii.* (de) to suffer (from).—**padecimiento,** *m.* suffering; ailment.

padrastro, *m.* stepfather.—**padre,** *m.* father; priest; principal author.—*pl.* parents, father and mother; ancestors.—*P. Eterno,* our Father, God Almighty.—**padrenuestro,** *m.* Lord's Prayer.—**padrino,** *m.* godfather; second (in a duel); best man; patron, sponsor.

paella, *f.* dish of rice with meat, chicken and shellfish.

paga, *f.* payment; wages, salary; pay.—**pagadero,** *a.* payable.—**pagador,** *n.* payer; paymaster; paying teller.—**pagaduría,** *f.* paymaster's office.

paganismo, *m.* paganism, heathenism.—**pagano,** *n. & a.* pagan, heathen.—*n.* sucker, dupe.

pagar, *vti.* [b] to pay; to pay for; to requite.—*p. contra entrega,* C.O.D.—*p. el pato,* to get the blame, be the scapegoat.—*p. una visita,* to visit, return a call.—*vri.* (de) to be pleased (with); to boast (of); to be conceited (about).—**pagaré,** *m.* (com.) promissory note; I.O.U.

página, *f.* page (of a book); folio.—**paginar,** *vt.* to page (a book, etc.), paginate.

pago, *m.* payment; requital.—*a.* (coll.) paid.

país, *m.* country, nation; land, region.—*del p.,* domestic, national.—**paisaje,** *m.* landscape.—**paisano,** *a.* from the same country.—*n.* fellow countryman(-woman); civilian; peasant.

paja, *f.* straw; chaff, trash.—*un quítame allá esas pajas,* an insignificant reason; a jiffy.—**pajar,** *m.* barn, straw loft.

pajarera, *f.* aviary; large bird cage.—**pajarería,** *f.* bird shop.—**pájaro,** *m.* bird; shrewd, sly fellow.—*p. carpintero,* woodpecker.—*p. de cuenta,* person of importance, big shot; shrewd, sly fellow.—*p. mosca,* hummingbird.—**pajarraco,** *m.* large bird; (coll.) shady character.

paje, *m.* page, valet.

pajizo, *a.* made of straw; straw-colored.

pajonal, *m.* (Am.) place abounding in tall grass.

pala, *f.* shovel; spade; scoop; trowel; blade of an oar; blade of the rudder; artifice; (coll.) fix, thrown game.

palabra, *f.* word.—*interj.* honestly! my word of honor!—*bajo p.,* on (one's) word.—*de p.,* by word of mouth.—*p. de matrimonio,* promise of marriage.—*pedir la p.,* to ask for the floor (at a meeting).—**palabrería,** *f.* wordiness, palaver, empty talk, verbosity, wind.—**palabrota,** *f.* coarse expression.

palacio, *m.* palace.

paladar, *m.* palate; taste, relish.—**paladear,** *vt.* to taste with pleasure, to relish.—**paladeo,** *m.* act of tasting or relishing.

paladín, *m.* champion.

palafrenero, *m.* stableboy, groom, ostler.

palanca, *f.* lever; bar, crowbar; pole for carrying a weight.

palangana, *f.* washbowl, basin.

palanqueta, *f.* small lever; (Am.) dumbbell.

palco, *m.* (theat.) box, loge; stand with seats.

palear, *vt.* (Am.) to shovel.

palenque, *m.* palisade; arena.

paleta, *f.* (cooking) ladle; (anat.) shoulder blade; (mason.) trowel; blade; (art) palette; little shovel.—

paletada, *f.* trowelful.—**paletilla**, *f.* shoulder blade.

palidecer, *vii.* [3] to pale, turn pale. —**palidez**, *f.* paleness, pallor.— **pálido**, *a.* pale, pallid, pasty.

palillo, *m.* toothpick; drumstick; small stick.—*pl.* castanets.

palio, *m.* cloak, mantle; pallium, pall.

palique, *m.* (coll.) chitchat, small talk.

paliza, *f.* beating, thrashing.

palizada, *f.* palisade; (fort.) stockade.

palma, *f.* palm tree; leaf of a palm tree; palm of the hand; emblem of victory or martyrdom.—*pl.* applause.—*ganar*, or *llevarse la p.*, to carry the day; to win the prize.— **palmada**, *f.* pat; clapping; slap. —**palmar**, *m.* palm grove.

palmario, *a.* clear, obvious, evident.

palmatoria, *f.* small candlestick.

palmear, *vt.* to clap (the hands); to pat.

palmera, *f.* palm tree.—**palmiche**, *m.* fruit of a palm tree.

palmo, *m.* span, measure of length. —*p. a p.*, foot by foot.—**palmotear**, *vi.* to clap hands.—**palmoteo**, *m.* hand clapping.

palo, *m.* stick; pole; timber, log; wood (material); (Am.) tree; blow with a stick; suit at cards; (Am.) a drink; (naut.) mast.—*pl.* blows, cudgeling.—*dar (de) palos*, to thrash, club, beat.

paloma, *f.* pigeon; dove; meek, mild person.—*p. mensajera*, carrier pigeon. —*p. torcaz*, wild pigeon.—**palomo**, *m.* cock pigeon.

palpable, *a.* palpable, obvious, evident.—**palpar**, *vt.* to feel (of); to touch; to see as self-evident; (med.) to palpate.—*vi.* to feel by touching; to grope in the dark.

palpitación, *f.* palpitation; throbbing.—**palpitante**, *a.* vibrating, palpitating.—**palpitar**, *vi.* to palpitate, throb, quiver.

palúdico, *a.* malarial.—**paludismo**, *m.* malaria.

pampa, *f.* pampa, prairie.—*estar a la p.*, (Am.) to be outdoors.—**pampeano, pampero**, *a.* of or from the pampas.—*n.* pampa man (woman).

pamplina, *f.* (coll.) trifle, frivolity.

pan, *m.* bread; loaf; wheat; leaf (of gold, silver).—*pl.* breadstuffs.— *p. integral*, whole-wheat bread.— *llamar al p. p. y al vino vino*, to call a spade a spade.

pana, *f.* corduroy, plush.

panadería, *f.* bakery.—**panadero**, *n.* baker.

panal, *m.* honeycomb; hornet's nest; a sweetmeat.

panameño, *n. & a.* Panamanian.

panamericano, *a.* Pan-American.

pandear, *vt.*, *vi. & vr.* to bend, warp, bulge out.—**pandeo**, *m.* bulge, bulging.

pandereta, *f.*, **pandero**, *m.* tambourine.

pandilla, *f.* gang, band.—**pandillero**, *n.* (Am.) gangster.

panecillo, *m.* roll (bread).

panel, *m.* (art, elec.) panel.

panetela, *f.* (Am.) sponge cake.

panfleto, *m.* tract, pamphlet; lampoon; libel.

paniaguado, *n.* protégé, henchman.

pánico, *m. & a.* panic(ky).

panocha, *f.* ear of grain.

panqué, panqueque, *m.* (Am.) pancake; cupcake.

pantaletas, *f. pl.* (Am.) panties.— **pantalón**, *m.* (gen. *pl.*) trousers; panties; slacks.—*p. corto*, shorts; Bermuda shorts.—**pantaloncitos**, *m. pl.* (Am.) panties.

pantalla, *f.* lamp shade; screen.

pantano, *m.* swamp, marsh, bog.— **pantanoso**, *a.* swampy, marshy, miry; full of difficulties.

pantera, *f.* panther.

pantomima, *f.* pantomime.

pantorrilla, *f.* calf (of leg).

pantufla, *f.* slipper.

panza, *f.* belly, paunch.—**panzada**, *f.* (coll.) bellyful.—**panzón, panzudo**, *a. & n.* big-bellied, paunchy (person).

pañal, *m.* diaper.—*estar en pañales*, to have little knowledge or experience.—**paño**, *m.* cloth, woolen material; wash cloth.—*pl.* clothes, garments.—*paños calientes*, half measures.—*paños menores*, underclothes.—**pañoleta**, *f.* triangular shawl.—**pañolón**, *m.* large square shawl.—**pañuelo**, *m.* handkerchief, kerchief.

papa, *m.* pope.—*f.* potato; (Am.) easy job; (coll.) food, grub; lie, fib.

papá, *m.* (coll.) dad, daddy, papa, pop.

papada, *f.* double chin; dewlap.

papagayo, *m.* macaw.

papal, *a.* papal.

papalote, *m.* (Am.) kite.

papamoscas, *m.* flycatcher, flyeater; (coll.) ninny.—**papanatas**, *m.* (coll.) simpleton, dolt, ninny.

paparrucha, *f.* (coll.) fake, humbug; nonsense, silliness.

papaya, *f.* papaya.

papel, *m.* paper; piece of paper; document; (theat.) part, role; char-

acter, figure.—*hacer buen* (*o mal*) *p.*, to cut a good (or bad) figure). —*p. de cartas*, stationery.—*p. de estraza*; brown wrapping paper.—*p. de inodoro*, or *p. higiénico*, toilet paper.—*p. de lija*, sandpaper.—*p. de seda*, tissue paper.—*p. secante*, blotting paper.—**papeleo**, *m.* red tape.—**papelera**, *f.* paper case; paper mill. —**papelería**, *f.* stationery; stationery shop.—**papelero**, *n.* paper maker; stationer.—**papeleta**, *f.* card, ticket, slip.—**papelucho**, *m.* worthless paper.

papera, *f.* goiter.—*pl.* mumps.

papilla, *f.* pap; guile, deceit.—*hacerse p.*, to break into small pieces.

paquete, *m.* packet, package; bundle of papers; (coll.) dandy, dude.

par, *a.* even (number).—*m.* pair, couple; peer; (elec.) cell.—*a la p.*, jointly, equally; (com.) par; at par; (horse racing) in a dead heat. —*de p. en p.*, (of a door, etc.) wide open.—*sin p.*, peerless, incomparable.

para, *prep.* for, to, in order to, toward, to the end that.—*estar p.*, to be on the point of, about to.—*p. mi capote*, to myself.—*¿p. qué?* what for?—*p. que*, so that, in order that.—*sin qué ni p. qué*, without rhyme or reason.

parabién, *m.* congratulation, felicitation, greeting.

parábola, *f.* parable; (geom.) parabola.—**parabólico**, *a.* parabolic.

parabrisa, *m.* windshield.

paracaídas, *m.* parachute.—**paracaidista**, *mf.* parachutist; (mil.) paratrooper.

parachoques, *m.* (auto) bumper.

parada, *f.* stop (as a train, etc.); (mil.) halt, halting; parade; review; stakes, bet; (fencing) parry.—*p. en firme* or *en seco*, dead stop.—**paradero**, *m.* halting place; (Am.) (R.R.) depot, station; whereabouts.

parado, *a.* unoccupied; (of a clock) stopped; shut down (as a factory); (Am.) standing.—*a. & n.* unemployed.

paradoja, *f.* paradox.

parafina, *f.* paraffin.

paraguas, *m.* umbrella.

paraguayo, *n. & a.* Paraguayan.

paragüero, *n.* umbrella maker, repairer or seller; (coll.) Sunday driver.—*m.* umbrella stand.

paraíso, *m.* paradise; heaven; (theat., coll.) upper gallery.—*p. terrenal*, Paradise, garden of Eden.

paraje, *m.* place, spot.

paralela, *f.* parallel line.—**paralelo**, *a.* parallel; similar.—*m.* parallel, resemblance; (geog.) parallel.

parálisis, *f.* paralysis.—**paralítico**, *n. & a.* paralytic; paralyzed.—**paralización**, *f.* paralyzation; (com.) stagnation.—**paralizado**, *a.* (com.) dull, stagnant.—**paralizar**, *vti.* [a] to paralyze; to impede, stop.

páramo, *m.* bleak plateau, moor; desert.

parangón, *m.* comparison.—**parangonar**, *vt.* to compare.

paraninfo, *m.* assembly hall in a university.

parapeto, *m.* (mil.) parapet.

parar, *vt.* to stop, detain; (fencing) to parry; (Am.) to stand, place in upright position.—*p. mientes en*, to consider carefully.—*vi.* to stop, halt; to come to an end; (en) to become, end (in); to stop or stay (at).—*ir a p. a* or *en*, to become, end in, finally to get to.—*vr.* to stop, halt; (Am.) to stand up.—*sin pararse*, without delay, instantly.—**pararrayos**, *m.* lightning rod.

parásito, *m. & a.* parasite; parasitic.

parasol, *m.* parasol.

parcela, *f.* parcel of land, lot.—**parcelar**, *vt.* to divide into lots.

parcial, *a.* partial.—*mf.* follower, partisan.—**parcialidad**, *f.* partiality, bias; party, faction.

parco, *a.* sparing, scanty; sober, moderate.

parche, *m.* patch, mending; (pharm.) plaster, sticking plaster; (mil.) drum-head; drum.

pardal, *m.* (ornith.) sparrow, linnet; crafty fellow.

pardo, *a.* brown; dark gray.—*n.* (Am.) mulatto.—**pardusco**, *a.* grayish, grizzly.

parear, *vt.* to match, mate, pair.

parecer, *vii.* [3] to appear, show up; to seem, look like.—*al p.*, apparently.—*vri.* to look alike, resemble. —*m.* opinion, thinking; look, mien; appearance.—**parecido**, *a.* (a) resembling, like, similar (to).—*bien* (*mal*) *p.*, good-(bad-) looking.—*m.* resemblance, likeness.

pared, *f.* wall.—*entre cuatro paredes*, confined; imprisoned.—*p. maestra*, main wall.—*p. medianera*, partition wall.

pareja, *f.* pair, couple; match; dancing partner.—*parejas mixtas*, (games) mixed doubles.—**parejo**, *a.* equal, even; smooth; (horse racing) neck and neck.

parentela, *f.* kinsfolk, relatives.—**parentesco**, *m.* kindred, relationship.

paréntesis, *m.* parenthesis.—*entre p.*, by the bye, by the way.

pargo, m. red snapper.

paria, *m.* outcast.

paridad, *f.* parity, equality.

pariente, *n.* relative, relation.

parihuela, *f.* handbarrow; litter; stretcher.

parir, *vt. & vi.* to give birth.—*poner a p.,* to constrain, force (a person).

parlamentar, *vi.* to parley; to converse.—**parlamentario,** *a.* parliamentary, parliamentarian.—*n.* member of parliament; envoy to a parley.—**parlamento,** *m.* parliament; legislative body; parley.

parlanchín, *n. & a.* chatterer, jabberer, talker; chattering, jabbering, talkative.—**parlero,** *a.* loquacious, talkative; chirping (birds); babbling (brooks).—**parlotear,** *vi.* to prattle, prate, chatter.—**parloteo,** *m.* chat, prattle, talk.

paro, *m.* lockout.—*p. forzoso,* unemployment.

parótida, *f.* parotid gland.—*pl.* mumps.

parpadear, *vi.* to wink; to blink, twinkle.—**parpadeo,** *m.* winking; blinking, twinkling.—**párpado,** *m.* eyelid.

parque, *m.* park; (Am.) ammunition. —**parquear,** *vt. & vi.* (Am.) to park (auto).

parra, *f.* grapevine.

párrafo, *m.* paragraph.

parranda, *f.* revel, carousal, spree.— **parrandear,** *vi.* to go on a spree. —**parrandero,** *a.* fond of carousing. —*n.* carouser, reveler.

parricida, *mf.* parricide (person).— **parricidio,** *m.* parricide (act).

parrilla, *f.* grill, broiler; toaster; (furnace) grate.

párroco, *m.* parish priest.—**parroquia,** *f.* parish; parish church; (com.) customers.—**parroquial,** *a.* parochial. —*f.* parochial church.—**parroquiano,** *n.* parishioner; (com.) customer, client.

parsimonia, *f.* moderation, calmness.

parte, *f.* part; portion; share; place; (law) party; (theat.) role.—*pl.* (coll.) the genitals.—*dar p.,* to inform, notify.—*de algún tiempo a esta p.,* for some time past.—*de mi p.,* for my part; on my side; in my name.—*de p. a p.,* from side to side, through.—*de p. de,* from, in the name of; in behalf of.—*en alguna p.,* somewhere.—*en ninguna p.,* nowhere.—*en todas partes,* everywhere.—*la mayor p.,* most.— *la tercera (cuarta, etc.) p.,* onethird (-fourth, etc.).—*p. de la oración,* part of speech.—*por mi p.,* as for me.—*por otra p.,* on the other hand.—*m.* communication, dispatch,

report, telegram, telephone message. —*adv.* in part, partly.

partera, *f.* midwife.

partición, *f.* division, partition, distribution.—**participación,** *f.* participation, share; communication; (com.) copartnership.—**participante,** *mf. & a.* participant, sharer; notifier; participating, sharing; notifying.—**participar,** *vt.* to notify, communicate.—*vi.* (de) to share (in); (en) to participate, take part (in). —**partícipe,** *mf.* participator, participant.—**participio,** *m.* participle.

partícula, *f.* particle.

particular, *a.* particular, peculiar, special; personal; private; individual; odd, extraordinary.—*m.* private person, individual; topic, point.—*en p.,* particularly.—**particularidad,** *f.* particularity, peculiarity; detail.

partida, *f.* departure; item in an account; entry; game; band, gang; (com.) shipment, consignment.—*p. de bautismo, (matrimonio, defunción),* certificate of birth (marriage, death).—*p. de campo,* picnic.—**partidario,** *n.* supporter; follower, retainer.—**partido,** *a.* divided; broken. —*m.* (pol.) party; advantage, profit; game, contest, match; odds, handicap; territorial division or district.—*sacar p. de,* to turn to advantage.—*tomar p.,* to take sides. —**partir,** *vt.* to split; to divide; to break, crush, crack.—*vi.* to depart, leave.—*a p. de,* starting from.—*vr.* to break; to become divided.

partitura, *f.* (mus.) score.

parto, *m.* childbirth.

parvedad, *f.* smallness, minuteness; light breakfast.

párvulo, *a.* very small; innocent; humble, low.—*n.* child.

pasa, *f.* raisin; (Am.) kinky hair of Negroes; (naut.) narrow channel.

pasable, *a.* passable, able to be traversed, crossed, etc.—**pasada,** *f.* passage, passing; pace, step.—*de p.,* on the way; hastily.—*mala p.,* (coll.) bad turn, mean trick.—**pasadero,** *a.* supportable, sufferable; passable, so-so, tolerably good.—*m.* stepping stone.—**pasadizo,** *m.* passageway, aisle; alley.—**pasado,** *a.* past; last (day, week, etc.); stale; (of fruit) spoiled; antiquated, out of date or fashion.—*p. mañana,* day after tomorrow.—*m.* past.—**pasador,** *m.* door bolt; window fastener; pin; woman's brooch.

pasaje, *m.* passage, passageway; fare; number of passengers in a ship; (naut.) strait, narrows.—**pasajero,** *a.*

passing, transient, transitory; provisional.—*n.* traveler, passenger.

pasamano, *m.* handrail, banister.

pasaporte, *m.* passport.

pasar, *vt.* to pass; to take across, carry over; to pass, hand; to go to, in, by, across, over, around, beyond, through; to filter; to surpass; to tolerate; to endure; to pass, spend (as time).—*p. a cuchillo,* to put to the sword.—*p. el rato,* to kill time.—*p. (la) lista,* to call the roll.—*pasarlo bien (mal),* to have a good (bad) time.—*p. por alto,* to overlook.—*p. por las armas,* to shoot, execute.—*¿qué (le) pasa?* what's the matter with (him)?—*vi.* to pass; to live; to get along; to pass, happen, turn out.—*p. de,* to exceed.—*p. de largo,* to pass by without stopping; to skim through.—*p. por,* to be considered as, to be taken for.—*p. sin,* to do without.—*vr.* to become spoiled, tainted or stale; to slip from one's memory; to go too far; to exceed; to be overcooked.

pasarela, *f.* gangplank; (theat.) runway.

pasatiempo, *m.* amusement, pastime.

pascua, *f.* Passover; Easter; Christmas; Twelfth-night; Pentecost.—*estar como una p.* or *unas pascuas,* to be as merry as a lark.—*felices Pascuas,* Merry Christmas.—*P. de Navidad,* Christmas.—*P. florida,* or *P. de Resurrección,* Easter.

pase, *m.* pass, permit; (fencing) thrust.

paseante, *mf.* walker, stroller.—**pasear,** *vi. & vr.* to take a walk; to ride, drive or sail for pleasure; to walk up and down, pace.—*vt.* to take out to walk (as a child).—**paseo,** *m.* walk; promenade; stroll; drive; ride; boulevard; parade.—*dar un p.,* to take a walk, ride, etc.—*echar* or *enviar a p.,* to dismiss or reject rudely or without ceremony.

pasillo, *m.* passage, corridor; aisle; short step.

pasión, *f.* passion.

pasivo, *a.* passive; inactive.—*m.* (com.) liabilities.

pasmar, *vt.* to stupefy; to stun; to amaze, astound.—*vr.* to wonder, marvel; (of plants) to freeze.—**pasmo,** *m.* astonishment; wonder, awe.—**pasmoso,** *a.* marvelous, wonderful.

paso, *m.* pace, step; pass, passage; passing; gait, walk; footstep.—*apretar el p.,* to hasten.—*de p.,* in passing; on the way.—*p. a nivel,* (RR.) grade crossing.—*p. de tortuga,* snail's pace.—*prohibido el p.,* no trespassing, keep out.—*salir del p.,* to get out of the difficulty; to get by.—*adv.* softly, gently.

pasquín, *m.* lampoon; anonymous satiric public poster.—**pasquinar,** *vt.* to ridicule, lampoon, satirize.

pasta, *f.* paste; dough; pie crust; noodles; board binding (for books).—*buena p.,* good disposition.

pastadero, *m.* pasture, grazing field.—**pastar,** *vi.* to pasture, graze.—*vt.* to lead (cattle) to graze.

pastel, *m.* pie; combine, plot; (art) pastel.—**pastelear,** *vi.* (coll.) (pol.) make a deal.—**pastelería,** *f.* pastry shop; pastry.—**pastelero,** *n.* pastry cook; (pol.) deal-maker.

pasteurizar, *vti.* [a] to pasteurize.

pastilla, *f.* tablet, lozenge, pastille, drop; cake (of soap).

pastizal, *m.* pasture ground.—**pasto,** *m.* pasture, grazing; grass for feed; pasture ground; food.—*a p.,* abundantly; excessively.—*a todo p.,* freely, abundantly and unrestrictedly.—**pastor,** *n.* shepherd(ess); pastor, clergyman.—**pastoral,** *f.* pastoral; idyl.—*a.* pastoral.—**pastorear,** *vt.* to pasture; to keep, tend (sheep).—**pastoreo,** *m.* pasturing.—**pastoril,** *a.* pastoral.

pastoso, *a.* pasty, soft, mellow, doughy, mushy.

pata, *f.* foot or leg of an animal; leg of a piece of furniture, an instrument, etc.; female duck.—*a* or *en cuatro patas,* on all fours.—*a la p. la llana,* plainly, unaffectedly.—*a p.,* (coll.) on foot.—*estirar la p.,* (coll.) to kick the bucket.—*meter la p.,* to put one's foot in.—*p. de gallina* or *de gallo,* crow's-foot wrinkles.—*patas arriba,* topsy-turvy, heels over head; upside down.—**patada,** *f.* kick.—**patalear,** *vi.* to kick about violently.—**pataleo,** *m.* kicking; pattering.—**pataleta,** *f.* (coll.) fainting fit; convulsion; tantrum.

patata, *f.* potato.

patatús, *m.* (coll.) swoon, fainting fit.

pateadura, *f.,* **pateamiento,** *m.* kicking, stamping of the feet.—**patear,** *vt. & vi.* to kick; to stamp the foot; to tramp.

patentar, *vt.* to patent.—**patente,** *a.* patent, manifest, evident.—*f.* patent; privilege, grant.—**patentizar,** *vti.* [a] to make evident.

paternal, *a.* paternal, fatherly.—**paternidad,** *f.* paternity, fatherhood.—**paterno,** *a.* paternal, fatherly.

patético, *a.* pathetic.—**patetismo,** *m.* dramatic quality; pathos.

patibulario, *a.* harrowing; criminal looking.—**patíbulo,** *m.* gallows.

patidifuso, *a.* (coll.) astounded.

patillas, *f. pl.* sideburns; side whiskers.

patín, *m.* skate; (aer.) skid; small patio; (theat.) orchestra.—*p. de ruedas,* roller skate.—**patinador,** *n.* skater.—**patinaje,** *m.* skating.—**patinar,** *vi.* to skate; (of vehicles) to skid.—**patinazo,** *m.* skid.

patio, *m.* yard, patio, courtyard.

patituerto, *a.* crook-legged, knock-kneed.—**patizambo,** *a.* knock-kneed, bowlegged.

pato, *m.* duck.—*pagar el p.,* to get the blame, be the scapegoat.

patochada, *f.* blunder; nonsense.

patología, *f.* pathology.—**patológico,** *a.* pathological.

patoso, *a.* (coll.) boring; awkward.

patraña, *f.* fabulous story; fake, humbug.

patria, *f.* native country, fatherland.

patrio, *a.* native; home.—**patriota,** *mf.* patriot.—**patriótico,** *a.* patriotic. —**patriotismo,** *m.* patriotism.

patrocinar, *vt.* to sponsor; to protect, favor.—**patrocinio,** *m.* sponsorship, auspices; protection, patronage.—**patrón,** *n.* patron(ess); host(ess); landlord (-lady); patron saint.—*m.* master, boss; pattern; standard; (naut.) skipper.—**patronato,** *m.* board of trustees; employers' association; foundation.—**patrono,** *n.* patron, protector; trustee; employer; patron saint.

patrulla, *f.* patrol; gang, squad.—**patrullar,** *vt.* to patrol.

paulatino, *a.* slow, gradual.

pausa, *f.* pause; rest, repose.—**pausado,** *a.* slow, calm, quiet.—*adv.* slowly.

pauta, *f.* guide lines; standard, rule, pattern.

pava, *f.* turkey hen; (Am.) joke, fun.—*pelar la p.,* to carry on a flirtation.

pavesa, *f.* embers, hot cinders.—*pl.* ashes.

pavimentación, *f.* paving; pavement. —**pavimentar,** *vt.* to pave.—**pavimento,** *m.* pavement.

pavo, *m.* turkey; gobbler.—*p. real,* peacock.—*p. silvestre,* wood grouse. —**pavonearse,** *vr.* to strut, show off.

pavor, *m.* fear, fright.—**pavoroso,** *a.* awful, frightful, terrible.

payasada, *f.* clownish joke or action. —**payaso,** *m.* clown.

paz, *f.* peace.—*en p.,* quits, even.

pazguato, *n.* dolt, simpleton.

peaje, *m.* (bridge, road, etc.) toll.

peana, *f.* pedestal stand; (mech.)

ground plate; step before an altar.

peatón, *m.* pedestrian, walker.

peca, *f.* freckle.

pecado, *m.* sin.—*p. capital, grave,* or *mortal,* deadly or mortal sin.—**pecador,** *n.* & *a.* sinner; sinning.—**pecaminoso,** *a.* sinful.—**pecar,** *vii.* [d] to sin.—*p. de listo,* to be too wise.

pececillo, *m.* minnow, little fish.

pecera, *f.* fishbowl, fish tank; aquarium.

pecoso, *a.* freckled.

peculado, *m.* (law) embezzlement.

peculiar, *a.* peculiar.—**peculiaridad,** *f.* peculiarity.

peculio, *m.* private property.

pechera, *f.* shirt bosom; shirt frill; chest protector; breast strap (of a harness).—**pecho,** *m.* chest, thorax; breast; bosom; teat; courage.— *abrir el p.,* to unbosom oneself.— *dar el p.,* to nurse, suckle; (coll.) to face it out.—*tomar a p.,* to take to heart.—**pechuga,** *f.* breast of a fowl; slope; (coll.) bosom.

pedagogía, *f.* pedagogy.—**pedagógico,** *a.* pedagogical.—**pedagogo,** *n.* pedagogue; teacher; educator.

pedal, *m.* pedal; (mech.) treadle.

pedazo, *m.* piece, fragment, bit.—*a pedazos,* or *en pedazos,* in bits, in fragments.

pedernal, *m.* flint.

pedestal, *m.* pedestal; stand; base.

pedestre, *a.* pedestrian; low, vulgar, common.

pedicuro, *n.* chiropodist.

pedido, *m.* demand, call; (com.) order.—**pedigüeño,** *a.* persistent in begging.—**pedir,** *vti.* [29] to ask for, request, beg, solicit; to demand; to wish, desire; to require; (com.) to order; to ask for in marriage.—*a p. de boca,* just right.—*p. prestado,* to borrow.

pedrada, *f.* throw of a stone; blow or hit with a stone.—**pedrea,** *f.* stone-throwing; stoning; hailstorm.—**pedregal,** *m.* stony ground.—**pedregoso,** *a.* stony, rocky.—**pedrería,** *f.* precious stones; jewelry.—**pedrusco,** *m.* rough piece of stone.

pega, *f.* joining, cementing together; (coll.) jest, practical joke; (ichth.) remora.—**pegajoso,** *a.* sticky; catching, contagious.—**pegar,** *vti.* [b] to stick, glue, cement; to fasten; to post (bills); to sew on; to pin; to patch; to attach; to infect with; to hit, beat, slap.—*no p. los ojos,* not to sleep a wink.—*p. fuego a,* to set fire to.—*p. un tiro,* to shoot.—*vii.* to make an impression on the mind; to join; to be con-

tiguous; to fit, match; to be becoming, fitting, appropriate.—*esa no pega*, (coll.) that won't go.—*vri.* to stick; adhere.—**pegote**, *m.* sticking plaster; coarse patch; sponger.

peina, *f.* = PEINETA.—**peinado**, *m.* hairdo.—**peinador**, *n.* hairdresser.—*m.* dressing gown, wrapper.—**peinar**, *vt.* to comb or dress (the hair); to touch or rub slightly.—**peine**, *m.* comb.—**peineta**, *f.* ornamental shell comb (to wear in the hair).

peladilla, *f.* sugar almond; small pebble.

pelado, *a.* plucked; bared; peeled, stripped; hairless; treeless; bare; penniless, broke.—*n.* penniless person.—*m.* Mexican peasant; haircut.—**peladura**, *f.* paring, peeling.—**pelafustán**, *m.* (coll.) nobody, idler, vagrant.—**pelagatos**, *m.* nincompoop, poor wretch.—**pelaje**, *m.* character or nature of the hair or wool; disposition.—**pelar**, *vt.* to cut the hair of; to pluck; to skin, peel, husk, shell; to cheat, rob; to break the bank.—*duro de p.*, exceedingly difficult, hard to crack.—*vr.* to get one's hair cut; to peel off, flake; to lose the hair (as from illness).

peldaño, *m.* step of a staircase.

pelea, *f.* fight; scuffle, quarrel.—**pelear**, *vi.* to fight; to quarrel; to struggle.—*vr.* to scuffle, come to blows.

pelele, *m.* stuffed figure, dummy; puppet; nincompoop.

peletería, *f.* furrier's trade or shop; (Am.) leather goods or shop; furrier.—**peletero**, *n.* furrier; (Am.) dealer in leather goods; skinner.

peliagudo, *a.* (coll.) arduous, difficult.

pelícano, *m.* pelican.

película, *f.* film; moving picture reel; moving picture.

peligrar, *vi.* to be in danger.—**peligro**, *m.* danger, peril.—*correr p.*, to be in danger.—**peligroso**, *a.* dangerous, perilous, risky.

pelillo, *m.* fine hair; trifle, slight trouble.—*echar pelillos a la mar*, to become reconciled.—**pelirrojo**, *a.* red-haired, red-headed.—**pelirrubio**, *a.* blond, light-haired.

pelmazo, *m.* crushed or flattened mass; undigested food in the stomach; nuisance, sluggard.

pelo, *m.* hair; fiber, filament; nap, pile (of cloth); hairspring (in watches and firearms); grain (in wood).—*de medio p.*, of little account; would-be important.—*de p. en pecho*, brave, daring.—*en p.*, bareback; unsaddled.—*no tener p. de tonto*, to be bright, quick, clever.—*no tener pelos en la lengua*, to

be outspoken.—*tomar el p. a*, to make fun of, pull one's leg.—*venir al p.*, to be to the point, fit the case to a tee.—**pelón**, *a.* hairless; bald.

pelota, *f.* ball; ball game; (Am.) baseball (game).—*en p.*, entirely naked; penniless.—**pelotazo**, *m.* blow or stroke with a ball.—**pelotear**, *vi.* to play ball; to throw (as a ball); to argue, dispute.—**pelotera**, *f.* quarrel, tumult, riot.—**pelotero**, *m.* (Am.) baseball player.—**pelotilla**, *f.* small ball; pellet.—**pelotón**, *m.* large ball; (mil.) platoon.

peluca, *f.* wig, toupee.—**peludo**, *a.* hairy, shaggy.—*m.* shaggy mat.—**peluquería**, *f.* hairdressing shop; barber shop.—**peluquero**, *n.* hairdresser; barber.—**pelusa**, *f.* down; floss, fuzz, nap; (coll.) envy.

pelleja, *f.* skin, hide.—**pellejo**, *m.* skin; rawhide; peel, rind.—*jugarse el p.*, to risk one's life.

pellizcar, *vti.* [d] to pinch; to nip; to clip.—**pellizco**, *m.* pinch; pinching; nip; small bit.

pena, *f.* penalty; punishment; affliction, sorrow, grief; (Am.) embarrassment.—*a duras penas*, with great difficulty, just barely.—*estar con (mucha) p.*, to be (very) sorry.—*merecer la p.*, to be worthwhile.

penacho, *m.* tuft of feathers, plumes, crest.

penado, *n.* convict.—**penal**, *m.* penitentiary, prison.—*a.* penal.—**penalidad**, *f.* trouble, hardship; (law) penalty.—**penalizar**, *vti.* [a] to penalize.—**penar**, *vi.* to suffer; to crave, long for.—*vt.* to impose penalty on.

penco, *m.* swaybacked nag.

pendencia, *f.* quarrel, fight.—**pendenciero**, *a.* quarrelsome, rowdy.

pender, *vi.* to hang, dangle; to be pending or suspended.—**pendiente**, *a.* pendent, hanging; dangling; pending.—*m.* earring, pendant; watch chain.—*f.* slope.

pendón, *m.* standard, banner.

péndulo, *m.* pendulum.

pene, *m.* penis.

penetración, *f.* penetration, penetrating; acuteness, sagacity.—**penetrante**, *a.* penetrating; keen, acute; deep.—**penetrar**, *vt.* to penetrate, pierce; to break or force in; to fathom, comprehend.

penicilina, *f.* penicillin.

península, *f.* peninsula.—**peninsular**, *a.* inhabiting or pert. to a peninsula.

penitencia, *f.* penitence; penance.—**penitenciaría**, *f.* penitentiary.—

penitente, *a.* penitent, repentant.— *mf.* penitent.

penoso, *a.* painful; laborious, arduous; distressing; embarrassing.

pensado, *a.* deliberate, premeditated. —*bien* p., wise, proper.—*mal* p., unwise, foolish.—*tener* p., to have in view, to intend.—**pensador,** *n.* thinker.—**pensamiento,** *m.* mind; thought, idea; thinking; epigram, maxim; (bot.) pansy.—**pensar,** *vii.* [1] to think; to reflect.—*vti.* to think over, or about, consider; to intend, contemplate.—**pensativo,** *a.* pensive, thoughtful.

pensión, *f.* pension; boarding-house; board; fellowship for study abroad. —**pensionado,** *n.* pensioner, pensionary; fellow (study).—**pensionar,** *vt.* to impose or to grant pensions on or to.—**pensionista,** *mf.* boarder, pensioner.

pentagrama, *m.* (mus.) ruled staff.

Pentecostés, *m.* Pentecost.

penúltimo, *a.* next to the last.

penumbra, *f.* dimness.

pabellón, *m.* pavilion; national colors, flag; (anat.) external ear.

penuria, *f.* destitution, indigence.

peña, *f.* rock; boulder.—**peñasco,** *m.* large rock.—**peñascoso,** *a.* rocky.— **peñón,** *m.* large rock; rocky cliff.

peón, *m.* day laborer; foot soldier; spinning top; pawn (in chess); pedestrian.

peonía, *f.* (bot.) peony.

peonza, *f.* top (toy).

peor, *adv.* & *a.* worse; worst.

pepa, *f.* (Am.) seed, stone, pit.

pepino, *m.* cucumber.—*no importarle un* p., not to give a fig.

pepita, *f.* pip or seed of fruit; nugget.

pequeñez, *f.* smallness; childhood; trifle; pettiness; mean act or conduct.—**pequeño,** *a.* little, small; of tender age; lowly, humble.—*n.* child.

pera, *f.* (bot.) pear; goatee.—*pedir peras al olmo,* to expect the impossible.—**peral,** *m.* pear tree.

percal, *m.* percale, calico.

percance, *m.* misfortune; mishap.

percatar, *vi.* & *vr.* to think, consider; to beware.—*p. de,* to notice.

percepción, *f.* perception.—**perceptible,** *a.* perceptible, perceivable.— **percibir,** *vt.* to perceive; to receive, collect.

percudir, *vt.* to tarnish, stain, soil.

percusión, *f.* percussion; collision.

percha, *f.* perch, pole; hat or clothes rack; roost; snare for birds.—**perchero,** *m.* clothes rack or hanger.

perdedor, *n.* loser.—**perder,** *vti.* [18] to lose; to forfeit; to squander away; to ruin; to miss (train, opportunity, etc.).—*echar a* p., to spoil, ruin.—*p. los estribos,* to lose one's poise; to become reckless.— *¡pierda Ud. cuidado!* don't worry! forget it!—*vii.* to lose.—*vri.* to get lost, lose one's way; to miscarry; to be lost, confounded; to be ruined; to go astray; to be spoiled or damaged (as fruits, crops, etc.); to disappear.—*perderse de vista,* to get out of sight; to be very shrewd. —**pérdida,** *f.* loss; detriment, damage; waste; (com.) leakage.—**perdidamente,** *adv.* desperately; uselessly.—**perdido,** *a.* lost; mislaid; misguided; profligate, dissolute.—*m.* (fig.) black sheep.

perdigón, *m.* young partridge; buckshot; pellet.—**perdigonada,** *f.* peppering of buckshot.—**perdiguero,** *n.* setter, retriever (dog).—**perdiz,** *f.* partridge.

perdón, *m.* pardon, forgiveness; remission.—*interj.* pardon! excuse me! —*con* p., by your leave.—**perdonar,** *vt.* to pardon, forgive; to remit (a debt); to excuse.

perdulario, *a.* reckless, heedless.—*n.* good-for-nothing, ne'er-do-well.

perdurable, *a.* lasting, everlasting.— **perdurar,** *vi.* to last long.

perecedero, *a.* perishable, not lasting. —**perecer,** *vii.* [3] to perish.

peregrinación, *f.,* **peregrinaje,** *m.* traveling; pilgrimage.—**peregrinar,** *vi.* to travel, roam.—**peregrino,** *a.* foreign; traveling, migratory; strange, odd, rare.—*n.* pilgrim.

perejil, *m.* parsley.

perenne, *a.* perennial, perpetual.

perentorio, *a.* urgent, decisive; peremptory.

pereza, *f.* laziness; slowness, idleness. —**perezoso,** *a.* lazy, indolent, idle. —*m.* (zool.) sloth.

perfección, *f.* perfection; perfect thing.—*a la* p., perfectly.—**perfeccionamiento,** *m.* perfecting, improvement, finish.—**perfeccionar,** *vt.* to improve, perfect.—**perfecto,** *a.* perfect.

perfil, *m.* profile, side view; outline.— **perfilar,** *vt.* to outline, profile.—*vr.* to place oneself sideways; to dress carefully.

perforación, *f.* perforation, hole, puncture; drilling, boring.—**perforador,** *a.* & *n.* perforator, driller; perforating, drilling.—**perforadora,** *f.* drill, rock drill.—**perforar,** *vt.* to perforate; to bore, drill.

perfumar, *vt.* to perfume.—**perfume,** *m.* perfume.—**perfumería,** *f.* per-

fumery; perfumer's shop.—**perfumista**, *mf.* perfumer.

pergamino, *m.* parchment, vellum; diploma.

pericia, *f.* skill, expertness.

perico, *n.* parakeet; small parrot.

perifollos, *m. pl.* ribbons, tawdry ornaments of dress.

perilla, *f.* small pear; pear-shaped ornament; knob; pommel of a saddle; goatee; lobe of the ear.—*de p.*, to the purpose.

perillán, *n.* rascal; sly, crafty person.

perímetro, *m.* perimeter.

periódico, *a.* periodic(al).—*m.* newspaper; periodical, journal.—**periodismo**, *m.* journalism.—**periodista**, *mf.* journalist.—**periodístico**, *a.* journalistic.—**período**, *m.* period, age; sentence; menstruation, period; (elec.) cycle; (pol.) term, tenure.

peripecia, *f.* situation, incident, episode.

peripuesto, *a.* dolled up; dressy.

periquete, *m.* (coll.) jiffy, instant.

periquito, *m.* parakeet, lovebird.

periscopio, *m* periscope.

peritaje, *m.* expertness; appraisal.—**perito**, *a.* skillful, able, experienced. —*n.* expert; appraiser.

perjudicar, *vti.* [d] to damage, impair, harm.—**perjudicial**, *a.* harmful. —**perjuicio**, *m.* damage.

perjurar, *vi.* to commit perjury; to swear.—*vr.* to perjure oneself.—**perjurio**, *m.* perjury.—**perjuro**, *a.* perjured, forsworn.—*n.* forswearer, perjurer.

perla, *f.* pearl; (fig.) jewel —*de perlas*, perfectly, to a tee.

permanecer, *vii.* [3] to stay, remain.— **permanencia**, *f.* stay, sojourn; duration, permanence.—**permanente**, *a.* permanent.—*f.* permanent (in hair).

permeable, *a.* porous, permeable; not waterproof.

permisible, *a.* permissible.—**permiso**, *m.* permission; permit.—*¡con p.!* excuse me!—**permitir**, *vt.* to permit, allow, let; to grant, admit.

permuta, *f.* barter; exchange.—**permutar**, *vt. & vi.* to exchange, barter.

pernera, *f.* trouser leg.—**perneta**, *f.—en pernetas*, barelegged.

pernicioso, *a.* pernicious; harmful.

pernil, *m.* hock (of animals).

perno, *m.* nut and bolt; spike; joint pin.

pernoctar, *vi.* to pass the night.

pero, *conj.* but; except, yet.—*m* (coll.) fault, defect.—*poner pero(s)*, to find fault.

perogrullada, *f.* (coll.) obvious truth, truism; platitude.

perol, *m.* kettle.

peroración, *f.* peroration.—**perorar**, *vi.* to deliver a speech or oration; to declaim.—**perorata**, *f.* (coll.) harangue, speech.

perpendicular, *f. & a.* perpendicular.

perpetrar, *vt.* to perpetrate, commit (a crime).

perpetuar, *vt. & vr.* to perpetuate.— **perpetuidad**, *f.* perpetuity.—**perpetuo**, *a.* perpetual, everlasting.

perplejidad, *f.* perplexity; quandary. —**perplejo**, *a.* uncertain, perplexed.

perra, *f.* bitch, female dog; slut; drunken state; tantrum.—**perrada**, *f.* mean, base action.—**perrera**, *f.* kennel.—**perrería**, *f.* pack of dogs; angry word; vile action.—**perro**, *m.* dog.—*p. de aguas* or *de lanas*, poodle.—*p. de presa*, or *dogo*, bulldog. —*p. viejo*, (coll.) cautious person; experienced person.—**perruno**, *a.* doggish, canine; currish.

persa, *a. & n.* Persian.

persecución, *f.* persecution; pursuit. —**perseguidor**, *n.* persecutor; pursuer.—**perseguir**, *vti.* [29-b] to pursue; to persecute.

perseverancia, *f.* perseverance.—**perseverante**, *a.* persevering.—**perseverar**, *vi.* to persevere, persist.

persiana, *f.* blind, shutter.

persignarse, *vr.* to cross oneself.

persistencia, *f.* persistence; obstinacy. —**persistente**, *a.* persistent; firm.— **persistir**, *vi.* to persist.

persona, *f.* person.—*en p.*, in person, personally.—**personaje**, *m.* personage; (theat., lit.) character.—**personal**, *a.* personal, private.—*m.* personnel, staff.—**personalidad**, *f.* personality; individuality; (law) person; legal capacity.—**personalizar**, *vti.* [a] to personalize; to become personal.—**personarse**, *vr.* to appear personally; (law) to appear as an interested party.— **personificar**, *vti.* [d] to personify.

perspectiva, *f.* perspective; view; prospect, outlook; appearance.

perspicacia, *f.* perspicacity, sagacity. —**perspicaz**, *a.* acute, sagacious, clear-sighted.

persuadir, *vt.* to persuade.—*vr.* to be persuaded.—**persuasión**, *f.* persuasion.—**persuasivo**, *a.* persuasive.

pertenecer, *vii.* [3] to belong, pertain; to concern.—**perteneciente**, *a.* belonging, pertaining.—**pertenencia**, *f.* possession, holding property.

pértiga, *m.* bar, pole, rod.

pertinente, *a.* pertinent, apt; (law) concerning, pertaining.

pertrechar, *vt.* & *vr.* (mil.) to supply, store, equip; to arrange, prepare.—**pertrechos,** *m. pl.* (mil.) stores; tools.

perturbación, *f.* perturbation, disturbance; agitation.—**perturbar,** *vt.* to perturb, disturb, unsettle; to confuse.

peruano, *n.* & *a.* Peruvian.

perversidad, *f.* perversity, wickedness. —**perversión,** *f.* perversion, perverting; depravity, wickedness.—**perverso,** *a.* perverse, wicked, depraved. —*n.* pervert.—**pervertir,** *vti.* [39] to pervert; to corrupt.—*vri.* to become depraved.

pesa, *f.* weight (in scales, clocks).— *pl.* bar bells.—**pesadez,** *f.* heaviness; slowness; drowsiness; trouble, pain, fatigue.—**pesadilla,** *f.* nightmare.— **pesado,** *a.* heavy; deep, sound (sleep); stuffy (air, atmosphere); cumbersome; tedious, tiresome; dull; slow; clumsy; fat, corpulent; importunate, annoying.—*n.* bore, tease.—**pesadumbre,** *f.* grief, affliction, sorrow; heaviness.—**pésame,** *m.* condolence, sympathy.—**pesantez,** *f.* gravity; heaviness.—**pesar,** *vi.* to weigh, have weight; to be weighty or important; to cause regret, sorrow or repentance; to preponderate. —*vt.* to weigh, to examine, consider.—*m* sorrow, grief, regret; repentance —*a p. de,* in spite of, notwithstanding —*a p mío,* or *a mi p,* in spite of me, against my wishes.— **pesaroso,** *a* sorrowful, regretful; sorry, sad.

pesca, *f.* fishing; fishery; catch, fish caught —**pescadería,** *f* fish market. —**pescadero,** *n.* fishmonger —**pescado,** *m.* fish (caught) —**pescador,** *n.* fisherman, fisher —**pescar,** *vti.* [d] & *vii.* to fish, to catch fish — *vti.* to find or pick up; to catch in the act, surprise

pescozón, *m.* slap on the neck. **pescuezo,** *m* neck; throat.

pesebre, *m.* manger, crib, rack.

pesimismo, *m* pessimism —**pesimista,** *mf.* & *a.* pessimist(ic).—**pésimo,** *a* very bad, very worst.

peso, *m* weight, heaviness, weighing, importance; burden, load; judgment, good sense; peso, monetary unit.—*caerse de su p.,* to be self-evident; to go without saying.—*en p.,* suspended in the air; bodily; totally.

pespunte, *m* backstitching.

pesquería, *f* fishing, fishing trip — **pesquero,** *a.* fishing.

pesquisa, *f.* inquiry, investigation, search.

pestaña, *f.* eyelash; (sewing) fringe, edging; (mech.) flange.—*quemarse las pestañas,* to burn the midnight oil.—**pestañear,** *vi.* to wink; to blink.—**pestañeo,** *m.* winking; blinking.

peste, *f.* pest, plague, pestilence; epidemic; foul smell, stink; (coll.) excess, superabundance.—*pl.* offensive words.—**pestilencia,** *f.* pest, plague, pestilence; foulness, stench. —**pestilente,** *a.* pestilent, foul.

pestillo, *m.* door latch; bolt of a lock.

petaca, *f.* cigar case; (Am.) leather trunk or chest; (Am.) suitcase.

pétalo, *m* petal.

petardo, *m* (artil.) petard; bomb.

petate, *m.* (Am.) sleeping mat; (coll.) luggage, baggage.—*liar el p.,* (coll.) to pack up and go.

petición, *f.* petition, request.

petimetre, *m.* fop, coxcomb, beau.

petirrojo, *m.* robin.

pétreo, *a.* rocky; stony, of stone.

petróleo, *m.* crude oil, (fuel, gas or diesel) oil.—**petrolero,** *a.* oil.—*n.* person in the oil industry, oil man; incendiary.—*m.* (naut.) oil tanker.

petulancia, *f.* petulance; insolence; flippancy.—**petulante,** *a.* petulant, insolent, pert.

petunia, *f.* petunia.

pez, *m.* fish (not caught).—*f.* pitch, tar.

pezón, *m* stem of fruits; leaf stalk; nipple of a teat.

pezuña, *f* hoof.

piada, *f.* chirping, peeping, peep.

piadoso, *a.* pious, godly; merciful.

piafar, *vi.* (of horses) to paw, to stamp

pianista, *mf* pianist.—**piano,** *m.* piano.—*p de cola,* grand piano.

piar, *vi.* to peep, chirp

piara, *f.* herd (of swine)

pica, *f.* pike, lance; stonecutter's hammer.—*poner una p en Flandes,* to achieve a triumph.

picacho, *m.* top, peak, summit.

picada, *f.* pricking, bite; (aer.) dive, diving —**picadero,** *m* riding school. —**picadillo,** *m.* hash, minced meat. **picador,** *m.* horse-breaker; horseman armed with a goad in bullfights; chopping block; paper pricker.—**picadura,** *f.* pricking; pinking; puncture, bite; sting; pipe tobacco.—**picante,** *a.* pricking, piercing; biting; spicy, racy, highly seasoned.—*m.* piquancy, pungency, acrimony.—**picapleitos,** *m* shyster, pettifogger; (coll.) litigious person. **picaporte,** *m.* spring latch; latchkey; (Am.) door knocker.

picar, *vti.* [d] to prick, pierce, puncture; to sting, bite (as insects); to mince, chop, hash; (of birds) to peck; (of fish) to bite; to nibble, pick at; to spur, goad, incite; to pique, vex.—*vii.* to sting, bite (as insects); (of fish) to bite; to itch, burn; to scorch, burn (as the sun); (aer.) to dive.—*p. alto,* to aim high. —*vri.* to be offended or piqued; to be moth-eaten; to stale, sour (as wine); to begin to rot (as fruit); to begin to decay (of teeth, etc.); (naut.) (of the sea) to get choppy.

picardía, *f.* knavery, roguery; malice, foulness; wanton trick, wantonness; lewdness.—**picaresco,** *a.* roguish, knavish, picaresque.—**pícaro,** *a.* knavish, roguish; vile, low; mischievous; crafty, sly.—*n.* rogue, knave, rascal.—**picarón,** *n.* great rogue, rascal.

picazón, *f.* itching, itch.

pico, *m.* beak or bill of a bird; sharp point; pick, pickaxe; spout; peak, top, summit; small balance of an account; (coll.) mouth; loquaciousness; (coll.) a lot of cash. —*costar un p.,* to be very expensive.—*p. de oro,* man of great eloquence.—*treinta y p.,* thirty odd.

picota, *f.* pillory, stocks; top, peak, point.

picotada, *f.,* **picotazo,** *m.* blow with the beak, peck—**picotear,** *vt. & vi* to strike with a beak, to peck, (Am.) to cut into small pieces.

pictórico, *a.* pictorial

pichón, *m.* young pigeon, squab.—*n.* (coll.) darling, dearest.

pie, *m.* foot; leg, stand, support, base; foot, bottom (of a page); motive, occasion —*al p.,* near, close to; at the foot.—*al p. de la letra,* literally, exactly —*a p.,* on foot.— *a p. juntillas,* firmly; most emphatically—*de p,* standing.—*en p.* = DE PIE; pending, undecided —*p. de amigo,* prop, shore.—*p de imprenta,* imprint, printer's mark.

piedad, *f* piety; mercy.

piedra, *f* stone, cobblestone, (med.) gravel; hail —*no dejar p sobre p,* to raze to the ground, to destroy entirely.—*p. angular,* cornerstone.— *p. de amolar* or *de afilar,* whetstone, grinding stone.—*p. falsa,* imitation (precious) stone.—*p. pómez,* pumice.

piel, *f.* skin; hide; leather; fur

pienso, *m.* fodder.

pierna, *f* leg.—*dormir a p. suelta,* to sleep soundly.

pieza, *f.* piece; part (of a machine, etc.); bolt or roll of cloth; room

(in a house); (theat.) play.—*de una p.,* solid, in one piece.

pifia, *f.* miscue at billiards; error, blunder.

pigmento, *m.* pigment.

pigmeo, *a.* dwarfish.—*n.* pygmy, dwarf.

pignorar, *vt.* to pledge, give as security.

pijama, *m.* or *f.* pajama.

pila, *f.* sink; (eccl.) font, holy water basin; pile, heap; stone trough or basin; (elec.) battery, cell.—*nombre de p.,* Christian or given name. —*pilar,* *m.* pillar, column, post; basin of a fountain.

píldora, *f.* pill, pellet.

pileta, *f.* (Am.) swimming pool.

pilón, *m.* mortar (for pounding); loaf (of sugar); watering trough; basin of a fountain; rider, sliding weight (of a balance).—*de p.,* to boot, in addition.

pilote, *m.* (eng.) pile.

pilot(e)ar, *vt.* to pilot.—**piloto,** *m.* (naut., aer.) pilot, navigator.

piltrafa, *f.* skinny flesh; hide parings.—*pl.* scraps of food.

pillaje, *m.* pillage, plunder, marauding.—**pillar,** *vt* to pillage, rifle, plunder; (coll.) to catch, grasp.— **pillería,** *f.* gang of rogues; piece of rascality.—**pillo,** *a.* roguish, knavish; shrewd, sly.—*n.* knave, rogue, rascal; petty thief —**pilluelo,** *n.* little rogue, urchin.

pimentón, *m.* Cayenne or red pepper; paprika.—**pimienta,** *f* pepper (spice).—**pimiento,** *m.* pepper (vegetable).

pimpollo, *m.* rosebud, spruce, lively youth; sprout, shoot

pináculo, *m.* pinnacle, summit.

pinar, *m* pine grove

pincel, *m.* fine paintbrush —**pincelada,** *f.* stroke with a brush, touch.

pinchar, *vt* to prick, puncture, pierce.—**pinchazo,** *m* prick, puncture, stab

pinche, *m* kitchen boy

pincho, *m.* thorn, prickle; goad; skewer

pingajo, *m.* (coll.) rag, tatter.

pingo, *m.* rag; (Am.) saddle horse. —*pl* worthless clothes, duds.

pingüe, *a.* plentiful, fat, greasy, oily.

pingüino, *m.* penguin.

pino, *m.* pine.

pin-pón, *m.* ping-pong.

pinta, *f* spot, mark; appearance, aspect, drop; pint. (See Table.)

pintada, *f.* (Am.) mackerel, guinea hen.

pintar, *vt.* to paint; to picture; to describe, portray; to fancy, im-

agine.—*vi.* to begin to ripen; to show, give signs of.—*vr.* to make up (one's face).—**pintarrajear,** *vt.* (coll.) to daub.

pintiparado, *a.* perfectly like, closely resembling; pat, fit.

pinto, *a.* (Am.) pinto, spotted.—**pintor,** *n.* painter.—*p. de brocha gorda,* house or sign painter; dauber.—**pintoresco,** *a.* picturesque. —**pintura,** *f.* painting; (art) picture, painting; color, paint, pigment; portrayal, description.

pinzas, *f.* tweezers, pincers; claws (of lobsters, etc.).

piña, *f.* pineapple; pine cone; cluster, gathering; game of pool.—**piñón,** *m.* the edible nut of the nut pine; (mech.) pinion.

pío, *a.* pious; mild, merciful.—*m.* peeping of chickens.

piojo, *m.* louse.—**piojoso,** *a.* lousy.

pionero, *n.* (neol.) pioneer.

pipa, *f.* cask, butt, hogshead; fruit seed; tobacco pipe.—**pipote,** *m.* keg.

pique, *m.* pique, resentment.—*a p. de,* in danger of, on the point of.—*echar a p.,* to sink (a ship).—*irse a p.,* (naut.) to founder, sink; fall.

piqueta, *f.* pickaxe; mason's hammer.

piquete, *m.* pricking; sting; small hole; stake, picket; (mil.) picket.

pira, *f.* pyre, funeral pile.

piragua, *f.* dugout, canoe.

pirámide, *f.* pyramid.

pirata, *m.* pirate.—**piratear,** *vi.* to pirate.—**piratería,** *f.* piracy.

piropear, *vt. & vi.* (coll.) to flatter; to compliment.—**piropo,** *m.* (coll.) flattery; compliment.

pirulí, *m.* lollipop.

pisada, *f.* footstep; footprint; treading.—**pisapapeles,** *m.* paperweight. —**pisar,** *vt.* to tread on, trample, step on; to press; to press on; to stamp on the ground.

pisaverde, *m.* (coll.) fop, coxcomb, dude.

piscina, *f.* swimming pool, fishpond.

piscolabis, *m.* (coll.) snack.

piso, *m.* floor; pavement, flooring; loft, flat, apartment; ground level; story; (Am.) fee for pasturage rights.—*p. bajo,* ground floor.—*p. principal,* second floor, first living floor.—**pisotear,** *vt.* to trample, tread under foot.—**pisotón,** *m.* heavy step or stamp of the foot.

pista, *f.* trail, track, trace, clue; race track, race course; circus ring; dancing floor; tennis court; (aer.) runway; landing strip.

pistilo, *m.* (bot.) pistil.

pistola, *f.* pistol.—**pistolera,** *f.* holster. —**pistoletazo,** *m* pistol shot

pistón, *m.* (mech.) piston; (mus.) piston of a brass instrument.

pita, *f.* agave plant, maguey; string, cord.

pitada, *f.* blow of a whistle.

pitanza, *f.* pittance; (coll.) daily food; salary.

pitar, *vi.* to blow a whistle; to hiss. —**pitazo,** *m.* sound or blast of a whistle.

pitillera, *f.* cigarette case.—**pitillo,** *m.* cigarette.

pito, *m.* whistle; (coll.) cigarette.—*no me importa* or *no se me da* or *me importa un p.,* (coll.) I don't care a bit.—*no tocar pitos en,* to have no part in.

pitón, *m.* (of deer, etc.) horn just starting to grow; spout, nozzle.

pivote, *m.* (mech.) king pin; pivot.

piyama, *m.* or *f.* = PIJAMA.

pizarra, *f.* slate; blackboard.—**pizarrín,** *m.* slate pencil.—**pizarrón,** *m.* blackboard.

pizca, *f.* (coll.) mite, speck, sprinkling, crumb, particle.

placa, *f.* plate; badge insignia; plaque, tablet.

pláceme, *m.* congratulation.

placentero, *a.* joyful, pleasant.—**placer,** *vti.* [30] to please.—*m.* pleasure.

placero, *a.* pertaining to the marketplace.—*n.* seller at a market; gadder.

plácido, *a.* placid, quiet, calm.

plaga, *f.* plague; calamity; scourge; pest.—**plagar,** *vti.* [b] to plague, infest.—*vri.* **(de)** to be full of, infested with.

plagiar, *vt* to plagiarize; (Am.) to kidnap.—**plagiario,** *n. & a.* plagiarist; plagiarizing.—**plagio,** *m.* plagiarism; (Am.) kidnapping.

plan, *m* plan; design, scheme.—*p. de estudios,* curriculum.

plana, *f.* page; copy; level ground, plain; (mason.) trowel —*enmendar la p. a,* to find fault with, criticize. —*p. mayor,* (mil.) staff.

plancha, *f.* plate, sheet; slab; flatiron, iron; (coll.) blunder, boner; (naut.) gangplank; photographic plate.—**planchador,** *n.* ironer.

planchar, *vt.* to iron, to press.

planeador, *m.* (aer.) glider.—**planear,** *vt. & vi.* to plan, design.—*vi.* (aer.) to glide.

planeta, *m.* planet.—**planetario,** *a.* planetary.—*m.* planetarium.

planicie, *f.* plain.

planilla, *f.* (Am.) list; payroll, (Mex.) list of candidates; ticket; (Cuba) application form, blank.

plano, *a* plane; level, smooth, even

—*m.* plan, blueprint; map; flat (of a sword, etc.); (geom.) plane; (aer.) plane, wing.—*de p.*, openly, clearly; flatly.—*primer p.*, foreground.

planta, *f.* sole of the foot; (bot.) plant; (eng.) plan, horizontal projection, top view; plant, works; site of a building.—**plantación,** *f.* plantation; planting.—**plantar,** *vt.* (agr.) to plant; to erect, set up, fix upright; to strike (a blow); to set, put, place; to leave in the lurch, disappoint; to jilt.—*vr.* (coll.) to stand upright; to stop, halt, balk.

plantear, *vt.* to plan, try; to put into action; to state or tackle (a problem); to raise (an issue).

plantel, *m.* nursery, nursery garden; establishment, plant; educational institution.

plantilla, *f.* first sole, insole (shoes); model, pattern; roster, staff; plan, design.

plantío, *m.* planting; plot, bed.

plañidero, *a.* mournful, weeping, moaning.—**plañido,** *m.* moan, lamentation, crying.—**plañir,** *vii.* [41] to lament, grieve; to whimper.

plasma, *m.* plasma.—**plasmar,** *vt.* to mold, shape.

plasta, *f.* soft mass; anything flattened; (coll.) anything poorly wrought.

plasticidad, *f.* plasticity.—**plástico,** *a.* & *m.* plastic.

plata, *f.* silver; silver coin; (Am.) money.—*en p.*, in plain language.

plataforma, *f.* platform.

platal, *m.* great quantity of money, great wealth.

platanal, platanar, *m.* banana grove or plantation.—**plátano,** *m.* banana (plant and fruit).

platea, *f.* (theat.) orchestra; pit.

platear, *vt.* to silver, plate with silver.—**platería,** *f.* silversmith's shop or trade.—**platero,** *m.* silversmith; jeweler.

plática, *f.* talk, chat, conversation; address, lecture; sermon.—**platicar,** *vii.* [d] to converse, talk, chat.

platillo, *m.* saucer; pan (of a balance); cymbal.

platino, *m.* platinum.

plato, *m.* dish, plate; dinner course.

platónico, *a.* Platonic.—**platonismo,** *m.* Platonism.

plausible, *a.* plausible.

playa, *f.* beach, shore.

plaza, *f.* plaza, square; marketplace; (com.) emporium, market; room, space; office, position, employment.

—*p. de toros,* bull ring, arena.—*sentar p.*, to enlist.

plazo, *m.* term, time, date, day of payment; credit.—*a plazos*, in installments, on credit.

plazoleta, plazuela, *f.* small square.

pleamar, *f.* high water, high tide.

plebe, *f.* common people, populace. —**plebeyo,** *n.* & *a.* plebeian.—**plebiscito,** *m.* (pol.) plebiscite; referendum.

plegable, plegadizo, *a.* pliable, folding.—**plegadura,** *f.* plait, fold; plaiting, folding, doubling; crease.— **plegar,** *vti.* [1-b] to fold; to plait; to crease.—*vri.* to fold; to bend; to submit, yield.

plegaria, *f.* prayer, supplication.

pleitear, *vi.* to plead, litigate; to wrangle.—**pleitista,** *mf.* litigious person.—*a.* litigious.—**pleito,** *m.* lawsuit; litigation; proceedings in a case; dispute, contest, debate, strife. —*poner p.* (*a*), to sue, bring suit (against).

plenario, *a.* complete, full; (law) plenary.—**plenilunio,** *m.* full moon. —**plenipotenciario,** *n.* & *a.* plenipotentiary.—**plenitud,** *f.* plenitude, fullness, abundance.—**pleno,** *a.* full, complete; joint (session).

pleuresía, *f.* pleurisy.

pliego, *m.* sheet (of paper).—*p. de condiciones*, specifications; tender, bid.—**pliegue,** *m.* fold, plait; crease.

plisar, *vt.* to pleat, plait.

plomada, *f.* plumb, lead weight, plummet.—**plomería,** *f.* lead roofing; leadware shop; plumbing.—**plomero,** *n.* plumber.—**plomizo,** *a.* leaden; lead-colored.—**plomo,** *m.* lead (metal); piece of lead; plummet; bullet; (coll.) dull person, bore.— *andar con pies de p.*, to proceed with the utmost caution.—*a p.*, true, plumb.—*caer a p.*, to fall down flat.

pluma, *f.* feather; plume; quill; writing pen; penmanship; (fig.) style.—*al correr de la*, or *a vuela p.*, written in haste.—**plumaje,** *m.* plumage; plume, crest.—**plumazo,** *m.* stroke of pen.—**plumero,** *m.* feather duster.—**plumón,** *m.* down, feather bed.—**plumoso,** *a.* feathered.

plural, *m.* & *a.* plural.—**pluralidad,** *f.* plurality.—**pluralizar,** *vti.* [a] to pluralize.

plus, *m.* (mil.) extra pay; bonus; extra.

población, *f.* population; populating; city, town, village.—**poblado,** *a.* populated, inhabited.—*m.* inhabited place, town, settlement.—**poblador,** *n.* settler.—**poblar,** *vti.* [12] & *vii.* to populate, settle; to inhabit; to

stock; to breed fast.—*vri.* to bud, leaf.

pobre, *a.* poor; needy; barren; pitiable, unfortunate.—*mf.* poor person; beggar.—**pobrete,** *m.* poor man.—**pobreza,** *f.* poverty; need; scarcity, dearth.

pocilga, *f.* pigsty, pigpen; dirty place.

pocillo, *m.* chocolate cup.

pócima, *f.*, **poción,** *m.* drink, draft; potion.

poco, *a.* little; scanty, limited; small.—*pl.* few, some.—*m.* a little, a bit, a small quantity.— *adv.* little, in a small degree; a short time.—*a p.*, immediately; shortly afterward.—*dentro de p.*, in a short time, soon.—*de p. más o menos*, of little account.—*p. a p.*, little by little, gradually, slowly.—*p. después*, shortly afterward.—*p. más o menos*, more or less.—*por p.*, almost, nearly.

poda, *f.* pruning, lopping; pruning season.—**podar,** *vt.* to prune, lop, trim.

podenco, *m.* hound (dog).

poder, *vti. & vii.* [31] to be able; can; may.—*a. más no p.*, or *hasta más no p.*, to the utmost, to the limit.—*no p. con*, not to be able to bear, manage, etc., to be no match for.—*no p. menos de*, to be necessary; cannot but, cannot fail to.—*puede que venga*, (or *que no venga*), he may come (or, he may not come).—*m.* power; faculty, authority; might; proxy; (law) power or letter of attorney.—**poderío,** *m.* power, might; dominion, jurisdiction; wealth.—**poderoso,** *a.* powerful, mighty; wealthy.

podre, *m.* pus; rotten substance.—**podredumbre,** *f.* decay; pus; putrid matter; corruption.—**podridero, podrimento,** *m.* = PUDRIDERO, PUDRIMENTO.—**podrido,** *pp.* of PODRIR, PUDRIR.—**podrir,** *vti.*, [33] *vii. & vri.* = PUDRIR.

poema, *m.* poem.—**poesía,** *f.* poetry; poetical composition, poem.—**poeta,** *m.* poet, bard.—**poética,** *f.* poetics.—**poético,** *a.* poetic(al).—**poetisa,** *f.* poetess.

polaco, *a.* Polish.—*m.* Polish language.—*n.* Pole.

polaina, *f.* legging.

polar, *a.* polar.—**polaridad,** *f.* polarity.

polea, *f.* pulley; tackle block, block pulley.

polen, *m.* pollen.

policía, *f.* police.—*mf.* policeman (-woman).—**policíaco, policial,** *a.* pertaining to police, police.

políglota, *a. & mf.* multilingual (person).

polígono, *m.* polygon; (artil.) practice ground.

polilla, *f.* moth; clothes moth.

polinesi(an)o, *n. & a.* Polynesian.

política, *f.* policy; politics.—**politicastro,** *n.* petty politician.—**político,** *a.* political; polite; suave.—*n.* politician.—*pariente p.*, in-law.—**politiquería,** *f.* (Am.) low politics; political talk and doings, political trash.—**politiquero,** *n.* (Am.) one that indulges in, or is fond of, common politics; political busybody.

póliza, *f.* (com.) policy; scrip; check, draft; voucher, certificate.

polizón, *n.* stowaway; vagrant.

polizonte, *m.* (coll.) cop, policeman.

polo, *m.* (geog. & astr.) pole; (sports) polo.

polonés, *a.* Polish.—*f.* polonaise.

polución, *f.* (med.) ejaculation, pollution.

polvareda, *f.* cloud of dust; (fig.) scandal.—**polvera,** *f.* (cosmetic) powder box.—**polvo,** *m.* dust; powder.—*pl.* toilet powder.—*en p.*, powdered.—**pólvora,** *f.* gunpowder.—**polvorear,** *vt.* to powder, sprinkle powder on.—**polvoriento,** *a.* dusty.—**polvorín,** *m.* (mil.) powder magazine.

polla, *f.* pullet; (cards) pool, (coll.) girl.—**pollada,** *f.* flock of young fowls; hatch, covey.—**pollera,** *f.* chicken roost, chicken coop; gocart; (Am.) skirt; hooped petticoat.—**pollería,** *f.* poultry shop or market.—**pollero,** *m.* poulterer; poultry yard.

pollino, *n.* donkey, ass.

pollo, *m.* chicken; (coll.) young person.—**polluelo,** *n.* little chicken, chick.

pomada, *f.* pomade.

pómez.—*piedra p.*, pumice.

pomo, *m.* small bottle, flask, flagon; pommel; doorknob.

pompa, *f.* pomp, ostentation; bubble.—**pomposidad,** *f.* pomposity, pompousness.—**pomposo,** *a.* pompous, turgid; magnificent, splendid; inflated.

pómulo, *m.* cheek bone.

ponche, *m.* punch.—**ponchera,** *f.* punch bowl.

poncho, *m.* (Am.) poncho; military coat.—*a.* lazy, soft; heedless.

ponderación, *f.* consideration, deliberation; exaggeration.—**ponderar,** *vt.* to weigh, ponder, consider; to exaggerate; to praise highly.

poner, *vti.* [32-49] to put, place, lay; to dispose, arrange, set (as the table); to impose, keep (as order); to oblige, compel; to wager, stake;

to appoint, put in charge; to write, set down; to lay eggs; to cause; to become or turn (red, angry, etc.). —*p. al corriente*, to inform.—*p. al día*, to bring up to date.—*p. como nuevo*, to humiliate, reprimand or treat harshly, dress down.—*p. coto a*, to stop, put a limit to.—*p. de manifiesto*, to make public.—*p. en claro*, to make clear; to clear up.— *p. en duda*, to question, doubt.— *p. en práctica*, to start doing, get (a project, etc.) underway.—*p. en ridículo*, to make ridiculous.—*p. en vigor*, to enforce.—*vri.* to apply oneself to; to set about; to put on (as a garment); to become, get (as wet, angry, dirty); to set (as the sun); to reach, get to, arrive.—*p. a*, to begin to, start to.—*p. a cubierto*, to shelter oneself from danger.— *p. colorado*, to blush.—*p. de acuerdo*, to reach an agreement.—*p. en camino*, to set out, start, take off. —*p. en pie*, to stand up.—*p. en razón*, to become reasonable.

poniente, *m.* west.

pontaje, pontazgo, *m.* bridge toll.

pontifical, *a.* pontifical, papal.— **pontífice,** *m.* pontiff.—*Sumo Pontífice,* Pope.

pontón, *m.* pontoon.

ponzoña, *f.* poison, venom.—**ponzoñoso,** *a.* poisonous.

popa, *f.* (naut.) poop, stern.

popelina, *f.* (neol.) poplin.

populachero, *a.* vulgar, common.— **populacho,** *m.* populace, mob, rabble.—**popular,** *a.* popular.—**popularidad,** *f.* popularity.—**popularizar,** *vti.* [a] to popularize, make popular.—*vri.* to become popular.—**populoso,** *a.* populous.

popurrí, *m.* (mus.) medley; potpourri; mess, confusion.

poquito, *a.* very little; weak of body and mind.—*m.* a wee bit.—*a poquitos,* little by little; a little at a time.

por, *prep.* by; for; through; as; across; about, nearly; per; after, for; for the sake of; in behalf of, on account of; in order to; by way of; in the name of; without, not yet, to be.—*p. cuanto,* inasmuch as, whereas.—*p. docena,* by the dozen.—*p. escrito,* in writing.—*p. la mañana (tarde, noche),* in the morning (afternoon, evening).—*p. más que,* or *p. mucho que,* however much, no matter how much; notwithstanding.—*p. poco,* almost.— *p. qué,* why.—*¿p. qué?* why?— *p. si,* or *p. si acaso,* in case; if by chance. —*p. si o p. no,* to be sure; to be

on the safe side.—*p. supuesto,* of course.

porcelana, *f.* porcelain; chinaware.

porcentaje, *m.* percentage.

porción, *f.* portion, part; lot.

porche, *m.* porch, portico; covered walk.

pordiosero, *n.* beggar.

porfía, *f.* tussle, dispute, competition, obstinate quarrel.—*a p.,* in competition; insistently.—**porfiado,** *a.* obstinate, stubborn, persistent; importunate.—**porfiar,** *vi.* to contend, wrangle, persist, insist; to importune.

pormenor, *m.* detail, particular.— **pormenorizar,** *vti.* [a] to detail, itemize.

poro, *m.* pore.—**porosidad,** *f.* porosity. —**poroso,** *a.* porous.

porque, *conj.* because, for, as; in order that.—**porqué,** *m.* reason, motive.

porquería, *f.* filth, squalor; vile, dirty act; nasty trick; trifle, worthless thing.—**porquerizo, porquero,** *n.* swineherd.

porra, *f.* bludgeon, club, truncheon; maul.—**porrazo,** *m.* blow, knock; fall; thump.

porta, *f.* porthole.

portaaviones, *m.* airplane carrier.

portada, *f.* portal, porch; frontispiece; cover (of a magazine, etc.); title page.

portador, *n.* bearer, carrier; (com.) holder, bearer.

portaféretro, *m.* pallbearer.

portal, *m.* porch, vestibule; portico.

portalámpara, *m.* (elec.) socket; lamp holder.

portalibros, *m.* book strap.

portalón, *m.* gangway.

portamonedas, *m.* purse.

portapliegos, *m.* large portfolio.

portaplumas, *m.* penholder.

portañuela, *f.* (Am.) fly of trousers.

portar, *vt.* to carry (as arms).—*vr.* to behave, act.—**portátil,** *a.* portable.—**portavoz,** *mf.* spokesman, representative; loudspeaker, megaphone.

portazgo, *m.* toll.

portazo, *m.* slam of a door.

porte, *m.* cost of carriage; freight; postage; bearing (of persons).— **portear,** *vt.* to carry or convey for a price.

portento, *m.* prodigy, wonder; portent.—**portentoso,** *a.* prodigious, marvelous.

porteño, *a. & n.* of or from Buenos Aires.

portería, *f.* porter's lodge or box; janitor's quarters.—**portero,** *n.* gate-

keeper, porter; superintendent, janitor.—**portezuela,** *f.* (vehicles) door.
pórtico, *m.* portico; porch.
portilla, *f.* opening, passage; (naut.) porthole.—**portillo,** *m.* opening, gap, breach; wicket, gate; pass between hills.—**portón,** *m.* front door or gate.
portorriqueño, *n.* & *a.* Porto Rican.
portugués, *n.* & *a.* Portuguese.—*m.* Portuguese language.
porvenir, *m.* future, time to come.
posada, *f.* inn; lodging house; lodging.—**posadero,** *n.* innkeeper.—*f. pl.* buttocks.
posar, *vi.* (art) to pose.—*vt.* to lay down.—*vr.* to land, alight, sit (on).
posdata, *f.* postscript.
poseedor, *m.* possessor, holder, owner.—**poseer,** *vti.* [e] to possess, own; to hold; to master (an art, language, etc.).—**posesión,** *f.* possession; ownership; property.—**posesionar,** *vt.* to give possession; to install, induct.—*vr.* to take possession.—**posesivo,** *n.* & *a.* (gram.) possessive.—**poseso,** *ppi.* of POSEER.—*a.* possessed (by evil spirits).
posguerra, *f.* postwar period.
posibilidad, *f.* possibility.—**posibilitar,** *vt.* to render possible, facilitate.—**posible,** *a.* possible.—*m. pl.* personal means.
posición, *f.* position; placing, placement; standing, status.
positivo, *a.* positive, certain; absolute, real; matter-of-fact; (math., elec., photog.) positive.
posma, *f.* (coll.) sluggishness, sloth, dullness.—*n.* (coll.) dull, sluggish person.
poso, *m.* sediment, dregs.
posponer, *vti.* [32-49] (a) to postpone, put off, defer; to subordinate; to put after.—**posposición,** *f.* postponement; subordination.—**pospuesto,** *ppi.* of POSPONER.
postal, *a.* postal.—*giro p.,* money order.—*f.* post card.
postdata, *f.* = POSDATA.
poste, *m.* post, pillar.
postergación, *f.* delaying; leaving behind.—**postergar,** *vti.* [b] to delay, postpone; to disregard someone's rights; to hold back, to pass over.
posteridad, *f.* posterity.—**posterior,** *a.* posterior, rear; later, subsequent.
postguerra, *f.* = POSGUERRA.
postigo, *m.* wicket; peep window; shutter.
postilla, *f.* scab on wounds.
postizo, *a.* artificial, not natural; false (teeth).—*m.* false hair.
postmeridiano, *a.* postmeridian (p.m.).

postración, *f.* prostration, proneness; kneeling; dejection.—**postrar,** *vt.* to prostrate; to weaken, exhaust.—*vr.* to prostrate oneself, kneel down; to be exhausted.
postre, *m.* dessert.—*a la p.,* at last.
postrer(o), *a.* last; hindmost.
postulado, *m.* postulate.—**postular,** *vt.* to postulate; to nominate a candidate.—*vr.* to become a candidate.
postura, *f.* posture, position, stance; bid (auction); wager, bet; egg-laying.
potable, *a.* potable, drinkable.
potaje, *m.* pottage; porridge; medley.
potasa, *f.* potash.
pote, *m.* pot, jar.
potencia, *f.* power; potency; dominion; faculty of the mind; power, strong nation; force, strength.—*en p.,* potentially.—**potencial,** *a.* & *m.* potential.—**potentado,** *m.* potentate.—**potente,** *a.* powerful.—**potestad,** *f.* power, dominion, jurisdiction; potentate.—**potestativo,** *a.* optional.
potingue, *m.* (coll.) medicinal concoction.
potra, *f.* filly; hernia.—**potranca,** *f.* filly.—**potrero,** *m.* pasture ground; cattle ranch.—**potril,** *m.* pasture for young horses.—**potro,** *m.* colt, foal.
poyo, *m.* stone seat against a wall.
poza, *f.* puddle.—**pozo,** *m.* (water) well.
práctica, *f.* practice; habit; practicing; exercise; manner, method, routine.—**practicable,** *a.* practicable, feasible.—**practicar,** *vti.* [d] to practice; to make; to perform, do, put in execution; to practice, go in for.—**práctico,** *a.* practical; skillful, experienced.—*m.* (naut.) harbor pilot.
pradera, *f.* prairie, meadow.—**prado,** *m.* lawn; field, meadow; pasture.
preámbulo, *m.* preamble; (coll.) evasion.
precario, *a.* precarious.
precaución, *f.* precaution.—**precaver,** *vt.* to prevent, obviate.—*vr.* (de) to guard, be on one's guard (against).
precedencia, *f.* precedence, priority.—**precedente,** *a.* prior, precedent.—*m.* precedent.—**preceder,** *vt.* to precede; to be superior to.
precepto, *m.* precept.—**preceptor,** *n.* teacher, tutor.
preciar, *vt.* to value, price, appraise.—*vr.* (de) to boast, brag (about); to take pride, glory (in).
precintar, *vt.* to strap, hoop, bind; to seal.
precio, *m.* price; importance, worth.—**preciosidad,** *f.* worth, preciousness;

rich or beautiful object, [a] beauty.
—**precioso,** a. precious; beautiful.

precipicio, m. precipice, chasm; violent fall.

precipitación, f. rash haste, unthinking hurry; (chem.) precipitation.—**precipitado,** a. headlong; hurried, hasty.—m. (chem.) precipitate.—**precipitar,** vt. to precipitate; to rush, hasten.—vr. to throw oneself headlong; to rush, hurry.

precisar, vt. to fix, set, determine; to compel, oblige; to be urgent or necessary.—**precisión,** f. necessity; compulsion; preciseness, exactness; precision, accuracy.—**preciso,** a. necessary; indispensable; precise, exact, accurate; distinct, clear; concise.

preconizar, vti. [a] to praise, eulogize.

predecesor, n. predecessor.

predecir, vti. [14-49] to foretell, predict, forecast.

predestinación, f. predestination.—**predestinar,** vt. to predestine, foreordain.

predeterminar, vt. to predetermine.

prédica, predicación, f. preaching; sermon.—**predicado,** m. predicate.—**predicador,** n. preacher.—**predicar,** vti. & vii. [d] to preach; to praise.

predicción, f. prediction.—**predicho,** ppi. of PREDECIR.

predilección, f. predilection.—**predilecto,** a. preferred, favorite.

predisponer, vti. [32-49] to prejudice, predispose; to prearrange.—**predisposición,** f. predisposition; prejudice.—**predispuesto,** ppi. of PREDISPONER.—a. predisposed, biased, inclined.

predominante, a. predominant, prevailing.—**predominar,** vt. & vi. to predominate, prevail; to rise above, overlook, command.—**predominio,** m. predominance, superiority.

prefabricado, a. prefabricated.

prefacio, m. preface, prologue.

preferencia, f. preference.—**preferente,** a. preferential; preferring; preferable.—**preferible,** a. preferable.—**preferir,** vti. [39] to prefer.

prefijar, vt. to predesignate, set beforehand.—**prefijo,** a. prefixed.—m. prefix.

pregón, m. hawker's cry.—**pregonar,** vt. to hawk, proclaim, cry out; to make known.—**pregonero,** n. hawker, town crier.

pregunta, f. question, query.—**preguntar,** vt. & vi. to ask, question, inquire.—vr. to wonder.—**preguntón,** a. inquisitive.

prejuicio, m. prejudice, bias.—**prejuzgar,** vti. [b] to prejudge.

prelación, f. preference.

prelado, m. prelate.

preliminar, a. preliminary.—m. preliminary; protocol.

preludio, m. introduction; (mus.) prelude.

prematuro, a. premature; untimely; unripe.

premeditación, f. premeditation, willfulness.—**premeditar,** vt. to premeditate.

premiar, vt. to reward, remunerate; to award a prize.—**premio,** m. prize; reward; recompense; (com.) premium, interest.

premisa, f. premise.

premura, f. urgency, pressure, haste.

prenda, f. pledge, token; piece of jewelry; garment; person dearly loved.—pl. endowments, natural gifts, talents.—soltar p., to commit oneself.—**prendarse** vr. (de), to fall in love with, take a great liking (to).

prendedor, m. breastpin; brooch; safety pin; tiepin.—**prender,** vti. [49] to seize, grasp, catch, apprehend; to fasten, clasp.—p. fuego a, to set on fire.—p. la luz, to turn on the light.—vii. to take root; to catch or take fire.—**prendería,** f. pawnshop.—**prendero,** m. pawnbroker.

prensa, f. press.—**prensar,** vt. to press.

preñada, a. pregnant (esp. of animals).—preñado de, full of.—**preñez,** f. pregnancy.

preocupación, f. worry, preoccupation, concern.—**preocupar,** vt. to worry, to preoccupy.—vr. to worry.

preparación, f. preparation; preparing; compound; medicine.—**preparar,** vt. to prepare, make ready.—vr. to be prepared, get ready, make preparations.—**preparativo,** a. preparatory.—m. pl. preparations, arrangements.—**preparatorio,** a. preparatory.

preponderancia, f. preponderance, sway.—**preponderar,** vi. to have control; to prevail.

preposición, f. preposition.

prepotencia, f. predominance.—**prepotente,** a. predominant.

prerrogativa, f. prerogative.

presa, f. capture, seizure; (mil.) booty; quarry, prey; (water) dam; morsel; tusk, fang; claw.

presagiar, vt. to presage, foretell.—**presagio,** m. presage, omen, prognostication.

presbiteriano, n. & a. Presbyterian.—**presbítero,** m. priest; presbyter.

prescindir, vi. (de) to dispense

(with), do (without); to set aside, ignore, omit.

prescribir, *vti.* [49] to prescribe, specify.—**prescrito,** *ppi.* of PRESCRIBIR.

presencia, *f.* presence; appearance.—*p. de ánimo,* coolness, presence of mind.—**presenciar,** *vt.* to witness, see; to attend.—**presentación,** *f.* presentation, exhibition; personal introduction.—**presentar,** *vt.* to present; to put on (a program, etc.); to display, show.—*vr.* to appear, present oneself, report; to turn up; to offer one's services.—**presente,** *a.* present, current.—*hacer p.,* to state; to remind of, call attention.—*tener p.,* to bear in mind.—*m.* present, gift; present (time).

presentimiento, *m.* presentiment; misgiving.—**presentir,** *vti.* [39] to have a presentiment of; to forebode, predict.

preservación, *f.* preservation, conservation.—**preservar,** *vt.* to preserve, guard, keep, save.

presidencia, *f.* presidency; presidential chair; chairmanship; presidential term.—**presidencial,** *a.* presidential.—**presidente,** *n.* president; chairman; any presiding officer.

presidiario, *m.* convict.—**presidio,** *m.* penitentiary.

presidir, *vt.* to preside over, or at; to govern, determine.

presilla, *f.* loop, fastener; clip.

presión, *f.* pressure.—**presionar,** *vt.* to press, urge.

preso, *ppi.* of PRENDER.—*a.* arrested; imprisoned.—*n.* prisoner; convict.

prestamista, *mf.* money lender.—**préstamo,** *m.* loan.

prestar, *vt.* to lend, loan.—*p. atención,* to pay attention.—*p. ayuda,* to help.—*p. un servicio,* to do a favor.—*vr.* to offer oneself or itself; to adapt oneself or itself.

presteza, *f.* quickness, promptness.—**prestidigitación,** *f.* legerdemain, sleight of hand; jugglery.—**prestidigitador,** *n.* juggler; magician.

prestigio, *m* prestige; influence; good name.—**prestigioso,** *a.* renowned; well-reputed.

presto, *a.* quick, swift, prompt; ready, prepared.—*adv.* soon; quickly.

presumible, *a.* presumable.—**presumido,** *a.* presumptuous, conceited.—**presumir,** *vti.* [49] to presume, surmise, conjecture.—*vii.* (de) to boast (of being), claim (to be); to be conceited.—**presunción,** *f.* presumption, conjecture; presumptuousness, conceit.—**presunto,** *ppi.* of

PRESUMIR.—*a.* presumed.—**presuntuosidad,** *f.* presumptuousness.—**presuntuoso,** *a.* presumptuous, conceited.

presuponer, *vti.* [32-49] to presuppose; to estimate; to budget.—**presuposición,** *f.* presupposition.—**presupuestario,** *a.* budgetary.—**presupuesto,** *ppi.* of PRESUPONER.—*m.* budget, estimate.—*a.* presupposed; estimated.

presuroso, *a.* prompt, quick.

pretender, *vti.* [49] to pretend; to aspire to; to seek, solicit; to try; to intend; to court.—*p. decir,* to mean, be driving at.—**pretensión,** *f.* pretension, claim; presumption.—**pretenso,** *ppi.* of PRETENDER.

preterir, *vti.* [50] to ignore, overlook.—**pretérito,** *m.* & *a.* preterit, past.

pretextar, *vt.* to give as a pretext.—**pretexto,** *m.* pretext, pretense, excuse.

pretil, *m.* railing, battlement.

pretina, *f.* girdle, waistband; belt; fly (of trousers).

prevalecer, *vii.* [3] to prevail.

prevención, *f.* prevention; foresight; warning; prejudice; police station.—**prevenir,** *vti.* [45] to prevent, avoid; to arrange, make ready; to foresee.—*vri.* to be ready, prepared, or on guard; to take precautions.—**preventivo,** *a.* preventive.

prever, *vti.* [46-49] to foresee, anticipate.—**previo,** *a.* previous, foregoing.—**previsión,** *f.* foresight.—**previsor,** *a.* far-seeing.—**previsto,** *ppi.* of PREVENIR.

prieto, *a.* blackish, very dark; tight.

prima, *f.* female cousin; (mus.) treble; (com.) premium; bounty.—**primacía,** *f.* primacy; superiority; priority.—**primario,** *a.* principal, primary.

primavera, *f.* spring (season); primrose.—**primaveral,** *a.* spring.

primer(o), *a.* first; former; leading; principal.—*de buenas a primeras,* suddenly.—*de primera,* of superior quality.—*adv.* first; rather, sooner.

primicia, *f.* first fruit.—*pl.* first production, maiden effort.

primitivo, *a.* primitive, original.

primo, *n.* cousin; (coll.) simpleton.—*coger a uno de p.,* to deceive someone easily.—*número p.,* prime number.—*p. carnal,* or *p. hermano,* first cousin.—*a.* first; superior, prime.—**primogénito,** *n.* & *a.* first-born.—**primogenitura,** *f.* state of being the first-born child; seniority.

primor, *m.* beauty; nicety.

primordial, *a.* primal.

primoroso, *a.* neat, fine, exquisite; beautiful; skillful.

princesa, *f.* princess.—**principado,** *m.* princedom.—**principal,** *a.* principal, main; first; famous.—*m.* (com.) principal, capital, stock; chief or head.—**príncipe,** *m.* prince.

principiante, *a.* beginning.—*mf.* beginner.—**principiar,** *vt.* to commence, begin, start.—**principio,** *m.* principle, tenet; beginning; start; original cause; rule of action.—*a principios de,* at the beginning of.—*al p.,* at first.—*en p.,* in principle.

pringoso, *a.* greasy, fatty.—**pringue,** *m.* or *f.* grease, fat; grease stain.

prior, *m.* (eccl.) prior, superior; rector, curate.—**prioridad,** *f.* priority, precedence.

prisa, *f.* haste, promptness; urgency. —*a p.,* quickly.—*darse p.,* to make haste, hurry.—*de p.,* quickly.—*estar de p.,* or *tener p.,* to be in a hurry.

prisión, *f.* seizure, capture; prison; imprisonment.—**prisionero,** *n.* prisoner.

prisma, *m.* prism.

prístino, *a.* pristine.

privación, *f.* privation; lack.—**privado,** *a.* private, secret; personal.—**privar,** *vt.* to deprive.—*vi.* to prevail, be in favor or in vogue.—*vr.* to deprive oneself.—**privativo,** *a.* privative; special, distinctive, particular; exclusive.

privilegiar, *vt.* to favor; to grant a privilege to.—**privilegio,** *m.* privilege; grant, concession.

pro, *m.* or *f.* profit, benefit, advantage.—*en p. de,* in behalf of, for the benefit of.

proa, *f.* bow, prow.

probabilidad, *f.* probability.—**probable,** *a.* probable.

probar, *vti.* [12] to try, test; to prove; to taste; to sample (as wine); to attempt, try; to try on (as a coat).—*p. fortuna,* to take one's chances.—*vii.* to suit, agree with.—*vri.* to try on (as a coat).

probeta, *f.* pressure gauge; test tube; beaker.

probidad, *f.* probity, honesty, integrity.

problema, *m.* problem.

probo, *a.* upright, honest.

procaz, *a.* impudent, bold, insolent.

procedencia, *f.* origin; source; place of sailing.—**procedente,** *a.* coming or proceeding (from); according to law.—**proceder,** *vi.* to proceed; to go on; to arise; to be the result; to behave; to act; to take action. —*m.* behavior, action.—**procedi-** miento, *m.* procedure; process; method; (law) proceeding.

prócer, *a.* tall, lofty, elevated.—*mf.* hero, leader, dignitary.

procesado, *a.* (law) related to court proceeding; included in the suit; prosecuted, indicted.—*n.* defendant. —**procesar,** *vt.* to sue; to indict.

procesión, *f.* procession.

proceso, *m.* process; course, development; (law) criminal case; proceedings of a lawsuit, trial.

proclama, *f.* proclamation; publication; banns of marriage.—**proclamación,** *f.* proclamation.—**proclamar,** *vt.* to proclaim; to acclaim.

procrear, *vt.* to father, procreate; to sire.

procuración, *f.* care, diligence; proxy, power or letter of attorney; procurement, procuring; office of an attorney.—**procurador,** *n.* (law) solicitor, attorney.—**procurar,** *vt.* to endeavor, try; to procure; (Am.) to look for.—*vi.* to act as a solicitor.

prodigalidad, *f.* prodigality, wastefulness; abundance.—**prodigar,** *vti.* [b] to lavish; to squander.

prodigio, *m.* prodigy; marvel.—**prodigioso,** *a.* prodigious, marvelous.

pródigo, *a.* prodigal, extravagant, wasteful; liberal, generous.—*n.* spendthrift.

producción, *f.* production; produce.—**producir,** *vti.* [11] to produce; to bring about; to yield.—*vri.* to explain oneself; to be produced; to come about; to break out.—**productivo,** *a.* productive; profitable, fruitful.—**producto,** *m.* product; article (of trade, etc.); produce.—**productor,** *a.* productive. —*n.* producer.

proeza, *f.* prowess, feat.

profanación, *f.* profanation, desecration.—**profanar,** *vt.* to profane, desecrate.—**profano,** *a.* profane; secular; irreverent; uninformed, ignorant.—*n.* layman; uninitiated person.

profecía, *f.* prophecy.

proferir, *vti.* [39] to utter, express, speak.

profesar, *vt.* to practice (a profession); to profess, declare; to show, manifest.—*vi.* to take vows.—**profesión,** *f.* profession, vocation.—**profesional,** *a.* professional.—**profesor,** *n.* professor.—**profesorado,** *m.* professorship; faculty; teaching profession.

profeta, *m.* prophet.—**profético,** *a.* prophetic(al).—**profetizar,** *vti.* [a] & *vii.* to prophesy.

proficiente, *a.* proficient, advanced.
profiláctico, *a.* prophylactic, preventive.—*m.* prophylactic.
prófugo, *n. & a.* fugitive from justice.
profundidad, *f.* depth; profoundness.—**profundizar**, *vti.* [a] to deepen; to go deep into.—**profundo**, *a.* deep; profound.
profusión, *f.* profusion; lavishness, prodigality.—**profuso**, *a.* profuse, plentiful; lavish.
progenie, *f.* progeny, offspring, issue.
progenitor, *m.* progenitor, ancestor.
programa, *m.* program.
progresar, *vi.* to progress; to advance.—**progresión**, *f.* progression.—**progresista**, *a. & mf.* progressive.—**progresivo**, *a.* advancing, progressive.—**progreso**, *m.* progress, civilization; advancement, development.—*pl.* progress, strides (in an undertaking, school, etc.).
prohibición, *f.* prohibition, forbidding.—**prohibir**, *vt.* to prohibit, forbid.—*se prohibe fumar*, no smoking.—**prohibitivo**, *a.* prohibitive, forbidding.
prohijar, *vt.* to adopt.
prójimo, *m.* fellow creature, neighbor.
prole, *f.* progeny, offspring.—**proletariado**, *m.* proletariat.—**proletario**, *a.* proletarian; belonging to the working classes.—*n.* proletarian.
prolífico, *a.* prolific, fruitful.
prólogo, *m.* prologue.
prolongación, *f.* prolongation, lengthening; extension.—**prolongar**, *vti. & vri.* [b] to prolong; to extend, continue.
promediar, *vt.* (com.) to average.—*vi.* to mediate.—**promedio**, *m.* average.
promesa, *f.* promise, offer; pious offering.—**prometedor**, *a.* promising.—**prometer**, *vt.* to promise; to bid fair.—*vi.* to show promise.—*vr.* to expect with confidence; to become engaged.—**prometido**, *n.* fiancé, fiancée, betrothed.—*m.* promise.
prominencia, *f.* elevation; prominence; protuberance.—**prominente**, *a.* prominent, outstanding; salient.
promiscuidad, *f.* promiscuity.—**promiscuo**, *a.* promiscuous.
promisorio, *a.* promissory.
promoción, *f.* promotion.
promontorio, *m.* promontory; anything bulky and unwieldy.
promotor, *n.* promoter, advancer.—**promover**, *vti.* [26] to promote; to advance.
pronombre, *m.* pronoun.
pronosticar, *vti.* [d] to prognosticate, foretell.—**pronóstico**, *m.* forecast, prediction; omen.

prontitud, *f.* promptness; quickness.—**pronto**, *a.* prompt, quick, fast; ready.—*m.* sudden impulse. *adv.* soon; promptly, speedily, quickly.—*de p.*, suddenly, without thinking.—*por lo p.*, for the time being.
pronunciación, *f.* pronunciation.—**pronunciar**, *vt.* to pronounce; to deliver, make (a speech).—*vr.* to declare oneself.
propagación, *f.* propagation; spreading, dissemination.—**propagador**, *n. & a.* propagator; propagating.—**propaganda**, *f.* propaganda.—**propagandista**, *mf.* propagandist.—**propagar**, *vti.* [b] to propagate; to spread, disseminate.—*vri.* to spread; to propagate; to multiply.
propalar, *vt.* to publish, divulge.
propasarse, *vr.* to go too far; to go to extremes.
propender, *vii.* [49] to tend, be inclined.
propensión, *f.* tendency, proclivity, proneness.—**propenso**, *ppi.* of PROPENDER.—*a.* inclined, disposed.
propiciar, *vt.* to propitiate.—**propicio**, *a.* propitious, favorable.
propiedad, *f.* ownership, proprietorship; property, holding; propriety, fitness; dominion, possession.—**propietario**, *n.* proprietor, owner, landlord.—*a.* proprietary.
propina, *f.* tip, gratuity.—**propinar**, *vt.* to deal (a beating, a kick, etc.).
propio, *a.* one's own; proper, appropriate; characteristic, typical.—*m.* messenger.
proponer, *vti.* [32-49] to propose, propound; to present or name (as candidate).—*vri.* to purpose, plan, intend.
proporción, *f.* proportion; opportunity, chance.—**proporcionado**, *a.* proportioned, fit, relevant.—**proporcional**, *a.* proportional.—**proporcionar**, *vt.* to proportion; to supply, provide, furnish; to adjust, adapt.
proposición, *f.* proposition; proposal; motion (in congress, etc.).
propósito, *m.* purpose, intention; aim, object.—*a p.*, for the purpose; fit; incidentally, by the way.—*a p. de*, in connection with, apropos of.—*de p.*, on purpose, purposely.—*fuera de p.*, irrelevant.
propuesta, *f.* proposal, offer; nomination.—**propuesto**, *ppi.* of PROPONER.
propugnar, *vt.* to advocate, defend strongly, promote.
propulsar, *vt.* to propel.—**propulsión**, *f.* propulsion.—*p. a chorro*, jet propulsion.—**propulsor**, *n. & a.* propeller; propelling.

prorrata, *f.* apportionment.—*a p.,* pro rata, in proportion.—**prorratear,** *vt.* to allot in proportion.—**prorrateo,** *m.* pro rata division.

prórroga, *f.* prolongation, extension (of time).—**prorrogable,** *a.* that may be prolonged or extended (in time).—**prorrogar,** *vti.* [b] to prolong, extend (in time).

prorrumpir, *vi.* to break forth, burst out.

prosa, *f.* prose.—**prosaico,** *a.* prosaic. —**prosista,** *mf.* prose writer.

proscribir, *vti.* [49] to proscribe, banish; to outlaw.—**proscripción,** *f.* proscription, banishment.—**poscrito,** *ppi.* of PROSCRIBIR.—*n.* exile; outlaw.

proseguir, *vti.* [29-b] to continue; to carry on with; to resume.—*vii.* to keep going, proceed.

prosodia, *f.* prosody.

prosperar, *vi.* to prosper, thrive.— **prosperidad,** *f.* prosperity, success. —**próspero,** *a.* prosperous; favorable.

prosternarse, *vr.* to prostrate oneself.

prostitución, *f.* prostitution.—**prostituir,** *vti.* [23-49-e] to prostitute, corrupt, debase.—*vri.* to sell one's honor; to turn prostitute.—**prostituto,** *ppi.* of PROSTITUIR.—*n.* prostitute; streetwalker.

protagonista, *mf.* protagonist, hero-(ine).

protección, *f.* protection; favor.—**protector,** *n.* protector.—**proteger,** *vti.* [c] to protect.—**protegido,** *n.* protégé.

proteína, *f.* protein.

protesta, *f.* protestation; protest.— **protestante,** *a.* protesting.—*mf.* & *a.* Protestant.—**protestantismo,** *m.* Protestantism.—**protestar,** *vt.* (com.) to protest; to assure, protest, asseverate; to profess (one's faith). —*p. contra,* to protest, deny the validity of.—*p. de,* to protest against.—**protesto,** *m.* (com.) protest (of a bill).

protocolo, *m.* protocol; registry, judicial record.

protoplasma, *m.* protoplasm.

prototipo, *m.* prototype, original; model.

protuberancia, *f.* protuberance.

provecho, *m.* benefit, advantage; profit, gain; proficiency, progress.— **provechoso,** *a.* profitable; beneficial, good; useful, advantageous.

proveedor, *n.* purveyor, provider; supplier.—**proveer,** *vti.* [49-e] to provide, furnish; to supply with provisions; (law) to decide.—*vri.*

(de) to provide oneself (with), get one's supply (of).

provenir, *vii.* [45] to come, originate, arise; to be due.

proverbial, *a.* proverbial.—**proverbio,** *m.* proverb.

providencia, *f.* providence, foresight; Providence; act of providing; (law) decision, sentence.—**providencial,** *a.* providential.

provincia, *f.* province.—**provincial,** *a.* provincial.—**provinciano,** *n.* & *a.* provincial.

provisión, *f.* provision; supply, stock; measure, means.—**provisional,** *a.* provisional, interim.—**provisorio,** *a.* provisional, temporary.—**provisto,** *ppi.* of PROVEER.—*a.* provided, stocked, supplied.

provocación, *f.* provocation, irritation.—**provocador,** *n.* provoker; inciter.—**provocar,** *vti.* [d] to provoke, excite, incite, anger; to promote; to tempt, arouse desire in.—**provocativo,** *a.* inciting; tempting; provoking, irritating.

proximidad, *f.* proximity.—**próximo,** *a.* next; nearest, neighboring; close.

proyección, *f.* projecting; projection. —**proyectar,** *vt.* to design; to project, plan, devise; to shoot or throw forth; (geom.) to project; to cast (as a shadow); to show (a movie).—*vr.* to be cast, fall (as a shadow).—**proyectil,** *m.* projectile, missile.—**proyectista,** *mf.* planner; designer.—**proyecto,** *m.* project, plan; design.—**proyector,** *m.* projector; searchlight.

prudencia, *f.* prudence; moderation. —**prudente,** *a.* prudent, cautious.

prueba, *f.* proof; evidence; trial, test; probation; sample; testing; temptation; trial, fitting.—*a p.,* on trial; according to the best standards.—*a p. de,* proof against.— *hacer la p.,* to try.—*poner a p.,* to try, put to the test.

prurito, *m.* itching; excessive desire.

prusiano, *n.* & *a.* Prussian.

psicoanálisis, *m.* psychoanalysis.— **psicoanalista,** *mf.* psychoanalist.— **psicoanalizar,** *vti.* [a] to psychoanalyze.—**psicología,** *f.* psychology. —**psicológico,** *a.* psychological.— **psicólogo,** *n.* psychologist.—**psicópata,** *mf.* psychopath.—**psicosis,** *f.* psychosis.—**psicótico,** *n.* & *a.* psychotic.—**psique,** *f.* psyche.—**psiquiatra,** *mf.* psychiatrist.—**psiquiatría,** *f.* psychiatry.—**psíquico,** *a.* psychic(al).

psitacosis, *f.* parrot fever.

púa, *f.* prick, barb; prong; thorn;

spine or quill (of porcupine); (coll.) tricky person.

pubertad, *f.* puberty.

publicación, *f.* publication.—**publicar,** *vti.* [d] to publish.—**publicidad,** *f.* publicity.—**público,** *a.* & *m.* public. —*en p.*, publicly.

puchero, *m.* cooking pot; stew; dinner, food; pouting.—*hacer pucheros,* (coll.) to pout.

pudiente, *a.* powerful; wealthy.

pudín, *m.* pudding.—*p. inglés con pasas,* plum pudding.

pudor, *m.* decorousness, modesty.— **pudoroso,** *a.* modest; bashful, shy.

pudrir, *vti., vii.* & *vri.* [33] to rot, decay.

pueblo, *m.* town, village; people; population; common people; nation.

puente, *m.* bridge.—*p. colgante,* suspension bridge.—*p. giratorio,* swing bridge.—*p. levadizo,* drawbridge.

puerco, *a.* filthy, dirty, foul; low, base, mean.—*n.* pig, hog; (fig.) dirty, base or low person.

pueril, *a.* childish, puerile.

puerta, *f.* door; doorway, gateway; gate; entrance.—*a p. cerrada,* privately, secretly.—*p. falsa,* back door, side door.—*p. franca,* open door, free entrance; free entry.

puerto, *m.* port; mountain pass; harbor; (fig.) shelter, refuge.

puertorriqueño, *n.* & *a.* (Am.) = PORTORRIQUEÑO.

pues, *conj.* because, for, as; since; then.—*p. bien,* now then, well then. —*p. no,* not at all, not so.—*p. que,* since.—*¿p. qué?* what? what about it? so what?—*p. sí,* yes, indeed, most certainly.—*¿y p.?* so? is that so? how is that?—*adv.* so; certainly; anyhow, just the same.

puesta, *f.* (astr.) set, setting; stake (at cards).—*p. de sol,* sunset.

puesto, *ppi.* of PONER.—*bien (mal) p.,* well (badly) dressed.—*p. que,* since, inasmuch as, as long as.—*m.* place; vendor's booth or stand; position, job; post, dignity, office; military post; blind for hunters; breeding stall.

pugilato, *m.* boxing; boxing bout.— **pugilista,** *mf.* boxer, pugilist, prize fighter.

pugna, *f.* combat, struggle; conflict. —*estar en p.,* to be in conflict, disagree.—**pugnar,** *vi.* to fight, struggle; (con) to conflict (with), be opposed (to); to persist.

puja, *f.* outbidding or overbidding at an auction; higher bid.—**pujante,** *a.* powerful, strong.—**pujanza,** *f.* push, might, strength.—**pujar,** *vi.* to outbid or overbid; to strive,

struggle.—**pujido, pujo,** *m.* grunt; strenuous effort.

pulcritud, *f.* neatness, tidiness.— **pulcro,** *a.* neat, trim.

pulga, *f.* flea.—*ser de* or *tener malas pulgas,* to be ill-tempered.—**pulgada,** *f.* inch.—**pulgar,** *m.* thumb.— **pulgón,** *m.* green fly, plant louse.

pulimentar, *vt.* to burnish, gloss, polish.—**pulimento,** *m.* polish; glossiness.—**pulir,** *vt.* to polish, burnish; to beautify; to render polite.—*vr.* to beautify or deck oneself; to become polished.

pulmón, *m.* lung.—**pulmonar,** *a.* pulmonary.—**pulmonía,** *f.* pneumonia.

pulpa, *f.* pulp, flesh; fruit or wood pulp.—**pulpería,** *f.* (Am.) retail grocery or general store; tavern.— **pulpero,** *n.* (Am.) grocer.

púlpito, *m.* pulpit.

pulpo, *m.* cuttlefish, octopus.

pulsación, *f.* pulsation, throb; pulse, beating.—**pulsar,** *vt.* to feel the pulse of; to finger (a string instrument); to explore, sound, or examine.—*vi.* to pulsate, beat.— **pulsera,** *f.* bracelet; wrist bandage. —*reloj de p.,* wrist watch.—**pulso,** *m.* pulse; beat; firmness or steadiness of hand; (Am.) bracelet.—*a p.,* freehand; with the strength of the hand.—*tomar el p.,* to feel the pulse.

pulular, *vi.* to swarm; to multiply with great rapidity; to bud, sprout.

pulverización, *f.* pulverization.—**pulverizador,** *m.* atomizer, spray; pulverizer.—**pulverizar,** *vti.* [a] to pulverize; to spray.

pulla, *f.* cutting remark, taunt, quip; hint.

puma, *m.* puma, American panther.

puna, *f.* (Am.) cold, desertlike tableland of the Andes; (Am.) desert; (Am.) mountain sickness.

pundonor, *m.* point of honor.

punición, *f.* punishment.

punta, *f.* point, sharp end; end, tip; apex, top; cape, promontory; touch, trace, suggestion; stub of a cigar or cigarette.—*de p.,* point first.—*de p. en blanco,* all dressed up; in full regalia.—*estar de p.,* to be on bad terms.—**puntada,** *f.* stitch; hint.— **puntal,** *m.* prop, support.—**puntapié,** *m.* kick.—**puntear,** *vt.* to play (the guitar); (art) to stipple; (sew.) to stitch.—**puntería,** *f.* aiming or pointing of a weapon; marksmanship.—**puntero,** *m.* pointer; chisel.—**puntiagudo,** *a.* sharp, spiky; pungent.—**puntilla,** *f.* lace edging; tack; joiner's nail.—*de,* or *en puntillas,* softly, gently; on tiptoe.—

puntilloso, *a.* sensitive, easily offended.—**punto,** *m.* point, dot; period in writing; point of a pen; sight in firearms; stitch; mesh; place; instant, moment; stop, rest, recess; end, object, aim.—*al p.,* immediately, at once.—*a p. de,* on the point of, about to.—*a p. fijo,* exactly.—*dos puntos,* colon.—*en p.,* on the dot, (of the hour) sharp.—*p. en boca,* silence.—*p. final,* stop; full stop.—*p. y coma,* semicolon.—*puntos suspensivos,* leaders.—**puntuación,** *f.* punctuation.—**puntual,** *a.* prompt, punctual.—**puntualidad,** *f.* punctuality.—**puntualizar,** *vti.* [a] to give a detailed account of.—**puntuar,** *vt.* to punctuate; to point.

punzada, *f.* prick, puncture; sharp pain.—**punzante,** *a.* pricking, sharp; poignant.—**punzar,** *vti.* [a] to punch, bore, perforate; to prick, puncture; to cause sharp pain; to grieve.

punzó, *a.* (Am.) deep scarlet red.

punzón, *m.* punch; puncher; driver, point, awl.

puñada, *f.* blow with the fist.—**puñado,** *m.* handful; a few.—**puñal,** *m.* dagger, poniard.—**puñalada,** *f.* stab (with a dagger); sharp pain.—**puñetazo,** *m.* = PUÑADA.—**puño,** *m.* fist; grasp; handful; cuff, wristband (of garment); hilt of a sword; haft (of a tool); handle (of an umbrella, etc.); head of a staff or cane.

pupila, *f.* (anat.) pupil.

pupilaje, *m.* room and board; boarding house.—**pupilo,** *n.* ward; boarding-school pupil; boarder.

pupitre, *m.* writing desk; school desk.

puré, *m.* thick soup, purée.—*p. de papas,* mashed potatoes.

pureza, *f.* purity, chastity; genuineness.

purga, *f.* physic, cathartic.—**purgación,** *f.* purge, purgation; gonorrhea, clap.—**purgante,** *a.* purging, purgative.—*m.* purgative, cathartic, physic.—**purgar,** *vti.* [b] to purge, purify; to expiate; to refine, clarify; to drain; to purge.—*vri.* to take a purgative; to clear oneself of guilt.—**purgatorio,** *m.* purgatory.

purificación, *f.* purification.—**purificador,** *n.* & *a.* purifier; purifying.—**purificar,** *vti.* [d] to purify.—*vri.* to be purified.

puritano, *a.* & *n.* Puritan.

puro, *a.* pure; unadulterated; mere, only, sheer.—*m.* cigar.

púrpura, *f.* purple shell; purple; dignity of a cardinal.—**purpúreo,** *a.* purple.—**purpurino,** *a.* purple.

purulento, *a.* purulent.—**pus,** *m.* pus.

pusilánime, *a.* faint-hearted, spineless.

pústula, *f.* pimple.

puta, *f.* whore, harlot.

puya, *f.* goad, goad stick.

Q

que, *rel. pron.* that; which; who, whom.—*el q.,* he who, the one who, the one that.—*lo q.,* what, which.—*por más q.,* no matter how.—*conj.* that, than; because, for.—*más q.,* more than.—*por mucho q.,* no matter how much.—*¿qué? interrog. pron.* what? which? how?—*¿para q.?* what for?—*¿por qué?* why?—*¿q. tal?* how goes it?—*interj.* what a! how!

quebrada, *f.* ravine; gorge; (Am.) gulch; stream.—**quebradizo,** *a.* brittle, fragile; frail, sickly.—**quebrado,** *a.* broken; (com.) bankrupt; rough, uneven (ground); (med.) ruptured.—*m.* (arith.) common fraction.—**quebrantar,** *vt.* to break, crush; to burst open; to pound; to transgress; to violate, break (as a contract); to vex; to weaken.—**quebranto,** *m.* (com.) loss, damage; breaking, crushing; grief, affliction.—**quebrar,** *vti.* [1] to break; to crush.—*vii.* (com.) to fail, become bankrupt.—*vri.* to be ruptured; to break (as a plate, a bone, etc.); to be broken.

quechua, *mf.* & *a.* Quechua; Quechuan (Indian and language).

quedar, *vi.* to remain; to stay, stop in a place; to be or be left in a state or condition.—*q. bien,* (*mal*), to acquit oneself well (badly); to come out well (badly).—*q. en,* to agree to; to have an understanding.—*vr.* to remain.—*quedarse atrás,* to get, or be left, behind.—*quedarse con,* to retain, keep.

quedo, *a.* quiet, still, noiseless; easy, gentle.—*adv.* softly, gently; in a low voice.

quehacer, *m.* occupation, business, work.—*pl.* chores; duties.

queja, *f.* complaint; grumbling, moan; grudge.—**quejarse,** *vr.* to complain; to grumble; (de) to regret, lament.—**quejido,** *m.* moan.—**quejoso,** *a.* complaining.—**quejumbroso,** *a.* grumbling; plaintive.

quema, *f.* burning, fire, conflagration.—*huir de la q.,* to get away from trouble, get out.—**quemado,** *a.* burnt, crisp; sunburned.—*m.* burnt down forest or thicket.—**quemadura,** *f.* burn, scald.—**quemar,** *vt.* to

burn; to scald; to scorch; to set on fire; to dispose of at a low price; to annoy.—*vi.* to burn, be too hot.—*vr.* to get burned, burn oneself; to be consumed by fire; to feel very hot.—**quemazón,** *f.* fire, conflagration; (coll.) smarting, burning; (Am.) bargain sale.

querella, *f.* complaint; quarrel; (law) plaint, complaint.—**querellante,** *mf. & a.* complainant; complaining.—**querellarse,** *vr.* to complain; (law) to file a complaint, bring suit.

querer, *vti.* [34] to will; to want, desire, wish; to like, love.—*q. decir,* to mean.—*vii.* to be willing.—*como quiera,* in any way.—*como quiera que,* since; however, no matter how.—*como quiera que sea,* in any case.—*como Ud. quiera,* as you like; let it be so.—*cuando quiera,* at any time, whenever.—*donde quiera,* anywhere, wherever.—*sin q.,* unwillingly; unintentionally.—*v. impers.* to look like (rain, etc.), threaten.—*m.* love, affection; will; desire.—**querido,** *a.* dear; beloved.—*n.* lover; mistress.

querosén, *m.* (Am.) kerosene.

querubín, *m.* cherub.

quesería, *f.* dairy.—**quesera,** *f.* cheese dish.—**quesero,** *n.* cheesemaker.—**queso,** *m.* cheese.

quicio, *m.* hinge of a door.—*sacar de q., to* unhinge; to exasperate.

quichua, *mf. & a.* = QUECHUA.

quid, *m.* main point, gist.

quidam, *m.* (coll.) person; a nobody.

quiebra, *f.* crack, fracture; gaping fissure; loss, damage; (com.) failure, bankruptcy.

quiebro, *m.* dodge, swerve; (mus.) trill.

quien, *pron.* (*pl.* QUIENES) who, whom, he who (*pl.* those who); whose.—**quienquiera** *pron.* (*pl.* QUIENES-QUIERA) whoever, whosoever, whomsoever.—**quién,** *interrog. pron.* (*pl.* QUIENES) who?

quieto, *a.* quiet, still; steady, undisturbed.—**quietud,** *f.* stillness, quietness; tranquility.

quijada, *f.* jaw, jawbone.

quijotesco, *a.* quixotic.

quilate, *m.* (jewelry) carat or karat; degree of excellence.

quilo, *m.* (med.) chyle.—*sudar el q.,* to work hard.

quilla, *f.* (naut.) keel.

quimbombó, *m.* (Am.) okra, gumbo.

quimera, *f.* fancy, absurd idea; quarrel.—**quimérico,** *a.* imaginary; wildly fanciful.

química, *f.* chemistry.—**químico,** *a.* chemical.—*n.* chemist.

quimono, *m.* kimono.

quina, *f.* = QUININA.

quincalla, *f.* (com.) hardware; small wares.—**quincallería,** *f.* hardware trade or store; small wares store.

quincena, *f.* fortnight.—**quincenal,** *a.* fortnightly, semi-monthly.

quinina, *f.* quinine.

quinta, *f.* country seat, villa; manor-house; (mil.) draft; (mus.) fifth.

quintaesencia, *f.* quintessence.

quintal, *m.* quintal. (See Table.)

quinteto, *m.* (mus.) quintet.

quíntuplo, *a.* quintuple, fivefold.

quiosco, *m.* kiosk.

quirófano, *m.* (surg.) operating room.

quiromancia, *f.* palmistry.—**quiromántico,** *n.* palmist.

quirúrgico, *a.* surgical.

quisquilla, *f.* bickering, trifling dispute; shrimp; (coll.) small man.—**quisquilloso,** *a.* fastidious; touchy, peevish.

quitamanchas, *m.* cleaner, spot remover.—*m.* dry cleaner.

quitanieves, *m.* snow plow.

quitar, *vt.* to take away; to subtract; to take off, remove; to separate, take out; to free from; to rob of, deprive of; to forbid, prohibit; (fencing) to parry.—*vr.* to abstain, refrain; to quit, move away, withdraw; to get rid of; to take off (a garment); to come out (as a stain).—**quite,** *m.* parry, dodge.

quitasol, *m.* sunshade, parasol.

quizá, quizás, *adv.* perhaps, maybe.

R

rabadilla, *f.* coccyx; rump.

rábano, *m.* radish.—*r. picante,* horse-radish.—*tomar el r. por las hojas,* (coll.) to be off the track.

rabí, *m.* rabbi.

rabia, *f.* rabies.—*tenerle r. a,* to have a grudge against.—**rabiar,** *vi.* to have rabies; to rage; to rave; to suffer racking pain.—*r. por,* to long eagerly for.—**rabieta,** *f.* tantrum.

rabínico, *a.* rabbinical.—**rabino,** *m.* rabbi.

rabión, *m.* rapids of a river.

rabioso, *a.* rabid; suffering from rabies; enraged.

rabo, *m.* tail; tail end, back, or hind part.—*con el r. entre las piernas,* (coll.) (fig.) with the tail between the legs, crestfallen.—*mirar con el r. del ojo,* to look askance, or out of the corner of the eye.

racial, *a.* racial, race.

racimo, *m.* bunch; cluster.

ración, *f.* ration; supply, allowance.

racional, *a.* rational; reasonable.

racionamiento, *m.* rationing.—**racionar**, *vt.* to ration.

racha, *f.* flaw; gust of wind; streak of luck.

radar, *m.* radar.

radiación, *f.* radiation.—**radiador**, *m.* radiator.—**radial**, *a.* radial; radio.—**radiante**, *a.* radiant, brilliant, beaming.—**radiar**, *vi.* to radiate.—*vt. & vi.* to radio; to broadcast.

radical, *a.* radical.—*mf.* (pol.) radical; (gram. & math.) root.

radicar, *vii.* [d] to take root; to be (in a place).—*vr.* to settle, establish oneself.

radio, *m.* radius; radio set; radiogram; radium; circuit, district.—*mf.* radio.—*r. de acción*, range.—**radioactividad**, *f.* radioactivity.—**radioactivo**, *a.* radioactive.—**radiodifundir**, *vt. & vi.* to broadcast.—**radiodifusión**, *f.* broadcast.—**radiodifusora**, **radioemisora**, *f.* broadcasting station.—**radioescucha**, *mf.* radio listener.—**radiografía**, *f.* X-ray, radiography.—**radiograma**, *m.* radiogram.—**radiólogo**, *n.* radiologist.—**radiorreceptor**, *m.* radio receiver.—**radiotransmisor**, *m.* radio transmitter.—**radioyente**, *mf.* radio listener.

raer, *vti.* [8] to scrape; to rub off, fray; to erase.

ráfaga, *f.* gust of wind; flash or gleam of light; burst (of an automatic weapon).—*r. de aire*, waft.

raíces, *pl.* of RAÍZ.—*bienes r.*, real estate.

raído, *a.* frayed, worn out, threadbare; shameless.

raigón, *m.* large strong root; root of a tooth.

rail, *m.* (RR.) rail.

raíz, *f.* root; base, foundation; origin.—*a r. de*, immediately, right after.—*de r.*, by the roots, from the root; entirely.—*echar raíces*, to take root, become settled or fixed.

raja, *f.* split, rent, crack; slice (as a fruit).—**rajadura**, *f.* cleft, crack; crevice.—**rajar**, *vt.* to split; to slice (food).—*vr.* to split, crack.—*vi.* (coll.) to chatter.—*a rajatabla(s)*, in a great haste.

ralea, *f.* race, breed, stock; kind, quality.—**ralo**, *a.* thin, sparse, not dense.

rallador, *m.* grater.—**rallar**, *vt.* to grate; (coll.) to vex.

rama, *f.* branch, twig, limb, bough.—*andarse por las ramas*, to beat around the bush.—*en r.*, raw.—**ramaje**, *m.* mass of branches; foliage.—**ramal**, *m.* branch, ramification; (RR.) branch road; strand of a rope; halter.—**ramalazo**, *m.* lash, stroke with a rope; mark left by a lash; blow; spot on the face caused by blows or disease.

ramera, *f.* prostitute, whore.

ramillete, *m.* bouquet; cluster.—**ramo**, *m.* bough; branch (of trade, science, art, etc.); branchlet; cluster, bouquet; line of goods.—**ramonear**, *vi.* to lop off twigs; to browse.

rampa, *f.* ramp.

ramplón, *a.* coarse, rude, vulgar, common.

rana, *f.* frog.

rancio, *a.* rank, rancid, stale.—*vino r.*, mellow wine.

ranchería, *f.* settlement; cluster of huts; camp.—**ranchero**, *m.* mess cook; small farmer; (Am.) rancher.—**rancho**, *m.* (mil.) mess, chow; messhall; hut; camp; (Am.) cattle ranch.

rango, *m.* rank, class, position, status.

ranura, *f.* groove, notch; slot.

rapacidad, *f.* rapacity.

rapadura, *f.* shaving; hair cut.—**rapapolvo**, *m.* (coll.) sharp reprimand, dressing down.—**rapar**, *vt.* to shave; to crop (the hair); to plunder, snatch, rob.

rapaz, *a.* rapacious, predatory.—*f. pl.* (RAPACES) birds of prey.—*n.* young boy (girl).

rape, *m.* (coll.) hurried shaving or hair cutting.—*al r.*, cropped, clipped, cut close or short.

rapidez, *f.* rapidity, swiftness.—**rápido**, *a.* rapid, swift.—*m.* rapids; express train.

rapiña, *f.* rapine, plundering.—*de r.*, (of birds) of prey.—**rapiñar**, *vt.* (coll.) to plunder; to steal.

raposa, *f.* vixen, fox; (fig.) cunning person.

rapsodia, *f.* rhapsody.

raptar, *vt.* to abduct; to kidnap (a woman).—**rapto**, *m.* kidnapping; abduction; ravishment; rapture, ecstasy.

raqueta, *f.* (sports) racket.

raquítico, *a.* rachitic, rickety; feeble, skinny.

rareza, *f.* rarity, uncommonness; queerness; freak; curiosity; oddness.—*por* or *de r.*, rarely, seldom.—**raro**, *a.* rare; scarce; thin, not dense; queer, odd.—*rara vez*, seldom.

ras, *m.* level, flush.—*al r. con* or *de*, even or flush with.—**rasante**, *a.* leveling, grazing.—*f.* (RR.) grade, grade line.—**rasar**, *vt.* to strike or level with a straight edge; to graze, touch lightly.

rascacielos, *m.* (coll.) skyscraper.—
rascar, *vti.* [d] to scratch; to rasp;
to scrape.—*vri.* to scratch oneself.
rasete, *m.* sateen.
rasgado, *a.* torn, open; generous.—
ojos rasgados, large eyes.—*m.* tear,
rip.—**rasgadura,** *f.* rent, rip.—
rasgar, *vti.* [b] to tear, rend, rip.—
rasgo, *m.* stroke, flourish; stroke
(of wit, kindness, etc.); feature (of
face); characteristic.—*a grandes
rasgos,* broadly, in outline.—**rasgón,**
m. rent, tear.
rasguñar, *vt.* to scratch.—**rasguño,**
m. scratch.
raso, *a.* clear; plain; flat.—*a campo
r.,* in the open air.—*m.* satin.—
soldado r., private.
raspadura, *f.* erasure; rasping, scrap-
ing; shavings.—**raspar,** *vt.* to
scrape, rasp; to erase; to steal.
rastra, sled; dray; (Am.) trailer;
(agr.) harrow, rake; anything dragging.—*a rastras,* dragging; by force,
unwillingly.—**rastreador,** *n.* tracer;
scout.—**rastrear,** *vt.* to trace, scent;
to track down, trail; (agr.) to
harrow, rake; to follow a clue to.
—*vi.* to fly very low.—**rastrero,** *a.*
creeping, dragging; trailing; flying
low; abject; low.—**rastrillar,** *vt.* to
hackle, dress (flax), comb; to rake.
—**rastrillo,** *m.* hackle, flax comb;
(agr.) rake.—**rastro,** *m.* track, scent,
trail; trace; (agr.) rake, harrow;
slaughterhouse; sign, token; vestige.
—**rastrojo,** *m.* stubble.
rata, *f.* rat.—*m.* (coll.) pickpocket.—
ratería, *f.* larceny, petty theft;
(coll.) meanness, stinginess.—**ratero,**
n. pickpocket.
ratificación, *f.* ratification, confirmation.—**ratificar,** *vti.* [d] to ratify,
confirm.
rato, *m.* short time, while.—*al poco r.,*
presently, very soon.—*a ratos,* from
time to time, occasionally.—*buen r.,*
a great while; a pleasant, good
time.—*mal r.,* a hard time.—*pasar
el r.,* to pass the time, while away
the time.
ratón, *m.* mouse; (Am.) hangover.—
ratonera, *f.* mousetrap, rat trap.
raudal, *m.* torrent; plenty, abundance.
raudo, *a.* rapid, swift.
raya, *f.* stroke, dash, streak, stripe,
line; crease (in trousers); parting
in the hair; (print.) dash, rule.—
tener a uno a r., to hold one at
bay; (ichth.) ray, skate.—**rayado,**
a. streaky.—**rayano,** *a.* neighboring,
contiguous, bordering.—**rayar,** *vt.* to
draw lines on; to rule; to scratch,
mar; to stripe, streak; to cross

out.—*vi.* to excel, surpass; to
border (on).—*r. el alba,* to dawn.
—**rayo,** *m.* ray, beam; spoke of a
wheel; thunderbolt; flash of lightning; lively, ready genius; great
power or efficacy of action.
rayón, *m.* (neol.) rayon.
raza, *f.* race, lineage; breed.—*de r.,*
pure-breed.
razón, *f.* reason; reasonableness;
right; account, explanation; information; (Am.) message; (math.)
ratio.—*a r. de,* at the rate of.—
con r. o sin ella, rightly or wrongly.
—*dar la r. a,* to agree with.—
entrar en r., to be, or become, reasonable, listen to reason.—*no tener
r.,* to be wrong or mistaken.—
perder la r., to become insane.—
r. social, (com.) firm, firm name.—
tener r., to be right.—**razonable,** *a.*
reasonable; moderate; fair, just.—
razonamiento, *m.* reasoning.—**razonar,** *vi.* to reason.
reabastecer, *vti. & vri.* [3] to supply
again.
reabrir, *vti. & vri.* [49] to reopen.
reacción, *f.* reaction.—**reaccionar,** *vi.*
to react.—**reaccionario,** *n. & a.* re-
actionary.
reacio, *a.* obstinate, stubborn; reluctant.
reacondicionar, *vt.* to recondition.
reactivo, *a.* reactive.—*m.* (chem.)
reagent; reactor.
readaptación, *f.* readjustment.—**readaptar,** *vt.* to readjust, adapt again.
reajuste, *m.* readjustment.
real, *a.* real, actual; royal, kingly.
—*m.* real, a silver coin; camp, encampment.
realce, *m.* excellence; luster, splendor;
raised work, embossment.—*dar r.,*
to enhance.
realeza, *f.* royalty, regal dignity.—
realidad, *f.* reality, fact; truth.—
en r., truly; really; in fact.—
realismo, *m.* realism; royalism.—
realista, *mf.* realist; royalist.—
realización, *f.* realization, fulfillment; (com.) sale.—**realizar,** *vti.*
[a] to realize, fulfill, carry out, perform; (com.) to sell out.
realzar, *vti.* [a] to raise, elevate; to
emboss; to brighten the colors of;
to make prominent; to heighten,
enhance.
reanimar, *vt.* to cheer, encourage; to
revive; reanimate.
reanudación, *f.* renewal; resumption.
—**reanudar,** *vt.* to renew, resume.
reaparecer, *vii.* [3] to reappear.—
reaparición, *f.* reappearance.
rearme, *m.* rearmament.

reasegurar, *vt.* (com.) to reinsure.—**reaseguro**, *m.* (com.) reinsurance.

reasumir, *vt.* to retake; to resume.

reata, *f.* rope, lariat; string of horses.

reavivar, *vt. & vr.* to revive, reanimate.

rebaja, *f.* (com.) discount; deduction, diminution.—**rebajar**, *vt.* to abate, lessen, diminish; to reduce, lower, cut down.—*vr.* to be dismissed; to lower oneself.

rebanada, *f.* slice.—**rebanar**, *vt.* to slice; to cut.

rebaño, *m.* herd; flock.

rebasar, *vt.* to exceed; to overflow.

rebatir, *vt.* to beat or drive back, repel; to refute.—**rebato**, *m.* alarm, alarm bell; call to arms; commotion; (mil.) sudden attack.

rebelarse, *vr.* to revolt, rebel.—**rebelde**, *a.* rebellious; stubborn.—*mf.* rebel; (law) defaulter.—**rebeldía**, *f.* rebelliousness, contumacy; stubbornness; (law) default.—**rebelión**, *f.* rebellion, revolt.

rebencazo, *m.* (Am.) blow with a whip.—**rebenque**, *m.* (Am.) whip.

reblandecer, *vti. & vri.* [3] to soften.—**reblandecimiento**, *m.* softening.

reborde, *m.* flange, border; rim.—**rebordear**, *vt.* to flange.

rebosar, *vi.* to overflow; **(de)** to abound (in); to teem (with).

rebotar, *vi.* to rebound.—*vt.* to cause to rebound; to repel; to vex.—**rebote**, *m.* rebound, rebounding, bounce, bound.—*de r.*, on the rebound; indirectly.

rebozar, *vti.* [a] to muffle up; to dip (food in flour, etc.).—*vri.* to muffle oneself up.—**rebozo**, *m.* muffler; woman's shawl.—*sin r.*, frankly, openly.

rebullir, *vii. & vri.* [27] to stir, begin to move; to boil up.

rebusca, *f.* search; research; searching; gleaning.—**rebuscar**, *vti.* [d] to search carefully; to glean; to dig up.

rebuznar, *vi.* to bray.—**rebuzno**, *m.* braying (of a donkey).

recabar, *vt.* to obtain by entreaty.

recado, *m.* message, errand; present, gift; regards; daily provision or marketing; voucher; equipment; precaution.

recaer, *vii.* [8-e] to fall back, relapse; to fall or devolve; to behoove.—**recaída**, *f.* relapse.

recalar, *vi.* to make, sight, or reach port.—*vt.* to soak, drench, saturate.

recalcar, *vti.* [d] to cram, pack, press; to emphasize, stress.—*vri.* to harp on a subject.

recalentar, *vti.* [1] to reheat; to overheat; to warm over; to superheat.—*vri.* to become overheated or superheated.

recamar, *vt.* to embroider with raised work.

recámara, *f.* dressing room; boudoir; (Mex.) bedroom; (artil.) breech of a gun.

recambiar, *vt.* to exchange or change again; (com.) to refill.

recapacitar, *vi.* to refresh one's memory; to think carefully.

recargar, *vti.* [b] to reload; to overload; to overcharge; to recharge.—*vri.* **(de)** to have in abundance, have an abundance (of).—**recargo**, *m.* overload; overcharge; surtax, additional tax, charge, etc.; extra charge.

recatado, *a.* prudent, circumspect, unobtrusive; shy; modest.—**recatar**, *vt.* to secrete, conceal.—*vr.* to act modestly; to be cautious.—**recato**, *m.* prudence, caution; modesty; bashfulness.

recaudación, *f.* collecting, collection.—**recaudador**, *n.* tax collector.—**recaudar**, *vt.* to gather; to collect (rents or taxes).—**recaudo**, *m.* collection of rents or taxes; precaution, care; (law) bail, bond, security.—*a buen r.*, well guarded, under custody, safe.

recelar, *vt.* to fear, suspect.—*vr.* **(de)** to fear, be afraid or suspicious (of), to beware (of).—**recelo**, *m.* misgiving, fear, suspicion.—**receloso**, *a.* suspicious, fearful, distrustful.

recental, *a.* suckling (lamb or calf).

recepción, *f.* reception, receiving, admission.—**recepcionista**, *mf.* receptionist.

receptáculo, *m.* receptacle.—**receptivo**, *a.* receptive.—**receptor**, *n.* receiver; abettor; (baseball) catcher.—**receptoría**, *f.* receiver or treasurer's office; (law) receivership.

recesar, *vi.* (Am.) to recess, suspend temporarily.—**receso**, *m.* recess; separation, withdrawal.

receta, *f.* prescription; recipe.—**recetar**, *vt.* to prescribe (medicines).

recibidor, *n.* receiver; (com.) receiving teller.—*m.* reception room; vestibule.—**recibimiento**, *m.* reception; greeting, welcome.—**recibir**, *vt.* to receive; to take, accept; to admit; to experience (an injury).—*vr.* **(de)** to graduate (as); to be admitted to practice (as).—**recibo**, *m.* reception; (com.) receipt.—*acusar r.*, (com.) to acknowledge receipt.—*estar de r.*, to be at home to callers.

recién, *adv.* (before *pp.*) recently, lately, newly.—*r. casados*, newlyweds.—*r. llegado*, newcomer.—*r. na-*

cido, newborn.—**reciente**, *a*. recent; new; modern; fresh.

recinto, *m*. enclosure; place (building, hall, etc.); precinct.

recio, *a*. strong, robust, vigorous; loud; rude; hard to bear; severe, rigorous (weather).—*adv*. strongly; rapidly; vigorously; loud.

recipiente, *a*. receiving.—*m*. receptacle; container; recipient.

reciprocar, *vti*. & *vri*. [d] to correspond.—**reciprocidad**, *f*. reciprocity. —**recíproco**, *a*. reciprocal, mutual.

recitación, *f*. recitation, recital.— **recital**, *m*. (mus.) recital.—**recitar**, *vt*. to recite; to rehearse.

reclamación, *f*. reclamation; (com.) complaint; claim.—**reclamante**, *mf*. & *a*. complainer; claimer; complaining; claiming.—**reclamar**, *vt*. to claim, demand; to decoy (birds); (law) to reclaim.—*vi*. to complain. —**reclamo**, *m*. decoy bird; lure (of birds); call; claim; complaint; advertisement.

reclinar, *vt*. to incline, recline, lean. —*vr*. to recline, lean back.— **reclinatorio**, *m*. pew; couch, lounge; prayer desk.

recluir, *vti*. [23-e] to shut up; to seclude.—**reclusión**, *f*. seclusion; place of retirement; arrest; jail, prison.—**recluso**, *ppi*. of RECLUIR.

recluta, *f*. (mil.) recruiting.—*m*. recruit.—**reclutamiento**, *m*. (mil.) recruiting.—**reclutar**, *vt*. (mil.) to recruit.

recobrar, *vt* & *vr*. to recover, recuperate, regain; to recoup.—**recobro**, *m*. recovery, recuperation; resumption.

recocer, *vti*. [26-a] to boil too much; to boil again; to reheat.—*vri*. to burn with rage

recodo, *m*. turn, winding, bend, angle.

recoger, *vti*. [c] to gather, pick; to pick up, take up; to take in, collect; to take in, shelter.—*vri*. to take shelter; to retire.—**recogida**, *f*. withdrawal; harvesting; (com.) retiral.—**recogimiento**, *m*. concentration, abstraction.

recolección, *f*. gathering, harvest; compilation; summary.—**recolectar**, *vt*. to gather, collect, harvest.

recomendable, *a*. commendable, laudable.—**recomendación**, *f*. recommendation; request; praise; merit; testimonial.—**recomendar**, *vti*. [1] to recommend; to commend; to entrust; to ask, request.

recompensa, *f*. compensation; recompense, reward.—*en r.*, in return. —**recompensar**, *vt*. to compensate; to recompense, reward

reconcentrar, *vt*. to concentrate; to dissemble.—*vr*. to concentrate (one's mind).

reconciliación, *f*. reconciliation.—**reconciliar**, *vt*. to reconcile.—*vr*. to become reconciled; to make up; to renew friendship.

reconocer, *vti*. [3] to recognize; to admit; (por) to acknowledge (as); to acknowledge; (mil.) to scout, reconnoiter.—**reconocimiento**, *m*. recognition; acknowledgment; gratitude; recognizance; examination, inquiry; (mil.) reconnoitering; (surv.) reconnaissance.

recontar, *vti*. [12] to recount; to relate.

reconvención, *f*. charge, accusation; reproach.—**reconvenir**, *vti*. [45] to accuse, reproach; (law) to countercharge.

recopilación, *f*. summary, compilation; (law) digest.—**recopilar**, *vt*. to compile, digest.

recordación, *f*. remembrance; recollection.—**recordar**, *vti*. [12] to remember, to remind.—*vri*. to remember.—**recordatorio**, *m*. reminder.

recorrer, *vt*. to go over; (mech.) to pass over, travel; to read over; to travel in or over; to overhaul.—*vi*. to resort; to travel.—**recorrido**, *m*. run; space or distance traveled or passed over, course; (auto) mileage.

recortar, *vt*. to cut away, trim, clip; to cut out; to cut to size; to outline (a figure).—**recorte**, *m*. cutting, paring; clipping (from newspaper, etc.), outline.—*pl*. trimmings, parings.

recostar, *vti*. [12] to lean, recline.— *vri*. to go or rest; to repose; to lean back (against), to recline.

recoveco, *m*. turning, winding; nook, cranny; sly approach.

recreación, *f*. recreation.—**recrear**, *vt*. to amuse, delight.—*vr*. to amuse oneself; to be pleased; to divert oneself.—**recreo**, *m*. recreation; place of amusement; (school) recess.

recrudecer, *vii*. & *vri*. [3] to increase; to recur.

rectángulo, *a*. rectangular; right-angled (triangle, etc.).—*m*. rectangle.

rectificar, *vti*. [d] to rectify; to correct, amend.

rectitud, *f*. straightness; righteousness, rightness, rectitude; accuracy, exactitude.—**recto**, *a*. straight; erect; righteous, just, fair; literal; right.—*m*. rectum.

rector, *n*. rector, curate; president (of a university, college, etc.); principal —**rectorado**, *m* rectorship; di

rectorship; rector's office.—**rectoría,** *f.* rectory, curacy; rectorship; rector's or director's office.

recua, *f.* herd of beasts of burden; multitude, pack of things.

recuento, *m.* recount; inventory.

recuerdo, *m.* remembrance; memory; recollection; souvenir; keepsake, memento.—*pl.* compliments, regards.

reculada, *f.* recoil, recoiling.—**recular,** *vi.* to recoil, back up; (coll.) to yield, give up, turn back.

recuperación, *f.* recovery, recuperation.—**recuperar,** *vt.* & *vr.* to recover, regain, recuperate.

recurrir, *vi.* to resort, apply; to revert.—**recurso,** *m.* recourse; resource, resort; return, reversion; memorial, petition; (law) appeal.—*pl.* resources, means.

recusar, *vt.* to reject, decline; to challenge (a juror).

rechazar, *vti.* [a] to repel, repulse, drive back; to reject; to rebuff.—**rechazo,** *m.* rebound; rebuff; recoil; rejection.

rechifla, *f.* hissing (in derision); hooting; mockery, ridicule.—**rechiflar,** *vt.* to hiss; to mock, ridicule.

rechinar, *vi.* to creak, squeak; to gnash the teeth.

rechoncho, *a.* (coll.) chubby, stocky.

red, *f.* net; network, netting; bag net; snare, trap; system (of RR., tel., etc.).

redacción, *f.* wording; editing; editorial rooms; editorial staff.—**redactar,** *vt.* to edit, be the editor of; to write, word.—**redactor,** *n.* editor.

redada, *f.* casting a net; catch, haul.

redarguir, *vti.* [23-e] to retort; (law) to impugn.

redecilla, *f.* hair net.

rededor, *m.* surroundings, environs.—*al* or *en r.,* around.

redención, *f.* redemption.—**redentor,** *n.* & *a.* redeemer; redeeming.

redil, *m.* sheepfold.

redimible, *a.* redeemable.—**redimir,** *vt.* to redeem, rescue, ransom; to liberate; (com.) to redeem, pay off.

rédito, *m.* (com.) revenue, interest, yield.

redoblar, *vt.* to double; to clinch; to repeat; (mil.) to roll (a drum).—**redoble,** *m.* (mil. & mus.) roll of a drum.

redoma, *f.* vial, flask.

redomado, *a.* artful, sly, crafty.

redonda, *f.* neighborhood, district.—*a la r.,* roundabout.—**redondamente,** *adv.* clearly, plainly, decidedly.—**redondear,** *vt.* to round, make round; to round off, to perfect.—*vr* to clear oneself of debts, to obtain good profits (of a business).—**redondel,** *m.* (coll.) circle; round cloak; bull ring, arena.—**redondez,** *f.* roundness, rotundity.—*r. de la Tierra,* face of the Earth.—**redondilla,** *f.* quatrain.—**redondo,** *a.* round, rotund; clear, straight; (fig.) nice, honest.—*en r.,* all around.—*negocio r.,* (fig.) profitable business.

reducción, *f.* reduction, decrease; discount.—**reducido,** *a.* limited; small; narrow; compact.—**reducir,** *vti.* [11] to reduce; to diminish, decrease; (a) to convert (into); to subdue; to condense, abridge.—*vri.* to adjust oneself, adapt oneself; to be compelled, to decide from necessity.

reducto, *m.* (fort.) redoubt.

redundancia, *f.* redundance.—**redundante,** *a.* redundant, superfluous.—**redundar,** *vi.* to overflow; to be redundant; (en) to redound (to), lead (to).

reduplicar, *vti.* [d] to duplicate again, redouble.

reedificar, *vti.* [d] to rebuild.

reelección, *f.* reëlection.—**reelecto,** *ppi.* of REELEGIR.—**reelegir,** *vti.* [29-49] to reëlect.

reembolsar, *vt.* to reimburse, refund, pay back.—**reembolso,** *m.* reimbursement, refund.

reemplazar, *vti.* [a] to replace; to substitute.—**reemplazo,** *m.* replacement; substitution; (mil.) substitute.

reenvasar, *vt* (com.) to refill

reestreno, *m.* (theat.) revival.

reexpedir, *vti.* [29] to forward (mail, etc.).

refacción, *f.* refreshment, luncheon; reparation; (Am.) spare part; financing.

refajo, *m.* underskirt, petticoat.

referencia, *f.* reference; narration.—**referéndum,** *m.* referendum.—**referente,** *a.* referring, relating.—**referir,** *vti.* [39] to refer, relate; to tell, narrate.—*vri.* (a) to refer (to), have relation (to)

refilón.—*de r.,* obliquely, askance.

refinamiento, *m* refinement; refining.—**refinar,** *vt* to refine, purify; to make polite or refined.—**refinería,** *f.* refinery

reflector, *a.* reflecting, reflective.—*m.* searchlight; reflector.—**reflejar,** *vt.* to reflect.—*vr.* to be reflected.—**reflejo,** *a.* reflected; (gram.) reflexive; (physiol.) reflex.—*m.* glare; reflection; light reflected.—**reflexión,** *f* reflection; thinking.—**reflexionar,**

vi. to think, reflect.—**reflexivo,** *a.* reflexive; reflective; thoughtful.

reflujo, *m.* ebb or ebb tide.

reforma, *f.* reform; reformation; alteration, correction, improvement. —**reformador,** *n.* & *a.* reformer; reforming.—**reformar,** *vt.* to reform; to amend, improve.—*vr.* to reform; to mend.—**reformatorio,** *a.* corrective, reforming.—*m.* reformatory.—**reformista,** *mf.* & *a.* reformer; reforming, reformist.

reforzar, *vti.* [12-a] to strengthen, reinforce.

refrán, *m.* proverb, saying.

refrenar, *vt.* to restrain, check; to rein, curb.

refrendar, *vt* to legalize, authenticate, countersign.

refrescante, *a.* cooling, refreshing.— **refrescar,** *vti.* [d] to refresh; to cool.—*vii.* & *vri.* (of the weather) to get cool; to take the fresh air; to take refreshment; to cool off.— **refresco,** *m.* refreshment.

refriega, *f.* affray, scuffle, fray.

refrigeración, *f.* refrigeration.—**refrigerador,** *a.* refrigerating, freezing, cooling.—*m.* refrigerator, freezer, ice box.—**refrigerar,** *vt.* to cool, refrigerate.—**refrigerio,** *m.* coolness; refreshment, refection.

refuerzo, *m.* reinforcement; strengthening; welt (of shoe); aid, help.

refugiado, *n.* refugee.—**refugiar,** *vt.* to shelter.—*vr.* to take shelter or refuge.—**refugio,** *m.* refuge, shelter.

refundir, *vt.* to remelt or recast; to rearrange, recast, reconstruct.—*vi.* to redound.

refunfuñar, *vt.* to growl, grumble, mutter.—**refunfuño,** *m.* grumbling, growl, snort.

refutar, *vt.* to refute.

regadera, *f.* watering pot, sprinkler. —**regadío,** *a.* & *m.* irrigated (land).

regalar, *vt.* to present, give as a present, make a present of; to regale, entertain; to gladden, cheer, delight.—*vr.* to feast sumptuously.

regalía, *f.* regalia, royal rights; (Am.) advance payment or royalty to owner of patent, etc.; privilege, exemption.

regalo, *m.* present, gift; pleasure; dainty; comfort, luxury

regañadientes.—*a* *r.,* reluctantly, grumbling.—**regañar,** *vi.* to growl, grumble; mutter; to quarrel.—*vt.* (coll.) to scold, reprimand.—**regaño,** *m.* scolding, reprimand.—**regañón,** *n.* growler, grumbler; scolder; scold.—*a.* growling, grumbling; scolding

regar, *vti.* [1-b] to water; to irrigate; to sprinkle; to scatter.

regata, *f.* regatta, boat race.—**regatear,** *vt.* to haggle about, beat down (the price), to resell at retail; to bargain; to dodge, dribble (soccer)—*vi.* to haggle; to wriggle; (naut.) to race.—**regateo,** *m.* chaffer, bargaining, haggling.

regazo, *m.* lap (of body).

regente, *a.* ruling, governing.—*mf.* regent; manager, director.—**regentear,** *vi.* to rule, boss, manage.— **regidor,** *a.* ruling, governing.—*m.* alderman or councilman.

régimen, *m.* regime; management, rule; (gram.) government; (med.) regimen, treatment.—*r. alimenticio,* diet.

regimiento, *m.* (mil.) regiment; administration, government; town council.

regio, *a.* royal, regal; sumptuous, magnificent.

región, *f.* region.—**regional,** *a.* regional, local.

regir, *vti.* [29-c] to rule, govern, direct; to manage.—*vii.* to be in force.

registrador, *n.* register; registrar, recorder, master or clerk of records; searcher, inspector.—*a.* registering. —**registrar,** *vt.* to inspect, examine; to search; to register, record.—*vr.* to register, be registered or matriculated.—**registro,** *m.* search, inspection, examination; census, registry, registration; enrollment; record, entry; enrolling office; certificate of entry; register book; bookmark; (mus.) register, organ stop; regulator (of a timepiece).

regla, *f.* rule, regulation, precept; order, measure, moderation; (drawing) ruler, straight edge; menstruation.—*en r.,* thoroughly, in due form, in order.—**reglamentar,** *vt.* to establish rules; to regulate by rule, law or decree.—**reglamento,** *m.* by-laws; rules and regulations.

regocijado, *a.* merry, joyful, festive.

regocijar, *vt.* to gladden, cheer, rejoice.—*vr* to rejoice, be merry.

regocijo, *m.* joy, gladness; merriment; rejoicing.

regodearse, *vr.* to take delight, re joice.—**regodeo,** *m.* joy, delight.

regordete, *a.* (coll.) chubby, plump.

regresar, *vi.* to return.—**regreso,** *m.* return, coming or going back.

reguero, *m.* trickle, drip; irrigating furrow

regulación, *f* regulation, adjustment —**regulador,** *a.* regulating, governing.—*m* (mech) regulator, gover

nor; register; controller (of electric car).—**regular**, *vt.* to regulate; to adjust.—*a.* regular; moderate, sober; ordinary; fairly good, so-so.—*por lo regular*, usually, as a rule.—**regularidad**, *f.* regularity; common usage, custom.—**regularizar**, *vti.* [a] to regularize.

rehacer, *vti.* [22-49] to remodel, make over, remake; do over; to renovate, mend, repair.—*vri.* to regain strength and vigor; (mil.) to rally, reorganize.—**rehecho**, *ppi.* of REHACER.

rehén, *m.* (gen. *pl.*) hostage.

rehuir, *vti., vii. & vri.* [23-e] to shun, avoid; to reject, decline, refuse.

rehusar, *vt.* to refuse, decline, reject, withhold.

reimpresión, *f.* reprint; reissue.—**reimprimir**, *vti.* [49] to reprint.

reina, *f.* queen.—**reinado**, *m.* reign.—**reinante**, *a.* reigning; prevailing.—**reinar**, *vi.* to reign; to prevail, predominate.

reincidir, *vi.* to relapse; to backslide.

reino, *m.* kingdom.

reintegrar, *vt.* to reintegrate, restore; (com.) to reimburse, refund.—*vr.* (de) to recover, recuperate.—**reintegro**, *m.* reimbursement, restitution.

reír, *vii. & vri.* [35] to laugh.—*r. a carcajadas*, to laugh loudly, guffaw.—*reírse de*, to laugh at; to mock.

reiterar, *vt.* to reiterate.

reja, *f.* grate, grating, railing; plowshare; plowing.—**rejilla**, *f.* small lattice or grating; latticed wicket; cane for backs and seats of chairs.

relación, *f.* relation, relationship, dealing; ratio; narration, account; (law) report, brief; (theat.) speech.—*pl.* relations, connections; acquaintance; courting, engagement.—*en* or *con r.* regarding (to or with).—**relacionar**, *vt.* to relate, connect; to make acquainted.—*vr.* to get acquainted, make connections; to be related.

relajación, *f.*, **relajamiento**, *m.* relaxation, laxity; slackening; hernia.—**relajar**, *vt.* to relax, slacken; to release from an obligation; to amuse, divert.—*vr.* to become relaxed, loosened, weakened; to grow vicious; to be ruptured.—**relajo**, *m.* (Am.) disorder, mix-up; (Am.) depravity; diversion.

relamer, *vt.* to lick again.—*vr.* to lick one's lips; to relish; to boast.

relámpago, *m.* lightning; flash; (fig.) quick person or action.—**relampaguear**, *vi.* to lighten; to flash, sparkle.—**relampagueo**, *m.* lightning; flashing.

relatar, *vt.* to relate, narrate.

relatividad, *f.* relativity.—**relativo**, *a.* relative.

relato, *m.* statement; narration; report, account.—**relator**, *n.* narrator.

releer, *vti.* [e] to read over again; to revise.

relegar, *vti.* [b] to relegate, banish; to set aside.

relente, *m.* night dew, night dampness.

relevador, *m.* (elec.) relay.

relevante, *a.* excellent, great, eminent.—**relevar**, *vt.* (mil.) to relieve, substitute; to emboss; to bring into relief; to relieve, release; to forgive, acquit; to exalt, aggrandize.—*vi.* (art) to stand out in relief.—**relevo**, *m.* (mil.) relief.—*carrera de relevos*, relay race.

relicario, *m.* locket; reliquary.

relieve, *m.* relief, raised work, embossment.—*poner de r.*, to bring out, throw into relief, emphasize.—*pl.* (of food) leavings; (fig.) highlights or high points.

religión, *f.* religion.—**religiosidad**, *f.* religiosity; religiousness.—**religioso**, *a.* religious; scrupulous.—*n.* religious, member of a religious order.

relinchar, *vi.* to neigh.—**relincho**, *m.* neigh, neighing.

reliquia, *f.* relic; remains; trace, vestige.

reloj, *m.* clock; watch.—*r. de arena*, hourglass.—*r. de pulsera*, wrist watch.—*r. de sol*, sundial.—*r. despertador*, alarm clock.—*estar como un r.*, (coll.) to be in perfect trim.—**relojero**, *n.* watchmaker.

reluciente, *a.* shining, glittering, bright.—**relucir**, *vii.* [3] to shine, glow, glitter; to be brilliant.

relumbrante, *a.* resplendent.—**relumbrar**, *vi.* to sparkle, shine, glitter.—**relumbrón**, *m.* luster, dazzling brightness; tinsel.—*de r.*, showy, pompous.

rellano, *m.* landing (of a stair).

rellenar, *vt.* to refill; to fill up; (cook.) to stuff; (sewing) to pad; (mason.) to point.—*vr.* to stuff oneself.—**relleno**, *a.* stuffed.—*m.* stuffing; filling; (mech.) packing, gasket; (sewing) padding, wadding.

remachar, *vt.* to clinch; to rivet; to secure, affirm.—**remache**, *m.* rivet; riveting; flattening, clinching.

remanente, *m.* remains, remnant, residue.—*a.* residual.

remangar, *vti.* [b] to tuck up (sleeves, etc.).

remanso, *m.* backwater; dead water; eddy.

remar, *vt. & vi.* to row, paddle.

rematado, *a.* sold (at auction); finished.—*estar r.*, (coll.) to be completely crazy.—**rematar**, *vt.* to end, finish; (com.) to auction; to give the finishing stroke; (sewing) to fasten off (a stitch).—*vr.* to be utterly ruined or destroyed; to become completely crazy.—**remate**, *m.* end, finish, conclusion; (com.) auction, public sale; (arch.) finial, pinnacle. —*de r.*, utterly, completely, hopelessly.—*r. de cuentas*, closing of accounts.

remedar, *vt.* to imitate, copy, mimic.

remediar, *vt.* to remedy; to help; to repair (mischief); to avoid.—*no poder r.*, not to be able to help (prevent).—**remedio**, *m.* remedy; medicine; help; amendment.—*no hay más r. (que)*, there's nothing else to do (but).—*no tener r.*, to be unavoidable; to be irremediable; to be no help for.—*sin r.*, inevitable; hopeless.

rememorativo, *a.* reminiscent, reminding, recalling.

remendar, *vti.* [1] to patch, mend, repair; to darn.—**remendón**, *n.* cobbler; botcher, patcher.

remero, *m.* rower, oarsman.

remesa, *f.* (com.) shipment; remittance.—**remesar**, *vt.* (com.) to ship; to send, remit.

remiendo, *m.* patch; mending piece; darning; repair.—*a remiendos*, by patchwork, piecemeal.

remilgado, *a.* affected, prudish, squeamish.—**remilgo**, *m.* affected nicety, prudery, squeamishness.

reminiscencia, *f.* reminiscence.

remirar, *vt.* to review, look at or go over again.—*vr.* (en) to take great pains with; to inspect or consider with pleasure.

remisión, *f.* remission, sending back, remitting, remittment; pardon, forgiveness; remissness, indolence; relaxation, abatement.—**remiso**, *a.* remiss, careless, slack.—**remitente**, *mf.* & *a.* remitter, sender; remitting, sending.—**remitir**, *vt.* to remit; to forward; to pardon; to refer; (law) to transfer, remit to another court. —*vt., vi.* & *vr.* to remit, abate.— *vr.* (a) to refer (to); to quote from.

remo, *m.* oar; leg (of quadruped); (coll.) arm or leg (of person).

remoción, *f.* removal, removing; dismissal.

remojar, *vt.* to steep, soak, drench. —**remojo**, *m.* steeping, soaking, soakage.

remolacha, *f.* (bot.) beet.

remolcador, *m.* tug, tugboat, tow-boat.—**remolcar**, *vti.* [d] to tow, tug, take in tow; to haul.

remolino, *m.* whirl, whirlwind; whirlpool; twisted tuft of hair; crowd, throng; commotion.

remolón, *a.* indolent, lazy, soft.—*n.* malingerer.

remolque, *m.* towing, towage; trackage; towline.—*a r.*, in tow.—*dar r.*, to tow.

remontar, *vt.* (Am.) to go up (river); to repair, resole, revamp (shoes).— *vt.* & *vr.* to elevate, raise, rise.— *vr.* to soar (as birds); to take to the woods; to go back to, date from.

rémora, *f.* hindrance, obstacle; cause of delay; (ichth.) remora.

remordimiento, *m.* remorse.

remoto, *a.* remote, far off; unlikely.

remover, *vti.* [26] to move, remove, stir, disturb; to dismiss.

rempujar, *vt.* to jostle, shove, push.— **rempujón**, *m.* jostle, push, shove.

remuneración, *f.* remuneration; gratuity, consideration.—**remunerar**, *vt.* to remunerate.

renacer, *vii.* [3] to be born again; to spring up again, grow again.—**renacimiento**, *m.* renaissance, renascence, new birth.

renacuajo, *m.* tadpole; (coll.) little squirt.

rencilla, *f.* grudge; heartburning.

renco, *a.* = RENGO.

rencor, *m.* rancor, animosity, grudge. —**rencoroso**, *a.* rancorous, spiteful.

rendición, *f.* rendition, surrendering; yielding; profit, yield, product.— **rendido**, *a.* obsequious; devoted; fatigued, tired out.

rendija, *f.* crevice, crack, cleft.

rendimiento, *m.* submission; yield; income; output; (mech.) efficiency. —**rendir**, *vti.* [29] to subdue, overcome; to surrender, yield, give up; to render, give back; to do (homage); (com.) to produce, yield; to fatigue, tire out.—*r. las armas*, to throw down the arms, to surrender. —*vri.* to become exhausted, tired, worn out; to yield, submit, give up, surrender.

renegado, *n.* renegade, apostate; wicked person.—**renegar**, *vti.* [1-b] to deny, disown; to detest.—*vii.* to turn renegade, apostatize; to blaspheme, curse; (de) to deny, renounce; to blaspheme, curse.

renegrido, *a.* blackish.

renglón, *m.* written or printed line; (com.) line of business, staple, item.—*a r. seguido*, immediately after; the next moment.—*pl.* lines, writings.

rengo, *a.* lame.—**renguear**, *vi.* to limp, hobble.

reno, *m.* reindeer.

renombrado, *a.* renowned, famous.—**renombre**, *m.* surname, family name; renown.

renovación, *f.* renovation, renewing; change, reform; replacement.—**renovador**, *n.* & *a.* renovator; renewing.—**renovar**, *vti.* [12] to renew; to renovate; to replace; to repeat.

renquear, *vi.* = RENGUEAR.

renta, *f.* profit; annuity; tax, contribution; revenue.—**rentar**, *vt.* to produce, bring, yield; to rent for.—**rentista**, *mf.* financier; bondholder; one who lives on a fixed income.

renuente, *a.* unwilling, reluctant.

renuevo, *m.* sprout, shoot.

renuncia, *f.* resignation; renunciation; renouncement; waiving.—**renunciamiento**, *m.* renouncement.—**renunciar**, *vt.* to renounce; to resign; to disown; to waive; to reject; to abandon, relinquish.—*vi.* to resign.

reñir, *vti.* & *vii.* [9] to wrangle, quarrel, fight; to fall out; to scold.

reo, *a.* guilty, criminal.—*mf.* criminal, culprit; (law) defendant.

reojo, *m.*—*mirar de r.*, to look askance.

reorganización, *f.* reorganization.—**reorganizar**, *vti.* [a] to reorganize; to reconstitute.

repantigarse, *vri.* [b] to stretch (oneself) in a chair.

reparación, *f.* reparation, repair, indemnity; atonement.—**reparador**, *n.* repairer; restorer; faultfinder.—**reparar**, *vt.* to repair, recondition; to restore; to observe, notice; to consider, heed; to make up for, indemnify for; to atone for.—**reparo**, *m.* repair, restoration; observation, warning, notice; difficulty; objection.—*poner reparos*, to make objections.

repartidor, *a.* distributing.—*n.* distributor; assessor of taxes.—**repartimiento**, *m.* division, distribution, apportionment; assessment.—**repartir**, *vt.* to divide, distribute, apportion; to assess.—**reparto**, *m.* = REPARTIMIENTO; (theat.) cast of characters; delivery (of goods, mail, etc.).

repasar, *vt.* to pass again; to reëxamine, revise; to glance over; to mend, darn; to review (as a lesson).—**repaso**, *m.* review (of a lesson); revision, reëxamination; final inspection; mending.

repecho, *m.* short, steep incline.

repelar, *vt.* to pull out the hair of.

repeler, *vt.* to repel, repulse; to refute, dispute.

repente, *m.* sudden movement or impulse.—*de r.*, suddenly.—**repentino**, *a.* sudden.

repertorio, *m.* repertory, repertoire.

repetición, *f.* repetition; (theat.) encore.—**repetir**, *vti.* & *vii.* [29] to repeat.—*vri.* to repeat oneself.

repicar, *vti.* [d] to peal, ring (bells); to mince, chop.—**repique**, *m.* ringing, pealing (bells).—**repiquetear**, *vt.* to ring, peal (bells); to tap (with fingers or shoes).—**repiqueteo**, *m.* ringing of bells; tapping, clicking.

repisa, *f.* mantelpiece; shelf, console; bracket.

replegar, *vti.* [1-b] to fold several times.—*vri.* (mil.) to fall back, retreat in order.

repleto, *a.* replete, very full.

réplica, *f.* reply, answer; retort, rejoinder; objection; exact copy, replica.—**replicar**, *vii.* [d] to reply, answer; to contradict, argue.

repliegue, *m.* doubling, folding; (mil.) orderly retreat.

repollo, *m.* cabbage; round head (of a plant).

reponer, *vti.* [32-49] to replace, put back; to reinstall; to restore.—*vri.* to recover lost health or property.

reportaje, *m.* (journalism) report, reporting.—**reportar**, *vt.* to control, restrain, check; to obtain, get, attain; to carry; to bring.—*vr.* to refrain, forbear, control oneself.—**repórter**, *mf.*, **reportero**, *n.* reporter.

reposado, *a.* quiet, restful.—**reposar**, *vi.* to rest, repose; to stand (on), be supported (by); to take a nap; to lie down; to lie (in the grave).—*vr.* to settle (as liquids).

reposición, *f.* replacement, reinstatement; recovery (in health); (theat.) revival.—**repositorio**, *m.* repository.

reposo, *m.* rest, repose; sleep; tranquillity.

repostería, *f.* confectionery, pastry shop.—**repostero**, *n.* pastry cook.

reprender, *vt.* to scold, reproach.—**reprensión**, *f.* reprimand, reproach.

represa, *f.* dam, dike, sluice; damming; stopping, holding back.

represalia, *f.* reprisal.

representación, *f.* representation; description; (theat.) performance, play; figure, image, idea.—*en r. de*, as a representative of.—**representante**, *a.* representing, representative.—*mf.* representative; agent.—**representar**, *vt.* to represent,

typify; (theat.) to perform, act.—*vr.* to image, picture to oneself, conceive.—**representativo,** *a.* representative.

represión, *f.* repression, check, control.—**represivo,** *a.* repressive, restrictive.

reprimenda, *f.* reprimand.—**reprimir,** *vt.* to repress, check, curb, quash.

reprobable, *a.* blameworthy.—**reprobación,** *f.* reproof.—**reprobado,** *a.* flunked.—**reprobar,** *vti.* [12] to reprove, disapprove, condemn; to damn; to flunk, fail.—**réprobo,** *n. & a.* reprobate.

reprochar, *vt.* to reproach, censure; to challenge (witnesses).—**reproche,** *m.* reproach, reproof; repulse, rebuff.

reproducción, *f.* reproduction; (art) copy.—**reproducir,** *vti. & vri.* [11] to reproduce. **reproductor,** *n. & a.* reproducer; reproducing.

reptil, *m.* reptile; crawler, creeper.

república, *f.* republic.—**republicano,** *a. & n.* republican.

repudiar, *vt.* to repudiate; to reject; to divorce.—**repudio,** *m.* repudiation; rejection; divorce.

repuesto, *ppi.* of REPONER.—*a.* recovered.—*m.* store, stock, supply.—*de r.,* extra; spare.

repugnancia, *f.* reluctance; aversion; loathing; disgust.—**repugnante,** *a.* loathsome; repulsive, disgusting.—**repugnar,** *vt.* to cause disgust; to do with reluctance.

repulgar, *vti.* [b] (sewing) to hem.

repulsa, *f.* refusal, rebuke, repulse.—**repulsión,** *f.* repulsion.—**repulsivo,** *a.* repelling.

reputación, *f.* reputation.—**reputar,** *vt.* to repute; to estimate, appreciate.

requebrar, *vti.* [1] to woo, court, make love to; to flatter, wheedle; to break again.

requemar, *vti.* to reburn; to overcook; to inflame (the blood).

requerimiento, *m.* summons; requisition, demand.—**requerir,** *vti.* [39] to summon; to notify; to require, need; to court, woo, make love to.

requesón, *m.* pot cheese, cottage cheese; curd.

requiebro, *m.* flattery, compliment; endearment.

requilorios, *m.* (coll.) useless ceremony; circumlocution.

requisa, *f.* tour of inspection; requisition.—**requisar,** *vt.* to make the rounds of; to requisition.—**requisito,** *m.* requisite, requirement.

res, *f.* head of cattle; beast.

resabio, *m.* unpleasant aftertaste; viciousness; bad habit.

resaca, *f.* surge, surf, undertow; (com.) redraft; (Am.) hangover.

resaltar, *vi.* to stand out; to jut out, project; to rebound; to come off, get loose; to be evident.

resarcimiento, *m.* compensation, reparation, indemnity.—**resarcir,** *vti.* [a] to compensate, indemnify, make amends to; to mend, repair; to recoup.

resbaladizo, *a.* slippery; glib; elusive; tempting, alluring.—**resbalar,** *vt. & vr.,* to slip, slide, glide; to skid; to err, go astray.—**resbalón,** *m.* slip, slipping; fault, error, break.—**resbaloso,** *a.* (Am.) slippery.

rescatar, *vt.* to ransom; to redeem, recover; to rescue; to exchange, barter, commute.—**rescate,** *m.* ransom; redemption; ransom money; exchange, barter.

rescindir, *vt.* to rescind, annul.—**rescisión,** *f.* cancellation, annulment.

rescoldo, *m.* embers, hot ashes; scruple, doubt, apprehension.

resecar, *vti. & vri.* [d] to dry up; to parch.—**reseco,** *a.* too dry; very lean.

resentimiento, *m.* resentment, grudge; impairment.—**resentirse,** *vri.* [39] to be impaired or weakened; to resent, be offended or hurt.

reseña, *f.* brief description; book review; sketch, summary, outline; (mil.) review.—**reseñar,** *vt.* to review, summarize, outline; (mil.) to review.

reserva, *f.* reserve, reticence; reservation; discretion; (mil.) reserve; *salvo—a r. de,* intending to.—*de r.,* extra, spare.—*en r.,* confidentially.—*guardar r.,* to act with discretion.—*sin r.,* openly, frankly.—**reservación,** *f.* reservation.—**reservar,** *vt.* to reserve, keep; to retain, hold; to postpone; to exempt; to conceal.—*vr.* to bide one's time; to keep for oneself; to beware, be cautious.

resfriado, *m.* cold (illness).—**resfriarse,** *vr.* to catch cold.—**resfrío,** *m.* = RESFRIADO.

resguardar, *vt.* to preserve, defend, protect.—*vr.* to take shelter; **(de)** to guard (against); protect oneself (from).—**resguardo,** *m.* security, safety, safeguard, defense, protection; (com.) guarantee, collateral.

residencia, *f.* residence, domicile.—**residencial,** *a.* residential.—**residente,** *a.* residing, resident, residential.—*mf.* dweller, inhabitant.—**residir,** *vi.* to reside, live; dwell; (fig.) to consist.

residuo, *m.* remainder, remnant; residue; (arith.) difference.—*pl.* refuse, leavings.

resignación, *f.* resignation; submission.—**resignar,** *vt.* to resign, give up.—*vr.* to resign oneself, be resigned.

resina, *f.* resin, rosin.—**resinoso,** *a.* resinous.

resistencia, *f.* resistance, endurance.—**resistente,** *a.* resisting; resistant, tough.—**resistir,** *vi.* to resist, offer resistance.—*vt.* to resist; to bear, stand; to endure.—*vr.* to put up a struggle, resist.

resma, *f.* ream (of paper).

resol, *m.* glare of the sun.

resolución, *f.* resolution; resoluteness; determination, courage; solution (of a problem).—*en r.,* in short.—**resolver,** *vti.* [47-49] to resolve, determine; to sum up; to solve (a problem).—*vri.* to resolve, determine; (med.) to resolve, be reduced.

resollar, *vii.* [12] to breathe noisily, pant; (coll.) to breathe; (coll.) to give signs of life.

resonancia, *f.* resonance.—*tener r.,* to cause a stir, attract attention.—**resonante,** *a.* resonant, resounding, sounding.—**resonar,** *vii.* [12] to resound, clatter.

resoplar, *vi.* to puff, breathe audibly; to snort.—**resoplido,** *m.* puff; snort.

resorte, *m.* (mech.) spring; resilience, spring, elasticity; means; motivation.

respaldar, *vt.* to indorse; to back; to answer for, guarantee.—*m.* back of a seat.—**respaldo,** *m.* back of a seat; backing; back of a sheet of paper; indorsement.

respectivo, *a.* respective.—**respecto,** *m.* relation, proportion; relativeness; respect.—*a este r.,* with respect to this.—*al r.,* relatively, respectively.—*con r. a, r. a,* or *r. de,* with respect to, with regard to.

respetabilidad, *f.* respectability.—**respetable,** *a.* respectable, considerable; worthy; honorable, reliable.—**respetar,** *vt.* to respect, revere, honor.—**respeto,** *m.* respect; deference, attention; observance.—*faltar al r. a,* to be disrespectful to.—**respetuoso,** *a.* respectful; respectable.

respingar, *vii.* [b] to kick, wince; to grunt; (coll.) to mutter; to talk back.—**respingo,** *m.* muttering, grumbling; gesture of unwillingness.

respirable, *a.* breathable.—**respiración,** *f.* respiration, breathing.—**respiradero,** *m.* vent, air hole; ventilator.—**respirar,** *vi. & vt.* to

rest, take rest or respite; to catch one's breath; to breathe freely; to exhale scents or odors.—**respiratorio,** *a.* respiratory.—**respiro,** *m.* breathing; moment of rest; respite; (com.) extension, time.

resplandecer, *vii.* [3] to glitter, glisten, shine.—**resplandeciente,** *a.* aglow.—**resplandor,** *m.* light, splendor, brilliance, radiance; glare.

responder, *vt. & vi.* to answer, reply; to respond; to acknowledge; to requite; to yield, produce; to have the desired effect; (com.) to correspond.—*vi.* **(de)** to answer (for), be responsible (for), vouch (for), guarantee.—**respondón,** *a.* saucy, pert, insolent.

responsabilidad, *f.* responsibility; reliability.—**responsable,** *a.* responsible; reliable.

responso, *m.* (eccl.) responsory for the dead.

respuesta, *f.* answer, reply; response, rejoinder; refutation.

resquebra(ja)dura, *f.* crack, cleft, fissure.—**resquebrajar,** *vt. & vr.* to crack, split.

resquicio, *m.* slit, crevice, crack; chance, opportunity.

resta, *f.* (arith.) subtraction; remainder, difference.

restablecer, *vti.* [3] to restore, reestablish, reinstate.—*vri.* to recover (from illness).—**restablecimiento,** *m.* reëstablishment; restoration; recovery.

restallar, *vi.* to crack (a whip); to crackle.

restante, *a.* remaining.—*m.* remainder.

restañar, *vt.* to stanch (wounds); to stop the flow of (blood).

restar, *vt.* to deduct; (arith.) to subtract.—*vi.* to be left, remain; (arith.) to subtract.

restauración, *f.* restoration.—**restaurante,** *m.* restaurant.—**restaurar,** *vt.* to restore; to recondition.

restitución, *f.* restitution.—**restituir,** *vti.* [23-e] to restore; to return, give back.—*vri.* to return, come back.

resto, *m.* remainder, balance, rest; limit for stakes at cards.—*pl.* remains.—*echar el r.,* to stake one's all; to do one's best.

restorán, *m.* (Am.) restaurant.

restregar, *vti.* [1-b] to rub, scrub.—**restregón,** *m.* scrubbing, hard rubbing.

restricción, *f.* restriction, limitation.—**restrictivo,** *a.* restrictive, restricting.—**restringir,** *vti.* [c] to restrain, restrict, confine.

resucitar, *vt.* to resuscitate, revive;

to renew.—*vi.* to rise from the dead, return to life.

resuelto, *ppi.* of RESOLVER.—*a.* resolute, determined, quick.

resuello, *m.* breath, breathing; puffing, snorting.

resulta, *f.* result, effect, consequence.—*de resultas,* in consequence.—**resultado,** *m.* result.—**resultar,** *vi.* to result, follow; to turn out; to turn out to be; (coll.) to work (well or badly).

resumen, *m.* summary, résumé.—*en r.,* in brief.—**resumir,** *vt.* to abridge; to summarize, sum up.—*vr.* to be reduced or condensed.

resurrección, *f.* resurrection.

retablo, *m.* series of historical pictures; (eccl.) altarpiece.

retador, *n.* challenger.—*a.* challenging.

retaguardia, *f.* rear, rear guard.

retahíla, *f.* string, series; line.

retar, *vt.* to challenge, dare.

retardado, *a.* retarded.—**retardar,** *vt.* to retard, slow up; to delay, detain.—*vr.* to fall behind, be slow.—**retardo,** *m.* retardation; delay.

retazo, *m.* piece, remnant; cutting; fragment, portion.

retemblar, *vii.* [1] to tremble, shake, quiver.

retención, *f.* retention, keeping or holding back.—**retener,** *vti.* [42] to retain, withhold; to detain.—**retentivo,** *a.* retentive, retaining.—**retentiva,** *f.* retentiveness, memory.

reticencia, *f.* reticence.—**reticente,** *a.* reticent.

retina, *f.* retina of the eye.

retinto, *a.* very black.

retintín, *m.* tinkling, jingle; (coll.) sarcastic undertone.

retirada, *f.* withdrawal; (mil.) retreat; retirement.—**retirado,** *a.* retired; isolated; distant; pensioned.—**retirar,** *vt.* to withdraw; to put aside, reserve; to repel.—*vr.* to withdraw; to retire; to recede; (mil.) to retreat.—**retiro,** *m.* retirement; retreat; secluded place.—*r. obrero,* social security.

reto, *m.* challenge; threat, menace.

retocar, *vti.* [d] to retouch; to touch up, finish.

retoñar, *vi.* to sprout; to reappear.—**retoño,** *m.* sprout, shoot.

retoque, *m.* retouching, finishing touch.

retorcer, *vti.* [26-a] to twist; to contort; to distort, misconstrue.—*vri.* to writhe, squirm.—**retorcimiento,** *m.* twisting; writhing.

retórica, *f.* rhetoric.—*pl.* (coll.) sophistries, quibbles, subtleties.

retornar, *vi.* & *vr.* to return, come back.—*vt.* to return; to give back.—**retorno,** *m.* return, coming back; repayment, requital.

retorta, *f.* (chem.) retort.—**retortero,** *m.*—*andar al r.,* to hover about.

retortijón, *m.* curling up, twisting up.—*r. de tripas,* cramps, bellyache.

retozar, *vii.* [a] to frisk, romp, frolic.—**retozo,** *m.* romping, frolic; wantonness.—**retozón,** *a.* frolicsome, rollicking.

retractación, *f.* retraction.—**retractar,** *vt.* & *vr.* to retract, to recant.

retraer, *vti.* [43] to bring again; to dissuade; (law) to redeem.—*vri.* to take refuge or shelter; to withdraw from, shun; to keep aloof, retire.—**retraimiento,** *m.* retirement; refuge; aloofness.

retranca, *f.* (Am.) brake.—**retranquero,** *m.* (Am., RR.) brakeman.

retransmitir, *vt.* to relay (a message, etc.); to broadcast again.

retrasar, *vt.* to defer, postpone; to delay; to set back (timepiece).—*vi.* to go back, decline.—*vr.* to be backward; to be behindhand, late, behind time; (of timepiece) to run slow.—**retraso,** *m.* delay, deferment, lateness.

retratar, *vt.* to portray; to imitate, copy; to photograph.—*vr.* to be reflected; to be depicted; to sit for a portrait or photograph.—**retratista,** *mf.* portrait painter; photographer.—**retrato,** *m.* portrait, picture; photograph; copy, resemblance; description.

retrechero, *a.* (coll.) wily; attractive, winsome.

retreparse, *vr.* to lean back; to recline in a chair.

retrete, *m.* toilet, water closet, privy.

retribución, *f.* retribution; recompense, fee.—**retribuir,** *vti.* [23-e] to remunerate, reward.

retroactividad, *f.* retroactivity.—**retroactivo,** *a.* retroactive.

retroceder, *vi.* to fall back, move backward; (auto) to back up; to recede.—**retroceso,** *m.* backward motion; (med.) relapse.

retrospectivo, *a.* retrospective.

retruécano, *m.* pun.

retumbante, *a.* resonant, resounding; pompous, bombastic.—**retumbar,** *vi.* to resound, rumble.

reuma, *m.,* **reumatismo,** *m.* rheumatism.

reunión, *f.* reunion; meeting; gathering.—**reunir,** *vt.* to unite; to reunite; to gather; to collect, accumulate; to join.—*vr.* to join, to unite; to meet, get together, assemble.

revalidar, *vt.* to ratify, confirm; to renew.

revancha, *f.* revenge.

revelación, *f.* revelation.—**revelador,** *n. & a.* revealer; revealing, telltale. —*m.* (photog.) developer.—**revelar,** *vt.* to reveal; (photog.) to develop.

revendedor, *n.* retailer; ticket speculator.—**revender,** *vt.* to resell; to retail.—**reventa,** *f.* resale.

reventar, *vii.* [1] to blow up, blow out; to burst forth; to explode; to sprout, shoot, blossom.—*vti.* to burst; to break; to crush, smash; to tire, wear out; to vex, annoy. —*vri.* to burst; to blow up, blow out; to break.—**reventón,** *a.* bursting.—*m.* bursting, blowout, explosion.

rever, *vti.* [46] to review, revise, look over again; (law) to try again.

reverdecer, *vii.* [3] to grow green again; to sprout again; to acquire new freshness and vigor.

reverencia, *f.* reverence; curtsy, bow; (eccl.) reverence (title).—**reverenciar,** *vt.* to venerate, revere; to hallow.—**reverendo,** *a.* reverend; worthy of reverence.—**reverente,** *a.* reverent.

reversible, *a.* (law) returnable, revertible; (phys.) reversible.—**reverso,** *m.* reverse (in coins); back, rear side.—*el r. de la medalla,* the opposite in every respect.

revertir, *vii.* [39] to revert.

revés, *m.* reverse, back, wrong side; backhand slap, shot or stroke; counterstroke; misfortune.—*al r.,* on the contrary, contrariwise; in the opposite or wrong way or direction; wrong side out.

revestimiento, *m.* (mason.) covering, facing, coat(ing); finish.—**revestir,** *vti.* [29] to dress, clothe; to cover, face; to line; (fig.) to cloak; (mason.) to coat, cover with a coating.—*vri.* to be invested with.

revisar, *vt.* to revise, review; to reëxamine, check.—**revisión,** *f.* revision, reviewing; reëxamination.—**revisor,** *m.* reviser, corrector; auditor; (RR.) conductor.—**revista,** *f.* (mil.) review, parade; review, magazine; (theat.) revue.—*pasar r.,* to review; to examine, go over.—**revistero,** *n.* reviewer.

revivir, *vi.* to revive.

revocable, *a.* revocable.—**revocación,** *f.* revocation; abrogation.—*r. de una sentencia,* (law) reversal.—**revocar,** *vti.* [d] to revoke, repeal, reverse; to whitewash, plaster.—**revoco,** *m.* whitewashing, plastering.

revolcar, *vti.* [12-d] to knock down,

tread or trample upon; (coll.) to floor (an opponent).—*vri.* to wallow; to be stubborn.

revolotear, *vi.* to flutter, fly about.— **revoloteo,** *m.* fluttering.

revoltijo, revoltillo, *m.* mess, mass, medley, jumble.—*r. de huevos,* scrambled eggs.—**revoltoso,** *a.* turbulent; rebellious; mischievous.— **revolución,** *f.* revolution.—**revolucionario,** *a. & n.* revolutionary; revolutionist.—**revolver,** *vti.* [47-49] to turn over, turn upside down; to stir; to agitate; to wrap up; to mix up.—*vri.* to move to and fro; to rebel; to change (as the weather).—**revólver,** *m.* revolver.

revuelco, *m.* rolling.—**revuelo,** *m.* fluttering; commotion, stir, disturbance.

revuelta, *f.* revolution, revolt; change. —**revuelto,** *ppi.* of REVOLVER.—*a.* mischievous; confused, mixed up; intricate, difficult; topsy-turvy.— *huevos revueltos,* scrambled eggs.

rey, *m.* king.

reyerta, *f.* dispute, wrangle, quarrel.

rezagado, *n.* straggler.—**rezagar,** *vti.* [b] to leave behind; to outstrip; to put off, defer.—*vri.* to fall behind, lag.—**rezago,** *m.* remainder, leftover.

rezar, *vti.* [a] to say, recite (prayers); to say, read, state (of books, etc.).—*vii.* to pray.—*r. con,* to concern, be the business or duty of.—**rezo,** *m.* prayer; praying, devotions.

rezongar, *vii.* [b] to grumble, mutter, growl.—**rezongón,** *n.* grumbler, mutterer, growler.

rezumadero, *m.* dripping place; cesspool.—**rezumar,** *vi. & vr.* to ooze, exude, percolate, filter through; (coll.) to transpire; to leak out.

ría, *f.* estuary.—**riachuelo,** *m.* rivulet, rill; small river.

ribazo, *m.* sloping bank; mound, hillock.

ribera, *f.* shore, beach, bank.

ribete, *m.* (sewing) binding; trimming; pretense.—**ribetear,** *vt.* to bind.

ricacho, ricachón, *n.* (coll.) vulgar, rich person.

ricino, *m.* castor-oil plant.

rico, *a.* rich, wealthy, abundant, plentiful; delicious, exquisite; cute (child).

ridiculez, *f.* ridiculous thing or action; ridiculousness.—**ridiculizar,** *vti.* [a] to ridicule.—**ridículo,** *a.* ridiculous.—*ponerse en r.,* or *quedar en r.,* to make oneself ridiculous.— *m.* ridicule.

riego, *m.* irrigation; watering.

riel, *m.* (RR.) rail.—*pl.* tracks.

rienda, *f.* rein of a bridle; (fig.) moderation, restraint.—*pl.* reins, ribbons; government, direction.—*a r. suelta,* with a free rein.—*soltar las riendas,* to act without restraint.

riesgo, *m.* risk.

rifa, *f.* raffle, scuffle, wrangle.—**rifar,** *vt.* to raffle.—*vi.* to quarrel.

rifle, *m.* rifle.

rigidez, *f.* rigidity; sternness.—*r. cadavérica,* rigor mortis.—**rígido,** *a.* rigid, stiff; rigorous, inflexible; puritanical.

rigor, *m.* rigor; sternness.—**rigoroso, riguroso,** *a.* rigorous; exact; absolute; strict, severe, puritanical.—**rigurosidad,** *f.* rigorousness; severity.

rima, *f.* rhyme; heap, pile.—*pl.* poems.—**rimar,** *vi.* to rhyme.

rimbombante, *a.* resounding; bombastic.

rincón, *m.* (inside) corner, nook; cozy corner.—**rinconera,** *f.* corner cupboard, stand, bracket.

ringla, ringlera, *f.* (coll.) row, file, line, tier; swath.

rinoceronte, *m.* rhinoceros.

riña, *f.* quarrel, scuffle, dispute.

riñón, *m.* kidney.—*tener cubierto el r.,* to be rich, to be well off.—**riñonada,** *f.* layer of fat about the kidneys; dish of kidneys.

río, *m.* river.

ripio, *m.* residue, rubbish; padding, useless words.—*no perder r.,* not to miss the least occasion.

riqueza, *f.* riches, wealth; richness; abundance; fertility.

risa, *f.* laugh, laughter.

risco, *m.* crag, cliff.

risible, *a.* laughable, ludicrous.—**risotada,** *f.* outburst of laughter, loud laugh.

ríspido, *a.* harsh, gruff.

ristra, *f.* string (of onions, garlic, etc.).

risueño, *a.* smiling; pleasing, agreeable.

rítmico, *a.* rhythmic.—**ritmo,** *m.* rhythm; rate (of increase, etc.).

rito, *m.* rite, ceremony.—**ritual,** *m.* (eccl.) ritual, ceremonial.—*a.* ritual.

rival, *mf.* rival.—**rivalidad,** *f.* rivalry.—**rivalizar,** *vii.* [a] to rival, compete.

rivera, *f.* brook, creek, stream.

rizar, *vti.* [a] to curl.—*vri.* to curl naturally.—**rizo,** *a.* naturally curled or frizzled.—*m.* curl, ringlet.—*rizar el r.,* (aer.) to loop the loop.

robar, *vt., vi. & vr.* to rob, steal; to abduct; to kidnap.

roble, *m.* oak; (fig.) very strong person or thing.

robo, *m.* robbery, theft; plunder, loot.

robustecer, *vti.* [3] to make strong.—**robustez,** *f.* robustness, ruggedness, hardiness—**robusto,** *a.* robust, vigorous, hale.

roca, *f.* (geol.) rock; cliff.—**rocalloso,** *a.* rocky.

roce, *m.* friction, rubbing; contact, familiarity.

rociada, *f.* sprinkling; reprimand.—**rociar,** *vi.* to fall (of dew).—*vt.* to sprinkle, to spray; to strew about.

rocin, *m.* decrepit nag.

rocío, *m.* dew; spray, sprinkle; light shower.

rocoso, *a.* rocky.

rodada, rodadura, *f.* wheel track, rut, tread.

rodaja, *f.* small wheel or disk; round slice.—**rodante,** *a.* rolling.—**rodapié,** *m.* (arch.) skirting; foot rail; dado.—**rodar,** *vii.* [12] to roll; to rotate, revolve, wheel; to run on wheels; to wander about; to go up and down.—*vt.* to shoot (a film, movie, etc.).

rodear, *vt. & vi.* to surround, encircle.—*vi.* to go around; to make a detour.—*vr.* to turn, twist, toss about.—**rodeo,** *m.* turn, winding; roundabout course, method or way; round-up, rodeo; circumlocution, beating around the bush; evasion, subterfuge; corral.

rodilla, *f.* knee.—*de rodillas,* on one's knees.—*doblar* or *hincar las rodillas,* to kneel down.—**rodillazo,** *m.* push or blow with the knee.—**rodillera,** *f.* knee guard; knee patch; bagging of trousers at the knee.

rodillo, *m.* roll, roller; (cook.) rolling pin.

roedor, *n. & a.* rodent.—**roer,** *vti.* [36] to gnaw, eat away; to corrode; to harass, annoy.

rogar, *vti.* [12-b] to request, beg, entreat.

rojez, *f.* redness, ruddiness.—**rojizo,** *a.* reddish, sandy; ruddy.—**rojo,** *a.* red; ruddy, reddish.—*m.* red color.

rol, *m.* list, roll, catalogue; muster roll.

roldana, *f.* sheave, pulley wheel; caster.

rollizo, *a.* plump, stocky.—*m.* log.

rollo, *m.* roll; roller, rolling pin.

romadizo, *m.* cold in the head, snuffles; hay fever.

romance, *m.* Romance (language); Spanish vernacular (language); Spanish ballad.—*en buen r.,* in plain language.

romanesco, *a.* Roman; characteristic of novels.—**románico,** *a.* (arch.)

Romanesque; Romance (language). —romano, n. & a. Roman.

romanticismo, m. romanticism.—**romántico,** a. romantic.—n. romanticist.—**romanza,** f. (mus.) romance.

rombo, m. (geom.) rhombus; lozenge, diamond.

romería, f. pilgrimage; picnic.

romero, m. (bot.) rosemary; pilgrim.

romo, a. obtuse; blunt.

rompecabezas, m. puzzle, riddle.— **rompehielos,** m. ice breaker; ice plow (of a boat).—**rompeolas,** m. breakwater, jetty.—**romper,** vti. [49] to break, smash, shatter; to fracture (bone); to tear; to pierce.—vii. to burst; to break; to burst forth; to fall out, quarrel; (of the day) to dawn; to begin, start; to sprout, bloom; to break out, spring out; (of light, sun, etc.) to break through.—vri. to break.—**rompiente,** a. breaking.—m. reef, shoal.— **rompimiento,** m. break, breakage, rupture; breach; quarrel.

ron, m. rum.

roncar, vii. [d] to snore; to roar; (coll.) to brag.—**ronco,** a. hoarse, raucous.

roncha, f. welt; blotch.

ronda, f. night patrol; rounds (by a night watch), beat; round (card game, drinks, cigars); serenade.— **rondar,** vt. & vi. to patrol, go the rounds; to walk the streets by night; to haunt, hover about; to impend.

ronquedad, ronquera, f. hoarseness.— **ronquido,** m. snore; raucous sound.

ronronear, vi. to purr.

ronzal, m. halter.

roña, f. filth, grime; scab (in sheep); stinginess; (Am.) ill-will; infection. —**roñoso,** a. scabby, leprous; dirty, filthy; rusty; (coll.) niggardly, stingy; (Am.) spiteful.

ropa, f clothes, clothing, garments. —a. quema r., at close range, pointblank; suddenly, unexpectedly.—r. blanca, linen.—**ropaje,** m. vestments; garb; (art) drapery.— **ropero,** m. wardrobe, closet.—**ropón,** m. wide, loose gown.

rorro, m. (coll.) babe in arms.

rosa, f. (bot.) rose; red spot on any part of the body; rose color.—r. náutica, or de los vientos, (naut.) mariner's compass.—**rosáceo,** a. rosecolored.—**rosado,** a. rose-colored; rose.—**rosal,** m. rose plant, rosebush. —**rosaleda,** f. rosary, rose garden.— **rosario,** m. rosary.

rosca, f. screw and nut; screw thread; ring-shaped biscuit or bread.

róseo, a. rosy.—**roseta,** f. small rose; rosette.—**rosetón,** m. large rosette; (arch.) rose window; rosette.

rosquilla, f. ring-shaped fancy cake.

rosillo, a. light red, roan (of horses).

rostro, m. face, countenance; rostrum.

rotación, f. rotation.—**rotar,** vi. to roll, rotate.—**rotativo,** a. rotary, revolving.—f. rotary printing press.— **rotatorio,** a. rotary, rotating.

roto, ppi. of ROMPER.—a. broken, chipped, shattered; torn; ragged; destroyed.—m. tear (in clothes); (Am.) man of the poorer classes; (Am.) hole.

rotonda, f. rotunda.

rótula, f. knee-joint.

rotulación, f. labeling.—**rotular,** vt. to label, put a title to.—**rótulo,** m. label, mark; show bill, placard.

rotundidad, f. roundness, rotundity.— **rotundo,** a. round, rotund; (of voice) full, sonorous; plain.

rotura, f. rupture, fracture; breakage, breach, opening.—**roturación,** f. breaking up new ground.—**roturar,** vt. to break up.

rozadura, f. friction; chafing.

rozagante, a. pompous, showy; trailing on the ground (as a gown).

rozamiento, m. friction; rubbing; disagreement, clashing.—**rozar,** vti. [a] to stub; to nibble; to gall, chafe; to graze, pass lightly over. —vii. to graze, rub.—vri. (con) to have to do with, be on familiar terms with.

rubí, m. ruby; red color.—**rubicundez,** f. ruddiness, rosiness.—**rubicundo,** a. reddish, ruddy.

rubio, a. blond(e), golden, fair.

rubor, m. blush, flush; bashfulness. —**ruborizarse,** vri. [a] to blush, to flush.—**ruboroso,** a. bashful.

rúbrica, f. mark, flourish; (after signature) rubric; title, heading.— de r., according to rules or custom. —**rubricar,** vti. [d] to sign with a flourish; to sign and seal.

rucio, a. (of animals) light silver gray.

rudeza, f. roughness, ruggedness, rudeness, coarseness.—**rudimentario,** a. rudimentary, undeveloped.—**rudimento,** m. rudiment, embryo; vestige.—pl. rudiments, elements.—**rudo,** a. rude, rough, unpolished; hard, rigorous; stupid.

rueca, f. distaff (for spinning).

rueda, f. wheel; circle of persons; round slice; turn, time, succession; rack (torture).—hacer la r., to cajole, wheedle; to court.

ruedo, m. bull ring, arena; rotation; circuit; circumference, edge of a

wheel or disk; round mat or rug;
(Am.) (sewing) hem of a skirt.

ruego, *m.* request, plea, petition,
supplication.

rufián, *m.* ruffian, rowdy, tough;
pimp, pander.—**rufianismo,** *m.*
rowdyism.

rufo, *a.* sandy (haired); curled.

rugido, *m.* roar; rumbling.—**rugir,**
vii. [c] to roar, bellow, howl.

ruido, *m.* noise; din; rumor; report.
—*hacer* or *meter r.*, to attract attention; to create a sensation; to
make a noise.—**ruidoso,** *a.* noisy,
loud; clamorous.

ruin, *a.* mean, vile, despicable; puny;
stingy; insidious; (of an animal)
vicious.—*m.* wicked, mean or vile
man.—**ruina,** *f.* ruin, downfall;
overthrow, fall.—*pl.* ruins, debris.
—**ruindad,** *f.* baseness; avarice;
base action.—**ruinoso,** *a.* decayed,
ramshackle; ruinous; worthless.

ruiseñor, *m.* nightingale.

rumano, *n. & a.* Rumanian.

rumbo, *m.* bearing, course, direction;
(coll.) pomp, show; generosity.—
con r. a, in the direction of; heading or sailing for.—**rumboso,** *a.*
pompous, magnificent; liberal, lavish.

rumiante, *m. & a.* ruminant.—**rumiar,**
vt. to ruminate.

rumor, *m.* rumor; sound of voices;
murmur—**rumorarse,** *vr.* (Am.) to
be said or rumored, be circulating
as a rumor.

runrún, *m* (coll.) rumor, report.

ruptura, *f.* rupture; fracture, breaking.

rural, *a* rural

ruso, *n. & a.* Russian.—*m* Russian
language.

rusticidad, *f* rustic nature; rudeness,
clumsiness.—**rústico,** *a.* rustic, rural;
coarse, clumsy; unmannerly —*en
rústica,* (bookbinding) in paper
covers, unbound —*n.* peasant.

ruta, *f.* route, way

rutilante, *a.* sparkling, starry

rutina, *f* routine, custom, habit.—
rutinario, *a.* routine.

S

sábado, *m.* Saturday.

sábana, *f* sheet (for a bed) —*pegár-
sele a uno las sábanas,* to rise late.

sabana, *f.* (Am.) savanna, grassy
plain.

sabandija, *f* small nasty reptile.—
pl. vermin

sabañón, *m* chilblain.

saber, *vti.* [37] to know; to be able,
know how to, can; to be aware of,

know about.—*vii.* to know; to be
very sagacious.—*a s.,* namely, to
wit.—*que yo sepa,* as far as I know,
to my best knowledge.—*¿quién
sabe?* perhaps, who knows?—*s. a,*
to taste of, taste like.—*s. de,* to
know, be familiar with; to hear of
or from, have news about.—*m.*
learning, knowledge, lore.—**sabiduría,** *f.* wisdom; learning, knowledge.—**sabiendas.**—*a s.,* knowingly,
consciously.—**sabihondo,** *a.* know-it-
all.—**sabio,** *n.* sage, wise person.—
a. wise, learned.

sablazo, *m.* blow with or wound from
a saber; (coll.) borrowing or spong-
ing.—**sable,** *m.* saber, cutlass.—
sablear, *vt.* (coll.) to sponge, borrow.—**sablista,** *mf.* (coll.) sponger,
one who asks for petty loans.

sabor, *m.* taste, flavor, savor.—
saborear, *vt.* to flavor, savor; to
give a relish or zest to.—*vt. & vr.*
to relish, enjoy; to smack one's
lips.

sabotaje, *m.* sabotage.—**sabotear,** *vt.*
& *vi.* to sabotage.

sabroso, *a.* savory, tasty, palatable,
delicious; pleasant.

sabueso, *m.* hound; bloodhound;
(fig.) bloodhound (detective).

sacabocado(s), *m.* (hollow) punch.—
sacacorchos, *m.* corkscrew.—**saca-
muelas,** *mf* (coll.) tooth extractor,
quack dentist.—**sacapuntas,** *m.* pencil sharpener —**sacar,** *vti.* [d] to
extract, draw out, pull out; to take
out; to put out; to take (a photo);
to bring out; to get, obtain; to
deduce, infer; to draw, win (a
prize); (games) to serve (the ball),
to kick off; to unsheathe (a sword),
to make, take (a copy).—*s. a bailar,*
to lead out for a dance.—*s. a luz,* to
print, publish.—*s. de quicio,* to
make one lose patience.—*s. (a uno)
de sus casillas,* (fig.) to drive crazy,
to exhaust one's patience.—*s. en
claro,* or *en limpio,* to conclude, arrive at the conclusion.—*s. la cara,*
to stand for, defend.—*s. la cuenta,*
to figure out

sacarina, *f* saccharin.

sacerdocio, *m.* priesthood —**sacerdote,**
m priest.—**sacerdotisa,** *f.* priestess.

saco, *m.* sack, bag; sackful, bagful;
coat, jacket; (mil.) sack, plunder.—
entrar a s, to plunder, loot.—*no
echar en s. roto,* not to forget, not
to ignore.—*s de noche,* hand bag,
satchel.

sacramento, *m* sacrament.

sacrificar, *vti.* [d] to sacrifice.—*vri.*
to sacrifice oneself, give up one's

life.—**sacrificio,** *m.* sacrifice, offering.

sacrilegio, *m.* sacrilege.—**sacrílego,** *a.* sacrilegious.

sacristán, *m.* sexton, sacristan.—**sacristía,** *f.* sacristy, vestry.

sacro, *a.* holy, sacred.—*m.* (anat.) sacrum.—**sacrosanto,** *a.* very holy, sacrosanct.

sacudida, *f.* shake, shaking, jerk.—**sacudimiento,** *m.* shake, shaking; shock, jerk, jolt.—**sacudir,** *vt.* to shake; jolt, jerk; to beat (to remove dust); to spank, drub; to shake off.—*vr.* to reject, drive away, shake off.

sádico, *a.* sadistic.—**sadismo,** *m.* sadism.

saeta, *f.* arrow, dart.

sagrado, *a.* sacred.

sahumar, *vt.* to perfume; to smoke; to fumigate.—**sahumerio,** *m* smoke; vapor, steam; fumigation; fuming.

sainete, *m.* (theat.) short farce; flavor sauce; tidbit.

sajón, *n. & a.* Saxon.

sal, *f.* salt; wit; grace, winning manners; (Am.) bad luck.

sala, *f.* living room, parlor; hall; courtroom, court of justice (room and judges); tribunal.—*s. de espera,* waiting-room.

salado, *a.* salty, salted; briny; witty; graceful, winsome; (Am.) unlucky; (Am) expensive.

salamandra, *f.* salamander

salar, *vt* to salt, to season or preserve with salt; to cure or corn (meat); to brine; (Am.) to bring bad luck; to spoil, ruin.

salario, *m.* wages, salary

salcochar, *vt.* (cook.) to boil with water and salt.

salchicha, *f.* sausage.—**salchichón,** *m* salami

saldar, *vt* (com.) to settle, liquidate, balance —**saldo,** *m.* (com.) balance, settlement, remnants sold at low price, sale.

saledizo, *a.* salient, projecting.—*m.* projection, ledge.

salero, *m.* saltcellar; salt pan, (coll) gracefulness, winning ways, charm —**saleroso,** *a.* (coll.) witty; lively, jolly, winsome

salida, *f* start, setting or going out, departure; exit; outlet; issue, result; subterfuge, pretext, witty remark; sally; projection, expenditure, outlay —*sin s.,* dead-end (street) —*s. del sol,* sunrise.—**saliente,** *a.* salient, projecting.—*f* projection, lug.

salino, *a.* saline.—*f.* salt works, salt mine

salir, *vii.* [38] to go or come out; to depart, leave; to get out, get off (of a vehicle); to rise (as the sun); to spring; to be issued or published; to come out, do (well, badly); to lead to; to open to; to say or do a thing unexpectedly or unseasonably; (theat.) to enter, appear.—*s. a,* to resemble, look like. —*s. adelante,* to be successful.—*s. al encuentro,* to come out to meet.— *s. de,* to dispose of; to part with; to get rid of.—*s. ganando,* to come out a winner, gain.—*vri.* to leak; to overflow.—*s. con la suya,* to accomplish one's end, to have one's way.

salitre, *m.* saltpeter, niter.

saliva, *f.* saliva, spittle.

salmo, *m.* psalm.

salmón, *m.* salmon.

salmuera, *f.* brine; pickle.

salobre, *a.* brackish, briny, saltish.

salón, *m.* salon, large parlor; living or assembly room.

salpicadura, *f.* splash, spatter, spattering.—**salpicar,** *vti.* [d] to spatter, sprinkle, splash.

salpimentar, *vti.* [1] to season with pepper and salt.

salpullido, *m.* (med.) rash.

salsa, *f.* sauce, dressing, gravy.—**salsera,** *f.* gravy dish, tureen.

saltamontes, *m.* grasshopper.—**saltar,** *vi.* to jump, leap, spring, hop; to skip, to bound, to snap, break in pieces; to come off (as a button) —*s. a la vista,* to be self-evident. *s. a tierra,* to land, debark.—*vt.* to leap or jump over; to skip.

salteado, *a.* assorted

salteador, *n.* highwayman(-woman); hold-up man, robber

saltimbanqui, *mf.* acrobat.—**salto,** *m.* jump, leap, skip, omission; gap. *a saltos,* leaping, by hops.—*dar un s.,* to jump, leap —*de un s ,* at one jump, in a flash.—*s. de agua,* waterfall, falls, cataract.—*s. mortal,* somersault.

saltón, *a.* jumping, hopping, protruding.—*ojos saltones,* bulging eyes. —*m* grasshopper.

salubre, *a.* salubrious, healthful.

salubridad, *f* salubrity, healthfulness.—**salud,** *f* health; public weal; welfare —*pl.* compliments, greetings. —*a su s,* to your health (in drinking).—**saludable,** *a.* healthy, salutary, wholesome.

saludar, *vt.* to greet, bow to, salute, hail.—**saludo,** *m.* bow, salute, salutation, greeting.—**salutación,** *f.* salutation, greeting, salute, bow.

salva, *f* (artil) salvo, salver, tray

salvación, *f.* salvation.

salvado, *m.* bran.

salvador, *n.* savior, rescuer, redeemer.

salvadoreño, *n.* & *a.* Salvadoran.

salvaguardar, *vt.* to safeguard, protect.—**salvaguardia,** *m.* safeguard, security, protection; guard; watchman.—*f.* safe-conduct, passport.

salvajada, *f.* savage word or action.—**salvaje,** *a.* savage, uncivilized; (of plants, animals) wild; rough, wild (country).—*mf.* savage.—**salvajismo,** *m.* savagery.

salvamento, *m.* salvage; safety; rescue.—*bote de s.,* lifeboat.—**salvar,** *vt.* to save, rescue; to avoid (a danger); to jump over, get over (ditch, creek, etc.), clear (an obstacle); to overcome (a difficulty); to excuse, make an exception of.—*s. las apariencias,* to keep up appearances.—*vr.* to be saved; to escape from danger.—**salvavidas,** *m.* life preserver; lifesaver.

¡salve! *interj.* hail!

salvedad, *f.* reservation, exception, qualification; salvo.

salvia, *f.* (bot.) sage.

salvo, *a.* saved, safe; excepted, omitted.—*adv.* save, saving, excepting, barring.—*s. que,* unless.—**salvoconducto,** *m.* safe-conduct; permit, pass.

san, *a. contr.* of SANTO.

sanar, *vt.* to heal, cure.—*vi.* to heal; to recover from sickness.—**sanatorio,** *m.* sanatorium, sanitarium; asylum (for mental illness); nursing home.

sanción, *f.* sanction; ratification.—**sancionar,** *vt.* to sanction, to ratify.

sandalia, *f.* sandal.

sandez, *f.* foolishness, stupidity.

sandía, *f.* watermelon.

sandio, *a.* foolish, stupid.

sandunga, *f.* gracefulness, charm.—**sandunguero,** *a.* (coll.) graceful, charming.

saneamiento, *m.* drainage (of land); sanitation; (law) waiver of lien.—**sanear,** *vt.* to drain, dry up (lands); (law) to indemnify.

sangrar, *vt.* to bleed; to drain.—*vi.* to bleed.—**sangre,** *f.* blood; lineage.—*a s. fría,* in cold blood.—*a s. y fuego,* by fire and sword.—*s. fría,* calmness, presence of mind.—**sangría,** *f.* bleeding; drain, drainage; pilferage.—**sangriento,** *a.* bloody, gory.—**sanguijuela,** *f.* leech.—**sanguinario,** *a.* sanguinary, bloody.—**sanguinolento,** *a.* bloody; blood-stained.

sanidad, *f.* health, healthfulness; health department.—**sanitario,** *a.*

sanitary, hygienic.—*m.* health officer.—**sano,** *a.* healthy, sound; honest.—*s. y salvo,* safe and sound.

sanseacabó, *m.* (coll.) that's all.

santabárbara, *f.* (naut.) magazine; powder room.

santiamén, *m.* (coll.) instant, moment, jiffy.

santidad, *f.* sanctity, sainthood, saintliness, holiness.—**santificar,** *vti.* [d] to sanctify, to consecrate, hallow; to keep.—**santiguar,** *vt.* to bless; to heal by blessing.—*vr.* to cross oneself.—**santo,** *a.* saintly, holy; saint; sacred.—*todo el s. día,* the whole day long.—*n.* saint; saint's day.—*s. y seña,* (mil.) password.—**santuario,** *m.* sanctuary.

saña, *f.* anger, rage, fury.—**sañudo,** *a.* furious, enraged.

sapo, *m.* toad.

saque, *m.* (sports) service; server (in tennis); kick-off (in football).

saqueador, *n.* looter, pillager.—**saquear,** *vt.* to plunder, loot, pillage.—**saqueo,** *m.* pillage, loot, plunder.

sarampión, *m.* measles.

sarao, *m.* dance; evening party.

sarape, *m.* (Am.) serape; blanket.

sarcasmo, *m.* sarcasm.—**sarcástico,** *a.* sarcastic.

sardina, *f.* sardine.

sargento, *m.* (mil.) sergeant.

sarmiento, *m.* vine shoot or branch.—**sarmentoso,** *a.* vinelike, gnarled, knotty.

sarna, *f.* itch, scabies, mange.—**sarnoso,** *a.* itchy; scabbed; mangy

sarpullido, *m.* = SALPULLIDO.

sarraceno, *n.* Saracen; Moor.—*a.* Saracen; Moorish.

sarro, *m* tartar on teeth.

sarta, *f.* string, series, row

sartén, *m.* & *f.* frying pan; skillet. *tener la s. por el mango,* to have the control or command.

sastre, *m.* tailor.—**sastrería,** *f.* tailor's shop.

satánico, *a.* satanic.

satélite, *m.* satellite; follower, henchman.

satén, *m.* sateen.

sátira, *f.* satire.—**satírico,** *a.* satirical; sarcastic.—**satirizar,** *vti.* [a] to satirize, lampoon.—**sátiro,** *m.* lewd man, satyr.

satisfacción, *f.* satisfaction; apology, excuse.—**satisfacer,** *vti.* [22-49] to satisfy; to pay in full, settle.—*s. una letra,* (com.) to honor a draft.—*vri.* to satisfy oneself; to be satisfied; to take satisfaction; to be convinced.—**satisfecho,** *ppi.* of SATISFACER.—*a.* satisfied, content; arrogant, conceited

saturación, *f.* saturation.—**saturar,** *vt.* to saturate.—*vr.* to become saturated; to fill, satiate.

sauce, *m.* willow, osier.

saurio, *m.* lizard.

savia, *f.* sap.

saxofón, saxófono, *m.* saxophone.

saya, *f.* skirt.—**sayuela,** *f.* (Am.) petticoat.

sazón, *f.* maturity, ripeness; season; taste, relish, flavor; occasion, opportunity.—*a la s.,* then, at that time.—*en s.,* ripe, in season.—**sazonar,** *vt.* (cook.) to season; to mature.—*vr.* to ripen, mature.

se, *3d. pers. refl. pron.* oneself, herself, itself, himself, themselves, each other, one another.—*(Replaces* le to him, to her, to you *(formal),* to them.

sebo, *m.* tallow, fat.

seca, *f.* drought; dry season.—*a secas,* simply; plain, alone.—**secador,** *a.* drying.—*m.* (Am.) dryer.—*f.* (Am.) clothes dryer.—**secante,** *f.* (geom.) secant.—*a.* drying.—*a. & m.* blotting (paper).—**secar,** *vti.* [d] to dry (out); to parch; to wipe dry; to tease, vex.—*vri.* to dry, dry up; to become lank, lean, or meager; to decay; to wither.

sección, *f.* act of cutting; section; division.—**seccionar,** *vt.* to section.

seco, *a.* dry; dried up; arid; dead (leaves); lean, meager; abrupt, curt; cold; sharp (noise).—*en s.,* high and dry; without cause or reason.—*parar en s.,* to stop suddenly.

secoya, *f.* sequoia.

secreción, *f.* (med.) secretion.—**secretar,** *vt.* (physiol.) to secrete.

secretaria, *f.* secretary's office; secretaryship.—**secretario,** *n.* secretary; actuary.—**secretear,** *vi.* (coll.) to whisper.—**secreteo,** *m.* (coll.) whispering.—**secreto,** *a.* secret; hidden.—*m.* secret; secrecy.—*s. a voces,* open secret.

secuaz, *mf.* follower, supporter, partisan.

secuela, *f.* sequel, result.

secuencia, *f.* sequence.

secuestrador, *n.* kidnapper.—**secuestrar,** *vt.* to kidnap, abduct; (law) to sequestrate.—**secuestro,** *m.* kidnapping, abduction; (law) sequestration.

secular, *a.* centenary; agelong; secular, lay.

secundar, *vt* to second, aid, favor.—**secundario,** *a.* secondary; subsidiary.—*m.* second hand (of timepiece).

sed, *f* thirst, longing, desire.—*tener s. de,* to be thirsty for; to thirst or hunger after.

seda, *f.* silk.—*como una s.,* sweet-tempered; smoothly.

sedal, *m.* fishline.

sedante, sedativo, *m. & a.* sedative.

sede, *f.* see, seat.

sedeño, *a.* silken, silky.—**sedería,** *f.* silks; silk shop.—**sedero,** *a.* silk.—*n.* silk weaver or dealer.

sedición, *f.* sedition.—**sedicioso,** *a.* seditious; mutinous.

sediento, *a.* thirsty; **(de)** eagerly desirous, anxious (for).

sedimento, *m.* sediment, dregs, settling; grouts, grounds.

sedoso, *a.* = SEDEÑO.

seducción, *f.* seduction, deceiving.—**seducir,** *vti.* [11] to seduce; to charm, captivate.—**seductivo,** *a.* seductive; enticing.—**seductor,** *a.* fascinating, attractive, tempting.—*n.* seducer; deceiver; delightful person.

segador, *n.* reaper; harvester.—*f.* harvester, mowing machine.—**segar,** *vti.* [1-b] to mow; to harvest; to cut off, mow down.

seglar, *a.* secular, lay.—*mf.* layman (-woman).

segmento, *m.* segment.

segregación, *f.* segregation, separation.—**segregar,** *vti.* [b] to segregate, separate; (med.) to secrete.

segueta, *f.* jig saw, marquetry saw.

seguida, *f.—en s.,* at once, immediately.—**seguidamente,** *adv.* right after that, immediately after.—**seguido,** *a.* continued, successive; straight, direct.—**seguidor,** *n.* follower.—**seguimiento,** *m.* pursuit, following; continuation.—**seguir,** *vti.* [29-b] to follow; to pursue; to prosecute; to continue; to keep on.—*vri.* to ensue, follow as a consequence.

según, *prep.* according to —*s. y como,* or *s. y conforme,* just as; it depends.—*conj.* as; according as.

segundero, *m.* second hand (of watch or clock).—**segundo,** *a. & n.* second.—*segunda intención,* double meaning.—*m.* (time) second.

seguridad, *f.* safety; security; certainty.—**seguro,** *a.* safe; secure; sure, certain, positive; dependable, trustworthy.—*m.* assurance; (mech.) click; safety catch (of a pistol); tumbler of a lock; (com.) insurance, assurance.—*a buen s.,* or *de s.,* certainly, undoubtedly.—*sobre s.,* without risk.

selección, *f.* selection, choice.—**seleccionar,** *vt* to select, choose.—

selecto, *a.* select, choice, distinguished.

selva, *f.* jungle, forest.

sellar, *vt.* to seal; to stamp; to conclude, finish; to cover, close.—**sello,** *m.* seal; stamp (sticker, mark or implement); signet.

semana, *f.* week.—*entre s.,* any weekday except Saturday.—**semanal,** *a.* weekly.—**semanario,** *m.* weekly publication.

semblante, *m.* mien, countenance, look, expression; aspect.—**semblanza,** *f.* portrait, biographical sketch.

sembrado, *m.* cultivated field, sown ground.—**sembradura,** *f.* sowing, seeding.—**sembrar,** *vti.* [1] to sow, seed; to scatter, spread.

semejante, *a.* similar, like; such, of that kind.—*m.* fellow creature, fellow man.—**semejanza,** *f.* resemblance, similarity, similitude.—*a s. de,* like.—**semejar,** *vi. & vr.* to be like; to resemble.

semen, *m.* semen, sperm; (bot.) seed. —**semental,** *a. & m.* breeding (horse).

semestre, *m.* semester.

semicircular, *a.* semicircular.—**semicírculo,** *m.* semicircle.

semidiós, *m.* demigod.—*f.* demigoddess.

semilla, *f.* seed.—**semillero,** *m.* seed bed, seed plot; nursery; hotbed.

seminario, *m.* seminary.—**seminarista,** *m.* seminarist.

sempiterno, *a.* eternal, everlasting.

senado, *m.* senate.—**senador,** *n.* senator.

sencillez, *f.* simplicity; plainness, naturalness; candor.—**sencillo,** *a.* simple; slight, thin; plain; harmless; natural, unaffected, unsophisticated; unadorned; single.

senda, *f.* path, footpath, way.—**sendero,** *m.* path, footpath, byway.

sendos, *a. pl.* one each, one for each.

senectud, *f.* old age, senility.—**senil,** *a.* senile.

seno, *m.* breast, bosom; womb; lap of a woman; cavity; sinus; bay; innermost recess; (math.) sine.

sensación, *f.* sensation.—**sensacional,** *a.* sensational.

sensatez, *f.* good sense, wisdom.—**sensato,** *a.* sensible, judicious, wise.

sensibilidad, *f.* sensibility; sensitiveness.—**sensible,** *a.* perceptible; sensitive, keen; regrettable; (photog.) sensitive, sensitized.—**sensiblería,** *f.* false sentimentality.—**sensitivo,** *a.* sensitive; sensual; appreciable.

sensual, *a.* sensuous; sensual; sexy.—**sensualidad,** *f.* sensuality, voluptuousness.

sentar, *vti.* [1] to seat; to establish, set up (a precedent, etc.).—*dar por sentado,* to take for granted.—*vii.* to fit, become, suit; to agree with (of food).—*vri.* to sit, sit down.

sentencia, *f.* (law) sentence, verdict, judgment; maxim.—*pronunciar s.,* to pass judgment.—**sentenciar,** *vt.* (law) to sentence; to pass judgment on.

sentido, *a.* sensitive, touchy; heartfelt; offended.—*m.* sense; meaning; direction, course.—*en el s. de que,* to the effect that; stating that.—*perder el s.,* to lose consciousness; to faint.—*sin s.,* meaningless; unconscious.

sentimental, *a.* sentimental; emotional, soulful.—**sentimentalismo,** *m.* sentimentality.—**sentimiento,** *m.* sentiment, feeling; sensation; grief, sorrow, regret.

sentina, *f.* (naut.) bilge; sewer.—*s. de vicios,* place of iniquity.

sentir, *vti.* [39] to feel, experience; to perceive by the senses; to grieve, regret, mourn; to be sorry for.—*vii.* to feel; to foresee.—*sin s.,* without noticing, inadvertently.—*vri.* to complain; to feel (well, bad, sad); to resent.—*m.* feeling; opinion, judgment.

seña, *f.* sign, mark, token; nod, gesture; signal.—*pl.* address; personal description.—**señal,** *f.* signal; sign, mark; indication; trace, vestige; scar; token.—**señalado,** *a.* distinguished, noted.—**señalamiento,** *m.* date, appointment.—**señalar,** *vt.* to stamp, mark; to point out; to name; to determine; to sign; to assign.—*vr.* to distinguish oneself, to excel; to call attention to oneself.

señor, *m.* mister, Mr.; sir; man, gentleman; lord, master.—*muy s. mío,* Dear Sir (in letters).—**señora,** *f.* lady; mistress; madam; dame.—**señorear,** *vt.* to master; to domineer, lord it over; to excel; to control (one's passions).—**señoría,** *f.* lordship.—**señorial,** *a.* lordly; manorial.—**señorío,** *m.* dominion, command; arrogance; lordship; domain, manor.—**señorita,** *f.* young lady; miss; Miss; (coll.) mistress of the house.—**señorito,** *m.* Master (title); (coll.) master of the house; (coll.) playboy.

señuelo, *m.* decoy, lure; bait; enticement.

separable, *a.* separable, detachable, removable.—**separación,** *f.* separation.—**separado,** *a.* separate, apart.—*por s.,* separate, separately.—

separar, *vt.* to separate; to divide; to detach; to remove, take away or off; to lay aside; to dismiss, discharge.—*vr.* to separate; to part company; to withdraw.

sepelio, *m.* burial.

septentrional, *a.* northern, northerly.

septiembre, *m.* September.

sepulcro, *m.* sepulcher, grave, tomb.—**sepultar,** *vt.* to bury, inter; to hide, conceal.—**sepultura,** *f.* burial; tomb, grave, sepulcher.—*dar s.,* to bury.—**sepulturero,** *n.* gravedigger, sexton.

sequedad, *f.* aridity, dryness; gruffness.—**sequía,** *f.* drought.

ser, *vii.* [40] to be; to exist; to happen.—*es tarde,* it is late.—*esto es,* that is to say.—*no sea que,* lest.—*¿qué ha sido de Juan?* what has become of John?—*sea lo que fuere, sea como fuere,* be that as it may; anyhow, anyway.—*son las dos,* it is two o'clock.—*soy yo,* it is I.—*m.* existence; being; essence.

serenar, *vt.* to calm down, pacify.—*vr.* (of weather) to clear up, become calm.

serenata, *f.* serenade.

serenidad, *f.* serenity, calmness; tranquility.—**sereno,** *a.* serene, calm; clear, cloudless.—*m.* night watchman; night dew.

serie, *f.* series; sequence.—*fabricación en s.,* mass production.

seriedad, *f.* seriousness, gravity; earnestness.—**serio,** *a.* serious, grave, dignified; grand, solemn; earnest; sincere.—*en s.,* seriously.

sermón, *m.* sermon; reprimand.—**sermonear,** *vt.* to sermonize; (coll.) to lecture, reprimand.—**sermoneo,** *m.* (coll.) repeated admonition, sermonizing.

serpentear, *vi.* to meander; to wind; to wriggle, squirm.—**serpentín,** *f.* coil (of a heater, etc.).—**serpentina,** *f.* (min.) serpentine; paper streamer.—**serpiente,** *f.* serpent, snake.—*s. de cascabel,* rattlesnake.

serranía, *f.* sierra; mountainous region.—**serrano,** *a.* mountain, highland.—*n.* mountaineer, highlander.

serrar, *vti.* [1] to saw.—**serrín,** *m.* sawdust.—**serrucho,** *m.* handsaw.

servible, *a.* serviceable, adaptable.—**servicial,** *a.* serviceable; obsequious; obliging, kind.—**servicio,** *m.* service; servants; (Am.) toilet, water closet; tea or coffee set.—*s. de mesa,* set of dishes.—**servidor,** *n.* servant.—*s. de Ud.,* at your service.—**servidumbre,** *f.* (staff of) servants or attendants; servitude; (law) right of way.—**servil,** *a.*

servile, slavish, abject; lowly, humble.—**servilismo,** *m.* servility, abjectness.

servilleta, *f.* napkin.

servio, *n. & a.* Serb, Serbian.

servir, *vii.* [29] to serve; to be of use.—*no s. para nada,* to be good for nothing.—*para s. a Ud.,* at your service.—*s. de,* to act as, to be used as.—*s. para,* to be for, be used or useful for; to be good for; to do for.—*vti.* to serve; to do a service or a favor to.—*vri.* to please; to help oneself (as at table).—*s. de,* to make use of; to employ.

sesgado, *a.* oblique, slanting, bias.—**sesgar,** *vti.* [b] to slope, slant; to cut on the bias.—*vii.* to take an oblique direction.—**sesgo,** *m.* bias, slope, obliqueness; turn (of an affair).

sesión, *f.* session, meeting; conference, consultation.—*levantar la s.,* to adjourn the meeting.

seso, *m.* brain; brains, intelligence.—*levantarse la tapa de los sessos,* to blow out one's brains.—*perder el s.,* to go crazy; (fig.) to lose one's head.—*sin seso(s),* scatterbrained.

sestear, *vi.* to take a nap.

sesudo, *a.* judicious, discreet, wise.

seta, *f.* mushroom.

seto, *m.* fence, inclosure.—*s. vivo,* hedge.

seudónimo, *m.* pseudonym, pen name.

severidad, *f.* severity, austerity, strictness; seriousness.—**severo,** *a.* severe, rigorous; rigid, strict; serious; puritanical.

sexagenario, *n. & a.* sexagenarian.

sex, *m.* sex.—**sexual,** *a.* sexual.

si, *adv.* yes; indeed.—*un s. es no es,* somewhat, a trifle.—*m.* yes, consent.—*3rd. pers. refl. pron.* (after prep.) himself, herself, yourself, itself, oneself, themselves, yourselves.—*dar de s.,* to stretch, give.—*metido en s.,* pensive, introspective.—**si,** *conj.* if; whether.—*por s. acaso,* just in case.—*s. bien,* although.

siamés, *n. & a.* Siamese, Thai.—*n. pl.* Siamese twins, Siamese.

sibila, *f.* prophetess.

siciliano, *n. & a.* Sicilian.

sicoanálisis, sicología, siquiatría, etc., V. PSICOANÁLISIS, PSICOLOGÍA, PSIQUIATRÍA, etc.

siderurgia, *f.* iron and steel industry.

sidra, *f.* cider.

siega, *f.* reaping, harvest, mowing.

siembra, *f.* sowing, seeding; seedtime; sown field.

siempre, *adv.* always.—*para* or *por s.* (*jamás*), forever (and ever).—*s. que,* provided; whenever.

sien, *f.* (anat.) temple.

sierpe, *f.* serpent, snake.

sierra, *f.* saw; mountain range.

siesta, *f.* siesta, afternoon nap; hottest part of the day.—**siestecita,** *f.* short nap, snooze.

sietemesino, *a.* & *n.* prematurely born (baby).—*m.* puny.

sifón, *m.* siphon; siphon bottle.

sigilo, *m.* secrecy, concealment, reserve.—**sigiloso,** *a.* silent, reserved.

siglo, *m.* century; age; period; the world, worldly matters.

significación, *f.* significance; sense, meaning; implication; importance.—**significado,** *m.* meaning, definition (of a word, etc.).—**significar,** *vti.* [d] to signify, mean; to indicate; to make known; to import, be worth.—**significativo,** *a.* significant.

signatario, *n.* & *a.* signatory.

signo, *m.* sign, mark, symbol; signal.

siguiente, *a.* following, next.

sílaba, *f.* syllable.—**silabario,** *m.* primer; reader, speller.

silba, *f.* (theat.) hiss, hissing (of disapproval).—**silbar,** *vi.* to whistle.—*vt.* & *vi.* (theat.) to hiss, boo.—**silbato,** *m.* whistle (instrument).—**silbido,** *m.* whistle, whistling sound; hiss.

silenciador, *m.* (auto) muffler; silencer (on gun, etc.).—**silencio,** *m.* silence; noiselessness; taciturnity; secrecy; stillness; quiet; (mus.) rest.—*guardar s.,* to keep quiet.—**silencioso,** *a.* silent, noiseless; still, quiet.

silueta, *f.* silhouette; (of person) figure.

silvestre, *a.* wild; uncultivated; rustic, savage.—**silvicultura,** *f.* forestry.

silla, *f.* chair; saddle; (eccl.) see.—*s. de montar,* riding saddle.—*s. de tijera,* camp chair.—**silletazo,** *m.* blow with a chair.—**sillín,** *m.* light riding saddle; saddle (on bicycle, etc.).—**sillón,** *m.* armchair; easy chair; sidesaddle.

sima, *f.* deep cavern; abyss.

simbólico, *a.* symbolical.—**simbolismo,** *m.* symbolism.—**simbolizar,** *vti.* [a] to symbolize, represent, typify.—**símbolo,** *m.* symbol; mark, device.

simetría, *f.* symmetry.—**simétrico,** *a.* symmetrical.

simiente, *f.* seed; germ; semen, sperm.

símil, *m.* resemblance, similarity; simile.—**similar,** *a.* similar, like, alike, resembling.—**similitud,** *f.* similitude, similarity.

simio, *n.* simian, ape.

simpatía, *f.* charm, attractiveness; congeniality; liking, friendly feeling; (med.) sympathy.—**simpático,** *a.* congenial; appealing; charming.—**simpatizar,** *vii.* [a] to be congenial with; to have a liking for; to be attracted by.

simple, *a.* simple; mere; foolish; artless, ingenuous; plain, unmixed, unadorned.—*mf.* simpleton.—**simpleza,** *f.* silliness, foolishness; silly thing; rusticity, rudeness.—**simplicidad,** *f.* simplicity.—**simplificación,** *f.* simplification.—**simplificar,** *vti.* [d] to simplify.—**simplón,** *m.* simpleton.

simulación, *f.* simulation, feigning.—**simulacro,** *m.* image, idol; show, semblance; pretense; sham battle.—**simulador,** *n.* simulator; malingerer.—*a.* simulative.—**simular,** *vt.* to simulate, pretend, sham.

simultaneidad, *f.* simultaneity.—**simultáneo,** *a.* simultaneous.

sin, *prep.* without; but for; besides, not including.—*s. embargo,* notwithstanding, nevertheless, however.—*s. que,* without.

sinagoga, *f.* synagogue.

sinapismo, *m.* mustard plaster; (coll.) nuisance, bore.

sincerar, *vt.* to justify.—*vr.* to excuse, justify, or vindicate oneself.—**sinceridad,** *f.* sincerity, good faith.—**sincero,** *a.* sincere.

síncope, *f.* (med.) swoon, fainting fit.

sincronizar, *vti.* [a] to synchronize.

sindéresis, *f.* common sense, discretion, good judgment.

sindicalismo, *m.* trade unionism.—**sindicato,** *m.* labor union.

síndico, *m.* trustee; (law) assignee, receiver.

sinfín, *m.* countless number.

sinfonía, *f.* symphony.—**sinfónico,** *a.* symphonic.

singular, *a.* singular; unique; unusual; odd; excellent.—**singularizar,** *vti.* [a] to single out; to distinguish.—*vri.* to be conspicuous; to be singled out; to distinguish oneself.

siniestro, *a.* sinister; left (side); vicious.—*m.* disaster; catastrophe.—*f.* left hand; left-hand side.

sino, *conj.* but; except, besides; solely, only.—*m.* fate, destiny.

sinónimo, *a.* synonymous.—*m.* synonym.

sinopsis, *f.* synopsis.

sinrazón, *f.* wrong, injury, injustice.

sinsabor, *m.* displeasure; trouble, grief, sorrow.

sinsonte, *m.* (Am.) mockingbird.

sintaxis, *f.* syntax.

síntesis, *f.* synthesis.—**sintético,** *a.* synthetical.—**sintetizar,** *vti.* [a] to synthesize; to sum up.

síntoma, *m.* symptom; sign.

sinnúmero, *m.* countless number.

sinvergüenza, *mf.* (coll.) scoundrel, rascal; brazen, shameless person.— *a.* shameless.

siquiera, *adv.* even, at least.—*conj.* even if; even.—*ni s.*, not even.

sirena, *f.* siren, mermaid; whistle, foghorn; temptress, vamp.

sirvienta, *f.* servant girl, maid.— **sirviente**, *m.* (domestic) servant; waiter.

sisa, *f.* petty theft; (sewing) dart.— **sisar**, *vt.* to pilfer, filch; (sewing) to take in.

sisear, *vi.* to hiss.—**siseo**, *m.* hiss, hissing.

sísmico, *a.* seismic.—**sismógrafo**, *m.* seismograph.

sistema, *m.* system.—**sistemático**, *a.* systematic.—**sistematización**, *f.* systematization.—**sistematizar**, *vti.* [a] & *vii.* to systematize.

sitial, *m.* seat of honor, presiding chair.

sitiar, *vt.* (mil.) to lay siege to; to surround, hem in, compass.—**sitio**, *m.* place, space, spot, room; stand; seat; location, site; country house; country seat, villa; (Cuba) small farm; (mil.) siege.—*quedar en el s.*, to die on the spot.

sito, *a.* situated, lying, located.— **situación**, *f.* situation; position; site, location; condition, circumstances.—**situar**, *vt.* to place, locate, situate; (com.) to remit or place (funds).—*vr.* to settle in a place; to station oneself.

so, *prep.* under.—*s. capa de*, or *s. color de*, under color of; on pretense of.—*s. pena de*, under penalty of.—*s. pretexto*, under the pretext of.—*interj.* whoa!

sobaco, *m.* armpit; (bot.) axil.

sobado, *a.* shopworn.

sobaquera, *f.* (tailoring) armhole.— **sobaquina**, *f.* bad odor of the armpit.

sobar, *vt.* to knead, to massage, squeeze, soften; to pummel, box; to handle (a person) with too much familiarity.

soberanía, *f.* sovereignty; rule, sway. —**soberano**, *a.* sovereign; supreme, royal; superior.—*n.* sovereign.

soberbia, *f.* excessive pride, haughtiness; presumption; magnificence, pomp; anger.—**soberbio**, *a.* overproud, arrogant, haughty; superb, grand; lofty, eminent.

sobornar, *vt.* to suborn, bribe.— **soborno**, *m.* subornation, bribe; incitement, inducement.

sobra, *f.* surplus, excess; leftover, leaving.—*de s.*, over and above; more than enough.—*estar de s.*, (coll.) to be one too many; to be superfluous.—**sobrante**, *a.* extra; excess; leftover.—*m.* surplus, remainder.—**sobrar**, *vt.* to surpass; to have in excess.—*vi.* to be in excess; to be intrusive; to remain, be left over.

sobre, *prep.* on, upon; over; above; about, concerning; about, more or less; to, toward, near.—*m.* envelope (for letters).

sobrealimentar, *vt.* to overfeed.

sobrecama, *f.* coverlet, bedspread.

sobrecargar, *vti.* [b] to overload, overburden; (com.) to overcharge.— **sobrecargo**, *m.* (naut.) purser, supercargo.

sobrecoger, *vti.* [c] to surprise, catch unaware; to startle.—*vri.* to become afraid or apprehensive.—**sobrecogimiento**, *m.* fear, apprehension.

sobrecoser, *vt.* (sewing) to fell, sew the edge of a seam flat.

sobreexcitación, *f.* overexcitement.— **sobreexcitar**, *vt.* to overexcite.

sobrehumano, *a.* superhuman.

sobrellevar, *vt.* to ease (another's burden); to carry, bear, endure; to overlook, be lenient about.

sobremanera, *adv.* beyond measure; exceedingly, most.

sobremesa, *f.* tablecloth; after-dinner chat.—*de s.*, during an after-dinner chat.

sobrenadar, *vi.* to float.

sobrenatural, *a.* supernatural.

sobrenombre, *m.* sobriquet; nickname.

sobrentender, *vti.* [18] to understand, deduce, infer.—*vri.* to be understood, go without saying.

sobrepasar, *vt.* to exceed, surpass.

sobrepeso, *m.* overweight.

sobreponer, *vti.* [32-49] to superimpose, overlap.—*vri.* to control oneself.—*s. a*, to master, overcome (difficulties, hardships).

sobreprecio, *m.* extra charge, raise.

sobreprenda, *f.* overdress.

sobrepujar, *vt.* to excel, beat, surpass.

sobresaliente, *a.* outstanding; projecting.—*mf.* substitute, understudy. —**sobresalir**, *vii.* [38] to excel, be prominent, stand out; to project, just out, flange.

sobresaltar, *vt.* to rush upon, assail; to frighten, startle.—*vi.* to stand out.—*vr.* to be startled.—**sobresalto**, *m.* assault; startling surprise; sudden dread or fear.

sobrescrito, *m.* envelope address.

sobreseer, *vti.* [e] to desist from a design; to relinquish a claim; (law) to stay a judgment, etc.

sobrestante, *m.* overseer; foreman; comptroller; inspector; supervisor.

sobresueldo, *m.* extra wages.

sobretodo, *m.* overcoat.

sobrevenir, *vii.* [45] to happen, take place; to follow.

sobreviviente, *mf.* & *a.* survivor; surviving.—**sobrevivir,** *vt.* & *vi.* to survive, outlive.

sobriedad, *f.* sobriety, frugality.

sobrina, *f.* niece.—**sobrino,** *m.* nephew.

sobrio, *a.* sober, temperate, frugal.

socarrón, *a.* cunning, sly, crafty.—**socarronería,** *f.* cunning, artfulness, craftiness.

socavar, *vt.* to excavate, undermine.

sociabilidad, *f.* sociableness, sociability.—**sociable,** *a.* sociable, companionable.—**social,** *a.* social.—**socialismo,** *m.* socialism.—**socialista,** *mf.* & *a.* socialist(ic).—**socialización,** *f.* socialization.—**socializar,** *vti.* [a] to socialize.—**sociedad,** *f.* society; social intercourse; (com.) society, corporation, company.—*s.* anónima, stock company.—**socio,** *n.* partner, copartner; companion; member, fellow.—**sociología,** *f.* sociology.

socorrer, *vt.* to assist, help, succor; to favor.—**socorrido,** *a.* furnished, well-supplied; (coll.) handy; hackneyed, trivial.—**socorro,** *m.* succor, aid, help.—*puesto de s.,* first-aid station.

soda, *f.* (chem.) = SOSA.

sodio, *m.* sodium.

sodomía, *f.* sodomy.

soez, *a.* mean, vile, base, coarse.

sofá, *m.* sofa.

sofisma, *m.* fallacy; sophism.—**sofisticar,** *vti.* [d] to falsify, pervert or distort by fallacy.

sofocación, *f.* suffocation; smothering, choking.—**sofocante,** *a.* suffocating, stifling.—**sofocar,** *vti.* [d] to choke, suffocate, smother; to quench, extinguish; to stifle; to oppress, harass; to importune, vex; to provoke; to make blush.—**sofoco,** *m.* suffocation; vexation; embarrassment.—**sofocón,** *m.* (coll.) vexation, chagrin.

sofreír, *vti.* [35-49] to fry lightly.

sofrenar, *vt.* to check (a horse) suddenly; to reprimand severely; to check (a passion).

sofrito, *ppi.* of SOFREÍR.

soga, *f.* rope, halter, cord.

soja, *f.* soy; soy bean.

sojuzgar, *vti.* [b] to conquer, subjugate, subdue.

sol, *m.* sun; sunlight; (mus.) sol.—*de s. a s.,* from sunrise to sunset. —*hacer s.,* to be sunny.—*tomar el s.,* to bask in the sun, sunbathe;

(naut.) to take the altitude on the sun.—**solana,** *f.* intense sunlight; sunny place.—**solanera,** *f.* sunburn; sunny place.

solapa, *f.* lapel; flap; pretense.—**solapado,** *a.* sly, artful, sneaky.—**solapar,** *vt.* to put lapels on; to overlap, lap; to cloak, conceal.—*vi.* to overlap (as a lapel).

solar, *m.* lot, ground plot; manor house, ancestral mansion.—*a.* solar. —**solariego,** *a.* manorial; of old lineage.

solaz, *m.* solace, consolation; relaxation, comfort; enjoyment.—**solazar,** *vti.* [a] to solace, comfort.—*vri.* to be comforted; to rejoice, have pleasure.

soldada, *f.* wages, salary.—**soldadesca,** *f.* soldiery; undisciplined troops.—**soldadesco,** *a.* soldierly.—**soldado,** *m.* soldier.—*s.* raso, private.

soldador, *m.* solderer; welder; soldering iron.—**soldadura,** *f.* soldering; welding; solder; correction.—**soldar,** *vti.* [12] to solder; to weld; to correct.

soleado, *a.* sunny.—**solear,** *vt.* to sun.

soledad, *f.* solitude, loneliness; lonely place.

solemne, *a.* solemn; imposing; ceremonious; (coll.) great, downright.—**solemnidad,** *f.* solemnity; religious pomp; grand ceremony.—*pl.* formalities.—**solemnizar,** *vti.* [a] to solemnize, celebrate with pomp.

soler, *vii.* [26-50] to be in the habit of, accustomed to, used to.

solera, *f.* vintage wine; lees or mother of wine; crossbeam.

solevantamiento, *m.* upheaval.

solfa, *f.* musical annotation, notes; music, harmony; (coll.) sound beating or flogging.—*estar,* or *poner en s.,* to appear (or present) in a ridiculous light.—**solfeo,** *m.* solfeggio; (coll.) beating, drubbing.

solicitar, *vt.* to solicit; to apply for; to woo, court.—**solícito,** *a.* solicitous, diligent, careful.—**solicitud,** *f.* solicitude; importunity; diligence; petition, application, request; (com.) demand.—*a s.,* on request, at the request (of).—*s. de ingreso,* application for admission.

solidaridad, *f.* solidarity; union.—**solidario,** *a.* solidary; mutually binding.—**solidarizarse,** *vri.* [a] to act together in a common cause.

solideo, *m.* skullcap.

solidez, *f.* solidity; firmess; strength; stability; compactness.—**solidificación,** *f.* solidification.—**solidificar,** *vti.* & *vri.* [d] to solidify.—**sólido,**

a. solid; firm; compact; strong.— *m.* (geom. & phys.) solid.

soliloquio, *m.* soliloquy, monologue.

solista, *mf.* (mus.) soloist.—**solitaria,** *f.* tapeworm.—**solitario,** *a.* solitary, lonely, isolated, secluded.—*m.* recluse, hermit; solitaire.

soliviantar, *vt.* to induce, incite, rouse.

solo, *a.* alone, unaccompanied; only, sole; unaided, unattended; solitary, lonely.—*a solas,* alone; unaided.—*m.* (mus.) solo.—**sólo,** *adv.* = SOLAMENTE.

solomillo, solomo, *m.* sirloin; loin of pork.

soltar, *vti.* [12] to untie, unfasten, loosen; to turn on (the water); to turn loose; to cast off, set free, discharge; to let go, drop; to throw down, throw out; to utter, let out (laughter, etc.).—*vri.* to get loose; to come off; to become expert; to lose restraint; to break out (laughing, crying, etc.).—*s. a,* to begin, start.

soltería, *f.* celibacy, bachelorhood.— **soltero,** *a.* single, unmarried.—*m.* bachelor, unmarried man.—*f.* spinster, unmarried woman.—**solterón,** *m.* old bachelor.—**solterona,** *f.* old maid.

soltura, *f.* freedom, abandon, ease; fluency; agility, nimbleness; laxity, licentiousness.

solubilidad, *f.* solubility.—**soluble,** *a.* soluble; solvable.—**solución,** *f.* loosening or untying; climax or denouement in a drama or epic poem; pay, satisfaction; (math., chem.) solution.—**solucionar,** *vt.* to solve; to meet (a difficulty).

solvencia, *f.* (com.) solvency.—**solventar,** *vt.* to settle (accounts); to solve.—**solvente,** *a.* solvent, dissolving; (com.) solvent.

sollozar, *vii.* [a] to sob.—**sollozo,** *m.* sob.

sombra, *f.* shade; shadow; darkness; spirit, ghost; protection; sign, vestige.—*buena s.,* wit; good luck.— **sombrear,** *vt.* to shade.—**sombrería,** *f.* hat factory or shop.— **sombrero,** *m.* hat.—*s. de copa,* or *de copa alta,* silk hat, high (silk) hat.—*s. de jipijapa,* Panama hat.— *s. hongo,* derby.—**sombrilla,** *f.* parasol, sunshade.—**sombrío,** *a.* gloomy, somber; overcast.

somero, *a.* superficial, shallow; concise, summary.

someter, *vt.* to subject; to submit, subdue; to put (to the test, etc.).— *vr.* to humble oneself; to submit; to surrender.—**sometimiento,** *m.* submission, subjection, subduing.

somnolencia, *f.* drowsiness, somnolence.

son, *m.* sound; tune; (Am.) popular song and dance.—*¿a son de qué?* why? for what reason?—*en s. de,* as, like, in the manner of.—*sin ton ni s.,* without rhyme or reason.

sonaja, *f.* jingles; tambourine; rattle. —**sonajero,** *m.* baby's rattle.

sonambulismo, *m.* sleepwalking.— **sonámbulo,** *n.* sleepwalker.

sonante, *a.* sounding, ringing.

sonar, *vti.* [12] to sound, to ring; (mus.) to play.—*vii.* to sound; to ring; (of clock) to strike; to be mentioned, talked about; **(a)** to sound or look (like); to seem; to sound familiar.—*vri.* to blow one's nose.

sonda, *f.* (naut.) sounding (line); lead, sounder, plummet; surgeon's probe.—**sondaje,** *m.* sounding.—**sondar, sondear,** *vt.* (naut.) to sound; to try, sound out (another's intentions); to explore, fathom; to probe.—**sondeo,** *m.* sounding; exploring.

soneto, *m.* sonnet.

sonido, *m.* sound; noise; report.— **sonoridad,** *f.* sonority, sonorousness. —**sonoro,** *a.* sonorous; sounding, clear, loud.

sonreír, *vii.* & *vri.* [35] to smile; to smirk.—**sonriente,** *a.* smiling.—**sonrisa,** *f.* smile; smirk.

sonrojar, *vt.* to make (one) blush.— *vr.* to blush.—**sonrojo,** *m.* blush; blushing.

sonrosado, *a.* pink, rosy.

sonsacar, *vti.* [d] to pilfer; to draw (one) out; to entice, allure; to elicit information.

sonsonete, *m.* singsong (voice).

soñador, *a.* dreamy.—*n.* dreamer.— **soñar,** *vti.* & *vii.* [12] to dream.— *s. con* or *en,* to dream of.—**soñoliento,** *a.* sleepy; somnolent; soporific.

sopa, *f.* soup; sop.—*hecho una s.,* (coll.) drenched, wet through to the skin.

sopapear, *vt.* (coll.) to chuck under the chin; to vilify, to abuse.— **sopapo,** *m.* chuck under the chin; (coll.) box, blow, slap; (mech.) stop valve.

sopera, *f.* soup tureen.

sopesar, *vt.* to test the weight of by lifting.

sopetón, *m.*—*de s.,* suddenly.

soplar, *vi.* to blow; (coll.) to tattle. —*vt.* to blow; to blow out; to fan; to fill with air, inflate; to rob or

steal in an artful manner; to prompt, tell what to say.—**soplete,** m. blowpipe; blow torch.—**soplido,** m. blowing; blast.—**soplo,** m. blowing; blast, gust, puff of wind; breath, instant; hint, tip, secret advice or warning; secret accusation. —**soplón,** n. talebearer, informer, telltale.

soponcio, m. fainting fit, swoon.

sopor, m. drowsiness, lethargic sleep. —**soporífero,** a. soporific.

soportable, a. bearable, endurable.

soportal, m. portico.—pl. arcades.

soportar, vt. to bear, put up with; to support.—**soporte,** m. support; rest; bearing.

soprano, m. soprano voice.—f. soprano singer.

sor, f. (eccl.) sister.

sorber, vt. to sip, suck; to imbibe, soak, absorb; to swallow.—**sorbete,** m. sherbet, water ice.—**sorbo,** m. imbibing; absorption; sip, draft, swallow, gulp.

sordera, f. deafness.

sordidez, f. sordidness.—**sórdido,** a. sordid.

sordina, f. (mus.) mute; damper (piano).

sordo, a. deaf; silent, noiseless, quiet; muffled, stifled; dull; unmoved, insensible.—n. deaf person.—**sordomudo,** a. & n., deaf and dumb; deaf mute.

sorna, f. slyness; ironic undertone, sneer.

sorprendente, a. surprising.—**sorprender,** vt. to surprise, astonish; to take by surprise.—**sorpresa,** f. surprise.—de s., by surprise.

sortear, vt. to draw or cast lots for; to raffle; to elude or shun cleverly. —**sorteo,** m. casting lots; drawing, raffle.

sortija, f. finger ring; curl of hair.

sortilegio, m. spell, charm; sorcery, sortilege.

sosa, f. (chem.) soda; (bot.) glasswort.

sosegar, vti. [1-b] to appease, calm, quiet; to lull.—vii. to rest, repose. —vri. to become quiet, calm or composed; to quiet down.

sosera, sosería, sosez, f. tastelessness; dullness.

sosiego, m. tranquillity, calm, quiet.

soslayar, vt. to do or place obliquely. —**soslayo,** m.—al s., or de s., askance; slanting.

soso, a. insipid; dull.

sospecha, f. suspicion.—**sospechar,** vt. & vi. to suspect.—**sospechoso,** a. suspicious; suspecting.

sostén, m. support (person or thing); prop; brassiére; upkeep.—**sostener,** vti. [42] to support, hold up; to maintain, keep; to assist, help; to encourage; to hold (a conference). —vri. to support or maintain oneself.—**sostenido,** a. supported; sustained.—m. (mus.) sharp.—**sostenimiento,** m. sustenance, maintenance; support.

sota, f. (cards) jack; hussy, jade.

sotabanco, m. garret, attic.

sotana, f. cassock.

sótano, m. cellar, basement.

sotavento, m. leeward, lee.

soterrar, vti. [1] to bury, put under ground; to hide.

soto, m. grove, thicket.

sóviet, m. soviet.—**soviético,** a. soviet.

soya, f. (Am.) = soja.

su, a. poss. (pl. sus), his, her, its, their, your, one's.

suave, a. smooth, soft; easy, tranquil; gentle, tractable, docile.— **suavidad,** f. softness, smoothness; ease; suavity; gentleness; lenity, forbearance.—**suavizar,** vti. [a] to soften, smooth, mitigate; to ease; to temper.

subarrendar, vti. [1] to sublet, sublease.

subasta, f. auction, auction sale.— poner en or sacar a pública s., to sell at auction.—**subastar,** vt. to sell at auction.

subconsciencia, f. subconscious.—**subconsciente,** a. subconscious.

subdirector, n. assistant director.

súbdito, mf. subject (of a state, etc.).

subdividir, vt. to subdivide.

subida, f. ascent, going up; climb; taking or carrying up; rise; increase; slope.—**subir,** vi. to rise; to come up, go up, climb, mount; to grow; to increase in intensity; (com.) to amount to.—vt. to raise, place higher; to take up, bring up; to set up.—vr. to go up; to climb; to rise.

súbito, a. sudden.—de s., suddenly.

subjetividad, f. subjectivity.—**subjetivo,** a. subjective.

subjuntivo, m. & a. (gram.) subjunctive.

sublevación, f. insurrection, revolt.— **sublevar,** vt. to incite to rebellion, raise in rebellion.—vr. to rise in rebellion.

sublimar, vt. to heighten, elevate, exalt; (chem.) to sublimate.—**sublime,** a. sublime.—**sublimidad,** f. sublimity.

submarino, a. & m. submarine.

subordinación, f. subordination; subjection.—**subordinado,** a. subordinate, subservient.—n. subordinate.—

subordinar, *vt.* to subordinate; to subject.

subproducto, *m.* by-product.

subrayar, *vt.* to underscore, underline; to emphasize.

subsanar, *vt.* to excuse; to mend, correct, repair; to obviate, get over.

subscribir, *vti. & vri.* [49] = SUSCRIBIR.—**subscripción**, *f.* = SUSCRIPCION.—**subscripto**, *ppi.* = SUSCRITO.—**subscriptor**, *n.* = SUSCRITOR.

subsecretaría, *f.* office and employment of an assistant secretary.—**subsecretario**, *n.* assistant secretary.

subsecuente, *a.* subsequent.

subsidiario, *a.* subsidiary; branch; auxiliary.—**subsidio**, *m.* subsidy, monetary aid.

subsiguiente, *a.* subsequent, succeeding.

subsistencia, *f.* livelihood, living; permanence, stability; subsistence.—**subsistir**, *vi.* to subsist, last; to live, exist.

substancia, *f.* = SUSTANCIA.—**substancial**, *a.* = SUSTANCIAL.—**substancioso**, *a.* = SUSTANCIOSO.—**substantivo**, *a. & m.* = SUSTANTIVO.

substitución, *f.* = SUSTITUCION.—**substituir**, *vti.* [23-e] = SUSTITUIR.—**substituto**, *pp.i.* of SUBSTITUIR = SUSTITUTO.

substracción, *f.* = SUSTRACCION.—**substraer**, *vti.* [43] = SUSTRAER.

subteniente, *m.* second lieutenant.

subterráneo, *a.* subterranean, underground.—*m.* any place underground; (Arg.) subway.

suburbano, *a. & n.* suburban(ite).

suburbio, *m.* outskirt; suburb.

subvención, *f.* subsidy, money aid.—**subvencionar**, *vt.* to subsidize.—**subvenir**, *vti.* [45] to aid, assist; to provide, supply.

subversión, *f.* subversion, overthrow.—**subversivo**, *a.* subversive, destructive.—**subvertir**, *vti.* [18] to subvert, destroy, ruin.

subyacente, *a.* underlying.

subyugación, *f.* subjugation, subjection.—**subyugador**, *n. & a.* subjugator; subjugating.—**subyugar**, *vti.* [b] to subdue, subjugate.

succión, *f.* suction, suck.

sucedáneo, *a. & m.* substitute.—**suceder**, *vi.* to succeed, follow; to happen.—**sucesión**, *f.* succession.—**sucesivo**, *a.* successive.—*en lo s.*, hereafter, in the future.—**suceso**, *m.* event, happening; issue, outcome.—**sucesor**, *n.* successor.

suciedad, *f.* nastiness, filthiness; dirt, filth.

sucinto, *a.* brief, succinct, concise.

sucio, *a.* dirty, nasty, filthy, squalid; soiled; untidy; low.

sucumbir, *vi.* to succumb; to submit, yield.

sucursal, *a.* subsidiary; branch.—*f.* branch of a commercial house.

sud, *m.* south; south wind.—**sudamericano**, *n. & a.* South American.

sudar, *vi.* to sweat, perspire; to ooze; to toil, labor.—**sudario**, *m.* shroud (for corpse).—**sudor**, *m.* sweat, perspiration.—**sudoroso**, *a.* sweating, perspiring freely.

sueco, *a.* Swedish.—*n.* Swede.—*m.* Swedish language.—*hacerse el s.*, to pretend not to hear.

suegra, *f.* mother-in-law.—**suegro**, *m.* father-in-law.

suela, *f.* sole (of shoe); shoe leather.—*de siete suelas*, downright.

sueldo, *m.* salary, stipend.

suelo, *m.* ground; soil; land, earth; pavement; floor, flooring; bottom.

suelto, *ppi.* of SOLTAR.—*a.* loose; light, expeditious; swift, able; free, bold, daring; fluent; odd, disconnected, unclassified; single (copy); blank (verse).—*s. de lengua*, outspoken.—*m.* editorial paragraph; newspaper item or paragraph; loose change.

sueño, *m.* sleep; sleeping; drowsiness, sleepiness; dream.—*conciliar el s.*, to get to sleep.—*descabezar or echar un s.*, to take a nap.—*en sueños*, dreaming; in dreamland.—*tener s.*, to be sleepy.

suero, *m.* whey; serum (of blood).

suerte, *f.* fortune, luck, chance; piece of luck; lot, fate; sort, kind; trick, feat (bullfighting).—*de s. que*, so that; and so.—*echar suertes*, to draw lots.—*tener s.*, to be lucky.—*tocarle a uno la s.*, to fall to one's lot.

suficiencia, *f.* sufficiency; capacity, ability; self-importance.—**suficiente**, *a.* sufficient; fit, competent.

sufijo, *a.* suffixed.—*m.* suffix.

sufragar, *vti.* [b] to defray, pay; to favor; to aid; (Am.) to vote for.—**sufragio**, *m.* suffrage; vote; favor, support, aid.—**sufragista**, *mf.* suffragette.

sufrible, *a.* tolerable, sufferable.—**sufrido**, *a.* patient, long-suffering.—*color s.*, color that does not show dirt.—*mal s.*, rude.—**sufrimiento**, *m.* suffering; sufferance.—**sufrir**, *vt.* to suffer, bear up; to undergo (a change, an operation, etc.); to sustain, resist (an attack); to permit, tolerate.—*vi.* to suffer.

sugerencia, *f.* insinuation, hint.—**sugerir**, *vti.* [39] to suggest, hint,

insinuate.—**sugestión**, *f.* suggestion, insinuation, hint.—**sugestionable**, *a.* easily influenced.—**sugestionar**, *vt.* to hypnotize; to influence.—**sugestivo**, *a.* suggestive; revealing (of a dress).

suicida, *a.* suicidal.—*mf.* suicide (person).—**suicidarse**, *vr.* to commit suicide.—**suicidio**, *m.* suicide (crime).

suizo, *n.* & *a.* Swiss.

sujeción, *f.* subjection; control; subordination; submission; connection.—**sujetapapeles**, *m.* paper clip.—**sujetar**, *vti.* [49] to subject, subdue; to hold fast, fasten, grasp.—*vri.* to control oneself; to submit; **(a)** to abide (by), to observe.—**sujeto**, *ppi.* of SUJETAR.—*a.* subject, liable; amenable.—*m.* subject; person; individual, fellow; (logic & gram.) subject.

sulfato, *m.* sulfate.

sulfurar, *vt.* to irritate, anger.—*vr.* to become furious.

suma, *f.* sum; addition; aggregate; amount; total; summary.—*en s.*, in short.—**sumando**, *m.* (math.) addend.—**sumar**, *vt.* to add; to amount to; to sum up, recapitulate.—*máquina de s.*, adding machine.—**sumario**, *a.* concise; plain, brief; (law) summary.—*m.* summary, abstract; (law) indictment.

sumarísimo, *a.* (law) swift, with dispatch.

sumergible, *a.* submersible.—*m.* submarine.—**sumergir**, *vti.* [c] to immerse; to submerge; to sink.—*vri.* to dive, to plunge; to submerge; to sink.—**sumersión**, *f.* submersion, immersion.—**sumidero**, *m.* sewer, drain, sink, gutter.

suministrar, *vt.* to supply, furnish, provide.—**suministro**, *m.* supply, providing.

sumir, *vt.* & *vr.* to sink; to plunge; to submerge.—**sumisión**, *f.* submission.—**sumiso**, *a.* submissive, humble, meek.

sumo, *a.* high, great, supreme.—*a lo s.*, at most.

suntuosidad, *f.* magnificence, sumptuousness.—**suntuoso**, *a.* sumptuous, magnificent.

supeditación, *f.* subjection; oppression.—**supeditar**, *vt.* to subdue, oppress; to reduce to subjection.

superar, *vt.* to overcome, conquer; to surpass; to exceed.

superávit, *m.* (com.) surplus.

superficial, *a.* superficial, shallow.—**superficialidad**, *f.* superficiality; shallowness.—**superficie**, *f.* surface; area.

superfluo, *a.* superfluous.

superhombre, *m.* superman.

superintendencia, *f.* superintendence, supervision.—**superintendente**, *n.* superintendent, manager; inspector; overseer, supervisor.

superior, *a.* superior; upper; better, finer; higher (algebra, math., studies).—*m.* superior.—*f.* mother superior.—**superioridad**, *f.* superiority.

superlativo, *m.* & *a.* superlative.

superponer, *vti.* [32-49] to superimpose.—**superposición**, *f.* superposition.—**superpuesto**, *ppi.* of SUPERPONER.

superstición, *f.* superstition.—**supersticioso**, *a.* superstitious.

supervisar, *vt.* (neol.) to supervise.—**supervisión**, *s.* (neol.) supervision.—**supervisor**, *m.* (neol.) supervisor.

supervivencia, *f.* survival.—**superviviente**, *mf.* & *a.* survivor; surviving.

suplantación, *f.* supplanting.—**suplantar**, *vt.* to supplant; to forge (as a check).

suplementario, *a.* supplementary.—**suplemento**, *m.* supply, supplying; supplement.

suplente, *a.* & *mf.* supply, substitute; substituting.

súplica, *f.* entreaty; supplication; request.—**suplicar**, *vti.* [d] to entreat; to supplicate; to petition.

suplicio, *m.* torture; execution; gallows; grief, suffering, anguish.

suplir, *vt.* to supply, furnish; to act as a substitute for; to make good, make up for.

suponer, *vti.* [32-49] to suppose, assume; to entail (expense, etc.).—*vii.* to have weight or authority.—**suposición**, *f.* supposition, assumption; imposition, falsehood.

supositorio, *m.* (med.) suppository.

supremacía, *f.* supremacy.—**supremo**, *a.* supreme; last, final.

supresión, *f.* suppression; omission; elimination.—**suprimir**, *vt.* to suppress; to cut out; to omit; to clear of.

supuesto, *ppi.* of SUPONER.—*s. que*, allowing that; granting that; since.—*por s.*, of course.—*m.* supposition; assumption.

supuración, *f.* suppuration.—**supurar**, *vi.* (med.) to suppurate.

sur, *m.* south; south wind.—**suramericano**, *a.* & *n.* = SUDAMERICANO.

surcar, *vti.* [d] to plow, furrow; to move through.—**surco**, *m.* furrow; rut; wrinkle.

surgir, *vii.* [49-c] to spout; to issue, come forth; to appear, arise; to sprout.

suri, *m.* (Am.) ostrich.

surtido, *a.* (com.) assorted.—*m.* assortment; stock, supply.—**surtidor,** *n.* purveyor, caterer.—*m.* jet, fountain.—**surtir,** *vt.* to supply, furnish, stock.—*s. efecto,* to have the desired effect, to work.—*vi.* to spout, spurt.

suscitar, *vt.* to stir up; to raise; to originate.—*vr.* to rise, start, originate.

suscribir, *vti.* [49] to subscribe; to sign; to endorse; to agree to.—*vri.* to subscribe (periodicals, etc.).—**suscrición,** *f.* subscription.—**suscrito,** *ppi.* of SUSCRIBIR.—**suscritor,** *n.* subscriber.

susodicho, *a.* aforementioned, aforesaid.

suspender, *vti.* [49] to suspend; to hang up; to stop, delay, interrupt; to discontinue; to fail (in exam); to adjourn (a meeting).—**suspensión,** *f.* suspension, interruption; reprieve; discontinuance.—**suspenso,** *ppi.* of SUSPENDER.—*m.* failing mark (in exam).

suspicacia, *f.* suspiciousness.—**suspicaz,** *a.* suspicious, distrustful.

suspirar, *vi.* to sigh.—*s. por,* to crave, long for.—**suspiro,** *m.* sigh; brief pause.

sustancia, *f.* substance; essence; (coll.) judgment, sense.—**sustancial,** *a.* substantial; essential.—**sustancioso,** *a.* juicy; nourishing; substantial.—**sustantivo,** *a.* substantive. —*m.* substantive, noun.

sustentación, *f.* support, sustenance.—**sustentar,** *vt.* to sustain, support, bear; to feed.—**sustento,** *m.* sustenance, maintenance; support.

sustitución, *f.* substitution.—**sustituir,** *vti.* [23-e] to substitute, replace.—**sustituto,** *n.* substitute; supply.—*ppi.* of SUSTITUIR.

susto, *m.* scare, fright, shock.—*dar un s.,* to frighten; to startle.

sustracción, *f.* subtraction.—**sustraer,** *vti.* [43] to subtract, remove, take off, deduct.—*vri.* to withdraw oneself; to elude.

susurrar, *vi.* to whisper; to murmur; to rustle; to hum gently (as the air).—*vr.* to be whispered about.—**susurro,** *m.* whisper, humming, murmur, rustle.

sutil, *a.* thin, slender; subtle, cunning; keen; light, volatile.—**sutileza,** *f.* thinness, slenderness, fineness; sublety, cunning; sagacity; nicety.

sutura, *f.* seam; suture.

suyo, *a.* & *pron. poss.* (*f.* **suya.**—*pl.* **suyos, suyas**) his, hers, theirs, one's; his own, its own, one's own, their own.—*de s.* intrinsically;

spontaneously.—*salirse con la suya,* to get one's own way.—*una de las suyas,* one of his pranks or tricks.

T

tabacalero, *a.* tobacco.—*n.* tobacco grower or dealer.—**tabaco,** *m.* tobacco; cigar.

tábano, *m.* (entom.) gadfly, horsefly.

tabaquera, *f.* cigar case; tobacco pouch.—**tabaquería,** *f.* cigar store.—**tabaquero,** *n.* cigar maker; tobacconist.

taberna, *f.* tavern, saloon, barroom.

tabernáculo, *m.* tabernacle.

tabernero, *m.* tavern keeper, barkeeper.

tabique, *m.* partition wall, partition.

tabla, *f.* (carp.) board; plank; slab; tablet, plate (of metal); pleat; table, list.—*pl.* (theat.) stage; draw, stalemate (in a game).—*a raja t.,* at any price, ruthlessly.—*hacer t. rasa de,* to ignore entirely; to set at nought.—*salvarse en una t.,* to have a narrow escape.—*t. de salvación,* last resource.—**tablado,** *m.* stage, scaffold, platform; (theat.) stage boards.—**tablero,** *m.* board; panel; sawable timber; drawing board; chessboard, checkerboard; (Am.) blackboard; shop counter; door panel.—*t. de distribución,* (elec.) switchboard.—**tableta,** *f.* tablet; writing pad; (pharm.) tablet, pastille, lozenge.—**tabletear,** *vt.* to rattle clappers.—**tableteo,** *m.* rattling sound of clappers.—**tablilla,** *f.* tablet, slab; bulletin board; (surg.) splint.—**tablón,** *m.* plank, thick board.—**tabloncillo,** *m.* flooring board.

tabú, *m.* taboo.

tabulador, *m.* (neol.) tabulator, computer.—**tabular,** *vt.* (neol.) to tabulate.

taburete, *m.* taboret; stool.

tacañería, *f.* stinginess.—**tacaño,** *a.* stingy, niggardly.

tácito, *a.* tacit, implied; silent. —**taciturno,** *a.* taciturn, reserved; sad, melancholy; silent.

taco, *m.* plug, stopper; (artil.) wad, wadding; billiard cue; (coll.) snack; (Am.) dandy; (Am.) heel (of shoe).—*echar tacos,* (coll.) to swear; to curse.

tacón, *m.* heel (of shoe).—**taconazo,** *m.* blow with a shoe heel.—**taconear,** *vi.* (coll.) to walk or strut loftily on the heels.—**taconeo,** *m.* noise made with the heels.

táctica, *f.* tactics.—**táctico,** *a.* tactical.

tacto, *m.* touch, sense of touch; tact, carefulness.

tacha, *f.* fault, defect, blemish, flaw. —**tachar,** *vt.* to censure, blame, charge; to find fault with; to cut out, cross out.

tachón, *m.* ornamental nail; trimming; crossing out (in writing). —**tachonar,** *vt.* (sew.) to adorn with trimming.

tachuela, *f.* tack, small nail.

tafetán, *m.* taffeta.—*t. inglés,* court plaster, sticking plaster.

tagarnina, *f.* (coll.) bad cigar.

tahalí, *m.* shoulder belt, sword belt.

tahur, *m.* gambler, gamester; sharper, card sharp.

taimado, *a.* sly, cunning, crafty.

taita, *m.* (Am.) (coll.) daddy, dad.

tajada, *f.* slice; (coll.) cut.—**tajar,** *vt.* to cut, cleave, chop.—**tajo,** *m.* cut; incision; cutting edge; steep cliff; chopping block.

tal, *a.* such, such as.—*t. cual,* such as; such as it is.—*pron.* such, such a one, such a thing.—*no hay t.,* there is no such thing.—*t. para cual,* two of a kind.—*t. por cual,* (a) nobody.—*adv.* thus, so, in such manner.—*con t. que, con t. de que,* provided, on condition, that.—*¿qué t.?* hello! how do you do?

talabarte, *m.* sword belt.—**talabartero,** *m.* saddler; harness maker.

taladrar, *vt.* to bore, drill; to pierce (the ears).—**taladro,** *m.* drill, bit, borer, auger; bore, drill hole.

tálamo, *m.* bridal chamber or bed.

talanquera, *f.* picket fence.

talante, *m.* mode or manner; mien; desire, will, disposition.—*de mal t.,* unwillingly, grudgingly.

talar, *vt.* to fell (trees).

talco, *m.* talc; talcum powder.

talega, *f.* bag, sack; money bag; diaper.—**talego,** *m.* bag or sack; clumsy, awkward fellow.

talento, *m.* talent; cleverness.—**talentoso,** *a.* smart, clever, talented.

talión, *m.* retaliation, requital.

talismán, *m.* talisman, charm, amulet.

talón, *m.* (anat., shoe) heel; (com.) check, draft; stub; coupon.—**talonario,** *m.* stub book.—*libro t.,* check book.

talud, *m.* slope, bank.

talla, *f.* carving, wood carving; (jewelry) cut, cutting; height, stature (of person).—*de t.,* (of person) prominent.—**tallar,** *vt.* to carve; to engrave; (jewelry) to cut; to appraise.—*vi.* (card games) to deal.

tallarín, *m.* noodle (for soup).

talle, *m.* form, figure; waist; (tailoring) fit, bodice.

taller, *m.* workshop, factory; atelier; studio.—*t. de reparaciones,* repair shop; (auto) service station.

tallo, *m.* (bot.) stem, stalk; shoot, sprout.

tamal, *m.* (Am.) tamale.

tamaño, *m.* size.—*t. natural,* full size. —*a.* so great; so big, so small; huge.

tambalear, *vi. & vr.* to stagger, totter, reel.—**tambaleo,** *m.* reeling, staggering, tottering.

también, *adv.* also, too; as well; likewise.

tambor, *m.* drum; drummer; band pulley, rope barrel.—**tambora,** *f.* bass drum.—**tamboril,** *m.* tabor, small drum.—**tamborilear,** *vi.* to drum.—*vt.* to praise, extol.—**tamborilero,** *m.* taborer, drummer.

tamiz, *m.* sieve, sifter; bolting cloth. —**tamizar,** *vti.* [a] to sift.

tampoco, *adv.* neither, not either; either (after negative).

tan, *adv. contr.* of TANTO: as so, so much, as well, as much.—*¡qué mujer t. bella!* what a beautiful woman.—*t. solo,* only, merely.

tanda, *f.* turn, rotation; task; gang of workmen, shift; relay; set, batch; each game of billiards.

tangente, *f. & a.* (geom.) tangent.— *salir* or *salirse por la t.,* to confuse the issue.

tangerina, *f.* tangerine.

tangible, *a.* tangible.

tanque, *m.* tank; (Am.) swimming pool.

tantear, *vt.* to try, test, measure; to feel out; to make an estimate of; to consider carefully; to scrutinize. —*vi.* to keep the score.—**tanteo,** *m.* estimate, calculation; test, trial; points, score (in a game).—*al t.,* by eye; as an estimate; by trial.

tanto, *a. & pron.* so much, as much. —*pl.* as many, so many.—*adv.* so, thus; so much, as much; so long, as long; so hard, so often.—*m.* undetermined sum or quantity; counter, chip; point (in games).—*a las tantas,* in the small hours.— *al t.,* posted about, up to date.—*en t.,* or *entre t.,* in the meantime.— *no ser para t.,* not to be so bad as that.—*otro t.,* as much; the same again.—*por lo t.,* therefore.—*t. así,* so much.—*t. más cuanto,* all the more because.—*t. mejor,* so much the better.—*t. peor,* so much the worse.—*t. por ciento,* percentage, rate.—*t. que,* so much that.—*treinta y tantos,* thirty odd.

tañer, *vti.* [41] to play (a musical

instrument).—**tañido,** m. playing;
tune; ringing.

tapa, f. lid, cover, cap; cover (of
book); heel lift (of shoe).—*t. de
los sesos,* top of the skull.—**tapa-
boca,** m. (coll.) slap on the mouth;
muffler, scarf.—**tapadera,** f. loose
lid, cover of a pot.—**tapar,** vt. to
hide, cover up, veil; to stop up,
plug; to close up, obstruct.—**tapa-
rrabo,** m. loin cloth.

tapete, m. cover for a table or chest;
small carpet, rug.—*t. verde,* gaming
table.

tapia, f. wall fence.—*más sordo que
una t.,* deaf as a post.—**tapiar,** vt.
to wall up; to wall in; to close or
block up.

tapicería, f. tapestry; tapestry making; upholstery; tapestry shop.—
tapicero, m. tapestry maker; up-
holsterer; carpet layer.

tapioca, f. tapioca.

tapiz, m. tapestry.—**tapizar,** vti. [a]
to hang with tapestry; to upholster.

tapón, m. cork, stopper; plug; (elec.)
fuse; (surg.) tampon.—**taponar,** vt.
to cork, plug; (surg.) to tampon.

tapujo, m. muffle; (coll.) pretext,
subterfuge.

taquigrafía, f. stenography.—**taquígrafo,** n. stenographer.

taquilla, f. letter file; booking office;
(theat., RR.) ticket office.—**taqui-
llero,** n. booking clerk; ticket seller.

tara, f. (com.) tare, weight of container; defect.

tarambana, mf. giddy person; madcap.

tararear, vt. & vi. to hum (a tune).
—**tararéo,** m. humming.

tarascada, f. bite, wound with the
teeth; (coll.) pert, rude answer.

tardanza, f. delay; slowness, tardiness.—**tardar,** vi. & vr. to delay,
tarry; to take a long time; to be
late.—*a más t.,* at the latest.—
tarde, f. afternoon.—*de t. en t.,*
now and then, once in a while.—
adv. late; too late.—**tardío,** a. late,
too late; slow, tardy.—**tardo,** a.
slow, sluggish; tardy; dull, thick.

tarea, f. task.

tarifa, f. tariff; price list, fare, rate.

tarima, f. stand; movable platform;
low bench, footstool.

tarjeta, f. card.—*t. postal,* post card.
—**tarjetero,** m. cardcase; index file;
wallet.

tarro, m. jar; (Am.) horn (of an
animal); (Am.) can, pot; (beer)
mug.

tarta, f. tart; cake.

tartamudear, vi. to stutter, stammer.
—**tartamudeo,** m., **tartamudez,** f.

stuttering, stammering.—**tartamudo,**
n. & a. stutterer, stammer; stuttering, stammering.

tartera, f. baking pan for pastry;
dinner pail.

tarugo, m. wooden peg or pin; stopper, plug; (fig.) blockhead.

tasa, f. measure, rule; standard;
rate; scot; valuation, appraisement.
—**tasación,** f. appraisement, appraisal, valuation.—**tasador,** n. appraiser.

tasajo, m. jerked beef.

tasar, vt. to appraise; to rate; to
stint.

tata, m. (Am., coll.) dad, daddy;
nursemaid; younger sister.

tatarabuelo, n. great-great-grand-
father(-mother).—**tataranieto,** n.
great-great-grandson(-daughter).

tatuaje, m. tattooing; tattoo.—**tatuar,**
vt. & vr. to tattoo.

taxi, taxímetro, m. taxi, taxicab.

taza, f. cup; cupful; bowl; basin of
a fountain; cup guard of a sword.—
tazón, m. large bowl; basin.

te, m. tea.

te, pers. & refl. pron. (obj. case of
TU) you, to you; yourself; thee.

tea, f. torch.

teatral, a. theatrical.—**teatro,** m.
theater; stage; dramatic art; scene.

tecla, f. key (of a piano, typewriter,
etc.).—*dar en la t.,* to find the way.
—**teclado,** m. keyboard.

técnica, f. technique; technical
ability.—**tecnicismo,** m. technical
term; technology.—**técnico,** a. technical.—n. technician.—**tecnología,** f.
technology.

tecolote, m. (Mex.) owl.

techado, m. roof, roofing; ceiling;
shed.—**techar,** vt. to roof; to cover
with a roof.—**techo,** m. = TECHUM-
BRE; (aer.) absolute ceiling.—
techumbre, f. ceiling; roof, roofing;
cover; shed.

tedio, m. boredom, tediousness.—
tedioso, a. tedious, boresome, boring,
tiresome.

teja, f. roof tile; (bot.) linden tree.—
tejado, m. roof; shed.—**tejamanil,**
m. shingle.—**tejar,** m. tile kiln.—vt.
to tile.

tejedor, n. weaver.—**tejemaneje,** m.
(coll.) skill, cleverness; (Am.)
scheming, trick.—**tejer,** vt. to
weave; (Am.) to knit; to devise.—
tejido, m. texture; weaving; fabric,
textile, web; (anat.) tissue.

tejón, m. (zool.) badger.

tela, f. cloth, fabric; pellicle, film.—
en t. de juicio, in doubt; under
careful consideration.—*t. de cebolla,*
onion skin; thin cloth.—*t. metálica,*

wire cloth.—**telar,** *m.* loom.—**tela-**
raña, *f.* cobweb.
telefonear, *vt. & vi.* to telephone.—
telefonema, *m.* telephone message.—
telefónico, *a.* telephonic.—**telefo-**
nista, *mf.* (telephone) operator.—
teléfono, *m.* telephone.
telegrafía, *f.* telegraphy.—**telegrafiar,**
vt. to telegraph; to wire.—**tele-**
gráfico, *a.* telegraphic.—**telegrafista,**
mf. telegrapher.—**telégrafo,** *m.* telegraph.—**telegrama,** *m.* telegram.
telepatía, *f.* telepathy.
telescópico, *a.* telescopic.—**telescopio,**
m. telescope.
televisión, *f.* television.—*receptor de*
t., television set.
telón, *m.* (theat.) curtain.—*bajar el*
t., to drop the curtain.—*t. de boca,*
drop curtain.
tema, *m.* theme, subject; text, thesis;
(mus.) theme, motive.—*f.* mania,
obsession.—**temario,** *m.* agenda.
temblar, *vii.* [1] to tremble, shake,
quake, quiver; to shiver.—**temble-**
quear, *vi.* (coll.) to tremble, shake,
shiver.—**temblor,** *m.* trembling,
tremor, thrill; quake.—*t. de tierra,*
earthquake.—**tembloroso,** *a.* trembling, tremulous, shivering, shaking.
temer, *vt. & vi.* to fear, dread.—
temerario, *a.* rash, imprudent;
reckless.—**temeridad,** *f.* temerity,
rashness, recklessness; foolhardiness.
—**temeroso,** *a.* dread; timid; timorous; fearful.—**temible,** *a.* dread,
terrible.—**temor,** *m.* dread, fear.
témpano, *m.* kettledrum; drumhead;
piece, block.—*t. de hielo,* iceberg.
temperamento, *m.* temperament, constitution; climate.—**temperatura,** *f.*
temperature.
tempestad, *f.* tempest, storm.—
tempestuoso, *a.* tempestuous,
stormy.
templado, *a.* moderate (esp. of climate); tempered; lukewarm; fair;
brave, firm; (mus.) tuned.—**tem-**
planza, *f.* temperance, moderation;
mildness (of temperature or climate).—**templar,** *vt.* to temper,
moderate; to temper, quench
(metals); (mus.) to tune.—*vr.* to
be moderate.—**temple,** *m.* temper
(of metals, of persons); courage;
disposition; (mus.) temperament.
templo, *m.* temple; church.
temporada, *f.* season; period (of
time); spell (of weather).
temporal, *a.* temporal; temporary;
secular, worldly.—*m.* tempest,
storm; long rainy spell.—**temporero,**
a. temporary (laborer).
tempranero, *a.* early.—**temprano,** *a.*
early.—*adv.* early; in good time.

ten, *m.*—*t. con t.,* tact, wisdom.
tenacidad, *f.* tenacity; tenaciousness,
perseverance.—**tenacillas,** *f.* small
tongs; pincers; sugar tongs; curling irons.—**tenaz,** *a.* tenacious;
strong, firm; stubborn; purposeful, persevering.—**tenaza(s),** *f.* claw
(as a lobster's).—*pl.* tongs, nip-
pers, pliers; (dent.) forceps.
tendal, *m.* tent, awning, tilt; piece of
canvas.
tendedero, *m.* drying place.—*f.* (Am.)
clothesline.—**tendencia,** *f.* tendency,
proclivity; trend, drift.—**tenden-**
cioso, *a.* tendentious.—**tender,** *vti.*
[18] to stretch, stretch out; to
spread out; to hang out (washing);
to lay (tablecloth, rails, etc.).—*vii.*
to have a tendency, tend.—*vri.* to
stretch out, lie full length.
tendero, *n.* retail shopkeeper.
tendido, *a.* lying, spread out.—*m.*
washing hung or spread out to dry.
—*pl.* uncovered seats in the bullring; bleachers.
tendón, *m.* tendon, sinew.
tenebroso, *a.* dark, gloomy.
tenedor, *m.* (table) fork; keeper;
(com.) holder.—*t. de libros,* bookkeeper.—**teneduría,** *f.* position of
bookkeeper.—*t. de libros,* bookkeeping.
tenencia, *f.* tenure, occupancy, possession, holding; (mil.) position of
a lieutenant.
tener, *vti.* [42] to have, possess; to
hold; to contain.—*no tenerlas todas*
consigo, to be worried, to be
anxious.—*t. a bien,* to please; to find
it convenient.—*t. cuatro años,* to be
four years old.—*t. cuidado de,* to
take care of.—*t. dos metros de*
ancho, to be two meters wide.—
t. en cuenta, to take into account.
—*t. gana* or *ganas,* to wish, desire
(to); to have in mind (to); to
feel like.—*t. gracia,* to be funny.—
t. gusto en, to be glad to.—*t. ham-*
bre (sed, etc.), to be hungry
(thirsty, etc.).—*t. presente,* to bear
in mind.—*t. prisa,* to be in a hurry.
—*t. razón,* to be right.—*t. suerte,* to
be lucky.—*vai.* to have.—*tengo*
dicho, I have said.—*tengo entendido,*
I understand.—*tengo escritas dos*
cartas, I have two letters written.—
tengo pensado, I intend.—*vri.* to
hold fast or steady; to stop, halt.—
t. en pie, to keep on one's feet,
remain standing.
tenería, *f.* tannery.
tenia, *f.* tapeworm.
teniente, *m.* lieutenant.
tenis, *m.* tennis.

tenor, *m.* (mus.) tenor; condition, nature; kind; literal meaning.

tensión, *f.* tension; (mech.) stress; strain; (elec.) voltage, tension.—**tenso,** *a.* tense, tight, taut, stretched.

tentación, *f.* temptation.

tentáculo, *m.* tentacle.

tentador, *n. & a.* tempter; tempting, tantalizing.—*el t.,* the devil.—**tentar,** *vti.* [1] to touch, feel with the fingers; to grope; to tempt; to attempt, try; to test; (surg.) to probe.—**tentativa,** *f.* attempt.—**tentativo,** *a.* tentative.

tentempié, *m.* (coll.) light luncheon, snack, refreshment.

tenue, *a.* thin, tenuous; worthless; (art) subdued.

teñir, *vti.* [9-49] to dye, tinge; to stain; (art) to darken (a color).

teologal, *a.* theologic(al).—**teología,** *f.* theology.—**teológico,** *a.* = TEOLO-GAL.

teorema, *m.* theorem.

teoría, *f.* theory.—**teórico,** *a.* theoretical.—*mf.* theorist.—**teorizar,** *vii.* [a] to theorize.

terapia, *f.* therapy.

tercer, *a.* third.—**tercería,** *f.* pandering, procuring.—**tercero,** *a.* third.—*n.* mediator; third person; go-between.

terciar, *vt.* to place sidewise; to sling diagonally; to divide into three parts; (mil.) to carry (arms.)—*vi.* to mediate, arbitrate; to go between; to join (in conversation).—**tercio,** *a.* third.—*m.* one-third; (Sp.) Foreign Legion; (Am.) (coll.) fellow, guy.—*hacer mal t.,* to do a bad turn.

terciopelo, *m.* velvet.

terco, *a.* stubborn.

tergiversar, *vt.* to misrepresent, distort.

terminación, *f.* termination; end, ending.—**terminal,** *a.* terminal, final, last.—*m.* (elec.) terminal.—**terminante,** *a.* ending, closing; final, decisive.—**terminar,** *vt. & vi.* to end, terminate, conclude.—**término,** *m.* end, ending, completion; term, word; boundary; manner, behavior; outlying district; period, limit; aim, goal; (math., log.) term.—*en buenos términos,* in kind language.—*en último t.,* finally; in the background.—*primer t.,* (art) foreground.—*t. medio,* average.

termita, *f.,* **termite,** *m.* termite.

termómetro, *m.* thermometer.—**termo(s),** *m.* thermos bottle.—**termóstato,** *m.* thermostat.

ternero, *n.* calf.—*f.* veal.

terneza, *f.* softness; tenderness; affection, caress.—*pl.* sweet nothings.

terno, *m.* set of three, trio; tern (in lottery); bad word; suit of clothes; (jewelry) set.

ternura, *f.* tenderness, softness, fondness.

terquedad, *f.* stubbornness, obstinacy.

terrado, *m.* terrace; flat roof of a house.

terral, *m.* land breeze.

terramicina, *f.* terramycin.

terraplén, *m.* (RR.) embankment; mound; terrace.

terrateniente, *mf.* landowner, landholder.

terraza, *f.* terrace; border in a garden; veranda.

terremoto, *m.* earthquake.—**terrenal,** *a.* worldly, earthly.—**terreno,** *a.* earthly, terrestrial; worldly, mundane.—*m.* land, ground, soil; terrain; piece of land, lot; field, sphere of action.—**terrestre,** *a.* terrestrial.

terrible, *a.* terrible.—**terrífico,** *a.* terrific, frightful.

territorio, *m.* territory; region.

terrón, *m.* clod; lump.

terror, *m.* terror.—**terrorismo,** *m.* terrorism.—**terrorista,** *mf. & a.* terrorist; terroristic.

terruño, *m.* native land; piece of ground.

terso, *a.* smooth, polished, glossy.—**tersura,** *f.* smoothness, polish; cleanliness, terseness.

tertulia, *f.* social gathering for entertainment; party; conversation; (Am.) (theat.) gallery.

tesis, *f.* thesis.

tesón, *m.* tenacity, firmness, endurance.—**tesonero,** *a.* (Am.) persistent, tenacious.

tesorería, *f.* treasury; treasurership.—**tesorero,** *n.* treasurer; bursar (of a college, univ.).—**tesoro,** *m.* treasure; treasury.

testa, *f.* (coll.) head; top or crown of the head; front, face; (coll.) brains, cleverness.

testaferro, *m.* man of straw, dummy, figurehead.

testamento, *m.* will, testament.—**testar,** *vi.* to make a will.—*vt.* to scratch out.

testarudez, *f.* hardheadedness, stubbornness, willfulness.—**testarudo,** *a.* stubborn, hardheaded.

testículo, *m.* testicle.

testificar, *vti.* [d] to attest, witness, testify.—**testigo,** *mf.* witness.—*t. de cargo,* witness for the prosecution.—*t. ocular,* eyewitness.—**testimoniar,** *vt.* to attest, bear witness to.—

testimonio, *m.* testimony; affidavit; attestation.

testuz, *m.* nape or forehead (of some animals).

teta, *f.* teat, breast; nipple; udder.

tétano, tétanos, *m.* tetanus, lockjaw.

tetera, *f.* teapot; (Am.) nursing bottle.—**tetilla,** *f.* teat.

tétrico, *a.* sad, sullen; dark, gloomy.

textil, *a.* textile.

texto, *m.* text; quotation; textbook.—**textual,** *a.* textual.

tez, *f.* complexion (of the face).

ti, *pron. 2d. pers. sing.* (after *prep.*) (*obj. case* of TU) you.

tía, *f.* aunt.—*no hay tu t.,* there's no use.

tibia, *f.* tibia, shin bone.

tibieza, *f.* tepidity, lukewarmness; coolness.—**tibio,** *a.* tepid, lukewarm; remiss.

tiburón, *m.* shark.

tibor, *m.* Chinese vase; (Am.) chamberpot.

tictac, *m.* tick, ticking (of a watch, etc.).

tiempo, *m.* time; (mus.) tempo; (gram.) tense; weather.—*andando el t.,* in time, in the long run.—*a su t.,* in due time.—*a t.,* timely, in or on time.—*cuanto t.,* how long.—*fuera de t.,* out of season; inopportunely.—*hace t.,* long ago.—*los buenos tiempos,* the good, old days.

tienda, *f.* shop, store; tent.—*ir de tiendas,* to go shopping.

tienta, *f.* (surg.) probe.—*andar a tientas,* to grope; to feel one's way.—*a tientas,* gropingly.

tiento, *m,* touch, act of feeling; blind man's stick; tact; steady hand; (coll.) blow, cuff; (coll.) swig.—*perder el t.,* to get out of practice, to get rusty.

tierno, *a.* tender, soft; delicate; affectionate; sensitive; young; green, unripe.

tierra, *f.* earth, world; land; soil; ground; native country.—*a t.,* ashore.—*besar la t.,* (coll.) to bite the dust.—*dar en t. con,* or *echar por t.,* to overthrow; to ruin, destroy.—*echar t. a,* to hush up, forget, drop (a matter).—*irse a t.,* to fall down, to topple over.—*t. firme,* mainland; firm, solid ground.—*tomar t.,* to land; to anchor.—*venirse a t.,* = IRSE A TIERRA.

tieso, *a.* stiff; tight, taut; stuck up; too grave or circumspect.

tiesto, *m.* potsherd; flowerpot.

tiesura, *f.* stiffness; rigidity.

tifo, *m.* typhus.—**tifoidea,** *a. & f.* typhoid (fever).

tifón, *m.* whirlwind; typhoon.

tifus, *m.* typhus.

tigre, *m.* tiger.—**tigresa,** *f.* tigress.

tijera, *f.* (usually in *pl.*) scissors; sawbuck.—*cama de t.,* folding bed, cot.—*silla de t.,* folding chair.—**tijeretada,** *f.,* **tijeretazo,** *m.* a cut with scissors, clip, snip.—**tijeretear,** *vt.* to cut with scissors; to snip, clip; to gossip.

tildar, *vt.* to cross or scratch out; to put a tilde over; to criticize.—*t. de,* to accuse of, or charge with being.—**tilde,** *f.* tilde, diacritic (~) of the letter *ñ;* blemish; jot.

timador, *n.* swindler.—**timar,** *vt.* to cheat, swindle.

timba, *f.* gambling party; gambling den; (Am.) guava paste or jelly.

timbrar, *vt.* to stamp.—**timbre,** *m.* seal; postage stamp; call or door bell; timbre, tone; crest (heraldry).—*t. de gloria,* glorious deed.

timidez, *f.* timidity; bashfulness.—**tímido,** *a.* timid, shy, bashful.

timo, *m.* (coll.) cheat, swindle.

timón, *m.* helm, rudder.—*t. de profundidad,* (aer.) elevator.—**timonear,** *vt. & vi.* (naut.) to helm; to steer.—**timonel,** *m.* helmsman, steersman; coxswain.

timorato, *a.* timorous, chicken-hearted.

tímpano, *m.* (anat.) eardrum; kettledrum.

tina, *f.* large earthen jar; vat; tub, wash tub; bathtub.—**tinaco,** *m.* wooden trough, tub, or vat.—**tinaja,** *f.* large earthen jar.—**tinajón,** *m.* very large earthen water jar, or tank.

tinglado, *m.* shed, shed roof; temporary board floor; machination, intrigue.

tiniebla, *f.* (usually in *pl.*) darkness.

tino, *m.* skill; steady and accurate aim; judgment; tact; knack.

tinta, *f.* ink; tint, hue, color.—*de buena t.,* from or on good authority.—*t. china,* India ink.—**tinte,** *m.* dyeing, staining; tint, hue; paint, color, stain; dye; (fig.) guise, color.—**tinterillo,** *m.* (Am.) shyster lawyer.—**tintero,** *m.* inkpot, inkwell.—*dejarse en el t.,* (coll.) to forget to mention.

tintinear, *vi.* to clink, tinkle, jingle.—**tintineo,** *m.* clink, tinkling.

tinto, *ppi.* of TEÑIR.—*a.* tinged; (dark) red; (Am.) black, strong (coffee).—**tintorería,** *f.* cleaner or dyer's shop.—**tintorero,** *n.* cleaner, dyer.—**tintura,** *f.* tincture; tint, color; stain; dye; smattering.

tiña, *f.* (med.) scab; ringworm.—

tiñoso, *a.* scabby, scurvy; stingy, mean.

tío, *m.* uncle; (coll.) good old man; fellow.

tiovivo, *m.* merry-go-round.

típico, *a.* typical, characteristic.

tiple, *m.* (mus.) treble, soprano voice; treble guitar.—*f.* soprano singer.

tipo, *m.* type, pattern; standard, model; (coll.) (of person) figure, physique; (Am.) (com.) rate; (print.) type; (zool.) class; (coll. contempt.) fellow, guy.—**tipografía,** *f.* printing; typography.—**tipógrafo,** *n.* typographer.

tira, *f.* long, narrow strip.

tirabuzón, *m.* corkscrew; corkscrew curl.

tirada, *f.* cast, throw; distance; (print.) edition, issue.—**tirador,** *n.* thrower; drawer; sharpshooter; marksman, good shot.—*m.* handle, knob.—**tirafondo,** *m.* wood screw.

tiranía, *f.* tyranny.—**tiranizar,** *vti.* [a] to tyrannize.—**tirano,** *a.* tyrannical.—*n.* tyrant.

tirante, *a.* drawing, pulling; taut, tense, stretched; strained (as relations).—*m.* trace, gear (of harness); brace, strap.—*pl.* suspenders, braces. —**tirantez,** *f.* tenseness, tightness; stretch; strain; tension.—**tirar,** *vt.* to throw, cast, pitch (as a ball); to cast off, throw away (as a garment); to print; to fire, shoot (as a gun); to draw (a line); to waste, squander.—*t. de,* to pull (on).—*vi.* to draw, pull; **(a)** to have a shade (of), border (on); to tend, incline (to).—*vr.* to throw oneself; to abandon oneself; to jump (at), spring (upon).

tiritar, *vi.* to shiver.

tiro, *m.* throw, shot; shot, discharge, report (of a firearm); target practice; range; team of draught animals; landing of a stairway; draught of a chimney.—*al t.,* (Am.) right away, immediately.—*a tiros,* with shots, by shooting.—*de t.,* draft (horse).—*de tiros largos,* in full dress, in full regalia.—*errar el t.,* to miss the mark; to be mistaken. —*ni a tiros,* (coll.) not for love or money, absolutely not.—*t. al blanco,* target shooting; shooting gallery.

tirón, *m.* pull, haul, tug; effort.— *de un t.,* at once, at one stroke.

tirotear, *vi. & vr.* to exchange shots, to skirmish.—**tiroteo,** *m.* skirmish; shooting.

tirria, *f.* (coll.) aversion, dislike, grudge.

tísico, *n. & a.* (med.) consumptive. —**tisis,** *f.* consumption, tuberculosis.

tisú, *m.* tissue, gold or silver tissue.

títere, *m.* puppet; whipper-snapper. —*no dejar t. con cabeza,* to upset everything; to leave no one to tell the tale.

titilar, *vi.* to twinkle, flicker.

titiritar, *vi.* to shiver with cold or fear.

titiritero, *n.* juggler, acrobat; puppeteer.

titubear, *vi.* to hesitate; to totter; to toddle (as a child); to stagger.— **titubeo,** *m.* hesitation; tottering.

titular, *vt.* to title, entitle, name, call.—*vr.* to call oneself.—*a.* titular; nominal.—*f.* headline (of a newspaper).—**título,** *m.* title; heading, headline; claim, privilege of right; (law) legal title to property; diploma; professional degree; (com.) certificate, bond.—*a t. (de),* under pretext (of); on the authority (of).

tiza, *f.* chalk; clay.

tiznar, *vt.* to smut, smudge; to stain, tarnish.—**tizne,** *m.* soot, coal smut; stain.

tizón, *m.* firebrand; (agr.) blight, rust; stain; mildew (of plants).

toalla, *f.* towel.—**toallero,** *m.* towel rack.

tobillo, *m.* ankle.

toca, *f.* hood, coif, bonnet, wimple.

tocado, *a.* (fig.) touched (in the head); perturbed; tainted.—*m.* hairdo, hairdress, coiffure.—**tocador,** *m.* dressing table; dressing room, boudoir; dressing case; player (of a musical instrument).—**tocante,** *a.*— *t. a,* respecting, concerning, with regard to.—**tocar,** *vti.* [d] to touch, feel; (mus.) to play; to toll, ring (a bell); to blow (a horn); to knock, rap.—*t. de cerca,* to concern, affect closely.—*t. fondo,* to strike ground.—*vii.* to touch; behoove, concern; to be one's turn; to call at a port; to border on; to be related.

tocayo, *n.* namesake.

tocino, *m.* bacon; salt pork.

tocólogo, *n.* obstetrician.

tocón, *m.* stump of a tree.

todavía, *adv.* still; yet; even.

todo, *a.* all, every, each; whole, entire.—*t. aquello que,* whatever.—*t. aquél que,* whoever.—*t. el mundo,* everybody.—*m.* all; whole; everything.—*pl.* everybody.—*ante t.,* first of all.—*con t.,* nevertheless, however.—*del t.,* entirely, wholly.—*en un t.,* together, in all its parts.— *jugar el t. por el t.,* to stake or risk all.—*sobre t.,* above all.—*adv* entirely, totally.—*así y t.,* in spite of

everything.—**todopoderoso,** *a.* almighty.

toga, *f.* robe or gown (worn by judges, professors, etc.); toga.

toldo, *m.* awning; tarpaulin; (Am.) Indian hut; tent.

tolerable, *a.* tolerable, bearable; permissible.—**tolerancia,** *f.* toleration; tolerance.—**tolerante,** *a.* tolerant.—**tolerar,** *vi.* to tolerate, endure, permit; to be indulgent; to overlook.

tolete, *m.* (Am.) club, cudgel.

toma, *f.* taking, receiving; take; (mil.) capture, seizure; dose (of a medicine); (hydraul.) intake; (elec.) outlet; tap (of a water main or electric wire).—**tomacorriente,** *m.* (Am.) (elec.) socket, plug.

tomaína, *f.* ptomaine.

tomar, *vt.* to take; to drink; to eat.—*t. asiento,* to take a seat, sit down.—*t. el pelo,* (coll.) to banter, make fun of.—*t. en cuenta,* to consider.—*t. la delantera,* to excel; to get ahead.—*vi.* to drink (liquor).—*vr.* to drink; to eat; to rust.

tomate, *m.* tomato.

tomillo, *m.* thyme.

tomo, *m.* volume, tome.—*de t. y lomo,* of weight and bulk; of importance.

ton, *m.*—*sin t. ni son,* without rhyme or reason.

tonada, *f.* tune, song.—**tonalidad,** *f.* tonality.

tonel, *m.* cask, barrel.—**tonelada,** *f.* ton.—**tonelaje,** *m.* tonnage, displacement; (com.) tonnage dues.

tónico, *a.* tonic; (gram.) accented or inflected.—*m.* tonic.—*f.* (mus.) keynote, tonic.—**tonificador, tonificante,** *a.* tonic, strengthening.—**tonificar,** *vti.* [d] (med.) to tone up.—**tono,** *m.* tone; tune; pitch; conceit; manner, social address.—*darse t.,* to put on airs.—*de buen t.,* stylish, fashionable, polite.

tonsila, *f.* (anat.) tonsil.

tontada, tontera, tontería, *f.* foolishness, silliness, nonsense.—**tonto,** *a.* silly, foolish, stupid.—*n.* fool, dunce, dolt.—*a tontas y a locas,* without order, haphazard.—*hacerse el t.,* to play dumb.

topacio, *m.* topaz.

topar, *vt.* to collide with; to meet with by chance; to find.—*vi.* to butt, strike; to stumble upon.—**tope,** *m.* butt, end; top, summit; (mech.) stop; (RR.) buffer; collision, knock.—*hasta el t.* or *los topes,* up to the top, or the brim.—**topetazo, topetón,** *m.* butt, knock, blow, collision.

tópico, *a.* topical.—*m.* commonplace, trite idea; topic.

topo, *m.* (zool.) mole; (coll.) awkward person.

toque, *m.* touch, touching; ringing (of bells); (mil.) bugle call; beat (of a drum).—*t. de diana,* reveille.

tórax, *m.* thorax.

torbellino, *m.* whirlwind; whirlpool; vortex; (fig.) hustling, restless person.

torcaz, torcaza, *f.* wild pigeon.

torcedura, *f.* twisting; sprain.—**torcer,** *vti.* [26-a] to twist, twine, wind (as strands); to sprain; to bend; to distort.—*no dar el brazo a t.,* to be obstinate.—*vii.* to turn (to right or left).—*vri.* to become twisted, bent or sprained; to go crooked or astray.—**torcimiento,** *m.* twist(ing); sprain; winding; bend.

tordillo, *a.* grayish, grizzled.—**tordo,** *a.* dappled (of horses).—*m.* (ornith.) thrush, throstle.

torear, *vi.* to fight bulls in the ring.—*vt.* to fight (bulls); to banter; to provoke.—**toreo,** *m.* bullfighting.—**torero,** *m.* bullfighter.—*a.* pertaining to bullfighters.

tormenta, *f.* storm, tempest; hurricane; misfortune.—**tormento,** *m.* torment, torture.—**tormentoso,** *a.* stormy; boisterous; turbulent.

tornado, *m.* tornado.

tornar, *vt.* to return, restore; to turn; to change, alter.—*vi.* to return, come back; to do again.—*vr.* (en) to change (into), to become.—**tornasol,** *m.* (bot.) sunflower; iridescence, sheen; litmus.—**tornasolado,** *a.* changeable, iridescent.

tornear, *vt.* & *vi.* to turn (in a lathe); to do lathe work.—**torneo,** *m.* turner.

tornillo, *m.* screw, bolt; vise, clamp.

torniquete, *m.* turnstile; turnbuckle; (surg.) tourniquet.

torno, *m.* lathe; winch, windlass; revolving dumbwaiter; turn; spindle.—*en t.,* round about.

toro, *m.* bull.—*los toros,* bullfighting.

toronja, *f.* grapefruit.

torpe, *a.* slow, heavy, torpid; dull, stupid; bawdy, lewd.

torpedear, *vt.* to torpedo.—**torpedeo,** *m.* torpedoing.—**torpedero,** *m.* torpedo boat.—**torpedo,** *m.* torpedo.

torpeza, *f.* heaviness, dullness; torpor; lewdness.

torre, *f.* tower; turret; steeple; (chess) castle or rook.

torrencial, *a.* torrential; overpowering.—**torrente,** *m.* torrent; rush; plenty.

torreón, *m.* fortified tower.—**torrero,** *m.* lighthouse keeper.

tórrido, *a.* torrid; parched, hot.

torsión, f. twist; twisting.

torso, m. trunk of the body or of a statue.

torta, f. cake, pie; loaf; (coll.) blow, slap.

tortícolis, m. stiff neck.

tortilla, f. omelet; (Am.) cornmeal cake, pancake.—hacer t., to smash to pieces.

tórtola, f. (ornith.) turtledove.

tortuga, f. turtle; tortoise.

tortuoso, a. tortuous, winding; sly, sneaky.

tortura, f. torture; grief.—torturar, vt. to torture.

torvo, a. fierce, stern, severe, grim.

tos, f. cough.—t. ferina or convulsiva, whooping cough.

tosco, a. coarse, rough; unpolished; slipshod.

toser, vi. to cough.

tosquedad, f. roughness, coarseness; rudeness; clumsiness.

tostada, f. [slice of] toast.—tostador, n. toaster; coffee roaster.—tostadura, f. toasting.—tostar, vti. [12] to toast; to roast; to tan (as the sun).

total, a. total; general.—m. total; totality; result, upshot.—en t., in short, to sum up.—totalidad, f. totality; whole.—totalitario, a. & n. totalitarian.—totalitarismo, m. totalitarianism.—totalizar, vti. [a] to sum up; to find the total of.

tóxico, a. toxic.—m. poison.—toxina, f. (med.) toxin.

toza, f. log; block of wood; piece of bark.

tozudo, a. stubborn, obstinate.

traba, f. tie, bond, brace, clasp, locking device; anything that binds together; ligament, ligature; hobble, clog; obstacle, hindrance.

trabajador, a. industrious; hard-working.—n. worker; laborer.—trabajar, vt. & vi. to work, labor; to shape, form; to endeavor.—trabajo, m. work, labor; piece of work; employment; obstacle, hindrance; trouble, hardship.—pasar trabajos, to have troubles, to experience hardships or privation.—trabajos forzados, hard labor.—trabajoso, a. difficult, hard; laborious.

trabalenguas, m. tongue twister.—trabar, vt. to seize, fetter, fasten; to impede; to link; to engage in, join in.—vr. to become locked, interlocked; to become confused, rattled.—trabazón, f. juncture, union, bond, connection.

tracción, f. traction; cartage; (mech.) tension.—tractor, m. tractor.

tradición, f. tradition.—tradicional, a. traditional.

traducción, f. translation; rendering.—traducir, vti. [11] to translate.—traductor, n. translator.

traer, vti. [43] to bring, fetch; to cause; to wear (as a garment); to carry.—t. a colación, to bring up for discussion.—t. a mal t., to go hard with one; to disturb, trouble, vex.—t. entre manos, to be engaged in, busy with.

tráfago, m. commerce, trade; drudgery; bustle, hustle.

traficar, vii. [d] to traffic, deal, trade; to travel, journey, roam.—tráfico, m. trade, business; traffic.

tragaderas, f. gullet.—tener buenas t., to be very gullible.—tragadero, m. gullet; pit.—tragaldabas, mf. glutton.—tragaluz, m. skylight, bull's-eye.—tragar, vti. [b] to swallow; to devour; to swallow up, engulf.—vri. to swallow; to dissemble.

tragedia, f. tragedy.—trágico, a. tragic.—n. tragedian.

trago, m. gulp, swallow; drink.—a tragos, by degrees, slowly.—echar un t., to take a drink.—mal t., calamity, misfortune.—tragón, n. & a. glutton(ous).—tragonería, f. gluttony.

traición, f. treason; treachery; betrayal.—a t., treacherously.—traicionar, vt. to betray.—traicionero, a. treacherous.—traidor, a. traitorous; treasonable; treacherous.—n. traitor; betrayer.

trailla, f. leash, lash; packthread; (agr.) leveling harrow; road leveler; road scraper.

traje, m. dress; suit; gown; apparel.—t. de baño, bathing suit.—t. de etiqueta, full dress, evening dress.—t. de montar, riding habit.—t. largo, evening dress.—t. sastre, (woman's) tailored suit.

trajín, m. transport, haulage; traffic; coming and going, bustle, commotion.—trajinar, vt. to carry from place to place.—vi. to bustle about; (coll.) to fidget.

trama, f. weft or woof of cloth; intrigue, scheme; (lit.) plot.—tramar, vt. to weave; to plot, scheme.

tramitación, f. procedure; transaction, action, carrying out.—tramitar, vt. to transact, carry through, conduct.—trámite, m. the carrying on (of administration, etc.), the transacting (of business, etc.); step; (law) proceeding.

tramo, m. parcel of ground; flight of stairs; stretch, span, section; panel (of a bridge).

tramoya, *f.* (theat.) stage machinery.
—**tramoyista,** *mf.* (theat.) stage
machinist; stage carpenter, stage-
hand.

trampa, *f.* trap, snare, pitfall; trapdoor; falling board of a counter;
flap or spring door; cheat, fraud,
deceit, trick; bad debt.—*hacer
trampa(s),* to cheat.—**trampear,** *vi.*
(coll.) to cheat; to swindle; to get
along, pull through.—*vt.* to defraud.

trampolín, *m.* springboard.

tramposo, *a.* tricky, deceitful.—*n.*
cheater, swindler.

tranca, *f.* crossbar, bolt (for door);
club, stick, truncheon; (Am., coll.)
drunken spell.—**trancar,** *vti.* [d] to
bar (a door).—**trancazo,** *m.* blow
with a club; (coll.) influenza.

trance, *m.* plight, predicament;
trance, rapture.—*a todo t.,* at all
costs, at any price.—*en t. de muerte,*
at the point of death.

tranco, *m.* long stride; threshold.—
a trancos, hurriedly, carelessly.

tranquilidad, *f.* tranquillity, peace,
quiet.—**tranquilizador,** *a.* quieting,
soothing, reassuring.—**tranquilizar,**
vti. [a] & *vri.* to calm, quiet down.
—**tranquilo,** *a.* tranquil, calm, quiet.

transacción, *f.* transaction, negotiation; compromise, settlement.
—**transar,** *vt. & vr.* (Am.) to compromise, adjust, settle.

transatlántico, *a.* transatlantic.—*m.*
ocean liner.

transbordador, *a.* transferring.—*m.*
transfer boat, car, etc.—**transbordar,** *vt.* to transfer.—**transbordo,**
m. transfer.

transcribir, *vti.* [49] to transcribe.—
transcripción, *f.* transcription.—
transcripto, *ppi.* of TRANSCRIBIR.

transcurrir, *vi.* (of time) to pass,
elapse.—**transcurso,** *m.* lapse, course.

transeúnte, *a.* transient; transitory.—
mf. pedestrian, passer-by.

transferencia, *f.* transference, transfer.—**transferible,** *a.* transferable.—
transferir, *vti.* [39] to transfer.

transformación, *f.* transformation.—
transformador, *n. & a.* transformer;
transforming.—*m.* (elec.) transformer.—**transformar,** *vt. & vr.* to
transform.—*vr.* to be or become
transformed.

tránsfuga, *mf.* deserter; fugitive;
turncoat.

transfusión, *f.* transfusion.

transición, *f.* transition.

transido, *a.* worn out; famished.

transigencia, *f.* tolerance.—**transi-
gente,** *a.* accommodating, pliable,
compromising; tolerant.—**transigir,**
vti. [c] to compromise, settle.—*vii.*
to give in, agree.

transitable, *a.* passable, practicable.—
transitar, *vi.* to go from place to
place (as traffic); to flow.—**transitivo,** *a.* transitive.—**tránsito,** *m.*
transit; traffic; passing; passage;
transition; death.—**transitorio,** *a.*
transitory.

translación, etc. = TRASLACION, etc.

transmisible, *a.* transmissible.—**transmisión,** *f.* transmission; (radio)
broadcast.—**transmisor,** *a.* trans-
mitting.—*m.* (elec.) transmitter.—*f.*
(radio) broadcasting station.—**transmitir,** *vt.* to transmit; to broadcast.

transparencia, *f.* transparency.—
transparentarse, *vr.* to be transparent; to show through.—**transparente,** *a.* transparent.—*m.* window
shade; stained glass window.

transpiración, *f.* perspiration.—**transpirar,** *vi.* to perspire; (fig.) to seep
through.

transponer, *vti.* [32-49] to transpose;
to transfer; to transplant.—*vri.* (of
sun, etc.) to set below the horizon;
to go behind; to be rather drowsy.

transportación, *f.* transportation,
transport.—**transportar,** *vt.* to
transport, carry; (mus.) to transpose.—*vr.* to be in a transport, to
be carried away.—**transporte,** *m.*
transport(ation), conveyance; cartage; fit; rapture, ecstasy.

transposición, *f.* transposition.—
transpuesto, *ppi.* of TRANSPONER.

transversal, *a.* transversal.—*sección t.,*
cross section.—**transverso,** *a.* transverse.

tranvía, *m.* streetcar, trolley car.

trapacear, *vi.* to cheat, defraud.—
trapacería, *f.* fraud, cheating.—
trapacero, *n. & a.,* **trapacista,** *mf.*
& a. cheat; cheating.

trapecio, *m.* trapezium; trapeze.

trapero, *n.* ragpicker; rag dealer.

trapezoide, *m.* trapezoid.

trapiche, *m.* grinding machine (in
sugar mills, etc.).—**trapichear,** *vi.*
(coll.) to contrive, shift.—**trapicheo,**
m. (coll.) contriving, shifting.

trapisonda, *f.* (coll.) bustle, clatter;
(coll.) deception, trickery; brawl,
scuffle; escapade.

trapo, *m.* rag; tatter; sails of a
ship; (coll.) bullfighter's cloak.—*a
todo t.,* with all one's might;
(naut.) all sails set.—*poner como un
t.,* to reprimand severely, to dress
down.—*soltar el t.,* (coll.) to burst
out (crying or laughing).

tráquea, *f.* trachea, windpipe.

traquetear, *vt. & vi.* to rattle; to
shake, jolt; to crack, crackle.—

traqueteo, *m.* shaking, jolting; cracking, creaking; (Am.) confused, noisy movement.—**traquido,** *m.* snapping, rattle; creaking, cracking.

tras, *prep.* after, behind; beyond; besides; in search of.—*t. de,* after, back of; besides, in addition to.

trasanteayer, trasantier, *adv.* three days ago.

trasatlántico, *a.* = TRANSATLANTICO.

trasbordador, etc. = TRANSBORDADOR, etc.

trascendencia, *f.* importance, consequence.—**trascendental,** *a.* transcendental; far-reaching; momentous, highly important.—**trascender,** *vii.* [18] to transcend; to spread beyond; to be pervasive; to become known, seep out.

trascribir, trascripción, etc. = TRANSCRIBIR, etc.

trascurrir, trascurso, etc. = TRANSCURRIR, etc.

trasegar, *vti.* [1-b] to upset, overturn; to change the place of; to pour into another vessel.

trasera, *f.* back part, rear.—**trasero,** *a.* hind, back, rear.—*m.* buttock; rump.

trasferencia, etc. = TRANSFERENCIA, etc.

trasfiguración, etc. = TRANSFIGURACIÓN, etc.

trasformación, etc. = TRANSFORMACIÓN, etc.

trásfuga = TRANSFUGA.

trasgo, *m.* goblin, sprite.

trasgredir, etc. = TRANSGREDIR, etc.

trashumante, *a.* (of flocks) nomadic.

trasiego, *m.* upsetting; transfer (of wine, etc.).

traslación, *f.* transfer, removal; translation, change of place.—**trasladar,** *vt.* to move, remove, transfer; to translate; to transcribe, copy.—**traslado,** *m.* transfer; transcription, copy.

trasmisible, etc. = TRANSMISIBLE, etc.

traslúcido, etc. = TRANSLUCIDO.—**traslucirse,** *vri.* [3] to be translucent.—**trasluz,** *m.* light seen through a transparent body; (art) transverse light.—*al t.,* against the light.

trasnochado, *a.* tired from lack of sleep; haggard; stale, worn-out; trite, hackneyed.—**trasnochador,** *n.* nighthawk; night owl.—**trasnochar,** *vi.* to stay out all night; to spend a sleepless night.

traspapelar, *vt.* to mislay.—*vr.* to become mislaid.

traspasar, *vt.* to pierce; to pass over; to cross over; to go beyond, exceed limits; to transfer (a business); to trespass.

traspié, *m.* slip, stumble.—*dar traspiés,* to stumble; to slip; to err.

trasplantar, *vt.* to transplant.—*vr.* to migrate.—**trasplante,** *m.* transplantation; migration.

trasponer = TRANSPONER.

trasportación, etc. = TRANSPORTACION, etc.

trasposición, etc. = TRANSPOSICION, etc.

traspunte, *mf.* (theat.) prompter.

trasquilar, *vt.* to shear (sheep); to lop; to cut down.

trastada, *f.* (coll.) inconsiderate act; bad turn.

trastazo, *m.* whack, thump, blow.

traste, *m.* fret of a guitar; utensils, implements. —*dar al t. con,* to spoil, ruin, destroy.

trasto, *m.* (pej.) piece of furniture; junk; (coll.) useless person, washout.—*pl.* tools, paraphernalia.

trastornar, *vt.* to upset; to turn upside down; to disorder, disarrange; to excite; to confuse, perplex, unsettle (the mind).—**trastorno,** *m.* upsetting; upheaval; disturbance, disorder, confusion; trouble; disarrangement.

trastrocar, *vti.* [12-d] to change the order of; to disarrange.—**trastrueco, trastrueque,** *m.* disarrangement; transposition; rearrangement.

trasudar, *vt.* to sweat, perspire slightly.

trasunto, *m.* faithful image, likeness; copy.

trasversal, etc. = TRANSVERSAL, etc.

trata, *f.* trade.—*t. de blancas,* white slavery.—**tratable,** *a.* sociable; compliant.—**tratado,** *m.* treaty; treatise. —**tratamiento,** *m.* treatment; manners; title or form of address.—**tratante,** *mf.* dealer, trader.—**tratar,** *vt.* to handle; to treat (a subject, a person, a patient, a substance); to deal with; (con) to have dealings with; to discuss; (de) to try, attempt; to address as, give the title of; to call, charge with being. —*vi.* to treat; to deal, trade.—*t. sobre* or *acerca de,* to treat of, deal with (a subject).—*t. de,* to treat (of a subject).—*t. en,* to deal in.—*vr.* to look after oneself; to be on good terms.—*tratarse de,* to concern, be a question of.—**trato,** *m.* treatment; social behavior; manner; pact, agreement, deal; trade, commerce; friendly intercourse; title or form of address.—*tener buen t.,* (coll.) to be pleasant, nice.—*tener mucho t.,* to be close friends.

traumático, *a.* (med.) traumatic.

través, *m.* bias, inclination; mis-

fortune.—*a(l) t. de*, across, through.
—*de t.*, crosswise.—**travesaño**, *m.*
crosspiece, crossbar; bolster; rung;
(RR.) tie.—**travesía**, *f.* crossing;
crossroad, cross passage; sea voyage.

travesura, *f.* prank, frolic; mischief;
lively fancy.—**travieso**, *a.* frolicsome,
mischievous.

trayecto, *m.* distance between two
points; run, stretch, way.—**trayectoria**, *f.* trajectory, path.

traza, *f.* looks, appearance; trick,
ruse; sign, indication.—**trazado**, *a.*
traced, outlined.—*m.* sketch, outline, plan; (act of) drawing.—
trazar, *vti.* [a] to design, plan out;
sketch, draw up; to trace, mark
out; to draw (as a line).—**trazo**,
m. outline; line, stroke (of a pen
or pencil).

trebejo, *m.* implement, tool, utensil.
trébol, *m.* clover, shamrock.
trecho, *m.* space, distance; lapse.—
de t. en t., at intervals.
tregua, *f.* truce; reprieve, respite.
tremebundo, *a.* dreadful, frightful,
fearful.
tremedal, *m.* quagmire, bog.
tremendo, *a.* tremendous; huge; excessive.
trementina, *f.* turpentine.
tremolar, *vt. & vi.* to wave (as a
flag).—**tremolina**, *f.* rustling of the
wind; (coll.) uproar.—**trémolo**, *m.*
(mus.) tremolo.—**trémulo**, *a.* tremulous, quivering, shaking.
tren, *m.* train; outfit; equipment;
following, retinue; show, pomp.—
t. de aterrizaje, (aer.) landing gear.
trencilla, *f.* braid.—**trenza**, *f.* braid;
plait; tress.—**trenzar**, *vti.* [a] to
braid; to plait.
trepador, *a.* climbing.—*m.* climber.—
f. (bot.) climber, creeper.—**trepar**,
vi. to climb, mount.—*vr.* (Am.) to
climb; to perch.
trepidación, *f.* trepidation; vibration,
trembling.—**trepidar**, *vi.* to shake,
vibrate, jar; to quake.
treta, *f.* trick, wile, craft; (fencing)
feint.
triángulo, *m.* triangle.
tribal, *a.* tribal.—**tribu**, *f.* tribe.
tribulación, *f.* tribulation, affliction.
tribuna, *f.* rostrum, platform; tribune; grandstand.—**tribunal**, *m.*
tribunal, court of justice.—**tribuno**,
m. orator; tribune.
tributación, *f.* tribute, contribution;
system of taxation.—**tributar**, *vt.*
to pay (taxes, etc.); to pay, render
(homage, respect).—**tributario**, *a.*
tributary.—*n.* taxpayer; tributary
river.—**tributo**, *m.* tribute; tax,
contribution; gift, offering.

triciclo, *m.* tricycle.
tricornio, *m.* three-cornered hat.
trifulca, *f.* (coll.) squabble, row.
trigal, *m.* wheat field.—**trigo**, *m.*
wheat.
trigonometría, *f.* trigonometry.
trigueño, *a.* brunette, swarthy, dark.
trilogía, *f.* trilogy.
trilla, *f.* (agr.) threshing.—**trillado**,
a. hackneyed, trite, commonplace.—
trillador, *n.* thresher.—**trilladora**, *f.*
thresher, threshing machine.—**trilladura**, *f.* (agr.) threshing.—**trillar**,
vt. (agr.) to thresh, beat; to frequent; to repeat.—**trillo**, *m.* (Am.)
footpath.
trimestral, *a.* quarterly.—**trimestre**,
m. quarter; quarterly payment.
trinar, *vi.* (mus.) to trill; to quaver;
to warble; (coll.) to fume (with
fury).
trincar, *vti.* [d] to tie, bind, make
fast.
trinchar, *vt.* to carve (food).
trinchera, *f.* (mil.) trench; deep cut,
ditch.
trineo, *m.* sleigh, sledge; sled, bobsled.
trinidad, *f.* Trinity, trinity.
trino, *a.* threefold, triple.—*m.* (mus.)
trill; warbling.
trío, *m.* trio.
tripa, *f.* gut, intestine; (coll.) belly.
—*pl.* insides, entrails.
triple, *a.* triple, treble.—**triplicar**, *vti.*
[d] to treble, triple.—**trípode**, *m.*
tripod.
tripulación, *f.* crew (or ship, etc.).—
tripulante, *mf.* one of the crew.
—*pl.* crew.—**tripular**, *vt.* to man
(ships).
triquina, *f.* trichina.
triquiñuela, *f.* (coll.) trickery, subterfuge.
triquitraque, *m.* crack, clashing; firecracker.
tris.—*en un t.*, almost, coming pretty
near.
triscar, *vii.* [d] to romp, frisk, frolic;
to walk lively, to hustle.
triste, *a.* sad, sorrowful; dismal.—
tristeza, *f.* sadness, sorrow, grief.—
tristón, *a.* rather sad, melancholy.
tritón, *m.* merman.
triturar, *vt.* to crush, grind, pound.
triunfador, *n.* conqueror, victor.—
triunfal, *a.* triumphal.—**triunfante**,
a. triumphant.—**triunfar**, *vi.* to
conquer; to triumph; to trump (at
cards); to win.—**triunfo**, *m.* triumph, victory; trump card.
trivial, *a.* trivial, trifling; trite, banal.
—**trivialidad**, *f.* triviality; triteness.

triza, *f.* fragment.—*hacer trizas,* to knock to pieces; to tear to bits.

trocar, *vti.* [12-d] to exchange; to change, alter; to interchange; to distort, pervert.—*vri.* to change; to be changed, transformed or re-formed.

trocha, *f.* (Am.) cross path, short cut; rough road, trail; military road.

trofeo, *m.* trophy; spoils of war; memorial.

troj(e), *f.* granary, barn.

trole, *m.* trolley.

tromba, *f.* waterspout.

trombón, *m.* trombone.

trombosis, *f.* (med.) thrombosis.

trompa, *f.* trumpet; (mus.) horn; trunk of an elephant; (Am.) thick lips; (RR.) cowcatcher, pilot (of a locomotive).—**trompada,** *f.,* **trompazo,** *m.* (coll.) heavy blow.—**trompeta,** *f.* trumpet; bugle.—*m.* trumpeter; bugler.—**trompetazo,** *m.* trumpet blast; bugle blast or call.—**trompetear,** *vi.* (coll.) to sound the trumpet.—**trompeteo,** *m.* sounding the bugle or trumpet.—**trompetilla,** *f.* small trumpet; ear trumpet; (Am. coll.) raspberry, Bronx cheer.

trompicón, *m.* stumbling.

trompo, *m.* spinning top.

tronada, *f.* thunderstorm.—**tronar,** *vii.* [12] to thunder, rumble; (coll.) to be ruined, come down in the world.—*por lo que pueda t.,* as a precaution, just in case.

tronco, *m.* trunk; stem, stalk; stock, origin; team of horses; unfeeling person.

tronchar, *vt. & vr.* to break off.—**troncho,** *m.* stalk.

tronera, *f.* (fort.) embrasure; loophole; porthole; pocket hole (billiards).—*m.* madcap, man about town.

tronido, *m.* thunder, loud report.

trono, *m.* throne.

tronquista, *m.* (U.S.) teamster; coachman.

tropa, *f.* troops, soldiers; multitude; (Am.) herd of cattle.—*pl.* forces, army.

tropel, *m.* rush, hurry, confusion; huddle; crowd.—*en t.,* tumultuously, in a throng.—**tropelía,** *f.* rush, hurry; injustice, outrage.

tropezar, *vii.* [1-a] to stumble; (con) to strike (against); to stumble, trip (over); to meet (with); to stumble, light (on), happen to find.—**tropezón,** *m.* stumbling; stumble; slip.—*a tropezones,* by fits and starts.

tropical, *a.* tropical.—**trópico,** *m.* tropic.

tropiezo, *m.* stumble; obstacle, hitch, stumbling block; slip, fault; quarrel, dispute.

troquel, *m.* die (as for coining).

trotar, *vt. & vi.* to trot.—**trote,** *m.* trot.—*al t.,* trotting, at a trot; (coll.) in haste.—**trotón,** *a.* trotting.—*n.* trotter.—*m.* horse.

trovador, *n.* troubadour, minstrel.

trozo, *m.* piece, fragment, part; selection (of music); passage (from a book, etc.).

truco, *m.* trick.

trucha, *f.* trout.

truchimán, *n.* (coll.) expert buyer; shrewd trader.

trueno, *m.* thunder.

trueque, *m.* exchange, barter.

trufa, *f.* truffle.

truhán, *n.* rascal, scoundrel, knave.—**truhanería,** *f.* rascality.

truncar, *vti.* [49-d] to truncate; to maim; to mutilate (a speech, quotation, etc.).

tú, *pron.* you (*sing.* fam. form); thou.—*tratar de tú,* to be on intimate terms with.—**tu,** *a.* (*pl.* tus) your (when on intimate terms); thy.

tubérculo, *m.* (bot.) tuber; (med.) tubercle.—**tuberculosis,** *f.* (med.) tuberculosis.—**tuberculoso,** *a. & n.* tubercular; sufferer from tuberculosis.

tubería, *f.* tubing; piping.—**tubo,** *m.* tube; pipe; lamp chimney.—**tubular,** *a.* tubular.

tuerca, *f.* (mech.) nut.

tuerto, *a.* one-eyed.—*n.* one-eyed person.—*m.* tort, wrong, injustice.

tueste, *m.* toast, toasting (by heat).

tuétano, *m.* marrow; pith.—*hasta los tuétanos,* to the marrow.

tufo, *m.* vapor, emanation; (coll.) offensive odor; conceit, airs, snobbishness.

tugurio, *m.* hovel; dive, saloon.

tul, *m.* tulle, net.

tulipán, *m.* (bot.) tulip.

tullir, *vti.* [27] to cripple, maim.—*vri.* to be crippled.

tumba, *f.* tomb, grave.—**tumbar,** *vt.* to fell, throw down; (coll.) to knock down.—*vi.* to tumble, fall down.—*vr.* (coll.) to lie down, tumble into bed.—**tumbo,** *m.* tumble, fall; somersault.

tumefacción, *f.* swelling.

tumor, *m.* tumor.—*t. maligno,* cancer.

túmulo, *m.* tomb.

tumulto, *m.* tumult; mob.—**tumultuario, tumultuoso,** *a.* tumultuous.

tuna, *f.* (bot.) prickly pear, tuna.

tunante, *n.* truant, rake; rascal, rogue.
tunda, *f.* (coll.) trouncing, whipping. —**tundir,** *vt.* to whip, thrash; to shear.
túnel, *m.* tunnel.
tungsteno, *m.* tungsten.
túnica, *f.* tunic; robe, gown.
tuno, *a.* roguish, cunning.—*m.* truant, rake, rascal.
tuntún, *m.*—*al buen t.*, (coll.) heedlessly, haphazard.
tupé, *m.* toupee; (coll.) nerve, cheek.
tupir, *vt.* to pack tight; to make thick or compact; to choke, obstruct; to block or stop up.—*vr.* to stuff or glut oneself.
turba, *f.* crowd, rabble, mob; peat.
turbación, *f.* confusion, embarrassment.—**turbador,** *n.* disturber.—*a.* disturbing.—**turbamulta,** *f.* mob.—**turbante,** *a.* disturbing.—*m.* turban. —**turbar,** *vt.* to disturb; to embarrass.—*vr.* to be disturbed, embarrassed.
turbina, *f.* turbine.
turbio, *a.* muddy, turbid; obscure (language).
turbión, *m.* windy shower; sweep, rush.—**turbonada,** *f.* squall, pelting shower.
turco, *a.* Turkish.—*n.* Turk.—*m.* Turkish language.
turgencia, *f.* (med.) swelling.—**turgente,** *a.* turgid, swollen.
turismo, *m.* tourism, touring.—**turista,** *mf.* & *a.* tourist; touring.
turnar, *vi.* & *vr.* to alternate; to take turns.—**turno,** *m.* turn, alternation.—*de t.*, open for service (of a store, etc.); on duty (of a person).
turquesa, *f.* turquoise.
turquí, *a.* deep blue.
turrón, *m.* nougat, almond paste.
turulato, *a.* (coll.) dumbfounded, stupefied.
tutear, *vt.* to use the familiar TU in addressing a person.
tutela, *f.* guardianship, tutelage, protection.
tutiplén.—*a t.*, (coll.) abundantly.
tutor, *n.* tutor.—**tutoría,** *f.* tutelage, guardianship.
tuyo, *a.* & *pron. poss.* (*f.* **tuya.**—*pl.* **tuyos, tuyas**) your(s) (*fam.* form corresp. to TU).

U

u, *conj.* (replaces o when preceding a word beginning with o or ho) or.
ubérrimo, *a.* very fruitful; exceedingly plentiful.
ubicación, *f.* situation, location, position.—**ubicar,** *vti.* & *vii.* [d] to locate; to lie; to be located or situated.—**ubicuidad,** *f.* ubiquity.
ubre, *f.* udder; teat.
ufanarse, *vr.* to boast, pride oneself. —**ufanía,** *f.* pride; conceit; joy, pleasure.—**ufano,** *a.* conceited, proud; gay, cheerful.
ujier, *m.* doorman; usher.
úlcera, *f.* ulcer; open sore.—**ulceración,** *f.* ulceration.—**ulcerar,** *vt.* to ulcerate.—*vr.* to become ulcerated.
ulterior, *a.* ulterior, farther; subsequent.
ultimar, *vt.* to end, finish, close.—**último,** *a.* last, latest; farthest; ultimate; final; latter; most valuable.
ultrajar, *vt.* to outrage, offend, abuse; to despise.—**ultraje,** *m.* outrage, insult; contempt; abuse.
ultramar, *m.* overseas.—**ultramarino,** *a.* oversea.—**ultrarrojo,** *a.* infra-red. —**ultrasónico,** *a.* ultrasonic.—**ultratumba,** *f.*—*de le u.* or *en u.,* beyond the grave.—**ultraviolado, ultravioleta** *a.* ultraviolet.
ulular, *vi.* to screech, hoot.
umbilical, *a.* umbilical.
umbral, *m.* threshold; (arch.) lintel; beginning, rudiment.
umbrío, *a.* shady.—**umbroso,** *a.* shady.
un (*f.* **una**) *art.* a, an.—*a.* (*abbr.* de UNO) one.
unánime, *a.* unanimous.—**unanimidad,** *f.* unanimity.—*por u.,* unanimously.
unción, *f.* unction; religious fervor.
uncir, *vti.* [a] to yoke.
ungimiento, *m.* unction.—**ungir,** *vti.* [c] to anoint.
ungüento, *m.* unguent, ointment.
único, *a.* only, sole; unique, rare, unmatched, unparalleled.
unidad, *f.* unity; unit.—**unificación,** *f.* unification.—**unificar,** *vti.* [d] to unify.
uniformar, *vt.* to standardize, make uniform; to put into uniform.—**uniforme,** *a.* & *m.* uniform.—**uniformidad,** *f.* uniformity.
unilateral, *a.* unilateral.
unión, *f.* union; harmony; concord; marriage; joining, joint; (com.) consolidation, merger.
unir, *vt.* to join, unite; to connect; to mix; bring together.—*vr.* to join, get together; to wed; (com.) to consolidate, merge.
unisonancia, *f.* state of being unisonal; monotony.—**unísono,** *a.* (mus.) unisonal; unisonous; unanimous.
unitario, *a.* & *n.* (eccl.) Unitarian; (pol.) supporter of centralization.

universal, *a.* universal.—**universidad,** *f.* university.—**universitario,** *a.* university.—**universo,** *m.* universe.

uno, *a.* (*f.* una) one; only, sole.—*pl.* some; nearly, about.—*u. que otro,* (only) a few.—*pron.* one, someone.—*pl.* some, a few (people).—*cada u.,* each one.—*u. a otro,* each other, mutually.—*u. y otro,* both.—*unos a otros,* one another.—*unos cuantos,* a few.—*unos y otros,* all, the lot (of them).—*n.* one (number).—*a una,* unanimously, of one accord.—*de u. en u.,* one by one; in single file.—*la una,* (time) one o'clock.—*u. por u.,* one after another; one by one, one at a time.

untar, *vt.* to anoint; to smear; to grease, oil; to bribe.—*u. las manos,* to grease the palm; to bribe.—*vr.* to be greased or smeared; to embezzle.—**unto,** *m.* grease, fat of animals; unguent, ointment.—**untuoso,** *a.* unctuous, greasy.—**untura,** *f.* unction; ointment, liniment.

uña, *f.* fingernail; toenail; hoof, claw; pointed hook of instruments.—*a u. de caballo,* at full gallop, in great haste.—*enseñar* or *mostrar las uñas,* to show one's true nature.—*hincar* or *meter la u.,* to overcharge; to sell at an exorbitant price; *largo de uñas,* filcher.—*ser u. y carne,* to be hand and glove, to be fast friends.—**uñero,** *m.* ingrowing nail.

uranio, *m.* uranium.

urbanidad, *f.* urbanity, civility, manners.—**urbanización,** *f.* urbanization.—**urbanizar,** *vti.* [a] to lay out (land) for a town; to polish, render polite.—**urbano,** *a.* urban; urbane, courteous.—**urbe,** *f.* large modern city, metropolis.

urdimbre, *f.* warp (of cloth).—**urdir,** *vt.* to warp (cloth); to plot, scheme.

urgencia, *f.* urgency.—**urgir,** *vii.* [c] to be urgent.

urinario, *a.* urinary.—*m.* urinal.

urna, *f.* urn, casket; glass case; ballot box.

urraca, *f.* magpie.

urticaria, *f.* (med.) hives.

uruguayo, *a. & n.* Uruguayan.

usanza, *f.* usage, custom.—**usar,** *vt.* to use; to make use of; to wear; to wear out.—*vr.* to be in use or fashion; to be customary.—**uso,** *m.* use; usage, custom; wearing, wear; wear and tear; (com., law) usance.—*a(l) u.,* according to usage.—*en buen u.,* in good condition.—*u. de razón,* discernment, understanding, thinking for oneself (esp. of a child).

usted, *pron.* (usually abbreviated **V.,**

Vd., U., Ud.) you.—*pl.* **ustedes** (abbrev. **VV., Vds., UU., Uds.)** you.—*de Ud.,* your, yours.

usual, *a.* usual, customary.—**usuario,** *n.* user.

usufructo, *m.* (law) usufruct; use, enjoyment; profit.—**usufructuar,** *vt.* to hold in usufruct; to enjoy the use.

usura, *f.* usury.—**usurario,** *a.* usurious.—**usurero,** *n.* usurer; money lender, loan shark.

usurpación, *f.* usurpation.—**usurpador,** *n. & a.* usurper; usurping.—**usurpar,** *vt.* to usurp.

utensilio, *m.* utensil; tool, implement.

uterino, *a.* uterine.—**útero,** *m.* (anat.) uterus, womb.

útil, *a.* useful; profitable.—*m. pl.* utensils, tools; outfit, equipment.—**utilidad,** *f.* utility; profit; usefulness.—**utilitario,** *a.* utilitarian.—**utilizable,** *a.* utilizable, available.—**utilizar,** *vti.* [a] to utilize.—*vri.* to be made profitable.

utopia, *f.* utopia,—**utópico,** *a.* utopian.

uva, *f.* grape.—*hecho una u.,* dead drunk.—*u. pasa,* raisin.

úvula, *f.* uvula.

uxoricida, *m.* uxoricide. (person).—*a.* uxoricidal.—**uxoricidio,** *m.* uxoricide (act).

V

vaca, *f.* cow.—*carne de v.,* beef.—*hacer una v.,* or *ir en una v.,* to pool money (two or more gamblers).—*v. lechera,* milch cow.

vacación, *f.* vacation.—*pl.* holidays, summer recess.—*de vacaciones,* on holidays.

vacada, *f.* herd of cows.

vacante, *a.* vacant; unoccupied.—*f.* vacancy.—**vacar,** *vii.* [d] to give up work or employment temporarily; to be vacant.

vaciado, *m.* plaster cast.—**vaciar,** *vt.* to empty; to pour out; to cast, mold; to hone, grind.—*vi.* to flow (into) (as rivers).—*vr.* to spill; to be drained; to become empty or vacant.—**vaciedad,** *f.* nonsense, silly remark.

vacilación, *f.* hesitation; vacillation; wavering.—**vacilante,** *a.* hesitating, irresolute; unstable.—**vacilar,** *vi.* to vacillate, fluctuate; to hesitate; to reel.

vacio, *a.* empty; hollow; vain, presumptuous; vacant, unoccupied.—*m.* void, empty space; vacuum; opening; hollowness; blank; gap.—*en el v.,* in vacuo.

vacuna, *f.* vaccine; vaccination; cowpox.—**vacunación,** *f.* vaccination.—**vacunar,** *vt.* to vaccinate.—**vacuno,** *a.* bovine.—**ganado v.,** (bovine) cattle.

vadear, *vt.* to wade through, ford.—**vado,** *m.* ford ot a river; expedient.

vagabundear, *vi.* (coll.) to wander, rove or loiter about.—**vagabundo,** *n.* vagabond, vagrant, rover; roamer, tramp.—*a.* roving, roaming, tramping, vagrant.—**vagancia,** *f.* vagrancy.—**vagar,** *vii.* [b] to rove, roam, loiter about, wander; to be idle.—*m.* leisure, idleness, loitering. —**vago,** *a.* roving, roaming, vagrant; vague; wavering; loose; (art) hazy; indistinct.—*n.* vagabond, loafer, vagrant, tramp.

vagón, *m.* (RR.) car; wagon.—**v. de cola,** caboose.—**vagoneta,** *f.* (RR.) small open car; (Am.) open delivery cart.

vaguear, *vi.* = VAGAR.

vaguedad, *f.* vagueness; vague statement.

vahído, *m.* vertigo, dizziness.

vaho, *m.* vapor, fume, steam; odor.

vaina, *f.* scabbard, sheath, case; (bot.) pod, capsule; (Am.) nuisance, annoyance.

vainilla, *f.* vanilla.

vaivén, *m.* fluctuation, oscillation, sway; unsteadiness, inconstancy; giddiness; rocking; (mech.) swing, seesaw.—*pl.* ups and downs.—**sierra de v.,** jig saw.

vajilla, *f.* table service, tableware, dinner set; crockery.—**v. de plata,** silverware.

vale, *m.* (com.) bond, promissory note, IOU; voucher; sales slip; bonus given to schoolboys.—**valedero,** *a.* valid, efficacious, binding. —**valedor** *n.* protector, defender; (Am.) chum, pal.

valenciano, *n.* & *a.* Valencian.

valentía, *f.* valor, courage, bravery; heroic exploit; brag, boast.—**valentón,** *a.* blustering, arrogant.—*m.* hector, bully.

valer, *vti.* [44] to protect, favor; to cost; to cause, bring upon or to (one) (discredit, fame); to amount to; to be worth, be valued at; to be equal to.—**hacer v.,** to assert (one's rights); to avail oneself of. —**ni cosa que lo valga,** nor anything of the kind, or like it.—**v. la pena,** to be worth while.—*vii.* to be valuable; to be worthy; to possess merit or value; to prevail, avail; (of coins) to be legal and current; to be valid or binding; to be important or useful; to be or serve

as a protection; to be equivalent to; to mean.—**hacer v.,** to turn to account.— (*impers.*) **más vale, más valiera,** it is better, it would be better.—**más vale tardé que nunca,** better late than never.—**v. por,** to be equal to, to be worth.—¡**válgame Dios!** good Heavens! bless me!—*vri.* to help oneself, take care of oneself.—**no poderse v.,** to be helpless.—**v. de,** to make use of, have recourse to.—*m.* value; merit, worth. —**valeroso,** *a.* brave, courageous.—**valía,** *f.* value, worth; favor, influence.—**validar,** *vt.* to validate.—**validez,** *f.* validity; soundness; vigor, strength.—**válido,** *a.* valid.

valiente, *a.* valiant, brave, courageous. —*mf.* brave person.

valija, *f.* valise, suitcase; mail bag; mail.

valimiento, *m.* benefit, advantage; favor, support; favoritism.—**valioso,** *a.* valuable; highly esteemed, of great influence; wealthy.—**valor,** *m.* value; price; worth; activity, power; valor, bravery; (fig.) cheek, nerve.—**valoración,** *f.* appraisement, valuation.—**valorar,** *vt.* **valorizar,** *vti.* [a] to appraise, value, price.

vals, *m.* waltz.

valuación, *f.* appraisement, valuation. —**valuar,** *vt.* to rate, price, value, appraise.

valva, *f.* valve (of a mollusk).—**válvula,** *f.* valve.

valla, *f.* fence, stockade; barrier, barricade; obstacle, impediment.—**valladar,** *m.* = VALLADO; obstacle.—**vallado,** *m.* stockade; inclosure; stone wall.

valle, *m.* valley; vale, dell.

¡**vamos!,** *interj.* well! come, now! go on! let's go!

vampiro, *m.* ghoul; vampire; (fig.) bloodsucker.

vanagloria, *f.* vainglory, boast, conceit.—**vanagloriarse,** *vr.* to be vainglorious; to glory; to boast.

vanguardia, *f.* vanguard.

vanidad, *f.* vanity; nonsense; shallowness.—**vanidoso,** *a.* vain, conceited.—**vano,** *a.* vain; hollow; inane, empty, shallow, insubstantial; unavailing.—*m.* opening in a wall (as for a door).

vapor, *m.* vapor, steam; mist; steamer, steamship.—**vaporización,** *f.* vaporization.—**vaporizador,** *m.* vaporizer.—**vaporoso,** *a,* vaporous, misty, cloudy.

vapulear, *vt.* (coll.) to whip, flog, beat.—**vapuleo,** *m.* (coll.) whipping, flogging, beating.

vaquería, *f.* dairy; stable for cows.—

vaquero, *n.* cowherd.—*m.* cowboy. —*a.* pertaining to a cowherd.— **vaqueta,** *f.* sole leather.

vara, *f.* twig; pole, staff; stick, rod, wand; yard, yardstick.—*v. alta,* sway, high hand.

varadero, *m.* shipyard.—**varar,** *vt.* to beach (a boat).—*vi. & vr.* (naut.) to run aground, be stranded; to be at a standstill.

variable, *a.* variable, changeable.—*f.* variable.—**variación,** *f.* variation.— **variado,** *a.* varying, varied; variegated.—**variante,** *a.* varying; deviating.—*f.* difference, discrepancy (in texts).—**variar,** *vt.* to vary, change; to shift; to variegate.—*vi.* to vary, change; to differ.

várice, varice, *f.* varicose vein.

varicela, *f.* (med.) chicken pox.

variedad, *f.* variety; change, variation.—*pl.* miscellany of things or items; variety show.

varilla, *f.* rod; spindle, pivot; wand; rib (of an umbrella, a fan, etc,); whalebone, stay.

vario, *a.* various, different; inconstant, changeable.—*pl.* various; some, several.

varón, *m.* male, man.—*santo v.,* (coll.) good but simple fellow.— **varonil,** *a.* manly; virile; vigorous.

vasco, vascongado, *n. & a.* Basque.

vaselina, *f.* vaseline.

vasija, *f.* vessel, container, receptacle (for liquids).—**vaso,** *m.* (drinking) glass; vessel, reeceptacle; glassful; vase.

vástago, *m.* stem, sapling, shoot; scion, offspring.

vasto, *a.* vast, huge, immense.

vate, *m.* bard, poet.—**vaticinar,** *vt.* to divine, predict, foretell.—**vaticinio,** *m.* prediction.

vatio, *m.* (elec.) watt.

¡vaya!, *interj.* go! come! indeed! certainly! well!

vecinal, *a.* neighboring, adjacent.— **vecindad,** *f.* neighborhood, vicinity. —*casa de v.,* tenement.—**vecindario,** *m.* population of a district, ward, etc.; neighborhood, vicinity.— **vecino,** *a.* neighboring, next, near by.—*n.* neighbor; resident; citizen.

veda, *f.* prohibition, interdiction by law; closed season (hunting, etc.). —**vedar,** *vt.* to prohibit, forbid; to impede.

vega, *f.* flat lowland; (Am.) tobacco plantation.

vegetación, *f.* vegetation.—**vegetal,** *a. & m.* vegetable, vegetal, plant.— **vegetar,** *vi.* to vegetate.

vehemencia, *f.* vehemence.—**vehemente,** *a.* vehement; persuasive; vivid; keen.

vehículo, *m.* vehicle.

veintena, *f.* score (twenty).

vejación, *f.,* **vejamen,** *m.* vexation, annoyance; oppression.—**vejar,** *vt.* to vex, tease, annoy; to oppress.

vejestorio, *m.* (coll.) valueless finery; shriveled old person.—**vejete,** *m.* (coll.) ridiculous old man.—**vejez,** *f.* old age.

vejiga, *f.* bladder; blister.

vela, *f.* candle; (naut.) sail; vigil, wakefulness; wake; watch, watchfulness.—*a toda v.,* with all sails up and full of wind; in full swing. —*en v.,* vigilantly, without sleep.— *hacerse a la v.,* to set sail.—**velada,** *f.* evening party or celebration.— **velador,** *n.* watchman(-woman), nightguard.—*m.* small round table. —**velamen,** *m.* (naut.) canvas; set of sails.—**velar,** *vi.* to watch; to be awake; to observe; to be vigilant; (por) to watch (over), protect.— *vt.* to veil; to cover, hide.

veleidad, *f.* fickleness; versatility.— **veleidoso,** *a.* fickle, inconstant.

velero, *a.* (naut.) swift-sailing.—*m.* sailboat, bark.

veleta, *f.* weathercock, vane.—*mf.* fickle person.

velo, *m.* veil; curtain.—*v. del paladar,* (anat.) soft palate, velum.

velocidad, *f.* velocity.—*a toda v.,* at full speed.—**velocímetro,** *m.* speedometer.

velorio, *m.* wake, watch (over a dead person); (Am.) boring party.

veloz, *a.* fast, quick, swift, rapid.

vello, *m.* down; nap; fuzz.

vellón, *m.* fleece, wool of one sheep; lock of wool; ancient copper coin.

velloso, *a.* downy, hairy, fuzzy.— **velludo,** *a.* = VELLOSO.—*m.* shag, velvet.

vena, *f.* vein; (min.) vein, seam, lode. —*estar en v.,* to be in the mood; to be inspired.—*v. de loco,* fickle disposition.

venablo, *m.* javelin, dart.

venado, *m.* deer, stag; venison.

venático, *a.* (coll.) cranky, erratic, daft.

vencedor, *a.* winning, victorious; conquering.—*n.* winner, victor; conqueror.—**vencer,** *vti.* [a] to conquer, subdue, defeat, vanquish; to surpass; to surmount, overcome; to win.—*vii.* to conquer; to win; (com.) to fall due, mature; to expire.—*vri.* to control oneself.—**vencido,** *a.* (com.) due; payable; conquered; defeated.—**vencimiento,** *m.* defeat; (com.) maturity, expiration.

venda, *f.* bandage.—**vendaje,** *m.* bandage; bandaging.—**vendar,** *vt.* to bandage.

vendaval, *m.* gale wind.

vendedor, *n.* seller, salesman (-woman); vendor.—**vender,** *vt.* & *vi.* to sell.—*v. al por mayor,* to sell at wholesale.—*v. al por menor,* or *v. al detalle,* to sell at retail.—*v. a plazos,* to sell on credit.—*vr.* to sell out, accept a bribe; to expose oneself to danger.—*v. caro,* to sell (be sold) dear.—*vendido, a.* sold; betrayed.—*estar v.,* to be duped; to be exposed to great risks.

vendimia, *f.* vintage.

venduta, *f.* (Am.) small vegetable store; (Am.) auction.

veneno, *m.* poison, venom.—**venenoso,** *a.* poisonous, venomous.

venerable, *a.* venerable.—**veneración,** *f.* veneration; worship.—**venerar,** *vt.* to venerate, revere; to worship.

venéreo, *a.* venereal.

venero, *m.* water spring; (min.) bed, lode; origin, source.

venezolano, *n.* & *a.* Venezuelan.

vengador, *n.* avenger; revenger.—*a.* avenging; revenging.—**venganza,** *f.* vengeance; revenge.—**vengar,** *vti.* [b] to avenge.—*vri.* (de) to take revenge (on).—**vengativo,** *a.* revengeful, vindictive, vengeful.

venia, *f.* pardon, forgiveness; leave, permission; bow with the head.

venial, *a.* venial; pardonable.

venida, *f.* arrival, return; flood, freshet; rashness, rush.—**venidero,** *a.* future, coming.—**venir,** *vii.* [45] to come; to arrive; to fit, suit; to occur (to one's mind).—*¡a qué viene eso?* what has that to do with the case?—*la semana que viene,* next week.—*si a mano viene,* perhaps.—*v. a buscar,* to come for, or to get. —*v. a las manos,* to come to blows. —*v. a menos,* to decay, to decline.— *v. a ser,* to get to be, become; to turn out to be.—*v. bien,* to suit, to be becoming.— *v. como anillo al dedo,* or *v. de perilla,* to come in the nick of time; to fit the case, be to the point.

venoso, *a.* venous; veined.

venta, *f.* sale; selling; roadside inn. —*de v.* or *en v.,* for sale.—*v. (al) por mayor,* wholesale.—*v. (al) por menor,* retail sale; retailing.—*v. pública,* public auction sale.

ventaja, *f.* advantage; gain, profit; handicap (in races, sports, etc.).— **ventajoso,** *a.* advantageous; profitable; advisable.

ventalla, *f.* valve; (bot.) pod.

ventana, *f.* window; (carp.) window frame.—*echar la casa por la v.,* to go to a lot of expense.—*v. de la nariz,* nostril.—**ventanilla,** *f.* window (vehicles, banks, theaters, etc.).— **ventanillo,** *m.* small window shutter; peephole.

ventarrón, *m.* stiff wind, gust.— **ventear,** *vt.* to smell; to scent, sniff (as dogs); to investigate, inquire; to air.

ventilación, *f.* ventilation.—**ventilador,** *m.* ventilator; (ventilating) fan.—**ventilar,** *vt.* to ventilate, air; to discuss.

ventisca, *f.* snowstorm, blizzard.— **ventisquero,** *m.* snowstorm, snowdrift; glacier; snow-capped mountain.

ventolera, *f.* gust of wind; whim, notion; scurry.

ventorrillo, *m.* poor inn or tavern.

ventosear, *vi.* to break wind.—**ventosidad,** *f.* flatulence, windiness.— **ventoso,** *a.* windy; flatulent.

ventrílocuo, *m.* ventriloquist.

ventura, *f.* happiness; luck, fortune; chance, hazard; risk.—*buena v.,* fortune told by cards, etc.—*por v.,* by chance; fortunately.—**venturoso,** *a.* lucky; successful, prosperous.

ver, *vti.* & *vii.* [46] to see; to look into, examine; to look; to look at. —*¡a v.!* let's see!—*no poder v. a,* to abhor or detest (can't bear).— *no tener que v. con,* to have nothing to do with.—*v. de,* to try to.—*v. el cielo abierto,* to see a great opportunity.—*vri.* to be seen; to be conspicuous; to find oneself (in a situation), be; to meet, have an interview; to see oneself or look at oneself (in a mirror); to see each other, one another; to meet one another.—*ya se vé,* it is obvious.— *m.* sense of sight, seeing.—*a mi modo de v.,* in my opinion, to my way of thinking.

vera, *f.* edge, border.—*a la v. de,* close, by the side of.

veracidad, *f.* veracity, truthfulness.

veraneante, *mf.* summer resident or vacationer.—**veranear,** *vi.* to summer.—**veraneo,** *m.* summering, summer vacation.—**veraniego,** *a.* summer.—**verano,** *m.* summer.

veras, *f. pl.* reality, truth.—*de v.,* really, in truth, in earnest.—**veraz,** *a.* veracious, truthful.

verbal, *a.* verbal; oral.

verbena, *f.* (bot.) verbena, vervain; night carnival (on a saint's day eve).

verbigracia, *adv.* for example, for instance.

verbo, *m.* verb.—*el Verbo,* the Word, second person of the Trinity.

verdad, *f.* truth, verity.—*a decir v.,* to tell the truth; in reality, in fact. —*a la v.,* truly, really, in truth.— *bien es v. que,* it is true that.—*decir cuatro verdades,* to speak one's mind freely.—*de v.* or *a la v.,* in earnest; real.—*en v.,* truly, really.—*¿no es v.?* isn't it? isn't that so?—*ser v.,* to be true.—*¿v.?* isn't it? isn't that so? is that so?—**verdadero,** *a.* true; real, actual; truthful.

verde, *a.* green; verdant; unripe; young, blooming; unseasoned (wood); off-color.—*están verdes, sour grapes.*—*m.* green (color); verdure; vert.—**verdear,** *vi.* to grow green; to look green.—**verdín,** *m.* mildew; verdigris.—**verdinegro,** *a.* dark green.—**verdor,** *m.* greenness; verdure, verdancy.—**verdoso,** *a.* greenish.

verdugo, *m.* executioner; shoot of a tree; lash, scourge; wale, welt; torturer, very cruel person.—**verdugón,** *m.* large wale or welt.

verdulera, *f.* market woman; (coll.) coarse, low woman.—**verdura,** *f.* verdure, verdancy; greenness.—*pl.* greens, vegetables.—**verdusco,** *a.* dark greenish.

vereda, *f.* path, trail; (Am.) sidewalk.

veredicto, *m.* verdict.

vergel, *f.* flower garden.

vergonzoso, *a.* bashful, shy; shameful, disgraceful.—**vergüenza,** *f.* shame; bashfulness, shyness; modesty; disgrace.—*pl.* private parts. —*tener v.,* to be ashamed; to be shy; to have shame.

vericueto, *m.* rough and pathless place.

verídico, *a.* truthful.—**verificación,** *f.* verification, confirmation.—**verificar,** *vti.* [d] to verify, confirm; to test, adjust (an instrument); to fulfil, accomplish, carry out.—*vri.* to be verified; to take place, occur.

verja, *f.* grate, grating; iron railing.

vernáculo, *a.* vernacular, native.

verosímil, *a.* credible, probable; true to life.—**verosimilitud,** *f.* verisimilitude, probability.

verraco, *m.* male hog or boar.

verruga, *f.* wart.

versado, *a.* versed, conversant.— **versar,** *vi.*—*v. acerca de* or *sobre,* to treat of, deal with.—*vr.* to become versed or conversant.

versátil, *a.* changeable, fickle, shifty. —**versatilidad,** *f.* versatility.

versículo, *m.* (eccl.) versicle.

versificación, *f.* versification.—**versificador,** *n.* versifier, verse maker.— **versificar,** *vti. & vii.* [d] to versify.

versión, *f.* version; translation.

verso, *m.* line (of poetry).—*pl.* poems.

vértebra, *f.* (anat.) vertebra.—**vertebrado,** *n. & a.* vertebrate.

vertedero, *m.* sink, dumping place; small dam; spillway.—**verter,** *vti.* [18] to pour, spill, shed, cast; to empty; to dump; to translate; to construe, interpret.—*vii.* to run, flow.

vertical, *a.* vertical.—*f.* vertical line. —**verticalidad,** *f.* verticality.

vértice, *m.* vertex; apex, top.

vertiente, *f.* watershed; slope.

vertiginoso, *a.* giddy.—**vértigo,** *m.* giddiness, dizziness, vertigo.

vesania, *f.* insanity.—**vesánico,** *a.* mentally deranged.

vesícula, *f.* blister, vesicle.—*v. biliar,* gall bladder.

vespertino, *a.* evening.—*m.* evening paper.

vestíbulo, *m.* vestibule, hall, lobby.

vestido, *m.* dress; apparel, clothing.— **vestidura,** *f.* vesture.—*pl.* (eccl.) vestments.

vestigio, *m.* vestige, trace; relic.— *pl.* remains.

vestimenta, *f.* clothes, garments.— **vestir,** *vti.* [29] to clothe, dress; to deck, adorn; to don, put on; to wear; to cover.—*vii.* to dress; to be dressy.—*vri.* to dress oneself; to be covered; to be clothed.—**vestuario,** *m.* apparel, wardrobe, clothes, clothing, dress; (eccl.) vestry; (theat.) wardrobe, dressing room.

veta, *f.* (min.) vein; grain (in wood).

vetar, *vt.* to veto.

veteado, *a.* striped, veined, grained, mottled.—**vetear,** *vt.* to grain, mottle.

veterano, *a.* (mil.) veteran; having had long experience.—*n.* veteran, old hand.

veterinario, *m.* veterinarian.

veto, *m.* veto; prohibition, interdict.

vetusto, *a.* very ancient.

vez, *f.* turn, time, occasion.—*a la v.,* at a time; at the same time; at one time.—*a la v. que,* while.— *alguna v.* (in a question) ever.— *alguna que otra v.,* once in a while, occasionally.—*algunas veces,* sometimes; some times.—*a su v.,* in his (one's) turn; on his (one's) part.— *a veces,* sometimes, occasionally.— *cada v.,* each time, every time.— *cada v. más,* more and more.—*cada v. que,* every time that, whenever. —*de una v.,* all at once; at one time.—*de v. en cuando,* occasionally, from time to time.—*en v. de,* instead of.—*otra v.,* again, once more; some other time.—*pocas* or *raras veces,* seldom, rarely; only a few

times.—*tal v.*, perhaps, maybe, perchance.—*todas las veces que*, whenever, as often as.—*una que otra v.*, once in a while, a few times.—*una v. que*, since, inasmuch as; after.

vía, *f.* way, road; route; carriage track; (RR.) track, line; gauge; manner, method; duct, conduit; passage.—*en v. de*, in the process of.—*por v. de*, by way of, as.—*v. muerta*, siding.—**viable**, *a.* viable; feasible, practicable.—**viaducto**, *m.* viaduct.

viajante, *a.* traveling.—*mf.* traveler.—*m.* traveling salesman.—**viajar**, *vi.* to travel, journey.—**viaje**, *m.* journey, voyage, travel, trip.—*v. de ida y vuelta*, round trip.—**viajero**, *n.* traveler, voyager; passenger.

vianda, *f.* food, viands.—*pl.* (Am.) vegetables for a stew.

viandante, *mf.* walker, pedestrian; tramp, vagabond.

víbora, *f.* viper; (fig.) perfidious person.

vibración, *f.* vibration.—**vibrar**, *vt.* to vibrate; to brandish; to throw, dart.—*vi.* to vibrate.—**vibratorio**, *a.* vibratory.

vicepresidente, *n.* vice president.—**vicesecretario**, *n.* assistant secretary.—**vicetesorero**, *n.* assistant treasurer.

viciar, *vt.* to vitiate, spoil; to adulterate; to pervert, corrupt; to falsify; to misconstrue.—*vr.* to become corrupt.—**vicio**, *m.* vice; (bad) habit; defect; craving.—*de v.*, by habit or custom.—**vicioso**, *a.* vicious; defective; licentious.

vicisitud, *f.* vicissitude.—*pl.* ups and downs.

víctima, *f.* victim.

victoria, *f.* victory, win, triumph.—**victorioso**, *a.* victorious, triumphant.

vid, *f.* (bot.) vine, grapevine.

vida, *f.* life; living, livelihood; activity, animation.—*darse buena v.*, to live comfortably.—*de por v.*, for life, during life.—*en v.*, while living, during life.—*ganarse la v.*, to earn one's living.—*v. airada*, licentious life, gay life.—*v. mía*, dearest, darling.

vidente, *a.* seeing.—*mf.* seer, prophet.

vidriar, *vt.* to glaze (earthenware).—**vidriera**, *f.* glass window or partition; (Am.) glass case, show case, show window.—**vidriero**, *n.* glazier; glassblower; glass dealer.—**vidrio**, *m.* glass; any article made of glass.—**vidrioso**, *a.* glassy; brittle; slippery (from sleet); peevish, touchy.

viejo, *a.* old, aged; ancient, anti-

quated; stale; worn-out; old-fashioned.—*n.* old man (woman).—*v. verde*, lecherous old man; girlish old woman.

viento, *m.* wind; bracing rope; scent of dogs; vanity.—*a los cuatro vientos*, in all directions.—*beber los vientos por*, to be crazy about.

vientre, *m.* abdomen; belly; bowels; womb; pregnancy.

viernes, *m.* Friday.—*V. Santo*, Good Friday.

viga, *f.* beam, girder; rafter.—*v. maestra*, chief supporting beam.

vigencia, *f.* currency; operation (of a law); life (of a ruling body, etc.).—**vigente**, *a.* (law) in force; standing.

vigía, *f.* watchtower; watch; watching; (naut.) shoal, rock.—*m.* watchman, lookout.—**vigilancia**, *f.* vigilance, watchfulness.—**vigilante**, *a.* vigilant, watchful.—*m.* watchman.—**vigilar**, *vt.* & *vi.* to watch (over); to keep guard; to look out (for); (coll.) to tail.—**vigilia**, *f.* vigil, wakefulness; (eccl.) vigil, fast.

vigor, *m.* vigor, stamina; validity.—*en v.*, in force, in effect.—**vigorizar**, *vti.* [a] to strengthen, invigorate; to encourage.—**vigoroso**, *a.* vigorous; substantial; trenchant.

viguería, *f.* set of girders or beams; timberwork.—**vigueta**, *f.* small beam; joist; beam.

vihuela, *f.* guitar.

vil, *a.* vile, low, despicable, soulless.—**vileza**, *f.* baseness, meanness, vileness; base act or conduct.—**vilipendiar**, *vt.* to scorn, revile, vilify.—**vilipendio**, *m.* contempt; reviling.

vilo, *m.*—*en v.*, in the air; insecurely; in suspense.

villa, *f.* village; villa, country house.

villancico, *m.* Christmas carol.

villanía, *f.* meanness; villainy, villainousness; vile, base deed.—**villano**, *a.* villainous; rustic, boorish.—*n.* villain.

villorrio, *m.* small village or hamlet.

vinagre, *m.* vinegar; acidity, sourness.—**vinagrera**, *f.* vinegar cruet.—**vinajera**, *f.* (eccl.) wine vessel for the Mass.—**vinatero**, *a.* pertaining to wine.—*n.* vintner, wine merchant.

vinculación, *f.* entail; binding; grounding.—**vincular**, *vt.* to entail; to tie, bond, unite; to ground or found upon.—**vínculo**, *m.* tie, bond; entail.

vindicar, *vti.* [d] to vindicate; to avenge; to assert (as rights), defend; (law) to reclaim.

vinícola, *a.* wine-growing.—**vino**, *m.*

wine.—*v. de Jerez*, sherry wine.—
v. tinto, red table wine.
viña, *f.*, **viñedo**, *m.* vineyard.
viñeta, *f.* (print. & photog.) vignette.
violáceo, *a.* violet-colored.
violación, *f.* violation; ravishment.
—**violado**, *pp.* of VIOLAR.—*a.* violet
(color).—**violador**, *m.* violator;
rapist.—**violar**, *vt.* to violate; to
rape; to desecrate; to tarnish.—
violencia, *f.* violence; compulsion,
force; rape, outrage.—**violentar**, *vt.*
to do violence to; to break into;
to distort.—*vr.* to force oneself (to
do something distasteful); to control one's unwillingness.—**violento**,
a. violent; impulsive; irascible;
forced, unnatural; exceedingly intense or severe.
violeta, *f.* (bot.) violet.
violín, *m.* violin; violinist.—**vio-**
linista, *mf.* violinist.—**violón**, *m.*
bass viol, double bass; bass-viol
player.—*tocar el v.*, to do or say
something absurd or nonsensical; to
talk through one's hat.—**violonce-**
lista, *mf.* (violon)cellist.—**violon-**
celo, *m.* (violon)cello.
viperino, *a.* viperish.
virago, *f.* mannish woman; shrew,
harpy.
virar, *vt.* to turn, turn around, change
direction; (naut.) to tack.—**virazón**,
f. sea breeze.
virgen, *f. & a.* virgin.—**virginal**,
virgíneo, *a.* virginal, virgin.—
virginidad, *f.* virginity.—**virgo**, *m.*
(anat.) hymen; (V.) (astr.) Virgo,
Virgin; virginity.
viril, *a.* virile, manly.—**virilidad**, *f.*
virility, manhood; vigor, strength.
virreinato, **virreino**, *m.* viceroyalty.—
virrey, *m.* viceroy.
virtual, *a.* apparent; virtual; potential.
virtud, *f.* virtue; power.—**virtuoso**, *a.*
virtuous, righteous; chaste.—*a. & n.*
(mus.) virtuoso.
viruela, *f.* (med.) pock; smallpox.
virulencia, *f.* virulence.—**virulento**, *a.*
virulent.—**virus**, *m.* (med.) virus.
viruta, *f.* wood shaving.
visa, *f.*, **visado**, *m.* visa.
visaje, *m.* grimace, grin, smirk.—
hacer visajes, to make wry faces.
visar, *vt.* to issue a visa; to countersign; to O.K.
víscera, *f.* vital organ.—*pl.* viscera.—
visceral, *a.* visceral.
viscosidad, *f.* viscosity, stickiness.—
viscoso, *a.* viscous, sticky.
visera, *f.* visor of a cap or helmet;
eyeshade.
visibilidad, *f.* visibility.—**visible**, *a.*
visible; evident; conspicuous.

visillo, *m.* window curtain or shade.
—**visión**, *f.* sight; vision; fantasy;
phantom, apparition; revelation;
(coll.) grotesque person, sight.—
visionario, *a. & n.* visionary.
visita, *f.* visit; call; visitor(s); visi-
tation, inspection.—*pagar una v.*, to
return or make a call.—*v. de cum-*
plido or *de cumplimiento*, formal
call.—**visitante**, *mf.* visitor; inspector.—**visitar**, *vt.* to visit; to call
on; to inspect, search, examine.—
vr. to visit one another, call on one
another.—**visiteo**, *m.* frequent visit-
ing or calling.
vislumbrar, *vt.* to glimpse, have a
glimmer of; to see imperfectly at
a distance; to know imperfectly;
to suspect, surmise.—**vislumbre**, *f.*
glimpse, glimmer; glimmering; conjecture, surmise; appearance, semblance.
viso, *m.* gloss, sheen (of fabric);
glass curtain; lady's slip.—*pl.*
aspect, appearance.
visón, *m.* mink.
víspera, *f.* eve, day before; forerunner; time just before.—*pl.*
vespers.
vista, *f.* sight, seeing, vision; view,
vista; eye, eyesight; glance, look;
aspect, looks; (law) trial.—*a la v.*,
at sight; in sight; before one's
eyes.—*a la v. de*, in the presence
of.—*a simple v.*, at first sight; with
the naked eye.—*estar a la v.*, to be
obvious.—*hacer la v. gorda*, to wink
at, overlook.—*hasta la v.*, good-by.
—*perder de v.*, to lose sight of.—
tener v. a, to face, look out on.—
v. cansada, farsightedness.—*m.* customs officer.—**vistazo**, *m.* glance.—
dar un v. a, to glance at, to look
over.—**visto**, *pp.* of VER.—*a.* obvious,
evident, clear; (law) whereas.—
bien v., proper or approved, good
form.—*mal v.*, improper or disap-
proved, bad form.—*v. bueno*
(*Vº.Bº.*), correct, approved, O.K.—*v.*
que, considering that, since.—**vistoso**,
a. showy; beautiful; flaring, loud.—
visual, *a.* visual; of sight.—*f.* line
of sight.
vital, *a.* vital; essential, necessary.—
vitalicio, *a.* lasting for life; during
life.—**vitalidad**, *f.* vitality.
vitamina, *f.* vitamin.
vitela, *f.* vellum, parchment.
vítor, *m.* cheer, applause.—*interj.*
hurrah!—**vitorear**, *vt.* to cheer,
acclaim.
vítreo, *a.* vitreous, glassy.—**vitrina**, *f.*
show case; (Am.) show window.
vitriolo, *m.* vitriol.

vituallas, *f. pl.* victuals, provisions, food.

viuda, *f.* widow.—**viudez,** *f.* widowhood.—**viudo,** *m.* widower.

vivac, vivaque, *m.* (mil.) bivouac; (Am.) police headquarters.

vivacidad, *f.* vivacity, liveliness; brilliance.—**vivaracho,** *a.* lively, frisky.—**vivaz,** *a.* lively, active; ingenious, bright, witty.

víveres, *m. pl.* provisions, foodstuffs.

vivero, *m.* hatchery; (bot.) nursery.

viveza, *f.* liveliness; vivacity; quickness; witticism; perspicacity.—**vívido,** *a.* vivid, bright.—**vivienda,** *f.* dwelling; housing; domicile.—**viviente,** *a.* living.—**vivificar,** *vti.* [d] to animate, enliven.—**vivir,** *vi.* to live, be alive; to last, endure.—*vt.* to live, experience; to dwell.—*¡viva!,* hurrah! long live!—*¿quién vive?* (mil.) who goes there?—*m.* life, living, existence.—*mal v.,* riotous living.—**vivo,** *a.* alive, live; lively; intense; (of color) vivid; acute, ingenious; quick, bright, smart; lasting, enduring.—*a lo v., al v.,* vividly.—*de viva voz,* by word of mouth.—*en v.,* living, alive.—*tocar en lo v.,* to cut or hurt to the quick.—*m.* (sewing) edging, piping.

vizcaíno, *a. & n.* Biscayan, Basque.

vizconde, *m.* viscount.—**vizcondesa,** *f.* viscountess.

vocablo, *m.* word, term.—**vocabulario,** *m.* vocabulary, lexicon.

vocación, *f.* vocation, calling; occupation.

vocal, *a.* vocal, oral; (gram.) vowel.—*f.* vowel.—*mf.* voting member of a governing body.—**vocalizar,** *vii.* [a] to vocalize.

vocear, *vi.* to cry out, shout.—*vt.* to cry, publish, proclaim; to call, hail.—**vocería,** *f.,* **vocerío,** *m.* clamor, outcry, shouting.—**vocero,** *n.* spokesman (for another).—**vociferar,** *vi.* to vociferate, shout.—**vocinglero,** *a.* vociferous; prattling, chattering.—*n.* loud babbler.

volador, *a.* flying.—*m.* skyrocket.—**voladora,** *f.* flywheel of a steam engine.—**voladura,** *f.* blast, explosion; blasting.—**volante,** *a.* flying, fluttering, unsettled.—*m.* steering wheel; balance wheel; handbill, circular; ruffle, frill; escapement (of a watch).—**volar,** *vii.* [12] to fly; to flutter, hover (as insects); to run or move swiftly; to vanish, disappear; to make rapid progress; to explode, burst.—*vti.* to blow up; to blast.—**volátil,** *a.* volatile; fickle; mercurial.—**volatinero,** *n.* tightrope walker; acrobat.

volcán, *m.* volcano.—**volcánico,** *a.* volcanic.

volcar, *vti.* [12-d] to upset, overturn; to tilt.—*vri.* to overturn.

volición, *f.* volition.—**volitivo,** *a.* volitional.

volt, *m.* volt.—**voltaje,** *m.* voltage.

voltear, *vt.* to turn; to revolve; to overturn; (arch.) to arch; to vault.—*vi.* to turn; to revolve; to roll over; to tumble (as an acrobat).—*vr.* to turn over; to upset; (coll.) to change one's party or creed.—**volteo,** *m.* whirl; whirling; turn; turning; overturning; felling; tumbling.—**voltereta,** *f.* tumble, somersault.

voltio, *m.* volt.

volubilidad, *f.* volubility.—**voluble,** *a.* easily moved about; voluble; fickle; versatile.

volumen, *m.* tome; volume, size, bulk; corpulence.—**voluminoso,** *a.* voluminous; bulky.

voluntad, *f.* will; goodwill, benevolence; desire; disposition; consent.—*a v.,* optional, at will.—*de (buena) v.,* with pleasure, willingly.—*de mala v.,* unwillingly.—**voluntariedad,** *f.* voluntariness; willfulness.—**voluntario,** *a. & n.* voluntary; volunteer.—**voluntarioso,** *a.* willful, self-willed.

voluta, *f.* (arch.) volute; spiral.

volver, *vti.* [47] to turn; to turn up, over, upside down, inside out; to return; to repay; to give back, restore; to send back.—*v. loco,* to drive crazy.—*vii.* to return, come, or go back; to come again; to turn (to the right, etc.).—*v. a cantar,* to sing again.—*v. atrás,* to come, or go, back.—*v. en sí,* to recover consciousness, come to.—*v. por,* to stand up for, to defend.—*vri.* to turn, become; to turn about, turn around; to change one's views.—*v. atrás,* to flinch; to back out.—*v. loco,* to lose one's mind.

vomitar, *vt.* to vomit, puke.—**vomitivo,** *m. & a.* emetic.—**vómito,** *m.* vomiting; vomit.

vorágine, *f.* vortex, whirlpool.

voraz, *a.* voracious, greedy; fierce (as fire).

vórtice, *m.* vortex, whirlpool, whirlwind; center of a cyclone.

vosotros, *pron. pl.* (*f.* **vosotras**) (fam.) you.

votación, *f.* voting, vote, balloting.—**votar,** *vi. & vt.* to vote; to vow.—*¡voto a tal!* goodness!—**voto,** *m.* vote; vow; votive offering; oath, curse.—*hacer votos por,* to pray for; to wish.

voz, *f.* voice; sound; clamor, outcry;

word, term; rumor, report.—*a media v.*, in a whisper.—*a una v.*, unanimously.—*a v. en cuello*, at the top of one's voice.—*a voces*, clamorously.—*correr la v.*, to be said, to be rumored; to spread the rumor.—*dar voces*, to scream, shout. —*secreto a voces*, open secret.—*ser v. común*, to be a common rumor.

vuelco, *m.* tumble, overturning, upset.

vuelo, *m.* flight; flying; sweep, space flown through; fullness of clothes; ruffle or frill; (arch.) projection, jut.—*al v.*, on the fly; quickly, in a moment; in passing.—*alzar or levantar v.*, to fly; to take off, depart.—*tomar v.*, to progress; to grow.

vuelta, *f.* turn; revolution (of a wheel, etc.); turning; return; reverse side; returning, giving back; (money) change; stroll, walk.—*a la v.*, on returning; round the corner; (turn) over (the page); (bookkeeping) carried over, carried forward. —*a la v. de*, within (time).— *dar la v. a*, to turn; to go around. —*dar una v.*, to take a stroll.—*dar vueltas*, to turn; to walk to and fro; to fuss about; to hang around. —*de la v.*, brought forward.—*de v.*, on returning.—*estar de v.*, to be back; to be knowing.—*no tener v. de hoja*, to be self-evident.—*poner de v. y media*, (coll.) to give a dressing down, or a going over, to. —**vuelto,** *ppi.* of VOLVER.—*m.* (Am.) (money) change.

vuestro, *pron. & a.* (coll.) your, yours.

vulcanización, *f.* vulcanization; mending (a tire, etc.).—**vulcanizar,** *vti.* [a] to vulcanize; to mend (a tire, etc.).

vulgar, *a.* vulgar, coarse; common, in general use.—**vulgaridad,** *f.* vulgarity; triteness.—**vulgarización,** *f.* vulgarization.—**vulgarizar,** *vti.* [a] to vulgarize, popularize.—*vri.* to become vulgar.—**vulgo,** *m.* common people; populace.

vulnerable, *a.* vulnerable.—**vulnerar,** *vt.* to harm, injure, damage.

X

xilófono, *m.* xylophone.

Y

y, *conj.* and.—*¡y bien? ¡y qué?* and then? so what?

ya, *adv.* already; now; at once; presently; in time; once, formerly. —*interj.* oh yes! I see.—*ya lo creo,*

naturally, of course.—*ya no*, no longer.— *ya que*, since, seeing that. —*ya se ve*, yes, indeed! it is clear, it is so.

yacaré, *m.* (Am.) alligator.

yacer, *vii.* [48] to lie in the grave; to lie, be located; to be lying down.— **yacimiento,** *m.* (geol.) bed; deposit, field.

yanqui, *n. & a.* American (of U.S.).

yarda, *f.* yard (measure).

yatagán, *m.* saber dagger.

yate, *m.* yacht.

yedra, *f.* = HIEDRA.

yegua, *f.* mare.—**yeguada,** *f.* herd of mares.

yelmo, *m.* helm, helmet.

yema, *f.* yolk (of an egg); bud; candied egg yolk; heart, center.— *dar en la y.*, to hit the nail on the head.—*y. del dedo*, fleshy tip of the finger.

yerba, *f.* = HIERBA.—**yerbabuena,** *f.* = HIERBABUENA.

yermo, *a.* barren, sterile.—*m.* wasteland, desert.

yerno, *m.* son-in-law.

yerro, *m.* error, mistake; fault.

yerto, *a.* stiff, motionless; rigid, tight.

yesca, *f.* tinder, touchwood, (fig.) fuel, incentive.—*pl.* tinderbox.

yeso, *m.* gypsum; plaster; plaster cast; chalk.

yo, *pron.* I.—*y. mismo*, I myself.— *m.* ego.

yodado, *a.* iodic.—**yodo,** *m.* iodine.

yugo, *m.* yoke; marriage tie.—*sacudir el y.*, to throw off the yoke.

yuguero, *m.* plowman.

yugular, *a.* jugular.

yunque, *m.* anvil; (anat.) incus.

yunta, *f.* couple, pair, yoke of draft animals.

yute, *m.* jute (fiber).

yuxtaponer, *vti.* [32-49] to juxtapose; to place next to each other.— **yuxtaposición,** *f.* juxtaposition.— **yuxtapuesto,** *ppi.* of YUXTAPONER.

Z

zafarrancho, *m.* turmoil, confusion.— *z. de combate*, (naut.) clearing for battle.

zafio, *a.* coarse, uncivil, ignorant, uncouth.

zafir(o), *m.* sapphire.

zafra, *f.* sugar crop; sugar making; sugar-making season.

zaga, *f.* rear, back.—*a la z. or en z.*, behind.—*no ir en z. a*, to be equal to.

zagal, *m.* shepherd boy; country lad. —**zagala,** *f.* shepherdess; lass,

maiden.—**zagalón**, *n.* overgrown boy or girl.

zaguán, *m.* entrance hall, vestibule.

zaguero, *a.* laggard, loitering.—*m.* back-stop (at the game of pelota).

zaherir, *vti.* [39] to censure, blame, reproach, upbraid.

zahorí, *mf.* seer, clairvoyant.

zahurda, *f.* pigsty, hogsty.

zaino, *a.* chestnut-colored (horse); vicious (animal); treacherous, wicked.

zalamería, *f.* flattery, wheedling.—**zalamero**, *n.* flatterer.—*a.* flattering.—**zalema**, *f.* bow, curtsy.—*pl.* flattery.

zamarra, *f.* sheepskin jacket.

zambo, *a.* knock-kneed; half-breed (Indian and Negro).

zambullida, *f.* dive, plunge.—**zambullir**, *vti.* [27] to plunge, immerse; to give a ducking to.—*vri.* to plunge, dip, dive.

zambullo, *m.* chamber pot; toilet.

zampar, *vt.* to stuff away; to conceal hurriedly; to devour eagerly.—*vr.* to rush in; to thrust oneself in or into; to scoff; to devour.

zanahoria, *f.* (bot.) carrot.

zanca, *f.* long shank or leg; large pin.—**zancada**, *f.* long stride.—**zancadilla**, *f.* sudden catch to trip one; trick, deceit.—**zancajear**, *vi.* & *vt.* to run, rush about.—**zanco**, *m.* stilt.—**zancudo**, *a.* long-legged. —*m.* (Am.) mosquito.

zanfona, *f.* hurdy-gurdy.

zanganada, *f.* impertinence.—**zanganear**, *vi.* to idle.—**zángano**, *m.* drone; (coll.) idler, sponger; (Am.) rascal; wag.

zangolotear, *vi.* (coll.) to shake violently; to fuss, fidget.—*vr.* to rattle, swing or slam.—**zangoloteo**, *m.* fuss, bustle; swinging, rattling.

zanguango, *a.* (coll.) lazy, sluggish; silly.—*m.* dunce, fool.—*f.* (coll.) feigned illness, malingering; wheedling, fawning.

zanja, *f.* ditch, trench.—**zanjar**, *vt.* to cut ditches in; to excavate; to settle amicably; to obviate, surmount.—**zanjón**, *m.* deep ditch; large drain.

zapa, *f.* spade; (fort.) sap.—**zapador**, *m.* mining engineer; miner.—**zapapico**, *m.* pickaxe.—**zapar**, *vt.* (fort.) to sap, mine; (fig.) to undermine.

zapateado, *m.* tap dance.—**zapatear**, *vt.* to strike with the shoe.—*vi.* to tap-dance.—**zapatería**, *f.* trade of shoemaker; shoemaker's shop.—**zapatero**, *m.* shoemaker; shoe dealer.—**zapateta**, *f.* caper, leap.—

zapatilla, *f.* slipper, pump.—**zapato**, *m.* shoe.

zafado, *a.* (Am.) brazen, shameless; (Am.) alert, wide-awake; (Am.) crazy, crackbrained.—**zafar**, *vt.* to loosen, untie.—*vr.* to loosen oneself or itself; to run away; to keep out of the way; to dodge; to slip away. —*z. de*, to get rid of; to avoid.

zaquizamí, *m.* garret; small wretched room.

zarabanda, *f.* saraband; bustle, noise.

zaragata, *f.* turmoil; scuffle, quarrel.

zaranda, *f.* sieve, sifter.

zarandajas, *f. pl.* trifles, odds and ends.

zarandear, *vt.* to winnow; to sift; to shake (coll.) to stir and move nimbly.—*vr.* to be in motion; to move to and fro; to stalk, strut.—**zarandeo**, *m.* sifting or winnowing; shaking; stalking, strut.

zarcillo, *m.* eardrop.

zarco, *a.* light blue (of eyes).

zarpa, *f.* claw, paw of an animal.—*echar la z.*, to grasp, grip.—**zarpar**, *vi.* (naut.) to weigh anchor; to sail. —**zarpazo**, *m.* blow with a paw; bang, thud, whack.

zarrapastroso, *a.* ragged, slovenly, shabby.—*n.* ragamuffin.

zarza, *f.* bramble; blackberry bush.—**zarzal**, *m.* bramble thicket.—**zarzamora**, *f.* blackberry.—**zarzaparrilla**, *f.* sarsaparilla.

zarzuela, *f.* Spanish musical comedy.

zascandil, *m.* (coll.) busybody.

zinc, *m.* zinc.

zipizape, *m.* (coll.) row, rumpus, scuffle.

zócalo, *m.* base of a pedestal; baseboard.

zocato, *a.* (of fruits) overripe.

zoco, *m.* market; market place.

zodíaco, *m.* zodiac.

zoilo, *m.* malicious critic.

zona, *f.* zone, belt; district, area, region.

zonzo, *a.* dull.—*n.* (Am.) simpleton, dunce.

zoología, *f.* zoology.—**zoológico**, *a.* zoologic(al).

zopenco, *a.* (coll.) doltish, dull.—*n.* dolt, blockhead, fool.

zopilote, *m.* (Am.) buzzard.

zoquetada, *f.* foolishness, foolish words or acts.—**zoquete**, *m.* (carp.) chump, chunk; bit of stale bread; (coll.) dolt, dunce; (Am.) slap.

zorra, *f.* (zool.) fox; foxy person; truck.—**zorro**, *a.* cunning, foxy.—*n.* fox; foxy person.

zorzal, *m.* (ornith.) thrush.

zote, *a.* dull and ignorant.—*m.* dolt.

zozobra, *f.* worry, anxiety; (naut.) foundering, sinking.—**zozobrar,** *vi.* (naut.) to sink. founder; to capsize; to be in great danger.

zueco, *m.* sabot, wooden soled shoe.

zumba, *f.* mule bell; banter, raillery; sarcasm.—**zumbar,** *vi.* to buzz, hum; to whiz; (of the ears) to ring.—**zumbido,** *m.* humming, buzzing, whiz; ringing in the ears.—**zumbón,** *a.* waggish; sarcastic.—*n.* wag, joker.

zumo, *m.* sap, juice.

zuncho, *m.* metal band or hoop.

zurcido, *m.* (sewing) darning.—**zurcir,** *vti.* [a] to darn, mend; (coll.) to concoct (lies).

zurdo, *a.* left-handed.—*n.* left-handed person.

zurra, *f.* beating, thrashing.—**zurrar,** *vt.* to thrash, flog.

zurrapa, *f.* sediment, dregs; rubbish, trash.

zurrón, *m.* shepherd's pouch; game bag; leather bag.

Zutano, *n.* (coll.) Mr. So-and-So.—*Fulano, Z. y Mengano,* Tom, Dick and Harry.

GEOGRAPHICAL NAMES THAT DIFFER IN ENGLISH AND SPANISH

A
Abisinia, Abyssinia.
Adriático, Adriatic.
Afganistán, Afghanistan.
Alejandría, Alexandria.
Alemania, Germany.
Alpes, Alps.
Alsacia y Lorena, Alsace-Lorraine.
Alto Volta, Upper Volta.
Amazonas, Amazon.
Amberes, Antwerp.
América del Norte, North America.
América del Sur, South America.
América Española, Spanish America.
América Meridional, South America.
Andalucía, Andalusia.
Antillas, Antilles, West Indies.
Apeninos, Apennines.
Arabia Saudita, Saudi Arabia.
Aragón, Arragon.
Argel, Algiers.
Argelia, Algeria.
Argentina, Argentine.
Asia Menor, Asia Minor.
Asiria, Assyria.
Atenas, Athens.
Atlántico, Atlantic.

B
Babilonia, Babylon.
Baja California, Lower California.
Báltico, Baltic.
Basilea, Basel.
Baviera, Bavaria.
Belén, Bethlehem.
Bélgica, Belgium.
Belgrado, Belgrade.
Belice, Beliza, Belize; British Honduras.
Berbería, Barbary.
Berlín, Berlin.
Berna, Bern.
Birmania, Burma.
Bizancio, Byzantium.
Bolonia, Bologna.
Bona, Bonn.
Borgoña, Burgundy.
Bósforo, Bosporus.
Brasil, Brazil.
Bretaña, Bretagne, Brittany.

Bruselas, Brussels.
Bucarest, Bucharest.
Burdeos, Bordeaux.

C
Cabo de Buena Esperanza, Cape of Good Hope.
Cabo de Hornos, Cape Horn.
Cachemira, Kashmir.
Calcuta, Calcutta.
Caldea, Chaldea.
Cambrige, Cambridge.
Camerón, Cameroons.
Canadá, Canada.
Canal de la Mancha, English Channel.
Canarias, Canary (Islands).
Caribe, Caribbean.
Carolina del Norte, North Carolina.
Carolina del Sur, South Carolina.
Cartagena, Carthagena.
Cartago, Carthage.
Caspio, Caspian (Sea).
Castilla (la Nueva, la Vieja), Castile (New C., Old C.).
Cataluña, Catalonia.
Cáucaso, Caucasus.
Cayena, Cayenne.
Cayo Hueso, Key West.
Ceilán, Ceylon.
Cerdeña, Sardinia.
Colonia, Cologne.
Columbia Británica, British Columbia.
Constantinopla, Constantinople.
Copen(h)ague, Copenhagen.
Córcega, Corsica.
Córdoba, Cordova.
Corea, Korea.
Corinto, Corinth.
Costa del Marfil, Ivory Coast.
Costa de Oro, Gold Coast.
Creta, Crete.
Croacia, Croatia.
Curasao, Curazao, Curaçao.

CH
Champaña, Champagne.

Checoslovaquia, Czechoslovakia.
Chile, Chili, Chile.
Chipre, Cyprus.

D
Dakota del Norte, North Dakota.
Dakota del Sur, South Dakota.
Dalmacia, Dalmatia.
Damasco, Damascus.
Danubio, Danube.
Dardanelos, Dardanelles.
Delfos, Delphi.
Dinamarca, Denmark.
Dresde, Dresden.
Duero (Río), Douro (River).
Dunquerque, Dunkirk.
Duvres, Dover.

E
Edimburgo, Edinburgh.
Egeo, Ægean.
Egipto, Egypt.
Elba, Elbe.
Escandinavia, Scandinavia.
Escocia, Scotland.
Escorial, Escurial.
Eslavonia, Slavonia.
Eslovaquia, Slovakia.
Eslovenia, Slovenia.
Esmirna, Izmir, Smyrna.
España, Spain.
Española, Hispaniola; Santo Domingo, Haiti.
Esparta, Sparta.
Espoleto, Spoleto.
Estados Federados de Malaya, Malay Federated States.
Estados Unidos de América, United States of America.
Estambul, Istanbul.
Estocolmo, Stockholm.
Estonia, Esthonia.
Estrasburgo, Strasbourg.
Estrecho de Magallanes, Strait of Magellan.
Etiopía, Ethiopia.
Eufrates, Euphrates.
Europa, Europe.

F
Fenicia, Phoenicia.
Filadelfia, Philadelphia.
Filipinas, Philippines.

237

Finlandia, Finland.
Flandes, Flanders.
Florencia, Florence.
Francfort del Mein, Frankfort-on-the-Main.
Francia, France.

G

Gales, Wales.
Galia, Gaul.
Galilea, Galilee.
Gante, Ghent.
Gascuña, Gascony.
Génova, Genoa.
Ginebra, Geneva.
Golfo Pérsico, Persian Gulf.
Gran Bretaña, Great Britain.
Grecia, Greece.
Groenlandia, Greenland.
Guadalupe, Guadeloupe.
Guaján, Guam, Guam.
Guayana, Guiana.

H

Habana, Havana.
Haití, Haiti.
Hamburgo, Hamburg.
Hauai, Hawai, Hawaii.
Haya (La), Hague.
Hébridas, Hebrides.
Hispano-América, Hispanoamérica, Spanish America.
Holanda, Holland.
Honduras Británicas, British Honduras.
Hungría, Hungary.

I

Indias (Occidentales, Orientales), Indies (West I., East I.).
Indostán, Hindustan, India.
Inglaterra, England.
Irlanda, Ireland.
Isla de San Salvador, Watling Island.
Islandia, Iceland.
Islas Baleares, Balearic Islands.
Islas Británicas, British Isles.
Islas Filipinas, Philippine Islands.
Islas Vírgenes, Virgin Islands.
Italia, Italy.

J

Japón, Japan.
Jericó, Jericho.
Jerusalén, Jerusalem.
Jonia, Ionia.
Jutlandia, Jutland.

K

Kartum, Khartoum.
Kenia, Kenya.
Kurdistán, Kurdistan.

L

Laponia, Lapland.
Lasa, Lhasa.
Lausana, Lausanne.
Leningrado, Leningrad.
Letonia, Latvia.
Líbano, Lebanon.
Libia, Libya.
Lieja, Liége.
Liorna, Leghorn.
Lisboa, Lisbon.
Lituania, Lithuania.
Lombardía, Lombardy.
Londres, London.
Lorena, Lorraine.
Lucerna, Lucerne.
Luisiana, Louisiana.
Luxemburgo, Luxemburg.

M

Madera, Madeira.
Malaca, Malay.
Mallorca, Majorca.
Mar de las Indias, Indian Ocean.
Mar del Norte, North Sea.
Mar Muerto, Dead Sea.
Mar Negro, Black Sea.
Mar Rojo, Red Sea.
Marañón, (upper reaches of the) Amazon.
Marruecos, Morocco.
Marsella, Marseilles.
Martinica, Martinique.
Meca, Mecca.
Mediterráneo, Mediterranian.
Méjico, Mexico.
Menfis, Memphis.
Menorca, Minorca.
Misisipí, Mississippi.
Misuri, Missouri.
Mobila, Mobile.
Mompeller, Montpellier.
Montañas Rocosas (o Rocallosas), Rocky Mountains.
Montes Apalaches, Appalachian Mountains.
Moscú, Moscow.
Mosela, Moselle.

N

Nápoles, Naples.
Navarra, Navarre.
Nazaret, Nazareth.
Niasalandia, Nyasaland, Nile.
Nilo, Nile.
Niza, Nice.
Normandía, Normandy.
Noruega, Norway.
Nueva Escocia, Nova Scotia.
Nueva Gales del Sur, New South Wales.
Nueva Inglaterra, New England.
Nueva Orleáns, New Orleans.
Nueva York, New York.
Nueva Zelandia, New Zealand.

Nuevo Brúnswick (Brúnsvick), New Brunswick.
Nuevo México (or Méjico), New Mexico.
Nuremberg, Nuremberg.

O

Oceanía, Oceania, Oceanica.
Océano Índico, Indian Ocean.
Olimpo, Olympus.
Omán, Masqat.
Ostende, Ostend.

P

Pacífico, Pacific.
Países Bajos, Low Countries, Netherlands.
Palestina, Palestine.
Panamá, Panama.
París, Paris.
Parnaso, Parnassus.
Paso de Calais, English Channel.
Pekín, Peking.
Peloponeso, Peloponnesus.
Pensilvania, Pennsylvania.
Perú, Peru.
Pirineos, Pyrenees.
Polinesia, Polynesia.
Polonia, Poland.
Pompeya, Pompeii.
Praga, Prague.
Provenza, Provence.
Providencia, Providence.
Provincias Vascas (or Vascongadas), Basque Provinces.
Prusia, Prussia.
Puerto (de) España, Port of Spain.
Puerto Príncipe, Port-au-Prince.
Puerto Rico, Porto Rico, Puerto Rico.

R

Reino Unido, United Kingdom.
Renania, Rhineland.
Rhin, Rin, Rhine.
Rocallosas, Rocosas, Rocky (Mountains).
Ródano, Rhone.
Rodas, Rhodes.
Rodesia, Rhodesia.
Roma, Rome.
Ruán, Rouen.
Rusia, Russia.

S

Saboya, Savoy.
Sajonia, Saxony.
Sena, Seine.
Servia, Serbia.
Seúl, Seoul.
Sevilla, Seville.
Sicilia, Sicily.
Sierra Leona, Sierra Leone.

Sión, Zion.
Siracusa, Syracuse.
Siria, Syria.
Somalia, Somaliland.
Sud-África, Sudáfrica, South Africa.
Sud-América, Sudamérica, South America.
Sudán, Sudan.
Suecia, Sweden.
Suiza, Switzerland.
Sur-América, Suramérica, South America.

T

Tabago, Tobago.
Tahití, Tahiti.
Tajo, Tagus.
Támesis, Thames.
Tanganica, Tanganyika.
Tánger, Tangier.
Tebas, Thebes.
Tejas, Texas.
Terranova, Newfoundland.

Thailandia, Thailand.
Tierra del Labrador, Labrador.
Tierra Santa, Holy Land.
Tirol, Tyrol.
Tokío, Tokyo.
Tolosa, Toulouse.
Toscana, Tuscany.
Tracia, Thrace.
Trento, Trent.
Troya, Troy.
Túnez, Tunis (City), Tunisia (Country).
Turquestán, Turkestan.
Turquía, Turkey.

U

Ucrania, Ukraine.
Unión Soviética, Soviet Union.
Unión Sudafricana, Union of South Africa.
URSS (Unión de Re-

públicas Socialistas Soviéticas), USSR (Union of Soviet Socialist Republics).

V

Varsovia, Warsaw.
Venecia, Venice.
Versalles, Versailles.
Vesuvio, Vesuvius.
Viena, Vienna.
Virginia Occidental, West Virginia.
Vizcaya, Biscay.

Y

Yugoeslavia, Yugoslavia, Jugoslavia.

Z

Zanzíbar, Zanzibar.
Zaragoza, Saragossa.
Zelandia, Zealand.
Zululandia, Zululand.

PROPER NAMES OF PERSONS, INCLUDING THOSE OF HISTORICAL, LITERARY, AND MYTHOLOGICAL PERSONAGES

(Only those which differ in English and Spanish are included)

A

Abelardo, Abelard.
Abrahán, Abraham.
Adán, Adam.
Adela, Adele.
Adelaida, Adelaide.
Adolfo, Adolf, Adolph.
Adriano, Hadrian.
Ágata, Agueda, Agatha.
Agustín, Augustine.
Alano, Allan, Allen.
Alberto, Albert.
Alejandro, Alexander.
Alfonso, Alphonso.
Alfredo, Alfred.
Alicia, Alice.
Alonso, Alphonso.
Ana, Ann(e), Anna, Hannah.
Andrés, Andrew.
Ángel, Angel.
Aníbal, Hannibal.
Antonio, Anthony.
Aquiles, Achilles.
Aristófanes, Aristophanes.
Aristóteles, Aristotle.
Arminio, Herman.
Arnaldo, Arnold.
Arquímedes, Archimedes.
Arturo, Arthur.

Atila, Attila.
Augusto, Augustus.

B

Baco, Bacchus.
Bartolomé, Bartholomew.
Basilio, Basil.
Beatricz, Beatrice.
Benita, Benedicta.
Benito, Benedicto.
Benjamín, Benjamin.
Bernardo, Bernard.
Berta, Bertha.
Bibiana, Vivian.
Bruto, Brutus.
Buda, Buddha.
Buenaventura, Bonaventura.

C

Calvino, Calvin.
Camila, Camille.
Camilo, Camillus.
Carlomagno, Charlemagne.
Carlos, Charles.
Carlota, Charlotte.
Carolina, Caroline, Carolyn.
Casandra, Cassandra.

Catalina, Catharine, Catherine, Katharine Katherine.
Catón, Cato.
Catulo, Catullus.
Cecilia, Cecile.
Cenón, Zeno.
César, Caesar.
Cicerón, Cicero.
Ciro, Cyrus.
Claudio, Claude.
Clemente, Clement.
Clodoveo, Clovis.
Colón, Columbus.
Confucio, Confucius.
Constancia, Constance
Constantino, Constantine.
Constanza, Constance.
Cristina, Christine.
Cristo, Christ.
Cristóbal, Christopher.

D

Dalila, Delilah.
Demóstenes, Demosthenes.
Diego, James.
Diógenes, Diogenes.
Dionisio, Dennis, Dionysius.

239

Domingo, Dominic.
Dorotea, Dorothy.

E

Edita, Edith.
Edmundo, Edmund.
Eduardo, Edward.
Elena, Ellen, Helen.
Elisa, Eliza.
Eloísa, Eloise.
Ema, Emma.
Emilia, Emily.
Emilio, Emil.
Eneas, Æneas.
Engracia, Grace.
Enrique, Henry.
Enriqueta, Henrietta.
Epicuro, Epicurus.
Erasmo, Erasmus.
Ernestina, Ernestine.
Ernesto, Ernest.
Escipión, Scipio.
Esopo, Æsop.
Esquilo, Æschylus.
Esteban, Stephen,
  Steven.
Ester, Esther, Hester.
Estrabón, Strabo.
Estradivario, Stradiva-
  rius.
Euclides, Euclid.
Eugenia, Eugénie.
Eugenio, Eugene.
Eva, Eve.
Ezequías, Hezekiah.
Ezequiel, Ezekiel.

F

Federica, Frederica.
Federico, Frederick.
Fedra, Phaedra.
Felicia, Felicia.
Felipa, Philippa.
Felipe, Filipo (de Mace-
  donia), Philip.
Felisa, Felicia.
Fernando, Ferdinand.
Florencia, Florence.
Francisca, Frances.
Francisco, Francis.

G

Galeno, Galen.
Gaspar, Jasper.
Geofredo, Jeffrey, Geof-
  frey.
Gerarda, Geraldine.
Gerardo, Gerard, Gerald.
Gerónimo, Jerome.
Gertrudis, Gertrude.
Gilberto, Gilbert.
Godofredo, Godfrey.
Graco, Gracchus.
Gregorio, Gregory.
Gualterio, Walter.
Guillermina, Wilhelmina.
Guillermo, William.
Gustavo, Gustave, Gus-
  tavus.

H

Haroldo, Harold.
Heriberto, Herbert.
Herodes, Herod.

Herodoto, Herodotus.
Hipócrates, Hippocrates.
Hipólito, Hippolytus.
Homero, Homer.
Horacio, Horace, Hora-
  tio.
Hortensia, Hortense.
Huberto, Hubert.
Humberto, Humbert.
Hunfredo, Humphrey.

I

Ignacio, Ignatius.
Ildefonso, Alphonso.
Inés, Inez, Agnes.
Inocencio, Innocent.
Isabel, Isabella, Eliza-
  beth.
Isidoro, Isidro, Isidor(e).

J

Jacobo, Jaime, James.
Javier, Xavier.
Jehová, Jehovah.
Jenofonte, Xenophon.
Jerjes, Xerxes.
Jerónimo, Jerome.
Jesucristo, Jesus Christ.
Joaquín, Joachim.
Jonás, Jonah.
Jonatán, Jonatás, Jona-
  than.
Jorge, George.
José, Joseph.
Josefa, Josefina, Jose-
  phine.
Juan, John.
Juana, Jane, Joan.
Juana de Arco, Joan of
  Arc.
Judit, Judith.
Julia, Juliet.
Julián, Juliano (el Em-
  perador), Julian.
Julieta, Juliet.
Julio, Julius.
Justiniano, Justinian.

L

Lázaro, Lazarus.
Leandro, Leander.
Lenora, Lenore, Leonora.
León, Leo, Leon.
Leonardo, Leonard.
Leonor, Eleanor, Elinor.
Leopoldo, Leopold.
Licurgo, Lycurgus.
Livio, Livy.
Lorenzo, Laurence, Law-
  rence.
Lucano, Lucan.
Lucas, Luke.
Lucía, Lucy.
Luciano, Lucian.
Lucrecia, Lucretia.
Lucrecio, Lucretius.
Luis, Lewis, Louis,
  Aloysius.
Luisa, Louise.
Lutero, Luther.

M

Magallanes, Magellan.
Magdalena, Magdalen.

Mahoma, Mohammed,
  Mahomet.
Manuel, Em(m)anuel.
Manuela, Emma.
Marcial, Martial.
Marco, Marcos, Mark.
Margarita, Margaret,
  Marjorie, Daisy.
María, Mary, Miriam.
Mariana, Marian, Mar-
  ion.
Marta, Martha.
Marte, Mars.
Mateo, Matthew.
Mauricio, Maurice,
  Morris.
Mercurio, Mercury.
Mesías, Messiah.
Miguel, Michael.
Miguel Angel, Michel-
  angelo.
Moisés, Moses.

N

Nabucodonosor, Nebu-
  chadnezzar.
Natán, Nathan.
Nataniel, Nathaniel.
Neptuno, Neptune.
Nerón, Nero.
Nicolás, Nicholas.
Noé, Noah.

O

Octavio, Octavius.
Oliverio, Oliver.
Orlando, Roland.
Otón, Otto.
Ovidio, Ovid.

P

Pablo, Paul.
Patricio, Patrick.
Paulina, Pauline.
Pedro, Peter.
Perseo, Perseus.
Pilatos, Pilate.
Píndaro, Pindar.
Pío, Pius.
Pitágoras, Pythagoras.
Platón, Plato.
Plauto, Plautus.
Plinio, Pliny.
Plutarco, Plutarch.
Pompeyo, Pompey.
Poncio, Pontius.
Prometeo, Prometheus.

Q

Quintiliano, Quintilian.
Quintín, Quentin.

R

Rafael, Raphael.
Raimundo, Raymond.
Ramón, Raymond.
Randolfo, Randolph.
Raquel, Rachel.
Rebeca, Rebecca.
Reinaldo, Reginald.
Renaldo, Ronald.
Renato, René.
Ricardo, Richard.

240

Roberto, Robert.
Rodolfo, Ralph, Rudolph.
Rodrigo, Roderick.
Rogelio, Rogerio, Roger.
Rolando, Roland.
Rómulo, Romulus.
Rosa, Rose.
Rosalía, Rosalie.
Rosario, Rosary.
Rubén, Reuben, Rubin.
Ruperto, Rupert.

S

Saladino, Saladin.
Salomé, Salome.
Salomón, Solomon.
Salustio, Sallust.
Sansón, Samson.
Santiago, James.
Sara, Sarah.
Satanás, Satan.
Saturno, Saturn.
Sila, Sulla.
Silvestre, Sylvester.
Sofía, Sophia.

Sófocles, Sophocles.
Solimán, Suleiman.
Suetonio, Suetonius.
Susana, Susan.

T

Tácito, Tacitus.
Tadeo, Thaddeus.
Tamerlán, Tamerlane.
Teócrito, Theocritus.
Teodoro, Theodore.
Teófilo, Theophilus.
Terencio, Terence.
Teresa, Theresa.
Tertuliano, Tertullian.
Tiberio, Tiberius.
Ticiano (el Ticiano), Titian.
Timoteo, Timothy.
Tito, Titus.
Tolomeo, Ptolemy.
Tomás, Thomas.
Trajano, Trajan.
Tristán, Tristram, Tristan.
Tucídides, Thucydides.

U

Ulises, Ulysses.
Urano, Uranus.
Urbano, Urban.
Urías, Uriah.

V

Valentina, Valentine.
Valeriano, Valerian.
Ventura, Bonaventura.
Veronés, Veronese.
Vespasiano, Vespasian.
Vespucio, Vespucci.
Vicente, Vincent.
Virgilio, Vergil, Virgil.

Y

Yugurta, Jugurtha.

Z

Zacarías, Zachary.
Zenón, Zeno.
Zoroastro, Zoroaster.
Zuinglio, Zwingli.

ABBREVIATIONS MOST COMMONLY USED IN SPANISH

A

a., área.
(a), alias.
@, arroba.
ab., abril.
A.C., antes de Cristo.
admón., administración.
admor., administrador.
afmo., afectísimo.
afto., afecto.
ag., agosto.
ap., aparte.
atto., atento.
Av., Avenida.

B

B.L.M., besa la mano.
bto., bulto; bruto.

C

c/, cargo; contra.
C.A., corriente alterna.
cap., capítulo.
C.C., corriente continua.
c. de., en casa de.
cg., centigramo(s).
Cía., Compañía.
cl., centilitro(s).
cm., centímetro(s).
Co., Compañía.
Const., Constitución.
corrte., corriente.
cta., cuenta.
cta. cte., cuenta corriente.

cts., céntimos.
c/u, cada uno.

D

D., don.
Da., doña.
D.C., después de Cristo.
dcha., derecha.
descto., descuento.
d/f, días fecha.
dg., decigramo(s).
Dg., decagramo(s).
dic., diciembre.
dl., decilitro(s).
Dl., decalitro(s).
dls., dólares ($).
dm., decímetro(s).
Dm., decámetro(s).
dna(s)., docena(s).
dom., domingo.
d/p, días plazo.
Dr., Doctor.
dup., duplicado.
d/v, días vista.

E

E., Este, oriente.
EE. UU., Estados Unidos.
E.M., Estado Mayor.
en., enero.
E.P.D., en paz descanse.
E.P.M., en propia mano.
etc., etcétera.
E.U., Estados Unidos.

E.U.A., Estados Unidos de América.
Exc., Excelencia.
Excmo., Excelentísimo.

F

f/, fardo(s).
fact., factura.
F.C., f.c., ferrocarril.
feb., febrero.
fol., folio.
Fr., Fray.
fra., fractura.

G

g., gramo(s).
gnte., gerente.
gob., gobierno.
gobr., gobernador.
gral., general.
gte., gerente.

H

hect., hectáreas.
Hg., hectogramo(s).
Hl., hectolitro(s).
Hm., hectómetro(s).
H.P., caballo(s) de fuerza.
id., ídem.
Ilmo., Ilustrísimo.
Ing., Ingeniero.
izda., izdo., izquierda, -do.

241

J

J.C., Jesucristo.
juev., jueves.
jul., julio.
jun., junio.

K

Kg., kg., kilogramo(s).
Kl., kl., kilolitro(s).
Km., km., kilómetro(s).
k.w., kilovatio.

L

L/, letra.
Ldo., Licenciado.
l., litro(s).
lb(s)., libra(s).
lun., lunes.

M

m., minuto(s); metro
    (s); mañana (A.M.).
M., Madre.
m/, mes; mi(s); mío(s).
Ma., María.
mar., marzo.
mart., martes.
m/f, mi favor.
mg., miligramo(s).
miérc., miércoles.
M/L, mi letra.
ml., mililitro(s).
mm., m/m, milímetro
    (s).
m/o, mi orden.
m/ o m/, más o menos.
Mons., Monseñor.

N

n., noche (P.M.)
N., Norte.
n/, nuestro.
Nª Sª, Nuestra Señora.
N.B., Nota bene.
n/cta., nuestra cuenta.
no., nro., número.
nov., noviembre.
N.S.J.C., Nuestro Señor
    Jesucristo.
nto., neto.

O

O., Oeste.

o/, orden.
ob., obpo., obispo.
oct., octubre.
O.E.A., Organización de
    Estados Americanos.
O.N.U., Organización de
    las Naciones Unidas.
onz., onza.
orn., orden.

P

P., Padre; pregunta.
pág., págs., página(s).
Part., Partida.
P.D., Posdata.
p.ej., por ejemplo.
P.O., por orden.
P.P., Porte pagado; por
    poder.
ppdo., próximo pasado.
pral., principal.
prof., profesor.
prov., provincia.
próx., próximo.
ps., pesos.
ptas., pesetas.
pte., parte.
pza., pieza.

Q

q., que.
Q.B.S.M., que besa su
    mano.
Q.D.G., que Dios guarde.
q.e.g.e., que en gloria
    esté.
q.e.p.d., que en paz des-
    canse.
q.e.s.m., que estrecha su
    mano.
qq., quintales.

R

R., Reverendo.
Rbí., Recibí.
Rda. M., Reverenda Ma-
    dre.
Rdo. P., Reverendo Pa-
    dre.
R.I.P., Requiescat in
    pace.
r.p.m., revoluciones por
    minuto.

rúst., rústica.

S

S., San(to); Sur.
s/, su(s); sobre.
S.A.R., Su Alteza Real.
S.C., s.c., su casa.
s/c, su cuenta.
s/cta., su cuenta.
sept., septiembre.
set., septiembre.
S.E. u O., salvo error u
    omisión.
S.M., Su Majestad.
S.N., Servicio Nacional.
Sr., Señor.
Sra(s)., Señora(s).
Sres., Señores.
Sría., Secretaría.
Srta., Señorita.
S.S., Su Santidad.
S.S.S., s.s.s., Su seguro
    servidor.
Sta., Santa; Señorita.
Sto., Santo.

T

t., tarde.
tít., título.
tpo., tiempo.
trib., tribunal.
tom., tomo.

U

U., Ud., usted.
Uds., UU., ustedes.

V

V., usted; venerable;
    véase.
Vers., Versículo.
Vd., usted.
Vds., ustedes.
V.E., Vuestra Excelencia.
vg., verbigracia.
v.gr., verbigracia.
vier., viernes.
Vto. Bno., Visto Bueno.
Vol., volumen; volun-
    tad.
vols., volúmenes.
vta., vto., vuelta, vuelto.

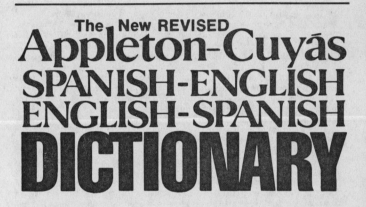

The New REVISED
Appleton–Cuyás
SPANISH-ENGLISH
ENGLISH-SPANISH
DICTIONARY

PREFACIO

Pocas frases introductorias son necesarias para presentar el *Nuevo Diccionario Appleton-Cuyás*. Es hijo del gran *Diccionario Appleton Español-Inglés Inglés-Español* de Arturo Cuyás, cuyo prestigio está sólidamente establecido en los mundos de habla española e inglesa. Se basa en la Cuarta Edición de esa obra, que contiene las revisiones y adiciones incorporadas a ella por el Profesor Lewis E. Brett y la Srta. Helen S. Eaton. El mismo rigor científico que caracterizó la labor tanto de Don Arturo Cuyás como la de aquellos lexicógrafos ha guiado la larga, minuciosa y cuidada tarea de preparación de este compendio.

Ahora bien, hay muchas gentes cuyas necesidades no justifican la adquisición de un diccionario de carácter tan exhaustivo como el Cuyás grande; tal es el caso de un gran número de las personas que tienen un interés general por el aprendizaje del español o el inglés. Por otra parte, hay también ciertas personas: estudiantes universitarios, traductores, hombres de negocios, viajeros, trabajadores sociales y otros que, a pesar de tal vez poseer ya el Cuyás grande, gustarían de tener una edición factible de llevarse sin estorbo para consulta inmediata y rápida en cualquier lugar donde se presente la necesidad. El objetivo principal que se persiguió a lo largo de toda la preparación de esta obra portátil fue el poder ofrecer en forma concisa y eficaz todo el contenido del diccionario original que fuese compatible con los propósitos y el tamaño del volumen que se proyectaba. Dentro del ámbito de su propósito, este diccionario responde a las necesidades expresivas básicas de todos los campos principales de la actividad humana y abarca todos los niveles del uso aceptado de expresión hablada y escrita de los dos idiomas. Tenemos la convicción de que, a base de la eficiente condensación de las definiciones y el empleo aprovechado del espacio disponible, el *Nuevo Diccionario Appleton-Cuyás* ofrece un número más elevado de vocablos y giros que ningún otro diccionario de tamaño semejante.

En la selección de la materia léxica se han utilizado, dándoles el valor auxiliar que tienen, todos cuantos cómputos de frecuencias y listas de palabras y modismos son accesibles hoy para ambas lenguas. Se han mantenido todos los términos y expresiones de alto índice de incidencia en el lenguaje hablado y escrito que aparecen en la obra original y se han añadido otros de incorporación reciente al uso común. El criterio para la selección de los términos ha sido la norma del uso culto medio que prevalece en ambas lenguas. Para esa norma en el continente americano se ha recurrido a la autoridad de los diccionarios de Santamaría y Malaret, amén de otras fuentes de información. En la parte española, la extensión del empleo de las variedades lingüísticas hispanoamericanas va indicada adecuadamente de la siguiente manera: (Am.) para los vocablos y giros de uso continental y (Mex.), (Arg.) etc., para aquellos que tienen sólo validez regional

Llamamos la atención del lector hacia ciertas secciones de especial utilidad que este diccionario contiene y que rara vez se encuentran juntas en ninguno de este tamaño, a saber: listas de números cardinales, ordinales y fraccionarios; tablas completas de verbos irregulares; claves de pronunciación, de carácter sencillo y claro; tablas de pesos, medidas y unidades termométricas; abreviaturas de uso común, y listas de nombres propios personales y geográficos.

Tuvimos la fortuna de contar, como colaboradores directos en esta empresa, con el Dr. Alberto Andino, antiguo Catedrático de Lengua y Literatura Españolas de la Universidad de Las Villas, Cuba, el Dr.

Fernando Figueredo, distinguido ex-miembro del Colegio de Abogados de Cuba, y el lexicógrafo Sr. Bernard Witlieb, Licenciado en Artes del Departamento de Inglés de la New York University. Suerte no menor fue el haber contado en todo momento con el sabio y experimentado consejo en materia editorial de la Srta. Catherine B. Avery, funcionaria de la casa Appleton-Century-Crofts.

New York University   E.G.D.
New York

ADVERTENCIAS AL CONSULTANTE

1. *Distribución y orden.* Para ahorrar espacio y poder incluir un mayor número de palabras hemos agrupado en familias todas aquellas que tienen una estrecha relación, ya de origen y significado, ya de ortografía, respetando, sin embargo, siempre, el orden alfabético. Todos los artículos principales van en negritas. Los modismos y giros van en itálica, alfabetizados por la primera palabra de la expresión. En las definiciones, la separación por medio de punto y coma indica áreas diferentes de significado; la coma, términos sinónimos dentro de cada área específica. Para ahorrar más espacio se ha omitido la parte común de las palabras que constituyen una misma familia. Las partes omitidas de las palabras que forman un grupo están referidas siempre al término que lo encabeza. Se llama la atención del consultante hacia el hecho de que el alfabeto inglés y el español no se corresponden exactamente: la ch, y la ll, por ejemplo, no son en aquél letras independientes. Por tanto, esto obliga a habituarse a una ordenación alfabética diferente en la que *achievement* precede a *acid* y *ally* a *almanac*.

2. Todos los verbos irregulares van indicados por abreviaturas (*vti., vii., vai.*). Los números que van a continuación de las abreviaturas hacen referencia a la *Tabla de Verbos Irregulares*, en la página x.

3. *Adverbios.* Todos los adverbios ingleses terminados en *-ly* se han omitido, excepto aquellos cuyo significado no tiene exacta correspondencia con el de sus equivalentes etimológicos en español.

4. *Abreviaturas.* Todas las abreviaturas empleadas en el texto para indicar limitaciones de uso, geográficas o de otra índole (ex. *Méx.*, México; *aer.*, aeronáutica; *med.*, medicina) se hallarán explicadas en la lista de *Abreviaturas usadas en la parte 1ª* en la página iv.

5. *Pronunciación.* La pronunciación y acentuación de todas las palabras inglesas va indicada entre corchetes por medio de una adaptación simplificada del Alfabeto Fonético Internacional. En las páginas xxix-xxx se incluye una Clave de las equivalencias españolas aproximadas de los sonidos ingleses representados por los símbolos fonéticos.

PRONUNCIACION INGLESA
CLAVE DE LOS SIMBOLOS FONETICOS

I. VOCALES

Símbolo	Grafías y Ejemplos	Equivalencia aproximada de sonido
[a]	a (father); e (sergeant); ea (heart); o (hot); ow (knowledge)	Como la a de pecado.
[ă]	a (legitimacy); ai (certain)	Entre e y a.
[a̧]	a (attire); ai (pageant)	Entre a y e.
[å]	a (forward, sofa)	Muy cercano a la a, pero más cerrado.
[æ]	a (man, that); ai (plaid); au (laugh)	Entre la a de caso y la e de guerra.
[ai]	ai (aisle); ay (aye); ei (height); ey (eye); i (life); ie (pie); uy (buy); y (by); ye (goodbye)	Como ai en vais.
[au]	ou (house); ow (cow)	Como au en causa.
[e]	a (any); ae (aeronautics); ai (chair); ay (prayer); e (let); ea (head); ei (heifer); eo (leopard); ie (friend); u (bury)	Como la e de cerro.
[ȩ]	e (adequate, courtesy)	Muy cercana a la e.
[e̱]	e (ardent); ea (sergeant)	Como la anterior.
[ei]	a (case); ai (train); au (gauge); ay (pay); e (fete)	Como ei en seis.
[i]	ae (alumnae); ay (quay); e (be); ea (clean); ee (sleep); ei (seize); eo (people); ey (key); i (machine); ie (fiend)	Como la i de vida.
[i̧]	a (average); ay (Sunday); e (subsequent); ea (tear); ee (cheer); ei (sovereign); ey (money); i (bit); ie (sieve); o (women); oi (chamois); u (business); ui (guilt); y (very)	Como la i de sin, pero más breve y abierta.
[iu]	eau (beautiful); eu (feud); ew (few); iew (view); u (mute); ue (cue); ui (suit)	Como iu en ciudad o yu en yugo.
[o]	o (obese, notation)	Como la o de sola.
[ǫ]	eo (dungeon); io (nation); o (atom)	Entre o y e.
[œ]	e (her); ea (earth); i (bird); o (word); ou (courage); u (burn); y (martyr)	Sonido parecido al de eu en francés (peur) o al de ö en aleman (schön).
[ou]	eau (beau); eo (yeoman); ew (sew); o (alone); oa (road); oe (foe); oo (brooch); ou (dough); ow (crow)	Como la o de loca seguida de una u leve.
[u]	eu (maneuver); ew (blew); o (do); oe (shoe); oo (food); ou (coupon); u (rude); ue (true); ui (juice)	Muy cercana a la u de suyo.
[u̧]	o (woman); oo (good); ou (could); u (bull)	Como la u de suyo, pero más cerrada.
[ǫ̧]	u (commensurate, corduroy)	Como iu en ciudad, pero más atenuado.

Símbolo	Grafías y Ejemplos	Equivalencia aproximada de sonido
[ǔ]	u (censure, natural)	Lo mismo que el anterior, pero más relajado.
[waj]	oi (choir); uay (Paraguayan)	Como ua en guapa seguido de una i muy relajada.
[wei]	ua (persuade)	Como ue en sueco seguido de una i muy relajada.
[yu]	eu (euphemism); ew (ewe); ou (you); u (unite)	Como iu en ciudad o yu en yugo.
[yǔ]	u (regular, secular)	Como iu en ciudad pero bastante más atenuado.
[ɔ]	a⁻(all); au (launch); aw (law); o (song); oa (broad); ou (fought)	Como la o de sol pero más prolongada.
[ɔi]	oi (oil); oy (toy); uoy (buoy)	Como oy en voy.
[ʌ]	o (come); oe (does); oo (flood); ou (young); u (just)	Sonido entre o y e. Parecido al de la o francesa en homme.

II. Consonantes

Símbolo	Grafías y Ejemplos	Equivalencia aproximada de sonido
[b]	baby; robber	Como la b de lumbre.
[ch]	church; furniture; righteous; christian; catch	Como la ch española.
[d]	did; ladder	Como la d de onda.
[dž]	arduous; grandeur; budge; adjacent; gem; judge	Sonido semejante al de la y de conyugal o al de g italiana en cortigiani.
[f]	far; rough; philosophy	Como la f española.
[g]	gag; wriggle	Como la g de gana.
[gz]	exact; example	Como la g de gana seguida de la s francesa de maison.
[h]	here; behave; who; whole	Como la j española pero más aspirada y más suave.
[hw]	what; when	Como la j de juez, pero más suave.
[k]	car; account; ache; back; kill; joke; antique	Como la c de calle.
[ks]	excuse; tax	Como la x de flexión.
[kw]	queen; acquaint	Como cu en cual o qu en que.
[l]	lard; lull; small	Como la l de lado.
[m]	man, mammal	Como la m española.
[n]	nun; banner	Como la n española.
[ŋ]	anchor; sink; sing; angle	Semejante al de la n de banco, pero más nasal.
[p]	top; pepper	Como la p española.
[r]	rat; merry	Parecida a la r suave española.
[s]	cent; sister; miss; quarts; façade	Como la s de sala, pero algo más tensa y larga.
[š]	ocean; chagrin; sure; conscience; fish; mission; partial; anxious	Como la ch francesa en chaise.
[t]	fixed; taunt; rattle; thyme	Próxima a la t española de parte.
[v]	of; vivid; over	Parecida a la v española, pero labiodental.
[w]	we; awake	Como la u española.
[y]	onion; year	Semejante a la y de ayer, pero más relajada.
[z]	riches; discern; dessert; desert; anxiety; zeal; dazzle	Como la s francesa de maison. Parecida a la s española de isla.
[ž]	mirage; pleasure; vision; azure	Como la g francesa de genre.
[ð]	this; with; mother	Muy semejante a la d de nada.
[θ]	thin; theater; truth	Como la z de Castilla en zorro.

SINOPSIS DE LA GRAMÁTICA INGLESA

I. CONSIDERACIONES GENERALES

El idioma inglés no es tan exacto como el español. No hay reglas fijas para la pronunciación ni para la colocación del acento ni acentos ortográficos para ayudar en la pronunciación de una palabra. Consecuentemente, hay que aprender de memoria la pronunciación de un gran número de vocablos. (Véase la sección PRONUNCIACIÓN INGLESA, págs. xxix–xxx.)

Se usan las mayúsculas en inglés como en español, y en los casos siguientes:
a) el pronombre sujeto I (*yo*) se escribe con mayúscula;
b) los nombres de los meses y días se escriben con mayúsculas;

    Saturday, July 17   *el sábado, 17 de julio*

c) los gentilicios y todos los adjetivos formados de nombres propios se escriben con mayúsculas;

    the Spaniards   *los españoles*

d) los títulos y tratamientos de cortesía se escriben con mayúsculas;

    Mr.   *señor*
    Mrs.   *señora*
    Miss   *señorita*

e) todas las palabras en un título de libro, película, etc. se escriben con mayúsculas, exceptuando las palabras cortas si no van al principio.

    From Here to Eternity

II. LAS PARTES DE LA ORACIÓN

A. Del artículo

1. El artículo indefinido en inglés carece de género; tiene las formas **a** y **an** (*un, una*). Cuando se antepone a una palabra comenzada en consonante se usa la forma **a**, y cuando se antepone a una palabra comenzada en vocal se usa la forma **an**. El plural de ambas formas es **some** (*unos, unas*).

    a book   *un libro*
    some books   *unos libros*
    an airplane   *un avión*
    some airplanes   *unos aviones*
    a pen   *una pluma*

Generalmente, se usa el artículo indefinido en inglés como en español, aunque no tan frecuentemente. Algunas diferencias se citan a continuación:
a) no es necesario repetir el artículo indefinido antes de cada nombre;

    I have a car, house and television   *Tengo un coche, una casa y una televisión*

b) se usa el artículo indefinido antes de substantivos de cantidad como a half (*medio*), a, one hundred (*cien*), a, one thousand (*mil*):

There are a hundred soldiers here *Hay cien soldados aquí*

c) se usa el artículo indefinido cuando el nombre predicado no está modificado;

John is a doctor   *Juan es médico*

d) se usa el artículo indefinido cuando se sobrentiende que la cantidad aludida es uno;

He is wearing a coat   *Lleva abrigo*

e) se usa el artículo indefinido cuando se habla de precios.

He sells eggs at twenty cents a   *Vende los huevos a veinte centavos la*
dozen   *docena*

2. El artículo definido en inglés carece de género: tiene una única forma the, que corresponde indistintamente a los artículos definidos españoles *el, los, la, las* y *lo.*

the book	*el libro*
the books	*los libros*
the pen	*la pluma*
the pens	*las plumas*

No es tan corriente su uso en inglés como en español.

Mr. Martin is ill	*El señor Martínez está enfermo*
Love is not enough	*El amor no es suficiente*
Spanish	*El español*
It is one o'clock	*Es la una*
He goes to church on Sundays	*Va a la iglesia los domingos*
This coming year	*El año que viene*
Last Sunday	*El domingo pasado*

Se usa el artículo definido antes del número en un título.

Charles the Fifth   *Carlos V*

B. Del nombre

1. El nombre carece de género en el idioma inglés y generalmente sólo cambia para indicar el número. Por eso el artículo definido es siempre el mismo.

the house	*la casa*
the houses	*las casas*
the pencil	*el lápiz*
the pencils	*los lápices*

2. El plural de los nombres ingleses generalmente se forma añadiendo -s al final de la palabra.

	SINGULAR		PLURAL
chair	*silla*	chairs	*sillas*
book	*libro*	books	*libros*

Se forman algunos plurales añadiendo -es después de las terminaciones -s, -sh, -x, -j, -z y -ch.

	SINGULAR		PLURAL
dress	*vestido*	dresses	*vestidos*
bush	*arbusto*	bushes	*arbustos*
box	*caja*	boxes	*cajas*
birch	*abedul*	birches	*abedules*

Se forma el plural de los nombres terminados en -y (después de una consonante o de -qu) cambiando la -y por -i y añadiendo -es.

SINGULAR		PLURAL	
enemy	*enemigo*	enemies	*enemigos*
lady	*señora*	ladies	*señoras*
soliloquy	*soliloquio*	soliloquies	*soliloquios*

Se forma el plural de los nombres que terminan en -y precedida de vocal añadiendo una -s al final de la palabra.

SINGULAR		PLURAL	
donkey	*burro*	donkeys	*burros*

Se forma el plural de los nombres que terminan en -f, -fe, y -ff como sigue.

a) añadiendo -s al final de la palabra;

SINGULAR		PLURAL	
roof	*techo*	roofs	*techos*
chief	*jefe*	chiefs	*jefes*
cuff	*puño de camisa*	cuffs	*puños de camisa*

b) cambiando -f a -v y añadiendo -es.

SINGULAR		PLURAL	
knife	*cuchillo*	knives	*cuchillos*
leaf	*hoja*	leaves	*hojas*

N. B. Staff, scarf y wharf tienen dos formas para el plural. staffs y staves; scarfs y scarves; wharfs y wharves.

Se forma el plural de los nombres que terminan en -o precedida de vocal añadiendo -s al final de la palabra.

SINGULAR		PLURAL	
radio	*radio*	radios	*radios*

Se forma el plural de los nombres que terminan en -o precedida de consonante añadiendo -es al final de la palabra.

SINGULAR		PLURAL	
hero	*héroe*	heroes	*héroes*
potato	*patata*	potatoes	*patatas*

Se forma el plural de los números y letras añadiendo un apóstrofo y una -s.

There are ten 5's in this column *Hay diez cincos en esta columna*
There are two s's in the word possible *Hay dos eses en la palabra possible*

Algunos nombres, como los nombres de tribus, pueblos, razas y animales, tienen la misma forma para el singular que para el plural.

SINGULAR		PLURAL	
Chinese	*chino*	Chinese	*chinos*
Portuguese	*portugués*	Portuguese	*portugueses*
Norse	*escandinavo*	Norse	*escandinavos*
sheep	*oveja*	sheep	*ovejas*
deer	*ciervo*	deer	*ciervos*

Algunos nombres forman el plural de manera irregular.

SINGULAR		PLURAL	
child	*niño*	children	*niños*
tooth	*diente*	teeth	*dientes*
mouse	*ratón*	mice	*ratones*

En el caso de las palabras compuestas, generalmente se forma el plural de éstas pluralizando a la palabra principal.

SINGULAR		PLURAL	
mother-in-law	*suegra*	mothers-in-law	*suegras*
man-of-war	*buque de guerra*	men-of-war	*buques de guerra*

C. Del adjetivo

1. El adjetivo inglés no tiene ni género ni número; generalmente, se antepone al substantivo que modifica.

the red house	*la casa roja*
the red houses	*las casas rojas*
the white pencil	*el lápiz blanco*
the white pencils	*los lápices blancos*
the beautiful girl	*la muchacha hermosa*
the beautiful girls	*las muchachas hermosas*

2. *La comparación de los adjetivos.* Hay tres grados de comparación en inglés, que son: el positivo, comparativo y superlativo. El positivo de una o dos sílabas forma el comparativo añadiendo el sufijo -er. Los positivos con más de dos sílabas forman el comparativo anteponiendo el adverbio more (*más*). Los positivos de una o dos sílabas forman el superlativo añadiendo el sufijo -est, y los de dos o más sílabas forman el superlativo anteponiendo el adverbio most (*el más*). Se usa el comparativo less para indicar la cualidad de menos, y least para indicar el menos; ambas formas se anteponen al positivo.

POSITIVO		COMPARATIVO		SUPERLATIVO	
hard	*duro*	harder	*más duro*	hardest	*el más duro*
long	*largo*	longer	*más largo*	longest	*el más largo*
bright	*claro*	brighter	*más claro*	brightest	*el más claro*
capable	*capaz*	more capable	*más capaz*	most capable	*el más capaz*
clever	*listo*	less clever	*menos listo*	least clever	*el menos listo*

Se forma el comparativo y el superlativo de los adjetivos que terminan en -y después de una consonante cambiando la -y por -i y añadiendo los sufijos -er y -est respectivamente.

POSITIVO		COMPARATIVO		SUPERLATIVO	
pretty	*bonito*	prettier	*más bonito*	prettiest	*el más bonito*
happy	*feliz*	happier	*más feliz*	happiest	*el más feliz*

En algunos casos es necesario modificar la ortografía del positivo para acomodar a los grados del comparativo y superlativo. Generalmente, cuando el adjetivo de una o dos sílabas termina en consonante precedida de vocal, la consonante se dobla.

POSITIVO		COMPARATIVO		SUPERLATIVO	
drab	*pardo*	drabber	*más pardo*	drabbest	*el más pardo*
fat	*gordo*	fatter	*más gordo*	fattest	*el más gordo*

A continuación se dan algunos adjetivos de comparación irregular:

POSITIVO		COMPARATIVO		SUPERLATIVO	
bad	*mal*	worse	*peor*	worst	*el peor*
ill	*mal*	worse	*peor*	worst	*el peor*
evil	*mal*	worse	*peor*	worst	*el peor*
good	*bueno*	better	*mejor*	best	*el mejor*
many	*muchos*	more	*más*	most	*los más*
much	*mucho*	more	*más*	most	*el más*

D. Del adverbio

1. Se usa el adverbio en inglés, como en español, para modificar un verbo, un adjetivo u otro adverbio.

He ran quickly	*Corrió rápidamente*
The very good man	*El hombre muy bueno*
He ran very quickly	*Corrió rapidísimamente*

2. Generalmente, se forma el adverbio añadiendo el sufijo -ly a un adjetivo. La terminación -ly corresponde a la terminación -mente en español Pero no todas las palabras terminadas en -ly son adverbios; algunas son adjetivos, como: **friendly** (*amigable*), **lovely** (*hermoso*), **kindly** (*bondadoso*), etc

ADJETIVO		ADVERBIO	
strong	*fuerte*	strongly	*fuertemente*
regular	*regular*	regularly	*regularmente*

3. Algunas veces los adverbios toman la misma forma que los adjetivos.

ADJETIVO		ADVERBIO	
a slow watch	*un reloj atrasado*	go slow	*ve lentamente*
a late train	*un tren tardío*	he arrived late	*él llegó tarde*

4. El adverbio, como el adjetivo, tiene tres grados de comparación, que son: el positivo, comparativo y superlativo. Generalmente, se forma el comparativo y superlativo añadiendo more (*más*) o less (*menos*) para el comparativo, y most (*el más*) o least (*el menos*) para el superlativo, antes del adverbio. No obstante, se forma el comparativo y superlativo de algunos adverbios añadiendo -er y -est respectivamente al final de la forma positiva.

POSITIVO		COMPARATIVO		SUPERLATIVO	
rapidly	*rápida- mente*	more rapidly	*más rápida- mente*	most rapidly	*más rápida- mente*
easily	*fácil- mente*	more easily	*más fácil- mente*	most easily	*más fácil- mente*
soon	*pronto*	sooner	*más pronto*	soonest	*más pronto*
easily	*fácil- mente*	less easily	*menos fácil- mente*	least easily	*menos fácil- mente*

Los siguientes adverbios tienen comparaciones irregulares.

POSITIVO		COMPARATIVO		SUPERLATIVO	
far	*lejos*	farther; further	*más lejos*	farthest; furthest	*el más lejos*
ill, bad	*mal*	worse	*peor*	worst	*el peor*
little	*poco*	less	*menos*	least	*el menos*
much	*mucho*	more	*más*	most	*el más*
well	*bien*	better	*mejor*	best	*el mejor*

E. Del pronombre

1. *Los pronombres personales.* Los pronombres personales se dividen según el caso y son: el sujeto, objeto y posesivo. En inglés, es necesario usar el pronombre sujeto, porque los verbos no indican a la persona gramatical; se usa el mismo pronombre para el objeto directo que para el objeto indirecto. No hay equivalente inglés para las formas españolas *usted, Vd. y ustedes, Vds.* Se usa la forma del pronombre sujeto de segunda persona **you** (*tu, vosotros*) siempre, ya sea cuando se hable a una o a varias personas.

He is going tomorrow	*Irá mañana*
I see him now	*Le veo ahora*
I gave it to him	*Se lo di*
Do you speak Spanish?	*¿Habla Vd. español?*

A continuación se citan los pronombres personales que se usan ya como sujeto, ya como objeto directo o indirecto.

SINGULAR

	SUJETO		OBJETO DIRECTO E INDIRECTO	
primera persona	I	*yo*	me	*me*
segunda persona	you	*tú*	you	*te*
tercera persona	he	*él*	him	*lo, le; se*
	she	*ella*	her	*la, le; se*
	it	*ello*	it	*lo*

PLURAL

	SUJETO		OBJETO DIRECTO E INDIRECTO	
primera persona	we	*nosotros*	us	*nos*
segunda persona	you	*vosotros*	you	*vos, os*
tercera persona	they	*ellos*	them	*los, las; les*

Los pronombres posesivos en inglés carecen de género. Se refieren y concuerdan en número con el poseedor y no con la cosa poseída.

This book is mine	*Este libro es el mío*
Those books are mine	*Esos libros son los míos*
That dog is his	*Aquel perro es el suyo*
Are these pencils yours, Peter?	*¿Son estos lápices los tuyos, Pedro?*

PRONOMBRES POSESIVOS

mine	*el mío, la mía, los míos, las mías*
yours	*el tuyo, la tuya, los tuyos, las tuyas; el vuestro, la vuestra, los vuestros, las vuestras*
his	*el suyo, los suyos*
hers	*la suya, las suyas*
ours	*el nuestro, la nuestra, los nuestros, las nuestras*
theirs	*el suyo, la suya, los suyos, las suyas*

Los adjetivos posesivos en inglés carecen de género. Concuerdan en número con el poseedor y no con la cosa poseída y preceden al substantivo que califican.

My books are in the drawer	*Mis libros están en la gaveta*
Our house is white	*Nuestra casa es blanca*

ADJETIVOS POSESIVOS

my	*mi, mis*
your	*tu, tus; vuestro, vuestros*
his	*su, sus*
her	*su, sus*
its	*su, sus*
our	*nuestro, nuestros*
their	*su, sus*

2. *Los pronombres relativos.* Los pronombres relativos sirven para referir a un nombre o pronombre que generalmente les precede en una oración. Los pronombres relativos se dividen en simples y compuestos.

a) Los pronombres relativos simples son:

who	*quien, que, cual, el que*
whom	*que, quien, el cual*
whose	*de quien, cuyo, del cual*
that	*que, cual, el que*
which	*que, quien, cual, el que*
what	*que, el que*

The man who came to dinner	*El hombre que vino a comer*
The man whom we saw is my brother	*El hombre que vimos es mi hermano*
The girl with whom he went to the movies is here	*La muchacha con quien fue al cine está aquí*
Give me what books you can	*Déme Vd. los libros que pueda*

b) Los pronombres relativos compuestos se forman añadiendo las terminaciones -ever y -soever a who, which y what (whoever, whichever, whatever) y se usan con carácter enfático.

c) Los pronombres relativos en inglés carecen de género y de número.

John and Charles, who are students, are on vacation	*Juan y Carlos, quienes son estudiantes, están de vacaciones*
Mary is the girl who sings	*María es la muchacha que canta*

d) Generalmente, who se refiere a una o algunas personas, which a una o algunas cosas, y that a ambas. Whom se puede usar tanto como objeto directo que indirecto. Whose se usa como posesivo.

Mary is the girl who sings	*María es la muchacha que canta*
Here is the book of which I spoke to you	*Aquí está el libro del cual te hablé*

Albert is the one that is playing the piano	*Alberto es el que toca el piano*
She is the girl to whom we gave the prize	*Ella es la muchacha a quien dimos el premio*
John, whose uncle is ill, is leaving tonight	*Juan, cuyo tío está enfermo, partirá esta noche*

3. *Los pronombres demostrativos.* Los pronombres demostrativos se usan para mostrar uno o varios objetos, a la vez que indican su proximidad o lejanía respecto a la persona que habla o de aquella a quien se habla. Los pronombres demostrativos en inglés carecen de género. Concuerdan en número con la cosa a la que se refieren.

SINGULAR		PLURAL	
this	*éste, ésta, esto;* cerca de la persona que habla	these	*éstos, éstas*
that	*ése, ésa, eso; aquél, aquélla, aquello;* lejos de la persona que habla	those	*ésos, ésas; aquéllos, aquéllas*

This is the pen	*Ésta es la pluma*
These are the books	*Éstos son los libros*
That is his	*Eso es suyo*
Those are hers	*Aquéllos son de ella*

4. *Los pronombres indefinidos.* Se usan los pronombres indefinidos en inglés como en español. A continuación se dan los pronombres indefinidos más usados en inglés:

all	*todo*	everybody	*todos*	nothing	*nada*
another	*otro*	everyone	*todos*	one	*uno*
any	*cualquier*	everything	*todo*	other	*otro*
anybody	*alguien, cualquiera*	few	*pocos*	some	*algunos*
anyone	*alguien, cualquiera*	many	*muchos*	somebody	*alguien*
anything	*algo, cualquier cosa*	neither	*ni uno ni otro*	someone	*alguien*
both	*ambos*	nobody	*ninguno, nadie*	something	*algo*
each	*cada uno, cada cual*	none	*ninguno, nadie*	such	*tal*
either	*uno u otro*	no one	*ninguno, nadie*		

One (*uno*) y other (*otro*) son los únicos que tienen plural.

These are the ones I like	*Estos son los que me gustan*
The others have already left	*Los otros ya se fueron*

5. *Los pronombres reflexivos o intensivos.* Los pronombres reflexivos, también llamados intensivos por su carácter enfático, carecen de género. Concuerdan en número con la persona a la que se refieren. Se forman de la unión del pronombre personal o del adjetivo posesivo con la terminación -self para el singular y -selves para el plural.

myself	*yo mismo; mí, mi mismo; me*
yourself	*tú mismo; Vd. mismo;ti, ti mismo; te, se*
himself	*él mismo; sí, sí mismo; se*
herself	*ella misma; sí, sí misma; se*
itself	*mismo; sí, sí mismo; se*
ourselves	*nosotros mismos; nos*
yourselves	*vosotros mismos; Vds. mismos; vos, os*
themselves	*ellos mismos; sí, sí mismos; se*

I did it myself	*Yo mismo lo hice*
It moves by itself	*Eso se mueve por sí mismo*
Did you do it yourself?	*¿Lo hizo Vd. mismo?*

F. Las palabras interrogativas

Las palabras interrogativas en inglés carecen de género y de número. A continuación se dan las de uso más frecuente.

how?	¿cómo?	where?	¿dónde?
how many?	¿cuántos?	which?	¿cuál?
how much?	¿cuánto?	who?	¿quién?
what?	¿qué?	why?	¿por qué?
when?	¿cuándo?		

How do you sell them?	¿A cómo los vende Vd.?
How many eggs are in that box?	¿Cuántos huevos hay en esa caja?
How much are they?	¿Cuánto cuestan?
What time is it?	¿Qué hora es?
When did you arrive?	¿Cuándo llegó Vd.?
Where are you going?	¿Dónde va Vd?
Which sister did he marry?	¿Con cuál de las hermanas se casó?
Who goes there?	¿Quién va?
Why do you weep?	¿Por qué llora Vd.?

G. Del verbo

1. Los verbos en inglés pueden ser regulares o irregulares, según la conjugación. Cada verbo consta de tres partes principales: el presente, el pretérito y el participio pasado.

2. El infinitivo se forma con to y el presente del verbo.

to change	cambiar	to play	jugar
to look	mirar	to use	usar

El infinitivo se puede usar como substantivo; también puede hacer oficio de adjetivo o adverbio.

To play in the park is fun	El jugar en el parque es divertido
I have plenty of books to read	Tengo muchos libros que leer
The student came to learn English	El alumno vino a aprender inglés

3. El participio presente o gerundio del verbo generalmente se forma añadiendo -ing al presente.

PRESENTE	PARTICIPIO PRESENTE
look	looking
play	playing

Los verbos que tienen el presente terminado en -e muda generalmente pierden la -e y añaden -ing para formar el participio presente.

PRESENTE	PARTICIPIO PRESENTE
change	changing
use	using

Los verbos que doblan la consonante final para formar el pretérito y el participio pasado también doblan la consonante final para formar el participio presente.

PRESENTE		PARTICIPIO PRESENTE
stop	parar	stopping
tip	ladear	tipping

El participio presente se puede usar con el verbo auxiliar to be para formar un tiempo progresivo.

I am playing cards	Estoy jugando a las cartas
I was playing football last week	Jugaba al fútbol la semana pasada

4. El pretérito y el participio pasado generalmente se forman añadiendo -d o -ed al presente.

PRESENTE	PRETÉRITO	PARTICIPIO PASADO
change	changed	changed
look	looked	looked
play	played	played
use	used	used

Sin embargo, muchos vergos en inglés tienen formas irregulares para el pretérito y para el participio pasado. A continuación se da una descripción de algunos verbos que forman el pretérito y el participio pasado de manera irregular. No se incluyen los que forman el pretérito y el participio pasado de manera regular, aunque éstos tengan a la vez una forma alterna, a menso que ésta sea la preferida.

a) Algunos verbos duplican la consonante final del presente para formar el pretérito y el participio pasado.

PRESENTE	PRETÉRITO	PARTICIPIO PASADO
abet	abetted	abetted
abhor	abhorred	abhorred
acquit	acquitted	acquitted

Los verbos de esta clase incluidos en este diccionario, a excepción de sus compuestos, se dan a continuación.

admit	concur	fit	jet	permit	scrap
allot	confer	flag	jig	pet	scrub
aver	control	flap	jot	pin	sham
bag	cop	flat	jut	plan	shin
ban	corral	flit	kid	plod	ship
bar	crab	flog	knot	plot	shop
bed	cram	flop	lag	plug	shrug
beg	crib	fog	lap	pop	shun
blab	crop	fret	log	prefer	sin
blot	dam	fur	lop	prod	skim
blur	defer	gad	lug	prop	skin
bob	deter	gag	man	propel	slam
bog	dim	gap	map	pun	slap
bootleg	din	gem	mar	quip	slip
brag	dip	grab	mob	quiz	slop
brim	dispel	grin	mop	rag	slot
bud	distil	grip	mud	ram	slug
bum	dog	grit	nab	rap	slum
can	don	grub	nag	recur	slur
cap	dot	gum	nap	refer	smut
chap	drag	gun	net	remit	snag
char	drip	gut	nip	rib	snap
chat	drop	handicap	nod	rig	snip
chip	drug	hem	occur	rip	snub
chop	drum	hop	omit	rob	sob
chum	emit	hug	outwit	rot	sod
clap	equip	impel	pad	rub	sop
clip	excel	incur	pan	rut	span
clog	expel	infer	pat	sag	spar
clot	extol	inter	patrol	sap	spat
club	fan	jab	peg	scan	spot
commit	fat	jam	pen	scar	spur
compel	fib	jar	pep	scram	squat

stab	strip	sum	thin	trap	war
star	strop	sun	throb	trim	wed
stem	strut	sup	tin	trot	whet
step	stub	tag	tip	tug	whip
stir	stud	tan	top	up	whir
stop	stun	tap	transfer	wad	whiz
strap	submit	tar	transmit	wag	wrap

b) Algunos verbos cambian la -y final del presente en -ied para formar el pretérito y el participio pasado.

PRESENTE	PRETÉRITO	PARTICIPIO PASADO
accompany	accompanied	accompanied
acetify	acetified	acetified
acidify	acidified	acidified

Los verbos de esta clase incluidos en este diccionario, a excepción de sus compuestos, se dan a continuación:

ally	dignify	hurry	occupy	shy
amnesty	dirty	identify	pacify	signify
amplify	diversify	imply	parry	solidify
apply	dizzy	indemnify	personify	specify
baby	dry	intensify	pillory	spy
beautify	eddy	inventory	pity	steady
belly	edify	jelly	ply	stratify
bloody	electrify	jolly	prophesy	study
body	empty	justify	pry	supply
bully	envy	levy	purify	tally
busy	espy	liquefy	putty	tarry
candy	falsify	lobby	qualify	terrify
carry	fancy	magnify	quarry	testify
certify	ferry	marry	query	tidy
classify	fortify	modify	rally	try
codify	fry	mortify	rectify	typify
comply	glorify	muddy	rely	unify
copy	gratify	multiply	remedy	vary
crucify	gully	mutiny	reply	weary
cry	harry	mystify	sally	worry
defy	horrify	notify	sanctify	
deny	humidify	nullify	satisfy	

c) Algunos verbos no cambian en la formación del pretérito y del participio pasado. Los verbos de esta clase incluidos en este diccionario, a excepción de sus compuestos, se dan a continuación:

PRESENTE	PRETÉRITO	PARTICIPIO PASADO	PRESENTE	PRETÉRITO	PARTICIPIO PASADO
bid (ofrecer)	bid	bid	let	let	let
burst	burst	burst	put	put	put
cast	cast	cast	read	read	read
cost	cost	cost	set	set	set
cut	cut	cut	shed	shed	shed
hit	hit	hit	spread	spread	spread
hurt	hurt	hurt	thrust	thrust	thrust

d) Algunos verbos añaden -ked al presente para formar el pretérito y el participio pasado. Los verbos de esta clase incluidos en este diccionario se dan a continuación.

PRESENTE	PRETÉRITO	PARTICIPIO PASADO	PRESENTE	PRETÉRITO	PARTICIPIO PASADO
frolic	frolicked	frolicked	picnic	picnicked	picnicked
mimic	mimicked	mimicked	shellac	shellacked	shellacked
panic	panicked	panicked	traffic	trafficked	trafficked

e) Algunos verbos irregulares no siguen regla fija en la formación del pretérito y del participio pasado. Los verbos de este grupo incluidos en este diccionario, a excepción de sus compuestos, se dan a continuación.

PRESENTE	PRETÉRITO	PARTICIPIO PASADO	PRESENTE	PRETÉRITO	PARTICIPIO PASADO
abide	abode	abode	forego	forewent	foregone
alight	alighted, alit	alighted, alit	foresee	foresaw	foreseen
			foretell	foretold	foretold
arise	arose	arisen	forget	forgot	forgotten
awake	awoke, awaked	awoke, awaked	forgive	forgave	forgiven
			forsake	forsook	forsaken
be	was, were	been	forswear	forswore	forsworn
bear	bore	born, borne	freeze	froze	frozen
beat	beat	beaten	get	got	got, gotten
become	became	become	give	gave	given
begin	began	begun	go	went	gone
behold	beheld	beheld	grind	ground	ground
bend	bent	bent	grow	grew	grown
beseech	besought, beseeched	besought, beseeched	hang	hung, hanged	hung, hanged
bid (ordenar)	bade	bidden	have	had	had
bind	bound	bound	hear	heard	heard
bite	bit	bitten	hide	hid	hid, hidden
bleed	bled	bled	hold	held	held
blow	blew	blown	keep	kept	kept
break	broke	broken	know	knew	known
breed	bred	bred	lay	laid	laid
bring	brought	brought	lead (dirigir)	led	led
build	built	built			
buy	bought	bought	leave	left	left
can	could		lend	lent	lent
catch	caught	caught	lie (echarse)	lay	lain
			light	lighted, lit	lighted, lit
chide	chide, chided	chid, chidden, chided	lose	lost	lost
			make	made	made
			may	might	
choose	chose	chosen	mean	meant	meant
cleave	cleft, cleaved, clove	cleft, cleaved, cloven	meet	met	met
			mistake	mistook	mistaken
			pass	passed	passed, past
cling	clung	clung	pay	paid	paid
come	came	come	pen (encerrar)	penned	pent
creep	crept	crept			
deal	dealt	dealt	quit	quit	quitted
dig	dug, digged	dug, digged	rend	rent	rent
dive	dove, dived	dove, dived	rid	rid, ridded	rid, ridded
do	did	done	ride	rode	ridden
draw	drew	drawn	ring	rang	rung
drink	drank	drunk	rise	rose	risen
drive	drove	driven	run	ran	run
eat	ate	eaten	say	said	said
fall	fell	fallen	see	saw	seen
feed	fed	fed	seek	sought	sought
feel	felt	felt	sell	sold	sold
fight	fought	fought	send	sent	sent
find	found	found	shake	shook	shaken
flee	fled	fled	shine	shone, shined	shone, shined
fling	flung	flung			
fly	flew	flown	shoe	shod	shod
forbear	forbore	forborne	shoot	shot	shot
forbid	forbade	forbidden	show	showed	shown

PRESENTE	PRETÉRITO	PARTICIPIO PASADO	PRESENTE	PRETÉRITO	PARTICIPIO PASADO
shrink	shrank, shrunk	shrunk, shrunken	swear	swore	sworn
			sweep	swept	swept
sing	sang	sung	swell	swelled	swelled, swollen
sink	sank, sunk	sunk, sunken			
			swim	swam	swum
sit	sat	sat	swing	swung	swung
slay	slew	slain	take	took	taken
sleep	slept	slept	teach	taught	taught
slide	slid	slid, slidden	tear	tore	torn
sling	slung	slung	tell	told	told
slink	slunk	slunk	think	thought	thought
sow	sowed	sown, sowed	thrive	throve, thrived	thrived, thriven
speak	spoke	spoken			
speed	sped, speeded	sped, speeded	throw	threw	thrown
			tread	trod	trodden, trod
spend	spent	spent			
spin	spun	spun	understand	understood	understood
spit	spat, spit	spat, spit	wake	woke, waked	woken, waked
spring	sprang, sprung	sprung			
			wear	wore	worn
stand	stood	stood	weave	wove	woven, wove
steal	stole	stolen			
stick	stuck	stuck	weep	wept	wept
sting	stung	stung	wet	wet, wetted	wet, wetted
stink	stank, stunk	stunk			
			win	won	won
strike	struck	struck, stricken	wind	winded, wound	winded, wound
string	strung	strung	wit	wist, wiste	wist
strive	strove, strived	striven, strived	wring	wrung	wrung
			write	wrote	written

5. Los tiempos del modo indicativo. Hay seis tiempos principales, que son: el presente, el pretérito, el futuro, el presente perfecto, el pretérito perfecto y el futuro perfecto. Los tiempos se forman de las partes principales del verbo. Obsérvese que el verbo inglés no cambia su terminación para indicar a la persona gramatical, por eso es necesario usar siempre los pronombres personales.

a) *El presente.* El presente se usa para expresar una acción o estado actual, una acción habitual o una verdad.

John works in the garden   *Juan trabaja en el jardín*

SINGULAR		PLURAL
primera persona	I play	we play
segunda persona	you play	you play
tercera persona	he, she plays	they play

b) *El pretérito.* El pretérito expresa una acción terminada en el pasado.

Columbus discovered America   *Colón descubrió América*

SINGULAR		PLURAL
primera persona	I played	we played
segunda persona	you played	you played
tercera persona	he, she played	they played

No hay ningún tiempo en inglés que corresponda al imperfecto en español. La idea del imperfecto se expresa por medio del pretérito del verbo auxiliar **to be** y el participio presente del verbo conjugado.

SINGULAR		PLURAL
primera persona	I was playing	we were playing
segunda persona	you were playing	you were playing
tercera persona	he, she was playing	they were playing

c) *El futuro.* El futuro expresa una acción realizada después del momento actual. En inglés es necesario usar el verbo auxiliar **will** para formar el tiempo futuro.

He will work tomorrow   *El trabajará mañana*

SINGULAR		PLURAL
primera persona	I will play	we will play
segunda persona	you will play	you will play
tercera persona	he, she will play	they will play

En inglés no se usa el futuro para expresar probabilidad.

d) *El presente perfecto.* El presente perfecto expresa una acción pasada que se prolonga hasta el presente. Se forma con el presente del verbo auxiliar **to have** y el participio pasado del verbo conjugado.

I have played football many times   *He jugado al fútbol muchas veces*

SINGULAR		PLURAL
primera persona	I have played	we have played
segunda persona	you have played	you have played
tercera persona	he, she has played	they have played

e) *El pretérito perfecto.* El pretérito perfecto expresa una acción completada antes de algún momento indicado en el pasado. Se forma con el pretérito del verbo auxiliar **to have** y el participio pasado del verbo conjugado.

He had played the year before   *El había jugado el año anterior*

SINGULAR		PLURAL
primera persona	I had played	we had played
segunda persona	you had played	you had played
tercera persona	he, she had played	they had played

f) *El futuro perfecto.* El futuro perfecto expresa una acción que habrá de completarse en algún momento indicado en el futuro. Este tiempo es de escaso uso en inglés.

SINGULAR		PLURAL
primera persona	I will have played	we will have played
segunda persona	you will have played	you will have played
tercera persona	he, she will have played	they will have played

6. Los verbos auxiliares **to be** y **to have**. La conjugación del verbo **to be** es irregular en el presente y en el pretérito.

a) *El presente* de **to be** y **to have**

SINGULAR	PLURAL	SINGULAR	PLURAL
I am	we are	I have	we have
you are	you are	you have	you have
he, she, it is	they are	he, she, it has	they have

b) *El pretérito* de **to be**

I was	we were
you were	you were
he, she, it was	they were

7. *El modo subjuntivo y sus tiempos.* El modo subjuntivo expresa una duda, deseo, reproche, concesión, suposición o una condición contraria a la realidad. El subjuntivo es de escaso uso en inglés. En su lugar se emplean otras construcciones que sirven para expresar la misma idea. Se puede usar el indicativo para expresar la idea del subjuntivo.

He commands that I leave	*Él manda que yo salga*

También se puede expresar la idea del subjuntivo por medio de las palabras **should, would, could might,** etc.

John should have come	*Juan debiera de haber venido*
He could have taken the train	*Él pudo haber tomado el tren*

Nótese que el modo potencial no existe en inglés. En su lugar se usa **would,** que equivale al presente, futuro o pretérito del subjuntivo, según las circunstancias.

If he had the money he would go	*Si él tuviera el dinero, iría*
Would you like to dance?	*¿Querría Vd. bailar?*

No se usa el subjuntivo en inglés para expresar probabilidad en el pasado.

It was probably three o'clock	*Serían las tres*

8. *El modo imperativo.* El modo imperativo expresa un mandato; sólo tiene el tiempo presente. Se forma con la segunda persona singular del verbo, sin el pronombre sujeto **you.**

go!	¡ve! ¡id!
come!	¡ven! ¡venid!

9. *La voz pasiva.* La voz pasiva se forma con el verbo auxiliar **to be** y el participio pasado del verbo conjugado.

The earth was seen clearly by the astronauts	*La tierra fue vista claramente por los astronautas*
This play has been performed many times	*Esta pieza teatral ha sido representada muchas veces*

H. De la conjunción

Las conjunciones son una parte invariable de la oración; se usan para enlazar dos o más palabras u oraciones. Las conjunciones se dividen en inglés, como en español, en *copulativas y disyuntivas.* Las conjunciones copulativas principales son: **and** (*y, e*), **but** (*pero, mas, sin embargo,* etc.) y **or** (*o, u*).

It was a black and white cat	*Era un gato negro y blanco*
John can play piano or guitar	*Juan toca piano o guitarra*

Las conjunciones disyuntivas principales son: **if** (*si, aunque,* etc.), **while** (*mientras que,* etc.), **although** (*bien que, aunque,* etc.), **though** (*bien que, aunque,* etc.), **when** (*cuando,* etc.), **until** (*hasta que*), **as** (*como; a medida que,* etc.), **since** (*desde que; puesto que,* etc.), **that** (*que; para que,* etc.) y **because** (*porque,* etc.).

I will play if you ask me	*Tocaré si Vd. me lo pide*
He didn't go out while it was raining	*Él no salió mientras que llovía*

I. De la preposición

La preposición sirve para denotar la relación entre dos palabras en una oración. Muchas preposiciones indican dirección o posición (over, *sobre, encima;* behind, *tras, detras de;* from, *de, desde;* to, *a, hasta, para;* above, *sobre, encima;* below, *bajo, debajo de;* out, *fuera de;* in, *en, mientras;* around, *cerca de, alrededor de;* through, *por, a través de;* beyond, *más allá de, tras;* across, *a través de;* beside, *al lado de, junto a,* etc.), y otras representan varios tipos de relación (of, *de;* except, *excepto, con excepción de;* for, *por, para;* besides, *además de, a más de,* etc.).

NUMEROS–NUMERALS

Números Cardinales	Cardinal Numbers	Números Ordinales	Ordinal Numbers	Fracciones	Fractions
1-uno, una	one	primero	first	—	—
2-dos	two	segundo	second	medio	half
3-tres	three	tercero	third	tercio	third
4-cuatro	four	cuarto	fourth	cuarto	fourth, quarter
5-cinco	five	quinto	fifth	quinto	fifth
6-seis	six	sexto	sixth	sexto	sixth
7-siete	seven	séptimo	seventh	séptimo	seventh
8-ocho	eight	octavo	eighth	octavo	eighth
9-nueve	nine	noveno, nono	ninth	noveno	ninth
10-diez	ten	décimo	tenth	décimo	tenth
11-once	eleven	undécimo	eleventh	onceavo	eleventh
12-doce	twelve	duodécimo	twelfth	doceavo	twelfth
13-trece	thirteen	décimotercio, o decimotercero	thirteenth	treceavo	thirteenth
14-catorce	fourteen	décimocuarto	fourteenth	catorceavo	fourteenth
15-quince	fifteen	décimoquinto	fifteenth	quinceavo	fifteenth
16-dieciséis, diez y seis	sixteen	décimosexto	sixteenth	dieciseisavo	sixteenth
17-diecisiete, diez y siete	seventeen	décimoséptimo	seventeenth	diecisieteavo	seventeenth
18-dieciocho, diez y ocho	eighteen	décimoctavo	eighteenth	dieciochoavo	eighteenth
19-diecinueve, diez y nueve	nineteen	décimonono, o decimonoveno	nineteenth	diecinueveavo	nineteenth
20-veinte	twenty	vigésimo	twentieth	veinteavo o vigésimo	twentieth
30-treinta	thirty	trigésimo	thirtieth	treintavo o trigésimo	thirtieth
40-cuarenta	forty	cuadragésimo	fortieth	cuarentavo o cuadragésimo	fortieth
50-cincuenta	fifty	quincuagésimo	fiftieth	cincuantavo o quincuagésimo	fiftieth
60-sesenta	sixty	sexagésimo	sixtieth	sesentavo o sexagésimo	sixtieth
70-setenta	seventy	septuagésimo	seventieth	setentavo o septuagésimo	seventieth
80-ochenta	eighty	octogésimo	eightieth	ochentavo o octogésimo	eightieth
90-noventa	ninety	nonagésimo	ninetieth	noventavo o nonagésimo	ninetieth
100-cien, ciento	one hundred	centésimo	(one) hundredth	centavo o céntimo centésimo	(one) hundredth
101-ciento uno	one hundred and one	centésimo primo o centésimo primero	(one) hundred and first		(one) hundred(th) and first

Números Cardinales	Cardinal Numbers	Números Ordinales	Ordinal Numbers	Fracciones	Fractions
200-dos-cientos	two hundred	ducentésimo	two-hundredth	ducentésimo	two-hundredth
300-tres-cientos	three hundred	tricentésimo	three-hundredth	tricentésimo	three-hundredth
400-cuatro-cientos	four hundred	cuadringen-tésimo	four-hundredth	cuadringenté-simo	four-hundredth
500-quinien-tos	five hundred	quingentésimo	five-hundredth	quingenté-simo	five-hundredth
600-seis-cientos	six hundred	sexagentésimo	six-hundredth	sexagentésimo	six-hundredth
700-sete-cientos	seven hundred	septingen-tésimo	seven-hundredth	septingenté-simo	seven-hundredth
800-ocho-cientos	eight hundred	octingenté-simo	eight-hundredth	octingenté-simo	eight-hundredth
900-nove-cientas	nine hundred	noningenté-simo	nine-hundredth	noningenté-simo	nine-hundredth
1000-mil	one thousand	milésimo	(one) thousandth	milésimo	(one) thousandth
10,000-diez mil	ten thousand	diezmilésimo	(one) ten thousandth	diezmilésimo	(one) ten thousandth
100,000-cien mil	one hundred thousand	cienmilésimo	(one) hundred thousandth	cienmilésimo	(one) hundred thousandth
1,000,000-un millon	one million	millonésimo	(one) millionth	millonésimo	(one) millionth
1,000,000,000 (000)-un billon	one billion (in Spain, one million millions)	billonésimo	(one) billionth	billonésimo	(one) billionth

TABLAS DE VERBOS IRREGULARES INGLESES

El número que aparece en corchetes a la derecha de un verbo irregular indica la clase a que pertenece en las tablas siguientes.

CLASE 1

Los verbos de esta clase duplican la consonante final del infinitivo para formar el pretérito y el participio pasado. Ejemplos:

Presente	Pretérito	Participio	Presente	Pretérito	Participio
annul	annulled	annulled	quiz	quizzed	quizzed
bag	bagged	bagged	etc.	etc.	etc.
cap	capped	capped			

CLASE 2

Los verbos pertenecientes a esta clase pueden, al formar el pretérito y el participio pasado, duplicar la consonante final del infinitivo o dejarla simple. Ambas formas son aceptadas en el uso. Ejemplos:

Presente	Pretérito	Participio
anvil	anviled, anvilled	anviled, anvilled
bias	biased, biassed	biased, biassed
focus	focused, focussed	focused, focussed
kidnap	kidnaped, kidnapped	kidnaped, kidnapped
patrol	patroled, patrolled	patroled, patrolled
travel	traveled, travelled	traveled, travelled
etc.	etc.	etc.

CLASE 3

Presente	Pretérito	Participio	Presente	Pretérito	Participio
bet	bet, betted	bet, betted	quit	quit, quitted	quit, quitted
dig	dug, digged	dug, digged			
dip	dipped, dipt	dipped, dipt	rid	rid, ridded	rid, ridded
			shred	shredded, shred	shredded, shred
drip	dripped, dript	dripped, dript	wed	wedded	wedded, wed
drop	dropped, dropt	dropped, dropt			
			wet	wet, wetted	wet, wetted
knit	knitted, knit	knitted, knit	whip	whipped, whipt	whipped, whipt
pen (en-cerrar)	penned, pent	penned, pent	wrap	wrapped, wrapt	wrapped, wrapt

CLASE 4

Presente	Pretérito	Participio
alight	alighted, alit	alighted, alit
awake	awoke, awaked	awoke, awaked
bend	bent, bended	bent, bended
blend	blended, blent	blended, blent
broadcast	broadcast, broadcasted	broadcast, broadcasted
burn	burned, burnt	burned, burnt
chide	chided, chid	chided, chid, chidden
cleave	cleft, cleaved, clove	cleft, cleaved, cloven
clothe	clothed, clad	clothed, clad
dream	dreamed, dreamt	dreamed, dreamt
dress	dressed, drest	dressed, drest
dwell	dwelt, dwelled	dwelt, dwelled
forecast	forecast, forecasted	forecast, forecasted
gild	gilded, gilt	gilded, gilt
gird	girded, girt	girded, girt
grind	ground, grinded	ground, grinded
heave	heaved, hove	heaved, hove
kneel	knelt, kneeled	knelt, kneeled
lean	leaned, leant	leaned, leant
leap	leaped, leapt	leaped, leapt
learn	learned, learnt	learned, learnt
light	lighted, lit	lighted, lit
misspell	misspelled, misspelt	misspelled, misspelt
mix	mixed, mixt	mixed, mixt
outwork	outworked, outwrought	outworked, outwrought
overwork	overworked, overwrought	overworked, overwrought
plead	pleaded, pled, plead	pleaded, pled, plead
smell	smelled, smelt	smelled, smelt
speed	sped, speeded	sped, speeded
spell	spelled, spelt	spelled, spelt
spill	spilled, spilt	spilled, spilt
spoil	spoiled, spoilt	spoiled, spoilt
stave	staved, stove	staved, stove
stay	stayed, staid	stayed, staid
sunburn	sunburned, sunburnt	sunburned, sunburnt
sweat	sweat, sweated	sweat, sweated
thrive	throve, thrived	thrived, thriven
unclothe	unclothed, unclad	unclothed, unclad
work	worked, wrought	worked, wrought

CLASE 5

Presente	Pretérito	Participio	Presente	Pretérito	Participio
bide	bode, bided	bided	dive	dived, dove	dived
crow	crowed, crew	crowed	wake	waked, woke	waked
dare	dared, durst	dared			

CLASE 6

Presente	Pretérito	Participio	Presente	Pretérito	Participio
hew	hewed	hewed, hewn	shave	shaved	shaved, shaven
melt	melted	melted, molten	shear	sheared	sheared, shorn
mow	mowed	mowed, mown	show	showed	showed, shown
pass	passed	passed, past	sow	sowed	sowed, sown
prove	proved	proved, proven	strew	strewed	strewed, strewn
saw	sawed	sawed, sawn	swell	swelled	swelled, swollen
sew	sewed	sewed, sewn	weave	wove	wove, woven

CLASE 7

Los verbos pertenecientes a esta clase cambian la *y* final del infinitivo en *ied* para formar el pretérito y el participio pasado. Si la *y* se pronuncia [ai], *ied* se pronuncia [aid]. Cuando se pronuncia [i] el preterito y el participio se pronuncian [id]. Ejemplos:

bury	buried	buried	fancy	fancied	fancied
certify	certified	certified	worry	worried	worried
dirty	dirtied	dirtied	etc.	etc.	etc.

CLASE 8

Todos los verbos pertenecientes a esta clase añaden *ked* al infinitivo para formar el pretérito y el participio pasado. Ejemplos:

frolic	frolicked	frolicked	panic	panicked	panicked
mimic	mimicked	mimicked	etc.	etc.	etc.

CLASE 9

Los verbos pertenecientes a esta clase no varian en la formación del pretérito y el participio pasado. Ejemplos:

cut	cut	cut	put	put	put
hit	hit	hit	etc.	etc.	etc.
let	let	let			

CLASE 10

abide	abode	abode	eat	ate	eaten
arise	arose	arisen	fall	fell	fallen
backbite	backbit	backbitten, backbit	feed	fed	fed
bear	bore	borne, born	feel	felt	felt
			fight	fought	fought
			find	found	found
beat	beat	beaten, beat	flee	fled	fled
			fling	flung	flung
become	became	become	fly	flew	flown
befall	befell	befallen	forbear	forbore	forborne
begin	began	begun	forbid	forbade, forbad	forbidden, forbid
behold	beheld	beheld			
beseech	besought	besought	forego	forewent	foregone
bid	bade, bid	bidden, bid	foresee	foresaw	foreseen
			foretell	foretold	foretold
bind	bound	bound	forget	forgot	forgotten, forgot
bite	bit	bitten, bit			
bleed	bled	bled	forgive	forgave	forgiven
blow	blew	blown	forsake	forsook	forsaken
break	broke	broken (roto), broke (arruinado)	forswear	forswore	forsworn
			freeze	froze	frozen
			get	got	gotten, got
			give	gave	given
			go	went	gone
breed	bred	bred	grow	grew	grown
bring	brought	brought	hang (colgar)	hung	hung
build	built	built			
buy	bought	bought	hear	heard	heard
catch	caught	caught	hide	hid	hidden, hid
choose	chose	chosen	hold	held	held
cling	clung	clung	inlay	inlaid	inlaid
come	came	come	keep	kept	kept
creep	crept	crept	know	knew	known
deal	dealt	dealt	lay	laid	laid
draw	drew	drawn	lead	led	led
drink	drank	drunk	leave	left	left
drive	drove	driven	lend	lent	lent

Presente	Pretérito	Participio	Presente	Pretérito	Participio
lie (echarse)	lay	lain	sing	sang, sung	sung
			sink	sank, sunk	sunk, sunken
lose	lost	lost			
make	made	made	sit	sat	sat
make-up	made-up	made-up	slay	slew	slain
mean	meant	meant	sleep	slept	slept
meet	met	met	slide	slid	slid, slidden
mislay	mislaid	mislaid			
mislead	misled	misled	sling	slung	slung
mistake	mistook	mistaken	slink	slunk	slunk
misunderstand	misunderstood	misunderstood	smite	smote	smitten, smit
outbid	outbid	outbidden, outbid	speak	spoke	spoken
			spellbind	spellbound	spellbound
outdo	outdid	outdone	spend	spent	spent
outgo	outwent	outgone	spin	spun	spun
outgrow	outgrew	outgrown	spit	spat, spit	spat, spit
outlay	outlaid	outlaid	spring	sprang, sprung	sprung
outrun	outran	outrun			
outshine	outshone	outshone	stand	stood	stood
overbear	overbore	overborne	steal	stole	stolen
overbid	overbid	overbidden, overbid	stick	stuck	stuck
			sting	stung	stung
overcome	overcame	overcome	stink	stank, stunk	stunk
overdo	overdid	overdone			
overdraw	overdrew	overdrawn	stride	strode	stridden
overeat	overate	overeaten	strike	struck	struck, stricken
overfeed	overfed	overfed			
overgrow	overgrew	overgrown	string	strung	strung
overhang	overhung	overhung	strive	strove	striven
overhear	overheard	overheard	swear	swore	sworn
overlay	overlaid	overlaid	sweep	swept	swept
overrun	overran	overrun	swing	swung	swung
oversee	oversaw	overseen	take	took	taken
overshoot	overshot	overshot	teach	taught	taught
oversleep	overslept	overslept	tear	tore	torn
overtake	overtook	overtaken	tell	told	told
overthrow	overthrew	overthrown	think	thought	thought
partake	partook	partaken	throw	threw	thrown
pay	paid	paid	tread	trod	trodden, trod
prepay	prepaid	prepaid			
rebuild	rebuilt	rebuilt	typewrite	typewrote	typewritten
remake	remade	remade			
rend	rent	rent	undergo	underwent	undergone
repay	repaid	repaid	underpay	underpaid	underpaid
resell	resold	resold	undersell	undersold	undersold
retake	retook	retaken	understand	understood	understood
ride	rode	ridden			
ring	rang	rung	undertake	undertook	undertaken
rise	rose	risen	undo	undid	undone
run	ran	run	uphold	upheld	upheld
say	said	said	waylay	waylaid	waylaid
see	saw	seen	wear	wore	worn
seek	sought	sought	weep	wept	wept
sell	sold	sold	win	won	won
send	sent	sent	wind	wound	wound
shake	shook	shaken	withdraw	withdrew	withdrawn
shine	shone, shined	shone, shined	withhold	withheld	withheld
			withstand	withstood	withstood
shoe	shod	shod	wring	wrung	wrung
shoot	shot	shot	write	wrote	written
shrink	shrank, shrunk	shrunk, shrunken			

CLASS 11 (Verbos auxiliares, anómalos y defectivos)

	Present	Preterit	Past Participle
to be	I am, you are, he is; (pl.) are	I was, you were, he was; (pl.) were	been
can	can	could	—
to do	I, you do, he does; (pl.) do	did	done
to have	I, you have, he has; (pl.) have	had	had

	Present		Preterit	Past Participle
may	may		might	—
must	must		—	—
ought	ought		ought	—
shall	shall		should	—
will	will		would	—

ABREVIATURAS USADAS EN LA PARTE IIª

a.	. . . .	adjetivo.
abrev.	. . . .	abreviatura.
adv.	. . . .	adverbio.
(aer.)	. . . .	aeronáutica.
(agr.)	. . . .	agricultura.
(alb.)	. . . .	albañilería.
(álg.)	. . . .	álgebra.
(Am.)	. . . .	América.
(anat.)	. . . .	anatomía.
(ant.)	. . . .	anticuado.
(apl.)	. . . .	aplícase.
(Arg.)	. . . .	Argentina.
(arit.)	. . . .	aritmética.
(arm.)	. . . .	armería.
(arq.)	. . . .	arquitectura.
art.	. . . .	artículo.
(arti.)	. . . .	artillería.
(astr.)	. . . .	astronomía, astrología.
(aut.)	. . . .	automovilismo.
aux.	. . . .	auxiliar.
(b.a.)	. . . .	bellas artes.
(biol.)	. . . .	biología.
(bot.)	. . . .	botánica.
(carp.)	. . . .	carpintería.
(carr.)	. . . .	carruajería.
(cir.)	. . . .	cirugía.
(coc.)	. . . .	cocina.
(com.)	. . . .	comercio.
comp.	. . . .	comparativo.
conj.	. . . .	conjunción.
contr.	. . . .	contracción.
(cost.)	. . . .	costura.
defect.	. . . .	defectivo.
(elec.), (eléc.)	. . . .	electricidad.
(esp.)	. . . .	especialmente.
(E.U.)	. . . .	Estados Unidos.
f.	. . . .	femenino.
(fam.)	. . . .	familiar.
(farm.)	. . . .	farmacia.
(f.c.)	. . . .	ferrocarriles.
(fig.)	. . . .	figurado.
(filos.)	. . . .	filosofía.
(fís.)	. . . .	física.
(fisiol.)	. . . .	fisiología.
(fon.)	. . . .	fonética.
(for.)	. . . .	voz forense.
(fort.)	. . . .	fortificación.
(fot.)	. . . .	fotografía.
(gen.)	. . . .	generalmente.
(geog.)	. . . .	geografía.
(geol.)	. . . .	geología.
(geom.)	. . . .	geometría.
ger.	. . . .	gerundio.
(gram.)	. . . .	gramática.
(heráld.)	. . . .	heráldica.
(hidr.)	. . . .	hidráulica.
(hist.)	. . . .	historia.
(hort.)	. . . .	horticultura.
(ict.)	. . . .	ictiología.
(igl.)	. . . .	iglesia.
imp.	. . . .	imperfecto.
impers.	. . . .	impersonal.
(impr.)	. . . .	imprenta.
indic.	. . . .	indicativo.

inf.	. . . .	infinitivo.
(ing.)	. . . .	ingeniería.
interj.	. . . .	interjección.
interrog.	. . . .	interrogativo.
(joy.)	. . . .	joyería.
(lóg.)	. . . .	lógica.
m.	. . . .	masculino.
(mar.)	. . . .	marina.
(mat.)	. . . .	matemáticas.
(mec.)	. . . .	mecánica.
(med.)	. . . .	medicina.
mf.	. . . .	masculino y femenino.
(mil.)	. . . .	milicia.
(miner.)	. . . .	minería, minerología.
(mús.), (mus.)	. . . .	música, musical.
(ópt.)	. . . .	óptica.
(orn.)	. . . .	ornitología.
pers.	. . . .	personal.
(pert.)	. . . .	perteneciente (a).
pl.	. . . .	plural.
(poét.)	. . . .	poética.
(pol.)	. . . .	política.
pos.	. . . .	posesivo.
pp.	. . . .	participio pasado.
pp. i.	. . . .	participio pasado irregular.
prep.	. . . .	preposición.
pret.	. . . .	pretérito.
pron.	. . . .	pronombre.
(quím.), (quim.)	. . . .	química.
(rad.)	. . . .	radiocomunicación,
refl.	. . . .	reflejo o reflexivo.
rel.	. . . .	relativo (gram.)
(rel.)	. . . .	relativo a.
s.	. . . .	substantivo.
sing.	. . . .	singular.
(sociol.)	. . . .	sociología.
subj.	. . . .	subjuntivo.
super.	. . . .	superlativo.
(teat.)	. . . .	teatro.
(técn.)	. . . .	técnica.
(tej.)	. . . .	tejidos.
(tlf.)	. . . .	telefonía.
(tlg.)	. . . .	telegrafía.
(Ú., ú.)	. . . .	Úsase, úsase.
(V., v.)	. . . .	Véa(n)se, véa(n)se.
va.	. . . .	verbo auxiliar.
vai.	. . . .	verbo auxiliar irregular.
(vg., v.g., v. gr.)	. . . .	por ejemplo.
vi.	. . . .	verbo intransitivo.
vii.	. . . .	verbo intransitivo irregular.
vr.	. . . .	verbo reflexivo o recíproco.
vri.	. . . .	verbo reflexivo o recíproco irregular.
vt.	. . . .	verbo transitivo.
vti.	. . . .	verbo transitivo irregular.
(vulg.)	. . . .	vulgarismo.
(zool.)	. . . .	zoología.

A

a [ə, ei], *art.* un, una.—*from A to Z,* de pe a pa.

aback [əbǽk], *adv.* detrás, atrás.—*to take a.,* desconcertar, coger de improviso.

abandon [əbǽndon], *vt.* abandonar, dejar.—*vr.* entregarse a (la bebida, etc.).—*s.* indiferencia, naturalidad; abandono, abandonamiento.

abase [əbéis], *vt.* abatir, humillar.

abash [əbǽʃ], *vt.* avergonzar, turbar; sonrojar.

abate [əbéit], *vt.* reducir, rebajar; impedir; condonar; anular.—*vr.* disminuirse, calmarse.

abbey [ǽbi], *s.* abadía.—**abbot** [ǽbot], *s.* abad.

abbreviate [əbríviei], *vt.* abreviar, reducir, compendiar.—**abbreviation** [əbrivijéiʃon], *s.* abreviatura; cifra; compendio.

abdicate [ǽbdikeit], *vt.* abdicar (al trono).

abdomen [ǽbdomen], *s.* abdomen, vientre.—**abdominal** [æbdámiṇəl], *a.* abdominal.

abduct [æbdʌkt], *vt.* secuestrar, raptar (a alguien).—**—ion** [æbdʌkʃon], *s.* robo, secuestro; (anat.) abducción.

aberration [æberéiʃon], *s.* error; desliz; aberración.

abet [əbét], *vti.* [1] favorecer, apoyar; instigar.

abeyance [əbéians], *s.* expectativa.—*in a.,* suspenso; latente.

abhor [æbhór], *vti.* [1] aborrecer, detestar, abominar.

abide [əbáid], *vti.* [10] esperar, tolerar, sufrir.—*vii.* habitar, permanecer.—*to a. by,* atenerse a.

ability [əbíliti], *s.* capacidad, talento.

abject [ǽbdʒekt], *a.* abatido, servil.—**—ion** [æbdʒékʃon], *s.* abyección; servilismo.

abjure [æbdʒúr], *vt.* abjurar, retractarse de; renunciar solemnemente a.—*vi.* retractarse; hacer renuncia solemne (del reino, etc.).

ablaze [əbléis], *adv.* en llamas.

able [éibl], *a.* capaz, apto, capacitado.—*a.-bodied,* robusto.—*to be a.,* poder, saber.

abnormal [æbnórmal], *a.* anormal, deforme.

aboard [əbórd], *adv.* a bordo.—*all a.!* ¡viajeros al tren!—*to go a.,* embarcarse.

abode [əbóud], *s.* morada, residencia.—*pret. y pp.* de TO ABIDE.

abolish [əbáliʃ], *vt.* abolir, revocar, anular.—**abolition** [æbolíʃon], *s.* abolición, revocación, anulación.

abominable [əbáminabl], *a.* abominable; aborrecible.—**abomination** [əbaminéiʃon], *s.* abominación, odio; maldad.

abortion [əbórʃon], *s.* aborto; fracaso.

abound [əbáund], *vi.* abundar.—*abounding in o with,* nutrido de.

bout [əbáut], *adv.* casi; poco más o menos; alrededor; por ahí (en el lugar, edificio, etc.).—*a.-face,* media vuelta (voz de mando).—*all a.,* por todas partes.—*prep.* de, acerca de; sobre, con respecto a; alrededor de; a eso de; por, en.—*to be a.,* estar para, al punto de.—*to think a.,* pensar en.—*to walk a. town,* pasear por el pueblo.

above [əbʌv], *adv.* susodicho, precitado; precedente.—*s.* lo anterior, lo precedente.—*adv. y prep.* sobre, arriba (de), superior (a), fuera de, anteriormente.—*a. all,* sobre todo.—*from a.,* de lo alto, del cielo; desde arriba.

abrasion [əbréiʒon], *s.* raspadura, desgaste.—**abrasive** [əbréisiv], *a.* raspante.—*s.* abrasivo.

abreast [əbrést], *adv.* de frente, en fila.—*four a.,* de cuatro en fondo.—*to keep a. of something,* estar al tanto de algo.

abridge [əbridʒ], *vt.* abreviar, condensar.—**—ment** [-mənt], *s.* compendio, resumen.

abroad [əbród], *adv.* en el extranjero, fuera de casa o del país; en público.—*to go a.,* salir del país, ir al extranjero.

abrupt [əbrʌpt], *a.* brusco, repentino; escarpado; grosero.

abscess [ǽbses], *s.* absceso.

absence [ǽbsens], *s.* ausencia, falta.—*in the a. of,* a falta de.—*leave of a.,* licencia, permiso.—**absent** [ǽbsent], *a.* ausente.—*a.-minded,* distraído, abstraído, absorto; en Babia.—*to a. oneself,* retirarse (de), ausentarse.

absolute [ǽbsolut], *a.* absoluto, categórico, positivo.

absolution [æbsolúʃon], *s.* absolución.

absolve [æbsálv], *vt.* absolver, dispensar, remitir los pecados.

absorb [æbsórb], *vt.* absorber; empapar; ocupar (el ánimo) intensamente.—**—ed** [-d], *a.* absorto, cautivado.—**—ent** [-ent], *s. y a.* absorbente.—**absorption** [æbsórpʃon], *s.* absorción.

abstain [æbstéin], *vi.* abstenerse, privarse.

abstemious [æbstímiʌs], *a.* sobrio, abstemio.

abstinence [ǽbstinens], *s.* abstinencia, ayuno.

abstract [ǽbstrækt], *s.* término abstracto; abstracción; sumario, extracto.—*a.* abstracto, distraído.—*vt.* [æbstrǽkt], abstraer; resumir, extractar; compendiar; separar.—**—ion** [æbstrǽkʃon], *s.* abstracción, recogimiento.

absurd [æbsǿrd], *a.* absurdo, ridículo, disparatado.— **—ity** [-iti], *s.* absurdo, disparate.

abundance [əbándəns], *s.* abundancia, exuberancia.—**abundant** [əbándənt], *a.* abundante, copioso.

abuse [əbiúz], *vt.* abusar de; insultar; ultrajar, maltratar.—*s.* [əbiús], abuso; injuria; maltrato; violación.— **abusive** [əbiúsiv], *a.* abusivo, insultante, injurioso.

abyss [əbís], *s.* abismo; sima.

academic(al) [ækədémik(əl)], *a.* académico; convencional; teórico.— **academy** [əkǽdemi], *s.* academia, instituto.

accede [æksíd], *vi.* acceder; subir o ascender (al trono).

accelerate [æksélereit], *vt.* acelerar, apresurar.—*vi.* darse prisa.—**acceleration** [ækseleréişon], *s.* aceleración.— **accelerator** [æksélereito(r)], *s.* acelerador.

accent [ǽksent], *s.* acento, dejo.—*vt.* [æksént], acentuar, recalcar.—**accentuate** [æksénchueit], *vt.* acentuar; hacer más patente.

accept [æksépt], *vt.* aceptar, admitir; reconocer.— **—able** [-əbl], *a.* aceptable, grato, admisible.— **—ance** [-əns], *s.* aceptación; buena acogida.

access [ǽkses], *s.* acceso, entrada; aumento; acceso o ataque (de tos, etc.).— **—ible** [æksésibl], *a.* accesible, asequible.— **—ion** [æksésǒn], *s.* aumento; subida (al trono); accesión; consentimiento.— **—ory** [æksésǒri], *a.* accesorio; secundario; adicional.—*s.* dependencia; cómplice.—*pl.* accesorios, repuestos, enseres; útiles (de cocina, etc.).

accident [ǽksident], *s.* accidente, casualidad; percance.— **—al** [æksidéntəl], *a.* accidental, casual.—*s.* (mus.) accidente.

acclaim [ækléim], *vt. y vi.* aclamar, aplaudir, proclamar.—*s.* aclamación. **—acclamation** [ækləméişon], *s.* aclamación, aplauso, proclamación.

acclimate [ækláimit], o **acclimatize** [ækláimŏtaiz], *vt. y vi.* aclimatar(se).

accommodate [əkámodeit], *vt.* acomodar, ajustar; componer; hacer un favor; alojar.—*to a. oneself*, conformarse, adaptarse.—**accommodation** [əkamodéişon], *s.* acomodamiento; favor; adaptación; ajuste; acuerdo.—*pl.* facilidades, comodidades, alojamiento.

accompaniment [əkámpəniment], *s.* acompañamiento.—**accompanist** [əkámpənist], *s.* acompañante.— **accompany** [əkámpəni], *vti.* [7] acompañar.

accomplice [əkámplis], *s.* cómplice.

accomplish [əkámpliş], *vt.* efectuar, cumplir; completar; lograr.— **—ment** [-ment], *s.* cumplimiento, enajenación, ejecución; proeza.—*pl.* conocimientos, habilidades; méritos.

accord [əkǿrd], *s.* acuerdo, convenio; concierto; armonía; (mus.) acorde.—*in a.*, de mutuo acuerdo.—*of one's own a.*, espontáneamente.—*vt.* acordar, conceder, otorgar.—*vi.* concordar; convenir, avenirse, concertar, estar de acuerdo.— **—ance** [-əns], **—ancy** [-ənsi], *s.* conformidad, armonía, acuerdo.—*in accordance with*, de acuerdo con.— **—ant** [-ənt], *a.* acorde, conforme, propio.— **—ing** [iŋ], *a.* conforme, acorde.—*a. as*, a medida que.—*a. to*, según.— **—ingly** [-iŋli], *adv.* en conformidad, en efecto; de consiguiente; por ende.

accordion [əkǿrdiǫn], *s.* acordeón.

accost [əkǿst], *vt.* dirigirse a, abordar (a alguien en la calle); acosar.

account [əkáunt], *vt.* tener por, considerar, estimar.—*vi.* dar cuenta y razón.—*to a. for*, dar razón o responder de.—*s.* relato, relación; importancia, valor; explicación, cuenta, razón; cálculo; consideración; aprecio; (com.) cuenta.—*a. book*, libro de cuentas.—*by all accounts*, según el decir o la opinión general.—*charge a.*, cuenta abierta o corriente.—*of a.*, de nota, de importancia.—*on a. of*, a causa de.—*on my own a.*, por mi cuenta, por mi cuenta y riesgo.—*on no a.*, de ninguna manera.— **—able** [-əbl], *a.* responsable; explicable.— **—ant** [-ənt], *s.* contador; tenedor de libros.— **—ing** [-iŋ], *s.* contabilidad, contaduría; estado de cuentas.—*to ask an a.*, pedir rendición de cuentas.

accredit [əkrédit], *vt.* acreditar; dar credenciales; dar crédito; atribuir a.

accrue [əkrú], *vi.* crecer, tomar incremento; acumularse.

accumulate [əkiúmiuleit], *vt. y vi.* acumular(se), amontonar(se), atesorar; crecer.—**accumulation** [əkiumiuléişon], *s.* acumulación, amontonamiento, hacinamiento.

accuracy [ǽkyurəsi], *s.* exactitud, precisión, esmero.—**accurate** [ǽkyurit], *a.* exacto, preciso; certero (en el tiro); exacto (en los cálculos).

accursed [əkǿrst], *a.* maldito; execrable; perverso, infame.

accusation [ækiuzéişon], *s.* acusación.— **accuse** [əkiúz], *vt.* acusar, denunciar, (in)culpar.

accustom [əkástom], *vt. y vi.* acostumbrar(se), habituar(se), hacer(se).

ace [eis], *s.* as (de naipes o dados); as (el más sobresaliente en su actividad); migaja, partícula.—*within an a. of*,

por poco, en un tris.—*a.* sobresaliente.

ache [eik], *s.* dolor.—*vi.* doler.

achieve [ɐchv], *vt.* realizar, ejecutar.——ment [-mɐnt], *s.* realización, logro; hazaña; proeza.

acid [ǽsid], *s.* y *a.* ácido.——ity [æsíditi], *s.* acidez, acedía.

acknowledge [æknálidž], *vt.* reconocer; confesar, admitir; testificar.—*to a. receipt,* acusar recibo.—acknowledgment [-mɐnt], *s.* reconocimiento; confesión; admisión; acuse de recibo; testificación.

acolyte [ǽkolait], *s.* acólito, monaguillo.

acorn [éikorn], *s.* bellota.

acoustic [ɐkústik], *a.* acústico.—*s. pl.* acústica; condiciones acústicas.

acquaint [ɐkwéint], *vt.* instruir, familiarizar; enterar, informar, advertir.—*to a. oneself with,* ponerse al corriente de, ponerse al tanto de.——ance [-ɐns], *s.* conocimiento; familiaridad.

acquiesce [ækwiés], *vi.* asentir, consentir, conformarse.——nce [ækwiéɐns], *s.* aquiescencia, asentimiento, resignación.

acquire [ɐkwáir], *vt.* adquirir, obtener, contraer (hábitos, etc.).—acquisition [ækwizíšɐn], *s.* adquisición, consecución.

acquit [ɐkwít], *vti.* [I] absolver, dispensar; exonerar, relevar; pagar.—*to a. oneself,* quedar bien; exonerarse.——tal [-ɐl], *s.* absolución.

acre [éikœr], *s.* acre (medida de superficie). Ver Tabla.

acrimonious [ækrimóuniɐs], *a.* acre.

acrobat [ǽkrobæt], *s.* acróbata.

across [ɐkrós], *adv.* a o de través; de una parte a otra; al otro lado; en cruz.—*prep.* a través de; al otro lado de; por.—*a. the way,* enfrente.

act [ækt], *s.* acción, acto, hecho; (teat.) acto, número; (for.) ley, decreto, acta.—*a. of God,* fuerza mayor.—*vi.* obrar, actuar, funcionar; representar (en el teatro); simular; portarse.—*to a. as,* servir de, estar de.—*to a. up,* jaranear.—*vt.* hacer o desempeñar el papel de.——ing [ǽktiŋ], *s.* acción; (teat.) representación.—*a.* interino.——ion [ǽkšɐn], *s.* acción, acto; operación, funcionamiento; movimiento; (teat.) argumento; (mil.) batalla; (mec.) mecanismo; (for.) demanda, proceso.—*to bring an a.,* entablar un pleito.—*to take a.,* proceder (contra).

activate [ǽktiveit], *vt.* activar.——active [ǽktiv], *a.* activo, diligente, ágil, eficaz.—activity [æktíviti], *s.* actividad, vigor.——*pl.* ocupaciones.

actor [ǽktɐ(r)], *s.* actor, comediante; (for.) demandante.—actress [ǽktris], *s.* actriz; (for.) actora, demandante.

actual [ǽkchuɐl], *a.* real, verdadero; efectivo; existente.

actuary [ǽkchuɐri], *s.* actuario (de seguros); escribano, registrador.

acumen [ɐkiúmin], *s.* cacumen.

acute [ɐkiút], *a.* agudo; ingenioso, perspicaz.

ad [æd], *s.* (fam.) anuncio, aviso.

adamant [ǽdɐmænt], *a.* firme, inflexible.

adapt [ɐdǽpt], *vt.* adaptar, ajustar, amoldar; refundir.——ation [ædæptéišɐn], *s.* adaptación, ajuste.

add [æd], *vt.* sumar, adicionar, totalizar, añadir.—*vi.* sumar.

addict [ǽdikt], *s.* adicto, aficionado.—*drug a.,* narcómano.——ed [ɐdíktid], *a.* adicto, entregado o afecto a; partidario de.

addition [ædíšɐn], *s.* adición, añadidura; aditamento, adjunto, suma.—*in a.,* por añadidura.—*in a. to,* además de.——al [-ɐl], *a.* adicional.

address [ɐdrés], *vt.* dirigir la palabra, arengar; dirigir o poner el sobre a una carta.—*s.* [ɐdrés, ǽdres], dirección, señas; sobrescrito; membrete; discurso; solicitud; memorial.——er [-œ(r)], *s.* remitente (de una carta, etc.).

adept [ɐdépt], *a.* adepto, perito.

adequacy [ǽdɐkwɐsi], *s.* adecuación, suficiencia.—adequate [ǽdɐkwit], *a.* adecuado, proporcionado, suficiente.

adhere [ædhír], *vi.* adherirse, unirse; pegarse.——nce [ædhírɐns], *s.* adhesión, apego, adherencia.—adhesion [ædhíšɐn], *s.* adhesión, adherencia.—adhesive [ædhísiv], *a.* adhesivo, sustancia adhesiva.—*a.* adhesivo, pegadizo, engomado (sello).—*a. tape* o *plaster,* esparadrapo.

adjacent [ædžéisɐnt], *a.* adyacente, contiguo.

adjective [ǽdžɐktiv], *s.* adjetivo.

adjoin [ædžóin], *vt.* juntar, unir.—*vt.* (co)lindar con, estar contiguo.——ing [-iŋ], *a.* contiguo, inmediato, adyacente.

adjourn [ædžœrn], *vt.* diferir, aplazar, clausurar, suspender o levantar la sesión.—*vi.* levantarse o suspenderse (una sesión).——ment [-mɐnt], *s.* aplazamiento, traslación, suspensión, clausura.

adjunct [ǽdžʌŋkt], *s.* aditamento, adjunto; ayudante; subalterno.—*a.* adjunto, auxiliar, subordinado.

adjust [ædžʌst], *vt.* ajustar, adaptar, acomodar, concertar; dirimir (disputas, etc.); regular.——ment [-mɐnt], *s.* arreglo, adaptación, ajuste; regulación.

administer [ædmínistœ(r)], *vt.* administrar; desempeñar (un cargo); suminis-

trar; dar; aplicar (remedios, un castigo, etc.).—*to a. an oath*, tomar juramento.—*vi.* servir, auxiliar.—
administration [ædmįnįstréįṣọn], *s.* administración; ministerio; gobierno; gerencia; manejo.—**administrative** [ædmįnįstreịtịv], *a.* administrativo; gubernativo.—**administrator** [ædmįnįstreịtọ(r)], *s.* administrador; albacea.
admirable [ǽdmįrạbl], *a.* admirable.
admiral [ǽdmįrạl], *s.* almirante.—**—ty** [-tį], *s.* almirantazgo; departamento o ministerio de marina.
admiration [ædmįréįṣọn], *s.* admiración.—**admire** [ædmáįr], *vt.* admirar; estimar; contemplar con placer.—*vi.* admirarse de; sentir admiración por.—**admirer** [ædmáįrœ(r)], *s.* admirador; enamorado, pretendiente.
admission [ædmįṣọn], *s.* admisión, entrada; acceso; precio de entrada; concesión, reconocimiento.—*a. fee*, cuota de entrada (en un club, etc.).—**admit** [ædmít], *vti.* [1] admitir, recibir; dar entrada; reconocer.—**admittance** [ædmítạns], *s.* admisión; entrada.
admonish [ædmánįṣ], *vt.* amonestar; advertir; prevenir.—**admonition** [ædmoníṣọn], *s.* amonestación; advertencia, prevención.
adolescence [ædolésẹns], *s.* adolescencia.—**adolescent** [ædolésẹnt], *s.* y *a.* adolescente.
adopt [ạdápt], *vt.* adoptar, prohijar.—**—ion** [ạdápṣọn], *s.* adopción, prohijamiento.
adorable [ạdórạbl], *a.* adorable—**adoration** [ædoréįṣọn], *s.* adoración; idolatría.—**adore** [ạdór], *vt.* adorar; idolatrar.
adorn [ạdórn], *vt.* adornar, ornamentar, embellecer, acicalar, aderezar.—**—ment** [-mẹnt], *s.* adorno, atavío, ornamento, adorno; acicalamiento.
adrenaline [ædrénạlįn], *s.* adrenalina.
adrift [ạdríft], *adv.* al garete; abandonado; a la deriva.
adroit [ạdróįt], *a.* diestro, hábil, listo.
adulation [ædʒuléįṣọn], *s.* adulación, lisonja.
adult [ạdÁlt], *a.* y *s.* persona mayor; adulto.
adulterate [ạdÁltœreịt], *vt.* adulterar, falsificar, viciar.—*a.* adulterado, falso; adúltero.—**adultery** [ạdÁltœrį], *s.* adulterio.
advance [ædvǽns], *vt.* avanzar; adelantar, promover; aventajar; acelerar; (com.) anticipar dinero, pagar adelantado, ofrecer; subir el precio de.—*vi.* avanzar, adelantarse; progresar; subir de valor o de precio.—*s.* avance; delantera; adelanto, progresso.—*pl.* propuestas; requerimientos amorosos; (com.) adelanto, anti-

cipo, préstamo; alza; precio adicional, —*a.* previo, anticipado.—*a. guard.* (mil.) avanzada.—*in a.*, anticipadamente; al frente; de antemano; (com.) por adelantado; anticipado.—**d** [-t], *a.* avanzado, adelantado, desarrollado.—*a. in years*, entrado en años; de edad madura.—**—ment** [-mẹnt], *s.* progreso, adelantamiento; promoción; mejora.
advantage [ædvǽntįdʒ], *s.* ventaja, beneficio, delantera.—*to one's a.*, con provecho para uno.—*to take a. of*, aprovecharse de, sacar partido de.—*vt.* adelantar, mejorar, favorecer; remunerar.—*vi.* medrar, sacar ventaja.—**—ous** [ædvạntéįdʒạs], *a.* provechoso, ventajoso, conveniente.
advent [ǽdvẹnt], *s.* venida, advenimiento.
adventure [ædvénchọr], *s.* aventura; casualidad; lance.—*vt.* aventurar, arriesgar.—*vi.* aventurarse (a), arriesgarse.—**r** [-œ(r)], *s.* aventurero.—**adventurous** [-ʌs], *a.* aventurero; aventurado, arriesgado; atrevido.
adverb [ǽdvœrb], *s.* adverbio.
adversary [ǽdvœrserį], *s.* adversario, enemigo, contrario.—**adverse** [ædvœrs], *a.* adverso, contrario, opuesto, enemigo.—**adversity** [ædvœrsịtį], *s.* adversidad, desgracia.
advertise [ǽdvœrtaịz], *vt.* anunciar, avisar, hacer propaganda o publicidad.—**—ment** [ædvœrtįzmẹnt], *s.* aviso, anuncio, reclamo.—**r** [ǽdvœrtaịzœ(r)], *s.* anunciante.—**advertising** [ǽdvœrtaịzịŋ], *s.* propaganda, publicidad.
advice [ædvaįs], *s.* consejo; aviso, notificación, parecer, advertencia.
advisable [ædvaịzạbl], *a.* aconsejable, prudente; conveniente.—**advise** [ædvaịz], *vt.* aconsejar; avisar, notificar, advertir, amonestar, denunciar; asesorar.—*vi.* consultar, aconsejarse, pedir o tomar consejo.—**adviser** [ædvaịzœ(r)], *s.* consejero, consultor.—*legal a.*, abogado, asesor.
advocate [ǽdvokeịt], *vt.* defender, abogar por, propugnar, interceder.—*s.* abogado; defensor, intercesor, partidario.
aerial [eịrịạl], *a.* aéreo, elevado; etéreo.—*s.* antena (radio, televisión).
aerodynamics [erodaịnǽmịks], *s.* aerodinámica.—**aeronaut** [éronot], *s.* aeronauta.—**aeronautics** [eronótịks], *s.* aeronáutica.—**aeroplane** [éroplein], *s.* aeroplano.
aesthetic [esθétịk], *a.* = ESTHETIC.—**s** [-s], *s.* = ESTHETICS.
afar [ạfár], *adv.* lejos, distante.—*s. off*, remoto.—*from a.*, desde lejos.

affable [ǽfabl], *a.* afable, atento.

affair [afér], *s.* asunto, negocio, lance; cosa.—*a. of honor,* duelo.—*love a.,* amorío.

affect [afékt], *vt.* afectar, hacer efecto o mella en, conmover; tomar la forma o el carácter de; fingir; tener afición a.— —ation [æfektéíʃɒn], *s.* afectación; melindre, remilgo.— —ed [-id], *a.* emocionado; relamido; inclinado, afecto a.— —ion [aféksɒn], *s.* afecto, devoción, ternura; emoción; inclinación; impresión; (med.) afección, dolencia.— —ionate [aféksɒnit], *a.* afectuoso, cariñoso, amoroso.— —ive [aféktiv], *a.* afectivo, conmovedor.

affidavit [æfidéivit], *s.* declaración jurada; testimonio.

affiliate [afílieit], *vt.* afiliar; prohijar, adoptar; asociar; (for.) legitimar.— *vi.* y *vr.* afiliarse, asociarse, unirse (a un partido, etc.).

affinity [afíniti], *s.* afinidad, atracción; semejanza; amor; conexión; parentesco matrimonial.

affirm [afórm], *vt.* afirmar, aseverar.— *vi.* afirmarse en alguna cosa; declarar formalmente ante un juez.— —ation [æfɔrméiʃɒn], *s.* afirmación, aserto.— —ative [afórmativ], *a.* afirmativo.— *s.* aserción; afirmativa.

affix [afíks], *vt.* anexar, fijar, pegar, unir; poner (firma o sello).—*s.* [áfiks], añadidura; (gram.) afijo, sufijo, prefijo.

afflict [aflíkt], *vt.* afligir, atormentar; castigar.— —ion [aflíksɒn], *s.* aflicción; angustia, duelo; achaque; desgracia.

affluence [ǽfluens], *s.* abundancia, opulencia; afluencia.—**affluent** [ǽfluent], *a.* opulento, afluente, abundante, copioso.—*s.* afluente, tributario.

afford [afórd], *vt.* dar, proporcionar, proveer; tener medios o recursos para una cosa, permitirse el lujo de.

affray [afréi], *s.* riña, pendencia.

affront [afránt], *vt.* afrentar, insultar.— *s.* afrenta, insulto, agravio.

afield [afíld], *adv.* lejos de casa; descarriado.—*far a.,* muy lejos.

afire [afáir], *adv.* ardiendo.

aflame [afléim], *adv.* en llamas.

afloat [aflóut], *a.* y *adv.* a flote, flotante, a nado; inundado.

afoot [afút], *a.* y *adv.* a pie; en movimiento.

afraid [afréid], *a.* acobardado, medroso, tímido.—*to be a.,* tener miedo, temer.

afresh [afréʃ], *adv.* nuevamente, desde el principio.

African [ǽfrikan], *s.* y *a.* africano; negro.

aft [æft], *adv.* a popa o en popa.

after [ǽftœ(r)], *prep.* después de; detrás de, tras (de); al cabo de; en pos de; por, en busca de; según.—*a. all,* después de todo, de todas maneras.— *the day a. tomorrow,* pasado mañana. —*to be a. something,* buscar algo.— *adv.* después, enseguida, seguidamente.—*soon a.,* poco después.— *conj.* después (de) que, así que.—*a.* posterior, siguiente; subsiguiente, resultante.—*a.-effect,* resultado, consecuencia.— —math [-mæθ], *s.* desenlace, consecuencia.— —noon [-nun], *s.* tarde.— —taste [-teist], *s.* resabio (sabor).— —ward(s) [-wɒrd(s)], *adv.* después.

again [agén], *adv.* otra vez, aún, nuevamente, además; asimismo.—*a. and a.,* muchas veces.—*come a.,* vuelva Ud.

against [agénst], *prep.* contra; enfrente de; junto a (una pared, etc.); en contraste con; listo para.—*a. the grain,* a contrapelo; de mal grado.— *a. time,* dentro de tiempo limitado.

age [eidʒ], *s.* edad; época, período, era, siglo; vejez, ancianidad; envejecimiento.—*a. old,* secular, milenario.—*full a.,* mayoría de edad.—*of a.,* mayor (de edad).—*under a.,* minoría, menor (de edad).—*vi.* envejecerse; deteriorarse.—*vt.* madurar.— —d [éidʒ(i)d], *a.* anciano, añejo.

agency [éidʒɒnsi], *s.* agencia; gestión, influencia, medio.—*free a.,* libre albedrío.—**agent** [éidʒɒnt], *s.* agente; representante, intermediario, apoderado; (for.) mandatario.

aggregate [ǽgrigeit], *a.* agregado; aglomerado; mezclado.—*s.* agregado, suma, conjunto; mezcla.—*in the a.,* en conjunto.—*vt.* y *vi.* agregar, sumar, juntar.

aggression [agréʃɒn], *s.* agresión, ataque; acometida.—**aggressive** [agrésiv], *a.* agresivo, acometedor.— **aggressor** [agrésɒ(r)], *s.* agresor.

agile [ædʒil], *a.* ágil, listo.—**agility** [adʒíliti], *s.* agilidad, ligereza, soltura.

agitate [ædʒiteit], *vt.* agitar, revolver, menear; inquietar, alborotar; maquinar.—*vi.* excitar la opinión pública.— **agitation** [ædʒitéiʃɒn], *s.* agitación; discusión; perturbación, ajetreo.— **agitator** [ædʒiteitɒ(r)], *s.* agitador; perturbador, alborotador; demagogo.

aglow [aglóu], *y a.* resplandeciente, encendido.

ago [agóu], *a.* y *adv.* pasado, en el pasado.—*a long time a.,* hace mucho tiempo.—*how long a.?* ¿cuánto tiempo hace?—*two years a.,* hace dos años.

agonize [ǽgonaiz], *vt.* angustiar; causar gran pena.—*vi.* agonizar; penar, sufrir intensamente, retorcerse de dolor.

—**agony** [ǽgonɪ], *s.* agonía; angustia, tormento, zozobra.

agrarian [əgréɾɪən], *a.* **y** *s.* agrario.— *s.* agrarista.

agree [əgrí], *vi.* concordar, coincidir, acordar; entenderse, avenirse; consentir; quedar o convenir en (precio, etc.); sentar (un precedente, etc.); sentarle a uno bien (ropa, clima, etc.); (gram.) concordar.— **-able** [-əbl], *a.* agradable; satisfactorio; simpático; complaciente.—*a. to,* de acuerdo con.— **-ment** [-mənt], *s.* acuerdo, convenio, ajuste, concierto, avenencia; consentimiento; armonía; conformidad; (gram.) concordancia.—*in s. (with),* acorde con.

agricultural [ægɾɪkÁlchʊɾəl], *a.* agrícola, agrario.—**agriculture** [ǽgɾɪkÁlchʊ(r)], *s.* agricultura.—**agriculturist** [ægɾɪkÁlchʊɾɪst], *s.* agricultor.

ahead [əhéd], *adv.* delante, al frente, a la cabeza; adelante; hacia delante.

aid [eɪd], *vt.* **y** *vi.* ayudar, socorrer, auxiliar, apoyar.—*s.* ayuda, auxilio, concurso, socorro; subsidio; (mil.) ayudante.—*first s.,* primeros auxilios (médicos).

ail [eɪl], *vt.* afligir, molestar (algún dolor).—*vi.* estar enfermo o indispuesto.— **-ment** [éɪlmənt], *s.* dolencia, enfermedad.

aim [eɪm], *vt.* apuntar (con un arma); dirigir, asestar, encarar.—*vi.* (con at) hacer puntería; aspirar a, pretender, proponerse, tirar a.—*to a. high,* picar alto.—*s.* puntería, encaro; blanco; designio, mira, propósito, finalidad.— *accurate a.,* tino.—*to miss one's a.,* errar el tiro.— **-less** [éɪmlɪs], *a.* sin objeto, sin rumbo, a la ventura.

air [er], *vt.* airear, ventilar, orear, aventar; secar (al aire o por calor); sacar a relucir, pregonar.—*s.* aire; atmósfera; brisa; semblante, ademán; (mús.) tonada.—*in the a.,* en vilo.— *in the open a.,* al aire libre; a la intemperie.—*to be on the a.,* estar trasmitiendo por radio.— *to put on airs,* darse tono o ínfulas.—*up in the a.,* indeciso; perplejo.—*a.* de aire, neumático; para aire; aéreo; aeronáutico, de aviación.—*a. brakes,* frenos neumáticos.—*a. carrier,* portaaviones.— *a. conditioning,* acondicionamiento del aire.—*a. cooling,* enfriamiento por aire.—*a. drill,* taladro neumático.— *a. duct,* canal de aire.—*a. force,* aviación militar, fuerzas aéreas.—*a. hostess,* aeromoza, azafata.—*a. lane,* vía aérea.—*a. line,* línea o empresa aérea. —*a. liner,* avión de una empresa o línea aérea.—*a. mail,* correo aéreo.— *a.-mail service,* servicio aeropostal.— *a. plant,* talleres de aviación.—*a.*

pocket, bache o cajón de aire.—*a. pressure,* presión atmosférica.—*a. proof,* hermético.—*a. raid,* ataque aéreo.—*a.-tight,* hermético.—*a. valve,* válvula (de admisión o salida) de aire.—*by a.-mail,* por vía aérea, por avión.— **-craft** [érkɾæft], *s.* máquina de volar (aeroplanos, dirigibles, etc.).— **-field** [-fild], *s.* campo de aviación.— **-plane** [-pleɪn], *s.* aeroplano, avión.— **-port** [-port], *s.* aeropuerto; aeródromo.— **-sickness** [-sɪknɪs], *s.* mareo en viaje aéreo.— **-way** [-weɪ], *s.* ruta de aviación, vía aérea.—*pl.* red aérea.— **-y** [-ɪ], *a.* aéreo, airoso; bien ventilado; etéreo, tenue; ligero; vanidoso, estirado.

aisle [áɪl], *s.* pasillo (de un teatro); nave (de una iglesia).

ajar [ədʒáɾ], *adv.* **y** *a.* entreabierto, entornado.—*to set a.,* entornar, entreabrir.

akimbo [əkɪmbou], *a.* **y** *adv.* en jarras.

akin [əkɪn], *a.* consanguíneo, emparentado, afín; análogo, semejante.

alabaster [æləbǽstœ(r)], *s.* alabastro.

alarm [əláɾm], *s.* alarma; rebato.—*a. clock,* (reloj) despertador.—*to sound the a.,* dar la alarma, tocar a rebato.— *vt.* alarmar; asustar; inquietar.—*vi.* dar la alarma; asustarse.

Alaskan [əlǽskən], *s.* natural de Alaska. —*a.* de o referente a Alaska.

alb [ælb], *s.* (igl.) alba.

Albanian [ælbéɪnɪən], *s.* **y** *a.* natural de Albania; lengua albanesa; albanés.

alcohol [ǽlkohol], *s.* alcohol.— **-ic** [ælkohólɪk], *a.* alcohólico.— **-ism** [-ɪzm], *s.* alcoholismo.

alcove [ǽlkouv], *s.* alcoba, nicho.

alderman [óldœrmən], *s.* regidor, concejal.

ale [eɪl], *s.* cerveza (inglesa).

alert [əlŕt], *a.* alerta, vigilante; cuidadoso.—*on the a.,* sobre aviso.—*s.* alarma.—*vt.* poner sobre aviso.

algebra [ǽldʒebɾə], *s.* álgebra.

Algerian [ældʒíɾɪən], *a.* **y** *s.* argelino.

alibi [ǽlɪbaɪ], *s.* excusa; coartada.

alien [éɪlyən], *a.* extraño, ajeno; extranjero, forastero.—*s.* extranjero, residente extranjero.— **-ate** [-eɪt], *vt.* enajenar, traspasar; quitar, indisponer; alejar (a una persona de otra).

alight [əláɪt], *vii.* [4] descender, bajar, apearse; (con on) posarse (sobre); (aer.) aterrizar, acuatizar (un hidroavión).—*a.* **y** *adv.* encendido; iluminado.

align [əláɪn], *vt.* alinear(se).— **-ment** [-mənt], *s.* alineación.

alike [əláɪk], *adv.* igualmente, del mismo modo; a la par.—*a.* semejante; igual.

alimony [ǽlɪmonɪ], *s.* (for.) alimentos,

pensión a la mujer en el divorcio o separación.

alive [aláiv], a. vivo, viviente; encendido; animado; sensible.

alkali [álkalai], s. (quím.) álcali.

all [ol], a. todo, todos; todo (el), todos (los).— s. y pron. todo, totalidad, conjunto; todos, todo el mundo; todo lo.—adv. completamente, enteramente.—above a., sobre todo, ante todo.—after a., después de todo, al fin y al cabo.—a. along, siempre, constantemente, sin cesar, por todo (el camino, tiempo, etc.).—a. around, en todo respecto.—a. at once, repentinamente; de un golpe; a un tiempo.— a. but, todo(s) menos, o sino; casi, por poco.—a. in, agotado, rendido de cansancio.—a. out, completamente; apagado (el fuego, un incendio).—a. out! ¡salgan todos!—a. out of, sin; desprovisto de.—a. over, terminado, acabado.—a. right, ciertamente, está bien, bueno.—a. round, por todas partes; completo; acabado, consumado; de idoneidad general.— a. set, listo dispuesto.—a. that, todo el (o lo) que, todos los que, cuanto(s). —a. the better (worse), tanto mejor (peor).—a. the same, a pesar de eso; lo mismo.—a. told, en (con)junto, por todo.—not at a., de ningún modo, nada de eso; no por cierto; no hay de que.—once and for a., una vez por todas; definitivamente; para siempre.

allay [aléi], vt. aliviar; calmar.

allegation [ælegéişon], s. alegación, argumento; (for.) alegato.—allege [aléd͠ž], vt. alegar; declarar; sostener; pretender; (for.) deducir.

allegiance [alíd͠žans], s. lealtad, homenaje, fidelidad.

allergic [alérd͠žik], a. alérgico.—allergy [élcerd͠ži], s. alergia.

alleviate [alívieit], vt. aliviar, mitigar; aligerar.

alley [éli], **alley-way** [éliwei], s. callejuela, callejón.—blind alley, callejón sin salida.—bowling alley, bolera, boliche.

alliance [alaíans], s. alianza.—allied [aláid], a. aliado, unido; relacionado.

alligator [æligeito(r)], s. caimán; yacaré.—a. pear, aguacate.

allocation [ælokéişon], s. colocación; asignación, distribución.

aloe [élou], s. (bot.) áloe.— —s [-z], (sing. y pl.) áloe o acíbar.

allot [alát], vti. [1] distribuir, repartir, asignar.

allow [aláu], vt. permitir, consentir, dejar, conceder; dar, admitir; (com.) rebajar, deducir.—vi. (con for) tener en cuenta.— —ance [-ans], s. concesión; asignación; ración; pensión,

mesada; permiso; indulgencia; descuento, bonificación, refacción; (tecn.) tolerancia, discrepancia permitida.—annual a., anualidad.—monthly a., mensualidad.—retirement a., jubilación, retiro.—to make a. for, tener en cuenta.

alloy [ælói], s. mezcla; (fund.) aleación; liga.—vt. alear, ligar (los metales).

allude [alíud], vi. aludir, referirse a.

allure [alíur], vt. halagar, atraer, seducir.—s. seducción, atractivo.—alluring [alíurin], a. seductivo, tentador.

allusion [alíuȝon], s. alusión.

ally [alái], vti. [7] unir.—vii. aliarse, coligarse.—s. aliado; pariente.

almanac [ólmanæk], s. almanaque, calendario.

almighty [olmáiti], a. todopoderoso, omnipotente.—s. (con the) Dios.

almond [ámond], s. almendra.—a. tree, almendro.

almost [ólmoust], adv. casi, por poco.

alms [ams], s. limosna.

aloft [alóft], adv. arriba, en alto, en los aires.

alone [alóun], a. y adv. solo, solitario; sólo, solamente.—all a., a solas.—to let a., dejar en paz, no molestar.

along [alón], prep. por; a lo largo de; al lado de.—adv. a lo largo de; adelante.—all a., todo el tiempo; de un extremo al otro.—these lines, en este sentido.—a. with, con, junto con. —come a., venga conmigo.—move a. ! ¡largo de aquí!—to get a. with, adelantar; ir tirando; llevarse (bien) con.— —shore [-ȝor], adv. a la orilla, a lo largo de la costa.— —side [-said], adv. y prep. a lo largo de, al lado, lado a lado.

aloof [alúf], adv. lejos, apartado, a distancia.—a. huraño, reservado.—to stand o keep a., mantenerse apartado; aislarse.— —ness [-nis], s. alejamiento, aislamiento.

aloud [aláud], adv. alto, en voz alta, recio.

alphabet [élfabet], s. alfabeto, abecedario, abecé.— —ical [ælfabétikal], a. alfabético.

already [olrédi], adv. ya, antes de ahora.

also [ólsou], adv. también, igualmente, además, asimismo.

altar [ólta(r)], s. altar, ara.—a. boy, monaguillo, acólito.—a. bread, pan de la eucaristía, hostia.

alter [ólta(r)], vt. alterar, cambiar, modificar, mudar, variar.—vi. alterarse, cambiarse, variar.— —ation [-éişon], s. alteración, cambio, mudanza; arreglo.

alternate [éltœrneit], vt. y vi. alternar; turnar; variar.—a. [éltœrnit], al-

terno; alternativo.—s. suplente, sustituto.—alternating [ɑ́ltœrneįtįʊ], a. alternante, alternativo, alterno.—a. current, corriente alterna.—alternative [ɑltœrnɑ́tįʊ], s. alternativa.—a. alternativo.

although [olðóų], conj. aunque, si (bien), bien que, no obstante, aun cuando.

altitude [ɑ́ltįtjud], s. altura, altitud; elevación.

altogether [oltugéðœ(r)], adv. en conjunto; enteramente, del todo.

alumnus [ɑlʌ́mnʌs], s. (pl. alumni [ɑlʌ́mnaį]), f. alumna [ɑlʌ́mnɑ], (pl. alumnae [ɑlʌ́mni]), ex-alumno; antiguo estudiante de una universidad o escuela.

aluminum [ɑljúminʌm], s. aluminio.

always [ólweįz], adv. siempre.

am [ɑm], (1ª pers. pres. ind. de TO BE), soy, estoy.

amalgamate [ɑmɑ́lgɑmeįt], vt. y vi. amalgamar, unir, incorporar.

amaranth [ɑ́mɑrɑnθ], s. bledo.

amass [ɑmɑ́s], vt. acumular, amasar (riquezas, etc.); apilar.

amateur [ɑ́mɑtjur], s. y a. aficionado, no profesional.

amaze [ɑméįz], vt. asombrar, pasmar, dejar atónito o maravillado.——ment [-mɑnt], s. asombro, pasmo, aturdimiento.—amazing [ɑméįzįŋ], a. asombroso, pasmoso, admirable.

ambassador [ɑmbɑ́sɑdǫ(r)], s. embajador.

amber [ɑ́mbœ(r)], s. ámbar; color de ámbar.—a. ambarino.

ambiguity [ɑmbįgiúįtį], s. ambigüedad.—ambiguous [ɑmbígįuʌs], a. ambiguo, equívoco; evasivo.

ambition [ɑmbíšǫn], s. aspiraciones; ambición, codicia.—ambitious [ɑmbíšʌs], a. lleno de aspiraciones; ambicioso, codicioso.

amble [ɑ́mbl], vi. andar; vagar.—s. (paso de) andadura.

ambulance [ɑ́mbįulɑns], s. ambulancia.

ambush [ɑ́mbųš], vt. acechar, poner celada, emboscar.—s. emboscada, celada.

amen [eįmɑ́n, ɑmɑ́n], interj. y s. amén.

amend [ɑmɑ́nd], vt. enmendar, rectificar, modificar, corregir, reformar.—vi. enmendarse, reformarse, restablecerse.——ment [-mɑnt], s. enmienda, reforma.

American [ɑmɑ́rįkɑn], s. y a. americano; norteamericano, estadounidense.

amethyst [ɑ́mɑθįst], s. amatista; color de amatista.

amiable [éįmįɑbl], a. amable, afable.

amicable [ɑ́mįkɑbl], a. amigable, amistoso.

amid [ɑmíd], amidst [ɑmídst], prep. entre, en medio de.

amiss [ɑmís], adv. mal, fuera de lugar o de razón; impropiamente; de más.—to take a., tomar a mal.—a. inoportuno, impropio, errado.

amity [ɑ́mįtį], s. amistad, concordia, armonía.

ammonia [ɑmóųnįậ], s. amoníaco.

ammunition [ɑmyunížǫn], s. munición, municiones.

amnesty [ɑ́mnɑstį], s. amnistía.—vt. amnistiar.

among [ɑmʌ́ŋ], amongst [ɑmʌ́ŋst], prep. entre, mezclado con, en medio de.

amorous [ɑ́morʌs], a. enamorado, amoroso, enamoradizo.

amortize [ɑmórtaįz], vt. amortizar.

amount [ɑmáųnt], s. cantidad; importe, suma; monto (capital más intereses).—vi. montar, ascender (a), valer; equivaler.

amperage [ɑmpírįdậ], s. amperaje.—ampere [ɑmpír], s. amperio.

amphibian [ɑmfíbįɑn], s. y a. anfibio.

amphitheater [ɑmfįθíɑtœ(r)], s. anfiteatro.

ample [ɑ́mpl], a. amplio; lato; abundante.

amplifier [ɑ́mplįfaįœ(r)], s. amplificador, megáfono.—amplify [ɑ́mplįfaį], vti. [7] amplificar; ampliar.

amputate [ɑ́mpįuteįt], vt. amputar, desmembrar.

amuse [ɑmiúz], vt. entretener, distraer, divertir.—to a. oneself, divertirse.——ment [-mɑnt], s. diversión, pasatiempo, entretenimiento.—amusing [ɑmiúzįŋ], a. divertido, recreativo; risible, gracioso.

an [ɑn], art. un, uno, una.

anachronism [ɑnɑ́kronįzm], s. anacronismo.

analogous [ɑnɑ́logʌs], a. análogo.—analogy [ɑnɑ́lodậį], s. analogía.

analysis [ɑnɑ́lįsįs], s. análisis.—analyze [ɑ́nɑlaįz].—vt. analizar.

anarchist [ɑ́nɑrkįst], s. anarchistic [ɑnɑrkístįk], a. anarquista.—anarchy [ɑ́nɑrkį], s. anarquía; confusión, desorden, caos.

anathema [ɑnɑ́θɑậậ], s. anatema; excomunión; maldición.

anatomy [ɑnɑ́tomį], s. anatomía, disección.

ancestor [ɑ́nsɑstǫ(r)], s. progenitor; antepasado.—ancestral [ɑnsɑ́strɑl], a. ancestral, hereditario.—ancestry [ɑ́nsɑstrį], s. ascendencia; linaje, prosapia, alcurnia.

anchor [ɑ́ŋkǫ(r)], vi. anclar; asegurar.—s. ancla, áncora; artificio de sujeción o amarre; escape de reloj.—to drop a., echar el ancla.—to ride at a.,

estar fondeado o anclado.—*to weigh s.*, zarpar.— —age [-idź], s. ancladero, fondeadero.

anchovy [énchouvi], s. anchoa, anchova.

ancient [éinsent), a. antiguo, vetusto.— *the Ancients*, la Antigüedad.

and [ænd], *conj.* y, e.—*a. so forth*, o a. *so on*, etcétera, y así sucesivamente.— *ifs, ands or buts*, dimes y diretes.

Andalusian [ændaliúźan], a. y s. andaluz.

Andean [ændían], a. y s. andino.

andirons [éndaiœrnz], s. *pl.* morillos.

anecdote [ænikdout], s. anécdota.

anemia [ænímiá], s. anemia.—**anemic** [ænímik], a. anémico.

anesthesia [ænesθíźiá], s. anestesia.— **anesthetic** [œnesθétik], a. y s. anestésico.

anew [anjú], *adv.* nuevamente.

angel [éindźel], s. ángel, serafín.— **ic** [ændźélik], a. angelical, angélico.

anger [ǽngœ(r)], s. enfado, enojo, ira, oólera.—*to provoke to a.*, encolerizar, enfadar.—*vt.* enfadar, enojar, encolerizar.

angina [ændźáina, ǽndźinǽ], s. angina. —*a. pectoris*, angina de pecho.

angle [ǽngl], *vt.* pescar con caña; intrigar; halagar con fin de lucro.—*s.* ángulo; esquina, rincón; avíos de pescar; punto de vista.— —r [ǽngloœ(r)], s. pescador (de caña).

angling [ǽngliŋ], s. pesca con caña.

angry [ǽngri], a. enojado, enfadado, encolerizado, bravo.—*to get a.*, enfadarse, enojarse, encolerizarse.

anguish [ǽngwiš], s. ansia, angustia, zozobra.

angular [ǽngiulǽ(r)], a. angular, anguloso.

aniline [ǽnilin], s. anilina.

animal [ǽnimal], s. y a. animal.

animate [ǽnimeit], *vt.* animar.—*a.* [ǽnimit], animado, viviente.—**animation** [ænimǽiśon], s. animación.— **animism** [ǽnimizm], s. animismo.— **animosity** [ænimásiti], s. animosidad, rencor.—**animus** [ǽnimʌs], s. ánimo, intención; animosidad.

anise [ǽnis], **anisette** [ænizét], s. anís.

ankle [ǽnkl], s. tobillo.—*a. strap*, correílla de zapato que cruza el pie un poco arriba del empeine.

annex [ǽnéks], *vt.* anexar, anexionar.— *s.* [ǽneks], anexo; añadidura; dependencia; ala o pabellón (de un edificio).— —ation [ænekséiśon], s. anexión, adición, unión.

annihilate [ǽnáijileit], *vt.* aniquilar; anonadar; demoler.—**annihilation** [ǽnaijiléiśon], s. aniquilación, anonadamiento.

anniversary [ænivóersari], s. aniversario. —*a.* anual.

annotate [ǽnoteit], *vt.* anotar; acotar, apostillar; comentar, glosar.—**annotation** [ænotéiśon], s. anotación, apunte; nota, notación; acotación, apostilla.

announce [anáuns], *vt.* anunciar, notificar, avisar; declarar.— —ment [-ment], s. aviso o anuncio; declaración, proclama.— —r [-œ(r)], s. anunciador, avisador.

annoy [anói], *vt.* molestar, incomodar, fastidiar.— —ance [-ans], s. molestia, incomodidad, disgusto, fastidio.— —ing [-iŋ], a. fastidioso, molesto, incómodo, importuno, engorroso.

annual [ǽnyual], a. anual.—**annuity** [aniúiti], s. anualidad; pensión o renta vitalicia; retiro.

annul [anʌl], *vti.* [1] anular, rescindir; derogar, revocar.— —ment [-ment], s. anulación, rescisión, cancelación, revocación, derogación.

anodyne [ǽnodain], a. y s. (med.) anodino, calmante.

anoint [anóint], *vt.* untar; ungir; administrar la extremaunción.

anonymous [anánimʌs], a. anónimo.

another [anʌðœ(r)], a. otro; distinto, diferente.—*pron.* otro, uno más.—*a. such*, otro que tal.—*one a.*, uno(s) a otro(s).

answer [ǽnsœ(r)], *vt.* y *vi.* responder, contestar; refutar; corresponder; obedecer; convenir; comparecer.—*to a. back*, replicar; refunfuñar.—*to a. for*, abonar, acreditar; salir fiador de; ser responsable de; hacer oficio de.—*to a. to the name of*, tener por nombre, llamarse.—*s.* respuesta, contestación; refutación, réplica; defensa; (mat.) solución, resultado.

ant [ænt], s. hormiga.—*a. hill*, hormiguero en forma de montículo.

antagonism [æntǽgonizm], s. antagonismo; contienda; oposición.—**antagonist** [æntǽgonist], s. antagonista, adversario.—**antagonize** [æntǽgonaiz], *vt.* y *vi.* contender, oponerse; contrariar; ser antagónico.

antarctic [æntárktik], a. antártico.

anteater [ǽntítœ(r)], s. oso hormiguero.

antecedent [æntisídent], a. y s. antecedente, precedente.

antechamber [ǽnticheimbœ(r)], s. antecámara, antesala.

antedate [æntidéit], *vt.* antedatar; retrotraer.

antelope [ǽnteloup], s. antílope; gacela, gamuza.

antenna [æntǽnǽ], s. (zool. y radio) antena.— —e [ænténi], *pl.* (zool.) antenas.

anthem [ǽnθem], s. himno; motete.

anthology [ænθálodʒi], *s.* antología, florilegio.

anthropology [ænθropálodʒi], *s.* antropología.

antiaircraft [æntjérkræft], *a.* antiaéreo.

antibiotic [æntjbaiátjk], *a.* y *s.* antibiótico.

antibody [ǽntjbadj], *s.* anticuerpo.

antic [ǽntjk], *s.* zapateta, cabriola.—*pl.* travesuras; actos ridículos.

anticipate [ænt[sípeit], *vt.* esperar, prever; prevenir, anticipar(se), adelantar(se) a; impedir.—**anticipation** [æntjsipéiʃon], *s.* anticipación, previsión; expectación.

anticommunist [æntjkámyunjst], *s.* y *a.* anticomunista.

antidote [ǽntjdout], *s.* antídoto, contraveneno.

antifreeze [ǽntjfriz], *s.* y *a.* anticongelante.

antiknock [ǽntjnak], *s.* y *a.* antidetonante.

antimony [ǽntjmouni], *s.* antimonio.

antinomy [æntínomj], *s.* antinomia; paradoja.

antipathy [æntípaθj], *s.* antipatía.

antipode [ǽntjpoud], *s.* antípoda.

antiquarian [æntjkwérian], *s.* y *a.* anticuario.—**antiquated** [ǽntjkweitjd], *a.* anticuado.—**antique** [æntík], *a.* antiguo.—*s.* antigüedad, antigualla.—*a. shop*, tienda de antigüedades.—**antiquity** [æntíkwitj], *s.* antigüedad; ancianidad; la Antigüedad.

anti-Semite [æntjsémait], *s.* antisemita.

antiseptic [æntjséptjk], *a.* antiséptico, desinfectante.

antiskid [ǽntjskjd], *a.* antideslizante.

antler [ǽntlœ(r)], *s.* asta (del ciervo, venado, etc.).

anus [éjnʌs], *s.* ano.

anvil [ǽnvjl], *s.* yunque.—*vti.* [2] formar o trabajar sobre el yunque; martillar.

anxiety [æŋgzáietj], *s.* ansiedad, anhelo; desasosiego, zozobra; cuidado; afán, ansia.

anxious [ǽŋkʌs], *a.* inquieto, impaciente, ansioso.

any [énj], *a.* y *pron.* cualquier(a), cualesquier(a); algún, alguno; todo.—*a. longer*, más tiempo, todavía; más.—*a. more*, más, aún; todavía.—*a. way*, de cualquier modo.—*at a. rate*, o *in a. case*, de cualquier modo, de todos modos.—*not a. longer, not a. more*, ya no, no más.— **-body** [-badj], **-one** [-wʌn], *pron.* alguno, alguien, cualquiera; todo el mundo, toda persona.— **-how** [-hau], **-way** [-wei], *adv.* de cualquier modo; en cualquier caso; de todos modos; sea lo que sea; sin embargo.— **-thing** [-θiŋ], *pron.* algo, alguna cosa, cualquier cosa; todo,

todo lo que.—*a. else*, cualquier otra cosa, algo más.—*to be a. but*, ser todo menos, no ser ni con mucho.— **-where** [-hwer], *adv.* donde quiera, en todas partes.—*a. near*, siquiera aproximadamente.—*not a.*, en ninguna parte.

apart [apárt], *adv.* aparte; separadamente; de por sí; además; prescindiendo de; en pedazos, en partes.—*to take a.*, desarmar, desmontar.

apartment [apártmɛnt], *s.* apartamento, piso; aposento, cuarto.—*a. building*, casa de apartamentos.

apathy [ǽpaθj], *s.* apatía, flema, dejadez.

aperitif [æperitíf], *s.* aperitivo.

aperture [ǽpœrchʊr], *s.* abertura, paso, rendija.

apex [éipeks], *s.* (*pl.* apices [ǽpjsiz]) ápice, cúspide, punta, cima.

apiece [apís], *adv.* por persona, por cabeza; cada uno; sendos.

ape [eip], *s.* simio; imitador.—*vt.* imitar, remedar.

aplomb [aplóm], *s.* aplomo, seguridad; verticalidad.

apogee [ǽpodʒi], *s.* apogeo; auge.

apologetic(al) [apalodʒétjk(ąl)], *a.* contrito; lleno de disculpas.—**apologize** [apálodʒaiz], *vt.* y *vi.* excusar(se), disculpar(se).—**apology** [apálodʒi], *s.* apología, excusa, disculpa, satisfacción.

apostasy [apástasi], *s.* apostasía.

apostle [apásl], *s.* apóstol.—**apostolic(al)** [æpostálik(ąl)], *a.* apostólico.—*Apostolic See*, (igl.) sede apostólica, la Santa Sede.

apostrophe [apástrofj], *s.* apóstrofe; apóstrofo.

apothecary [apáθɛkeri], *s.* boticario.

appall [apɔ́l], *vt.* espantar, aterrar; consternar.— **-ing** [-iŋ], *a.* espantoso, aterrador.

apparatus [æpærétʌs], *s.* instrumento, aparato; aparejo.

apparel [apǽrɛl], *s.* ropa; vestiduras; aparejo y demás accesorios de un barco.—*vti.* [2] vestir; adornar; proveer.

apparent [apérɛnt], *a.* aparente, visible, manifiesto.—*a. horizon*, horizonte sensible.—*a. time*, tiempo solar.—*heir a.*, heredero forzoso.

apparition [æparíʃon], *s.* aparición, aparecimiento; aparecido, fantasma, espectro.

appeal [apíl], *vi.* apelar o recurrir a; pedir o suplicar; mover, excitar; despertar atención o simpatía; poner por testigo; exhortar a.—*vt.* apelar de, llevar a un tribunal superior.—*s.* súplica, instancia; llamamiento, exhortación; apelación, recurso; simpatía, atracción.

appear [ặpír], *vi.* aparecer(se), mostrarse, personarse; brotar, surgir; semejar; comparecer.—*to a. to be*, aparentar, representar.— —ance [-ặns], *s.* apariencia, aspecto, facha; aparición, comparecencia.

appease [ặpíz], *vt.* apaciguar, pacificar; calmar.— —ment [-mặnt], *s.* conciliación, apaciguamiento.— —r [-œ(r)], *s.* apaciguador.

appellable [ặpélặbl], *a.* apelable.— **appellancy** [ặpélặnsi], *s.* apelación.— **appellation** [æpeléíjặn], *s.* nombre (apelativo); denominación, título, tratamiento.—**appellative** [ặpélặtiv], *s.* sobrenombre; apellido.

append [ặpénd], *vt.* añadir, anexar; atar, colgar.— —age [-idž], *s.* pertenencia, dependencia, accesorio; colgajo, apéndice.— —ectomy [æpendéktomi], *s.* apend(ic)ectomía.— —icitis [ặpendisáitis], *s.* apendicitis.— —ix [ặpéndiks], *s.* (*pl.* appendices [ặpéndisiz]) apéndice.

appetite [ǽpặtait], *s.* apetito, hambre, apetencia, gana; deseo, anhelo.— **appetizer** [ǽpặtaizœ(r)], *s.* aperitivo.

applaud [ặplód], *vt.* aplaudir, aclamar. —applause [ặplóz], *s.* aplauso, aclamación.

apple [ǽpl], *s.* manzana, poma.— *Adam's a.*, nuez, bocado de Adán.— *a. of discord*, manzana de la discordia. —*a. of one's eye*, niña del ojo.—*a. orchard*, manzanal, pomal.—*a. pie o tart*, pastel(illo) de manzana.—*a.-pie order*, orden perfecto.—*a. tree*, manzano.— —jack [-džæk], *s.* aguardiente de manzana.— —sauce [-sos], *s.* compota de manzana.

appliance [ặpláiặns], *s.* aparato, instrumento, utensilio.—**applicable** [ǽpljkặbl], *a.* aplicable.—**applicant** [ǽpljkặnt], *s.* solicitante, aspirante, candidato.—**application** [æpljkéíjặn], *s.* aplicación; uso, empleo; instancia, solicitud.—*a. blank, a. form*, formulario, planilla.—**applied** [ặpláid], *a.* aplicado; adaptado, utilizado.—*a. for*, pedido, encargado.— —apply [ặpláj], *vti.* y *vii.* [7] aplicar, poner, fijar; ser aplicable o pertinente.

appoint [ặpóint], *vt.* nombrar, elegir; comisionar, destinar; asignar; equipar, amueblar.—ment [-mặnt], *s.* nombramiento; puesto, empleo; cita; acuerdo.—*pl.* mobiliario; accesorios.

appraise [ặpréiz], *vt.* (a)valuar, valorar, justipreciar, aforar, tasar; estimar, apreciar.— —ment [-mặnt], *s.* tasación.— —r [-œ(r)], *s.* tasador.

appreciable [ặpríšjặbl], *a.* apreciable.— **appreciate** [ặpríšjeit], *vt.* apreciar,

---

valuar, tasar.—appreciation [ặpríšjéíjặn], *s.* valuación, tasa.

apprehend [æprjhénd], *vt.* y *vi.* comprender, entender; temer, recelar; aprehender, capturar.—**apprehension** [æprjhénšặn], *s.* aprensión, recelo, desconfianza; aprehensión, captura. —**apprehensive** [æprjhénsjv], *a.* aprensivo, receloso; penetrante, perspicaz.

apprentice [ặpréntjs], *s.* aprendiz, novicio, principiante.—*vt.* contratar como aprendiz.— —ship [-šjp], *s.* aprendizaje, noviciado.

approach [ặpróuch], *vt.* y *vi.* aproximar(se), acercar(se); hacer propuesta, insinuación.—*s.* acercamiento; acceso; proximidad.

approbation [æprobéíjặn], *s.* aprobación.

appropriate [ặpróuprieit], *vt.* apropiar(se), destinar; posesionarse.—*a.* apropiado, apto, pertinente.—**appropriation** [ặprouprjéíjặn], *s.* apropiación, suma consignada.

approval [ặprúvặl], *s.* aprobación; visto bueno; consentimiento.—*on a.*, a prueba.—**approve** [ặprúv], *vt.* aprobar, sancionar, confirmar.—*vi.* (seguido de *of*), aprobar, sancionar.

approximate [ặpráksjmit], *a.* aproximado, aproximativo.—*vt.* y *vi.* [ặpráksjmeit], aproximar(se), acercar(se).

apricot [éíprikat], *s.* albaricoque, (Am.) chabacano.

April [éíprjl], *s.* abril.

apron [éíprặn], *s.* delantal, mandil; plancha de protección; cubierta.— *tied to the a. strings*, dominado por la mujer o la madre.

apt [æpt], *a.* apto, idóneo, capaz; propenso.— —itude [ǽptjtjud], —ness [ǽptnjs], *s.* aptitud, capacidad; tendencia, disposición.

aquamarine [ǽkwặmặrín], *s.* (min.) aguamarina.—**aquarium** [ặkwériặm], *s.* acuario, pecera.—**aquatic** [ặkwǽtjk], *a.* acuático.—**aqueduct** [ǽkwjdẶkt], *s.* acueducto.

Arab [ǽrặb], *s.* árabe.— —ian [ặréibjặn], *a.* árabe, arábigo.— —ic [ǽrặbjk], *s.* árabe, lengua arábiga.—*a.* arábigo.

Aragonese [ærặgoníz], *a.* y *s.* aragonés.

arbiter [árbitœ(r)], *s.* árbitro.—**arbitrary** [árbitreri], *a.* arbitrario, despótico.—**arbitrate** [árbitreit], *vt.* y *vi.* arbitrar, terciar.—**arbitration** [arbitréíjặn], *s.* arbitraje.—**arbitrator** [árbjtreito(r)], *s.* árbitro.

arbor [árbọ(r)], *s.* (mec.) árbol, eje; tambor; (bot.) emparrado, glorieta.

arc [ark], *s.* arco.— —ade [arkéid], *s.* arcada; arquería.

arch [arch], *vt.* y *vi.* arquear(se), enar-

car(se), encorvar(se); abovedarse.—
s. arco, bóveda.—a. travieso; astuto.
archangel [árkéjndžel], s. arcángel.
archbishop [árchbjšop], s. arzobispo.—
—ric [-rik], s. arzobispado.
archer [árchœ(r)], s. arquero, flechero.—
—y [-i], s. tiro de arco.
archetype [árkitajp], s. arquetipo.
arching [árchin], a. arqueado.—s.
arqueo, curvatura.
archipelago [arkipélágou], s. archipiélago.
architect [árkitekt], s. arquitecto, artífice.— —ure [árkitekchů(r)], s. arquitectura.
archive [árkajv], s. archivo, documento
archivado.—archivist [árkjvjst], s.
archivista, archivero.
archway [árchwej], s. arcada; pasadizo
bajo un arco.
arctic [árktik], a. ártico, septentrional;
frígido.—s. región ártica, círculo
ártico.
ardent [árdent], a. ardiente; apasionado.—ardor [árdo(r)], s. ardor,
calor; pasión, ansia.
arduous [árdžuʌs], a. arduo, difícil;
alto, escabroso, enhiesto.
are [ar], 2da. pers. sing., 1ra., 2da. y
3ra. pl., pres. ind. de TO BE.
area [ériǎ], s. área; extensión; región,
zona; terreno.
arena [ǎrinǎ], s. arena, liza, ruedo.
Argentine(an) [ardžéntin, ardžent[n-
ian], s. y a. argentino.
argue [árgju], vt. y vi. debatir, disputar,
discutir, argüir, argumentar; sostener; demostrar, indicar.—argument
[árgiument], s. controversia, disputa;
alegación.
arid [érid], a. árido, seco.— —ity [ǎríd-
iti], s. aridez, sequedad.
arise [ǎrájz], vii. [10] levantarse, subir;
surgir; proceder, provenir (de); suscitarse; originarse, sobrevenir; resucitar.—arisen [ǎrízen], pp. de TO ARISE.
aristocracy [ærjstákrǎsi], s. aristocracia.
—aristocrat [ærístokræt], s. aristócrata.—aristocratic(al)[ærjstokrétjk-
(ǎl)], a. aristocrático.
arithmetic [ǎríθmetjk], s. aritmética.—
—al [ærjθmétjkǎl], a. aritmético.—
—ian [ǎrjθmetíšan], s. aritmético.
ark [ark], s. arca.—A. of the Covenant,
Arca de la Alianza.—Noah's a., Arca
de Noé.
arm [arm], s. brazo; rama, canal; arma.
—pl. armas, blasón.—s. band, brazalete.—a. bone, canilla o caña del
brazo.—a. in a., de bracete, del brazo.
—a.'s reach, alcance del brazo.—vt.
armar; fortalecer; proveer de medios
o elementos.—vi. armarse.
armament [ármamcnt], s. armamento;
equipo.

armchair [ármcher], s. sillón.
armful [ármful], s. brazada, brazado.
armistice [ármjstjs], s. armisticio.
armless [ármljs], a. desarmado; manco.
armor [ármo(r)], s. armadura, arnés;
coraza, blindaje.—a.-clad, blindado,
acorazado.—vt. acorazar, blindar.—
—ed [-d], a. blindado, acorazado.—
—y [-i], s. cuartel; armería; heráldica.
armpit [ármpjt], s. sobaco.
army [armi], s. ejército, tropas; multitud, muchedumbre.
aroma [ǎróumǎ], s. aroma, fragancia.—
—tic(al) [æromætjk(al)], a. aromático.
arose [ǎróuz], pret. de TO ARISE.
around [ǎráund], adv. alrededor o en
derredor, a la redonda; a la vuelta;
allá, por todos lados; de un lado para
otro.—the other way a., al contrario,
viceversa, al revés.—prep. al volver
de, alrededor de, cerca de, en torno
de.—a. here, por aquí.—a. the corner,
a la vuelta de la esquina.
arouse [ǎráuz], vt. despertar; mover,
excitar, alborotar.
arraign [ǎréjn], vt. procesar criminal-
mente; acusar, denunciar.— —ment
[-mcnt], s. proceso, instrucción de
cargos.
arrange [ǎréjndž], vt. arreglar, acomodar, preparar; colocar, ordenar; convenir, concertar; (mus.) arreglar,
adaptar.—vi. prevenir, hacer arreglos;
concertarse, convenir.— —ment
[-mcnt], s. colocación; orden, arreglo,
distribución; preparativo, medida,
providencia, convenio.
array [ǎréj], s. orden de batalla, formación; pompa, adorno; conjunto,
colección.—vt. poner en orden de
batalla; ataviar, adornar.
arrears [ǎrírz], s. pl. atrasos, cantidades
vencidas y no pagadas.—in a., atrasado en el pago.
arrest [ǎrést], s. prisión, arresto, reclusión; detención; captura.—vt. impedir, detener, atajar, reprimir; arrestar, prender, recluir; atraer; fijar la
atención.— —ing [-iṇ], a. impresionante, llamativo.
arrival [ǎrájvǎl], s. arribo, llegada; logro, consecución.—arrive [ǎrájv], vi.
llegar, arribar.
arrogance [érogans], s. arrogancia.—
arrogant [érogant], a. arrogante.
arrow [érou], s. flecha, saeta.—a.
wound, flechazo.
arsenal [ársinǎl], s. arsenal.
arsenic [ársinjk], s. y a. arsénico.
arson [árson], s. incendio premeditado.—
—ist [-jst], s. incendiario.
art [art], s. arte, habilidad, destreza;
artificio; oficio, gremio.—fine arts,
bellas artes.

artery [ártęri], *s.* arteria.

artesian [artíżąn], *a.* artesiano.—*a. well,* pozo artesiano.

artful [ártfụl], *a.* artero, ladino; diestro.

artichoke [ártįchoụk], *s.* alcachofa.

article [ártįkl], *s.* artículo (gr., lit., leg., com.).—*a. of clothing,* prenda de vestir.—*leading a.,* artículo de fondo.

articulate [artíkiuleịt], *vt.* articular, enunciar; enlazar.—*vi.* articular, enunciar; estar unido por articulación.—*a.* [artíkiụlịt], articulado; claro, de expresión inteligible.—**articulation** [artįkiuléịśọn], *s.* coyuntura, articulación; pronunciación.

artifice [ártįfịs], *s.* artificio; ardid.—**r** [artífịsœ(r)], *s.* artífice; inventor; artesano.—**artificial** [artįfíşạl], *a.* artificial; imitado; ficticio, afectado, artificioso.

artillery [artílęri], *s.* artillería.

artisan [ártįżąn], *s.* artesano.—**artist** [ártịst], *s.* artista; artífice; actor.—**artistic** [artístịk], *a.* artístico.

arum [éram], *s.* aro, (Am.) malanga.

Aryan [érịạn], *s.* y *a.* ario (pueblo e idioma).

as [æz], *adv., conj.* y *pron. rel.* como; a medida que, mientras (que), según, conforme; cuando, en el momento en que, al; hasta donde va, en lo que contiene.—*a. for,* en cuanto a, por lo que respecta a.—*a. from,* a partir de. —*a. if,* como si.—*a. it were,* por decirlo así.—*a. late a.,* tan recientemente como, apenas, no más.—*a. many a.,* tantos como, cuantos; hasta.—*a. much a. to say,* como quien dice.—*a. of,* con fecha de.—*a. per,* según, de acuerdo con.—*a. soon a. possible,* cuanto antes.—*a. such,* como tal.—*a. well,* también, además.—*a. well a.,* también como, lo mismo que; así como.—*a. yet,* todavía, aún, hasta ahora.

asbestic [æsbéstịk], *a.* incombustible.—**asbestos** [æsbéstọs], *s.* asbesto, amianto.

ascend [ạsénd], *vt.* subir.—*vi.* ascender, subir.—**ancy** [-ạnsị], —**ency** [-ęnsị], *s.* predominio, ascendiente.—**ascension** [ạsénśọn], *s.* ascensión.—**ascent** [ạsént], *s.* subida, ascensión; ascenso.

ascertain [æscęrtéịn], *vt.* averiguar, indagar.—*vi.* cerciorarse (de).

ascribe [ạskráịb], *vt.* atribuir, imputar.

ascetic [ạsétịk], *s.* asceta.—*a.* ascético.—**ism** [ạsétịsịzm], *s.* ascetismo.

aseptic [ạséptịk], *a.* aséptico.

ash [æś], *s.* ceniza, cenizas.—*a. tray,* cenicero.—*A. Wednesday,* miércoles de ceniza.—**es** [æśịz], *s.* restos mortales.

ashamed [ạśéịmd], *a.* avergonzado,

corrido.—*to be a.,* darle a uno vergüenza.

ashore [ạśór], *adv.* en tierra, a tierra.— *to go a.,* desembarcar.

Asian [éịżạn], **Asiatic** [eịżịétịk], *a.* y *s.* asiático.

aside [ạsáịd], *adv.* a un lado; aparte.—*s.* aparte (en obras teatrales).

ask [æsk], *vt.* y *vi.* preguntar; pedir, rogar; invitar, convidar.—*to a. one down, in, up,* rogar a uno que baje, entre, suba.

askance [ạskǽns], *adv.* de soslayo, recelosamente.—*to look a.,* no aprobar; mirar recelosamente.—**askew** [ạskiú] *adv.* de lado, de través.

asleep [ạslíp], *adv.* y *a.* dormido, durmiendo; entumecido.—*to fall a.,* dormirse.

asparagus [æspérạgʌs], *s.* espárrago.

aspect [ǽspekt], *s.* aspecto; apariencia.

asperity [æspérịtị], *s.* aspereza; rudeza, acrimonia.

asphalt [ǽsfolt], *s.* asfalto.

aspirant [ạspáịrạnt], *s.* y *a.* aspirante.— **aspiration** [ạspịréịśọn], *s.* aspiración; anhelo.—**aspire** [ạspáịr], *vi.* aspirar, ambicionar, pretender.

aspirin [ǽspịrịn], *s.* aspirina.

ass [æs], *s.* asno, burro, etc.

assail [ạséịl], *vt.* asaltar, atacar.—**ant** [-ạnt], —**er** [-œ(r)] *s.* y *a.* asaltante, atracador.

assassin [ạsǽsịn], *s.* asesino.—**ate** [-eịt], *vt.* asesinar.—**ation** [-éịśọn], *s.* asesinato.

assault [ạsólt], *s.* asalto, ataque; violación; atraco.—*vt.* asaltar, atacar, violar.

assay [ạséị], *vt.* ensayar; probar, aquilatar.—*s.* prueba, contraste, ensayo.

assemble [ạsémbl], *vt.* juntar; convocar, congregar; montar maquinaria.—*vi.* reunirse, juntarse.—**assembly** [ạsémblị], *s.* reunión, asamblea.—*a. line production,* producción en serie.

assent [ạsént], *vi.* asentir, convenir.—*s.* asentimiento.

assert [ạsœrt], *vt.* afirmar, asegurar; hacer valer.—*to a. oneself,* hacerse valer.—**ion** [ạsœrśọn], *s.* aserto, afirmación.

assess [ạsés], *vt.* tasar, valorar, asignar impuestos.—**ment** [-mẹnt], *s.* tasación, avaluación; impuesto.

asset [ǽset], *s.* cualidad, ventaja.—*pl.,* activo, haber, capital.

assiduous [ạsídżụʌs], *a.* asiduo.

assign [ạsáịn], *vt.* asignar, señalar; adscribir; consignar, traspasar.—**ment** [-mẹnt], *s.* asignación, señalamiento, cesión.

assimilate [ạsímịleịt], *vt.* y *vi.* asimilar(se); comparar(se).

assist [ạsíst], *vt.* asistir, ayudar.—*vi.*

ayudar; asistir, concurrir.— —ance [-ạns], *s.* auxilio, socorro, asistencia; concurso, ayuda.— —ant [-ạnt], *s.* y *a.* ayudante, auxiliar.

associate [ạsóu̯s̩ie̩it], *vt.* y *vi.* asociar(se), unir(se).—*a.* [ạsóu̯s̩iit], asociado.—*s.* compañero; (con)socio, colega; cómplice.—association [ạsou̯s̩ié̩iȿọn], *s.* asociación; unión; sociedad; conexión, relación.

assort [ạsórt], *vt.* surtir con variedad; clasificar.— —ed [-i̩d], *a.* variado, surtido, mezclado.— —ment [-me̩nt], *s.* surtido variado, colección.

assume [ạsúm], *vt.* tomar, asumir, suponer, dar por sentado.—*vi.* arrogarse, atribuirse.— —d [-d], *a.* supuesto; fingido.—assumption [ạsʌmȿọn], *s.* suposición, supuesto.

assurance [ạs̩úra̩ns], *s.* seguridad, certeza; confianza; seguro.—assure [ạs̩úr], *vt.* afirmar; infundir confianza; asegurar (contra riesgos).—assured [ạs̩úrd], *s.* y *a.* asegurado (contra riesgos); cierto, seguro.

asterisk [æste̩ris̩k], *s.* asterisco.

astern [ạstœrn], *adv.* por la popa, a popa.

asthma [æzmạ], *s.* asma.

astonish [ạstáni̩ȿ], *vt.* asombrar.— —ed [-t], *a.* atónito.— —ing [-i̩ŋ], *a.* sorprendente, asombroso.— —ment [-me̩nt], *s.* pasmo, asombro, sorpresa.

astound [ạstáu̯nd], *vt.* y *vi.* pasmar, aturdir, confundir.

astraddle [ạstrǽdl], *adv.* y *a.* a horcajadas.

astray [ạstré̩i], *adv.* y *a.* desviada o descarriadamente.—*to go a.*, desviarse, perderse.—*to lead a.*, llevar por el mal camino.

astride [ạstráid], *adv.* a horcajadas.

astrologer [æstrálodȝœ(r)], *s.* astrólogo. —astrology [ạstrálodȝi], *s.* astrología.

astronomer [ạstránomœ(r)], *s.* astrónomo.—astronomic(al) [æstronám̩ik(ạl)], *a.* astronómico.—astronomy [ạstránomi], *s.* astronomía.

Asturian [æstúriạn], *s.* y *a.* asturiano, astur.

asylum [ạsáilʌm], *s.* asilo, casa de beneficencia; amparo.—*insane a.*, manicomio.

at [æt], *prep.* a; en; con; de; por.— *angry a. me*, enfadado conmigo.—*a. his command*, por orden suya.—*a. last*, por fin.—*a. once*, inmediatamente.—*a. one stroke*, de un golpe.—*a. Rome*, en Roma.—*a. the door*, a o en la puerta.—*a. work*, trabajando.

ate [eit], *pret.* de TO EAT.

atheism [é̩iθiizm], *s.* ateísmo.—atheist [é̩iθiist], *s.* ateo.—atheistic(al) [eiθiístik(ạl)], *a.* ateo, ateístico.

athlete [ǽθlit], *s.* atleta.—athletic

[æθlétik], *a.* atlético.—athletics [æθlétiks], *s.* deportes, atletismo; gimnasia.

Atlantic [ætlǽntik], *a.* atlántico.—*s.* el mar Atlántico.

atlas [ǽtlạs], *s.* atlas.

atmosphere [ǽtmọsfir], *s.* atmósfera.— atmospheric(al) [ætmọsférik(ạl)], *a.* atmosférico.—atmospherics [ætmọsfériks], *s.* estática (rad.).

atom [ǽtọm], *s.* átomo.—*a. bomb*, bomba atómica.—*a. splitting*, fisión nuclear.— —ic(al) [atámik(ạl)], *a.* atómico.—*atomic fission*, fisión atómica.— —ization [ætọmaizé̩iȿọn], *s.* pulverización.— —ize [ǽtomaiz], *vt.* atomizar, pulverizar, rociar.— —izer [ǽtomaizœ(r)], *s.* pulverizador.

atone [ạtóu̯n], *vt.* y *vi.* expiar, purgar; reparar.— —ment [-me̩nt], *s.* expiación, etc.

atop [ạtáp], *adv.* y *prep.* encima (de).

atrocious [ạtróu̯ȿạs], *a.* atroz.—atrocity [atrásiti], *s.* atrocidad.

attach [ạtǽch], *vt.* unir, juntar; atar; pegar; enganchar; prender, coger; sujetar; asignar, atribuir; acompañar; embargar bienes.— —e [ạtaȿé̩i], *s.* agregado (diplomático).— —ed [ạtǽcht], *a.* fijo; anejo; adicto, devoto.— —ment [ạtǽchme̩nt], *s.* adhesión, apego, devoción; unión; cariño; embargo (de bienes).

attack [ạtǽk], *vt.* y *vi.* atacar, acometer, asaltar, embestir.—*s.* ataque, agresión, atentado; acceso (de tos, etc.).

attain [ạté̩in], *vi.* lograr, alcanzar, llegar a.— —able [-ạbl], *a.* asequible, accesible.— —ment [-me̩nt], *s.* logro, consecución; dote, cualidad.

attempt [ạtémpt], *vt.* y *vi.* intentar, atentar; aventurar; tentar; procurar; probar, pretender.—*s.* prueba, ensayo; tentativa; atentado; conato.

attend [ạténd], *vt.* y *vi.* atender, cuidar; servir; acompañar; asistir o concurrir a; presenciar.—*well-attended*, muy concurrido (espectáculo, etc.).— —ance [-ạns], *s.* presencia, asistencia; comparecencia; público, concurrencia.— —ant [-ạnt], *s.* acompañante; sirviente; asistente.—*a.* concomitante, acompañante.

attention [ạténȿọn], *s.* atención; cortesía, fineza; agasajo.—*to pay o give a.*, prestar atención; hacer caso.—attentive [ạténtiv], *a.* atento, solícito, cortés.—attentiveness [ạténtivni̩s], *s.* cuidado, cortesía; atención.

attest [ạtést], *vt.* atestiguar, atestar, certificar; autenticar; dar testimonio o fe.

attic [ǽtik], *s.* desván, buhardilla; ático.

attire [ǝtái(r)], *vt.* vestir, ataviar, ador- nar.—*s.* atavío, traje, ropa.

attitude [ǽtitiud], *s.* actitud, ademán, postura.

attorney [ǝtǝ́rni], *s.* abogado; apode- rado.—*a. general*, fiscal nacional.— *district a.*, fiscal del distrito.

attract [ǝtrǽkt], *vt.* y *vi.* atraer; cauti- var.— **—ion** [ǝtrǽkȿǝn], *s.* atracción; atractivo, aliciente.— **—ive** [ǝtrǽk- tiv], *a.* atractivo; cautivador; simpá- tico.— **—iveness** [ǝtrǽktivnis], *s.* atracción, atractivo.

attribute [ǝtríbiut], *vt.* atribuir, impu- tar, achacar.—*s.* [ǽtribiut], atributo, característica, distintivo.

attrition [ætríȿǝn], *s.* roce, rozadura, frotación; atrición.

attune [ǝtiún], *vt.* armonizar, afinar.

auburn [ɔ́bœrn], *a.* castaño rojizo.

auction [ɔ́kȿǝn], *s.* subasta, almoneda, remate.—*vt.* subastar, rematar.— **—eer** [-ír], *s.* subastador; pregonero, rematador.—*vt.* vender en pública subasta.

audacious [ɔdéiȿʌs], *a.* audaz, osado; descarado.—**audacity** [ɔdǽsiti], *s.* audacia, osadía.

audible [ɔ́dibl], *a.* audible.—**audience** [ɔ́diens], *s.* auditorio, concurso, con- currencia, público; los oyentes o circunstantes; audición; audiencia o entrevista.—**audit** [ɔ́dit], *s.* interven- ción y ajuste de cuentas.—*vt.* inter- venir, revisar una cuenta.—**auditor** [ɔ́ditǝ(r)], *s.* oyente; interventor.— **auditorium** [ɔditɔ́riʌm], *s.* auditorio, salón de actos o de espectáculos.

auger [ɔ́gœ(r)], *s.* barrena; taladro.—*a. bit*, broca o mecha de taladro.

aught [ɔt], *s.* algo; cero; nada.—*adv.* absolutamente.

augment [ɔgmént], *vt.* y *vi.* aumentar, crecer.— **—ative** [-ǝtiv], *a.* aumenta- tivo.

august [ɔgʌ́st], *a.* augusto, majestuoso. —**A.** [ɔ́gʌst], *s.* agosto (mes).

aunt [ænt, ant], *s.* tía.

aureola [ɔriólǝ], *s.* aureola, corona.

aureomycin [ɔrioumáisin], *s.* aureomi- cina.

auricular [ɔríkyʊlǝ(r)], *a.* auricular; oíble; confidencial, secreto, dicho al oído.

auspices [ɔ́spisiz], *s. pl.* auspicios; dirección.—**auspicious** [ɔspíȿʌs], *a.* favorable, propicio.

austere [ɔstír], *a.* austero.— **—ness** [-nis], **austerity** [ɔstériti], *s.* austeri- dad.

Australian [ɔstréilyǝn], *a.* y *s.* austra- liano.

Austrian [ɔ́strian], *a.* y *s.* austríaco.

authentic(al) [ɔθéntik(ǝl)], *a.* autén-

tico.— **—ity** [ɔθentísiti], *s.* autentici- dad.

author [ɔ́θǝ(r)], *s.* autor.— **—ess** [-is], *s.* autora.

authoritative [ɔθǝ́riteitiv], *a.* autorizado. **—authority** [ɔθǝ́riti], *s.* autoridad.— **authorization** [ɔθǝrizéiȿǝn], *s.* auto- rización.—**authorize** [ɔ́θǝraiz], *vt.* autorizar, facultar.

authorship [ɔ́θǝrȿip], *s.* autoría, pater- nidad literaria.

auto [ɔ́tou], *s.* automóvil, auto.

autocracy [ɔtákrǝsi], *s.* autocracia.— **autocrat** [ɔ́tokræt], *s.* autócrata.

autograph [ɔ́tográf], *a.* y *s.* autógrafo.— *vt.* autografiar.

automat [ɔ́tomæt], *s.* mecanismo auto- mático; restaurante de servicio auto- mático.— **—ic(al)** [ɔtomǽtik(ǝl)], *a.* automático.— **—ism** [ɔtǽmǝtizm], *s.* automatismo.— **—on** [ɔtǽmǝtan], *s.* autómata.

automobile [ɔ́tomoubil], *s.* automóvil.

autonomous [ɔtánomʌs], *a.* autónomo. **—autonomy** [ɔtánomi], *s.* autonomía.

autopsy [ɔ́tapsi], *s.* autopsia.

autumn [ɔ́tʌm], *s.* otoño.

auxiliary [ɔgzílyǝri], *a.* auxiliar.

avail [ǝvéil], *vt.* aprovechar, beneficiar, valer.—*vi.* valer, servir, ser útil.—*to a. oneself of*, aprovecharse de.—*s.* provecho, utilidad.— **—able** [-abl], *a.* aprovechable, disponible.

avalanche [ǽvǝlænch], *s.* alud.

avarice [ǽvǝris], *s.* avaricia, codicia.— **avaricious** [ævǝríȿʌs], *a.* avaro, ava- riento.

avenge [ǝvéndʒ], *vt.* y *vi.* vengar(se).

avenue [ǽveniu], *s.* avenida, calzada; alameda.

aver [ǝvǝ́r], *vt.* asegurar, afirmar.

average [ǽveridʒ], *s.* promedio; término medio.—*on an a.*, como promedio.— *a.* medio, común, corriente, típico.— *vt.* calcular el promedio o término medio; prorratear.

averse [ǝvǝ́rs], *a.* adverso, contrario; renuente.—**aversion** [ǝvǝ́rʒǝn], *s.* aversión.

avert [ǝvǝ́rt], *vt.* desviar, apartar; prevenir, conjurar.

aviary [éivieri], *s.* pajarera.

aviation [eiviéiȿǝn], *s.* aviación.—**avia- tor** [éivieitǝ(r)], *s.* aviador.

avid [ǽvid], *a.* ávido, codicioso; ansioso. **—ity** [ǝvíditi], *s.* avidez, codicia; ansia.

avocado [ævokádou], *s.* aguacate.

avocation [ævokéiȿǝn], *s.* vocación; distracción, diversión.

avoid [ǝvɔ́id], *vt.* evitar, eludir, esqui- var, evadir; zafarse de. **—able** [-abl], *a.* evitable, eludible.— **—ance** [-ǝns], *s.* evitación.

await [ǝwéit], *vt.* y *vi.* aguardar esperar.

awake [ạwéịk], vti. y vii. [4], awaken [ạwéịkẹn], vt. y vi. despertar(se).— s. despierto, desvelado.—awakening [ạwéịkẹnịŋ], s. despertar, despertamiento.

award [ạwórd], vt. y vi. otorgar, conferir; premiar; adjudicar.—s. premio; sentencia, adjudicación.

aware [ạwér], a. consciente; enterado, sabedor; sobre aviso.

awash [ạwáš], a. y adv. a flor de agua.

away [ạwéị], adv. y a. lejos; a lo lejos; ausente, fuera.—far a., muy lejos.—right a., ahorita.—to go a., alejarse.—to take a., quitar.—interj. ¡fuera de aquí! ¡lárguese usted!

awe [o], s. temor; pasmo; pavor.—a.-inspiring, imponente.—a.-struck, despavorido, aterrado, espantado.—to stand in a. of, temer; reverenciar.—vt. aterrar, infundir miedo o respeto.

awful [óful], a. tremendo; terrible.

awhile [ạhwáịl], adv. un rato, algún tiempo.

awkward [ókwạrd], s. torpe, desmañado, desgarbado; embarazoso.—-ness [-nịs], s. torpeza, desmaña.

awl [ol], s. lezna; punzón; lengüeta.

awning [ónịŋ], s. toldo.

awoke [ạwóụk], pret. y pp. de TO AWAKE.

ax(e) [æks], s. hacha.

axiom [æksịọm], s. axioma, postulado, sentencia.

axis [æksịs], s. (pl. axes [æksịz]) eje.

axle [æksl], s. eje, árbol.

aye, ay [aị], adv. sí.—s. voto afirmativo.

Aztec [æztek], a. y s. azteca.

azure [ǽžụr], a. y s. azur, azul celeste.

B

babble [bæbl], vt. y vi. balbucear; charlar; murmurar (un arroyo).—s. charla, balbuceo, charlatanería; susurro, murmullo.—-r [bǽblœ(r)], s. charlatán, hablador; trapalero.—babbling [bǽblịŋ], a. murmurante, balbuciente.—s. cháchara, garrulería, balbucencia.

babe [beịb], s. criaturita, nene, bebé.

baboon [bæbún], s. mandril.

baby [béịbị], s. criatura, crío, nene, nena, pequeñuelo, bebé, (Am.) guagua.—a. de niño; de, para o como nene; pequeño; de tierna edad; infantil.—b. blue, azul claro.—b. carriage, cochecillo de nene.—b. grand piano, piano de media cola.—b. talk, modo infantil de hablar, media lengua.—b. tooth, diente de leche.—vti. [7] tratar como niño; mimar.

baccalaureate [bækạlórịịt], s. bachillerato.

bachelor [bǽchẹlọ(r)], s. soltero, célibe; bachiller.

bacilli [bæsịlaị], s. pl. bacilos, bacterias.—bacillus [bæsịlʌs], s. bacilo, bacteria.—bacillary [bǽsịleri], a. bacilar.

back [bæk], s. espalda; lomo, espinazo (de un animal); respaldo; dorso, revés (de la mano); reverso; parte posterior o de atrás, trasera; lomo (de un cuchillo, de un libro); (teat.) foro; (dep.) zaguero, defensa.—behind one's b., por detrás, a espaldas de uno.—in the b. of one's mind, en lo recóndito del pensamiento.—on one's b., a cuestas, boca arriba, de espaldas.—to turn one's b. (on), volver la espalda; negar ayuda (a).—with one's b. to the wall, entre la espada y la pared.—a. trasero, posterior, inferior; dorsal; atrasado, pasado (apl. al tiempo); lejano.—b. pay, sueldo atrasado.—adv. atrás, detrás; de nuevo; de vuelta.—b. and forth, de un lado a otro.—to come b., volver, regresar.—to give b., devolver.—interj. ¡atrás!—vt. hacer retroceder; apoyar, respaldar; endosar.—vi. (a veces con up) recular, retroceder, ciar.—to b. down, to b. out, volverse atrás; abandonar una empresa.—-ache [bǽkeịk], s. dolor de espalda.—backbit [bǽkbịt], pret. y pp. de TO BACKBITE.—-bite [-baịt], vti. y vii. [10] difamar, murmurar; morder.—-biter [-baịtœ(r)], s. murmurador, difamador, detractor.—-biting [-baịtịŋ], s. murmuración, difamación, calumnia.—backbitten [bǽkbịtẹn], pp. de TO BACKBITE.—-board [-bord], s. respaldo, espaldar.—-bone [-boụn], s. espinazo; nervio; fundamento.—-breaking [-breịkịŋ], a. agobiante, abrumador.—-fire [-faịr], s. contracandela; explosión prematura.—vi. salir el tiro por la culata.—-ground [-graụnd], s. trasfondo; antecedentes; base, fondo; lejanía.—-shop [-šap], s. trastienda; rebotica.—-side [-saịd], s. envés, vuelta, espalda; nalgas.—-stitch [-stịch], s. pespunte, punto atrás.—vt. y vi. pespuntar.—-ward [-wạrd], a. vuelto o dirigido hacia atrás; retrógrado, atrasado; retraído; tardo, tardío.—to go b. and forward, ir y venir.—-wardness [-wạrdnịs], s. atraso; torpeza; retraimiento.—-wards [-wạrdz], adv. atrás, de espaldas.—to go b., retroceder, ir para atrás.

bacon [béịkọn], s. tocino.

bacteria [bæktírịạ], s. pl. bacterias.—bacterial [bæktírịạl], a. bacteriano, bactérico.

bad [bæd], a. mal(o), perverso, depravado; dañoso; enfermo, indispuesto; dañado, podrido.—b. blood, animosi-

dad, encono.—*b. coin,* moneda falsa.
—*b. time,* mal rato.—*very b.,* pésimo.

bade [bæd], *pret.* de TO BID.

badge [bædʒ], *s.* condecoración, insignia, placa, distintivo.

badger [bǽdʒœ(r)], *vt.* molestar, cansar, fatigar.—*s.* tejón.

baffle [bǽfl], *vt.* desconcertar; contrariar; frustrar, impedir.—**baffling** [bǽfliŋ], *a.* desconcertante, desconcertador.

bag [bæg], *s.* saco, costal, talega; bolsa, zurrón; presa; saquito de mano.— *to be in the b.,* (fam.) ser cosa segura.— *to hold the b.,* (fam.) pagar los vidrios rotos.—*vti.* [1] ensacar, entalegar; cazar, cobrar (la caza).—*vii.* hacer bolsa o pliegue (la ropa).— **—gage** [bǽgidʒ], *s.* equipaje, maletas.—*b. check,* contraseña de equipaje.

bail [beil], *s.* caución, fianza; fiador; cubo o vertedor para achicar (agua). —*on b.,* bajo fianza.—*to go b. for,* salir fiador de.—*vt.* dar fianza, caucionar; poner en libertad bajo fianza; achicar.—*vi.*—*to b. out,* (aer.) arrojarse de un avión.

bailiff [béilif], *s.* alguacil.

bait [beit], *vt.* cebar; atraer, tentar; molestar, acosar.—*s.* cebo, carnada; anzuelo, señuelo; pienso.—*to take the b.,* tragar el anzuelo, caer en un lazo.

baize [beiz], *s.* bayeta.—*green b.,* tapete verde.

bake [beik], *vt.* cocer o asar al horno, calcinar.—*vi.* hornear (como oficio); cocerse el horno.— **—d** [-t], *a.* horneado; cocido al horno.—*b. eggs,* huevos al plato.— **—r** [béikœ(r)], *s.* panadero, hornero; pastelero.— **—ry** [-œri], *s.* horno, tahona, panadería, pastelería.—**baking** [-iŋ], *s.* hornada; cocción.

balance [bǽlans], *s.* balanza; equilibrio; balance, contrapeso; (com.) balance, saldo.—*b. wheel,* balancín, volante.— *vt.* equilibrar; balancear; contrapesar; (com.) saldar; pesar, considerar.—*vi.* equilibrarse; contrarrestarse; (com.) saldarse; balancearse, mecerse.— **balancing** [bǽlansiŋ], *s.* equilibrio; balanceo.—*a.* compensador.—*b. flap,* (aer.) alerón.

balcony [bǽlkoni], *s.* balcón; (teat.) galería, anfiteatro.

bald [bɔld], *a.* calvo; escueto; pelado, desnudo; desabrido.— **—head** [bɔ́ldhed], *s.* persona calva.— **—ness** [-nis], *s.* calvicie.

bale [beil], *s.* fardo; tercio (de tabaco); bala, paca (de algodón, de papel).— *vt.* embalar, empaquetar.

Balearic [bæliǽrik], *a.* balear.

baling [béiliŋ], *s.* embalaje; enfardeladura.

balk [bɔk], *vt.* frustrar, desbaratar.—*vi.* plantarse, encabritarse (un caballo); resistirse.—*s.* obstáculo, impedimento, fracaso; (carp.) viga.

ball [bɔl], *s.* bola, pelota, globo; yema (del dedo); baile; bala (de cañón).— *b. bearing,* caja de bolas, cojinete.— *b. game,* juego de pelota, de beisbol.— *b. of yarn,* ovillo.—*to b. up,* embrollar, confundir.

ballad [bǽlad], *s.* balada, romance; copla, canción.

ballast [bǽlast], *s.* lastre; (f.c.) balasto. —*b. bed,* firme (de carretera).— *washed b.,* guijarro.—*vt.* lastrar; (f.c.) balastar.— **—ing** [-iŋ], *s.* lastre; balasto.

balloon [balún], *s.* globo (aerostático).— **—ist** [-ist], *s.* aeronauta.

ballot [bǽlot], *s.* cédula o boleta para votar; voto; votación.—*b. box,* urna electoral.—*vt.* y *vi.* votar.— **—ing** [-iŋ], *s.* votación.

balm [bam], *s.* bálsamo, ungüento fragante.— **—y** [bámi], *a.* balsámico, fragante; calmante; alocado, tonto.

ban [bæn], *s.* bando, edicto, proclama, pregón; excomunión.—*vti.* [1] prohibir, proscribir; excomulgar.

banal [béinal], *a.* trivial, vulgar.

banana [banǽnə], *s.* plátano, banano, guineo.—*b. plantation,* platanal, platanar.—*b. tree,* banano, plátano bananero.

band [bænd], *s.* banda, faja, tira; correa, cinta, franja, lista; abrazadera, zuncho; banda, pandilla, cuadrilla; (mús.) banda, charanga.—*vt.* y *vi.* juntar, congregar; fajar, atar.— *to b. together,* asociarse; formar pandilla.

bandage [bǽndidʒ], *s.* vendaje, venda, faja.—*vt.* vendar.

bandit [bǽndit], *s.* bandido, bandolero.— **—ry** [-ri], *s.* bandolerismo, bandidaje.

bane [bein], *s.* ruina, azote, daño.— **—ful** [béinful], *a.* pernicioso, dañino, ponzoñoso, funesto.

bang [bæŋ], *vt.* golpear con ruido, hacer estrépito.—*vi.* dar estampido; saltar. —*s.* golpe; estampido; portazo; ruido de un golpe; flequillo.—*with a b.,* con un golpe violento; con estrépito; de repente.—*interj.* ¡pum!

banish [bǽniʃ], *vt.* desterrar, deportar; confinar.— **—ment** [-mənt], *s.* destierro, deportación; confinamiento.

banister [bǽnistœ(r)], *s.* baranda, pasamano.

bank [bæŋk], *s.* orilla, ribera, margen; loma, cuesta; banco, bajío; (com.) banco, casa de banca.—*b. book,* libreta de banco.—*b. note,* billete de banco.—*vt.* represar, estancar; amontonar, apilar; depositar en un banco.

—*vi.* ocuparse en negocios de banca; ser banquero.—*vt.* y *vi.* (aer.) ladear(se).—*to b. on*, contar con, confiar en.— —**er** [bǽŋkœ(r)], *s.* banquero; cambista.— —**ing** [-iŋ], *s.* banca, operaciones de banco.—*a.* bancario.— —**rupt** [-rʌpt], *s.* y *a.* quebrado, en quiebra, insolvente.—*vt.* quebrar, arruinar.— —**ruptcy** [-rʌptsi], *s.* bancarrota, quiebra.—*to go into b.*, declararse en quiebra.

banner [bǽnœr], *s.* bandera, estandarte.

banns [bænz], *s. pl.* amonestaciones.

banquet [bǽŋkwit], *s.* banquete, festín.—*vt.* y *vi.* banquetear.

banter [bǽntœ(r)], *vt.* y *vi.* zumbar(se), dar matraca, chotear, embromar.—*s.* zumba, burla, chunga.— —**er** [-œ(r)], *s.* zumbón, burlón.

baptism [bǽptizm], *s.* bautismo, bautizo.— —**al** [bæptízmal], *a.* bautismal. —*b. name*, nombre de pila.—**baptize** [bǽptajz], *vt.* bautizar.

bar [bar], *s.* barra; varilla; barra o pastilla (de chocolate, etc.); palanca; impedimento; barrera; cantina, bar, mostrador de taberna; reja, barrote; tribunal; abogacía, foro, cuerpo de abogados; (for.) foro, estrados; recinto de los acusados; (mus.) barra, raya de compás; (metal.) barra, lingote.—*b. association*, colegio de abogados.—*b. bell*, palanqueta de gimnasio.—*to be admitted to the b.*, recibirse de abogado.—*vti.* [1] trancar; estorbar, obstruir; prohibir; excluir.—*prep.* excepto, salvo.—*b. none*, sin excepción.

barb [barb], *s.* púa; lengüeta (de saeta, anzuelo).

barbarian [barbérian], *a.* y *s.* bárbaro, barbárico.—**barbarism** [bárbarizm], *s.* barbarie; barbarismo.—**barbarity** [barbǽriti], *s.* barbaridad, ferocidad. —**barbarous** [bárbarʌs], *a.* bárbaro, inculto; cruel.

barbecue [bárbikju], *vt.* hacer barbacoa. —*s.* barbacoa; churrasco.

barbed [barbd], *a.* barbado, armado con lengüetas o púas.—*b. wire*, alambre de púas.

barber [bárbœ(r)], *s.* barbero, peluquero.—*b. shop*, barbería, peluquería.

bard [bard], *s.* bardo, poeta.

bare [ber], *a.* desnudo; raso; pelado; liso; sencillo; desarmado; descarnado; descubierto; público; desamueblado; vacío; mero, solo.—*b. of money*, sin un cuarto, sin un real.—*vt.* desnudar, descubrir, despojar.— —**back** [bérbæk], *a.* y *adv.* (montado) al pelo, sin silla.— —**boned** [-bound], *a.* muy flaco, descarnado.— —**faced** [-fejst], *a.* descarado, insolente, atrevido.— —**facedness** [-fejstnis], *s.* descaro,

desfachatez.— —**foot** [-fut], *a.* descalzo.— —**headed** [-hedjd], *a.* sin sombrero, descubierto.— —**legged** [-lɛgid], *a.* sin medias.— —**ly** [-li], *adv.* mera, sola, escasamente.— —**necked** [-nɛkt], *a.* descotado, con escote.— —**ness** [-nis], *s.* desnudez; flaqueza; miseria.

bargain [bárgin], *s.* convenio, concierto; ganga; negocio, trato de compra o venta; artículo muy reducido de precio.—*at a b.*, baratísimo; en una ganga.—*b. driver*, regateador.—*to strike a b.*, cerrar un trato; hallar una ganga.—*vt.* y *vi.* concertar, negociar; regatear.—*to b. away*, permutar; vender regalado.— —**ing** [-iŋ], *s.* regateo; trato.

barge [bardʒ], *s.* lanchón, barcaza.

baritone [bǽritoun], *s.* barítono.

bark [bark], *s.* corteza; ladrido; velero. —*vt.* descortezar, raspar, raer; curtir o teñir en una infusión de corteza.— *vi.* ladrar; vociferar.—*to b. up the wrong tree*, tomar el rábano por las hojas, ir descaminado.

barkeeper [bárkipœ(r)], *s.* tabernero cantinero.

barley [bárli], *s.* cebada.

barmaid [bármejd], *s.* cantinera, moza de taberna, (Am.) mesera.

barn [barn], *s.* granero, pajar, troje; henil; establo (para ganado).

barnacle [bárnakl], *s.* lapa, percebe.

barnyard [bárnyard], *s.* corral.

barometer [barámetœ(r)], *s.* barómetro. —**barometrical** [bærométrikal], *a.* barométrico.

barrack [bǽrak], *s.* barraca, cabaña.— *pl.* cuartel.—*vt.* y *vi.* acuartelar(se).

barrel [bǽrel], *s.* barril, cuba, bocoy, tonel; tambor de reloj; cañón (de arma de fuego).—*vti.* [2] embarrilar.

barren [bǽren], *a.* estéril, árido, infecundo.— —**ness** [-nis], *s.* esterilidad, infecundidad, aridez.

barricade [bǽrikéjd], *s.* barricada, barrera, empalizada.—*vt.* cerrar con barricadas; obstruir el paso.

barrier [bériœ(r)], *s.* barrera; valla; obstáculo, estacada, atasco; límite.

bartender [bártendœ(r)], *s.* cantinero, tabernero.

barter [bártœ(r)], *vt.* permutar, trocar, cambiar.—*s.* permuta, cambio, trueque.— —**er** [-œ(r)], *s.* traficante, cambalachero.

base [bejs], *a.* bajo, ruín, villano; básico; (mus.) bajo, grave.—*b. court*, tribunal inferior.—*s.* basa, base, cimiento, fundamento, pedestal; zócalo; (mus.) bajo, grave; (beisbol) base.—*vt.* basar, apoyar, fundamentar.— —**ball** [béjsbɔl], *s.* beisbol o basebol; pelota de beisbol.— —**board** [-bɔrd], *s.* zócalo, plancha que sirve

de base; rodapié.— —born [-born], **a**. plebeyo; bastardo.— —less [-lis], **a**. desfondado; sin fundamento.— —ment [-mɛnt], **s**. sótano; basamento.— —ness [-nis], **s**. bajeza, vileza; ruindad.

bashful [bǽ͡ʃful], **a**. vergonzoso, tímido, corto.— —ness [-nis], **s**. vergüenza, timidez, cortedad.

basic [béjsik], **a**. básico, fundamental.

basilica [basílika], **s**. basílica.

basin [béjsin], **s**. (al)jofaina, bacía, palangana; cubeta; pila (de agua bendita); taza, pilón; estanque, represa, dársena; charca; cuenca de un río.

basis [béjsis], **s**. base; fundamento.

bask [bæsk], **vt**. y **vi**. asolearse, calentarse al sol, tomar el sol.

basket [bǽskit], **s**. cesto, canasta; cesta; (aer.) barquilla.— —**ball** [-bɔl], **s**. baloncesto, basketbol.

Basque [bæsk], **a**. y **s**. vasco, vascongado; (lengua) vascuence.

bass [bejs], **a**. (mus.) bajo, grave.—**b**. *drum*, bombo.—**b**. *horn*, tuba.—**b**. *string*, bordón.—**b**. *viol*, violón, contrabajo.—**s**. [bæs] (ict.) perca; [bejs] bajo (apl. a la voz).

bastard [bǽstard], **s**. bastardo, hijo natural.—**a**. bastardo; falso, espurio.— —y [-i], **s**. bastardía.

baste [bejst], **vt**. hilvanar; echar grasa sobre el asado; (fam.) azotar.—**basting** [béjstiŋ], **s**. hilván; (fam.) paliza.

bastion [bǽschɔn], **s**. bastión, baluarte.

bat [bæt], **s**. bate de beisbol; garrote; murciélago; guata.—**vti**. y **vii**. [1] golpear; batear; pestañear.

batch [bæch], **s**. hornada; tanda; grupo.

bath [bæθ], **s**. baño, cuarto de baño; bañadera.— —e [bejð], **vt**. bañar, lavar.—**vi**. bañarse.— —er [béjð͡œ(r)], **s**. bañista.— —**house** [bǽθha͡us], **s**. casa de baño.— —**ing** [béjðiŋ], **s**. baño.—**a**. de baño.—**b**. *resort*, balneario.—**b**. *suit*, traje de baño; (Am.) trusa.—**b**. *trunks*, calzón de baño.— —**robe** [bǽθro͡ub], **s**. bata de baño, albornoz.— —**room** [-rum], **s**. cuarto de baño.— —**tub** [-tʌb], **s**. bañadera, bañera.

baton [bætán], **s**. bastón de mando; (mus.) batuta.

battalion [bætǽlyɔn], **s**. batallón.

batter [bǽtœ(r)], **vt**. y **vi**. golpear, batir, majar.—**b**. *down*, demoler.—**s**. batido, masa culinaria; golpeadura.

battery [bǽtœrj], **s**. (arti. y mec.) batería; (elec.) pila; batería, acumulador; asalto, agresión.

battle [bǽtl], **s**. batalla, combate; lucha.—**b**. *cruiser*, crucero de combate.—**vi**. y **vt**. batallar, combatir; luchar.— —**field** [-fild], —**ground** [-gra͡und], **s**. campo de batalla.— —**ment** [-mɛnt],

s. muralla almenada.— —**ship** [-ʃip], **s**. acorazado.

bawl [bɔl], **vt**. pregonar.—**vi**. gritar, chillar, desgañitarse.—**s**. gritería.— —er [bɔl͡œ(r)], **s**. vocinglero, alborotador, chillón.

bay [bej], **a**. bayo.—**vt**. y **vi**. ladrar, aullar.—**s**. bahía, ensenada, cala, rada; ladrido, aullido; caballo bayo; laurel.—*at b.*, acorralado; a raya.—*b. window*, mirador, ventana saliente.

bayonet [béjɔnit], **s**. bayoneta.—**vt**. cargar o herir con bayoneta.

bazaar [bazár], **s**. bazar, feria.

be [bi], **vii**. [11] ser, existir; estar, encontrarse, hallarse, verse, quedar(se); haber; hacer; tener.—*he is no more*, ya no existe.—*it is cold, hot, etc.*, hace frío, calor, etc.—*there is no one there*, no hay nadie allí.—*to be American, Spanish, etc.*, ser americano, español, etc.—*to be astonished, surprised, etc.*, quedar(se) atónito, sorprendido, etc.—*to be cold, hungry, right, two years old, etc.*, tener frío, hambre, razón, dos años, etc.—*to be healthy, sick, etc.*, estar sano, enfermo, etc.—*to be in a serious situation, without money, etc.*, encontrarse, hallarse, verse en una situación seria, sin un centavo.

beach [bich], **s**. playa, costa, orilla.—**vt**. y **vi**. arrastrar a la playa; varar; encallar en la playa.

beacon [bíkɔn], **s**. faro; baliza, boya; fanal; señal luminosa.—**vt**. abalizar; iluminar, guiar.

bead [bid], **s**. cuenta (de rosario, collar), abalorio; burbuja; espuma; gota (de sudor); saliente.—*pl.* rosario.—**vt**. adornar con abalorios; redondear los bordes (de un tubo ensanchado).—**vi**. formar espuma; burbujear.— —**ing** [bídiŋ], **s**. abalorio; listón; moldura convexa; pestaña, reborde.

beadle [bídl], **s**. pertiguero o macero, muñidor, bedel, alguacil, ministril.

beak [bik], **s**. pico; hocico; (fam.) rostro; cabo; espolón (de buque).— —ed [-t], **a**. picudo.— —er [bíkœ(r)], **s**. vaso, copa.

beam [bim], **s**. rayo, destello; viga, tablón; (mar.) bao; manga de un buque; brazo de romana.—*on the b.*, ir bien encaminado.—*radio b.*, radio faro.—**vi**. destellar, fulgurar; rebosar de alegría.—**vt**. enviar; emitir, irradiar; radiar.— —**ing** [bímiŋ], **a**. radiante; brillante; alegre.— —y [-i], **a**. radiante; alegre, vivo; macizo; (mar.) ancho de manga.

bean [bin], **s**. frijol, haba, habichuela, alubia, judía; grano, semilla; (fam.) cabeza, chola, cayuca.—*string b.*, habichuela verde, ejote, poroto.

bear [ber], **vti**. [10], sostener, sustentar;

llevar; aguantar, soportar, sobrellevar; sufragar; producir; parir, dar a luz.—*to b. company*, acompañar.—*to b. in mind*, tener en cuenta.—*to b. out*, confirmar, corroborar.—*to b. with*, tener paciencia con.—*to b. witness*, dar testimonio.—*s.* oso; (com.) bajista (en la Bolsa).— **able** [bérɐbl], *a.* sufrible, soportable.— **er** [-œ(r)], *s.* portador; mensajero; soporte.— **ing** [-iŋ], *s.* cojinete, caja de bolas; paciencia, sufrimiento; porte, presencia; relación, conexión; cosecha, gestación.—*pl.* orientación, rumbo; línea de flotación.—*to find one's b.,* orientarse.—*a.* de apoyo, de contacto; productivo.—*fruit b.,* fructífero.

beard [bird], *s.* barba o barbas; (bot.) arista.

beast [bist], *s.* bestia; animal; cuadrúpedo; hombre brutal.—*b. of burden,* acémila.

beat [bit], *vti.* [10] batir; revolver; sacudir; pegar; golpear; ganar, vencer; aventajar; marcar (el compás); (caz.) dar una batida; sonar (el tambor).—*to b. a retreat,* batirse en retirada.—*vii.* latir, pulsar; batir (el sol, las olas); golpear repetidamente; sonar.—*to b. around the bush,* andar(se) con rodeos.—*to b. it,* (fam.) poner pies en polvorosa.—*s.* golpe; palpitación, latido; toque de tambor; ronda.—*a.* (fam.) fatigado, rendido de cansancio.—*pret. y pp.* de TO BEAT.—**beaten** [bitɐn], *pp.* de TO BEAT.—*a.* trillado; batido, vencido.— **er** [-œ(r)], *s.* martillo, maza; molinillo; batidor, agitador, sacudidor.— **ing** [-iŋ], *s.* paliza, zurra, tunda; latido, palpitación, pulsación; golpeo.

beatitude [biǽtitjud], *s.* beatitud; bienaventuranza.—*the Beatitudes,* las bienaventuranzas.

beau [bou], *s.* pretendiente, acompañante, novio.

beautician [bjutíʃɐn], *s.* peluquero, peluquera.—**beautiful** [bjútiful], *a.* bello, hermoso, precioso.—**beautify** [bjútifai], *vti.* [7] hermosear, embellecer, acicalar.—*vii.* hermosearse, pulirse, maquillarse.—**beauty** [bjúti], *s.* belleza, beldad, hermosura, preciosidad.—*b. parlor,* salón de belleza.

beaver [bívœ(r)], *s.* castor; piel de castor.— **board** [-bord], *s.* cartón de fibras para tabiques.

becalm [bikám], *vt.* calmar, sosegar; encalmarse (tiempo o viento).

became [bikéim], *pret.* de TO BECOME.

because [bikóz], *conj. y adv.* porque, pues, que.—*b. of,* a causa de.

beckon [békɐn], *vt.* llamar o mandar con (o por) señas.—*vi.* hacer señas

o ademanes.—*s.* seña, ademán, llamada.

become [bikám], *vii.* [10] devenir; hacerse; llegar a ser; ponerse; volverse; convertirse en; quedarse (cojo, sordo, etc.).—*vti.* sentar bien, caer bien (trajes, vestidos, colores).—*pp.* de TO BECOME.—**becoming** [bikámiŋ], *a.* propio, conveniente; favorecedor (vestido, color).

bed [bed], *s.* cama, lecho; (geol.) capa, estrato, yacimiento; cauce (de río); (mec.) asiento, lecho, fondo; armadura, base, cimiento; (ing.) firme.— *double b.,* cama de matrimonio, cama camera.—*to go to b.,* acostarse.—*vti.* [1] acostar.— **bug** [bédbʌg], *s.* chinche.— **clothes** [-klouðz], *s. pl.* ropa de cama; (Am.) cobijas.

bedlam [bédlɐm], *s.* casa de orates; bullicio; desbarajuste.

Bedouin [béduin], *s.* beduino; vago.

bedplate [bédpleit], *s.* (mec.) bancaza, platina.

bedraggled [bidrǽgld], *a.* enlodado.

bedridden [bédridɐn], *a.* postrado en cama.—**bedroom** [bédrum], *s.* alcoba, dormitorio; (Mex.) recámara.—**bedside** [bédsaid], *s.* lado de cama; cabecera.—**bedspread** [bédspred], *s.* colcha, cobertor.—**bedspring** [bédspriŋ], *s.* colchón de muelle.—**bedtime** [bédtaim], *s.* hora de acostarse.

bee [bi], *s.* abeja; (fam.) reunión, tertulia.—*b. line,* línea recta.

beech [bich], *s.* (bot.) haya.— **nut** [bíchnʌt], *s.* nuez de haya, hayuco.

beef [bif], *s.* carne de res; res; queja.— *vi.* (fam.) jactarse; quejarse.

beehive [bíhaiv], *s.* colmena.—**beekeeper** [bíkipœ(r)], *s.* apicultor, colmenero.—**beekeeping** [bíkipiŋ], *s.* apicultura.

been [bin], *pp.* de TO BE.

beer [bir], *s.* cerveza.

beet [bit], *s.* remolacha, (Mex.) betabel.

beetle [bitl], *s.* escarabajo.—**beetling** [bítliŋ], *s.* saliente, colgante; estampación.

before [bifór], *adv.* delante, al frente; antes, con prioridad; (mar.) de proa. — *b.-mentioned,* antemencionado, susodicho.—*prep.* delante de, enfrente de; ante, en presencia de; antes de.— *b. the wind,* viento en popa.—*conj.* antes (de) que, primero...— **hand** [-hænd], *adv.* de antemano; previamente, con antelación.—*a.* acomodado, con recursos.

befriend [bifrénd], *vt.* favorecer, patrocinar; brindar amistad.

beg [beg], *vii.* [1] mendigar, pordiosear, vivir de limosna.—*vti.* rogar, suplicar, pedir.—*to b. (leave) to,* permitirse.

began [bigǽn], *pret.* de TO BEGIN.

beggar [bégǎr], *s.* pordiosero, mendigo.- **—ly** [-li], *a.* pobre, miserable.—*adv.* pobremente.—**begging** [bégin], *s.* mendicidad, mendicación, pordioseo.

begin [bigín], *vti.* y *vii.* [10] comenzar, principiar, empezar; iniciar; (for.) incoar (un pleito).- **—ner** [-œ(r)], *s.* principiante; novicio, novato; (com.) meritorio.- **—ning** [-in], *s.* comienzo, iniciación, principio, origen; génesis. —*from b. to end*, de cabo a rabo, de pe a pa.

beguile [bigáil], *vt.* engañar, seducir; defraudar; pasar el tiempo.

begun [bigán], *pp.* de TO BEGIN.

behalf [bihǽf], *s.*—*in o on behalf of*, por; a favor, en nombre de; en pro de; de parte de.

behave [bihéiv], *vt.* y *vi.* proceder, obrar, conducirse; (com)portarse (bien o mal).—*b. yourself!* ¡pórtate bien!— **behavior** [bihéivyǫr], *s.* conducta, comportamiento; funcionamiento.

behead [bihéd], *vt.* decapitar, degollar.- **—ing** [-in], *s.* decapitación, degüello.

beheld [bihéld], *pret.* y *pp.* de TO BEHOLD.

behind [biháind], *adv.* atrás, detrás; en o a la zaga.—*to fall b.*, atrasarse, retrasarse.—*prep.* tras; detrás de; después de.—*b. one's back*, a espaldas de uno.—*b. the scenes*, entre bastidores.—*b. the time*, atrasado de noticias.—*s.* (coll.) nalgas, trasero.

behold [bihóuld], *vti.* [10] mirar, ver, contemplar.—*interj.* ¡he aquí! ¡mire Ud.!— **—er** [-œ(r)], *s.* espectador.

being [bíin], *ger.* de TO BE.—*for the time b.*, por el momento; por ahora.—*s.* ser, ente, criatura; existencia, vida.

belch [belch], *vi.* eructar; vomitar.— *vt.* arrojar; vomitar.—*s.* eructo.

belfry [bélfri], *s.* campanario.

Belgian [béldžǎn], *s.* y *a.* belga.

belief [bilíf], *s.* fe, creencia, crédito; confianza; credo; opinión.—**believable** [bilívǎbl], *a.* creíble.—**believe** [bilív], *vt.* y *vi.* creer; pensar; opinar. —*to b. in*, creer en; tener fe en.— **believer** [bilívœ(r)], *s.* creyente, fiel.

bell [bel], *s.* campana; campanilla; timbre; cencerro; cascabel.—*b. boy*, botones.—*b. clapper*, badajo.—*b. ringer*, campanero.—*b. tower*, campanario.— *to b. the cat*, ponerle el cascabel al gato.

belligerent [bilídžęrent], *s.* beligerante. —*a.* belicoso, guerrero.

bellow [bélou], *vi.* bramar, berrear; mugir, rugir; vociferar.—*s.* bufido, bramido, rugido.—*—s* [-z], *s. pl.* fuelle(s).

bellwether [bélweδœ(r)], *s.* (carnero o morueco) manso.

belly [béli], *s.* vientre; barriga, tripa, panza; estómago.—*vii.* [7] pandear.- **—ache** [-eik], *s.* dolor de vientre.-

—ful [-ful], *s.* panzada, hartazgo.

belong [bilón], *vi.* pertenecer; tocar; corresponder.- **—ing** [-in], *a.* perteneciente.—*s.* pertenencia, propiedad. —*pl.* bienes; efectos; bártulos.

beloved [bilÁv(i)d], *a.* querido, amado. —*s.* persona amada.

below [bilóu], *adv.* abajo, bajo, debajo, más abajo.—*prep.* bajo, debajo de; después de.—*b.-stated*, más adelante, o más abajo mencionado.

belt [belt], *s.* cinto o cinturón, faja, cincho; correa; tira; (mec.) correa de trasmisión; área, perímetro.—*b. shaft*, árbol de transmisión.—*vt.* fajar; ceñir; poner correa a (una máquina).

bench [bench], *s.* banco, banca; escaño; (for.) tribunal.—*b. warrant*, auto de prisión.

bend [bend], *vti.* y *vii.* [4] encorvar(se), curvar(se), doblar(se), plegar(se), torcer(se); inclinar(se); doblegar(se); someter(se).—*s.* comba(dura), encorvadura, curvatura, curva; recodo; codillo.—*to b. one's efforts*, redoblar uno sus esfuerzos.

beneath [biníθ], *adv.* abajo, debajo.— *prep.* bajo, debajo de; por bajo.

benediction [benidíkšǫn], *s.* bendición.

benefactor [bénǐfæktǫr(r)], *s.* benefactor, bienhechor.

benefice [bénifis], *s.* beneficio, prebenda.- **—nce** [binéfisens], *s.* beneficencia; caridad.- **—nt** [binéfisent], *a.* benéfico, caritativo.—**beneficial** [benifíšǎl], *a.* beneficioso, provechoso, ventajoso.—**benefit** [bénifit], *s.* beneficio; lucro; provecho, ventaja.—*vt.* beneficiar, aprovechar.—*vi.* sacar provecho.

benevolence [binévolęns], *s.* benevolencia.—**benevolent** [binévolęnt], *a.* benévolo.

benign [bináin], *a.* benigno; afable.- **—ity** [binígniti], *s.* benignidad, bondad.

bent [bent], *pret.* y *pp.* de TO BEND.—*a.* curvo, encorvado, torcido; inclinado. —*s.* encorvadura, curvatura; inclinación, propensión, tendencia.

bequeath [bikwíð], *vt.* legar, donar (en testamento).- **—er** [-œ(r)], *s.* el que lega o dona (en testamento).— **bequest** [bikwést], *s.* manda, donación o legado.

berate [biréit], *vt.* reprender, reñir, regañar.

beret [beréi], *s.* boina.

berry [béri], *s.* baya (fresa, mora, etc.); grano (de café, etc.).

berth [bœrθ], *s.* litera, camarote; atracadero, dársena.—*vt.* y *vi.* atracar, llevar al puerto; dar camarote, pasaje o empleo a.

beseech [bisích], *vti.* [10] suplicar, rogar, implorar.

beset [bisét], *vti.* [9] acosar, perseguir; bloquear; rodear.—*pret.* y *pp.* de TO BESET.—*a.* acosado; engastado.

beside [bisáid], *adv.* cerca, al lado, a la mano.—*prep.* al lado de; junto a; en comparación de.—*b. himself*, fuera de sí.—*b. the point*, que no viene al caso.—*s* [-z], *adv.* también, además. —*prep.* además de; sobre, por encima de; excepto.

besiege [bisídʒ], *vt.* sitiar; asediar, acosar.— *r* [-œ(r)], *s.* sitiador; asediador.

besought [bisót], *pret.* y *pp.* de TO BESEECH.

best [best], *a.* y *adv. super.* de GOOD y WELL: mejor, del mejor modo, óptimo, óptimamente, superior(mente). —*b. man*, padrino de boda.—*b. seller*, el que más se vende, el favorito (apl. a libros).—*the b. part of*, casi todo, la mayor parte de.—*you know b.*, Ud. sabe mejor que nadie.—*s.* [el, lo] mejor, [los] mejores, etc.—*at (the) b.*, a lo más, cuando más, aun en el mejor caso.—*to do one's b.*, hacer lo posible.—*to make the b. of*, sacar el mejor partido de.—*to the b. of my knowledge*, según mi leal saber y entender.—*vt.* aventajar, vencer, ganar a.

bestial [béschạl], *a.* bestial, brutal.— *ity* [beschiǽliti], *s.* bestialidad, brutalidad.— *ize* [béschạlaiz], *vt.* embrutecer.

bestow [bistóu], *vt.* conceder, conferir; otorgar; agraciar; donar.—*to b. in abundance*, colmar (de).— *al* [-ạl], *s.* otorgamiento; dádiva, presente.

bet [bet], *s.* apuesta.—*it's a good b.*, es cosa segura.—*vti.* y *vii.* [3] apostar. —*you b.*, (fam.) claro, ya lo creo. —*pret.* y *pp.* de TO BET.

betray [bitréi], *vt.* traicionar, vender; revelar, descubrir; engañar; dejar ver.— *al* [-ạl], *s.* traición, perfidia; engaño; seducción.— *er* [-œ(r)], *s.* traidor; seductor.

betroth [bitróθ], *vt.* y *vi.* desposar(se), contraer matrimonio o esponsales, comprometerse, dar palabra de casamiento.— *al* [-ạl], *s.* esponsales, desposorio, compromiso, noviazgo.— *ed* [-t], *s.* prometido, novio, futuro.

better [bétœ(r)], *a.* y *adv. comp.* de GOOD y WELL: mejor, de mejor modo; más bueno o bien; superior(mente).— *b. half*, cara mitad, costilla, media naranja (esposo o esposa).—*the b. part of*, casi todo.—*to be b.*, estar mejor.—*to know b.*, saber que no se deben hacer ciertas cosas.—*s.* superioridad, ventaja; persona superior

(a uno).—*all* o *so much the b.*, tanto mejor.—*our betters*, nuestros superiores.—*vt.* mejorar; aventajar.— *vi.* mejorarse, progresar.— *ment* [-mẹnt], *s.* mejora; adelantamiento; superación.

betting [bétiṇ], *s.* apuesta. ¶

between [bitwín], *adv.* en medio, de por medio, entre los dos.—*prep.* entre.—*b. now and then*, de acá para allá.

beverage [bévirạdʒ], *s.* bebida.

beware [biwér], *vi.* (Ú. sólo en *inf.*) guardarse, cuidarse de, estar alerta contra.—*interj.* ¡cuidado! ¡mucho ojo!

bewilder [biwíldœ(r)], *vt.* aturdir, azorar; desorientar.— *ment* [-mẹnt], *s.* aturdimiento; azoramiento; perplejidad.

bewitch [biwích], *vt.* embrujar, encantar, hechizar, embelesar.— *er* [-œ(r)], *s.* brujo, encantador.— *ing* [-iṇ], *a.* hechicero, encantador.

beyond [biyánd], *adv.* más allá, más lejos; allende.—*s.* lo que está más allá; la otra vida.—*prep.* más allá de, tras; después de; sobre; superior a; susceptible de.—*b. (a) doubt*, fuera de duda.—*b. the seas*, ultramarino.

bias [báias], *s.* sesgo, oblicuidad; preferencia; prejuicio.—*a.* sesg(ad)o, diagonal, terciado.—*vti.* [2] influir, predisponer, torcer.—*biased* o *biassed* [báiast], *a.* parcial.

bib [bib], *s.* babero.

Bible [báibl], *s.* Biblia, historia sagrada. —*Biblical* [bíblikạl], *a.* bíblico.

bicarbonate [baikárbonịt], *s.* bicarbonato.

bicker [bíkœ(r)], *vi.* altercar, reñir, disputar.— *er* [-œ(r)], *s.* camorrista.— *ing* [-iṇ], *s.* altercado o disputa ociosa.

bicycle [báisikl], *s.* bicicleta, velocípedo. —*vi.* andar o montar en bicicleta.

bid [bid], *s.* postura, licitación; oferta; envite.—*vti.* [10] ofrecer, pujar licitar; envidar; mandar; rogar; invitar. —*to b. farewell, good-bye*, despedirse, decir adiós.—*vii.* hacer una oferta. —*pret.* y *pp.* de TO BID.— *der* [-œ(r)], *s.* postor, licitador.—*the highest b.*, el mejor postor.— *ding* [-iṇ], *s.* orden, mandato; invitación; licitación, postura.

bide [baid], *vii.* [5] residir, quedarse; esperar.—*to b. one's time*, reservarse para mejor ocasión.

bidet [bidéi], *s.* bidé, bidel.

bier [bir], *s.* féretro.

big [big], *a.* grande, gordo, grueso; importante, considerable; abultado, fatuo.—*b. brother*, hermano mayor. —*b. game*, caza mayor.—*b. shot*,

(fam.) pez gordo, personaje influyente.

bigamist [bígamist], **s.** bígamo; bígama.—**bigamous** [bígamas], **a.** bígamo.—**bigamy** [bígami], **s.** bigamia.

bigness [bígnis], **s.** grandeza; tamaño, volumen.

bigot [bígot], **s.** fanático, persona intolerante.— **—ry** [-ri], **s.** fanatismo, intolerancia.

bile [bail], **s.** bilis, hiel; cólera, mal genio.

bilge [bildž], **vi.** (mar.) abrirse una vía de agua, hacer agua; combar.—**vt.** (mar.) quebrar el pantoque (de un buque); hacer combar.—**s.** (mar.) pantoque, sentina; barriga de barril.

bilingual [bailíŋgwal], **a.** bilingüe.

bilious [bílyas], **a.** bilioso.

bilk [bilk], **vt.** defraudar.

bill [bil], **s.** billete de banco; cuenta, factura; letra; giro; proyecto de ley; ley; certificado, documento; declaración; lista; cartel; pico (de ave); (teat.) programa.—**b. broker,** corredor o agente de cambios.—**b. of exchange,** letra de cambio.—**b. of fare,** menú.—**b. of indictment,** acusación oficial escrita.—**b. of lading,** conocimiento de embarque.—**b. of rights,** declaración de derechos, ley fundamental.—**b. of sale,** escritura de venta.—**vt.** cargar en cuenta; anunciar por carteles; facturar, adeudar.—**vi.** juntar el pico (las aves).— **—board** [bílbord], **s.** cartelera.— **—ed** [-d], **a.** picudo.— **—fold** [-fould], **s.** billetera, cartera para billetes.

billiard [bílyard], **s.** carambola.—**pl.** billar.

billow [bílou], **s.** oleada, ola grande; golpe de mar; onda.—**vi.** ondular o hincharse como una ola.— **—y** [-i], **a.** ondeante, ondulante.

billy goat [bíli gout], **s.** chivo, cabrón.

bin [bin], **s.** receptáculo; depósito.—**coal b.,** carbonera.

bind [baind], **vt.** [10] atar; juntar; ligar; ceñir; obligar; vendar; ribetear; encuadernar, empastar; compeler.—**to b. over,** obligar a comparecer ante el juez.— **—er** [báindœ(r)], **s.** encuadernador; portafolio, archivador; atadero.— **—ing** [-iŋ], **a.** atadura; venda, tira, cinta; encuadernación; ribete.—**half b.,** media pasta.—**paper b.,** encuadernación en rústica.—**a.** obligatorio; válido.

binoculars [binákyülãrs], **s. pl.** gemelos, binóculos.

biochemical [baioukémikal], **a., biochemist** [baioukémist], **s., biochemistry** [baioukémistri], **s.** bioquímica.

biographer [baiágrœfœ(r)], **s.** biógrafo.—**biographical** [baiografíkal], **a.** biográfico.—**biography** [baiágrafi], **s.** biografía.

biologic(al) [baioládžik(al)], **a.** biológico.—**biologist** [baiálodžist], **s.** biólogo.—**biology** [baiálodži], **s.** biología.

birch [bœrch], **s.** abedul; disciplina.—**vt.** azotar, fustigar.

bird [bœrd], **s.** ave, pájaro; (fam.) persona, tipo raro o singular.—**b. of prey,** ave de rapiña.—**b.'s eye view,** vista de pájaro.— **—call** [-col], **s.** reclamo.— **—lime** [-laim], **s.** liga (de caza).— **—seed** [-sid], **s.** alpiste.

biretta [birétä], **s.** (igl.) birreta, birrete, bonete.

birth [bœrθ], **s.** nacimiento; origen; parto, alumbramiento; linaje.—**b. certificate,** partida de nacimiento.—**by b.,** de nacimiento.—**to give b. to,** dar a luz, parir.— **—day** [bœrθdei], **s.** cumpleaños, natalicio.— **—place** [-pleis], **s.** suelo natal.

Biscayan [biskéian], **s. y a.** vizcaíno, vasco.

biscuit [bískit], **s.** galleta; bizcocho.

bishop [bíšap], **s.** obispo; alfil (en el ajedrez).— **—ric** [-rik], **s.** obispado.

bit [bit], **s.** trozo; pizca; pedacito; poquito; momento; taladro, broca; bocado del freno.—**not a b.,** ni pizca.—**to smash to bits,** hacer añicos.—**pret. y pp.** de TO BITE.

bitch [bich], **s.** perra; (vulg.) ramera, zorra.

bite [bait], **vti. y vii.** [10] morder, mordiscar; picar (un insecto, un pez, la pimienta).—**s.** mordedura, dentellada; mordisco; tentempié; picadura.— **—r** [báitœ(r)], **s.** mordedor.— **—biting** [báitiŋ], **a.** penetrante; mordaz; picante; caústico; mordedor.— **—bitten** [bíten], **pp.** de TO BITE.

bitter [bítœ(r)], **a.** agrio, amargo(so); áspero; agudo, mordaz; encarnizado; cortante.—**s. pl.** amargo.— **—ness** [-nis], **s.** amargor; acíbar, hiel; rencor; encono.

bitumen [bitjúmen], **s.** betún.—**bituminous** [bitjúminAs], **a.** bituminoso, abetunado.

blab [blæb], **vii.** [1] revelar.—**vti.** chismear.—**b. o blabber** [blǽbœ(r)], **s.** hablador; chismorreo.

black [blæk], **s.** negro; luto.—**a.** negro; oscuro; sombrío; tétrico.—**b. and blue,** amoratado.—**in b. and white,** por escrito.— **—berry** [blǽkberi], **s.** (zarza)mora.— **—bird** [-bœrd], **s.** mirlo.— **—board** [-bord], **s.** pizarrón, pizarra.— **—en** [-ɛn], **vt.** ennegrecer; teñir de negro; embetunar; difamar.—**vi.** ennegrecerse, oscurecerse.— **—head** [-hed], **s.** espinilla.— **—ish** [-iš], **a.** negruzco, bruno.— **—mail** [-meil], **s.** chantaje.— **—mailer** [-meil

œ(r)], *s.* chantajista.— —ness [-nį͡s] *s.* negrura, oscuridad.— —out [-aųt], *s.* apagón.— —smith [-smjθ], *s.* herrero.

blade [bleid], *s.* hoja (de navaja, espada, etc.); hoja (de hierba); pala (de remo, etc.); paleta (de hélice, turbina o ventilador).

blame [bleįm], *vt.* (in)culpar; censurar. —*s.* (in)culpación; reproche, censura; culpa.— —less [bléįmljs], *a.* inocente; inculpado.

blanch [blænch], *vt.* blanquear; hacer palidecer.—*vi.* palidecer.— —ing [blénchįŋ], *s.* blanqueo.

bland [blænd], *a.* blando, suave.

blank [blæŋk], *a.* en blanco; vacío; pálido; inexpresivo.—*s.* espacio en blanco; laguna, hueco; forma o papel en blanco, planilla; esqueleto.—*b.-verse,* verso libre o suelto.

blanket [blǽŋkįt], *s.* manta, frazada, cobija.—*vt.* cubrir con manta.

blaspheme [blæsfím], *vt.* y *vi.* blasfemar; vilipendiar.—**blasphemy** [blǽsfįmį], *s.* blasfemia.

blast [blæst], *s.* ráfaga, bocanada; explosión, detonación; onda explosiva.—*b. furnace,* alto horno.—*vt.* volar, hacer saltar; maldecir.

blaze [bleįʒ], *s.* llama, llamarada; hoguera; fogata; ardor; arranque (ira, etc.).—*vt.* templar (acero); encender, inflamar; proclamar.—*vi.* arder con llama; resplandecer.

bleach [blich], *vt.* blanquear al sol; descolorar; aclarar (el pelo).—*vi.* ponerse blanco; desteñirse; palidecer. —*s.* blanqueamiento.— —er [blícḥœ(r)], *s.* blanqueador.—*pl.* gradería, gradas o tendido de sol (deportes).

bleak [blik], *a.* desierto, desolado, yermo; helado.—*b. region,* páramo, puna.—*s.* dardo.

blear(ed) [blír(d)], **bleary** [blírį], *a.* nublado; bañado en lágrimas; legañoso, lacrimoso.

bleat [blit], *s.* balido.—*vi.* balar.

bled [bled], *pret.* y *pp.* de TO BLEED. —**bleed** [blid], *vii.* [10] sangrar, desangrarse.—*vti.* sangrar a (persona, planta); arrancarle a uno el dinero, chuparle la sangre.—*to b. white,* desangrar a, arrancar hasta el último centavo.

blemish [blémįš], *vt.* dañar, manchar, empañar; infamar.—*s.* tacha, defecto, borrón.

blend [blend], *vti.* [4] mezclar, combinar; templar.—*vii.* mezclarse, fundirse; armonizar.—*s.* mezcla; matiz.— —er [bléndœ(r)], *s.* batidora, licuadora.

bless [bles], *vt.* bendecir.— —ed [blésįd], *a.* bendecido, bendito; bienaventu-

rado.— —ing [-iŋ], *s.* bendición; gracia, favor.—**blest** [blest], *a.* = BLESSED.

blew [blu], *pret.* de TO BLOW.

blight [blaįt], *s.* tizón, pulgón(parásito); contratiempo, malogro; ruina.—*vt.* y *vi.* destruir(se), agostar(se), frustrar(se).

blind [blaįnd], *vt.* cegar; deslumbrar; ofuscar; encubrir; tapar; engañar.— *a.* ciego.—*b. alley,* callejón sin salida. —*b. flying,* vuelo a ciegas.—*b. man,* ciego (*b. woman,* ciega).—*s.* cualquier cosa que impide ver o quita la luz.

blindage [bláįndįdâ] *s.* blindaje.

blindfold [bláįndfoųld], *s.* venda para los ojos.—*a.* con los ojos vendados. —*vt.* vendar los ojos; ofuscar.— **blinding** [bláįndįŋ], *a.* deslumbrador, cegador.—*s.* acción de cegar.— **blindness** [bláįndnįs], *s.* ceguera, ceguedad.

blink [blįŋk], *vi.* pestañear, parpadear; destellar.—*vt.* guiñar; mirar con los ojos entreabiertos.—*s.* pestañeo, guiño o guiñada; destello.— —er [blíŋkœ(r)], *s.* pestañeador; aparato trasmisor de señales luminosas.

bliss [blįs], *s.* gloria; bienaventuranza, felicidad; arrobamiento, deleite.— —ful [blísfųl], *a.* dichoso.

blister [blístœ(r)], *s.* ampolla, vejiga, burbuja.—*vt.* y *vi.* levantar ampollas; ampollar(se).

blizzard [blįʒârd], *s.* ventisca, tormenta de nieve.

bloat [bloųt], *vi.* hincharse, abotagarse.— —ed [blóųtįd], *a.* tumefacto, hinchado.

block [blak], *s.* bloque, trozo; obstáculo, obstrucción; lote; tableta o bloc de papel; plancha o estampa de impresión; horma; fajo; cuadra, manzana. —*vt.* bloquear; tapar; estorbar; planchar sobre horma; parar (una pelota, una jugada).—*to b. out,* esbozar, bosquejar.—*to b. the way,* impedir el paso.— —ade [-éįd], *s.* bloqueo, asedio.— —head [blákhed], *s.* tonto, estúpido, mentecato.

blond(e) [bland], *a.* y *s.* rubio, (Am.) huero, catire.

blood [blʌd], *s.* sangre; linaje o parentesco; savia.—*b. clot,* coágulo.—*b. count,* análisis cuantitativo de sangre. —*b.-curdling,* horripilante.—*b. pudding* o *sausage,* morcilla.—*b. relative,* pariente, consanguíneo.—*to get one's b. up,* encendérsele a uno la sangre.— —less [blʌdljs], *a.* exangüe, desangrado.— —shed [šed], *s.* efusión o derramamiento de sangre.— —shot [šat], *a.* inyectado de sangre.— —sucker [-saкœ(r)], *s.* sanguijuela, usurero.— —thirsty [-θœrstį], *a.* san-

guinario.— —y [-i], *a.* ensangrentado, sangriento, sanguinario.—*vti.* [7] ensangrentar.

bloom [blum], *s.* flor; floración; florecimiento; lozanía.—*vi.* florecer.— —**ing** [blúmiŋ], *a.* en flor; floreciente; fresco, lozano.

blossom [blásǫm], *s.* flor; floración.—*vi.* florecer.— —**y** [-i], *a.* lleno de flores, floreciente.

blot [blat], *s.* borrón; mancha, mancilla; tacha.—*vti.* [1] emborronar; manchar; mancillar; empañar; secar con papel secante.—*to b. out*, tachar, borrar.—*vii.* correrse la tinta; pasarse (el papel).— —**ch** [-ch], *s.* mancha; borrón; pústula.—*vt.* marcar o cubrir con manchas o ronchas.

blouse [blaųs], *s.* blusa.

blow [bloų], *s.* golpe; contratiempo; vendaval; (re)soplido; trompada; trompetazo; fanfarrón—*at a b.*, de un solo golpe.—*to come to blows*, venir a las manos.—*without striking a b.*, sin dar un golpe, sin esfuerzo. —*vti.* [10] (re)soplar; hacer sonar (un instrumento de viento); ventear; divulgar; gastar con profusión; fanfarronear, alardear.—*to b. up*, estallar, reventar.—*vt.* inflar; volar con dinamita.—*to b. one's nose*, sonarse las narices.— —**er** [blóųœ(r)], *s.* soplador; soplete.— —**ing** [-iŋ], *s.* soplo, soplido.—*s.* soplador.—**blown** [bloųn], *pp.* de TO BLOW.—*a.* jadeante, rendido; soplado, inflado.— —**out** [-aųt], *s.* reventón, escape violento de aire, gas, etc.— —**pipe** [-paip], *s.* soplete.— —**torch** [-torch], *s.* lámpara de soldar, soplete.— —**up** [-ʌp], *s.* explosión; acceso de ira.— —**y** [-i], *a.* ventoso.

bludgeon [blʌ́dʒǫn], *s.* porra, garrote, estaca.

blue [blu], *s.* azul.—*pl.* melancolía.—*a.* azul; triste, melancólico.—*vt.* azular; teñir de azul; añilar.—*vi.* ponerse azul.— —**bell** [blúbel], *s.* campanilla (flor).— —**print** [-print], *s.* ferroprusiato (impresión de planos, etc.).

bluff [blʌf], *a.* francote, brusco; escarpado.—*s.* escarpadura; fanfarronada; fanfarrón; farsa; farsante; embaucador.—*vt.* conseguir algo a fuerza de descaro; alardear, baladronar; pretender; simular lo que no se tiene.— —**er** [blʌ́fœ(r)], *s.* baladrón, fanfarrón, embaucador.

bluing [blúiŋ], *s.* azul o añil para la ropa.—**bluish** [blúiš], *a.* azulado, azulino.

blunder [blʌ́ndœ(r)], *vt.* desatinar, disparatar, meter la pata.—*s.* disparate, patochada.

blunt [blʌnt], *a.* embotado, romo;

brusco, descortés; lerdo.—*vt.* embotar; calmar o mitigar.— —**ness** [blʌ́ntnis], *s.* embotadura; franqueza.

blur [blœr], *s.* trazo borroso o confuso; borrón, mancha.—*vti.* [1] hacer borroso; embotar, entorpecer; empañar; manchar.—*vii.* ponerse borroso; nublarse; empañarse.

blush [blʌš], *vi.* ruborizarse, sonrojarse; abochornarse.—*s.* rubor; bochorno; sonrojo.

bluster [blʌ́stœ(r)], *s.* ventolera; tumulto; jactancia; fanfarronada.—*vi.* soplar con furia; fanfarronear; enfurecerse.— —**er** [-œ(r)], *s.* fanfarrón.

boar [bor], *s.* verraco.—*wild b.*, jabalí.

board [bord], *s.* tabla; tablero; mesa; comida(s); hospedaje; tribunal, consejo, junta; cartón; bordo; borda(da). —*pl.* escenario, tablas.—*b. and lodging*, o *room and b.*, cuarto y comida, pensión completa.—*vt.* abordar; subir (a un tren, etc.); entablar, entarimar; dar manutención por dinero.—*vi.* estar a pupilaje.— —**er** [bórdœ(r)], *s.* huésped, pupilo.— —**ing** [-iŋ], *s.* tablazón; tabique de tablas; pupilaje; abordaje.—*b. house*, casa de huéspedes; pupilaje.

boast [boųst], *vi.* alardear, cacarear; blasonar; jactarse.—*vt.* decantar; ponderar; ostentar.—*s.* jactancia, ostentación; baladronada; cacareo.— —**er** [bóųstœ(r)], *s.* fanfarrón.— —**ful** [-fųl], *a.* jactancioso.— —**fulness** [-fųlnis], *s.* jactancia.

boat [boųt], *s.* buque, navío; bote, lancha, chalupa.—*vt.* poner o llevar a bordo.—*vi.* navegar, remar, ir en bote.— —**house** [bóųthaųs], *s.* cobertizo para botes.— —**ing** [-iŋ], *s.* ir o pasear en bote; manejo de un bote; transporte en bote.— —**man** [-man], *s.* barquero, botero, etc.

bob [bab], *vii.* [1] moverse con sacudidas o de arriba abajo; cabecear.—*s.* corcho (en la pesca); meneo; borla; plomo de plomada; disco de un péndulo; melena.

bobbin [bábin], *s.* bobina, canilla, broca.

bobsleigh [bábslei], *s.* trineo.

bode [boųd], *vt.* presagiar, pronosticar, presentir.—*vi.* predecir; prometer.— *to b. ill* (o *well*), ser de mal (o buen) agüero.—*pret.* de TO BIDE.

bodice [bádis], *s.* corpiño, jubón, cuerpo de vestido.

bodily [bádili], *a.* corpóreo, corporal, físico.—*adv.* corporalmente; en persona; en conjunto; en peso.— **body** [bádi], *s.* cuerpo; conjunto; gremio; cadáver; fuselaje; carrocería; parte principal o central; persona. —*vti.* [7] dar cuerpo o forma a;

representar.— —guard [-gard], *s.* guardaespaldas.

bog [bag], *s.* pantano, fangal, atolladero; ciénaga.—*vti.* y *vii.* [1] hundir(se), atollar(se), atascar(se).

bogey [bóugi], *s.* espantajo; fantasma; duende, coco.

Bohemian [bouhímiən], *a.* y *s.* bohemio.

boil [boil], *vt.* y *vi.* hervir; cocer, salcochar; agitarse, hervirle a uno la sangre.—*s.* hervor, ebullición; divieso, tumorcillo.— —er [bóilœ(r)], *s.* olla; marmita; caldera; caldera de vapor.— —ing [-iŋ], *a.* hirviente.

boisterous [bóistœræs], *a.* turbulento, ruidoso, revuelto.

bold [bould], *a.* arrojado, valiente; descarado; escarpado; bien delineado.— —face [bóuldfeis], *s.* descaro; persona desfachatada; letra negra, negrita o negrilla.— —ness [-nis], *s.* arrojo, etc.; descaro.

Bolivian [bolívian], *s.* y *a.* boliviano.

bolster [bóulstœ(r)], *s.* travesaño, almohada larga; cabezal; larguero, soporte, refuerzo.—*vt.* sostener, reforzar, apoyar, auxiliar.

bolt [boult], *s.* cerrojo, pestillo, falleba; perno; clavija; proyectil; dardo; rayo; suceso repentino; pieza o rollo de paño.—*vt.* echar el cerrojo; escudriñar; engullir; arrojar, echar.—*vi.* saltar de repente; lanzarse; desbocarse; resistirse.

bomb [bam], *s.* bomba; suceso inesperado y perturbador.—*b. shelter,.* refugio contra bombardeos.—*vt.* bombardear.— —ard [bambárd], *vt.* bombear, bombardear.— —ardier [bambärdír], *s.* bombardero.— —ardment [bambárdment], *s.* bombardeo, cañoneo.

bombast [bámbæst], *s.* ampulosidad.— —ic [bambǽstik], *a.* ampuloso, altisonante, campanudo.

bomber [bámœ(r)], *s.* avión de bombardeo; bombardero (avión o aviador).— —ing [-iŋ], *s.* bombardeo.— —proof [-pruf], *a.* a prueba de bombas.— —sight [-sait], *s.* mira o visor de bombardeo.

bond [band], *s.* lazo, vínculo; unión; ligazón; bono, obligación; fiador; fianza.—*pl.* cadenas, cautiverio.—*vt.* unir; dar fianza; hipotecar; poner mercancías en depósito afianzado.— —age [bándiʒ], *s.* cautiverio, esclavitud; obligación.— —holder [-houldœ(r)], *s.* accionista; rentista.— —sman [-zman], *s.* fiador, garante.

bone [boun], *s.* hueso; espina de pez.—*pl.* osamenta.—*vt.* deshuesar.— —ache [bóuneik], *s.* dolor de huesos.— —d [-d], *a.* deshuesado.— —head [-hed], *s.*, —headed [-hedid], *a.* mentecato,

imbécil.— —less [-lis], *a.* sin huesos.

boner [bóunœ(r)], *s.* (fam.) patochada, disparate.

bonfire [bánfair], *s.* hoguera, fogata.

bonito [bonítou], *s.* (ict.) bonito.

bonnet [bánit], *s.* gorra, gorro; sombrero de mujer; toca; solideo, bonete.

bonus [bóunʌs], *s.* bonificación; prima; gratificación.

bony [bóuni], *a.* huesudo; óseo.

boo [bu], *s.* abucheo, grita, rechifla.— *vt.* y *vi.* dar grita, abuchear.— *interj.* ¡fuera!, ¡bu!

boob [bub], *s.*, booby [búbi], *s.* y *a.* bobo, gaznápiro, papanatas.

book [buk], *s.* libro.—*b. stand* o *stall*, puesto de libros.—*b. worm*, (fig.) ratón de biblioteca.—*vt.* asentar, inscribir; sacar, comprar o reservar (pasaje, localidades, etc.); contratar o apalabrar (a un artista, conferenciante, etc.).— —binder [búkbaindœ(r)], *s.* encuadernador.— —binding [-baindiŋ], *s.* encuadernación.— —case [-keis], *s.* librero, estante para libros.— —ing [-iŋ], *s.* registro, asiento; compra o venta de billetes.— —keeper [-kipœ(r)], *s.* tenedor de libros.— —keeping [-kipiŋ], *s.* teneduría de libros.— —let [-lit], *s.* folleto.— —maker [-meikœ(r)], —ie [-i], *s.* corredor de apuestas.— —seller [-selœ(r)], *s.* librero, vendedor de libros.— —store [-stor], *s.* librería.

boom [bum], *s.* estampido; alza en el mercado; auge o prosperidad repentina.—*vi.* dar estampido; resonar; estar en auge; medrar.—*vt.* favorecer, fomentar.

boon [bun], *s.* dádiva, don; gracia; dicha, bendición.—*a.* jovial, festivo.

boor [bur], *s.* patán, rústico.— —ish [búriʃ], *a.* rústico, agreste; tosco; guajiro, jíbaro.— —ishness [-iʃnis], *s.* rusticidad; grosería.

boost [bust], *vt.* empujar; levantar; alzar desde abajo; fomentar, promover.—*s.* alza; ayuda, asistencia.— —er [bústœ(r)], *s.* impulsador; elevador de potencial o de tensión.

boot [but], *vt.* y *vi.* aprovechar, valer, servir; calzarse uno las botas; dar patadas a.—*s.* bota; ganancia.—*to b.*, por añadidura, de pilón, de contra, de ñapa.— —black [-blæk], *s.* limpiabotas.

bootee [búti], *s.* botín (calzado).

booth [buθ], *s.* garita, casilla; puesto o mesilla de venta; cabina; reservado (restaurantes, etc.).

bootleg [bútleg], *vti.* y *vii.* [1] contrabandear (esp. en licores).—*a.* de contrabando.

booty [búti], *s.* botín, despojo, presa.

border [bórdœ(r)], *s.* frontera; orilla;

borde; margen; límite, confín; orla, ribete, cenefa.—*vi.* lindar; ` rayar, acercarse.—*vt.* orlar, ribetear, guarnecer; confinar.

bore [bor], *vt.* taladrar; barrenar, horadar; sondear; aburrir, dar la lata. —*s.* taladro, barreno; agujero hecho con taladro o barreno; calibre; diámetro interior de un cilindro.—*pret.* de TO BEAR.— **d** [-d], *a.* taladrado; aburrido.— **dom** [bórdǫm], *s.* fastidio; aburrimiento, tedio.——**r** [-œ(r)], *s.* horadador; barrena; taladro; perforadora; cualquier animal que horada; pelmazo, latoso.—**boring** [bórin̩], *a.* pesado, aburrido, latoso.—*s.* perforación; sondeo.—*pl.* partículas que se desprenden al taladrar o barrenar.

born [born], *a.* nacido; de nacimiento; por naturaleza.—*pp.* de TO BEAR. —*to be b.,* nacer.— **borne**[born], *pp.* de TO BEAR.

borough [bárou], *s.* barrio; villa; municipio incorporado; distrito administrativo de una ciudad.

borrow [bárou], *vt.* pedir o tomar prestado; tomar fiado; apropiarse, copiar.— **er** [-œ(r)], *s.* prestatario, el que pide o toma prestado.

bosom [búzǫm], *s.* seno, pecho, corazón; buche, pechera; amor, inclinación. —*a.* íntimo, querido; secreto.

boss [bɔs], *s.* amo, capataz, patrón; jefe, cabecilla; cacique.—*vt.* mandar; dominar; regentear; dirigir.— **ism** [bósizm], *s.* caciquismo, caudillismo.— **y** [-i], *a.* mandón, autoritario.

botany [bátani] *s.* botánica.

both [bouθ], *a.* y *pron.* ambos, entrambos.—*b. my father and his,* tanto mi padre como el suyo.

bother [báðœ(r)], *vt.* y *vi.* incomodar(se), molestar(se); marear.—*s.* molestia, incomodidad; lata, pejiguera.

bottle [bátl], *s.* botella; frasco.—*vt.* embotellar.

bottom [bátǫm], *s.* fondo; suelo; lecho de un río, lago, etc.; parte inferior, lo más bajo; fundamento; trasero, nalgatorio; hez; asiento de una silla; pie (de página).—*vt.* poner fondo o asiento; cimentar, basar.—*vi.* apoyarse.— **less** [-lis], *a.* sin asiento; insondable.

bough [bau], *s.* rama, ramo.

bought [bot], *pret.* y *pp.* de TO BUY.

bouillon [búlyan], *s.* caldo.

boulder [bóuldœ(r)], *s.* peña, roca, pedrusco.

bounce [bauns], *vi.* rebotar; brincar, saltar; lanzarse; echar bravatas; fanfarronear.—*vt.* hacer (re)botar; echar a cajas destempladas, despedir.—*s.*

(re)bote; salto, brinco; acto de arrojar a alguien violentamente.— **r** [báunsœ(r)], *s.* (coll.) guardián fornido a cargo de echar del lugar (cabaret, etc.) a los perturbadores.

bound [baund], *s.* límite, término, lindero; bote, brinco, corcovo.—*vt.* deslindar; parcelar; hacer saltar; confinar.—*vi.* saltar, (re)botar; corvetear.—*pret.* y *pp.* de TO BIND.—*a.* atado, sujeto; confinado; moral o legalmente obligado; encuadernado; destinado; resuelto (a).— **ary** [báundari], *s.* límite, lindero, frontera; término.—*a.* limítrofe, divisorio.— **less** [-lis], *a.* ilimitado, infinito.

bounteous [báuntiʌs], **bountiful** [báuntifuḷ], *a.* liberal, generoso; copioso.— **bounteousness** [báuntiʌsnis], **bountifulness** [báuntifuḷnis], *s.* munificencia, liberalidad, generosidad; copiosidad.—**bounty** [báunti], *s.* generosidad, liberalidad; merced, gracia; subvención; prima.—*b. money* (mil.), enganche.

bouquet [bukéi], *s.* ramo, ramillete; aroma.

bout [baut], *s.* encuentro, combate; asalto de esgrima o boxeo; ataque de enfermedad; vez, turno.

bow [bau], *s.* saludo, reverencia; zalema; proa.—*vi.* inclinarse; hacer una reverencia; agobiarse; ceder, someterse.—*s.* [bou], arco (flecha, violín, etc.); curva; lazada; lazo (de corbata, cinta, etc.).

bowels [báuęlz], *s.* intestinos, tripas; entrañas; mondongo.

bower [báuœ(r)], *s.* glorieta, emparrado, cenador, enramada.

bowl [boul], *s.* escudilla, cuenco; concavidad; tazón de fuente; palangana, jofaina; bola, bocha; ponchera.—*pl.* juego de bolos.—*vi.* bolear, jugar a los bolos, al boliche, etc.

bowman [bóumạn], *s.* arquero.

box [baks], *s.* caja, cajón; estuche; cofre, arca; palco de teatro; apartado (de correos); casilla; compartimento; taquilla; establo; manotazo, revés. —*vt.* encajonar, embalar; abofetear. —*vi.* boxear.— **er** [báksœ(r)], *s.* boxeador; embalador.— **ing** [-in̩], *s.* encajonamiento, empaque; madera para encajonar; boxeo, pugilismo; marco de puerta o de ventana.—**box tree, boxwood** [bákswuḍ], *s.* boj.

boy [boi], *s.* muchacho, niño, chico; hijo varón; mozo; criado; grumete.

boycott [bóikat], *s.* boicot, boicoteo. —*vt.* boicotear.

boyhood [bóihuḍ], *s.* niñez; pubertad, adolescencia.

brace [breis], *vt.* ligar, asegurar; re-

forzar; fortalecer; ensamblar: empatar; atirantar; bracear; cercar, rodear; encerrar en una llave o corchete.—vi. animarse.—s. abrazadera; berbiquí; tirante; corchete, llave; braguero; ligadura.- —let [bréjslit], s. brazalete.

bracket [brǽkjt], s. soporte, brazo o sostén (de lámpara, candelabro, etc.) asegurado en la pared; consola, repisa; ménsula; grupo, clase, nivel, categoría.—pl. corchetes; paréntesis angulares.—vt. poner entre paréntesis; unir; poner en una misma clase.

brackish [brǽkjš], a. salobre, salado.

brag [brǽg], s. jactancia, fanfarronada; fanfarrón.—vii. [1] jactarse (de); fanfarronear; alardear; farolear.- —gart [brǽgart], s. matasiete.

braid [breid], vt. trenzar, entrelazar; galonear.—s. galón, trencilla; trenza.

brain [brein], s. cerebro, seso.—pl. sesos; inteligencia, juicio.—to rack one's b., devanarse los sesos.- —y [bréini], a. sesudo, inteligente.

brake [breik], s. freno, retranca; grada, rastra; palanca.—b. lining, forro de freno.—b. shoe, zapata de freno.—vt. frenar; gradar.- —man [bréjkman], s. guardafrenos, retranquero.

bramble [brémbl], s. zarza.

bran [brǽn], s. salvado, afrecho.

branch [brǽnch], s. rama; ramo; dependencia; división o sección; ramal, brazo; afluente; sucursal; bifurcación, ramal; arma (de las fuerzas armadas).—a. dependiente, tributario.—vi. ramificarse; echar astas o ramas.—to b. off, bifurcarse.

brand [brǽnd], s. sello o marca de fábrica; calidad; hierro de marcar reses; estigma, baldón.—b. name, marca conocida.—b.-new, nuevecito, flamante.—vt. herrar, marcar ganado, calimbar; tildar; infamar.- —ing [bréndiŋ], s. herradero, hierra.—b. iron, hierro de marcar ganado.

brandish [brǽndjš], vt. blandir; cimbrar, florear.—s. floreo, molinete.

brandy [brǽndi], s. coñac; aguardiente.

brass [brǽs], s. latón; cualquier objeto de latón; descaro; calderilla (dinero); cobres (instrumentos de música).— b. band, banda, charanga.—vt. revestir de latón.

brassière [brazír], s. sostén, corpiño, ajustador.

brat [brǽt], s. rapaz, mocoso; niño travieso y díscolo.

bravado [bravádou], s. bravata, baladronada.

brave [breiv], a. bravo, valiente; bizarro.—vt. desafiar, arrostrar.- —ry [bréiveri], s. valor; bizarría, heroísmo.

brawl [brol], s. alboroto, pendencia,

camorra; quimera; trapisonda.—vi. alborotar, armar camorra.—vt. decir a gritos.

bray [brei], vi. rebuznar.—s. rebuzno.- —ing [bréiiŋ], s. rebuzno.

braze [breiz], vt. broncear; soldar; endurecer.- —n [bréizen], a. (como) de latón; broncíneo; bronco; descarado.

brazier [bréizœ(r)], s. brasero.

Brazilian [brazílian], a. y s. brasileño, brasilero.

breach [brich], s. brecha, abertura; rotura, fractura; quebrantamiento; infracción, violación; rompimiento.— b. of promise, violación de palabra de matrimonio.—vt. hacer brecha.

bread [bred], s. pan.—b. crumb, miga de pan.—vt. empanar; empanizar. —breaded cutlet, chuleta empanizada.

breadth [bredθ], s. anchura, ancho; envergadura; latitud; amplitud.- —wise [brédθwaiz], adv. a lo ancho.

break [breik], vti. [10] romper, quebrantar, partir; infringir, violar (la ley, etc.); abrir brecha en; domar; arruinar; interrumpir; cambiar (un billete, etc.); moderar, amortiguar; exceder; descomponer.—to b. away, escaparse, fugarse.—to b. down, abatirse; (mec.) averiarse.—to b. in, forzar, romper o abrir empujando hacia adentro; domar (animales); entremeterse.—to b. into a house, escalar, allanar una casa.—to b. out, estallar.—to b. up, dividir en partes. —vii. romperse, quebrarse, frustrarse; descomponerse; rayar el día; brotar, florecer; dispersarse.—s. rotura, ruptura; abertura, grieta; comienzo, principio; intervalo, pausa; interrupción; baja en el mercado; casualidad, chiripa.- —able [bréikabl], a. quebradizo, frágil.- —age [-idž], s. fractura, rotura; indemnización por daños (tránsito, etc.).- —down [-daun], s. derrumbamiento; trastorno; interrupción o paralización de un servicio; avería; agotamiento.- —er [-œ(r)], s. rompiente (ola); infractor.

breakfast [brékfast], s. desayuno.—vi. desayunarse.

bream [brim], s. (ict.) besugo.

breast [brest], s. pecho, seno; teta; mama; pechuga.—vt. amamantar; arrostrar resueltamente.- —bone [bréstboun], s. esternón.

breath [breθ], s. aliento, respiración, resuello; soplo; pausa, respiro; instante.—b.-taking, conmovedor, sorprendente.- —e [brið], vi. y vt. respirar, alentar; vivir; tomar aliento; soplar; aspirar; exhalar.- —r [brið-œ(r)], s. respirador; viviente; inspi-

rador; tregua.— —ing [bríðịŋ], *s.*
respiración; respiro, resuello.— —less
[bréθlịs], *a.* sin resuello; jadeante;
muerto.— —lessness [-lịsnịs], *s.* jadeo,
desaliento; muerte.

bred [bred], *pret.* y *pp.* de TO BREED.

breech [brich], *s.* (arti.) recámara,
culata, cierre.

breeches [bríchịs], *s.pl.* calzones, bragas.

breed [brid], *vti.* [10] engendrar; criar;
empollar; parir; producir; educar.
—*vii.* multiplicarse.—*s.* casta, raza,
progenie; prole.— —er [brídœ(r)],
s. criador, ganadero; padre, reproductor o semental.— —ing [-ịŋ], *s.*
cría, crianza; educación, maneras.

breeze [briz], *s.* brisa, airecillo.—
breezy [brízị], *a.* airoso, ventilado;
animado, vivo.

breviary [bríviẹrị], *s.* breviario.

brevity [brévịtị], *s.* brevedad; concisión.

brew [bru], *vt.* hacer cerveza; preparar
té; fermentar licores; fraguar, urdir,
tramar.—*vi.* amenazar; formarse,
prepararse.—*s.* cerveza; mezcla.—
—er [brúœ(r)], *s.* cervecero.— —ery
[-œrị], *s.* fábrica de cerveza, cervecería.— —ing [-ịŋ], *s.* elaboración de
cerveza; señales de borrasca.

briar [bráị§(r)], *s.* rosal silvestre; zarza;
brezo (para pipas).

bribe [braịb], *s.* cohecho, soborno.—*vt.*
sobornar, cohechar.— —ry [brájbẹrị],
s. cohecho, soborno.

brick [brịk], *s.* ladrillo(s).—*vt.* enladrillar.— —bat [bríkbæt], *s.* tejoleta,
pedazo de ladrillo; insulto.— —layer
[-leịœ(r)], *s.* albañil.

bridal [bráịdạl], *a.* nupcial.—*s.* boda,
fiesta nupcial.—**bride** [braịd], *s.* novia, desposada.—**bridegroom** [bráịd-
grum], *s.* novio.—**bridesmaid** [bráịdz-
meịd], *s.* madrina de boda.

bridge [brịdʒ], *s.* puente; caballete de
la nariz; juego de naipes.—*b. toll,*
peaje, pontazgo.—*draw b.,* puente
levadizo.—*vt.* tender un puente; atravesar.—*to b. a gap,* llenar un vacío.

bridle [bráịdl], *s.* brida, freno; frenillo.
—*vt.* enfrenar; reprimir; embridar.
—*vi.* erguirse.

brief [brif], *a.* breve, conciso; fugaz.—*s.*
epítome, resumen, memorial, informe;
alegato.—*to hold no b. for,* no estar
defendiendo o no ser defensor de.
—*vt.* abreviar; dar instrucciones bre-
ves.— —case [brífkeịs], *s.* cartera.—
—ing [-ịŋ], *s.* órdenes o instrucciones.

brigade [brịgéịd], *s.* brigada.—**brigadier** [brịgạdír], *s.* brigadier, general
de brigada.

bright [braịt], *a.* brillante, claro, lus-

troso; subido (colores); eximio; vivo,
inteligente; halagüeño.— —en [bráịt-
ẹn], *vt.* pulir; alegrar, consolar;
ennoblecer; mejorar.—*vi.* aclarar,
despejarse (el cielo); animarse.—
—ness [-nịs], *s.* lustre, lucidez;
resplandor, claridad; agudeza.

brilliance [brílyạns], **brilliancy** [bríl-
yạnsị], *s.* brillantez, brillo; resplandor; esplendor.—**brilliant** [brílyạnt],
a. brillante; talentoso; excelente.—
s. brillante; diamante.

brim [brịm], *s.* borde, margen; labio
de un vaso; ala de sombrero.—*vti.* [1]
llenar hasta el borde.—*to b. over,* rebosar; desbordar, derramar.

brimstone [brímstoụn], *s.* azufre.

brine [braịn], *s.* salmuera; agua car-
gada de sal.—*vt.* salar.

bring [brịŋ], *vti.* [10] traer; llevar;
conducir; persuadir; aportar; causar,
producir.—*to b. about,* efectuar, poner
por obra; lograr; dar lugar a; causar.
—*to b. forth,* producir; parir; dar
a luz.—*to b. forward,* empujar; llevar
una suma a otra cuenta.—*to b. out,*
presentar; publicar; poner en escena;
descubrir.—*to b. over,* persuadir; convertir; traer.—*to b. up,* criar, educar.

brink [brịŋk], *s.* orilla, margen; extremidad.—*on the b. of,* a pique de,
al borde de.

brisk [brịsk], *a.* vivo, activo; enérgico;
rápido; estimulante.— —ness [brísk-
nịs], *s.* vivacidad, despejo; gallardía.

bristle [brísl], *s.* cerda.—*vt.* erizar,
poner tieso.—*vi.* erizarse.

British [brítị§], *a.* británico, inglés.
—*the B.,* el pueblo inglés.

brittle [brítl], *a.* quebradizo; frágil;
vidrioso.— —ness [-nịs], *s.* fragilidad.

broach [broụch], *s.* broca, mecha;
punzón.—*vt.* mencionar por primera
vez; introducir; hacer público; espetar; traer a colación.

broad [brod], *a.* ancho; amplio; claro;
general; tolerante; indelicado; pronunciado, marcado; pleno.

broadcast [bródkæst], *vti.* y *vii.* [4]
transmitir, perifonear; propalar;
esparcir; sembrar a voleo; (radio)-
difundir.—*pret.* y *pp.* de TO BROAD-
CAST.—*s.* (radio)difusión, transmisión; siembra al voleo.—*adv.* por
todas partes.—*a.* radioemitido, radiado; esparcido, difundido.— —er
[-œ(r)], *s.* radiodifusor(a), estación
radiodifusora.— —ing [-ịŋ], *s.* (radio)-
difusión; transmisión; siembra al
voleo.—*a.* (radio)difusor(a), (radio)-
emisor(a).

broadcloth [bródkloθ], *s.* paño fino de
lana o algodón.

broaden [bródẹn], *vt.* y *vi.* ensanchar(se).

brocade [brokéjd], s. brocado.—vt. decorar con brocado.

broccoli [brákolj], s. bróculi, brécol, brecolera.

brochure [brošúr], s. folleto.

broil [brojl], s. carne, etc. asada al fuego o a la parrilla; calor intenso; pendencia; tumulto; alboroto.—vt. asar sobre las ascuas o en parrillas. —vi. asarse; asarse de calor.— —er [brójlœ(r)], s. parrilla(s); pollo propio para asar; camorrista.——ing [-jŋ], a. extremadamente cálido, abrasador.

broke [brouk], pret. de TO BREAK.—a. tronado, sin blanca, sin un real.— broken [bróukęn], pp. de TO BREAK. —a. quebrado, roto; imperfecto; interrumpido; domado; mal pronunciado; debilitado; arruinado.— —r [bróukœ(r)], s. corredor, cambista; agente de bolsa.— —rage [bróukœridź], s. corretaje, correduría.

bronchial [bráŋkjąl], a. bronquial.

bronze [branz], s. bronce.—vt. broncear.

brooch [broųch], s. broche, pasador.

brood [brud], a. clueca.—b. mare, yegua madre o paridera.—s. cría; pollada, nidada; camada; melancolía.—vt. empollar, incubar.—vi. preocuparse, ensimismarse.—to b. over, cavilar.

brook [bruk], s. arroyo, riachuelo; cañada, quebrada.—vt. sufrir, aguantar.— —let [brúklįt], s. arroyuelo.

broom [brum], s. escoba; retama.— —stick [brúmstįk], s. palo de escoba.

broth [broθ], s. caldo.

brothel [bróθęl], s. burdel, lupanar.

brother [bráðœ(r)], s. hermano.—b.-in-law, cuñado.—vt. hermanar; tratar como a un hermano.— —hood [-hųd], s. hermandad; hermanazgo; confraternidad; cofradía.——like [-lajk], a. fraternal.— —ly [-lį], a. fraternal, fraterno.—adv. fraternalmente.

brought [brot], pret. y pp. de TO BRING.

brow [brau], s. ceja; frente; sien; arco superciliar.

brown [braųn], a. pardo, castaño, moreno, carmelita.—s. color pardo, castaño o carmelita.—vt. poner moreno o tostado; broncear; quemar (el sol).— —ish [bráųnįš], a. pardusco.

browse [braųz], vt. y vi. ramonear; tascar; rozar; curiosear; hojear (un libro).

bruise [bruz], vt. magullar; golpear; machacar; machucar; abollar; majar. —s. magulladura, etc.

brunette [brunét], s. y a. morena o trigueña.

brush [braš], s. cepillo; escobilla; brocha; pincel; matorral; escaramuza; haz de leña menuda.—vt. (a)cepillar; frotar, restregar; pintar con brocha. —vi. moverse apresuradamente.—to

b. aside, echar a un lado.—to b. away, restregar duro.—to b. up (on), repasar, refrescar; retocar.— —wood [bráŠwųd], s. broza, maleza.

brusk [brask], a. brusco, rudo.

brutal [brútąl], a. brutal.— —ity [brutǽljtį], s. brutalidad.— —ize [brútalajz], vt. embrutecer; tratar cruelmente.—vi. embrutecerse.—brute [brut], s. bruto, bestia.—a. bruto, brutal.—brutish [brútįš], a. bruto, brutal; embrutecido.

bubble [bábl], s. burbuja, pompa; ampolla; bagatela; engañifa.—vi. burbujear; hacer espuma; bullir; murmurar el río; ampollarse.—to b. over, rebosar; estar en efervescencia. —to b. up, ampollarse.—bubbly [báblį], a. burbujeante, espumoso.

bubo [bjúbou], s. bubón.— —nic [bjubánįk], a. bubónico.

buck [bak], s. gamo; macho cabrío; macho de ciervo, alce, reno, etc.; corveta o respingo; topada.—to pass the b., (coll.) rehuir una responsabilidad.—vi. encabritarse, respingar.

bucket [bákįt], s. cubo, pozal, balde; contenido de un balde; excavadora de cucharón.

buckle [bákl], s. hebilla.—vt. abrochar con hebilla.—vi. doblarse, combarse.

bud [bad], s. yema, botón, capullo; brote, retoño.—vii. [1] brotar, retoñar; echar capullos.

buddy [bádį], s. camarada, compañero.

budge [badź], vt. mover.—vi. moverse, menearse; hacer lugar.

budget [bádźit], s. presupuesto.—vt. hacer presupuesto.

buff [baf], s. piel de ante, búfalo, etc.; color crema; pulidor.—a. de ante; de color crema.—vt. pulir, bruñir.

buffer [báfœ(r)], s. pulidor; amortiguador de choques.—b. state, estado o país que sirve de valla entre dos naciones rivales.

buffet [buféj], s. aparador; repostería; ambigú; [báfįt], bofetada; (fam.) sopapo; embote.—vt. abofetear; luchar contra.

buffoon [bafún], s. bufón.— —ery [-ęrį], s. bufonada.

bug [bag], s. insecto; bicho; sabandija; (fam.) microbio.

bugaboo [bágabu], bugbear [bágber], s. coco, espantajo, bu.

buggy [bágį], s. coche ligero, calesa; vagón de cola.—a. lleno de chinches u otros insectos.

bugle [bjúgl], s. corneta de órdenes; trompeta; clarín.— —r [bjúglœr], s. trompetero, corneta.

build [bįld], vti. y vii. [10] edificar, construir, fabricar.—s. estructura; forma; figura (de una persona).—

—er [bĭldœ(r)], s. constructor; maestro de obras.— —ing [-ĭŋ], s. edificio, casa, obra, local.—a. constructor, para construcciones; relativo a casas o edificios.—built [bĭlt], pret. y pp. de TO BUILD.

bulb [bʌlb], s. bulbo; ampolleta; bomb(ill)a, foco; pera de goma; ensanche, protuberancia.

Bulgarian [bʌlgérĭan], s. y a. búlgaro.

bulge [bʌldž], s. pandeo, comba.—vt. y vi. pandear(se); abultar(se).— bulgy [bʌldžĭ], a. combo, pandeado; saliente.

bulk [bʌlk], s. bulto, volumen; masa; parte principal; la mayor parte; el grueso.—vi. hincharse; aumentar (bulto, peso, importancia).— —y [bʌlkĭ], a. abultado, voluminoso.

bull [bŭl], s. toro; bula pontificia; disparate; alcista.—b.'s eye, diana, centro del blanco; tiro perfecto.— —dog [bŭldog], s. perro dogo.— —dozer [-doŭzœ(r)], s. máquina razadora.

bullet [bŭlĭt], s. bala.

bulletin [bŭlĭtĭn], s. boletín.—b. board, tablón o tablilla de anuncios.

bullfight [bŭlfaĭt], s. corrida de toros.— —er [-œ(r)], s. torero.— —ing [-ĭŋ], s. toreo.

bullfrog [bŭlfrag], s. rana toro.

bullock [bŭlǫk], s. buey.

bullpen [bŭlpen], s. toril.—bullring [bŭlrĭŋ], s. plaza de toros.

bully [bŭlĭ], s. matón, bravucón, valentón.—a. magnífico, excelente.— vti. [7] intimidar.—vii. bravear, fanfarronear.

bulwark [bŭlwɐrk], s. baluarte, bastión; defensa.

bum [bʌm], vti. [1] (fam.) sablear, obtener (algo) graciosamente.—vii. (fam.) holgazanear; vivir parasitariamente.—s. (fam.) vago; golfo; atorrante.—a. (fam.) de calidad ínfima.

bumblebee [bʌmblbĭ], s. abejorro, moscardón.

bump [bʌmp], s. tope(tazo); chichón, protuberancia.—vt. chocar contra.— to b. off, (coll.) matar, despachar.— —er [bʌmpœ(r)], s. parachoques, defensa; lo que da golpes.—a. lleno; excelente; abundante.

bumpy [bʌmpĭ], a. desigual, con baches.

bun [bʌn], s. buñuelo; friturita, bollo.

bunch [bʌnch], s. haz, manojo, atado; mazo, montón; racimo; ramillete; grupo; bulto.—vt. agrupar, juntar. —vi. arracimarse, amacollarse.

bundle [bʌndl], s. atado, lío; haz, mazo; fardo, bulto.—vt. liar, atar; empaquetar, envolver.—to b. up, abrigarse, taparse bien.

bungle [bʌŋgl], vt. chapucear, echar a

perder.—vi. hacer chapucerías.—s. chapucería.— —r [bʌŋglœ(r)], s. chapucero, chambón.—bungling [bʌŋglĭŋ], a. chapucero.

bunion [bʌnyǫn], s. juanete.

bunk [bʌŋk], s. tarima, litera; embuste; (fam.) baladronada, palabrería.

buoy [bóĭ, búĭ], s. boya.—vt. aboyar. —vi. aboyarse, flotar, boyar.— —ancy [-ansĭ], s. flotabilidad; flotación; alegría, animación; fuerza ascensional.— —ant [-ant], a. boyante.

burden [bœrdęn], s. carga, peso, gravamen; capacidad, tonelaje.—vt. cargar, agobiar, gravar.— —some [-sʌm], a. gravoso, oneroso, molesto.

bureau [bĭuroŭ], s. buró, escritorio; oficina, despacho; agencia, negociado; ramo, división, departamento.— —cracy [bĭurákrasĭ], s. burocracia.— —crat [bĭurokræt], s. burócrata.— —cratic [bĭurokrǽtĭk], a. burocrático.

burglar [bœrglɐr], s. ladrón (de viviendas).— —y [-ĭ], s. robo con escalo; hurto.

burial [bérĭal], s. entierro, inhumación, sepelio.

burlap [bœrlæp], s. arpillera.

burlesque [bœrlésk], s. parodia; (E.U. teat.) espectáculo de variedades de carácter burlesco.—a. burlesco, paródico.—vt. chufar, parodiar.

burly [bœrlĭ], a. corpulento, fornido; nudoso.

Burmese [bœrmĭz], a. y s. birmano.

burn [bœrn], vti. y vii. [4] quemar(se), abrasar(se), incendiar(se); calcinar(se).—vi. arder.—s. quemadura; marca de hierro candente.— —er [bœrnœ(r)], s. quemador, mechero, hornilla.

burnish [bœrnĭš], vt. bruñir, pulir.—vi. tomar lustre.—s. bruñido.— —er [-œ(r)], s. bruñidor.

burrow [bœroŭ], s. madriguera, cueva. —vt. hacer cueva(s) en.—vi. encuevarse; minar, horadar.

burst [bœrst], vti. y vii. [9] reventar(se), romper(se); abrir(se) violentamente. —to b. into flames, inflamarse.—to b. into tears, romper a llorar.—pret. y pp. de TO BURST.—s. reventón, estallido; ataque, arrebato.

bury [bérĭ], vti. [7] enterrar, inhumar; sepultar; ocultar.

bus [bʌs], s. ómnibus, autobús, guagua, camión.

bush [bŭš], s. arbusto; matorral; terreno cubierto de malezas, maniagua. —to beat around the b., andar(se) con rodeos.

bushel [bŭšęl], s. medida de áridos. Ver Tabla.

business [bĭznĭs], s. negocio(s); cuestion de negocios; oficio, trabajo, profesión;

comercio.—*b. man*, negociante, hombre de negocios o de empresas.

bust [bʌst], *s.* busto; pecho (de mujer); parranda, borrachera.

bustle [bʌsl], *vi.* bullir, trajinar, ajetrearse.—*s.* bullicio, trajín; polisón.

busy [bízi], *a.* ocupado; activo; atareado.—*b. street*, calle concurrida, de mucho tráfico.—*vti.* [7] ocupar, emplear.— —*body* [-badi], *s.* entremetido; chismoso.

but [bʌt], *conj., prep.* y *adv.* pero, mas; sin embargo; excepto, menos; sólo, solamente, no más que; sino; que no; sin que; sin.—*b. for*, a no ser por. —*none b.*, solamente.—*s.* objeción, pero.

butcher [búchœ(r)], *s.* carnicero.—*b.'s shop*, carnicería.—*vt.* matar reses; dar muerte cruel, hacer una carnicería.— —*y* [-i], *s.* carnicería, matanza; oficio de carnicero; matadero.

butler [bʌtlœ(r)], *s.* mayordomo.

butt [bʌt], *s.* culata (de rifle, etc.); colilla, cabo; mango, cabo; fin, límite; blanco (de las miradas, etc.); topetazo.—*b. of ridicule*, hazmerreír. —*vt.* topar; mochar.—*vi.* embestir.

butter [bʌtœ(r)], *s.* mantequilla, manteca (de nata de leche).—*vt.* untar con mantequilla o manteca; adular.

butterfly [bʌtœ(r)flai], *s.* mariposa.

buttermilk [bʌtœ(r)milk], *s.* suero de mantequilla.—*buttery* [bʌtœri], *s.* bodega; despensa.—*a.* mantecoso; adulador.

buttock [bʌtɔk], *s.* nalga, trasero.—*pl.* posaderas.

button [bʌtɔn], *s.* botón; tirador de puerta.—*vt.* abotonar.—*vi.* abotonarse.— —*hole* [-houl], *s.* ojal, presilla.—*vt.* abrir ojales; importunar.

buy [bai], *vti.* [10] comprar.—*to b. off*, sobornar.—*s.* compra.— —*er* [báiœ(r)], *s.* comprador, marchante.

buzz [bʌz], *s.* zumbido; susurro.—*b. saw*, sierra circular.—*vi.* zumbar; susurrar.

buzzard [bʌzɑrd], *s.* buitre, aura, zopilote, carancho.

buzzing [bʌzin], *s.* zumbido.

by [bai], *prep.* por; a, en; para, por, junto a, cerca de, al lado de; según, de acuerdo con.—*adv.* cerca, al lado; aparte, a un lado.—*b. and b.*, pronto, luego.—*b. day*, de día.—*b. God!* ¡por Dios!—*b. itself*, por sí mismo.—*b. means of*, mediante.—*b. much*, con mucho.—*b. the dozen*, por docenas.— *b. the way*, apropósito, de paso, ya que viene al caso, etc.—*b. then*, para entonces.—*b. this time*, ahora, ya.— *b. way of*, por vía de.—*days gone b.*, días pasados.— —*gone* [báigon], *a.* pasado.—*let bygones be bygones*, olvi-

demos lo pasado; pelillos a la mar.— —*law* [-lo], *s.* estatuto o reglamento.— —*path* [-pæθ], *s.* senda.— —*product* [-pradʌkt], *s.* producto accesorio, derivado, residual.— —*stander* [-stændœ(r)], *s.* espectador, circunstante, presente.

C

cab [kæb], *s.* taxi; coche; (f.c.) casilla del maquinista; casilla del chofer de un camión.—*c. stand*, parada de taxis; punto de coches.

cabal [kabál], *s.* cábala.

cabaret [kæbaréi], *s.* cabaret, café cantante.

cabbage [kæbidʒ], *s.* berza, col, repollo.

cabby [kæbi], *s.* (fam.), **cabdriver** [kæbdraivœ(r)], *s.* cochero; chofer de taxi.

cabin [kæbin], *s.* cabaña, barraca, choza; (mar.) cabina, camarote.

cabinet [kæbinit], *s.* escaparate, vitrina; armario; (pol.) gabinete; caja o mueble (de radio, T.V.).—*c. council*, consejo de ministros o del gabinete.— *a.* ministerial; secreto, reservado.— —*maker* [-meikœ(r)], *s.* ebanista.— —*making* [-meikin], *s.* ebanistería.

cable [kéibl], *s.* cable; (mar.) amarra, maroma; telégrafo submarino; cablegrama.—*c. railroad*, funicular.—*vt.* y *vi.* cable(grafi)ar; proveer de o atar con cables.— —*gram* [-græm], *s.* cablegrama, cable.

cacique [kasík], *s.* cacique.

cackle [kækl], *vi.* cacarear; chacharear. —*s.* cacareo; cháchara.

cadaver [kadévœ(r)], *s.* cadáver.— —*ous* [-ʌs], *a.* cadavérico.

cadence [kéidens], *s.* cadencia, ritmo.

cadet [kadét], *s.* cadete.

cafeteria [kæfetíriã], *s.* cafetería.

cage [keidʒ], *s.* jaula.—*vt.* enjaular.

cajole [kadʒóul], *vt.* lisonjear, engatusar.

cake [keik], *s.* torta, bizcocho, pastel, bollo, hojaldre; pastilla o pan de jabón, de cera, etc.; terrón.—*vi.* apelmazarse, formar costra.

calabash [kælabæʃ], *s.* calabacín; calabaza.

caboose [kælabus], *s.* (fam.) calaboso.

calamitous [kalémitʌs], *a.* calamitoso. —**calamity** [kalémiti], *s.* calamidad.

calcium [kælsiʌm], *s.* calcio.

calculate [kælkiuleit], *vt.* calcular.—**calculation** [kælkiuléiʃon], *s.* cálculo, cómputo.—**calculator** [kælkiuleitɔ(r)], *s.* calculista; calculador, (máquina) calculadora.—**calculus** [kælkiulʌs], *s.* cálculo.

caldron [kóldron], *s.* caldero, paila.

calendar [kælindã(r)], *s.* calendario;

almanaque.—*c. year*, año natural; año civil.—*vt.* poner en el calendario o en una lista.

calf [kæf], *s.* becerro, ternero; piel de becerro; pantorrilla.—*c. bound*, encuadernado en piel.— *-skin* [kǽf-skịn], *s.* piel de becerro curtida.

caliber [kǽlịbœ(r)], *s.* calibre; diámetro; (fig.) mérito.—**calibrate** [kǽlịbrejt], *vt.* calibrar.—**calibration** [kælịbréj-şǫn], *s.* calibración.

calipers [kǽlịpœrs], *s.* calibrador, calibre.

calk [kɔk], *vt.* calafatear; rellenar; tapar.— —**er** [kókœ(r)], *s.* calafate, calafateador.— —**ing** [kókịǹ], *s.* calafateo, calafateadura.

call [kɔl], *vt.* llamar; visitar; denominar; apellidar; citar.—*vi.* gritar.—*to c. again*, volver.—*to c. at*, (mar.) hacer escala, tocar (en un puerto).—*to c. back*, mandar volver; retirar.—*to c. for*, pedir; ir por; ir a buscar.—*to c. forth*, producir.—*to c. in*, hacer entrar.—*to c. names*, insultar.—*to c. off*, suspender; desistir de.—*to c. out*, gritar; hacer salir.—*to c. together*, convocar.—*to c. up*, recordar; llamar por teléfono.—*s.* llamada; llamamiento; citación; reclamo; vocación; señal, aviso; visita; (mil.) toque; (com.) demanda.—*on c.*, disponible; (com.) a solicitud, al pedir.—*to make o pay a c.*, hacer una visita.—*within c.*, al alcance de la voz.— —**er** [kólœ(r)], *s.* visitante.— —**ing** [-ịǹ], *s.* vocación; llamamiento; visita.

callous [kǽlʌs], *a.* calloso, córneo, encallecido; (fig.) duro, insensible.—**callus** [kǽlʌs], *s.* callo, dureza.

calm [kam], *s.* calma, serenidad, tranquilidad.—*a.* calmado, tranquilo, sereno.—*vt.* tranquilizar; apaciguar, calmar; aplacar.—*to c. down*, calmarse, serenarse.— —**ness** [kámnịs], *s.* = CALM.— —**y** [-ị], *a.* tranquilo, apacible.

calorie [kǽlorị], *s.* caloría.

calumny [kǽlʌmnị], *s.* calumnia, difamación.

calves [kævz], *s. pl.* de CALF.

calyx [kéjlịks], *s.* (bot.) cáliz.

cam [kæm], *s.* (mec.) leva.

came [kejm], *pret.* de TO COME.

camel [kǽmẹl], *s.* camello.

camellia [kạmílịạ], *s.* (bot.) camelia.

cameo [kǽmjoụ], *s.* camafeo.

camera [kǽmẹrạ], *s.* cámara fotográfica.— —**man** [-mæn], *s.* fotógrafo; operador cinematográfico.

camomile [kǽmomạjl], *s.* manzanilla.

camouflage [kǽmụflaẑ], *s.* camuflaje; disfraz de protección.—*vt.* camuflar, disfrazar, encubrir.

camp [kæmp], *s.* campo, campamento. —*vt.* acampar.

campaign [kæmpéjn], *s.* campaña (mil., pol., etc.).—*vi.* hacer campaña o propaganda.

camphor [kǽmfǫ(r)], *s.* alcanfor.—*c. ball*, = MOTH BALL.—*vt.* alcanforar.

campus [kǽmpʌs], *s.* (E.U.) terreno o campo de un colegio o universidad.

can [kæn], *s.* (envase de) lata.—*c. opener*, abrelatas.—*vti.* [1] enlatar, envasar o conservar en latas; (fam.) despedir (de un empleo).—*v. def. i.* [11] poder, saber.

Canadian [kạnéjdiạn], *s.* y *a.* canadiense.

canal [kạnǽl], *s.* canal; conducto.—*vti.* [2] canalizar; acanalar.

canary [kạnérị], *s.* canario; color de canario.

cancel [kǽnsẹl], *vti.* [2] cancelar, revocar, rescindir; tachar; anular; suprimir.— —**lation** [kænsẹléjṣǫn], *s.* cancelación, rescisión; supresión.

cancer [kǽnsœ(r)], *s.* cáncer.— —**ous** [-ʌs], *a.* canceroso.

candid [kǽndịd], *a.* candoroso, sincero.

candidacy [kǽndịdạsị], *s.* candidatura.— —**candidate** [kǽndịdejt], *s.* candidato.

candied [kǽndịd], *a.* garapiñado.

candle [kǽndl], *s.* vela, bujía; cirio; unidad lumínica.— —**stick** [-stịk], *s.* palmatoria, candelero.

candor [kǽndǫ(r)], *s.* candor, candidez, franqueza; sinceridad.

candy [kǽndị], *s.* confite, caramelo, bombón, dulce.—*vti.* [7] almibarar, confitar, garapiñar.

cane [kejn], *s.* caña; bastón.—*c. field* o *plantation*, cañaveral.—*c. juice*, guarapo.—*sugar c.*, caña de azúcar.—*vt.* bastonear, apalear.

canine [kéjnạjn], *a.* canino, perruno.

canned [kænd], *a.* enlatado.

cannibal [kǽnịbạl], *s.* caníbal, antropófago.— —**ism** [-ịẓm], *s.* canibalismo.

cannon [kǽnǫn], *s.* cañón; (billar) carambola.—*c. bone*, canilla, caña.— *c. shot*, cañonazo.—*vt.* y *vi.* cañonear.— —**ade** [kænǫnéjd], *s.* cañoneo.—*vt.* cañonear.

cannot [kǽnat], *fusión* de CAN (poder) y NOT.

canny [kǽnị], *a.* astuto.

canoe [kạnú], *s.* canoa, piragua; (Mex.) chalupa.—*vt.* y *vi.* llevar o pasear en canoa.

canon [kǽnǫn], *s.* canon; regla o precepto; (igl.) canon o cánones; canónigo.— —**ize** [-ạjz], *vt.* canonizar.

canopy [kǽnopị], *s.* dosel; palio; toldo; pabellón.

can't [kænt], *contr.* de CANNOT.

cant [kænt], *s.* jerga; beatería, gazmoñería.

cantaloupe [kǽntəloup], s. variedad de melón.

canteen [kæntín], s. cantina, taberna; cantimplora.

canter [kǽntœ(r)], s. medio galope.

canticle [kǽntɪkl], s. cántico, canto.

canton [kǽntɒn], s. cantón, distrito.

canvas [kǽnvəs], s. lona; lienzo, cuadro; vela, velamen.

canvass [kǽnvəs], s. examen; investigación; escrutinio; encuesta; pesquisa.

canyon [kǽnyɒn], s. garganta, cañón, desfiladero.

cap [kǽp], s. gorro, gorra; birrete; tapa; cima, cumbre; cápsula fulminante; casquillo, coronilla.—vti. [1] cubrir con gorra; poner tapa; poner cima o remate.

capability [keɪpəbílɪtɪ], s. capacidad, idoneidad, aptitud.—capable [kéɪpəbl], a. capaz; apto, idóneo, competente.

capacious [kəpéɪʃʌs], a. capaz, espacioso.—capacitate [kəpǽsɪteɪt], vt. capacitar.—capacity [kəpǽsɪtɪ], s. capacidad, cabida, espacio; inteligencia, disposición, suficiencia; poder.

cape [keɪp], s. (geog.) cabo; promontorio; capa.

caper [kéɪpœ(r)], s. cabriola; voltereta; alcaparra.—to cut a c., hacer una cabriola.—vi. dar brincos, retozar.

capillary [kǽpɪlerɪ], a. capilar.

capital [kǽpɪtəl], s. capital; principal; excelente, magnífico.—c. letter, mayúscula.—c. punishment, pena de muerte.—s. capital (ciudad), cabecera (de un territorio o distrito); capitel; (com.) capital; fondos; caudal.—to make c. (out) of, sacar partido de.—ism [-ɪzm], s. capitalismo.— ist [-ɪst], s. capitalista.— istic [-ɪstɪk], a. capitalista (sistema, teoría, etc.).— ization [-ɪzéɪʃɒn], s. capitalización; empleo de mayúsculas.— ize [-aɪz], vt. capitalizar; principiar una palabra con mayúscula.

capitol [kǽpɪtɒl], s. capitolio.

caprice [kəprís], s. capricho, antojo; fantasía.—capricious [kəpríʃʌs], a. caprichoso.

capsize [kǽpsaɪz], vi. zozobrar, dar la vuelta.—vt. hacer zozobrar, volcar.

capsule [kǽpsjul], s. cápsula, celdilla, vaina.

captain [kǽptɪn], s. capitán.—vt. capitanear.— ship [-ʃɪp], s. capitanía.

captious [kǽpʃʌs], a. capcioso; quisquilloso.

captivate [kǽptɪveɪt], vt. cautivar, captar, fascinar.—captivating [kǽptɪveɪtɪŋ], a. cautivador, encantador, atractivo, seductivo.—captivation [kǽptɪvéɪʃɒn], s. encanto, fascinación. —captive [kǽptɪv], s. y a. cautivo.—

captivity [kæptívɪtɪ], s. cautiverio, cautividad, prisión.—captor [kǽptɒ(r)], s. captor, aprehensor.—capture [kǽpchŭ(r)], s. captura, apresamiento, prisión; presa.—vt. capturar, apresar, prender; (mil.) tomar.

car [kar], s. coche, auto, automóvil; carro, vagón (de f.c.); (Am.) ascensor, elevador.

caracole [kárəkoul], s. (equit.) caracoleo.—vi. caracolear.

carafe [kərǽf], s. garrafa, cantimplora.

caramel [kǽrəmel], s. caramelo.

carat [kǽrət], s. quilate.

carbine [kárbaɪn], s. carabina.

carbon [kárbɒn], s. copia de papel carbón; carbono; carbón (de lámpara de arco).—c. dioxide, ahidrido carbónico. —c. paper, papel carbón.— ic [karbánɪk], a. carbónico.— ization [karbɒnɪzéɪʃɒn], s. carbonización.— ize [kárbɒnaɪz], vt. carbonizar.

carbuncle [kárbʌŋkl], s. (joy.) carbúnculo o carbunclo; (med.) carbunc(l)o.

carburetor [kárbjuretɒ(r)], s. carburador.

carcass, carcase [kárkəs], s. res muerta; esqueleto; despojo; caparazón (de ave); (mar.) casco o armazón.

card [kard], s. tarjeta, papeleta; naipe, carta; postal; ficha.—to have a c. up one's sleeve, tener algo (plan, etc.) en reserva.— board [kárdbɒrd], s. cartulina, cartón.

cardiac [kárdɪæk], a. cardíaco.

cardinal [kárdɪnəl], a. cardinal, fundamental; rojo vivo; cardenalicio.—s. cardenal.

care [ker], s. cuidado; atención, cautela; esmero; ansiedad; cargo, custodia.— vi. tener cuidado, ansiedad o interés por; querer; importarle a uno; estimar, apreciar; hacer caso.

career [kərír], s. carrera, profesión.

carefree [kérfrí], a. alegre, sin cuidados. —careful [kérfʊl], a. cuidadoso, esmerado; cauteloso, prudente.—to be c., tener cuidado.—carefulness [kérfʊlnɪs], s. cuidado, cautela, atención. —careless [kérlɪs], a. descuidado, negligente, indiferente; desatento.— to be c., descuidar.—carelessness [kérlɪsnɪs], s. descuido, indiferencia, desaliño.

caress [kərés], vt. acariciar, halagar.—s. caricia, halago, cariño.

caretaker [kérteɪkœ(r)], s. curador, guardián, vigilante.

carfare [kárfer], s. dinero para el pasaje (urbano).

cargo [kárgou], s. carga, flete, cargamento.

Carib [kérɪb], s. caribe.— bean [kærɪbɪən], a. caribe, del mar Caribe.

caricature [kǽrikachụr], *s.* caricatura.
　—vt. caricaturizar.—**caricaturist**
　[-ịst], *s.* caricaturista.

carload [kárloụd], *s.* carga de un furgón
　o vagón (f.c.)

Carmelite [kármẹlait], *s.* carmelita
　(monje o monja).

carnal [kárnạl], *a.* carnal; sensual,
　lascivo.

carnation [karnéịṣọn], *s.* clavel; color
　encarnado.

carnival [kárnịvạl], *s.* carnaval.

carnivore [kárnịvor], *s.* carnívoro.—
　carnivorous [karnívọrʌs], *a.* carní-
　voro, carnicero.

carob [kérọb], *s.* algarrobo.

carol [kérọl], *s.* villancico de Navidad;
　canto alegre.—*vti.* [2] cantar villanci-
　cos.

carouse [karáụz], *vi.* jaranear, andar de
　parranda; (fam.) correrla; embria-
　garse.—*s.* parranda; juerga; franca-
　chela.

carp [karp], *s.* (ict.) carpa.

carpenter [kárpentœ(r)], *s.* carpintero.
　—vi. carpintear.—**carpentry** [kár-
　pentrị], *s.* carpintería.

carpet [kárpịt], *s.* alfombra.—*vt.* alfom-
　brar, entapizar.— *—ing* [-ịŋ], *s.* tela
　o tejido para alfombras; alfombrado.

carriage [kérịdẓ], *s.* carruaje, coche;
　conducción, acarreo, transporte;
　porte, aire de una persona; tren de
　aterrizaje.—**carrier** [kérịœ(r)], *s.*
　(trans)portador; arriero; carretero,
　cargador; empresa de transporte;
　mensajero; portaaviones; portador,
　agente transmisor de gérmenes; (rad.)
　onda de transmisión.—*c. pigeon*,
　paloma mensajera o correo.

carrion [kérịọn], *s.* carroña.

carrot [kérọt], *s.* zanahoria.

carry [kérị], *vti.* [7] llevar, conducir,
　transportar, acarrear; cargar; traer,
　llevar encima; contener; comprender;
　entrañar; dirigir; aprobar (una mo-
　ción); ganar (las elecciones); tomar;
　aguantar, sostener; portarse.—*to c.
　away*, llevarse, entusiasmar, arreba-
　tar.—*to c. off*, llevarse, retirar; ganar.
　—to c. out, llevar a cabo; sacar.—*to c.
　through*, llevar a cabo, completar.—
　vii. portear (como oficio); tener
　alcance (voz, tiro, etc.).

cart [kart], *s.* carro, carromato, carreta.
　—c. load, carretada.—*vt.* acarrear.-
　—er [-œ(r)], *s.* carretero.

cartilage [kártịlịdẓ], *s.* cartílago,
　ternilla.

carton [kártọn], *s.* (caja de) cartón fino.

cartoon [kartún], *s.* (pint.) cartón,
　boceto; caricatura.—*vt.* y *vi.* carica-
　turizar.— *—ist* [-ịst], *s.* caricaturista.

cartridge [kártrịdẓ], *s.* (armas) cápsula,
　casquillo; cartucho.—*c. belt*, canana,
　cartuchera.

cartwright [kártrait], *s.* carretero.

carve [karv], *vt.* y *vi.* esculpir; tallar;
　labrar; trinchar carne.— *—n* [kárvẹn],
　a. esculpido, entallado, grabado.— *—r*
　[kárvœ(r)], *s.* escultor; grabador, ta-
　llista; trinchante.—**carving** [kárvịŋ],
　s. escultura, talla; arte de trinchar.—
　c. knife, trinchante.

cascade [kæskéịd], *s.* cascada, catarata.

case [kɛis], *s.* caso; ejemplo; suceso;
　situación; causa, pleito, proceso; caja;
　vaina, funda, cubierta; bastidor.
　—c. shot, metralla.—*in c.*, caso (de)
　que, por si (acaso).—*in any c.*, de
　todos modos.—*in the c. of*, en cuanto
　a, respecto a.—*such being the c.*,
　siendo así.—*vt.* embalar, encajonar;
　enfundar.

cash [kæš], *s.* efectivo, dinero contante
　y sonante; (cont.) caja.—*c. balance*,
　saldo (en) efectivo.—*c. on delivery*,
　(C.O.D.), pago contra entrega.—*c.
　payment*, pago al contado.—*c. regis-
　ter*, caja registradora; contadora.—
　in c., en efectivo.—*adv.* al contado.—
　vt. cambiar, cobrar, hacer efectivo
　(un cheque, etc.).— *—book* [kǽšbụk],
　s. libro de caja.— *—ier* [kæšír], *s.*
　cajero.—*c.'s check*, cheque de caja.

cashmere [kǽšmir], *s.* (tej.) casimir,
　cachemir(a).

casing [kéịsịŋ], *s.* envoltura, cubierta,
　funda; forro; marco de ventana o
　puerta.—*pl.* tripas para embutidos.

cask [kæsk], *s.* barril, tonel, bocoy;
　cuba.

casket [kǽskịt], *s.* cofrecito, estuche,
　joyero; ataúd, féretro.

casserole [kǽsẹroụl], *s.* cacerola.

cassock [kǽsọk], *s.* sotana.

cast [kæst], *vti.* [9] tirar, botar, emitir,
　lanzar; echar; tumbar, derribar;
　dirigir (la mirada o el pensamiento);
　vaciar, moldear (metales); calcular;
　(teat.) repartir (papeles); depositar
　(una boleta electoral).—*to c. anchor*,
　anclar, fondear.—*to c. aside*, dese-
　char.—*to c. down*, abatir, descorazo-
　nar.—*to c. forth*, exhalar, despedir.—
　to c. in one's teeth, echar en cara.—*to
　c. in the rôle of*, adjudicar el papel de.
　—to c. lots, echar suerte.—*to c. off*,
　desamarrar, largar.—*to c. out*, echar
　fuera, arrojar.—*pret.* y *pp.* de TO
　CAST.—*a.* vaciado, fundido.—*c. iron*,
　hierro fundido.—*c. net*, atarraya.—*s.*
　lanzamiento, tirada; fundición;
　molde; mascarilla; aspecto, estampa;
　tinte; (teat.) reparto de papeles;
　actores (en un drama).

castanets [kæstạnɛ́ts], *s. pl.* castañuelas,
　palillos.

castaway [kǽstạwei], *s.* náufrago.

caste [kæst], *s.* casta.—*to lose c.*, desprestigiarse.

Castilian [kæstſlįan], *s.* y *a.* castellano.

castle [kéɛl], *s.* castillo; torre o roque de ajedrez.—*c. builder*, soñador.

castor [kǽstǫ(r)], *s.* castor; paño o sombrero de castor.—*c. oil*, aceite de ricino.

casual [kǽʒual], *a.* casual, fortuito, ocasional; de paso.— —*ness* [-nįs], *s.* descuido, inadvertencia; indiferencia. — —*ty* [-tį], *s.* accidente, desastre; víctima (de un accidente); muerte violenta; (mil.) baja; pérdida; (for.) caso fortuito.

cat [kæt], *s.* gato.—*to bell the c.*, poner el cascabel al gato.—*to let the c. out of the bag*, revelar un secreto.—*to rain cats and dogs*, llover a cántaros.

catacombs [kǽtǫkoumz], *s. pl.* catacumbas.

Catalan [kǽtǫlan], *s.* y *a.* catalán.

catalog, catalogue [kǽtǫlag], *s.* catálogo.—*vt.* catalogar.

Catalonian [kætǫlóunįan], *a.* y *s.* catalán.

cataract [kǽtǫrækt], *s.* catarata.

catarrh [kǫtár], *s.* catarro.

catastrophe [kǫtǽstrofį], *s.* catástrofe; cataclismo.

catcall [kǽtkɔl], *s.* silbido, rechifla.

catch [kæch], *vti.* [10] coger, agarrar; contraer, atrapar; pescar; sorprender.—*to c. in the act*, pescar in fraganti.—*to c. on*, comprender; popularizarse.—*to c. one's eye*, llamarle a uno la atención.—*vii.* engancharse; engranar; prenderse (fuego).—*to c. hold of*, agarrarse a, asirse de.—*to c. up (with)*, alcanzar a, emparejarse (con); ponerse al día.—*s.* presa, captura; botín; redada; gancho, enganche; pestillo; cogida (de la pelota); trampa. — —*er* [kéchœ(r)], *s.* cogedor; agarrador; receptor (de beisbol).— —*ing* [-įŋ], *s.* engranaje.—*a.* contagioso, pegadizo; seductor.

catechism [kǽtekįzm], *s.* catecismo.— **catechize** [kǽtekaįz], *vt.* catequizar.

category [kǽtǫgorį], *s.* categoría, clase.

cater [kéįtœ(r)], *vi.* y *vt.* abastecer, proveer, surtir (de víveres); complacer o halagar a uno en sus gustos.— —*er* [-œ(r)], *s.* proveedor, abastecedor, surtidor, despensero.

caterpillar [kǽtœrpįlǎ(r)], *s.* oruga, gusano.

catgut [kǽtgʌt], *s.* cuerda de tripa.

cathartic [kǫθártįk], *a.* purgante.—*s.* purga, purgante.

cathedral [kǫθídrǎl], *s.* catedral.

Catholic [kǽθǫlįk], *a.* y *s.* católico.—*a.* (c.) católico, universal.— —*ism* [kǫθáljįzm], *s.* catolicismo.

catsup [kǽtsʌp], *s.* salsa de tomate.

cattle [kǽtl], *s.* ganado, ganado vacuno, res.—*c. barn*, establo.—*c. bell*, cencerro, esquilón.—*c. raising*, ganadería.—*c. ranch*, hacienda de ganado, ganadería, rancho; (Am.) estancia.— *c. thief*, abigeo, cuatrero.—*c. tick*, garrapata.— —*man* [-mæn], *s.* ganadero.

Caucasian [kokéįʒan], *s.* y *a.* caucásico.

caught [kɔt], *pret.* y *pp.* de TO CATCH.

cauliflower [kólįfiauœ(r)], *s.* coliflor.

caulk [kɔk], *vt.* -. CALK.

cause [koz], *s.* causa, origen, razón; (for.) proceso.—*vt.* causar; motivar; originar.

cauterize [kótœraįz], *vt.* cauterizar.

caution [kóʃǫn], *s.* cautela; cuidado; advertencia.—*vt.* advertir, precaver, prevenir.— **cautious** [kóʃʌs], *a.* cauto, precavido, prudente.

cavalier [kævǫlír], *s.* caballero; jinete; galán.—*a.* caballeresco; altivo, desdeñoso.— **cavalry** [kǽvǫlrį], *s.* caballería; caballos.— **cavalryman** [kǽvǫlrįman], *s.* jinete; soldado de caballería.

cave [keįv], *s.* cueva, gruta, caverna.— *c. in*, hundimiento.—*vi.* hundirse, desplomarse.— **cavern** [kǽvœrn], *s.* caverna, gruta.

cavity [kǽvįtį], *s.* cavidad, hueco; caries.

caw [kɔ], *s.* graznido.—*vi.* graznar.

cay [kei, ki], *s.* cayo; isleta.

cayman [kéįman], *s.* caimán.

cease [sįs], *vi.* cesar (de), desistir o dejar de, parar (de).—*vt.* cesar, parar, suspenderse.— —*less* [sįslįs], *a.* incesante.

cedar [sídǎ(r)], *s.* cedro.

cede [sįd], *vt.* ceder, traspasar, transferir.

ceiling [sílįŋ], *s.* techo interior, cielo raso; (aer.) altura máxima; límite de visibilidad.

celebrant [sélębrant], *s.* celebrante.— **celebrate** [sélębreįt], *vt.* celebrar; festejar; alabar.—*vi.* celebrar; echar una cana al aire.— **celebrated** [sélębreįtįd], *a.* célebre, famoso.— **celebration** [selębréįʃǫn], *s.* celebración.— **celebrity** [sęlébrįtį], *s.* celebridad, renombre.

celerity [sęlérįtį], *s.* celeridad, prontitud.

celery [sélęrį], *s.* apio.

celestial [sęléschǎl], *a.* celeste; celestial.

celibacy [sélįbǎsį], *s.* celibato, soltería.

cell [sel], *s.* celda, calabozo; célula; pila eléctrica.

cellar [sélǎ(r)], *s.* sótano, bodega.

cello [chélou], *s.* violoncelo.

cellophane [sélofeįn], *s.* celofán.

celluloid [séljuloįd], *s.* celuloide; película de cinema.

cellulose [séljulous], *s.* celulosa.

Celt [selt], *s.* Celta.— **-ic** [séltik], *a.* céltico.

cement [sęmént], *s.* cemento.—*vt.* cementar; recubrir con cemento; unir; pegar.—*vi.* pegarse; unirse.

cemetery [sémęterį], *s.* cementerio, necrópolis.

censor [sénsǫ(r)], *s.* censor; crítico.—*vt.* censurar, someter a la censura (cartas periódicas, etc.).— **-ship** [-ṣip], *s.* censura.—**censure** [sénṣǫ(r)], *s.* censura, reprimenda, crítica.—*vt.* censurar, reprender, criticar.

census [sénsas], *s.* censo, empadronamiento, registro; catastro.—*vt.* empadronar, hacer el censo.

cent [sent], *s.* centavo.—*per c.,* por ciento.

center [séntœ(r)], *s.* centro.—*a.* central; céntrico.—*vt.* centrar, centralizar.—*vi.* concentrarse; estar o colocarse en el centro.— **-piece** [-pis], *s.* centro de mesa.

centigrade [séntįgreįd], *s.* centígrado.

centipede [séntipid], *s.* ciempiés.

central [séntrąl], *a.* central, céntrico.—*s.* central (de teléfono).— **-ize** [-aįz], —*vt.* centralizar.— **-izer** [-aįzœ(r)], *s.* centralizador.

centrifugal [sentrífįugąl], *a.* centrífugo.

centripetal [sentrípetąl], *a.* centrípeto.

century [sénchǫrį], *s.* siglo; centuria.

cereal [síriąl], *s.* cereal, grano.—*a.* cereal.

ceremonial [serẹmóųnįąl], *a.* y *s.* ceremonial; rito.—**ceremonious** [serẹmóųnįąs], *a.* ceremonioso; ceremonioso.—**ceremony** [serẹmouni], *s.* ceremonia, ceremonial; cumplido, etiqueta.

certain [sœrtạn], *a.* cierto, alguno; seguro; positivo.—*for c.,* de fijo, con seguridad.— **-ty** [-tį], *s.* certeza, certidumbre; seguridad.

certificate [sœrtífįkįt], **certification** [sœrtįfikéįṣǫn], *s.* certificado, testimonio; (for.) atestado, certificación, partida.—*certificate of residence,* carta de vecindad.—*certificate of stock,* bono, obligación.—**certify** [sœrtįfaį], *vti.* [7] certificar, atestiguar, responder de o por.

cervix [sœrvįks], *s.* (anat.) cerviz, nuca.

cessation [seséįṣǫn], *s.* cese, cesación, paro.

cession [séṣǫn], *s.* cesión, traspaso.

cesspool [séspul], *s.* pozo negro, cloaca.

chafe [cheįf], *vt.* excoriar, rozar; irritar.—*vi.* irritarse.—*s.* excoriación, rozadura; irritación.

chaff [chæf], *s.* hollejo, cáscara.—*vt.* y *vi.* embromar.

chagrin [ṣągrín], *s.* mortificación, disgusto.—*vt.* mortificar, enfadar.

chain [cheįn], *s.* cadena.—*pl.* (fig.)

prisiones; esclavitud.—*c. of mountains,* cordillera.—*vt.* encadenar; esclavizar.

chair [cher], *s.* silla; asiento; cátedra; sillón de la presidencia; (por extensión) presidencia, presidente (de una junta, etc.).—*folding c.,* silla de tijeras, silla plegable.—*rocking c.,* mecedora.—*to take the c.,* presidir (una junta).— **-man** [chérmạn], *s.* presidente de una junta, persona que preside.

chalice [chǽlįs], *s.* cáliz.

chalk [chǫk], *s.* tiza, yeso.—*c. for cheese,* gato por liebre.—*vt.* enyesar; dibujar o marcar con tiza; poner tiza (al taco).— **-y** [chókį], *a.* yesoso; blanco.

challenge [chǽlįndẓ], *vt.* desafiar, retar; disputar, contradecir; (for.) tachar, recusar; (mil.) dar el quién vive.—*s.* desafío, reto; (for.) recusación, tacha; (mil.) quién vive.— **-r** [-œ(r)], *s.* retador, desafiador; (for.) demandante.

chamber [chéįmbœ(r)], *s.* cámara; gabinete, alcoba, dormitorio; tribunal o sala de justicia; (mec.) depósito, cilindro.— **-lain** [-lįn], *s.* camarero; chambelán.— **-maid** [-meįd], *s.* camarera, doncella de cuarto.

chameleon [kąmílįon], *s.* (zool.) camaleón.

chamois [ṣǽmį], *s.* gamuza.

champ [chæmp], *s.* (fam.) campeón.

champagne [ṣæmpéįn], *s.* champaña.

champion [chémpįǫn], *s.* campeón, adalid; defensor.—*vt.* defender.— **-ship** [-ṣip], *s.* campeonato.

chance [chæns], *s.* azar, casualidad; fortuna; ocasión, oportunidad; riesgo; probabilidad.—*by c.,* por casualidad; de chiripa.—*there is no c.,* no hay esperanza.—*to take chances,* correr un albur, aventurarse.—*a.* casual, fortuito.—*vi.* acontecer.—*to c. to have,* tener por casualidad.—*to c. upon,* topar (con).—*vt.* arriesgar.

chancellery [chǽnsęlęrį], *s.* cancillería.—**chancellor** [chǽnselǫ(r)], *s.* canciller; ministro; magistrado; rector de universidad.

chandelier [ṣændęlír], *s.* araña o lámpara de techo.

change [cheįndẓ], *vt.* cambiar, alterar, modificar; substituir, reemplazar.—*to c. one's mind,* mudar de parecer.—*vi.* mudar, cambiar, alterarse.—*s.* cambio, alteración, mudanza; substitución, trueque; muda (de ropa, voz, etc.); vuelto; menudo; moneda suelta; novedad.—*c. of life,* menopausia.—*for a c.,* para variar, por cambiar.— **-able** [chéįndẓąbl], *a.* variable; in-

constante; alterable; (tej.) tornasolado.- —less [-ljs], a. inmutable.

channel [chǽnẹl], s. canal; cauce; ranura; estría.—vti. [2] acanalar, estriar; conducir.

chant [chænt], vt. y vi. cantar (salmos, etc.).—s. canto llano; salmodia.

chaos [kéjas], s. caos; gran confusión o desorden.—**chaotic** [kejátjk], a. caótico.

chap [chæp], vti. [1] rajar, agrietar.— vii. rajarse, cuartearse.—s. grieta, raja, hendidura; (fam.) chico; tipo.

chapel [chǽpẹl], s. capilla.

chaperon [ʃǽpẹrouŋ], s. acompañante, señora de compañía o respeto.—vt. acompañar a una o más señoritas en lugares públicos.

chaplain [chǽpljn], s. capellán.—army c., capellán castrense.

chaps [chæps], s. pl. (Am.) chaparreras, zamarros.

chapter [chǽptœ(r)], s. capítulo; cabildo; filial (de una asociación).—c. and verse, con sus pelos y señales.

char [char], vti. y vii. [1] carbonizar(se), chamuscar(se).

character [kǽrjktœ(r)], s. carácter, genio; reputación; sujeto; (lit.) personaje; (teat.) papel; (fam.) tipo raro u original.— —istic [-jstjk], a. característico, propio.—s. característica, rasgo típico.— —ize [-ajz], vt. caracterizar.

charcoal [chárkoul], s. carbón de leña.— c. pencil, carboncillo de dibujo.

charge [chardʒ], vt. cargar (armas, acumuladores, etc.); instruir; encargar; gravar; cobrar (precio); cargar en cuenta; acusar; atacar; embestir.— vi. pedir (precio); cargarse; cargar (a la bayoneta).—s. carga, embestida; carga (de un acumulador, etc.); cargo; custodia; encargo, encomienda; persona o cosa de que uno está encargado; impuesto; acusación, cargo.— pl. honorarios, gastos.—c. account, cuenta abierta.—to take c. of, encargarse de.

chariot [chǽrjọt], s. carro antiguo de guerra o de carreras; cuádriga.

charitable [chǽrjtạbl], a. caritativo, benéfico.—**charity** [chǽrjtj], s. caridad; limosna.

charlatan [ʃárlạtạn], s. charlatán, curandero.

charm [charm], s. encanto, hechizo; embeleso; talismán.—vt. hechizar; encantar, embelesar, prendar.— —ing [chármjŋ], a. encantador; fascinante, atractivo; seductor.

chart [chart], vt. poner en una carta náutica; cartografiar; trazar en un diagrama.—s. carta náutica; mapa; plano; gráfica.

charter [chártœ(r)], s. cédula, título, carta de fuero o privilegio; estatuto; constitución.—vt. estatuir; fletar un barco; alquilar un tren, etc.—c., member, socio fundador.

charwoman [chárwụmạn], s. fregatriz, mujer de la limpieza.

chase [chejs], vt. cazar; perseguir.—to c. away, ahuyentar, espantar.—s. caza; persecución; ranura, muesca.- —r [chéjsœ(r)], s. cazador; perseguidor; (aer.) avión de caza.

chasm [kǽzm], s. abismo, precipicio, sima.

chassis [ʃǽsj], s. armazón, bastidor, marco; chasis.

chaste [chejst], a. casto; honesto; puro.

chastise [chæstájz], vt. castigar, corregir.- —ment [-mẹnt], s. castigo, corrección.

chastity [chǽstjtj], s. castidad, pureza, honestidad.

chat [chæt], vii. [1] charlar, platicar.— s. charla, plática, palique.

chattels [chǽtẹlz], s. pl. enseres, bienes muebles.

chatter [chǽtœ(r)], vi. castañetear o rechinar (los dientes); parlotear, charlar, (fam.) hablar por los codos; (mec.) vibrar.—s. charla, cháchara; vibración.

chauffeur [ʃoufœ́r], s. chófer o chofer, conductor de automóvil.

cheap [chip], a. barato; de pacotilla.— to feel c., avergonzarse, sentirse inferior.— —en [chípẹn], vt. y vi. abaratar(se), despreciar(se).— —ness [-njs], s. baratura, modicidad; vulgaridad.

cheat [chit], vt. engañar, embaucar; defraudar; timar.—s. trampa, fraude, engaño; timador.- —er [chítœ(r)], s. estafador, embustero; tramposo, fullero.- —ing [-jŋ], s. engaño, fraude.

check [chek], vt. refrenar, reprimir; comprobar, confrontar, cotejar, verificar y marcar; registrar, facturar o depositar (equipajes, etc.); dar a guardar (el sombrero, etc.), recibiendo una contraseña; dar jaque (ajedrez). —to c. out, desocupar (el cuarto de un hotel, etc.).—vi. detenerse; corresponder; rajarse; dar jaque.—s. cheque; póliza; comprobación, prueba; contraseña, talón de reclamo (de equipajes, etc.); cuenta (de restaurante); detención; rechazo; obstáculo; contratiempo; jaque (en el ajedrez); ficha (en el juego); grieta (en el hormigón); muesca.—c. mark, marca, contraseña.—c. up, examen, comprobación.- —book [chékbụk], s. talonario, chequera.- —er [-œ(r)], s. cuadro, casilla; verificador; cada pieza del juego de damas.—pl. juego de damas.- —erboard [-œ(r)bord], s.

tablero de damas.— —ing [-iŋ], *s.* comprobación.—*c. account,* cuenta corriente (en un banco).— —**mate** [-mejt], *vt.* dar (jaque) mate; desconcertar, derrotar.—*s.* (jaque) mate.— —**room** [-rum], *s.* guardarropa.

cheek [chik], *s.* carrillo, mejilla, cachete; montante, larguero; (fam.) tupé, descaro; jamba (de puerta o ventana).— —**bone** [chíkboun], *s.* pómulo.

cheer [chir], *s.* alegría; jovialidad; consuelo.—*pl.* vivas, aplausos.—*vt.* alentar, alegrar; vitorear, aplaudir.— *vi.* alegrarse.—*c. up!* ¡ánimo! ¡valor!— —**ful** [chírful], *a.* alegre, animado, jovial.— —**fulness** [-fulnis], *s.* alegría, jovialidad.

cheese [chiz], *s.* queso.— —**cake** [chízkejk], *s.* quesadilla.— —**cloth** [-klɔθ], *s.* estopilla de algodón.

chemical [kémikal], *a.* químico.—*s.* producto químico.

chemise [șemíz], *s.* camisa de mujer.

chemist [kémist], *s.* químico; farmaceútico.— —**ry** [-ri], *s.* química.

cherish [chériș], *vt.* apreciar, fomentar; abrigar, acariciar.

cherry [chéri], *s.* cereza; cerezo (árbol y madera).—*a.* hecho de cereza o de cerezo; de color de cereza.

cherub [chérab], *s.* querubín.

chess [ches], *s.* ajedrez.— —**board** [chésbord], *s.* tablero de ajedrez.

chest [chest], *s.* pecho, torax; arca, cofre.—*c. of drawers,* cómoda, buró.

chestnut [chésnʌt], *s.* (bot.) castaña; castaño (árbol, madera; color).

chevron [șévron], *s.* (mil.) galón, insignia.

chew [chu], *vt. y vi.* mas(ti)car; rumiar; (fig.) meditar.—*to c. the rag,* (fam.) charlar, estar dale que dale.—*s.* mascada; mordisco, bocado.— —**ing** [chúiŋ], *s.* masticación; rumia.—*c. gum,* chicle, goma de mascar.

chick [chik], *s.* polluelo, pollito; pajarito; (fam.) chica, pollita.— —**en** [chíken], *s.* pollo, gallina (como alimento).—*c.-hearted,* cobarde, gallina.—*c. pox,* varicela, viruela loca.— —**pea** [-pi], *s.* garbanzo.

chief [chif], *s.* jefe; cabecilla; caudillo; cacique; (com.) principal.—*a.* principal; primero, en jefe.— —**tain** [chíftin], *s.* jefe, comandante; caudillo, capitán; cabeza.

chiffon [șifán], *s.* gasa.

chignon [șíŋyan], *s.* moño, castaña.

chilblain [chílblejn], *s.* (med.) sabañón.

child [chajld], *s.* niño o niña; hijo o hija; criatura; chiquillo.—*with c.,* embarazada, encinta.— —**birth** [chájldbœrθ], *s.* parto, alumbramiento.— —**hood** [chájldhud], *s.* infancia, niñez.— —**ish**

[-iș], *a.* pueril, frívolo.—*c. action,* chiquillada, niñería.— —**less** [-lis], *a.* sin hijos.— —**ren** [chíldren], *s. pl.* de CHILD.

Chilean [chílian], *s. y a.* chileno.

chili, chilli [chíli], *s.* (bot.) (Am.) chile, ají picante, mole.

chill [chil], *a.* frío, desapacible.—*s.* frío, (es)calofrío; enfriamiento; estremecimiento.—*chills and fever,* fiebre intermitente.—*vt.* enfriar, resfriar, helar; desanimar.—*vi.* dar escalofríos, calofriarse.— —(i)ness [chíl(i)nis], *s.* frialdad, calidad de frío.— —**y** [-i], *a.* frío, fresco; friolento.

chime [chajm], *s.* juego de campanas; campaneo, repique; armonía, conformidad.—*vt.* tocar, tañer las campanas.—*vi.* repicar (las campanas); sonar con armonía.

chimney [chímni], *s.* chimenea.—*c. corner,* hogar, chimenea.—*c. flue,* cañón, tiro de la chimenea.

chimpanzee [chimpænzí], *s.* chimpancé.

chin [chin], *s.* barba, barbilla, mentón. —*c. cloth,* babero, babador.—*c. strap,* barboquejo.—*c. up!* ¡ánimo!

china [chájna], *s.* porcelana, loza fina, vajilla fina.—*c. cabinet,* chinero, vitrina.— —**man** [-man], *s.* chino.— —**ware** [-wer], *s.* = CHINA.

chine [chajn], *s.* espinazo; lomo.

Chinese [chajníz], *s.* chino (lengua y persona).—*a.* chino.—*C. lantern,* farolillo.

chink [chiŋk], *s.* grieta, resquicio.—*vt. y vi.* (hacer) sonar, (hacer) tintinar (copas, monedas, etc.).

chip [chip], *vti.* [1] desmenuzar, picar, astillar.—*vii.* quebrarse, desconcharse.—*s.* fragmento, astilla; desconchadura; viruta; ficha; tanto (en el juego).—*a c. off the old block,* de tal palo tal astilla.—*potato chips,* papas a la inglesa, rueditas de papas.

chipmunk [chípmʌnk], *s.* especie de ardilla.

chiropodist [kajrápodist], *s.* pedicuro, callista, quiropedista.

chirp [chœrp], *vi.* chirriar, gorjear, piar. —*s.* chirrido; gorjeo; canto.

chisel [chízel], *s.* cincel; escoplo; buril. —*vti. y vii.* [2] cincelar; burilar; (fam.) engañar, embaucar.— —(l)er [-œ(r)], *s.* (fam.) engañador; ventajista.

chivalrous [șívalrʌs], *a.* caballeroso, cortés, caballeresco.— —**chivalry** [șívalri], *s.* caballerosidad, cortesía, galantería.

chlorine [klórin], *s.* cloro.—**chloroform** [klóroform], *s.* cloroformo.—**chlorophyll** [klórofil], *s.* clorofila.

chock [chak], *s.* calzo, cuña; choque.—

vt. afianzar, soportar, calzar.—*c.-full*, colmado, atestado, de bote en bote.

chocolate [chákljt], *s.* chocolate; bombón.—*c. pot*, chocolatera.

choice [chojs], *s.* elección; selección; preferencia, opción; cosa elegida; lo selecto, lo más escogido; variedad.— *a.* escogido, selecto, exquisito.

choir [kwajr], *s.* coro, masa coral.

choke [chouk], *vt.* y *vi.* estrangular(se); ahogar(se); sofocar(se); atragantar(se), atorar(se); obturar(se) (el carburador).—*s.* estrangulación; ahogo; sofoco; estrangulador o ahogador (del automóvil).

cholera [kálęrȝ], *s.* cólera; cólera morbo. —**choleric** [kálęrjk], *a.* colérico, irascible.

choose [chuz], *vti.* [10] escoger, preferir, seleccionar, optar por; desear.

chop [chap], *vti.* [1] tajar, cortar; picar carne; desbastar; hender.—*to c. off*, tronchar.—*vii.* dar cuchilladas.—*s.* proción, parte; tajada; chuleta o costilla.—*pl.* quijadas (de animal).

choral [kórạl], *s.* y *a.* (mus.) coral.—*c. society*, orfeón, masa coral.

chord [kord], *s.* cordón, cuerda; (mus.) acorde.

chore [chor], *s.* quehacer, faena, tarea.

chorus [kórᴀs], *vt.* y *vi.* corear; componer o cantar música coreada; cantar o hablar a coro; hacer coro a.—*s.* (teat.) coro; estribillo.—*c. girl*, corista.—*in c.*, al unísono.

chose [chouz], *pret.* de TO CHOOSE.— **chosen** [chóuzęn], *pp.* de TO CHOOSE.

chrism [krjzm], *s.* (igl.) crisma.

Christ [krajst], *s.* Cristo.—*the C. child*, el niño Jesús.—**christen** [krjsęn], *vt.* bautizar.—**Christendom** [krjsęndǫm], *s.* cristiandad, cristianismo.—**christening** [krjsęnjȵ], *s.* bautismo, cristianismo; bautizo.—*a.* bautismal.— **Christian** [krjschạn], *a.* y *s.* cristiano. —*C. name*, nombre de pila o de bautismo.—**Christianism** [krjschạnjzm], **Christianity** [krjschjénjtj], *s.* cristianismo, cristiandad.—**Christmas** [krjsmạs], *s.* Navidad.—*C. carol*, villancico, cántico de Navidad.—*C. Eve*, nochebuena.

chronic [kránjk], *a.* crónico, inveterado.

chronicle [kránjkl], *s.* crónica.—*vt.* escribir, registrar o narrar en forma de crónica.—*r* [kránjklœ(r)], *s.* cronista, historiador.

chronologic(al) [kranǫládȝjk(ạl)], *a.* cronológico.

chronometer [kronámętœ(r)], *s.* cronómetro.

chrysalis [krjsạljs], *s.* (ent.) crisálida.

chrysanthemum [krjsénθȩmᴧm], *s.* crisantemo.

chubby [chábj], *a.* regordete, gordinflón, rechoncho.

chuck [chᴧk], *vt.* desechar, tirar lo inútil; acariciar la barbilla.—*s.* mamola; echada, tirada; golpecito, caricia.—*c. hole*, bache.—*c. steak*, bisté de falda.—*le* [chᴧkl], *vi.* reír entre dientes.—*s.* risa ahogada, risita.

chum [chᴧm], *vii.* [1] (fam.) ser camarada.—*s.* (fam.) camarada, compinche.

chunk [chᴧȵk], *s.* pedazo corto y grueso, trozo; (fam.) persona fornida.— *y* [chᴧȵkj], *a.* trabado, fornido, rechoncho.

church [chœrch], *s.* iglesia; templo; culto público, el clero.—*c. calendar*, santoral.—*man* [chœrchmạn], *s.* sacerdote, clérigo.—*yard* [chœrchyard], *s.* cementerio (de parroquia).

churn [chœrn], *s.* mantequera.—*vt.* agitar, menear, revolver; batir manteca.—*vi.* agitarse, revolverse.—*ing* [chœrnjȵ], *s.* batido; cantidad de manteca batida de una vez.

chute [ŝut], *s.* conducto; canal; tubo; sumidero; vertedero; paracaídas.

chyle [kajl], *s.* (fis.) quilo.

cider [sájdœ(r)], *s.* sidra.

cigar [sigár], *s.* cigarro, tabaco, puro, habano.—*c. case*, petaca.—*c. holder*, boquilla.—*c. lighter*, mechero, encendedor.—*c. store*, tabaquería, estanco.—*ette* [sjgarét], *s.* cigarrillo, pitillo, cigarro.—*c. case*, pitillera, cigarrera.

cinch [sjnch], *vt.* cinchar; apretar.—*s.* cincha; (fam.) ganga, cosa fácil o segura.

cinder [sjndœ(r)], *s.* ceniza; carbón; brasa; rescoldo.—*pl.* pavesas, cenizas; carbón a medio quemar.—*vt.* reducir a cenizas.

cinema [sjnęmặ], *s.* cine, cinematógrafo.

cinnamon [sjnạmǫn], *s.* canela; árbol de la canela.

cipher [sájfœ(r), *s.* cifra; (arit.) cero; nulidad.—*vt.* calcular; cifrar con clave.—*vi.* numerar.

circle [sœrkl], *s.* círculo; circunferencia, redondel, esfera; círculo (social); rueda, corro.—*vt.* circundar, cercar, rodear.—*vi.* dar vueltas, remolinear.

circuit [sœrkjt], *s.* circuito; vuelta, rodeo; radio; distrito; partido, jurisdicción.—*c. breaker*, interruptor automático.

circular [sœrkjulạ(r)], *a.* circular; redondo.—*c. letter*, circular.—*c. plate*, disco.—*s.* circular; carta, aviso o folleto circular.—**circulate** [sœrkjulejt], *vt.* propalar, propagar; poner en circulación.—*vi.* circular; propagarse. —**circulation** [sœrkjuléjṣǫn], *s.* circulación; propaganda.—**circulatory**

[sœrkjulątori], *a.* circulatorio, circular.

circumcise [sœrkAmsaiz], *vt.* circuncidar.—**circumcision** [sœrkAmsíẓon], *s.* circuncisión.

circumference [sœrkÁmfęręns], *s.* circunferencia, periferia; perímetro.

circumscribe [sœrkAmskráib], *vt.* circunscribir, fijar, limitar.

circumspect [sœrkAmspekt], *a.* circunspecto, discreto.

circumstance [sœrkAmstæns], *s.* circunstancia, incidente, acontecimiento.—*under no circumstances,* jamás; de ningún modo.—*under the circumstances,* en las circunstancias presentes, siendo así las cosas.—**circumstantial** [sœrkAmstǽnsąl], *a.* circunstancial, accidental, incidental.—*c. evidence,* prueba de indicios.

circus [sœrkAs], *s.* circo.

cistern [sįstœrn], *s.* cisterna, aljibe.

citadel [sítądęl], *s.* ciudadela.

citation [saitéiẓon], *s.* cita, mención; (for.) citación, emplazamiento.—**cite** [sait], *vt.* citar, referirse a; (for.) citar a juicio.

citizen [sítiẓęn], *s.* ciudadano, vecino.——**ship** [-ṣip], *s.* ciudadanía; nacionalidad.—*c. papers,* carta de ciudadanía o nacionalidad.

city [síti], *s.* ciudad, población, urbe; municipio.—*a.* municipal; citadino, urbano.—*c. council,* ayuntamiento.—*c. district,* barrio.—*c. hall,* ayuntamiento, casa consistorial.

civic [sívįk], *a.* cívico.——**ism** [sívįsįzm], *s.* civismo.——**s** [sívįks], *s.* cívica, ciencia del gobierno civil.—**civil** [sívįl], *a.* civil, ciudadano; cortés, urbano.—*c. procedure,* enjuiciamiento civil.—*c. service,* ramo civil de la administración pública.—**civilian** [sivíl-yąn], *s.* paisano (no militar), civil.—*pl.* la población civil.—*a.* civil.—**civility** [sivíliti], *s.* civilidad, cortesía, urbanidad.—**civilization** [sivilizéiṣon], *s.* civilización.—**civilize** [sívilaiz], *vt.* civilizar.

clad [klæd], *a.* vestido, aderezado.

claim [kleim], *vt.* demandar, pedir en juicio; reclamar; denunciar (una mina); sostener, pretender, alegar.—*to c. to be,* echárselas de.—*s.* demanda; reclamación, petición; pretensión, título, derecho; denuncia minera.——**ant** [kléimąnt], ——**er** [-œ(r)], *s.* reclamante.

clairvoyance [klervóiąns], *s.* videncia, clarividencia.—**clairvoyant** [klervóiant], *a.* clarividente.

clam [klæm], *s.* almeja.

clamor [klǽmǫ(r)], *s.* clamor(eo), gritería, vocería, algarabía; estruendo.—*vi.* clam(ore)ar, gritar, vociferar.—

——**ous** [-As], *a.* clamoroso, ruidoso, estruendoso.

clamp [klæmp], *s.* tornillo de banco; grampa; abrazadera; pinzas, tenazas; montón (de mineral, ladrillos, etc.); pisadas recias.—*vt.* empalmar; afianzar; sujetar.—*vi.* pisar recio.

clan [klæn], *s.* clan; tribu; cuerpo o sociedad exclusivista.

clang [klæŋ], *s.* retintín; campanada; campanillazo.—*vt. y vi.* (hacer) sonar, resonar o retumbar.

clap [klæp], *vti.* [1] batir; cerrar de golpe; aplaudir.—*to c. the hands,* batir palmas.—*vti.* aplaudir, dar palmadas, palm(ot)ear.—*s.* ruido o golpe seco; palmada, aplauso; (fam.) gonorrea.

claret [klǽrit], *s.* clarete, vino tinto.

clarinet [klǽrinet], *s.* clarinete.

clarity [klǽriti], *s.* claridad.

clash [klæŝ], *vi.* chocar, entrechocarse, encontrarse; discordar, oponerse.—*vt.* batir, golpear.—*s.* choque; encontrón, colisión; antagonismo, discordia.

clasp [klæsp], *s.* broche, presilla, traba, hebilla, abrazadera; cierre; (mec.) grapa; apretón, abrazo.—*vt.* abrochar, enganchar; asir, agarrar; asegurar; abrazar, ceñir; apretar (la mano).

class [klæs], *s.* clase; condición, rango; (mil.) promoción; clase en las escuelas; (fam.) elegancia.—*vt.* clasificar, calificar, ordenar.

classic [klǽsįk], *s. y a.* clásico.——**al** [-ąl], *a.* clásico.

classification [klæsifikéiṣon], *s.* clasificación.—**classify** [klǽsifai], *vti.* [7] clasificar, ordenar.

classmate [klǽsmeit], *s.* condiscípulo.—**classroom** [klǽsrum], *s.* aula, clase.

clatter [klǽtœ(r)], *vi.* resonar ruidosamente, matraquear, guachapear; charlar.—*s.* ruido, estruendo; gritería; alboroto, bulla.

clause [klǫz], *s.* cláusula.

clavicle [klǽvikl], *s.* clavícula.

claw [klǫ], *s.* garra, zarpa, uña; pinza o tenaza (del cangrejo); gancho, garfio.—*c. hammer,* martillo de orejas.—*vt.* desgarrar; arañar; rasgar, despedazar.—*vi.* arañar.

clay [klei], *s.* arcilla, greda, barro.

clean [klin], *a.* limpio; puro; despejado; aseado; nítido; simétrico.—*c.-bred,* de pura raza.—*c.-handed,* con las manos limpias, sin culpa.—*to show a c. pair of heels,* tomar las de Villadiego.—*vt.* limpiar, asear; desengrasar, desenlodar.—*vi.* (gen. con up) limpiar(se), asear(se).——**er** [klínœ(r)], *s.* limpiador; mondador; tintorero; quitamanchas; depurador (de aire, etc.).——**ing** [-įŋ], *s.* aseo, limpieza; desengrase.——**liness** [klénlį-

nis], *s.* limpieza, aseo, aliño; compostura; tersura.— —ly [klénli], *a.* limpio, aseado; puro, delicado.— —ness [-nis], *s.* limpieza, aseo; pureza.—cleanse [klenz], *vt.* limpiar, purificar; purgar, depurar.—cleanser [klénzœ(r)], *s.* limpiador, purificador.

clear [klir], *a.* claro, lúcido, transparente; despejado, (d)escampado; inocente; (com.) neto; sin deudas; puro; evidente.—*c.-headed*, inteligente, listo.—*c. profit*, beneficio neto.—*c.-sighted*, clarividente, perspicaz.—*c. track*, vía libre.—*s.* claro, espacio entre objetos.—*vt.* despejar, quitar estorbos; aclarar; justificar; salvar (un obstáculo); absolver; desenredar; desmontar, tumbar; obtener una ganancia líquida.—*to c. the table*, levantar la mesa.—*vi.* aclarar(se), serenar(se); liquidar cuentas.—*to c. off* o *up*, despejarse o escampar (el cielo).—*to c. out*, irse, escabullirse.— —ance [klírans], *s.* despejo; despacho de aduana; beneficio líquido; (com.) venta de liquidación; (mec., ing.) juego, espacio libre.—*c. papers*, certificación del pago de derechos de aduana.— —ing [-iŋ], *s.* aclaramiento, despejo; desmonte; claro, raso; justificación.—*c. house*, banco de liquidación.— —ness [-nis], *s.* claridad; luz; despejo.

cleave [kliv], *vti.* [4] partir, rajar, tajar; penetrar.—*vii.* resquebrar, henderse; pegarse, adherirse.— —r [klívœ(r)], *s.* partidor; cuchilla o cortante de carnicero.

clef [klef], *s.* (mus.) clave, llave.

cleft [kleft], *pret.* y *pp.* de TO CLEAVE.— *a.* agrietado, partido.—*s.* grieta, fisura, rajadura, rendija.

clemency [klémensi], *s.* clemencia, misericordia.—clement [klémęnt], *a.* clemente, misericordioso.

clench [klench], *vt.* agarrar; apretar o cerrar el puño; remachar.—V. CLINCH.—*s.* agarradera.— —er [klénchœ(r)], *s.* agarrador; remachador; (fig.) argumento sin réplica.

clergy [klǿrdʒi], *s.* clero.— —man [-mąn], *s.* clérigo; cura, sacerdote.— cleric [klérik], *s.* clérigo.—*a.* clerical. —clerical [klérikal], *a.* clerical; eclesiástico; burocrático, oficinesco.—*s.* clérigo.—*pl.* ropa clerical.—clerk [klœrk], *s.* oficial de secretaría; escribiente; empleado de oficina; clérigo; escolar; escribano, actuario.

clever [klévœ(r)], *a.* diestro, hábil; avisado, listo; inteligente.— —ness [-nis], *s.* talento; destreza, maña, habilidad.

cliché [klišéi], *s.* (impr.) clisé; frase hecha, lugar común.

click [klik], *s.* golpe seco; seguro, gatillo; gatillazo; chasquido de lengua.— *vt.* y *vi.* (hacer) sonar con uno o más golpes secos; hacer tictac; piñonear (un arma de fuego); (fam.) tener buen éxito.

client [kláient], *s.* cliente; parroquiano. — —ele [-él], *s.* clientela.

cliff [klif], *s.* farallón, risco, acantilado, precipicio.

climate [kláimit], *s.* clima.

climax [kláimæks], *s.* clímax.

climb [klaim], *vt.* trepar, subir, escalar. —*vi.* trepar, subir, encaramarse, elevarse.—*s.* subida, ascenso.— —er [kláimœ(r)], *s.* trepador, escalador; enredadera; oportunista.— —ing [-iŋ], *s.* trepa, subida.—*a.* trepante, trepador.

clime [klaim], *s.* clima.

clinch [klinch], *vt.* remachar; agarrar; afianzar.—*vi.* agarrarse; (fam.) abrazarse estrechamente.—*s.* remache; forcejeo, lucha cuerpo a cuerpo (esp. en el boxeo); (fam.) abrazo estrecho.— —er [klínchœ(r)], *s.* remachador; clavo remachado; argumento decisivo.

cling [kliŋ], *vii.* [10] asirse, adherirse, pegarse.— —ing [klíŋiŋ], *a.* colgante, pendiente; adhesivo.

clinic [klínik], *s.* clínica.— —al [-al], *a.* clínico.

clinker [klíŋkœ(r)], *s.* escoria.—*vi.* formar escorias.

clip [klip], *vti.* [1] trasquilar; tijeretear; cercenar; podar; pellizcar; agarrar.— *s.* tijeretazo; recorte; trasquila; cantonera; grapa, pinza, sujetapapeles; pasador o broche (de presión).— —per [klípœ(r)], *s.* trasquilador; cercenador, recortador; maquinilla para cortar el pelo.—*pl.* tijeras de trasquilar.— —ping [-iŋ], *s.* trasquileo; recorte; cercenadura; tijereteo.—*pl.* recortes.

clique [klik], *s.* camarilla, compadraje.

cloak [klouk], *s.* capa, manto.—*vt.* encapotar; embozar; ocultar.— —room [klóukrum], *s.* guardarropa.

clock [klak], *s.* reloj (de mesa o pared). —*c. dial* o *face*, esfera.—*vt.* medir o contar el tiempo de un acto.— —maker [klákmeikœ(r)], —smith [-smiθ], *s.* relojero.— —wise [-waiz], *a.* y *adv.* en el sentido de las agujas del reloj.— —work [-wœrk], *s.* maquinaria del reloj.

clod [klad], *s.* terrón; necio, gaznápiro.

clog [klag], *vti.* [1] embarazar; obstruir, entorpecer; amontonar.—*vii.* apiñarse, atestarse; amontonarse; atorarse; obstruirse; atascarse.—*s.* traba, obstáculo; carga; chanclo, zueco.— *c. dance*, zapateado.

cloister [klóistœ(r)], *s.* claustro; monas-

terio.—vt. enclaustrar.— —ed [-d], a. enclaustrado.

close [klouz], vt. cerrar; tapar; terminar; levantar (una sesión); finiquitar (una cuenta).—vi. cerrar(se); unirse; terminar; fenecer.—to c. with, cerrar (con el adversario).—s. fin, terminación; caída (de la tarde); clausura; cierre; coto; parcela.—a. [klous], cerrado; apretado; justo; íntimo (amistad); sofocante; mal ventilado; cercano, próximo; tupido, compacto; inmediato; sucinto; oculto; reservado; restringido; tacaño; casi empatado; parejo; reñido (combate, etc.).—at c. range, a quema ropa, a boca de jarro.—adv. cerca, de cerca; estrechamente.—c. by, muy cerca.—c. to, junto a; arrimado o pegado a; a raíz de.— —d [klouzd], a. cerrado; concluso.—c. chapter, asunto concluído.— —ness [klóusnis], s. contigüidad; estrechez; falta de ventilación; firmeza; soledad; fidelidad (de copia o traducción).—close-out [klóuzaut], s. (com.) liquidación.—closet [klázit], s. armario, alacena; excusado, retrete.—a. secreto, confidencial.—vt. encerrar a uno para conferenciar a puerta cerrada.—close-up [klóusʌp], s. fotografía de primer plano.—closing [klóuziŋ], s. cierre; final, conclusión; clausura; remate (de cuentas).—a. de cierre; último; de clausura.—closure [klóuẑɹ(r)], s. clausura; cierre; fin, conclusión.

clot [klat], s. coágulo, grumo.—vii. [1] coagularse, engrumecerse.

cloth [kloθ], s. tela, paño, género, tejido.—c. binding, encuadernación en tela.—clothe [klouð], vti. [4] vestir; cubrir, arropar; revestir.—to c. with authority, investir de autoridad.—clothed [klouðd], pret. y pp. de TO CLOTHE.— —es [klouðz], s. pl. vestido, vestuario, indumentaria; ropaje, ropa de toda especie.—c. chest, ropero.—c. hanger, perchero.—c. moth, polilla.—c. rack, perchero.— —esline [klóuðzlajn], s. tendedera.— —espin [klóuðzpin], s. pinzas para colgar ropa; (Cuba) palitos de tendedera.—clothier [klóuðjœ(r)], s. comerciante o fabricante de ropa; pañero, ropero.—clothing [klóuðiŋ], s. vestidos, ropa; vestuario, indumentaria.

cloud [klaud], s. nube; nublado, nubarrón; muchedumbre, multitud.—under a c., desacreditado, sospechoso.—in the clouds, abstraído; en las nubes.—vt. anublar, nublar; enturbiar; abigarrar; empañar.—vi. nublarse, obscurecerse.— —iness [kláudjnis], s. nebulosidad, obscuridad.— —less [-lis], a. sin nubes, despejado,

claro.— —y [-i), a. nublado, encapotado; nebuloso; turbio; obscuro; lóbrego; (fot.) velado.

clove [klouv], s. clavo de especia.—c. of garlic, diente de ajo.—pret. de TO CLEAVE.—cloven [klóuvɐn], pp. de TO CLEAVE.

clover [klóuvœ(r)], s. trébol.—to be o live in c., vivir en la abundancia.

clown [klaun], s. payaso, bufón; gracioso.— —ish [kláuniŝ], a. rudo, zafio, grosero.

cloy [klɔj], vt. empalagar; hastiar, hartar.

club [klʌb], s. porra, garrote, tranca; tolete; club, círculo; centro de reunión; palo o maza de golf.—pl. bastos (de baraja).—c. law, la ley del más fuerte; gobierno tiránico.—c. steak, pequeño biftec.—vii. [1] contribuir a gastos comunes; unirse o juntarse para un mismo fin.—vti. aporrear, golpear con garrote, apalear.

cluck [klʌk], vt. y vi. cloquear.—s. cloqueo.

clue [klu], s. indicio, pista; norte, guía.

clump [klʌmp], s. tarugo; terrón; aglutinación, masa, grupo; pisada recia.—vt. y vi. aglutinar(se); andar torpemente con fuertes pisadas.

clumsy [klʌmzi], a. desmañado, chapucero; incómodo; difícil de manejar.

clung [klʌŋ], pret. y pp. de TO CLING.

cluster [klʌstœ(r)], s. racimo; ramillete; grupo; caterva; enjambre.—vi. agruparse, arracimarse.—vt. apiñar, amontonar.

clutch [klʌch], vt. agarrar; apretar; embragar.—to c. at, tratar de empuñar.—s. agarro, presa; uña, garra; nidada; embrague.

clutter [klʌtœ(r)], s. baraúnda, batahola; desorden, confusión.—V. CLATTER.—vi. alborotar, hacer ruido o estrépito.—vt. poner en desorden, trastornar.

coach [kouch], s. coche, carruaje; carroza; automóvil; (f.c.) vagón; maestro particular; (dep.) entrenador.—vt. adiestrar; aleccionar; entrenar.—vi. (dep.) entrenarse; servir de entrenador.— —er [kóuchœ(r)] s. preceptor; entrenador.— —man [-man], s. cochero.

coagulate [kouǽgjulejt], vt. y vi. coagular(se), cuajar(se).

coal [koul], s. carbón, hulla, antracita.—c. bin, carbonera.—c. brick, briqueta, carbón prensado.—c. dust, cisca.—c. tar, alquitrán de hulla.—vt. y vi. echar carbón; hacer carbón; proveer(se) de carbón.

coalition [koualíŝɐn], s. coalición, liga.

coarse [kors], a. basto, ordinario; tosco-vulgar; burdo.—c. file, lima de des-

bastar.— —ness [kɔ́rsnis], *s.* tosquedad; vulgaridad, grosería, rudeza.

coast [koṵst], *s.* costa, litoral.—*c. guard*, guarda de costas, servicio costanero; guardacostas.—*the c. is clear*, no hay moros en la costa.—*vt.* (mar.) costear.—*vi.* navegar a lo largo de la costa; deslizarse cuesta abajo.— —er [kóṵstœ(r)], *s.* piloto práctico; barco de cabotaje; habitante de la costa; deslizador.— —line [-lain], *s.* costa, litoral.

coat [koṵt], *s.* americana, chaqueta, saco; abrigo; pelo, lana, pelaje de los animales; funda, caperuza; revestimiento; capa o mano (de pintura, etc.).—*c. hanger*, perchero.—*c. of arms*, escudo de armas.—*to turn one's c.*, cambiar de casaca.—*vt.* vestir, revestir; dar una mano o capa de; azogar.— —ing [kóṵtiŋ], *s.* revestimiento, capa, mano (de pintura); enlucido.

coax [koṵks], *vt. y vi.* persuadir con halagos, engatusar.

cob [kab], *s.* tusa o carozo de maíz; jaca.

cobble [kábl], *s.* guijarro.

cobbler [káblœ(r)], *s.* zapatero de viejo, remendón; chapucero.

cobweb [kábweb], *s.* telaraña.

cocaine [koṵkéin], *s.* cocaína.

coccyx [káksiks], *s.* (anat.) coxis, rabadilla.

cock [kak], *s.* gallo; macho de ave; espita (de agua, etc.); percusor o martillo de armas de fuego.—*c.-eyed*, bizco; (fam.) extravagante, loco.—*c. robin*, petirrojo.—*vt.* montar o amartillar (un arma de fuego); ladear (el sombrero).—*vi.* engreírse, gallear.

cockatoo [kakatú], *s.* cacatúa.

cockfight(ing) [kákfait(iŋ)], *s.* riña o pelea de gallos.—cockfighter [kákfaitœ(r)], *s.* gallero.

cockpit [kákpit], *s.* (aer.) carlinga del avión; parte baja de popa de la cubierta (de un yate); cámara.

cockroach [kákroṵch], *s.* cucaracha.

cockscomb [kákskoṵm], *s.* cresta (de gallo); gorro de bufón; (Am.) moco de pavo.—cockspur [kákspœ(r)], *s.* espuela (de gallo), espolón.

cocktail [kákteil], *s.* coctel; aperitivo.—*c. shaker*, coctelera.

cocky [káki], *a.* arrogante, engreído.

cocoa [kóṵkoṵ], *s.* cacao molido o en polvo; bebida de cacao.

coconut [kóṵkonat], *s.* coco; cocotero.—*c. plantation*, cocal.

cocoon [koṵkún], *s.* capullo (del gusano de seda, etc.).

cod [kad], *s.* bacalao, abadejo.

coddle [kádl], *vt.* mimar, consentir.

code [koṵd], *s.* código; clave.

codeine [kóṵdin], *s.* codeína.

codfish [kádfiš], *s.* = COD.

codify [kádifai], *vt.* codificar, compilar leyes.

coefficient [koṵifíšent], *s.* coeficiente.

coerce [koṵérs], *vt.* forzar, obligar.— coercion [koṵéršon], *s.* coerción, coacción.

coexist [koṵigzíst], *vi.* coexistir.— —ence [-ens], *s.* coexistencia.

coffee [kófi], *s.* café.—*c. plantation*, cafetal.—*c. tree*, cafeto, café.— —house [-haus], *s.* café (establecimiento).— —pot [-pat], *s.* cafetera.

coffer [kófœ(r)], *s.* arca, cofre.

coffin [kófin], *s.* ataúd, féretro.

cog [kag], *s.* (mec.) diente o punto de rueda.— —wheel [kághwil], *s.* rueda dentada.

cohabitation [kouhæbitéišon], *s.* contubernio, cohabitación.

coherence [kohírens], coherency [kohírensi], *s.* coherencia.—coherent [kohírent], *a.* coherente.

cohesion [koṵhížon], *s.* cohesión, adhesión, unión.—cohesive [koṵhísiv], *a.* cohesivo, coherente, adherente.

coif [kóif], *s.* cofia, toca.

coiffure [kwafyúr], *s.* tocado, peinado.

coil [kojl], *s.* bobina, carrete; rosca; rollo; espiral de alambre.—*vt.* enrollar.—*vi.* enrollarse; enroscarse.

coin [kojn], *s.* moneda acuñada.—*vt.* acuñar; inventar, forjar (palabras, mentiras).— —age [kójnidž], *s.* acuñación; moneda; sistema monetario; invención.

coincide [koṵinsáid], *vi.* coincidir; estar de acuerdo.—coincidence [koṵínsidens], *s.* coincidencia.

coke [koṵk], *s.* cok (carbón).

colander [kʌ́lándœ(r)], *s.* colador; espumadera, escurridor.

cold [koṵld], *a.* frío; helado; indiferente.—*c. cream*, crema cosmética.—*c. cuts*, fiambres variados.—*c.-hearted*, insensible, impasible.—*s.* frío, frialdad; enfriamiento; resfriado, catarro, constipado.—*to catch c.*, resfriarse, acatarrarse.— —ness [kóṵldnis], *s.* frialdad; tibieza, indiferencia, despego.

colic [kálik], *s.* cólico.

coliseum [kalisíʌm], *s.* coliseo.

collaborate [kʌlǽboreit], *vt.* colaborar.— —collaboration [kʌlæboréišon], *s.* colaboración.—collaborator [kʌlǽboreitœ(r)], *s.* colaborador.

collapse [kʌlǽps], *s.* derrumbamiento; desplome; fracaso; colapso.—*vi.* derrumbarse, desplomarse; fracasar; sufrir un colapso.

collar [kálɑ(r)], *s.* cuello (de camisa, etc.); collar de perro; collera; aro.—*vt.* poner cuello, aro; agarrar del cuello, acogotar.

collateral [kǫlǽtęrǫl], *a.* colateral.—*s.* garantía, resguardo.

collation [kǫléjṣǫn], *s.* cotejo; (igl.) colación; merienda, colación.

colleague [kǎlig], *s.* colega.

collect [kǫlékt], *vt.* colectar, recaudar; coleccionar; (re)copilar.—*c. on delivery* (*C.O.D.*), entrega contra reembolso, cóbrese al entregar.—*to c. one's self*, volver en sí, reponerse.—*s.* [kálekt], colecta.— **—ion** [kǫléкṣǫn], *s.* colección; colecta; montón; recaudación; cobranza; reunión.— **—ive** [kǫléktjv], *s.* (gram.) nombre colectivo.—*a.* colectivo.— **—or** [kǫléktǫ(r)], *s.* coleccionista; colector; recaudador; cobrador.

college [kǎlidʒ], *s.* colegio universitario; escuela o facultad profesional.—*a.* de colegio; estudiantil.

collet [kǎljt], *s.* (mec.) collar, mandril; (joy.) engaste.

collide [kǫláid], *vi.* chocar, topar; contradecir, estar en conflicto.

collision [kǫlíʒǫn], *s.* colisión, choque; antagonismo.

colloquial [kǫlóuḳwiǫl], *a.* familiar, dialogal.— **—ism** [-ɪzm], *s.* expresión familiar.

Colombian [kǫlámbjǫn], *s. y a.* colombiano.

colon [kóulǫn], *s.* (gram.) dos puntos (:); (anat.) colon.

colonel [kǎrnǫl], *s.* coronel.

colonial [kǫlóuniǫl], *a.* colonial.— **—ist** [kálǫnjst], *s.* colono.— **—ize** [kálǫnajz], *vt.* colonizar, poblar.—*vi.* establecerse en colonia.— **—colony** [kálǫnj], *s.* colonia.

color [kálǫ(r)], *s.* color; colorido; (naipes) palo.—*pl.* colores nacionales.—*c.-blind*, daltoniano.—*vt.* color(e)ar; teñir; iluminar; embellecer.—*vi.* ruborizarse.— **—ed** [-d], *a.* de color; persona negra; engañoso, disfrazado; adornado.— **—ful** [-fụl], *a.* lleno de colorido; pintoresco.— **—ing** [-iŋ], *s.* colorante, color; coloración; estilo o aire particular; colorido.— **—less** [-ljs], *a.* descolorido; incoloro.

colossal [kǫlásǫl], *a.* colosal, descomunal.

colt [kóụlt], *s.* potro.

Columbian [kǫlámbjǫn], *a.* colombino, relativo a Colón.

column [kálʌm], *s.* columna.— **—ist** [kálʌm(n)jst], *s.* periodista encargado de una sección permanente.

comb [kóụm], *s.* peine; peineta; rastrillo; cresta de ave; panal de miel.—*vt.* peinar; cardar; rastrillar; escudriñar.

combat [kámbæt], *s.* combate.—*vt. y vi.* combatir.— **—ant** [kámbǫtǫnt], *s. y a.*

combatiente, luchador.— **—ive** [kʌmbǽtjv], *a.* combativo.

combination [kambjnéjṣǫn], *s.* combinación.— **—combine** [kǫmbájn], *vt. y vi.* combinar(se); mezclar(se); unir(se).

come [kʌm], *vii.* [10] venir, llegar; ir, acudir; provenir; aparecer, salir; acontecer.—*come in!* ¡entre(n)! ¡adelante!—*to c. about*, suceder.—*to c. across*, topar con.—*to c. back*, volver; retroceder.—*to c. by*, obtener; pasar junto a.—*to c. down*, bajar; descender. —*to c. down with*, enfermar de.—*to c. in*, entrar.—*to c. off*, desaparecer.— *to c. on*, seguir, progresar.—*to c. out*, salir, mostrarse.—*to c. over*, venir, cruzar.—*to c. through*, salir bien.—*to c. upon*, acometer, topar con.—*pp.* de TO COME.— **—back** [kámbæk], *s.* rehabilitación; regreso al puesto u oficio; respuesta aguda; motivo de queja.— **—down** [-daụn], *s.* revés de fortuna; humillación, chasco.

comedian [kǫmídjǫn], *s.* comediante, actor cómico.—*comedy* [kámędj], *s.* comedia.

comet [kámjt], *s.* cometa.

comfort [kámfǫrt], *s.* comodidad; consuelo; bienestar.—*vt.* confortar; consolar.— **—able** [-ǫbl], *a.* cómodo; consolador; adecuado.— **—er** [-œ(r)], *s.* edredón.— **—ing** [-iŋ], *a.* confortante.

comic [kámjk], *a.* cómico, gracioso, chistoso.—*a. y s.* bufo.—*s. pl.* tiras cómicas, historietas.

coming [kámjŋ], *s.* venida, llegada.—*a.* próximo, venidero.

comma [kámǎ], *s.* coma (,).

command [kǫmǽnd], *vt.* mandar, ordenar, disponer; acaudillar, capitanear. —*vi.* imperar; imponerse.—*s.* mando; mandato, orden; comandancia; comando.— **—er** [-œ(r)], *s.* comandante, jefe supremo.— **—ment** [-mǫnt], *s.* mandato, precepto.—*the Commandments*, los Mandamientos.

commemorate [kǫmémǫrejt], *vt.* conmemorar.— **—commemoration** [kǫmemoréjṣǫn], *s.* conmemoración.

commence [kǫméns], *vt. y vi.* comenzar, iniciar.— **—ment** [-mǫnt], *s.* comienzo; inauguración; acto de distribución de diplomas.

commend [kǫménd], *vt.* encomendar, recomendar; alabar.— **—able** [-ǫbl], *a.* loable.— **—ation** [kamǫndéjṣǫn], *s.* elogio, alabanza.

comment [kámɛnt], *vt. y vi.* comentar; glosar, anotar.—*s.* comentario.— **—ary** [kámęntęrj], *s.* comentario.— **—ator** [kámęntejtǫ(r)], *s.* comentarista.

commerce [kámœrs], *s.* comercio; trato.

—**commercial** [kọmœ́ršạl], *a.* comercial.

commiseration [kọmizẹréjšọn], *s.* piedad, conmiseración.

commissary [kámjserj], *s.* comisario, delegado.—**commission** [kọmíšọn], *s.* comisión; misión; encargo; nombramiento.—*commissioned officer*, oficial del ejército.—**commissioner** [kọmíšọnœ(r)], *s.* comisario; comisionado.

commit [kọmít], *vti.* [1] cometer, perpetrar; encargar, encomendar.—*to c. one's self*, comprometerse.—*to c. to memory*, aprender de memoria.—*to c. to prison*, encarcelar, encerrar.—*to c. to writing*, poner por escrito.—**ment** [-mẹnt], *s.* compromiso, obligación.

committee [kọmítj], *s.* comité, comisión, delegación.

commodity [kọmádjtj], *s.* comodidad; artículo de consumo; mercancía, género.

common [kámọn], *a.* común, corriente; vulgar, trivial; público, general, comunal; inferior.—*c. law*, derecho consuetudinario.—*c. sense*, sentido común.—*c. soldier*, soldado raso.—*s. pl.* ejido; refectorio; campo común.—**ness** [-njs], *s.* comunidad; frecuencia; vulgaridad.—**place** [-plejs], *a.* común, vulgar.—*s.* lugar común.—**weal** [-wil], *s.* el bien público.—**wealth** [-welθ], *s.* estado; nación; comunidad de naciones; cosa pública.

commotion [kọmóųšọn], *s.* conmoción.

commune [kọmjún], *vi.* comulgar; conversar, ponerse en contacto.—**communicate** [kọmjúnjkejt], *vti.* comunicar, dar parte de; contagiar; dar la comunión.—*vi.* comunicarse; tomar la comunión.—**communication** [kọmjunjkéjšọn], *s.* comunicación.—**communion** [kọmjúnyọn], *s.* comunión.

communism [kámyunjzm], *s.* comunismo.—**communist** [kámyunjst], *a.* y *s.* comunista.

community [kọmjúnjtj]. *s.* comunidad; vecindad; sociedad.

commuter [kọmjútœ(r)], *s.* abonado al ferrocarril; (elec.) conmutador.

compact [kámpækt], *s.* pacto, convenio; polvera de bolsillo; compresa.—*a.* [kọmpækt], compacto, conciso.

companion [kọmpǽnyọn], *s.* compañero; acompañante.—**ship** [-šjp], *s.* compañerismo; compañía.—**company** [kámpạnj], *s.* compañía; sociedad; visita.—*ship's c.*, tripulación.—*present c. excepted*, mejorando lo presente.

comparable [kámpạrạbl], *a.* comparable.—**comparative** [kọmpǽrạtjv], *a.* comparativo, relativo; comparado.—**compare** [kọmpér], *vt.* comparar; comprobar, cotejar; equiparar.—*vi.* poderse comparar; ser comparable;

ser igual.—*beyond c.*, sin igual o rival, sin par.—**comparison** [kọmpǽrjsọn], *s.* comparación, cotejo; equiparación; símil; metáfora.

compartment [kọmpártmẹnt], *s.* compartimiento; departamento; división, sección.

compass [kÁmpạs], *s.* compás de dibujo; brújula; circunferencia; alcance, ámbito.

compassion [kọmpǽšọn], *s.* compasión.—**ate** [-jt], *a.* compasivo, misericordioso.—*vt.* [-ejt], compadecer.

compatible [kọmpǽtjbl], *a.* compatible.

compatriot [kọmpéjtrjọt], *s.* y *a.* compatriota.

compel [kọmpél], *vti.* [1] compeler, obligar; dominar, someter.

compendium [kọmpéndiʌm], *s.* compendio, resumen.

compensate [kámpensejt], *vt.* compensar; indemnizar.—*vi.* compensar; (con *for*) igualar, equivaler.—**compensation** [kampenséjšọn], *s.* compensación; remuneración.

compete [kọmpít], *vi.* competir, rivalizar; (con *for*) disputarse.—**nce** [kámpẹtẹns], —**ncy** [kámpẹtẹnsj], *s.* competencia, suficiencia; subsistencia.—**nt** [kámpẹtẹnt], *a.* competente, adecuado, calificado.—**competition** [kampẹtíšọn], *s.* competición; rivalidad; certamen, concurso, oposición.—**competitive** [kọmpétjtjv], *a.* competidor, que compite.—**competitor** [kọmpétjtọ(r)], *s.* competidor, rival, opositor.

compilation [kampjléjšọn], *s.* compilación, recopilación.—**compile** [kọmpájl], *vt.* compilar, recopilar.

complacence [kọmpléjsẹns], **complacency** [kọmpléjsẹnsj], *s.* complacencia; presunción.—**complacent** [kọmpléjsẹnt], *a.* complaciente; satisfecho de sí mismo.

complain [kọmpléjn], *vi.* quejarse, lamentarse; querellarse.—**t** [-t], *s.* queja; lamento; querella; enfermedad.

complement [kámplẹmẹnt], *s.* complemento; accesorio.—*vt.* complementar, completar.

complete [kọmplít], *a.* completo.—*vt.* completar, rematar; perfeccionar.—**ness** [-njs], *s.* perfección, minuciosidad.—**completion** [kọmplíšọn], *s.* terminación; cumplimiento; completamiento.

complex [kámpleks], *a.* complejo, complicado.—*s.* complejo; obsesión.

complexion [kọmplékšọn], *s.* tez; cutis.

complexity [kọmpléksjtj], **complexness** [kọmpléksnjs], *s.* complejidad.

compliance [kọmplájạns], *s.* sumisión; complacencia; acatamiento; anuen-

cia.—*in c. with*, de acuerdo con, accediendo a.—**compliant** [kɔmpláiant], *a.* dócil, obediente; complaciente.

complicate [kámplikeit], *vt.* complicar, enredar.—*a.* complicado.— —d [kámplikeitid], *a.* complicado, enredado.— **complication** [kamplikéišən], *s.* complicación.

compliment [kámpliment], *s.* galantería, lisonja; piropo; fineza; cumplido.— *pl.* recados, memorias.—*vt.* piropear; cumplimentar; obsequiar.—*vi.* hacer cumplimientos.

comply [kɔmpláı], *vii.* [7] obedecer a; cumplir con.

component [kɔmpóunənt], *a. y s.* componente.

compose [kɔmpóuz], *vt.* componer; conciliar, sosegar.— —d [-d], *a.* sosegado, sereno; compuesto (de).— —r [-œ(r)], *s.* autor, compositor.—**composite** [kɔmpázit], *a.* compuesto; mixto.—*s.* compuesto, cosa compuesta; mixtura.—**composition** [kampozíšən], *s.* composición; tema; componenda.

composure [kɔmpóuƺü(r)], *s.* compostura, calma, sangre fría.

compote [kámpout], *s.* compota, dulce.

compound [kámpaund], *s.* compuesto; mezcla; palabra compuesta; cuerpo compuesto.—*a.* compuesto; mezclado.—*vt.* [kámpáund], componer, combinar, mezclar.—*vi.* avenirse, transigir.

comprehend [kamprihénd], *vt.* comprender; abarcar, incluir.—**comprehensible** [kamprihénsibl], *a.* comprensible, inteligible.—**comprehension** [kamprihénsən], *s.* comprensión. —**comprehensive** [kamprihénsiv], *a.* compre(he)nsivo, inclusivo; amplio; perspicaz.

compress [kɔmprés], *vt.* comprimir, apretar, condensar.—*s.* [kámpres], compresa.— —ion [kɔmpréšən], *s.* compresión.

comprise [kɔmpráiz], *vt.* incluir, contener, comprender; constar de.

compromise [kámpromaiz], *s.* compromiso, arreglo, avenencia.—*vt.* comprometer.—*vi.* avenirse, transigir, transar.

comptroller [kɔntróulœ(r)], *s.* interventor, contralor.

compulsion [kɔmpʌ́lšən], *s.* compulsión, apremio.—**compulsive** [kɔmpʌ́lsiv], *a.* compulsivo.—**compulsory** [kɔmpʌ́lsɔri], *a.* obligatorio.

compunction [kɔmpʌ́ŋkšən], *s.* compunción, remordimiento, escrúpulo.

computation [kampiutéišən], *s.* computación, cálculo.—**compute** [kɔmpiút], *vt.* computar, calcular.—**computer**

[kɔmpiútœ(r)], *s.* calculista; computador; máquina calculadora.

comrade [kámræd], *s.* camarada, compañero.— —**ship** [-šip], *s.* camaradería.

concave [kánkeiv], *a.* cóncavo.—**concavity** [kankæviti], *s.* concavidad.

conceal [kɔnsíl], *vt.* ocultar, esconder, encubrir.— —**ment** [-mɛnt], *s.* ocultación; encubrimiento.

concede [kɔnsíd], *vt.* conceder, admitir. —*vi.* asentir; convenir.

conceit [kɔnsít], *s.* presunción, engreimiento, ínfulas; vanagloria; concepto.— —**ed** [-id], *a.* vanidoso, engreído.

conceivable [kɔnsívabl], *a.* concebible. —**conceive** [kɔnsív], *vt. y vi.* concebir.

concentrate [kánsentreit], *vt.* (re)concentrar.—*vi.* reunirse.—*s.* substancia concentrada.— —d [kánsentreitid], *a.* concentrado.—**concentration** [kansentréišən], *s.* (re)concentración; recogimiento.

concept [kánsept], *s.* concepto.— —**ion** [kɔnsépšən], *s.* concepción.

concern [kɔnsœ́rn], *vt.* concernir; afectar; interesar; inquietar.—*s.* interés; inquietud; asunto; incumbencia; compañía, firma; importancia, consecuencia.—*of what c. is it to you?* ¿qué le importa? ¿qué más le da a Ud.?— —**ed** [-d], *a.* inquieto, preocupado; interesado; comprometido.—*as far as I am c.*, en cuanto a mí.— —**ing** [-iŋ], *prep.* por lo concerniente a, respecto a.

concert [kánsœrt], *s.* concierto.—*vt.* [kɔnsœ́rt], concertar.

concession [kɔnséšən], *s.* concesión, privilegio.— —**ary** [-eri], *s.* concesionario.—*a.* otorgado por concesión.

conch [kaŋk, kanch], *s.* caracol marino; concha; (arq.) concha.

conciliate [kɔnsílieit], *vt.* conciliar; apaciguar.—**conciliation** [kɔnsíliéišən], *s.* conciliación.—**conciliatory** [kɔnsíliatori], *a.* conciliatorio.

concise [kɔnsáis], *a.* conciso, sucinto.— —**ness** [-nis], *s.* concisión, laconismo.

conclude [kɔnklúd], *vt. y vi.* concluir(se).—**conclusion** [kɔnklúƺən], *s.* conclusión; decisión; deducción.—**conclusive** [kɔnklúsiv], *a.* concluyente; decisivo.

concord [kánkord], *s.* concordia; armonía; concordancia.— —**ance** [kankórdəns], *s.* concordancia, conformidad.

concrete [kánkrit], *a.* fraguado; cuajado; de hormigón.—*s.* concreto; hormigón; cemento.—*c. steel* o *reinforced c.*, hormigón armado.

concur [kɔnkœ́r], *vii.* [1] concurrir;

convenir con, estar de acuerdo; unirse, juntarse.

concussion [konkΛ́şọn], *s.* sacudida, golpe, conmoción.

condemn [kọndém], *vt.* condenar; expropiar.— **—ation** [kandemnéjşọn], *s.* condenación; confiscación.— **—atory** [kọndémnạtọrị], *a.* condenatorio.

condensation [kandenséjşọn], *s.* condensación.—**condense** [kọndéns], *vt.* y *vi.* condensar(se); reducirse.—**condenser** [kọndénsœ(r)], *s.* condensador.

condescend [kandịsénd], *vi.* condescender.—**condescencion** [kandịsénşọn], *s.* condescendencia.

condiment [kándịment], *s.* condimento.

condition [kọndíşọn], *s.* condición; estado; requisito; nota o calificación provisional.—*vt.* estipular; acondicionar; reprobar (en un examen).— **—al** [-ạl], *a.* condicional.

condole [kọndóụl], *vi.* condolerse, dar el pésame.— **—nce** [kọndóụlẹns], *s.* condolencia, pésame.

condor [kándọ(r)], *s.* cóndor.

conduce [kọndjús], *vi.* conducir a, favorecer, tender a.—**conducive** [kọndjúsịv], *a.* conducente, conveniente, apropiado.

conduct [kọndΛkt], *vt.* conducir, guiar; (mus.) dirigir.—*vr.* conducirse, comportarse.—*vi.* ser conductor; llevar la batuta.—*s.* [kándΛkt], conducta, comportamiento; manejo, conducción.— **—ion** [kọndΛ́kşọn], conducción.— **—or** [kọndΛ́ktọ(r)], *s.* conductor; director de orquesta; revisor o inspector de boletines.—**conduit** [kándịt], *s.* conducto, tubería, cañería.

cone [koụn], *s.* cono; cucurucho; barquillo.—*pine c.*, piña (del pino).

confection [kọnfékşọn], *s.* confección, hechura; confite, confitura.— **—er** [-œ(r)], *s.* confitero.— **—ery** [-erị], *s.* dulces, confites; confitería, repostería.

confederacy [kọnfédœrạsị], *s.* confederación.—**confederate** [kọnfédœrejt], *vt.* y *vi.* confederar(se).—*a.* y *s.* [kọnfédœrịt], confederado.—**confederation** [kọnfedœréjşọn], *s.* confederación.

confer [kọnfœr], *vii.* [1] conferenciar, tratar.—*vti.* conferir, otorgar.— **—ence** [kánfœrẹns], *s.* conferencia, deliberación, entrevista; el acto de conferir.

confess [kọnfés], *vt.* y *vi.* confesar(se).— **—ion** [kọnféşọn], *s.* confesión.— **—ional** [kọnféşọnal],—**ionary** [kọnféşọnerị], *s.* confes(i)onario.— **—or** [kọnféşọ(r)], *s.* confesor.

confidant [kanfịdǽnt], *s.* confidente.—

confide [kọnfáịd], *vt.* y *vi.* confiar(se), fiar(se).—**confidence** [kánfịdẹns], *s.* confianza; confidencia.—**confident** [kánfịdẹnt], *a.* cierto, seguro; confiado.—*s.* confidente.—**confidential** [kanfịdénşạl], *a.* confidencial.

confine [kọnfáịn], *vt.* y *vi.* confinar.—*to be confined in bed*, guardar cama.—*s.* *pl.* [kánfaịnz], confín, límite.— **—ment** [kọnfáịnment], *s.* confinamiento, encierro; restricción; ahogo.

confirm [kọnfœ́rm], *vt.* confirmar.— **—ation** [kanfœrméjşọn], *s.* confirmación; ratificación.

confiscate [kánfịskejt], *vt.* confiscar.

conflagration [kanflagréjşọn], *s.* conflagración.

conflict [kánfịkt], *s.* conflicto, choque, oposición.—*vi.* [kọnflíkt], luchar, estar en pugna.— **—ing** [kọnflíktịŋ], *a.* antagónico; contradictorio.

confluence [kánfluẹns], *s.* confluencia.

conform [kọnfórm], *vt.* y *vi.* conformar(se), ajustar(se).— **—ity** [kọndži-niélịtị], *s.* conformidad, concordancia; resignación.

confound [kọnfáụnd], *vt.* confundir, aturrullar; trabucar.— **—ed** [-ịd], *a.* maldito, condenado.

confront [kọnfrΛnt], *vt.* afrontar; confrontar; carear.

confuse [kọnfjús], *vt.* confundir.— **—d** [-d], *a.* confuso; confundido, turbado.—**confusing** [kọnfjúzịŋ], *a.* confuso, desconcertante.—**confusion** [kọnfjúžọn], *s.* confusión, desorden.

congeal [kọndžíl], *vt.* y *vi.* congelar(se), helar(se); cuajar(se).

congenial [kọndžínjạl], *a.* congenial; agradable, simpático.— **—ity** [kọndžiniélịtị], **—ness** [-nịs], *s.* simpatía, congenialidad.

congest [kọndžést], *vt.* y *vi.* congestionar(se), apiñar(se).— **—ed** [-ịd], *a.* congestionado, apiñado.— **—ion** [kọndžéschọn], *s.* congestión; apiñamiento.

congratulate [kọngrǽchulejt], *vt.* felicitar, congratular.—*to c. on*, felicitar por.—**congratulation** [kọngrǽchuléjşọn], *s.* felicitación, congratulación.

congregate [kángrịgejt], *vt.* y *vi.* congregar(se).—**congregation** [kaŋgrigéjşọn], *s.* congregación; asamblea, reunión; grey.

congress [káŋgrịs], *s.* convención, congreso, asamblea; (C.) Congreso, Parlamento.— **—ional** [kọngrésọnạl], *a.* perteneciente o relativo al congreso.— **—man** [káŋgrịsman],—**woman** [káŋgrịswụman], *s.* congresista, diputado; miembro de un congreso.

congruent [káŋgruẹnt], *a.* congruente.

conjecture [kọndžékohụr], *s.* conjetura.—*vt.* conjeturar.

conjugate [kándžugejt], *vt.* conjugar.—

49 CON—CON

conjugation [kandzugéiṣǫn], *s.* conjugación.—**conjunction** [kǫndʒʎnkṣǫn], *s.* conjunción; unión, liga.

conjuration [kandʒuréiṣǫn], *s.* conjuro; sortilegio, encantamiento.—**conjure** [kǫndʒúr], *vt.* rogar o pedir con instancia, conjurar; [kándʒu(r)], exorcizar.—*vi.* [kándʒu(r)], conjurar; escamotear, hacer juegos de mano.

connect [kǫnékt], *vt.* y *vi.* conectar(se), unir(se), acoplar(se); relacionar(se); comunicar(se); entroncar(se); empalmar(se).— **—ion** [kǫnékṣǫn], *s.* conexión; enlace; relación, parentesco.

connivance [kǫnáivǫns], *s.* connivencia.—**connive** [kǫnáiv], *vi.* hacer la vista gorda, tolerar.—**conniver** [kǫnáivœ(r)], *s.* consentidor, cómplice.

connoisseur [kanisǿr], *s.* conocedor, perito.

conquer [kánkœ(r)], *vt.* conquistar; vencer.—*vi.* triunfar.— **—ing** [-iŋ], *a.* conquistador, victorioso.— **—or** [-ǫ(r)], *s.* conquistador, vencedor.—**conquest** [kánkwest], *s.* conquista.

conscience [kánṣens], *s.* conciencia (moral).—**conscientious** [kanṣjénṣʌs], *a.* concienzudo.—**conscious** [kánṣʌs], *a.* consciente.—**consciousness** [kánṣʌsnis], *s.* conocimiento, sentido; conciencia.

conscript [kǫnskrípt], *vt.* reclutar, alistar.—*a.* y *s.* [kánskript], conscripto, recluta.— **—ion** [kǫnskrípṣǫn], *s.* conscripción, reclutamiento.

consecrate [kánṣekreit], *vt.* consagrar, santificar; ungir; dedicar; canonizar.—**consecration** [kanṣekréiṣǫn], *s.* consagración; dedicación; canonización.

consecutive [kǫnṣékyutiv], *a.* consecutivo, sucesivo.

consent [kǫnṣént], *s.* consentimiento, permiso, aquiescencia.—*by common c.*, de común acuerdo.—*vi.* consentir, acceder.

consequence [kánṣekwens], *s.* consecuencia; importancia.—**consequent** [kánṣekwent], *a.* y *s.* consecuente, consiguiente.

conservation [kanṣœrvéiṣǫn], *s.* conservación, preservación.—**conservative** [kǫnṣǿrvǫtiv], *s.* y *a.* conservador.—**conservatory** [kǫnṣǿrvǫtori], *s.* conservatorio, academia; invernadero.—**conserve** [kǫnṣǿrv], *vt.* conservar, preservar; hacer conserva.—*s.* [kánṣœrv], conserva, dulce.

consider [kǫnṣídœ(r)], *vt.* considerar; tratar con respeto.—*vi.* pensar, reflexionar.— **—able** [-ǫbl], *a.* considerable; notable.— **—ate** [-it], *a.* considerado, (muy) mirado.— **—ation** [-éiṣǫn], *s.* consideración, miramiento;

deliberación.— **—ing** [-iŋ], *prep.* en atención a, considerando que, visto que, etc.

consign [kǫnṣáin], *vt.* consignar; confiar, traspasar; relegar.— **—ment** [-mǫnt], *s.* (com.) consignación, partida, envío.

consist [kǫnṣíst], *vi.* consistir (en), constar (de).— **—ence** [-ǫns], **—ency** [-ǫnsi], *s.* consistencia; consecuencia; firmeza, estabilidad.— **—ent** [-ǫnt], *a.* consecuente, conveniente; armonizable; coherente, consistente, denso.

consistory [kǫnṣístori], *s.* consistorio; asamblea, congreso.

consolation [kanṣoléiṣǫn], *s.* consuelo.—**console** [kǫnṣóul], *vt.* consolar.—*s.* [kánṣoul], consola.

consolidate [kǫnṣálideit], *vt.* y *vi.* consolidar(se); unir(se); fundir(se).—**consolidation** [kǫnṣalidéiṣǫn], *s.* consolidación; unión; fusión.

consoling [kǫnṣóuliŋ], *a.* consolador.

consonant [kánṣonǫnt], *s.* y *a.* consonante.

consort [kánṣort], *s.* consorte, cónyuge.—*vi.* [kǫnṣórt], asociarse; armonizar.—*vt.* asociar, casar.

conspicuous [kǫnspíkyuʌs], *a.* conspicuo, eminente, notorio, manifiesto.

conspiracy [kǫnspírǫsi], *s.* conspiración, complot.—**conspirator** [kǫnspírǫtǫ(r)], *s.* conspirador.—**conspire** [kǫnspáir], *vi.* conspirar.—*vt.* maquinar, tramar.

constable [kánstǫbl], *s.* alguacil, agente de policía; condestable.

constancy [kánstǫnsi], *s.* constancia; lealtad.—**constant** [kánstǫnt], *a.* constante.—*s.* (mat.) constante.

constellation [kansteléiṣǫn], *s.* constelación.

consternation [kanstœrnéiṣǫn], *s.* consternación.

constipate [kánstipeit], *vt.* estreñir.—**constipation** [kanstipéiṣǫn], *s.* estreñimiento.

constituent [kǫnstítchuǫnt], *s.* elemento, ingrediente o componente.—*a.* constitutivo; constituyente (asamblea, etc.).—**constitute** [kánstitiut], *vt.* constituir, establecer.—**constitution** [kanstitiúṣǫn], *s.* constitución; complexión, naturaleza (de una persona); estatutos.—**constitutional** [kanstitiúṣǫnǫl], *a.* constitucional; constituyente.—*s.* (fam.) paseo higiénico.

constrain [kǫnstréin], *vt.* constreñir, compeler, forzar.— **—t** [-t], *s.* fuerza, constreñimiento.

construct [kǫnstrʎkt], *vt.* construir; fabricar.— **—ion** [kǫnstrʎkṣǫn], *s.* construcción.— **—ive** [kǫnstrʎktiv], *a.* constructivo; provechoso, de utilidad positiva.

construe [kɔnstrū], *vt.* interpretar, explicar; inferir; construir, componer.

consul [kánsʌl], *s.* cónsul.— **—ar** [kánsiulǎ(r)], *a.* consular.— **—ate** [kánsiulit], *s.* consulado.

consult [kɔnsʌlt], *vt.* consultar.—*vi.* asesorarse, consultarse, aconsejarse (con); conferenciar.— **—ant** [-ǝnt], **—er** [-œ(r)], *s.* consultante, consultor.— **—ation** [kansʌltéiʃǝn], *s.* consulta(ción), junta; deliberación.

consume [kɔnsiúm], *vt.* y *vi.* consumir(se).— **—r** [kɔnsiúmœ(r)], *s.* consumidor.

consummate [kánsʌmeit], *vt.* consumar, acabar, completar.—*a.* [kansámit], consumado.—**consummation** [kansʌméiʃǝn], *s.* consumación.

consumption [kɔnsʌmpʃǝn], *s.* consunción; consumo, gasto; tisis.—**consumptive** [kɔnsʌmptiv], *a.* consuntivo, destructivo.—*s.* y *a.* tísico.

contact [kántækt], *s.* contacto.—*pl.* relaciones.—*vt.* y *vi.* tocar(se), poner(se) en contacto.

contagion [kɔntéidʒǝn], *s.* contagio; infección, peste.—**contagious** [kɔntéidʒʌs], *a.* contagioso.

contain [kɔntéin], *vt.* contener, caber, tener cabida para; abarcar; reprimir; ser exactamente divisible.— **—er** [-œ(r)], *s.* recipiente, vasija, envase.

contaminate [kɔntǽmineit], *vt.* contaminar; viciar.—**contamination** [kɔntæminéiʃǝn], *s.* contaminación.

contemplate [kántempleit], *vt.* contemplar; proyectar, tener la intención de.—**contemplation** [kantempléiʃǝn], *s.* contemplación, especulación; intención, proyecto.

contemporary [kɔntémporeri], *a.* y *s.* contemporáneo, coetáneo.

contempt [kɔntémpt], *s.* desprecio, menosprecio, desdén.—*c. of court*, (for.) contumacia; rebeldía.— **—ible** [-ibl], *a.* despreciable, desdeñable.— **—uous** [kɔntémpchuʌs], *a.* desdeñoso, despreciativo.

contend [kɔnténd], *vt.* sostener o afirmar.—*vi.* contender.— **—er** [-œ(r)], *s.* contendiente, competidor.

content [kɔntént], *a.* contento, satisfecho.—*vt.* (com)placer, contentar.— *s.* contento, satisfacción; [kántent], cantidad, proporción; volumen.—*pl.* contenido.—*table of contents*, índice general.— **—ed** [kɔnténtid], *a.* contento, placentero.

contention [kɔnténʃǝn], *s.* contención, contienda; argumento; aseveración; tema.

contentment [kɔnténtment], *s.* contentamiento, satisfacción.

contest [kántest], *s.* contienda, debate; certamen, competencia; litigio.—*vt.*

[kɔntést], disputar; discutir; litigar.—*vi.* contender; competir; rivalizar con.—**contestant** [kɔntéstǝnt], *s.* contendiente, opositor; litigante.

context [kántekst], *s.* contexto.

contiguous [kɔntígiuʌs], *a.* contiguo.

continent [kántinent], *s.* continente.—*a.* casto, continente.— **—al** [kantinéntǝl], *a.* continental.

contingency [kɔntíndʒensi], *s.* contingencia.—**contingent** [kɔntíndʒent], *a.* y *s.* contingente.

continual [kɔntíniuǝl], *a.* continuo, incesante.—**continuance** [kɔntíniuǝns], *s.* (for.) aplazamiento; continuación.—**continuation** [kɔntiniuéiʃǝn], *s.* continuación, prolongación.—**continue** [kɔntíniu], *vt.* continuar; mantener, prolongar; (for.) aplazar.—*vi.* continuar; durar; proseguir.—**continuity** [kantiniúiti], *s.* continuidad; coherencia.—**continuous** [kɔntíniuʌs], *a.* continuo, ininterrumpido.

contour [kántur], *s.* contorno; curva de nivel.—*vt.* contorn(e)ar, perfilar.

contraband [kántrǎbænd], *s.* contrabando.— *a.* prohibido, ilegal.— **—ist** [-ist], *s.* contrabandista.

contract [kántrækt], *s.* contrato, convenio, pacto, ajuste; contrata.—*vt.* [kɔntrǽkt], contratar, pactar; contraer (enfermedad, deuda, etc.).—*vi.* contraerse, encogerse; comprometerse por contrato.— **—ion** [kɔntrǽkʃǝn], *s.* contracción, encogimiento, estrechamiento.— **—or** [kɔntrǽktǝ(r)], *s.* contratista.

contradict [kantrǎdíkt], *vt.* contradecir, desmentir, llevar la contraria a.— **—ion** [kantrǎdíkʃǝn], *s.* contradicción.— **—ory** [kantradíktori], *a.* contradictorio; contrario.

contrary [kántreri], *a.* contrario; testarudo, porfiado.—*c.-minded*, de diversa opinión.—*s.* contrario.—*on the c.*, al contrario.

contrast [kántræst], *s.* contraste, contraposición.—*vt.* y *vi.* [kɔntrǽst], contrastar.

contribute [kɔntríbiut], *vt.* y *vi.* contribuir.—**contribution** [kantribiúʃǝn], *s.* contribución; colaboración literaria, donativo.—**contributor** [kɔntríbiutǝ(r)], *s.* colaborador, contribuidor.

contrite [kántrait], *a.* contrito.—**contrition** [kɔntríʃǝn], *s.* contrición.

contrivance [kɔntráivʌns], *s.* idea, plan, invención; artefacto, dispositivo; traza, artificio; estratagema.—**contrive** [kɔntráiv], *vt.* idear, inventar; tramar, urdir.—*vi.* darse maña o trazas (de); maquinar.

control [kɔntróul], *s.* mando, dirección, dominio; influencia predominante;

regulación, inspección; restricción.—
pl. mandos, controles.—*a.* regulador;
de gobierno; de comprobación.—*vti.*
[1] controlar, gobernar, dirigir, regular; tener a raya; tener predominan-
cia en; reprimir, restringir.— —ler
[-œ(r)], *s.* interventor, registrador,
contralor; aparato de manejo y
control.

controversy [kántrovœrsi], *s.* controversia, debate.

contumacy [kántjumạsi], *s.* contumacia,
terquedad.

contusion [kontúẓọn], *s.* contusión.

convalesce [kanvalés], *vi.* convalecer.—
—**nce** [kanvalésẹns], *s.* convalecencia.— —**nt** [kanvalésẹnt], *a.* y *s.*
convaleciente.

convene [kọnvín], *vt.* convocar, citar;
emplazar.—*vi.* reunirse.—**convenience** [kọnvínyẹns], **conveniency**
[kọnvínyẹnsi], *s.* comodidad, conveniencia.—*at one's earliest convenience*, en la primera oportunidad
que uno tenga, tan pronto como sea
posible.—**convenient** [kọnvínyẹnt],
a. conveniente.

convent [kánvẹnt], *s.* convento, monasterio.

convention [kọnvénŝọn], *s.* convención,
congreso; convenio; costumbre; convencionalismo.— —**al** [-ạl], *a.* convencional.

conversant [kánvœrsạnt], *a.* versado,
experto, entendido.—**conversation**
[kanvœrséiŝọn], *s.* conversación, plática.—**converse** [kọnvœrs], *vi.* conversar.—*a.* [kánvœrs], inverso, contrario.—*s.* (fam.) conversa; (lóg.)
inversa, recíproca.

conversion [kọnvœrẓọn], *s.* conversión.
—**convert** [kọnvœrt], *vt.* convertir;
transmutar; reducir a; cambiar
(valores).—*vi.* convertirse, transformarse.—*s.* [kánvœrt], neófito, con-
verso. **convertible** [kọnvœrtibl], *a.*
convertible, conversible.

convex [kánveks], *a.* convexo.

convey [kọnvéi], *vt.* conducir, acarrear,
transportar; transferir; transmitir;
comunicar; dar a entender.— —**ance**
[-ạns], *s.* vehículo, conducción;
transmisión; traspaso; escritura de
traspaso.

convict [kánvikt], *s.* reo convicto;
presidiario.—*vt.* [kọnvikt], condenar;
probar la culpabilidad.— —**ion** [kọn-
víkŝọn], *s.* convicción; fallo condenatorio.

convince [kọnvíns], *vt.* convencer.—
convincing [kọnvínsiŋ], *a.* convincente.

convocation [kanvokéiŝọn], *s.* convocación, llamamiento.—**convoke** [kọn-
vóuk], *vt.* convocar, citar.

convoy [kọnvói], *vt.* escoltar, convoyar.
—*s.* [kánvoi], convoy, escolta.

convulsion [kọnválŝọn], *s.* convulsión.
—**convulsive** [kọnválsiv], *a.* convulsivo.

coo [ku], *s.* arrullo.—*vi.* arrullar, decir
ternezas.

cook [kụk], *vt.* y *vi.* cocinar, cocer, guisar.—*to c. up*, tramar, urdir.—*what's
cooking?* (fam.) ¿qué se trama? ¿qué
pasa?—*s.* cocinero, cocinera.— —**ery**
[kúkœri], *s.* arte de la cocina.— —**ie**
[i], —**y** [i], *s.* gallet(it)a, bizcochito.—
—**ing** [iŋ], *s.* arte culinario; cocción.
—*a.* de la cocina.—*c. pan*, cacerola,
cazuela.

cool [kul], *a.* fresco; frío, indiferente;
sereno.—*c.-headed*, sereno.—*s.* frescura.—*vt.* enfriar, refrescar.—*to c.
one's heels*, hacer antesala, esperar
mucho tiempo.—*vi.* enfriarse, calmarse.— —**er** [kúlœ(r)], *s.* enfriadera;
enfriadero; refrigerante; nevera.—
—**ing** [-iŋ], *a.* refrescante, refrigerante.—*s.* enfriamiento, refrigeración.— —**ness** [-nis], *s.* frialdad;
sangre fría; tibieza, despego.

coon [kun], *s.* mapache o coatí.—*old c.*,
viejo marrullero.

coop [kup], *s.* jaula.—*chicken c.*, gallinero.—*vt.* (in o up) enjaular, encerrar.

coöperate [koápẹreit], *vi.* cooperar.—
coöperation [koapẹréiŝọn], *s.* cooperación.—**coöperative** [koápẹrạtiv], *a.*
cooperativo, cooperante.—*s.* cooperativa.—**coöperator** [koápẹreitọ(r)], *s.*
cooperador.

coördinate [koórdineit], *vt.* coordinar.—
s. [koórdinit], igual, semejante;
coordenada.—*a.* coordenado; relativo
a las coordenadas.—**coördination**
[koordinéiŝọn], *s.* coordinación.

cop [kap], *s.* (fam.) polizonte.—*vti.* [1]
hurtar.

copartner [koupártnœ(r)], *s.* (con)so-
cio; copartícipe.

cope [koup], *vi.* hacer frente a, habérselas con.—*I cannot c. with this*, no
puedo con esto.

copilot [koupáilọt], *s.* copiloto, segundo
piloto.

copious [kóupiʌs], *a.* copioso, abundante.

copper [kápœ(r)], *s.* cobre; (fam.)
policía.—*a.* de cobre, cobrizo.—
—**smith** [kápœrsmiθ], *s.* calderero.

copulation [kapyụléiŝọn], *s.* cópula o
coito; unión.

copy [kápi], *s.* copia; ejemplar (de una
obra); imitación; número de un
periódico.—*c. book*, copiador (para
cartas, cuentas, etc.); libreta, cuaderno.—*vti.* y *vii.* [7] copiar; imitar.—
—**right** [-rait], *s.* derechos de propiedad (literaria, etc.).—*vt.* obtener la

propiedad literaria.— **—righted** [raj-tid], *a.* derechos registrados.

cord [kord], *s.* cordel, cuerda; tendón.

cordial [kórdźạl], *s.* cordial, tónico.—*a.* cordial, sincero.— **—ity** [kordźélịtị], *s.* cordialidad.

cordovan [kórdovạn], *s.* cordobán.— (C.), *a.* y *s.* cordobés.

corduroy [kórdᶙroj], *s.* pana.

core [kọr], *s.* centro, corazón, parte central; fondo, núcleo.—*vt.* quitar el corazón o centro; despepitar (fruta).

cork [kork], *s.* corcho; tapón de corcho.—*vt.* tapar con corcho.— **—screw** [kórkskru], *s.* tirabuzón, sacacorchos.

corn [korn], *s.* maíz; grano, cereal; callo (de los pies o manos).—*c. cob*, mazorca.—*vt.* salar, curar; granular.— **—ed** [-d], *a.* acecinado, curado.—*c. beef*, cecina.

corner [kórnœ(r)], *s.* esquina; rincón; recodo; aprieto o apuro; monopolio.—*c. bracket*, rinconera.—*to cut corners*, echar por el atajo, atajar; economizar.—*to drive into a c.*, poner entre la espada y la pared.—*vt.* arrinconar, acorralar, poner en aprieto; copar; monopolizar.— **—ed** [-d], *a.* anguloso, esquinado; acorralado, en aprietos; copado.— **—stone** [-stoᶙn], *s.* piedra angular; primera piedra.— **—wise** [-wajz], *adv.* diagonalmente.

cornet [kornét], *s.* corneta; cornetín.

cornice [kórnịs], *s.* cornisa.

corny [kórnị], *a.* de maíz; de trigo; calloso; (coll.) afectado, exageradamente sentimental; inferior, de mala calidad o gusto; manido.

corolla [korálạ], *s.* (bot.) corola.— **—ry** [kárọlerị], *s.* corolario.

coronation [karonéịşọn], *s.* coronación.

coroner [káronœ(r)], *s.* médico forense.

corporal [kórporạl], *a.* corporal, corpóreo.—*s.* (mil.) cabo.

corporation [korporéịşọn], *s.* corporación; sociedad mercantil; cuerpo, sociedad, gremio.

corps [koᶙr], *s.* cuerpo o grupo organizado.—*army c.*, cuerpo de ejército.

corpse [korps], *s.* cadáver.

corpuscle [kórpʌsl], *s.* corpúsculo.

corral [korrél], *vt.* acorralar.—*s.* corral.

correct [korékt], *vt.* corregir; reprender; castigar; reparar, remediar.—*a.* exacto; correcto.— **—ion** [korékşọn], *s.* enmienda, corrección.— **—ional** [korékşọnạl], *a.* correccional, penal.— **—ness** [koréktnịs], *s.* corrección.— **—or** [-ọ(r)], *s.* revisor, corrector.

correlate [kórelejt], *vt.* correlacionar.—*vi.* tener correlación.—**correlative** [korélạtịv], *a.* y *s.* correlativo.—**correlation** [koreléịşọn], *s.* correlación.

correspond [korẹspánd], *vi.* corresponder; mantener correspondencia.— **—ence** [-ẹns], **—ency** [-ẹnsị], *s.* correspondencia; reciprocidad.— **—ent** [-ẹnt], *a.* correspondiente.—*s.* corresponsal, correspondiente.

corridor [kárịdọ(r)], *s.* corredor, galería, pasillo.

corroborate [koráborejt], *vt.* corroborar, confirmar.—**corroboration** [koraboréịşọn], *s.* corroboración.

corrode [koróᶙd], *vt.* y *vi.* corroer(se).—**corrosive** [koróᶙsịv], *a.* corrosivo; mordaz.

corrugation [karugéịşọn], *s.* corrugamiento; contracción.

corrupt [korʌpt], *a.* corrompido; depravado.—*vt.* corromper.—*vi.* corromperse, podrirse.— **—ion** [korʌpşọn], *s.* corrupción.

cortege [kortéź], *s.* comitiva, séquito.

cortisone [kórtịsoᶙn], *s.* cortisona.

corvette [korvét], *s.* (mar.) corbeta.

cosmetic [kazmétịk], *a.* y *s.* cosmético.

cosmic(al) [kázmịk(ạl)], *a.* cósmico.

cosmopolitan [kazmopálịtạn], **cosmopolite** [kazmápolajt], *a.* y *s.* cosmopolita.

cost [kost], *s.* costo, coste, costa; precio, importe.—*at all costs*, a toda costa.—*vi.* [9] costar.—*pret.* y *pp.* de TO COST.— **—liness** [kóstlịnịs], *s.* suntuosidad, carestía.— **—ly** [-lị], *a.* costoso, caro.

costume [kástịum], *s.* vestuario; disfraz.

cot [kat], *s.* cabaña, choza; catre, camilla.

coterie [kóᶙterị], *s.* camarilla, claque.

cottage [kátịdź], *s.* casita, cabaña, choza; casa de campo.—*c. cheese*, requesón.

cotton [kátọn], *s.* algodón (planta y fibra); ropa o género de algodón.—*c. belt*, (E.U.), región algodonera.—*c. wool*, algodón en rama.—*c. yarn*, hilaza.

couch [kauch], *s.* diván.

cough [kọf], *s.* tos.—*c. drop*, pastilla para la tos.—*whooping c.*, tosferina.—*vi.* toser.—*to c. up*, expectorar; (fam.) pagar.— **—ing** [kófịŋ], *s.* acceso de tos.

could [kud], *pret.* de CAN.

council [káunsịl], *s.* concilio; consejo; concejo.—*city c.*, consejo municipal.—*c. of war*, consejo de guerra.—**man** [-mạn], *s.* concejal.— **(l)or** [-ọ(r)], *s.* concejal; consejero.

counsel [káunsẹl], *s.* consejo; deliberación; dictamen; abogado consultor.—*vti.* [2] aconsejar, recomendar; asesorar.— **—(l)or** [-ọ(r)], *s.* consultor; asesor.—*c. at law*, abogado.

count [kaunt], *vt.* contar, numerar, calcular.—*vi.* valer.—*to count on o*

upon, contar con, confiar en.—s. cuenta, cómputo; conde; acusación, cargo.

countenance [káuntęnąns], s. semblante, cara; talante, aspecto.—out of c., desconcertado.—to give c. apoyar, favorecer.—vt. aprobar; apoyar.

counter [káuntœ(r)], s. mostrador, tablero; ficha; contador.—adv. contra, al contrario, en contra.—to run c. to, oponerse, violar.—a. contrario. —vt. contradecir; rechazar; prevenir. —vi. oponerse.

counteract [kauntœrǽkt], vt. contrariar; neutralizar, contrarrestar.

counterattack [kauntœratǽk], vt. y vi. contraatacar, hacer un contraataque. —s. contraataque.

counterbalance [kauntœrbǽląns], vt. contrapesar, compensar.—s. [káuntœrbǽląns], contrapeso, equilibrio, compensación.

counterfeit [káuntœrfįt], vt. falsificar.— s. falsificador, moneda falsa.—a. falsificado.—**counterfeiter** [káuntœrfįtœ(r)], s. falsificador, monedero falso.

countermand [kauntœrmǽnd], s. contraorden.—vt. revocar.

countermarch [káuntœrmarch], s. contramarcha.

counterpart [káuntœrpart], s. contraparte.

counterpoint [káuntœrpojnt], s. contrapunto.

counterrevolution [kauntœrrevoliúšon], s. contrarrevolución.

counterstroke [káuntœrstrouk], s. contragolpe.

countess [káuntįs], s. condesa.

countless [káuntlįs], a. innumerable, sin cuento.

country [kántri], s. país, nación; región, tierra, patria; campo.—a. campestre. — —man [-mąn], s. compatriota, coterráneo; campesino, aldeano.— —side [-sajd], s. campo; distrito rural.

county [káunti], s. condado, jurisdicción.—c. seat, cabecera de distrito o jurisdicción.

couple [kǽpl], s. pareja, par.—vt. acoplar, (a)parear.—vi. acoplarse, formar pareja.—**coupling** [kǽpliŋ], s. acoplamiento; cópula; unión, junta.

courage [kǽrįdƷ], s. coraje, valor.— —ous [kʌréjdƷʌs], a. corajudo, valiente, valeroso.— —ousness [kʌréjdƷʌsnįs], s. valor, brío.

courier [kúrjœ(r)], s. mensajero, propio.

course [kors], s. curso; marcha; rumbo, dirección; progreso.—in due c., a su tiempo.—matter of c., cosa de cajón, de rutina.—of c., por supuesto, desde luego, etc.

court [kort], s. tribunal de justicia, juzgado, corte, audiencia; pista, cancha, campo de juego (tenis, etc.); séquito; patio, plazoleta; cortejo, galanteo.—to pay c. to, hacer la corte a.—to put out of c., demostrar la falsedad de.—vt. cortejar, galantear; atraerse, captar.

courteous [kœ́rtjʌs], a. cortés.—**courtesy** [kœ́rtęsi], s. cortesía; reverencia.

courtier [kórtjœ(r)], s. cortesano; palaciego.

courtship [kórtšip], s. cortejo, galanteo.

courtyard [kórtyard], s. patio, atrio.

cousin [kázin], s. primo o prima.— first c., primo hermano o carnal.

couturier [kutųrỵé], s. modisto.

cove [kouv], s. cala, ensenada.

covenant [kávęnąnt], s. contrato, convenio, pacto; escritura de contrato.

cover [kávœ(r)], vt. cubrir; tapar, ocultar; cobijar, proteger; forrar; abarcar; recorrer (distancias, etc.); empollar; ponerse el sombrero; (con up) encubrir.—s. cubierta, tapa; forro; envoltura; capa, pretexto; albergue; cubierto; funda; cobertor, tapete.— c. charge, (precio de) cubierto (en restaurantes, etc.).—to take c., buscar abrigo.- —ing [-iŋ], s. funda, cubierta; envoltura; ropa, abrigo.— —t [kávœrt], a. encubierto, disimulado.

covet [kávįt], vt. codiciar.- —ous [-ʌs], a. codicioso.

cow [kau], s. vaca; hembra de otros cuadrúpedos grandes (elefantes, etc.).— —vt. acobardar, intimidar.

coward [káuạrd], a. y s. cobarde.- —ice [-įs], —liness [-lįnįs], s. cobardía.

cowbell [káubel], s. cencerro.—**cowboy** [káuboj], s. vaquero, montero.

cower [káuœ(r)], vi. agacharse; aplastarse de miedo.

cowhide [káuhajd], s. cuero, vaqueta.

cowpox [káupaks], s. vacuna.—**cowshed** [káušed], s. establo de vacas.

coxcomb [kákskoum], s. petimetre.

coy [koj], **coyish** [kójįš], a. recatado, modesto; tímido.

cozy, cozey [kóuzi], a. cómodo, agradable.

crab [kræb], s. cangrejo; (fig.) cascarrabias.—c. apple, manzana silvestre. —a. agrio, áspero.—vii. [1] regañar, estar de mal humor; pescar crustáceos.

crack [kræk], s. grieta, rajadura; crujido, chasquido; trueno, estampido; chanza.—at the c. of dawn, al romper el día.—a. de calidad superior.—c. shot, tirador certero.—vt. romper; rajar; chasquear, restallar; crujir; trastornar.—to c. jokes, gastar bromas.—vi. agrietarse; rajarse, partirse; traquetear.- —ed [-t], a. agrietado,

cuarteado; chiflado; (voz) cascada, desapacible.— —er [krǽkœ(r)], s. galleta, bizcocho; triquitraque.— —le [krǽkl], vt. hacer crujir.—vi. crujir, crepitar, restallar.—s. crujido, crepitación.

cradle [kréidl], s. cuna.—vt. acunar.—vi. mecerse en la cuna.

craft [kræft], s. artificio; maña, habilidad; arte u oficio; gremio; embarcación, embarcaciones.— —sman [krǽftsmən], s. artífice, artesano.— —y [-i], a. astuto, taimado.

crag [kræg], s. despeñadero, risco.— —gy [krǽgi], a. escarpado.

cram [kræm], vti. y vii. [1] rellenar(se), hartar(se), atracar(se); cebar(se); (fig.) preparar(se) rápidamente para un examen.

cramp [kræmp], s. calambre; grapa.—a. contraído, apretado.—vt. comprimir, apretar; estrechar; sujetar con grapa.

cranberry [krǽnberi], s. arándano agrio de los pantanos.

crane [krein], s. grulla; grúa.—vt. levantar con la grúa; estirar, extender (el cuello).—vi. estirarse, alargarse.

cranium [kréiniʌm], s. cráneo.

crank [krænk], s. manija, manubrio; biela; cigüeña, manivela; maniático, caprichoso; capricho, chifladura.— c. axle, cigüeñal.— —case [krǽnkkeis], s. cárter del cigüeñal.— —shaft [-šæft], s. cigüeñal.— —y [-i], a. chiflado.

cranny [krǽni], s. grieta, resquicio.

crape [kreip], s. = CREPE.

crash [kræš], vi. romperse, caerse estrepitosamente, estrellarse; estallar; quebrar; aterrizar violentamente.—vt. romper o despedazar estrepitosamente, estrellar; echar a pique.—to c. the gate, colarse.—s. estallido, estampido, estrépito; quiebra; aterrizaje violento; choque, estrellamiento.

crate [kreit], s. canasto, jaula de embalaje; huacal.—vt. embalar (en huacales, etc.).

crater [kréitœ(r)], s. cráter.

cravat [krəvǽt], s. corbata; chalina.

crave [kreiv], vt. anhelar, desear; apetecer vehementemente.—vi. pedir o desear con vehemencia, suspirar por.

craven [kréivin], a. cobarde.

crawl [krol], vi. arrastrarse, andar a gatas; serpear; humillarse; ir a paso de tortuga.—s. arrastramiento; natación marinera.

crayon [kréiɔn], s. lápiz de color, creyón; tiza; dibujo al pastel.

craze [kreiz], vt. y vi. enloquecer(se).—s. locura, manía; moda.— —d [-d], a.

enloquecido, loco.—crazy [kréizi], a. loco.

creak [krik], vi. crujir, rechinar, chirriar.—s. crujido, rechinamiento.

cream [krim], s. crema, nata.—cold c., crema cosmética.—vi. criar nata.—vt. desnatar.— —ery [krímœri], s. lechería.— —y [-i], a. cremoso.

crease [kris], s. pliegue; arruga; raya (del pantalón, etc.).—vt. y vi. plegar(se); arrugar(se).

create [kriéit], vt. crear o criar.—creation [kriéišɔn], s. creación.—creative [kriéitiv], a. creador.—creativeness [kriéitivnis], s. facultad creadora.—creator [kriéitɔ(r)], s. creador.—the C., el Creador, Dios.—creature [kríchʊ(r)], s. criatura.

creche [kréis], s. (igl.) belén, nacimiento.

credence [krídəns], s. creencia; crédito.—credentials [krədénsəlz], s. pl. cartas credenciales.

credit [krédit], s. crédito, fe; (com.) activo, haber.—on c., al fiado, a plazos.—vt. creer; atribuir; reconocer; acreditar; abonar en cuenta; dar al fiado.— —able [-əbl], a. estimable, loable.— —ed [-id], a. acreditado.— —or [-ɔ(r)], s. acreedor.

credulous [krédjuləs], a. crédulo.

creed [krid], s. credo, creencia.

creek [krik], s. cala; riachuelo, arroyo.

creep [krip], vii. [10] arrastrarse; gatear; trepar; moverse cautelosamente; someterse abyectamente.—s. arrastramiento.—pl. hormigueo; pavor.— —er [krípœ(r)], s. reptil; enredadera; trepadora, trepador.

cremate [krímeit], vt. incinerar.

cremation [krɨméišɔn], s. incineración.

creole [kríoʊl], s. y a. criollo.

crepe [kreip], s. crespón, cendal.

crept [krept], pret. y pp. de TO CREEP.

crepuscular [krepʌ́skjulə(r)], a. crepuscular.—crepuscule [krepʌ́skjul], s. crepúsculo.

crescent [krésənt], a. creciente.—s. (cuarto) creciente; media luna.

cress [kres], s. mastuerzo, berro.

crest [krest], s. cresta, penacho; cima; blasón.— —fallen [kréstfolən], a. cabizbajo, abatido.

cretonne [krítan], s. (tej.) cretona.

crevice [krévis], s. hendedura, grieta, rendija.

crew [kru], s. tripulación o dotación; marinería; cuadrilla de obreros.—pret. de TO CROW.

crib [krib], s. pesebre; camita de niño; granero; arcón; casucha; plagio.—vti. [1] hurtar; plagiar; enjaular; estribar.

cricket [kríkit], s. grillo; cri(c)quet.

crime [kraim], s. crimen, delito.—

criminal [krímjnąl], *a.* y *s.* criminal.

crimp [krimp], *vt.* rizar, encrespar, engrifar.—*a.* rizado.—*s.* rizo.

crimson [krímzǫn], *a.* y *s.* carmesí.

cripple [krípl], *s.* cojo o manco; tullido. —*vt.* lisiar, derrengar, baldar.

crisis [kráįsjs], (*pl.* **crises** [kráįsiz]) *s.* crisis.

crisp [krisp], *a.* quebradizo; tostado; crespo; vivo, animado.—*vt.* encrespar; hacer frágil.— —y [kríspi], *a.* crespo, frágil; fresco.

criterion [kraįtíriǫn], *s.* criterio.

critic [krítjk], *s.* crítico; censor; crítica.— —al [-ąl], *a.* crítico, criticón; difícil; decisivo.— —ism [krítjsjzm], *s.* crítica; juicio crítico; censura.— —ize, —ise [krítjsaįz], *vi.* criticar.—*vt.* censurar, fiscalizar.

croak [krouk], *vi.* graznar; croar; gruñir.—*s.* graznido, canto de ranas.

crock [krak], *s.* vasija de barro.— —ery [krákœrj], *s.* loza, cacharros.

crocodile [krákodaįl], *s.* cocodrilo; caimán.

crook [kruk], *s.* falsario, estafador; fullero; maleante; gancho, curva- (tura).—*vt.* y *vi.* encorvar(se); torcer- (se).— —ed [krúkjd], *a.* encorvado; torcido; pícaro.

crop [krap], *s.* cosecha; látigo; buche de ave.—*vti.* [1] segar, cosechar.—*vii.* dar frutos.

croquette [kroukét], *s.* (coc.) croqueta.

crosier [króȷ̆žœ(r)], *s.* báculo pastoral.

cross [krȯs], *s.* cruz (sentidos recto y figurado); cruce; querella, encuentro; cruzamiento (de razas).—*a.* relativo o perteneciente a la cruz; atravesado, transversal; cruzado; malhumorado. —*c.-eyed*, bizco.—*crossword puzzle*, crucigrama.—*vt.* cruzar, atravesar; marcar con una cruz; cruzar (razas); eliminar tachando; poner el trazo transversal a una letra; santiguarse; hacerse cruces.—*vi.* cruzarse.— —bar [krósbar], *s.* travesaño.— —beam [-bim], *s.* viga transversal.

crossing [krȯsjŋ], *s.* cruce, intersección; paso, vado; travesía, acción de cruzar; cruzamiento (razas); santigua- miento.—**crossroad** [krósroųd], *s.* cruce de dos caminos.

crouch [kraųch], *vi.* agacharse, agaza- parse; rebajarse.

crow [krou], *s.* cuervo; canto del gallo. —*c.'s foot*, pata de gallo (arrugas).— *vii.* [5] cantar el gallo.—*vi.* cantar victoria, alardear.— —bar [króųbar], *s.* barra o palanca de hierro.

crowd [kraud], *s.* gentío, multitud; apiñamiento.—*vt.* amontonar, apiñar. —*vi.* apiñarse.— —ed [kráųdjd], *a.* apiñado; lleno de bote en bote.

crown [kraųn], *s.* corona; diadema;

guirnalda; monarca; soberanía; coro- nilla; copa de sombrero; cima.—*vt.* coronar.

crucible [krúsjbl], *s.* crisol.

crucifix [krúsjfiks], *s.* crucifijo.—**cru- cify** [krúsjfaį], *vti.* [7] crucificar.

crude [krud], *a.* crudo; imperfecto; tosco.— —ness [krúdnjs], *s.* crudeza, tosquedad.

cruel [krúęl], *a.* cruel.— —ty [-tj], *s.* crueldad.

cruet [krúįt], *s.* ampoll(et)a; vinajera; vinagrera.—*c. stand*, convoy de mesa.

cruise [kruz], *vi.* cruzar, viajar de cru- cero; andar de un lado a otro.—*s.* crucero, viaje.—*cruising speed*, veloci- dad de crucero.— —r [krúzœ(r)], *s.* (mar.) crucero.

crumb [krʌm], *s.* migaja, migajón; pizca.—*vt.* desmig(aj)ar; desmenuzar. — —le [krʌmbl], *vt.* desmigar, desme- nuzar.—*vi.* desmoronarse.

crumple [krʌmpl], *vt.* arrugar.—*vi.* contraerse, apabullarse.

crunch [krʌnch], *vi.* crujir; mascullar.— *vt.* tascar; cascar.—*s.* crujido.

crusade [krūséjd], *s.* cruzada.— —r [krūséįdœ(r)], *s.* cruzado.

crush [krʌš], *vt.* romper por compresión; aplastar, machacar; estrujar; majar; abrumar.—*vi.* aplastarse; romperse o deformarse por compresión.—*s.* estru- jamiento o deformación por com- presión o choque.

crust [krʌst], *s.* costra; postilla; corteza (pan, queso, etc.); mendrugo; cara- pacho, concha.—*vt.* encostrar, incrus- trar.—*vi.* encostrarse.

crustacean [krʌstéįšjạn], *a.* y *s.* crus- táceo.

crusty [krʌstj], *a.* costroso; sarroso; brusco, malhumorado.

crutch [krʌch], *s.* muleta; arrimo; muletilla; horquilla; horcajadura, entrepierna.

cry [kraį], *vti.* y *vii.* [7] gritar; llorar; exclamar; lamentarse; vocear; prego- nar.—*s.* grito; lloro, llanto; pregón.— *a far c. from*, muy lejos de.— —ing [kráįjŋ], *a.* llorón; gritón; enorme; urgente.

crypt [kript], *s.* gruta, cripta.— —ic [kríptjk], *a.* enigmático, oculto.

crystal [krístạl], *s.* cristal; cristal de roca; cristal de reloj.—*a.* de cristal.— —line [-įn], *a.* cristalino.— —lization [-įzéįšǫn], *s.* cristalización.— —lize [-aįz], *vt.* y *vi.* cristalizar(se).

cub [kʌb], *s.* cachorro (de fiera).

Cuban [kiúbạn], *a.* y *s.* cubano.

cube [kiub], *s.* cubo.—*c. root*, raíz cúbica.—**cubic** [kiúbjk], *a.* cúbico.

cuckold [kʌkǫld], *s.* marido cornudo, cabrón, cuclillo.—*vt.* encornudar.

cuckoo [kúku], *s.* cuco; cucú (canto).— *a.* (fam.) chiflado.

cucumber [kjúkʌmbœ(r)], *s.* pepino.— *cool as a c.*, fresco como una lechuga.

cud [kʌd], *s.* rumia.—*c.-chewing*, rumiante.—*to chew the c.*, rumiar; charlar.

cuddle [kʌdl], *vt.* abrazar con ternura; acariciar, mimar.—*vi.* abrazarse; estar abrazados.—*s.* abrazo.

cudgel [kʌ́dʒ̧el], *s.* garrote, estaca, porra, cachiporra.

cue [kju], *s.* señal, indicación; (teat.) pie, apunte; indirecta, sugestión.— *billiard c.*, taco de billar.

cuff [kʌf], *s.* trompada; puño de camisa; bocamanga; vuelta del pantalón.—*c. buttons* o *links*, gemelos.—*pl.* manillas, esposas.—*vt.* abofetear; maniatar.—*vi.* darse puñetazos.

culinary [kjúli̦neri̦], *a.* culinario.

culminate [kʌlmi̦nejt], *vi.* culminar.— **culmination** [kʌlmi̦néjş̂ǫn], *s.* culminación.

culprit [kʌlpri̦t], *s.* reo, delincuente, culpable.

cult [kʌlt], *s.* culto, devoción; secta.

cultivate [kʌ́lti̦vejt], *vt.* cultivar.— **cultivation** [kʌlti̦véjş̂ǫn], *s.* cultivo.— **cultivator** [kʌ́lti̦vejtǫ(r)], *s.* labrador, cultivador; máquina cultivadora.

culture [kʌlchu̦(r)], *s.* cultura; cultivo (de bacterias, etc.).— **—d** [-d], *a.* culto, cultivado.

cumbersome [kʌ́mbœ(r)sʌm], *a.* pesado, engorroso.

cumulus [kjúmyu̦lʌs], *s.* montón; (meteor.) cúmulo.

cunning [kʌ́ni̦ŋ], *a.* astuto; socarrón; sutil; sagaz; gracioso, mono (aplícase a los niños).—*s.* astucia; sagacidad.

cup [kʌp], *s.* taza, jícara, pocillo; cubeta; cáliz; trago; (deportes) copa.— **—board** [kʌ́bǫrd], *s.* aparador.

cupola [kjúpolǎ], *s.* (arq.) cúpula, domo.

cur [kœr], *s.* perro callejero; canalla, bellaco.

curate [kjúri̦t], *s.* cura.—**curator** [kjúrejtǫ(r)], *s.* conservador (de museo).

curb [kœrb], *s.* borde o encintado (de la acera); freno, restricción; barbada; brocal de pozo.—*vt.* refrenar, contener; poner freno o coto a.

curd [kœrd], *s.* cuajada; requesón.—*vt.* y *vi.* cuajar(se), coagular(se).— **—le** [kœrdl], *vt.* y *vi.* cuajar(se), coagular-(se); helar(se).

cure [kjur], *s.* cura, curación; remedio.—*vt.* curar; vulcanizar.—*vi.* vulcanizarse; curarse; sanarse.

curfew [kœ́rfju], *s.* toque de queda.

curio [kjúrjou], *s.* objeto curioso y raro. **— —sity** [kjurjásji̦ti], *s.* curiosidad; rareza.— **—us** [kjúrjʌs], *a.* curioso; entremetido; cuidadoso; raro.

curl [kœrl], *s.* bucle, rizo; ondulación.— *vt.* rizar; fruncir.—*vi.* enroscarse; rizarse.

curlew [kœ́rlju], *s.* chorlito.

curly [kœ́rli̦], *a.* rizado, crespo.

currant [kœ́ranț], *s.* grosella.

currency [kœ́rę̦nsj̦], *s.* moneda corriente; dinero en circulación; uso corriente; valor corriente.—**current** [kœ́rę̦nt], *a.* corriente, común; actual, en curso.—*c. account*, cuenta corriente.—*c. events*, asuntos de actualidad.—*s.* corriente (de aire, agua, etc.).—*direct c.*, corriente continua.

curriculum [kʌríkyu̦lʌm], *s.* plan de estudios.

curse [kœrs], *vt.* maldecir.—*vi.* renegar; blasfemar.—*s.* maldición; terno.— **—d** [kœrsj̦d], *a.* maldito.

curt [kœrt], *a.* brusco; conciso.— **—ail** [kœrtéjl], *vt.* cortar; abreviar; restringir.

curtain [kœ́rti̦n], *s.* cortina; (teat.) telón.—*pl.* cortinaje.

curvature [kœ́rvach̦u̦(r)], *s.* curvatura, encorvamiento.—**curve** [kœrv], *vt.* curvar, combar, encorvar.—*vi.* encorvarse; torcerse.—*s.* curva; curvadura, comba.—**curved** [kœrvd], *a.* curvo; encorvado; combado.

cushion [kúş̂ǫn], *s.* cojín; almohadilla; almohadón; amortiguador.—*vt.* acojinar, suavizar, amortiguar.

cusp [kʌsp], *s.* cúspide.

custard [kʌ́stǎrd], *s.* flan, natillas.—*c. apple*, guanábana, anona.

custody [kʌ́stǫdj̦], *s.* custodia, guardia.

custom [kʌ́stǫm], *s.* costumbre; usanza; clientela o parroquia.—*c.-made*, hecho especialmente.—*pl.* derechos de aduana o arancelarios.—**—ary** [-ę̦rj̦], *a.* habitual, acostumbrado.— **—er** [-œ(r)], *s.* parroquiano, cliente.— **—shouse** [-ş̂aǔs], *s.* aduana.

cut [kʌt], *vti.* [9] cortar; dividir, partir; rebanar; grabar; labrar, tallar; segar; desbastar; recortar; negar el saludo a; cortar los naipes; rebajar, reducir (sueldos, gastos, etc.); cortar (trajes). —*to c. across*, cruzar, atravesar, cortar al través.—*to c. a figure*, descollar; hacer buen papel.—*to c. asunder*, separar cortando, despedazar.—*to c. away*, recortar.—*to c. capers*, hacer cabriolas.—*to c. down*, tumbar; talar; mermar, rebajar, cercenar.—*to c. off*, cercenar; aislar; interceptar (la comunicación); interrumpir; suspender los abastecimientos; desheredar.—*to c. up*, trinchar; despedazar. —*vii.* hacer un corte o incisión; ser cortante.—*pret.* y *pp.* de TO CUT.—*s.* corte; cortadura, incisión; tajo; ofensa; cosa o palabra hiriente; ausencia (de una clase, etc.); pedazo,

cosa cortada; atajo; rebaja (sueldos, gastos, etc.); clisé, grabado; talla.—*a*. cortado.—*c. and dried*, preparado, convenido de antemano.

cute [kiut], *a*. lindo, mono, gracioso; listo.

cuticle [kiútjkl], *s*. cutícula; película.

cutler [kʌtlœ(r)], *s*. cuchillero.— —**y** [-i], *s*. cuchillería, cuchillos; tienda del cuchillero.

cutlet [kʌtljt], *s*. chuleta.

cutter [kʌtœ(r)], *s*. cortador; herramienta o máquina para cortar.— **cutting** [kʌtjŋ], *a*. cortante; de cortar; incisivo, mordaz.—*s*. cortadura; corte; incisión.

cuttlefish [kʌtlfiŝ], *s*. (ict.) pulpo.

cycle [sájkl], *s*. ciclo; bicicleta.—*vi*. andar en bicicleta.—**cycling** [sájkljŋ], *s*. ciclismo.

cyclone [sájkloun], *s*. ciclón.

cyclotron [sájklotran], *s*. ciclotrón.

cylinder [sjlindœ(r)], *s*. cilindro; rodillo; tambor.

cymbal [símbal], *s*. címbalo, platillo.

cynic [sínjk], *s*. cínico.— —**al** [-al], *a*. cínico.— —**ism** [sínjsjzm], *s*. cinismo.

cypress [sájpres], *s*. ciprés.

Czech [chɛk], *s. y a*. checo.— —**oslovak-(ian)** [-oslovák(jan)], *s. y a*. checo(e)-slovaco.

D

dabble [dæbl], *vt*. rociar; mojar.—*to d. in*, meterse en.— —**r** [dæblœ(r)], *s*. aficionado, diletante.

dad [dæd], **daddie, daddy** [dædj], *s*. papá, papaíto; (Am.) papacito, tata.

dado [déjdou], *s*. (arq.) rodapié.

daffodil [dæfodjl], *s*. narciso.

dagger [dægœ(r)], *s*. daga, puñal.

daily [déjli], *a*. diario, cotidiano, diurno. —*s*. periódico diario.—*adv*. diariamente.

daintiness [déjntjnjs], *s*. delicadeza, elegancia.—**dainty** [déjntj], *a*. delicado, elegante, refinado; sabroso; melindroso.—*s*. bocado exquisito, golosina.

dairy [dérj], *s*. lechería; quesería; vaquería.

daisy [déjzj], *s*. margarita; (fam.) primor.

dale [dejl], *s*. valle; cañada.

dam [dæm], *s*. (re)presa, embalse, dique; central hidroeléctrica.—*vti*. [1] represar, embalsar.

damage [dæmjdź], *s*. daño, perjuicio, deterioro; pérdida; avería.—*pl*. daños y perjuicios.—*vt*. dañar, averiar, deteriorar; perjudicar, damnificar.— *vi*. dañarse, averiarse.

dame [déjm], *s*. dama, señora; (col.) tía, fulana.

damn [dæm], *vt*. maldecir; reprobar. —*d. it!* ¡maldito sea!—*vi*. renegar, maldecir.—*s*. maldición.

damp [dæmp], *a*. húmedo, mojado.—*s*. humedad; desaliento.—*d*. o **dampen** [dæmpɛn], *vt*. humedecer, mojar; desanimar, desalentar; amortiguar. —*vi*. humedecerse.— —**er** [-œ(r)], *a*. registro, regulador de tiro de chimenea; sordina; desalentador; amortiguador.— —**ness** [-njs], *s*. humedad, relente.

damsel [dæmzɛl], *s*. damisela, doncella.

dance [dæns], *vi*. bailar, danzar.—*s*. danza, baile.— —**r** [dænsœ(r)], *s*. bailarín(a); bailador(a).

dandelion [dændjlajon], *s*. (bot.) diente de león.

dandruff [dændrʌf], *s*. caspa.

dandy [dændj], *s*. dandi, petimetre, lechuguino.—*a*. (fam.) excelente, magnífico.

Dane [dejn], *s*. danés, dinamarqués. —*great D.*, perro danés.

danger [déjndźœ(r)], *s*. peligro, riesgo.— —**ous** [-ʌs], *a*. peligroso, arriesgado; grave, de cuidado.

dangle [dæŋgl], *vt*. colgar, suspender. —*vi*. pender, bambolearse; andar al retortero.

Danish [déjnjŝ], *a*. danés, dinamarqués. —*s*. danés; lengua danesa.

dapple(d) [dæpl(d)], *a*. rodado, tordo, con manchas, salpicado.

dare [der], *vii*. [5] osar, atreverse, arriesgarse.—*vti*. retar, desafiar; provocar.—*s*. reto, desafío.— —**devil** [dérdevjl], *a. y s*. temerario, osado. —**daring** [dérjn], *a*. osado, temerario; denodado.—*s*. osadía, bravura.

dark [dark], *a*. oscuro; trigueño, moreno; sombrío, tenebroso; siniestro. —*to be left in the d.*, dejar en ayunas, en la ignorancia.—*to grow d.*, anochecer, oscurecer.—*to keep it d.*, ocultar algo.—*s*. oscuridad; tinieblas; noche; anochecer; ignorancia, secreto.— —**en** [dárkn], *vt*. oscurecer, ensombrecer; cegar; nublar; denigrar, manchar.—*vi*. oscurecerse, nublarse.— —**ness** [-njs], *s*. oscuridad, sombra, tinieblas; ofuscación; ceguera; ignorancia.

darling [dárljn], *a*. querido, amado.—*s*. querido, el predilecto.—*my d.*, vida mía, amor mío.—*you are a d.*, eres un encanto.

darn [darn], *vt*. zurcir, remendar; (fam.) maldecir.—*s*. zurcido.—*I don't give a d.*, me importa un bledo.

darnel [dárnɛl], *s*. (bot.) cizaña.

darning [dárnjn], *s*. zurcido, remiendo.

dart [dart], *s*. dardo, saeta; banderilla; movimiento rápido; (cost.) sisa.— *d. thrower*, banderillero.—*vt*. lanzar,

flechar.—*vi.* lanzarse, precipitarse.

dash [dæŝ], *vt.* arrojar, tirar, lanzar; estrellar, romper; magullar; frustrar (esperanzas); rociar, salpicar; sazonar.—*to d. out,* tachar.—*to d. to pieces,* hacer añicos.—*vi.* chocar, estrellarse; lanzarse; saltar.—*s.* arremetida; ataque; choque, embate; guión, raya; energía; condimento; poquito, pizca; carrera corta.— —**board** [dǽŝbord], *s.* (aut.) tablero de instrumentos.

data [déjtạ, dǽtạ], *s.* (*pl.* de DATUM [déjtʌm]) datos, antecedentes.

date [dejt], *s.* fecha; cita, compromiso; época; (bot.) dátil.—*d. palm,* palma datilera.—*down to d.,* hasta la fecha, hasta ahora.—*out of d.,* anticuado, pasado de moda.—*up to d.,* hasta ahora; al día.—*vt.* datar, fechar; computar; dar cita a uno.—*vi.* (con *from*) datar (de), remontarse a.

datum [déjtʌm], *s.* dato.

daub [dob], *vt.* embadurnar; untar; pintarrajear.

daughter [dótœ(r)], *s.* hija.—*d.-in-law,* nuera.

dawn [don], *vi.* amanecer, alborear, clarear; asomar, mostrarse.—*to d. (up)on,* ocurrírsele a uno, caer en la cuenta.—*s.* alba, aurora, madrugada; albores.— —**ing** [dónịŋ], *s.* alborada.

day [dej], *s.* día.—*d. after tomorrow,* pasado mañana.—*d. bed,* sofá cama. —*d. before yesterday,* anteayer.—*d. in, d. out,* día tras día, sin cesar.—*d. laborer,* jornalero.—*days of obligation,* fiestas de guardar.—*d.-star,* lucero del alba.—*d. wages,* jornal.—*every other d.,* cada dos días.— —**book** [déjbụk], *s.* libro de cuentas diarias.— —**break** [-brejk], *s.* amanecer.— —**dream** [-drím], *s.* ensueño, ilusión. —*vi.* soñar despierto.— —**light** [-lajt], *s.* luz del día, luz natural.—*d. saving time,* hora de verano (E.U.).

daze [dejz], *vt.* ofuscar, aturdir, trastornar.—*s.* deslumbramiento, ofuscamiento.

dazzle [dǽzl], *vt.* deslumbrar, ofuscar, encandilar; camuflar.—*s.* deslumbramiento.

deacon [dikọn], *s.* diácono.

dead [ded], *a.* muerto; inerte; marchito. —*d. center,* punto muerto.—*d. end,* callejón sin salida.—*d. eye,* tirador certero.—*d. pan (face),* (cara) inalterable.—*d. stop,* parada en seco.—*d. weight,* carga onerosa; tara.—*s. pl.* los muertos.—*the d. of night,* lo más profundo de la noche.—*adv.* entera o absolutamente; del todo; repentinamente.—*d. drunk,* borracho perdido.—*d. tired,* agotado.— —**en** [dédn], *vt.* amortiguar; quitar brillo,

sonido, etc.— —**line** [-lajn], *s.* línea vedada; término, plazo final.— —**lock** [-lak], *s.* detención, paro, estancamiento.— —**ly** [-lị], *a.* mortal; fatal; fulminante; implacable.— —**ness** [-nịs], *s.* inercia; amortiguamiento.

deaf [def], *a.* sordo.—*d.-mute,* sordomudo.— —**en** [défn], *vt.* ensordecer.— —**ening** [-ẹnịŋ], *a.* ensordecedor.— —**ness** [-nịs], *s.* sordera; ensordecimiento

deal [dil], *s.* trato, negocio; pacto o convenio; mano (en el juego de naipes); porción; parte.—*a great d.,* mucho, una gran cantidad.—*vti.* [10] distribuir, repartir; dar (los naipes); asestar (un golpe).—*to d. out,* dispensar.—*vii.* negociar, traficar, gestionar; mediar; dar (en el juego de baraja).— —**er** [dílœ(r)], *s.* comerciante, negociante, agente de comercio; el mano (en el juego de baraja).— —**ing** [-iŋ], *s.* conducta; trato; negocio.—*pl.* negocios; transacciones. —**dealt** [delt], *pret.* y *pp.* de TO DEAL.

dean [din], *s.* deán; decano.

dear [djr], *a.* querido, amado; costoso, caro.—*s.* persona querida, bien amado.—*d. me!* ¡válgame Dios!—*d. sir(s),* muy señor(es) mío(s), o nuestro(s).

dearth [dœrθ], *s.* carestía, escasez.

death [deθ], *s.* muerte; defunción, fallecimiento; mortandad.—*d. certificate,* partida de defunción.—*d. dealing,* mortífero.—*d. rate,* mortalidad.—*d. rattle,* estertor.—*d. struggle,* agonía. —*d. wound,* herida mortal.—*to be in the d. house,* estar en capilla.— —**less** [déθlịs], *a.* inmortal.— —**watch** [-wach], *s.* velorio.

debarkation [djbarkéjŝọn], *s.* = DISEMBARKATION.

debase [djbéjs], *vt.* rebajar, deshonrar.

debatable [djbéjtạbl], *a.* discutible, disputable.—**debate** [djbéjt], *s.* discusión, debate, disputa.—*vt.* disputar, controvertir; considerar.—*vi.* deliberar, discutir.

debenture [djbénchụ(r)], *s.* bono; obligación; pagaré del gobierno.

debit [débịt], *s.* débito, cargo; egreso; debe (de una cuenta).—*d. balance,* saldo deudor.—*vt.* adeudar, cargar en cuenta.

debris [dạbrí], *s.* escombros, restos, ruinas; despojos.

debt [det], *s.* deuda, débito; obligación. —*to run into d.,* endeudarse, entramparse.— —**or** [détọ(r)], *s.* deudor.

debut [dạbjú], *s.* estreno; presentación de una señorita en sociedad.

decade [dékejd], *s.* decenio, década.

decadence [djkéjdẹns], *s.* decadencia.

—**decadent** [dikéidẹnt], *a.* decadente, decaído.

decapitate [dikǽpiteit], *vt.* decapitar, degollar.—**decapitation** [dikæpitéi-ṣọn], *s.* decapitación.

decay [dikéi], *vi.* decaer, declinar; deteriorarse; carcomerse; cariarse; pudrirse, dañarse; picarse.—*s.* decaimiento, decadencia; ruina; caries; podredumbre.

decease [disís], *s.* fallecimiento, defunción.—*vi.* morir, fallecer.— —**d** [-t], *s.* y *a.* difunto, finado.

deceit [disít], *s.* engaño, fraude, falacia, trampa.— —**ful** [-fụl], *a.* engañoso, falso; mentiroso.—**deceive** [disív], *vt.* engañar, embaucar, defraudar.

December [disémbœ(r)], *s.* diciembre.

decency [dísẹnsi], *s.* decencia; pudor.

decennial [disénial], *a.* decenal.

decent [dísẹnt], *a.* decente; razonable, módico.

deception [disépṣọn], *s.* engaño, fingimiento, impostura.

decide [disáid], *vt.* y *vi.* decidir, determinar, resolver.— —**d** [-id], *a.* decidido, resuelto.

decimal [désimạl], *s.* y *a.* decimal.— **decimate** [désimeit], *vt.* diezmar.

decipher [disáifœ(r)], *vt.* descifrar, interpretar; aclarar.

decision [disíẓọn], *s.* decisión, resolución; entereza; (for.) fallo, auto, providencia.—**decisive** [disáisiv], *a.* decisivo; terminante, perentorio.

deck [dek], *vt.* ataviar, engalanar.—*s.* cubierta (de un buque); baraja.

declaim [dikléim], *vi.* declamar, perorar.

declaration [deklạréiṣọn], *s.* declaración; exposición; manifiesto.—**declare** [diklér], *vt.* y *vi.* declarar, manifestar; deponer.

declension [díklénṣọn], *s.* (gram.) declinación.

decline [dikláin], *vt.* rehusar; (gram.) declinar.—*vi.* rehusar, negarse (a); declinar, decaer.—*s.* declinio; declive.—**declivity** [diklívitị], *s.* declive.

décolletage [deikaltáž], *s.* escote; traje escotado.

decompose [dikọmpóuz], *vt.* descomponer; pudrir.—*vi.* pudrirse, corromperse.—**decomposition** [dikampozí-ṣọn], *s.* descomposición; corrupción, putrefacción.

decorate [dékoreit], *vt.* decorar, adornar; condecorar.—**decoration** [dekoréiṣọn], *s.* decoración; adorno, ornamento, condecoración, insignia. —**decorative** [dékorạtiv], *a.* decorativo, ornamental.—**decorator** [dékoreitọ(r)], *s.* decorador.

decorous [dékórʌs], *a.* decoroso.

decorum [dikórʌm], *s.* decoro, honor; corrección.

decoy [dikói], *vt.* atraer con señuelo o añagaza.—*s.* señuelo, añagaza, reclamo.

decrease [dikrís], *vi.* decrecer.—*vi.* y *vt.* disminuir, reducir, mermar.—*s.* disminución; merma; menguante; decadencia.

decree [dikrí], *vt.* y *vi.* decretar, mandar.—*s.* decreto, edicto, mandato, ley.

decrepit [dikrépit], *a.* decrépito, caduco.

dedicate [dédikeit], *vt.* dedicar; aplicar. —**dedication** [dedikéiṣọn], *s.* dedicación, dedicatoria.

deduce [didiús], *vt.* deducir, inferir; derivar.

deduct [didʌ́kt], *vt.* deducir, restar, su(b)straer, rebajar, descontar.— —**ion** [didʌ́kṣọn], *s.* deducción; su(b)stracción; descuento, rebaja; conclusión.

deed [did], *s.* acto, hecho; hazaña; (for.) escritura.

deep [dip], *a.* profundo, hondo; abstruso, recóndito; intenso (color); (mus.) grave; sagaz.—*d. blue*, turquí. —*d. sea*, alta mar.—*d.-sea fishing*, pesca mayor, pesca de profundidad.— *adv.* profundamente.—*d.-seated*, arraigado.—*d. in thought*, abstraído.—*s.* profundidad(es); piélago, mar.— —**en** [dípn], *vt.* profundizar, ahondar; oscurecer; entristecer.—*vi.* hacerse más hondo, más profundo o más intenso.— —**ness** [-nịs], *s.* profundidad, hondura; intensidad.

deer [dir], *s.* venado, ciervo.

deface [diféis], *vt.* afear, desfigurar, mutilar.

default [difólt], *s.* omisión; incumplimiento de una obligación; insolvencia; falta; (for.) rebeldía.—*vt.* y *vi.* faltar; no pagar; (for.) no comparecer.— —**er** [-œ(r)], *s.* desfalcador; rebelde.

defeat [difít], *s.* derrota; frustración; (for.) anulación.—*vt.* derrotar, vencer; frustrar; anular.— —**ist** [-ịst], *s.* y *a.* derrotista.

defect [difékt], *s.* defecto, falta, tacha.— —**ion** [difékṣọn], *s.* deserción; defección; abandono.— —**ive** [diféktiv], *a.* defectuoso; falto de inteligencia; (gram.) defectivo.

defend [difénd], *vt.* defender, proteger.— —**ant** [-ạnt], *a.* acusado; que defiende.—*s.* demandado, acusado, procesado.— —**er** [-œ(r)], *s.* defensor, protector.—**defense** [diféns], *s.* defensa, protección.—*d. attorney*, abogado defensor.—**defenseless** [difénslịs], *a.* indefenso; inerme.—**defensive** [difénsiv], *a.* defensivo.—*s.* defensiva.

defer [difœ́r], *vti.* [1] diferir, aplazar, retrasar; remitir.—*vii.* demorarse;

(con to) ceder, acatar, consentir.-
—ence [défĕrens], s. deferencia, acatamiento, respeto.
defiance [difáians], s. desafío, reto;
oposición.—defiant [difáiant], a. retador, provocador.
deficiency [difíśensi], s. deficiencia,
defecto.—deficient [difíśent], a. deficiente; defectuoso.
defile [difáil], vi. (mil.) desfilar.—vt.
manchar, profanar, viciar, corromper.
—s. desfiladero.
define [difáin], vt. definir; limitar;
fijar; determinar.—definite [définit],
a. definido, exacto, categórico, preciso.—definition [definíśon], s. definición.—definitive [difínitiv], a. definitivo, decisivo, terminante.
deflate [difléit], vt. desinflar; reducir
(valores, etc.).—deflation [difléiśon],
s. deflación; desinflación.
deflect [diflékt], vt. y vi. desviar(se),
apartar(se), ladear(se).
deflower [difláуœ(r)], vt. desflorar;
violar.
deform [difórm], vt. deformar, desfigurar, afear.- —ation [diformeíśon]
s. deformación, desfiguración.- —ed
[difórmd], a. deformado, desfigurado;
deforme, contrahecho.- —ity [difór-
miti], s. deformidad; deformación;
fealdad.
defraud [difród], vt. defraudar, estafar.-
—er [-œ(r)], s. defraudador, estafador.
defray [difréi], vt. costear, sufragar.
defrost [difróst], vt. descongelar, deshelar.
deft [deft], a. diestro, hábil.- —ness
[déftnis], s. destreza, habilidad.
defunct [difʌŋkt], a. y s. difunto.
defy [difái], vti. [7] desafiar, retar.
degenerate [didźénereit], vi. degenerar.
—s. y a. [didźénerit], degenerado.
degradation [degradéiśon], s. degradación; degeneración; corrupción.—
degrade [digréid], vt. degradar; rebajar.—vi. degenerar; envilecerse.
degree [digrí], s. grado; título; cuantía.
—by degrees, gradualmente, poco a
poco.—to take a d., graduarse.
deign [dein], vt. y vi. dignarse, condescender.
deity [díiti], s. deidad, divinidad.
dejected [didźéktid], a. acongojado,
abatido.—dejection [didźékśon], s.
melancolía, abatimiento, desaliento;
deposición.
delay [diléi], vt. dilatar, demorar, retardar; entretener.—vi. tardar, demorarse.—s. dilación, tardanza, demora.
delectable [diléktabl], a. delicioso,
deleitable.—delectation [dilektéiśon],
s. deleite, deleitación.

delegate [délegeit], vt. delegar, comisionar.—a. y s. delegado, comisario.—delegation [delegéiśon], s. delegación, comisión.
delete [dilít], vt. tachar, borrar,
suprimir.
deliberate [dilíbereit], vt. y vi. deliberar,
reflexionar.—a. [dilíberit], delibe-
rado, premeditado; cauto. —deliberation [dilibeŕéiśon], s. deliberación,
reflexión, premeditación.
delicacy [délikasi], s. delicadeza; suavidad; ternura; fragilidad; manjar,
golosina.—delicate [délikit], a. delicado, frágil; suave; fino; tierno;
exquisito.—delicatessen [delikatés-
en], s. manjares delicados, esp.
fiambres; tienda donde se venden.
delicious [dilíśʌs], a. delicioso, sabroso,
rico.
delight [diláit], s. deleite, delicia,
encanto.—vt. deleitar, encantar, recrear.—vi. deleitarse, recrearse, complacerse (en).— —ed [-id], a. encantado, contentísimo.—to be d. to, tener
mucho gusto en; alegrarse muchísimo de.- —ful [-ful], a. delicioso,
encantador.
delineate [dilíneit], vt. delinear, trazar,
diseñar.—delineator [dilíneito(r)], s.
delineante.
delinquency [dilíŋkwensi], s. delincuencia.—delinquent [dilíŋkwent], s.
y a. delincuente.
delirious [dilíriʌs], a. delirante, des-
variado.—to be d., delirar, desvariar.
—delirium [dilíriʌm], s. delirio,
desvarío; devaneo.
deliver [dilívœ(r)], vt. entregar; libertar;
pronunciar (conferencia, discurso,
etc.); descargar, asestar (un golpe);
despachar (un pedido); transmitir
(energía, etc.).—to d. a baby, dar
a luz.- —ance [-ans], s. rescate,
liberación.- —er [-œ(r)], s. libertador; repartidor, mensajero.- —y [-i],
s. entrega; distribución o reparto;
remesa; liberación, rescate; dicción,
forma de expresión; cesión; parto;
(mec.) descarga, proyección.—d. man,
recadero, mensajero.
dell [del], s. cañada.
delude [diliúd], vt. engañar, alucinar.
deluge [déliudź], s. diluvio, inundación;
calamidad.—vt. inundar.
delusion [diliúźon], s. error; ilusión;
decepción, engaño.
demagogue [démagag], s. demagogo.—
demagogy [démagadźi], s. demagogia.
demand [dimænd], vt. demandar; exigir,
reclamar.—s. demanda; exigencia.—
on d., a la presentación; a solicitud.
—to be in d., tener demanda, ser
solicitado.- —ing [-iŋ], a. exigente.

demeanor [dịmínọ(r)], *s.* conducta, comportamiento, proceder; porte, semblante.

demented [dịméntịd], *a.* demente.

demerit [dịmérịt], *s.* demérito, desmerecimiento.

demijohn [démịdẓan], *s.* botellón.

demise [dịmáịz], *s.* defunción, fallecimiento.

demobilize [dimóụbịlaịz], *vt.* desmovilizar.

democracy [dịmákrạsị], *s.* democracia. —**democrat** [démokrᴂt], *s.* demócrata.—**democratic** [demokrᴂtịk], *a.* democrático.

demolish [dịmálịs̱], *vt.* demoler, derribar.— —**er** [-œ(r)], *s.* demoledor. —**demolition** [demolịs̱ọn], *s.* demolición, derribo, arrasamiento.

demon [dímọn], *s.* demonio, diablo.

demonstrate [démọnstreịt], *vt.* demostrar, probar.— demonstration [demọnstréịs̱ọn], *s.* demostración, muestra; prueba; manifestación pública.— **demonstrative** [dịmánstrạtịv], *a.* demostrativo; efusivo.—demonstrator [démọnstreịto(r)], *s.* manifestante.

demoralize [dịmarạlịzéịs̱ọn], *s.* desmoralización.—demoralize [dịmárạlaịz], *vt.* desmoralizar.

den [dεn], *s.* cueva, guarida, cuchitril, pocilga; gabinete (de estudio).

dengue [déŋgeị], *s.* (med.) dengue.

denial [dịnáịạl], *s.* negación, negativa, desmentida; denegación.

denominate [dịnámịneịt], *vt.* denominar, nombrar.—*a.* denominado.—**denomination** [dịnamịnéịs̱ọn], *s.* denominación, título, designación; confesión religiosa.—denominator [dịnámịneịtọ(r)], *s.* (arit.) denominador.

denote [dịnóụt], *vt.* denotar, señalar.

denouement [deịnúman], *s.* desenlace.

denounce [dịnáụns], *vt.* denunciar, delatar.

dense [dεns], *a.* denso, espeso, tupido; estúpido.—**density** [dénsịtị], *s.* densidad, espesura; estupidez.

dent [dεnt], *s.* abolladura; mella; hendidura.—*vt.* y *vi.* abollar(se), mellar(se).

dental [déntạl], *a.* dental.—*d. floss,* hilo dental.—*d. plate,* dentadura postiza.—**dentist** [déntịst], *s.* dentista, odontólogo.—**dentistry** [déntịstrị], *s.* odontología.—**denture** [dénchụ(r)], *s.* dentadura postiza.

denunciation [dịnʌnsịéịs̱ọn], *s.* denuncia, acusación.

deny [dịnáị], *vtị.* [7] negar; denegar; desmentir; negarse a.—*vti.* negar.

deodorant [dióụdọrạnt], *s.* desodorante.

depart [dịpárt], *vi.* irse, partir, salir;

apartarse, desviarse; morir.—*the departed,* los difuntos.

department [dịpártmẹnt], *s.* departamento; compartimiento; sección (en una tienda, etc.); oficina, negociado; ministerio; distrito.—*d. store,* grandes almacenes, bazar.

departure [dịpárchụ̈(r)], *s.* partida, salida, ida, marcha; desviación.

depend [dịpénd], *vi.* depender.—*to d. on* o *upon,* depender de; contar con; confiar en; necesitar (de); ser mantenido por.— —**able** [-ạbl], *a.* formal, seguro, digno de confianza.— —**ence** [-ẹns], *s.* dependencia; confianza; sostén, apoyo.— —**ency** [-ẹnsị], *s.* dependencia.— —**ent** [-ẹnt], *a.* y *s.* dependiente, subalterno.—*s.* familiar mantenido.

depict [dịpíkt], *vt.* pintar; representar; describir.

deplorable [dịplórạbl], *a.* deplorable; lastimoso.—**deplore** [dịplór], *vt.* deplorar.

deploy [dịplóị], *vt.* y *vi.* (mil.) desplegar(se).—*s.* despliegue.

depopulate [dịpápyuleịt], *vt.* y *vi.* despoblar(se).

deport [dịpórt], *vt.* deportar.—*vr.* (com)portarse, conducirse.— —**ation** [-éịs̱ọn], *s.* deportación.— —**ment** [-mẹnt], *s.* conducta, comportamiento.

depose [dịpóụz], *vt.* deponer; destronar; (for.) declarar, atestiguar.—*vi.* deponer, testificar.

deposit [dịpázịt], *vt.* depositar.—*vi.* depositarse.—*s.* depósito; sedimento; (geol., min.) yacimiento, filón.— **deposition** [depozịs̱ọn], *s.* deposición, testimonio; destitución.—**depositor** [dịpázịtọ(r)], *s.* depositante.

depot [dípoụ], *s.* depósito, almacén; paradero de tren.

deprave [dịpréịv], *vt.* depravar, pervertir.— —**d** [-d], *a.* depravado. —**depravity** [dịprᴂvịtị], *s.* depravación.

depreciate [dịpríṣịeịt], *vt.* depreciar, abaratar; menospreciar.—*vi.* abaratarse; depreciarse.

depress [dịprés], *vt.* deprimir, abatir; abaratar, rebajar el precio de; hundir.— —**ion** [dịpréṣọn], *s.* depresión, abatimiento; concavidad; hondonada.

deprivation [deprịvéịs̱ọn], *s.* privación; pérdida.—**deprive** [dịpráịv], *vt.* privar, despojar.

depth [depþ], *s.* profundidad; hondura; fondo; espesor, grueso (de una cosa); viveza (color); gravedad (sonido); penetración.—*d. bomb,* carga de profundidad.

deputy [dépịutị], *s.* diputado; delegado, agente.

derail [dịréịl], *vt.* y *vi.* descarrilar(se).—

—ment [-mɛnt], *s.* descarrilamiento.

derelict [dérɛlikt], *a.* negligente.—*s.* persona sin amparo; golfo, indigente.

deride [dịráịd], *vt.* ridiculizar, escarnecer, burlarse o mofarse de.— —**r** [dịráịdœ(r)], *s.* burlón.—**derision** [dịríʒǫn], *s.* mofa, escarnio.—**derisive** [dịráịsịve], *a.* burlesco.

derive [dịráịv], *vt.* deducir (una conclusión); derivar.—*vi.* derivar, provenir, emanar.

derrick [dérịk], *s.* grúa, cabria; armazón de un pozo de petróleo.

descend [dịsénd], *vt.* y *vi.* descender, bajar; (con **to**) rebajarse a; (con **up** o **upon**) invadir, caer en o sobre.— —**ant** [-ǫnt], *s.* descendiente.— —**ent** [-ɛnt], *a.* descend(i)ente; originario (de).—**descent** [dịsént], *s.* descenso, bajada; descendimiento; declive; alcurnia, descendencia, sucesión.

describe [dịskráịb], *vt.* describir, pintar. —**description** [dịskrípʃǫn], *s.* descripción; trazado; clase.—**descriptive** [dịskríptịv], *a.* descriptivo.

desert [dézœrt], *s.* desierto, yermo; páramo.—*a.* desierto, yermo, desolado.—*vt.* [dịzœ́rt] desamparar, abandonar.—*vt.* y *vi.* desertar.— —**er** [dịzœ́rtœ(r)], *s.* desertor.— —**ion** [dịzœ́rʃǫn], *s.* deserción, abandono.— —**s** [dịzœ́rt(s)], *s.* mérito, merecimiento.—*to get one's d.*, llevar su merecido.—**deserve** [dịzœ́rv], *vt.* merecer.—*vi.* tener merecimientos.— **deserving** [dịzœ́rvịŋ], *a.* meritorio; merecedor o digno.—*s.* mérito, merecimiento.

design [dịzáịn], *vt.* diseñar, delinear; concebir; proyectar.—*vi.* hacer proyectos, diseños, planos.—*s.* diseño; proyecto; disposición, arreglo, construcción; plan; propósito, designio; plano.—*by* o *through d.*, adrede, intencionalmente.— —**er** [-œ(r)], *s.* dibujante; diseñador; proyectista.— *custom d.* figurinista.—*stage d.*, escenógrafo.— —**ing** [-ịŋ], *a.* insidioso, astuto, intrigante.

designate [dézịgneịt], *vt.* designar, destinar; señalar.—**designation** [dezịgnéịʃǫn], *s.* designación, señalamiento, nombramiento.

desirable [dịzáịrǫbl], *a.* deseable, apetecible, conveniente.—**desire** [dịzáịr], *s.* deseo, anhelo, ansia, antojo.—*vt.* desear, anhelar, ansiar.—*vi.* sentir deseo.—**desirous** [dịzáịrʌs], *a.* deseoso, anheloso.

desist [dịsíst], *vi.* desistir.

desk [dɛsk], *s.* escritorio, pupitre, buró. —*d. pad*, carpeta.

desolate [désoleịt], *vt.* desolar, arrasar; despoblar; desconsolar.—*a.* [désǫlịt], desolado; solitario; triste.—**desola-**

tion [desoléịʃǫn], *s.* desolación; desconsuelo; soledad; aflicción.

despair [dịspér], *s.* desesperanza, desesperación.—*vi.* desesperar, perder toda esperanza.— —**ing** [-ịŋ], *a.* desesperante; sin esperanza.

despatch, *s.*, *vt.* = DISPATCH.

desperado [despœréịdoʋ], *s.* foragido; prófugo; malhechor.—**desperate** [déspœrịt], *a.* desesperado; arrojado, arriesgado o temerario.—**desperation** [despœréịʃǫn], *s.* desesperación; furor.

despicable [déspịkǫbl], *a.* despreciable, vil.—**despise** [dịspáịz], *vt.* despreciar, menospreciar.

despite [dịspáịt], *s.* despecho, inquina. —*prep.* a pesar de, a despecho de.

despoil [dịspóịl], *vt.* despojar, expoliar.

despondence, despondency [dịspándǫns(i)], *s.* desaliento, abatimiento. —**despondent** [dịspándǫnt], *a.* desalentado, abatido, desesperanzado.

despot [déspǫt], *s.* déspota.— —**ic** [despátịk], *a.* despótico.— —**ism** [déspǫtịzm], *s.* despotismo; absolutismo.

dessert [dịzœ́rt], *s.* postre.

destination [destịnéịʃǫn], *s.* destino; paradero.—**destine** [déstịn], *vt.* destinar; dedicar.—**destiny** [déstịnị], *s.* destino, hado, sino.

destitute [déstịtịut], *a.* destituido, necesitado; (con **of**) falto, desprovisto de.—**destitution** [destịtịúʃǫn], *s.* indigencia, privación.

destroy [dịstróị], *vt.* destruir, destrozar, desbaratar, acabar con.— —**er** [-œ(r)], *s.* destructor; (mar.) destructor, cazatorpedero.—**destruction** [dịstrʌ́kʃǫn], *s.* destrucción, ruina, destrozo.— **destructive** [dịstrʌ́ktịv], *a.* destructor; destructivo; dañino.

detach [dịtéch], *vt.* separar, despegar o desprender; (mil.) destacar.— —**ed** [-t], *a.* suelto, separado; imparcial; desinteresado.— —**able** [-ǫbl], *a.* separable, desmontable, de quita y pon.— —**ment** [-mɛnt], *s.* separación; indiferencia; desinterés, despego; (mil.) destacamento.

detail [dịtéịl], *vt.* detallar, particularizar, promenorizar.—*s.* detalle, pormenor; (mil.) destacamento.

detain [dịtéịn], *vt.* detener; retardar, atrasar; retener.

detect [dịtékt], *vt.* descubrir; averiguar; (rad.) rectificar.— —**ion** [dịtékʃǫn], *s.* averiguación, descubrimiento; rectificación.— —**ive** [-ịv], *s.* detective, agente de policía secreta o particular.— —**or** [-ǫ(r)], *s.* descubridor; indicador de nivel; rectificador; (elec.) detector.

deter [dịtœ́r], *vti.* [1] disuadir; desanimar, acobardar

detergent [dɪtɚ́rdᴣᴇnt], a. y s. detergente.

deteriorate [dɪtɪ́rɪoreɪt], vt. y vi. deteriorar(se), desmejorar(se).—**deterioration** [dɪtɪrɪoréɪʃǫn], s. deterioro, desperfecto, desmejora.

determination [dɪtɚrmɪnéɪʃǫn], s. determinación, decisión.—**determinative** [dɪtɚ́rmɪnắtɪv], a. determinativo, determinante.—**determine** [dɪtɚ́rmɪn], vt. determinar, decidir; (for.) definir.—vi. resolverse, decidirse.—**determined** [dɪtɚ́rmɪnd], a. determinado, decidido, resuelto.

detest [dɪtést], vt. detestar, aborrecer.—**-able** [-ǎbl], a. detestable, aborrecible.

detonate [détoneɪt], vi. detonar, estallar.—vt. hacer estallar.—**detonating** [détoneɪtɪŋ], a. detonante.—**detonation** [detonéɪʃǫn], s. detonación.—**detonator** [détoneɪtǫ(r)], s. detonador.

detour [dɪtúr], s. desviación, desvío, rodeo.—vt. y vi. (hacer) desviar o rodear.

detract [dɪtrǽkt], vt. disminuir o quitar.—vi. detractar.—**-or** [-ǫ(r)], s. detractor.—**-ion** [dɪtrǽkʃǫn], s. detracción.

detriment [détrɪmᴇnt], s. detrimento; perjuicio.

deuce [djus], s. dos (en naipes o dados); pata (en otros juegos); (fam.) diantre, demontre.

devaluate [dɪvǽlyueɪt], vt. depreciar, desvalorizar.—**devaluation** [dɪvǽlyuéɪʃǫn], s. depreciación, desvalorización.—**devalue** [dɪvǽlyu], vt. depreciar.

devastate [dévǎsteɪt], vt. devastar, asolar.—**devastating** [dévǎsteɪtɪŋ], a., **devastator** [dévǎsteɪtǫ(r)], s. devastador, asolador.—**devastation** [devǎstéɪʃǫn], s. devastación, desolación, ruina.

develop [dɪvélǫp], vt. desenvolver, desarrollar; mejorar; fomentar; explotar (minas, etc.); revelar (fotos).—vi. progresar; avanzar; desarrollarse.—**-er** [-œ(r)], s. (fot.) revelador.—**-ment** [-mᴇnt], s. desarrollo, evolución, progreso; fomento; explotación; revelado.

deviate [dívɪeɪt], vt. y vi. desviar(se), apartar(se).—**deviation** [dɪvɪéɪʃǫn], s. desviación; deriva; desvío, extravío.

device [dɪváɪs], s. artefacto, artificio; invento; proyecto; expediente, recurso; ardid; dibujo, patrón; lema, divisa.—pl. deseo, inclinación.

devil [dévɪl], s. diablo; demonio; manjar muy picante.—between the d. and the deep sea, entre la espada y la pared.—the D., Satanás.—the d. take the hindmost, el que venga atrás, que arree.—-ish [-ɪʃ], a. diabólico; perverso; travieso.—-try [-trɪ], —ment [-mᴇnt], s. diablura; travesura; maldad.

devious [dívɪʌs], a. desviado, descarriado; tortuoso.

devise [dɪváɪz], vt. idear, trazar; proyectar; (for.) legar.—vi. urdir, maquinar.

devoid [dɪvóɪd], a. libre, exento; desprovisto (de).

devote [dɪvóut], vt. dedicar; consagrar.—vr. dedicarse, consagrarse (a).—**-d** [-ɪd], a. devoto, ferviente; leal, afecto.—**devotion** [dɪvóuʃǫn], s. devoción, piedad; dedicación; lealtad, afecto.

devour [dɪváʉr], vt. devorar, engullir.

devout [dɪváʉt], a. piadoso, devoto.

dew [dju], s. rocío; relente, sereno.—vt. rociar; refrescar.— —**drop** [djúdrap], s. gota de rocío.

dewlap [djúlæp], s. papada.

dewy [djúj], a. lleno de rocío.

dexterity [dekstérɪtɪ], s. destreza, habilidad, maña, tino.—**dexterous** [dékstɚrʌs], a. diestro, hábil.

diabolic(al) [dɪabálɪk(ǎl)], a. diabólico.

diagnose [daɪægnóus], vt. diagnosticar.—**diagnosis** [daɪægnóusɪs], s. diagnosis.

diagonal [daɪǽgonǎl], a. y s. diagonal.

diagram [dáɪagræm], s. diagrama; gráfico.

dial [dáɪǎl], s. esfera de reloj; cuadrante; disco del teléfono; indicador.—vt. sintonizar; marcar (en el disco de llamada), (Am.) discar.—sun d., reloj de sol.

dialect [dáɪǎlekt], s. dialecto.

dialogue [dáɪǎlag], s. diálogo.

diameter [daɪémetœ(r)], s. diámetro.

diamond [dáɪmǫnd], s. diamante; brillante; oros (de baraja); (geom.) rombo.

diaper [dáɪapœ(r)], s. pañal, braguita.

diaphragm [dáɪafræm], s. diafragma.

diarrhea [daɪǎríǎ], s. diarrea.

diary [dáɪǎrɪ], s. diario.

dice [daɪs], s. (pl. de DIE) dados.—d. box, cubilete.—vt. cortar en forma de cubos menudos.

dictate [dɪkteɪt], vt. y vi. dictar; mandar, imponer(se).—s. dictamen.—**dictation** [dɪktéɪʃǫn], s. dictado; mando arbitrario.—**dictator** [dɪkteɪtǫ(r)], s. dictador.—**dictatorial** [dɪktǎtórɪǎl], a. dictatorial.—**dictatorship** [dɪktéɪtǫrʃɪp], s. dictadura.

diction [dɪ́kʃǫn], s. dicción; locución.—**-ary** [-erɪ], s. diccionario.

did [dɪd], pret. de TO DO.

die [daɪ], vi. morir(se), expirar, fallecer; marchitarse.

die [daɪ], s. (pl. dice [daɪs]) dado (para

jugar); (*pl.* dies [dajz]) cuño, troquel; molde.—*the d. is cast,* la suerte está echada.

diet [dájet], *s.* dieta, régimen alimenticio; dieta (asamblea).—*vt.* poner a dieta.—*vi.* estar a dieta.

differ [dífœ(r)], *vi.* diferir; diferenciarse, distinguirse.—*to d. from,* o *with,* no estar de acuerdo con.— —ence [-ęns], *s.* diferencia; distinción (de personas, etc.); discrepancia; desacuerdo; (arit.) residuo.—*it makes no d.,* no importa.— —ent [-ęnt], *a.* diferente, distinto.— —ential [-énšal], *s.* diferencial.— —entiate [-énšjejt], *vt.* y *vi.* diferenciar(se), distinguir(se).

difficult [dífjkʌlt], *a.* difícil; penoso.— —y [-j], *s.* dificultad; tropiezo; reparo.—*pl.* aprieto, apuro.

diffuse [dífjúz], *vt.* difundir; desparramar.—*vi.* difundirse; disiparse.— *a.* [dífjús] difundido, esparcido; difuso.—*diffusion* [dífjúžon], *s.* difusión; dispersión; prolijidad.

dig [dig], *vti.* [3] cavar, excavar; ahondar; escarbar.—*to d. out,* desentrañar. —*to d. up,* desenterrar.—*vii.* cavar; (fam.) matarse a trabajar.—*s.* empuje; (fam.) observación sarcástica.

digest [dájdžest], *s.* compendio, resumen; recopilación.—*vt.* [dajdžést], recopilar, abreviar y clasificar; digerir.—*vi.* digerirse; asimilarse.— —ible [dajdžéstjbl], *a.* digerible, digestible.— —ion [dajdžéschǫn], *s.* digestión; asimilación.— —ive [dajdžéstjv] *a.* y *s.* digestivo.

dignified [dígnjfajd], *a.* serio, grave; digno.—*dignify* [dígnjfaj], *vti.* [7] dignificar, honrar, exaltar.—*dignitary* [dígnjteri], *s.* dignatario.—*dignity* [dígnjtj], *s.* dignidad; nobleza, majestuosidad; rango o cargo elevado.

digress [dajgrés], *vi.* divagar.— —ion [dajgréšǫn], *s.* divagación o digresión.

dike [dajk], *s.* dique, represa; zanja; malecón.—*vt.* represar; canalizar.

dilapidate [dilápidejt], *vt.* dilapidar.— —d [-jd], *a.* destartalado, arruinado.

dilate [dajléjt], *vt.* dilatar, ensanchar. —*vi.* dilatarse, extenderse.

dilemma [djlémǫ], *s.* dilema.

diligence [dílidžęns], *s.* diligencia; coche diligencia.—*diligent* [dílidžęnt], *a.* diligente, aplicado; activo.

dilute [djljút], *vt.* desleír, diluir; aguar. —*vi.* desleírse, diluirse.—*a.* diluido.

dim [dim], *a.* oscuro; borroso; empañado; deslustrado; (fot.) velado.— *vti.* [1] oscurecer; empañar, deslustrar; amortiguar o reducir la intensidad de una luz.—*vii.* oscurecerse, etc.

dime [dajm], *s.* (E.U. y Canadá) moneda de diez centavos.

dimension [djménšǫn], *s.* dimensión, extensión, tamaño.

diminish [djmínjš], *vt.* disminuir, (a)minorar; rebajar, degradar.—*vi.* disminuir(se), menguar, (a)minorarse, decrecer.—*diminution* [djmjnjúšǫn], *s.* di(s)minución, rebaja, reducción. —*diminutive* [djmínyǫtjv], *a.* diminuto; diminutivo.—*s.* (gram.) diminutivo.

dimness [dímnjs], *s.* ofuscamiento; penumbra.

dimple [dímpl], *s.* hoyuelo.—*vt.* y *vi.* formar o formarse hoyuelos.

din [din], *s.* estrépito, alboroto.—*vti.* [1] ensordecer; aturdir.—*vii.* alborotar; (re)sonar con estrépito.

dine [dajn], *vi.* comer (la comida principal), cenar.— —r [dájnœ(r)], *s.* comedor; comensal.—*dining-car* [dájnjŋkar], *s.* coche comedor.—*dining room* [dájnjŋ rúm], *s.* comedor.

dinghy [díŋgi], *s.* lancha o bote pequeño.

dingy [díndži], *a.* empañado, deslustrado; manchado, sucio; oscuro.

dinner [dínœ(r)], *s.* comida (principal), cena; cubierto.—*d. jacket,* smoking, media etiqueta.—*d. set,* vajilla.

diocese [dájǫsis], *s.* diócesis.

dip [dip], *vti.* [3] sumergir; bañar, humedecer, mojar, zambullir; saludar con la bandera; (mar.) achicar.—*vii.* sumergirse, zambullirse; hundirse; hojear (en un libro, etc.); inclinarse hacia abajo.—*s.* inmersión, zambullida; baño corto; inclinación, caída, pendiente.

diphtheria [difθíriǫ], *s.* difteria.

diphthong [dífθǫŋ], *s.* diptongo.

diploma [diplóumǫ], *s.* diploma; título.

diplomacy [diplóumǫsi], *s.* diplomacia; tacto.—*diplomat* [díplomæt], *s.* diplomático.—*diplomatic* [diplomætjk], *a.* diplomático.

dipper [dípœ(r)], *s.* cazo, cucharón.

dire [dajr], *a.* extremo, angustioso; horrendo; de mal agüero.

direct [djrékt], *a.* directo; derecho; en línea recta (descendencia, sucesión, etc.).—*vt.* dirigir; encaminar; gobernar.—*vi.* dirigir; servir de guía.— —ion [djrékšǫn], *s.* dirección; rumbo; gobierno, administración; instrucción.—*d. finder,* (rad.) radiogoniómetro.— —ive [-jv], *a.* directivo.—*s.* instrucción, mandato.— —or [-ǫ(r)], *s.* director; gerente; administrador; vocal de una junta directiva; director de orquesta.—*board of directors,* consejo de administración.—*a.* (mat.) director, directriz.— —ory [-ǫrj], *s.* directorio; guía comercial.

dirt [dœrt], *s.* basura; mugre; tierra; lodo; polvo; bajeza.—*dirty* [dœrtj], *a.* sucio; manchado; enlodado; inde-

cente; puerco; vil.—*d. trick*, (fam.) perrada.—*vti.* [7] emporcar, ensuciar.

disability [dis̯əblĭtĭ], *s.* incapacidad; inhabilidad, impotencia.—**disable** [dis̯éjbl], *vt.* imposibilitar; inhabilitar; (for.) incapacitar legalmente.

disadvantage [dis̯ədvéntĭdž], *s.* desventaja, detrimento.—*at a d.*, en situación desventajosa.

disagree [dis̯əgrí], *vi.* disentir, discrepar, diferir, desavenirse; estar en pugna.—*to d. with*, no estar de acuerdo con; no sentar bien a.——**able** [-əbl], *a.* desagradable; descortés, desapacible.——**ment** [-męnt], *s.* desacuerdo, desavenencia; discordia; disensión; discrepancia.

disappear [dis̯əpír], *vi.* desaparecer(se).——**ance** [-əns], *s.* desaparición.

disappoint [dis̯əpóint], *vt.* chasquear; decepcionar, desilusionar; defraudar una esperanza.—*to be disappointed*, verse contrariado; estar desilusionado o decepcionado.——**ment** [-męnt], *s.* desengaño, desilusión, decepción, contratiempo; chasco.

disapproval [dis̯əprúvəl], *s.* desaprobación, censura.—**disapprove** [dis̯əprúv], *vt.* y *vi.* desaprobar.

disarm [dis̯árm], *vt.* desarmar; (fig.) apaciguar, sosegar.—*vi.* deponer las armas; licenciar tropas.——**ment** [-əmęnt], *s.* desarme.

disarrange [dis̯əréjndž], *vt.* desarreglar, descomponer, desordenar.——**ment** [-męnt], *s.* desarreglo, desorden.

disassemble [dis̯əsémbl], *vt.* desarmar, desmontar (un reloj, una máquina).

disaster [dis̯éstœ(r)], *s.* desastre; siniestro.—**disastrous** [dis̯éstrʌs], *a.* desastroso, funesto.

disband [dis̯bénd], *vt.* licenciar las tropas.—*vi.* dispersarse, desbandarse.

disburse [dis̯bœrs], *vt.* desembolsar, pagar, gastar.——**ment** [-męnt], *s.* desembolso; gasto.—*pl.* (com.) egresos.

disc [dis̯k], *s.* (anat.) disco; = DISK.

discard [dis̯kárd], *vt.* descartar; despedir.—*vi.* descartarse (en el juego).—*s.* [dis̯kard] descarte (en el juego).

discern [dizœ́rn], *vt.* y *vi.* discernir, percibir, distinguir.——**ment** [-męnt], *s.* discernimiento; criterio.

discharge [dis̯chárdž], *vt.* descargar; disparar; cumplir, desempeñar, ejecutar; despedir; exonerar, eximir, dispensar; arrojar, vomitar; (mil.) licenciar.—*vi.* descargarse; vaciarse; desaguar.—*s.* descarga; disparo; (com.) descargo; carta de pago; desempeño; remoción, despido; (mil.) licencia absoluta; absolución, exoneración; derrame, desagüe.

disciple [dis̯áipl], *s.* discípulo

discipline [dísiplin], *s.* disciplina; enseñanza; castigo; materia de estudio.—*vt.* disciplinar, instruir; castigar.

disclose [dis̯klóuz], *vt.* descubrir, destapar; revelar, publicar.—**disclosure** [dis̯klóuźư(r)], *s.* descubrimiento; revelación.

discolor [dis̯kÁlǫ(r)], *vt.* y *vi.* descolorar(se), desteñir(se).——**ation** [-éjșǫn], *s.* descoloramiento.

discomfort [dis̯kÁmfǫrt], *s.* incomodidad; malestar, molestia.—*vt.* incomodar; molestar.

disconcert [dis̯kǫnsœ́rt], *vt.* desconcertar, confundir.

disconnect [dis̯kǫnékt], *vt.* desconectar; desunir o separar.——**ed** [-id], *a.* desconectado; inconexo, incoherente.

disconsolate [dis̯kánsolit], *a.* desconsolado, inconsolable, desolado.

discontent [dis̯kǫntént], *s.* descontento, desagrado.—*a.* descontento; quejoso, disgustado.—*vt.* descontentar, desagradar.——**ed** [-id], *a.* descontent(adiz)o; disgustado.——**ment** [-męnt], *s.* descontento, mal humor.

discontinue [dis̯kǫntínyu], *vt.* y *vi.* interrumpir, descontinuar; suspender; desabonarse.

discord [dis̯kǫrd], *s.* discordia; desacuerdo, (mus.) disonancia.—*to sow d.*, cizañar.—*vi.* [dis̯kǫ́rd], discordar.——**ance** [dis̯kǫ́rdəns], ——**ancy** [dis̯kǫ́rdənsi], *s.* discordia; discordancia; disensión.——**ant** [dis̯kǫ́rdənt], *a.* discorde, desconforme; discordante, disonante.

discount [dis̯káunt], *vt.* descontar; rebajar, deducir; dar poca importancia a.—*s.* descuento, rebaja.—*d. rate*, tipo de descuento.

discourage [dis̯kœ́ridž], *vt.* desalentar; desaprobar, oponerse a.——**d** [-d], *a.* desanimado, desalentado.——**ment** [-męnt], *s.* desaliento, desánimo, obstáculo.

discourse [dis̯kǫrs], *s.* discurso; plática, conversación; disertación.—*vi.* [dis̯kǫ́rs], [dis̯cǔrrir, discursar; disertar; conversar, razonar.—*vt.* hablar de; proferir, expresar.

discourteous [dis̯kœ́rtĭʌs], *a.* descortés, grosero.—**discourtesy** [dis̯kœ́rtȩsi], *s.* descortesía.

discover [dis̯kÁvœ(r)], *vt.* descubrir.——**er** [-œ(r)], *s.* descubridor.——**y** [-i], *s.* descubrimiento, hallazgo.

discredit [dis̯krédit], *s.* descrédito, desconfianza; deshonra, oprobio.—*vt.* desacreditar; desautorizar, desvirtuar.

discreet [dis̯krít], *a.* discreto, prudente, juicioso.——**ness** [-nįs], *s.* = DISCRETION.

DIS—DIS
66

discrepancy [dĭskrépansĭ], *s.* discrepancia, diferencia; variación.

discretion [dĭskréšọn], *s.* discreción, juicio, prudencia.

discriminate [dĭskrímĭnejt], *vt.* discriminar, prejuzgar; discernir, distinguir.—*a.* [dĭskrímĭnĭt], definido, distinguible; discernidor.—**discrimination** [dĭskrĭmĭnéišọn], *s.* discriminación, prejuicio; discernimiento; distinción, diferencia.

discuss [dĭskás], *vt.* discutir, debatir; tratar.— **ion** [dĭskášọn], *s.* discusión, debate; exposición, ventilación.

disdain [dĭsdéjn], *vt.* desdeñar, despreciar.—*vi.* desdeñarse, esquivarse.—*s.* desdén, desprecio, esquivez.— **ful** [-fŭl], *a.* desdeñoso; altivo, altanero.

disease [dĭzíz], *s.* enfermedad, afección, dolencia.—*vt.* enfermar, hacer daño.— **d** [-d], *a.* enfermo; morboso.

disembark [dĭsembárk], *vt.* y *vi.* desembarcar(se).— **ation** [-éišọn], *s.* desembarco o desembarque.

disembowel [dĭsembáṵel], *vti.* [2] destripar, desentrañar, sacar las entrañas.

disengage [dĭsengéjdž], *vt.* desunir, desasir; (mec.) desembragar; desenganchar.—*vi.* soltarse, desligarse, zafarse.

disentangle [dĭsentæŋgl], *vt.* desenredar, desenmarañar, desembrollar.

disfigure [dĭsfígyṵ(r)], *vt.* desfigurar, afear.

disgorge [dĭsgórdž], *vt.* desembuchar; vomitar.

disgrace [dĭsgréjs], *s.* ignominia, vergüenza; deshonra, estigma.—*vt.* deshonrar; desacreditar.— **ful** [-fŭl], *a.* vergonzoso, oprobioso.

disguise [dĭsgájz], *vt.* disfrazar, enmascarar; desfigurar; encubrir.—*s.* disfraz, máscara; embozo.

disgust [dĭsgást], *s.* repugnancia; asco, náusea; disgusto.—*vt.* repugnar; fastidiar, hastiar.— **ed** [-id], *a.* disgustado, fastidiado.— **ing** [-iŋ], *a.* repugnante, asqueroso; odioso.

dish [dĭš], *s.* plato, fuente; manjar.—*pl.* vajilla, loza.—*d. drainer* o *rack*, escurreplatos.

dishearten [dĭshártẹn], *vt.* desanimar, descorazonar.

dishevel [dĭšévẹl], *vti.* [2] desgreñar, desmelenar.

dishonest [dĭsánjst], *a.* falto de honradez, pícaro; fraudulento, falso.— **y** [-ĭ], *s.* improbidad, picardía; fraude.

dishonor [dĭsánọ(r)], *s.* deshonor, deshonra; afrenta.—*vt.* deshonrar; afrentar.— **able** [-ạbl], *a.* deshonroso, ignominioso; deshonrado, infamado.

dishwasher [dĭšwášœ(r)], *s.* máquina de lavar platos; lavaplatos.

disillusion [dĭsĭljúžọn], *vt.* desilusionar, desengañar.— **ment** [-mẹnt], *s.* desilusión, desengaño, decepción.

disinfect [dĭsĭnfékt], *vt.* desinfectar.— **ant** [-ạnt], *a.* y *s.* desinfectante.— **ion** [dĭsĭnfékšọn], *s.* desinfección.

disinherit [dĭsĭnhérĭt], *vt.* desheredar.

disinterment [dĭsĭntérmẹnt], *s.* exhumación, desenterramiento.

disjoin [dĭsdžójn], *vt.* desunir, apartar, disgregar.— **t** [-t], *vt.* descoyuntar, dislocar.— **ted** [-tĭd], *a.* dislocado, descoyuntado; sin ilación.

disk [dĭsk], *s.* disco; rodaja.

dislike [dĭslájk], *s.* aversión, antipatía.—*vt.* tener aversión, no gustar de.

dislocate [dĭslokejt], *vt.* dislocar, descoyuntar.—**dislocation** [dĭslokéišọn], *s.* dislocación, luxación.

dislodge [dĭsládž], *vt.* desalojar, echar fuera.—*vi.* mudarse.

disloyal [dĭslójạl], *a.* desleal.— **ty** [-tĭ], *s.* deslealtad.

dismal [dĭzmạl], *a.* lúgubre, triste.—*s.* pantano.

dismantle [dĭsmǽntl], *vt.* desguarnecer; desmantelar; desmontar.

dismay [dĭsméj], *s.* desaliento, desmayo; consternación.—*vt.* desanimar, espantar, aterrar.

dismiss [dĭsmís], *vt.* despedir, destituir; descartar; despachar; dar de baja.— **al** [-ạl], *s.* despido, remoción, destitución.

dismount [dĭsmáunt], *vt.* desmontar; desarmar.—*vi.* apearse, descabalgar.

disobedience [dĭsobídjens], *s.* desobediencia.—**disobedient** [dĭsobídjent], *a.* desobediente.—**disobey** [dĭsobéj], *vt.* y *vi.* desobedecer.

disorder [dĭsórdœ(r)], *s.* desorden; irregularidad; alboroto; enfermedad.—*vt.* desordenar; inquietar, perturbar.— **ly** [-lĭ], *a.* desordenado, desarreglado; escandaloso, perturbador.—*d. house*, burdel.—*adv.* desordenadamente, etc.

disown [dĭsóụn], *vt.* repudiar, negar, desconocer; renunciar, renegar de.

disparity [dĭspárĭtĭ], *s.* disparidad.

dispatch [dĭspéch], *vt.* despachar, expedir; remitir.—*s.* despacho; mensaje, comunicación.

dispel [dĭspél], *vti.* [1] dispersar; disipar, desvanecer.

dispensary [dĭspénsạrĭ], *s.* dispensario.—**dispensation** [dĭspenséišọn], *s.* dispensa, exención; designio divino.—**dispense** [dĭspéns], *vt.* distribuir, repartir; administrar (justicia); dispensar, eximir.

dispersal [dĭspérsạl], *s.* dispersión.—**disperse** [dĭspérs], *vt.* dispersar;

esparcir.—*vi.* dispersarse; disiparse.
—*a.* disperso.—**dispersion** [dispǽr-
șǫn], *s.* dispersión; esparcimiento;
difusión.

displace [displéjs], *vt.* desalojar, desplazar, quitar el puesto a.- —**ment**
[-mǫnt], *s.* remoción, desalojo, desplazamiento.

display [displéj], *vt.* desplegar, extender;
exhibir, lucir.—*s.* despliegue; ostentación, exhibición.—*d. window*, escaparate, vidriera.—*on d.*, en exhibición.

displease [displíz], *vt. y vi.* desagradar,
disgustar.—**displeasure** [displéžŭ(r)],
s. desagrado, disfavor.

disposal [dispóuzal], *s.* disposición;
colocación, arreglo; venta (de bienes);
donación.—**dispose** [dispóuz], *vt.*
arreglar, disponer; inclinar el ánimo;
ordenar, mandar.—*vi.* disponer.—*to
d. of*, acabar con; deshacerse de; dar,
vender, traspasar; disponer de.—
disposition [dispozíșǫn], *s.* disposición; arreglo, ordenación; índole.

dispossess [dispǫsés], *vt.* desposeer,
desalojar; (for.) desahuciar, lanzar.

disprove [disprúv], *vt.* refutar.

dispute [dispjút], *vt.* refutar, impugnar.
—*vi.* disputar, discutir.—*s.* disputa,
discusión; litigio, pleito.

disqualify [diskwálifaj], *vti.* [7] descalificar, inhabilitar.

disregard [disrigárd], *vt.* desatender,
hacer caso omiso de; desairar, despreciar.—*s.* desatención, descuido,
omisión; desprecio, desaire.

disrespect [disrispékt], *s.* desatención,
falta de respeto.—*vt.* desacatar, desairar; faltar el respeto a.- —**ful**
[-fǔl], *a.* irrespetuoso, irreverente.

disrupt [disrápt], *vt.* romper; rajar,
reventar; hacer pedazos; desorga-
nizar, desbaratar.- —**ion** [disrápșǫn],
s. desgarro, rotura; desorganización
o rompimiento.—**ive** [disráptiv], *a.*
destructor, disolvente.

dissatisfaction [disætjsfǽkșǫn], *s.* descontento, disgusto.—**dissatisfy** [dis-
ǽtjsfaj], *vti.* [7] desagradar, descontentar.

dissect [disékt], *vt.* disecar, anatomizar;
analizar.- —**ion** [disékșǫn], *s.* disección, disecación, anatomía; análisis.

dissension [disénșǫn], *s.* disensión,
discordia.—**dissent** [disént], *vi.* disentir, disidir.—*s.* disensión, desavenencia.

dissertation [discertéjșǫn], *s.* disertación.

dissimulation [disimyŭléjșǫn], *s.* disimulo, disfraz; tolerancia afectada.

dissipate [dísipejt], *vt. y vi.* disipar(se),
dispersar(se); desintegrar(se), des-
vanecer(se), evaporar(se).—*vt.* desperdiciar, derrochar.- —**d** [dísipej-

tjd], *a.* disipado, disoluto.—**dissipation** [disipéjșǫn], *s.* disipación; libertinaje.

dissociate [disóușiejt], *vt.* disociar, dividir, separar.

dissolute [dísoljut], *a.* disoluto, libert-
tino, licencioso.—**dissolution** [diso-
ljúșǫn], *s.* disolución.—**dissolve** [di-
zálv], *vt.* disolver; disipar; dispersar;
desleír; derogar, revocar, anular.
—*vi.* disolverse; descomponerse; desvanecerse; languidecer.

dissonance [dísonąns], *s.* disonancia;
desconcierto, discordia.—**dissonant**
[dísonąnt], *a.* disonante, discordante; contrario, discorde.

distaff [dístæf], *s.* rueca.—*d. o d. side*,
sexo débil.

distance [dístąns], *s.* distancia; alejamiento; lejanía, lontananza; trecho;
intervalo.—*at a d.*, de lejos.—*in the
d.*, en lontananza, a lo lejos.—*to keep
one's d.*, guardar las distancias.—*vt.*
alejar, apartar; espaciar; tomar la
delantera.—**distant** [dístąnt], *a.* distante, alejado; esquivo, frío.

distaste [distéjst], *s.* fastidio, aversión,
disgusto.- —**ful** [-fǔl], *a.* enfadoso,
desagradable.

distend [disténd], *vt. y vi.* tender(se),
ensanchar(se), dilatar(se), hin-
char(se); distender(se).

distill [distíl], *vt. y vi.* destilar.- —**ation**
[distiléjșǫn], *s.* destilación.- —**ery**
[-œrj], *s.* destilería.

distinct [dístįnkt], *a.* distinto, claro,
preciso; diferente.—*d. from*, distinto
a.- —**ion** [distįnkșǫn], *s.* distinción;
discernimiento; diferencia; honor.—
—**ive** [distįnktjv], *a.* distintivo, característico.—**distinguish** [distíngwiș],
vt. distinguir, discernir, diferenciar;
honrar.—**distinguished** [distíngwjȿt],
a. distinguido; prestigioso; especial,
señalado.

distort [distórt], *vt.* (ro)torcer; deformar; falsear, tergiversar.- —**ion**
[distórșǫn], *s.* distorsión; esguince;
deformación, tergiversación.

distract [distrǽkt], *vt.* distraer; perturbar, interrumpir.- —**ion** [dis-
trǽkșǫn], *s.* distracción; perturbación; diversión, pasatiempo.

distress [distrés], *s.* pena, dolor;
angustia; desgracia, miseria; embargo, secuestro.—*vt.* angustiar, afligir; poner en aprieto; embargar,
secuestrar.

distribute [distríbjut], *vt.* distribuir.
—*vi.* hacer distribución.- —**r** [dis-
tríbjutœ(r)], **distributor** [distríbju-
tǫ(r)], *s.* distribuidor, repartidor.
—**distribution** [distribjúșǫn], *s.* distribución, reparto.

district [dístrjkt], *s.* distrito, comarca,

territorio; barriada, barrio; región; jurisdicción.

distrust [dịstrʌst], *vt.* desconfiar, recelar.— *-s.* desconfianza, recelo; descrédito.— —**ful** [-fụl], *a.* desconfiado, receloso; suspicaz.

disturb [dịstə́rb], *vt.* alborotar, (per)turbar; distraer, interrumpir; desordenar, revolver.— —**ance** [-ạns], *s.* disturbio, conmoción, alboroto, desorden.— —**er** [œ(r)], *s.* perturbador.

disuse [dịsyús], *s.* desuso.—*to fall into d.*, caer en desuso, perder vigencia. —*vt.* [dịsyúz], desusar; cesar de usar; desechar.

ditch [dịch], *s.* zanja; cuneta; trinchera; foso; acequia.—*vt.* zanjar; abandonar, desembarazarse de; (fam.) dar calabazas a.

ditto [dị́tou], *s.* ídem; lo mismo; marca (") o abreviatura (id.); duplicado, copia fiel.—*vt.* duplicar, copiar.—*adv.* como ya se dijo; asimismo.

divan [dájvæn, dịvǽn], *s.* diván.

dive [dajv], *vii.* [5] za(m)bullirse, echarse o tirarse de cabeza; bucear; enfrascarse, profundizar; (aer.) picar.— *-s.* za(m)bullidura, buceo; enfrascamiento; tugurio; (aer.) picada.— —**r** [dájvœ(r)], *s.* buceador, buzo. —**diving** [dájvịŋ], *s.* za(m)bullida, buceo; deporte del salto de palanca y trampolín; (aer.) picada.—*d. board*, trampolín.

diverge [dịvə́rdʒ], *vi.* divergir, diferir, desviarse.— —**nce** [dịvə́rdʒəns], —**ncy** [dịvə́rdʒənsị], *s.* divergencia.— —**nt** [dịvə́rdʒənt], *a.* divergente.

divers [dájvœrz], *a.* varios, diversos.

diverse [dịvə́rs], *a.* diverso, variado, distinto.—**diversify** [dịvə́rsịfaj], *vti.* [7] diversificar, variar.—**diversion** [dịvə́rʒọn], *s.* desviación; diversión, entretenimiento.—**diversity** [dịvə́rsịtị], *s.* diversidad, variedad; diferencia.—**divert** [dịvə́rt], *vt.* desviar; divertir.—**diverting** [dịvə́rtịŋ], *a.* divertido, entretenido, recreativo.

divide [dịvájd], *vt.* dividir; desunir, separar; repartir, compartir.—*vi.* dividirse.— —**nd** [dịvịdend], *s.* dividendo.

divine [dịvájn], *a.* divino; teólogo.—*vt.* adivinar; vaticinar.—**divinity** [dịvínịtị], *s.* divinidad; deidad; atributo divino; teología.

division [dịvíʒọn], *s.* división; distribución, repart(imient)o; ramo, negociado, departamento; sección; desunión, desacuerdo.

divorce [dịvórs], *s.* divorcio.—*vt.* y *vi.* divorciar(se).— —**e** [dịvorsí], *s.* persona divorciada.

divulge [dịvʌ́ldʒ], *vt.* divulgar, propalar.

dizziness [dịzịnịs], *s.* vértigo, vahído; desvanecimiento.—**dizzy** [dịzị], *a.* vertiginoso, desvanecido.—*vti.* [7] causar vértigos; aturdir.

do [du], *vti.* [11] hacer; ejecutar; obrar; finalizar; producir; despachar; cumplir; arreglar; cocer, guisar.—*vii.* hacer; comportarse; proceder; hallarse.—*how d. you d.?* ¿cómo está Ud.?—*that will d.*, eso basta, bastará.

docile [dásịl], *a.* dócil, sumiso.

dock [dak], *s.* dique, dársena; muelle, desembarcadero; banquillo de los acusados.—*vt.* cortar, cercenar; reducir, rebajar; (mar.) poner en dique.—*vt.* y *vi.* atracar, entrar en muelle.— —**er** [dákœ(r)], *s.* estibador, trabajador de muelle.

docket [dákit], *s.* minuta, sumario; rótulo, marbete.

dockyard [dákyard], *s.* astillero, arsenal.

doctor [dáktọ(r)], *s.* médico; doctor. —*vt.* medicinar, tratar; falsificar, adulterar; componer.— —**ate** [-ịt], *s.* doctorado.

doctrine [dáktrịn], *s.* doctrina, dogma; teoría.

document [dákyụmənt], *s.* documento. —*vt.* [dákyụment], documentar; probar con documentos.— —**al** [dakyụméntạl], *a.*, —**ary** [dakyụméntạrị], *a.* documental.—*s.* (película) documental.— —**ation** [dakyụmentéjʃọn], *s.* documentación.

dodge [dadʒ], *vt.* esquivar, soslayar, evadir.—*vi.* escabullirse; dar un quiebro o esquinazo; hurtar el cuerpo.

doe [dou], *s.* hembra del gamo, de la liebre, del conejo, del canguro y del antílope.— —**skin** [dóuskịn], *s.* ante; tejido fino de lana.

dog [dog], *s.* perro; macho de los cánidos (zorro, lobo, chacal, etc.); calavera, tunante.—*d.-cheap*, baratísimo.—*d.-tired*, cansadísimo.—*to put on the d.*, darse ínfulas.—*vti.* [1] seguir los pasos; espiar, perseguir.— —**fight** [dógfajt], *s.* riña de perros; combate entre aviones de caza.—**dogged** [dógịd], *a.* terco, tenaz.— —**house** [-haụs], *s.* caseta de perro.—*in the d.*, en desgracia.

dogma [dógmạ], *s.* dogma.— —**tic** [dogmǽtịk], *a.* dogmático.

doily [dójlị], *s.* mantelillo individual.

doings [dúịŋs], *s. pl.* acciones, obras; acontecimientos, cosas que ocurren.

dole [doụl], *s.* distribución, reparto; porción; sopa boba; limosna; ración.—*vt.* repartir, distribuir, dar (limosna).— —**ful** [dóụlfụl], *a.* dolorido; lúgubre, triste.

doll [dal], *s.* muñeca, muñeco.—*to d. up*, acicalarse, emperifollarse.— —**y**

[dáli], *s.* muñequita; plataforma rodante.

dolphin [dálfin], *s.* delfín.

domain [doméin], *s.* dominio; heredad.

dome [doum], *s.* cúpula.

domestic [doméstik], *a.* doméstico, familiar; del país, nacional; interno, interior.—*s.* doméstico, sirviente.— —**ate** [-eit], *vt.* domesticar; hacer adquirir costumbres caseras.

domicile [dámisil], *s.* domicilio.

dominant [dáminant], *a.* dominante.— **dominate** [dámineit], *vt.* y *vi.* dominar.—**domination** [daminéi§on], *s.* dominación, dominio, imperio.— **domineer** [daminír], *vt.* y *vi.* dominar, tiranizar.—**domineering** [daminírin], *a.* dominante, tiránico, mandón.— **dominion** [domínyon], *s.* dominio; territorio; distrito; posesión, propiedad.

don [dan], *vti.* [1] vestirse, ponerse, calarse.—*s.* caballero; don (título).

donate [dóuneit], *vt.* donar, contribuir. —**donation** [dounéi§on], *s.* donación, donativo, dádiva.

done [dʌn], *pp.* de TO DO.—*a.* hecho, ejecutado; acabado: bien cocido o asado.—*d. for,* agotado, rendido; perdido.—*d. up,* envuelto; fatigado.

donkey [dánki], *s.* asno, burro.

donor [dóuno(r)], *s.* donante, donador.

doom [dum], *vt.* sentenciar a muerte; predestinar a la perdición.—*s.* sentencia, condena; sino, destino; perdición, ruina.— —**sday** [dúmzdei], *s.* día del juicio final.

door [dor], *s.* puerta; portezuela; entrada.—*d. mat,* felpudo.— —**bell** [dórbel], *s.* timbre o campanilla de llamada.— —**keeper** [-kipœ(r)], —**man** [-man], *s.* portero.— —**knob** [-nab], *s.* tirador o perilla de puerta.— —**plate** [-pleit], *s.* placa de puerta.— —**sill** [-sil], *s.* umbral.— —**step** [-step], *s.* escalón de la puerta.— —**way** [-wei], *s.* entrada; portal.

dope [doup], *s.* estupefaciente, narcótico; menjurje; (fam.) datos, informes; tonto, estúpido.—*d. addict,* o *fiend,* narcómano.—*d. racket,* tráfico ilícito de drogas.—*vt.* narcotizar; pronosticar; conjeturar.—**dopy** [dóupi], *a.* (fam.) narcotizado, aletargado.

dormitory [dórmitori], *s.* dormitorio (colectivo).

dormouse [dórmaus], *s.* (zool.) lirón.

dorsal [dórsal], *a.* dorsal, espinal.

dosage [dóusid£], *s.* dosificación.—**dose** [dous], *s.* dosis; (fig.) mal trago.—*vt.* administrar una dosis.—*vi.* medicarse con frecuencia.

dot [dat], *s.* punto.—*on the d.,* en punto, a la hora exacta.—*to a d.,* perfectamente, absolutamente.—*vti.* [1] puntear; poner punto (a una letra).

dotage [dóutid£], *s.* chochera; cariño excesivo.—**dote** [dout], *vi.* chochear.

double [dʌbl], *a.* doble, duplicado; falso, engañoso.—*d. bed,* cama de matrimonio.—*d. boiler,* baño María. —*d.-breasted,* (sast.) cruzado, de dos filas.—*d.-cross,* traición hecha a un cómplice.—*d. chin,* papada.—*d. dealer,* falso, traidor.—*d. entry,* partida doble.—*d. meaning,* doble sentido; equívoco; segunda intención. —*adv.* doblemente.—*s.* doble, duplo; (teat., cine) doble.—*vt.* doblar, duplicar.—*vi.* doblarse, duplicarse; volver atrás.

doubt [daut], *vt.* y *vi.* dudar; desconfiar. —*s.* duda.—*if o when in d.,* en caso de duda.— —**ful** [dáutful], *a.* dudoso.— —**less** [-lis], *a.* indudable, cierto; confiado.—*adv.* sin duda, indudablemente, probablemente.

douche [duš], *s.* jeringa o lavado vaginal; ducha, (Am.) regadera.—*vt.* y *vi.* duchar(se).

dough [dou], *s.* pasta, masa; (fam.) plata, dinero.— —**nut** [dóunʌt], *s.* buñuelo, rosca.— —**y** [-i], *a.* pastoso.

dove [dʌv], *s.* paloma, tórtola.— [douv], *pret.* de TO DIVE.

dowel [dáuel], *s.* clavija, espiga.

down [daun], *adv.* abajo; hacia abajo; al sur.—*d. below,* allá abajo.—*d. from,* desde.—*d. to,* hasta.—*d. to date,* hasta la fecha.—*to boil d.,* reducir la ebullición.—*to cut d.,* recortar, rebajar.—*to go o come d.,* bajar.—*to lie d.,* acostarse.—*interj.* ¡abajo!—*d. with the King!* ¡muera el Rey!—*prep.* en sentido descendente; por, al largo de, hacia abajo.—*d. the street,* calle abajo.—*a.* pendiente, descendente; abatido, alicaído; de abajo; atrasado, atrás.—*d. and out,* fuera de combate; vencido; arruinado.—*d. payment,* primer plazo, paga al contado.—*to be d. on,* tener inquina a.—*s.* plumón; bozo; lana fina o pelo suave, pelusa; revés de fortuna, baja, caída; colina, duna. —*d. bed,* colchón de plumas.—*vt.* derribar; vencer; tragar, creer sin previo examen.— —**cast** [dáunkæst], *a.* alicaído, cabizbajo.— —**fall** [-fol], *s.* caída; ruina.— —**grade** [-greid], *a.* y *adv.* cuesta abajo.—*s.* bajada, descenso.— —**hearted** [-hartid], *a.* abatido, descorazonado.— —**hill** [-hil], *a.* pendiente, en declive.—*s.* declive, bajada.—*adv.* cuesta abajo.— —**pour** [-por], *s.* aguacero, chaparrón.— —**right** [-rait], *a.* vertical; claro, categórico; absoluto, completo.—*adv.* claramente, completamente.— —**stairs**

[-stérz], *adv.* abajo, en el piso de abajo.—*s.* piso inferior, primer piso.—**—town** [-taun], *a.* y *adv.* de o en la parte baja de la ciudad; del centro.

dowry [dáuri], *s.* dote; arras.

doze [douz], *vi.* dormitar, descabezar el sueño.—*s.* sueño ligero; sopor, adormecimiento.

dozen [dΛzen], *s.* docena.

drab [dræb], *a.* pardusco; monótono; ordinario, sin atractivos.—*s.* color entre gris pardo y amarillento.

draft [dræft], *s.* corriente de aire; tiro (de chimenea, etc.); succión; trago; (mar.) calado; tracción; carretada; trazado, dibujo; plan, plano; borrador, minuta; proyecto, propuesta (de ley, reglamento, etc.); letra de cambio, libranza, orden de pago; (mil.) reclutamiento, leva; destacamento.—*d.* ale o *beer,* cerveza de tonel o de barril.—*d. dodger,* emboscado; prófugo del servicio militar.—*vt.* proyectar, bosquejar; hacer un borrador o diseño, esquema, plan; reclutar; redactar.— **—sman** [dræftsman], *s.* dibujante, delineante, diseñador.

drag [dræg], *vti.* [1] arrastrar, tirar; rastrear, rastrillar.—*to d. in,* traer por los cabellos.—*to d. on* o *out,* prolongar.—*vii.* arrastrarse por el suelo; ir tirando; atrasarse, ir en zaga; pasar con penosa lentitud, ser interminable.—*s.* rastra; draga; rémora, cosa que retarda o dificulta.

drain [drein], *vt.* drenar, desaguar; desecar; escurrir; colar; achicar; agotar; consumir, disipar.—*to d. off,* vaciar.—*vi.* desaguarse, vaciarse, escurrirse.—*s.* desagüe, escurridor; sumidero, alcantarilla; consumo; agotamiento.—*a.* de desagüe.— **—age** [dréinidʒ], *s.* drenaje, desagüe.— **—er** [-œ(r)] *s.* colador, coladero.

drake [dreik], *s.* pato o ánade macho.

drama [drámʒ], *s.* drama.— **—tic** [drʒmétik], *a.* dramático.— **—tics** [drʒmétiks], *s.* dramática.— **—tist** [drémʒtist], *s.* dramaturgo.— **—tize** [drémʒtaiz], *vt.* dramatizar.

drank [dræŋk], *pret.* de TO DRINK.

drape [dreip], *vt.* revestir, entapizar, colgar (cortinas, etc.); formar pliegues artísticos.— **—ry** [dréipœri], *s.* cortinaje, ropaje, colgaduras, tapicería, etc.

draught [dræft], *s., vt. =* DRAFT.

draw [dro], *vti.* [10] tirar; atraer; estirar; sacar; inferir, deducir; desenvainar; hacer salir; chupar o mamar; aspirar, respirar; cobrar (un sueldo); sacarse (un premio); echar (suertes); procurarse, proporcionarse; correr o descorrer (cortinas, etc.);

dibujar; trazar; redactar, extender (un cheque, etc.); devengar (intereses, etc.); retirar (fondos); girar, librar; tender (un arco); destripar (aves).—*to d. along,* arrastrar.—*to d. aside,* llevar aparte.—*to d. back,* hacer retroceder.—*to d. in,* atraer, seducir, embaucar.—*to d. up,* redactar.—*vii.* tirar; atraer gente; (dep.) empatar; dibujar.—*to d. away,* alejarse.—*to d. back,* retroceder.—*to d. near,* acercarse.—*to d. up,* pararse, detenerse.—*s.* tracción; atracción; empate; sorteo.— **—back** [dróbæk], *s.* desventaja, inconveniente.— **—bridge** [-bridʒ], *s.* puente levadizo o giratorio.— **—er** [-œ(r)], *s.* gaveta, cajón.—*pl.* calzoncillos.— **—ing** [-iŋ], *s.* dibujo; sorteo; giro; cobranza; extracción.—*d. account,* cuenta corriente.— **—drawn** [dron], *pp.* de TO DRAW.

dread [dred], *s.* miedo, pavor.—*a.* terrible, espantoso.—*vt.* y *vi.* temer, tener miedo a.— **—ful** [drédful], *a.* terrible, espantoso.

dream [drim], *s.* sueño, ensueño.—*vti.* y *vii.* [4] soñar; ver en sueños; fantasear, forjar(se).—*to d. of,* soñar con.— **—er** [drímœ(r)], *s.* soñador.— **—y** [-i], *a.* contemplativo, soñador; propio de un sueño.

dreary [dríri], *a.* triste, melancólico; monótono, pesado.

dredge [dredʒ], *vt.* dragar; rastrear; polvorear.—*s.* draga; rastra.

dregs [dregz], *s. pl.* heces; sedimento; desperdicios; hez, gentuza.

drench [drench], *vt.* empapar; mojar; remojar.—*s.* empapada; mojadura.

dress [dres], *vti.* [4] vestir; ataviar; adornar; curar (heridas); preparar, arreglar; aliñar, aderezar; curtir; amortajar; arreglar (el pelo).—*to d. down,* poner como nuevo (a alguien).—*vii.* vestirse; ataviarse; adornarse; alinearse.—*to d. up,* vestirse de etiqueta, prenderse de veinticinco alfileres.—*s.* vestido; traje; indumentaria.—*d. ball,* baile de etiqueta o de trajes.—*d. suit,* traje de etiqueta.

drew [dru], *pret.* de TO DRAW.

dried [draid], *a.* seco; secado; desecado.— **—drier** [dráiœ(r)], *s.* secador, secadora; secadero; secante; desecante.

drift [drift], *s.* rumbo, tendencia; impulso; deriva; montón (de nieve, arena).—*to get the d. of,* comprender lo esencial de algo; enterarse sólo a medias.—*vi.* (aer., mar.) derivar, ir a la deriva; vagar; apilarse, amontonarse o esparcirse con el viento.— **—wood** [dríftwud], *s.* madera flotante; madera de playa.

drill [dril], *vt.* taladrar, barrenar, horadar; fresar; sembrar, plantar en

hileras o surcos; ejercitar, dar instrucción (ejército, etc.), entrenar.—*vi.* (mil.) hacer la instrucción, practicar, ejercitarse.—*s.* taladro, fresa, barrena; práctica, ejercicio; disciplina; adiestramiento; (tela de) dril.

drink [drɪŋk], *vti. y vii.* [10] beber.—*s.* bebida; trago, copa.— —**able** [drɪŋkəbl], *a.* potable.— —**er** [-œ(r)], *s.* bebedor; borrachín.

drip [drip], *vti. y vii.* [3] gotear.—*s.* gota; goteo; gotera.

drive [drajv], *vti.* [10] guiar, conducir, manejar (automóviles, etc.); impulsar, empujar; echar, arrojar; inducir; forzar (a); arrear; meter, clavar, hincar.—*vii.* andar o ir de paseo (automóvil, etc); saber guiar, manejar o conducir vehículos.—*to d. at*, aspirar a, tender a; querer decir.—*to d. away*, ahuyentar, alejarse (en un vehículo).—*s.* paseo en automóvil; capacidad de mando, energía; calzada para vehículos; presión, exigencia; tendencia, anhelo; campaña pública; conducción de vehículos.—*d.-in*, cine al aire libre para automovilistas; cafetería que sirve directamente en el automóvil.

drivel [drɪvḷ], *vti.* [2] babear; bobear.—*s.* baba; ñoñería; cháchara.

driven [drɪvḍn], *pp.* de TO DRIVE.— **driver** [drájvœ(r)], *s.* el que conduce, maneja o gobierna un vehículo (chofer, cochero, carretero, etc.); rueda motriz.—*driver's seat*, asiento del chofer.—*pile d.*, martinete.—**driveway** [drájvwej], *s.* vía de acceso a un garage; calzada.

drizzle [drɪzl], *vi.* lloviznar.—*s.* llovizna.

drone [droun], *s.* zángano; haragán; zumbido.—*vi.* haraganear; zumbar; hablar en tono monótono.

droop [drup], *vi.* inclinarse, caer; colgar, pender; decaer, desanimarse; languidecer, marchitarse.

drop [drap], *s.* gota; zarcillo; caída, declive, pendiente; pastilla; (com.) baja, caída.—*d. curtain*, telón de boca.—*d. hammer*, martinete.—*vti.* [3] verter a gotas; soltar, dejar caer; desprenderse de; renunciar a, desistir de; despedir, echar.—*to d. a letter*, echar una carta en el buzón.—*to d. a line*, escribir unas líneas.—*to d. in*, hacer una visita inesperadamente.—*to d. out*, desaparecer; separarse.—*vii.* gotear; descender; detenerse.— —**let** [dráplɪt], *s.* gotita.

drought [drajt], **drouth** [drajθ], *s.* sequía; aridez, sequedad.

drove [drouv], *s.* manada, recua, hato,

piara; gentío.—*pret.* de TO DRIVE.— —*r* [dróμvœ(r)], *s.* ganadero.

drown [drajn], *vt. y vi.* ahogar(se); anegar(se); sumergir(se).

drowse [drajz], *vt. y vi.* adormecer(se), amodorrar(se).—**drowsiness** [dráuzinịs], *s.* modorra, somnolencia, pesadez.—**drowsy** [dráuzị], *a.* soñoliento, amodorrado; soporífero.

drudge [drʌdʒ], *vi.* afanarse, fatigarse.—*s.* ganapán, esclavo del trabajo.

drug [drʌg], *s.* droga, medicamento; narcótico; artículo de poca venta.—*d. addict o fiend*, narcómano.—*d. store*, farmacia, botica, droguería.—*vti.* [1] mezclar con drogas; narcotizar.—*vii.* tomar drogas.—**druggist** [drʌgist], *s.* droguero, farmacéutico.

drum [drʌm], *s.* tambor; redoblante; cuñete; cuerpo de columna; tímpano (del oído).—*vti. y vii.* [1] tocar el tambor; tamborilear; repetir, machacar; teclear.—**drummer** [-œ(r)], *s.* tambor, tamborilero; viajante de comercio.

drunk [drʌŋk], *pp.* de TO DRINK.—*s.* borrachín; parranda, borrachera.—*a.* ebrio, borracho.— —**ard** [drʌŋkərd], *s.* borracho, borrachín.— —**en** [-œn], *a.* ebrio, borracho.— —**enness** [-œnnịs], *s.* embriaguez; ebriedad.

dry [draj], *a.* árido, seco.—*d. cell*, pila o elemento seco.—*d. cleaner*, tintorería.—*d. cleaning*, limpieza en seco.—*d. goods*, lencería; víveres.—*vti.* [7] secar, desecar; enjugar; desaguar; dar sed; acecinar.—*vii.* secarse, enjugarse.—*to d. up*, secarse completa y rápidamente.— —**er** [drájœ(r)], *s. =* DRIER.— —**ness** [-nịs], *s.* sequedad, aridez.

dubious [djúbịʌs], *a.* dudoso; incierto; ambiguo.

duchess [dʌchịs], *s.* duquesa.

duck [dʌk], *s.* pato, ánade; acción de agacharse.—*vt.* chapuzar; evitar (un golpe, deber, etc.).—*vi.* agacharse, chapuzar(se).— —**ling** [dʌklịŋ], *s.* patito.

ductile [dʌktịl], *a.* dúctil.

dud [dʌd], *s.* (fam.) persona o cosa floja o inútil; fiasco; bomba o granada que no estalla.—*pl.* (fam.) ropa.

dude [djud], *s.* petimetre, lechuguino.

due [dju], *a.* cumplido, vencido; pagadero; apto, propio, conveniente, oportuno; legítimo; esperado, que debe llegar.—*d. bill*, pagaré.—*adv.* exactamente.—*s.* deuda u obligación; derechos, tributo.—*to get one's d.*, llevar su merecido castigo.

duel [djúęl], *s.* duelo, desafío; certamen.—*vi.* batirse en duelo.

duet [djuét], *s.* dúo, dueto.

dug [dʌg], *pret. y pp.* de TO DIG.—*s.*

teta, ubre.- —out [-aʊt], s. chabola; (mar.) piragua.

duke [djuk], s. duque.

dull [dʌl], a. embotado, obtuso, sin punta, sin filo; apagado, sordo; lerdo; insípido, soso, insulso; flojo, perezoso; lánguido; (colores) desvaído, mate; insensible; triste; deslustrado, empañado; opaco, nebuloso; soñoliento; (com.) inactivo, muerto.—vt. y vi. embotar(se); entorpecer(se); ofuscar(se); empañar(se).— —ard [dʌlɡrd], a. estúpido.— —ness [-nis], s. embotamiento; estupidez; aburrimiento; somnolencia, pesadez.

dumb [dʌm], a. mudo; callado; estúpido.—d. motions, señas.—d. show, pantomima.- —ness [dʌmnis], s. mudez; silencio; estupidez.

dummy [dʌmi], a. imitado, fingido, contrahecho.—s. maniquí; testaferro; figurón; proyecto de formato de una publicación; objeto simulado; zoquete, estúpido.

dump [dʌmp], vt. vaciar de golpe; descargar; vender a precios inferiores a los corrientes.—s. vaciadero; vaciamiento.—pl. melancolía, morriña.- —ing [dʌmpiŋ], s. vaciamiento; inundación del mercado con artículos de precios rebajados; competir comercialmente con precios ínfimos.

dunce [dʌns], s. zopenco, tonto.

dune [djun], s. duna.

dung [dʌŋ], s. estiércol, boñiga.—d. heap o yard, estercolero, muladar.

dungeon [dʌndʒɒn], s. calabozo, mazmorra.

dunghill [dʌŋhil], s. estercolero, muladar.

dunk [dʌŋk], vt. (coll.) mojar, ensopar; tirar al agua.

dupe [djup], s. incauto, primo.—vt. engañar, embaucar.

duplicate [djuplikeit], vt. duplicar.—s. [djuplikit], duplicado, copia.—in d., por duplicado.—a. duplicado, doble, en pares.—duplicity [djuplisiti], s. duplicidad, engaño, segunda intención.

durability [djurəbiliti], s. durabilidad, duración; permanencia.—duration [djureiʃɒn], s. duración.—during [djuriŋ], prep. durante, mientras.

dusk [dʌsk], a. oscuro (poet.).—s. crepúsculo vespertino; oscuridad.—d.-to-dawn, del anochecer, a la madrugada.- —y [dʌski], a. oscuro; moreno, pardo.

dust [dʌst], s. polvo; cenizas, restos mortales.—d. brush, plumero.—d. cloud, polvareda.—vt. sacudir o quitar el polvo; (es)polvorear.—to d. one's jacket, zurrar a uno.- —er [dʌstœ(r)],

s. paño del polvo; plumero; guardapolvos.- —y [-i], a. empolvado, polvoriento.

Dutch [dʌch], s. y a. holandés.—D. tile, azulejo.—D. treat, convite a escote.—to go D., ir a medias.- —man [dʌchman], s. holandés.

duty [djuti], s. deber, obligación; incumbencia; impuesto, derechos de aduana; trabajo, servicio (mec.).—d. free, libre de derechos.—in d. bound, moralmente obligado.—off d., libre, franco de servicio.—on d., de guardia o de servicio.

dwell [dwel], vii. [4] habitar, morar.

dwarf [dwɔrf], s. enano, pigmeo.—a. diminuto, enano.

dwindle [dwindl], vi. menguar, disminuirse; degenerar; decaer; consumirse.—vt. mermar.

dye [dai], vt. teñir.—s. tinte.- —r [dáiœ(r)], s. tintorero.

dying [dáiiŋ], a. moribundo; mortecino; mortal.—s. muerte.

dynamic [dainémik], a. dinámico; enérgico.

dynamite [dáinamait], s. dinamita.—vt. volar con dinamita, dinamitar.

dynamo [dáinamou], s. dínamo, generador.

dynasty [dáinasti], s. dinastía.

dysentery [dísenteri], s. disentería.

E

each [ich], a. cada, todo.—pron. cada uno, cada cual, todos.—e. for himself, cada cual por su cuenta, o por su lado.—e. other, mutuamente; unos a otros.—adv. por persona, por cabeza, cada cual.

eager [igœ(r)], a. ansioso, anhelante, deseoso.- —ness [-nis], s. ansia, anhelo, afán, ahinco; vehemencia.

eagle [igl], s. águila.- —t [iglit], s. aguilucho.

ear [ir], s. oreja; oído; espiga.—by the ears, en pugna abierta.—e. muff, orejera.—to be all ears, (fam.) aguzar los oídos o las orejas.- —drum [irdram], s. tímpano.

earl [œrl], s. conde.

early [œrli], a. primitivo, primero; tempran(er)o; próximo.—e. bird, (fig.) madrugador.—the e. part of, el principio de.—adv. temprano, pronto, antes de la hora; al principio. —as e. as possible, lo más pronto posible.

earn [œrn], vt. ganar; merecer.

earnest [œrnist], a. serio, formal.—s. seriedad, buena fe; prenda, señal.- —ness [-nis], s. seriedad; sinceridad; celo.

earnings [ɔ́rnɪ̄ŋz], *s. pl.* salario, sueldo, paga, jornal; ganancias.

earphone [ɪ́rfoŭn], *s.* auricular; audífono.

earring [ɪ́rɪ̄ŋ], *s.* pendiente, arete.

earth [ɔɔrθ], *s.* tierra (materia; planeta); mundo; suelo.— **—enware** [ɔ́rθɛ̄nwer], *s.* loza de barro, cacharros.— **—ly** [-lɪ̄], *a.* terreno; terrenal, mundano.— **—quake** [-kweĭk], *s.* temblor de tierra, terremoto.——**ward** [-wǎrd], *s.* y *adv.* hacia la tierra.— **—worm** [-wœrm], *s.* lombriz de tierra.— **—y** [-ĭ], *a.* terroso; mundano, primario.

ease [iz], *s.* tranquilidad; comodidad, alivio, descanso; facilidad, desenvoltura, naturalidad.—*at e.*, descansadamente, a sus anchas.—*with e.*, con facilidad.—*vt.* aliviar, mitigar, aligerar, desembarazar, facilitar.—*vi.* disminuir, apaciguarse, suavizarse.

easel [ízɛ̄l], *s.* caballete de pintor; atril.

east [ist], *s.* este, levante, oriente.—*a.* oriental; del este.—*E. Indian*, indio, hindú.—*adv.* hacia el este.

Easter [ístœ(r)], *s.* Pascua florida o de Resurrección.—*E. Saturday*, Sábado Santo.—*E. Sunday*, Domingo de Resurrección.

eastern [ístœrn], *a.* oriental.—**Easterner** [ístœrnœ(r)], *s.* oriental; habitante del este (de los E.U.).

easy [ízɪ̄], *a.* fácil; cómodo; suelto; libre; tranquilo; aliviado.—*e. chair*, butaca, poltrona.—*e. going*, lento; calmado, sereno.—*adv.* e *interj.* despacio, qued(it)o.

eat [it], *vti.* [10] comer, tomar.—*to e. away*, *into* o *through*, corroer.—*to e. breakfast, lunch, dinner, supper*, desayunarse, almorzar, comer, cenar.—*to e. one's heart out*, sufrir en silencio.—*to e. one's words*, retractarse.—*to e. up*, devorar, tragar.—*vti.* comer, alimentarse, sustentarse.—**eaten** [ítɛ̄n], *pp.* de TO EAT.

eaves [ivz], *s. pl.* alero.— **—drop** [ívzdrap], *vti.* [1] escuchar solapadamente, fisgonear.

ebb [eb], *vi.* menguar la marea; decaer.—*s.* menguante, marea baja, reflujo; decadencia.—*e. of life*, vejez.—*e. tide*, marea menguante.

ebony [ɛ́bɒnĭ], *s.* ébano.

eccentric [ikséntrĭk], *s.* persona excéntrica o rara; (mec.) excéntrica.—*a.* also **—al** [-ɐl], *a.* (geom. y mec.) excéntrico; extravagante, estrafalario.

ecclesiastic [iklizĭ̄ǽstĭk], *s.* eclesiástico.—*e.*, **—al** [-ɐl], *a.* eclesiástico.

echo [ɛ́koŭ], *s.* eco.—*vi.* repercutir, resonar.—*vt.* repetir con aprobación; hacer eco.

eclipse [iklíps], *s.* eclipse.—*vt.* eclipsar.

economic(al) [ĭkonámĭk(ɐl)], *a.* económico; moderado, módico.—**economics** [ĭkonámĭks], *s.* economía política.—**economist** [ĭkánomĭst], *s.* economista.—**economize** [ĭkánomaĭz], *vt.* y *vi.* economizar, ahorrar.—**economy** [ĭkánomĭ], *s.* economía, ahorro.

ecstasy [ɛ́kstɐsĭ], *s.* éxtasis, arrobamiento.

Ecuadorian [ekwɐdórĭɐn], *a.* y *s.* ecuatoriano.

eddy [ɛ́dĭ], *s.* remanso; remolino.—*vi.* arremolinarse; remansarse.

edge [edʑ], *s.* filo; canto; borde, orilla, margen.—*on e.*, de canto; impaciente, ansioso.—*to set the teeth on e.*, dar dentera.—*vt.* afilar; incitar; (cost.) orlar.—*vi.* avanzar de lado, escurrirse.— **—wise** [ɛ́dʑwaĭz], *adv.* de filo o de canto.—**edging** [ɛ́dʑĭ̄ŋ], *s.* orla(dura), pestaña.

edible [ɛ́dĭbl], *a.* y *s.* comestible.

edict [ídĭkt], *s.* edicto, mandato; bando.

edifice [ɛ́dĭfĭs], *s.* edificio.—**edify** [ɛ́dĭfaĭ], *vti* [7] edificar; instruir moralmente.

edit [ɛ́dĭt], *vt.* redactar; editar; dirigir (un periódico); corregir (manuscritos).— **—ion** [idíʃɒn], *s.* edición; tirada.— **—or** [-ɒ(r)], *s.* redactor; director de un periódico o revista; editor.— **—orial** [-órĭɐl], *a.* editorial.—*e. rooms* o *staff*, redacción.—*s.* editorial, artículo de fondo.

educate [ɛ́djukeĭt], *vt.* educar; instruir.—**education** [edjukéĭʃɒn], *s.* educación; enseñanza, instrucción.—**educational** [edjukéĭʃɒnɐl], *a.* docente; educativo.—*e. institution*, plantel, centro docente.—**educator** [ɛ́djukeĭtɒ(r)], *s.* educador.

eel [il], *s.* anguila.

effect [ɛfékt], *s.* efecto; impresión; eficiencia.—*pl.* efectos, bienes.—*in e.*, vigente; en realidad.—*into e.*, en vigor, en práctica.—*of no e.*, sin resultado; vano.—*to the e. that*, de que, en el sentido de que.—*vt.* efectuar, realizar, llevar a cabo.— **—ive** [-ĭv], *a.* efectivo, eficaz; vigente.

effeminate [ɛfémĭnĭt], *a.* afeminado.

efficacy [ɛ́fĭkɐsĭ], *s.* eficacia.

efficiency [ɛfíʃɛnsĭ], *s.* eficiencia; eficacia; (mec.) rendimiento.—**efficient** [ɛfíʃɛnt], *a.* eficiente; eficaz, competente; (mec.) de gran rendimiento.

effigy [ɛ́fĭdʑĭ], *s.* efigie.

effort [ɛ́fɒrt], *s.* esfuerzo, empeño.

effrontery [ɛfrántœrĭ], *s.* desfachatez, descaro.

effusion [ɛfĭúʑɒn], *s.* efusión, derrame; expansión.—**effusive** [ɛfĭúsĭv], *a.* expansivo, efusivo, comunicativo.

egg [eg], *s.* huevo.—*e. dealer*, huevero.

—e.-*laying*, postura.—*hard boiled e.*, huevo duro.—*poached e.*, huevo escalfado.—*soft-boiled e.*, huevo pasado por agua.- —nog [égnag], *s.* ponche de huevo.- —plant [-plænt], *s.* berenjena.

egotism [ígouţizm], *s.* egolatría, egotismo.—**egotist** [ígouţist], *s.* ególatra, egotista.

Egyptian [idŽípŞan], *a.* y *s.* egipcio.

either [íŎœ(r), áiŎœ(r)], *a.* y *pron.* uno u otro, cualquiera de los dos.—*conj.* o, ora, ya.—*adv.* (después de **not,** nor) tampoco.

ejaculate [idŽǽkyuleit], *vt.* exclamar, proferir; (med.) eyacular.—**ejaculation** [idzækyuléiŞon], *s.* exclamación; eyaculación, polución.

eject [idŽékt], *vt.* arrojar, lanzar, expulsar.- —ion [idzékŞon], *s.* expulsión, evacuación.

elaborate [ilǽboreit], *vt.* elaborar; explicar detalladamente.—*a.* [ilǽborit], elaborado, trabajado, detallado, esmerado; recargado.—**elaboration** [ilæboréiŞon], *s.* elaboración; obra acabada.

elapse [ilǽps], *vi.* mediar, pasar, transcurrir.

elastic [ilǽstik], *a.* elástico.—*s.* cinta de goma, elástico.- —ity [ilæstísiti], *s.* elasticidad.

elate [iléit], *vt.* exaltar; alborozar; elevar.- —d [-id], *a.* exaltado, alborozado.

elbow [élbou], *s.* codo; recodo, ángulo; brazo de sillón.—*at one's e.*, a la mano, muy cerca.—*e. room*, espacio suficiente, holgura.—*vt.* dar codazos.—*to e. one's way*, abrirse paso a codazos.—*vi.* codear; formar recodos o ángulos.

elder [éldœ(r)], *a.* mayor, de más edad; antiguo, anterior.—*s.* anciano; señor mayor; dignatario.—*pl.* ancianos, mayores, antepasados.- —ly [-li], *a.* mayor, de edad madura o avanzada.—**eldest** [éldist], *a.* mayor de todos, [el] de más edad.—*e. son*, hijo primogénito.

elect [ilékt], *vt.* elegir, escoger.—*a.* y *s.* electo o elegido.- —ion [ilékŞon], *s.* elección.- —or [-ǫ(r)], *s.* elector.- —oral [-ǫral], *a.* electoral.- —orate [-ǫrit], *s.* electorado.

electric(al) [iléktrik(al)], *a.* eléctrico; (fig.) supersensible.—*e. bulb*, bombilla, (Am.) bombillo.—*e. eye*, célula fotoeléctrica.—*e. fixtures*, aparatos eléctricos.—*e. powerhouse*, central eléctrica.—*e. tape*, cinta aisladora adhesiva.—*e. wiring*, instalación eléctrica.—**electrician** [ilektríŞan], *s.* electricista.—**electricity** [ilektrísiti], *s.* electricidad.—**electrification** [ilektri-fikéiŞon], *s.* electrización; electrificación.—**electrify** [iléktrifai], *vti.* [7] electrizar; electrificar.—**electrocute** [iléktrokiut], *vt.* electrocutar.—**electrocution** [ilektrokiúŞon], *s.* electrocución.—**electronics** [ilektránjks], *s.* electrónica.

elegance [éligans], *s.* elegancia.—**elegant** [éligant], *a.* elegante.

element [élimęnt], *s.* elemento; componente.—*pl.* nociones, rudimentos.- —al [eliméntal], —ary [eliménteri], *a.* elemental, primordial, rudimentario.

elephant [élifant], *s.* elefante.

elevate [éliveit], *vt.* elevar; alzar, exaltar.—**elevation** [eliivéiŞon], *s.* elevación; exaltación; altura; eminencia.—**elevator** [éliveitǫ(r)], *s.* ascensor; elevador.—*e. shaft*, caja o pozo del ascensor.—*grain e.*, silo.

eligible [élidŽibl], *a.* elegible.

eliminate [ilímineit], *vt.* eliminar, suprimir.—**elimination** [iliminéiŞon], *s.* eliminación, supresión.—**eliminatory** [ilíminatori], *a.* eliminatorio.

elk [elk], *s.* alce o ante.

elm [elm], *s.* olmo.

elocution [elokiúŞon], *s.* elocución; declamación.

elope [ilóup], *vi.* fugarse, huir con un amante.- —ment [-męnt], *s.* fuga amorosa.

eloquence [élokwęns], *s.* elocuencia, oratoria, (fam.) labia.—**eloquent** [élokwęnt], *a.* elocuente.

else [els], *a.* otro, diferente; más. —*anything e.*, algo más; cualquiera otra cosa.—*nobody e.*, no one e., ningún otro.—*adv.* y *conj.* más, además; en vez de.—*how e.?*, ¿de qué otro modo?.—*or e.*, o bien, o en su lugar, de otro modo, en otro caso; si no.- —where [élswer], *adv.* en, a o de otra parte.

elude [iljúd], *vt.* eludir, evadir, evitar, sortear.—**elusive** [iljúsiv], **elusory** [iljúsori], *a.* evasivo, esquivo, fugaz.

emaciate(d) [iméişieit(id)], *a.* demacrado, macilento, flaco; extenuado.

emancipate [imǽnsipeit], *vt.* emancipar.—**emancipation** [imænsipéiŞon], *s.* emancipación.—**emancipator** [imǽn-sipeitǫ(r)], *s.* emancipador, libertador.

embalm [embám], *vt.* embalsamar.- —ment [-męnt], *s.* embalsamamiento.

embankment [embǽŋkmęnt], *s.* dique; terraplén.

embarcation [embarkéiŞon], *s.* = EM-BARKATION.

embargo [embárgou], *s.* embargo, detención, prohibición.—*vt.* embargar, detener.

embark [embárk], *vt.* y *vi.* embar-

car(se).— —ation, [-éɪʂǫn], *s.* embarque.

embarrass [embǽrǝs], *vt.* turbar, desconcertar; embarazar.— —ment [-mǝnt], *s.* turbación; embarazo, estorbo; (com.) apuros, dificultades.

embassy [émbǡsɪ], *s.* embajada.

embed [embéd], *vti.* [1] encajar, empotrar.

embellish [embélɪʂ], *vt.* embellecer.— —ment [-mǝnt], *s.* embellecimiento.

ember [émbœr], *s.* ascua, pavesa. —*pl.* rescoldo.

embezzle [embézl], *vt.* desfalcar.— —ment [-mǝnt], *s.* desfalco.— —r [embézlœr], *s.* desfalcador.

embitter [embítœr], *vt.* emargar.

emblem [émblem], *s.* emblema, símbolo.

embody [embádɪ], *vti.* [7] dar cuerpo, encarnar; incorporar; incluir, englobar.—*vii.* unirse, incorporarse.

embolus [émbolǝs], *s.* (med.) émbolo.

emboss [embós], *vt.* repujar, realzar, estampar en relieve.— —ment [-mǝnt], *s.* realce, relieve.

embrace [embréɪs], *vt.* abrazar; abarcar, rodear.—*vi.* abrazarse.—*s.* abrazo.

embrasure [embréɪʐûr], *s.* (fort.) tronera, aspillera; (arq.) alféizar.

embroider [embróɪdœr], *vt.* bordar, recamar.—*vi.* hacer labor de bordado.— —er [-œr], —ess [-ɪs], *s.* bordador; bordadora.— —y [-ɪ], *s.* bordado, bordadura, labor.

embroil [embróɪl], *vt.* embrollar, enredar.— —ment [-mǝnt], *s.* embrollo, intriga.

embryo [émbrɪou], *s.* embrión.— —nic [embriánɪk], *a.* embrionario.

emendation [imendéɪʂǫn], *s.* enmienda, corrección.

emerald [émgrǝld], *s.* esmeralda.

emerge [ɪmœ́rdʐ], *vi.* emerger, brotar, surgir.

emergency [ɪmœ́rdʐensɪ], *s.* emergencia, aprieto o necesidad urgente.—*e. hospital,* hospital de urgencia, casa de socorros.—*e. landing,* aterrizaje forzoso.—emergent [ɪmœ́rdʐent], *a.* emergente; urgente.

emery [émerɪ], *s.* esmeril.

emigrant [émɪgrant], *a.* emigrante. —*s.* emigrante, emigrado.—emigrate [émɪgreɪt], *vi.* emigrar, expatriarse. —emigration [emɪgréɪʂǫn], *s.* emigración.

eminence [émɪnens], *s.* altura, cima, eminencia.—eminent [émɪnent], *a.* eminente.

emissary [émɪserɪ], *s.* emisario.— emission [imíʂǫn], *s.* emisión, salida. —emit [imít], *vti.* [1] emitir.

emotion [imóuʂǫn], *s.* emoción.— —al [-ǝl], *a.* emocional, emotivo, sensible; sentimental.

emperor [émpœrǫr], *s.* emperador.

emphasis [émfǡsɪs], *s.* énfasis.—emphasize [émfǡsaɪz], *vt.* enfatizar, poner énfasis; recalcar, acentuar.

empire [émpaɪr], *s.* imperio.

employ [emplóɪ], *vt.* emplear; usar; dedicar.—*s.* empleo; ocupación, oficio.— —ee [-í], *s.* empleado.— —er [-œr], *s.* patrón, patrono.— —ment [-mǝnt], *s.* empleo, colocación; uso, aplicación.

empower [empáuœr], *vt.* autorizar, facultar, dar poder.

empress [émprɪs], *s.* emperatriz.

empty [émptɪ], *a.* vacío, desocupado; vacante; vano; vacuo, frívolo. —*e.-headed,* tonto.—*vti.* [7] vaciar, desocupar, evacuar.—*vii.* vaciarse; desaguar, desembocar.

emulsion [imʌ́lʂǫn], *s.* emulsión.

enable [enéɪbl], *vt.* habilitar, capacitar, permitir.

enact [enǽkt], *vt.* promulgar, dar (una ley); decretar; (teat.) hacer el papel de.

enamel [enǽmel], *vti.* [2] esmaltar.— *s.* esmalte.

encamp [enkǽmp], *vt. y vi.* (mil.) acampar.— —ment [-mǝnt], *s.* campamento.

enchant [enchǽnt], *vt.* encantar, hechizar; fascinar, embelesar.— —er [-œr], *s.* encantador, hechicero.— —ment [-mǝnt], *s.* encantamiento, hechicería, hechizo; encanto.— —ress [-rɪs], *s.* maga; encantadora, seductora, hechicera.

encircle [ensœrkl], *vt.* cercar, rodear.

enclose [enklóuz], *vt.* cercar; rodear, circundar; encerrar; incluir, adjuntar o enviar adjunta una cosa.—enclosure [enklóuʐûr], *s.* vallado, tapia; cercado; recinto; lo adjunto (en carta, etc.), contenido.

encompass [enkʌ́mpǡs], *vt.* circundar, rodear, encerrar; abarcar.

encounter [enkáuntœr], *s.* encuentro; choque; combate.—*vt. y vi.* encontrar; salir al encuentro de; topar o tropezar con.

encourage [enkœ́erɪdʐ], *vt.* animar, alentar; fomentar.— —ment [-mǝnt], *s.* aliento, ánimo; fomento.

encyclopedia [ensaɪklopídɪa], *s.* enciclopedia.

end [end], *s.* fin; extremidad; punta; remate; desenlace, final; fondo; propósito, objeto.—*at loose ends,* en desorden, desarreglado.—*at the e. of,* al cabo de.—*e. line,* línea de límite. —*no e. of,* un sinfín de, muchísimo(s), la mar de.—*to make both ends meet,* pasar con lo que se tiene.—*to no e.,* sin efecto, en vano.—*vt. y vi.* acabar, concluir, terminar, finalizar.

endear [endír], *vt.* hacer(se) querer.

endeavor [endévǫ(r)], *s.* esfuerzo, conato, empeño, tentativa.—*vt.* intentar, pretender, tratar de.—*vi.* esforzarse, hacer un esfuerzo (por).

ending [éndiɳ], *s.* fin, conclusión; terminación; desenlace.

endive [éndaiv], *s.* (bot.) escarola.

endless [éndlis], *a.* sin fin; interminable, perpetuo.

endorse [endórs], *vt.* = INDORSE.—**endorsement** [endórsmęnt], *s.* = INDORSEMENT.

endow [endáu], *vt.* dotar; fundar.——**ment** [-męnt], *s.* dotación; fundación.

endurance [endiúrąns], *s.* paciencia; resistencia; duración.—*to be beyond* o *past e.*, ser insoportable o inaguantable.—**endure** [endiúr], *vt.* soportar, sufrir, resistir, tolerar.—*vi.* durar, perdurar; tener paciencia.

enema [énęmǎ], *s.* (med.) enema, lavativa.

enemy [énęmi], *s.* enemigo, adversario.

energetic(al) [encerdžétik(ąl)], *a.* enérgico, vigoroso.—**energy** [éncerdži], *s.* energía, vigor, carácter.

enervate [éncervejt], *vt.* enervar, debilitar; desvirtuar, embotar.

enfold [enfóuld], *vt.* = INFOLD.

enforce [enfórs], *vt.* dar fuerza o vigor; poner en vigor; cumplimentar, observar o ejecutar (una ley); hacer hincapié en.——**ment** [-męnt], *s.* ejecución de una ley; observancia forzosa.

engage [engéidž], *vt.* ajustar, apalabrar, comprometer; contratar; emplear; entretener; atraer; (mil.) librar o trabar batalla o combate, entrar en lucha con; (mec.) engranar con.—*vi.* obligarse, dar palabra, comprometerse; ocuparse, entregarse a; pelear.——**d** [-d], *a.* ocupado; comprometido; comprometido para casarse; engranado.——**ment** [-męnt], *s.* contrato; compromiso, noviazgo; cita; engranaje; batalla, acción.

engender [endžéndœ(r)], *vt.* engendrar, procrear.—*vi.* engendrarse, producirse.

engine [éndžin], *s.* máquina; locomotora; motor; instrumento.——**er** [-ɾ], *s.* ingeniero; maquinista.—*vt.* manejar, dirigir.—*vi.* hacer de ingeniero o maquinista.——**ering** [-ɾiɳ], *s.* ingeniería; manejo.

English [íɳgliš], *s.* y *a.* inglés.—*E. Channel*, Canal de la Mancha.—*s.* idioma inglés.——**man** [-mąn], *s.* inglés.——**woman** [-wumąn], *s.* inglesa.

engrave [engréjv], *vt.* grabar; cincelar, esculpir.——**r** [-œ(r)], *s.* grabador.

—**engraving** [engréjviɳ], *s.* grabado; lámina, estampa.

enhance [enhéns], *vt.* mejorar, acrecentar; realzar.

enigma [inígmǎ], *s.* enigma, intríngulis.

enjoin [endžóin], *vt.* mandar, ordenar; imponer.—*to e. from*, (for.) prohibir.

enjoy [endžói], *vt.* gozar de; gustar de, gustarle a uno; disfrutar de; saborear.—*to e. oneself*, gozar, divertirse.——**able** [-ąbl], *a.* deleitable, agradable.——**ment** [-męnt], *s.* goce, disfrute, placer; usufructo.

enlarge [enlárdž], *vt.* agrandar, ensanchar; ampliar o amplificar.—*vi.* ensancharse o agrandarse; explayarse (en).——**ment** [-męnt], *s.* agrandamiento, ensanchamiento; ampliación.——**r** [-œ(r)], *s.* (fot.) ampliador(a).

enlighten [enláitęn], *vt.* iluminar, instruir, ilustrar, alumbrar, esclarecer.

enlist [enlíst], *vt.* alistar; enrolar; reclutar.—*vi.* enrolarse; sentar plaza.——**ment** [-męnt], *s.* alistamiento, enganche, enrolamiento, reclutamiento.

enliven [enláiven], *vt.* animar, alentar, avivar.

enmity [énmiti], *s.* enemistad.

ennoble [enóubl], *vt.* ennoblecer.

enormity [inórmiti], *s.* enormidad; atrocidad.—**enormous** [inórmʌs], *a.* enorme; atroz.

enough [inʌf], *a.* bastante, suficiente.—*to be e.*, bastar.—*s.* lo suficiente.—*interj.* ¡basta! ¡no más!—*adv.* bastante, harto.

enquire [enkwáir], *vt.* = INQUIRE.—**enquirer** [enkwáirœ(r)], *s.* = INQUIRER.

enrage [enréjdž], *vt.* enfurecer, encolerizar.

enrapture [enrǽpch𝔲(r)], *vt.* arrobar, embelesar, extasiar.

enrich [enrích], *vt.* enriquecer.——**ment** [-męnt], *s.* enriquecimiento.

enroll [enróul], *vt.* y *vi.* alistar(se), enrolar(se); matricular(se); envolver(se); enrollar(se).—*vi.* alistarse, enrolarse; inscribirse, matricularse.——**ment** [-męnt], *s.* alistamiento, enrolamiento; matrícula, registro.

ensign [énsąin], *s.* bandera, enseña, pabellón; [énsin] alférez; subteniente.—*e. bearer*, abanderado.

enslave [ensléjv], *vt.* esclavizar.

ensue [ensiú], *vi.* suceder, sobrevenir.

entail [entéil], *s.* vinculación.—*vt.* vincular, perpetuar; acarrear, imponer.

entangle [entǽɳgl], *vt.* enredar, embrollar, enmarañar.——**ment** [-męnt], *s.* enredo, embrollo, complicación.

enter [éntœ(r)], *vt.* entrar a, por o en; penetrar; asentar, registrar; hacerse

miembro de, ingresar en.—*vi.* entrar,
introducirse; (teat.) salir al escenario,
entrar en escena.
enterprise [éntœrprajz], *s.* empresa.
—**enterprising** [éntœrprajziŋ], *a.*
emprendedor.
entertain [entœrtéjn], *vt.* entretener,
divertir; festejar, agasajar (en casa).
—*to s. hopes, ideas,* abrigar o acariciar esperanzas o ideas.— —**er** [-œ(r)],
s. artista de variedades; anfitrión.—
—**ment** [-mẹnt], *s.* entretenimiento.
enthrone [enθróun], *vt.* entron(iz)ar.
enthusiasm [enθiúzjæzm], *s.* entusiasmo.—**enthusiast** [enθiúzjæst], *s.*
entusiasta.—**enthusiastic(al)** [enθiu-
zjæstik(ạl)], *a.* entusiástico, entusiasta; entusiasmado.
entice [entájs], *vt.* atraer, seducir,
halagar; engatusar.
entire [entájr], *a.* entero, cabal, completo, íntegro, todo.— —**ty** [-tị], *s.*
entereza, integridad, totalidad; todo.
entitle [entájtl], *vt.* titular; intitular;
dar derecho; autorizar.
entity [éntiti], *s.* entidad; ente, ser.
entrails [éntrejlz], *s.* entrañas, vísceras;
tripas.
entrance [éntrạns], *s.* entrada; ingreso;
portal, puerta.—*e. hall,* zaguán. vestíbulo.—*no e.,* se prohibe la entrada.
entrance [entréns], *vt.* extasiar, hechizar.
entreat [entrít], *vt.* rogar, suplicar,
implorar, instar.— —**y** [-ị], *s.* ruego,
súplica, instancia.
entree [ántrej], *s.* entrada; privilegio
de entrar; (coc.) principio o entrada.
entrench [entrénch], *vt.* y *vi.* atrin-
cherar(se).—*s. on* o *upon,* invadir,
infringir.— —**ment** [-mẹnt], *s.* atrincheramiento, trinchera.
entrust [entrást], *vt.* (con **to** o **with**)
entregar, encargar (de), (con)fiar,
depositar.
entry [éntri], *s.* entrada; acceso; ingreso; asiento, anotación; registro;
partida; bervete (catálogo, diccionario, etc.).
entwine [entwájn], *vt.* entrelazar,
entretejer.
enumerate [injúmẹrejt], *vt.* enumerar.
—**enumeration** [injumẹréjṣǫn], *s.*
enumeración; catálogo.
envelop [envélǫp], *vt.* envolver.— —**e**
[énvẹloup], *s.* envoltura; cubierta;
sobre(carta).
enviable [énviạbl], *a.* envidiable.—
envious [énviạs], *a.* envidioso.
environment [envájrǫnmẹnt], *s.* cercanía; ambiente o medio ambiente.
—**environs** [envájrǫns], *s. pl.* alrededores, suburbios, afueras.
envoy [énvoj], *s.* enviado.

envy [énvi], *vti.* [7] envidiar; codiciar.
—*s.* envidia.
epaulet [épolet], *s.* (mil.) charretera.
epic [épik], *a.* épico.—*s.* epopeya.
epidemic [epidémjk], *a.* epidémico.—
s. epidemia, peste, plaga.
epigram [épigræm], *s.* epigrama.
epileptic [epiléptjk], *a.* y *s.* epiléptico.
epilogue [épilag], *s.* epílogo.
Epiphany [ipífạni], *s.* (igl.) Epifanía.
episcopal [ipískǫpạl], *a.* episcopal.
episode [épisoud], *s.* episodio.
epistle [ipísl], *s.* epístola.—**epistolary**
[ipístoleri], *a.* epistolar.
epitaph [épitæf], *s.* epitafio.
epithet [épiθet], *s.* epíteto.
epitome [ipítǫmi], *s.* epítome.—**epitomize** [ipítǫmajz], *vt.* abreviar, epito-
mar.
epoch [épǫk], *s.* época, era.—*s.-making,*
trascendental, que forma época.
equal [íkwạl], *a.* igual; parejo; adecuado.—*s.* igual; cantidad igual.—*vt.*
igualar; emparejar; igualarse a, ponerse al nivel de; ser igual a.— —**ity**
[ikwáliti], *s.* igualdad; uniformidad;
paridad.— —**ization** [ikwạlizéjṣǫn], *s.*
igualación, compensación.— —**ize**
[íkwạlajz], *vt.* igualar; compensar.
equanimity [ikwạnímitị], *s.* ecuanimidad.
equation [ikwéjṣǫn], *s.* ecuación; igualdad.
equator [ikwéjtǫ(r)], *s.* ecuador.— —**ial**
[ikwạtórjạl], *a.* ecuatorial.
equilibrium [ikwilíbrjạm], *s.* equilibrio.
equip [ikwíp], *vti.* [1] equipar.— —**ment**
[-mẹnt], *s.* equipo, habilitación;
conjunto de aparatos, accesorios, etc.
equitable [ékwitạbl], *a.* equitativo.—
equity [ékwiti], *s.* equidad, justicia.
equivalence [ikwívạlẹns], *s.* equivalencia.—**equivalent** [ikwívạlẹnt], *a.*
y *s.* equivalente.
equivocal [ikwívǫkạl], *a.* equívoco,
ambiguo.—**equivocate** [ikwívǫkejt],
vi. usar palabras o frases equívocas.
era [írạ], *s.* era, época.
eradicate [irédikejt], *vt.* desarraigar;
destruir, extirpar.—**eradication** [iræd-
ikéjṣǫn], *s.* desarraigo, extirpación.
erase [iréjs], *vt.* borrar, raspar.— —**r**
[-œ(r)], *s.* borrador, goma de borrar;
raspador.—**erasure** [iréjṣǫ(r)], *s.* borradura, raspadura.
erect [irékt], *vt.* erigir, edificar; montar,
instalar; erguir, alzar.—*a.* erecto,
erguido; vertical.
ermine [œ́rmin], *s.* armiño.
erosion [iróuẓǫn], *s.* erosión; desgaste;
corrosión.
erotic [erátik], *a.* erótico.
err [œr], *vi.* errar; equivocarse; descarriarse, pecar.— —**and** [érạnd], *s.*
recado, mandado, diligencia.—*s. boy,*

mandadero, recadero.— —ant [érᴀnt], a. errante.—*knight e.*, caballero andante.— —atic [irǽtjk], a. irregular; excéntrico; errático.— —oneous [eróu̯njᴀs], a. errado, erróneo.— —or [érǫ(r)], s. error, yerro, equivocación; pecado.

erupt [irʌ́pt], vi. salir con fuerza; hacer erupción.— —ion [irʌ́pṣǫn], s. erupción; irrupción.

escalator [éskᴀlei̯tǫ(r)], s. escalera móvil.

escapade [eskᴀpéi̯d], s. travesura; correría, aventura; fuga.—escape [eskéi̯p], vi. escaparse o librarse de; fugarse, huir.—vt. evadir, evitar, esquivar.—*to e. notice*, pasar inadvertido.—s. escapada; fuga o escape.

escarpment [eskárpmẹnt], s. escarpa, acantilado.

escort [éskort], s. escolta; acompañante.— —vt. [eskórt] escoltar; acompañar.

Eskimo [éskjmou̯], s. y a. esquimal.

espionage [éspjǫnjdž], s. espionaje.

esplanade [esplᴀnéi̯d], s. explanada, paseo.

espy [espái̯], vti. [7] divisar, columbrar.— —vii. mirar alrededor, observar.

esquire [eskwái̯r], s. escudero.—Esq., (abrev.) Sr. D.—*country e.*, hacendado.

essay [eséi̯], vt. ensayar.—e. [ései̯] ensayo literario; tentativa.— —ist [ései̯ist], s. ensayista.

essence [ésẹns], s. esencia.—*in e.*, esencialmente.—essential [esénṣal], a. esencial; indispensable.—s. esencial, substancia.—*to stick to essentials*, ir al grano.

establish [estǽbljṣ], vt. establecer.— —vr. establecerse, radicarse.— —ment [-mẹnt], s. establecimiento; fundación; institución; pensión o renta vitalicia.

estate [estéi̯t], s. bienes, propiedades; patrimonio, herencia; finca, hacienda; estado, clase o condición.—*country e.*, finca rústica.—*real e.*, bienes raíces.

esteem [estím], vt. estimar, apreciar; tener en o por, creer.—s. estimación, aprecio; mérito; juicio, opinión.— estimable [éstjmᴀbl], a. estimable; calculable.—estimate [éstjmei̯t], vt. estimar, apreciar, valorar; calcular aproximadamente.—s. [éstjmit] estimación, cálculo; opinión; presupuesto aproximado.—estimation [estjméi̯ṣǫn], s. estima, aprecio; opinión; suposición; valuación; presupuesto.

esthetic [estéti̯k], a. estético.— —s [-s], s. estética.

estrange [estréi̯ndž], vt. extrañar, alejar; enajenar.

estuary [éschi̯u̯eri̯], s. estuario, estero, ría.

etch [ech], vt. y vi. grabar al agua fuerte.— —er [échœ(r)], s. grabador, aguafortista.— —ing [-jŋ], s. grabado al agua fuerte.

eternal [itɚ́rnᴀl], a. eterno.—eternity [itɚ́rnjti], s. eternidad.

ether [íθœ(r)], s. éter.— —eal [iθírjᴀl], a. etéreo.

ethical [éθjkᴀl], a. ético, moral.— ethics [éθjks], s. ética, moral.

Ethiopian [iθjóu̯pjᴀn], s. y a. etíope.

ethnic [éθnjk], a. étnico.

etiquette [étjket], s. etiqueta.

etymology [etjmálodžj], s. etimología.

eucalyptus [yucᴀlíptᴀs], s. eucalipto.

eulogy [yúlǫdžj], s. elogio, panegírico.

Eurasian [yuréi̯žjᴀn], s. y a. eurasio, eurasiático.

European [yuropíᴀn], s. y a. europeo.

evacuate [ivǽkyuei̯t], vt. evacuar.— vi. vaciarse; retirarse.—evacuation [ivækyuéi̯ṣǫn], s. evacuación.

evade [ivéi̯d], vt. evadir, eludir, esquivar.

evaluate [ivǽlyuei̯t], vt. evaluar, tasar.— —evaluation [ivælyuéi̯ṣǫn], s. evaluación.

evangelic(al) [ivænddžélik(ᴀl)], a. evangélico.

evaporate [ivǽporei̯t], vt. y vi. evaporar(se); desvanecer(se).—evaporation [ivæporéi̯ṣǫn], s. evaporación.

evasion [ivéi̯žǫn], s. evasión; evasiva.— —evasive [ivéi̯sjv], a. evasivo.

eve [iv], s. noche; vigilia; víspera.— *Christmas E.*, Nochebuena.

even [ívẹn], a. llano, plano, nivelado, liso; igual, uniforme, imparcial; apacible; cabal, justo; constante; (número) par; parejo (con).—*of e. date*, de la misma fecha.—*to be e. with*, estar en paz, mano a mano con. —*to get e. with*, desquitarse.—adv. aun, hasta, incluso.—*e. as*, así como. —*e. if*, aun cuando, aunque.—*e. now*, ahora mismo.—*e. so*, así; aun así.—*e. though*, aunque.—*not e.*, ni siquiera.—vt. igualar, emparejar, allanar, nivelar; liquidar.

evening [ívnjŋ], s. tarde; (primeras horas de la) noche.—*last e.*, anoche. —a. de la tarde; vespertino.

event [ivént], s. acontecimiento, suceso; caso; consecuencia, resultado.—*at all events, in any e.*, sea lo que fuere, en todo caso, de cualquier modo.— —ful [-fᴜl], a. memorable, lleno de acontecimientos.— —ual [ivénchuᴀl], a. último, final; consiguiente; eventual, fortuito.— —uality [ivenchuǽljti], s. eventualidad.

ever [évœ(r)], adv. siempre; alguna vez, en cualquier tiempo; nunca.— *—as e.*, como siempre.—*e. since*, desde que; desde entonces.—*for e.*

and e., por siempre jamás, por los siglos de los siglos.—*hardly e.*, casi nunca.—*nor e.*, ni nunca.— —*green* [-grin], *a.* siempre verde.—*s.* planta de hoja perenne.— —*lasting* [-lǽstiŋ], *a.* perpetuo, perdurable, duradero. —*s.* eternidad.— —*more* [-mɔr], *adv.* eternamente; por siempre jamás.

every [évrị], *a.* cada; todo, todos los. —*e. once in a while*, de vez en cuando. —*e. one of them*, todos, todos sin excepción.—*e. other*, cada dos, uno sí y otro no.— —*body* [-badị], *pron.* todos, todo el mundo; cada uno, cada cual.— —*day* [-deị], *a.* de cada día, diario, cuotidiano.— —*one* [-wʌn], *pron.* todo el mundo; todos.— —*thing* [-θiŋ], *pron.* todo.— —*where* [-hwɛr], *adv.* en o por todas partes, donde-quiera.

evict [ivíkt], *vt.* desalojar, desahuciar; expulsar.— —*ion* [ivíkṣọn], *s.* desa-lojamiento; desahucio; expulsión.

evidence [évịdẹns], *s.* evidencia; demos-tración; prueba; testimonio.—**evi-dent** [évịdẹnt], *a.* evidente, claro, manifiesto.

evil [ívịl], *a.* malo; maligno, perverso; nocivo; aciago.—*e. deed*, mal hecho. —*e. eye*, mal de ojo.—*s.* mal; infortu-nio; maldad.—*the E. One*, el diablo. —*adv.* mal; malignamente.— —*doer* [-duœ(r)], *s.* malhechor, persona perversa.

evoke [ivóụk], *vt.* evocar.

evolution [evoljúṣọn], *s.* evolución, desarrollo; maniobra.— —*ism* [-ịzm], *s.* evolucionismo.—**evolve** [iválv], *vt.* desenvolver, desarrollar; producir por evolución.—*vi.* desarrollarse; evolucionar.

ewe [yu], *s.* oveja.

exacerbation [egzæsœrbéịṣọn], *s.* exa-cerbación; agravación; exasperación.

exact [egzǽkt], *a.* exacto; justo; pun-tual.—*vt.* exigir, imponer.— —*ing* [-iŋ], *a.* exigente.

exaggerate [egzǽdʒẹreịt], *vt. y vi.* exage-rar, ponderar.—**exaggeration** [egz-ædʒẹréịṣọn], *s.* exageración.

exalt [egzólt], *vt.* exaltar, enaltecer; regocijar; reforzar.— —*ation* [-éịṣọn], *s.* exaltación; enaltecimiento; rego-cijo.

exam [egzǽm], *s.* examen.— —*ination* [-inéịṣọn], *s.* examen; investigación; reconocimiento; ensayo, prueba; (for.) interrogatorio.— —*ine* [-in], *vt.* examinar; indagar; reconocer; preguntar, inquirir; analizar.— —*iner* [-inœ(r)], *s.* examinador, inspector.

example [egzǽmpl], *s.* ejemplo, ejem-plar; lección, escarmiento.

exasperate [egzǽspẹreịt], *vt.* exasperar; irritar; agravar.—**exasperation** [egz-æspẹréịṣọn], *s.* exasperación; agra-vación.

excavate [ékskạveịt], *vt.* excavar, (so)cavar; vaciar, ahondar.—**excava-tion** [ekskạvéịṣọn], *s.* excavación; des-monte; zanja.

exceed [eksíd], *vt.* exceder; aventajar, sobrepujar; (sobre)pasar; rebasar. —*vi.* excederse, propasarse; pre-ponderar.— —*ing* [-iŋ], *a.* excesivo; extraordinario.

excel [eksél], *vti. y vii.* [1] aventajar, superar; ser superior a; sobresalir.— —*lence* [éksẹlẹns], *s.* excelencia.— —*lent* [éksẹlẹnt], *a.* excelente.

except [eksépt], *vt.* exceptuar, excluir, omitir.—*prep.* excepto, con excep-ción de, fuera de.— —*ing* [-iŋ], *prep.* a excepción de, salvo, exceptuando.— —*ion* [eksépṣọn], *s.* excepción, salve-dad; objeción.—*to take e.*, objetar, oponerse, desaprobar.— —*ional* [ek-sépṣọnạl], *a.* excepcional.

excess [eksés], *s.* exceso; excedente; inmoderación o destemplanza; des-orden; demasía; sobrante.—*a.* exce-sivo, sobrante; suplemental, de recargo.— —*ive* [-iv], *a.* excesivo.

exchange [ekschéịndʒ], *vt.* cambiar; canjear, permutar; trocar, inter-cambiar.—*s.* cambio, trueque, per-muta; canje; (com.) lonja, bolsa; cambio (de la moneda).—*bill of e.*, letra de cambio.—*e. rate*, tipo de cambio.—*stock e.*, bolsa de cambios.

excite [eksáịt], *vt.* excitar; provocar, suscitar, estimular.— —*d* [-id], *a.* excitado, acalorado.— —*ment* [-mẹnt], *s.* excitación; estimulación; agitación; acaloramiento.—**exciting** [-iŋ], *a.* excitante, estimulante, incitante; emocionante.

exclaim [ekskléịm], *vt. y vi.* excla-mar, clamar.—**exclamation** [eksklạ-méịṣọn], *s.* exclamación.—*e. point*, signo de admiración.

exclude [eksklúd], *vt.* excluir.—**exclu-sion** [eksklúʒọn], *s.* exclusión.— **exclusive** [eksklúsịv], *a.* exclusivo; privativo; selecto.—*e. of*, exclusive, sin contar.—**exclusiveness** [eksklú-sịvnịs], *s.* exclusividad; exclusiva.

excommunicate [ekskọmjúníkeịt], *vt.* excomulgar.—*a. y s.* excomulgado. —**excommunication** [ekskọmjunịkéị-ṣọn], *s.* excomunión.

excrement [ékskrịmẹnt], *s.* excremento, heces.

excursion [ekskǽrʒọn], *s.* excursión, romería; expedición.

excusable [ekskịúzạbl], *a.* excusable, disculpable.—**excuse** [ekskịúz], *vt.* excusar, disculpar; sincerar, justifi-car; eximir; paliar; despedir.—*s.* [ekskịús], excusa; pretexto.

execration [eksikréiŝǫn], *s.* abominación.

execute [éksikiut], *vt.* ejecutar, llevar a cabo; legalizar, formalizar; ajusticiar.—execution [eksikiúŝǫn], *s.* ejecución, cumplimiento; mandamiento judicial; legalización; ajusticiamiento. —executioner [eksikiúŝǫnœ(r)], *s.* verdugo.—executive [egzékyutiv], *a.* ejecutivo.—*s.* poder ejecutivo; funcionario ejecutivo.—executor [egzékyutǫ(r)]. *s.* ejecutor; albacea.

exempt [egzémpt], *vt.* eximir, franquear. —*a.* exento; libre, franco, inmune.— —ion [egzémpŝǫn], *s.* exención, franquicia, inmunidad.

exercise [éksœrsaiz]. *s.* ejercicio.—*vt.* ejercer; ejercitar; adiestrar; preocupar, causar ansiedad.—*vi.* adiestrarse, ejercitarse; hacer ejercicio.

exert [egzœrt], *vt.* esforzar; ejercer. —*vr.* empeñarse, esforzarse.— —ion [egzœrŝǫn]. *s.* esfuerzo, empeño, ejercicio.

exhale [ekshéil], *vt.* exhalar, espirar. —*vi.* vah(e)ar; disiparse, desvanecerse.

exhaust [egzóst], *vt.* agotar, vaciar; gastar, consumir; debilitar, cansar. —*s.* vapor de escape; tubo de escape; (fis. y mec.) vacío.— —ion [egzóschǫn], *s.* agotamiento; debilitación, postración; (mec.) vaciamiento.— —ive [-iv], *a.* exhaustivo; agotador; completo, cabal.

exhibit [egzíbit], *vt.* exhibir; presentar, manifestar; exponer, mostrar.—*vi.* dar una exhibición.—*s.* exhibición; manifestación; (for.) pruebas en un juicio.— —ion [eksibiŝǫn], *s.* exhibición, exposición; manifestación; ostentación.

exhilarate [egzílareit], *vt.* alegrar, regocijar o alborozar; animar, estimular.

exile [égzail], *s.* destierro, expatriación; desterrado, expatriado.—*vt.* desterrar, expatriar.

exist [egzíst], *vi.* existir, subsistir, vivir.— —ence [-ǫns], *s.* existencia, vida, subsistencia; ente, ser.— —ent [-ǫnt], —ing [-iŋ], *a.* existente, actual, presente.

exit [éksit], *s.* salida; (teat.) mutis, vase.—*vi.* salir.

exodus [éksǫdʌs], *s.* éxodo.

exonerate [egzánęreit] *vt.* exonerar; relevar.

exorbitance [egzórbitǫns], *s.* exorbitancia, exceso.—exorbitant [egzórbitʌnt], *a.* exorbitante excesivo.

exotic [egzátik], *a.* exótico.

expand [ekspǽnd], *vt.* y *vi.* extender(se), expandir(se).—expanse [ekspǽns], *s.* extensión, espacio.—expansion [eks-

pǽnŝǫn], *s.* expansión, dilatación; desarrollo.—expansive [ekspǽnsiv], *a.* expansivo, efusivo.

expatriate [ekspéitrieit], *vt.* y *vr.* expatriar(se), desnaturalizar(se), desterrar(se).—*s.* y *a.* [ekspéitriit] expatriado, desterrado.

expect [ekspékt], *vt.* esperar; contar con.— —ance [-ʌns], —ancy [-ʌnsi], *s.* expectativa.— —ant [-ʌnt], *a.* expectante; embarazada, encinta.— —ation [-éiŝǫn], *s.* expectación, expectativa, esperanza.

expectorate [ekspéktǫreit], *vt.* y *vi.* expectorar, escupir.

expedience [ekspídiǫns], expediency [ekspídiǫnsi], *s.* conveniencia.—expedient [ekspídiǫnt], *a.* oportuno, conveniente; prudente, propio.—*s.* expediente, medio, recurso.

expedition [ekspidíŝǫn], *s.* expedición.— —ary [-ęri], *a.* y *s.* expedicionario.

expel [ekspél], *vti.* [1] expeler, expulsar; despedir.

expend [ekspénd], *vt.* gastar, consumir; desembolsar.— —iture [-ichǫ(r)], *s.* gasto, desembolso.—expense [ekspéns], *s.* gasto, coste, costa, costo; desembolso.—*at any e.*, a toda costa. —expensive [ekspénsiv], *a.* costoso; caro, dispendioso.

experiment [ekspérimǫnt], *s.* experimento.—*vi.* experimentar.— —al [eksperiméntʌl], *a.* experimental.—experience [ekspíriǫns], *s.* experiencia; conocimiento; pericia; lance, incidente personal.—*vt.* experimentar; sentir.—experienced [ekspíriǫnst], *a.* experimentado, perito; hábil; avezado; amaestrado o aleccionado. —expert [ekspœrt], *a.* experto; pericial.—*s.* [ékspœrt], experto, perito.

expiate [ékspieit], *vt.* expiar.

expiration [ekspiréiŝǫn], *s.* expiración; vencimiento; espiración; muerte.— expire [ekspáir], *vt.* espirar, expeler. —*vi.* expirar, terminar; fallecer, morir.

explain [ekspléin], *vt.* explicar.—explanation [eksplǫnéiŝǫn], *s.* explicación.—explanatory [eksplǽnʌtǫri], *a.* explicativo.

explode [eksplóud], *vt.* volar, hacer estallar o explotar; refutar, confundir.—*vi.* estallar, hacer explosión; reventar.

exploit [ekspláit], *s.* haz..ña, proeza. —*vt.* [ekspláit], explotar, sacar partido de; abusar.— —ation [eksplaitéiŝǫn], *s.* explotación, aprovechamiento.— —er [eksplóitœ(r)], *s.* explotador.

exploration [eksplǫréiŝǫn], *s.* exploración.—explorator [éksplǫreitǫ(r)], ex-

plorer [eksplórœ(r)], *s.* explorador.
—**explore** [eksplór], *vt.* explorar; averiguar; sondear.—*vi.* dedicarse a exploraciones.

explosion [eksplóuʒǫn], *s.* explosión, voladura; detonación, reventón.—**explosive** [eksplóusiv], *a.* y *s.* explosivo.

exponent [ekspóunǫnt], *s.* exponente.

export [ekspórt], *vt.* exportar.—*s.* [éksport] exportación.

expose [ekspóuz], *vt.* exponer, exhibir; poner en peligro; revelar, sacar a luz; desenmascarar.—**exposé** [ekspozéj], *s.* revelación comprometedora o escandalosa.—**exposition** [ekspozíʃon], *s.* exposición, exhibición.—**exposure** [ekspóuʒü(r)], *s.* exposición; acción de exponer(se); estar expuesto a (la intemperie); orientación, situación; revelación.

expound [ekspáund], *vt.* exponer, explicar.

express [eksprés], *vt.* expresar, manifestar; enviar por expreso.—*vi.* expresarse.—*a.* expreso; claro, explícito; especial; hecho de encargo; llevado por expreso; pronto, rápido. —*adv.* por expreso; expresa o especialmente.—*s.* tren, autobús, ascensor, etc. expreso o exprés; expreso; servicio de transporte de mercancías.— —**ion** [ekspréʃǫn], *s.* expresión; semblante, talante; dicción, locución, giro.- —**ive** [eksprésiv], *a.* expresivo.

expropriate [ekspróuprijeit], *vt.* enajenar, expropiar.

exquisite [ékskwizit], *a.* exquisito.

extend [eksténd], *vt.* extender; amplificar; prolongar; ampliar.—*vi.* extenderse, prolongarse; dar de sí.- —**ed** [-id], *a.* extenso, prolongado; diferido.—**extension** [ksténʃǫn], *s.* extensión; dilatación; expansión; prolongación; prórroga.—**extensive** [eksténsiv], *a.* extens(iv)o.—**extent** [ekstént], *s.* extensión; alcance; grado, punto, límite.—*to a certain e.*, hasta cierto punto.—*to a great e.*, en sumo grado, grandemente.—*to the full e.*, en toda su extensión, completamente.

exterior [ekstíriǫ(r)], *a.* exterior, externo; manifiesto.—*s.* exterior; exterioridad, aspecto.

exterminate [ekstŕœrmineit], *vt.* exterminar.—**extermination** [ekstœrminéiʃǫn], *s.* exterminio.—**exterminator** [ekstœrmineitǫ(r)], *s.* exterminador.

external [ekstŕœrnəl], *a.* externo, exterior; extranjero.—*s.* exterior; exterioridad.

extinct [ekstíŋkt], *a.* extinto; extinguido, apagado.- —**ion** [ekstíŋkʃǫn],

s. extinción.—**extinguish** [ekstíŋgwiʃ], *vt.* extinguir; apagar; sofocar; suprimir, destruir; oscurecer.—**extinguisher** [ekstíŋgwiʃœ(r)], *s.* extintor de incendios; apagador; matacandelas.

extol [ekstóul], *vti.* [1] ensalzar, enaltecer, elogiar.

extort [ekstórt], *vt.* extorsionar; sacar u obtener por fuerza; arrebatar; exigir dinero sin derecho.- —**ion** [ekstórʃǫn], *s.* extorsión; exacción.

extra [ékstrə], *a.* extraordinario; suplementario; de repuesto o de reserva. —*e. charge*, recargo.—*s.* exceso; recargo, sobreprecio; gasto extraordinario.—*adv.* excepcionalmente, en exceso.

extract [ekstrékt], *vt.* extraer; extractar.—*s.* [ékstrækt], extracto; resumen.

extradite [ékstrədait], *vt.* entregar o reclamar por extradición—**extradition** [ekstrədíʃǫn], *s.* extradición.

extraordinary [ekstrórdinɛri], *a.* extraordinario.

extravagance [ekstrǽvəgəns], **extravagancy** [ekstrǽvəgənsi], *s.* lujo desmedido, derroche; extravagancia; disparate.—**extravagant** [ekstrǽvəgənt], *a.* extravagante.

extreme [ekstrím], *a.* extremo, extremado; riguroso, estricto.—**extremity** [ekstrémiti], *s.* extremidad; rigor; necesidad, apuro.—*pl.* medidas extremas; extremidades.

exult [egzʌlt], *vi.* saltar de alegría, regocijarse. —**ant** [-ənt], *a.* regocijado, alborozado; triunfante.- —**ation** [-éiʃǫn], *s.* regocijo, transporte; triunfo.

eye [ai], *s.* ojo.—*before one's eyes*, en presencia de uno, a la vista. —*by e.*, a ojo.—*e. shade*, visera, guardavista.—*e. socket*, órbita o cuenca del ojo.—*half an e.*, ojeada, vistazo.—*to keep an e. on*, vigilar. —*to make eyes at*, mirar amorosamente o con codicia; comerse con los ojos.—*to see e. to e.*, ser del mismo parecer.—*to shut one's eyes to*, hacer la vista gorda.—*with an e. to*, con la intención de, pensando en, con vistas a.—*vt.* mirar de hito en hito; clavar la mirada a; hacer ojos o agujeros a.- —**ball** [áibol], *s.* globo del ojo.- —**brow** [-brau], *s.* ceja.- —**glass** [-glæs], *s.* ocular; anteojo. —*pl.* lentes, espejuelos, gafas, anteojos.- —**lash** [-læʃ], *s.* pestaña.- —**lid** [-lid], *s.* párpado.- —**sight** [-sait], *s.* vista; alcance de la vista.- —**sore** [-sor], *s.* cosa que ofende la vista.- —**strain** [-strein], *s.* vista fatigada. —**tooth** [-tuθ], *s* colmillo.-

—wash [-waš], s. colirio, loción para los ojos; (fam.) patraña.- —witness [-wítnįs], s. testigo presencial.

F

fable [féibl], s. fábula, ficción.
fabric [fǽbrįk], s. tejido, género; fábrica, edificio; textura.- —ate [-eįt], vt. fabricar; construir; inventar, mentir.- —ation [-éįšǫn], s. fabricación; edificio; invención, mentira.
fabulous [fǽbyuʌls], a. fabuloso, ficticio.
façade [fǽsád], s. (arq.) fachada.
face [feįs], s. cara, rostro; faz; lado; superficie; fachada, frente; aspecto; apariencias; prestigio; esfera (de reloj); descaro; mueca.—f. card, figura (en la baraja).—f. down(ward), boca abajo.—f. powder, polvos de arroz o de tocador.—f. value, (com.) valor nominal; significado literal.— in the f. of, ante; luchando contra, a pesar de.—to lose f., desprestigiarse.— vt. volverse o mirar hacia; arrostrar, afrontar, enfrentarse o encararse con; (for.) responder (a un cargo); cubrir, forrar.—to f. out, persistir en o sostener descaradamente.—to f. the music, (fam.) hacer frente a las consecuencias.—vi. volver la cara; dar o mirar (a, hacia).—to f. about, voltear la cara; cambiar de frente.- —t [fǽsįt], s. faceta.
facetious [fasíšʌs], a. jocoso, chistoso, humorístico.
facial [féįšʌl], a. facial.
facilitate [fǽsįlįteįt], vt. facilitar, allanar, expedir.—facility [fǽsįlįtį], s. facilidad; destreza.—pl. medios (de transporte, etc.).
fact [fǽkt], s. hecho; realidad.—in f., en efecto, en realidad; de hecho.—in the very f., en el mero hecho.—matter of f., hecho positivo.—the f. remains that, ello es que, es un hecho, a pesar de todo.
faction [fǽkšǫn], s. facción, bando; alboroto.—factious [fǽkšʌs], a. faccioso, sedicioso, revoltoso.
factor [fǽktǫ(r)], s. elemento, factor; agente comisionado.
factory [fǽktorį], s. fábrica, taller, manufactura.
factual [fǽkchuʌl], s. exacto; real.
faculty [fǽkʌltį], s. facultad; aptitud; claustro de profesores.
fad [fǽd], s. novedad, moda; manía.
fade [feįd], vt. marchitar; desteñir.—vi. destañirse, descolorarse; marchitarse; (rad.) apagarse la intensidad.—f.-out, desaparición u oscurecimiento gradual.—to f. away, desvanecerse, desa-

parecer.—fading [féidįŋ], s. pérdida gradual de intensidad, sonido, etc.; (rad.) fluctuación en la intensidad de las señales.
faggot, fagot [fǽgǫt], s. haz, manojo, gavilla de leña; (fam.) marica.
fail [feįl], vt. abandonar, dejar; frustrar; (fam.) reprobar, suspender (en los estudios).—vi. faltar; fallar; fracasar; frustrarse; consumirse, decaer; (com.) quebrar; salir mal, ser reprobado (en examen, etc.).—s. falta; defecto; fracaso.—without f., sin falta.- —ure [féįlyǫ(r)], s. fracaso, malogro; suspenso (en un examen); falta, omisión, descuido; (com.) quiebra, bancarrota; (mec.) avería, defecto (de motor, etc.).
faint [feint], vi. desmayarse; desfallecer. —a. lánguido, abatido; indistinto, tenue; desfallecido.—f.-hearted, medroso, pusilánime.—s. desmayo, desfallecimiento.—fainting fit o spell, síncope, desmayo.—in a f., desmayado.- —ness [féįntnįs], s. falta de claridad; languidez, desaliento.
fair [fer], a. claro, despejado; rubio; limpio; favorable, próspero; bello; justo, imparcial; razonable; regular, pasable.—f. and square, honrado a carta cabal.—f. complexion, tez blanca.—f. name, nombre honrado, sin tacha.—f. play, proceder leal, juego limpio.—f. sex, bello sexo.—f. trade, comercio recíproco.—f. weather, buen tiempo, bonanza.—f. wind, viento favorable.—to give f. warning, prevenir, avisar de antemano.—to make a f. copy, poner en limpio.— adv. justamente, honradamente; claramente; bien.—f.-minded, imparcial, justo.—s. feria; exposición.- —ness [férnįs], s. hermosura, belleza; honradez; justicia, imparcialidad.- —y [-į], s. hada, duende; (fam.) afeminado.—a. de hadas, de duendes. —f. tale, cuento de hadas.- —yland [-įlænd], s. país de las hadas.
faith [feįθ], s. fe; confianza; creencia, religión; fidelidad.—to break f. with, faltar a la palabra dada a.—upon my f., a fe mía.- —ful [féįθfuˌl], a. fiel; leal; exacto; justo, recto.- —fully [-fuˌlį], adv. fielmente, firmemente; puntualmente.- —fulness [-fuˌlnįs], s. fidelidad; honradez; exactitud.- —less [-lįs], a. infiel, desleal, pérfido.
fake [feįk], s. (fam.) falsificación, fraude, impostura; imitación, copia; patraña, farsa. V. FAKER.—vt. y vi. (fam.) falsificar; fingir, contrahacer. —a. falso, fraudulento.- —r [féįkœ(r)], s. (fam.) farsante; falsario, imitador; embustero.
falcon [fólkǫn], s. halcón.

fall [fol], *vii.* [10] caer(se); bajar, decrecer, disminuir; decaer.—*to f. asleep*, dormirse.—*to f. back*, retroceder, retirarse.—*to f. back on*, o *upon*, recurrir a, echar mano de.—*to f. behind*, rezagarse.—*to f. down*, postrarse; caerse.—*to f. due*, (com.) vencer(se).—*to f. for*, (fam.) prendarse de; ser engañado por.—*to f. in*, (mil.) alinearse; expirar, caducar.—*to f. in line*, formar cola; seguir la corriente.—*to f. in love*, enamorarse.—*to f. in price*, abaratarse.—*to f. in with*, convenir, estar de acuerdo con.—*to f. out*, desavenirse, reñir.—*to f. short*, faltar; errar el tiro.—*to f. sick*, enfermar.—*to f. through*, fracasar, malograrse.—*s.* caída, bajada, descenso; salto de agua; otoño; ruina; desnivel; desembocadura de un río; (com.) baja de precios; (mús.) cadencia; disminución del sonido.— *a.* otoñal.—**fallen** [fólɛn], *pp.* de TO FALL.

fallow [fǽlou], *a.* descuidado, abandonado.—*s.* barbecho.—*vt.* barbechar.

false [fols], *a.* falso, fingido, engañoso; postizo; (mus.) desafinado, discordante.—*f. bottom*, fondo falso.—*f. claim*, pretensión infundada.—*f.-faced*, hipócrita, falso.—*f.-hearted*, pérfido.—*f. step*, desliz; imprudencia.—*f. teeth*, dentadura postiza.— —**hood** [fólshud], *s.* falsedad, embuste.— —**ness** [-nɪs], *s.* falsedad, perfidia.— —**tto** [-étou], *s.* (mús.) falsete.— **falsification** [folsɪfɪkéɪʃɔn], *s.* falsificación.—**falsify** [fólsɪfaɪ], *vti.* [7] falsificar; falsear.—*vii.* mentir.

falter [fóltœ(r)], *vt.* balbucear.—*vi.* vacilar; tartamudear.—*s.* vacilación, temblor.

fame [feɪm], *s.* fama.—*vt.* afamar; celebrar.— —**d** [-d], *a.* afamado, famoso, renombrado; célebre.

familiar [fɑ̃mɪljǎ(r)], *a.* familiar, íntimo; confianzudo.—*f. with*, acostumbrado a; versado o ducho en, conocedor de, al tanto de.—*s.* familiar.— —**ity** [fɑmɪljɛ́rɪtɪ], *s.* familiaridad, intimidad; confianza, llaneza; (con *with*) conocimiento (de).— **family** [fémɪlɪ], *s.* familia.—*a.* familiar, casero, de la familia.—*f. man*, padre de familia.—*f. name*, apellido.—*f. tree*, árbol genealógico.—*in the f. way*, (fam.) encinta, embarazada.

famine [fǽmɪn], *s.* hambre, carestía.— **famished** [fǽmɪʃt], *a.* famélico, hambriento.

famous [féɪmʌs], *a.* famoso, afamado, célebre; (fam.) excelente.

fan [fæn], *s.* abanico; ventilador; aventador; aficionado, entusiasta,

admirador.—*vti.* [1] abanicar; ventilar; aventar.

fanatic [fɑnǽtɪk], *s.* y *a.* fanático.— —(al) [-(ɑl)], *a.* fanático.— —**ism** [fɑnǽtɪsɪzm], *s.* fanatismo.

fanciful [fǽnsɪful], *a.* imaginativo, caprichoso; fantástico.—**fancy** [fǽnɪ], *s.* fantasía, imaginación, antojo, capricho; afición, afecto.—*to take a f. to*, aficionarse a; coger cariño a.—*a.* fantástico; de fantasía; elegante; de lujo, costoso.—*f. ball*, baile de trajes.—*f. dress*, disfraz.—*vti.* [7] imaginar; gustar de, aficionarse a; antojarse, fantasear.—*vii.* tener un antojo o capricho; creer o imaginar algo sin prueba.

fang [fæŋ], *s.* colmillo (de animal, fiera); diente (de serpiente, del tenedor). — —**ed** [-d], *a.* colmilludo.

fantastic [fæntǽstɪk], *a.* fantástico; caprichoso; ilusorio, imaginario.— **fantasy** [fǽntasɪ], *s.* fantasía.

far [far], *adv.* lejos; a lo lejos; en alto grado.—*as f. as*, *so f. as*, hasta; en la medida que, en cuanto a, según.—*by f.*, con mucho.—*f. and wide*, por todas partes.—*f. away*, muy lejos.—*f. flung*, vasto, extenso.—*f. from*, ni con mucho.—*f. off*, a lo lejos; muy lejos; distante, remoto.—*so f.*, *thus f.*, hasta ahora; hasta aquí; hasta ahí.—*a.* lejano, distante, remoto.—*a f. cry (from)*, muy lejos de.

faraway [fárawei], *a.* lejano, alejado; abstraído, distraído.

farce [fars], *s.* (teat.) farsa; comedia, engaño.

fare [fer], *vi.* pasarlo, irle a uno (bien o mal); acontecer.—*s.* pasaje o tarifa (precio); pasajero; comida, plato.— *bill of f.*, menú.— —**well** [térwel], *interj.* ¡adiós! ¡vaya con Dios!—*a.* de despedida.—*f. performance*, función de despedida.—*s.* despedida, adiós.

farm [farm], *s.* finca de labor, granja; (Am.) chácara.—*f. hand*, peón o mozo de labranza, bracero.— —**er** [fármœ(r)], *s.* labrador, granjero, agricultor.—*tenant f.*, colono.— —**house** [-haus], *s.* granja.— —**ing** [-ɪŋ], *s.* cultivo, labranza; agricultura.—*a.* agrícola; de labranza.— —**stead** [-sted], *s.* granja, alquería.

farther [fárðœ(r)], *adv.* más lejos, a mayor distancia; además de, demás de.—*f. on*, más adelante.—*a.* más lejano; ulterior.— —**most** [-moust], *a.* más lejano o remoto.—**farthest** [fárðɪst], *a.* más lejano o remoto; más largo o extendido.—*adv.* lo más lejos, a la mayor distancia.

fascinate [fǽsɪneɪt], *vt.* fascinar, hechizar.—**fascinating** [fǽsɪneɪtɪŋ], *a.*

fascinador, hechicero.—**fascination**
[fæsjnéişǫn], *s.* fascinación, hechizo.

fashion [fǽşǫn], *s.* moda, estilo; elegancia; manera.—*f. plate,* figurín.—*f. shop,* tienda de modas.—*in f.,* de moda.—*out of f.,* pasado de moda.—*to be the f.,* ser (de) moda.—*vt.* adaptar; formar; idear.— —**able** [-ǫbl], *a.* de moda; elegante, de buen tono.

fast [fæst], *vi.* ayunar, hacer abstinencia.—*s.* ayuno, abstinencia, vigilia.—*a.* firme, seguro, fuerte; fijo, indeleble; apretado; constante, fiel; profundo (sueño); veloz, ligero, rápido; adelantado (reloj); derrochador; disoluto.—*adv.* fuertemente, firmemente; estrechamente; para siempre; aprisa, rápidamente.—*f. by,* cerca de, junto a.— —**en** [fǽsn], *vt.* afirmar, asegurar, sujetar; pegar; atar, amarrar; trabar, unir; abrochar.—*vi.* fijarse; agarrarse, pegarse.

fastidious [fæstídjas], *a.* escrupuloso, melindroso; descontentadizo; quisquilloso.

fasting [fǽstiŋ], *s.* ayuno, abstinencia.

fat [fæt], *a.* gordo; obeso; graso, mantecoso; opulento, rico; lucrativo.—*s.* gordura; grasa, manteca, sebo.—*vti. y vii.* [1] engordar.

fatal [féjtǫl], *a.* fatal; mortal; inevitable. — —**ism** [-izm], *s.* fatalismo.— —**ist** [-ist], *s.* fatalista.— —**ity** [fejtǽliti], *s.* fatalidad; desgracia; muerte.

fate [fejt], *s.* hado, destino, sino; suerte, fortuna; parca.— —**d** [féjtid], *a.* predestinado; fatal, aciago.

father [fáðœ(r)], *s.* padre.—*f.-in-law,* suegro.—*vt.* engendrar; prohijar; tratar como hijo.—*to f. on o upon,* achacar, atribuir a.— —**hood** [-hud], *s.* paternidad.— —**land** [-lænd], *s.* (madre)patria, suelo natal.— —**less** [-lis], *a.* huérfano de padre; bastardo. — —**ly** [-li], *a.* paternal, paterno.— *adv.* paternalmente.

fathom [fǽðǫm], *s.* braza.—*vt.* sondar, sondear; profundizar.— —**less** [-lis], *a.* insondable, impenetrable.

fatigue [fǫtíg], *s.* fatiga, cansancio; (mil.) faena.—*pl.* (mil.) traje de faena.—*vt. y vi.* fatigar(se), cansar(se).

fatness [fǽtnis], *s.* gordura.—**fatten** [fǽtn], *vt.* engordar, cebar.—*vi.* engordar, echar carnes.—**fattening** [fǽtniŋ], *s.* ceba, engorde (del ganado). —*a.* engordador.

faucet [fósit], *s.* grifo, llave, espita.

fault [folt], *s.* falta, culpa; defecto, tacha; (geol.) falla; (elec.) fuga de corriente.—*at f. o in f.,* culpable, responsable.—*to a f.,* excesivamente, con exceso.—*to find f. with,* culpar; hallar defecto en.— —**finder** [fólt-fajndœ(r)], *s.* censurador, criticón.—

—**less** [-lis], *a.* sin tacha, impecable.-
—**y** [-i], *a.* defectuoso, imperfecto.

favor [féjvǫ(r)], *vt.* hacer un favor; agraciar, favorecer; patrocinar, sufragar.—*s.* favor; fineza, cortesía; auspicio, apoyo; (com.) carta, grata, atenta.—*in f. of,* a favor de; (com.) pagadero a.—*to be in f. with,* disfrutar del favor de.—*to lose f.,* caer en desgracia.- —**able** [-ǫbl], *a.* favorable, propicio.- —**ed** [-d], *a.* favorecido; valido.—**well** (*ill*)-*f.,* bien (mal) parecido.- —**ite** [-it], *a.* favorito, preferido.—*s.* favorito, protegido.— —**itism** [-itizm], *s.* favoritismo.

fawn [fǫn], *s.* cervato, cervatillo; color de cervato.—*vi.* halagar, adular.

fear [fir], *s.* temor, miedo, pavor, recelo. —*vt. y vi.* temer, recelar.- —**ful** [fírful], *a.* miedoso; tímido, temeroso; horrendo, espantoso, terrible.- —**less** [-lis], *a.* intrépido; sin temor, arrojado.- —**lessness** [-lisnis], *s.* intrepidez, arrojo.

feasible [fízibl], *a.* factible, hacedero, practicable, viable.—*adv.* de modo factible.

feast [fist], *s.* fiesta; festejo, función; (fam.) comilona.—*vt.* festejar, agasajar.—*vi.* comer opíparamente.

feat [fit], *s.* acción; hazaña, proeza; juego de manos.—*pl.* suertes.

feather [féðœ(r)], *s.* pluma; plumaje; (carp.) lengüeta, barbilla.—*a f. in one's cap,* un triunfo, un timbre de orgullo para uno.—*f. duster,* plumero. —*to show the white f.,* volver las espaldas, huir.—*vt.* emplumar.—*to f. one's nest,* hacer su agosto; sacar tajada.- —**brain** [-brejn], *s.* imbécil, tonto.- —**less** [-lis], *a.* desplumado; implume.- —**weight** [-wejt], *a. y s.* ligero de peso; (dep.) peso pluma.- —**y** [-i], *a.* plumado; ligero.

feature [fíchü(r)], *s.* rasgo, carácter distintivo; (teat.) pieza o película principal.—*pl.* facciones, fisonomía. —*vt.* destacar, poner en primer plano; exhibir, mostrar (como lo más importante).

February [fébruerj], *s.* febrero.

fecund [fíkand], *a.* fecundo, fértil.— —**ity** [fjkánditi], *s.* fecundidad; fertilidad, abundancia.

fed [fed], *pret. y pp.* de TO FEED.

federal [fédœrǫl], *a.* federal.—**federate** [fédœrejt], *vt. y vi.* (con)federar(se). —**federation** [fedœréjşǫn], *s.* (con)federación, liga.

fee [fi], *s.* honorarios; derechos; cuota.

feeble [fíbl], *a.* débil; enfermizo; flojo, endeble; delicado.

feed [fid], *vti.* [10] alimentar, mantener, dar de comer a; dar pienso.—*vii.* comer, alimentarse; pacer, pastar.—

s. forraje, pienso, comida.—*f.* bag, morral.—*f.* cock o tap, grifo de alimentación.—*f.* pump, bomba de alimentación.—*f.* rack, pesebre, comedero.— —er [fídœ(r)], *s.* alimentador; cebador (de ganado).— —ing [-iŋ], *s.* alimentación; forraje, pasto.—*a.* alimenticio, de alimentación.—*f.* bottle, biberón.

feel [fíl], *vti.* [10] sentir; experimentar; tocar, palpar; percibir.—*to f. one's way,* ir a tientas.—*to f. the effects of,* resentirse de.—*vii.* sentirse, encontrarse.—*to f. angry, happy,* etc., estar enfadado, contento, etc.—*to f. ashamed, joyous,* etc., avergonzarse, alegrarse, etc.—*to f. bad,* sentirse mal; estar triste, entristecerse.—*to f. cold, warm, hungry, thirsty,* tener frío, calor, hambre, sed.—*to f. for,* condolerse de.—*to f. like (having o doing),* sentir deseos de, tener gana(s) de, querer.—*s.* tacto; sensación, percepción.— —er [fílœ(r)], *s.* el que toca o palpa; tentativa; tentáculo, antena.— —ing [-iŋ], *s.* tacto; sensación; sentimiento, sentido, emoción, sensibilidad; ternura, compasión; presentimiento, sospecha.—*to hurt one's feelings,* herir el amor propio, tocar en lo vivo.—*a.* sensible, tierno, conmovedor.

feet [fit], *s. pl.* de FOOT.

felicitate [fílisiteit], *vt.* felicitar, cumplimentar.—**felicitation** [fílisitéisɔn], *s.* felicitación, enhorabuena.—**felicity** [fílisiti], *s.* felicidad, bienaventuranza, dicha; ocurrencia oportuna.

fell [fel], *pret.* de TO FALL.—*vt.* derribar, tumbar, cortar (un árbol); (cost.) sobrecoser.

fellow [félou], *a.* asociado; compañero de o en.—*f. boarder,* compañero de pupilaje.—*f. citizen,* conciudadano.— *f. countryman,* compatriota.—*f. man, being o creature,* prójimo, semejante. —*f. member,* compañero, colega.—*f. partner,* consocio.—*f. scholar, f. student,* condiscípulo.—*f. traveler,* compañero de viaje; (pol.) simpatizante. —*s.* compañero, camarada; socio o individuo de un colegio, sociedad, etc.; (fam.) hombre, sujeto, tipo.—*a good f.,* (fam.) buen chico.—*a young f.,* un joven, un muchacho.— —ship [-ṣip], *s.* confraternidad, compañerismo; asociación; sociedad; colegiatura; beca.—*f. holder,* becario, becado.

felony [félɔni], *s.* crimen, delito, felonía.

felt [felt], *s.* fieltro.—*pp.* y *pret.* de TO FEEL.—*a.* de fieltro.

female [fímeil], *s.* hembra (mujer, animal, o planta).—*a.* hembra;

femenino.—*f.* dog, donkey, etc., perra, burra, etc.

feminine [féminin], *a.* femenino, femenil; afeminado.—*s.* (gram.) (género) femenino.—**femininity** [femínìniti], *s.* feminidad.

femur [fímœ(r)], *s.* fémur.

fence [fens], *s.* cerca, cerc(ad)o, valla, vallado; estacada; seto; (fam.) comprador de efectos robados; (mec.) resguardo.—*f.* season, tiempo de veda.—*to be on the f.,* estar indeciso. —*vt.* (gen. con in) cercar, vallar.—*vi.* esgrimir.— —r [fénsœ(r)], *s.* esgrimista.—**fencing** [fénsiŋ], *s.* esgrima; materiales para cercar; valladar.—*f.* foil, florete.

fender [féndœ(r)], *s.* guardafango, guardabarros; guardafuegos de chimenea; (mar.) defensas.

fennel [fénęl], *s.* (bot.) hinojo.

ferment [fœrmént], *vt.* (hacer) fermentar.—*vi.* fermentar.—*s.* [fœrment] fermento; levadura; fermentación.— —ation [-éiṣɔn], *s.* fermentación.

fern [fœrn], *s.* helecho.

ferocious [fìróuṣas], *a.* feroz, brutal, fiero.—**ferocity** [fìrásiti], *s.* ferocidad, ensañamiento, fiereza salvaje.

ferret [férit], *s.* (zool.) hurón; (cost.) listón, ribete.—*vt.* (con out) indagar, averiguar; escudriñar.

ferry [féri], *vti.* y *vii.* [7] transportar de una a otra orilla; cruzar una vía de agua en embarcación; (aer.) transportar (tropas) por avión. —*s.* medio de transporte a través de una vía de agua; embarcadero.— **ferryboat** [féribout], *s.* barca chata; transbordador, barco de transbordo.

fertile [fœrtil], *a.* fértil, fecundo.— **fertility** [fœrtíliti], *s.* fertilidad.— **fertilization** [fœrtilizéiṣɔn], *s.* fertilización, abono; (biol.) fecundación.— **fertilize** [fœrtilaiz], *vt.* fertilizar, fecundar; abonar.—**fertilizer** [fœrtilaizœ(r)], *s.* abono, fertilizador.

fervent [fœrvęnt], *a.* ferviente, fervoroso; ardiente.—**fervor** [fœrvɔ(r)], *s.* fervor, devoción; ardor, calor.

fester [féstœ(r)], *vi.* enconarse, ulcerarse, supurar.—*s.* llaga, úlcera.

festival [féstival], *s.* fiesta, festival, festividad.—**festive** [féstiv], *a.* festivo, regocijado.—**festivity** [festíviti], *s.* regocijo, júbilo; fiesta, festividad.

fetch [fech], *vt.* ir a buscar; traer; coger; aportar.—*vi.* moverse, menearse.—*s.* tirada, alcance; estratagema; aparecido.

fete [feit], *vt.* festejar.—*s.* fiesta.

fetter [fétœ(r)], *vt.* engrillar, encadenar; impedir.—*s.* traba, grillete.—*pl.* grillos, prisiones.

fetus [fítas], *s.* feto.

feud [fjud], *s.* contienda, enemistad entre familias, tribus, etc.; feudo.

fever [fívœ(r)], *s.* fiebre; calentura.— **—ish** [-iš], *a.* febril, calenturiento.

few [fju], *a., pron.* o *s.* pocos; no muchos, contados.—*a f.,* (alg)unos, unos cuantos, unos pocos.

fiancé [fjanséi], *s.* prometido, novio.— **—e** [fjanséi], *s.* prometida, novia.

fib [fib], *s.* embuste, filfa, bola.—*vii.* [1] contar embustes.

fiber [fáibœ(r)], *s.* fibra, filamento.— **fibrous** [fáibrʌs], *a.* fibroso.

fickle [fíkl], *a.* voluble, inconstante, veleidoso.

fiction [fíkšɔn], *s.* ficción; literatura novelesca; novela.—**fictitious** [fiktíšʌs], *a.* ficticio.

fiddle [fídl], *s.* (fam.) violín.—*fit as a f.,* en buena condición física.—*vi.* (fam.) tocar el violín.—*to f. away,* malgastar el tiempo.— **—r** [-œ(r)], *s.* (fam.) violinista.

fidelity [fidélti], *s.* fidelidad; veracidad.

fidget [fídʒit], *vt.* inquietar.—*vi.* ajetrearse, afanarse; moverse nerviosamente.—*s.* (gen. *pl.*) afán, agitación, inquietud, impaciencia.— **—y** [-i], *a.* inquieto, agitado.

field [fild], *s.* campo (en todas sus acepciones).—*f. artillery,* artillería de campaña.—*f. glass,* gemelos de campaña, anteojo de largo alcance.—*f. hospital,* hospital de sangre.—*f. kitchen,* cocina de campaña.

fiend [find], *s.* demonio, diablo; monstruo.—*dope f.,* narcómano.— **—ish** [fíndiš], *a.* diabólico, malvado.

fierce [firs], *a.* fiero, feroz; bárbaro; furioso; vehemente.— **—ness** [fírsnis], *s.* fiereza, ferocidad; vehemencia.

fiery [fáiri], *a.* ardiente; vehemente; feroz, furibundo.

fig [fig], *s.* higo.—*f. tree,* higuera.

fight [fait], *vti.* [10] pelear, combatir o luchar con (contra); librar (una batalla); lidiar (toros).—*to f. off,* rechazar.—*to f. out,* llevar la lucha hasta lo último.—*vii.* batallar, luchar, pelear; torear, lidiar.—*to f. against odds,* luchar con desventaja.—*s.* batalla, lucha, combate, lidia; pelea, riña.— **—er** [fáitœ(r)], *s.* guerrero; peleador; lidiador, luchador, combatiente.—*f. plane,* avión de combate o de caza.— **—ing** [-iŋ], *a.* combatiente; agresivo; luchador.—*s.* combate, riña, pelea.

figure [fígyŋ(r)], *s.* figura; forma; talle; representación; personaje; (arit.) cifra, número; (com.) precio, valor.—*f. of speech,* tropo; metáfora.—*f. skating,* patinaje artístico.—*to cut a f.,* descollar.—*vt.* figurar, delinear; representar; calcular.—*to f. out,* hallar por cálculo, resolver.—*to f. up,* computar, calcular.—*vi.* figurar; (fam.) figurarse, imaginarse; calcular; (mús.) florear.

filament [fílamęnt], *s.* filamento; hilacha.

file [fail], *s.* lima; escofina; archivo; carpeta o cubierta (para archivar papeles); legajo; actas; protocolo (de notario, etc.); fila, hilera.—*f. case,* archivador; fichero.—*f. card,* ficha o tarjeta (de fichero).—*vt.* limar; archivar; acumular; presentar, registrar, anotar; protocolar.—*vi.* marchar en filas.—*to f. past,* desfilar.

filial [fíliąl], *a.* filial.—**filiation** [filiéišɔn], *s.* filiación.

filibuster [fílibʌstœ(r)], *vi.* (E.U.) hacer obstrucción en un cuerpo legislativo prolongando el debate.—*s.* obstruccionista u obstrucción parlamentaria; filibustero, pirata.

filigree [fíligri], *s.* filigrana.

filing [fáiliŋ], *s.* limado, acción de limar; acción de archivar; (gen. *pl.*) limaduras, limalla.—*f. card,* ficha, tarjeta para archivo.

Filipino [filipínou], *s.* y *a.* filipino.

fill [fil], *vt.* llenar; rellenar; desempeñar, ocupar (un puesto); preparar (una receta); despachar (un pedido); hinchar, inflar; empastar (un diente).— *to f. in,* terraplenar; rellenar; insertar. —*to f. out,* completar; llevar a cabo. —*to f. up,* colmar; llenar un impreso; tapar.—*to f. up the time,* emplear el tiempo.—*vi.* (a menudo con **up**) llenarse, henchirse; saciarse.—*s.* terraplén; hartura; abundancia.

fillet [fílet], *s.* filete; solomillo; cinta o tira de adorno.

filling [fíliŋ], *s.* relleno; envase; empaquetadura; terraplén; empaste dental. —*f. station,* estación de gasolina.

film [film], *s.* película; telilla, velo; membrana; nube en el ojo.—*vt.* cubrir con película; rodar una película; fotografiar.

filter [fíltœ(r)], *vt.* filtrar, colar.—*vi.* (in)filtrarse.—*s.* filtro.

filth [filθ], *s.* suciedad, inmundicia, porquería, mugre.— **—y** [fílθi], *a.* sucio, puerco, asqueroso; inmundo.

fin [fin], *s.* aleta (de pez); barba de ballena.

final [fáinąl], *a.* final, terminante, definitivo, decisivo.—*s.* final.— **—ist** [-ist], *s.* finalista en un torneo deportivo.— **—ity** [fáinéliti], *s.* finalidad; decisión, determinación.— **—ly** [fáinąli], *adv.* finalmente, en fin, en conclusión, por último.

finance [finéns], *s.* finanza.—*pl.* finanzas; fondos.—*vt.* financiar.— **financial** [finénšąl], *a.* financiero,

monetario.—**financier** [fɪnænsíɾ], *s.*
financiero, financista, hacendista.—
financing [fɪnǽnsiŋ], *s.* financiamiento, (Am.) refacción.

find [faɪnd], *vti.* [10] encontrar, hallar.
—*to f. fault with,* censurar o criticar a.
—*to f. out,* descubrir; averiguar,
enterarse (de).—*vii.* (for.) juzgar,
fallar.—*s.* hallazgo, descubrimiento;
encuentro.— **—er** [fáɪndœ(r)], *s.* el
que encuentra; (fot.) visor, enfocador.
— **—ing** [-iŋ], *s.* descubrimiento;
hallazgo; (for.) fallo, sentencia.

fine [faɪn], *a.* fino; refinado; excelente,
admirable; primoroso; guapo, ga-
llardo; claro; agradable.—*f. arts,*
bellas artes.—*f. weather,* tiempo
despejado.—*s.* multa.—*vt.* afinar,
refinar; multar.—*to be fined,* incurrir
en multa.—*adv.* finamente; (fam.) de
primera; muy bien (apl. a la salud).
—*f.-tongued,* zalamero.—*interj.* ¡bien!
¡magnífico!.- **—ness** [fáɪnnɪs], *s.*
fineza, delicadeza; primor, excelencia;
perfección; finura (de arena, cemento,
etc.).—**—ry** [fáɪnœɾi], *s.* gala, adorno,
atavío.

finger [fɪŋgœ(r)], *s.* dedo (de las manos).
—*little f.,* (dedo) meñique.—*middle f.,*
dedo (del) corazón.—*to have a f. in
the pie,* meter la cuchara; tener
participación en un asunto.—*to have
at one's fingers' ends o f. tips,* tener o
saber al dedillo.—*vt.* tocar, manosear;
hurtar; (mus.) pulsar, teclear.-
—nail [-neɪl], *s.* uña del dedo.-
—print [-prɪnt], *s.* huella dactilar;
impresión digital.—*vt.* tomar las
impresiones digitales de.— **—printing**
[-prɪntiŋ], *s.* dactiloscopía.

finish [fɪnɪʃ], *vt.* acabar, terminar, rematar; pulir, retocar, perfeccionar.—*to
f. off,* rematar.—*to f. up,* darle la
última mano a; retocar; terminar.—
vi. acabar, finalizar; fenecer.—*s.* fin,
término, remate; pulimento, última
mano, acabado.—*f. line,* (dep.) meta.
— **—ed** [-t], *a.* acabado, perfeccionado,
pulido.- **—ing** [-iŋ], *s.* consumación;
perfección; última mano, repaso.—*a.*
último, de remate; de acabar.—*f.
blow,* golpe de gracia.—*f. coat,* (pint.)
última mano.

Finn [fɪn], *s.* finlandés, finlandesa.-
—ish [fɪnɪʃ], *a.* y *s.* finlandés.

fir [fœr], *s.* abeto; pino.

fire [faɪr], *s.* fuego; lumbre; incendio,
quema; chispa; ardor, pasión.—*f.
alarm,* alarma de incendios.—*f. department,* servicio de bomberos.—*f.
engine,* bomba de incendios.—*f.
escape,* escalera de incendios.—*f.
extinguisher,* matafuego.—*f. works,*
fuegos de artificio.—*to catch f.,*
encenderse, inflamarse.—*to set f.,* to

set on *f.,* pegar fuego a, incendiar.—
to take f., encenderse; acalorarse.—
under f., (mil., fig.) expuesto al fuego;
atacado; censurado.—*vt.* incendiar;
encender; disparar; enardecer; (fam.)
despedir, echar (empleados).—*to f.
up,* encender.—*vi.* encenderse; inflamarse; disparar, hacer fuego; enardecerse.—*to f. up,* enfurecerse.— **—arm**
[fáɪrarm], *s.* arma de fuego.- **—brand**
[-brænd], *s.* tea, tizón; incendiario.-
—bug [-bʌg], *s.* (fam.) incendiario.—
—cracker [-krækœ(r)], *s.* triquitraque, buscapiés, cohete.- **—fly**
[-flaɪ], *s.* luciérnaga.- **—house**
[-haʊs], *s.* estación o cuartel de
bomberos.- **—man** [-man], *s.* bombero; fogonero.- **—place** [-pleɪs], *s.*
hogar, chimenea.- **—proof** [-pruf], *a.*
incombustible, a prueba de fuego,
refractario.—*vt.* hacer refractario o
incombustible.- **—side** [-saɪd], *s.*
hogar, fogón; vida doméstica.—*a.*
casero, íntimo.- **—wood** [-wʊd], *s.*
leña.- **—works** [-wœrks], *s.* fuegos
artificiales.—**firing** [fáɪriŋ], *s.* descarga, tiroteo.—*f. squad,* (mil.)
pelotón o piquete de fusilamiento.

firm [fœrm], *a.* firme; fijo, estable;
sólido; persistente; tenaz, inflexible.
—*s.* (com.) casa o empresa de comercio; firma, razón social.

firmament [fœrmamənt], *s.* firmamento.

firmness [fœrmnɪs], *s.* firmeza; estabilidad, fijeza, solidez; entereza, tesón.

first [fœrst], *a.* primero; primario;
primitivo.—*f.-aid kit,* botiquín de
urgencia o de primeros auxilios.—*f.-
born,* primogénito.—*f. cousin,* primo
hermano.—*f. floor,* planta baja.—*f.-
hand,* de primera mano.—*f. lady,*
primera dama.—*f. name,* nombre de
pila.—*adv.* primero; en primer lugar;
al principio; antes; por, o la, primera
vez.—*at f.,* al principio, al pronto.—
f. of all, en primer lugar, ante todo.—
f. or last, tarde o temprano.—*f.-rate,*
de primera clase.

fiscal [fɪskal], *a.* fiscal.

fish [fɪʃ], *s.* pez; pescado.—*f. bait,* cebo
o carnada.—*f. hatchery,* vivero,
criadero.—*f. market,* pescadería.—*f.
pole,* caña de pescar.—*f. story,* cuento
increíble.—*f. tank,* pecera.—*neither
f. nor fowl,* ni carne ni pescado.—
shell-f., marisco.—*vt.* y *vi.* pescar.—
—bone [fɪʃboʊn], *s.* espina de pescado.- **—erman** [-œrman], *s.* pescador.- **—ery** [-œri], *s.* industria pes-
quera; pesquero.- **—hook** [-hʊk], *s.*
anzuelo; garfio; bichero.- **—ing** [-iŋ],
s. pesca, pesquería.—*a.* de pescar;
pesquero (barco, industria).—*f. line,*
sedal o tanza de pescar.—*f. reel,*
carrete.—*f. rod,* caña o vara de pes-

car.—*f.* *tackle*, avíos de pescar.—
—**monger** [-mʌŋgœ(r)], *s.* pescadero.
— —**worm** [-wœrm], *s.* lombriz para
pescar.— —**y** [-i], *a.* que huele o sabe
a pescado; abundante en peces;
(fam.) sospechoso.

fissure [fĭʃŋ(r)], *s.* fisura, grieta, rajadura.—*vi.* agrietararse.

fist [fĭst], *s.* puño; (impr.) llamada,
manecilla, ▰.— —**icuffs** [fĭstĭkʌfs],
s. puñetazos; riña a puñetazos.

fit [fĭt], *s.* ataque, convulsión; arranque,
arrebato; corte, talle; ajuste, encaje;
conveniencia, adaptación.—*by fits
(and starts)*, a tontas y a locas.—*a.*
apto, idóneo, a propósito, adecuado,
conveniente; capaz; apropiado; en
buena salud, bien.—*f. to be tied,*
(fam.) loco de atar.—*vt.* [1] ajustar,
encajar, acomodar; adaptar; surtir,
equipar; preparar; (cost.) entallar
un vestido, probar.—*to f. out*, equipar;
armar.—*to f. up*, ajustar, componer;
ataviar; amueblar.—*vii.* convenir;
ajustarse, entallarse, venir, sentar o
caer bien o mal.—*to f. into*, encajar
en.— —**ness** [fĭtnĭs], *s.* aptitud,
idoneidad, disposición; conveniencia;
adaptabilidad.— —**ting** [-iŋ], *a.*
propio, adecuado, conveniente.—*s.*
ajuste; unión o conexión de tubería;
(cost.) corte, prueba.—*pl.* guarniciones, accesorios; avíos o herrajes.

fix [fĭks], *vt.* fijar; asegurar; señalar
(una fecha); arreglar; reparar, componer; (fam.) ajustar las cuentas.—
to f. up, componer, arreglar; equipar.
—*s.* apuro, aprieto.— —**ed** [-t], *a.* fijo,
estable, permanente.— —**ture** [fĭks-
chʊ(r)], *s.* cosa fija o enclavada en
un sitio; adorno; empleado inamovible.—*pl.* muebles y enseres; aparatos y accesorios eléctricos.

flabby [flǽbĭ], *a.* flojo, fofo, blando.

flag [flǽg], *s.* bandera; pabellón; banderola.—*vi.* [1] izar bandera; hacer
señales con banderola; enlosar.—*vii.*
flaquear; decaer, debilitarse.

flagpole [flǽgpoul], *s.* asta de bandera.

flagrant [flǽgrǝnt], *a.* notorio, escandaloso; flagrante.

flagship [flǽgʃip], *s.* nave capitana.—
flagstaff [flǽgstæf], *s.* asta de bandera.—**flagstone** [flǽgstoun], *s.* losa
grande de embaldosar; laja.

flair [flɛr], *s.* sagacidad; aptitud,
propensión.

flake [flejk], *s.* escama; copo de nieve;
hojuela, laminilla.—*f. of ice*, carámbano.—*vt. y vi.* formar hojuelas o
escamas.—*flaky* [fléjki], *a.* escamoso.

flame [flejm], *s.* llama(rada), flama;
ardor, pasión.—*f. thrower*, lanza-
llamas.—*vt.* quemar, chamuscar.—*vi.*
arder, flamear, llamear; brillar,

fulgurar; inflamarse.— —**less** [fléjm-
lĭs], *a.* sin llama.—**flaming** [fléjmiŋ],
a. flamante, llameante; encendido,
inflamado; apasionado.

flamingo [flǝmĭŋgou], *s.* (orn.) flamenco.

flange [flændʒ], *s.* borde, reborde,
pestaña, oreja.—*f. joint*, junta de
pestañas.—*f. nut*, tuerca de reborde.
—*vt.* rebordear, poner pestaña o
reborde.—*vi.* sobresalir, hacer reborde.

flank [flæŋk], *s.* ijar, ijada; flanco,
costado.—*a.* de lado, de costado o
por el flanco.—*vt.* estar a cada lado
de; (mil.) flanquear.—*vi.* (con **on**)
lindar con.

flannel [flǽnǝl], *s.* franela, bayeta.

flap [flæp], *s.* (sast.) cartera; faldeta,
faldón; aleta; ala de sombrero; hoja
plegadiza de mesa; oreja de zapato;
revés, cachete; (cir.) colgajo.—*f.
door*, trampa.—*f.-eared*, orejudo.—*f.-
mouthed*, hocicudo, morrudo.—*vti.*
[1] batir (las alas), sacudir, pegar;
agitar.—*to f. the wings*, aletear.—*vii.*
batir; colgar.

flare [flɛr], *vt.* chamuscar; acampanar.
—*vi.* brillar; fulgurar; resplandecer.
—*to f. up*, encenderse; encolerizarse.
—*s.* llama, llamarada, fulgor; luz de
Bengala; cohete de señales; brillantez.—*f. up*, llamarada; arrebato
de cólera; jarana.

flash [flæʃ], *s.* llamarada, destello, resplandor; fogonazo; (period.) breve
despacho telegráfico; (cine) incidencia.—*f. of lightning*, relámpago.—*f. of
the eye*, ojeada, vistazo.—*f. of wit*,
agudeza, ingenio.—*vt.* encender;
enviar o despedir con celeridad;
hacer brillar.—*vi.* relampaguear;
brillar, fulgurar, destellar; pasar o
cruzar como un relámpago.— —**ing**
[flǽʃiŋ], *a.* centelleante; relampa-
gueante.—*s.* centelleo; relampagueo.—
—**light** [-lajt], *s.* linterna eléctrica de
bolsillo o portátil; reflector de luz
intermitente (de un faro); (fot.) luz
instantánea.— —**y** [-i], *a.* charro,
llamativo.

flask [flæsk], *s.* frasco grande; matraz;
caneca.

flat [flæt], *s.* apartamento, piso; (mús.)
bemol.—*f. of the hand*, palma de la
mano.—*a.* plano, llano, liso; chato,
aplastado; extendido; categórico;
insulso, insípido; (mús.) bemol;
desafinado; monótono; menor o
disminuído.—*f.-bottomed*, de fondo
plano.—*f.-footed*, de pies planos;
(fam.) resuelto, determinado.—*f.-
nosed*, chato, ñato.—*f. rate*, tipo o
tarifa fijos; precio alzado.—*f. tire,*
pinchazo; neumático desinflado.—
adv. terminantemente; resueltamente;

(com.) sin interés.—*vti.* [1] (mús.)
bemol(iz)ar; achatar.—*vii.* (mús.)
desafinar por lo bajo; aplastarse.—
—boat [flétboụt], *s.* bote o barco de
fondo plano.— —car [-kar], *s.* (f.c.)
(vagón de) plataforma.— —iron
[-aịọrn], *s.* plancha (de planchar).—
—ly [-lị], *adv.* categóricamente,
rotundamente.— —ness [-nịs], *s.*
llanura, lisura, insipidez, insulsez.—
—ten [-n], *vt.* aplastar, achatar,
aplanar; deprimir; enderezar (un
avión).—*vi.* aplanarse; (aer.) enderezarse.

flatter [flétœ(r)], *vt.* y *vi.* adular, lisonjear.— —er [-œ(r)], *s.* adulador;
lisonjero, zalamero.— —y [-ị], *s.*
adulación, lisonja, halago.

flattop [fléttap], *s.* (fam.) portaaviones.

flaunt [flont], *vt.* y *vi.* ostentar, lucir;
desplegar, ondear.—*s.* ostentación.

flavor [fléịvọ(r)], *s.* sabor; sazón.—*vt.*
saborear; sazonar.

flaw [flɔ], *s.* defecto, falta, mancha;
grieta, pelo, paño, paja; ráfaga,
racha.—*vt.* afear; estropear; agrietar.
—*vi.* agrietarse; estropearse.—less
[flɔ́lịs], *a.* entero; intachable, irrepro-
chable; perfecto.

flax [flæks], *s.* lino.

flay [fleị], *vt.* desollar, despellejar.

flea [flii], *s.* pulga.

fled [fled], *pret.* y *pp.* de TO FLEE.—flee
[flii], *vti.* [10] huir de, evitar.—*vii.*
huir; fugarse; desaparecer.

fleece [fliis], *s.* vellón, lana.—*Golden F.*,
Toisón de Oro.—*vt.* esquilar; despojar, esquilmar.—fleecy [flisị], *a.*
lanudo.

fleet [fliit], *s.* armada, escuadra; flota,
flotilla.—*a.* veloz, rápido.— —ing
[flítịŋ], *a.* fugaz, efímero.

Flemish [flémịş], *a.* y *s.* flamenco.—*s.*
idioma flamenco.

flesh [fleş], *s.* carne; pulpa (de las
frutas).—*f. and blood*, carne y hueso;
sangre, parentela, progenie.—*f.
wound*, herida superficial.—*in the f.*,
vivo; en persona.—*to put on f.*, echar
carnes.— —y [fléşị], *a.* gordo, carnoso;
pulposo; suculento.

flew [flu], *pret.* de TO FLY.

flexibility [flėksịbfḷịtị], *s.* flexibilidad.—
flexible [flėksịbl], *a.* flexible.—flexion
[flėkṣọn], *s.* flexión.

flick [flịk], *vt.* golpear o sacudir leve-
mente.—*vi.* revolotear.—*s.* golpecito.
— —er [flịkœ(r)], *vi.* flamear; fluctuar,
vacilar; aletear; revolotear.—*s.* llama
vacilante; pestañeo, parpadeo.

flier [flájœ(r)], *s.* volador; aviador;
fugitivo; (mec.) volante; hoja o papel
volante; cosa veloz.

flight [flaịt], *s.* vuelo; escuadrilla aérea;
bandada de pájaros; ímpetu, arran-

que; huída, evasión.—*f. of stairs*,
tramo de escalera.

flimsy [flímzị], *a.* débil, endeble; baladí,
frívolo.

flinch [flịnch], *vi.* vacilar; acobardarse;
retroceder.—*s.* titubeo.

fling [flịŋ], *vti.* [10] arrojar, tirar,
lanzar, echar.—*to f. about*, desparramar, esparcir.—*to f. away*, desechar.
—*to f. open*, abrir de repente.—*to f.
out*, arrojar con fuerza; hablar violentamente, echar chispas.—*to f. up*,
abandonar, dejar.—*vii.* lanzarse.—*s.*
tiro; lanzamiento; indirecta; tentativa.—*to go on a f.*, echar una cana
al aire.

flint [flịnt], *s.* pedernal.

flirt [flœrt], *vi.* coquetear, (neol.) flirtear; dejarse tentar (por una idea,
etc.).— —ation [-éịşọn], *s.* coqueteo,
galanteo.

flit [flịt], *vii.* [1] revolotear; volar; deslizarse velozmente.

float [floụt], *vt.* poner, mantener o
llevar a flote; (com.) emitir, poner en
circulación.—*vi.* flotar, sobrenadar.—
s. flotador; boya; balsa salvavidas;
corcho de una caña de pescar;
carroza.—*a.* de flotador.

flock [flak], *s.* hato, manada, rebaño;
grey; bandada; congregación; multitud; pelusilla.—*vi.* congregarse.

flog [flag], *vti.* [1] azotar.— —ging
[flágịŋ], *s.* azotaina, paliza.

flood [flʌd], *s.* diluvio; avenida, creciente, inundación; torrente; plétora.
—*f. light*, reflector.—*f. tide*, pleamar.
—*vt.* inundar; anegar; abarrotar.—*vi.*
desbordar.— —gate [flʌ́dgeịt], *s.* compuerta.

floor [flọr], *s.* suelo; piso; pavimento.—
boarded f., entarimado.—*first f.*,
ground f., planta baja.—*to have the f.*,
tener la palabra.—*vt.* derribar, tirar
al suelo; entarimar; echar el piso;
derrotar; dejar turulato.

flop [flap], *vti.* [1] batir, sacudir.—*vii.*
aletear; caer flojamente; colgar;
caerse, venir abajo.—*to f. down*, tum-
barse, dejarse caer.—*to f. up*, voltear-
(se).—*s.* fracaso, fiasco.

florist [flórịst], *s.* florista.

floss [flɔs], *s.* seda floja; penacho del
maíz.—*dental f.*, hilo dental.

flounce [flaụns], *s.* volante, fleco, cairel.

flounder [flaụndœ(r)], *s.* (ict.) lenguado.
—*vi.* forcejear torpemente; tropezar y
caer; revolcarse.

flour [flaụr], *s.* harina.—*vt.* enharinar.
—*vi.* pulverizarse.

flourish [flǽrịş], *vt.* florear, blandir;
embellecer.—*vi.* florecer; medrar,
prosperar; (mus.) florear.—*s.* rasgo;
rúbrica; floreo, adorno; (esgr.)
molinete.

floury [fláuri], *a.* harinoso.

flout [flaut], *vt.* burlarse de, mofarse de.

flow [flou], *vi.* fluir; manar; correr; seguirse; ondear; flotar; abundar; crecer (la marea).—*to f. away,* deslizarse, pasar.—*to f. from* o *out,* brotar, salir, nacer, manar de.—*to f. into,* desembocar.—*to f. with,* rebosar de.—*vt.* inundar; derramar; hacer fluir. —*s.* corriente; torrente; flujo; desagüe; abundancia.

flower [fláuœ(r)], *s.* flor; planta en flor; flor y nata.—*f. pot,* tiesto.—*f. vase,* florero, búcaro.—*vi.* florecer.— *y* [-i], *a.* florido, ornado.

flowing [flóuin], *a.* corriente, fluente, fluido; suelto; colgante.—*s.* derrame; salida; corriente; flujo; fluidez.

flown [floun], *pp.* de TO FLY.—*a.* vidriado.

flu [flu], *s.* (fam.) influenza, gripe.

fluctuate [flákchueit], *vi.* fluctuar; oscilar, ondear.—**fluctuation** [flakchuéišon], *s.* fluctuación.

flue [flu], *s.* cañón de chimenea; tubo de caldera; pelusa, borra; conducto; cañón de órgano.

fluency [flúensi], *s.* fluidez; afluencia; labia.—**fluent** [flúent], *a.* facundo; suelto, corriente; copioso; flúido.

fluff [flaf], *s.* pelusa, lanilla, vello, plumón.—*vt.* mullir, esponjar.— *y* [flÁfi], *a.* cubierto de plumón o vello; mullido, esponjoso.

fluid [flúid], *s.* flúido; líquido; gas.—*a.* flúido; líquido; gaseoso.—*ity* [fluíditi], —**ness** [flúidnis], *s.* fluidez.

flung [flan], *pret.* y *pp.* de TO FLING.

flunk [flank], *s.* fracaso.—*vt.* reprobar, suspender; fracasar en un examen.— (*e)y* [flÁnki], *s.* lacayo; adulón.

fluorescence [fluorésens], *s.* fluorescencia.—**fluorescent** [fluorésent], *a.* fluorescente.

flush [flaš], *vi.* sonrojarse, abochonarse; inundarse; nivelar(se).—*vt.* limpiar con un chorro de agua.—*a.* nivelado, parejo; copioso.—*s.* rubor; animación; flujo rápido; abundancia; flux (de naipes).

flute [flut], *s.* flauta; estria de una columna; rizado, pliegue.—*vt.* estriar, acanalar; rizar, plegar.

flutter [flÁtœ(r)], *vt.* agitar, menear, sacudir; aturdir.—*vi.* agitarse, menearse; aletear, revolotear; flamear, ondular.—*s.* agitación; vibración; palpitación; aleteo; ondulación.

flux [flaks], *s.* flujo; diarrea.

fly [flai], *vti.* [10] hacer volar; elevar (una cometa, etc.); enarbolar; evitar, huir de; dirigir (un avión); cruzar o atravesar en avión.—*vii.* volar; lanzarse, precipitarse; pasar rápidamente; escaparse; desaparecer, desvanecerse.—*to f. around,* ir de un lado a otro.—*to f. at,* arrojarse o lanzarse sobre.—*to f. away,* irse volando, escaparse.—*to f. from,* huir de.—*to f. into a passion* o *rage,* montar en cólera; irse del seguro.—*to f. off,* desprenderse súbitamente; separarse, sublevarse.—*to f. open,* abrirse repentinamente.—*to f. out,* dispararse, salir a espetaperros.—*s.* mosca; vuelo; bragueta.- —**away** [fláiawei], *a.* tremolante; inconstante.- —**er** [-œ(r)], *s.* = FLIER.- —**ing** [-in], *a.* volante, volador, volátil; flameante, ondeante; rápido, veloz; breve.—*s.* aviación; vuelo.- —**leaf** [-lif], *s.* guarda de un libro.

foam [foum], *s.* espuma.—*vt.* hacer espuma.—*vi.* espumar, echar espuma(rajos).- —**y** [fóumi], *a.* espumoso.

focus [fóukas], *s.* foco; distancia focal. —*out of f.,* desenfocado.—*vti.* y *vii.* [2] enfocar(se); concentrar(se).

fodder [fádœ(r)], *s.* forraje, pienso.—*vt.* dar forraje a.

foe [fou], *s.* enemigo.

fog [fag], *s.* niebla, neblina, bruma; velo; confusión, perplejidad.—*vti.* [1] oscurecer; velar.—*vii.* ponerse brumoso; velarse.- —**gy** [fági], *a.* brumoso, neblinoso; velado.

foil [foil], *vt.* frustrar, contrarrestar.—*s.* hoja delgada de metal; oropel; chapa; hoja de oro o plata; florete; rastro; contraste.

fold [fould], *s.* doblez, pliegue; redil; hato, rebaño.—*vt.* doblar, plegar; encerrar, envolver; meter en redil.— *to f. the arms,* cruzar los brazos.—*vi.* doblarse, plegarse.- —**er** [fóuldœ(r)], *s.* plegador, plegadera; carpeta; cuadernillo, circular.- —**ing** [-in], *a.* plegadizo.—*f. bed,* catre de tijera.— *f. chair,* silla plegadiza.—*f. screen,* biombo.—*s.* plegado, doblamiento; repliegue.

foliage [fóuliidž], *s.* follaje, frondosidad, fronda.

folk [fouk], *s.* gente; nación, raza, pueblo.—*pl.* parientes, parentela.—*a.* de o perteneciente al pueblo; que tiene fuentes populares.—*f. music,* música tradicional del pueblo.—*f. tale,* conseja.

follow [fálou], *vt.* seguir; venir después de; perseguir; ejecutar, poner por obra; resultar de; ejercer.—*to f. out,* llevar hasta el fin.—*to f. suit,* jugar el mismo palo (en los naipes); seguir el ejemplo; seguir la corriente.—*to f. up,* llevar hasta el fin; continuar.—*vi.* ir detrás; seguirse.—*to f. on,* perseverar.- —**er** [-œ(r)], *s.* seguidor; acompañante; secuaz.—*pl.* comitiva, séquito.- —**ing** [-in], *a.* siguiente; próximo.—

s. adhesión; séquito; oficio, profesión.

folly [fáli], *s.* tontería, locura, desatino.

foment [fomént], *vt.* fomentar.

fond [fand], *a.* aficionado, enamorado; tierno, cariñoso; querido, acariciado.— *to be f. of,* ser amigo de o aficionado a; ser afecto a, estar encariñado con.— —**le** [fándl], *vt.* mimar, acariciar, hacer fiestas a.— —**ness** [fándnis], *s.* afecto, ternura; apego, inclinación.

font [fant], *s.* pila de bautismo o de agua bendita; fuente; (impr.) fundición, torta.

food [fud], *s.* alimento, comida, sustento. — —**stuff** [fúdstʌf], *s.* producto o sustancia alimenticia.—*pl.* víveres, comestibles.

fool [ful], *s.* tonto, necio; inocente, bobo; badulaque; (teat.) gracioso; bufón.—*vt.* chasquear; embromar; engañar.—*to f. away,* malbaratar; perder el tiempo.—*vi.* tontear, divertirse, chancear.— —**ery** [fúlœri], *s.* tontería.— —**ish** [-iš], *a.* tonto; disparatado; badulaque; bobo.— —**ishness** [-išnis], *s.* simpleza, tontería, disparate.

foot [fut], *s.* (*pl.* **feet** [fit]) pie; pata; base.—*by f.,* a pie.—*f. by f.,* paso a paso.—*f.-loose,* sin trabas u obligaciones, andariego.—*f. soldier,* soldado de infantería.—*on f.,* de pie; a pie; progresando.—*to put one's f. in it,* meter la pata.— —**ball** [fútbɔl], *s.* football, balompié, balón.— —**ing** [-iŋ], *s.* base, fundamento; cimiento; posición firme.—*on the same f.,* en pie de igualdad.— —**lights** [-laits], *s.* candilejas; el teatro, las tablas.— —**man** [-man], *s.* lacayo.— —**note** [-nout], *s.* nota al pie de una página.— —**pace** [-peis], *s.* descanso de escaleras; paso lento.— —**path** [-pæθ], *s.* senda para peatones.— —**print** [-print], *s.* pisada, rastro.— —**step** [-step], *s.* huella, pisada, paso.— —**stool** [-stul], *s.* escabel, taburete.— —**walk** [-wɔk], —**way** [-wei], *s.* senda de peatones; acera.— —**wear** [-wer], *s.* calzado.— —**work** [-wœrk], *s.* juego o manejo de los pies (boxeo, baile, etc.)

fop [fap], *s.* petimetre, pisaverde, lechuguino.

for [for], *prep.* por; para; durante, por espacio de; de; con, a pesar de, no obstante.—*as f.,* en cuanto a.—*as f. me,* por mi parte.—*but f.,* a no ser, sin.—*f. all that,* no obstante, con todo, a pesar de eso.—*f. good,* para siempre.—*what f.?* ¿para qué?—*conj.* porque, puesto que, pues; en efecto.

forage [fáridʒ], *vt.* y *vi.* forrajear, proveer(se) de forraje; apacentar(se); saquear.—*s.* forraje.

forbad o **forbade** [forbǽd], *pret.* de TO FORBID.

forbear [forbér], *s.* antepasado, antecesor.—*vti.* y *vii.* [10] abstenerse de, tener paciencia; reprimirse.

forbid [forbíd], *vti.* [10] prohibir; impedir, estorbar; excluir de.—**forbidden** [forbíden], *pp.* de TO FORBID.— —*a.* prohibido, vedado, ilícito.— —**ding** [-iŋ], *a.* prohibitivo; repulsivo, aborrecible, repugnante.

forbore [forbór], *pret.* de TO FORBEAR.— —**forborne** [forbórn], *pp.* de TO FORBEAR.

force [fors], *s.* fuerza; necesidad; personal; cuerpo (de tropas, de policía, etc.).—*pl.* fuerzas (militares o navales).—*by f. of,* a fuerza de.—*in f.,* vigente, en vigor.—*vt.* forzar, obligar; violar; impulsar; embutir.—*to f. along,* hacer avanzar o adelantar.— *to f. away,* obligar a alejarse.—*to f. back,* rechazar, hacer retroceder.—*to f. the issue,* hacer que el asunto se discuta o decida pronto, que se vaya al grano sin demora.— —**ed** [-t], *a.* forzado, forzoso; fingido.— —**ful** [fórsful], *a.* enérgico, potente, violento.—**forcible** [fórsibl], *a.* fuerte, enérgico; violento; de peso.

ford [ford], *s.* vado.—*vt.* vadear.

fore [for], *a.* anterior, delantero; proel.— —*adv.* delante, hacia delante; de proa.—*s.* delantero, frente.— —**arm** [fórarm], *s.* antebrazo.—*vt.* [forárm], armar de antemano.— —**bode** [-bóud], *vt.* y *vi.* pronosticar, presagiar; presentir.— —**boding** [-bóudiŋ], *s.* presentimiento, corazonada.— —**c.** agorero.— —**cast** [fórkæst], *vti.* y *vii.* [4] pronosticar, prever, predecir; proyectar, trazar.—*pret.* y *pp.* de TO FORECAST.— —*s.* pronóstico, predicción; proyecto, plan.— —**doom** [-dum], *s.* predestinación, sino.— —**father** [-faðœ(r)], *s.* ascendiente, antepasado.— —**finger** [-fiŋgœ(r)], *s.* dedo índice.— —**foot** [-fut], *s.* mano o pata delantera.— —**front** [-frʌnt], *s.* vanguardia, primera fila.— —**go** [-góu], *vii.* [10] privarse de, renunciar a; ceder, abandonar.— —**gone** [-gón], *a.* predeterminado; inevitable, seguro.—*pp.* de TO FOREGO.— —**ground** [-graund], *s.* primer plano.— —**head** [-id], *s.* frente; parte delantera.

foreign [fárin], *a.* extranjero; exterior; extraño; advenedizo; remoto.—*f. commerce,* comercio exterior.—*f. exchange,* cambio extranjero.—*f. to the case,* ajeno al caso.— —**er** [-œ(r)], *s.* extranjero, extraño, forastero.

forelock [fórlak], *s.* guedeja.

foreman [fórman], *s.* capataz; encargado; mayoral; presidente del jurado.

foremost [fórmoųst], *a.* delantero,
primero; principal, más notable.

forenoon [fórnun], *s.* [la] mañana.

forerunner [forránœ(r)], *s.* precursor;
presagio, pronóstico.

foresaid [fórsed], *a.* antedicho, susodicho.

foresaw [forsó], *pret. y pp.* de TO
FORESEE.—foresee [forsí], *vti.* [10]
prever.—*vii.* tener previsión.—fore-
seen [forsín], *pp.* de TO FORESEE.—
foresight [fórsajt], *s.* previsión,
perspicacia.

forest [fárist], *s.* selva, bosque, floresta.
—*f. ranger,* guardabosques.—*vt.* arbo-
lar.

forester [fáristœ(r)], *s.* silvicultor;
guardamonte; habitante del bosque.
—forestry [fáristri], *s.* silvicultura;
ingeniería forestal.

foretell [fortél], *vti. y vii.* [10] predecir,
adivinar.— —er [-œ(r)], *s.* profeta.—
foretold [fortóųld], *pret. y pp.* de
TO FORETELL.

forever [forévœ(r)], *adv.* siempre; para
o por siempre; a perpetuidad.—*f. and
a day,* o *f. and ever,* eternamente, por
siempre jamás.

forewarn [forwórn], *vt.* prevenir, advertir, avisar.

forewent [forwént], *pret.* de TO FOREGO.

foreword [fórwœrd], *s.* prefacio.

forfeit [fórfit], *s.* prenda perdida; multa;
decomiso; pérdida legal de cosa o
derecho por incumplimiento de
obligaciones.—*pl.* juego de prendas.
—*a.* confiscado, perdido por incumplimiento.—*vt.* perder algo por
incumplimiento de obligaciones.

forgave [forgéjv], *pret.* de TO FORGIVE.

forge [fordž], *s.* fragua; forja; herrería.
—*vt.* forjar, fraguar; falsificar, falsear;
inventar; tramar.—*to f. ahead,* abrirse
paso, avanzar.— —ry [fórdžœri], *s.*
falsificación.

forget [forgét], *vti. y vii.* [10] olvidar(se
de).—*f. it,* no piense más en eso; no
se preocupe, descuide Ud.—*to f. oneself,* excederse, propasarse; ser distraído; ser abnegado.— —ful [-fųl], *a.*
olvidadizo.— —fulness [-fųlnis], *s.*
olvido, descuido; calidad de olvidadizo.—*f.-me-not* [-minat], *s.* (bot.)
nomeolvides.

forgive [forgív], *vti.* [10] perdonar, dispensar, condonar.—forgiven [for-
gíven], *pp.* de TO FORGIVE.— —ness
[-nis], *s.* perdón; clemencia, misericordia.—forgiving [forgíviŋ], *a.* magnánimo, clemente, de buen corazón,
perdonador.

forgot [forgát], *pret.* de TO FORGET.—
forgotten [forgáten], *pp.* de TO
FORGET.

fork [fork], *s.* tenedor; horquilla; bifur-

cación; confluencia de un río.—*vt.*
cargar heno con la horquilla.—*vi.*
bifurcarse.

forlorn [forlórn], *a.* abandonado;
infeliz, desdichado.—*f. hope,* empresa
desesperada.

form [form], *s.* forma; figura; hechura;
hoja, modelo que ha de llenarse;
condición; estado; práctica, ritual,
formalidad; estilo; horma, matriz,
patrón; porte, modales.—*vt.* formar,
construir, labrar, modelar; idear,
concebir; constituir, integrar.—*vi.*
formarse.— —al [fórmal], *a.* formal.—
—ality [-éliti], *s.* formalidad, etiqueta, cumplimiento.— —alize
[-alajz], *vt.* formalizar.— —at [-æt], *s.*
formato.— —ation [-éjšon], *s.* formación; desarrollo; arreglo.

former [fórmœ(r)], *a.* primero; precedente, anterior; antiguo; ex-, que fue.
—*the f.,* aquél, aquélla, aquéllos, etc.—
—ly [-li], *adv.* antiguamente, antes,
en tiempos pasados.

formula [fórmyųla], *s.* fórmula, receta.—
—te [fórmyųlejt], *vt.* formular.

forsake [forséjk], *vti.* [10] abandonar,
desamparar; separarse de; renegar de;
desechar; dar de mano a.—forsaken
[forséjken], *pp.* de TO FORSAKE.—*a.*
abandonado.—forsook [forsúk], *pret.*
de TO FORSAKE.

forswear [forswér], *vti.* [10] abjurar;
renunciar o negar solemnemente.—
vii. perjurar(se).—forswore [forswór],
pret. de TO FORSWEAR.—forsworn
[forswórn], *pp.* de TO FORSWEAR.

fort [fort], *s.* fuerte, fortaleza, fortín.

forth [forθ], *adv.* delante; adelante;
fuera, afuera; a la vista, pública-
mente; hasta lo último.—*and so f.,* y
así sucesivamente; etcétera.— —coming [-kámiŋ], *a.* venidero, futuro,
próximo.—*s.* aparición, acercamiento,
proximidad.— —with [-wiδ], *adv.*
inmediatamente.

fortification [fortifikéjšon], *s.* fortificación; fortalecimiento; fortaleza.—
fortify [fórtifaj], *vti.* [7] fortificar;
fortalecer; reforzar; corroborar.—*vii.*
construir defensas.

fortitude [fórtitjud], *s.* fortaleza, fuerza,
ánimo.

fortnight [fórtnajt], *s.* quincena, dos
semanas.— —ly [-li], *a.* quincenal,
bisemanal.—*adv.* quincenalmente.—
s. revista bisemanal.

fortress [fórtris], *s.* fortaleza, plaza
fuerte.

fortunate [fórchunit], *a.* afortunado,
dichoso.—fortune [fórchun], *s.* fortuna; dicha; sino; caudal, bienes.—*f.
teller,* adivino.—*vt.* dotar con una
fortuna.

forum [fóram], *s.* plaza; foro; tribunal; reunión para debatir un asunto.

forward [fórwərd], *adv.* adelante, en adelante, hacia adelante, más allá.— *a.* delantero; adelantado; precoz; anterior; activo; desenvuelto; emprendedor; radical.—*s.* delantero.—*vt.* reenviar; trasmitir, remitir; activar; fomentar.

foster [fástœ(r)], *vt.* criar, nutrir; dar alas, alentar.—*a.* putativo, adoptivo.

fought [fot], *pret.* y *pp.* de TO FIGHT.

foul [faul], *a.* sucio, impuro; fétido; viciado (aire); detestable, vil; injusto, sin derecho; contrario, desagradable; obsceno; lleno de errores y correcciones.—*f.-dealing*, dolo, mala fe.—*f. language*, lenguaje soez.—*f.-mouthed*, mal hablado.—*f. play*, juego sucio o desleal.—*f. weather*, mal tiempo.—*s.* acción de ensuciar; violación de las reglas establecidas.—*vt.* ensuciar; trabar; violar las reglas.—*vi.* ensuciarse; trabarse; chocar.

found [faund], *pret.* y *pp.* de TO FIND.— *vt.* cimentar, fundamentar; fundar, instituir; apoyar en; fundir, derretir.— —**ation** [-éişən], *s.* fundación, establecimiento; fundamento, base; dotación; cimiento.—*f. stone*, primera piedra.— —**er** [fáundœ(r)], *s.* fundador; fundidor.—*vt.* (mar.) hacer zozobrar.—*vi.* irse a pique, zozobrar; fracasar.— —**ry** [-ri], *s.* fundición (fábrica).

fountain [fáuntin], *s.* fuente; manantial; fontanar; pila.—*f. pen*, pluma estilográfica.— —**head** [-hed], *s.* fuente, origen.

fowl [faul], *s.* gallo, gallina; pollo; aves en general.—*pl.* aves de corral.

fox [faks], *s.* zorra, raposa; zorro, taimado.— —**hole** [fákshoul], *s.* trinchera individual.— —**y** [-i], *a.* taimado, astuto.

foyer [fóiœ(r)], *s.* recibidor; salón de descanso.

fraction [frékşən], *s.* fracción, quebrado; fragmento.—*vt.* fraccionar.— —**al** [-əl], *a.* fraccionario; fraccionado.

fracture [frékchə(r)], *s.* fractura, rotura, ruptura, quiebra.—*vt.* y *vi.* fracturar(se), quebrar(se).

fragile [frédʒil], *a.* frágil.— —**ness** [-nis], **fragility** [frədʒíliti], *s.* fragilidad.

fragment [frégmənt], *s.* fragmento; trozo.— —**ary** [-ɛri], *a.* fragmentario.

fragrance [fréigrəns], *s.* fragancia.— **fragrant** [fréigrənt], *a.* fragante.

frail [freil], *a.* frágil; endeble.—*s.* canasta, espuerta.— —**ty** [fréilti], *s.* fragilidad; debilidad.

frame [freim], *vt.* enmarcar, encuadrar; formar, construir; armar; forjar, idear; arreglar clandestinamente (el resultado de un juego, etc.); acusar o hacer condenar con falsas pruebas. —*s.* marco; armazón; estructura; figura; armadura, esqueleto; bastidor. —*f. of mind*, estado de ánimo.— —**up** [fréimʌp], *s.* conspiración, fraude.

franc [trænk], *s.* franco (moneda).

franchise [frénchaiz], *s.* derecho político; franquicia, privilegio; concesión; exención.

frank [frænk], *a.* franco, sincero; francote, campechano.—*s.* franquicia postal.—*vt.* franquear (una carta).

frankfurter [frénkfœrtœ(r)], *s.* salchicha alemana.

frankness [frénknis], *s.* franqueza.

frantic [fréntik], *a.* frenético, furioso.

fraternal [frətœrnəl], *a.* fraternal, fraterno.—**fraternity** [frətœrniti], *s.* (con)fraternidad; hermandad; gremio estudiantil.—**fraternize** [frétœrnaiz], *vi.* y *vt.* (con)fraternizar, hermanar(se).

fraud [frod], *s.* fraude; farsante, trampista.— —**ulent** [fródʒulent], *a.* fraudulento.

fray [frei], *s.* riña, refriega; raedura, desgaste.—*vt.* ludir, raer.—*vi.* deshilacharse.

freak [frik], *s.* capricho, antojo; rareza; monstruo, fenómeno.—*f. of nature*, aborto de la naturaleza.—*a.* raro; anormal.— —**ish** [fríkiş], *a.* caprichoso, antojadizo; raro.

freckle [frékl], *s.* peca.—*f.-faced*, pecoso. —*vt.* motear.—*vi.* ponerse pecoso.— —**d** [-d], *a.* pecoso; moteado.

free [fri], *a.* libre; franco; vacante; exento; gratuito; desocupado; liberal; generoso.—*f. of charge*, gratis.—*f. on board*, franco a bordo, libre a bordo.— *vt.* librar, libertar; eximir; desembarazar.—*adv.* libremente, gratis.— —**dom** [frídəm], *s.* libertad; exención, inmunidad; libre uso.

Freemason [frímeişən], *s.* masón.

freeze [friz], *vti.* [10] congelar, helar.— *vii.* helarse; helar, escarchar.—*s.* helada.— —**r** [frízœ(r)], *s.* congelador, refrigerador; heladora, sorbetera.— **freezing** [frízi̦ŋ], *a.* congelante, frigorífico; glacial.—*s.* helamiento, congelación.

freight [freit], *vt.* fletar; cargar.—*s.* carga, cargazón; flete.—*by f.*, como carga.—*f. car o train*, carro, tren de mercancías.—*f. elevator*, montacargas.— —**er** [fréitœ(r)], *s.* buque de carga.

French [french], *a.* y *s.* francés.—*s.* idioma francés.— —**man** [frénchmən], *s.* francés.— —**woman** [-wumən], *s.* francesa.

frenzy [frénzi], *s.* frenesí.

frequency [fríkwənsi], *s.* frecuencia.—*f.*

modulation, frecuencia modulada, modulación de frecuencia.—**frequent** [fríkwęnt], *a.* frecuente.—*vt.* [frikwént], frecuentar; concurrir a.

fresh [freš], *a.* fresco; reciente; nuevo; refrescante; desahogado, entremetido.—*f. air*, aire puro; aire libre.—*f. from*, acabado de llegar, sacar, etc.—*f. hand*, novicio.—*f. water*, agua dulce.—**—en** [fréšęn], *vt.* refrescar, refrigerar.—*vi.* refrescarse, avivarse.— **—ly** [-lǐ], *adv.* frescamente, con frescura; nuevamente, recientemente.— **—man** [-mǎn], *s.* estudiante de primer año; novato, novicio.— **—ness** [-nǐs], *s.* frescura, frescor; lozanía, verdor; descaro.

fret [fret], *vti.* [1] rozar, raer; desgastar; enojar, irritar; adornar con calados.—*vii.* apurarse, inquietarse; incomodarse, impacientarse; agitarse.—*s.* roce; raedura; desgaste; irritación, enojo; hervor; relieve, realce; traste de guitarra.—*f. saw*, segueta, sierra caladora.— **—ful** [frétfŭl], *a.* displicente, irritable, enojadizo; inquieto; incómodo, molesto.

friar [frájǎ(r)], *s.* fraile.

fricassee [frĭkǎsí], *s.* fricasé.—*vt.* hacer fricasé.

friction [frĭkšǫn], *s.* fricción; frotación; roce; desavenencia.—*f. tape*, (elec.) cinta aisladora adherente.

Friday [frájdǐ], *s.* viernes.

friend [frend], *s.* amigo, amiga.— **—less** [fréndlǐs], *a.* desamparado, desvalido, sin amigos.— **—liness** [-lǐnǐs], *s.* amistad.— **—ly** [-lǐ], *a.* amistoso, amigable, cordial.—*adv.* amistosamente.— **—ship** [-šǐp], *s.* amistad.

fright [frajt], *s.* susto, espanto, pavor; espantajo.— **—en** [frájtęn], *vt.* espantar, asustar, amilanar.—*to f. away*, ahuyentar.— **—ful** [-fŭl], *a.* espantoso, terrible.— **—fulness** [-fŭlnǐs], *s.* espanto, terror.

frigid [frĭdžǐd], *a.* frío, frígido; indiferente.— **—ity** [frĭdžǐdǐtǐ], *s.* frialdad, frigidez; indiferencia.

fringe [frĭndž], *s.* fleco, pestaña; orla, borde.—*vt.* guarnecer con flecos; orlar.

frisk [frĭsk], *vi.* saltar, brincar, retozar.—*vt.* registrar los bolsillos, cachear.—*s.* retozo; brinco, salto.— **—y** [frĭskǐ], *a.* retozón, vivaracho.

fritter [frĭtœ(r)], *s.* fritura, fruta de sartén.—*to f. away*, desperdiciar o malgastar a poquitos.

frivolity [frĭválǐtǐ], *s.* frivolidad.— **—ous** [frĭvǫlǎs], *a.* frívolo.

fro [frou], *adv.* atrás, hacia atrás.—*to and f.*, de una parte a otra, de acá y allá.

frock [frak], *s.* vestido (de mujer).—*f. coat*, levita.

frog [frag], *s.* rana; alamar.—*f. in the throat*, carraspera.

frolic [frálǐk], *s.* juego, retozo, travesura.—*a.* alegre, juguetón, travieso.—*vii.* [8] juguetear, retozar, triscar.—**frolicked** [frálǐkt], *pret.* y *pp.* de TO FROLIC. **—some** [-sʌm], *a.* retozón, travieso.

from [fram], *prep.* de; desde; de parte de; a fuerza de; a partir de; a causa de.—*f. memory*, de memoria.—*f. now on*, de ahora en adelante, en lo sucesivo.—*f. nature*, del natural.

frond [frand], *s.* fronda.— **—age** [-ǐdž], *s.* frondosidad, follaje, frondas.

front [frʌnt], *s.* frente (m.); frontispicio, fachada, portada.—*in f.*, delante, enfrente.—*in f. of*, delante de, ante.—*shirt f.*, pechera.—*a.* anterior, delantero; frontero; frontal.—*f. door*, puerta principal.—*f. row*, delantera, primera fila.—*vt.* hacer frente a.—*to f. towards*, mirar hacia; dar o caer a.—*vi.* estar al frente de.

frontier [frʌntír], *s.* frontera.—*a.* fronterizo.

frost [frost], *s.* escarcha; helada.—*f. -bitten*, helado.—*vt.* cubrir de escarcha.—*vi.* escarchar, helar, congelarse.— **—y** [fróstǐ], *a.* escarchado; helado.

froth [froθ], *s.* espuma; bambolla.—*vi.* espumar, hacer espuma; echar espuma.— **—y** [fróθǐ], *a.* espumoso; frívolo, vano.

frown [fraun], *s.* ceño, entrecejo.—*vi.* fruncir el entrecejo.—*to f. at, on*, o *upon*, desaprobar, mirar con ceño.— **—ing** [fráunǐŋ], *a.* ceñudo.

froze [frouz], *pret.* de TO FREEZE.

frozen [fróuzęn], *pp.* de TO FREEZE.

fructification [frʌktǐfǐkéišǫn], *s.* fructificación; fruto.

frugal [frúgǎl], *a.* frugal.— **—ity** [frugǽlǐtǐ], *s.* frugalidad.

fruit [frut], *s.* fruta; fruto; provecho; resultado.—*f. tree*, árbol frutal.—*ful* [frútfŭl], *a.* fructífero, feraz; productivo; prolífico, fecundo; fructuoso, provechoso.— **—ion** [frušǫn], *s.* fruición.— **—less** [-lǐs], *a.* infructuoso, estéril, vano.

frustrate [frʌstrejt], *vt.* frustrar.— **frustration** [frʌstréišǫn], *s.* frustración.

fry [fraj], *s.* fritada; brete, sofocón; cría, pececillos recién nacidos; enjambre, muchedumbre.—*small f.*, chiquellería, gente menuda.—*vt.* y *vii.* [7] freír(se), achicharrar(se).—*frying pan*, sartén.

fudge [fʌdž], *s.* jarabe o dulce de chocolate; embuste, cuento.

fuel [fjúęl], *s.* combustible; pábulo,

aliciente.—*vt.* y *vi.* abastecer(se) de combustible.

fugitive [fiúdžitiv], *a.* y *s.* fugitivo.

fulfill [fulfíl], *vt.* colmar, llenar; realizar. - —ment [-ment], *s.* cumplimiento, desempeño, ejecución, realización; colmo.

full [ful], *a.* lleno; completo, cabal, repleto; pleno; cumplido; amplio; rotundo; harto, ahito; maduro, perfecto.—*f. age*, mayoría de edad.—*f.-blooded*, de sangre pura, pura raza.—*f.-length*, de cuerpo entero.—*f. name*, nombre y apellido.—*f. scope*, carta blanca, rienda suelta.—*f. speed*, a toda velocidad.—*f. stop*, punto final; detención total de un vehículo.—*f. time*, tiempo o período completo, horas normales de trabajo.—*adv.* enteramente, del todo; de lleno; totalmente, en pleno; derechamente. —*f.-blown*, abierta del todo (una flor).—*f.-grown*, maduro, crecido; completamente desarrollado.- —ness [fúlnis], *s.* plenitud, abundancia; hartura, saciedad; complemento.

fume [fjum], *s.* tufo, gas, emanación; vapores, gases, emanaciones deletéreas.—*vt.* fumigar, sahumar, exhalar. —*vi.* exhalar vapores; encolerizarse.

fumigate [fjúmigeit], *vt.* fumigar, sahumar.—**fumigation** [fjumigéiṣon], *s.* fumigación; sahumerio.

fun [fʌn], *s.* broma, chanza, burla; diversión.

function [fʌ́ŋkṣon], *s.* función, ejercicio, ocupación; ceremonia, acto; potencia, facultad.—*vi.* funcionar.- —al [-al], *a.* funcional.- —ary [-eri], *s.* funcionario.

fund [fʌnd], *s.* fondo (dinero).—*pl.* fondos.—*vt.* consolidar (una deuda).

fundament [fʌ́ndament], *s.* fundamento.- —al [fʌndaméntal], *a.* fundamental.—*s.* fundamento.

funeral [fjúneral], *a.* funeral, funerario, fúnebre.—*f. home* o *parlor*, funeraria. —*f. procession*, cortejo fúnebre.—*s.* funeral(es), exequias; entierro; duelo. —**funereal** [fjunírial], *a.* fúnebre.

fungus [fʌ́ŋgʌs], *s.* (*pl.* fungi [fʌ́ndžai]) hongo.

funnel [fʌ́nel], *s.* embudo; cañón de chimenea.—*vti.* y *vii.* [2] encauzar(se); concentrar(se).

funny [fʌ́ni], *a.* cómico, divertido, gracioso, ocurrente, chusco; (fam.) extraño, curioso.—*f. business*, treta; picardía, fraude.

fur [fœr], *s.* piel, pelo (de los animales); sarro.—*vti.* [1] cubrir, forrar o adornar con pieles.—*vii.* formarse incrustaciones.

furious [fjúriʌs], *a.* furioso, enfurecido.

furl [fœrl], *vt.* plegar, recoger.

furlough [fœrlou], *s.* (mil.) licencia.—*vt.* licenciar.

furnace [fœrnis], *s.* horno (industrial).—*blast f.*, alto horno.

furnish [fœrniṣ], *vt.* surtir, suministrar; aparejar, equipar; amueblar.

furniture [fœrnichur], *s.* mobiliario; muebles; ajuar; adornos, accesorios; avíos.

furrow [fœrou], *s.* surco; zanja; arruga; muesca; mediacaña.—*vt.* surcar; estriar; arar.

further [fœrðœ(r)], *a.* ulterior, más distante; más amplio; nuevo, adicional.—*adv.* más; más lejos, más allá; además; además de eso.—*vt.* fomentar, adelantar, promover.- —ance [-ans], *s.* adelantamiento, promoción.- —more [-mór], *adv.* además; otrosí.—**furthest** [fœrðist], *a.* y *adv.* (el) más lejano, (el) más remoto; (lo) más lejos.

furtive [fœrtiv], *a.* furtivo, secreto.

fury [fjúri], *s.* furia; frenesí.

fuse [fjuz], *vt.* y *vi.* fundir(se).—*s.* espoleta; mecha; fusible.

fuselage [fjúzelidž], *s.* fuselaje.

fusion [fjúžon], *s.* fusión, fundición; unión.

fuss [fʌs], *s.* bulla, bullicio; melindre; agitación o actividad inútil.—*f. budget*, persona exigente o fastidiosa. —*vi.* inquietarse por pequeñeces; hacer melindres.- —y [fʌ́si], *a.* inquieto; remilgado, exigente.

futile [fjútil], *a.* fútil.—**futility** [fjutíliti], *s.* futilidad.

future [fjúchu(r)], *a.* futuro.—*s.* futuro, porvenir.—*in f.*, en lo sucesivo; de aquí en adelante.—*in the near f.*, en fecha próxima.

fuzz [fʌz], *vi.* soltar pelusa o borra.—*s.* pelusa, borra, vello.- —y [fʌ́zi], *a.* velloso, cubierto de pelusa; crespo.

G

gabardine [gæbərdín], *s.* gabardina (tejido y sobretodo).

gabble [gæbl], *vt.* y *vi.* charlar; graznar (los gansos).—*s.* algarabía; charla; graznido.

gable [géibl], *s.* (arq.) aguilón, remate triangular de edificio o pared; pared lateral.—*g. end*, alero.—*g. roof*, tejado de dos aguas.

gad [gæd], *vii.* [1] callejear.- —about [gǽdabaut], *a.* callejero.—*vi.* corretear, callejear.—*s.* placero, persona callejera. —fly [-flai], *s.* tábano.

gadget [gǽdžit], *s.* (fam.) dispositivo, artefacto, artificio.

gaff [gæf], *s.* arpón o garfio; (mar.) botavara.

gag [gæg], *vti.* [1] amordazar; hacer

callar; provocar náuseas; (teat.) meter morcilla.—*vii.* arquear, dar náuseas.—*s.* mordaza; asco; (teat.) morcilla; (fam.) chuscada; payasada; chiste.

gage, *s.* **y** *vt.* = GAUGE.—**gager,** *s.* = GAUGER.

gaiety [géiẹti], *s.* jovialidad, alegría, alborozo; viveza.—**gaily** [géili], *adv.* alegremente, jovialmente.

gain [gein], *s.* ganancia, beneficio, provecho.—*vt.* ganar, adquirir; lograr, conseguir.—*vi.* ganar.—*to g. weight,* echar carnes, engordar.— —**ful** [géinfụl], *a.* lucrativo, ventajoso.— —**ings** [-iŋz], *s. pl.* ganancias.

gait [geit], *s.* marcha, paso, andadura. —*at a good g.,* a buen paso.

gale [geil], *s.* ventarrón, viento fuerte; (fig.) algazara.

Galician [galíṣạn], *s.* y *a.* gallego.

gall [gọl], *s.* hiel, bilis; amargura; odio, rencor; (fam.) descaro.—*g. bladder,* vesícula biliar.—*vt.* y *vi.* irritar, hostigar.

gallant [gǽlạnt], *a.* galante, cortés; galanteador; gallardo, bizarro; valeroso, valiente.—*s.* galán.— —**ry** [-ri], *s.* valentía, gallardía, valor; galantería.

gallery [gǽlẹri], *s.* galería; tribuna; pasadizo; (teat.) paraíso, cazuela, gallinero; público que ocupa el paraíso.

galley [gǽli], *s.* (mar.) galera; (mar.) cocina; (imp.) galera.—*g. slave,* galeote.

gallon [gǽlọn], *s.* galón. Ver Tabla.

gallop [gǽlọp], *s.* galope.—*vi.* galopar. —*vt.* hacer galopar.

gallows [gǽlouz], *s.* horca; patíbulo.

galore [galór], *adv.* en abundancia.

galosh [galáś], *s.* galocha, choclo, chanclo, zueco.

galvanize [gǽlvạnaiz], *vt.* galvanizar.

gamble [gǽmbl], *vt.* jugar, aventurar o perder una cosa en el juego.—*vi.* jugar por dinero.—*s.* (fam.) jugada.- —**r** [gǽmblœ(r)], *s.* jugador, tahur. —**gambling** [gǽmbliŋ], *s.* juego (por dinero).—*g. house,* garito, casa de juego.

gambol [gǽmbọl], *vi.* brincar, saltar; cabriolar; juguetear.—*s.* cabriola, brinco, travesura.

game [geim], *s.* juego; pasatiempo; partido o partida de juego; caza (piezas, vivas o muertas).—*g. warden,* guardabosque.—*to make g. of,* burlarse de, mofarse de.—*vt.* y *vi.* jugar; jugar fuerte.—*a.* relativo a la caza o al juego; dispuesto a pelear; valeroso.—*to die g.,* morir peleando.- —**cock** [géimkak], *s.* gallo de pelea.-

—**keeper** [-kipœ(r)], *s.* guardamonte, guardabosque.

gander [gǽndœ(r)], *s.* ánsar, ganso.

gang [gæŋ], *s.* cuadrilla, pandilla; juego (de herramientas, etc.); grupo.—*vt.* y *vi.* formar cuadrilla.

gangplank [gǽŋplæŋk], *s.* pasarela, pasamano, plancha.

gangrene [gǽŋgrin], *vt.* y *vi.* gangrenar(se).—*s.* gangrena.

gangster [gǽŋstœ(r)], *s.* pandillero, pistolero.

gangway [gǽŋwei], *s.* (mar.) pasamano, portalón, tilla.

gap [gæp], *s.* portillo, abertura, brecha; vacío, laguna; barranca, hondonada. —*vti.* [1] hacer una brecha en.

gape [geip], *vi.* quedarse boquiabierto; embobarse; bostezar.—*s.* bostezo; boqueada; brecha, abertura.

garage [garáź], *s.* garaje; taller mecánico o de reparaciones.

garb [garb], *s.* vestido, vestidura; apariencia exterior, aspecto.—*vt.* vestir, ataviar.

garbage [gárbịdź], *s.* basura, desperdicios.

garden [gárdn], *s.* jardín; huerta, huerto.—*g. of Eden,* paraíso terrenal. —*g. stuff,* hortalizas, legumbres, verduras.—*vt.* y *vi.* cultivar jardines o huertos.— —**er** [-œ(r)], *s.* jardinero; hortelano.— —**ing** [-iŋ], *s.* jardinería; horticultura.

gargle [gárgl], *vt.* y *vi.* gargarizar, hacer gárgaras.—*s.* gárgara, gargarismo.

garland [gárlạnd], *s.* guirnalda.

garlic [gárlịk], *s.* ajo.

garment [gármẹnt], *s.* prenda de vestir; vestido.—*pl.* ropa, vestimenta.

garnish [gárnịś], *vt.* (coc.) aderezar; guarnecer, ataviar; (for.) prevenir, notificar; aprestar.—*s.* (coc.) aderezo; guarnición, adorno.

garnet [gárnịt], *s.* granate.

garret [gǽrịt], *s.* buhardilla, desván.

garrison [gǽriṣọn], *s.* (mil.) guarnición. —*vt.* (mil.) guarnecer; guarnicionar.

garrote [garóut], *s.* garrote.—*vt.* agarrotar, dar garrote a; estrangular para robar.

garter [gártœ(r)], *s.* liga (para las medias).

gas [gæs], *s.* gas; gasolina.—*g. burner,* mechero de gas.—*g. meter,* contador de gas.—*g. range,* o *g. stove,* fogón o cocina de gas.—*g. station,* estación o puesto de gasolina.—*tear g.,* gas lacrimógeno.—*vt.* [1] (mil.) asfixiar, envenenar o atacar con gas. —**eous** [gǽsịʌs], *a.* gaseoso; aeriforme.

gash [gæś], *vt.* dar una cuchillada.—*s.* cuchillada; incisión grande.

gasket [gǽskịt], *s.* (mec.) relleno, empaquetadura.

gaslight [gǽslait], *s.* luz de gas; mechero de gas.—**gasoline** [gǽsolin], *s.* gasolina.

gasp [gæsp], *vt.* jadear, boquear; emitir sonidos entrecortados.—*s.* boqueada, jadeo.

gate [geit], *s.* portón; entrada; puerta; (f.c.) barrera; cancela; compuertas de esclusa; garganta, paso.— —**keeper** [géjtkipœ(r)], *s.* portero; (f.c.) guardabarrera.— —**way** [-wei], *s.* entrada, paso (con portillo).

gather [gǽðœ(r)], *vt.* reunir, recoger; coger; acumular; recolectar; juntar, congregar; (cost.) fruncir; colegir, deducir.—*to g. breath*, tomar aliento. —*vi.* unirse, reunirse, juntarse, congregarse; amontonarse, acumularse; concentrarse.—*s.* (cost.) pliegue, frunce.— —**ing** [-iŋ], *s.* asamblea; reunión; agrupación; (re)colección, acopio; fruncimiento; (cost.) fruncido.

Gaucho [gáuchou], *s.* gaucho.

gaudy [gódi], *a.* vistoso; llamativo, chillón.

gauge [geidž], *s.* medida; calibre; calibrador; indicador; (mar.) calado; (m.v.) manómetro; (f.c.) ancho de vía; aforo, arqueo.—*g. pressure*, presión manométrica.—*vt.* calibrar; medir; estimar, apreciar.

gaunt [gɔnt], *a.* flaco, delgado, demacrado.

gauntlet [góntlit], *s.* manopla; guantelete.

gauze [gɔz], *s.* gasa, cendal.

gave [geiv], *pret.* de TO GIVE.

gavel [gǽvęl], *s.* mazo; (agr.) haz, gavilla.

gawk [gɔk], *vi.* (fam.) bobear, cometer torpezas.—*s.* bobo, torpe.— —**y** [góki], *s.* papanatas.—*a.* bobo, tonto, torpe, desgarbado.

gay [gei], *a.* alegre, festivo, ufano, llamativo; ligero de cascos, calavera. —**gayety,** *s.* ═ GAIETY.

gaze [geiz], *vi.* mirar con fijeza, clavar la mirada.—*s.* contemplación, mirada fija o penetrante.

gazette [gązét], *s.* gaceta.

gazelle [gązél], *s.* gacela.

gear [gir], *s.* engranaje; mecanismo de tra(n)smisión, de distribución o de gobierno; juego; rueda dentada; (mar.) aparejo; equipo, pertrechos, aperos; atavíos.—*g. box* o *case*, caja de engranajes; (aut.) caja de velocidades.—*g. shifting*, cambio de velocidad o de marcha.—*g. wheel*, rueda dentada.—*in g.*, engranado. —*landing g.*, tren de aterrizaje.—*out of g.*, desengranado.—*to put in g.*, relacionar; engranar, embragar.—*to throw out of g.*, desengranar, des-

embragar.—*vt.* aparejar; equipar; montar, armar; engranar, embragar. —*vi.* engranar.

geese [gis], *s. pl.* de GOOSE.

gelatin(e) [džélątin], *s.* gelatina.

gem [džem], *s.* gema; alhaja.—*vti.* [1] adornar con piedras preciosas.

gendarme [žándarm], *s.* gendarme, polizonte armado.

gender [džéndœ(r)], *s.* (gram.) género.

general [džénęrąl], *a.* general, frecuente. —*g. delivery*, lista de correos.—*s.* (mil.) general.—*in g.*, en general, por regla general.— —**ity** [dženęréliti], *s.* generalidad.— —**ize** [džénęrąlaiz], *vt.* generalizar.

generate [džénęreit], *vt.* engendrar; producir, causar.—**generation** [dženęréišǫn], *s.* generación; reproducción. —**generator** [džénęreitǫ(r)], *s.* generador, dínamo.

generosity [dženęrásiti], *s.* generosidad, larguеza.—**generous** [džénęrąs], *a.* generoso; noble, magnánimo; amplio.

genial [džínią l], *a.* genial, afable, alegre.— —**ity** [dž iniǽliti], *s.* afabilidad.

genital [džénitą l], *a.* genital.—*pl.* genitales, partes pudendas.

genius [džínyʌs], *s.* genio; prototipo.

genteel [dzentil], *a.* cortés, gentil; gallardo, airoso, elegante; cursi.

gentile [džéntail], *s.* y *a.* gentil, pagano.

gentle [džéntl], *a.* suave, dulce, benévolo; dócil, manso; bien nacido.— —**man** [-mąn], *s.* caballero; señor.— —**manliness** [-mąnlinis], *s.* caballerosidad, hidalguía.— —**manly** [-mąnli], *a.* caballeroso.— —**men** [-męn], *s. pl.* de GENTLEMAN; señores; (en cartas) muy señores míos (nuestros).—*g.'s agreement*, pacto de caballeros.— —**ness** [-nis], *s.* dulzura, suavidad; docilidad, mansedumbre; urbanidad. —**gently** [džéntli], *adv.* dulcemente, suavemente; poco a poco, despacio.

genuine [džényuin], *a.* genuino, auténtico; sincero.

geographer [dži ágrạfœ(r)], *s.* geógrafo. —**geographic(al)** [džiográfik(ąl)], *a.* geográfico.—**geography** [dži ágrạfi], *s.* geografía.—**geologist** [dži álodžist], *s.* geólogo.—**geology** [dži álodži], *s.* geología.—**geometric(al)** [dži ométrik(ą l)], *a.* geométrico.—**geometry** [džiámetri], *s.* geometría.

geranium [džęréiniʌm], *s.* geranio.

German [džœ́rmąn], *s.* y *a.* alemán.—*s.* lengua alemana.—*G. measles*, roséola.

germ [džœrm], *s.* germen; microbio.— —**icide** [džœ́rmisaid], *s.* germicida.

germinate [džœ́rmineit], *vi.* germinar. —**germination** [džœrminéišǫn], *s.* germinación.

gerund [džérʌnd], *s.* (gram.) gerundio.

gestation [dȝestéiʃọn], *s.* gestación.

gesture [dȝéschụ(r)], *s.* gesto, ademán, signo.—*vi.* accionar; gesticular o hacer gestos.

get [get], *vti.* [10] conseguir, obtener, adquirir; agarrar, atrapar; ganar; llevar (premio, ventaja, etc.); recibir; procrear; hacer que; incitar; procurar, lograr; ir por, traer; entender.—*to g. back*, recobrar.—*to g. down*, descolgar, bajar; tragar.—*to g. on*, ponerse (ropa).—*to g. out*, publicar, editar, sacar.—*to g. the worse* o *the worst*, llevar la peor parte, quedar mal parado.—*to g. wind of*, recibir aviso de, tener noticia de.—*vii.* ganar dinero; llegar; ponerse o volverse; hacerse, ser; hallarse, estar; introducirse, meterse.—*g. out!* ¡fuera! ¡largo de aquí!—*g. up!* ¡arre!—*to g. along*, ir pasando.—*to g. along well (badly) with*, llevarse bien (mal) con.—*to g. married*, casarse.—*to g. off*, salir de un asunto; escapar; salir; bajar(se), apearse.—*to g. on*, adelantar; ponerse encima de; subir; montar; entrar en un coche.—*to g. out*, salir, salirse.—*to g. out of order*, desajustarse, descomponerse.—*to g. out of the way*, apartarse o hacerse a un lado.—*to g. ready*, disponerse, aprestarse.—*to g. rid of*, zafarse o librarse de, acabar con, quitar de encima.—*to g. through*, pasar, penetrar; terminar.—*to g. together*, juntarse, reunirse; cooperar.—*to g. up*, levantarse; subir.—*to g. well*, curar, sanar, ponerse bueno.— **—away** [gétawei], *s.* ida, partida; escape; arranque (de un auto).—**—ter** [-œ(r)], *s.* persona que consigue o logra.— **-up** [-ʌp], *s.* arreglo, disposición; atavío; traje.

ghastly [gáestli], *a.* lívido, cadavérico; horrible, espantoso.—*adv.* horriblemente; mortalmente.

ghost [goụst], *s.* fantasma, espectro, sombra; espíritu.—*the Holy G.*, el Espíritu Santo.—*not a g. of a doubt*, ni sombra de duda.—*to give up the g.*, entregar el espíritu, morir(se).- **—ly** [góụstli], *a.* espectral, fantástico, de duendes o aparecidos.

giant [dȝáiạnt], *a.* gigantesco, gigante. —*s.* gigante.

giblets [dȝíblịts], *s. pl.* menudillos.

giddiness [gídịnịs], *s.* vértigo, vahído; desvarío.—**giddy** [gídị], *a.* vertiginoso; voluble, inconstante; atolondrado.

gift [gift], *s.* regalo, dádiva; donación; don, dote, talento.- **—ed** [gíftịd], *a.* talentoso, genial; agraciado.

gigantic [dȝạigǽntịk], *a.* gigantesco.

giggle [gígl], *vi.* reírse sin motivo;

reírse por nada.—*s.* risa nerviosa, risita.

gild [gild], *vti.* [4] dorar.

gill [gil], *s.* agalla, branquia.

gilt [gilt], *pret. y pp.* de TO GILD.—*a.* dorado, áureo.—*s.* dorado; oropel; falso brillo.

gin [dȝin], *s.* ginebra (licor de enebro).

ginger [dȝíndȝœ(r)], *s.* jengibre.—*g. ale*, cerveza de jengibre.- **—bread** [-bred], *s.* pan de jengibre.—*a.* recargado, de mal gusto.

gipsy [dȝípsị], *s.* = GYPSY.

giraffe [dȝịrǽf], *s.* jirafa.

gird [gœrd], *vti.* [4] ceñir; rodear.- **—le** [gœrdl], *s.* faja; ceñidor; cinto.—*vt.* ceñir, cercar, fajar, circundar.

girl [gœrl], *s.* muchacha, niña; (fam.) sirvienta, criada.- **—hood** [gœrlhụd], *s.* doncellez; vida o edad de muchacha; la juventud femenina.- **—ish** [-ịʃ], *a.* juvenil; propio de niña o joven.

girt [gœrt], *pret. y pp.* de TO GIRD.—*a.* (mar.) amarrado.

girth [gœrθ], *s.* cincha; faja, cinto; gordura; circunferencia, periferia. —*vt.* cinchar, ceñir.

gist [dȝist], *s.* substancia, quid.

give [giv], *vti.* [10] dar, donar; conceder, otorgar.—*to g. advice*, dar consejo; asesorar.—*to g. a lift to one*, ayudar a uno a levantarse o a levantar algo; llevarle (en coche, etc.).—*to g. a piece of one's mind to*, decir las verdades del barquero, decir cuántas son cinco.—*to g. away*, regalar; deshacerse de; vender regalado; divulgar un secreto.—*to g. back*, restituir, devolver.—*to g. birth*, dar a luz, parir; producir.—*to g. chase*, perseguir.—*to g. ear to*, prestar oídos a.—*to g. forth*, publicar, divulgar. —*to g. oneself away*, (fam.) enseñar la oreja.—*to g. oneself up*, rendirse; abandonarse, desesperarse.—*to g. out*, publicar, divulgar; proclamar.—*to g. over*, abandonar; desistir de; desahuciar.—*to g. pause*, dar en qué pensar; hacer pensar.—*to g. place*, dejar el puesto (a).—*to g. rise to*, dar lugar a, ocasionar.—*to g. the slip*, dar esquinazo; echar.—*to g. up*, renunciar a; entregar; resignar.—*to g. up the ghost*, morir, darse por vencido. —*to g. voice to*, decir, expresar.—*to g. warning*, prevenir, advertir.—*to g. way*, ceder, retroceder; ceder su puesto.—*vi.* dar libremente, ser dadivoso; dar de sí, aflojarse; ceder. —*to g. in*, ceder, acceder; asentir. —*to g. up*, desistir, cejar; darse por vencido; perder la esperanza.—*s.* acción de dar de sí o ceder físicamente (como una cuerda); elasticidad.

—**g.-and-take** [gívₐnteik], **s.** concesiones mutuas, componenda.—**given** [gívₑn], **pp.** de TO GIVE.—**a.** dado; citado, especificado; (mat.) conocido.—**g. name,** nombre bautismal.—**g. that,** suponiendo que, sabiendo que.—**g. to,** adicto o aficionado a.—**giver** [gívœ(r)], **s.** donante, donador.

gizzard [gízₐrd], **s.** molleja (de ave).

glacial [gléisial], **a.** glacial; (geol.) glaciario.—**glacier** [gléiʂœ(r)], **s.** glaciar, ventisquero.

glad [glæd], **a.** alegre, contento, gozoso. —**to be g.,** alegrarse, tener gusto.— —**den** [glǽdn], **vt.** alegrar, regocijar, recrear.

glade [gleid], **s.** claro, raso o pradera (en un bosque).

gladiolus [glædióulʌs], **s.** (bot.) gladiolo, espadaña.

gladness [glǽdnis], **s.** alegría, placer, gozo.

glamor [glǽmₒ(r)], **s.** encanto, hechizo, embrujo; embeleso.—**vt.** encantar, hechizar.— —**ous** [-ʌs], **a.** encantador, hechicero.

glance [glæns], **s.** mirada, ojeada, vistazo; vislumbre; fulgor.—**at first g.,** a primera vista.—**vt.** mirar de o al soslayo, o de refilón.—**vi.** dar un vistazo o una ojeada; centellear; tocar o herir oblicuamente.

gland [glænd], **s.** glándula.

glare [gler], **vi.** relumbrar, brillar; tener colores chillones; (con **at**) mirar echando fuego por los ojos.—**s.** resplandor; resol; mirada feroz y penetrante.—**a.** liso, lustroso y resbaladizo.—**glaring** [glériŋ], **a.** deslumbrador; evidente, notorio; penetrante, furioso.

glass [glæs], **s.** vidrio; cristal; vaso; copa; espejo; lente, catalejo.—**pl.** anteojos, gafas, espejuelos, lentes. —**g. blower,** soplador de vidrio.—**g. cutter,** diamante de vidriero.—**a.** de vidrio.—**g. window,** vidriera, escaparate.— —**ful** [glǽsful], **s.** vaso (su contenido).— —**ware** [-wer], **s.** vajilla de cristal, cristalería—**wort** [-wœrt], **s.** (bot.) sosa, matojo.— —**y** [-i], **a.** vítreo, vidrioso.—**glaze** [gleiz], **vt.** poner vidrios a una ventana; vidriar; glasear; (cerá.) esmaltar.—**s.** superficie lisa y lustrosa; lustre; capa de hielo. —**glazier** [gléiʂœ(r)], **s.** vidriero.

gleam [glim], **s.** destello, fulgor, viso, centelleo.—**vi.** centellear, fulgurar, destellar.

glean [glin], **vt.** espigar; recoger, juntar.

glee [gli], **s.** alegría, gozo, júbilo; (mús.) canción para voces solas. —**g. club,** cantoría, coro; orfeón.

glib [glib], **a.** suelto de lengua, locuaz.

glide [glaid], **vi.** resbalar, deslizarse; (aer.) planear.—**s.** deslizamiento; (aer.) planeo.— —**r** [gláidœ(r)], **s.** el o lo que se desliza; (aer.) planeador, deslizador.

glimmer [glímœ(r)], **vi.** rielar, centellear.—**s.** luz trémula; vislumbre, viso.

glimpse [glimps], **s.** ojeada, vistazo; vislumbre.—**vt.** vislumbrar.—**vi.** ojear.

glint [glint], **vi.** brillar, destellar.—**s.** destello, relumbre.

glisten [glisn], **vi.** brillar, resplandecer.

glitter [glítœ(r)], **vi.** resplandecer, centellear, rutilar, brillar.—**s.** brillo, resplandor, centelleo.

global [glóubₐl], **a.** global; esférico. —**globe** [gloub], **s.** esfera, globo. —**globetrotter** [glóubtratœ(r)], **s.** trotamundos.—**globular** [glábyulₐ(r)], **s.** globular, esférico.—**globule** [glábyul], **s.** glóbulo.

gloom [glum], **gloominess** [glúminis], **s.** oscuridad, lobreguez, tenebrosidad, tinieblas; melancolía, tristeza.— **gloomy** [glúmi], **a.** tenebroso, sombrío, lóbrego; nublado, triste, melancólico.

glorify [glórifai], **vti.** [7] glorificar, exaltar, alabar.—**glorious** [glórjʌs], **a.** glorioso; (fam.) excelente, magnífico. —**glory** [glóri], **s.** gloria.—**vii.** [7] gloriarse, vanagloriarse, jactarse.

gloss [glɔs], **s.** lustre, brillo; pulimento; apariencia; glosa; comentario.—**vt.** pulir, pulimentar, satinar.—**vt. y vi.** glosar, comentar.— —**ary** [glásₐri], **s.** glosario.— —**y** [glɔ́si], **a.** lustroso, satinado; (fot.) brillante.

glove [glʌv], **s.** guante.—**to be hand and g.,** ser uña y carne.—**to deal with gloves,** tratar con mucho miramiento.—**to handle without gloves,** tratar sin contemplaciones.—**vt.** enguantar.

glow [glou], **vi.** brillar o lucir suavemente; fosforecer; ponerse incandescente; enardecerse.—**s.** brillo sin llama; incandescencia; calor intenso; vehemencia.— —**ing** [glóuiŋ], **a.** incandescente, encendido; ardiente. —**worm** [-wœrm], **s.** luciérnaga, (Am.) cocuyo.

glue [glu], **s.** cola, engrudo o goma de pegar.—**vt.** encolar; engomar.— —**y** [glúi], **a.** pegajoso, viscoso.

glutton [glátₒn], **s.** glotón, tragón, comelón.— —**ous** [-ʌs], **a.** glotón, goloso.— —**y** [-i], **s.** glotonería, gula.

gnash [næʃ], **vt.** rechinar o crujir los dientes.

gnat [næt], **s.** (Am.) jején; mosquito.

gnaw [nɔ], **vt.** roer; carcomer; corroer.— —**er** [nɔ́œ(r)], **s.** roedor.

go [gou], *vii.* [10] ir, irse; andar; marcharse, partir; (mec.) funcionar; acudir; sentar, caer bien.—*to g. abroad*, ir al extranjero.—*to g. across*, cruzar.—*to g. after*, seguir a.—*to g. ahead*, adelantar, proseguir.—*to g. along*, seguir, proseguir; irse, marcharse.—*to g. around*, alcanzar para todos.—*to g. astray*, extraviarse.—*to g. away*, desaparecer; irse, marcharse. —*to g. back*, regresar; volverse atrás. —*to g. in for*, dedicarse a.—*to g. into*, entrar en.—*to g. near*, acercarse. —*to g. off*, irse, largarse; dispararse. —*to g. on*, avanzar, continuar, proseguir.—*to g. out*, salir; apagarse. —*to g. to pot*, arruinarse.—*to g. under*, quedar arruinado; hundirse; ser vencido; pasar por debajo de.—*to g. up*, subir, ascender.—*to g. without saying*, sobreentenderse.—*s.* usanza; energía, empuje; buen éxito.—*is it a g.?* ¿está resuelto? ¿estamos convenidos?—*it is no g.*, es inútil, esto no marcha.—*on the g.*, en actividad.

goad [goud], *s.* aguijón, puya.—*g. spur*, acicate.—*g. stick*, garrocha, rejo.—*vt.* aguijonear; estimular.

goal [goul], *s.* meta, fin, objeto, objetivo, propósito; (dep.) gol, tanto.

goat [gout], *s.* cabra; chiva.—*billy o male g.*, cabrón, chivo, macho cabrío.—*to be the g.*, cargar con la culpa ajena.- **—ee** [goutí], *s.* pera, perilla.

gobble [gábl], *vt.* engullir, tragar.—*vi.* hacer ruido con la garganta como los pavos.—*s.* voz del pavo.- **—r** [gáblœ(r)], *s.* glotón, tragón; pavo.

go-between [góubitwin], *s.* mediador; alcahuete.

goblet [gáblit], *s.* copa de mesa, vaso de pie.

goblin [gáblin], *s.* trasgo, duende.

gocart [góukart], *s.* carretilla.

god, God [gad], *s.* dios, Dios.—*G. be with you*, vaya usted con Dios.—*G. forbid*, no lo quiera Dios.—*G. willing*, Dios mediante, si Dios quiere.- **—child** [gádchajld], *s.* ahijado, ahijada.- **—dess** [-is], *s.* diosa.- **—father** [-faðœ(r)], *s.* padrino.- **—less** [-lis], *a.* ateo, impío.- **—lessness** [-lisnis], *s.* impiedad, ateísmo.- **—like** [-lajk], *a.* divino.- **—liness** [-linis], *s.* piedad, santidad.- **—ly** [-li], *a.* divino; devoto, piadoso.- **—mother** [-mʌðœ(r)], *s.* madrina.- **—parents** [-perents], *s.* padrinos.- **—ship** [-ʃip], *s.* divinidad.- **—son** [-sʌn], *s.* ahijado.

go-getter [góugétœ(r)], *s.* buscavidas.

going [góuiŋ], *a.* y *ger.* de TO GO; activo,

que funciona.—*a g. concern*, una empresa que funciona o marcha.—*s.* paso, andar; marcha, ida; partida; estado del camino.—*g. out*, salida.

goiter [gójtœ(r)], *s.* bocio, papera, (Am.) buche.

gold [gould], *s.* oro; color de oro.—*g. standard*, patrón de oro.—*g. work*, orfebrería.- **—en** [góulden], *a.* áureo, de oro, dorado; rubio, amarillento.- **—finch** [-finch], *s.* cardelina; jilguero amarillo.- **—fish** [-fiʃ], *s.* pececillo(s) de colores; carpa dorada.- **—smith** [-smiθ], *s.* orfebre.

gondola [gándolà], *s.* góndola; (aer.) barquilla o cabina; (f.c.) vagón de mercancías.—**gondolier** [gandolír], *s.* gondolero.

gone [gon], *pp.* de TO GO.—*a.* ido; perdido, arruinado; pasado.—*a.* apagado.

gong [gaŋ], *s.* batintín, gong.

gonorrhea [ganoríà], *s.* gonorrea.

good [gud], *a.* bueno; apto, conveniente; genuino, válido, valedero; digno. —*a g. deal*, mucho, bastante.—*a g. turn*, un favor, una gracia.—*as g. as*, casi.—*g. afternoon*, buenas tardes. —*g. enough*, suficientemente bueno, pasadero, suficiente.—*g. evening*, buenas tardes; buenas noches.—*G. Friday*, Viernes Santo.—*g. for nothing*, inútil, sin valor; haragán. —*g.-looking*, guapo, bien parecido.— *g. morning*, buenos días.—*g. nature*, bondad, buen corazón.—*g. night*, buenas noches.—*s.* bien; provecho, ventaja.—*pl.* géneros, mercancías, efectos.—*for g.*, para siempre.—*for g. and all*, terminantemente, una vez por todas.—*it's no g.*, no vale, es inútil.—*interj.* ¡bueno! ¡muy bien!- **—by, —bye** [gudbái], *s.* e *interj.* adiós; hasta la vista; vaya usted con Dios.- **—liness** [gúdlinis], *s.* belleza, gracia, elegancia.- **—ness** [-nis], *s.* bondad, benevolencia; fineza.—*interj.* ¡Ave María! ¡Dios mío!- **—y** [-i], *a.* y *s.* bonachón, Juan Lanas.- *—g.-g.*, santurrón, beato.—*pl.* dulces.

goose [gus], *s.* ganso, oca; necio.— *g. flesh*, carne de gallina (aplicado a la piel humana).- **—berry** [gúzberi], *s.* grosella.

gore [gor], *s.* cuajarón de sangre; (cost.) cuchillo, nesga; pedazo triangular de terreno.—*vt.* herir con los cuernos; poner nesga o cuchillo.

gorge [gordʒ], *s.* garganta, barranco, desfiladero; cuello de un vestido; trago, bocado; asco.—*vt.* engullir, tragar; atiborrar; hartar, saciar.—*vi.* hartarse, saciarse.

gorgeous [górdʒʌs], *a.* vistoso, magnífico, suntuoso.

gorilla [gorílà], *s.* gorila.

gory [góri], *a.* sangriento, sanguinolento.
gospel [gáspel], *s.* evangelio; cosa cierta e indudable.—*g. truth,* verdad palmaria.- —(l)er [-œ(r)], *s.* evangelista.
gossip [gásip], *s.* chismografía, murmuración; chismoso; chisme.—*vi.* chismear, murmurar.- —ing [-iŋ], —y [-i], *a.* chismoso, murmurador.
got [gat], *pret.* y *pp.* de TO GET.
goth [gaθ], *s.* godo.—**Gothic** [gáθik], *a.* gótico.—*s.* lengua goda.
gotten [gátn], *pp.* de TO GET.
gouge [gaudż], *s.* gubia; ranura, canal, estría.—*vt.* escoplar; arrancar, sacar, vaciar; engañar.
gourd [gord], *s.* calabaza; (Am.) güiro.
gout [gaut], *s.* gota, artritis.- —y [gáuti], *a.* gotoso.
govern [gávœrn], *vt.* y *vi.* gobernar; regir.- —ess [-is], *s.* institutriz.- —ment [-ment], *s.* gobierno, gobernación; administración, dirección; régimen.- —or [-Ǫ(r)], *s.* gobernador; regulador.
gown [gaun], *s.* traje de mujer; túnica; toga, vestidura talar.—*dressing g.,* bata.—*vt.* y *vi.* togar(se).
grab [græb], *vti.* [1] asir, agarrar; arrebatar; posesionarse.—*s.* agarrón, toma, asimiento; presa; arrebatiña; copo; gancho, garfio; (fam.) robo.
grace [greis], *s.* gracia, garbo; favor, concesión, privilegio; talante.—*good graces,* favor, amistad, bienquerencia. —*to say g.,* bendecir la mesa.—*with a bad (good) g.,* de mala (buena) gana.- —ful [gréisful], *a.* gracioso, agraciado; garboso; fácil, natural; decoroso.- —fulness [-fulnis], *s.* donosura, garbo, elegancia.
gracious [gréiśAs], *a.* bondadoso, benigno; afable; gracioso, grato.— *g. me!* o *good*(ness) *g.!* ¡válgame Dios! ¡caramba!
gradation [greidéiśǫn], *s.* graduación; grado; serie; escalonamiento; (mús. y pint.) gradación.—**grade** [greid], *s.* grado; clase; nota o calificación; declive.—*at g.,* a nivel.—*down g.,* cuesta abajo.—*g. crossing,* paso a nivel.—*g. school,* escuela primaria.— *highest g.,* de primera clase o calidad. —*up g.,* cuesta arriba.—*vt.* clasificar u ordenar; graduar; (ing.) nivelar. —**gradual** [grédżual], *a.* gradual; graduado.—**graduate** [grédżueit], *vt.* graduar.—*vi.* graduarse, (Am.) recibirse de bachiller.—*a.* [grédżuit], graduado, (Am.) que ha recibido el grado.—*s.* el que ha recibido un grado académico.—**graduation** [gradżuéiśǫn], *s.* graduación, obtención del grado.
graft [græft], *s.* injerto; tejido injertado;

parte donde se hace el injerto; malversación; (Am.) peculado; latrocinio; soborno político.—*vt.* y *vi.* injertar; malversar; traficar con puestos públicos; cometer peculado.
grain [grein], *s.* grano; fibra o veta de la madera, el mármol, etc.—*pl.* cereales, granos en general.—*across the g.,* transversalmente a la fibra.
gram [græm], *s.* gramo.
grammar [grémǎ(r)], *s.* gramática; elementos de una ciencia.—*g. school,* escuela pública de enseñanza elemental.- —ian [gramérian], *s.* gramático.—**grammatical** [gramétikǎl], *a.* gramatical.
granary [grénari], *s.* granero.
grand [grænd], *a.* grande, grandioso; magnífico; ilustre, augusto.- —aunt [grændænt], *s.* tía abuela.- —child [-chaild], *s.* nieto, nieta.- —daughter [-dɔtœ(r)], *s.* nieta.- —ee [grændí], *s.* noble, grande.- —father [-faðœ(r)], *s.* abuelo.- —ma [-ma], *s.* (fam.) abuelita.- —mother [-mʌðœ(r)], *s.* abuela.- —nephew [-nefju], *s.* sobrino nieto.- —ness [-nis], *s.* grandiosidad.- —niece [-nis], *s.* sobrina nieta.- —pa [-pa], *s.* (fam.) abuelito.- —parent [-perent], *s.* abuelo, abuela.- —sire [-sair], *s.* antepasado.- —son [-sʌn], *s.* nieto.- —stand [-stænd], *s.* tribuna, tendido, gradería de asientos para espectadores.- —uncle [-ʌŋkl], *s.* tío abuelo.
grange [greindż], *s.* granja, cortijo, alquería, hacienda; asociación de agricultores.- —r [gréindżœ(r)], *s.* granjero.
granite [grénit], *s.* granito.
granny [gréni], *s.* (fam.) abuelita; comadre; viejecita.
grant [grænt], *vt.* conceder; permitir; ceder, transferir; asentir, convenir en.- —*to take for granted,* dar por supuesto. —*s.* concesión, donación; otorgamiento, subvención, franquicia, asentimiento; documento que confiere un privilegio o concesión.—*granting that,* dado que, supuesto que.
granulate [grényuleit], *vt.* granular; granear.—*vi.* granularse; (med.) encarnar.—**granule** [grényul], *s.* granito, gránulo.
grape [greip], *s.* uva; vid.- —fruit [gréipfrut], *s.* toronja.- —shot [-śat], *s.* (art.) metralla.- —vine [-vain], *s.* vid, parra; noticia que circula por vías secretas.
graph [græf], *s.* gráfica; diagrama.—*vt.* construir la gráfica de, representar gráficamente.- —ic(al) [gréfik(ǎl)], *a.* gráfico.- —ite [-ait], *s.* grafito.
grapple [grépl], *vt.* agarrar, asir; amarrar.—*vi.* agarrarse; (mar.)

atracarse, abordarse.—*s.* lucha, riña.

grasp [græsp], *vt.* empuñar, asir; apresar, apoderarse de, usurpar; ver, entender.—*vi.* agarrarse fuertemente.—*s.* asimiento; presa; usurpación; puñado; garras; comprensión.

grass [græs], *s.* hierba; pasto, césped.—*g. grown*, cubierto de hierba.—*vt.* cubrir de hierba; apacentar.—*vi.* pacer; cubrirse de hierba.— **—hopper** [grǽshapœ(r)], *s.* saltamontes, langosta.— **—y** [-i], *a.* herboroso; herbáceo.

grate [greit], *s.* reja, verja, enrejado; parrilla.—*vt.* enrejar, poner enrejado; (coc.) rallar; raspar; frotar, hacer rechinar; emparrillar.—*vi.* rozar; raer; rechinar, chirriar.—*to g. on*, molestar, irritar.

grateful [gréitfʊl], *a.* agradecido; grato, gustoso.— **—ness** [-nis], *s.* gratitud, agrado.

grater [gréitœ(r)], *s.* rallador, rallo, raspador.

gratify [grǽtifai], *vti.* [7] satisfacer, complacer, dar gusto; gratificar.

grating [gréitiɳ], *a.* rechinante, chirriante, discordante; irritante, áspero.—*s.* reja, rejilla, verja, enrejado; emparrillado; escurridero; chirrido, rechinamiento; retícula (de microscopio, etc.); ralladura.

gratis [gréitis], *adv.* gratis.—*a.* gratuito.

gratitude [grǽtitiud], *s.* gratitud, reconocimiento.

gratuitous [gratjúitʌs], *a.* gratuito; injustificado.—**gratuity** [gratjúiti], *s.* gratificación; propina.

grave [greiv], *s.* sepultura, sepulcro, tumba; acento grave.—*a.* grave, serio; solemne; (mus.) bajo, profundo.— **—clothes** [gréivklouðz], *s. pl.* mortaja.— **—digger** [-digœ(r)], *s.* sepulturero, enterrador.

gravel [grǽvel], *s.* cascajo, grava; (med.) cálculos.

graveyard [gréivyard], *s.* cementerio.

gravitate [grǽviteit], *vi.* gravitar.—**gravitation** [grævité]ʃøn], *s.* gravitación.—**gravity** [grǽviti], *s.* gravedad; seriedad; importancia.

gravy [gréivi], *s.* salsa o caldillo de un guiso de carne.

gray [grei], *vt.* y *vi.* ponerse gris o cano; encanecer.—*a.* gris, pardo; tordo, rucio; cano, encanecido.—*g.-haired*, o *-headed*, canoso; envejecido.—*s.* color gris; animal gris.— **—ish** [gréiiʃ], *a.* pardusco, grisáceo; entrecano; tordillo.

graze [greiz], *vt.* apacentar, pastorear; rozar.—*vi.* pacer, pastar; rozarse.

grease [gris], *s.* grasa; pringue; lubrificante.—*vt.* engrasar; ensuciar con grasa; lubrificar; sobornar;

(fam.) untar la mano.— **—r** [grísœ(r)], *s.* engrasador; lubricante, lubrificante.— **—greasy** [grísi], *a.* grasiento, pringoso.

great [greit], *a.* gran, grande; magno; admirable; excelente; espléndido.—*a g. deal*, mucho, gran cantidad.—*a g. many*, muchos.—*a g. way off*, muy lejos.—*a g. while*, un largo rato.— **—g.-grandchild** [-grǽndchaild], *s.* biznieto.—**g.-grandfather** [-grǽndfaðœ(r)], *s.* bisabuelo.—**g.-grandmother** [-grǽndmʌðœ(r)], *s.* bisabuela.— **—ness** [gréitnis], *s.* grandeza; grandiosidad; magnitud, extensión; fausto.

Grecian [gríʃən], *s.* y *a.* griego.

greed [grid], *s.* voracidad, gula; codicia, avidez.— **—ily** [grídili], *adv.* vorazmente; codiciosamente; vehementemente, con ansia.— **—y** [-i], *a.* voraz; anhelante, ávido, codicioso.

Greek [grik], *s.* griego; (fam.) lenguaje o cosa ininteligible.—*a.* griego.

green [grin], *a.* verde (de color y de sazón); fresco; inexperto, bisoño.—*g. corn*, maíz tierno; trigo nuevo.—*g.-eyed*, ojiverde, celoso.—*g. goods*, verduras.—*g. hand*, novicio.—*s.* color verde; verdor, verdura; prado o pradera; césped.—*pl.* verduras, hortalizas.—*vt.* pintar o teñir de verde.—*vi.* verdear.— **—house** [grínhaus], *s.* invernadero.— **—ish** [-iʃ], *a.* verdoso, verdusco.— **—ly** [-li], *adv.* nuevamente, recientemente; sin madurez.— **—ness** [-nis], *s.* verdor; vigor, frescura; falta de experiencia; novedad.

greet [grit], *vt.* saludar, dar la bienvenida.—*vi.* encontrarse y saludarse.— **—ing** [gríʃtiɳ], *s.* salutación, saludo.—*pl.* ¡salud! ¡saludos!

grenade [grenéid], *s.* (mil.) granada.

grew [gru], *pret.* de TO GROW.

grey [grei], *a.* gris; pardo; canoso.—*v.* GRAY.— **—hound** [gréihaund], *s.* galgo; lebrel.— **—ish** [-iʃ], *a.* *v.* GRAYISH.

grid [grid], *s.* red; parrilla; reja, rejilla.— **—dle** [gridl], *s.* tapadera de fogón; tortera.— **—iron** [grídaiœrn], *s.* parrillas; andamiaje; (dep.) campo marcado para el futbol americano.

grief [grif], *s.* pesar, aflicción, dolor, sentimiento.—*g.-stricken*, desconsolado, apesadumbrado.—*to come to g.*, pasarlo mal; malograrse.

grievance [grívans], *s.* injusticia, perjuicio; motivo de queja, agravio.— **—grieve** [griv], *vt.* afligir, lastimar; apesadumbrar.—*vi.* apesadumbrarse, dolerse, penar.— **—grievous** [grívas], *a.* penoso, doloroso, oneroso; fiero, atroz, cruel.

griffin [grífin], **griffon** [grífon], *s.* (mit. griega) grifo.

grill [gril], *vt.* asar en parrillas; atormentar con fuego o calor; interrogar severamente y sin tregua.— *s.* parrilla; manjar asado en parrilla; restaurante.- **—room** [grílrum], *s.* restaurante especializado en asados a la parrilla.

grim [grim], *a.* torvo, ceñudo; horrendo; inflexible; formidable.

grimace [griméjs], *s.* mueca, gesto, mohín, visaje.—*vi.* hacer muecas, hacer visajes.

grime [grajm], *s.* tizne, mugre, porquería.—*vt.* ensuciar, tiznar.— **grimy** [grájmi], *a.* tiznado, sucio, manchado.

grimness [grímnis], *s.* horror, espanto, grima.

grin [grin], *vii.* [1] hacer muecas mostrando los dientes; sonreír satisfecha, aprobativa o sarcásticamente. —*s.* mueca (de ira, dolor, etc.); sonrisa expresiva (de satisfacción, etc.).

grind [grajnd], *vti.* [4] moler, quebrantar, triturar; pulverizar; picar carne; hacer crujir o rechinar (los dientes); afilar, amolar; vaciar; rallar, estregar; pulir, esmerilar; mascar; dar vueltas a un manubrio; acosar, oprimir; (fam.) dar lata o matraca.—*vii.* hacer molienda; rozar; pulirse o deslustrarse con el roce. —*s.* molienda; (fam.) trabajo pesado.- **—er** [grájndœ(r)], *s.* molinero; moledor; esmerilador; piedra de molino o de amolar; molino; amolador; muela.- **—ing** [-iŋ], *s.* molienda; afilamiento; esmerilado; pulimiento; rechinamiento.—*a.* opresivo.

grip [grip], *s.* apretón de mano; agarrón, asimiento; presa; saco de mano; mango, puño, agarradera; capacidad de agarrar, comprender o retener. —*to be at grips*, estar en un cuerpo a cuerpo.—*vti.* [1] agarrar, empuñar. —*vii.* agarrarse con fuerza.

gripe [grajp], *vt.* agarrar, empuñar; pellizcar; (mec.) morder; dar cólico; afligir.—*vi.* agarrar fuertemente; padecer cólico; quejarse, refunfuñar de vicio.—*s.* grapa, abrazadera; puño, mango, manija, agarradera; aprieto.—*pl.* retortijón, cólico.

grippe [grip], *s.* gripe, influenza.

grisly [grízli], *a.* espantoso, terrible.

gristle [grísl], *s.* cartílago, ternilla.

grit [grit], *s.* arena, cascajo; firmeza; entereza; valor.—*pl.* sémola.—*vti.* y *vii.* [1] (hacer) rechinar o crujir (los dientes, etc.).

grizzle [grízl], *s.* color gris; mezclilla.

—grizzly [grízli], *a.* grisáceo, pardusco.—*g. bear*, oso gris.

groan [groun], *vi.* gemir; **lanzar** quejidos.—*s.* gemido, quejido.

grocer [gróusœ(r)], *s.* especiero, abacero, bodeguero.- **—y** [-i], *s.* abacería, especiería, tienda de comestibles, bodega.—*pl.* especierías, víveres, comestibles.

groom [grum], *s.* novio (en el acto de la boda); mozo de mulas; lacayo. —*vt.* cuidar, almohazar los caballos; peinar y vestir, acicalar.- **—sman** [grúmzman], *s.* padrino de boda.

groove [gruv], *s.* muesca, ranura, estría; surco; rutina.—*g. and tongue*, (carp.) ranura y lengüeta, unión machihembrada; machihembrar.

grope [group], *vt.* y *vi.* tentar, **andar a** tientas; buscar tentando.

gross [grous], *a.* craso; grueso; espeso, denso; indecoroso, obsceno; tosco, grosero; estúpido; (com.) bruto. —*g. profit*, ganancia bruta.—*g. weight*, peso bruto.—*s.* gruesa (doce docenas); grueso, la mayor parte; la totalidad, el conjunto.

grotto [grátou], *s.* gruta; antro, covacha.

grouch [grauch], *s.* gruñón, descontento. —*to have a g.*, estar de mal humor.

ground [graund], *pret.* y *pp.* de TO GRIND.—*g. glass*, vidrio esmerilado.—*g. meat*, carne picada (molida).—*s.* tierra, terreno, suelo; territorio; base, fundamento; razón, motivo, causa; (pint.) fondo o campo; baño, capa; (elec. y radio) toma de tierra; (mil.) campo de batalla.—*pl.* poso, sedimento, heces; jardín, parque, terrenos; cancha.—*g. floor*, planta baja.—*to break g.*, desmontar, roturar; empezar un trabajo.—*to come o fall to the g.*, caer al suelo; fracasar.—*to gain g.*, ganar terreno. —*to give o to lose g.*, perder terreno; retroceder, atrasar.—*to take the g.*, (mar.) encallar.—*vt.* fundar, apoyar, establecer; poner en tierra; (elec. y rad.) conectar con tierra.—*vi.* encallar, varar.- **—less** [gráundlis], *a.* infundado.

group [grup], *s.* grupo, agrupación, conjunto.—*vt.* y *vi.* agrupar(se), reunir(se).

grouse [graus], *s.* (orn.) chocha; (Am.) guaco.—*vi.* (fam.) quejarse.

grove [grouv], *s.* arboleda, bosquecillo, enramada.

grow [grou], *vti.* [10] cultivar; criar. —*vii.* crecer; aumentar; desarrollarse; nacer, darse (frutas, plantas, etc.). —*to g. crazy*, volverse loco.—*to g. dark*, anochecer, oscurecer.—*to g. late*, hacerse tarde.—*to g. less*, disminuir. —*to g. old*, envejecer.—*to g. on* o

upon, ir apoderándose de; ganar o aventajar a; hacerse cada vez más querido, admirable, etc.—*to g. up*, crecer, hacerse hombre.—*to g. young again*, remozarse.

growl [grau̯l], *vi.* gruñir, rezongar.—*vt.* decir gruñendo.—*s.* gruñido, rezongo.

grown [grou̯n], *pp.* de TO GROW.—*a.* crecido, espigado; cubierto o lleno de hierbas, malezas, etc.—*g.-up*, crecido, adulto.—**growth** [grou̯θ], *s.* crecimiento, desarrollo; aumento; producto, producción; tumor, excrecencia.

grub [grʌb], *s.* (ent.) gorgojo; larva; (fam.) manducatoria.—*vti.* y *vii.* [1] rozar; cavar; emplearse en oficios bajos; (fam.) manducar.

grudge [grʌdʒ], *vt.* envidiar, codiciar; escatimar, dar de mala gana.—*s.* rencor, inquina; renuencia, mal grado.

gruesome [grúsʌm], *a.* macabro; horripilante.

gruff [grʌf], *a.* ceñudo, áspero; grosero; (b)ronco (voz).—*-ness* [grʌ́fnis], *s.* aspereza, mal humor.

grumble [grʌ́mbl], *vi.* refunfuñar, rezongar, quejarse.—*s.* regaño, refunfuñadura.—*-r* [grʌ́mblœ(r)], *s.* refunfuñador, rezongador, malcontento.

grunt [grʌnt], *vi.* gruñir; refunfuñar.—*s.* gruñido.

guano [gwánou̯], *s.* guano.

Guarani [gwaraní], *s.* guaraní.

guarantee [gærʌntí], *vt.* garantizar; afianzar, responder de o por; dar fianza.—*s.* garantía, fianza; persona de quien otra sale fiadora.

guard [gard], *vt.* y *vi.* guardar, custodiar; vigilar; estar prevenido; guardarse.—*to g. against*, guardarse de.—*s.* guarda, guardia; guardián, custodio; protección, defensa; vigilancia; centinela; cautela; estado de defensa; guarnición de un vestido o de una espada; conductor de tren.—*on g.*, alerta; en guardia.—*a.* de guardia, de protección.—*-ian* [gárdiʌn], *s.* guardián, custodio; tutor.—*a.* que guarda, tutelar.—*g. angel*, ángel de la guarda.—*-ianship* [-iʌnṣip], *s.* tutela; protección, custodia.

Guatemalan [gwatẹmálʌn], *a.* and *s.* guatemalteco.

guava [gwávẹ], *s.* guayaba; guayabo.

guerrilla [gerílẹ], *s.* guerrilla; guerrillero.

guess [ges], *vt.* y *vi.* conjeturar, suponer; adivinar, acertar.—*s.* conjetura, suposición; adivinación.

guest [gest], *s.* huésped, invitado; forastero, visita; pensionista.

guffaw [gʌfɔ́], *s.* carcajada, risotada.—*vi.* reír a carcajadas.

guidance [gáidʌns], *s.* guía, dirección,

conducta.—**guide** [gaid], *vt.* guiar, dirigir, encaminar; adiestrar; arreglar, gobernar.—*guided missile*, proyectil dirigido.—*s.* guía, mentor; baquiano; (mec.) corredera; (impr.) mordante.—**guidebook** [gáidbụk], *s.* guía del viajero.

guild [gild], *s.* gremio; cofradía, hermandad; corporación; colegio profesional (de médicos, abogados, etc.); sociedad benéfica.

guile [gail], *s.* dolo o engaño; estratagema.

guilt [gilt], *s.* delito; culpa, culpabilidad; pecado.—*-less* [gíltlis], *a.* inocente, libre de culpa.—*-y* [-i], *a.* reo; culpable.

guinea pig [gíni píg], *s.* conejillo de Indias.

guitar [gitár], *s.* guitarra.—*-ist* [-ist], *s.* guitarrista.

gulch [gʌlch], *s.* quebrada, cañada.

gulf [gʌlf], *s.* golfo; seno; sima, vorágine.—*G. Stream*, corriente del golfo (de México).

gull [gʌl], *vt.* engañar, timar, estafar.—*s.* gaviota; bobo, primo.

gullet [gʌ́lit], *s.* fauces; gaznate; zanja, trinchera profunda.

gullible [gʌ́libl], *a.* crédulo, simple.

gully [gʌ́li], *vti.* [7] formar canal.—*s.* zanja honda; barranco, barranca; hondonada.

gulp [gʌlp], *vt.* engullir, tragar; sofocar (un sollozo).—*vi.* entrecortar el resuello.—*s.* trago, sorbo.

gum [gʌm], *s.* goma; encía.—*chewing g.*, chicle, goma de mascar.—*vti.* [1] engomar; pegar con goma.

gumbo [gʌ́mbou̯], *s.* (Am.) quimbombó.

gummy [gʌ́mi], *a.* gomoso, engomado.

gun [gʌn], *s.* arma de fuego (cañón; fusil; escopeta; pistola o revólver); disparo de arma de fuego.—*vti.* [1] hacer fuego.—*vii.* cazar con escopeta o rifle.—*-boat* [gʌ́nbou̯t], *s.* cañonero.—*-man* [-mʌn], *s.* pistolero, bandido armado.—*-ner* [-œ(r)], *s.* artillero; ametrallador.—*-powder* [-pau̯dœ(r)], *s.* pólvora.—*-smith* [-smiθ], *s.* armero.

gurgle [gœ́rgl], *vi.* borbotar, gorgotear.—*s.* gorgoteo; borbotón; gluglú.

gush [gʌṣ], *vt.* derramar, verter.—*vi.* brotar, fluir, manar a borbotones, chorrear; (fam.) ser extremoso.—*s.* chorro, borbotón; (fam.) efusión, extremo.

gust [gʌst], *s.* ráfaga, bocanada; acceso, arrebato.

gusto [gʌ́stou̯], *s.* entusiasmo, satisfacción, celo.

gut [gʌt], *s.* intestino, tripa; cuerda de tripa; (mar.) estrecho.—*pl.*

(fam.) entrañas; valor ánimo.—*vti.*
[1] destripar; desentrañar.

gutter [gátœ(r)], *s.* canal, canalón;
gotera; cuneta; arroyo de la calle;
albañal; acequia; estría, canal de
ebanistería.—*vt.* acanalar, estriar;
construir albañales, etc.—*vi.* acana-
larse; manar, gotear.

guy [gai], *s.* cable de retén, tirante,
viento; (fam.) tipo, sujeto, tío;
adefesio, mamarracho.—*vt.* sujetar
con vientos; hacer burla o mofa.

gymnasium [džimnéizjam], *s.* gimnasio.
—**gymnast** [džimnæst], *s.* gimnasta.
—**gymnastic(al)** [džimnǽstik(al)], *a.*
gimnástico.—**gymnastics** [džimnǽs-
tiks], *s.* gimnasia, gimnástica.

gynecology [gainekálodži], *s.* ginecología.

H

haberdasher [hǽbœrdæšœ(r)], *s.* camisero, mercero, tendero.— —**y** [-i],
s. camisería, mercería.

habit [hǽbit], *s.* hábito, costumbre;
vicio; vestido.—*by* o *from* (*force of*)
h., de vicio.—*to be in the h. of*, soler,
acostumbrar.

habitable [hǽbitabl], *a.* habitable.—
habitation [hǽbitéišon], *s.* habitación, domicilio, morada.—**habitat**
[hǽbitæt], *s.* (biol.) ámbito natural
de un animal o planta.

habitual [habíchual], *a.* habitual, acostumbrado.—**habituate** [habíchueit],
vt. y *vi.* habituar(se).

hack [hæk], *s.* caballo de alquiler,
rocín; tos seca; plumífero, autor
mercenario; taxi.—*h. stand*, punto
o parada de taxis.—*h. saw*, sierra
para cortar metal.—*vt.* tajar, picar.
—*vi.* cortar; toser con tos seca;
alquilarse.

hackle [hǽkl], *s.* rastrillo; plumas de
cuello de ciertas aves; mosca para
pescar.—*vt.* rastrillar; tajar; mutilar.

hackneyed [hǽknid], *a.* trillado, gastado.

had [hæd], *pret.* de TO HAVE.

haggard [hǽgard], *a.* trasnochado,
macilento, ojeroso, flaco.

haggle [hǽgl], *vt.* tajar.—*vi.* regatear.

hail [heil], *s.* granizo; saludo: grito,
llamada.—*H. Mary*, Ave María.—
within h., al habla, al alcance de la
voz.—*interj.* ¡salve! ¡salud!—*vt.* saludar; aclamar; llamar.—*vi.* granizar;
vocear.—*to h. from*, ser oriundo de.—
—**storm** [héilstorm], *s.* granizada.

hair [her], *s.* pelo; vello; cabello;
cabellera; cerda; hebra, filamento;
pelusa.—*against the h.*, a contrapelo.
—*h. net*, redecilla.—*h.-raising*, espeluznante, horripilante.—*h. remover*,

depilatorio.—*h. stroke*, rasgo muy
fino.—*to a h.*, exactamente, perfectamente.— —**brush** [hérbrʌš], *s.* cepillo
de cabeza.— —**cloth** [-kloθ], *s.* tela
de crin.— —**cut** [-kʌt], *s.* pelado,
corte de pelo.— —**do** [-du], *s.*
peinado.— —**dresser** [-dresœ(r)], *s.*
peluquero, peluquera, peinador o
peinadora.— —**dressing** [-dresiŋ], *s.*
peinado.— —**less** [-lis], *a.* pelón; sin
pelo, lampiño.— —**pin** [-pin], *s.*
horquilla, (Am.) gancho del pelo.—
—**y** [-i], *a.* peludo, velludo.

Haitian [héitian], *a.* y *s.* haitiano.

hake [heik], *s.* (ict.) merluza.

hale [heil], *a.* sano, robusto, fuerte.
—*vt.* tirar de, arrastrar; llevar por
la fuerza.

half [hæf], *s.* mitad; medio.—*h. and h.*,
mitad y mitad; de medio a medio;
en partes iguales.—*a.* y *adv.* medio;
semi.—*h.-baked*, a medio cocer, asar,
etc.—*h. binding*, (enc.) media pasta.
—*h.-blood* o *h.-breed*, mestizo,
(Am.) cholo.—*h.-closed*, entornado.
—*h. hour*, media hora; de media
hora.—*h.-mast*, media asta (la bandera); poner a media asta.—*h.-
open(ed)*, entreabierto.—*h.-past one*,
two, etc., la una, las dos, etc. y media.
—*h.-witted*, tonto, imbécil.—*to h.-
open*, entreabrir.— —**way** [hǽfwei], *a.*
y *adv.* equidistante, a medio camino;
parcial(mente).

halibut [hǽlibʌt], *s.* (ict.) mero.

hall [hol], *s.* pasillo, corredor; vestíbulo,
zaguán; salón (para reuniones, funciones, etc.); edificio (de un colegio
u universidad).—*city h.*, o *town h.*,
ayuntamiento, alcaldía.

hallo [halóu], *interj.* ¡hola! ¡oiga!

hallow [hǽlou], *vt.* consagrar; reverenciar.

Hallowe'en [hælouín], *s.* víspera de
Todos los Santos.

hallucination [hæljusinéišon], *s.* alucinación.

halo [héilou], *s.* halo, nimbo, aureola.

halt [holt], *vi.* vacilar; parar, hacer
alto.—*vt.* parar, detener.—*s.* parada,
alto.—*interj.* ¡alto!

halter [hóltœ(r)], *s.* cabestro, ronzal,
jáquima; dogal.

halve [hæv], *vt.* dividir o partir en dos
partes iguales; (carp.) machihem-
brar.— —**s** [-z], *s. pl.* de HALF.

ham [hæm], *s.* jamón, pernil; corva.
—*pl.* (fam.) nalgas.

hamburger [hǽmbœrgœ(r)], *s.* emparedado de carne picada, (Am.)
hamburguesa, frita.

hamlet [hǽmlit], *s.* aldea, caserío,
villorrio.

hammer [hǽmœ(r)], *s.* martillo; martinete.—*vt.* martillar; machacar; cla-

var; forjar.—*to h.* *one's brains,*
devanarse los sesos.—*vi.* martillar,
dar golpes; repiquetear.— —head
[-hɛd], *s.* pez martillo, cornuda.
hammock [hǽmɔk], *s.* hamaca.
hamper [hǽmpœ(r)], *s.* canasta, cesto,
cuévano.—*vt.* embarazar, estorbar;
encestar, encanastar.
hand [hænd], *s.* mano; palmo; ajecu-
ción; mano de obra; manecilla o
aguja del reloj; operario, obrero,
bracero; carácter de letra; firma;
mano (en los naipes).—*at h.,* o *near
at h.,* a la mano, cerca.—*by h.,* a
mano; con biberón.—*h. and glove,*
uña y carne.—*h. in h.,* parejas; junto;
de acuerdo.—*h. over head,* inconside-
radamente.—*hands off,* no tocar; no
meterse.—*hands off policy,* política
de no intervención.—*h. to h.,* cuerpo
a cuerpo, a brazo partido.—*in h.,*
de contado.—*on the one h.,* por una
parte.—*on the other h.,* por otra
parte; en cambio; al contrario.—*to
h.,* a la mano; listo.—*to set the h.
to,* emprender; firmar.—*vt.* dar,
entregar, poner en manos (de alguien).—*to h. down,* transmitir;
entregar; dictar (un fallo).—*to h.
over,* entregar, alargar.—*a.* de mano;
hecho a mano; manual.—*h. glass,*
lente de aumento, lupa.— —ball
[hǽndbɔl], *s.* pelota, juego de pelota.-
—bag [-bæg], *s.* maletín; bolsa de
mano.- —bill [-bil], *s.* volante.-
—book [-buk], *s.* manual; prontuario;
guía.- —cuff [-kʌf], *s.* manilla.—
pl. esposas.—*vt.* maniatar, esposar.-
—ful [-ful], *s.* puñado, manojo.
handicap [hǽndikæp], *vti.* [1] (dep.)
emparejar ventajas entre compe-
tidores; poner obstáculos.—*s.* (dep.)
ventaja en carreras o torneos; desventaja, impedimento, obstáculo.—
handicapped [hǽndikæpt], *a.* impedido; que sufre de algún impedimento
físico o mental.
handiwork [hǽndiwœrk], *s.* artefacto;
trabajo manual.
handkerchief [hǽŋkœrchif], *s.* pañuelo.
handle [hǽndl], *vt.* tocar, manosear;
manipular, manejar; tratar; dirigir;
comerciar en; poner mango a.—*vi.*
usar las manos o trabajar con ellas;
ser manejado.—*s.* mango, puño, asa,
manigueta, manubrio, tirador; (Am.)
cacha (de arma).—**handling** [hǽnd-
liŋ], *s.* manejo; manoseo; maniobra;
manipulación.
handmade [hǽndmejd], *a.* hecho a
mano.—**handmaid** [hǽndmejd], *s.*
criada de mano, asistenta.—**handrail**
[hǽndrejl], *s.* pasamano, baranda,
barandilla.—**handsaw** [hǽndsɔ], *s.*
serrucho, sierra de mano.—**hand-**

shake [hǽndšejk], *s.* apretón de
manos.
handsome [hǽndsʌm], *a.* hermoso;
guapo; bien parecido; generoso.
handwriting [hǽndrajtiŋ], *s.* carácter
de letra; escritura cursiva, caligrafía.
handy [hǽndi], *a.* manuable, fácil de
manejar; próximo, a la mano; cómodo; diestro, hábil.—*h.-man,* factótum.—*to come in h.,* venir al pelo,
caer bien.
hang [hæŋ], *vt.* ahorcar.—*vi.* ser
ahorcado.—*vti.* [10] colgar, suspender; fijar (en la pared); empapelar;
poner colgaduras.—*to h. out,* enarbolar; colgar.—*to h. up,* levantar;
colgar.—*vii.* colgar, pender, caer.—
to h. around, rondar, haraganear.—*to
h. up,* colgar el auricular.—*s.* caída
(de un vestido, cortina, etc.); (fam.)
maña, destreza; quid.
hangar [hǽŋǵ(r)], *s.* hangar.
hanger [hǽŋœ(r)], *s.* perchero, colga-
dero.—**hanging** [hǽŋiŋ], *s.* muerte
en la horca.—*pl.* colgaduras, tapices,
cortinaje.—*a.* colgante.—**hangman**
[hǽŋman], *s.* verdugo.—**hangover**
[hǽŋouvœ(r)], *s.* malestar que sigue
a una borrachera, (Am.) goma,
cruda, ratón.
hank [hæŋk], *s.* madeja.
happen [hǽpn], *vi.* acontecer, suceder,
pasar, acaecer, sobrevenir; hallarse
por casualidad en.—*to h. on,* encontrarse o tropezar con.—*whatever
happens,* suceda lo que suceda.—
—ing [-iŋ], *s.* suceso, acontecimiento.
happily [hǽpili], *adv.* feliz o dichosa-
mente; afortunadamente.—**happiness**
[hǽpinis], *s.* felicidad, dicha, alegría.—**happy** [hǽpi], *a.* feliz, dichoso,
alegre, contento; afortunado.
harangue [hærǽŋ], *s.* arenga, perorata.
—*vt.* arengar a.
harass [hǽras], *vt.* acosar, atosigar;
(mil.) hostigar, hostilizar.
harbinger [hárbindžœ(r)], *s.* heraldo.
harbor [hárbɔ(r)], *s.* puerto; asilo,
abrigo, albergue.—*h. master,* capitán
del puerto.—*h. pilot,* práctico.—*vt.*
abrigar; hospedar.—*vi.* ampararse,
refugiarse.
hard [hard], *a.* duro, endurecido; difícil,
arduo; penoso; fuerte, recio; riguroso,
severo; inflexible.—*h. drink,* bebida
fuertemente alcohólica; licor.—*h.
labor,* trabajo forzado.—*h. luck,* mala
suerte.—*h. of hearing,* duro de oído.
—*h. rubber,* ebonita, vulcanita.—
h. sausage, salchichón.—*h. to deal
with,* intratable, intransigente.—*h. water,* agua
cruda.—*h. words,* palabras injuriosas.
—*adv.* mucho; con ahinco, con impaciencia; difícilmente; con fuerza,
fuertemente; duramente.—*h.-bitten,*

(fam.) endurecido, aguerrido.—*h.-boiled*, duro, insensible.—*h.-boiled egg*, huevo duro.—*h. by*, inmediato, muy cerca.—*h.-hearted*, empedernido.—*to rain h.*, llover a cántaros.——**en** [hárdn], *vt.* y *vi.* endurecerse.——**ening** [-niŋ], *s.* endurecimiento.——**ly** [-li], *adv.* difícilmente, apenas, a duras penas, escasamente; duramente.——**ness** [-nis], *s.* dureza, endurecimiento; crudeza (del agua).——**ship** [-ŝip], *s.* penalidad, trabajo; privaciones.——**ware** [-wer], *s.* ferretería, quincallería; herraje, conjunto de accesorios metálicos.—*h. store*, ferretería, quincallería.——**wareman** [-wermạn], *s.* ferretero, quincallero.——**y** [-i], *a.* fuerte, robusto; bravo, intrépido.

hare [her], *s.* liebre. ——**brained** [hérbreind], *a.* cabeza de chorlito, ligero de cascos.——**lip** [-lip], *s.* labio leporino.

harlot [bárlot], *s.* ramera, prostituta.

harm [harm], *s.* daño, perjuicio, mal. —*vt.* dañar, perjudicar; ofender, herir.——**ful** [hármful], *a.* dañoso, dañino, nocivo, perjudicial.——**less** [-lis], *a.* inocuo; inofensivo; ileso; sano y salvo.

harmonic [harmánik], *s.* (mús.) armónico, tono secundario.—*pl.* armonía.—*a.* armónico.——**a** [-ạ], *s.* (mús.) armónica.——**harmonious** [harmóuniạs], *a.* armónico; armonioso; proporcionado.——**harmonize** [hármonaiz], *vt.* armonizar, concertar.—*vi.* armonizarse, congeniar; armonizar, convenir, corresponder.——**harmony** [hármoni], *s.* armonía, acuerdo.

harness [hárnis], *s.* arreos, guarniciones (de caballerías); arnés; (mec.) aparejo; (fig.) servicio activo.—*vt.* enjaezar; poner los arreos.

harp [harp], *s.* arpa.—*vi.* tocar el arpa. —*to h. on* o *upon*, repetir, machacar; porfiar.

harpoon [harpún], *s.* arpón.

harpy [hárpi], *s.* arpía.

harrow [hérou], *s.* grada, rastrillo; rodillo para desterronar.—*vt.* gradar, rastrillar; perturbar, atormentar.

harry [héri], *vti.* [7] asolar, saquear; acosar, molestar.

harsh [harŝ], *a.* áspero; tosco.——**ness** [hárŝnis], *s.* aspereza; severidad.

harvest [hárvist], *s.* cosecha; siega, agosto; fruto, recolección.—*h. fly*, cigarra, chicharra.—*h. time*, mies.—*vt.* recoger la cosecha, segar; cosechar.——**er** [-œ(r)], *s.* cosechero, segador; segadora, máquina de segar.

hash [hæŝ], *s.* picadillo, jigote.—*vt.* picar, hacer picadillo.

haste [heist], *s.* prisa.—*in h.*, de prisa.——

n [héisn], *vt.* apresurar, activar; precipitar.—*vi.* darse prisa, apresurarse.——**hasty** [héisti], *a.* apresurado; precipitado.

hat [hæt], *s.* sombrero.—*bowler h.*, sombrero hongo.—*h. box*, sombrerera. —*h. rack*, perchero.—*Panama h.*, jipijapa.—*silk h.* o *top h.*, sombrero de copa.—*soft h.*, sombrero flexible.

hatch [hæch], *vt.* criar, empollar, incubar; fraguar, tramar, maquinar.—*s.* cría; nidada; pollada; compuerta; portezuela; trampa; escotilla.——**ery** [hæchœri], *s.* incubadora; vivero.

hatchet [hæchit], *s.* hacha pequeña, hachuela.—*to bury the h.*, hacer las paces.

hatchway [hæchwei], *s.* escotilla.

hate [heit], *vt.* odiar, aborrecer.—*s.* odio, aborrecimiento.——**ful** [héitful], *a.* aborrecible, odioso.——**hatred** [héitrid], *s.* odio, aborrecimiento.

hatter [hætœ(r)], *s.* sombrerero.

haughtiness [hótinis], *s.* arrogancia, altanería, altivez; ínfulas, humos. ——**haughty** [hóti], *a.* arrogante; altivo, altanero.

haul [hol], *vt.* tirar de, arrastrar; transportar; (mar.) halar.—*to h. down the colors*, arriar la bandera.—*to h. the wind*, (mar.) ceñir el viento. —*s.* tirón o estirón, arrastre, transporte; redada; (fam.) buena pesca; botín, ganancia.

haunch [honch], *s.* anca; pernil, pierna, pata.

haunt [hont], *vt.* frecuentar; rondar, vagar por; perseguir, causar obsesión; molestar.—*s.* guarida, nidal; lugar que uno frecuenta.——**ed** [hóntid], *a.* embrujado, encantado.

have [hæv], *vai.* [11] haber.—*vti.* tener; contener; tomar (comer, beber); recibir (carta, noticia, etc.).—*to h. in hand*, estar ocupado en, tener entre manos.—*to h. on*, tener puesto (traje, etc.).—*to h. one's way*, salirse uno con la suya.—*to h. something done*, mandar hacer algo.—*to h. to*, tener que.

haven [héivn], *s.* puerto, fondeadero, abra; abrigo, asilo.

haversack [hævœrsæk], *s.* mochila.

havoc [hævọk], *s.* estrago, ruina.—*to play h. with*, hacer estragos.

Hawaiian [hawáiyạn], *a.* y *s.* hawaiano.

hawk [hok], *s.* halcón; gavilán.—*h.-nosed*, de nariz aguileña.—*vt.* y *vi.* pregonar mercancías; cazar con halcón. ——**sbill** [hóksbil], *s.* carey.

hawthorn [hóθorn], *s.* espino, oxiacanta.

hay [hei], *s.* heno; paja de heno u otras hierbas para forraje.——**fork** [héifork], *s.* horca, tridente.——**loft**

[-lɔft], *s.* henil, pajar.— —stack [-stæk], *s.* almiar; montón de heno.

hazard [hǽzǝrd], *s.* azar, albur; peligro, riesgo; obstáculo (en el golf, etc.). —*vt.* arriesgar, aventurar.— —ous [-ʌs], *a.* arriesgado, peligroso.

haze [hejz], *s.* niebla, bruma.—*vi.* abrumarse la atmósfera.—*vt.* dar novatadas (en los colegios).

hazel [héjzl], *s.* avellano.—*a.* castaño claro, avellanado; de avellano.— —nut [-nʌt], *s.* avellana.

hazing [héjziŋ], *s.* novatada (en los colegios).—hazy [héjzi], *a.* nublado, brumoso; confuso, vago.

he [hi], *pron. pers.* él.—*h.-bear*, oso (macho).—*h.-goat*, macho cabrío.— *h.-man*, (fam.) hombre cabal, todo un hombre.—*h. who, h. that*, el que, aquel que, quien.

head [hed], *s.* cabeza; cima; parte superior o principal; cabecera (de cama, mesa, río); jefe, caudillo; director; punta (de flecha, etc.); puño (de bastón).—*a h.*, por barba, por persona.—*at the h. (of)*, al frente (de).—*h. over heels*, precipitadamente. —*heads or tails*, cara o cruz.—*to bring to a h.*, ultimar.—*to come to a h.*, llegar a un estado definitivo o a una crisis; (med.) madurar.—*a.* principal; de o para la cabeza; de frente; (mar.) de proa.—*h. cold*, romadizo, coriza.—*vt.* encabezar; dirigir, presidir; descabezar; poner título; podar.—*to h. off*, detener, prevenir.—*vi.* (con *for*) dirigirse a.— —ache [hédejk], *s.* jaqueca, dolor de cabeza.— —board [-bǝrd], *s.* cabecera de cama.— —dress [-dres], *s.* cofia, tocado, redecilla.— —first [-fǝrst], *adv.* de cabeza.— —iness [-inis], *s.* terquedad, obstinación; encabezamiento del vino.— —ing [-iŋ], *s.* título, encabezamiento; membrete.— —less [-lis], *a.* descabezado, degollado; acéfalo.— —light [-lajt], *s.* (aut.) faro o farol delantero; (f.c.) farol, fanal.— —line [-lajn], *s.* titular, cintillo; título, encabezamiento.— —long [-lɔŋ], *a.* temerario, arrojado, precipitado.—*adv.* de cabeza, precipitadamente, irreflexivamente.— —master [-mǽstœ(r)], *s.* director de escuela.— —mistress [-místris], *s.* directora.— —quarters [-kwǝrtœrz], *s.* (mil.) cuartel general; jefatura (de policía, etc.); oficina principal de operaciones.— —stone [-stoun], *s.* lápida mortuoria.— —strong [-strɔŋ], *a.* terco, testarudo, obstinado.— —way [-wej], *s.* (mar.) salida, marcha de un buque; avance; progreso; adelanto, ventaja.—*to make h.*, adelantar, progresar.— —y [-i], *a.*

temerario, arrojado; violento, impetuoso.

heal [hil], *vt.* curar; componer.—*vi.* sanar; recobrar la salud.—*to h. up*, cicatrizarse.— —ing [híliŋ], *a.* sanativo, curativo.—*s.* cura, curación, cicatrización.

health [helθ], *s.* salud; sanidad.— —ful [hélθfµl], *a.* sano, saludable, salubre.— —iness [-inis], *s.* salubridad, sanidad.— —y [-i], *a.* sano; saludable.

heap [hip], *s.* montón, pila, acumulación; multitud.—*in heaps*, a montones.—*vt.* amontonar, apilar, acumular.—*h. up*, colmar.

hear [hir], *vti.* [10] oír; oír decir; escuchar; tener noticia de.—*vti.* oír.—*to h. from someone*, saber de, tener noticias de alguien.—heard [hœrd], *pret.* y *pp.* de TO HEAR.— —er [hírœ(r)], *s.* oyente.— —ing [-iŋ], *s.* sentido del oído; audiencia; (for.) vista (de un pleito o causa); examen de testigos; audición.— —say [-sej], *s.* rumor, fama.—*by h.*, de oídas.

hearse [hœrs], *s.* coche o carroza fúnebre.

heart [hart], *s.* corazón; ánimo; (fig.) entraña(s).—*at h.*, en el fondo, esencialmente; en verdad.—*by h.*, de memoria.—*from one's h.*, de todo corazón, con sinceridad.—*h. and soul*, en cuerpo y alma.—*h.-rending*, doloroso, desgarrador.—*to take h.*, cobrar ánimo.—*to take to h.*, tomar a pechos.— —ache [hártejk], *s.* dolor de corazón; angustia, congoja, pesar.— —beat [-bit], *s.* latido del corazón, palpitación; profunda emoción.— —broken [-broµkn], *a.* acongojado, transido de dolor, (fig.) muerto de pesar; desengañado.— —burn [-bœrn], *s.* (med.) acedía, acidez.— —en [-n], *vt.* animar, confortar.— —felt [-felt], *a.* cordial, sincero; sentido.

hearth [harθ], *s.* hogar, fogón, chimenea.

heartily [hártili], *adv.* cordialmente, de corazón.—heartless [hártlis], *a.* sin corazón; cruel; pusilánime.—hearty [hárti], *a.* cordial, sentido, sincero; sano, vigoroso; gustoso, grato.

heat [hit], *s.* calor; ardor, vehemencia; celo (de los animales); hornada; colada; (dep.) carrera o corrida eliminatoria.—*vt.* y *vi.* calentar(se), caldear(se); acalorar(se).— —er [hítœ(r)], *s.* calentador; aparato de calefacción.

heathen [híðen], *s.* y *a.* gentil, pagano, idólatra.

heating [hítiŋ], *s.* calefacción.—*a.* caluroso; de calefacción (superficie, área, etc.).—*h. pad*, almohadilla o bolsa eléctrica.

heave [hiv], *vti.* [4] alzar, levantar

(con esfuerzo); (mar.) izar; lanzar, arrojar; exhalar, prorrumpir.—*vii.* levantarse y bajarse alternativamente; suspirar hondo; palpitar; jadear, trabajar penosamente; tener náuseas; (mar.) virar.—*to h. in sight*, (mar.) aparecer, asomar.—*s.* alzadura, levantamiento; náusea, arqueada.

heaven [hévn], *s.* cielo, paraíso.—*pl.* firmamento, las alturas.—*for h.'s sake!* ¡por Dios!—**—ly** [-li], *a.* celeste; celestial.—*adv.* celestialmente.— **—ward** [-wərd], *adv.* hacia el cielo, hacia las alturas.

heaviness [hévinis], *s.* pesantez, pesadez, peso; abatimiento; opresión, carga.—**heavily** [hévili], *adv.* pesadamente; lentamente; tristemente; excesivamente.—**heavy** [hévi], *a.* pesado; grueso; opresivo; molesto; denso, espeso; pesaroso; indigesto.—*h. duty*, servicio o trabajo fuerte (de una máquina).—*h. rain*, chaparrón, aguacero.—**heavyweight** [héviweit], *a.* (dep.) de peso pesado o máximo.—*s.* (boxeo) peso completo.

Hebrew [híbru], *a. y s.* hebreo; israelita; judío.—*s.* lengua hebrea.

hedge [hedž], *s.* seto, vallado.—*vt.* cercar con seto, vallar; circundar; rodear.— **—hog** [hédžhag], *s.* (zool.) erizo.

heed [hid], *vt.* atender.—*vi.* prestar atención, hacer caso.—*s.* cuidado, atención.

heel [hil], *s.* talón o calcañar; tacón; talón de una media.—*heels over head*, patas arriba, —*vt.* poner talón a (zapatos y medias).—*to be well heeled*, (fam.) estar bien provisto de dinero.—*vi.* escorarse.—*to h. over*, zozobrar.

heifer [héfœ(r)], *s.* vaquilla, novilla.

height [hait], *s.* altura, elevación; estatura, talla.—*the h. of folly*, el colmo de la locura.— **—en** [háitn], *vt.* realzar, elevar; exaltar; avivar.

heinous [héinʌs], *a.* atroz, nefando, horrible.

heir [er], *s.* heredero.—*h. apparent*, heredero forzoso.— **—ess** [éris], *s.* heredera.— **—loom** [-lum], *s.* reliquia de familia.

held [held], *pret. y pp.* de TO HOLD.

helicopter [héjikaptœ(r)], *s.* helicóptero.

helium [híljʌm], *s.* (quim.) helio.

hell [hel], *s.* infierno.— **—ish** [héliš], *a.* infernal.

hello [helóu], *interj.* ¡hola!; (al teléfono) ¡diga! (Am.) ¡bueno!

helm [helm], *s.* (mar.) timón; yelmo.

helmet [hélmit], *s.* casco, yelmo.

help [help], *vt.* ayudar, auxiliar, socorrer; aliviar; remediar.—*I can't h.*

it, no puedo evitarlo.—*to h. one to*, servir a uno (carne, sopa, etc.); proporcionar.—*vi.* ayudar, contribuir; servir (en la mesa).—*I can't h. saying*, no puedo (por) menos de decir.—*s.* ayuda, auxilio, socorro; remedio; fuerza de trabajo (criados, obreros, empleados, dependientes).—*there is no h. for it*, eso no tiene remedio.— **—er** [hélpœ(r)], *s.* asistente, ayudante.— **—ful** [-ful], *a.* útil, servicial; provechoso; saludable.— **—ing** [-iŋ], *s.* ayuda; porción (de comida) que uno se sirve o le sirven.— **—less** [-lis], *a.* desvalido; imposibilitado; inútil; irremediable.— **—lessness** [-lisnis], *s.* desamparo; impotencia.

hem [hem], *s.* (cost.) dobladillo, jaretón, borde.—*vti.* [1] dobladillar, bastillar; (gen. con **in**) rodear, encerrar.—*vii.* fingir tos.—*interj.* ¡ejem!

hemisphere [hémisfir], *s.* hemisferio.— **hemispheric(al)** [hemisférik(ʌl)], *a.* hemisférico.

hemlock [hémlak], *s.* (bot.) abeto; cicuta.

hemorrhage [hémoridž], *s.* hemorragia.— **hemorrhagic** [hemorédžik], *a.* hemorrágico.

hemorrhoids [hémoroidz], *s. pl.* hemorroides, almorranas.

hemp [hemp], *s.* (bot.) cáñamo.—*h. cord*, bramante.—*h. sandal*, alpargata.

hen [hen], *s.* gallina; hembra de ave.—*h.-pecked*, dominado por su mujer.

hence [hens], *adv.* de aquí; desde aquí; de ahí que, por tanto, en consecuencia.— **—forth** [hénsforθ], *adv.* (de aquí) en adelante, en lo sucesivo.

henchman [hénchmʌn], *s.* secuaz, paniaguado.

her [hœr], *pron.* la, le, a ella, (después de *prep.*) ella.—*a.* su, de ella.

herald [hérʌld], *s.* heraldo.—*vt.* anunciar, pregonar, proclamar.— **—ry** [-ri], *s.* heráldica, blasón.

herb [(h)œrb], *s.* hierba, yerba.

herd [hœrd], *s.* manada, rebaño, hato; piara; multitud.—*vi.* ir en manadas.—*vt.* reunir el ganado en rebaños.— **—sman** [hœrdzmʌn], *s.* pastor.

here [hir], *adv.* aquí; acá; por aquí; ahora, en este momento, en este punto; ¡presente!—*h. it is*, he aquí; aquí tiene Ud.—*h.'s to you!*, ¡a la salud de Ud!—*that is neither h. nor there*, eso no viene al caso.— **—abouts** [-ʌbáuts], *adv.* por aquí, por aquí cerca.— **—after** [-æftœ(r)], *adv.* (de aquí) en adelante, en lo sucesivo, en lo futuro.—*s.* el más allá.— **—by** [-bái], *adv.* por éstas, por la presente, por este medio.

hereditary [hiréditeri], *a.* hereditario.
—**heredity** [hiréditi], *s.* (biol.) herencia.

heresy [héresi], *s.* herejía.—**heretic** [héretįk], *s.* hereje.—*a.* herético.

heritage [héritįdž], *s.* herencia.

hermit [hœrmit], *s.* ermitaño.- —**age** [-idž], *s.* ermita.

hernia [hœrnįǎ], *s.* hernia.

hero [híroų], *s.* héroe; protagonista.- —**ic(al)** [hiróųik(ạl)], *a.* heróico, épico.- —**ine** [héroįn]. *s.* heroína, protagonista.- —**ism** [héroįzm], *s.* heroísmo, heroicidad; proeza.

heron [hérǫn], *s.* garza.

herring [hérįŋ]. *s.* arenque.

hers [hœrz]. *pron. pos.* suyo, suya, (de ella); el suyo, la suya, los suyos, las suyas (de ella).- —**elf** [hœrsélf], *pron.* ella misma. ella, sí misma.

hesitant [hézitạnt]. *a.* vacilante, indeciso.—**hesitate** [hézitejt], *vi.* vacilar, titubear.—**hesitation** [hezitéįšǫn], *s.* titubeo, vacilación.

heterogeneous [hetẹrǫdžínįʌs], *a.* heterogéneo.

hew [hiu], *vti.* [6] tajar, cortar, picar piedra; desbastar; labrar.—*to h. in pieces,* destrozar, destroncar.—*vti.* golpear.—*to h. right and left,* acuchillar a diestra y siniestra.

hey [hej], *interj.* ¡eh! ¡oiga! ¡digo!

hi [haj], *interj.* ¡hola!

hibernate [hájbœrnejt], *vi.* invernar.— **hibernation** [hajbœrnéįšǫn], *s.* invernada.

hiccough, hiccup [híkʌp], *s.* hipo.—*vi.* hipar, tener hipo.

hickory [híkǫri], *s.* nogal americano.

hid [hid], *pret.* y *pp.* de TO HIDE.

hidden [hídn], *pp.* de TO HIDE.—*a.* oculto, escondido, secreto.—**hide** [hajd], *vti.* [10] esconder, ocultar. —*vti.* esconderse, ocultarse; (con **out**) estarse escondido.—*s.* escondite; cuero, piel, pellejo.—**hideaway** [hájdạwej], *s.* escondite, escondrijo; fugitivo.

hideous [hídiʌs], *a.* horrible, espantoso, feo.

hierarchy [hájẹrarki], *s.* jerarquía.

hieroglyphic [hajẹrǫglífįk], *s.* y *a.* jeroglífico.

high [haj], *a.* alto; de alto; elevado; encumbrado o eminente, superior; solemne; supremo, sumo; vivo, intenso; arrogante; poderoso.—*h. altar,* altar mayor.—*h. and dry,* en seco.—*h. blood pressure,* hipertensión arterial.—*h.-brow,* intelectual.— *h. hat,* sombrero de copa.—*H. Mass,* misa cantada o mayor.—*h. priest,* sumo sacerdote.—*h. rank,* categoría, alto rango.—*h. school,* escuela se-

cundaria.—*h. sea,* mar gruesa.—*h. seas,* alta mar.—*h. words.* palabras ofensivas o ásperas.—*in h. gear,* (aut.) en directa.—*in h. terms,* en términos lisonjeros.—*it is h. time to.* ya es hora de.—*adv.* alto; en lo alto; altamente; muy, sumamente; a grande altura; arrogantemente; a precio elevado; lujosamente.—*h. and low,* de arriba abajo; por doquiera. —*h.-handed,* despótico, arbitrario.— *h.-minded,* magnánimo, noble, idealista.—*h.-priced,* caro.—*h.-seasoned,* picante.—*h.-sounding,* altisonante.— *s.* alza, subida; punto o lugar alto; valor o precio máximo.— —**ball** [hájbol], *s.* whiskey, ron, etc., mezclado con soda y hielo.- —**land** [-lạnd], *s.* región montañosa.—*pl.* tierras altas, montañas.- —**lander** [-lạndœ(r)], *s.* montañés de Escocia.— —**landish** [-lạndįš], *a.* montañés.— —**light** [-lajt], *vt.* realzar, hacer destacar, subrayar.—*s.* punto de destaque, o de resalto.- —**ly** [-lį], *adv.* altamente; levantadamente, elevadamente; sumamente; arrogantemente; ambiciosamente; encarecidamente.— —**ness** [-nįs], *s.* altura, elevación; celsitud; Alteza (título).- —**way** [-wej], *s.* carretera, calzada; camino real; vía pública.

hike [hajk], *s.* (fam.) caminata; marcha; excursión.—*vi.* dar una caminata o paseo largo; ir de excursión.—*vt.* levantar, arrastrar; aumentar de pronto.- —**r** [hájkœ(r)], *s.* excursionista.

hill [hil], *s.* collado, colina, cerro, cuesta, otero, altozano.—*vt.* aporcar. —*vi.* amontonarse.- —**man** [hílmạn], *s.* serrano, arribeño.- —**ock** [-ǫk], *s.* altillo, loma, montecillo, otero.- —**side** [-sajd], *s.* ladera, flanco de una colina.- —**top** [-tap], *s.* cima, cumbre de una colina.- —**y** [-į], *a.* montañoso, montuoso.

hilt [hilt], *s.* puño, empuñadura.—*up to the h.,* a fondo; por completo.

him [him], *pron.* le, (a, para, con, etc.) él.- —**self** [himsélf], *pron.* él, él mismo, se, sí, sí mismo.—*by h.,* solo, por sí, por su cuenta.—*for h.,* por su cuenta, por cuenta propia.—*he said to h.,* él mismo; en persona.—*he said to h.,* se dijo a sí mismo.

hind [hajnd], *a.* trasero, zaguero, posterior.—*h. foremost,* lo de atrás delante.—*s.* cierva.- —**brain** [hájndbrejn], *s.* cerebelo; parte posterior del encéfalo.- —**er** [híndœ(r)], *vt.* impedir, estorbar, obstaculizar; oponerse.—*a.* [hájndœ(r)], posterior, trasero.- —**ermost** [-œrmoųst], —**most** [-moųst], *a.* postrero, último.

hindrance [híndrəns], *s.* impedimento, obstáculo, estorbo.

Hindu [híndu], *s.* y *a.* hindú, indostánico.

hinge [hindź], *s.* gozne, gonce, bisagra; punto principal o capital.—*vt.* engoznar, poner goznes.—*vi.* girar sobre goznes.—*to h. on*, depender de.

hint [hint], *vt.* insinuar, indicar, sugerir.—*vi.* echar una indirecta.—*to h. at*, aludir a.—*s.* indirecta, sugestión, insinuación.

hip [hip], *s.* cadera.

hire [hair], *vt.* alquilar, dar o tomar en arriendo; arrendar; emplear; contratar; sobornar.—*to h. out*, alquilar(se).—*s.* alquiler, arriendo; salario; paga; jornal; soborno.

his [hiz], *a.* y *pron.* su, sus (de él); suyo, etc.; el suyo, la suya, los suyos, las suyas (de él).

Hispanic [hispǽnik], *a.* hispánico, hispano.

hiss [his], *vt.* y *vi.* silbar, (re)chiflar; sisear.—*s.* silbido, silba; siseo.

historian [histórjən], *s.* historiador.—**historic(al)** [histárik(əl)], *a.* histórico.—**history** [hístorj], *s.* historia.

hit [hit], *vti.* [9] dar, pegar, golpear; atinar, acertar; encontrar, dar con o en; denunciar.—*to h. it off*, avenirse, simpatizar; hacer buenas migas.—*vi.* rozar, chocar; acaecer o acontecer felizmente, salir bien; encontrar por casualidad; acertar.—*h. or miss*, al azar; atolondradamente.—*to h. against*, dar contra alguna cosa, chocar.—*to h. on o upon*, dar con, hallar; ocurrírsele a uno; acordarse de.—*pret.* y *pp.* de TO HIT.—*s.* golpe, choque, coscorrón; rasgo de ingenio.

hitch [hich], *vt.* atar, ligar; enganchar; mover a tirones.—*vi.* moverse a saltos; enredarse; congeniar, llevarse bien con otro.—*s.* alto, parada; tropiezo, dificultad; tirón.- —**hike** [híchhaik], *vi.* (fam.) viajar a pie pidiendo pasaje gratuito a los vehículos que pasan.

hither [híðœ(r)], *adv.* acá, hacia acá. —*a.* citerior.- —**most** [-moust], *a.* más cercano o próximo.- —**to** [-tu], *adv.* hasta ahora, hasta aquí.

hive [haiv], *s.* colmena; enjambre; emporio.—*pl.* urticaria.—*vt.* enjambrar; atesorar, acumular.—*vi.* vivir juntos como en colmena.

hoard [hord], *vt.* y *vi.* acaparar; atesorar, acumular y guardar.—*s.* provisión; montón; acumulación; tesoro escondido.- —**er** [hórdœ(r)], *s.* acaparador; atesorador.

hoarse [hors], *a.* ronco.- —**ness** [hórsnis], *s.* ronquera, carraspera.

hoary [hóri], *a.* blanco, blanquecino; cano, canoso; escarchado; venerable.

hobble [hábl], *vt.* poner trabas.—*vi.* cojear.—*s.* cojera, traba; dificultad, atolladero.

hobby [hábi], *s.* chifladura, afición, pasatiempo; trabajo que se hace por afición.

hobgoblin [hábgablin], *s.* duende, trasgo.

hock [hak], *s.* vino del Rin; corvejón, jarrete (del caballo, etc.); (anat.) corva.—*in h.*, (E.U., fam.) empeñado. —*vt.* (E.U., fam.) empeñar, dar en prenda.

hodgepodge [hádźpadź], *s.* mezcolanza, baturrillo.

hoe [hou], *s.* azada, azadón, escardillo. —*vt.* azadonar.

hog [hag], *s.* cochino, cerdo; (fam.) persona sucia, tragona o egoísta; (aer.) vuelta hacia abajo.- —**gish** [hágiś], *a.* porcino; egoísta; comilón.- —**gishness** [-iśnis], *s.* porquería, cochinada; glotonería; egoísmo.- —**shead** [hágzhed], *s.* pipa, tonel.

hoist [hoist], *vt.* alzar, elevar; izar, enarbolar.—*s.* cabria, pescante, grúa, montacargas; levantamiento, ascención.—*h. bridge*, puente levadizo.

hold [hould], *vti.* [10] tener, asir, coger, agarrar; retener, reservar; detener, contener; sostener, apoyar; tener de reserva; restringir; encerrar; mantener; tener cabida o capacidad para; opinar, juzgar, reputar, entender; poseer, ocupar, disfrutar; celebrar (sesión, reunión); continuar, seguir; conservar; guardar, observar; obligar; hacer (responsable, etc.).— *to h. a bet o wager*, apostar.—*to h. a candle to*, (fam.) poder compararse con.—*to h. at bay*, tener a raya. —*to h. back*, retener; contener.— *to h. down*, oprimir, tener sujeto; conservar, no perder.—*to h. forth*, expresar, publicar; mostrar.—*to h. in*, sujetar, refrenar, contener.—*to h. off*, apartar, alejar.—*to h. out*, ofrecer, proponer; extender.—*to h. over*, tener suspendido o en suspenso; diferir, aplazar; prolongar una nota musical.—*to h. sway*, gobernar, mandar.—*to h. up*, levantar, alzar; apoyar, sostener; asaltar para robar, atracar.—*vii.* valer, ser válido, estar en vigor; mantenerse firme, sostenerse, aguantar; seguir, proseguir; estar en posesión; refrenarse, abstenerse; aplicarse, ser aplicable.—*s.* presa, asimiento; asa, mango; influencia, dominio; freno; refugio; posesión; custodio; celda; (mus.) calderón.- —**er** [hóuldœ(r)], *s.* tenedor, posesor; mantenedor; asidero, mango, asa; porta-(*lamp h.*,

portalámpara, etc.); sostén: propietario; arrendatario; inquilino.— **h.** *of a bill,* tenedor de una letra. —**h.** *of a share,* accionista.- —**up** [-ʌp], *s.* atraco, asalto.

hole [houl], *s.* agujero, orificio; cavidad, hueco, hoyo; bache; perforación; pozo, charco (de un río, arroyo, etc.); cueva, madriguera, guarida (de animales); (fam.) atolladero, aprieto, brete.—*vt.* agujerear, taladrar, perforar; meter una bola de billar en la tronera.—*vi.* encuevarse; hacer un agujero u hoyo.

holiday [hálidei], *s.* día festivo, festividad.—*pl.* vacaciones, asueto.—*a.* alegre, festivo.

holiness [hóulinis], *s.* santidad, beatitud.—*His H.,* Su Santidad.

hollow [hálou], *a.* hueco, vacío; cóncavo; hundido; sordo (ruido); falso, insincero.—*h.-chested,* de pecho hundido.—*h.-hearted,* solapado. —**h.** *punch,* sacabocados.—**h.** *ware,* ollas, pucheros, marmitas.—*s.* cavidad, depresión, concavidad; canal, ranura; hueco, hoyo; valle; cañada. —*vt.* excavar; ahondar; ahuecar.- —**ness** [-nis], *s.* cavidad, oquedad, vaciedad; doblez, falsía.

holly [háli], *s.* acebo; agrifolio.- —**hock** [-hak], *s.* malva loca u hortense.

holster [hóulstœr(r)], *s.* pistolera, funda (de pistola).

holy [hóuli], *a.* santo, pío; puro, inmaculado; sacro, sagrado; consagrado, santificado; bendito.—*h. cross,* santa cruz.—*h. cup,* cáliz.—*h. orders,* órdenes sacerdotales.—*H. Ghost,* Espíritu Santo.—*h. rood,* crucifijo; santa cruz.—*h. water,* agua bendita. —*H. Week,* Semana Santa.—*H. Writ,* la Sagrada Escritura.

homage [hámidž], *s.* homenaje, reverencia, culto.—*to do* o *pay h.,* acatar, rendir homenaje.

home [houm], *s.* hogar, casa; morada; domicilio, residencia, habitación; asilo, albergue, refugio; (dep.) meta, límite o término.—*at h.,* en casa; en el país de uno; con toda comodidad; en su elemento.—*to hit* o *strike h.,* llegar al alma, herir en lo vivo.—*a.* doméstico, de casa, casero; nativo, natal; regional, del país; certero, que llega a la meta.—*adv.* a casa; en casa; al país o en la tierra de uno; en su lugar. —**land** [hóumlænd], *s.* patria, tierra natal.- —**less** [-lis], *a.* sin casa ni hogar; mostrenco.- —**like** [-laik], *a.* como en casa; sosegado y cómodo.- —**liness** [-linis], *s.* simpleza, sencillez; fealdad, mal aspecto.- —**ly** [-li], *a.* casero, doméstico; sencillo, llano; feo; rús-

tico, inculto, vulgar.- —**made** [-méid], *a.* casero, hecho en casa; fabricado en el país.- —**sick** [-sik], *a.* nostálgico.- —**sickness** [-siknis], *s.* nostalgia, añoranza.- —**stead** [-sted], *s.* casa de habitación y sus terrenos, heredad; hogar.- —**ward** [-wård], *adv.* hacia casa, hacia su país; de vuelta.—*h.-bound,* de regreso.- —**work** [-wœrk], *s.* trabajo, tarea, estudio, etc. para hacer en la casa.

homicidal [hámisaidəl], *a.* homicida. —**homicide** [hámisaid], *s.* homicidio; homicida.

homogeneity [houmodženíiti], *s.* homogeneidad.—**homogeneous** [houmodžíniəs], *a.* homogéneo.—**homogenize** [homádženaiz], *vt.* homogenizar.

homosexual [homoséksuəl], *a.* homosexual, por el propio sexo, por individuos del mismo sexo.—*s.* homosexual; marica.

Honduran [handúrən], *a.* **y** *s.* hondureño.

hone [houn], *s.* piedra de afilar.—*vt.* afilar, asentar, pulir, esmerilar.

honest [ánist], *a.* honrado, probo, recto; sincero; equitativo; honesta (mujer).- —**ly** [-li], *adv.* honradamente; de veras; francamente; honestamente.- —**y** [-i], *s.* honradez, probidad; franqueza; honestidad; bonhomía.

honey [háni], *s.* miel de abejas; dulzura; querido, querida, mi cariño, etc.- —**comb** [-koum], *s.* panal de miel.- —**ed** [-d], *a.* dulce, meloso, melifluo.- —**moon** [-mun], *s.* luna de miel.- —**suckle** [-sʌkl], *s.* madreselva.

honk [hank], *s.* pitazo, bocinazo (automóvil); graznido.—*vt.* y *vi.* pitar o sonar la bocina; graznar.

honor [ánor(r)], *s.* honor, honra; honradez, rectitud; cargo, dignidad; lauro.—*pl.* distinción (en estudios, etc.).—*h. bright,* (fam.) de veras, a fe de caballero.—*on* o *upon my h.,* por mi fe, por mi palabra.—*your H.,* usía, vuestra señoría.—*vt.* honrar; laurear, condecorar; respetar.- —**able** [-əbl], *a.* honorable; pundonoroso; honrado; honorífico, honroso, (**H.**) honorable (tratamiento).- —**ary** [-eri], *a.* honorario, honorífico; honroso.

hood [hud], *s.* capucha, capucho, caperuza; muceta; fuelle de carruaje; (aut.) cubierta del motor; cubierta, tapa; campana del hogar.—*vt.* cubrir con caperuza, capucha, etc.; tapar, ocultar.

hoodoo [húdu], *s.* mal de ojo.—*vt.* hacer mal de ojo; traer mala suerte.

hoof [huf], *s.* casco, uña (del caballo,

etc.); pezuña; animal ungulado.—
on the h., en pie (ganado), vivo.

hook [huk], *s.* gancho, garabato, garfio;
anzuelo; grapón; garra; corchete;
atractivo, aliciente; (mús.) rabo de
una corchea.—*vt.* enganchar; atraer,
engatusar; dar una cornada, coger;
pescar; encorvar.—*to h. up*, conectar;
enganchar.— **—ed** [-t], *a.* engan-
chado; encorvado, ganchudo, gan-
choso.— **—up** [húkʌp], *s.* (rad.)
trasmisión en cadena; cadena de
emisoras.— **—y** [-i], *a.* ganchudo.—
to play h., hacer novillos o rabona,
no ir a la escuela o a la clase.

hooligan [húligan], *s.* rufián, truhán.—
a. de rufianes, truhanesco.— **—ism**
[-izm], *s.* truhanería, rufianismo.

hoop [hup], *s.* aro; fleje, zuncho;
(mec.) collar(ín); anilla, argolla;
sortija; miriñaque; grito.—*vt.* poner
aro a; enzunchar; ceñir.—*vi.* gritar;
ojear.

hoot [hut], *vi.* gritar, ulular, huchear;
dar grita; sonar la bocina o el pito.—
vt. ridiculizar, recibir con risotada,
abuchear.—*s.* grita, ruido, clamor,
chillido.— **—ing** [hútiŋ], *s.* grita,
rechifla, abucheo.

hop [hap], *vti.* [1] saltar, brincar;
(fam.) alzar el vuelo en (un avión),
poner en marcha.—*vii.* saltar en
un pie, andar a saltitos; cojear.—*s.*
salto, brinco; (fam.) baile; lúpulo;
(aer.) trayecto de vuelo; (fam.)
vuelo.—*pl.* (com.) lúpulo.

hope [houp], *s.* esperanza; expectativa.
—*in hopes*, en o con la esperanza.—*vt.*
y vi. esperar, tener esperanza.—*to h.
against h.*, esperar lo imposible.—
—ful [hóupful], *a.* esperanzado, confiado; que da esperanza o promete.
—*s.* (fam.) joven que promete.—
—fully [-fuli], *adv.* con esperanza.-
—less [-lis], *a.* desahuciado; desesperante, desespera(nza)do; incurable; irremediable.— **—lessness**
[-lisnis], *s.* desesperanza; falta de
esperanza o remedio.

horde [hord], *s.* horda; enjambre; hato
o manada; muchedumbre.

horizon [horáizon], *s.* horizonte.— **—tal**
[harizántal], *a.* y *s.* horizontal.-
—tality [harizantáliti], *s.* horizonta-
lidad.

hormone [hórmoun], *s.* hormona.

horn [horn], *s.* cuerno, asta; tentáculo;
palpo o antena; (mus.) trompa;
corneta de monte o cuerno de caza;
bocina.—*pl.* cornamenta.—*vt.* poner
cuernos; dar una cornada; dar una
cencerrada.

hornet [hórnit], *s.* avispón, moscardón.

horrible [háribl], *a.* horrible, horroroso.— **horrid** [hárid], *a.* horrible,

hórrido; ofensivo, dañoso.—**horrify**
[hárifai], *vti.* [7] horrorizar.—**horrifying** [hárifaiiŋ], *a.* horripilante.
—horror [háro(r)], *s.* horror.—*h.
-stricken*, horrorizado.

horse [hors], *s.* caballo; (mil.) caballería; potro (de carpintero, gimnasia, etc.); caballete, burro, banco.
—*h. breaker*, domador de caballos.
—*h. dealer*, chalán.—*h. race*, carrera
de caballos.—*h. racing*, carreras de
caballos.—*h. sense*, (fam.) gramática
parda, sentido común.—*h. show*,
concurso hípico.—*h. thief*, cuatrero.—
—back [hórsbæk], *s.* lomo de caballo
o asiento del jimete.—*to ride h.*,
montar a caballo.— **—fly** [-flai], *s.*
tábano.— **—hide** [-haid], *s.* piel de
caballo.— **—laugh(ter)** [-læf(tœ(r))],
s. risotada, carcajada.— **—man** [-man],
s. jinete.— **—manship** [-manʃip], *s.*
equitación.— **—power** [-pauœ(r)], *s.*
caballo de fuerza.— **—radish** [-rædiʃ],
s. rábano picante o rústico.— **—shoe**
[-ʃu], *s.* herradura.— **—tail** [-teil], *s.*
cola de caballo.— **—whip** [-hwip], *s.*
látigo, fuete, fusta.—*vti.* [1] dar
fuetazos, azotar con el látigo, etc.—
—woman [-wuman], *s.* amazona.
—horsiness [hórsinis], *s.* afición a
los caballos.—**horsy** [hórsi], *a.* caballar, caballuno; hípico, aficionado a
caballos.

hose [houz], *s.* calceta; medias o
calzas; manguera, manga de bomba
o de riego; tubo flexible de goma.—
h. reel, carretel de manguera.—

hosiery [hóuʒœri], *s.* calcetería.

hospice [háspis], *s.* hospicio.

hospitable [háspitabl], *a.* hospitalario.-
—ness [-nis], *s.* hospitalidad.—
hospital [háspital], *s.* hospital.—
hospitality [haspitáliti], *s.* hospitalidad.

host [houst], *s.* hospedero, huésped;
anfitrión; hueste; multitud; (H.) (igl.)
hostia.

hostage [hástidʒ], *s.* rehén.

hostess [hóustis], *s.* posadera, meso-
nera; anfitriona; (aer.) azafata.

hostile [hástil], *a.* hostil, enemigo,
adverso.— **hostility** [hastíliti], *s.* hostilidad.—*pl.* (actos de) guerra.

hot [hat], *a.* caliente, cálido; caluroso;
ardiente, fogoso; picante, acre;
violento, furioso; (fam.) intolerable;
en caliente; (fam.) cercano (de algo
que se busca).—*h.-blooded*, apasionado.—*h. dog*, (fam.) = FRANK-
FURTER.—*h.-headed*, fogoso, exaltado.

hotel [hotél], *s.* hotel.—*h. keeper* o
manager, hotelero, fondista.

hothouse [háthous], *s.* estufa, invernadero.

hound [haund], *s.* sabueso, podenco;

hombre vil.—*vt.* cazar con perros; soltar los perros; seguir la pista; perseguir; azuzar.

hour [aυr], *s.* hora.—*pl.* horas (rezos). —*h. hand,* horario (del reloj).—**-ly** [áυrli], *adv.* a cada hora; por horas; frecuentemente.—*a.* frecuente, por horas.

house [haυs], *s.* casa, domicilio, vivienda; familia, linaje; casilla (tablero de damas y ajedrez); casa comercial, razón social; cámara de un cuerpo legislativo; (teat.) sala, público; (mec.) caja, cubierta.—*H. of Commons,* (*Lords, Peers, Representatives*), Cámara de los Comunes, (Lores, Pares, Cámara de Representantes).—*vt.* albergar, alojar; poner a cubierto; almacenar.— **-breaker** [háυsbrejkœ(r)], *s.* ladrón que escala una casa o la violenta para entrar.— **-hold** [-hoυld], *s.* casa, familia.— **-keeper** [-kipœ(r)], *s.* ama de gobierno o de llaves; mujer de casa.— **-keeping** [-kipiŋ], *s.* manejo de casa, incluyendo la cocina.—*a.* doméstico, casero, provisto de facilidades para cocinar.— **-top** [-tap], *s.* tejado, techo, azotea.— **-wife** [-waif], *s.* ama de casa; madre de familia.— **-work** [-wœrk], *s.* tareas domésticas. **-housing** [háυziŋ], *s.* alojamiento, vivienda; almacenaje.

hove [hoυv], *pret. y pp.* de TO HEAVE.

hovel [hável], *s.* cobertizo, choza, cabaña, casucha, tugurio.

hover [hávœ(r)], *vt.* cubrir con las alas.—*vi.* revolotear; cernerse (las aves, y fig.), rondar; estar suspenso; dudar.— **-ing** [-iŋ], *s.* revoloteo.

how [haυ], *adv.* cómo; cuán, cuánto; a cómo.—*h. about it?* ¿qué le parece? ¿y si lo hiciéramos?—*h. do you do?* ¿cómo le va? ¿cómo está usted?— *h. early?* ¿cuándo, a más tardar?— *h. far?* ¿a qué distancia? ¿hasta dónde?—*h. late?* ¿a qué hora? ¿hasta qué hora? ¿cuándo?—*h. long?* ¿cuánto tiempo? ¿cuánto demorará?—*h. many?* ¿cuántos?—*h. much?* ¿cuánto? —*h. now?* ¿y bien? ¡pues qué? ¿qué significa eso?—*h. often?* ¿con qué frecuencia? ¿cuántas veces?—*h. pretty!* ¡qué bonito!—*h. so?* ¿cómo así? —*h. soon?* ¿cuándo? ¿con qué rapidez?—*h. well!* ¡qué bien!—*s.* cómo, modo, manera.— **-beit** [haυbíjt], *adv.* sea como fuere, así como así; no obstante.— **-ever** [haυévœ(r)], *adv.* como quiera que, de cualquier modo; por muy.—*conj.* no obstante, sin embargo.

howitzer [háυjtsœ(r)], *s.* (arti.) obús.

howl [haυl], *vi.* aullar, dar alaridos; ulular; rugir; bramar.—*vt.* gritar;

condenar o echar a gritos.—*s.* aullido; alarido; gemido; rugido; bramido.

hub [hΛb], *s.* cubo de la rueda; por extensión, centro, eje; calzo.— **-bub** [hΛbΛb], *s.* grita, alboroto, bulla.

huckster [hΛkstœ(r)], *s.* vendedor ambulante; sujeto ruin.

huddle [hΛdl], *vt.* amontonar desordenadamente; atrabancar.—*vi.* acurrucarse; apiñarse.—*s.* tropel, confusión; (fam.) junta o reunión secreta.

hue [hiu], *s.* matiz, tinte; grita, clamor. —*h. and cry,* alarma, vocerío.— *many-hued,* matizado.

hug [hΛg], *vti.* [1] abrazar; abrazarse a; navegar muy cerca de la costa.— *to h. one's self,* congratularse.—*s.* abrazo apretado.

huge [hiudž], *a.* inmenso, enorme, vasto, colosal.— **-ness** [hiúdžnįs], *s.* enormidad, inmensidad.

hulk [hΛlk], *s.* casco de barco; barco viejo; armatoste.— **-ing** [hΛlkiŋ], *a.* tosco, grueso.

hull [hΛl], *s.* cáscara, corteza; vaina de legumbre; casco (de un buque); flotador (de aeroplano); armazón.—*vt.* mondar, descascarar; desvainar; deshollejar.

hum [hΛm], *vti.* [1] canturrear, tararear.—*vii.* zumbar; susurrar.—*s.* zumbido; susurro; voz inarticulada (¡hum!); (fam.) engaño, filfa, chasco.

human [hiúman], *a.* humano.—*h. race,* género humano.—*s.* mortal, ser humano.— **-e** [hiuméjn], *a.* humano, benévolo, compasivo; humanitario.— **-itarian** [hiumænįtérjan], *a.* humanitario.—*s.* filántropo.— **-itarianism** [hiumænįtérjanįzm], *s.* humanitarismo.— **-ity** [hiumæniti], *s.* humanidad.—*pl.* humanidades.— **-ize** [hiúmanajz], *vt. y vi.* humanizar(se).— **-kind** [hiúmankaind], *s.* humanidad, género humano.

humble [hΛmbl], *a.* humilde, modesto. —*vt.* humillar, someter.—*vi.* bajar o doblar la cerviz.— **-ness** [-nįs], *s.* humildad.

humbug [hΛmbΛg], *s.* farsa, patraña, fraude; farsante.

humdrum [hΛmdrΛm], *a.* monótono, pesado, cansado.—*s.* fastidio, lata, aburrimiento; posma.

humid [hiúmid], *a.* húmedo.— **-ify** [hiumídjfaį], *vti.* [7] humedecer.— **-ity** [hiumídįti], *s.* humedad.

humiliate [hiumíljejt], *vt.* humillar.— **-humiliation** [hiumįljéįşơn], *s.* humillación.—**-humility** [hiumíljiti], *s.* humildad, sumisión.

humming [hΛmiŋ], *s.* zumbido; susurro; canturreo, tarareo.—*a.* zumbador; (fam.) muy activo, intenso, grande, etc.—**hummingbird** [hΛmiŋ-

bœrd], **s.** colibrí, pájaro mosca, tominejo.

humor [hjúmǫ(r)], **s.** humor, carácter, índole; humorada, fantasía, capricho; humorismo; agudeza, chiste, jocosidad; (med.) humor.—*to be in a bad h.* o *out of h.*, estar de mal humor.— *vt.* contemporizar, seguir el humor, dar gusto; consentir, mimar.- —**ous** [-ʌs], **a.** humorístico.

hump [hʌmp], **s.** giba, joroba.—*vi.* encorvarse, doblar la espalda.- —**back** [hʌmpbæk], **s.** giba, joroba; jorobado.- —**backed** [-bækt], **a.** jorobado, giboso, corcovado.- —**y** [-i], **a.** giboso.

hunch [hʌnch], **vt.** empujar, dar empellones; doblar la espalda.—*vi.* moverse o avanzar a tirones o a sacudidas; abalanzarse.—**s.** giba, corcova; pedazo o trozo grueso; (fam.) corazonada, presentimiento.- —**back** [hʌnchbæk], **s.** joroba; jorobado.- —**backed** [-bækt], **a.** jorobado.

hundred [hʌndrẹd], **a.** cien(to).—**s.** ciento; (arit.) centena, centenar.— *by hundreds*, a (o por) centenares.— *by the h.*, por ciento(s); por centenares.- —**fold** [-fould], **s.** céntuplo.- —**th** [-θ], **a.** y **s.** centésimo, céntimo; ciento (ordinal).- —**weight** [-weit], **s.** quintal. Ver Tabla.

hung [hʌŋ], *pret.* y *pp.* de TO HANG (colgar).

Hungarian [hʌŋgériạn], **a.** y **s.** húngaro.- —**s.** lengua húngara.

hunger [hʌ́ŋgœ(r)], **s.** hambre.—*h. strike*, huelga de hambre.—*vt.* hambrear.—*vi.* hambrear, tener hambre. —*to h. for*, anhelar, tener hambre de. —**hungry** [hʌ́ŋgri], **a.** hambriento; deseoso; estéril, pobre.—*to be o feel h.*, tener hambre, estar hambriento.

hunk [hʌŋk], **s.** (fam.) buen pedazo; rebanada gruesa.

hunt [hʌnt], **vt.** cazar; perseguir, seguir; recorrer buscando.—*to h. up*, buscar.—*to h. up and down*, buscar por todas partes.—*vi.* cazar; hacer un registro minucioso; buscar.—*to h. after*, buscar, anhelar.—*to h. counter*, ir contra la pista.—**s.** caza, cacería; acosamiento.- —**er** [hʌntœ(r)], **s.** cazador, montero; podenco; caballo de caza.- —**ing** [-iŋ], **s.** montería, caza, cacería.—*h.-box*, pabellón de caza.- —**ress** [-ris], **s.** cazadora.- —**sman** [-smạn], **s.** montero, cazador.

hurdle [hœrdl], **s.** valla (portátil); (fig.) obstáculo.—*pl.* (dep.) carrera de obstáculos.

hurdy-gurdy [hœrdi gœrdi], **s.** organillo; zanfona.

hurl [hœrl], **vt.** tirar, lanzar, arrojar,

echar; proferir.—*vr.* lanzarse, abalanzarse.—**s.** tiro, lanzamiento.

hurrah [hụrá], *interj.* ¡viva! ¡hurra!— *vt.* y *vi.* aclamar, vitorear.

hurricane [hœrikein], **s.** huracán, ciclón.

hurried [hœrid], **a.** precipitado, apresurado, hecho de prisa.—**hurry** [hœri], *vti.* y *vii.* [7] apresurar(se); dar(se) prisa; obrar a la carrera o con precipitación.—*to h. after*, correr detrás o en pos de.—*to h. away*, salir precipitadamente.—*to h. back*, volver de prisa; apresurarse a volver.—*to h. off*, huir, salir o hacer marchar de prisa.—*to h. on*, apresurar, precipitar; impulsar; precipitarse, apresurarse.—*to h. over*, (hacer) pasar rápidamente; despachar, expedir.—*to h. up*, apresurarse, darse prisa.—**s.** prisa, premura, precipitación, apuro.—*there is no h. about it*, no corre prisa.—*to be in a h.*, tener prisa.

hurt [hœrt], *vti.* [9] dañar, hacer mal o daño, lastimar, herir; injuriar, ofender; perjudicar.—*to h. one's feelings*, herirle a uno el amor propio, ofenderlo.—*vii.* doler.—*pret.* y *pp.* de TO HURT.—**s.** lesión, herida, contusión; mal, daño, perjuicio, detrimento.—*a.* lastimado, herido, perjudicado.

husband [hʌ́zbạnd], **s.** marido, esposo.- —**ry** [-ri], **s.** labranza, agricultura.

hush [hʌ́ʃ], **vt.** apaciguar, aquietar; hacer callar.—*to h. up*, tapar, ocultar; mantener secreto.—*vi.* estar quieto, callar, enmudecer, estar callado.—**s.** silencio, quietud.—*h. money*, dinero para soborno o cohecho.—*very h.-h.*, muy secreto.

husk [hʌsk], **s.** cáscara, vaina, pellejo, hollejo; bagazo; desperdicio.—*vt.* descascarar, desvainar, pelar, mondar, despellejar, deshollejar.- —**y** [hʌ́ski], **a.** cascarudo; ronco.—**a.** y **s.** (fam.) fuerte, fornido.—**s.** perro esquimal; un dialecto esquimal.

hussy [hʌ́si], **s.** sota, mujerzuela.

hustle [hʌ́sl], **vt.** mezclar, confundir; empujar, atropellar, sacudir.—*vi.* andar a empellones; (fam.) patear, moverse con actividad.—*h. and bustle*, vaivén.

hut [hʌt], **s.** choza, cabaña, barraca; cobertizo; (Am.) bohío.

hyacinth [hájạsinθ], **s.** jacinto.

hybrid [hájbrid], **a.** y **s.** híbrido.

hyena [hajínạ], **s.** hiena.

hydrant [hájdrạnt], **s.** boca de riego.— **hydraulic(al)** [hajdrólik(ạl)], **a.** hidráulico.—**hydrocarbon** [hajdrocárbon], **s.** hidrocarburo.—**hydrogen** [hájdrodžin], **s.** hidrógeno.—**hydroplane** [-plein], **s.** hidroplano.

hygiene [háidźin], hygienics [haidźiéniks], s. higiene.

hymen [háimen], s. himeneo; himen.

hymn [him], s. himno.

hyphen [háifen], s. raya, guión.

hypocrisy [hipákrisi], s. hipocresía.— hypocrite [hípokrit], s. hipócrita.— hypocritical [hipokrítikal], a. hipócrita.

hypothesis [haipáθesis], s. hipótesis, supuesto.

hysteria [histíria], s. histeria.—hysteric(al) [histérik(al)], a. histérico.— hysterics [histériks], s. = HYSTERIA.

I

I [ai], pron. pers. yo.

Iberian [aibírian], a. ibérico.—a. y s. ibero.

ice [ais], s. hielo; sorbete.—i. box, nevera, refrigerador.—i. breaker, buque rompehielos.—i. cream, helado, mantecado.—i. water, agua helada.—vt. helar; cubrir con escarcha (un pastel); enfriar con hielo.— —berg [áisbœrg], s. témpano flotante de hielo.— —d [-t], a. congelado; enfriado con hielo.

Icelander [áislandœ(r)], s. islandés.— Icelandic [aisléndik], a. y s. islandés. —s. lengua islandesa.

iceman [áismæn], s. nevero, vendedor de hielo.—icicle [áisikl], s. carámbano.—iciness [áisinis], s. frigidez; calidad de glacial.—icing [áisin], s. (dulcería) alcorza, adorno de azúcar. —icy [áisi], a. helado, frío, álgido.

idea [aidíá], s. idea.— —l [aidíal], s. y a. ideal; prototipo.— —lism [aidíalizm], s. idealismo.— —list [aidíalist], s. idealista.— —lize [aidíalaiz], vt. idealizar.

identical [aidéntikal], a. idéntico.— identification [aidentifikéíšon], s. identificación.—identify [aidéntifai], vti. [7] identificar.—identity [aidéntiti], s. identidad.

ideological [aidioládźikal], a. ideológico. —ideology [aidiálodźi], s. ideología.

idiocy [ídioṣi], s. idiotez; imbecilidad.

idiom [ídiom], s. modismo, idiotismo; habla, lenguaje.

idiot [ídiot], s. idiota.— —ic [idiátik], a. idiota.

idle [áidl], a. ocioso; sin colocación (dinero, etc.); perezoso, haragán; inútil, vano, frívolo.—i. pulley, polea de guía; polea de tensión.—i. wheel, rueda de transmisión.—vi. holgazanear o haraganear; holgar, estar ocioso; (aut.) funcionar el motor sin embragar.—vt. (generalmente con away) gastar ociosamente; dejar sin trabajo.— —ness [-nis], s. ocio-

sidad, ocio; pereza, holgazanería, haraganería; inutilidad.- —r [áidlœ(r)], s. holgazán, perezoso.—idly [áidli], adv. ociosamente; desidiosamente; inútilmente.

idol [áidol], s. ídolo.- —ater [aidálatœ(r)], s. idólatra.- —atry [aidálatri], s. idolatría.- —ize [áidolaiz], vt. idolatrar.

if [if], conj. si; supuesto que; con tal que; aunque; aun cuando.—as i., como si.—s. hipótesis, suposición; condición.

ignite [ignáit], vt. encender, pegar fuego.—vi. encenderse, inflamarse. —ignition [igníšon], s. ignición; encendido (del motor).

ignoble [ignóubl], a. innoble, indigno; bajo.

ignorance [ígnorans], s. ignorancia; falta de cultura.—ignorant [ígnorant]. a. ignorante.—ignore [ignór], vt. desconocer, pasar por alto, no hacer caso de; desairar; ignorar.

illegal [ilígal], a. ilegal, ilícito.- —ity [iligæliti], s. ilegalidad.

illegible [ilédźibl], a. ilegible.

illegitimacy [ilidźítimaṣi], s. ilegitimidad.—illegitimate [ilidźítimit], a. ilegítimo.

ill [il], a. enfermo; malo; dañino.—i. breeding, grosería, mala educación.— i. nature, mala disposición; malevolencia.—i. turn, mala jugada.—i. will, mala voluntad, malquerencia, ojeriza.—s. calamidad; mal.—adv. mal, malamente.—i. at ease, intranquilo, ansioso, inquieto; confundido.—i.-bred, malcriado, descortés.—i.-contrived, mal pensado, mal dispuesto.—i.-disposed, descontento; malintencionado.—i.-favored, feo, repulsivo.—i.-natured, avieso.—i.-shaped, malhecho.—i.-spoken of, de mala reputación.—i.-tempered, de malas pulgas, de mal genio.—i.-will, rencor, malquerencia.—to i.-treat, maltratar.— to take (it) i., tomar a mal.

illicit [ilísit], a. ilícito; ilegal.

illiteracy [ilíteraṣi], s. analfabetismo; ignorancia.—illiterate [ilíterit], a. y s. analfabeto; ignorante.

illness [ílnis], s. enfermedad, mal.

illogical [iládźikal], a. ilógico.

illuminate [iljúminejt], vt. iluminar, alumbrar; aclarar, esclarecer.—illumination [iljuminéíšon], s. iluminación, alumbrado; (b.a.) iluminación en colores.

illusion [iljúźon], s. ilusión.—to cause i., ilusionar.—illusive [iljúsiv], a. ilusorio, ilusivo.—illusory [iljúsori], a. ilusorio; engañoso.

illustrate [ilʌstrejt], vt. ilustrar, explicar, esclarecer con ejemplos.—illus-

tration [iᴧstréiɕɘn], *s.* ejemplo, aclaración; (b.a.) grabado, ilustración, lámina.—**illustrator** [[ᴧstrejtǫ(r)], *s.* ilustrador.—**illustrious** [ilᴧstrɪᴧs], *a.* ilustre, preclaro.

image [ímidɮ], *s.* imagen.— —**ry** [-ri], *s.* fantasía; conjunto de imágenes.—**imaginable** [imǽdɮinᴀbl], *a.* imaginable.—**imaginary** [imǽdɮineri], *a.* imaginario.—**imagination** [imædɮinéiɕɘn], *s.* imaginación; inventiva.—**imaginative** [imǽdɮineitiv], *a.* imaginativo; imaginario.—**imagine** [imǽdɮin], *vt.* imaginarse, figurarse. —*vi.* imaginar.

imbecile [ímbisil], *a.* y *s.* imbécil.—**imbecility** [imbisíliti], *s.* imbecilidad.

imbibe [imbáib], *vt.* embeber, absorber; empapar(se), saturarse de.

imitate [ímiteit], *vt.* imitar, remedar.—**imitation** [imitéiɕɘn], *s.* imitación.— *a.* de imitación.—**imitator** [ímiteitǫ(r)], *s.* imitador.

immaculate [imǽkyulit], *a.* inmaculado, sin mancha; impecable.

immaterial [imatíriᴀl], *a.* inmaterial, incorpóreo.—*to be i.*, no importar, ser indiferente.

immature [imachúr], *a.* inmaturo, verde; prematuro.

immediate [imídiit], *a.* inmediato, cercano; próximo.— —**ly** [-li], *adv.* inmediatamente, en seguida, en el acto.

immense [iméns], *a.* inmenso, vasto.—**immensity** [iménsiti], *s.* inmensidad.

immerse [imǫrs], *vt.* sumergir; anegar, sumir.—**immersion** [imǫ́rɕɘn], *s.* inmersión, sumersión; bautismo por inmersión.

immigrant [ímigrᴀnt], *a.* y *s.* inmigrante.—**immigrate** [ímigreit], *vi.* inmigrar.—**immigration** [imigréiɕɘn], *s.* inmigración.

imminent [íminᴇnt], *a.* inminente.

immobile [imóubil], *a.* inmóvil, inmovible.—**immobility** [imoubíliti], *s.* inmovilidad.—**immobilize** [imóubilaiz], *vt.* inmovilizar.

immodest [imádist], *a.* inmodesto; indecoroso, indecente; atrevido.— —**y** [-i], *s.* inmodestia; indecencia, impudicia.

immoral [imárᴀl], *a.* inmoral, licencioso, depravado.— —**ity** [imorǽliti], *s.* inmoralidad.

immortal [imórtᴀl], *a.* y *s.* inmortal.— —**ity** [imortǽliti], *s.* inmortalidad.— —**ize** [imórtᴀlaiz], *vt.* inmortalizar.

immovable [imúvᴀbl], *a.* inmóvil, inmovible, inamovible; impasible; inmutable; (for.) inmueble.—*s. pl.* inmuebles, bienes raíces.

immune [imiún], *a.* y *s.* inmune.—**immunity** [imiúniti], *s.* inmunidad.

—immunization [imiunizéiɕɘn], *s.* inmunización.—**immunize** [ímiunaiz], *vt.* inmunizar.

imp [imp], *s.* diablillo, trasgo.

impact [ímpækt], *s.* impacto, choque.

impair [impér], *vt.* empeorar, dañar, perjudicar, menoscabar, deteriorar.— —**ment** [-mᴇnt], *s.* empeoramiento, deterioro, menoscabo.

impart [impárt], *vt.* impartir, comunicar, dar.

impartial [impárɕᴀl], *a.* imparcial.— —**ity** [imparɕiǽliti], *s.* imparcialidad.

impassable [impǽsᴀbl], *a.* intransitable, impracticable; insuperable.

impassion [impǽɕɘn], *vt.* apasionar; conmover o afectar fuertemente.— —**ed** [-d], *a.* apasionado, vehemente, extremoso.

impassive [impǽsiv], *a.* impasible.

impatience [impéiɕᴇns], *s.* impaciencia.—**impatient** [impéiɕᴇnt], *a.* impaciente.

impeach [impích], *vt.* acusar (a un funcionario ante un tribunal); poner en tela de juicio; interpelar, residenciar.— —**ment** [-mᴇnt], *s.* acusación; imputación, residencia.

impeccable [impékᴀbl], *a.* impecable.

impede [impíd], *vt.* impedir, estorbar, dificultar.—**impediment** [impédimᴇnt], *s.* impedimento; obstrucción, traba, cortapisa.

impel [impél], *vti.* [1] impeler, impulsar; abalanzar.

impending [impéndiŋ], *a.* inminente; pendiente; amenazante.

impenetrable [impénitrᴀbl], *a.* impenetrable.

impenitent [impénitᴇnt], *a.* impenitente.

imperative [impérᴀtiv], *a.* imperativo, imperioso, imprescindible.— *s.* mandato perentorio; (gram.) imperativo.

imperceptible [impǫrséptibl], *a.* imperceptible.

imperfect [impǫrfikt], *a.* imperfecto, defectuoso.— —**ion** [impǫrfékɕɘn], *s.* imperfección, defecto.

imperial [impíriᴀl], *a.* imperial.— —**ism** [-izm], *s.* imperialismo.— —**ist** [-ist], *s.* imperialista.

imperious [impíriᴧs], *a.* imperioso.

impersonal [impǫrsᴏnᴀl], *a.* impersonal.

impersonate [impǫrsᴏneit], *vt.* personificar; (teat.) representar; imitar.—**impersonation** [impǫrsᴏnéiɕɘn], *s.* personificación; (teat.) representación, papel; imitación.

impertinence [impǫrtinᴇns], **impertinency** [impǫrtinᴇnsi], *s.* impertinencia; insolencia.—**impertinent** [impǫrtinᴇnt], *a.* impertinente; insolente, atrevido.

imperturbable [impœrtœ́rbạbl], *a.* imperturbable.

impervious [impœ́rvịʌs], *a.* impermeable, impenetrable, refractario.

impetuosity [impechụʌ́sịti], *s.* ímpetu, impetuosidad.—**impetuous** [impéchụʌs], *a.* impetuoso.—**impetus** [ímpịtʌs], *s.* ímpetu.

impiety [impáịeti], *s.* impiedad, irreligiosidad.—**impious** [ímpịʌs], *a.* impío.

implacable [impléịkạbl], *a.* implacable, inexorable.

implement [ímplịmẹnt], *s.* herramienta, utensilio; instrumento (de guerra, etc.).—*pl.* utensilios, útiles, aperos, enseres.—*vt.* poner por obra, poner en ejecución, cumplir.

implicate [ímplịkeịt], *vt.* implicar, envolver; enredar.—**implication** [implịkéịșọn], *s.* deducción; complicación.

implicit [implísịt], *a.* implícito, sobrentendido, tácito.—*i. faith*, fe ciega.

implore [implór], *vt.* implorar, suplicar, rogar.

imply [impláị], *vti.* [7] querer decir; significar, denotar, importar.

impolite [impoláịt], *a.* descortés; grosero.

import [impórt], *vt.* (com.) importar; denotar, significar; interesar.—*vi.* convenir, tener importancia.—*s.* [ímport], sentido, significación; importancia, valor.—*pl.* (com.) artículos importados.—**ance** [impórtạns], *s.* importancia.—**ant** [impórtạnt], *a.* importante.—**ation** [importéịșọn], *s.* (com.) importación; artículo importado.—**er** [impórtœ(r)], *s.* importador.

importune [importịún], *vt.* y *vi.* importunar, instar, porfiar, machacar.

impose [impóụz], *vt.* imponer; obligar a aceptar.—*to i. on* o *upon,* abusar de; engañar.—**imposing** [impóụzịŋ], *a.* imponente; solemne, tremendo.—**imposition** [impozíșọn], *s.* imposición; impuesto, carga.

impossibility [impasịbílịti], *s.* imposibilidad.—**impossible** [impásịbl], *a.* imposible.

impostor [impástọ(r)], *s.* impostor, embaucador.—**imposture** [impáschụ(r)], *s.* impostura.

impotence [ímpotẹns], *s.* impotencia.—**impotent** [ímpotẹnt], *a.* impotente.

impoverish [impávœrịș], *vt.* empobrecer, depauperar.—**ment** [-mẹnt], *s.* empobrecimiento, depauperación.

impracticable [impráktịkạbl], *a.* impracticable, intransitable; intratable; irrazonable.

impregnate [imprégneịt], *vt.* impregnar;

fecundizar, empreñar.—*a.* impregnado; embarazada, preñada.

impress [imprés], *vt.* imprimir, grabar, estampar; marcar; impresionar.—*s.* [ímpres], impresión, señal, huella.—**ion** [impréșọn], *s.* impresión; marca, señal.—**ionable** [impréșọnạbl], *a.* impresionable, susceptible.—**ive** [imprésịv], *a.* impresionante; grandioso, imponente.

imprint [imprínt], *vt.* imprimir, estampar.—*s.* [ímprint], impresión, marca, huella; pie de imprenta.

imprison [imprízọn], *vt.* encarcelar, aprisionar.—**ment** [-mẹnt], *s.* prisión, encarcelación.

improbable [imprábạbl], *a.* improbable.

improper [imprápœ(r)], *a.* impropio; incorrecto.

improve [imprúv], *vt.* mejorar; perfeccionar.—*vi.* mejorarse; mejorar.—**ment** [-mẹnt], *s.* mejora; mejoramiento; adelanto, progreso; mejoría.

improvisation [impravịzéịșọn], *s.* improvisación.—**improvise** [improváịz], *vt.* improvisar.

imprudence [imprúdẹns], *s.* imprudencia, indiscreción.—**imprudent** [imprúdẹnt], *a.* imprudente.

impudence [ímpịudẹns], *s.* desfachatez, descaro; impudicia.—**impudent** [ímpịudẹnt], *a.* descarado; impúdico.

impulse [ímpʌls], *s.* impulso; estímulo.—**impulsive** [impʌ́lsịv], *a.* impulsivo.

impure [impịúr], *a.* impuro.—**impurity** [impịúrịti], *s.* impureza.

in [in], *prep.* en, de, por, con, mientras, dentro de.—*i. haste,* de prisa.—*i. so far as,* o *insofar as,* en cuanto (a), hasta donde.—*adv.* dentro, adentro; en casa.—*i. here, there, etc.,* aquí dentro, allí dentro, etc.—*to be all i.,* estar rendido, agotado.—*to be i.,* haber llegado; estar (en casa, en la oficina, etc.).—*to be i. with someone,* gozar del favor de alguien.

inability [inạbílịti], *s.* inhabilidad, incapacidad, ineptitud.

inaccessible [inæksésịbl], *a.* inaccesible.

inaccurate [inǽkyụrịt], *a.* inexacto, erróneo.

inactive [inǽktịv], *a.* inactivo, inerte.—**inactivity** [inæktívịti], *s.* inactividad, ociosidad.

inadequate [inǽdịkwịt], *a.* inadecuado.

inadmissible [inædmísịbl], *a.* inadmisible.

inadvertence [inædvœ́rtẹns], *s.* inadvertencia.—**inadvertent** [inædvœ́rtẹnt], *a.* inadvertido, accidental; descuidado.

inalienable [inéịlyẹnạbl], *a.* inalienable.

inanimate [inǽnịmịt], *a.* inanimado; exánime.

inasmuch as [inạzmʌ́ch ạz], *adv.* en

cuanto; tanto como; como quiera que, puesto que, visto que, por cuanto.

inaugural [inógiuṛal], *a.* inaugural. —**inaugurate** [inógiuṛeit], *vt.* inaugurar; investir.—**inauguration** [inogiuṛéiṣon], *s.* inauguración, estreno; toma de posesión.

inborn [ínborn], *a.* innato, ingénito.

Inca [iṇkạ], *s.* inca.—*a.* inca, incaico.

incalculable [inkǽlkiuạbl], *a.* incalculable.

incandescent [inkǽndéṣent], *a.* incandescente, candente.

incapable [inkéipạbl], *a.* incapaz.— **incapacitate** [inkạpǽsiteit], *vt.* incapacitar, inhabilitar.—**incapacity** [inkạpǽsiti], *s.* incapacidad.

incarnate [inkárneit], *vt.* encarnar.—*a.* [inkárnit], encarnado; personificado. —**incarnation** [inkarnéiṣon], *s.* encarnación.

incendiary [inséndieri], *a.* y *s.* incendiario.

incense [ínsens], *s.* incienso.—*vt.* [inséns], exasperar, irritar; incensar.

incentive [inséntiv], *s.* incentivo, estímulo, aliciente.—*a.* incitativo.

incessant [inséssant], *a.* incesante.

inch [inch], *s.* pulgada.—*by inches*, paso a paso, con gran lentitud.— *every i.*, cabal, en todo respecto.—*i. by i.*, palmo a palmo, pulgada por pulgada.—*within an i. of*, a dos dedos de.—*a.* de una pulgada.—*vi.* (con *along*) avanzar poquito a poquito.

incident [ínsident], *s.* incidente; acontecimiento, episodio.—*al* [ínsidental], *a.* incidental, incidente, contingente; concomitante.—*s. pl.* gastos imprevistos; circunstancias imprevistas.

incinerator [insíneṛeito(r)], *s.* incinerador, crematorio.

incision [insíẓon], *s.* incisión; muesca. —**incisor** [insáiẓo(r)], *a.* y *s.* (diente) incisivo.

incite [insáit], *vt.* incitar, instigar.

inclination [inklinéiṣon], *s.* inclinación; pendiente, declive.—**incline** [inkláin], *vt.* inclinar, ladear.—*vi.* inclinarse, ladearse; hacer reverencia; sentir inclinación o predilección.—*s.* [ínklain], declive, pendiente, cuesta; rampa.

inclose [inklóuz], *vt.* = ENCLOSE.— **inclosure** [inklóuẓ̱o(r)], *s.* = ENCLOSURE.

include [inklúd], *vt.* incluir, encerrar; comprender, abarcar.—**inclusion** [inklúẓon], *s.* inclusión, contenido.— **inclusive** [inklúṣiv], *a.* inclusivo.

incoherent [inkohíṛent], *a.* incoherente, inconexo.

income [ínkʌm], *s.* renta, entrada, ingreso, rédito.—*i. tax return*, declaración del impuesto sobre la renta.

incomparable [inkámpạṛabl], *a.* incomparable, sin igual.

incompetence [inkámpitens], *s.* incompetencia.—**incompetent** [inkámpitent], *a.* incompetente.

incomplete [inkọmplít], *a.* incompleto.

incomprehensible [inkamprihénsibl], *a.* incomprensible.

incongruous [inkáŋgruʌs], *a.* incongruente, discordante, mal adaptado; inconsecuente.

inconsiderate [inkonsídœrit], *a.* desconsiderado; desatento.

inconsistency [inkonsístensi], *s.* incompatibilidad, contradicción, inconsecuencia.—**inconsistent** [inkonsístent], *a.* incompatible, contradictorio, inconsecuente.

inconstancy [inkánstansi], *s.* inconstancia.—**inconstant** [inkánstant], *a.* inconstante, vario.

inconvenience [inkọnvíniens], *s.* inconveniencia, inconveniente; incomodidad, molestia.—*vt.* incomodar, estorbar, molestar.—**inconvenient** [inkọnvíniant], *a.* inconveniente, inoportuno, molesto, incómodo.

incorporate [inkórporeit], *vt.* incorporar; formar corporación.—*vi.* incorporarse, unirse, asociarse.—*a.* [inkórporit], incorporado; inmaterial.

incorrect [inkọrékt], *a.* incorrecto.

increase [inkrís], *vt.* y *vi.* aumentar(se); acrecentar(se); incrementar; arreciar (en intensidad, sonido, etc.).—*s.* [ínkris], aumento, incremento, crecimiento, acrecentamiento.—**increasingly** [inkrísiŋli], *adv.* crecientemente; con creces; cada vez más.

incredible [inkrédibl], *a.* increíble.— **incredulity** [inkridiúliti], *s.* incredulidad.—**incredulous** [inkrédẓiulʌs], *a.* incrédulo.

increment [ínkriment], *s.* incremento, aumento, crecimiento.

incriminate [inkrímineit], *vt.* incriminar, acusar.

incubation [inkiubéiṣon], *s.* incubación. —**incubator** [ínkiubeito(r)], *s.* incubadora; empolladora.

incumbency [inkámbensi], *s.* posesión o goce de un empleo; duración del mismo; incumbencia.—**incumbent** [inkámbent], *a.* obligatorio; sostenido por, colocado sobre, apoyado en.

incur [inkœ́r], *vti.* [1] incurrir (en); atraerse.—*to i. a debt*, contraer una deuda.

incurable [inkiúṛabl], *a.* incurable, irremediable.—*s.* incurable.

incursion [inkœ́rẓon], *s.* incursión, correría.

indebted [indétid], *a.* adeudado, endeudado o en deuda; (fam.) entrampado; obligado, reconocido.—

—ness [-nịs], s. deuda; pasivo; obligación.

indecency [indísẹnsị], s. indecencia.— indecent [indisẹnt], a. indecente, indecoroso.

indecision [indịsíẓọn], s. indecisión, irresolución.

indecorous [indékọrʌs], a. indecoroso.

indeed [indíd], adv. verdaderamente, realmente, de veras, a la verdad, claro está.—interrog. ¿de veras? ¿es posible?

indefatigable [indịfǽtịgạbl], a. incansable.

indefensible [indịfénsịbl], a. indefendible, insostenible.

indefinite [indéfịnịt], a. indefinido, vago.

indelible [indélịbl], a. indeleble.

indelicate [indélịkịt], a. indecoroso, falto de delicadeza.

idemnify [indémnịfaị], vti. [7] indemnizar.—indemnity [indémnịtị], s. indemnización.

indent [indént], vt. dentar, endentar; (impr.) sangrar.—s. mella, diente, muesca.

independence [indịpéndẹns], s. independencia.—independent [indịpéndẹnt], a. independiente.

indescribable [indịskrájbạbl], a. indescriptible.

indeterminate [indịtɶ́rmịnịt], a. indeterminado, vago.

index [índeks], s. índice; elenco.—i. card, tarjeta o ficha para archivos. —vt. ordenar o archivar alfabéticamente; poner en un índice; indicar.

Indian [índịạn], a. indio; indígena.—I. ink, tinta china.—I. Ocean, Océano Índico.—I. summer, veranillo de San Martín.—s. indio, indo; piel roja.

indicate [índịkejt], vt. indicar, significar.—indication [indịkéjṣọn], s. indicación, indicio.—indicative [indịkạtịv], a. y s. indicativo.

indict [indájt], vt. (for.) acusar ante el juez; procesar, encausar, enjuiciar.— —ment [-mẹnt], s. (for.) sumario; denuncia, acusación; procesos(amient)o.

indifference [indífẹrẹns], s. indiferencia; apatía, despego.—indifferent [indífẹrẹnt], a. indiferente; apático.

indigenous [indídẓẹnʌs], a. indígena, nativo.

indigestion [indịdẓéschọn], s. indigestión.

indignant [indígnạnt], a. indignado.— —ly [-lị], adv. con indignación.— indignation [indịgnéjṣọn], s. indignación.—indignity [indígnịtị], s. indignidad, ultraje o afrenta, improperio.

indigo [índịgoụ], s. añil, índigo.

indirect [indịrékt], a. indirecto.

indiscreet [indịskrít], a. indiscreto.— indiscretion [indịskréṣọn], s. indiscreción.

indispensable [indịspénsạbl], a. indispensable, imprescindible; de rigor.

indispose [indịspóụz], vt. indisponer.— —d [-d], a. indispuesto; ligeramente enfermo.—indisposition [indịspozíṣọn], s. indisposición; malestar.

indistinct [indịstị́nkt], a. indistinto.

individual [indịvídẓụạl], a. individual. —s. individuo, particular, persona, sujeto.— —ity [indịvịdẓụǽlịtị], s. individualidad, personalidad.

indivisible [indịvíẓịbl], a. indivisible.

Indo-Chinese [índoụ chạjníz], a. y s. indochino.

indoctrinate [indáktrịnejt], vt. adoctrinar.

indolence [índolẹns], s. indolencia, desidia.—indolent [índolẹnt], a. indolente, desidioso.

indomitable [indámịtạbl], a. indomable.

indoor [índor], a. interno, interior, de casa.— —s [índorz], adv. (a)dentro; en casa; bajo techo.

indorse [indórs], vt. (com.) endosar; respaldar; garantizar; apoyar.— —e [-í], s. endosatario.— —ment [-mẹnt], s. endoso; respaldo; aval, garantía.— —r [indórsœ(r)], s. endosante.

induce [indjús], vt. inducir, persuadir.— —ment [-mẹnt], s. inducción; aliciente; persuasión.

induct [indʌ́kt], vt. instalar; iniciar.— —ion [indʌ́kṣọn], s. (elec. y lóg.) inducción.—i. valve, válvula de admisión.

indulge [indʌ́ldẕ], vt. mimar, consentir; gratificar; conceder indulgencia a; (com.) dar plazo o prorrogar el plazo a.—vi. (con in) entregarse a; gustar de.— —nce [indʌ́ldẕẹns], s. indulgencia; exceso, complacencia, favor; (com.) prórroga.— —nt [indʌ́ldẕẹnt], a. indulgente.

industrial [indʌ́strịạl], a. industrial.— —ist [-ịst], s. industrial.— —ization [-ịzéjṣọn], s. industrialización.— —ize [-ajz], vt. industrializar.—industrious [indʌ́strịʌs], a. industrioso, diligente, aplicado, laborioso.—industry [índʌstrị], s. industria; laboriosidad.

ineffective [inẹféktịv], a. ineficaz, inefectivo.—ineffectual [inẹfékchụạl], a. ineficaz; fútil.—inefficacy [inéfịkạsị], inefficiency [inẹfíṣẹnsị], s. ineficacia; futilidad.—inefficient [inẹfíṣẹnt], a. ineficaz.

ineligible [inélịdẕịbl], a. inelegible.

inept [inépt], a. inepto.— —itude [-ịtjud], s. ineptitud, inhabilidad.

inequality [inịkwálịtị], s. desigualdad, disparidad.

inert [inert], *a.* inerte.— **ia** [inérsiạ], *s.* inercia.

inestimable [inéstimạbl], *a.* inestimable, inapreciable.

inevitable [inévitạbl], *a.* inevitable, ineludible.

inexpensive [inekspénsiv], *a.* barato, poco costoso.

inexperience [inekspírięns], *s.* inexperiencia, impericia.— **d** [-t], inexpert [inekspćert], *a.* inexperto, bisoño, novel.—**inexpertness** [inekspćertnis], *s.* impericia.

inexplicable [inéksplikạbl], *a.* inexplicable.

inexpressible [ineksprésibl], *a.* indecible, inexpresable, inenarrable.

infallibility [infælibíliti], *s.* infalibilidad. —**infallible** [infælibl], *a.* infalible.

infamous [infạmʌs], *a.* infame; infamante.—**infamy** [ínfạmi], *s.* infamia, ignominia.

infancy [ínfạnsi], *s.* infancia.—**infant** [ínfạnt], *s.* infante, niñito, criatura, nene.—*a.* infantil; menor de edad; de niños; naciente.—**infantile** [ínfạntil], *a.* infantil.

infantry [ínfạntri], *s.* infantería.— **man** [-mạn], *s.* soldado de infantería.

infect [infékt], *vt.* infectar, contagiar.— **ion** [infékṣọn], *s.* infección, contagio.— **ious** [infékṣʌs], *a.* contagioso, infeccioso.

infelicity [infilísiti], *s.* infelicidad, infortunio; falto de tino.

infer [infćer], *vti.* [1] inferir, colegir. —*vi.* sacar consecuencias o inferencias.— **ence** [ínfẹrẹns], *s.* inferencia.— **entially** [ínfẹrénṣạli], *adv.* por inferencia.

inferior [infírịọ(r)], *s.* and *a.* inferior; subordinado, subalterno.— **ity** [infịriáriti], *s.* inferioridad.

infernal [infćernạl], *a.* infernal.— **inferno** [infćernou], *s.* infierno.

infest [infést], *vt.* infestar, plagar.

infidel [ínfidel], *s.* infiel; pagano; librepensador.—*a.* infiel; librepensador; de infieles, de los infieles.— **ity** [infidéliti], *s.* infidelidad, descreimiento; infidelidad conyugal.

infield [ínfild], *s.* campo y jugadores situados dentro del cuadro (baseball); campos inmediatos a los edificios (en una granja, etc.).

infighting [ínfaitịn], *s.* boxeo cuerpo a cuerpo.

infiltrate [infíltreit], *vt.* y *vi.* infiltrar(se); meter(se); introducir(se) en pequeño número por varias partes.—**infiltration** [infiltréiṣọn], *s.* infiltración.

infinite [ínfinit], *a.* infinito; innumerable; perfecto.—*s.* infinito.—**infinitive** [infínitiv], *s.* y *a.* infinitivo.—

infinity [infíniti], *s.* infinidad, inmensidad; (mat.) infinito; sinfín.

infirm [infćerm], *a.* enfermizo, achacoso; poco firme; (for.) anulable.— **ary** [-ạri], *s.* hospital, enfermería, casa de salud.— **ity** [-iti], *s.* enfermedad, dolencia, achaque; flaqueza, fragilidad.— **ly** [-li], *adv.* débilmente.

inflame [infléim], *vt.* inflamar, encender; enardecer; provocar, irritar.—*vi.* arder; inflamarse, hincharse.—**inflammable** [inflǽmạbl], *a.* inflamable.— **inflammation** [inflạméiṣọn], *s.* inflamación.

inflate [infléit], *vt.* inflar, hinchar.— **inflation** [infléiṣọn], *s.* inflación monetaria; hinchazón; inflación.

inflect [inflékt], *vt.* torcer, doblar; modular; (gram.) declinar, conjugar.— **ion** [inflékṣọn], *s.* inflexión, dobladura; acento, modulación; flexión, conjugación, declinación, desinencia.

inflexibility [infleksibíliti], *s.* inflexibilidad.—**inflexible** [infléksibl], *a.* inflexible.

inflict [inflíkt], *vt.* infligir, imponer.— **ion** [inflíkṣọn], *s.* imposición, aplicación; pena, castigo.

influence [ínfluẹns], *s.* influencia, valimiento, influjo; ascendiente.—*vt.* influir; inducir; ejercer presión sobre. —**influential** [influénṣạl], *a.* influyente.

influenza [influénzạ], *s.* influenza, trancazo, gripe.

influx [ínflʌks], *s.* (in)flujo; afluencia; instilación, intromisión; desembocadura, entrada.

infold [infóuld], *vt.* envolver; incluir; abrazar; abarcar.

inform [infórm], *vt.* informar, comunicar; poner al corriente; instruir; dar forma a, modelar; animar.—*vi.* soplar, delatar.—*to i. against*, denunciar a, delatar a.— **al** [-ạl], *a.* de confianza, sin ceremonia.— **ality** [informǽliti], *s.* informalidad, irregularidad.— **ation** [informéiṣọn], *s.* informe, información, aviso; conocimiento(s); (for.) acusación, delación.— **er** [infórmœ(r)], *s.* delator; denunciante; (fam.) soplón, chivato.

infraction [infrǽkṣọn], *s.* infracción, transgresión; fractura incompleta.

infrequent [infríkwẹnt], *a.* raro, poco frecuente.

infringe [infríndʒ], *vt.* infringir, violar. —*to i. upon*, violar.— **ment** [-mẹnt], *s.* infracción, violación.

infuriate [infjúrieit], *vt.* enfurecer, irritar.

ingenious [indʒíniʌs], *a.* ingenioso; hábil.— **ness** [-nis], *s.* ingeniosidad, ingenio.—**ingenuity** [indʒinjúiti], *s.* ingeniosidad, inventiva.

ingenuous [indźɛ́nyųʌs], *a.* ingenuo, cándido.— —**ness** [-nįs], *s.* ingenuidad, candidez.

ingoing [íngoųįn], *a.* entrante, que entra.—*s.* entrada, ingreso.

ingot [íngot], *s.* lingote; barra.

ingrained [ingréjnd], *a.* inculcado, arraigado, inveterado.

ingratiate [ingréjśįejt], *vt.* hacer aceptable.—*to i. oneself with*, insinuarse, hacerse a la buena voluntad de, conquistarse el favor de.—**ingratiating** [ingréjśįejtįn], *a.* insinuante.

ingratitude [ingrǽtįtjud], *s.* ingratitud.

ingredient [ingrídįȩnt], *s.* ingrediente.

inhabit [inhǽbįt], *vt.* habitar, poblar. —*vi.* residir.— —**able** [-ȩbl], *a.* habitable.— —**ant** [-ȩnt], *s.* habitante, poblador, residente.

inhalation [inhȩléjśȩn], *s.* inspiración; (med.) inhalación.—**inhale** [inhéjl], *vt.* inspirar, inhalar, aspirar.

inhere [inhír], *vi.* ser inherente.— —**nt** [inhȩ́rȩnt], *a.* inherente, inmanente; innato, esencial.

inherit [inhérįt], *vt.* heredar.—*vi.* suceder como heredero.— —**ance** [-ȩns], *s.* herencia, patrimonio.— —**or** [-ǫ(r)], *s.* heredero.— —**ress** [-rįs], —**rix** [-rįks], *s.* heredera.

inhibit [inhíbįt], *vt.* inhibir, prohibir.— —**ion** [inhįbíśȩn], *s.* inhibición, prohibición.

inhospitable [inháspįtȩbl], *a.* inhospitalario, inhóspito.

inhuman [inhįúmȩn], *a.* inhumano.— —**e** [inhįuméjn], *a.* inhumanitario.— —**ity** [inhįumǽnįtį], *s.* inhumanidad.

inimical [inímįkȩl], *a.* hostil, enemigo.

inimitable [inímįtȩbl], *a.* inimitable.

initial [iníśȩl], *a.* inicial, incipiente. —*s.* (letra) inicial.—*vti.* [2] poner las iniciales, firmar con iniciales.— —**ly** [-į], *adv.* en primer lugar; en los comienzos; por modo inicial.—**initiate** [iníśįejt], *vt.* iniciar, entablar.—*a. y s.* adepto, iniciado.—**initiation** [inįśįéjśȩn], *s.* iniciación.—**initiative** [iníśįȩtįv], *a.* iniciativo.—*s.* iniciativa; originalidad.

inject [indźɛ́kt], *vt.* inyectar; introducir.— —**ion** [ındźɛ́ksȩn], *s.* inyección; enema, lavativa.

Injunction [indźʌ́nksȩn], *s.* mandato, mandamiento; requerimiento; prohibición; precepto.

injure [índźur], *vt.* injuriar; perjudicar; averiar, lastimar, lesionar.— **injurious** [indźúrįȩs], *a.* injurioso; perjudicial; lesivo.—**injury** [índźurį], *s.* daño, avería, desperfecto; perjuicio, detrimento, menoscabo, lesión.

injustice [indźʌ́stįs], *s.* injusticia.

ink [įnk], *s.* tinta.—*vt.* entintar, dar tinta, pasar o linear en tinta.— —**ling**

[íŋklįn], *s.* insinuación; sospecha; vislumbre, indicio, noción vaga.— —**stand** [-stænd], *s.* escribanía; tintero.— —**well** [-wɛl], *s.* tintero; frasco de tintero.

inland [ínlȩnd], *a.* interior; del país, nacional, regional.—*s.* el interior de un país.—*adv.* tierra adentro.— —**er** [-œ(r)], *s.* el que habita tierra adentro.

in-law [ínlɔ], *s.* (fam.) pariente político.

inlay [inléj], *vti.* [10] embutir; incrustar; hacer ataujía o mosaico.—*s.* [ínlej], taracea, embutido.

inlet [ínlet], *s.* entrada; abra, caleta, ensenada; estero, estuario; boca de entrada.

inmate [ínmejt], *s.* enfermo hospitalizado; recluso; presidiario.

inmost [ínmoųst], *a.* más íntimo, recóndito, profundo.

inn [in], *s.* fonda, mesón, posada.

innate [inéjt], *a.* innato, ingénito, connatural.

inner [ínœ(r)], *a.* interno, interior.—*i. spring mattress*, colchón de muelles. —*i. tube* o *tire*, cámara de rueda de automóvil.

inning [íníŋ], *s.* entrada, turno (baseball y otros juegos).—*pl.* tierras ganadas al mar.

innkeeper [ínkipœ(r)], *s.* posadero, mesonero, fondista.

innocence [ínosȩns], *s.* inocencia.— **innocent** [ínosȩnt], *s. y a.* inocente.

innovate [ínovejt], *vt.* innovar.—**innovation** [inovéjśȩn], *s.* innovación; novedad.

innuendo [inyųéndoų], *s.* indirecta, insinuación.

innumerable [injúmȩrȩbl], *a.* innumerable.

inoculate [inákįulejt], *vt. y vi.* inocular; fertilizar (el suelo) con bacterias; infundir; infectar, inficionar.—**inoculation** [inakįuléjśȩn], *s.* inoculación; contaminación, infección; fertilización con bacterias.

inoffensive [inофénsįv], *a.* inofensivo.

inopportune [inapǫrtjún], *a.* inoportuno, intempestivo; inconveniente.

inorganic [inǫrgǽnįk], *a.* inorgánico.

inquire [inkwájr], *vt. y vi.* inquirir, preguntar, averiguar.—*to i. about*, *after* o *for*, preguntar por.—*to i. into*, investigar, examinar, informarse.— *to i. of*, dirigirse a.—**inquiry** [inkwájrį], *s.* pregunta, indagación, investigación, estudio.

inquisition [inkwįzíśȩn], *s.* escudriñamiento, investigación; (I.) (igl.) Inquisición, Santo Oficio.—**inquisitive** [inkwízįtįv], *a.* curioso, preguntón.— **inquisitiveness** [inkwízįtįvnįs], *s.* curiosidad, manía de preguntar.

insane [inséin], *a.* loco, demente; de o para locos.—**insanity** [insǽniti], *s.* locura, insania, demencia.

inscribe [inskráib], *vt.* inscribir; grabar; dedicar; apuntar.—**inscription** [inskrípʃǫn], *s.* inscripción; rótulo; registro; dedicatoria.

inscrutable [inskrútạbl], *a.* inescrutable, insondable.

insect [ínsekt], *s.* insecto, bicho.—**icide** [inséktisaid], *s.* insecticida.

insecure [insikiúr], *a.* inseguro.—**insecurity** [insikiúriti], *s.* inseguridad, incertidumbre; riesgo.

insensibility [insensibíliti], *s.* insensibilidad.—**insensible** [insénsibl], *a.* insensible; imperceptible; impasible.

inseparable [insépạrạbl], *a.* inseparable.

insert [ínsœrt], *s.* cosa insertada, intercalada, etc.—*vt.* [insœrt], insertar; introducir, encajar; intercalar.—**ion** [insœrʃǫn], *s.* inserción; (cost.) entredós.

inshore [ínʃór], *a.* cercano a la orilla.—*adv.* hacia la orilla o cerca de ella.

inside [ínsáid], *a.* interior, interno.—*s.* el interior; contenido; forro.—*pl.* (fam.) entrañas, interioridades.—*adv.* dentro, adentro, en el interior.—*i. out,* de dentro afuera; al revés.—*prep.* dentro de.— —r [insáidœ(r)], *s.* individuo bien informado o con información de primera mano.

insidious [insídias], *a.* insidioso, solapado, capcioso.

insight [ínsait], *s.* discernimiento, perspicacia; comprensión; conocimiento, idea; penetración.

insignia [insígniạ], *s. pl.* insignias.

insignificance [insignífikạns], *s.* insignificancia.—**insignificant** [¿insignífikạnt], *a.* insignificante.

insinuate [insínyueit], *vt.* insinuar, sugerir.—*to i. oneself,* insinuarse, introducirse, congraciarse.—*vi.* echar pullas o indirectas.—**insinuation** [insinyuéiʃǫn], *s.* insinuación; sugestión; indirecta, pulla.

insipid [insípid], *a.* insípido.

insist [insíst], *vi.* insistir; persistir; hacer hincapié.— —**ence** [-ens], *s.* insistencia, porfía.— —**ent** [-ent], *a.* insistente, persistente; porfiado.

insolence [ínsolens], *s.* insolencia.—**insolent** [ínsolent], *a.* insolente.

insomnia [insámniạ], *s.* insomnio.

inspect [inspékt], *vt.* inspeccionar, reconocer, registrar, revis(t)ar.— —**ion** [inspékʃǫn], *s.* inspección, reconocimiento, registro.— —**or** [inspéktǫ(r)], *s.* inspector, registrador, interventor, revisor.

inspiration [inspiréiʃǫn], *s.* inspiración; estro, numen.—**inspire** [inspáir], *vt.* inspirar; animar, alentar; autorizar

(por funcionario público); sugerir, insinuar.—*vi.* inspirar.

instability [instạbíliti], *s.* inestabilidad.

install [instól], *vt.* instalar, montar; colocar.— —**ation** [-éiʃǫn], *s.* instalación; montaje.— —**er** [-œ(r)], *s.* montador.—**instal(l)ment** [instólment], *s.* instalación; entrega; plazo.—*i. plan,* pago por cuotas o plazos.

instance [ínstạns], *s.* ejemplo; caso; instancia, ruego, solicitación; ocasión, lugar.—*for i.,* por ejemplo.—*in the first i.,* desde el principio.—*vt.* poner por caso; ejemplificar; citar, mencionar.

instant [ínstạnt], *a.* inminente, inmediato, perentorio; corriente, presente, actual.—*s.* instante, momento, (fam.) santiamén.— —**aneous** [-éinias], *a.* instantáneo.

instead [instéd], *adv.* en lugar, en vez, en cambio (de); en lugar de eso, ello, él, etc.

instep [ínstep], *s.* empeine o garganta del pie; parte anterior de la pata trasera.

instigate [ínstigeit], *vt.* instigar, fomentar, incitar, provocar.—**instigation** [instigéiʃǫn], *s.* instigación.

instinct [ínstiŋkt], *s.* instinto.— —**ive** [instíŋktiv], *a.* instintivo.

institute [ínstitiut], *vt.* instituir, fundar; iniciar.—*s.* instituto.—**institution** [institiúʃǫn], *s.* institución; comienzo, establecimiento.

instruct [instrʌkt], *vt.* instruir; dar instrucciones.— —**ion** [instrʌkʃǫn], *s.* instrucción; conocimiento, saber.—*pl.* instrucciones; órdenes, consigna.— —**ive** [-iv], *a.* instructivo, aleccionador.— —**or** [-ǫ(r)], *s.* instructor.

instrument [ínstrument], *s.* instrumento; agente.— —**al** [instruméntạl], *a.* instrumental; influyente, servicial; conducente.—*to be i.,* contribuir a.

insubordinate [insʌbórdinịt], *a.* insubordinado, refractario.—**insubordination** [insʌbordinéiʃǫn], *s.* insubordinación.

insufficiency [insʌfíʃensi], *s.* insuficiencia.—**insufficient** [insʌfíʃent], *a.* insuficiente; incapaz, inepto.

insulate [ínsuleit], *vt.* aislar.—**insulation** [insuléiʃǫn], *s.* aislamiento.—**insulator** [ínsuleitǫ(r)], *s.* aislador.

insult [ínsʌlt], *s.* insulto.—*vt.* [insʌlt], insultar.

insuperable [insiúpẹrạbl], *a.* insuperable.

insurance [inʃúrạns], *s.* aseguramiento, seguro; prima o premio del seguro.—*i. agent,* agente de seguros.—*i. company,* compañía de seguros.—*i. policy,* póliza de seguro.—**insure** [inʃúr], *vt.* (com.) asegurar; afianzar;

dar o tener seguridad de; lograr.—
vi. asegurarse.

insurgence [inscérdżęns], *s.* insurrección, rebelión.—**insurgent** [inscérdżęnt], *a.* y *s.* insurgente, insurrecto.

insurrection [inscerékṣǫn], *s.* insurrección.

intact [intǽkt], *a.* intacto, íntegro, entero.

intake [ínteik], *s.* entrada, recaudación.

integral [íntigrạl], *a.* íntegro; integrante, inherente; (mat.) entero (número, función, etc.).—**integrity** [intégriti], *s.* integridad, entereza.

intellect [íntelekt], *s.* intelecto; persona o gente de talento.— —**ual** [intelékchụạl], *s.* y *a.* intelectual.—**intelligence** [intélidżęns], *s.* inteligencia; información, noticia; correspondencia mutua; policía secreta.—**intelligent** [intélidżęnt], *a.* inteligente.

intemperance [intémpœrạns], *s.* intemperancia; destemplanza.—**intemperate** [intémpœrit], *s.* destemplado; intemperante; desmedido.

intend [inténd], *vt.* intentar, proponerse; destinar; aplicar, determinar; querer decir; tener por objeto.

intendancy [inténdạnsi], *s.* intendencia.—**intendant** [inténdạnt], *s.* intendente, procurante.

intense [inténs], *a.* intenso; extremado, sumo; esforzado.—**intensification** [intensjfikéiṣǫn], *s.* intensificación.—**intensify** [inténsifai], *vti.* y *vii.* [7] intensificar(se).—**intensity** [inténsiti], *s.* intensidad.—**intensive** [inténsjv], *a.* intenso, intensivo.

intent [intént], *a.* atento; asiduo; decidido, resuelto a, empeñado en.—*s.* intento, designio, intención, propósito.—*to all intents and purposes,* en realidad, en el fondo.—**ion** [inténṣǫn], *s.* intención; designio, fin, propósito deliberado; (cir.) procedimiento de curación.—**ional** [inténṣǫnạl], *a.* intencional.

inter [intœr], *vti.* [1] enterrar, sepultar.

intercede [intœrsíd], *vi.* interceder.

intercept [intœrsépt], *vt.* interceptar; atajar.— —**ion** [intœrsépṣǫn], *s.* atajo.

intercession [intœrséṣǫn], *s.* intercesión.

interchange [intœrchéindż], *vt.* alternar; cambiar, trocar; permutar.—*vi.* alternarse, trocarse.—*s.* [íntœrcheindż], intercambio; comercio, tráfico.

intercourse [íntœrkors], *s.* comercio, tráfico; intercambio; correspondencia, trato; coito, trato sexual.

interdict [intœrdikt],   **interdiction** [intœrdíkṣǫn], *s.* veto, veda, prohibición; interdicción, **interdicto**, entredicho.

interest [íntœrist], *vt.* interesar.—*s.* interés; provecho; simpatía; rédito; participación en una empresa.—*the interests,* las grandes empresas, los intereses creados, los capitalistas.—**ed** [-id], *a.* interesado.— —**ing** [-iŋ], *a.* interesante, atractivo.—*in an i. condition,* en estado interesante, encinta.

interfere [intœrfír], *vi.* inmiscuirse, interponerse, meterse; intervenir; impedir, estorbar; (fís.) interferir; (vet.) tropezar un pie con otro (los caballos),- —**nce** [intœrfíręns], *s.* ingerencia, intromisión; obstáculo, impedimiento; (fís., rad.) interferencia.

interim [íntœrim], *a.* interino, intermedio, ínterin.

interior [intíriǫ(r)], *a.* interior, interno.—*s.* parte de adentro, interior.

interjection [intœrdżékṣǫn], *s.* interjección; interposición.

interlace [intœrléis], *vt.* entrelazar.

interlock [intœrlák], *vt.* y *vi.* trabar, engranar; unirse, entrelazarse; cerrar.—*s.* traba, trabazón; (cine) sincronización; sincronizador.

interlude [íntœrljud], *s.* intervalo; entreacto, intermedio, entremés; (mus.) interludio.

intermediary [intœrmídjeri], *a.* y *s.* intermediario.—**intermediate** [intœrmídjit], *a.* medianero, intermedio.—*vi.* [intœrmídjeit], mediar, intervenir, intermediar.

interminable [intœrmjnạbl], *a.* interminable.

intermingle [intœrmíŋgl], *vt.* entremezclar.—*vi.* mezclarse.

intermission [intœrmíṣǫn], *s.* interrupción, tregua; intermitencia; intermedio, entreacto.

intermittent [intœrmítęnt], *a.* intermitente.

intermix [intœrmíks], *vt.* entremezclar, entreverar, interpolar.—*vi.* entremezclarse, compenetrarse.

intern [intœrn], *vt.* encerrar, poner a buen recaudo; internar; meter en un campo de concentración.—*s.* [íntœrn], interno, practicante de hospital.— —**al** [intœrnạl], *a.* interno, interior; doméstico; íntimo.

international [intœrnǽṣǫnạl], *a.* internacional.- —**ize** [-aiz], *vt.* internacionalizar.

interne [íntœrn], *s.* = **INTERN**.

interposal [intœrpóuzạl], *s.* interposición, mediación, intervención.—**interpose** [intœrpóuz], *vt.* interponer; (cine) reemplazar gradualmente una

figura por otra, o cambiar la una en la otra.—*vi.* interponerse.

interpret [intœrprit], *vt.* interpretar, descifrar; representar, ilustrar.— —**ation** [-éişǫn], *s.* interpretación.— —**er** [-œ(r)], *s.* intérprete, traductor.

interrogate [intérǫgeit], *vt.* interrogar, preguntar.—*vi.* hacer preguntas.— **interrogation** [interǫgéişǫn], *s.* interrogatorio, pesquisa.—*i. point,* signo de interrogación (?), interrogante. —**interrogative** [interágǫtiv], *a.* interrogativo.—*s.* palabra interrogativa.

interrupt [interápt], *vt.* interrumpir.— —**ion** [interápşǫn], *s.* interrupción.— —**or** [-ǫ(r)], *s.* interruptor, disyuntor.

intersect [intersékt], *vt.* cortar.—*vi.* (geom.) cortarse.— —**ion** [intersékşǫn], *s.* intersección; cruce, bocacalle.

intertwine [intœrtwáin], **intertwist** [intœrtwist], *vt.* entretejer, entrelazar.

interval [intœrvǫl], *s.* intervalo; blanco, claro, hueco; (mus.) intervalo.

intervene [intœrvín], *vi.* intervenir; interponerse; sobrevenir.—**intervention** [intœrvénşǫn], *s.* intervención; mediación; interposición.

interview [íntœrvju], *s.* entrevista.—*vt.* entrevistar(se con).— —**er** [-œ(r)], *s.* entrevistador; reportero que hace entrevistas.

intestine [intéstin], *a.* interior, intestino, doméstico; interno.—*s.* (anat.) intestino, tripa.

intimacy [íntimǫsi], *s.* intimidad, confianza.—**intimate** [íntimit], *a.* íntimo; familiar; profundo (conocimiento).—*s.* amigo íntimo, confidente.—*vt.* [íntimeit], insinuar, intimar.—**intimation** [intiméişǫn], *s.* insinuación, indirecta, pulla; indicio.

into [íntu], *prep.* en, dentro, adentro, hacia el interior.—*i. the bargain,* por añadidura.

intolerable [intálerǫbl], *a.* intolerable, insufrible.—**intolerance** [intálerǫns], *s.* intolerancia.—**intolerant** [intálerǫnt], *a.* intolerante.

intonation [intonéişǫn], *s.* entonación.

intoxicate [intáksikeit], *vt.* embriagar. —**intoxication** [intaksikéişǫn], *s.* embriaguez, beodez; (med.) intoxicación, envenenamiento.

intransitive [intrǽnsitiv], *a.* (gram.) intransitivo.

intrepid [intrépid], *a.* intrépido, impávido.

intricate [íntrikit], *a.* intrincado, enredado.

intrigue [intríg], *s.* intriga; galanteo, lío amoroso.—*vi.* intrigar; tener intrigas amorosas.— —**r** [intrígœ(r)], *s.* intrigante.

introduce [introdjús], *vt.* introducir; implantar; presentar (una persona

a otra); poner en uso.—*to i. a bill,* presentar un proyecto de ley,— **introduction** [introdákşǫn], *s.* introducción; prefacio; implantación; presentación.

intrude [intrúd], *vi.* intrusarse, entremeterse, inmiscuirse.—*vt.* meter, forzar.— —**r** [intrúdœ(r)], *s.* intruso, entremetido.—**intrusion** [intrúʒǫn], *s.* intrusión, entremetimiento.—**intrusive** [intrúsiv], *a.* intruso; (geol.) de intrusión; intrusivo.

intrust [intrást], *vt.* = ENTRUST.

intuition [intjuíşǫn], *s.* intuición.— **intuitive** [intjúitiv], *a.* intuitivo.

inundate [ínǝndeit], *vt.* inundar, anegar.

invade [invéid], *vt.* invadir.— —**r** [invéidœ(r)], *s.* invasor.

invalid [invélid], *a.* inválido, nulo.— *a. y s.* [ínvǝlid], inválido, lisiado.— *vt.* lisiar, incapacitar.— —**ate** [invélideit], *vt.* invalidar, anular.

invaluable [invélyuǝbl], *a.* inestimable, inapreciable.

invariable [invériǝbl], *a.* invariable.

invasion [invéiʒǫn], *s.* invasión.

invective [invéktiv], *s.* invectiva, vituperio.—*a.* ultrajante, injurioso.

invent [invént], *vt.* inventar; idear.— —**ion** [invénşǫn], *s.* invención, invento.— —**ive** [-iv], *a.* inventivo.— —**or** [-ǫ(r)], *s.* inventor.

inventory [ínventori], *s.* inventario.— *vti.* [7] inventariar.

inverse [invœrs], *a.* inverso, invertido. —**invert** [invœrt], *vt.* invertir; volver al revés; trastocar; trasponer.— *inverted commas,* comillas.

invest [invést], *vt.* (com.) invertir, emplear o imponer dinero; (re)vestir; investir, conferir; (mil.) sitiar, cercar.

investigate [invéstigeit], *vt.* investigar. —**investigation** [investigéişǫn], *s.* investigación.—**investigator** [invéstigeitǫ(r)], *s.* investigador.

investment [invéstmǫnt], *s.* (com.) inversión; (mil.) sitio, cerco; investidura; cubierta; envoltura.—**investor** [invéstǫ(r)], *s.* (com.) inversionista.

inveterate [invétǫrit], *a.* inveterado, empedernido.

invigorate [invígǫreit], *vt.* vigorizar, fortificar.

invincible [invínsibl], *a.* invencible.

invisibility [invizibíliti], *s.* invisibilidad. —**invisible** [invízibl], *a.* invisible.

invitation [invitéişǫn], *s.* invitación, convite.—**invite** [inváit], *vt.* convidar, invitar; atraer; provocar, tentar; instar.—**inviting** [inváitiŋ], *a.* atractivo; incitante.

invocation [invokéişǫn], *s.* invocación; (for.) mandamiento.

invoice [ínvois], *s.* (com.) factura.—*vt.* facturar.

invoke [invóuk], *vt.* invocar; (for.) expedir suplicatorio, exhorto o mandamiento.

involuntary [inválʌnteri], *a.* involuntario.

involve [inválv], *vt.* envolver, enrollar; implicar; entrañar, comprender; complicar, enredar; involucrar; (mat.) elevar a una potencia, hallar una potencia de.

inward(s) [ínwərd(z)], *adv.* hacia adentro, hacia lo interior; adentro. —inward, *a.* interior, interno.—*s.* el interior.—*pl.* entrañas.

iodin(e) [áiodain], *s.* yodo o iodo.

iota [aióutə], *s.* jota, punto, tilde.

irascible [airǽsibl], *a.* irascible.

irate [áireit], *a.* airado, iracundo.—**ire** [air], *s.* ira, furia.

iridescent [iridésent], *a.* iridiscente, tornasolado.

iris [áiris], *s.* (anat.) iris; arco iris; flor de lis.

Irish [áiriʃ], *a.* y *s.* irlandés.—*s.* lengua irlandesa.

irk [œrk], *vt.* fastidiar, molestar.— **—some** [œrksʌm], *a.* fastidioso, enfadoso.

iron [áiœrn], *s.* hierro; plancha (de planchar); herramienta.—*a.* férreo, de hierro; relativo al hierro.—*vt.* planchar; aherrojar.

ironic(al) [airánik(əl)], *a.* irónico.

ironing [áiœrniŋ], *s.* planchado, acción de planchar; ropa por planchar.—*s.* de planchar.

irony [áironi], *s.* ironía.

irradiate [iréidieit], *vt.* irradiar; inspirar; esparcir.—*vi.* lucir, brillar.—**irradiation** [ireidiéiʃən], *s.* irradiación.

irrational [irǽʃɒnəl], *a.* irracional; absurdo, ilógico; (álg.) irracional.

irregular [irégyʊlə(r)], *a.* irregular.— **—ity** [iregyʊlǽriti], *s.* irregularidad.

irrelevancy [irélɪvənsi], *s.* inaplicabilidad.—**irrelevant** [irélɪvənt], *a.* inaplicable, impertinente.

irreligious [irilídʒəs], *a.* irreligioso.

irresponsible [irispánsibl], *a.* irresponsable.

irreverence [irévərens], *s.* irreverencia. —**irreverent** [irévərent], *a.* irreverente.

irrevocable [irévɒkəbl], *a.* irrevocable; inapelable.

irrigate [írigeit], *vt.* regar.—**irrigation** [irigéiʃən], *s.* riego; irrigación.

irritable [írɪtəbl], *a.* irritable. —**—ness** [-nis], *s.* irritabilidad.—**irritate** [íriteit], *vt.* irritar, exacerbar.—**irritation** [iritéiʃən], *s.* irritación.

island [áilənd], *s.* isla, ínsula.— **—er** [-œ(r)], *s.* isleño.—**isle** [ail], *s.* isla,

ínsula.—**islet** [áilit], *s.* isleta, cayo.

isolate [áisoleit], *vt.* aislar, apartar; incomunicar.—**isolation** [aisoléiʃən], *s.* aislamiento; incomunicación.— **isolationism** [aisoléiʃənizm], *s.* aislacionismo.

Israeli [izréili], *a.* y *s.* israelita.— **—te** [ízrielait], *s.* israelita.

issue [íʃu], *s.* (impr.) edición, tirada, impresión; número (de una revista, etc.); prole; (com.) emisión de valores; (for.) beneficios, rentas; salida, egreso; (med.) flujo; fuente, nacimiento, evento, consecuencia; decisión; tema de discusión.—*vt.* echar, arrojar; dar; dictar, expedir; (com.) librar, emitir; dar a luz, publicar.—*vi.* salir, fluir, provenir; nacer; resultar; resolverse.

isthmus [ísmʌs], *s.* istmo.

it [it], *pron.* neutro él, ella, eso, ello, lo, la, le.—*i. is late*, es tarde.—*i. rains*, llueve.—*what time is i.?* ¿qué hora es?

Italian [itǽlyən], *a.* y *s.* italiano.—*s.* lengua italiana.—**Italic** [itǽlik], *a.* (impr.) bastardilla, itálica (letra); (I.) itálico, italiano.—**italicize** [itǽlisaiz], *vt.* poner en letra itálica o bastardilla; subrayar, dar énfasis.—**italics** [itǽliks], *s. pl.* (impr.) letra itálica, bastardilla o cursiva.

itch [ich], *s.* comezón, picazón; prurito. —*vi.* picar, sentir picazón o comezón; antojarse; desear vehementemente.— **—y** [íchi], *a.* sarnoso; picante.

item [áitem], *adv.* ítem; otrosí, aun más.—*s.* partida; artículo; párrafo; detalle; renglón. **—ize** [-aiz], *vt.* detallar, especificar, particularizar, pormenorizar.

itinerary [aitínerəri], *s.* itinerario, ruta; relación de un viaje; guía de viajeros. —*s.* itinerario, hecho en viaje.

its [its], *a.* posesivo neutro su, sus (de él, de ella, de ello).—**elf** [itsélf], *pron.* (él) mismo, (ella) misma; sí mismo, sí misma; sí; se.—*it moves of i.*, eso se mueve por sí mismo.

ivory [áivəri], *s.* marfil.—*pl.* cosas hechas de marfil.—*a.* ebúrneo.

ivy [áivi], *s.* hiedra o yedra; cazus.

J

jab [dʒæb], *vti.* [1] pinchar, punzar.—*s.* punzada, pinchazo.

jack [dʒæk], *s.* macho del burro y otros animales; (mec.) gato, cric; sota de la baraja; (mar.) bandera de proa.—*j.-of-all-trades*, aprendiz de todo y oficial de nada.—*j.-o'-lantern*, fuego fatuo; linterna hecha de una calabaza, con cara grotesca.—*j. plane*, (carp.) garlopa.—*j.-pot*, premio gordo, premio

mayor.—*j. rabbit,* liebre americana.— *vt.* alzar un objeto con el gato.

jackal [dʒǽkḁl], *s.* chacal.

jackass [dʒǽkæs], *s.* asno, borrico, burro; (fig.) estúpido, necio.

jackdaw [dʒǽkdo], *s.* grajo.

jacket [dʒǽkiṭ], *s.* chaqueta, chamarra; envoltura; forro; sobrecubierta.

jackknife [dʒǽknajf], *s.* navaja de bolsillo.

jade [dʒejd], *s.* (min.) jade; rocín, jamelgo; mujerzuela, sota.—*vt.* cansar.—*vi.* desalentarse.

jagged [dʒǽgịd], *a.* mellado, dentado, serrado.

jail [dʒejl], *s.* cárcel.—*vt.* encarcelar.— **—er** [dʒéjlœ(r)], *s.* carcelero.

jam [dʒæm], *s.* compota, conserva; agolpamiento; atascamiento; atascadero; situación peliaguda.—*vti.* [1] apiñar; apretar, apachurrar, estrujar; atorar; (rad.) causar interferencia en. —*vii.* atorarse, trabarse, agolparse.

Jamaican [dʒạméjkạn], *a.* y *s.* jamaiquino.

jamb [dʒæm], *s.* montante, batiente (de puerta, etc.).

jammed [dʒæmd], *a.* atorado, trabado; de bote en bote, repleto.

janitor [dʒǽnịtọ(r)], *s.* portero; conserje

January [dʒǽnyụerị], *s.* enero.

Jap [dʒæp], (fam.), **Japanese** [dʒæpạníz], *a.* y *s.* japonés, nipón.

jar [dʒar], *vti.* [1] sacudir, agitar, hacer vibrar o trepidar.—*vii.* chirriar, hacer ruido desagradable; vibrar, trepidar. —*s.* jarro o jarra; pote, tarro; vibración; sacudida; chirrido.

jargon [dʒárgọn], *s.* jerga, jerigonza; caló.

jasmin(e) [dʒǽsmịn], *s.* jazmín.

jasper [dʒǽspœ(r)], *s.* (min.) jaspe.

jaundice [dʒóndịs], *s.* ictericia; predisposición.—*vt.* causar ictericia; predisponer.— **—d** [-t], *a.* ictérico, cetrino.

jaunt [dʒont], *vi.* corretear, ir y venir.— *s.* excursión, caminata.— **—iness** [dʒóntịnịs], *s.* ligereza, garbo.— **—y** [-i], *a.* airoso, garboso.

Javanese [dʒavạnís], *s.* y *s.* javanés.

javelin [dʒǽvlịn], *s.* jabalina, venablo.

jaw [dʒo], *s.* quijada, mandíbula; (mec.) mordaza.—*a.* de las quijadas; de mordaza.— **—bone** [dʒóboụn], *s.* maxilar, quijada, mandíbula (esp. la inferior).

jay [dʒej], *s.* (fam.) rústico; simplón; (orn.) grajo.— **—walker** [dʒéjwok-œ(r)], *s.* (fam.) peatón descuidado o imprudente.

jazz [dʒæz], *s.* música popular sincopada.—*vt.* (frecuentemente con up) animar, alegrar, tocar o bailar el jazz. - **—y** [dʒǽzị], *a.* chillón; de última moda.

jealous [dʒélʌs], *a.* celoso, envidioso.— *to be j.,* tener celos.—*to become j.,* encelarse, ponerse celoso.— **—y** [-i], *s.* celos; envidia.

jean [dʒin], *s.* (tej.) sarga, mezclilla.— *pl.* ropa, esp. pantalones, hecha de esta tela.

jeer [dʒịr], *vt.* y *vi.* mofar, befar, escarnecer, burlarse.—*s.* befa, mofa, burla, escarnio, choteo.

jelly [dʒélị], *s.* jalea; gelatina.—*vti.* y *vii.* [7] convertir(se) en jalea o gelatina.— **—jellyfish** [dʒélịfịʃ], *s.* medusa, aguamala.

jeopardize [dʒépạrdajz], *vt.* arriesgar, exponer.— **jeopardy** [dʒépạrdị], *s.* riesgo, peligro.

jerk [dʒœrk], *s.* tirón, sacudida; espasmo muscular; (fam.) estúpido, idiota.—*vt.* dar un tirón; sacudir; traquetear; hacer tasajo.—*vi.* moverse a tirones.—*jerked beef,* tasajo.— **—y** [dʒœrkị], *a.* espasmódico; (fam.) estúpido, atontado.

jersey [dʒœrzị], *s.* tejido de punto.

jest [dʒest], *vi.* bromear, chancearse.— *s.* chanza, broma, guasa.— **—er** [dʒéstœ(r)], *s.* bufón; burlón, guasón.

Jesuit [dʒéʒụịt], *s.* jesuíta.

jet [dʒet], *s.* chorro; surtidor; (min.) azabache.—*j. plane,* avión de chorro o de retropropulsión.—*j. propulsion engine,* motor de retropropulsión o de chorro.—*vii.* [1] salir en chorro.

jetty [dʒétị], *s.* malecón, rompeolas; muelle, espolón.—*a.* de azabache; negro.

Jew [dʒu], *s.* judío, israelita.

jewel [dʒúẹl], *s.* joya, alhaja; gema, piedra preciosa.—*j. box,* joyero.—*vti.* [2] enjoyar, adornar con piedras preciosas.

Jewish [dʒúịʃ], *a.* judaico, judío.

jiffy [dʒífị], *s.* (fam.) instante, periquete.—*in a j.,* en un santiamén.

jig [dʒig], *s.* jiga (música y danza).—*j. saw,* sierra de vaivén o de marquetería.—*vti.* [1] cantar o tocar una jiga; sacudir de abajo hacia arriba.— *vii.* bailar una jiga.

jilt [dʒịlt], *vt.* despedir o dar calabazas; (fam.) plantar, dejar plantado.—*vi.* coquetear.

jingle [dʒíŋgl], *vt.* y *vi.* sonar o resonar. —*s.* retintín, sonido metálico; (rad., T.V., etc.) anuncio musical.—*j. bell,* cascabel.

job [dʒab], *s.* tarea, faena; empleo, ocupación, trabajo; empresa.—*by the j.,* a destajo.— **—ber** [dʒábœ(r)], *s.* corredor o comisionista al por mayor.

jockey [dʒáki], *s.* jinete (en las carreras de caballos).—*vt.* y *vi.* trampear, engañar; maniobrar hábilmente para sacar alguna ventaja.

jocose [dʒokóus], **a.** jocoso.

join [dʒoin], **vt.** juntar, unir, ensamblar, acoplar; asociar; afiliarse o unirse a.— *to j. battle*, librar batalla.—*to j. company*, incorporarse.—*to j. the colors*, (fam.) alistarse, enrolarse.—*vi.* asociarse, unirse.— **—t** [-t], **s.** juntura, junta, unión, empalme, ensambladura, acopladura; conexión, enganche; coyuntura, articulación; nudillo; gozne, bisagra; charnela; cuarto de un animal; encuentro de un ave.— *out of j.*, dislocado, descoyuntado.—**a.** unido, agrupado, colectivo; copartícipe; asociado; mixto; conjunto.— *j. property*, propiedad mancomunada. —*j. stock company*, sociedad anónima.

joke [dʒouk], **s.** broma, burla, chanza, chiste, chuscada.—*in j.*, en chanza, de broma.—*vi.* bromear, chancear-(se), gastar bromas.— **—r** [dʒóuk-œ(r)], **s.** burlón, bromista, guasón; (naipes) comodín; equívoco o falla de ley o contrato a cuyo amparo pueden ser burlados legalmente.—**jokingly** [dʒóukinli], **adv.** por burla, en chanza.

jolly [dʒáli], **a.** alegre, festivo, jovial; jaranero; divertido; (fam.) excelente, magnífico.—**adv.** (fam.) muy, sumamente.—*vt.* y *vi.* [7] (fam.) engatusar, lisonjear; seguir el humor (a).

jolt [dʒoult], **vt.** y *vi.* traquetear, sacudir, dar sacudidas.—**s.** sacudida, traqueteo.

jonquil [dʒánkwil], **s.** (bot.) junquillo.

jostle [dʒásl], **vt.** y *vi.* empujar, empellar, codear.—**s.** empellón, empujón.

jot [dʒat], **s.** pizca, jota (cosa mínima). —*I don't care a j.* (about), me importa un bledo.—*vt.* [1] (con *down*) tomar notas, apuntar.

journal [dʒérnal], **s.** diario, periódico diario; revista (publicación); acta; diario (apuntes personales); (com.) diario (libro).— **—ism** [-izm], **s.** periodismo, diarismo, la prensa.— **—ist** [-ist], **s.** periodista.— **—istic** [-ístik], **a.** periodístico.— **—ize** [-aiz], *vt.* (com.) pasar al diario.—*vi.* apuntar en un diario.

journey [dʒérni], **s.** jornada; viaje por tierra; camino, tránsito, pasaje.—*vi.* viajar, recorrer un trayecto.

joust [dʒast, dʒaust], **s.** justa, torneo.— *vi.* justar.

jovial [dʒóuvial], **a.** jovial.

jowl [dʒaul], **s.** carrillo; quijada; papada.

joy [dʒoi], **s.** alegría, júbilo, regocijo; felicidad.— **—ful** [dʒóiful], **a.** alegre, gozoso; placentero.— **—ous** [-ʌs], **a.** alegre, gozoso.

jubilant [dʒúbilant], **a.** jubiloso, alborozado, regocijado, alegre.—**jubilee** [dʒúbili], **s.** jubileo.

Judaic(al) [dʒudéiik(al)], **a.** judaico.— **Judaism** [dʒúdijzm], **s.** judaísmo.

judge [dʒadʒ], **s.** juez; magistrado; perito.—*vt.* juzgar; sentenciar, fallar. —*vi.* juzgar.—**judgment** [dʒádʒment], **s.** juicio, criterio, discernimiento; sentir, opinión, dictamen; (for.) fallo; sentencia; ejecutoria.

judicial [dʒudíʃal], **a.** judicial.—**judiciary** [dʒudíʃieri], **a.** judiciario; judicial.—**s.** administración de justicia; judicatura; magistratura; poder judicial.—**judicious** [dʒudíʃas], **a.** juicioso, cuerdo, sensato, sesudo, atinado.

jug [dʒag], **s.** botijo; jarro, cacharro, cántaro, porrón; reclamo del ruiseñor; (fam.) chirona (cárcel).

juggle [dʒagl], **vi.** hacer juegos de manos, escamotear; engañar, hacer trampas.—**s.** juego de manos, escamoteo; impostura, engaño.— **—r** [dʒágle(r)], **s.** prestidigitador; malabarista; impostor.— **—ry** [dʒágleri], **s.** prestidigitación; juegos malabares; engaño, trampa.

Jugoslav [yúgoslav], **s.** = YUGOSLAV. —**Jugoslavian** [yúgoslávian], **Jugoslavic** [yúgoslávik], **a.** = YUGOSLAVIAN, YUGOSLAVIC.

jugular [dʒágyula(r)], **a.** and **s.** yugular.

juice [dʒus], **s.** zumo; jugo, substancia. —**juiciness** [dʒúsinis], **s.** jugosidad, suculencia.—**juicy** [dʒúsi], **a.** jugoso, suculento.

July [dʒuláj], **s.** julio.

jumble [dʒámbl], **vt.** arrebujar, (fam.) emburujar; confundir.—*vi.* mezclarse, revolverse, confundirse.—**s.** mezcla, revoltillo, embrollo, mezcolanza; bollito delgado y dulce.

jumbo [dʒámbou], **a.** (fam.) coloso, cosa o animal enorme.—**s.** colosal, gigantesco.

jump [dʒamp], **vt.** saltar por encima de o al otro lado de; hacer saltar; saltarse, omitir; comer un peón (en el juego de damas).—*to j. the track*, descarrilar.—*vi.* saltar, brincar; cabriolar; subir rápidamente (precios, etc.); (con *with*) convenir, concordar.—*to j. at*, apresurarse a aprovechar.—*to j. on*, arremeter; (fam.) poner como nuevo.—*to j. over*, saltar por encima de.—*to j. to a conclusion*, sacar precipitadamente una conclusión.—**s.** salto, cabriola, brinco; (dep.) pista de saltos (esquí); (fam.) ventaja.—*on the j.*, de un salto, al vuelo.—*to get o have the j. on*, tomar la delantera a, adelantársele a uno.— **—er** [dʒámp-œ(r)], **s.** saltador; blusa de obrero o de mujer; zamarra de pieles; narria, rastra.— **—y** [-i], **a.** nervioso o excitable en exceso.

Junction [dʒʌŋkʃǫn], *s.* conexión, junta, unión; acopladura; bifurcación; entronque, empalme, confluencia de vías.—**juncture** [dʒʌŋkchȳ(r)], *s.* junta, juntura; coyuntura, articulación; ocasión, oportunidad; trance, momento o circunstancia críticos; exigencia.

June [dʒun], *s.* junio.

jungle [dʒʌŋgl], *s.* jungla, selva, bosque virgen, (Am.) manigua; maraña, matorral.

junior [dʒúnyǫ(r)], *s.* joven; estudiante de tercer año (en escuela superior, colegio o universidad).—*a.* más joven; hijo (Jr.); menor; más nuevo o reciente.—*j. college,* colegio para los dos primeros años universitarios. —*j. high school,* escuela secundaria inferior (intermedia entre la elemental y la secundaria).—*j. partner,* socio menos antiguo o socio menor.

junk [dʒʌŋk], *s.* (mar.) junco; chicote; hierro viejo, chatarra; cecina; (fam.) basura, hojarasca.—*vt.* (fam.) descartar por inservible.

juridic(al) [dʒuŗídik(ǫl)], *a.* jurídico, judicial.—**jurisdiction** [dʒuŗisdíkṣǫn], *s.* jurisdicción; potestad; fuero; competencia.—**jurisprudence** [dʒuŗisprúdĕns], *s.* jurisprudencia.—**jurist** [dʒúŗist], *s.* jurista, jurisconsulto.— **juristic** [dʒuŗístik], *a.* jurídico.— **juror** [dʒúŗǫ(r)], *s.* (for.) jurado (individuo).—**jury** [dʒúŗi], *s.* (for.) jurado (cuerpo e institución).

just [dʒʌst], *a.* justo, honrado, recto, justiciero; justificado; legal; legítimo; exacto, cabal.—*adv.* justamente, exactamente; casi; sólo, no más que; apenas; simplemente; hace un momento.—*j. about,* poco más o menos; o poco menos.—*j. as,* al momento que; cuando; no bien; lo mismo que, semejante a.—*j. beyond,* un poco más allá.—*j. by,* al lado, al canto, aquí cerca.—*j. now,* ahora mismo, hace poco.—*j. so,* ni más ni menos.—*to have j. time enough,* tener el tiempo preciso.—*to have j. arrived,* acabar de llegar.— —**ice** [dʒʌstis], *s.* justicia; razón, derecho; (for.) juez; magistrado.— —**ifiable** [-ịfaịǫbl], *a.* justificable.— —**ification** [-ịfịkéiṣǫn], *s.* justificación; descargo, defensa; razón de ser.—**justify** [-ịfaị], *vti.* [7] justificar.

jut [dʒʌt], *vii.* [1] sobresalir, resaltar; combarse; proyectar.—*s.* salidizo, proyección.

jute [dʒut], *s.* yute, cáñamo de Indias.

juvenile [dʒúvĕnịl], *a.* juvenil, joven.— *s.* mocito, joven; (teat.) galancete.

juxtapose [dʒʌkstapóuṣ], *vt.* yuxta-poner.—**juxtaposition** [dʒʌkstạpouẓị-ṣǫn], *s.* yuxtaposición.

K

kaleidoscope [kạláịdoskoup], *s.* calidoscopio.

kangaroo [kæŋgarú], *s.* canguro.

karat [kérạt], *s.* (joy.) quilate.

keel [kil], *s.* quilla.—*vt.* volcar una embarcación poniéndola quilla arriba; volcar.—*vi.* (naut.) dar de quilla; volcarse.—*to k. over,* (fam.) volcarse, zozobrar; desplomarse; desmayarse.

keen [kin], *a.* afilado; aguzado; agudo, sutil; perspicaz; ansioso; mordaz.— —**ness** [kínnịs], *s.* agudeza; sutileza, perspicacia; anhelo.

keep [kip], *vti.* [10] conservar; quedarse con; guardar; tener (criados, secretario, un perro); tener (cuentas, libros); cumplir (la palabra, una promesa); detener, mantener.—*to k. an eye on,* vigilar.—*to k. back,* detener; ocultar; impedir.—*to k. down,* sujetar.—*to k. from,* mantener lejos de; impedir (cambiando el giro).—*to k. in,* mantener dentro; no dejar salir.—*to k. in mind,* recordar; tener en cuenta.—*to k. informed (of),* tener al corriente o al tanto (de).—*to k. on,* mantener; continuar.—*to k. one's distance,* mantenerse dentro de propios límites, no tomarse libertades.—*to k. one's hands off,* no tocar, no meterse en.— *to k. one's temper,* contenerse; obrar con calma.—*to k. one's word,* cumplir su palabra, tener palabra.—*to k. out,* no dejar entrar; excluir.—*to k. up,* mantener, conservar.—*vii.* mantenerse, sostenerse; continuar; permanecer.—*to k. along,* continuar, proseguir.—*to k. at home,* quedarse en casa. —*to k. away,* mantenerse apartado, no acercarse.—*to k. from,* abstenerse de; no meterse en.—*to k. in,* permanecer dentro; estarse en casa.—*to k. off,* no entrar a; no tocar; mantenerse fuera o lejos de.—*to k. on,* seguir, proseguir.—*to k. out of,* no meterse en, evitar.—*to k. out of the way,* estarse o hacerse a un lado.—*to k. up,* mantenerse firme; persistir; no cejar.— *s.* manutención, subsistencia.—*for keeps,* para siempre; para guardar, para quedarse con ello.— —**er** [kípœ(r)], *s.* guarda, guardián, custodio; carcelero.— —**ing** [-ịŋ], *s.* custodia, mantenimiento; cuidado, preservación.—*in k. with,* en armonía con, al mismo tenor que.— —**sake** [-seịk], *s.* regalo, recuerdo.

keg [keg], *s.* cuñete, barrilito, pipote.

kennel [kénĕl], *s.* perrera.

kept [kept], *pret. y pp.* de TO KEEP.

kerchief [kérchif], *s.* pañuelo.

kernel [kérnęl], *s.* grano de cereal; médula, núcleo.

kerosene [kérosin], *s.* petróleo destilado, querosén, (Am.) kerosina.

kettle [kétl], *s.* caldera, marmita, olla.— **—drum** [-drʌm], *s.* (mús.) timbal, atabal.

key [ki], *s.* llave; clave; fundamento; tono (de la voz); (mec.) llave; (elec.) conmutador; tecla (del piano, de máquina de escribir, etc.); (mar.) cayo, isleta.—*in k.,* templado, de acuerdo, en armonía.—*k. ring,* llavero.—*pass k.,* llave maestra.—*a.* principal; fundamental; estratégico. —*vt.* poner llaves; afinar.— **—board** [kíbɔrd], *s.* teclado.— **—hole** [-houl], *s.* ojo de la cerradura.— **—note** [-nout], *s.* (mus.) nota tónica; principio fundamental, piedra angular.— **—stone** [-stoun], *s.* clave, llave de arco.

khaki [kékị], *s.* kaki, caqui (tela y color).

kibitzer [kíbjtsœ(r)], *s.* (fam.) mirón, espectador molesto en los juegos de naipes; entremetido.

kick [kịk], *vt.* acocear, dar patadas a.— *to k. the bucket,* (fam.) estirar la pata, irse para el otro mundo.—*vi.* cocear, patear, dar o tirar coces; oponerse; quejarse.—*s.* patada, coz; puntapié; oposición; queja; estímulo, aliento.

kid [kịd], *s.* cabrito, chivato; cabritilla (piel); (fam.) niño; muchachito, chico, chica.—*vti.* y *vii.* [1] (fam.) embromar, tomar el pelo; bromear.

kidnap [kídnæp], *vti.* [2] secuestrar, raptar, (Am.) plagiar.— **—(p)er** [-œ(r)], *s.* secuestrador, raptor, (Am.) plagiario.— **—(p)ing** [-ịŋ], *s.* secuestro, rapto, (Am.) plagio.

kidney [kídnị], *s.* riñón.—*k. bean,* judía, alubia, habichuela.

kill [kịl], *vt.* matar; destruir; amortiguar; suprimir.—*s.* acción de matar; (caza) pieza muerta.—*k.-joy,* aguafiestas.— **—er** [kịlœ(r)], *s.* matador, homicida; (fam.) matón.— **—ing** [-ịŋ], *a.* matador, destructivo; irresistible. —*s.* acto de matar, matanza.

kiln [kịl], *s.* horno, estufa; horno de cerámica.

kilogram [kịloụgræm], *s.* kilo(gramo). Ver Tabla.—**kilometer** [kịlómitœ(r)], *s.* kilómetro.—**kilowatt** [kịlowat], *s.* kilovatio.

kimono [kịmóụnoụ], *s.* quimono, bata.

kin [kịn], *s.* parentesco; parentela, familia.—*the next of k.,* los parientes (más) próximos.—*a.* pariente, allegado.

kind [kạịnd], *s.* bondadoso, benévolo; amable; afectuoso.—*k. regards,* cordial saludo; sentimientos de consideración.—*s.* género, clase, casta, índole, calidad.—*nothing of the k.,* nada de eso; no hay tal.

kindergarten [kịndœrgartịn], *s.* escuela de párvulos, jardín de la infancia.

kindle [kíndl], *vt.* encender; inflamar, enardecer.—*vi.* prender; inflamarse. —**kindling** [kíndlịŋ], *s.* inflamación; encendimiento.—*k. wood,* leña menuda.

kindly [kájndlị], *adv.* amable o bondadosamente; cordialmente.—*tell me k.,* tenga la amabilidad de decirme.—*a.* bondadoso, benévolo; favorable.— **kindness** [kájndnịs], *s.* bondad, benevolencia, amabilidad, atención, favor.

kindred [kíndrịd], *s.* parentesco, consanguinidad; parentela.—*a.* emparentado, deudo, consanguíneo, afín; congénere.

king [kịŋ], *s.* rey; rey (en el ajedrez); dama (en el juego de damas).— **—dom** [kíŋdǫm], *s.* reino.— **—ly** [-lị], *a.* real, regio; majestuoso.—*adv.* regiamente, majestuosamente.— **—ship** [-šịp], *s.* majestad; monarquía; reinado.

kinky [kíŋkị], *a.* ensortijado, crespo; (fam.) chiflado.

kinsfolk [kínzfoụk], *s.* parentela.—**kinship** [kínšịp], *s.* parentesco.—**kinsman** [kínzmǫn], *s.* pariente, deudo.— **kinswoman** [kínzwǫmǫn], *s.* parienta.

kiosk [kíásk], *s.* kiosco o quiosco.

kiss [kịs], *vt.* besar.—*to k. the rod,* someterse a un castigo.—*s.* beso, ósculo.

kit [kịt], *s.* tineta; cubo; equipo, avíos, juego o caja de herramientas, medicinas, piezas componentes de un mecanismo, etc.; gatito.—*soldier's k.,* mochila.

kitchen [kíchęn], *s.* cocina.—*k. boy,* pinche.—*k. garden,* huerta.—*k. range* o *stove,* cocina económica.— **—ette** [-ét], *s.* cocina reducida o pequeña.— **—ware** [-wer], *s.* utensilios de cocina, batería de cocina.

kite [kạịt], *s.* cometa, papalote; milano.

kitten [kítn], *s.* gatito.—*vi.* parir la gata.— **—ish** [-įš], *a.* retozón.— **kitty** [kítị], *s.* gatito, minino; (en el juego) puesta.

knack [næk], *s.* tino, don, destreza, acierto, arte; treta; chuchería.

knapsack [næpsæk], *s.* mochila; alforja, morral.

knave [neịv], *s.* bribón, bellaco; sota de los naipes.— **—ry** [néịvœrị], *s.* picardía, bribonada, bellaquería.

knead [nid], *vt.* amasar, sobar.—*k. trough,* artesa, amasadura.

knee [ni], *s.* rodilla; codillo (de cuadrúpedo); (mec.) codo, angular, escuadra; (mar.) curva.—*k. deep,*

metido hasta la rodilla.—*k. high*, hasta la rodilla.—**kneel** [nil], *vii.* [4] arrodillarse, ponerse de hinojos, hincar la rodilla, postrarse.

knell [nɛl], *s.* doble, toque de difuntos; clamoreo; mal agüero.—*vt.* y *vi.* doblar, tocar a muerto.

knew [nju], *pret.* de TO KNOW.

knicknack [níknæk], *s.* chuchería, baratija, juguete.

knife [naif], *s.* cuchillo; navaja; bisturí. —*vt.* acuchillar; (fam.) frustrar o arruinar por intrigas.

knight [nait], *s.* caballero (medieval o de las órdenes militares); campeón; caballo (del ajedrez).—*k. commander*, comendador.—*k. errant*, caballero andante.—*k. errantry*, caballería andante.—*vt.* armar caballero; conferir el título de Sir.— —**hood** [náit-hud], *s.* caballería, rango o dignidad de caballero.— —**ly** [-li], *a.* caballeresco.—*adv.* caballerosamente.

knit [nit], *vti.* y *vii.* [3] hacer malla, media o calceta; atar, enlazar, entretejer; contraer; unirse, trabarse; soldarse (un hueso); tejer a punto de aguja.—*to k. one's brow*, fruncir las cejas, arrugar el entrecejo.—**knitting** [nítin], *s.* labor o trabajo de punto. —**knitwear** [nítwer], *s.* artículo(s) de punto.

knives [naivz], *s. pl.* de KNIFE.

knob [nab], *s.* prominencia, bulto, protuberancia; nudo en la madera; borlita o borlilla; perilla, tirador (de puerta, gaveta, etc.).

knock [nak], *vt.* y *vi.* golpear; tocar, llamar a una puerta; (fam.) criticar, hablar mal de.—*to k. down*, derribar, tumbar; atropellar (con un auto, etc.); (mec.) desarmar, desmontar.— *to k. out*, hacer salir a golpes; acogotar; destruir; dejar o poner fuera de combate.—*s.* golpe; aldabonazo, llamada; (fam.) crítica.— —**er** [nák-œ(r)], *s.* golpeador; llamador, aldaba, aldabón.

knoll [noul], *s.* loma, otero; cumbre o cima; doble de campanas.

knot [nat], *s.* nudo; lazo, vínculo.—*vti.* y *vii.* [1] anudar(se).— —**ty** [-i], *a.* nudoso; duro, áspero; intrincado, difícil.

know [nou], *vti.* [10] conocer; saber; discernir.—*to k. how to* (*swim, sing, etc.*), saber (nadar, cantar, etc.).—*to k. the ropes*, conocer los detalles, estar al tanto, (fig.) saber el juego.—*vii.* saber.—*as far as I k.*, que yo sepa.— *to be in the k.*, estar informado o en el secreto.—*to k. best*, ser el mejor juez, saber lo que más conviene.—*to k. better*, saber que no es así; saber lo que debe hacerse o como debe uno por-

tarse.—*to k. of*, saber de, tener noticia o conocimiento de; conocer de oídas.— —**ingly** [nóuinli], *adv.* hábilmente, sabiamente; a sabiendas, con conocimiento de causa.— —**ledge** [nálidʒ], *s.* conocimiento, saber, sapiencia; ciencia, erudición.—*to the best of my k.*, según mi leal saber y entender.—**known** [noun], *pp.* de TO KNOW.

knuckle [nákl], *s.* nudillo, artejo, articulación de los dedos; jarrete de ternero o cerdo; (mec.) charnela.—*vi.* someterse; abandonar la partida.— *to k. down*, o *to*, consagrarse o emprender con vehemencia.—*to k.* (*under*) *to*, doblegarse ante; ceder a.

Korean [korían], *a.* y *s.* coreano.

L

label [léibel], *s.* marbete, rótulo, etiqueta; marca.—*vti.* [1] rotular o marcar; apodar; designar, clasificar.

labial [léibial], *a.* labial.

labor [léibo(r)], *s.* trabajo; [el] obrerismo; mano de obra; labor; obra.— *l. union*, sindicato o gremio obrero.— *vi.* trabajar; estar de parto.—*vt.* elaborar; hacer trabajar, activar.

laboratory [lǽb(o)ratori], *s.* laboratorio.

labored [léibord], *a.* hecho con dificultad; forzado.—**laborer** [léibɔrœ(r)], *s.* peón, jornalero, bracero; obrero, operario, trabajador.—**laborious** [labóriʌs], *a.* laborioso, trabajoso, ímprobo; diligente, industrioso.

labyrinth [lǽbirinθ], *s.* laberinto.

lace [leis], *s.* encaje; cordón, cinta; cordón del corsé o del zapato.—*vt.* atar, abrochar (corsé, zapatos, vestidos, etc.) con lazos o cordones; enlazar; galonear; entrelazar.

lack [læk], *vt.* y *vi.* carecer, necesitar, faltar.—*s.* falta, carencia, escasez, necesidad.— —**ing** [lǽkin], *a.* falto, carente, defectuoso.—*to be l. in*, hacerle falta a uno; carecer de.

lackey [lǽki], *s.* lacayo.—*vt.* y *vi.* servir como lacayo; ser criado.

laconic [lakánik], *a.* lacónico.

lacquer [lǽkœ(r)], *vt.* dar laca; barnizar. —*s.* laca, barniz.

lacy [léisi], *a.* de o parecido al encaje.

lad [læd], *s.* mozo, mozalbete, chico.

ladder [lǽdœ(r)], *s.* escalera o escala (de mano).

laden [léidn], *a.* cargado, abrumado, oprimido.

ladle [léidl], *s.* cucharón, cazo; (fund.) caldero.—*vt.* sacar o servir con cucharón.

lady [léidi], *s.* señora, dama.—*l.-killer*, tenorio, conquistador.— —**like** [-laik], *a.* delicado, tierno, elegante; afemi-

nado.- —love [-lʌv], s. amada, mujer querida.

lag [læg], s. retraso; retardación de movimiento.—*vii.* [1] retrasarse, rezagarse, quedarse atrás.- —gard [lǽgård], a. tardo, perezoso, holgazán.—s. rezagado, holgazán.

lagoon [lăgún], s. laguna, charca.

laic [léjik], a. laico, lego, secular, seglar. —s. lego, seglar.

laid [lejd], *pret.* y *pp.* de TO LAY.

lain [lejn], *pp.* de TO LIE (echarse).

lair [ler], s. cubil, guarida.

lake [lejk], s. lago.

lamb [læm], s. cordero, borrego.- —kin [lǽmkjn], s. corderito.

lame [lejm], a. cojo, renco; lisiado, estropeado.—*vt.* lisiar, estropear.- —ness [léjmnjs], s. cojera; defecto, imperfección.

lament [lămént], *vt.* y *vi.* lamentar(se). —s. lamento.- —able [lǽmentabl], a. lamentable, deplorable, desconsolador.- —ation [læmentéjšǫn], s. lamento, lamentación.

laminate [lémjnejt], *vt.* y *vi.* (metal.) laminar.

lamp [læmp], s. lámpara; farol; linterna. —l. burner, mechero.—l. post, farola de la calle.—l. shade, pantalla de lámpara.- —black [lǽmblæk], s. negro de humo.

lampoon [læmpún], s. pasquín, sátira.— *vt.* pasquinar, satirizar.

lance [læns], s. lanza; pica.—*vt.* lancear, dar una lanzada; abrir con bisturí.— —r [lénsœ(r)], s. lancero.- —t [lénsjt], s. (cir.) lanceta.

land [lænd], s. tierra; terreno; suelo; país, nación; región, territorio.—l. breeze, terral.—l. surveying, agrimensura.—l. surveyor, agrimensor.—*vt.* desembarcar; echar en tierra.—*vi.* desembarcar; tomar tierra; (aer.) aterrizar; amarar (un avión).- —holder [lǽndhoujldœ(r)], s. hacendado, terrateniente.— —ing [-jŋ], s. descanso, rellano de escalera; desembarco, desembarque; desembarcadero; aterrizaje; amaraje.—a. de desembarque, de aterrizaje.—l. craft, barcaza militar de desembarque.—l. forces, tropas de desembarco.—l. gear, tren de aterrizaje.- —lady [-lejdj], s. casera, ama, patrona; arrendadora, propietaria.- —lord [-lord], s. propietario o dueño de tierras o casas; arrendador; casero, patrón.—mark [-mark], s. mojón, señal; (mar.) marca; punto o acontecimiento culminante.- —owner [-ounœ(r)], s. hacendado, terrateniente, propietario.- —scape [-skejp], s. paisaje.- —slide [-slajd], s. derrumbamiento, derrumbe.—l. victory,

victoria aplastante (esp. en elecciones).

lane [lejn], s. senda, vereda; calle, callejuela; ruta; pista o carrilera (de tránsito).

language [léŋgwjdž], s. lengua, idioma; lenguaje.

languette [léŋgwet], s. (mus.) lengüeta.

languid [léŋgwid], a. lánguido.— languish [léŋgwjš], *vi.* languidecer, consumirse.—languishing [léŋgwjšjŋ], s. languidez.—a. lánguido, decaído.— languor [léŋgǫ(r)], s. desfallecimiento, languidez, debilidad.

lank [læŋk], a. flaco, seco; alto y delgado.—l. hair, cabellos largos y lacios.- —y [léŋkj], a. larguirucho, langaruto, delgaducho.

lantern [léntœrn], s. linterna, farol; (mar.) faro, fanal.—l. jack, fuego fatuo.

lap [læp], s. falda; regazo; (dep.) vuelta completa de la pista; lamedura.—l. dog, perrillo faldero.—*vti.* [1] lamer; envolver; sobreponer, solapar.

lapel [lăpél], s. (sast.) solapa.

Laplander [lǽplændœ(r)], s. lapón.

lapse [læps], s. lapso; intervalo de tiempo, transcurso; desliz, equivocación, falta; (for.) prescripción, caducidad de la instancia.—in the l. of time, con el transcurso del tiempo, andando el tiempo.—*vi.* pasar, transcurrir; decaer, deslizarse; caer en desliz o error; (for.) prescribir, caducar.

larceny [lársenj], s. ratería, hurto.

lard [lard], s. manteca (de cerdo), (tocino) gordo.—*vt.* mechar.— —er [lárdœ(r)], s. despensa.

large [lardž], a. grande; amplio.—at l., en libertad, suelto; extensamente; sin limitación, libre.- —ly [lárdžlj], adv. grandemente; ampliamente; en gran manera.- —ness [-njs], s. grandor, gran tamaño; extensión, amplitud.

lariat [lérjat], s. lazo, reata, mangana.

lark [lark], s. alondra, calandria; (fam.) francachela, parranda, holgorio.

larva [lárvǎ], s. (pl. larvae [lárvi]) larva.

laryngitis [lærjndžájtjs], s. laringitis, afonía, ronquera.—larynx [lérjŋks], s. laringe.

lascivious [lǎsívjʌs], a. lascivo.

lash [læš], s. látigo, flagelo; azote, latigazo; chasquido; pestaña (del ojo).—*vt.* dar latigazos; azotar, flagelar; reprochar; atar; (mar.) amarrar, trincar.—*vi.* chasquear el látigo.

lass [læs], s. doncella, moza, muchacha, chica.

lassitude [lǽsitjud], *s.* lasitud, languidez.

lasso [lǽsou], *vt.* (en)lazar.—*s.* lazo, mangana, (Am.) guaso.

last [læst], *a.* último; final, supremo; pasado.—*l. evening,* ayer por la noche, anoche.—*l. night,* anoche.—*l. word,* palabra o decisión final; (fam.) última moda.—*next to the l.,* penúltimo.—*adv.* por la última vez, por último, al fin.—*at l.,* por fin, al cabo.—*s.* fin, término; (lo, el) último; (zap.) horma.—*to the l.,* hasta el fin, hasta lo último.—*vi.* durar, perdurar, permanecer, subsistir.—*vt.* (zap.) ahormar, poner en la horma.— —ing [lǽstiŋ], *a.* duradero, perdurable.— —ly [-li], *adv.* en conclusión, por fin, finalmente, por último.

latch [læch], *s.* aldaba, pestillo, cerrojo, picaporte.—*l. key,* llavín.—*vt.* cerrar con aldaba o pestillo.

late [leit], *a.* tardío; tardo; último, postrero; reciente; difunto.—*l. arrival,* recién llegado.—*adv.* tarde; poco ha, últimamente.—*l. in the year,* al fin del año.—*to be l.,* llegar tarde, retrasarse, estar atrasado; ser tarde.—*too l.,* (demasiado) tarde.— —ly [léitli], *adv.* poco ha, no ha mucho; recientemente, últimamente.

latent [léitent], *a.* latente.

later [léitœ(r)], *adv. y a.* (comp. de LATE) más tarde; luego, después, posterior. —*l. on,* más trade, después.

lateral [lǽteral], *a.* lateral.

latest [léitist], *a. y adv.* (superl. de LATE) último; novísimo.—*at the l.,* a más tardar.

lathe [leið], *s.* torno.—*l. bed,* banco del torno.

lather [lǽðœ(r)], *vt.* enjabonar (para afeitar).—*vi.* hacer espuma.—*s.* jabonadura, espuma de jabón.

Latin [lǽtin], *a. y s.* latino.—*s.* latín.

latitude [lǽtitjud], *s.* latitud; amplitud; libertad.

latrine [lætrín], *s.* letrina.

latter [lǽtœ(r)], *a.* posterior, más reciente, moderno.—*the l.,* éste, ésta, esto.

lattice [lǽtis], *s.* enrejado, celosía.

laud [lod], *s.* (canto de) alabanza; loa. —*vt.* alabar, loar, elogiar.— —able [lódabl], *a.* laudable, loable.

laugh [læf], *vi.* reír(se).—*to l. loudly,* reírse a carcajadas.—*vt.* ahogar en o con risa.—*s.* risa; risotada.— —able [lǽfabl], *a.* risible, irrisorio; divertido. — —ing [-iŋ], *s.* risa, reír.— —ter [-tœ(r)], *s.* risa.

launch [lonch], *vt.* botar o echar al agua (un barco); dar principio a, acometer; lanzar.—*vi.* lanzarse.—*s.* lancha,

chalupa.— —ing [lónchiŋ], *s.* lanzamiento; (mar.) botadura.

launder [lóndœ(r)], *vt.* lavar y planchar la ropa.—**laundress** [lóndris], *s.* lavandera.—**laundry** [lóndri], *s.* lavadero; lavandería; tren de lavado; ropa lavada o para lavar.—**laundryman** [lóndrimən], *s.* lavandero.

laureate [lórijt], *a.* laureado.—**laurel** [lórel], *s.* laurel, lauro; honor, distinción.

lava [lǽvə], *s.* lava.

lavatory [lǽvatori], *s.* lavatorio, lavabo, lavamanos; lavadero.

lavender [lǽvendœ(r)], *s.* espliego, lavanda.

lavish [lǽviʃ], *a.* pródigo, gastador; profuso.—*vt.* disipar, malbaratar, prodigar.— —ness [-nis], *s.* prodigalidad, profusión.

law [lo], *s.* ley; derecho; leyes (en general); justicia, jurisprudencia.—*l. abiding,* observante de la ley.—*l. of nations,* derecho internacional; derecho de gentes.—*l. school,* Facultad de Derecho.—**breaker** [lóbreikœ(r)], *s.* transgresor, infractor.— —**ful** [-ful], *a.* legal, lícito; permitido, válido.— —**less** [-lis], *a.* ilegal; desaforado, desmandado, de mal vivir.— —**maker** [-meikœ(r)], *s.* legislador.— —**making** [-meikiŋ], *s.* legislación.—*a.* legislativo.

lawn [lon], *s.* césped, prado.—*l. mower,* cortadora de césped.

lawsuit [lósjut], *s.* pleito, litigio, juicio. —**lawyer** [lóyœ(r)], *s.* abogado, letrado.—*l.'s bill,* minuta.—*l.'s office,* bufete.

lax [læks], *a.* suelto, flojo; laxo, relajado.— —**ative** [lǽksʌtiv], *a. y s.* laxante, purgante suave.— —**ity** [-iti], —**ness** [-nis], *s.* aflojamiento, flojedad; relajamiento; relajación.

lay [lei], *pret.* de TO LIE (echarse).

lay [lei], *vti.* [10] poner, colocar; tender (tuberías, rieles, etc.), instalar; derribar; poner (un huevo), la mesa, etc.); enterrar; calmar; imponer (cargas, tributos).—*to l. against,* acusar de, achacar a.—*to l. apart* reservar, poner aparte.—*to l. aside,* desechar; arrinconar; abandonar.—*to l. off,* trazar, delinear; despedir.—*to l. out,* gastar, emplear; exhibir; trazar; proyectar.—*vi.* poner (las gallinas, etc.); apostar; (mar.) situarse, colocarse.—*to l. off,* parar (en el trabajo). —*to l. over,* demorarse, detenerse; sobrepasar.—*a.* laico, lego, seglar; profano, incompetente.—*s.* caída; contorno; (fam.) oficio, ocupación; canción, balada.— —**er** [léiœ(r)], *s.* capa, estrato, mano; gallina ponedora.— —**ing** [-iŋ], *s.* colocación; pos-

tura (del huevo).— **man** [-man], *s.* lego, seglar.— **off** [-of], *s.* despedida o despido (de obreros).— **out** [-aut], *s.* plan, disposición, arreglo, trazado.— **over** [-ouvœ(r)], *s.* parada temporal en un lugar.

lazily [léizili], *adv.* perezosamente.— **laziness** [léizinis], *s.* pereza, holgazanería.— **lazy** [léizi], *a.* perezoso, holgazán; pesado.—*l. bones*, perezoso, dormilón.

lead [lid], *s.* primacía, primer lugar; dirección, mando; delantera; (teat.) papel principal, protagonista; [led], plomo; mina o grafito del lápiz; (mar.) sonda, escandallo; plomada.—*l. poisoning*, (med.) cólico saturnino.— *vti.* [10] [lid], llevar de la mano; guiar, dirigir; mandar, acaudillar; ir a la cabeza de; enseñar, amaestrar; llevar (buena, mala vida); inducir.— *to l. a new life*, enmendarse.—*to l. astray*, descarriar, seducir.—*to l. off* o *out*, desviar; principiar.—*vii.* guiar, enseñar el camino; sobresalir; ir adelante; conducir; dominar; ser mano en el juego de naipes.—*to l.* (*up*) *to*, conducir a, dar a.— **en** [lédn], *a.* plomizo; aplomado; pesado.

leader [lídœ(r)], *s.* jefe, (neol.) líder; guía, conductor; guión; caballo delantero; (imp.) puntos suspensivos. — **ship** [-śip], *s.* jefatura, (neol.) liderato; dirección, primacía.— **leading** [lídin], *a.* director; principal; dominante, sobresaliente.—*l. edge*, (aer.) borde de ataque.—*l. lady*, (teat.) primera actriz.—*l. man*, jefe, cabecilla; (teat.) galán, protagonista.

leaf [lif], *s.* hoja.—*l. tobacco*, tabaco en rama.—*vi.* echar hojas; hacerse frondoso.—*vt.* hojear (un libro).— **less** [lífis], *a.* deshojado.— **let** [-lit], *s.* (impr.) folleto, volante, circular; (bot.) hojuela.— **y** [-i], *a.* frondoso; de forma de hoja.

league [lig], *s.* liga, confederación, alianza; sociedad o asociación; legua (unas 3 millas).—*vt.* y *vi.* aliar(se); asociar(se), confederar(se).

leak [lik], *s.* gotera en un techo; fuga o escape de gas, vapor, etc.; (mar.) vía de agua.—*vi.* gotear; (mar.) hacer agua; salirse; dejar escapar (el agua, vapor, etc.), escurrirse.—*to l. out*, (fig.) divulgarse, saberse, traslucirse.— **age** [líkidź], *s.* goteo, escape, fuga, salida; (com.) avería, merma, derrame.

lean [lin], *vii.* [4] apoyarse, recostarse, inclinarse; ladearse, encorvarse.— *vti.* apoyar, reclinar; inclinar; encorvar. —*a.* flaco; magro; enjuto, delgado.

leap [lip], *vii.* [4] saltar, brincar, dar un salto o brinco.—*vti.* (hacer) saltar,

cubrir el macho a la hembra.—*s.* salto, brinco; cabriola, zapateta.— *by leaps and bounds*, a saltos; a pasos agigantados.—*l. year*, año bisiesto.

learn [lœrn], *vti.* y *vii.* [4] aprender; enterarse de, saber; instruirse.— **ed** [lœrnid], *a.* docto, erudito, sabio.— **ing** [-in], *s.* saber, ciencia; instrucción; aprendizaje.

lease [lis], *s.* arriendo, contrato de arrendamiento.—*l. holder*, arrendatario.—*vt.* arrendar, alquilar, dar o tomar en arriendo.

leash [liś], *s.* traílla, correa.

least [list], *a.* (*super.* de LITTLE) mínimo; ínfimo; (el) más pequeño.— *not in the l.*, de ninguna manera, bajo ningún concepto.—*adv.* menos.—*s.* (lo) menos.—*at l.*, al menos, por lo menos.

leather [léðœ(r)], *s.* cuero, piel, curtido. —*a.* de cuero.—*l. belt*, correa, cinturón.—*l. strap*, correa.— **n** [-n], *a.* de cuero.

leave [liv], *s.* licencia, permiso, venia.— *l.-taking*, despedida.—*on l.*, (mil.) con licencia.—*vti.* [10] dejar; abandonar; salir o partir de; separarse de.— *to l. alone*, dejar quieto o en paz; no meterse con.—*to l. off*, cesar, suspender; dejar (un vicio, una costumbre). —*to l. out*, omitir, excluir.—*to l. word*, dejar dicho.—*vii.* irse, marcharse, salir, partir.

leaven [lévn], *s.* levadura, fermento.— *vt.* fermentar.— **ing** [-in], *s.* fermento.

leaves [livz], *s. pl.* de LEAF.

leaving [lívin], *s.* partida, marcha.—*pl.* sobras, desechos, desperdicios.

lecherous [léchœrʌs], *a.* lujurioso, lascivo.—**lechery** [léchœri], *s.* lujuria, lascivia.

lecture [lékchu(r)], *s.* disertación, conferencia; lectura, instrucción; sermoneo, represión.—*l. hall* o *room*, aula, cátedra, salón de conferencias.—*vi.* reprender, (fam.) sermonear, regañar. — **r** [lékchuœ(r)], *s.* conferenciante, conferencista; lector (de universidad o iglesia).

led [led], *pp.* y *pret.* de TO LEAD.

ledge [ledź], *s.* borde; repisa, saledizo.

ledger [lédźœ(r)], *s.* (com.) libro mayor; traviesa de andamio.

lee [li], *s.* sotavento, socaire.—*l. side*, banda de sotavento.—*under the l.*, a sotavento.

leech [lich], *s.* sanguijuela.

leer [lir], *s.* mirada de soslayo o de reojo.—*vi.* mirar de soslayo, maliciosa o lascivamente.— **ingly** [lírinli], *adv.* de soslayo.— **y** [-i], *a.* (fam.) astuto; receloso.

leeward [líwₐrd, (mar.) lúₐrd], *a.* sotavento.

left [left], *pret. y pp. de* TO LEAVE.—*l. behind*, rezagado.—*l. off*, desechado.—*to be l.*, quedar(se).—*a.* izquierdo.—*l. hand*, izquierdo (lado, etc.); con la mano izquierda.—*l.-handed*, zurdo; torpe, desmañado; insincero, malicioso.—*l. wing*, (pol.) bando izquierdista o radical, las izquierdas.—*s.* mano izquierda, lado izquierdo; (pol.) izquierda(s).—*at, on, o to the l.*, a la izquierda.— *ist* [léftjst], *a. y s.* izquierdista.— *over* [-oɥvœ(r)], *s.* sobrante, sobra, rezago.—*a.* sobrante, sobrado.

leg [leg], *s.* pierna; pata o pie (animales y objetos); trayecto, jornada.—*not to have a l. to stand on*, no tener razón o argumento válidos.—*on o upon its legs*, en pie, firmemente establecido.—*on one's last legs*, acabándose; agonizante; sin recursos.—*to pull someone's leg*, tomarle el pelo a uno.

legacy [légəsi], *s.* legado, manda.

legal [lígₐl], *a.* legal, legítimo, lícito.—*l. tender*, moneda de curso legal.— *ity* [ligálitj], *s.* legalidad, legitimidad.— *ization* [-izéjʃən], *s.* legalización.— *ize* [-aiz], *vt.* legalizar; refrendar.

legate [légit], *s.* legado, enviado.— **legation** [ligéjʃən], *s.* legación, misión, embajada.

legend [lédʒₑnd], *s.* leyenda; letrero, inscripción.— *ary* [-eri], *a.* legendario.

legerdemain [ledʒœrdiméjn], *s.* juego de manos, prestidigitación.

legging [légiɳ], *s.* polaina.

legible [lédʒibl], *a.* legible.

legion [lídʒən], *s.* legión.— *ary* [-eri], *a. y s.* legionario.

legislate [lédʒisleit], *vi.* legislar.—**legislation** [ledʒisléjʃən], *s.* legislación.— **legislative** [lédʒisleitiv], *a.* legislativo.— **legislator** [lédʒisleitₒ(r)], *s.* legislador.—**legislature** [lédʒisleichₒ(r)], *s.* legislatura, asamblea, cuerpo legislativo.

legitimate [lidʒítimit], *a.* legítimo.—*vt.* [lidʒítimeit], legitimar; legalizar.

leisure [líʒₒ(r)], *s.* ocio, ociosidad; comodidad.—*l. hours*, horas libres o desocupadas, ratos perdidos.—*to be at l.*, estar desocupado.— *ly* [-li], *a.* pausado, deliberado.—*adv.* despacio; cómoda o desocupadamente; a sus anchas.

lemon [lémₒn], *s.* limón.—*l. tree*, limonero, limón.— *ade* [-éjd], *s.* limonada.

lend [lend], *vti.* [10] prestar, dar prestado.—*to l. a hand*, dar una mano, ayudar.— *er* [léndœ(r)], *s.* prestador, prestamista.

length [leɳθ], *s.* longitud, largo(r); extensión, distancia; duración de tiempo; alcance (de un tiro, etc.); (mar.) eslora.—*at full l.*, a lo largo, de todo el largo.—*at l.*, al fin, finalmente; extensamente.— **en** [léɳₒn], *vt. y vi.* alargar(se), prolongar(se).— **ways** [-wejz], **wise** [-wajz], *adv.* longitudinalmente; a lo largo; de largo a largo.— **y** [-i], *a.* largo; larguísimo.

leniency [línjₑnsi], *s.* indulgencia, lenidad.—**lenient** [línjₑnt], *a.* indulgente, clemente.

lens [lenz], *s.* lente; cristalino (del ojo).

lent [lent], *pret. y pp. de* TO LEND.— (L.), *s.* cuaresma.

lentil [léntil], *s.* (bot.) lenteja.

leopard [lépₐrd], *s.* leopardo.

leper [lépœ(r)], *s.* leproso.—**leprosy** [léprₒsi], *s.* lepra.—**leprous** [léprʌs], *a.* leproso, lazarino.

lesion [líʒₒn], *s.* lesión.

less [les], *a.* (*comp. de* LITTLE) menor, menos, inferior.—*adv.* menos; en grado más bajo.—*l. and l.*, cada vez menos.—*s.* (el o lo) menos.—*prep.* menos; sin.

lessee [lesí], *s.* arrendatario, inquilino.

lessen [lésn], *vt.* aminorar, disminuir, mermar; rebajar.—*vi.* mermar, disminuirse; rebajarse, degradarse.— **lesser** [lésœ(r)], *a.* (*comp. de* LITTLE) menor, más pequeño.

lesson [lésₒn], *s.* lección.

lessor [lésₒ(r)], *s.* arrendador.

lest [lest], *conj.* para que no, por miedo de, no sea que.

let [let], *vti.* [9] dejar, permitir; arrendar, alquilar.—*l. alone*, cuanto más, ni mucho menos.—*l. us go!* ¡vamos! ¡vámonos!—*to l. alone*, dejar en paz.—*to l. be*, no molestar; no meterse con.—*to l. down*, dejar caer; bajar; abandonar.—*to l. go*, soltar.—*to l. in*, dejar entrar, admitir.—*to l. know*, hacer saber, avisar.—*to l. off*, disparar, descargar; dispensar, indultar.—*to l. out*, dejar salir, soltar; arrendar; divulgar (un secreto).—*to l. the cat out of the bag*, revelar un secreto.—*vii.* alquilarse o arrendarse.—*pret. y pp. de* TO LET.

lethal [líθₐl], *a.* mortal, mortífero.

lethargic [liθárdʒik], *a.* letárgico.—**lethargy** [léθₐrdʒi], *s.* letargo, apatía.

letter [létœ(r)], *s.* letra; carta.—*l. box*, buzón; apartado.—*l. carrier*, cartero.—*l. of license*, moratoria, espera.—*to the l.*, al pie de la letra, a la letra.—*vt.* rotular; poner letras, título o letreros a.— **head** [-hed], *s.* membrete.— **ing** [-iɳ], *s.* letrero, inscripción, rótulo.

lettuce [létis], *s.* lechuga.

leukemia [ljukímiǎ], *s.* leucemia.
Levant [livént], *s.* Levante, Oriente.—
—**ine** [-in], *a.* y *s.* levantino.
level [lévęl], *a.* plano, llano, igual,
parejo; a nivel.—*l. crossing*, (f.c.)
paso a nivel.—*l.-headed*, juicioso,
discreto.—*s.* nivel (instrumento;
altura); puntería.—*on the l.*, abiertamente, sin dolo.—*adv.* a nivel, a ras.
—*vti.* [2] igualar, allanar; nivelar;
apuntar; emparejar.—*vii.* apuntar
(un arma); nivelar, hacer nivela-
ciones.
lever [lévœ(r)], *s.* palanca; escape de
reloj.—*control l.*, palanca de mando.-
—**age** [-idz], *s.* apalancamiento;
(fig.) ventaja.
Levite [lívait], *s.* levita.
levity [lévitị], *s.* liviandad; veleidad.
levy [lévị], *s.* leva, reclutamiento;
impuesto, recaudación; (for.) embargo.—*vti.* [7] imponer, recaudar;
reclutar; (for.) embargar.
lewd [ljud], *a.* lujurioso, lascivo.—
—**ness** [ljúdnịs], *s.* lujuria, lascivia.
lexicography [lęksịkágrafị], *s.* lexicografía.—**lexicon** [léksịkọn], *s.* léxico,
vocabulario, diccionario.
liability [laiabílịtị], *s.* riesgo; obligación,
responsabilidad.—*pl.* (com.) pasivo,
obligaciones a pagar.—**liable** [láịabl],
a. sujeto, expuesto; obligado, responsable; propenso.
liar [láịǎr], *s.* embustero, mentiroso.
libel [láịbęl], *s.* libelo; difamación.—*vti.*
[2] difamar.— —(l)ous [-ʌs], *a.* difamatorio.
liberal [líbęral], *a.* liberal, generoso;
(pol.) liberal.— —**ism** [-izm], *s.* liberalismo.— —**ity** [libęrélịtị], *s.* liberalidad.
liberate [líbęreit], *vt.* libertar, librar.—
liberation [libęréịsọn], *s.* liberación.—
liberator [líbęreịtọ(r)], *s.* libertador.
libertine [líbœrtịn], *a.* y *s.* libertino,
disoluto.
liberty [líbœrtị], *s.* libertad; liberación
de presos o cautivos; licencia, permiso.—*to take undue liberties*, propasarse.
librarian [laịbrérịạn], *s.* bibliotecario.—
library [láịbrerị], *s.* biblioteca.
libretto [librétọu], *s.* libreto.
Libyan [líbịạn], *s.* y *a.* libio; líbico.
lice [laịs], *s. pl.* de LOUSE.
license, licence [láịsęns], *s.* licencia,
permiso; título (universitario); licencia, libertinaje.—*driver's l.*, licencia
de conducción (de automóviles).—*l.
plate*, (aut., etc.) placa, matrícula o
chapa.—*vt.* licenciar, dar licencia o
permiso; autorizar.—**licentiate** [laị-
sénšịịt], *s.* licenciado.—**licentious**
[laịsénsʌs], *a.* licencioso, desenfrenado, disoluto.

licit [lísịt], *a.* lícito.
lick [lik], *vt.* lamer; (fam.) cascar, dar
una tunda o zurra; vencer.—*to l. the
dust*, morder el polvo.—*vi.* flamear.—
s. lamedura, lengüetada; lamedero;
(fam.) mojicón, bofetón.— —**ing**
[líkịŋ], *s.* tunda, paliza; derrota.
licorice [líkorịs], *s.* anís.
lid [lid], *s.* tapa, tapadera; párpado.
lie [laị], *s.* mentira, embuste.—*to give
the l. to*, desmentir, dar un mentís.—
white l., mentira inocente, mentirilla.
—*vi.* mentir.—*vii.* [10] echarse, estar
tendido; yacer; descansar, hallarse
(sobre una superficie); estar ubicado,
radicar.
lien [lin], *s.* (for.) embargo; derecho de
retención.
lieutenant [ljụténạnt], *s.* teniente;
lugarteniente.—*l. commander*, capitán
de fragata.
life [laịf], *s.* vida; modo de vivir; vivacidad, animación.—*for l.*, de por vida;
vitalicio.—*from l.*, del natural.—*still
l.*, naturaleza muerta, bodegón.—*a.*
de la vida; vitalicio.—*l. annuity*,
renta vitalicia.—*l. belt*, cinturón
salvavidas.—*l. imprisonment*, cadena
perpetua.—*l. preserver*, salvavidas.—
l. sentence, cadena perpetua.—*l.-size*,
de tamaño natural.—*boat* [láịfbout],
s. bote o lancha salvavidas, o de
salvamento.—*guard* [-gard], *s.*
salvavidas (persona).— —**less** [-lịs],
a. sin vida, muerto, inanimado; deshabitado.— —**lessness** [-lịsnịs], *s.*
falta de vida; falta de animación o
vigor.— —**like** [-laịk], *a.* que parece
vivo, natural.— —**long** [-loŋ], *a.* de
toda la vida, perpetuo.— —**saver**
[-seịvœ(r)], *s.* bañero, salvavidas
(persona).— —**time** [-taịm], *s.* curso
de la vida; toda la vida.—*a.* vitalicio,
de por vida.
lift [lift], *vt.* alzar, levantar, elevar;
(fam.) hurtar; plagiar.—*to l. up*,
alzar; soliviar.—*to l. (up) the hand*,
prestar juramento levantando la
mano; orar; hacer un esfuerzo.—*vi.*
disiparse (la niebla).—*s.* elevación;
alza; aparejo o gancho de alzar;
ascensión.—*to give one a l.*, ayudar a
uno; alentar o animar a uno; llevar a
uno gratis en un vehículo.
ligament [lígamęnt], (anat.) ligamento.
light [laịt], *s.* luz; claridad, resplandor;
lumbre; alumbrado; día, alba.—*in
this l.*, desde este punto de vista.—*a.*
ligero, leve; sutil; llevadero, fácil;
fútil, frívolo, superficial; ágil, liviano;
inconstante, mudable; alegre, vivo;
incontinente; claro (colores; piel).—
l.-haired, pelirrubio.—*l.-headed*, ligero
de cascos; atolondrado.—*l.-headed-
ness*, atolondramiento, aturdimiento.

—*l.-hearted*, alegre, festivo.—*l.-witted*, chalado, cascabelero.—*-ti*. [4] encender, alumbrar, iluminar.—*-vi*. encenderse; iluminarse; descender, posarse; apearse.— —en [láitn], *vt*. iluminar, alumbrar; aclarar; aligerar; aliviar; regocijar.—*vi*. ponerse ligero; relampaguear, centellear.— —er [-œ(r)], *s*. (comp. de LIGHT).—*s*. encendedor.——house [-haus], *s*. faro. — —ing [-iŋ], *s*. alumbrado, luz; iluminación.— —ness [-nis], *s*. levedad, ligereza; agilidad; frivolidad, liviandad.— —ning [-niŋ], *s*. relámpago; relampagueo.

likable [láikȧbl], *a*. amable, simpático, agradable.—**like** [laik], *a*. semejante; análogo, igual; lo mismo que, equivalente.—*it looks l. rain*, parece que va a llover.—*to feel l. going*, tener ganas de ir.—*s*. semejanza; semejante, igual. —*pl*. gustos, simpatías, aficiones.— *adv*. **y** *prep*. como, semejante a; a (la) manera de, a guisa de, en son de; al igual que, del mismo modo que, a semejanza de; (fam.) probablemente. —*l. as*, como, así como.—*l. mad*, como loco, furiosamente.—*l. this*, así, de este modo.—*that is (just) l. him*, eso es muy propio de él.—*what are they l.?* ¿cómo son ellos?—*vt*. gustarle a uno; gustar de; tener gusto en o afición a; aprobar; querer, simpatizar con.—*to l. best, better*, gustarle (a uno) más.—*vi*. gustar, agradar.—*as you l.*, como usted quiera, como a usted guste.—*if you l.*, si le parece (bien).— *she had l. to die o have died*, (fam.) por poco se muere.—**likelihood** [láiklihud], *s*. probabilidad; verosimilitud; apariencia.—**likely** [láikli], *a*. probable, verosímil, fácil; prometedor; apto, idóneo, a propósito.—*adv*. probablemente.—*l. enough*, no sería extraño.—**liken** [láikn], *vt*. asemejar, comparar.—**likeness** [láiknis], *s*. semejanza, parecido; igualdad; apariencia, aire; retrato.—**likewise** [láikwaiz], *adv*. también, asimismo, además, igualmente; otrosí.—**liking** [láikiŋ], *s*. afición, gusto, agrado, inclinación; simpatía; preferencia.

lilac [láilȧk], *s*. (bot.) lila.—*a*. de color de lila.

Lilliputian [lilipiúsȧn], *a*. **y** *s*. liliputiense, enano.

lily [líli], *s*. (bot.) lirio, azucena; flor de lis.—*l.-livered*, cobarde, ruin.

limb [lim], *s*. miembro (del cuerpo); rama (de árbol); miembro, individuo; limbo; borde, orilla.—*vt*. desmembrar. — —er [límbœ(r)], *a*. flexible, blando. —*vi*. (up) ponerse flexible.— —erness [límbœrnis], *s*. flexibilidad.

lime [laim], *s*. cal; liga (para cazar);

(bot.) lima.— —**light** [láimlait], *s*. luz de calcio; proscenio.

limit [límit], *s*. límite, fin; frontera, lindero; ámbito; limitación, restricción; colmo.—*vt*. limitar.— —ation [-éisȯn], *s*. limitación.— —less [-lis], *a*. ilimitado.

limp [limp], *s*. cojera.—*a*. débil, flojo; fláccido.—*vi*. cojear, renquear.— —er [límpœ(r)], *s*. cojo.

limpid [límpid], *a*. limpio, cristalino, límpido.— —ity [limpíditi], —ness [límpidnis], *s*. limpidez, diafanidad.

line [lain], *s*. línea; tubería, cañería; raya; veta; renglón; sedal (de pescar); frontera, límite; (com.) renglón, ramo, clase; surtido, artículos; (f.c., etc.) recorrido, trayecto; método, plan; línea de conducta; hilera, fila; verso; especialidad.—*along these lines*, en este sentido.—*in a l.*, en línea.— *in l.*, alineado; de acuerdo; dispuesto. —*in one's line*, dentro de la especialidad o conocimientos de uno.—*on the lines of*, conforme a, a tenor de.— *out of one's line*, ajeno a la especialidad o tarea de uno; asunto de que uno no entiende.—*vt*. trazar líneas, rayar; alinear; ir a lo largo o en los bordes u orillas de.—*to l. out*, marcar con rayas.—*to l. up*, alinear.—*vi*. alinearse; estar alineado; (up) formar fila, estar en fila o haciendo cola; formar, ponerse en formación.——age [línijá], *s*. linaje, alcurnia.— —ar [líniȧ(r)], *a*. lineal; longitudinal; (zool. y bot.) linear.— —d [laind], *a*. rayado; forrado.

linen [línen], *s*. lienzo, lino; holanda; género de lino; lencería, ropa blanca.

liner [láinœ(r)], *s*. barco o avión de una línea establecida; delineador; rayador; forrador; forro.

linger [língœ(r)], *vi*. demorarse, ir despacio; subsistir, persistir.—*vt*. (out o away) prolongar, demorar.

linguist [língwist], *s*. lingüista; políglota.— —ic [lingwístik], *a*. lingüístico.— —ics [lingwístiks], *s*. lingüística.

lining [láiniŋ], *s*. forro; revestimiento; material para forros; (aut.) forro o banda de frenos; encofrado.

link [liŋk], *s*. eslabón; vínculo; enganche; cada una de las partes de un sistema articulado.—*pl*. cancha de golf.—*vt*. **y** *vi*. eslabonar(se), enlazar(se).— —age [líŋkidá], *s*. eslabonamiento, encadenamiento; sistema articulado.

linnet [línit], *s*. jilguero, pardillo.

linoleum [linóuliȧm], *s*. linóleo.

linotype [láinotaip], *s*. linotipo; linotipia.—**linotypist** [-ist], *s*. linotipista.

linseed [línsid], *s.* linaza.—*l. oil,* aceite de linaza.

lint [lint], *s.* hilas; pelusilla de la ropa.

lion [láiǫn], *s.* león.— —**ess** [-is], *s.* leona.— —**ize** [-aiz], *vt.* poner por las nubes.

lip [lip], *s.* labio.—*to give l.-service,* defender de dientes a fuera, de boquilla. — —**stick** [lípstik], *s.* creyón o lápiz de los labios.

liquefy [líkwifai], *vti.* y *vii.* [7] liquidar, liquidarse; derretir, fundirse.

liqueur [likœ(r)], *s.* licor; bebida cordial.

liquid [líkwid], *s.* líquido.—*a.* líquido; (com.) realizable.—**liquidate** [líkwideit], *vt.* liquidar.—**liquidation** [likwidéişon], *s.* liquidación.

liquor [líkǫ(r)], *s.* bebida alcohólica.

lisp [lisp], *vt.* y *vi.* cecear; balbucir o balbucear.—*s.* ceceo; balbuceo, balbucencia.

list [list], *s.* lista; nómina; registro; matrícula; (tej.) orilla, borde; lista, tira; filete, orla; tabloncillo; (mar.) escora, inclinación.—*pl.* liza, palestra. —*vt.* registrar, matricular, inscribir; poner en lista; catalogar; (com.) cotizar, facturar; (mil.) alistar; guarnecer con listones o cenefas.—*vi.* (mar.) escorar.

listen [lisn], *vi.* escuchar, oir; atender, prestar oídos a.—*to l. in,* ser radioyente, escuchar en el radio; oir subrepticiamente o arreglar un instrumento (radio, teléfono, etc.) con ese fin.— —**er** [-œ(r)], *s.* oyente.— *radio l.,* radioyente.

listless [lístlis], *a.* desatento; indiferente, descuidado.— —**ness** [-nis], *s.* descuido, indiferencia.

litany [lítani], *s.* (igl.) letanía.

liter [lítœ(r)], *s.* litro. Ver Tabla.

literacy [lítœraşi], *s.* capacidad de leer y escribir.—**literal** [lítœral], *a.* literal.— **literalism** [lítœralizm], *s.* exactitud literal; realismo extremo.—**literally** [lítœrali], *adv.* literalmente.—**literary** [lítœreri], *a.* literario.—**literate** [lítœrit], *a.* que sabe leer y escribir.— **literature** [lítœrachur], *s.* literatura.

lithography [liǫágrafi], *s.* litografía.

litigate [lítigeit], *vt.* y *vi.* litigar.— **litigation** [litigéişon], *s.* litigio.

litre [lítœ(r)], *s.* = LITER.

litter [lítœ(r)], *s.* litera; camilla, parihuela, andas; camada, cría; yacija (para animales); tendalera, cosas esparcidas desordenadamente por el suelo; desechos, residuos.—*vt.* esparcir (colillas, desechos, etc.); desordenar, desaliñar; preparar una yacija (para un animal).—*vi.* parir (los animales).

little [lítl], *a.* pequeño; poco.—*a. l. (bit),* un poco, un poquito.—*a l. sugar,* un poquito de azúcar.—*a l. while,* un rato, un ratico.—*adv.* poco.—*l. by l.,* poco a poco.—*s.* poco; porción o parte pequeña.

live [liv], *vt.* vivir, llevar (tal o cual vida).—*vi.* vivir, existir; habitar, morar, residir; mantenerse, subsistir. —*a.* [laiv], vivo, viviente; de la vida, vital; encendido, en ascua; activo, listo; de interés actual.— —**lihood** [láivlihud], *s.* vida, subsistencia.— —**liness** [láivlinis], *s.* vida, vivacidad, viveza, animación; agilidad, actividad.— —**ly** [láivli], *a.* vivo, vivaz, vivaracho; gallardo, airoso; rápido; animado.—*adv.* enérgicamente; vivamente; aprisa.— —**r** [lívœ(r)], *s.* (anat., zool.) hígado; vividor.

livery [lívœri], *s.* librea.

lives [laivz], *s. pl.* de LIFE.

livestock [láivstak], *s.* ganado, ganadería.

livid [lívid], *a.* lívido.

living [lívin], *s.* vida; modo de vivir; subsistencia, mantenimiento; vida, potencia vital.—*the l.,* los vivos, los seres vivientes.—*a.* vivo, viviente, con vida; animado; contemporáneo. —*l. room,* sala.—*l. wage,* salario decoroso.

lizard [lízard], *s.* lagarto; lagartija; saurio.

llama [láma], *s.* (zool.) llama.

load [loud], *s.* carga; peso; (o)presión.— *loads of,* (fam.) montones de, gran cantidad o número.—*vt.* y *vi.* cargar; recargar.

loaf [louf], *s.* (of bread), pan en sus diversas formas (hogaza, caña, flauta, panecillo, etc.).—*l. of sugar,* pilón de azúcar.—*vi.* haraganear, holgazanear. — —**er** [lóufœ(r)], *s.* holgazán, vago, zángano; zapato deportivo (sin cordones).

loan [loun], *s.* préstamo; (com.) empréstito.—*l. shark,* (fam.) usurero, garrotero.—*vt.* prestar (dinero).

loath [louǫ], *a.* poco dispuesto, renuente. — —**e** [louð], *vt.* detestar, abominar.— *vi.* tener hastío, sentir fastidio, disgusto o aborrecimiento.— —**some** [lóuðsam], *a.* aborrecible, repugnante, asqueroso.

loaves [louvz], *s. pl.* de LOAF.

lobby [lábi], *s.* vestíbulo; salón de entrada; paso, pasillo; pórtico; camarilla (política).—*vti.* y *vii.* [7] politiquear.

lobster [lábstœ(r)], *s.* langosta (de mar), bogavante.

local [lóukal], *a.* local; vecinal; regional. —*l. horizon,* horizonte sensible o visible.—*l. train,* tren ordinario o de escalas.— —**ity** [lokæliti], *s.* situación; localidad; lugar.— —**ization** [-izéişon],

s. localización.- —**ize** [-aiz], **vt.** localizar.—**locate** [lóukeit], **vt.** y **vi.** ubicar(se).—**location** [lokéişon], **s.** ubicación; sitio, localidad; situación, posición.

lock [lak], **s.** cerradura; llave o pestillo (de las armas de fuego); chaveta; esclusa, compuerta; abrazo estrecho y apretado; bucle, guedeja.—**l. nut,** (mec.) contratuerca.—**l. stitch,** punto de cadeneta.—**l. washer,** (mec.) arandela de seguridad.—**under l. and key,** bajo llave.—**vt.** cerrar con llave; poner cerradura; juntar, entrelazar, atar, trabar; abrazar; fijar, trincar; cerrar. —**to l. in,** encerrar, poner bajo llave. —**to l.** (one) **out,** cerrar la puerta a uno; dejar en la calle o sin trabajo.— **to l. up,** encerrar, encarcelar.—**vi.** cerrarse con llave; unirse; trabarse; sujetarse.- —**et** [lákit], **s.** relicario, medallón, guardapelo.- —**jaw** [-dżo], **s.** tétano(s).- —**out** [-aut], **s.** cierre de una fábrica, paro forzoso patronal.- —**smith** [-smiθ], **s.** cerrajero.— —**up** [-ʌp], **s.** calabozo; cárcel; encarcelamiento.

locomotive [loukomóutiv], **s.** locomotora.—**l. engineer,** maquinista.

locust [lóukʌst], **s.** langosta, langostón, saltamontes; cigarra.

locution [lokiúşon], **s.** locución.

lodge [ladż], **vt.** alojar, albergar; colocar; plantar, introducir, fijar; dar a guardar.—**to l. a complaint,** dar una queja.—**vi.** hospedarse; tenderse, echarse.—**s.** casa de guarda; pabellón; portería; logia.- —**r** [ládżœ(r)], **s.** inquilino, huésped.—**lodging** [ládżin], **s.** posada, hospedería; hospedaje, alojamiento; morada, residencia.

loft [loft], **s.** ático, sobrado, desván; almacén.- —**iness** [lóftinis], **s.** altura; nobleza; altanería.- —**y** [-i], **a.** alto, encumbrado; noble, elevado; sublime; eminente, altivo, soberbio.

log [log], **s.** leño, palo; tronco, madero; (mar.) corredera.—**l. book,** cuaderno de bitácora.—**l. cabin, l. hut,** cabaña rústica.—**vti.** [1] cortar (madera) y transportarla; apuntar en el cuaderno de bitácora; indicar en la corredera.— **vii.** cortar, aserrar y transportar trozas; extraer madera.

loge [louż], **s.** palco; anfiteatro.

logic [ládżik], **s.** lógica.- —**al** [-ạl], **a.** lógico.- —**ian** [lodżíşan], **s.** lógico.

loin [loin], **s.** lomo; ijada; ijar.

loiter [lóitœ(r)], **vi.** remolonear, holgazanear.—**vt.** (away) malgastar (tiempo).- —**er** [-œ(r)], **s.** vagabundo, holgazán.

loll [lal], **vi.** apoyarse, recostarse, tenderse; pender, colgar (la lengua de

un animal).—**vt.** dejar colgar (la lengua).

lollipop [lálipap], **s.** caramelo en palito, pirulí.

lone [loun], **a.** solitario, solo; soltero.- —**liness** [lóunlinis], **s.** soledad; tristeza del aislamiento.- —**ly** [-li], **a.** solitario; triste, desamparado.- —**some** [-sʌm], **a.** solitario, desierto; triste.

long [loŋ], **a.** largo; de largo; extenso, prolongado; tardío, dilatorio; excesivo, de más; distante; (com.) recargado, esperando alza de precios.— **how l.?** ¿de qué largo (medida)?— **in the l. run,** a la larga.—**it is a l. way,** dista mucho, está muy lejos.—**l. dozen,** docena de fraile, trece.—**l. hundred,** ciento veinte.—**l.-suffering,** paciencia, resignación, aguante.—**l. suit,** fuerte, especialidad de una persona.—**l. time,** mucho tiempo, largo rato.—**adv.** a gran distancia; mucho; (durante) mucho tiempo.—**all o the whole day, year, etc. l.,** todo el santo día, todo el año, etc.—**as l. as,** mientras.—**before** o **ere l.,** en breve, antes de mucho.—**how l.?** ¿cuánto tiempo?—**how l. is it since?** ¿cuánto (tiempo) hace que?—**l. after,** mucho (tiempo) después.—**l. ago,** hace mucho (tiempo).—**l.-drawn,** lento, pesado, prolongado.—**l. live!** ¡viva!— **l.-lived,** longevo.—**l.-range,** de largo alcance.—**l.-sighted,** sagaz, previsor.— **l.-standing,** de larga duración.— **l.-term,** (com.) a largo plazo.—**not l. ago** o **since,** no hace mucho.—**not l. before,** poco tiempo antes.—**so l. as,** mientras que, en tanto que.—**s.** longitud, largo.—**pl.** (com.) los que guardan acciones en espera de alza.—**vi.** (for, o to) anhelar, suspirar (por), codiciar, apetecer, ansiar; añorar.— —**er** [lóŋgœ(r)], **a.** más largo.—**adv.** más tiempo, más rato.—**how much l.?** ¿cuánto tiempo más?—**no l.,** ya no, no más.- —**evity** [lɔndżéviti], **s.** longevidad.- —**ing** [lóŋiŋ], **s.** deseo vehemente, anhelo, ansia, ansiedad. —**a.** anhelante, ansioso, vehemente.- —**itude** [lándżitjud], **s.** longitud.

longshoreman [lóŋşorman], **s.** estibador, cargador del muelle.

look [luk], **vt.** mirar, pasar la vista a; causar o expresar con la mirada o el ademán.—**to l. daggers,** echar chispas; (at) mirar echando chispas.—**to l. in the face,** mirar cara a cara, sin vergüenza.—**to l. one's age,** representar uno los años que tiene.—**to l. over,** mirar ligeramente o por encima.—**to l. up,** buscar, averiguar; (fam.) visitar a uno.—**vi.** mirar, ver; parecer, aparentar; poner cuidado o tener

cuidado; lucir (bien, mal); tener cara de.—*as it looks to me*, a mi ver.—*to l. about*, observar, mirar alrededor.—*to l. about one*, estar alerta, vigilar.— *to l. after*, cuidar, atender a, mirar por; prestar atención; inquirir, investigar.—*to l. alike*, parecerse.—*to l. alive*, darse prisa.—*to l. at*, mirar; tender la vista a; considerar.—*to l. back*, reflexionar; mirar atrás.—*to l. bad*, tomar mal cariz; parecer feo; tener mala cara.—*to l. down upon*, despreciar.—*to l. for*, buscar; esperar. —*to l. into*, estudiar, examinar, averiguar.—*to l. like*, parecerse a; tener cara o traza de; dar o haber señales de.—*to l. on*, considerar; estimar, juzgar; mirar, ver; ser espectador.— *to l. out of*, asomarse a.—*to l. sharp*, tener ojo avizor.—*to l. through*, examinar, inspeccionar, hacer un registro de.—*to l. to*, cuidar de, velar por; atender a; hacer responsable; esperar de; acudir a.—*to l. up to*, respetar, estimar.—*s.* mirada, ojeada, vistazo.—*pl.* aspecto, apariencia, semblante, traza.—*to have a l. at*, mirar, echar una ojeada a.— —**ing** [lúkiŋ], *s.* miramiento; busca; examen.—*a.* de o para mirar.—*good (bad)-l.*, bien (mal) parecido.— —**out** [-aut], *s.* vigía, vigilancia; observación; mirador; centinela.—*that's his l.*, (fam.) eso le concierne (a él); allá él, con su pan se lo coma.—*to be on the l.*, estar a la mira.

loom [lum], *s.* telar; arte de tejer; presencia, aparición—*vi.* asomar, aparecer exageradamente; destacarse, descollar; (re)lucir.— —**ing** [lúmiŋ], *s.* espejismo.

loon [lun], *s.* bobo, tonto.— —**y** [lúni], *s. y a.* (fam.) bobo, loco rematado.

loop [lup], *s.* gaza, lazo, bucle; ojal, presilla, alamar; onda; punto; curva, vuelta; (mec.) abrazadera, anilla; (aer.) rizo.—*vt.* asegurar con presilla; hacer gazas en; formar festones o curvas en.—*to l. in*, (elec.) intercalar (en un circuito).—*to l. the l.*, (aer.) rizar el rizo, dar una vuelta vertical. —*vi.* andar haciendo curvas; formar gaza.— —**hole** [lúphoul], *s.* abertura, mirador; aspillera, tronera; escapatoria, excusa.

loose [lus], *vt.* desatar, desprender; aflojar; aliviar; soltar, libertar, librar; desenredar; desocupar.—*to l. one's hold*, soltar.—*a.* suelto; desatado; flojo, holgado; vago, indefinido; libre, disoluto; negligente.—*s.* libertad, soltura.—*on the l.*, (fam.) libre; sin trabas; de parranda.— —**n** [lúsn], *vt.* aflojar, soltar, desunir; laxar, relajar; librar.—*vi.* desunirse, aflojarse, desa-

tarse.— —**ness** [-nis], *s.* aflojamiento, flojedad, holgura; relajamiento; soltura; flujo de vientre; vaguedad.

loot [lut], *vt. y vi.* saquear.—*s.* botín; saqueo, pillaje.

lop [lap], *vti.* [1] (des)mochar, podar; cercenar.—*vii.* colgar, pender, caer flojamente.—*s.* desmochadura; ramas podadas.—*l.-eared*, de orejas gachas.

loquacious [lokwéiŝəs], *a.* locuaz.— **loquacity** [lokwǽsiti], *s.* locuacidad.

lord [lord], *s.* señor; dueño, amo; lord (*pl.* lores).—*L.'s Prayer*, Padrenuestro.—*Our L.*, Nuestro Señor.—*vt. y vi.* gobernar, señorear, mandar imperiosamente.—*to l. it over*, dominar (en), señorear, imponerse a.— —**ly** [lórdli], *a.* señoril; imperioso.—*adv.* señorilmente; altiva o imperiosamente.— —**ship** [-ŝip], *s.* señorío, dominio, poder; señoría, excelencia. —*your l.*, usía, vuecencia.

lore [lor], *s.* erudición, saber, ciencia.

lorgnette [lornyét], *s.* impertinentes; gemelos de teatro con mango.

lose [luz], *vti.* [10] perder.—*to l. face*, desprestigiarse.—*to l. heart*, descorazonarse.—*to l. oneself*, perderse, extraviarse.—*to l. one's temper*, encolerizarse.—*to l. sight of*, perder de vista.—*vii.* perder, tener una pérdida; atrasar (un reloj).—*to l. out*, (fam.) llevarse chasco, ser derrotado.— —**r** [lúzœ(r)], *s.* perdedor.— —**losing** [lúziŋ], *a.* perdedor, perdidoso; vencido.—**loss** [los], *s.* pérdida; perjuicio, daño; privación.—*at a l.*, perdiendo, con pérdida; perplejo, indeciso, en duda.—*at a l. to*, sin acertar a.—*it's your l.*, (fam.) usted se lo pierde.— **lost** [lost], *pret. y pp.* de TO LOSE.—*a.* perdido, extraviado, descarriado; desorientado; perplejo; malogrado; desperdiciado.—*l. and found (office)*, departamento de objetos perdidos.

lot [lat], *s.* solar, terreno; lote, porción, parte; grupo (de personas); suer.e, hado, sino.—*a l.*, (fam.) mucho.—*a l. of*, (fam.) gran número de, gran cantidad de.—*by lots*, echando suertes, a la suerte.—*lots of*, (fam.) mucho, muchos.—*to draw o to cast lots*, echar suertes.—*to fall to one's l.*, tocarle a uno en suerte.

lotion [lóuŝən], *s.* loción.

lottery [látœri], *s.* lotería, rifa.— **lotto** [látou], *s.* lotería.

loud [laud], *a.* ruidoso; recio, fuerte; chillón; (fam.) urgente; llamativo; subido de color.—*l. laugh*, risotada, carcajada.—*l.-voiced*, estentóreo.— *adv.* ruidosamente; en alta voz; a gritos.— —**ness** [láudnis], *s.* ruido, sonoridad; (fam.) vulgaridad, mal gusto.

—**loud-speaker** [láųd spíkœ(r)], *s.* altavoz, altoparlante; megáfono.

lounge [laųndź], *vi.* holgazanear; repatingarse; ponerse uno a sus anchas.— *s.* salón de fumar o descansar; sofá, canapé.

louse [laųs], *s.* piojo.—**lousy** [láųzi], *a.* piojoso.

lovable [lávąbl], *a.* amable.—**love** [lav], *vt.* amar, querer; (fam.) gustar mucho de, tener gran afición a.—*vi.* amar; gustarle a uno mucho.—*s.* amor, cariño, afecto, devoción; pasión amatoria o sexual; el ser amado.— *for l. or money*, por buenas o por malas; a cualquier precio.—*in l. with*, enamorado de.—*l. affair*, intriga amorosa, amorío.—*l. bird*, periquito. —*not l. or money*, por nada del mundo.—*to make l. to*, enamorar, galantear, cortejar.—**loveliness** [lávlinįs], *s.* amabilidad, agrado, encanto; belleza.—**lovely** [lávli], *a.* amable, cariñoso; hermoso, bello; (fam.) agradable, atractivo; ameno.—**lover** [lávœ(r)], *s.* amante; galán; aficionado.—**lovesick** [lávsįk], *a.* enamorado, herido de amor.—**loving** [lávįŋ], *a.* amante, amoroso, cariñoso, afectuoso; aficionado; apacible.

low [loų], *a.* bajo; abatido; gravemente enfermo; malo (dieta, opinión, etc.); módico (precio); muerto, grosero; vil, rastrero; pobre, humilde, débil, debilitado.—*in l. gear*, (aut.) en primera. —*l. comedy*, farsa, sainete.—*l.-down*, (fam.) bajo, vil.—*l. spirits*, abatimiento.—*l. tide*, bajamar.—*l. trick*, mala pasada.—*l. water*, marea baja. —*adv.* bajo; en la parte inferior; a precio bajo; vilmente; sumisamente; en voz baja; en tono profundo.— *l.-minded*, ruin.—*vi.* mugir, berrear. —*s.* mugido, berrido; punto o lugar bajo; valor o precio mínimo; (aut.) primera velocidad.—*l.-down*, (fam.) información confidencial o de primera mano; los hechos verdaderos.— —**born** [lóųborn], *a.* de humilde cuna.- —**bred** [-bred], *a.* malcriado; vulgar.- —**brow** [-braų], *a.* poco intelectual.- —**er** [-œ(r)], *vt.* humillar, abatir, deprimir; bajar, poner más bajo; rebajar, disminuir; [láųœ(r)], mirar amenazadoramente. —*to l. the flag*, abatir la bandera.—*vi.* menguar, disminuirse.—*a.* más bajo; inferior.- —**erclassman** [lóųœrklǽsmąn], *s.* estudiante de primero o segundo año.- —**ering** [lóųœriŋ], *a.* encapotado, nebuloso; amenazador.- —**land** [lóųląnd], *s.* tierra baja.- —**liness** [-linįs], *s.* humildad; bajeza, vileza.- —**ly** [-li], *a.* humilde; vil, bajo.—*adv.* humildemente; vilmente.

loyal [lóiąl], *a.* leal, fiel, constante.—**ty** [-ti], *s.* lealtad, fidelidad.

lozenge [lázęndź], *s.* pastilla; rombo.

lubricant [liúbrikąnt], *s. y a.* lubri(fi)cante.—**lubricate** [liúbrikeit], *vt.* lubri(fi)car, engrasar.

lucid [liúsid], *a.* luciente; diáfano; brillante; lúcido; cuerdo.- —**ity** [liusíditi], —**ness** [liúsidnįs], *s.* lucidez; claridad mental; transparencia; brillantez; cordura.

luck [lak], *s.* azar, casualidad; suerte, dicha.—*to be in l.*, estar de buena suerte.—*to be out of l.*, estar de malas. - —**ily** [lákili], *adv.* por fortuna, afortunadamente, por dicha.- —**y** [-i], *a.* afortunado, dichoso; propicio. — *l. break*, (fam.) chiripa, coyuntura favorable.

lucrative [liúkrątiv], *a.* lucrativo.

ludicrous [liúdįkras], *a.* ridículo, risible.

lug [lag], *s.* (fam.) tirón, estirón; cosa tirada; cosa lenta y pesada; (mec.) oreja, argolla; saliente; agarradera.— *vt.* tirar de, halar.

luggage [lágidź], *s.* equipaje; (fam.) trastos.

lukewarm [liúkworm], *a.* tibio, templado; indiferente, frío.

lull [lal], *vt.* arrullar; aquietar.—*vi.* calmarse, sosegarse.—*s.* momento de calma o de silencio.- —**aby** [láląbai], *s.* arrullo; canción de cuna, nana.

lumber [lámbœ(r)], *s.* madera aserrada; maderaje; armatoste; trastos o muebles viejos.—*vt.* amontonar trastos viejos.—*vi.* andar pesadamente; avanzar con ruido sordo.- —**ing** [-iŋ], *a.* pesado.- —**jack** [-dźæk], *s.* leñador, hachero.

luminary [liúminęri], *s.* astro; lumbrera.

lump [lamp], *s.* masa, bulto, burujón; protuberancia, chichón; hinchazón; pitón; terrón.—*a l. in the throat*, un nudo en la garganta.—*by the l.*, a bulto, en globo, a ojo, por junto.— *in a o in the l.*, todos juntos, sin distinción.—*l. of sugar*, terrón de azúcar.—*l. sum*, suma redonda.—*vt.* amontonar; comprar a bulto, en globo.—*to l. it*, (fam.) soportarlo, tragar saliva.—*vi.* trabajar como estibador; apelotonarse, aterronarse.- —**y** [lámpi], *a.* aterronado.

lunacy [liúnąsi], *s.* locura.—**lunar** [liúną(r)], *a.* lunar; lunario; lunado; lunático.—**lunatic** [liúnątįk], *s. y a.* loco, lunático.

lunch [lanch], **luncheon** [lánchon], *s.* almuerzo, comida ligera del mediodía; merienda, refrigerio.—*vi.* almorzar; merendar.

lung [laŋ], *s.* pulmón.

lunge [landź], *s.* estocada; arremetida.

—*vi.* dar una estocada, tirarse a fondo; arremeter, abalanzarse.

lurch [lœrch], *s.* sacudida, vaivén; bandazo, guiñada.—*to leave in the l.*, plantar, dejar en las astas del toro o en la estacada.—*vi.* andar tambaleando; dar bandazos.

lure [ljur], *s.* añagaza, señuelo; cebo.—*vt.* atraer, inducir, tentar.

lurid [ljúrįd], *a.* cárdeno; espeluznante, siniestro.

lurk [lœrk], *vi.* acechar; moverse furtivamente; emboscarse.

luscious [lẢsẢs], *a.* sabroso, delicioso; meloso; empalagoso.

lush [lẢš], *a.* suculento, jugoso; fresco y lozano; exuberante.

lust [lẢst], *s.* lujuria, concupiscencia; codicia; anhelo vehemente.—*vi.* (for o after) codiciar.

luster [lẢstœ(r)], *s.* lustre, brillo.—*pl.* realce, lucimiento; araña de cristal; lustro.—*vt.* lustrar.—**lustrous** [lẢstras], *a.* lustroso, brillante.

lusty [lẢsti], *a.* lozano, vigoroso.

lute [ljut], *s.* laúd.

Lutheran [ljúθœrąn], *s. y a.* luterano.

luxuriant [lẢkšúriąnt], *a.* exuberante; superfluo; frondoso; lujuriante.—**luxurious** [lẢkšúriʌs], *a.* lujoso; sibarítico; exuberante; frondoso.—**luxury** [lẢkšuri], *s.* lujo; gastos superfluos; cosa que deleita los sentidos.

lye [lai], *s.* lejía.

lying [láiįɲ], *a.* falso, mentiroso; echado, yacente; sito, situado.—*l. down*, acostado.—*l.-in*, parto.—*l.-in hospital*, hospital de maternidad.—*l.-in woman*, mujer parida.—*s.* mentira, embuste.

lynch [lįnch], *vt.* linchar.

lynx [lįɲks], *s.* lince.

lyre [lair], *s.* (mus.) lira.—**lyric(al)** [lįrik(ạl)], *a.* lírico.—**lyric** [lįrik], *s.* poema lírico.—**lyricism** [lįrisįzm], *s.* lirismo.—**lyrist** [láirist], *s.* tocador de lira; poeta lírico.

M

ma [ma], *s.* (fam.) mamá.

ma'am [mæm], *s. contr.* de MADAM, señora.

macabre [mạkábr], *a.* macabro.

macaroni [mækạróunį], *s. pl.* macarrones.

macaroon [mækạrún], *s.* almendrado.

macaw [mạkó], *s.* guacamayo.

mace [meįs], *s.* maza, porra.—*m. bearer*, macero.

macerate [mǽsẹreįt], *vt.* macerar.—**maceration** [mǽsẹréįšọn], *s.* maceración.

machinate [mǽkįneįt], *vt. y vi.* maquinar.—**machination** [mækįnéį-

šọn], *s.* maquinación, intriga.—**machine** [mạšín], *s.* máquina, aparato; vehículo, automóvil, avión, etc.—*m. gun*, ametralladora.—*to m.-gun*, ametrallar, atacar con ametralladora.—*m.-made*, hecho a máquina.—**machinery** [mạšínœrį], *s.* maquinaria; mecanismo, aparato; organización, sistema.—**machinist** [mạšínįst], *s.* maquinista, mecánico; tramoyista.

mackerel [mǽkẹrẹl], *s.* caballa, (Am.) macarela, pintada.

mad [mæd], *a.* loco, demente; furioso, rabioso; insensato; enojado, encolerizado.—*to go m.*, enloquecerse, volverse loco.

madam [mǽdạm], *s.* celestina; dueña de un burdel; señora.

madame [mǽdạm, mǽdǽm], *s.* señora.

madbrain [mǽdbreįn], **madcap** [mǽdkæp], *a. y s.* fogoso; temerario; calavera, tarambana.—**madden** [mǽdn], *vt. y vi.* enloquecer(se), enfurecer(se).

made [meįd], *pret. y pp.* de TO MAKE.—*a.* hecho, fabricado.—*m.-over*, rehecho; reformado.—**made-up** [méįdẢp], *a.* artificial; ficticio; maquillado, pintado; (con of) compuesto (de).

madhouse [mǽdhaus], *s.* manicomio.—**madman** [mǽdmạn], *s.* loco, orate.—**madness** [mǽdnįs], *s.* locura, demencia; furia, rabia.

Madrilenian [mædrilínįạn], *a. y s.* madrileño.

magazine [mægạzín], *s.* revista; (arti.) cámara o depósito para los cartuchos en las armas de repetición; almacén militar.—*m. rifle*, rifle de repetición.—*powder m.*, polvorín; santabárbara.

magic [mǽdžįk], *s.* magia; prestidigitación.—*a.* mágico, encantador.—*m. wand*, varita mágica, varita de virtud.—*-ian* [mạdžíšạn], *s.* mago, mágico, prestidigitador.

magistrate [mǽdžįstreįt], *s.* magistrado; juez.

magnanimous [mægnǽnįmʌs], *a.* magnánimo.

magnate [mǽgneįt], *s.* magnate.

magnet [mǽgnįt], *s.* imán, magneto.—*-ic* [mægnétįk], *a.* magnético; atractivo.—*-ism* [mǽgnįtįzm], *s.* magnetismo.—*-ize* [mǽgnįtaįz], *vt.* magnetizar, imantar.—*vi.* imantarse.

magnificence [mægnífįšẹns], *s.* magnificencia.—**magnificent** [mægnífįšẹnt], *a.* magnífico.

magnify [mǽgnįfaį], *vti.* [7] aumentar, amplificar, ampliar.—*magnifying glass*, vidrio de aumento, lupa.

magnitude [mǽgnįtjud], *s.* magnitud.

magpie [mǽgpaį], *s.* urraca; (fig.) hablador, cotorra.

mahogany [mɐhágani], *s.* caoba, caobo.
Mahometan [mɐhámitɐn], *s.* **y** *a.* mahometano.
maid [mejd], *s.* doncella, soltera; criada, sirvienta, doméstica; (Am.) mucama.
—*m. of honor,* dama de honor.
—**en** [méjdn], *s.* doncella, virgen, joven soltera.—*a.* soltera.—*m. name,* apellido de soltera.
mail [mejl], *s.* correo; correspondencia; cota de malla.—*m. bag,* valija.—*m. carrier,* cartero.—*vt.* echar al correo; enviar por correo.— **box** [méjlbaks], *s.* buzón.——**man** [-mæn], *s.* cartero.
maim [mejm], *vt.* estropear, lisiar, tullir.
main [mejn], *a.* principal; esencial; de mayor importancia.—*m. floor,* planta baja.—*m. office,* (com.) casa matriz.—*m. street,* calle principal, calle mayor.—*m. wall,* pared maestra.—*the m. thing,* lo principal, lo esencial.—*s.* cañería maestra, conducto; océano, alta mar.—*in the m.,* mayor o principalmente, en conjunto.—**land** [méjnlɐnd], *s.* continente, tierra firme.——**stay** [-stej], *s.* sostén, apoyo.
maintain [mejntéjn], *vt.* mantener, guardar; sostener, afirmar.—**maintenance** [méjntɐnɐns], *s.* mantenimiento; manutención; sostén, sustento, sostenimiento; conservación (de vía, máquina, camino, etc.).
maize [mejz], *s.* maíz.
majestic [mɐdʒéstik], *a.* majestuoso.—**majesty** [médʒisti], *s.* majestad; majestuosidad.
major [méjdʒɐ(r)], *a.* mayor, más grande; principal.—*s.* comandante, mayor; mayor de edad; curso de especialización (en universidad o colegio).—*m.-domo,* mayordomo.—*m. general,* general de división.—*vi.* (con in) especializarse en un estudio o asignatura.— **ity** [mɐdʒáriti], *s.* mayoría, el mayor número (de); (for.) mayoría, mayor edad.
make [mejk], *vti.* [10] hacer; confeccionar; formar; poner (triste, alegre); decir, pronunciar (un discurso, etc.); dar, prestar (excusas, juramento); cometer (error, equivocación).—*to m. a clean breast of,* confesar, admitir francamente un error.—*to m. a fool of,* engañar; poner en ridículo.—*to m. a hit,* (fam.) causar buena impresión.—*to m. fun of,* burlarse de.—*to m. good,* abonar, subsanar.—*to m. haste,* darse prisa.—*to m. known,* hacer saber; dar a conocer.—*to m. love to,* enamorar, cortejar, hacer el amor a.—*to m. money,* ganar dinero.—*to m. no difference,* no importar, ser indiferente.—*to m. off with,* llevarse

arrebatar.—*to m. one's way,* avanzar; progresar; abrirse paso; salir bien.—*to m. room for,* dar paso a; dejar campo, lugar o puesto para; dar lugar o puesto a.—*to m. sense,* tener sentido (una frase); parecer acertado; (con of) comprender.—*to m. sure,* cerciorar, asegurar.—*to m. the most of,* aprovecharse de.—*to m. up,* inventar (cuentos); conciliar, apaciguar; saldar, ajustar.—*to m. up for,* compensar, indemnizar.—*to m. up one's mind,* resolverse, determinar.—*to m. way,* abrir paso.—*vii.* (con at, for, o toward) dirigirse o encaminarse a, abalanzarse a; (con for o to) contribuir a, servir para.—*to m. merry,* divertirse; regodearse.—*to m. sure,* asegurarse, cerciorarse.—*s.* hechura, forma, figura; fabricación, manufactura; marca, nombre de fábrica.— —**believe** [-biljv], *a.* fingido, falso, de mentirijillas.—*s.* artificio, fingimiento.—*vt.* fingir.— —**r** [méjkœ(r)], *s.* hacedor; artífice; fabricante; autor; librador (de cheque, pagaré, etc.); otorgante (de escritura).— —**up** [-ʌp], *s.* conjunto; carácter, modo de ser; (teat.) caracterización; afeite, maquillaje.—*vti.* **y** *vii.* [10] maquillar(se).
malady [mélɐdi], *s.* mal, enfermedad.
maladjustment [mælɐdʒʌ́stmɐnt], *s.* ajuste defectuoso; inadaptación; discordancia.
malaria [mɐlériɐ], *s.* malaria, paludismo.
Malay(an) [mɐléi(ɐn)], *a.* **y** *s.* malayo, de Malaca.
male [mejl], *a.* masculino; macho; varonil.—*s.* varón, hombre; animal macho.
malediction [mælidíkʃɐn], *s.* maldición.
malefactor [mélifæktɐ(r)], *s.* malhechor.
malevolent [mɐlévolɐnt], *a.* malévolo, maligno.
malice [mélis], *s.* malicia, malignidad.—*m. aforethought,* (for.) premeditación.—**malicious** [mɐlíʃɐs], *a.* malicioso, maligno, maléfico.—**malign** [mɐláin], *a.* maligno; pernicioso, perjudicial.—*vt.* difamar; calumniar.—**malignant** [mɐlígnɐnt], *a.* maligno; malévolo; perverso; (med.) maligno, pernicioso.
malinger [mɐlíŋgœ(r)], *vi.* fingirse enfermo.— **er** [-œ(r)], *s.* remolón; (fam.) maula.
malleable [méliɐbl], *a.* maleable; dúctil; dócil.
mallet [mélit], *s.* mazo, maceta.
malt [mɔlt], *s.* malta.—*malted milk,* leche malteada.
mam(m)a [mámɐ, mɐmá], *s.* mamá.
mammal [mémɐl], *s.* mamífero.

mammoth [mémœ6], s. enorme, gigantesco.—s. mamut.

mammay [mémij], s. mamita, mamá; (E.U.) niñera o criada negra.

man [mæn], s. hombre; varón; peón (de ajedres o damas).—m. and wife, marido y mujer.—m. Friday, auxiliar competente.—m. of all work, (fam.) factótum.—m. of straw, testaferro.—m. of war, buque de guerra.—to a m., hasta el último hombre.—vt. [1] tripular, dotar; armar; poner guarnición a.

manacle [ménækl], s. manilla.—pl. esposas.—vt. maniatar, poner esposas a.

manage [ménjdá], vt. manejar, dirigir, administrar; gestionar, procurar; manipular.—vi. arreglarse, componérselas; darse uno maña.—able [-əbl], a. manejable, dócil, tratable.—ment [-ment], s. manejo, gobierno, dirección, administración; (com.) gerencia; proceder, conducta; empresa (de teatro, etc.).—r [ménjdáœ(r)], s. administrador, director; empresario; superintendente; (com.) gerente.

manatee [mænatí], s. manatí, vaca marina.

mandate [méndejt], s. mandato; mandado, encargo.—vt. asignar por mandato.—mandatory [méndatori], s. (for.) preceptivo, obligatorio.—s. mandatario.

mane [mejn], s. crin o crines; melena (de león).

maneuver [manúvœ(r)], s. maniobra.—vt. y vi. maniobrar.

manful [ménful], a. viril, varonil; resuelto.

manganese [mænganís], s. manganeso.

mange [mejndá], s. sarna, roña.

manger [méjndáœ(r)], s. pesebre.

mangle [méngl], vt. mutilar, destrozar, estropear, lacerar; planchar con máquina.—s. planchadora mecánica.

mango [méngou], s. (bot.) mango.

mangrove [méngrouv], s. mangle.

mangy [méjndái], a. sarnoso, roñoso.

manhood [ménhud], s. hombría; edad viril; virilidad; masculinidad; los hombres.

mania [méjniá], s. manía.—c [méjniæk], a. y s. maníaco, maniático, loco.

manicure [ménikjur], s. manicura.—vi. hacer la manicura.—manicurist [ménikjurist], s. manicuro, manicura, manicurista.

manifest [ménifest], a. manifiesto, claro.—s. (com.) manifiesto.—vt. manifestar; poner o declarar en el manifiesto.—vi. hacer una manifestación o demostración pública.—ation [-éjàon], s. manifestación.—e [mæniféstou], s. manifiesto, proclama.

manifold [ménifould], a. múltiple, numeroso; diverso.—s. copia o duplicado; (aut.) tubo múltiple, agregado.

manikin [ménikin], s. maniquí; muñeco; hombre pequeño.

manipulate [manípyuleit], vt. manipular; manejar.—manipulation [manipyuléjàon], s. manipulación.

mankind [mænkájnd], s. (la) humanidad, (el) género humano; [mænkájnd], los hombres, el sexo masculino.—manliness [ménlinis], s. virilidad, hombría; valentía, ánimo.—manly [mænli], a. varonil; viril; animoso.

manner [ménœ(r)], s. manera, modo; modo de ser; suerte, jaez, género, especie; aire, ademán, porte.—pl. modales; costumbres; educación.—after the m. of, como, a la manera de, a la, a lo.—by no m. of means, de ningún modo.—in a m., en cierto modo, hasta cierto punto.—in a m. of speaking, como quien dice, por decirlo así.—ism [-ízm], s. amaneramiento, manerismo.

mannish [ménià], a. hombruno, machuno.—m. woman, virago, (fam.) marimacho.

manor [méng(r)], s. feudo; finca o casa solariega.

mansion [ménàon], s. mansión; morada, residencia.

manslaughter [ménslotœ(r)], s. homicidio sin premeditación, o culposo.

mantel(piece) [méntl(pis)], s. repisa o tablero de chimenea; manto de la chimenea.

mantilla [mæntíá], s. mantilla; mantón.

mantle [méntl], s. manto, capa; palio.

manual [ményuál], a. manual; manuable.—s. manual.

manufacture [mænyufékchg(r)], s. fabricación, elaboración; manufactura.—vt. manufacturar, fabricar.—vi. manufacturar, ser fabricante.—r [-œ(r)], s. fabricante, industrial.—manufacturing [-ig], s. manufacturero, industrial, fabril.—s. fabricación, manufactura, elaboración.

manure [manjúr], vt. abonar, estercolar.—s. abono, estiércol.

manuscript [ményuskript], a. y s. manuscrito.

many [méni], a., pron. y s. muchos, muchas.—a great m., muchos, muchísimos.—as m., igual número, otros tantos.—as m. as, tantos como; cuantos; más que; hasta.—how m.? ¿cuántos?—one, two, etc., too m., uno, dos, etc., de más o de sobra.—so m., tantos.—the m., la mayoría,

la mayor parte de la gente; las masas, la muchedumbre.—*too m.*, demasiados.—*twice as m.*, dos veces más.

map [mæp], *s.* mapa, carta geográfica; plano (de una ciudad).—*m. maker*, cartógrafo.—*vti.* [1] delinear mapas; (a veces con *out*) proyectar, hacer planes.

maple [méipl], *s.* arce, (Am.) meple.

mar [mar], *vti.* [1] echar a perder, estropear, desfigurar.

marauder [maródœ(r)], *s.* merodeador.—*marauding* [maródiŋ], *s.* merodeo, pillaje.

marble [márbl], *s.* mármol; canica o bolita de vidrio o mármol.—*pl.* juego de canicas o bolitas.—*a.* marmóreo, de mármol.

march [march], *vt.* poner en marcha, hacer marchar.—*vi.* marchar, caminar.—*to m. in*, entrar.—*to m. off*, irse, marcharse.—*to m. out*, salir o hacer salir.—*s.* marcha; progreso, adelanto; (mil. mús.) marcha, pasodoble; (M.) marzo.

marchioness [márṣonis], *s.* marquesa.

mare [mer], *s.* yegua.

margarine [márdžarin], *s.* margarina, mantequilla artificial.

margin [márdžin], *s.* margen, borde, orilla; reserva; sobrante.—*vt.* marginar, apostillar; poner borde o margen.—*al* [-al], *a.* marginal.

marigold [mérigould], *s.* (bot.) caléndula, maravilla.

marine [marín], *a.* marino, marítimo, naval.—*s.* infante de marina; marina (mercante).—*M. Corps*, Infantería de Marina.—*r* [mœrinœ(r)], *s.* marinero, nauta.

marital [mérital], *a.* marital, matrimonial.

maritime [méritaim], *a.* marítimo.

marjoram [márdžoram], *s.* mejorana.

mark [mark], *s.* marca; signo; seña o señal; huella, impresión; nota; calificación; marco (moneda); blanco o diana.—*birth m.*, antojo, lunar.—*question m.*, punto de interrogación (?).—*up to the m.*, (fam.) enteramente satisfactorio, perfectamente bueno o bien.—*vt.* marcar, señalar; acotar; advertir, notar.—*to m. down*, poner por escrito, anotar; marcar a un precio más bajo.—*to m. out*, elegir o escoger; cancelar, borrar.—*er* [márkœ(r)], *s.* marcador; marca; jalón.

market [márkit], *s.* mercado; plaza; feria.—*m. price*, precio corriente.—*m. woman*, verdulera.—*on the m.*, de o en venta.—*vt.* llevar al, o vender en el mercado; hallar mercado para.—*vi.* comprar o vender en un mercado; hacer compras en un mercado

o tienda de víveres.—*ing* [-iŋ], *s.* gasto de plaza; compra o venta en el mercado.

marksman [márksman], *s.* buen tirador.—*ship* [-ṣip], *s.* buena puntería.

marmalade [mármaleid], *s.* mermelada o conserva de naranja.

marmot [mármot], *s.* (zool.) marmota.

maroon [marún], *s.* y *a.* castaño o rojo oscuro.—*vt.* abandonar a uno en una costa desierta.

marquee [markí], *s.* marquesina.

marquetry [márkitri], *s.* marquetería.

marquis [márkwis], *s.* marqués.—*e* [markíz], *s.* marquesa.

marriage [méridž], *s.* matrimonio; casamiento, boda, nupcias; enlace.—*m. articles*, capitulaciones matrimoniales.—**married** [mérid], *a.* casado; matrimonial, conyugal.—*m. couple*, cónyuges, marido y mujer.—*to get m.*, casarse.

marrow [mérou], *s.* tuétano, médula, meollo; substancia, esencia.

marry [méri], *vti.* [7] casar, desposar, unir en matrimonio; casarse con.—*vii.* casarse, contraer matrimonio.

marsh [marš], *s.* pantano, ciénaga, marisma.

marshal [márṣal], *s.* mariscal; (E.U.) alguacil; jefe de policía en algunas ciudades.—*vti.* [2] ordenar, poner en orden; mandar, guiar.

marshmallow [márṣmælou], *s.* altea; pastilla de altea.

marshy [márṣi], *a.* pantanoso, cenagoso.

mart [mart], *s.* mercado; emporio.

martial [márṣal], *a.* marcial.

martyr [mártœ(r)], *s.* mártir.—*vt.* martirizar; atormentar.—*dom* [-dom], *s.* martirio.—*ize* [-aiz], *vt.* martirizar.

marvel [márvel], *s.* maravilla, prodigio.—*vii.* [2] maravillarse, admirarse.—*(l)ous* [-As], *a.* maravilloso, prodigioso; milagroso; increíble; (fam.) excelente.

mascot [méskat], *s.* mascota, amuleto.

masculine [méskjulin], *a.* masculino; varonil.—**masculinity** [mæskjulíniti], *s.* masculinidad.

mash [mæš], *s.* amasijo, masa.—*vt.* amasar, majar.—*mashed potatoes*, puré de papas o patatas.

mask [mæsk], *s.* máscara, careta, antifaz; disfraz.—*death m.*, mascarilla.—*masked ball*, baile de máscaras.—*vt.* enmascarar, disfrazar; encubrir.—*vi.* andar disfrazado.

mason [méison], *s.* albañil; (M.) masón.—*ry* [-ri], *s.* albañilería; mampostería; (M.) masonería.

masquerade [mæskœréid], *s.* mascarada, comparsa de máscaras; máscara, disfraz.—*vi.* enmascararse, disfrazarse.

mass [mæs], *s.* masa, montón, mole; bulto, volumen; (M.) misa.—*M. book*, libro de misa; misal.—*m. meeting*, reunión en masa, mitin popular. —*m. production*, producción o fabricación en serie.—*the masses*, el pueblo, las masas.—*vt.* juntar, reunir en masa, amasar.

massacre [mǽsəkœ(r)], *s.* masacre, matanza, carnicería.—*vt.* matar atrozmente, destrozar, hacer una carnicería.

massage [məsáʒ], *s.* masaje, fricción. —*vt.* dar masaje.—**massagist** [məsáʒist], *s.* masajista.—**masseur** [mæsœ́r], *s.* masajista (hombre).— **masseuse** [mæsœ́z], *s.* masajista (mujer).

massif [mǽsif], *s.* macizo.—**massive** [mǽsiv], *s.* macizo, abultado, sólido.

mast [mæst], *s.* mástil, palo mayor.—*pl.* arboladura.

master [mǽstœ(r)], *s.* amo, dueño, señor; maestro; director; señorito; perito, experto.—*m. builder*, maestro de obras; contratista.—*M. of Arts*, licenciado, maestro en artes.—*a.* maestro, superior.—*vt.* amaestrar, domar; dominar; conocer a fondo. —*ful* [-ful], *a.* dominante; experto; excelente.— *ly* [-li], *a.* magistral; maestro.—*adv.* con maestría; magistralmente.— *piece* [-pis], *s.* obra maestra.— *y* [-i], *s.* dominio, poder; maestría, destreza; conocimiento.

mastiff [mǽstif], *s.* mastín.

mat [mæt], *s.* estera, esterilla, felpudo; rejilla; colchón gimnástico; orla, diafragma.—*a.* mate, sin lustre.

match [mæch], *s.* fósforo, cerilla; pareja; igual, semejante; (dep.) partido, juego, contienda; concurso, certamen. —*drawn m.*, empate.—*m. point*, (dep.) tanto o punto decisivo.—*to meet one's m.*, encontrar la horma de su zapato.—*vt.* hermanar, aparear; igualar a, equiparar; competir con. —*vi.* armonizar, hacer juego, casar.- —*less* [mǽchlis], *a.* incomparable, sin igual, sin par.— **maker** [-meikœ(r)], *s.* casamentero; organizador de encuentros deportivos.

mate [meit], *s.* consorte, cónyuge; compañero, compañera; macho o hembra entre los animales; mate (ajedrez); (mar.) piloto.—*vt.* casar; aparear (animales).—*vi.* aparearse, copular (los animales).

material [mətírial], *a.* material; sustancial, esencial.—*s.* material o ingrediente; materia o asunto; género, tejido.— *ize* [-aiz], *vt.* materializar; dar cuerpo, exteriorizar.—*vi.* hacerse visible o corpóreo; realizarse o

verificarse (planes, etc.); **cuajar**; tomar forma; aparecer.

maternal [mətérnal], *a.* maternal, materno.—**maternity** [mətérniti], *s.* maternidad.

mathematic(al) [mæθimǽtik(al)], *a.* matemático.—**mathematician** [mæθimətíʃan], *s.* matemático.—**mathematics** [mæθimǽtiks], *s.* matemática(s).

matinée [mǽtinéi], *s.* matiné, función de tarde.

mating [méitiŋ], *s.* apareamiento; casamiento.—*m. season*, época de celo (de los animales).

matriculate [mətríkyuleit], *vt. y vi.* matricular(se).—*s. y a.* matriculado. —**matriculation** [mətríkyuléiʃan], *s.* matrícula, matriculación.

matrimonial [mætrimóuniạl], *a.* matrimonial; conyugal, marital.—**matrimony** [mǽtrimoni], *s.* matrimonio.

matrix [méitriks], *s.* (*pl.* **matrices** [méitrisiz]) matriz; molde.

matron [méitron], *s.* matrona; ama de llaves; vigilante, celadora (de asilo, cárcel de mujeres, etc.); enfermera jefe; acomodadora.

matter [mǽtœ(r)], *s.* materia; substancia; asunto, cuestión; material; cosa, negocio; importancia; pus.—*as a m. of fact*, a decir verdad; de hecho; en realidad.—*m. of course*, cosa natural, de rutina.—*m. of fact*, realidad, hecho cierto.—*m.-of-fact*, positivista, práctico, prosaico; sensato.—(*it is*) *no m.*, no importa.—*no m. how* (*much, good, etc.*), por (bueno, mucho, muy bueno, etc.) que.—*small m.*, cosa sin importancia; menudencia.—*to make matters worse*, para colmo de desdichas.—*what is the matter?* ¿qué pasa? ¿qué ocurre?—*vi.* importar; convenir, hacer al caso.—*what does it m.?* ¿qué importa?

matting [mǽtiŋ], *s.* estera; orla o marco de cartón (para cuadros, grabados, etc.).

mattress [mǽtris], *s.* colchón; jergón.

mature [mətiúr], *a.* maduro; (com.) vencido, pagadero.—*vt.* madurar, sazonar.—*vi.* madurar(se), sazonarse; (com.) vencer, cumplirse un plazo. —**maturity** [-iti], *s.* madurez; (com.) vencimiento.

maul [mol], *vt.* apalear, aporrear; maltratar.—*s.* mazo.

maxim [mǽksim], *s.* máxima, adagio; axioma.

maximum [mǽksimʌm], *s. y a.* máximo.

may [mei], *vai.* [11] poder, tener facultad o permiso, ser posible o permitido. —*m. I come in?* ¿se puede entrar?— *m. you have a good trip*, que tenga Ud.

buen viaje.—s. (M.) mes de mayo.—*M. day,* el primero de mayo.

Mayan [máyạn], a. y s. maya, de los mayas.

maybe [méịbị], adv. acaso, quizá, tal vez.

mayonnaise [meịọnéịz], s. mayonesa.

mayor [méịọ(r)], s. alcalde.— **—ess** [-ịs], s. alcaldesa.

maze [meịz], s. laberinto; perplejidad, confusión.—*to be in a m.,* estar perplejo.

me [mi], pron. pers. me, mí.—*do me the favor,* hágame Ud. el favor.—*for me,* para mí.—*with me,* conmigo.

meadow [médoụ], s. pradera, vega, prado.

meager [mígœ(r)], a. escaso, pobre, insuficiente; magro, flaco.— **—ness** [-nịs], s. escasez; delgadez; pobreza.

meal [mil], s. comida; harina.—*m. time,* hora de comer.— **—ly** [mílị], a. harinoso.

mean [min], a. humilde; mediano; inferior; bajo, vil; malo, desconsiderado; de mal humor; despreciable; tacaño, mezquino; insignificante; medio; intermedio.—*m.-spirited,* ruin, bajo.—*s.* medio; mediocridad, medianía; término medio.—*pl.* modos; fondos, medios, recursos.— *by all means,* sin duda, por supuesto; por todos los medios posibles.—*by means of,* por medio de; mediante. —*by no means,* de ningún modo. —*to live on one's means,* vivir de sus rentas.—*vti.* [10] significar, querer decir; pensar, proponerse, pretender; destinar a; envolver, encerrar; decir de veras.—*I didn't m. to do it,* lo hice sin pensar, o sin querer.—*I m. it,* hablo en serio o formalmente.—*what do you m.?* ¿qué quiere Ud. decir? ¿qué se propone Ud.?—*you don't m. it!* ¡calla!— **—ing [mínịŋ], a.** significativo.—*well-m.,* de buena fe, bien intencionado.—*s.* intención; sentido, significado, significación.- **—ingless** [mínịŋlịs], a. sin sentido, vacío.— **—ness [mínnịs], s.** bajeza; vileza; miseria, mezquindad; mal genio.— **meant [ment], pret. y pp.** de TO MEAN. —*to be m. for,* o *to,* servir para; haber nacido para; tener por objeto.—*who is m.?* ¿de quién se trata?— **—time** [míntaịm], **—while [mínhwaịl], adv.** mientras tanto, entretanto, por de (o lo) pronto.—*s.* ínterin.—*in the m.,* mientras tanto, en el ínterin, hasta entonces.

measles [mízlz], s. pl. sarampión.

measurable [méẓụrạbl], a. mensurable; apreciable; moderado.— **measurably** [méẓụrạblị], **adv.** perceptiblemente, hasta cierto grado; con moderación.

—measure [méẓụ(r), s. medida; compás, cadencia; proyecto de ley; (mús.) compás.—*pl.* medios.—*beyond m.,* con exceso, sobremanera.—*in a great m.,* en gran manera; en gran parte.—*in some m.,* hasta cierto punto, en cierto modo.—*vt.* medir; calibrar, graduar; (mar.) arquear, cubicar (un barco).—*vi.* medir, tener tal o cual dimensión.—**measured** [méẓụrd], a. acompasado, medido; moderado; rítmico.—**measurement** [méẓụrmẹnt], s. medición; dimensión; medida; (mar.) arqueo, cubicación.

meat [mit], s. carne; sustento (en general); substancia, jugo.—*cold meats,* fiambres.—*m. ball,* albóndiga. —*m. market,* carnicería.— **—y [mítị], a.** carnoso; jugoso, substancioso.

mechanic [mịkénịk], a. y s mecánico.— **—al [-ạl], a.** mecánico, maquinal. —*m. pencil,* lapicero.— **-s [-s], s.** mecánica.—**mechanism [mékạnịzm], s.** mecanismo; maquinaria.—**mechanization [mekạnịzéịẓọn], s.** mecanización; maquinismo; (mil.) motorización.—**mechanize [mékạnaịz], vt.** mecanizar; (mil.) motorizar.

medal [médạl], s. medalla; condecoración.— **—lion [mịdélyọn], s.** medallón.

meddle [médl], vi. (gen. con with o in) meterse, entremeterse.— **—r [médlœ(r)], s.** entremetido.- **—some** [médlsam], a. entremetido, oficioso.

median [mídịạn], a. mediano, del medio.

mediate [mídịeịt], vt. y vi. mediar, intervenir, intermediar.—*a.* [mídịịt] mediato, medio; interpuesto.— **mediation [mịdịéịẓọn], s.** mediación, intercesión; intervención; tercería.— **mediator [mídịeịtọ(r)], s.** mediador, intercesor, medianero.

medical [médịkạl], a. médico, medicinal. —*m. corps,* cuerpo de sanidad.— *m. kit,* botiquín.—**medicate [médịkeịt], vt.** medicinar.—**medication** [medịkéịẓọn], s. medicación; medicamento.—**medicine [médịsịn], s.** medicina, medicamento, remedio; medicina (arte o ciencia).—*m man,* exorcista, curandero (indio).— **medicinal [mịdísịnạl], a.** medicinal.

medieval [mịdịívạl], a. medi(o)eval.

mediocre [mídịọkœ(r)], a. mediocre, mediano; vulgar, trivial.—**mediocrity [mịdịákrịtị], s.** mediocridad; medianía.

meditate [médịteịt], vt. y vi. meditar, reflexionar.—**meditation [medịtéịẓọn], s.** meditación, reflexión.— **meditative [médịteịtịv], a.** meditativo, meditabundo.

Mediterranean [medịtẹréịnịạn], a. mediterráneo.

medium [mídiʌm], **s.** medio, instrumento; médium o medio (en el espiritismo); medio ambiente.—*at* **s** *m.*, uno con otro, por término medio.—*a.* mediano, intermedio; (coc.) no muy cocido, término medio.

medley [médli], **s.** miscelánea, mezcla, mezcolanza; (mus.) popurrí.

meek [mik], *a.* manso, humilde, dócil.— **—ness** [míknis], **s.** mansedumbre, humildad, docilidad.

meet [mit], *vti.* [10] encontrarse con; encontrar, topar o chocar con; satisfacer, llenar (requisitos); pagar, saldar (un pagaré, etc.); sufragar (los gastos, etc.); ir a esperar (un tren, vapor, persona, etc.); combatir o pelear con; conocer o ser presentado.—*to m. a charge*, refutar, responder a una acusación.—*to m. the eye*, saltar a la vista.—*vii.* encontrarse, verse; reunirse, chocarse; tocarse; confluir.—*till we m. again*, hasta la vista, hasta más ver(nos). —*to m. halfway*, partir la diferencia.— **—ing** [mítiŋ], **s.** mitin; reunión, sesión; junta, asamblea; entrevista; encuentro, duelo o desafío.—*to call a m.*, convocar a junta.

megaphone [mégǎfoun], **s.** megáfono, portavoz, bocina.

melancholy [mélʌnkoli], **s.** melancolía, tristeza.—*a.* melancólico.

mellow [mélou], *a.* maduro; sazonado; meloso; tierno, blando, suave.—*vt.* y *vi.* sazonar(se); madurar(se); ablandar(se), suavizar(se).

melodious [melóudiʌs], *a.* melodioso. —**melody** [mélodi], **s.** melodía.

melon [mélon], **s.** melón.

melt [melt], *vti.* y *vii.* [6] derretir(se), fundir(se); deshelar(se); disolver(se). —*to m. into tears*, deshacerse en lágrimas.

member [mémbœ(r)], **s.** miembro, socio, asociado.— **—ship** [-ʃip], **s.** asociación, calidad de miembro o socio; número de socios o miembros; personal.—*m. dues*, cuota.

membrane [mémbrein], **s.** membrana.

memento [miméntou], **s.** recordatorio, memoria, recuerdo.—**memo** [mémou], **s.** *abrev.* de MEMORANDUM.— **memoir** [mémwar], **s.** memoria, informe, relación.—*pl.* memorias; (auto)biografía.—**memorable** [mémorǎbl], *a.* memorable.—**memorandum** [memorǽndʌm], **s.** memorándum, memoria, nota, apuntación.—*m. book*, memorándum, libreta, prontuario. —**memorial** [mimórjǎl], *a.* conmemorativo.—**s.** monumento conmemorativo; memorial, instancia, petición; (for.) nota, apuntamiento.—**memorize** [mémoraiz], *vt.* aprender

de memoria, memorizar.—**memory** [mémori], **s.** memoria, recuerdo; memoria, retentiva.—*from m.*, de memoria.

men [men], **s.** *pl.* de MAN.

menace [ménis], *vt.* y *vi.* amenazar. —**s.** amenaza, reto.

mend [mend], *vt.* remendar; repasar; zurcir; arreglar, componer; enmendar. —*vi.* enmendarse, reformarse.—**s.** remiendo; reparación; reforma.—*on the m.*, mejorando(se).

menial [mínjal], *a.* y **s.** servil, bajo.

menstruate [ménstrueit], *vi.* menstruar. —**menstruation** [menstruéiʃon], **s.** menstruación.

mental [méntal], *a.* mental.—*m. test*, examen de capacidad mental.— **mentality** [mentǽliti], **s.** mentalidad.

mention [ménʃon], **s.** mención, alusión. —*vt.* mencionar, mentar, aludir a. —*don't m. it!* ¡no hay de qué! ¡de nada!—*not to m.*, por no decir nada de; además.

menu [ményu], **s.** menú.

meow [miáu], **s.** y *vi.* = MEW.

mercantile [mérkǎntil], *a.* mercantil, comercial.—**mercantilism** [mérkǎntilizm], **s.** mercantilismo.

mercenary [mérseneri], *a.* interesado, mercenario.—**s.** mercenario.

merchandise [mérchǎndaiz], **s.** mercancía(s), mercadería.—**merchant** [mérchǎnt], **s.** mercader, comerciante; tendero.—*a.* mercante, mercantil.—*m. marine*, marina mercante.

merciful [mérsiful], *a.* misericordioso, compasivo.—**merciless** [mérsilis], *a.* despiadado, desalmado, inhumano.

mercurial [mœrkjúrial], *a.* mercurial; (fig.) vivo, volátil.—**mercury** [mérkjuri], **s.** mercurio, azogue.

mercy [mérsi], **s.** misericordia, clemencia, compasión; merced, gracia, perdón.—*m. killing*, eutanasia.—*m. stroke*, golpe de gracia.

merge [mœrdž], *vt.* y *vi.* unir(se), fundir(se), fusionar(se).—**—r** [mérdžœ(r)], **s.** unión, consolidación, fusión comercial.

meridian [mirídian], **s.** meridiano; mediodía; (fig.) cenit.—*a.* meridiano.

meringue [meréŋ], **s.** merengue.

merit [mérit], **s.** mérito; merecimiento. —*on its (his, etc.) own merits*, por sí mismo.—*vt.* merecer, ser digno de.— **—orious** [-óriʌs], *a.* meritorio, benemérito.

mermaid [mérmeid], **s.** sirena.— **merman** [mérmæn], **s.** tritón.

merrily [mérili], *adv.* alegremente, con júbilo.—**merriment** [mériment], **s.** alegría, júbilo, gozo, regocijo; diversión.—**merry** [méri], *a.* alegre,

festivo, divertido; feliz; gozoso; risueño.—m.-go-round, tiovivo, caballitos.—m. Christmas, felices Pascuas.—to make m., divertirse, ir de parranda.—merrymaker [mérimejkœ(r)], s. flestero, parrandero.—merrymaking [mérimejkiŋ], s. fiesta, parranda, holgorio.—s. regocijado, parrandero.

mesh [meʃ], s. malla; punto u obra de malla; redecilla; (mec.) engranaje.—pl. red, trampas, lazos.—vt. enredar, coger con red; (mec.) endentar.—vi. enredarse; (mec.) endentar, engranar.

mess [mes], s. ración; rancho (comida); (fam.) lío, confusión.—vt. dar rancho; (a veces con up) desarreglar, desordenar, confundir; ensuciar.—vi. comer en rancho o hacer rancho; arrancharse; hacer un revoltijo.—to m. about o around, ocuparse en fruslerías, entrometerse.

message [mésidʒ], s. mensaje; recado, parte, aviso.—messenger [mésəndʒœ(r)], s. mensajero, mandadero, propio, recadero.

messy [mési], s. sucio, puerco; desordenado, revuelto.

met [met], pret. y pp. de TO MEET.

metal [métəl], s. metal.—s. metálico, de metal.—lic [metélik], s. metálico.—lize [métəlajz], vt. metalizar.—lurgic(al) [metælœr-dʒik(əl)], s. metalúrgico.—lurgy [métəlœrdʒi], s. metalurgia.

metamorphose [metəmórfouz], vt. metamorfosear.—metamorphosis [metəmórfəsis], s. metamorfosis.

metaphor [métəfo(r)], s. metáfora.

meteor [mítiɔ(r)], s. meteoro; estrella fugaz.—ological [-oládʒikəl], s. meteorológico.—ologist [-álodʒist], s. meteorólogo.—ology [-álodʒi], s. meteorología.

method [méθəd], s. método, procedimiento; orden, regularidad; técnica.—ic(al) [meθádik(əl)], s. metódico, sistemático.

meticulous [mitíkyulʌs], s. meticuloso.

metre [mítœ(r)], s. = METER.

metric(al) [métrik(əl)], s. métrico.

metro [métrou], s. medida (poética y de longitud. Ver Tabla.); contador (de gas, agua, etc.).

metronome [métronoum], s. metrónomo.

metropolis [metrápolis], s. metrópoli; urbe.—metropolitan [metropálitan], s. metropolitano, de la capital.—s. ciudadano de una metrópoli.

mettle [métl], s. temple, brío, coraje; vivacidad, fuego.—some [-sʌm], s. brioso, vivo, fogoso.

mew [mju], s. maullido; gaviota.—pl.

establo, caballeriza.—vi. maullar, mayar.—ing [mídiŋ], s. maullido; muda (de las aves).—s. maullador; que está en la muda.

Mexican [méksikan], s. y s. mejicano.

mezzanine [mézanin], s. entresuelo.

mice [majs], s. pl. de MOUSE.

microbe [májkroub], s. microbio.

microphone [májkrofoun], s. micrófono.

microscope [májkroskoup], s. microscopio.—microscopic(al) [majkroskápik(əl)], s. microscópico.

mid [mid], s. medio.—(in) m. air, (en) el aire.—m.-course, media carrera o medio camino.—m.-sea, alta mar.—day [míddej], s. mediodía.—s. del mediodía.— dle [mídl], s. medio, intermedio, mediano; de en medio.—M.-Age, medieval.—m.-aged, de edad madura.—M. Ages, Edad Media.—m.-class, de la clase media.—m. class, clase media, burguesía.—m. finger, dedo del corazón.—m. ground, posición intermedia.—m.-sized, de mediana estatura o tamaño.—s. centro, medio, mitad.—about o towards the m. of, a mediados de.—m. of, mediados de.—m. of the road, posición intermedia.—m.-of-the-road, moderado, enemigo de extremos.—dleman [mídlmæn], s. intermediario; (com.) corredor; revendedor; agente de negocios.—dlemost [mídlmoust], s. del medio; en el medio o más cercano a él.—dleweight [mídlwejt], s. (dep.) de peso medio (hasta 160 lbs.).—s. peso medio.— dling [mídliŋ], s. mediano, regular, pasadero.

middy [mídi], s. (fam.) guardiamarina; blusa marinera.

midget [mídʒit], s. enanillo, liliputiense; chiquillo vivaracho.

midnight [mídnajt], s. medianoche.—s. nocturno; negro.

midriff [mídrif], s. (anat.) diafragma; parte media del cuerpo.

midshipman [mídʃipman], s. guardiamarina.

midst [mídst], s. medio, centro; (fig.) seno; presión, rigor.—in our, their, your m., en medio de nosotros, ellos, ustedes.—in the m. of, en medio de, entre; rodeado de; en lo más (reñido, agitado, etc.).—adv. en medio.—prep. (poét.) entre.

midstream [mídstrím], s. el medio de una corriente.

midsummer [mídsʌmœ(r)], s. la mitad del verano, pleno verano.

midway [mídwej], s. mitad del camino, medio camino.—s. situado a mitad del camino.—adv. en medio del camino; a mitad del camino.

midwife [mídwaif], *s.* partera, comadrona.

mien [min], *s.* semblante, aire, talante, facha.

might [mait], *pret. y pres. opcional* de MAY.—*s.* poder, poderío, fuerza. —*with m. and main*, con todas sus fuerzas, a más no poder.— —*ily* [máitili], *adv.* poderosamente.— —*y* [-i], *a.* potente, poderoso; fuerte, vigoroso; enorme; eficaz, importante.

migraine [máigrein], *s.* jaqueca, migraña.

migrant [máigrant], *s.* emigrante; ave migratoria o de paso.—*a.* nómada; (e)migratorio.—**migrate** [máigreit], *vi.* emigrar; trasplantarse.—**migration** [maigréişon], *s.* (e)migración; trasplante.—**migratory** [máigratori], *a.* (e)migratorio; nómada.

mike [maik], *s.* (fam.) micrófono = MICROPHONE.

milch [milch], *a.* lechera.—*m. cow*, vaca lechera.

mild [maild], *a.* suave, moderado, manso; benigno, blando, indulgente; leve, ligero.

mildew [míldju], *s.* moho; tizón (de las plantas).—*vi.* enmohecerse; atizonarse.

mildness [máildnis], *s.* suavidad, lenidad; apacibilidad; mansedumbre, indulgencia.

mile [mail], *s.* milla. Ver Tabla.— —**age** [máilidž], *s.* longitud en millas; peaje por milla; número de millas (millaje) recorridas o recorribles.

militant [mílitant], *a.* militante, combatiente; belicoso, guerrero.—**military** [míliteri], *a.* militar; guerrero, marcial; castrense; soldadesco; de guerra.—*m. coup* o *uprising*, pronunciamiento, cuartelazo.—*s.* ejército, milicia, soldadesca, tropa(s), los militares.—**militia** [milíşa], *s.* milicia. —**militiaman** [milíşaman], *s.* miliciano.

milk [milk], *s.* leche.—*m. diet*, dieta o régimen lácteo.—*vt.* ordeñar; (fam.) extraer de.— —*er* [mílkœ(r)], *s.* ordeñador; vaca (etc.) de leche.— —**maid** [-meid], *s.* lechera.— —**man** [-mæn], *s.* lechero.— —*y* [-i], *a.* lácteo; lechoso; blando, tierno, tímido.—*M. Way*, Vía Láctea.

mill [mil], *s.* molino; taller, fábrica; milésimo de un dólar; milésima parte; (fam.) pugilato.—*to go through the m.*, saber una cosa por experiencia. —*vt.* moler, desmenuzar; aserrar; fabricar; acordonar (moneda), estriar; fresar.—*to m. around*, arremolinarse.

miller [mílœ(r)], *s.* molinero; mariposa con manchas blancas.

milliner [mílinœ(r)], *s.* modista de sombreros.— —*y* [mílineri], *s.* artículos para sombreros femeninos; sombrerería femenina; ocupación en este sector; tienda de sombreros femeninos.

milling [mílin], *s.* molienda; acordonamiento, acuñación (moneda); cordoncillo de la moneda; fresado.—*m. around*, remolino.—*a.* de moler, fresar, etc.—*m. cutter* o *tool*, fresa. —*m. machine*, fresadora.—*m. saw*, sierra.

million [mílyon], *s.* millón.— —**aire** [-ér], *s. y a.* millonario.

millpond [mílpand], *s.* represa de molino.—**millstone** [mílstoun], *s.* muela, rueda de molino.

milt [milt], *s.* (anat.) bazo.

mime [maim], *s.* mimo; truhán; pantomima, farsa.

mimic [mímik], *vti.* [8] remedar.—*s.* imitador, remedador.—*a.* mímico, imitativo, burlesco.—**mimicked** [mímikt], *pret. y pp.* de TO MIMIC.— —*ry* [-ri], *s.* mímica; bufonería; monería, remedo; mimetismo.

mince [mins], *vt.* desmenuzar; picar (carne), hacer picadillo; medir (las palabras); atenuar.—*minced oath*, eufemismo.—*vi.* ser afectado al hablar, andar, etc.—*not to m. words*, hablar sin rodeos.— —*meat* [mínsmit], *s.* relleno de carne para pasteles.— *to make m. of*, destruir, aniquilar. —**mincingly** [mínsinli], *adv.* a pedacitos; a pasitos; con afectación.

mind [maind], *s.* mente, entendimiento, pensamiento, inteligencia; espíritu, ánimo; gusto, inclinación, afecto; memoria; voluntad, gana; intención, resolución; opinión, criterio.—*of one m.*, unánimes.—*of sound m.*, en su cabal juicio.—*out of m.*, olvidado. —*out of one's m.*, loco; fuera de juicio.—*to bear in m.*, tener en cuenta, tener presente.—*to call to m.*, recordar, traer a la memoria.—*to change one's m.*, mudar de parecer.—*to give someone a piece of one's m.*, decirle a alguien cuántas son cinco, ponerlo como nuevo.—*to have a m. to*, tener gana de, querer; proponerse.—*to have in m.*, recordar; tener en consideración; pensar en.—*to keep in m.*, tener presente o en cuenta.—*to make up one's m.*, decidirse.—*to my m.*, a mi juicio, a mi ver.—*with one m.*, unánimemente.—*vt.* notar, observar; atender a; cuidar; cuidarse de; tener inconveniente en; hacer caso a, o de. —*to m. one's business*, meterse uno en lo que le importa.—*vi.* atender,

obedecer, hacer caso; tener cuidado.
—*I don't m.*, no me importa.—
never m., no importa; no se moleste,
no se preocupe.— —ful [májndful],
a. atento, cuidadoso.
mine [majn], *pron. pos.* mío, mía, míos,
mías; el mío, etc.; lo mío.—*of m.*,
mío, mía.
mine [majn], *s.* mina (en todas sus
acepciones).—*vt.* minar; destruir;
zapar; extraer mineral.— —r
[májnœ(r)], *s.* minero; zapador.
—ral [mínęral], *s.* y *a.* mineral.—
—alogy [mínœrálǫdži], *s.* mineralogía.
mingle [míŋgl], *vt.* mezclar; confundir.
—*vi.* mezclarse, incorporarse.
miniature [mínjæchyr], *s.* miniatura.—
a. en miniatura; diminuto.
minimize [mínjmajz], *vt.* atenuar, quitar
importancia; reducir al mínimo;
achicar; menospreciar.—**minimum**
[mínjmʌm], *s.* y *a.* mínimo.
mining [májnjŋ], *s.* minería; acto de
sembrar minas explosivas.—*a.* minero, de mina.
minister [mínjstœ(r)], *s.* ministro;
clérigo, pastor.—*vt.* y *vi.* dar,
ministrar, suministrar.—*vi.* atender,
auxiliar; socorrer.—**ministry** [mín-
jstri], *s.* ministerio; sacerdocio; clero.
mink [miŋk], *s.* visón; piel de visón.
minnow [mínou], *s.* pececillo de agua
dulce usado como cebo.
minor [májnǫ(r)], *a.* menor; secundario,
inferior; leve.—*m. key*, tono menor.
—*s.* menor de edad.— —**ity**
[majnárjti], *s.* minoridad, menoría
(de edad); minoría.
minstrel [mínstrel], *s.* juglar, trovador,
cantor; bardo.
mint [mint], *s.* casa de moneda; menta,
hierbabuena; pastilla de menta.—
a m. of money, un dineral.—*vt.* acuñar.
minus [májnʌs], *prep.* menos; falto de;
sin.—*a.* (mat. y elec.) negativo;
deficiente.—*m. sign*, signo de restar
(—).—*to be, come out, etc. m.*
(*something*), salir perdiendo (algo).
—*s.* cantidad negativa; deficiencia;
signo menos.
minute [majnjút], *a.* menudo, minúsculo; nimio, minucioso.—*s.* [mínjt],
minuto, momento, instante; (geom.
etc.) minuto; minuta, nota, apunte.
—*pl.* actas, minutas; memoria autén-
tica.—*m. book*, minutario, libro de
actas.—*m. hand*, minutero.—*this
(very) m.*, ahora mismito.
miracle [mírąkl], *s.* milagro; maravilla.
—**miraculous** [mirǽkyulʌs], *a.* milagroso.
mirage [miráž], *s.* espejismo.
mire [majr], *s.* lodo, cieno, fango;
lodazal.—*vt.* enlodar.—*vi.* atascarse.

mirror [mírǫ(r)], *s.* espejo; ejemplar,
modelo.—*vt.* reflejar.
mirth [mœrθ], *s.* alegría, regocijo.—
—ful [mœrθful], *a.* alegre, gozoso.—
—less [-ljs], *a.* triste, abatido;
sardónico.
miry [májri], *a.* cenagoso, fangoso.
misadventure [mjsadvénchǖ(r)], *s.*
desventura, desgracia.
miscarriage [mjskǽrjdž], *s.* aborto,
malparto; fracaso, malogro; extravío,
desmán.—**miscarry** [mjskǽri], *vii.*
[7] frustrarse, malograrse; abortar,
malparir; extraviarse.
miscellaneous [mjseléjnjʌs], *a.* misceláneo, mezclado; diverso.
mischief [mjschjf], *s.* mal, daño; injuria,
agravio; diablura, barrabasada; persona traviesa.—**mischievous** [mjs-
chjvʌs], *a.* dañino; malicioso o
malévolo; chismoso o enredador;
travieso.
misdeed [mjsdíd], *s.* fechoría, delito.
misdemeanor [mjsdjmínǫ(r)], *s.* mala
conducta; (for.) falta, delito de menor
cuantía.
miser [májzœ(r)], *s.* avaro, tacaño.—
—able [mízęrabl], *a.* miserable;
pobre; sin valor; despreciable; lastimero.— —ly [májzœrlj], *a.* avariento,
tacaño, mezquino.— —y [mízeri], *s.*
miseria, desgracia; aflicción; calamidad.
misfortune [mjsfórchun], *s.* desgracia,
desdicha, contratiempo, percance,
infortunio, revés.
misgiving [mjsgívjŋ], *s.* recelo, duda,
presentimiento; desconfianza, temor.
mishap [mjshǽp], *s.* desgracia, accidente, contratiempo.
misinterpret [mjsjntœrprjt], *vt.* y *vi.*
interpretar mal, tergiversar.— —ation
[-éjšǫn], *s.* tergiversación.
misjudge [mjsdžʌdž], *vt.* y *vi.* errar,
juzgar mal.
mislead [mjslíd], *vti.* [10] extraviar,
descaminar, descarriar, despistar;
conducir a conclusiones erróneas;
alucinar, engañar, seducir, pervertir.—
—ing [-jŋ], *a.* engañoso; de falsas
apariencias.—**misled** [mjsléd], *pret.*
y *pp.* de TO MISLEAD.—*a.* engañado,
seducido, etc.
mismanagement [mjsmǽnjdžment], *s.*
mal manejo, mala administración,
desconcierto.
misplace [mjspléjs], *vt.* colocar mal o
fuera de sitio; trastocar, traspapelar.
misprint [mjsprínt], *vt.* imprimir con
erratas.—*s.* error de imprenta, errata.
mispronounce [mjspronáuns], *vt.* y *vi.*
pronunciar mal.—**mispronunciation**
[mjspronʌnsjéjšǫn], *s.* pronunciación
incorrecta.
misrepresent [mjsreprjzént], *vt.* des-

figurar, tergiversar, disfrazar, falsificar.— —ation [-éiş ǫn], s. falsedad, noticia o relación falsa, tergiversación.

miss [mis], s. señorita; (abrev.) Srta., Sta.

miss [mis], vt. errar (el tiro, el golpe, etc.); no acertar con, no comprender; equivocar; perder (el tren, la función, etc.); echar de menos; pasar sin, abstenerse, carecer de; pasar por alto, dejar de hacer.—to m. the mark, errar el blanco o el tiro.—vi. frustrarse, salir mal; marrar, errar, faltar; fallar.—to m. out, (fam.) llevarse chasco; llegar tarde.—s. malogro, fracaso; tiro fallido.

misshapen [misşéipn], a. disforme, deformado.

missile [mísil], a. arrojadizo.—s. proyectil; arma arrojadiza.

missing [mísiŋ], a. extraviado, perdido; desaparecido; ausente.

mission [mísǫn], s. misión.— —ary [-eri], s. misionario, misionero.—a. misional.—m. station, (igl.) misión.

missive [mísiv], s. misiva, carta, comunicación escrita.

misspell [misspél], vti. [4] deletrear mal, escribir con mala ortografía.

mist [mist], s. niebla, neblina, bruma; vapor, vaho; llovizna.—vt. empañar. —vi. lloviznar.

mistake [mistéik], vti. [10] equivocar, comprender mal; trabucar, tomar una cosa por otra.—vii. errar, equivocarse.—s. equivocación, yerro, desacierto; errata.—mistaken [mistéikn], pp. de TO MISTAKE.—a. erróneo, incorrecto, desacertado.

mister [místœ(r)], s. señor.—Mister (Mr.), Sr.

mistletoe [místou], s. muérdago.

mistook [mistúk], pret. de TO MISTAKE.

mistress [místris], s. señora; dueña, ama; querida.—Mistress (Mrs.) [mísiz], Sra.

mistrust [mistrÁst], s. desconfianza. —vt. desconfiar de, dudar de; sospechar, recelar.— —ful [-ful], a. desconfiado, receloso.

misty [místi], a. brumoso; nublado; empañado; vago, impreciso.

misunderstand [misandœrsténd], vti. [10] entender mal, tomar en sentido erróneo.—misunderstood [misandœrstúd], pret. y pp. de TO MISUNDERSTAND.—s. mal entendido o comprendido.

misuse [misyús], s. mal uso; abuso; maltrato.—vt. [misyúz], abusar de; maltratar; estropear; usar mal o impropiamente.

mite [mait], s. pizca, triza, mota; óbolo; gorgojo.

miter [máitœ(r)], s. mitra; tiara del Papa; dignidad de obispo.

mitigate [mítigeit], vt. mitigar, calmar. —vi. calmarse, mitigarse.

mitt [mit], s. mitón; guante de beisbol.

mitten [mítn], s. mitón.—pl. (fam.) guantes de boxeo; (fam.) las manos.

mix [miks], vti. y vii. [4] mezclar(se), unir(se).—to m. up, incorporar, asociar; confundir; envolver.—s. mezcla; proporciones de los ingredientes de una mezcla.—m.-up, (fam.) lío, confusión; agarrada.— —ture [míksch ų(r)], s. mezcla; mixtura; mezcolanza.

moan [moųn], s. quejido, gemido, lamento.—vt. lamentar, llorar, deplorar.—vi. gemir, quejarse; lamentarse.

moat [moųt], s. foso.—vt. rodear con fosos.

mob [mab], s. chusma, populacho, gentuza; (fam.) turbamulta; multitud.—vti. [1] atropellar.—vii. formar tropel, tumulto, alboroto.

mobile [móųbil], a. movedizo, movible, móvil; inconstante, variable.— **mobility** [mobíliti], s. movilidad; volubilidad.—**mobilization** [mobiliźéişǫn], s. movilización.—**mobilize** [móųbilaiz], vt. movilizar, poner en pie de guerra; poner en movimiento.

moccasin [mákasin], s mocasín o mocasina (calzado); mocasín (serpiente).

mock [mak], vt. mofar, escarnecer; remedar; engañar, burlar.—to m. at, burlarse o mofarse de, hacer mofa de. —s. mofa, burla, befa; remedo.—a. ficticio falso, imitado; cómico, burlesco.— —ery [mákœri], s. mofa, burla, irrisión; remedo; parodia. —ing [-iŋ], a. burlón.—**ingbird** [-iŋbœrd], s. (Am.) sinsonte.

mode [moųd], s. modo, manera, procedimiento; moda; uso, costumbre; (gram. fil. mús.) modo; (mús.) modalidad.— **—l** [mádęl], s. modelo, ejemplar o patrón; prototipo; muestra; horma; patrón, figurín; modelo vivo.—a. modelo, ejemplar. —vti. [2] modelar; moldear.—vii. servir de modelo, modelar.— **-l(l)ing** [mádęliŋ], s. modelado.—a. modelador.

moderate [mádęrit], a. moderado; regular, ordinario; razonable, sobrio; módico (en precio).—s. moderado.— vt. y vi. [mádęreit], moderar(se), calmar(se); presidir.—**moderation** [mádęréişǫn], s. moderación; sobriedad; presidencia, acto de presidir.

modern [mádœrn], a. moderno.— —ize [-aiz], vt. modernizar.

modest [mádist], a. modesto; recatado,

pudoroso.— —y [-ĭ], *s.* modestia; recato, pudor.

modification [madĭfĭkéĭšọn], *s.* modificación.—modifier [mádĭfaĭọ(r)], *s.* modificador.—modify [mádĭfaĭ], *vti.* [7] modificar, cambiar.

modiste [moudíst], *s.* modista.

modulate [mádẓuleĭt], *vt.* y *vi.* modular.

Mogul [móugʌl], *s.* mogol; (m.) capitán de industria.

mohair [móuḥer], *s.* pelo de la cabra de Angora; tela de este material.

Mohammedan [mouḥǽmedạn], *s.* y *a.* mahometano.

moist [moĭst], *a.* húmedo; lloroso; lluvioso.— —en [móĭsn], *vt.* humedecer, mojar ligeramente.— —ure [móĭschọ(r)], *s.* humedad.

molar [móulạ(r)], *a.* molar.—*s.* muela.

molasses [molǽsĭz], *s.* melaza, miel de purga.—*m. candy*, (Am.) melcocha.

mold [mould], *s.* molde, matriz; moho; tierra vegetal.—*vt.* moldear, vaciar, amoldar.—*vi.* enmohecerse.— —er [móuldœ(r)], *vi.* convertirse en polvo, desmoronarse, consumirse.—*vt.* convertir en polvo, consumir, desgastar.— —ing [-ĭṇ], *s.* moldura; amoldamiento; moldeamiento, vaciado.— —y [-ĭ], *a.* mohoso, enmohecido.

mole [moul], *s.* lunar o mancha en la piel; muelle, malecón, espolón; topo. —*m.-eyed*, cegato.

molecule [mǽlĭkĭul], *s.* molécula.

molest [molést], *vt.* molestar, vejar; faltar al respeto (a una mujer); meterse con, dañar.

mollusk [mǽlʌsk], *s.* molusco.

molt [moult], *vt.* mudar la pluma.— —ing [móultĭṇ], *s.* muda.

molten [móultẹn], *pp.* de TO MELT.—*a.* fundido, derretido (metales).

moment [móumẹnt], *s.* momento, instante; importancia, peso.— —ary [-erĭ], *a.* momentáneo.— —ly [-lĭ], *adv.* por momentos.— —ous [moméntʌs], *a.* importante, grave, trascendental.— —um [moméntʌm], *s.* impulso, ímpetu; (mech.) cantidad de movimiento.

monarch [mánạrk], *s.* monarca.— —y [-ĭ], *s.* monarquía.

monastery [mánạsterĭ], *s.* monasterio, convento.—monastic [mọnǽstĭk], *a.* monástico.

Monday [mándĭ], *s.* lunes.

monetary [mánĭterĭ], *a.* monetario, pecuniario.—money [mánĭ], *s.* dinero; moneda; sistema monetario.— *m. changer, dealer, o jobber*, cambista. —*m.-exchange house*, casa de cambio. —*m. lender*, prestamista, usurero. —*m.-maker*, cosa con que se gana dinero; persona que gana y acumula dinero, acaudalada; persona metalizada.—*m. order*, giro postal.

Mongol [máṇgọl], *s.* mongol.— —ian [maṇgóulĭạn], *s.* mongólico.—*s.* mongol.— —ic [maṇgálĭk], *a.* = MONGOLIAN.

mongrel [máṇgrẹl], *a.* y *s.* mixto, mestizo.—*s.* (perro) de raza indefinida.

monk [mʌṇk], *s.* monje, fraile.

monkey [máṇkĭ], *s.* mono, macaco, mico.—*m. wrench*, llave inglesa.— *to play the m.*, hacer monadas.—*vt.* y *vi.* (fam.) remedar; hacer payasadas o monerías.—*to m. with*, meterse con; bregar con.— —shine [-šaĭn], *s.* (fam.) monería.

monogram [mánogræm], *s.* monograma.

monologue [mánolag], *s.* monólogo, soliloquio.

monopolize [monápolaĭz], *vt.* monopolizar, acaparar.—monopoly [monápolĭ], *s.* monopolio, estanco.

monosyllable [manọsĭlạbl], *s.* monosílabo.

monotonous [monátọnʌs], *a.* monótono, machacón.—monotony [monátọnĭ], *s.* monotonía.

monster [mánstœ(r)], *s.* monstruo.—*a.* enorme, prodigioso, extraordinario. —monstrosity [manstrásĭtĭ], *s.* monstruo; monstruosidad.—monstrous [mánstrʌs], *a.* monstruoso; descomunal.

month [mʌnθ], *s.* mes.— —ly [mánθlĭ], *a.* mensual.—*adv.* mensualmente.—*s.* publicación mensual.—*pl.* las reglas, menstruo.

monument [mányumẹnt], *s.* monumento; memoria, recuerdo; hito.— —al [manyuméntạl], *a.* monumental; conmemorativo; grandioso.

moo [mu], *vi.* mugir.—*s.* mu, mugido.

mood [mud], *s.* disposición de ánimo, talante, genio, humor; (gram.) modo. —y [múdĭ], *a.* caprichoso; irritable, de mal humor; cavĭloso; triste, taciturno.

moon [mun], *s.* luna; satélite; mes lunar.—*m.-blind*, cegato, corto de vista.—*m.-mad, m.-struck*, lunático, loco.— —light [múnlaĭt], *s.* luz de la luna.—*a.* iluminado por la luna.— —lit [-lĭt], *a.* iluminado por la luna.— —rise [-raĭz], *s.* salida de la luna.— —set [-set], *s.* puesta de la luna.— —shine [-šaĭn], *s.* claridad de la luna; desatino; (fam.) música celestial; licor destilado ilegalmente.— —y [-ĭ], *a.* claro como la luna; lunático; simplón; soñador.

moor [mur], *s.* páramo; brezal; (M.) moro, marroquí, sarraceno.—*vt.* (mar.) amarrar, aferrar, afirmar con anclas.—*vi.* (mar.) anclar, atracar;

estar anclado.– **—ish** [múrįš], *s.* pantanoso, cenagoso; árido; (M.) moro; morisco.

moose [mus], *s.* alce, ante.

mop [map], *s.* (Am.) trapeador; greña, mechón, cabellera revuelta; mueca. —*vti.* [1] limpiar el piso, trapear.— *to m. up*, acabar con el resto del enemigo.—*mopping-up*, (mil.) operación de limpieza.

mope [moųp], *vt.* abatir.—*vi.* abatirse, desanimarse, estar tétrico, taciturno o apático.—*s.* hombre abatido o desanimado.—*pl.* apatía, murria.

moral [márǎl], *a.* moral, ético; virtuoso; honrado, recto.—*s.* moralidad, moraleja.—*pl.* costumbres, conducta; moral social.– **—e** [morél], *s.* moral, estado de ánimo, espíritu.– **—ism** [márǎlįzm], *s.* enseñanza moral.— **—ist** [márǎlįst], *s.* moralista.– **—ity** [morélįti], *s.* ética, moral; moralidad; moraleja.– **—ize** [márǎlaįz], *vt. y vi.* moralizar.

morbid [mórbįd], *a.* mórbido, morboso, malsano.

more [mor], *a.* más, adicional.—*adv.* más, en mayor grado; además.—*s.* mayor cantidad o número.—*m. and m.*, cada vez más.—*m. or less*, poco más o menos.—*no m.*, no más; ya no; se acabó.—*so much the m.*, tanto más, cuanto más.—*the m.*, tanto más.— **—over** [-óųvœ(r)], *adv.* además, por otra parte.

morning [mórnįŋ], *s.* mañana (primera parte del día).—*good m.!* ¡buenos días!—*a.* matutino, matinal, de mañana.

Moroccan [morákǎn], *a. y s.* marroquí.

morphine [mórfin], *s.* morfina.

morsel [mórsęl], *s.* bocado, manjar; presa.

mortal [mórtǎl], *s.* mortal, ser humano. —*a.* mortal; fatal, letal.– **—ity** [mortélįti], *s.* mortalidad; mortandad; humanidad.—*m. rate*, mortalidad.

mortar [mórtǎ(r)], *s.* mortero, almirez; (arti.) mortero, obús.—*m. piece*, (alb.) mortero, mezcla.

mortgage [mórgįdž], *s.* hipoteca, gravamen.—*m. loan*, préstamo hipotecario.—*vt.* hipotecar, gravar.

mortify [mórtįfaį], *vti.* [7] mortificar, humillar, abochornar.

mortuary [mórchųerį], *s.* depósito de cadáveres.—*a.* mortuorio.

mosaic [mozéįįk], *a. y s.* mosaico.

Moslem [mázlem], *s. y a.* musulmán.

mosque [mask], *s.* mezquita.

mosquito [mǫskítoų], *s.* mosquito.—*m. net*, mosquitero.

moss [mos], *s.* musgo, moho; tremedal, ciénaga.—*vt.* cubrir de musgo.– **—y** [mósį], *a.* musgoso.

most [moųst], *a.* más; lo más, los más, el mayor número (de); casi todo(s); la mayor parte (de).—*for the m. part*, principalmente, generalmente.—*adv.* más, lo más, sumamente, muy; (fam.) casi.—*s.* lo principal, la mayor parte, el mayor número, lo más, el mayor valor.—*at (the) m.*, a lo más, a lo sumo, cuando más.– **—ly** [móųstlį], *adv.* en su mayor parte, casi todo(s), principalmente.

mote [moųt], *s.* mota (de polvo).

moth [moϑ], *s.* polilla.—*m. ball*, bola de alcanfor u otra sustancia contra la polilla.—*m.-eaten*, apolillado.

mother [mʌðœ(r)], *s.* madre.—*m. country*, madre patria, metrópoli. —*m.-in-law*, suegra.—*m.-of-pearl*, nácar, madreperla.—*a.* materno, maternal; nativo, natal; vernáculo, nacional; metropolitano.—*M. Superior*, madre superiora (monjas).— *m. tongue*, lengua materna.—*vt.* servir de madre a.—*vi.* criar madre (vino, etc.).—**—hood** [-hųd], *s.* maternidad.— **—less** [-lįs], *a.* huérfano de madre.— **—ly** [-lį], *a.* maternal, materno.—*adv.* maternalmente.

motif [motíf], *s.* motivo, asunto, tema.

motility [motílįtį], *s.* movilidad.— **motion** [móųšǫn], *s.* movimiento; signo, señal, seña; moción, proposición; (for.) pedimento.—*m. picture*, cine; fotografía cinematográfica; película.—*on the m. of*, a propuesta de.—*to set in m.*, poner en marcha. —*vi.* hacer señas.—**motionless** [móų-šǫnlįs], *a.* inmóvil; yerto.

motivate [móųtįveįt], *vt.* motivar.— **motive** [móųtįv], *a.* motor, motriz. —*m. power*, fuerza motriz.—*s.* motivo, móvil, porqué; pie, tema, idea.

motley [mátlį], *a.* abigarrado; mezclado, variado, diverso; vestido de colorines. —*s.* traje de payaso; mezcla de colores; mezcolanza.

motor [móųtǫ(r)], *s.* motor.—*a.* motriz, motor; de motor.—*m. boat o launch*, gasolinera, lancha automóvil.—*vi.* ir en automóvil.– **—car** [-kar], *s.* automóvil, auto.– **—coach** [-koųch], *s.* autobús, ómnibus.– **—cycle** [-saįkl], *s.* motocicleta.– **—ist** [-įst], *s.* automovilista, motorista.– **—ization** [moųtǫrįzéįšǫn], *s.* motorización.— **—ize** [-aįz], *vt.* motorizar.– **—man** [-mǎn], *s.* motorista, conductor (de tranvía o tren eléctrico).

mottle [mátl], *vt.* motear, vetear, manchar.—*s.* mota, veta, mancha.

motto [mátoų], *s.* mote, lema, divisa.

mould [moųld], *s., vt. y vi.* MOLD.— **moulder** [móųldœ(r)], *vi. y vt.* **=** MOLDER.—**moulding** [móųldįŋ], *s.* **=**

MOLDING.—**mouldy** [móuldi], a. =
MOLDY.

moult [moult], vi. = MOLT.—**moulting**
[móultin], s. = MOLTING.

mound [maund], s. montón de tierra;
montículo; baluarte; túmulo.—vt.
amontonar; atrincherar, fortalecer.

mount [maunt], s. monte, montaña;
baluarte; terraplén; montadura;
caballería; montura; apeadero; (mil.)
monta, toque de clarín.—vt. cabalgar;
armar, montar; subir, alzar, elevar;
enaltecer; engastar, montar (joyas);
(teat.) poner en escena; preparar una
cosa para usarla o exhibirla.—vi.
ascender, elevarse; montar a caballo;
subir, montar, ascender (una cuenta,
etc.).— —**ain** [máuntin], s. monte,
montaña.—a. montés, montañés; de
montaña.—m. chain, sierra, cordillera, cadena de montañas.—m.
climber, alpinista.—m. climbing,
alpinismo.— —**aineer** [-inír], s. montañés, serrano.— —**ainous** [-inʌs], a.
montañoso.

mourn [mourn, morn], vt. lamentar,
llorar, sentir.—vi. lamentarse, dolerse; vestir o llevar luto.—to m. for,
llevar luto por; lamentar, llorar.—
—**ful** [mórnful], a. triste, plañidero,
apesadumbrado; fúnebre, lúgubre.—
—**ing** [-in], s. luto; duelo; dolor,
aflicción.—in m., de luto, de duelo;
fúnebre.—m. band, brazal de luto.

mouse [maus], s. ratón.— —**trap**
[máustræp], s. ratonera.

moustache [mastáʃ], s. = MUSTACHE.

mouth [mauθ], s. boca; abertura;
embocadura o desembocadura de un
río.— —**ful** [máuθful], s. bocado;
buchada; migaja, pizca.— —**piece**
[-pis], s. boquilla, embocadura;
vocero, portavoz.

movability [muvǎbíliti], s. movilidad.—
movable [múvǎbl], a. movible; móvil;
movedizo.—s. pl. muebles, menaje,
mobiliario, efectos.—**move** [muv], s.
movimiento; paso; jugada, lance,
turno de jugar.—on the m., en
marcha, en movimiento; de viaje.
—to get a m. on, (fam.) darse prisa,
empezarse a mover.—to make a m.,
dar un paso; hacer una jugada.—vt.
mover; remover; trasladar, mudar;
hacer una moción; conmover; persuadir.—to m. to, causar (cólera,
etc.), poner (colérico, etc.).—vi.
moverse; mudarse; ir, andar, caminar,
ponerse en marcha; obrar, entrar en
acción; avanzar, progresar; mover el
vientre; hacer una jugada.—to m.
away, alejarse; irse; trasladarse;
mudar de casa.—to m. in, entrar;
entrar a habitar una casa.—**movement** [múvment], s. movimiento;

moción; maniobra; paso, acto, acción,
incidente; defecación, evacuación.—

movie [múvi], s. (fam.) función de
cine; película.—pl. cine.—**moving**
[múvin], a. conmovedor, emocionante, patético.—m. parts, piezas
que se mueven (en un mecanismo).
—s. movimiento, moción; traslado,
mudanza.

mow [mou], vti. [6] segar, guadañar,
cortar la hierba.— —**er** [móuœ(r)],
s. segador; segadora mecánica.

Mr. [místœ(r)], s. = MISTER.—**Mrs.**
[mísiz], s. = MISTRESS.

much [mʌch], a. mucho, abundante,
copioso.—adv. mucho; muy; con
mucho, en gran manera.—as m. as,
tanto como.—as m. more, otro tanto
más.—how m.? ¿cuánto?—m. as, por
más que, a pesar de.—m. the same,
casi lo mismo.—m. too, demasiado.—
not so m. as, no tanto como; ni
siquiera.—so m., tanto.—this m. more,
esto más, tanto así más.—s. mucho.

muck [mʌk], s. abono, estiércol; cieno;
porquería, basura.

mucous [mjúkʌs], a. mucoso, mocoso.
—**mucus** [mjúkʌs], s. moco, moco-
sidad.

mud [mʌd], s. fango, lodo, barro.
—m. wall, tapia.—vt. enlodar,
embarrar; ensuciar, enturbiar.— —**dle**
[mʌdl], vt. embrollar, confundir; revolver; atontar.—to m. through, hacer
algo malamente, salir del paso a duras
penas.—s. embrollo, confusión.— —**dy**
[mʌdi], a. lodoso, sucio, turbio; tonto,
confuso.—vti. [7] enturbiar, ensuciar;
entontecer, turbar.

muff [mʌf], s. manguito (para las
manos); chabacanería, torpeza;
(baseball) fallar la bola.—vt. desperdiciar (una ocasión); dejar escapar
(la pelota); (fam.) hacer algo
torpemente.

muffin [mʌfin], s. panecillo, bollito.

muffle [mʌfl], vt. embozar; encubrir;
apagar o atenuar un sonido.—to m.
up, embozarse.— —**d** [-d], a. apagado,
sordo.— —**r** [mʌflœ(r)], s. bufanda;
(aut.) silenciador; (mús.) sordina.

mug [mʌg], s. tarro (para cerveza);
(fam.) cara, boca; mueca; vaso con
asa.

mulatto [mulǽtou], a. y s. mulato.

mulberry [mʌlberi], s. mora.—m. tree,
moral.

mule [mjul], s. mulo, mula.— —**teer**
[mjuletír], s. arriero.

mull [mʌl], s. muselina clara; cabo,
promontorio.—vi. rumiar, cavilar;
afanarse mucho sin resultado.

multilingual [mʌltilíngwal], a. políglota.

multiple [mʌltipl], s. múltiplo.—a.
múltiple; (mat.) múltiplo.—**multipli-**

cation [mʌltiplikéiʂɒn], s. multiplicación.—m. table, tabla de multiplicar.—multiplicity [mʌltiplísiti], s. multiplicidad, sinnúmero.—multiply, vti. y vii. [7] multiplicar(se).

multitude [mʌltitiud], s. multitud; vulgo.

mum [mʌm], interj. ¡chitón! ¡silencio! —a. callado, silencioso.—m.'s the word, punto en boca.—to keep m., callarse.

mumble [mʌmbl], vt. y vi. rezongar, musitar, hablar o decir entre dientes; murmurar, refunfuñar; (fam.) mascullar.

mummy [mʌmi], s. momia.

mumps [mʌmps], s. (med.) paperas, parótidas.

munch [mʌnch], vt. mascar enérgicamente, mascullar.

municipal [miunísipal], a. municipal.—ity [miunisipǽliti], s. municipio; municipalidad.

munificence [miunífisens], s. munificencia.—munificent [miunífisent], a. munífico, generoso, liberal.

munitions [miunísɒnz], s. pl. municiones, pertrechos; equipo.

mural [miúral], a. mural; escarpado, vertical.—s. cuadro mural.

murmur [mérmœ(r)], s. murmullo, susurro; murmuración.—vi. murmurar, susurrar; refunfuñar.

murder [mérdœ(r)], s. asesinato, homicidio.—vt. asesinar; estropear.—vi. cometer homicidio.—er [-œ(r)], s. asesino, homicida.—ess [-is], s. asesina.—ous [-ʌs], a. asesino, sanguinario.

murky [mérki], a. oscuro, lóbrego.

muscat [mʌskat], s. moscatel (uva y pasa).—muscatel [mʌskatél], s. moscatel (vino y uva).

muscle [mʌsl], s. músculo; fuerza muscular.—muscular [mʌskiulǎ(r)], a. muscular; musculoso; atlético.

Muse [miuz], s. musa; (m.) meditación o abstracción profunda; éxtasis, numen.—(m.) vi. meditar, reflexionar, estar absorto.—to m. on, over o upon, meditar en.

museum [miuzíʌm], s. museo.

mush [mʌʂ], s. masa blanda y espesa; masa espesa de harina de maíz; (fam.) sentimentalismo exagerado; (rad.) ruido como de chisporroteo.

mushroom [mʌʂrum], s. seta, hongo.—a. hecho con setas u hongos; efímero.—vi. recoger setas; (fig.) desarrollarse y extenderse rápidamente.

mushy [mʌʂi], a. pastoso; exageradamente sentimental.

music [miúzik], s. música.—m. hall, salón de conciertos; café cantante.

—m. stand, atril; tablado para una orquesta.—al [-al], a. musical.—m. comedy, zarzuela, comedia musical.—ian [miuzíʂan], s. músico.

musk [mʌsk], s. almizcle.—a. almizclero.

muskmelon [mʌskmelɒn], s. melón.—muskrat [mʌskræt], s. rata almizclera.

Muslim [mʌzlim], s. y a. = MOSLEM.

muslin [mʌzlin], s. muselina; percal; percalina.—a. de muselina; de percal.

muss [mʌs], s. (fam.) desorden, confusión; arrebatiña.—vt. (fam.) desordenar, manosear, arrugar; ensuciar.

mussel [mʌsel], s. mejillón.

must [mʌst], voi. [11] deber, tener que; haber que; deber (de).—he m. have gone, debió ir, debe (de) haber ido.—it m. be very late, será muy tarde.—she m. have missed the train, habrá perdido el tren.—s. mosto; moho.

mustache [mʌstǽʂ], s. bigote, mostacho.

mustard [mʌstǎrd], s. mostaza.

muster [mʌstœ(r)], vt. reunir; (mil.) juntar para pasar lista, revista, etc.—to m. in o into service, (mil.) alistar.—to m. up, tomar (valor, fuerza, etc.).—vi. (mil.) juntarse; pasar lista.—s. (mil.) revista; lista, reseña; alarde, muestra.—to pass m., llenar los requisitos.

musty [mʌsti], a. mohoso; añejo; rancio; pasado; mustio, triste.

mutability [miutabíliti], s. inconstancia, veleidad.—mutable [miútabl], a. inconstante, veleidoso.—mutation [miutéiʂɒn], s. mutación.

mute [miut], a. mudo; callado, silencioso; sordo.—s. mudo; letra muda; (mus.) sordina.

mutilate [miútileit], vt. mutilar; truncar.—mutilation [miutiléiʂɒn], s. mutilación.

mutinous [miútinʌs], a. amotinado, sedicioso, turbulento.—mutiny [miútini], vii. [7] amotinarse.—s. motín, amotinamiento.

mutter [mʌtœ(r)], vt. y vi. murmurar, rezongar, gruñir; bisbisar, decir entre dientes.—s. refunfuñadura, gruñido.—er [-œ(r)], s. rezongador, gruñón.

mutton [mʌtɒn], s. carne de carnero.—m. broth, caldo de carnero.—m. chop, chuleta de carnero.

mutual [miúchual], a. mutuo, recíproco.—m. friend, amigo común.

muzzle [mʌzl], s. morro, hocico; bozal; boca de arma de fuego.—vt. abozalar, poner bozal; amordazar.—vi. hocicar.

my [mai], a. pos. mi, mis.

myopia [maióupiǎ], s. miopía.—myopic [maiápik], a. miope, corto de vista.

myriad [mírịạd], *s.* miríada; diez mil; millares, un gran número.—*a.* innumerable, numeroso.

myrrh [mœr], *s.* mirra, goma resinosa.

myrtle [mœrtl], *s.* mirto, arrayán.

myself [maịsélf], *pron.* yo mismo; me, mí, mí mismo.—*I myself did it*, yo mismo lo hice.—*I said to myself*, me dije a mí mismo o para mí.

mysterious [mịstịrịạs], *a.* misterioso. —**mystery** [místẹrị], *s.* misterio; arcano.

mystic [mịstịk], *a.* y *s.* místico.— **mystify** [místịfaị], *vti.* [7] confundir, desconcertar; intrigar; mixtificar.

myth [mịθ], *s.* mito; fábula; ficción.- —**ical** [mịθịkạl], *a.* mítico; fabuloso; imaginario.- —**ological** [mịθọládẹị- kạl], *a.* mitológico.- —**ology** [mịθálodẹị], *s.* mitología.

N

nab [næb], *vti.* [1] (fam.) prender, atrapar, agarrar, echar mano a, echar el guante a.

nag [næg], *s.* jaco, rocín, caballejo; (fam.) penco, jamelgo.—*vti.* y *vti.* [1] (a veces con **at**) regañar, machacar, sermonear.

nail [neịl], *s.* uña.—*n. file*, lima para las uñas.—*n. polish*, esmalte de uñas.— *n. scratch*, arañazo.—*vt.* clavar, clavetear.—**brush** [neịlbrᴀ̂ŝ], *s.* cepillo para las uñas.

naive [naív], *a.* ingenuo, cándido.

naked [néịkịd], *a.* desnudo; descubierto; descamisado; patente.—*stark n.*, en cueros, (fam.) en pelota.—*the n. truth*, la verdad pura y simple.—*(with the) n. eye*, (a) simple vista.- —**ness** [-nịs], *s.* desnudez.

name [neịm], *s.* nombre; apellido; (fam.) gracia; fama, renombre.—*by u of the n. of*, llamado, nombrado.— *Christian n.*, nombre de pila.—*in God's name*, por el amor de Dios.—*in n.*, de nombre.—*n. day*, día del santo, onomástico.—*to call names*, injuriar. —*what is your n.?* ¿cómo se llama usted?—*vt.* nombrar, apellidar; designar; llamar, poner nombre; mentar, mencionar; fijar.- —**less** [néịmlịs], *a.* sin nombre, anónimo.- —**ly** [-lị], *adv.* especialmente; a saber, o sea, es decir.- —**sake** [-seịk], *s.* tocayo; homónimo.

nap [næp], *s.* siesta; (tej.) lanilla, pelusa.—*vii.* [1] dormitar, echar una siesta, cabecear el sueño; estar desprevenido.

nape [neịp], *s.* nuca, cogote, testuz.

naphtha [næfθạ], *s.* nafta.- —**lene** [-lin], *s.* naftalina.

napkin [næpkịn], *s.* servilleta.

narcissus [narsịsᴀs], *s.* narciso.

narcotic [narkátịk], *s.* y *a.* narcótico.

narrate [næréịt], *vt.* y *vi.* narrar, relatar. —**narration** [næréịŝọn], *s.* narración, relato.—**narrative** [nǽrạtịv], *a.* narrativo.—*s.* narración, narrativa, relato.—**narrator** [næréịtọ(r)], *s.* narrador.

narrow [nǽrouị], *a.* angosto, estrecho; limitado; tacaño, mezquino; próximo, cercano, intolerante.—*n. gauge*, (f.c.) de vía estrecha.—*n.-minded*, estrecho de miras.—*n. pass*, desfiladero.—*to have a n. escape*, salvarse en una tabla.—*s. pl.* pasaje angosto; desfiladero; estrecho.—*vt.* estrechar, contraer, encoger; limitar.—*vi.* estrecharse, encogerse, reducirse.- —**ly** [-lị], *adv.* estrechamente; por poco, escasamente.- —**ness** [-nịs], *s.* angostura; estrechez, pobreza.

nastiness [nǽstịnịs], *s.* mala intención, malevolencia; suciedad, porquería; obscenidad.

nasty [nǽstị], *a.* malévolo; sucio, asqueroso; ofensivo; obsceno, indecente; (tiempo) inclemente.

natal [néịtạl], *a.* nativo; natal.

nation [néịŝọn], *s.* nación; pueblo, gente.- —**al** [nǽŝọnạl], *a.* nacional.— *n. debt*, deuda pública.—*s.* ciudadano; súbdito.- —**alism** [nǽŝọnạlizm], *s.* nacionalismo.- —**ality** [nǽŝọnǽliṭị], *s.* nacionalidad; origen, tradición.- —**alization** [nǽŝọnạlịzéịŝọn], *s.* nacionalización; naturalización.- —**alize** [nǽŝọnạlaịz], *vt.* nacionalizar; naturalizar.

native [néịtịv], *a.* nativo, natal, natural, oriundo; indígena; del país, patrio.— *n. country o land*, patria, país natal, terruño.—*s.* natural, nativo, indígena.—**nativity** [neịtịvịtị], *s.* nacimiento, natividad; (N.) Navidad.

natural [nǽchụrạl], *a.* natural; nativo; sencillo, sin afectación; normal, ordinario, ilegítimo, bastardo.—*s.* (mús.) becuadro; tecla blanca.— —**ism** [-ịzm], *s.* naturalismo.- —**ist** [-ịst], *s.* naturalista.- —**ization** [-ịzéịŝọn], *s.* naturalización; nacionalización.—*n. papers*, carta de naturaleza.—**ize** [-aịz], *vt.* naturalizar; nacionalizar.- —**ly** [-lị], *adv.* naturalmente; desde luego.- —**ness** [-nịs], *s.* naturalidad; sencillez.—**nature** [néị-chụ(r)], *s.* naturaleza; natural, índole, genio; especie, género, clase; naturalidad.

naught [not], *s.* nada; cero.—*to set at n.*, hacer tabla rasa de.

naughtiness [nótịnịs], *s.* maldad, perversidad; picardía, travesura.— **naughty** [nótị], *a.* desobediente,

díscolo; pícaro, travieso; libre, picaresco.

nausea [nɔ́şįȧ], *s.* náusea, asco.— —**te**
[nɔ́şįeįt], *vt.* dar asco o disgusto,
apestar.— —**ting** [nɔ́şįeįtįŋ], *a.* nauseabundo, asqueroso, apestoso.

nautical [nɔ́tįkȧl], *a.* náutico, marino.

naval [néįvȧl], *a.* naval; de marina.—
n. base o *station,* base o apostadero
naval.

nave [neįv], *s.* (arq.) nave.

navel [néįvȩl], *s.* ombligo.

navigable [nǽvigȧbl], *a.* navegable.—
navigate [nǽvigeįt], *vt. y vi.* navegar.
—**navigation** [nǽvigéįşȩn], *s.* navegación; náutica.—**navigator** [nǽvi-
geįtọ(r)], *s.* navegante; piloto; tratado de náutica.—**navy** [néįvi], *s.*
armada, marina de guerra, flota.—*n.
blue,* azul marino.—*n. yard,* astillero;
arsenal.

nay [neį], *adv.* no; de ningún modo;
más aún, y aún.—*s.* voto negativo;
negación.

near [nįr], *prep.* cerca de, junto a,
próximo a, por, hacia.—*adv.* cerca;
proximamente; (fam.) casi.—*n. at
hand,* a (la) mano, cerca.—*a.* cercano,
próximo, inmediato; allegado; íntimo,
estrecho; a punto de, por poco.—*vt.
y vi.* acercar(se).— —**by** o **n.-by**
[nɪ́rbaị], *prep.* cerca de.—*adv.* cerca,
a (la) mano.—*a.* cercano, contiguo,
próximo.— —**ly** [-lį], *adv.* cerca,
cerca de; estrechamente; casi; de
cerca; próximamente, aproximadamente.— —**ness** [-nįs], *s.* proximidad,
cercanía.— —**sighted** [-sáįtįd], *a.*
miope, corto de vista.— —**sightedness**
[-sáįtįdnįs], *s.* miopía.

neat [nit], *a.* limpio, aseado, pulcro;
pulido; mondo, lirondo; nítido, claro;
esmerado.— —**ness** [nítnįs], *s.* aseo,
pulcritud, nitidez, limpieza; elegancia, delicadeza.

nebula [nébyųlȧ], *s.* (astr.) nebulosa;
nube en el ojo.—**nebulous** [nébyųlʌs],
a. nebuloso.

necessarily [néseserįlį], *adv.* necesaria-
mente.—**necessary** [néseseri], *a.*
necesario, preciso, forzoso.—*to be n.,*
ser menester, hacer falta.—*s.* lo
necesario.—*pl.* necesidades, cosas
necesarias o imprescindibles.—**necessitate** [nįsésįteįt], *vt.* hacer necesario.
—**necessity** [nįsésįti], *s.* necesidad;
indigencia.—*pl.* artículos de primera
necesidad, requisitos indispensables.

neck [nȩk], *s.* cuello, garganta; pescuezo; gollete (de botella); (cost.)
escote; istmo, cabo, península; desfiladero.—*n. and n.* (dep.) parejos en
una carrera.—*n. of land,* lengua de
tierra.—*in* u *on the n. of,* a raíz de.—

—**lace** [nȩklįs], *s.* collar, gargantilla.—
—**tie** [-taį], *s.* corbata.

nectarine [nektȧrín], *s.* abridor (variedad de durazno).

need [nid], *s.* necesidad; carencia, falta;
pobreza, miseria.—*if n. be,* si hubiere
necesidad, si fuere necesario.—*vt.*
necesitar; hacer falta.—*vi.* ser necesario; estar en la necesidad, carecer de
lo necesario.— —**ful** [nídfųl], *a.*
necesario; necesitado.

needle [nídl], *s.* aguja.—*n. case,*
alfiletero.

needless [nídlįs], *a.* inútil, innecesario,
superfluo.—*n. to say,* excusado es
decir.

needlework [nídlwœrk], *s.* costura;
labor, bordado de aguja.

needy [nídį], *a.* necesitado, menesteroso.

ne'er [nɛr], *adv. contr.* de NEVER.—
n.-do-well [nɛ́rduwȩl], *s.* haragán,
perdulario.

nefarious [nįférįʌs], *a.* nefando, malvado.

negation [nįgéįşȩn], *s.* negación, negativa.—**negative** [négȧtįv], *a.* negativo.—*s.* negativa; denegación; veto;
negación; (foto.) negativo.

neglect [nįglékt], *s.* descuido, negligencia; abandono, dejadez.—*vt.* descuidar, desatender; abandonar.— —**ful**
[-fųl], *a.* negligente, descuidado.—
negligence [néglįdžȩns], *s.* negligencia.—**negligent** [néglįdžȩnt], *a.* negligente.

negotiable [nįgóųşįȧbl], *a.* negociable.—
negotiate [nįgóųşįeįt], *vt.* negociar;
gestionar, agenciar; (fam.) vencer,
superar.—*vi.* negociar.—**negotiation**
[nįgóųşįéįşȩn], *s.* negociación; negocio, gestión.

Negro [nígroų], *s. y a.* negro.

neigh [neį], *vi.* relinchar.—*s.* relincho.

neighbor [néįbọ(r)], *s.* vecino; prójimo.
— —**hood** [-hųd], *s.* vecindad; vecindario; barrio; cercanías, alrededores.
—*in the n. of,* (fam.) casi, como,
aproximadamente.— —**ing** [-įŋ], *a.*
vecino, vecinal, colindante, próximo
o cercano.

neither [níðœ(r), náįðœ(r)], *a.* ningún,
ninguno de los dos.—*conj.* ni; tampoco, ni siquiera.—*n. he nor she,* ni
él ni ella.—*pron.* ninguno, ni uno ni
otro, ni el uno ni el otro.

Neo-Latin [niolǽtįn], *s. y a.* neolatino.

neologism [nįálȯdžįzm], *s.* neologismo.

nephew [néfįu], *s.* sobrino.

nerve [nœrv], *s.* nervio; vigor, fibra;
valor, ánimo; (fam.) desfachatez,
descaro.—*pl.* excitabilidad nerviosa.
—*n.-racking,* horripilante.— —**nervous**
[nœ́rvʌs], *a.* nervioso.—*n. breakdown,*
crisis neurótica.—**nervousness** [nœ́r-

vʌsnĭs], *s.* nerviosidad; estado nervioso o irritable.

nest [nest], *s.* nido; nidada; madriguera.—*vi.* anidar; anidarse.

nestle [nésl], *vt.* abrigar, poner en un nido.—*vi.* anidar(se).

net [net], *s.* red; redecilla; malla; (fig.) trampa; (tej.) tul.—*vti.* [1] enredar o coger con red; cubrir con redes o mallas; coger; obtener; producir una ganancia líquida.—*a.* (com.) neto, líquido; de punto de malla.—*n.* amount, importe neto.—*n.* balance, saldo líquido o neto.—*n.* profit, ganancia o utilidad líquida, beneficio líquido.— **-ting** [-iŋ], *s.* red; tejido de malla.

nettle [nétl], *s.* (bot.) ortiga.—*vt.* picar; irritar, provocar.

network [nétwœrk], *s.* red, malla; (rad., T.V., f.c., etc.) cadena, red, sistema.

neurasthenia [njurʌsꝋínĭặ], *s.* neurastenia.

neurosis [njuróusĭs], *s.* neurosis.—**neurotic** [njurátĭk], *a.* neurótico.

neuter [njútœ(r)], *a.* neutro; neutral.— **neutral** [njútrʌl], *a.* neutral; neutro; indiferente.—*s.* neutral.—*in n.,* (aut.) en punto muerto.—**neutrality** [njutrǽlĭtĭ], *s.* neutralidad.—**neutralize** [njútrʌlaɪz], *vt.* neutralizar.

never [névœ(r)], *adv.* nunca, jamás; no, de ningún modo.—*n.* again, nunca más, otra vez no.—*n.* ending, interminable, sin fin.—*n.* fear, no hay cuidado, no hay miedo.—*n.* mind, no importa.— **-more** [nevœrmór], *adv.* jamás, nunca más.— **-theless** [nevœrðĕlés], *adv.* y *conj.* no obstante, con todo, sin embargo, a pesar de eso.

new [nju], *a.* nuevo; moderno; fresco, reciente, recién; distinto.—*what's n.?* ¿qué hay de nuevo?— **-born** [njúbórn], *a.* recién nacido.— **-comer** [njúkʌmœ(r)], *s.* recién llegado.— **-fangled** [njúfǽŋgld], *a.* recién inventado.— **-ly** [njúlĭ], *adv.* nuevamente, recientemente, recién.—*n.* arrived, recién llegado; advenedizo.— **-lywed** [-ljwed], *s.* recién casado, recién casada.— **-ness** [-nĭs], *s.* novedad; innovación.— **-s** [-z], *s.* noticia, nueva; noticias; noticia fresca.—*no n. is good n.,* la falta de noticias es buena noticia.—*what's the n.?* ¿qué hay de nuevo? ¿qué noticias hay?— **-sboy** [-zbɔɪ], *s.* chiquillo vendedor de periódicos.— **-smonger** [-zmʌŋgœ(r)], *s.* gacetista, noticiero.— **-spaper** [-zpeɪpœ(r)], *s.* periódico, diario.—*n.* man, periodista; reportero, repórter.—*n.* serial, folletín.— **-sreel** [-zril], *s.* noticiario cinematográfico.— **-sstand** [-zstænd], *s.*

quiosco o puesto de periódicos, revistas, etc.

New Zealander [nɪu zílặndœ(r)], *s.* neozelandés.

next [nekst], *a.* siguiente; entrante; próximo, contiguo, inmediato; subsiguiente, futuro, venidero.—*n.* door, la puerta (o casa) al lado.—*n.* month, (week, year), el mes (la semana, el año) entrante, próximo o que viene.—*n.* time, otra vez, la próxima vez.—*the n.* life, la otra vida.—*to be n.,* seguir en turno, tocarle a uno.—*adv.* luego, después, inmediatamente después, en seguida, a renglón seguido.—*n.* best, lo mejor a falta de eso.—*n.* to, junto a, al lado de; después de; casi.—*n.* to impossible, punto menos que imposible.—*what n.?* ¿y ahora (o luego) qué?

nibble [nĭbl], *vt.* mordiscar, mordisquear; pacer.—*vi.* picar, morder (como el pez); (at) criticar.—*s.* mordisco, bocadito.

Nicaraguan [nĭkặrágwặn], *a.* y *s.* nicaragüense.

nice [naɪs], *a.* fino, sutil; delicado; diligente, solícito; esmerado, pulcro, refinado; agradable, lindo; simpático, gentil, amable.— **-ly** [náɪslɪ], *adv.* muy bien, con delicadeza, finamente.—*to get along n.* with, llevarse bien con.— **-ness** [-nɪs], *s.* finura, delicadeza, amabilidad; esmero; refinamiento; sutileza.— **-ty** [náɪsẹtɪ], *s.* primor, cuidado; finura, delicadeza; remilgo; pormenor.

niche [nĭch], *s.* nicho.

nick [nĭk], *s.* muesca, mella, corte, picadura; momento oportuno; jugada favorable.—*in the n.* of time, en el momento justo.

nickel [nĭkẹl], *s.* níquel; (fam.) moneda de cinco centavos (E.U.).—*n.* steel, acero níquel.—*to n.-plate,* niquelar.

nickname [nĭknejm], *s.* mote, apodo.—*vt* motejar, apodar.

nicotine [nĭkotin], *s.* nicotina.

niece [nis], *s.* sobrina.

niggard [nígặrd], *a.* y *s* tacaño, mezquino.— **-ly** [-lɪ], *a.* = NIGGARD.—*adv.* mezquinamente, etc.

night [naɪt], *s.* noche.—*last n.,* anoche.—*n.* before last, anteanoche.—*tomorrow n.,* mañana por la noche.—*a.* nocturno; de noche.—*n.* clothes, ropa de dormir.—*n.* club, café cantante, cabaret.—*n.* owl, buho, lechuza, mochuelo; (fam.) trasnochador.—*n.* shift, turno de noche.—*n.* watch, sereno, guardia nocturno; guardia nocturna; acción de trasnochar.—*n.* watchman, sereno.— **-cap** [náɪtkæp], *s.* gorro de dormir.— **-fall** [-fɔl], *s.* anochecida, anochecer, caída de la

tarde.— —gown [-gaʊn], s. camisa de dormir.— —hawk [-hɔk], s. chotacabras; (fam.) trasnochador.— —ingale [-iŋgeɪl], s. ruiseñor.— —ly [-lɪ], adv. por las noches, todas las noches.—a. nocturno, de noche.— —mare [-mer], s. pesadilla.— —shirt [-ʃœrt], s. camisa de dormir.— —time [-taɪm], s. noche.—in the n., de noche.

nimble [nɪmbl], a. vivo, listo, ágil, veloz, expedito.—n.-witted, despierto, inteligente.—nimbly [nɪmblɪ], adv. ligeramente, ágilmente.

nip [nɪp], vt. [1] pellizcar; asir, sujetar; recortar, desmochar; helar, escarchar; marchitar.—to n. in the bud, cortar en flor.—to n. off, desmochar.—s. pellizco; pedacito; trago, traguito; dentellada; helada, escarcha; cogida; daño repentino (plantas y sembrados).—n. and tuck, (dep.) empate.

nipple [nɪpl], s. pezón; tetilla; mamadera; (mec.) tubo roscado de unión.

Nipponese [nɪpaníz], s. y a. nipón, japonés.

nit [nɪt], s. liendre.

nitrate [nájtreɪt], s. nitrato.—nitric [nájtrɪk], a. nítrico, azoico.—nitrogen [nájtrodʒɪn], s. nitrógeno, ázoe.

no [noʊ], adv. no.—no longer, ya no.—n. more, nada más.—n. sooner, no bien. —a. ninguno, ningún.—n.-account, (fam.) sin valor, deleznable.—n. fooling, sin broma, fuera de broma.—n. matter, no importa.—n. matter how much, por mucho que.—n. one, nadie, ninguno.—n. payment, no delivery, sin pago no hay (o habrá) entrega.— n. smoking, se prohibe fumar.—to n. purpose, sin objeto.—with n. money, sin dinero.—s. no, voto negativo.

nobility [nobɪlɪtɪ], s. nobleza; hidalguía. —noble [noʊbl], a. y s. noble; hidalgo.—nobleman [noʊblman], s. noble, hidalgo.—nobleness [noʊblnɪs], s. nobleza, caballerosidad.— noblesse [noblés], s. nobleza.—nobly [noʊblɪ], adv. noblemente.

nobody [noʊbadɪ], pron. nadie, ninguno.—n. else, nadie más, ningún otro.—s. persona insignificante, (fam.) quídam.

nocturnal [naktœrnal], a. nocturno, nocturnal.—nocturne [náktœrn], s. nocturno.

nod [nad], vti. [1] hacer una seña afirmativa o llamativa con la cabeza; inclinar (una rama, etc.).—vii. cabecear, inclinar la cabeza; descabezar un sueño, dormitar.—s. cabeceo; cabezada; señal afirmativa con la cabeza; inclinación de cabeza.—to get the n., recibir el visto bueno.

node [noʊd], s bulto, protuberancia,

chichón; nudo; tumor, dureza, nódulo; nodo.

noise [nɔɪz], s. ruido; sonido; estrépito; bullicio, gritería.—it's being noised about that, corre el rumor de que, se rumora que.— —less [nɔɪzlɪs], a. silencioso, sin ruido.—noisily [nɔ́izilɪ], adv. ruidosamente.—noisy [nɔ́ɪzɪ], a. ruidoso, turbulento, estrepitoso.

nomad [noʊmæd], a. nómada; trashumante.—s. nómada.— —ic [noǽdɪk], a. = NOMAD.

nominal [nɑmɪnal], a. nominal.—nominate [nɑmɪneɪt], vt. nombrar o nominar como candidato, designar; señalar.—nomination [namɪnéɪʂon], s. nombramiento, nominación; propuesta.—nominative [nɑmɪnatɪv], a. y s. (gram.) nominativo.

nonchalance [nɑnʂalans], s. indiferencia.—nonchalant [nɑnʂalant], a. indiferente, impasible.

noncommittal [nankomɪ́tal], a. reservado, evasivo.

nondescript [nɑndɪskrɪpt], a. indefinido, inclasificable.

none [nʌn], pron. nadie, ninguno; nada; nada de.—adv. no, de ninguna manera, absolutamente no.—n. the less, no obstante, sin embargo; no menos. —to be n. the better (worse), no hallarse mejor (peor), no salir o quedar mejor (peor) librado, no ganar (perder).

nonexistent [nanɪgzɪ́stent], a. inexistente.

nonrusting [nanrʌ́stiŋ], a. inoxidable.

nonsense [nɑnsens], s. disparate, desatino; tontería, absurdo; (fam.) música celestial.—interj. ¡qué disparate! ¡bah! —nonsensical [nansénsɪkal], a. disparatado, desatinado.

nonunion [nanyúnyon], a. no agremiado u opuesto a los sindicatos obreros; de fuera de los sindicatos obreros.

noodle [núdl], s. tallarín, fideo, pasta alimenticia; tonto, mentecato; (fam.) cabeza.

nook [nʊk], s. rincón; escondrijo.

noon [nun], s. mediodía; las doce del día; (poét.) medianoche; (fig.) culminación, apogeo.—a. meridional. —day [núndej], s. mediodía (mitad del día).—a. meridional, de mediodía.

noose [nus], s. lazo corredizo, dogal.— n. snare, trampa.—vt. lazar; coger con lazo corredizo o trampa; abrumar.

nor [nor], conj. ni.—n. I, yo tampoco.

Nordic [nórdɪk], a. y s. nórdico.

norm [norm], s. norma, modelo, tipo.— —al [nórmal], a. normal, regular, corriente; típico, ejemplar; perpendicular.—s. norma, estado normal. —alize [-alaɪz], vt. normalizar, regularizar.

north [norθ], s. norte, septentrión.—s.

septentrional.—*N. American*, norteamericano.—*adv.* al norte, hacia el norte.— **—east** [nɔrθíst], *s.* y *a.* nordeste.— **—erly** [nɔ́rðɔrli], **—ern** [nɔ́rðɔern], *a.* septentrional, norteño, nórtico; nordista; del norte o hacia el norte.—*northern lights*, aurora boreal.— **—erner** [nɔ́rðɔ̃ernɔ(r)], *s.* habitante del norte.— **—land** [nɔ́rθlænd], *s.* tierra o región del norte.— **—west** [nɔrθwést], *s.* y *a.* noroeste o norueste.— **—western** [nɔrθwéstœrn], *a.* del noroeste.

Norwegian [nɔrwídʒi̥an], *s.* y *a.* noruego.

nose [nouz], *s.* nariz; (animal) hocico; olfato; sagacidad.—*n. dive*, (aer.) picada.—*vt.* y *vi.* oler, olfatear; entremeterse.—*to n. about*, husmear, curiosear.—*to n.-dive*, (aer.) picar.— *to n. out*, descubrir; vencer por poco.

nostalgia [nɔstáldʒä], *s.* nostalgia.— **nostalgic** [nɔstáldʒik], *a.* nostálgico.

nostril [nástril], *s.* ventana de la nariz; nariz.

not [nat], *adv.* no; ni, ni siquiera.—*is it n.?* ¿no es así? ¿no es eso? ¿verdad? —*n. a little*, no poco, bastante.—*n. any*, ninguno.—*n. at all*, nada; de ningún modo; de nada (contestación a *thank you*).—*n. even*, ni siquiera.— *n. one*, ni uno (sólo).—*n. so much as*, ni siquiera.—*n. to*, sin, por no.

notability [nóutabíliti], *s.* notabilidad. **—notable** [nóutabl], *a.* notable.—*s.* notabilidad, personaje eminente.

notary (**public**) [nóutari (páblik)], *s.* notario (público).— **notation** [notéiṣn], *s.* notación; anotación; numeración escrita.

notch [nach], *s.* muesca, corte; ranura; mella.—*vt.* hacer muescas; dentar; mellar.

note [nout], *s.* nota; marca, señal; anotación, apunte; comunicación, nota diplomática; esquela; aviso, conocimiento; distinción, importancia; (mus.) nota; (com.) billete; letra; vale, pagaré.—*vt.* marcar, distinguir; observar, advertir; apuntar, anotar, asentar, registrar.— **—book** [nóutbuk], *s.* libreta, cuaderno.— **—d** [nóutid], *a.* notable, afamado, insigne.— **—worthy** [-wœrði], *a.* notable, digno de atención.

nothing [náθiŋ], *s.* nada; cero; nadería, friolera.—*for n.*, gratis; inútilmente, sin provecho.—*good for n.*, inservible; despreciable.—*n. but*, sólo, no más que.—*n. else*, ninguna otra cosa; nada más.—*n. less than*, lo mismo que, no menos que.—*n. much*, no mucho, poca cosa.—(*there is*) *n. to o in it*, eso no vale nada, no asciende a nada.—*sweet nothings*, ternezas.—

that is n. to me, eso nada me importa. —*there is n. else to do o n. for it but*, no hay más remedio (que).—*adv.* de ningún modo, en nada.

notice [nóutis], *s.* nota, observación; atención; aviso, anuncio, noticia, informe, notificación; mención; artículo, suelto; llamada; consideración, cortesía.—*at the shortest n.*, al momento, tan pronto como sea posible. —*on short n.*, con poco plazo o tiempo, con poco tiempo de aviso.— *to take n.*, prestar atención; hacer caso; notar, observar.—*until further n.*, hasta más aviso.—*vt.* notar, reparar en, caer en la cuenta de; atender a, cuidar de; hacer mención de.— **—able** [-abl], *a.* digno de atención, notable; perceptible.— **—notification** [noutifikéiṣɔn], *s.* notificación; cita.— **notify** [nóutifai], *vti.* [7] notificar, avisar; prevenir; requerir, citar.

notion [nóuṣɔn], *s.* noción; idea; parecer, opinión; preocupación; intención, inclinación.—*pl.* mercería, novedades, baratijas.—*notions counter*, sección de mercería (en una tienda).

notoriety [noutɔráieti], *s.* notoriedad, mala reputación.— **notorious** [notóriʌs], *a.* notorio; escandaloso, sensacional; de mala fama.— **notoriousness** [notóriʌsnis], *s.* notoriedad, mala reputación.

notwithstanding [natwiðsténdiŋ], *adv.* no obstante, sin embargo.—*prep.* a pesar de, a despecho de.—*conj.* aun cuando, aunque, bien que; por más que.—*n. that*, aunque.

nought [nɔt], *s.* nada; cero; la cifra 0.

noun [naun], *s.* (gram.) nombre, sustantivo.

nourish [nœriṣ], *vt.* nutrir, alimentar; alentar, fomentar.— **—ment** [-mɛnt], *s.* alimento; nutrición, alimentación; pábulo, fomento.

novel [návɛl], *a.* novel, original; reciente, moderno.—*s.* novela.— **—ist** [-ist], *s.* novelista.— **—ty** [-ti], *s.* novedad; innovación.—*pl.* novedades, artículos de fantasía.

November [novémbɔ(r)], *s.* noviembre.

novice [návis], *s.* novicio, novato, aprendiz.— **novitiate** [novíṣieit], *s.* (igl.) noviciado.

now [nau], *adv.* ahora; ya; hoy día, actualmente; al instante; después de esto; ahora bien, esto supuesto.— *from n. on*, de aquí en adelante.—*just n.*, ahora mismo, poco ha.—*n. and again o then*, de vez en cuando.—*n. rich, n. poor*, ya rico, ya pobre; tan pronto rico como pobre; ora rico, ora pobre.—*n. then*, y bien, ahora bien, bien, pues bien.—*conj.* (con

that) ya que, ahora que, puesto que.—
s. actualidad, momento presente.—
—adays [náuedeiz], *adv.* hoy (en) día.

nowhere [nóuhwer], *adv.* en ninguna
parte.—*n. else,* en ninguna otra
parte.—*n. near,* ni con mucho.—

nowise [nóuwaiz], *adv.* de ningún
modo, de ninguna manera, de modo
alguno.

noxious [nákSᴧs], *a.* nocivo.

nozzle [názl], *s.* pitón, pulverizador (de
manguera); pico (de cafetera); hocico,
nariz; (fam.) nariz de persona.

nucleus [njúkljᴧs], *s.* núcleo.

nude [njud], *a.* desnudo; escueto.—*s.*
(b.a.) desnudo, figura humana des-
nuda.

nudge [nᴧdž], *vt.* tocar ligera o disimu-
ladamente con el codo.—*s.* codazo
ligero.

nudism [njúdizm], *s.* nudismo, desnudismo (culto o práctica).—**nudist**
[njúdist], *s.* y *a.* desnudista.—**nudity**
[njúditi], *s.* desnudez.

nugget [nᴧgit], *s.* (min.) pepita.

nuisance [njúsᴧns], *s.* incomodidad,
molestia, estorbo; lata, fastidio;
(for.) perjuicio o incomodidad cau-
sado a tercero; persona fastidiosa,
pelmazo.

null [nᴧl], *a.* nulo, sin fuerza legal.—
—**ification** [-ifikéiSon], *s.* anulación,
invalidación.—**nullify** [nᴧlifai], *vti.*
[7] anular, invalidar.

numb [nᴧm], *a.* aterido, entumecido,
entorpecido; torpe.—*vt.* entumecer,
entorpecer, adormecer.

number [nᴧmbœ(r)], *vt.* numerar, contar; computar; incluir, ascender a.—
s. número, cifra, guarismo; porción,
cantidad, multitud; (gram.) número;
número o ejemplar (de periódico).—
—**less** [-lis], *a.* innumerable, sin
número.

numbness [nᴧmnis], *s.* entumecimiento,
adormecimiento.

numeral [njúmerᴧl], *a.* numeral, numérico, numerario.—*s.* número, cifra,
guarismo; nombre o adjetivo numeral.—**numeric(al)** [njumérik(ᴧl)], *a.*
numérico.—**numerous** [njúmerᴧs], *a.*
numeroso; muchos.

nun [nᴧn], *s.* monja.

nunnery [nᴧnœri], *s.* convento de monjas.

nuptial [nᴧpSᴧl], *a.* nupcial.—*n. song,*
epitalamio.—*pl.* nupcias, bodas.

nurse [nœrs], *s.* enfermera, enfermero;
aya, nana.—*wet n.,* ama de cría,
nodriza.—*vt.* criar, amamantar; cuidar o asistir enfermos; cultivar (una
planta).—**maid** [nœrsmeid], *s.*
niñera, (Am.) manejadora.—**ry**
[nœrsœri], *s.* cuarto de los niños;
institución o lugar para párvulos o

lactantes; semillero; vivero (de plantas).—*n. school,* escuela de párvulos (previa al kindergarten).—*n.
tales,* cuentos infantiles o de hadas.— **rymaid** [nœrsœrimeid], *s.* =
NURSEMAID.—**nursing** [nœrsiŋ], *s.*
crianza, lactancia; asistencia, profesión de enfermera.—*n. bottle,*
biberón.—*n. home,* clínica; sanatorio
o asilo (de ancianos).

nurture [nœrchu(r)], *s.* nutrición, alimentación; educación, crianza; fomento.—*vt.* nutrir, alimentar; criar;
educar; fomentar, promover.

nut [nᴧt], *s.* nuez; tuerca; cejilla de
violín o guitarra; (fam.) chiflado,
loco; maniático; (fam.) cabeza.—
—**meg** [nᴧtmeg], *s.* nuez moscada.—

nutrient [njútrient], *a.* nutritivo.—
—**nutriment** [njútriment], *s.* alimento.
—**nutrition** [njutríSon], *s.* nutrición,
alimentación.—**nutritious** [njutríSᴧs],
nutritive [njútritiv], *a.* nutricio,
nutritivo, sustancioso.

nutshell [nᴧtSel], *s.* cáscara de nuez o
avellana.—*in a n.,* en sustancia, en
pocas palabras.

nutty [nᴧti], *a.* abundante en nueces;
con sabor a nueces; (fam.) loco,
chiflado.

nymph [nimf], *s.* ninfa.

O

oak [ouk], *s.* roble, encina.—*o. grove,*
encinar, robledo.

oar [or], *s.* remo.—*vt.* y *vi.* remar,
bogar.— **sman** [órzmᴧn], *s.* remero.

oasis [oéisis], *s.* oasis.

oat(s) [out(s)], *s.* avena.

oath [ouθ], *s.* juramento; blasfemia,
terno.—*on o upon o.,* bajo juramento.
—*to take o make an o.,* jurar, prestar
juramento.

oatmeal [óutmil], *s.* harina de avena;
gachas de avena.

obedience [obídjens], *s.* obediencia.—
obedient [obídjent], *a.* obediente.

obeisance [obéisᴧns], *s.* cortesía, reverencia; homenaje; deferencia.

obelisk [ábelisk], *s.* obelisco; (impr.)
cruz.

obese [obís], *a.* obeso, gordo.—**obesity**
[obísiti], *s.* obesidad, gordura.

obey [obéi], *vt.* obedecer.—*vi.* ser
obediente.

obituary [obíchueri], *a.* y *s.* obituario,
necrología.

object [ábdžekt], *s.* objeto, cosa; obje-
jeto, propósito; blanco, punto;
(gram.) complemento.—*o. ball,* mingo
(en el billar).—*vt.* [obdžékt], objetar,
poner reparos.—*vi.* oponerse, poner
objeción, tener inconveniente.— **ion**
[obdžékSon], *s.* objeción, reparo; in-

conveniente.- —ive [ǫbdǽktiv], *a.* objetivo.—*o. case*, (gram.) caso complementario.—*s.* (ópt., mil.) objetivo; objeto, propósito.

obligate [ábligeit], *vt.* obligar, comprometer, empeñar; constreñir.—**obligation** [abligéiʃǫn], *s.* obligación, compromiso, deber.—*pl.* (com.) obligaciones y compromisos; pasivo.—*to be under o. to one*, deber favores a uno.—**obligatory** [ǫblígatǫri], *a.* obligatorio, forzoso.—**oblige** [ǫbláiʤ], *vt.* obligar, constreñir; complacer, servir, hacer un favor.—*I am very much obliged to you*, muchas gracias, le quedo muy agradecido.—*much obliged*, muchas gracias.—**obliging** [ǫbláiʤiŋ], *a.* servicial, obsequioso, condescendiente, cortés.

oblique [ǫblík], *a.* oblicuo.

obliterate [ǫblítereit], *vt.* borrar, tachar; destruir, arrasar.

oblivion [ǫblíviǫn], *s.* olvido.—**oblivious** [ǫblíviʌs], *a.* olvidadizo, desmemoriado; abstraído, absorto.

obnoxious [ǫbnákʃʌs], *a.* ofensivo, odioso, detestable.

obscene [ǫbsín], *a.* obsceno, indecente, pornográfico.—**obscenity** [ǫbséniti], *s.* obscenidad, indecencia.

obscure [ǫbskiúr], *a.* oscuro.—*vt.* oscurecer; ocultar.—**obscurity** [ǫbskiúriti], *s.* oscuridad.

obsequies [ábsikwiz], *s. pl.* exequias, funeral(es), honras fúnebres.

obsequious [ǫbsíkwiʌs], *a.* obsequioso, zalamero; servil.

observance [ǫbzǽrvʌns], *s.* observancia, cumplimiento; rito o ceremonia. —**observant** [ǫbzǽrvʌnt], *a.* observador; observante.—**observation** [abzœrvéiʃǫn], *s.* observación.—**observatory** [ǫbzǽrvatǫri], *s.* observatorio; atalaya, mirador.—**observe** [ǫbzǽrv], *vt.* observar; notar; reparar; velar, vigilar; guardar (una fiesta).—**observer** [ǫbzǽrvœ(r)], *s.* observador.

obsolete [ábsolit], *a.* anticuado; desusado.— **—ness** [-nis], *s.* desuso.

obstacle [ábstǫkl], *s.* obstáculo; traba, tropiezo.

obstetrician [abstetríʃǫn], *s.* tocólogo, especialista en obstetricia, partero, comadrón.—**obstetrics** [ǫbstétriks], *s.* obstetricia, tocología.

obstinacy [ábstinǫsi], *s.* obstinación, porfía, terquedad, tozudez.—**obstinate** [ábstinit], *a.* obstinado, terco, porfiado.

obstruct [ǫbstrʌkt], *vt.* obstruir, impedir, estorbar.—**obstruction** [ǫbstrʌ́kʃǫn], *s.* obstrucción, impedimento, estorbo.

obtain [ǫbtéin], *vt.* obtener, adquirir,

conseguir, alcanzar, lograr.—*vi.* prevalecer, reinar.- **—able** [-ǫbl], *a.* obtenible, asequible.

obtuse [ǫbtiús], *a.* obtuso (ángulo, etc.); romo, sin punta; lerdo, torpe.

obviate [ábvieit], *vt.* obviar, evitar.—**obvious** [ábviʌs], *a.* obvio, evidente, claro.

occasion [ǫkéiʒǫn], *s.* ocasión; acontecimiento; oportunidad, lugar, coyuntura; causa.—*as o. requires*, en caso necesario, cuando llegue la ocasión.—*on o.*, en su oportunidad o a su debido tiempo.—*on the o. of*, con motivo de.—*to give o.*, dar pie.—*vt.* ocasionar, causar, acarrear.— **—al** [-ǫl], *a.* ocasional, casual; alguno que otro; poco frecuente.— **—ally** [-ǫli], *adv.* a veces, de vez en cuando, ocasionalmente.

occident [áksiḑent], *s.* occidente, ocaso, oeste; (O.) Europa y América, hemisferio occidental.- **—al** [aksidéntǫl], *a.* occidental.

occlusion [ǫklúʒǫn], *s.* obstrucción; (med.) oclusión.

occult [ǫkʌ́lt], *a.* oculto, secreto, arcano.

occupancy [ákiɥpʌnsi], *s.* ocupación, tenencia, inquilinato.—**occupant** [ákiɥpʌnt], *s.* ocupante; inquilino.—**occupation** [akiɥpéiʃǫn], *s.* ocupación, trabajo; oficio, empleo.—**occupy** [ákiɥpai], *vti.* [7] ocupar, llenar, emplear (tiempo); dar empleo, ocupación o trabajo a.

occur [ǫkœ́r], *vii.* [1] ocurrir; suceder, acontecer, acaecer; ocurrirse, venir a la imaginación o a la memoria.— **—rence** [-ǫns], *s.* ocurrencia; suceso, caso, acontecimiento.

ocean [óuʃǫn], *s.* océano.—*o. liner*, transatlántico.—**oceanic** [ouʃiénik], *a.* oceánico.

o'clock [ǫklák], *contr.* de OF THE CLOCK. —*it is eight o.*, son las ocho.

octave [áktiv], *s.* (mús.) octava.

October [aktóubœ(r)], *s.* octubre.

octopus [áktǫpʌs], *s.* (zool.) pulpo.

ocular [ákiɥlǫ(r)], *a.* ocular, visual.—**oculist** [ákiɥlist], *s.* oculista, oftalmólogo.

odd [ad], *a.* impar; non; suelto; casual, accidental; extraordinario, singular, raro; extraño.—*twenty o.*, veinte y tantos, veinte y pico.— **—ity** [áditi], *s.* singularidad, rareza.— **—s** [adz], *s. pl.* desigualdad, diferencia, disparidad; partido o apuesta desigual; ventaja, exceso; disputa.—*by all o.*, con mucho; sin duda.—*o. and ends*, retazos.—*the o. are that*, las probabilidades son, es lo más probable que.

ode [oud], *s.* oda.

odious [óudiʌs], *a.* odioso, abominable.

odor [óudǫ(r)], *s.* olor.—*bad o.*, mal

olor, hedor.— —ous [-ʌs], a. oloroso.

odyssey [ádisi], s. odisea, viaje largo y accidentado.

o'er [oụr], contr. de OVER.

of [av], prep. de; a; en.—it tastes o. wine, sabe a vino.—o. course, por supuesto, desde luego.—o. late, últimamente.— o. mine, mío, mía.—to dream o., soñar con.—to think o., pensar en.

off [ɔf], adv. lejos, a distancia, fuera; de menos.—day o., día libre.—far o., lejos (de).—hands o., no tocar.—o. and on, de vez en cuando, algunas veces; a intervalos.—six miles o., a seis millas de distancia.—to be badly (o well) o., andar mal (bien) de dinero.—to be o., irse, marcharse, salir.—to put o., diferir, aplazar.—to see someone o., despedir a alguien.— to turn o. the water (the light, the gas), cortar el agua (la luz, el gas).—two dollars o., un descuento de dos dólares.—prep. lejos de; fuera de; de; desde; frente a, cerca de.—an o. day, un día libre; un día desafortunado.— o. the track, (fam.) despistado, por los cerros de Úbeda.

offend [ɔfénd], vt. ofender, agraviar.— vi. pecar.—to o. against, faltar a.— —er [-œ(r)], s. delincuente, transgresor, reo, pecador.—**offense** [ɔféns], s. ofensa; agravio, injuria, falta; delito. —no o., sin ofender a usted; no lo dije por tanto.—to take o., sentirse, agraviarse, ofenderse.—**offensive** [ɔfénsiv], a. ofensivo.—s. ofensiva, ataque.

offer [ɔ́fœ(r)], vt. y vi. ofrecer(se).—s. oferta, ofrecimiento, promesa; declaración de amor; propuesta.— —ing [-iŋ], s. ofrecimiento, oferta; ofrenda.

offhand [ɔ́fhǽnd], a. y adv. improvisado, de repente; sin pensarlo, de improviso.

office [ɔ́fis], s. oficio; ministerio o cargo; oficina, despacho; negociado, departamento.—pl. servicio, favor; buenos oficios.—doctor's o., consultorio médico.—lawyer's o., bufete.—o. boy, mandadero, mensajero (de oficina).— —holder [-houldœ(r)], s. empleado público, funcionario, burócrata.— —r [ɔ́fisœ(r)], s. oficial; funcionario; guardia, agente de policía.—vt. mandar (como oficial o jefe); proveer de oficiales y jefes.—**official** [ɔfíʃəl], a. oficial.—s. oficial público; funcionario autorizado o ejecutivo.—**officiate** [ɔfíʃieit], vi. oficiar, celebrar (la misa); ejercer o desempeñar un cargo. —**officious** [ɔfíʃʌs], a. oficioso, entremetido, intruso.

offset [ɔ́fset], s. balance, compensación, equivalencia.—a. fuera de su lugar; desalineado; (impr.) calcado en

láminas de caucho.—vti. [9] [ɔfsét], compensar, contrapesar; terraplenar. —vii. [ɔ́fset], (impr.) repetir; emplear el procedimiento offset.—pret. y pp. de TO OFFSET.

offspring [ɔ́fspriŋ], s. hijo(s), vástago(s), prole, progenie o descendencia.

often [ɔ́fn], adv. frecuentemente, a menudo, muchas veces.—as o. as, siempre que, tantas veces (o tan a menudo) como.—how o.? ¿cuántas veces? ¿con qué frecuencia?—not o., rara vez.—so o., tantas veces.—too o., con demasiada frecuencia.

ogre [óugœ(r)], s. ogro, monstruo.

oil [ɔil], s. aceite; petróleo; óleo.—o. can, bidón o lata de aceite.—o. cup, (mec.) lubri(fi)cadora, copilla.—o. painting, pintura o cuadro al óleo; arte de pintar al óleo.—o. tanker, barco petrolero.—vt. aceitar, engrasar, lubri(fi)car; (fam.) untar (la mano), sobornar.—cloth [ɔ́ilklɔθ], s. encerado, hule.— —y [-i], a. aceitoso, oleoso, oleaginoso; grasiento.

ointment [ɔ́intment], s. ungüento, untura.

O.K., OK, okay [óukéi], a. (fam.) correcto; conforme; bueno, que sirve.— adv. bien.—it is O.K., está bien.— s. (V°.B°.) visto bueno.—vt. aprobar; dar o poner el visto bueno a.

okra [óukrǎ], s. (bot.) (Am.) quimbombó.

old [ould], a. viejo, anciano; antiguo; añejo.—how o. is he? ¿cuántos años tiene?—of o., de antiguo, de atrás.— o. age, vejez, ancianidad.—o. bachelor, solterón.—o. boy, (fam.) chico, (Am.) viejo (expresión de amistad).—o.- fashioned, chapado a la antigua; anticuado.—o. lady, anciana; (fam.) madre, esposa.—o. maid, solterona.— o. man, anciano, viejo; (fam.) padre, marido.—o.-timer, antiguo residente.

olive [áliv], s. (bot.) olivo, aceituno; aceituna, oliva.—o.-colored, aceitunado.—o. grove, olivar.—o. oil, aceite de oliva.—a. aceitunado; verde olivo.

Olympic [olímpik], a. olímpico.—O. games, olimpíadas, juegos olímpicos.

omelet [ámlit], s. tortilla (de huevos).

omen [óumin], s. agüero, augurio, presagio.—vt. presagiar, augurar.—

ominous [áminʌs], a. ominoso, siniestro, nefasto de mal agüero.

omission [omíʃon], s. omisión.—**omit** [omít], vti. [1] omitir; prescindir de; pasar por alto, olvidar.

omnibus [ámnibʌs], s. ómnibus; (Mex.) camión, (Arg.) colectivo, (Cuba) guagua.

omnipotent [amnípotent], a. omnipotente.

on [an], prep. sobre, encima de; en;

a, al; bajo; por; contra.—*o. account (of),* a cuenta (de).—*o. an average,* por término medio.—*o. a sudden,* de golpe, de repente.—*o. hand,* entre manos.—*o. leaving,* al salir.—*o. my part,* por mi parte.—*o. my responsibility,* bajo mi responsabilidad.—*o. purpose,* a propósito, adrede.—*o. record,* registrado; que consta.—*o. the contrary,* por el contrario.—*o. the road,* de viaje, viajando.—*o. the table,* sobre la mesa.—*to draw o. my bank,* girar contra mi banco.—*a. y adv.* puesto; encendido; funcionando; en contacto.—*and so o.,* y así sucesivamente; etcétera.—*o. and off,* a intervalos, de vez en cuando.—*o. and o.,* continuamente, sin cesar.—*to have one's hat o.,* tener el sombrero puesto. —*to turn o. the light (the radio, etc.),* encender la luz (el radio, etc.).

once [wʌns], *adv. y s.* una vez; en otro tiempo.—*at o.,* en seguida, al instante, inmediatamente; a un mismo tiempo, simultáneamente.—*o. and again,* varias veces.—*o. for all,* por última vez, de una vez para siempre.—*o. in a while,* de cuando en cuando.—*o. upon a time,* había una vez, érase que se era.—*this o.,* (siquiera) esta vez.—*a. de otro tiempo, pasado, que fue.— conj.* una vez que, tan pronto como.

one [wʌn], *a.* un, uno; solo, único; cierto; igual.—*it is all o. to me,* lo mismo me da; me es lo mismo.—*o. day,* cierto día, un día; algún día, un día de éstos.—*o.-eyed,* tuerto.—*o.-handed,* manco; con una sola mano.— *o.-sided,* parcial, injusto, (for.) leonino; unilateral; de un solo lado; desigual.—*o. way,* de una sola dirección; (f.c., avión, etc.) billete o boleto de ida o sencillo.—*s. y pron.* uno.—*a better o.,* uno mejor.—*all o.,* lo mismo. —*o. and all,* todos, todos sin excepción.—*o. and the same,* idéntico.—*o. another,* uno(s) a otros.—*o. by o.,* uno a uno, uno por uno.—*o. (for) each,* sendos, uno para cada uno.—*o. or two,* unos pocos.—*o.'s,* de uno, su.— *that o.,* ése; aquél.—*the white o.,* el blanco.—*this o.,* éste.

onerous [ánerʌs], *a.* oneroso, gravoso, molesto, cargoso.

oneself [wʌnsélf], *pron.* se, sí, sí mismo, (a) uno mismo.—*by o.,* solo, por sí solo.—*with o.,* consigo.

onion [ʌnyʌn], *s.* cebolla.— **—skin** [-skin], *s.* papel cebolla.

onlooker [ánlʊke(r)], *s.* espectador, observador; (fam.) mirón.

only [óunli], *a.* único, sólo.—*adv.* (tan) sólo, solamente, únicamente; no más que (o de).—*if o.,* ojalá, si.—*not o.*

. . . *but also,* no sólo . . . *sino* también.—*conj.* sólo que, pero.

onset [ánset], *s.* embestida, arremetida, carga; arranque.

onto [ántu], *prep.* a; encima de, sobre, en.

onward [ánwɑrd], *a.* avanzado; progresivo.— **—(s)** [-(z)], *adv.* adelante, hacia adelante; en adelante.

ooze [uz], *vt. y vi.* escurrir(se); exudar(se), rezumar(se); manar, fluir.—*s.* cieno, limo.

opal [óupʌl], *s.* ópalo.

opaque [opéik], *a.* opaco; sin brillo, mate.

open [óupn], *vt.* abrir; destapar; desplegar; empezar, iniciar; entablar.—*vi.* (a veces con out) abrirse, entreabrirse; desplegarse; empezar.—*to o. on o upon,* caer, dar o mirar a.—*to o. with,* empezar con.—*a.* abierto; sincero, franco; descubierto; expuesto a un ataque; público, descampado.— *in the o. air,* al aire libre, a la intemperie.—*in the o. field,* a campo raso.— *o.-minded,* razonable, liberal.—*o.-mouthed,* boquiabierto.—*o. port,* puerto franco.—*o. question,* cuestión discutible; asunto en duda.—*o. sea,* alta mar.—*o. season,* temporada de caza, pesca.—*o. secret,* secreto a voces. —*o. winter,* invierno templado.—*wide o.,* de par en par.—*s.* claro, raso, lugar abierto.—*can opener,* abrelatas.—*in the o.,* a campo raso; al aire libre, a la intemperie; al descubierto, abiertamente.— **—ing** [-iŋ], *s.* abertura, brecha; boca, orificio; salida; claro, campo abierto; inauguración, apertura; empleo vacante.—*a.* preliminar, inicial; inaugural.—*o. performance,* (teat.) estreno.

opera [ápeɹ̱], *s.* ópera.—*o. house,* teatro de la ópera.

operable [ápeɹabl], *a.* operable.— **—operate** [ápeɹeit], *vt.* operar, hacer funcionar, mover; (min.) explotar; manejar.—*vi.* (con in, on o upon) obrar, operar; producir efecto; funcionar; (cir.) operar; (com.) operar, especular; (mil.) operar, maniobrar. —*operated by,* (mec.) accionado por. **—operating** [ápeɹéitiŋ], *a.* operante, actuante; operatorio.— *o. room,* quirófano.—**operation** [apeɹéiṣ̱n], *s.* operación; funcionamiento; manejo, manipulación.—**operator** [ápeɹeito(r)], *s.* operario; maquinista; telegrafista; telefonista; asesor, asesorista; cirujano; empresario de minas; (fam.) manipulador.

operetta [apeɹétɑ̱], *s.* opereta, zarzuela.

opiate [óupiit], *s.* narcótico.—**opium** [óupiʌm], *s.* opio.—*o. den,* fumadero de opio.

opinion [ǫpínyǫn], *s.* opinión, concepto, parecer; dictamen.— **—ated** [-eitid], *a.* terco, porfiado, obstinado.

opossum [ǫpásʌm], *s.* zarigüeya, oposúm.

opponent [ǫpóunǫnt], *s.* antagonista, contrincante, contrario; opositor.—*a.* antagónico; opuesto, contrario; oponente.

opportune [apǫrtjún], *a.* oportuno, a propósito, conveniente.—**opportunity** [apǫrtjúniti], *s.* oportunidad; ocasión.

oppose [ǫpóuz], *vt.* oponer; hacer frente a, oponerse a; objetar; resistir.— *vi.* oponerse.—**opposite** [ápǫzit], *a.* opuesto, contrario; frontero, adverso, de cara, de enfrente, al otro lado.— *prep.* del otro lado de; enfrente de, frente a.—*s.* contrario.—*the o.,* lo opuesto, lo contrario.—**opposition** [apǫzíšǫn], *s.* oposición.

oppress [ǫprés], *vt.* oprimir, agobiar; tiranizar.— **—ion** [ǫpréšǫn], *s.* opresión; tiranía; agobio, ahogo.— **—ive** [ǫprésiv], *a.* opresivo, opresor; agobiador, abrumador; sofocante.— **—or** [ǫprésǫ(r)], *s.* opresor, tirano.

optic(al) [áptik(ǫl)], *a.* óptico.—**optician** [aptíšǫn], *s.* óptico.—**optics** [áptiks], *s.* óptica.

optimism [áptimizm], *s.* optimismo.— **optimist** [áptimist], *s.,* **optimistic** [aptimístik], *a.* optimista.

option [ápšǫn], *s.* opción, facultad de escoger; alternativa; (com.) opción, plazo para determinar.— **—al** [-ǫl], *a.* opcional, optativo, discrecional.

opulence [ápyulǫns], *s.* opulencia, abundancia.—**opulent** [ápyulǫnt], *a.* opulento.

or [ǫr], *conj.* o, u; si no, de lo contrario. —*o. else,* o bien.

oracle [árakl], *s.* oráculo.

oral [órǫl], *a.* oral; verbal, hablado; bucal.—*s.* examen oral.

orange [árǫndž], *s.* naranja; color naranja, anaranjado.—*o. blossom,* azahar.—*o. grove,* naranjal.—*o. pekoe,* té negro de Ceilán.—*o. tree,* naranjo. —*a.* perteneciente a las naranjas; anaranjado.— **—ade** [-éid], *s.* naranjada.

orang-utan [orǫŋutæn], *s.* orangután.

oration [oréišǫn], *s.* oración, discurso.— **orator** [árǫtǫ(r)], *s.* orador.—**oratory** [árǫtǫri], *s.* oratoria, elocuencia; oratorio, capilla.

orb [ǫrb], *s.* orbe.

orbit [órbit], *s.* órbita.

orchard [órchǫrd], *s.* huerto, vergel.

orchestra [órkistrǝ], *s.* orquesta; (teat.) patio de butacas, (Am.) platea.—*o. seat,* luneta, butaca de platea.

orchid [órkid], *s.* orquídea.

ordain [ordéin], *vt.* ordenar, mandar;

decretar; (igl.) conferir órdenes sagradas.

ordeal [ǫrdíl], *s.* prueba muy difícil; ordalía.

order [órdœ(r)], *s.* orden; (com.) orden, pedido.—*pl.* órdenes sagradas o sacerdotales; sacramento.—*in (good) o.,* en regla, en orden, en buen estado.— *in o. to o that,* para, a fin de que, para que, porque, con (el) objeto de. —*in working o.,* en buen estado.— *money o.,* giro postal.—*on the o. of,* de la clase de.—*o. of knighthood,* orden de caballería.—*out of o.,* descompuesto; que no funciona; desordenado, desarreglado.—*to give o place an o.,* hacer un pedido.—*to o.,* a propósito, especialmente; (com.) a la orden, por encargo especial, según se pida, a la medida.—*vi.* dar órdenes. —*vt.* ordenar, mandar; poner en orden; mandar hacer; encargar, pedir (mercancías, un coche, el almuerzo, etc.).—*to o. away,* despedir a uno, decirle que se vaya.—*to o. in,* mandar entrar; mandar traer.—*to o. out,* mandar salir; mandar llevar; echar.— **—ly** [-li], *a.* ordenado, metódico; bien arreglado; obediente, disciplinado; tranquilo.—*s.* ordenanza, asistente.— *adv.* ordenadamente, metódicamente, en orden.—**ordinal** [órdinǫl], *a.* ordinal.—*s.* numeral ordinal; (igl.) libro ritual.—**ordinance** [órdinǫns], *s.* ordenanza, ley, reglamento; rito, ceremonial; ordenación, disposición.

ordinary [órdineri], *a.* ordinario, común, corriente; tosco, burdo; mediano.

ordnance [órdnǫns], *s.* (mil.) artillería, cañones.—*o. stores o supplies,* pertrechos de guerra.

ore [oųr], *s.* mineral en bruto, ganga.

organ [órgǫn], *s.* órgano.—*barrel o.,* organillo.— **—ic(al)** [orgǽnik(ǫl)], *a.* orgánico; organizado; sistematizado; constitutivo o fundamental.— **—ism** [-izm], *s.* organismo.— **—ist** [-ist], *s.* (mus.) organista.— **—ization** [-izéišǫn], *s.* organización; estructura orgánica; constitución; organismo; cuerpo, entidad, compañía, corporación.— **—ize** [-aiz], *vt.* organizar.— *vi.* organizarse, constituirse.— **—izer** [-aizœ(r)], *s.,* **—izing** [-aizin], *a.* organizador.

organdy [órgandi], *s.* organdí.

orgasm [órgæzm], *s.* orgasmo.

orgy [órdži], *s.* orgía.

orient [óurjent], *s.* oriente, este, levante.—*the O.,* el Oriente.—*vt.* orientar.— **—al** [orjéntǫl], *a.* y *s.* oriental.— **—ate** [óurjenteit], *vt.* orientar.— **—ation** [orjentéišǫn], *s.* orientación.

orifice [árifis], *s.* orificio, abertura.

origin [óridžin], *s.* origen.— **—al** [ǫrí-

dźinąl], *a.* original; primitivo, primero, originario.—*s.* original; prototipo.— —ality [ǫrįdźįnéliti], *s.* originalidad.— —ally [ǫrídźįnąli], *adv.* originariamente, en el principio; originalmente.— —ate [ǫrídźįnejt], *vt.* originar.—*vi.* originarse, dimanar.— —ator [ǫrídźįnejtǫ(r)], *s.* originador, iniciador.

oriole [óųrįoųl], *s.* oropéndola.

ornament [órnąmęnt], *s.* ornamento, adorno.—*vt.* [órnąment], ornamentar, adornar.— —al [ornąméntąl], *a.* ornamental, decorativo.—*s.* cosa, planta, etc. de adorno.—**ornate** [ornéjt], *a.* ornado, ornamentado, adornado; recargado.

ornithology [ornįθálǫdźį], *s.* ornitología.

orphan [órfąn], *a.* y *s.* huérfano.—*vt.* dejar huérfano a.— —age [-idź], *s.* orfandad; orfanato(rio).

orthodox [órθodaks], *a.* ortodoxo; convencional.— —y [-i], *s.* ortodoxia.

orthographic(al) [orθográfįk(ąl)], *a.* ortográfico.—**orthography** [orθágrąfį], *s.* ortografía.

oscillate [ásįlejt], *vt.* balancear, hacer oscilar.—*vi.* oscilar, fluctuar.—**oscillation** [asįléjšǫn], *s.* oscilación, fluctuación, vaivén.

osier [óųżœ(r)], *s.* sauce; mimbre.—*a.* de mimbre.

osmosis [asmóųsįs], *s.* ósmosis.

ostensible [asténsįbl], *a.* aparente; pretendido.—**ostentation** [astentéjšǫn], *s.* ostentación, jactancia, alarde.— **ostentatious** [astentéjšąs], *a.* ostentoso, fastuoso; jactancioso.

ostracism [ástrąsįzm], *s.* ostracismo.— **ostracize** [ástrąsajz], *vt.* aislar; desterrar, condenar al ostracismo.

ostrich [ástrįch], *s.* avestruz; (Am.) ñandú, suri.

other [Áðœ(r)], *a.* y *pron.* otro, otra (otros, otras).—*each o.*, uno a otro, el uno al otro, unos a otros.—*every o. day*, en días alternos, un día sí y otro no.—*o. than*, otra cosa que; más que.—*some o. day*, cualquier otro día.— —**wise** [-wajz], *adv.* de otra manera, de otro modo; de lo contrario, si no; o bien.—*a.* otro, diferente.

otter [átœ(r)], *s.* nutria; piel de nutria.

ought [ot], *vai.* [11] deber; convenir.— *it o. to be so*, así debería (o debiera) ser.—*you o. not to go*, usted no debe (debiera, debería) ir.—*you o. to know*, usted debería saberlo.—*pret.* de OUGHT.

ought [ot], *s.* y *adv.* algo, alguna cosa; nada; cero.—*for o. I know*, por lo que yo puedo comprender, en cuanto yo sé.

ounce [ауns], *s.* onza. Ver Tabla.

our(s) [aųr(z)], *a.* y *pron. pos.* (el, los)

nuestro(s), (la, las) nuestra(s).—*a friend of ours*, un amigo nuestro.— **ourselves** [aųrsélvz], *pron.* nosotros mismos, nosotras mismas; a nosotros mismos; nos (reflexivo).

oust [aųst], *vt.* desposeer, desanuciar, desalojar, echar fuera, despedir.

out [aųt], *adv.* fuera, afuera; hacia fuera.—*prep.* fuera de; más allá de.— *a.* exterior; ausente; fuera de moda; errado (cálculos, etc.); cesante; (declarado) en huelga.—*a way o.*, escapatoria.—*four o. of five*, de cada cinco, cuatro.—*o. and away*, con mucho.—*o. and o.*, cabal, completo; declarado; redomado.—*o. at interest*, puesto a interés.—*o. at the elbows*, andrajoso, roto por los codos.—*o. loud*, en voz alta.—*o. of*, fuera de; más allá de; sin; por.—*o. of fear*, por miedo.—*o. of money*, sin dinero.—*o. of print*, agotado (libros).—*time is o.*, el tiempo (la hora) ha pasado; el plazo ha expirado.—*to be o.*, estar fuera o ausente; no estar en boga; quedar cesante; quedarse cortado; salir perdiendo; estar apagado o extinguido; haberse agotado o acabado; haberse publicado, haber salido (libro, periódico, etc.); estar reñidos.—*to be o. of*, no tener más, habérsele acabado a uno.—*to run o. of*, acabársele a uno, quedarse sin.—*interj.* ¡fuera!—*o. with it!* ¡fuera con ello! hable sin rodeos.—*s.* exterior, parte de afuera; esquina, lugar exterior; exterioridad; cesante; dimisionario; (fam.) pero, defecto; (impr.) olvido, omisión.—*pl.* (pol.) la oposición.

outbalance [aųtbǽląns], *vt.* sobrepujar, exceder.

outbid [aųtbíd], *vti.* [10] mejorar, pujar, ofrecer más dinero (en subasta, etc.). —*pret.* y *pp.* de TO OUTBID.—**outbidden** [aųtbídn], *pp.* de TO OUTBID.

outbreak [aųtbrejk], *s.* erupción, brote; ataque violento; pasión; tumulto, disturbio; principio (de una guerra, epidemia, etc.).

outburst [aųtbœrst], *s.* explosión, erupción, estallido; acceso; arranque.

outcast [aųtkæst], *a.* desechado, inútil; proscripto; perdido.—*s.* paria.

outcome [aųtkʌm], *s.* resultado.

outcry [aųtkraj], *s.* clamor(eo); grita; alboroto, gritería; protesta.

outdid [aųtdíd], *pret.* de TO OUTDO.

outdistance [aųtdístąns], *vt.* dejar atrás, adelantarse a.

outdo [aųtdú], *vti.* [10] exceder, sobrepujar, descollar, eclipsar, vencer.— *to o. oneself*, superarse, excederse a sí mismo.—**outdone** [aųtdÁn], *pp.* de TO OUTDO.

outdoor [aųtdor], *a.* externo, fuera de la

casa, al aire libre.— —s [-z], s. el campo raso, el mundo de puertas afuera.—adv. fuera de casa, a la intemperie.

outer [áu̯tœ(r)], a. exterior, externo.— —most [-mou̯st], a. extremo; [lo] más exterior.

outfit [áu̯tfi̯t], s. equipo, apresto, tren; ropa, vestido, traje; habilitación; pertrechos; avíos.—vti. [1] equipar, habilitar, pertrechar.

outgo [au̯tgóu̯], vti. [10] aventajar, vencer.—s. [áu̯tgou̯], gasto, expendio.— —ing [áu̯tgou̯i̯n], s. ida, salida, partida.—a. saliente, que cesa; que sale, de salida; extrovertido.—outgone [au̯tgón], pp. de TO OUTGO.

outgrew [au̯tgrú], pret. de TO OUTGROW. —outgrow [au̯tgróu̯], vti. [10] crecer más que; pasar de la edad de, ser ya viejo para, ser demasiado grande para; curarse de con la edad o con el tiempo.—outgrown [au̯tgróu̯n], pp. de TO OUTGROW.—he has o. his crib, la cuna ya le queda pequeña.—outgrowth [áu̯tgrou̯θ], s. excrecencia; resultado, consecuencia.

outhouse [áu̯thau̯s], s. accesoria; retrete situado fuera de la casa.

outing [áu̯ti̯n], s. salida; paseo, caminata, excursión.

outlaid [au̯tléi̯d], pret. y pp. de TO OUTLAY.

outlandish [au̯tlǽndi̯ʃ], a. extraño, ridículo; de aspecto extranjero o exótico; remoto.

outlast [au̯tlǽst], vt. durar más que; sobrevivir a.

outlaw [áu̯tlo], s. forajido, facineroso; proscrito; fuera de la ley; rebelde.— vt. proscribir; declarar fuera de la ley.

outlay [áu̯tlei̯], s. desembolso, gasto, salida.—vti. [10] [au̯tléi̯], gastar; desplegar.

outlet [áu̯tlet], s. salida; orificio de salida; escape; desagüe; sangrador; toma (de agua, corriente eléctrica, etc.).

outline [áu̯tlai̯n], s. contorno, perfil; croquis, esbozo, bosquejo, plan general, reseña.—vt. bosquejar, delinear, esbozar, reseñar, trazar.

outlive [au̯tlív], vt. sobrevivir a, durar más que.

outlook [áu̯tlu̯k], s. vista, perspectiva, aspecto; punto de vista; probabilidades.—pl. actitud; atalaya, vigía, garita; centinela.

outlying [áu̯tlai̯i̯n], a. distante, remoto; lejos del centro; extrínseco; exterior.

outnumber [au̯tnʌ́mbœ(r)], vt. exceder en número, ser más que.

outpatient [áu̯tpei̯ʃe̯nt], s. enfermo externo.

outpost [áu̯tpou̯st], s. (mil.) avanzada, avanzadilla.

outpouring [áu̯tpori̯n], s. chorro, chorreo, efusión; desahogo.

output [áu̯tpu̯t], s. producción total, rendimiento; capacidad, fuerza; (mec., elec.) potencia neta o útil.

outrage [áu̯trei̯dʒ], vt. ultrajar; maltratar; violar, desflorar.—s. ultraje; desafuero; atrocidad; violación, rapto.— —ous [au̯tréi̯dʒʌs], a. ultrajante, injurioso; atroz; desaforado.

outran [au̯trǽn], pret. de TO OUTRUN.

outright [áu̯trai̯t], a. completo; directo; sincero, franco.—adv. [áu̯trái̯t], completamente; abiertamente; sin reserva; sin tardanza, al momento.

outrun [au̯trʌ́n], vti. [10] correr más que; pasar, ganar, exceder.—pp. de TO OUTRUN.

outset [áu̯tset], s. principio; salida; estreno.

outshine [au̯tʃái̯n], vti. [10] dejar deslucido, eclipsar.—outshone [au̯tʃóu̯n], pret. y pp. de TO OUTSHINE.

outside [áu̯tsái̯d], a. exterior, externo; superficial; extremo; ajeno, neutral. —s. exterior, parte de afuera, superficie; apariencia; extremo.—at the o., (fam.) a lo sumo, a más tirar.—adv. afuera, fuera.—o. of, (fam.) con excepción de.—prep. fuera de; (fam.) excepto.— —r [áu̯tsái̯dœ(r)], s. forastero, extraño; intruso.

outsize [áu̯tsai̯z], s. prenda de vestir de tamaño fuera de lo común.—a. de tamaño extraordinario; (fam.) inmenso.

outskirt [áu̯tskœrt], s. borde, linde.— pl. afueras, suburbios, arrabales, inmediaciones.

outspoken [áu̯tspóu̯kn], a. abierto, franco(te).—to be o., (fam.) no tener pelos en la lengua.

outspread [au̯tspréd], vti. y vii. [9] extender(se), difundir(se); desplegar(se).—pret. y pp. de TO OUTSPREAD.—a. [áu̯tspred], (ex)tendido; desplegado.—s. extensión; despliegue; expansión.

outstanding [au̯tstǽndi̯n], a. saliente; destacado, descollante, sobresaliente, prominente; que resiste; (com.) pendiente, no pagado.

outstretch [au̯tstréch], vt. extender, alargar, estirar.

outstrip [au̯tstríp], vti. [1] pasar, rezagar; aventajar, ganar.

outward [áu̯twa̯rd], a. exterior, visible; aparente, superficial; extraño; extrínseco; corpóreo.—adv. fuera, afuera, exteriormente; superficialmente; (mar.) de ida; para el extranjero.

outweigh [au̯twéi̯], vt. preponderar;

pesar más que; exceder en valor o importancia.

outwent [autwént], *pret.* de TO OUTGO.

outwit [autwít], *vti.* [1] ser más listo que; llevar ventaja a; engañar con habilidad.

outwork [autwœrk], *vti.* [4] trabajar más que; acabar.—*s.* (mil.) obra exterior.

outworn [autwórn], *a.* ajado, gastado, usado; anticuado.

oval [óuval], *s.* óvalo.—*a.* oval, ovalado.

ovary [óuvari], *s.* ovario.

ovation [ovéisǫn], *s.* ovación.

oven [ʌvn], *s.* horno.

overall [óuvœrol], *a.* global, total, de conjunto.—*s. pl.* traje de mecánico, mono(s); (Am.) overol, overoles.

over [óuvœ(r)], *prep.* sobre, encima, por encima de; allende, al otro lado de; a causa o por motivo de; a pesar de; más de; mientras, durante; por, en.—*o. all*, total, de extremo a extremo.—*o. night*, durante la noche, hasta el otro día.—*adv.* al otro lado; al lado, parte o partido contrario; enfrente; encima; al revés; más, de más, de sobra; otra vez, de nuevo; demasiado, excesivamente; acabado, terminado; a la vuelta, al dorso.— *to be (all) o.*, haber pasado; haberse acabado, terminar(se).—*to be left o.*, quedar, sobrar.—*to be o. and above*, sobrar.—*a.* acabado, terminado; demasiado; sobrante, en exceso de; superior; exterior.—*it is all o.*, ya pasó; se acabó.

overate [ouvœréit], *pret.* de TO OVEREAT.

overbear [ouvœrbér], *vti.* [10] sojuzgar; oprimir, subyugar; agobiar, vencer.— *vti.* llevar demasiado fruto.— *-ing* [-iŋ], *a.* despótico, imperioso, dominante, arrogante.

overbid [ouvœrbíd], *vti.* [10] ofrecer más que, pujar.—*vi.* ofrecer demasiado.—*pret.* y *pp.* de TO OVERBID.— *s.* [óuvœrbid], puja.—**overbidden** [ouvœrbídn], *pp.* de TO OVEBBID.

overboard [óuvœrbord], *adv.* (mar.) al mar, al agua.—*man o.!* ¡hombre al agua!

overbore [ouvœrbór], *pret.* de TO OVERBEAR.—**overborne** [ouvœrbórn], *pp.* de TO OVERBEAR.

overburden [ouvœrbœrdn], *vt.* sobrecargar; oprimir.

overcame [ouvœrkéim], *pret.* de TO OVERCOME.

overcast [ouvœrkæst], *vti.* [9] anublar, oscurecer; entristecer; cicatrizar; sobrehilar.—*vti.* anublarse.—*pret.* y *pp.* de TO OVERCAST.—*a.* [óuvœrkæst], nublado, encapotado; sombrío.

overcharge [ouvœrchárdž], *vt.* cobrar

demasiado; recargar el precio; sobrecargar.—*s.* [óuvœrchardž], cargo excesivo; cargo adicional; recargo; carga eléctrica excesiva.

overcoat [óuvœrkout], *s.* sobretodo, gabán, abrigo.

overcome [ouvœrkʌm], *vti.* [10] vencer, rendir; sojuzgar, subyugar; superar, vencer, salvar (obstáculos).—*vii.* sobreponerse; ganar, vencer; hacerse superior.—*pp.* de TO OVERCOME.—*a.* agobiado, confundido.

overconfidence [ouvœrkánfidǫns], *s.* presunción, excesiva confianza.— **overconfident** [ouvœrkánfidǫnt], *a.* demasiado confiado.

overcrowd [ouvœrkráud], *vt.* apiñar, atestar.

overdid [ouvœrdíd], *pret.* de TO OVERDO. —**overdo** [ouvœrdú], *vti.* [10] hacer más de lo necesario; extralimitarse.— *vti.* agobiar, abrumar de trabajo; exagerar; (coc.) recocer, requemar.— **overdone** [ouvœrdʌn], *a.* demasiado trabajado; (coc.) recocido, requemado, demasiado asado.—*pp.* de TO OVERDO.

overdose [óuvœrdous], *s.* dosis excesiva.

overdraft [óuvœrdræft], *s.* descubierto bancario, giro en exceso.—**overdraw** [ouvœrdró], *vti.* [10] girar en descubierto; exagerar (en el dibujo, la descripción, etc.).—**overdrawn** [ouvœrdrón], *pp.* de TO OVERDRAW.

overdress [ouvœrdrés], *vt.* adornar con exceso.—*vi.* vestirse con exceso.—*s.* [óuvœrdres], sobreprenda.

overdrew [ouvœrdrú], *pret.* de TO OVERDRAW.

overdue [óuvœrdjú], *a.* vencido y no pagado, retrasado en el pago.

overeat [ouvœrít], *vii.* [10] comer con exceso, hartarse.—**overeaten** [ouvœrítn], *pp.* de TO OVEREAT.

overestimate [ouvœréstimeit], *vt.* presuponer; estimar en valor excesivo; tener en más de lo justo.—*s.* [ouvœréstimit], estimación exagerada.

overexcite [ouvœrikséit], *vt.* sobreexcitar.— **-ment** [-mǫnt], *s.* sobreexcitación.

overexposure [ouvœrikspóužǫ(r)], *s.* (fot.) exceso de exposición.

overfed [ouvœrféd], *pret.* y *pp.* de TO OVERFEED.—**overfeed** [ouvœrfíd], *vti.* [10] sobrealimentar.

overflow [ouvœrflóu], *vi.* rebosar, desbordarse.—*vt.* inundar.—*s.* [óuvœrflou], inundación; rebosamiento, derrame; exceso, superabundancia; escape, sumidero.

overgrew [ouvœrgrú], *pret.* de TO OVERGROW.—**overgrow** [ouvœrgróu], *vti.* [10] cubrir con plantas o hierbas; crecer más que.—*vii.* crecer o desa-

rollarse con exceso.—**overgrown** [oцvɔergróцn], *pp.* de TO OVERGROW. —*a.* grandullón.

overhang [oцvɔerhǽn], *vti.* [10] sobresalir horizontalmente por encima de; colgar, suspender; mirar a, dar a, caer a; ser inminente, amenazar.— *vii.* colgar o estar pendiente.—*s.* [óцvɔerhæn], (arq.) alero; vuelo.

overhaul [oцvɔerhɔ́l], *vt.* repasar, registrar, recorrer; componer, remendar; desarmar y componer; alcanzar.—*s.* [óцvɔerhɔl], recorrido, revisión, reparación; alcance.

overhead [oцvɔerhéd], *adv.* arriba, en lo alto; más, o hasta más, arriba de la cabeza.—*a.* [óцvɔerhed], de arriba; de término medio; de techo.—*o. charges*, gastos generales fijos (alquiler, etc.).—*s.* gastos generales.

overhear [oцvɔerhír], *vti.* [10] alcanzar a oír; oír por casualidad o espiando.— **overheard** [oцvɔerhɔ́rd], *pret. y pp.* de TO OVERHEAR.

overheat [oцvɔerhít], *vt.* recalentar; abochornar; acalorar, achicharrar.

overhung [óцvɔerhʌn], *pret. y pp.* de TO OVERHANG.—*a.* colgado o suspendido por arriba.

overjoy [oцvɔerdʒɔ́j], *vt.* alborozar, regocijar.

overlaid [oцvɔerléjd], *pret. y pp.* de TO OVERLAY.

overland [óцvɔerlænd], *a. y adv.* por tierra.

overlap [oцvɔerlǽp], *vti.* [1] sobreponer, sobremontar, superponer.—*vii.* superponerse.—*s.* [óцvɔerlæp], superposición.

overlay [oцvɔerléj], *vti.* [10] cubrir, extender sobre; dar una capa o mano (pintura, etc.); echar un puente sobre.—*s.* [óцvɔerlej], capa o mano.

overload [oцvɔerlóцd], *vt.* sobrecargar, recargar.—*s.* [óцvɔerloцd], sobrecarga.

overlook [oцvɔerlúk], *vt.* mirar desde lo alto; tener vista a, dar, o caer a; dominar (con la vista); examinar; cuidar de; pasar por alto, disimular, tolerar; hacer la vista gorda; no hacer caso de; no notar.

overnight [oцvɔernájt], *adv.* durante la noche; toda la noche; de la noche a la mañana.—*a.* [óцvɔernajt], de una noche; de la noche; de la noche anterior.

overpower [oцvɔerpáцɔe(r)], *vt.* sobreponerse a, vencer, superar; sujetar; embargar (los sentidos).

overproduction [oцvɔerprodʌ́kʂɔn], *s.* exceso de producción, superproducción.

overran [oцvɔerrǽn], *pret.* de TO OVERRUN.

overrate [oцvɔerréjt], *vt.* encarecer; exagerar el valor de.

overreach [oцvɔerrích], *vt.* ser más listo que; engañar; alargar demasiado; tirar alto.—*to o. oneself*, excederse, ir más allá de lo necesario.

overrule [oцvɔerrúl], *vt.* (for.) denegar, no admitir; predominar, dominar; gobernar.

overrun [oцvɔerrʌ́n], *vti.* [10] invadir, infestar; saquear; excederse; desbordarse.—*vii.* rebosar, estar muy abundante.—*pp.* de TO OVERRUN.

oversaw [oцvɔersɔ́], *pret.* de TO OVERSEE.

oversea(s) [óцvɔersí(z)], *adv.* allende los mares.—*a.* de ultramar, ultramarino; extranjero.

oversee [oцvɔersí], *vti.* [10] inspeccionar, vigilar; descuidar, pasar por alto.—**overseen** [oцvɔersín], *pp.* de TO OVERSEE.—**-r** [óцvɔersiœ(r)], *s.* sobrestante, capataz; superintendente, veedor, inspector; mayoral.

overset [oцvɔersét], *vti.* [9] volcar, voltear, derribar; trastornar, arruinar.—*vii.* volcarse, caerse; desarreglarse.—*pret. y pp.* de TO OVERSET.

overshoe [óцvɔerʂu], *s.* chanclo; zapato de goma.

oversight [óцvɔersajt], *s.* inadvertencia, descuido; vigilancia, cuidado.

oversleep [oцvɔerslíp], *vii.* [10] dormir demasiado; no despertarse a tiempo.

oversleeve [óцvɔersliv], *s.* manguito.

overslept [oцvɔerslépt], *pret. y pp.* de TO OVERSLEEP.

overstate [oцvɔerstéjt], *vt.* exagerar.

overstep [oцvɔerstép], *vti.* [1] traspasar, transgredir, excederse, extralimitarse, propasarse.

overstock [oцvɔersták], *vt.* abarrotar.— *s.* [óцvɔerstak], surtido excesivo.

overt [óцvɔert], *a.* abierto, público, patente, evidente.—*o. act*, (for.) acción premeditada; acto hostil.

overtake [oцvɔertéjk], *vti.* [10] dar alcance, alcanzar; atajar; (fam.) atrapar.—**overtaken** [oцvɔertéjkn], *pp.* de TO OVERTAKE.

overthrew [oцvɔerθrú], *pret.* de TO OVERTHROW.—**overthrow** [oцvɔerθróц], *vti.* [10] echar abajo, abatir, demoler, derribar; derrocar, destronar; vencer.—*s.* [óцvɔerθroц], derribo, derrocamiento; caída; derrota, ruina; subversión; destronamiento; (dep.) lanzamiento o boleo demasiado alto. —**overthrown** [oцvɔerθróцn], *pp.* de TO OVERTHROW.

overtime [óцvɔertajm], *s.* horas extraordinarias de trabajo; tiempo suplementario; pago por trabajo hecho fuera de las horas regulares.—*adv.* fuera del tiempo estipulado.—*a.* en

exceso de las horas regulares de trabajo.

overtook [ou̯vœrtúk], *pret.* de TO OVERTAKE.

overture [óu̯vœrchur], *s.* insinuación, proposición o propuesta formal; (mús.) obertura.

overturn [ou̯vœrtǽrn], *vt.* volcar; echar abajo; trastornar.—*vi.* volcarse; (mar.) zozobrar.—*s.* [óu̯vœrtœrn], vuelco, volteo; trastorno.

overweight [óu̯vœrwei̯t], *s.* exceso de peso; sobrepeso.—*a.* [ou̯vœrwéi̯t], que pesa demasiado.

overwhelm [ou̯vœrhwélm], *vt.* abrumar, agobiar, anonadar; sumergir, hundir. — —**ing** [-iŋ], *a.* abrumador, (fam.) aplastante.—*s.* abrumamiento, anonadación.

overwork [ou̯vœrwǽrk], *vti.* [4] hacer trabajar excesivamente, esclavizar.— *vii.* trabajar demasiado.—*s.* [óu̯vœrwœrk], trabajo excesivo o hecho fuera de las horas reglamentarias.— **overworked** [ou̯vœrwǽrkt], *a.* recargado, muy elaborado; agobiado de trabajo.

owe [ou̯], *vt.* deber, adeudar; (to) ser deudor de; estar obligado a.—*owing to*, debido a, con motivo de, por causa de.—*to be owing to*, ser debido, imputable o atribuible a.—*vi.* estar endeudado, deber.

owl [au̯l], *s.* lechuza, buho, mochuelo.

own [ou̯n], *a.* propio, particular, de mi, su, etc. propiedad.—*a house of his o.*, una casa de su propiedad.—*to be on one's o.*, no depender de otro, trabajar por su (propic) cuenta.—*to hold one's o.*, mantenerse firme.—*vt.* poseer, ser dueño de, tener; reconocer, confesar. —*owned by*, propiedad de —*to o. up*, confesar de plano.- —**er** [óu̯nœ(r)], *s.* propietario, amo, dueño.- —**ership** [-œrśip], *s.* propiedad, pertenencia.

ox [aks], *s.* (*pl.* **oxen** [áksn]) buey.— *o. driver*, boyero.

oxidation [aksidéi̯śọn], *s.* oxidación.— **oxygen** [áksidžen], *s.* oxígeno.

oyster [ói̯stœ(r)], *s.* ostra, (Am.) ostión.

ozone [óu̯zou̯n], *s.* ozono.

P

pa [pa], *s.* (fam.) papá,

pace [pei̯s], *s.* paso; modo de andar. —*vt.* recorrer o medir a pasos; marcar el paso.-*ri.* pasear, andar, marchar.- —**maker** [péi̯smei̯kœ(r)], *s.* el que marca el paso o da el ejemplo.

pacific [paṣffik], *a.* pacífico.—**pacifier** [pǽṣifai̯œ(r)], *s.* pacificador, apaciguador; chupete (para niños).— **pacify** [pǽṣifai̯], *vti.* [7] pacificar, apaciguar, calmar.

pack [pæk], *s.* lío, fardo; paquete; cajetilla o paquete de cigarrillos; jauría; manada; cuadrilla (de pícaros).—*p. animal*, acémila, animal de carga.—*p. cloth*, arpillera.—*p. train*, recua, reata.—*vt.* empacar, empaquetar; embalar, envasar; apretar; cargar (una acémila).—*to p. off*, o *to send packing*, enviar, despedir, despachar; poner de patitas en la calle.—*vi.* empaquetar; hacer el baúl, arreglar el equipaje.—*to p. away* u *off*, largarse.- —**age** [pǽkidž], *s.* fardo, bulto, lío; paquete.—*vt.* empacar, empaquetar.- —**er** [-œ(r)], *s.* embalador, empaquetador, empacador, envasador.- —**et** [-it], *s.* paquete, cajetilla; fardo pequeño.- —**ing** [-iŋ], *s.* embalaje; envase; (mec.) empaquetadura, relleno.—*p. plant*, planta empacadora; frigorífico.

packsaddle [pǽksædl], *s.* albarda.

pact [pækt], *s.* pacto, convenio, tratado.

pad [pæd], *s.* cojinete o cojincillo, almohadilla; (sast.) hombrera, relleno; bloc (de papel); pata (de ciertos animales).—*vti.* [1] forrar, rellenar.—*vii.* caminar (penosa o cansadamente).- —**ding** [-iŋ], *s.* (cost.) relleno, almohadilla; algodón guata; ripio (en un escrito).

paddle [pædl], *vt.* y *vi.* bogar o remar con canalete; chapotear.—*s.* canalete, remo corto.—*p. wheel*, rueda de paletas.

padlock [pǽdlak], *s.* candado.—*vt.* echar el candado, cerrar con candado.

pagan [péi̯gạn], *s.* pagano.- —**ism** [-izm], *s.* paganismo.

page [pei̯dž], *s.* página, plana; paje, criado.—*vt.* paginar; vocear, buscar llamando (en los hoteles)

pageant [pǽdžạnt], *s.* procesión, manifestación imponente; pompa, celebridad; (teat.) espectáculo.

paginate [pǽdžinei̯t], *vt.* paginar, foliar.

paid [pei̯d], *pret.* y *pp.* de TO PAY.

pail [pei̯l], *s.* cubo, balde.

pain [pei̯n], *vt.* doler; causar dolor; apenar, afligir.—*vi* doler.—*s.* dolor. —*on p. of*, so pena de.—*to be in p.*, tener dolor, estar con dolor.- —**ful** [péi̯nful], *a.* penoso; doloroso; arduo, laborioso.—*to be p.*, doler.- —**less** [-lis], *a.* sin pena, sin dolor.- —**s** [-z], *s. pl.* trabajo; esmero, cuidado; ansiedad; dolores de(l) parto.- —**staking** [-ztei̯kiŋ], *a.* cuidadoso, industrioso; esmerado.—*s.* esmero.

paint [pei̯nt], *vt.* pintar; pintarse el rostro.—*to p. the town red*, (fam.) ir de parranda, correrla.—*vi.* pintar, ser pintor; pintarse, maquillarse, darse colorete.—*s.* pintura; color; colorete, arrebol.- —**brush** [péi̯nt-

braš], s. brocha, pincel.——er [-œ(r)], s. pintor (artista y obrero).— —ing [-iŋ], s. pintura, arte pictórica; cuadro.

pair [per], s. par; pareja.—vt. y vi. (a)parear(se), hermanar(se).

pajamas [pɐdžámɐz], s. pl. pijama; (Am.) piyama.

pal [pæl], s. (fam.) compañero, compinche.

palace [pǽliš], s. palacio.

palatable [pǽlɐtɐbl], a. sabroso, apetitoso; agradable.—palatal [pǽlɐtɐl], a. y s. palatal.—palate [pǽlit], s. paladar, cielo de la boca.

palaver [pɐlǽvœ(r)], s. palabrería, labia; embustes.

pale [peil], a. pálido; descolorido.—to grow p., ponerse pálido.—vi. palidecer; perder el color.— —ness [péilnis], s. palidez, descoloramiento.

palette [pǽlit], s. (pint.) paleta.—p. knife, espátula.

palisade [pælišéid], s. (em)palizada, estacada.—pl. risco.

pall [pol], s. paño mortuorio; (igl.) palio.—vt. quitar el sabor; hartar, empalagar.—vi. hacerse insípido, perder el sabor.— —bearer [pólberœ(r)], s. portaféretro.

pallet [pǽlit], s. jergón, cama pobre.

pallid [pǽlid], a. pálido, descolorido.

pallium [pǽliɐm], s. (igl.) palio.

pallor [pǽlo(r)], s. palidez.

palm [pam], s. palma, palmera; palma de la mano.—p. grove, palmar.—P. Sunday, domingo de Ramos.—vt. escamotear; (con off, on o upon) engañar, defraudar con.— —ist [pámist], s. quiromántico.— —istry [-istri], s. quiromancia.— —y [-i], a. floreciente, próspero.

palpable [pǽlpɐbl], a. palpable, evidente.

palpate [pǽlpeit], vt. palpar.

palpitate [pǽlpiteit], vi. palpitar, latir.—palpitation [pælpitéišɐn], s. palpitación, latido.

pamper [pǽmpœ(r)], vt. mimar, consentir.

pamphlet [pǽmflit], s. folleto, panfleto; impreso.

pan [pæn], s. cacerola, cazuela; perol; caldero.—frying p., sartén.—vii. [1] (con out) (fam.) dar buen resultado o provecho.—vti. (fam.) criticar o poner como nuevo.

Panamanian [pænɐméiniɐn], s. y a. panameño.

Pan-American [pǽnɐmérikɐn], a. panamericano.

pancake [pǽnkeik], s. hojuela, torta delgada, (Am.) panqué o panqueque.

pane [pein], s. hoja de vidrio o cristal

de ventana o vidriera; entrepaño de puerta, etc.

panel [pǽnɐl], s. panel; entrepaño, tablero; (cost.) paño en un vestido; (for.) jurado.—vti. [2] artesonar, formar tableros.

pang [pæŋ], s. angustia, congoja, dolor, tormento.—pl. ansias.

panic [pǽnik], a. y s. pánico.—p.-stricken, sobrecogido de terror, preso de pánico.—vti. [8] consternar, sobrecoger de terror.—panicked [pǽnikt], pret. y pp. de TO PANIC.— —ky [pǽniki], a. aterrorizado.

pansy [pǽnzi], s. (bot.) pensamiento; (fam.) marica.

pant [pænt], vi. jadear, resollar; palpitar.—to p. for o after, suspirar por, desear con ansia.

panther [pǽnθœ(r)], s. pantera, leopardo; (Am.) puma.

panties [pǽntiz], s. pl. (fam.) pantalones de mujer, (Am.) pantaletas, pantaloncitos.

panting [péntiŋ], a. jadeante.—s. jadeo; (med.) disnea.

pantomime [pǽntomaim], s. pantomima; mímica.

pantry [pǽntri], s. despensa.

pants [pænts], s. pl. (fam.) pantalones; calzoncillos.

pap [pæp], s. (coc.) papilla; gachas.

papa [pápɐ, papá], s. (fam.) papá.

papacy [péipɐsi], s. papado, pontificado.—papal [péipɐl], a. papal, pontifical.

papaya [pɐpáyɐ], s. (Am.) lechosa, papaya.

paper [péipœ(r)], s. papel; memoria; disertación, ensayo; diario, periódico; (com.) valor negociable.—pl. papeles, documentos, credenciales.—on p., escrito; por escrito; en teoría.—p. clip, grapa, sujetapapeles.—p. currency o money, papel moneda.—p. hanger, empapelador.—p. knife, plegadera.—a. de papel; para papel; escrito.—vt. empapelar.— —back [-bæk], s. libro de bolsillo.— —weight [-weit], s. pisapapeles.

paprika [pǽprikɐ], s. pimentón.

par [par], s. equivalencia, paridad; (com.) par.—p. value, valor a la par, valor nominal.—to be on a p. with, ser igual a, correr parejas con.

parable [pǽrɐbl], s. parábola.

parachute [pǽrɐšut], s. paracaídas.—parachutist [pǽrɐšutist], s. paracaidista.

parade [pɐréid], s. (mil.) parada; desfile, procesión; paseo público.—p. ground, plaza de armas.—vt. y vi. formar en parada; pasar revista; desfilar; pasear; ostentar.

paradise [pǽrɐdais], s. paraíso.

paradox [pǽrɐdaks], s. paradoja.

paraffin [pǽrǝfin], *s.* parafina.
paragraph [pǽrǝgrǽf], *s.* párrafo.—*vt.* dividir en párrafos.
Paraguayan [pærǝgwéiǝn, pærǝgwáiǝn], *a.* y *s.* paraguayo.
parakeet [pǽrǝkit], *s.* periquito, perico.
parallel [pǽrǝlel], *a.* paralelo.—*p. bars*, paralelas (gimnasia).—*s.* linea paralela; (geog.) paralelo.—*vti.* [2] ser paralelo o igual a; cotejar.
paralysis [pǝrǽlisis], *s.* parálisis.—**paralytic** [pærǝlítik], *s.* y *a.* paralítico.—**paralyzation** [pærǝlizéiſǝn], *s.* parálisis; paralización.—**paralyze** [pǽrǝlaiz], *vt.* paralizar.—**paralyzed** [pǽrǝlaizd], *a.* paralítico.
paramount [pǽrǝmaunt], *a.* superior, supremo, principalísimo.
paramour [pǽrǝmur], *s.* amante, querido; manceba.
parapet [pǽrǝpet], *s.* parapeto, baluarte.
paraphernalia [pærǝfœrnéiliǝ], *s. pl.* avíos, trastos.
parasite [pǽrǝsait], *s.* parásito; (fam.) gorrista, gorrón.—**parasitic(al)** [pærǝsítik(ǝl)], *a.* parásito.
parasol [pǽrǝsol], *s.* parasol, quitasol.
paratrooper [pǽrǝtrupœ(r)], *s.* soldado paracaidista.—**paratroops** [pǽrǝtrups], *s. pl.* tropas de paracaídas.
parcel [pársǝl], *s.* paquete; bulto; partida.—*p. of ground o land*, parcela o lote de terreno, solar.—*p. post*, servicio de paquetes postales.—*vti.* [2] (con out o into) partir, dividir; empaquetar; parcelar, dividir en parcelas.
parch [parch], *vt.* y *vi.* (re)secar(se); tostar(se), quemar(se).—*to be parched with thirst*, morirse de sed.
parchment [párchmǝnt], *s.* pergamino.
pardon [párdǝn], *vt.* perdonar; indultar; disculpar, dispensar.—*p. me!* ¡perdone Ud.! ¡Ud. dispense!—*s.* perdón, absolución, indulto.—*I beg your p.!* ¡Ud. dispense! ¡perdone Ud.! ¿cómo decía Ud.?
pare [per], *vt.* cortar, recortar; mondar, pelar.
parent [pérǝnt], *s.* padre o madre; autor, origen.—*pl.* padres.—**age** [-idʒ], *s.* ascendencia, alcurnia, origen.—**al** [pǝréntǝl], *a.* paternal o maternal.
parenthesis [pǝrénθǝsis], *s.* paréntesis.—**parenthetical** [pærǝnθétikǝl], *a.* entre paréntesis.
paring [périŋ], *s.* peladura, mondadura; recorte.
parish [pǽriſ], *s.* parroquia.—*p. priest*, (cura) párroco.—**ioner** [pǝríſǝnœ(r)], *s.* feligrés.
parity [pǽriti], *s.* paridad, semejanza,

igualdad; (com.) paridad, cambio a la par.
park [park], *s.* parque.—*vt.* y *vi.* estacionar(se) (un coche), (Am.) parquear.—**ing** [párkiŋ], *s.* estacionamiento (de un vehículo).—*no p.*, prohibido estacionarse.—*p. place*, plaza de estacionamiento, (Am.) parqueo.
parley [párli], *vi.* (mil.) parlamentar; discutir; conferenciar.—*s.* (mil.) parlamento; conferencia.
parliament [párlimǝnt], *s.* parlamento.—**ary** [parliméntǝri], *a.* parlamentario.
parlor [párlǝ(r)], *s.* sala de recibo; salón.
parochial [pǝróukiǝl], *a.* parroquial; de criterio estrecho, limitado.
parole [pǝróul], *s.* libertad bajo palabra de un prisionero.—*vt.* poner en libertad bajo palabra.
parotid [pǝrátid], *a.* parotídeo.—*s.* parótida.
parricide [pǽrisaid], *s.* parricida; parricidio.
parrot [pǽrǝt], *s.* cotorra, loro.—*p. fever*, psitacosis.—*vt.* y *vi.* repetir o hablar como loro.
parry [pǽri], *vti.* y *vii.* [7] (esgr.) parar, rechazar, quitar.—*s.* parada, quite.
parsley [pársli], *s.* perejil.
parsnip [pársnip], *s.* chirivía.
parson [pársǝn], *s.* clérigo; pastor, cura (igl. protestante).
part [part], *s.* parte; pedazo, trozo; región, lugar; (teat.) papel; raya del cabello.—*pl.* prendas, cualidades.—*p. and parcel*, parte integrante; uña y carne, carne y hueso.—*p. owner*, condueño.—*p.-time*, por horas, parcial (trabajo).—*to do one's p.*, cumplir uno con su obligación; hacer cuanto pueda.—*to take p.* (in), participar o tomar parte (en).—*vt.* separar, dividir.—*to p. company*, separarse.—*to p. one's hair*, hacerse la raya.—*to p. with*, deshacerse de.—*vi.* separarse; despedirse.—*to p. with*, desprenderse o deshacerse de.
partial [párſǝl], *a.* parcial; amigo; aficionado.—**ity** [parſ(i)ǽliti], *s.* parcialiadad; afición.—**ly** [párſǝli], *adv.* parcialmente, en parte; parcialmente, con parcialidad.
participant [partísipǝnt], *a.* y *s.* participante, (co)partícipe.—**participate** [partísipeit], *vt.* y *vi.* participar.—**participation** [partisipéiſǝn], *s.* participación.
participle [pártisipl], *s.* participio.
particle [pártikl], *s.* partícula; pizca.
particular [partíkyulǝ(r)], *a.* particular, peculiar; preciso, exacto; delicado, escrupuloso; detallado; exigente, quis-

quilloso.—*s.* particular, particula-ridad, detalle, pormenor.—*in p.,* particularmente, en particular, espe-cíficamente.—*to go into particulars,* entrar en detalles.

parting [pártiŋ], *s.* separación; partida; despedida; bifurcación (de una vía o camino); raya del pelo.—*to be at the p. of the roads* u *of the ways,* haber llegado al tiempo de decidir o de tomar cada uno su camino.—*a.* divisorio; de despedida; último, al partir.

partisan [pártizan], *a.* y *s.* partidario; adepto.—*s.* (mil.) guerrillero.

partition [partíʃǫn], *s.* partición, re-partimiento; división, separación; demarcación; (alb.) tabique; (carp.) mampara.—*p. wall,* tabique; pared medianera.—*vt.* partir, dividir; re-partir, distribuir.

partly [pártli], *adv.* en parte, en cierto modo.

partner [pártnœ(r)], *s.* socio; compa-ñero; pareja (de baile, tenis, etc.).— —**ship** [-ʃip], *s.* (com.) compañía; sociedad; consorcio.—*to enter into a p. with,* asociarse con.

partridge [pártridʒ], *s.* perdiz.

party [párti], *s.* partido político; reunión o fiesta privada; partida (de campo, teatro, etc.); (for.) parte, parte interesada; partida, facción; cómplice.

pass [pæs], *vti.* [6] pasar; pasar de; pasar por; aprobar (un proyecto, a un alumno); promulgar (una ley); traspasar (un negocio); ser aprobado (en un examen, una materia); admitir, dar entrada.—*to p. by,* pasar por; pasar de largo.—*to p. each other,* o *one another,* cruzarse.—*to p. over,* atravesar, cruzar, salvar; traspasar; omitir, pasar por alto; excusar.—*to p. sentence,* dictar o pronunciar sen-tencia.—*to p. the buck,* (fam.) echarle la carga o el muerto a otro.—*to p. the time away,* gastar o pasar el tiempo.—*vii.* pasar; correr, trans-currir (el tiempo, etc.); ser aprobado (un proyecto, un alumno); ser admitido; (esgr.) dar una estocada, hacer un pase.—*to p. away,* fallecer. —*to p. through,* pasar por; atravesar; colarse.—*s.* paso; desfiladero; pase (billete, permiso; de manos, de es-grima, en el juego); (mil.) licencia, salvoconducto; aprobación (en un examen).— —**able** [pæsạbl], *a.* pasa-ble, transitable; pasadero, regular.— —**age** [-idʒ], *s.* pasaje; paso, tránsito; travesía; pasillo, pasadizo; callejón; pasaje (de un libro, etc.); trámite y aprobación de un proyecto de ley.—

—**ageway** [-idzwei], *s.* pasadizo, pasaje.

passbook [pǽsbụk], *s.* libro de cuenta y razón; libreta de banco.

passenger [pǽsɛndʒœ(r)], *s.* pasajero. —*pl.* pasajeros, el pasaje.—**passer-(-by)** [pǽsœ(r) bái], *s.* transeúnte, viandante.

passion [pǽʃǫn], *s.* pasión; cólera.—*p. flower,* pasionaria.—*P. Week,* semana de Pasión, semana santa.- —**ate** [-it], *a.* apasionado.

passive [pǽsiv], *a.* pasivo; inerte.—*s.* (gram.) voz pasiva.- —**ness** [-nịs], *s.* pasividad; inercia.

passivity [pæsívitị], *s.* pasividad; inercia.

passkey [pǽski], *s.* llave maestra; llavín.

Passover [pǽsǫuvœ(r)], *s.* pascua (de los hebreos).

passport [pǽspǫrt], *s.* pasaporte.— **password** [pǽswœrd], *s.* contraseña; (mil.) santo y seña.

past [pæst], *pp.* de TO PASS.—*a.* pasado, último; ex, que fue (presidente, director, etc.).—*p. master of,* experto o sobresaliente en.—*p. participle,* participio pasivo.—*p. tense,* pre-térito.—*s.* (lo) pasado; antecedentes, historia; (gram.) pretérito; pasado. —*in the p.,* antes, en tiempos pasados. —*prep.* más de, después de (tiempo); más allá de, fuera de (lugar).—*half (quarter, etc.) p. two,* las dos y media (cuarto, etc.).—*p. remedy,* irreme-diable.

paste [peist], *s.* pasta; engrudo.—*vt.* empastar, pegar con engrudo.— —**board** [péịstbǫrd], *s.* cartón.

pastel [pæstél], *s.* (b.a.) pastel; pintura al pastel.

pasteurization [pæstœrịzéịʃǫn], *s.* pas-te(u)rización.—**pasteurize** [pǽstœr-aịz], *vt.* paste(u)rizar.

pastille [pæstíl], *s.* pastilla, tableta.

pastime [pǽstaịm], *s.* pasatiempo, dis-tracción.

pastor [pǽstǫ(r)], *s.* pastor espiritual, cura, párroco, clérigo.- —**al** [-ạl], *a.* pastoril, pastoral; (igl.) pastoral. —*s.* pastoral; idilio; (igl.) (carta) pastoral.

pastry [péịstri], *s.* pastelería, pasteles, pastas.—*p. cook,* pastelero.—*p. shop,* pastelería, repostería.

pasture [pǽschụ(r)], *s.* pasto, pastura. —*p. ground* o *lands,* pradera, dehesa, prado, pastizal.—*vt.* pastar, apa-centar, pastorear.—*vi.* pastar, pacer.

pasty [péịsti], *a.* pastoso; pálido.

pat [pæt], *a.* oportuno, propio, (fam.) pintiparado, al pelo; fijo, firme.—*to have* o *know p.,* (fam.) saber al dedillo.—*adv.* justamente, convenien-temente, a propósito.—*s.* golpecito.

palmadita; caricia; porción pequeña de mantequilla.—*p. on the back*, (fam.) felicitación, enhorabuena.—*vti.* [1] dar palmaditas a, acariciar, pasar la mano sobre.

patch [pæch], *vt.* remendar.—*vi.* echar remiendos.—*s.* parche; remiendo; material para remiendos; sembrado (de trigo, etc.).—*p. of land* o *ground*, pedazo de terreno.

pate [peįt], *s.* coronilla.

patent [pǽtẹnt], *a.* patente, palmario, manifiesto; de patente, patentado.— *p. leather*, charol.—*s.* patente.— *p. pending*, patente solicitada.—*vt.* patentar.

paternal [pạtǿrnạl], *a.* paternal, paterno.—**paternity** [pạtǿrnịtị], *s.* paternidad; linaje.

path [pæθ], *s.* senda, sendero; vereda; camino; trayectoria.

pathetic [pạθétịk], *a.* patético, conmovedor.

pathological [pæθọládʒịkạl], *a.* patológico.—**pathology** [pạθálọdʒị], *s.* patología.—**pathos** [péįθạs], *s.* rasgo conmovedor; sentimiento; patetismo.

pathway [pǽθweį], *s.* senda, vereda.

patience [péįšẹns], *s.* paciencia.—**patient** [péįšẹnt], *a.* paciente.—*s.* paciente, enfermo.

patriot [péįtrịọt], *s.* patriota.— **—ic** [peįtrịátịk], *a.* patriótico.— **—ism** [péįtrịọtịzm], *s.* patriotismo.

patrol [pạtróul], *s.* patrulla; ronda. —*vti.* y *vii.* [2] patrullar; hacer la ronda.

patron [péįtrọn], *s.* patrón, patrocinador, protector; padrino; cliente, parroquiano.— **—age** [-įdʒ], *s.* (igl.) patronato; patrocinio; clientela habitual; (pol.) control de nombramientos por el partido de gobierno.— **—ess** [-ịs], *s.* patrona, protectora; patrocinadora, madrina.— **—ize** [-aįz], *vt.* patrocinar, apadrinar; tratar con condescendencia; ser parroquiano habitual de.

pattern [pǽtœrn], *s.* modelo, norma; patrón, molde, plantilla, diseño.— *vt.* copiar, imitar.—*to p. oneself after*, tomar como modelo a, seguir el ejemplo de.

paunch [ponch], *s.* panza, barriga, vientre.— **—y** [pónchị], *a.* barrigón, panzudo.

pauper [pópœ(r)], *s.* indigente, pobre de solemnidad.

pause [poz], *s.* pausa.—*vi.* pausar, cesar, parar, detenerse.

pave [peįv], *vt.* pavimentar, adoquinar, enlosar, embaldosar.—*paved road*, carretera pavimentada, camino asfaltado.—*to p. the way*, facilitar, preparar el terreno, abrir el camino.—

—ment [péįvmẹnt], *s.* pavimento, adoquinado, piso; pavimentación.

pavilion [pạvílyọn], *s.* pabellón; glorieta; cenador.

paving [péįvịŋ], *s.* pavimento; pavimentación; materiales de pavimentación.

paw [po], *s.* garra, zarpa.—*vt.* y *vi.* patear, piafar; (fam.) manosear.

pawn [pon], *vt.* empeñar, pignorar, dar en prenda.—*s.* prenda, empeño; peón de ajedrez.- **—broker** [pónbroųkœ(r)], *s.* prestamista, prendero.- **—shop** [-šap], *s.* casa de empeños.

pay [peį], *vti.* [10] pagar, remunerar; costear; abonar, saldar; producir ganancia o provecho a.—*to p. a call* o *a visit*, hacer una visita.—*to p. a compliment*, hacer un cumplido; (fam.) piropear.—*to p. attention*, prestar atención; fijarse o reparar (en), hacer caso (de).—*to p. back*, devolver, reembolsar; pagar en la misma moneda.—*to p. court*, hacer la corte, enamorar.—*to p. for*, pagar, costear.—*to p. off*, pagar; pagar por completo; vengarse de, ajustarle a uno las cuentas.—*to p. one's respects*, presentar u ofrecer sus respetos.—*to p. up*, pagar por completo.—*to p. the piper*, pagar el pato, pagar los vidrios rotos.—*vii.* pagar (a veces con *off*) compensar, tener cuenta, ser provechoso; valer la pena.—*to p. dearly*, costarle a uno caro.—*s.* paga, sueldo, salario, jornal; recompensa. —*bad (good) p.*, mal (buen) pagador, (fam.) mala (buena) paga.—*p. roll*, nómina, lista de jornales.- **—able** [péįạbl], *a.* pagadero; reembolsable.- **—ee** [peį], *s.* (com.) tenedor, persona a quien se paga o debe pagarse una letra, cheque.- **—master** [-mæstœ(r)], *s.* pagador.—*p.'s office*, pagaduría.- **—ment** [-mẹnt], *s.* pago, paga.—*p. in advance*, anticipo, pago adelantado.—*p. in full*, pago total.

pea [pi], *s.* guisante, chícharo.—*p. gun* o *shooter*, cerbatana.—*sweet p.*, guisante de olor.

peace [pis], *s.* paz.—*public p.*, orden público.- **—able** [písạbl], *a.* pacífico, tranquilo.- **—ful** [-fụl], *a.* tranquilo, pacífico, apacible.

peach [pich], *s.* melocotón, durazno; (fam.) persona o cosa admirable.—*p. tree*, melocotonero; duraznero.

peacock [píkak], *s.* pavo real.

peak [pik], *s.* cima, cumbre, pico, picacho; cúspide.—*s.* y *a.* máximo.

peal [pil], *s.* repique de campanas; estruendo, estrépito.—*p. of laughter*, carcajada, estrepitosa.—*p.-ringing*,

repiqueteo.—*vt.* y *vi.* repicar, repiquetear.

peanut [pínʌt], *s.* cacahuete, (Am.) maní.—*p. vendor*, manisero.

pearl [pœrl], *s.* perla.—*p. button*, botón de nácar.—*p.-colored*, perlino.— —ly [pǿrlị], *a.* perlino; nacarado.

peasant [pézạnt], *s.* y *a.* labrador, campesino; rústico, aldeano; (Am.) guajiro, jíbaro.

pebble [pébl], *s.* guijarro, china.

pecan [pịkán], *s.* (bot.) pacana (árbol y nuez).

peck [pɛk], *s.* medida de áridos, celemín; picotazo, picotada.—*vt.* picotear, picar.—*vi.* picotear.

peculiar [pịkịúlyạ(r)], *a.* peculiar; singular, raro.- —ity [pịkịulérịtị], *s.* peculiaridad, particularidad.

pedagogue [pédạgąg], *s.* pedagogo.— **pedagogy** [pédạgoụdžị], *s.* pedagogía.

pedal [pédạl], *s.* pedal.—*vii.* [2] pedalear.

peddle [pédl], *vt.* vender de puerta en puerta.—*vi.* ser vendedor ambulante. - —r [pédlœ(r)], *s.* baratillero, vendedor ambulante.

pedestal [pédestạl], *s.* pedestal, peana.

pedestrian [pịdéstrịạn], *s.* peatón, transeúnte.—*a.* pedestre.

pedigree [pédịgri], *s.* genealogía; linaje, estirpe; raza, casta.

peek [pik], *vi.* atisbar.—*s.* atisbo.

peel [pil], *vt.* (a veces con *off*) descortezar, pelar, mondar.—*vi.* desconcharse, descascararse, pelarse.—*s.* corteza, cáscara; piel.- —ing [pílịŋ], *s.* peladura, mondadura; desconchado.

peep [pip], *vi.* atisbar, mirar a hurtadillas; asomar; piar.—*not to p.*, (fam.) no chistar.—*s.* atisbo; mirada, ojeada; pío, piada.- —hole [píphoụl], *s.* mirilla.

peer [pịr], *vi.* atisbar, husmear; escudriñar; asomar, aparecer.—*s.* par, igual; Par del Reino.- —less [pírlịs], *a.* sin par, incomparable.

peg [pɛg], *s.* espiga, taco; tarugo; (mar.) cabilla; (mus.) clavija; (coll.) (beisbol) tiro.—*p. leg*, pierna o pata de palo.—*to take someone down a p.*, humillar, bajarle a uno los humos. —*vti.* [1] estaquillar, clavar; estacar, jalonear; tirar o lanzar (la pelota). —*vii.* (gen. con *away*) afanarse; trabajar con ahinco.

pelican [pélịkạn], *s.* pelícano, alcatraz.

pellet [pélịt], *s.* píldora, pelotilla; bola, bolita; perdigón.

pelt [pɛlt], *s.* pellejo, piel, cuero; trastazo.—*vt.* apedrear, llover (piedras o algo análogo) sobre.—*vi.* arrojar alguna cosa; caer con fuerza (la lluvia, etc.).

pen [pɛn], *s.* pluma (para escribir); corral.—*p. name*, seudónimo.—*p. stroke*, plumazo.—*vti.* [1] escribir con pluma; [3] (a veces con *up*) encerrar, acorralar, enjaular.

penal [pínạl], *a.* penal.- —ize [-aịz], *vt.* penalizar, castigar; perjudicar.- —ty [pénạltị], *s.* pena, castigo; sanción, multa.

penance [pénạns], *s.* penitencia.

pencil [pénsịl], *s.* lápiz.—*mechanical p.*, lapicero.—*p. sharpener*, sacapuntas. —*vti.* [2] dibujar o escribir con lápiz.

pendant [péndạnt], *s.* medallón, colgante; pendiente; araña (de luces). —*a.* = PENDENT.

pending [péndịŋ], *a.* pendiente.—*prep.* durante; hasta.

pendulum [péndẓụlʌm], *s.* péndulo.

penetrate [pénẹtreịt], *vt.* y *vi.* penetrar. —*penetrating* [pénẹtreịtịŋ], *a.* penetrante.—*penetration* [penẹtréịšọn], *s.* penetración.

penguin [péngwịn], *s.* pingüino.

penicillin [penịsịlịn], *s.* penicilina.

peninsula [pịnínsụlạ], *s.* península.— —r [-(r)], *a.* peninsular.

penis [pínịs], *s.* pene, miembro viril.

penitence [pénịtẹns], *s.* penitencia; contrición.—*penitent* [pénịtẹnt], *a.* y *s.* penitente.—*penitentiary* [penịténšạrị], *a.* penitenciario; de castigo, penal.—*s.* penitenciaría, presidio.

penknife [pénnaịf], *s.* cortaplumas.

penmanship [pénmạnšịp], *s.* escritura, caligrafía.

pennant [pénạnt], *s.* gallardete, banderola; (fig.) campeonato.

penniless [pénịlịs], *s.* sin un real; en la miseria; sin dinero.—*penny* [pénị], *s.* (E.U.) centavo.

pension [pénšọn], *s.* pensión; jubilación; retiro.—*vt.* (a veces con *off*) pensionar, jubilar.

pensive [pénsịv], *a.* pensativo, meditabundo.

Pentecost [péntịkọst], *s.* (pascua de) Pentecostés.

penthouse [pénthaụs], *s.* terraza, apartamento en la azotea; cobertizo.

peony [píọnị], *s.* peonía.

people [pípl], *s.* pueblo; gente; personas; los habitantes (de un país). —*p. say*, dicen, se dice, dice la gente.—*the common p.*, el pueblo, el vulgo, la plebe.—*the p.*, el público, la gente.—*vt.* poblar.

pep [pɛp], *s.* (fam.) brío; energía, vigor.—*vti.* [1] (con *up*) (fam.) animar, estimular.

pepper [pépœ(r)], *s.* (bot.) pimienta; pimiento.—*green p.*, ají, pimiento. —*p.-and-salt cloth*, tejido de mezclilla. —*red p.*, chile, pimentón.—*vt.* sazonar con pimienta; acribillar.- —mint

[-mint], *s.* menta.— —y [-i], *a.* picante; mordaz; irascible.

per [pœr], *prep.* por.—*p.* annum, al año.—*p.* cent, por ciento.

perambulator [pœrémbiuleito(r)], *s.* cochecito de niño.

percale [pœrkéil], *s.* percal.

perceive [pœrsív], *vt.* percibir; percatar(se) (de); comprender, entender.

percentage [pœrséntidž], *s.* (com.) tanto por ciento, porcentaje.

perceptible [pœrséptibl], *a.* perceptible, sensible.—perception [pœrsépşọn], *s.* percepción.

perch [pœrch], *s.* (ict.) perca; percha (para las aves).—*vi.* posarse, encaramarse.

perchance [pœrchéns], *adv.* acaso, tal vez, quizá, por ventura.

percolate [pœrkọleit], *vt.* y *vi.* (tras)colar, (in)filtrar, pasar, rezumarse.— percolator [pœrkọleito(r)], *s.* cafetera filtro.

percussion [pœrkÁşọn], *s.* percusión.

peremptory [pœrémptori], *a.* perentorio; terminante, definitivo.

perennial [pœrénial], *a.* perenne; continuo, incesante, perpetuo.—*s.* planta de hoja perenne.

perfect [pœrfíkt], *a.* perfecto; completo.—*s.* (gram.) tiempo perfecto. —*vt.* [pœrfékt], perfeccionar, mejorar.— —ion [[pœrfékşọn], *s.* perfección.

perforate [pœrforeit], *vt.* perforar.— perforation [pœrforéişọn], *s.* perforación.

perform [pœrfórm], *vt.* ejecutar, hacer, realizar; desempeñar, cumplir.—*vi.* (teat.) desempeñar un papel, representar.— —ance [-ạns], *s.* ejecución; desempeño, cumplimiento; actuación, funcionamiento; obra, hecho, hazaña; (teat.) función, representación.— *first p.*, (teat.) estreno.— —er [-œ(r)], *s.* ejecutor, ejecutante; actor, actriz.

perfume [pœrfium], *s.* perfume; aroma. — —r [pœrfiúmœ(r)], *s.* perfumador, perfumista.

perhaps [pœrhéps], *adv.* tal vez, quizá(s), acaso, por ventura.

peril [péril], *s.* peligro, riesgo.—*vti.* [2] poner en peligro.—*vii.* peligrar; correr peligro.— —ous [-Aş], *a.* peligroso, arriesgado.

perimeter [pœrímetœ(r)], *s.* perímetro.

period [píriọd], *s.* período; época, tiempo; término, fin, conclusión; (impr.) punto; menstruación.— —ic(al) [piriádik(ạl)], *a.* periódico.— —ical [piriádikạl], *s.* periódico, publicación periódica.

periscope [périskoup], *s.* periscopio.

perish [périš], *vi.* perecer, sucumbir.— —able [-ạbl], *a.* perecedero.—*pl.*

mercancías de fácil descomposición.

perjure [pœrdžur], *vt.* perjurar.— perjury [pœrdžuri], *s.* perjurio.—*to commit p.*, jurar en falso.

perk [pœrk], *vt.* erguir, levantar (la cabeza, la oreja).—*vi.* (con up) animarse, avivarse, levantar la cabeza.— —y [pœrki], *a.* animado, despabilado.

permanence [pœrmạnẹns], *s.* permanencia.—permanent [pœrmạnẹnt], *a.* permane(cie)nte, duradero; indeleble. —*s.* ondulado permanente.

permeate [pœrmieit], *vt.* penetrar; estar difundido en.

permissible [pœrmísibl], *a.* permisible, lícito.—permission [pœrmíşọn], *s.* permiso, licencia.—permit [pœrmít], *vti.* [1] permitir, autorizar.—*s.* [pœrmit], permiso, licencia, pase.

pernicious [pœrníşAs], *a.* pernicioso, nocivo.

peroration [perọréişọn], *s.* peroración.

perpendicular [pœrpendíkyulä(r)], *a.* perpendicular; vertical.—*s.* perpendicular.

perpetrate [pœrpẹtreit], *vt.* perpetrar, cometer.—perpetrator [pœrpẹtreito(r)], *s.* perpetrador; el que comete un delito.

perpetual [pœrpéchuạl], *a.* perpetuo.— perpetuate [pœrpéchueit], *vt.* perpetuar.—perpetuity [pœrpẹtúiti], *s.* perpetuidad.

perplex [pœrpléks], *vt.* confundir, aturdir.— —ed [-t], *a.* perplejo, confuso.— —ity [-iti], *s.* perplejidad, confusión, duda.

persecute [pœrsẹkjut], *vt.* perseguir; acosar.—persecution [pœrsẹkjúşọn], *s.* persecución.—persecutor [pœrsẹkjuto(r)], *s.* perseguidor.

perseverance [pœrsẹvírạns], *s.* perseverancia; persistencia.—persevere [pœrsẹvír], *vi.* perseverar; persistir.

Persian [pœržạn], *s.* y *a.* persa.

persist [pœrsíst], *vi.* persistir, insistir.— —ence [-ẹns], *s.* persistencia, insistencia.— —ent [-ẹnt], —ing [-iŋ], *a.* persistente, insistente.

person [pœrsọn], *s.* persona.— —age [-idž], *s.* personaje.— —al [-ạl], *a.* personal; en persona (acción, comparecencia, etc.).— —ality [pœrsọnéliti], *s.* personalidad; alusión personal; personaje.—personify [pœrsánifai], *vti.* [7] personificar.— —nel [pœrsọnél], *s.* personal.

perspective [pœrspéktiv], *s.* perspectiva.

perspicacious [pœrspikéişAs], *a.* perspicaz, sagaz.—perspicacity [pœrspikésiti], *s.* perspicacia, penetración.

perspiration [pœrspiréişọn], *s.* sudor, transpiración.—perspire [pœrspáir],

vt. y *vi.* sudar, transpirar.—**perspiring** [pœrspáiriŋ], *a.* sudoroso.

persuade [pœrswéjd], *vt.* persuadir, inducir.—**persuasion** [pœrswéjƶɒn], *s.* persuasión; creencia, opinión.—**persuasive** [pœrswéjsiv], *a.* persuasivo.

pert [pœrt], *a.* atrevido, descarado, insolente; listo, despierto.

pertain [pœrtéin], *vi.* pertenecer; atañer.—*pertaining to*, perteneciente, tocante a.

pertinent [pœrtinɛnt], *a.* pertinente, a propósito, atinado.

perturb [pœrtœrb], *vt.* perturbar, inquietar.

perusal [pœrúƶəl], *s.* lectura cuidadosa. —**peruse** [pœrúz], *vt.* leer con cuidado; examinar, escudriñar.

Peruvian [pœrúviən], *s.* y *a.* peruano.

pervade [pœrvéjd], *vt.* penetrar, llenar. —**pervasive** [pœrvéjsiv], *a.* penetrante.

perverse [pœrvœrs], *a.* perverso.— **pervert** [pœrvœrt], *vt.* pervertir, corromper; falsear.—*s.* [pœrvœrt], perverso, depravado; desviado sexual.

pessimism [pésimiƶm], *s.* pesimismo. —**pessimist** [pésimist], *s.*, **pessimistic** [pesimístik], *a.* pesimista.

pest [pest], *s.* peste, plaga; persona o cosa molesta o nociva; molestia; (fam.) lata.—**-er** [péstœ(r)], *vt.* molestar, incomodar, importunar.— **-ilence** [-ilɛns], *s.* plaga, pestilencia.—**-ilent** [-ilɛnt], *a.* pestilente.

pet [pet], *s.* cualquier animal domesticado y mimado; favorito; niño mimado.—*a.* mimado; favorito.—*p. name*, diminutivo o epíteto cariñoso. —*vti.* [1] mimar, acariciar.—*vti.* acariciarse (los amantes)

petal [pétəl], *s.* pétalo.

petard [pitárd], *s.* petardo; especie de triquitraque.—*hoist on one's own p.*, cogido en las propias redes.

petition [pitíʃɒn], *s.* petición, demanda, súplica; instancia, solicitud.—*vt.* suplicar, rogar; pedir.

petroleum [pitróuljam], *s.* petróleo.

petticoat [pétikout], *s.* refajo; enagua(s).

pettiness [pétinis], *s.* pequeñez, mezquindad.—**petty** [péti], *a.* insignificante, mezquino, despreciable; subordinado, inferior.—*p. cash*, (com.) caja chica.—*p. larceny*, hurto, ratería.—*p. officer*, suboficial, oficial subalterno de marina.

petulance [péchulans], *s.* mal genio, impaciencia; petulancia.—**petulant** [péchulant], *a.* quisquilloso, enojadizo; petulante.

petunia [pitjúniš], *s.* petunia.

pew [pju], *s.* reclinatorio; banco de iglesia.

phalanx [féilæŋks], *s.* falange.

phantom [fǽntɒm], *s.* fantasma.

pharmacist [fármasist], *s.* farmacéutico, boticario.—**pharmacy** [fármasi], *s.* farmacia, botica.

pharynx [fériŋks], *s.* faringe.

phase [feiz], *s.* fase.

pheasant [féƶant], *s.* faisán.

phenomena [fináменə], *s.* *pl.* de PHENOMENON.— **-l** [fináменəl], *a.* fenomenal.—**phenomenon** [fináменən], *s.* fenómeno.

philanthropist [filǽnθropist], *s.* filántropo.—**philanthropy** [filǽnθropi], *s.* filantropía.

philharmonic [filharmánik], *a.* filarmónico.

philosopher [filásofœ(r)], *s.* filósofo.— **philosophic(al)** [filosáfik(al)], *a.* filosófico.—**philosophy** [filásofi], *s.* filosofía.

phone [foun], *s.* teléfono.—*vt.* y *vi.* telefonear.

phonetics [fonétiks], *s.* fonética.

phonograph [fóunogræf], *s.* fonógrafo, gramófono.

phony [fóuni], *a.* (fam.) falso, falsificado.

phosphate [fásfeit], *s.* fosfato.—**phosphorus** [fásfɒras], *s.* (quím.) fósforo.

photo [fóutou], *s.* retrato, foto, fotografía.— **-graph** [fóutɒgræf], *vt.* fotografiar, retratar.—*s.* fotografía, retrato.— **-grapher** [fɒtágrafœ(r)], *s.* fotógrafo.— **-graphic** [fotɒgrǽfik], *a.* fotográfico.— **-graphy** [fɒtágrafi], *s.* fotografía (arte).— **-meter** [fotámɛtœ(r)], *s.* fotómetro.— **-stat** [fóutɒstæt], *s.* fotocopia.

phrase [freiz], *s.* frase; expresión o locución.—*vt.* frasear; expresar, formular.

physic [fízik], *s.* purgante; medicina.— **-al** [-al], *a.* físico.— **-ian** [fizíʃan], *s.* médico, facultativo.— **-ist** [fízisist], *s.* físico.— **-s** [fíziks]. *s.* física.

physiologic(al) [fizioládƶik(al)], *a.* fisiológico.—**physiology** [fiziálodƶi], *s.* fisiología.

physique [fizík], *s.* físico, figura, presencia.

pianist [piǽnist], *s.* pianista.—**piano** [piǽnou], *s.* piano.—*p. stool*, banqueta de piano.—*p. tuner*, afinador.

piccolo [píkolou], *s.* flautín.

pick [pik], *vt.* picar, picotear; abrir (una cerradura) con ganzúa; escoger, elegir; coger; recoger; mondar o limpiar; descañonar (un ave).—*to p. out*, escoger, entresacar.—*to p. pockets*, robar carteras.—*to p. up*, alzar, recoger; coger; recobrar (el ánimo, las carnes).—*to p. up speed*, acelerar la marcha, aumentar la velocidad. —*vi.* picar, comer bocaditos.—*to p.*

up, restablecerse, recobrar la salud; cobrar carnes; desarrollar velocidad. —*s.* (zapa)pico (herramienta); ganzúa; lo más escogido, la flor y nata; cosecha.— **—ax(e)** [píkæks], *s.* zapapico, piqueta.— **—et** [-it], *s.* piquete; estaca.—*p. fence*, cerca de estacas puntiagudas.—*vt.* y *vi.* cercar con estacas; (mil.) colocar de guardia; estacionar o poner piquetes de vigilancia y propaganda.

pickle [píkl], *s.* escabeche; salmuera; encurtido; (fam.) lío, enredo, brete, apuro.—*vt.* escabechar; encurtir.— *pickled fish*, pescado en escabeche.

pickpocket [píkpakit], *s.* carterista. ratero.—**pickup** [píkʌp], *s.* (aut.) aceleración; camioneta; (radio) reproductor de tono.

picnic [píknik], *s.* jira campestre, romería.—*vii.* [8] ir de romería.— **picnicked** [píknikt], *pret.* y *pp.* de TO PICNIC.

picture [píkchу(r)], *s.* pintura, cuadro; retrato, fotografía; (fig.) estampa, imagen; lámina, grabado; película, film.—*pl.* (fam.) cine.—*p. frame*, marco, cuadro.—*to be out of the p.*, no figurar ya en el asunto.—*vt.* pintar, dibujar; describir; imaginar.— **—sque** [pikchуrésk], *a.* pintoresco.

pie [pai], *s.* pastel; empanada.—*to have a finger in the p.*, tener parte en el asunto; meter cuchara.

piece [pis], *s.* pieza, pedazo, trozo; sección, parte; cualquier moneda; (teat.) pieza: ficha (del dominó o de las damas).—*of a p.*, de la misma clase, del mismo tenor.—*p. of advice*, consejo.—*p. of furniture*, mueble.—*p. of ground o land*, parcela, solar.—*p. work*, destajo.—*to go to pieces*, desarmarse, desbaratarse.—*vt.* remendar. —*to p. on*, pegar o poner a.

pier [pir], *s.* muelle, embarcadero; espigón; (arq.) pila, machón; entrepaño de pared.

pierce [pirs], *vt.* agujerear, taladrar; acribillar; atravesar, traspasar.— *pierced with holes*, acribillado.—*vi.* penetrar, internarse, entrar a la fuerza.—**piercing** [pírsin], *a.* penetrante, cortante.

piety [páieti], *s.* piedad, devoción, religiosidad.

pig [pig], *s.* cochino, cerdo, puerco, marrano.—*a p. in a poke*, trato a ciegas.—*p.-headed*, terco, cabezudo.

pigeon [pídżọn], *s.* paloma, palomo; pichón.— **—hole** [-houl], *s.* casilla, casillero.—*vt.* encasillar, poner en una casilla; (fig.) archivar; dar carpetazo (a un proyecto de ley, etc.).

piggy [pígi], *s.* lechón, cochinito, cochinillo.—*p. bank*, alcancía.

pigment [pígmẹnt], *s.* pigmento, color.

pigmy [pígmi], *s.* = PYGMY.

pigpen [pígpen], *s.* zahúrda, pocilga, chiquero, (coll.) cochiquero.—**pigskin** [pígskin], *s.* piel de cochino o de cerdo; pelota de fútbol.—**pigsty** [pígstai], *s.* = PIGPEN.—**pigtail** [pígteil], *s.* cola de cerdo; trenza, coleta.

pike [paik], *s.* pica, garrocha; (ict.) especie de lucio o sollo; (fam.) carretera; camino o carretera por peaje.

pile [pail], *s.* pila, montón, rimero; pilote; pelillo, pelusa.—*pl.* hemorroides, almorranas.—*p. driver*, *p. engine*, martinete para clavar pilotes. —*vt.* hincar pilotes en; amontonar, apilar; acumular.—*vi.* amontonarse, acumularse.

pilfer [pílfœ(r)], *vt.* y *vi.* ratear, hurtar, birlar, sisar.

pilgrim [pílgrim], *s.* peregrino.— **—age** [-idż], *s.* peregrinación.

pill [pil], *s.* píldora; sinsabor, mal trago; (fam.) posma, persona fastidiosa.

pillage [pílidż], *s.* pillaje, saqueo.—*vt.* pillar, saquear.—*vi.* rapiñar.

pillar [pílạ(r)], *s.* columna, pilar.—*from p. to post*, de la Ceca a la Meca.

pillbox [pílbaks], *s.* caja para píldoras; (mil.) fortín de ametralladoras.

pillory [pílọri], *s.* cepo, picota.—*vti.* [7] empicotar; exponer a la vergüenza pública.

pillow [pílou], *s.* almohada; almohadón; cojín.—*vt.* poner sobre una almohada. — **—case** [-keis], *s.* funda de almohada.

pilot [páilọt], *vt.* pilotear, timonear; dirigir, guiar.—*s.* piloto; práctico (de puerto); guía.

pimp [pimp], *s.* chulo, alcahuete.—*vi.* alcahuetear.

pimple [pímpl], *s.* grano, barro.

pin [pin], *s.* alfiler; prendedor, broche; (mec.) perno, pasador, espiga; bolo; (mar.) cabilla; (mus.) clavija.—*I don't care a p.*, no se me da un bledo, no me importa un pito.—*p. money*, (dinero para) alfileres.—*vti.* [1] prender con alfileres; fijar, clavar; enclavijar.—*to p. one's faith to u on*, confiar absolutamente en.—*to p. up*, asegurar o prender con alfileres o tachuelas.

pincers [pínsœrz], *s. pl.* pinzas, tenacillas; alicates, tenazas.

pinch [pinch], *vt.* pellizcar; apretar con pinzas o tenazas; estrechar; escatimar; (fam.) prender, arrestar. —*vi.* pellizcar; apretar.—*my shoes p. me*, me aprietan los zapatos.—*s.* pellizco; pizca; aprieto, apuro; dolor, punzada.—**pinch-hit** [pínch hit], *vii.* [9] batear por otro, batear de

emergente; (fig.) servir en lugar de otro en caso de necesidad.—*pret.* y *pp.* de TO PINCH-HIT.—**pinch-hitter** [pínch hítœ(r)], *s.* bateador emergente.

pincushion [pínkụṣọn], *s.* acerico, alfiletero.

pine [paịn], *s.* pino y su madera.— *p. cone*, piña (de pino).—*p. grove*, pinar.—*p. kernel* o *nut*, piñón.—*vi.* (con **away**) desfallecer, languidecer, consumirse; (con **for**) anhelar.— —**apple** [pájnæpl], *s.* piña, ananá(s).

ping [piṇ], *s.* silbido o zumbido de una bala.—*p.-pong*, pin-pón, tenis de mesa.

pining [pájnịṇ], *s.* languidez, nostalgia.

pinion [pínyọn], *s.* (mec.) piñón; ala de ave.—*p. drive*, transmisión por engranajes.—*vt.* atar las alas; atar los brazos.

pink [piṇk], *s.* clavel; color de rosa, rosado.—*in the p. (of condition)*, en el apogeo, en el mejor estado posible. —*a.* (son)rosado; (pol. fam.) radical, algo rojo.

pinking [pínkịṇ], *s.* (cost.) picadura.

pinnacle [pínạkl], *s.* (arq.) pináculo, remate; cima, cumbre.

pint [paịnt], *s.* cuartillo, pinta (medida de líquidos).Ver Tabla.

pinto [píntoụ], *a.* pintado, pinto.—*s.* caballo o frijol pinto.

pinwheel [pínhwil], *s.* molinete (juguete).

pioneer [paịọnír], *s.* pionero, colonizador; precursor.—*vt.* y *vi.* colonizar; promover.

pious [pájʌs], *a.* pío, piadoso, devoto.

pipe [paịp], *s.* tubo, caño; tubería; cañería; pipa de fumar, cachimba; (mús.) cañón (de órgano) (mús.) caramillo, flauta.—*pl.* gaita; tubería.—*p. line*, tubería, cañería; oleoducto.—*p. stock*, tarraja.—*vt.* conducir por medio de cañerías o tubos; instalar cañerías en.—*vi.* pitar; gritar.—*to p. down*, (fam.) callarse.- —*r* [pájpœ(r)], *s.* flautista; gaitero. —**piping** [pájpiṇ], *a.* agudo.—*p. hot*, en (o muy) caliente, hirviendo.—*s.* (fam.) llanto, gemido; cañería, tubería; (cost.) vivo, cordoncillo.

pippin [pípịn], *s.* camuesa.

pique [pik], *s.* pique, resentimiento, rencilla.—*vt.* picar, irritar; exacerbar (interés, curiosidad, etc.).—*vi.* (aer.) picar, descender en picada.—*vr.* (gen. con **on** o **upon**) preciarse, jactarse; picarse, ofenderse.

piracy [pájrạṣi], *s.* piratería.—**pirate** [pájrịt], *s.* pirata.—*vt.* y *vi.* piratear.

pistil [pístịl], *s.* pistilo.

pistol [pístọl], *s.* pistola; revólver.— *p. holster*, funda, cartuchera.

piston [pístọn], *s.* pistón, émbolo.— *p. ring*, aro del pistón.—*p. rod*, vástago del émbolo.—*p. travel*, carrera del émbolo.

pit [pịt], *s.* hoyo; hoya; foso; abismo; hueso de ciertas frutas; (teat.) platea.

pitch [pịch], *s.* grado de inclinación, pendiente, declive; paso (de tornillo, hélice, etc.); (mús.) tono; diapasón; (beisbol) lanzamiento, tiro; pez, betún, brea, alquitrán; resina.—*p. dark*, oscuro como boca de lobo.— *p. pine*, pino tea.—*vt.* tirar, arrojar; (beisbol) lanzar la pelota al bateador; armar (tienda, etc.); embrear, embetunar; graduar el tono, dar el diapasón.—*to p. tents*, (mil.) acampar. —*vi.* caerse de cabeza; establecerse; cabecear (el buque).—*to p. in*, (fam.) poner manos a la obra.—*to p. into*, (fam.) arremeter a, embestir; sermonear.—*to p. (up)on*, escoger.- —*er* [píchœ(r)], *s.* jarro, cántaro; (beisbol) el lanzador.—**fork** [-fork], *s.* (agr.) horca, horquilla; tridente.

piteous [pítịʌs], *a.* lastimero, lastimoso.

pitfall [pítfọl], *s.* trampa, hoyo cubierto; peligro latente.

pith [piϑ], *s.* meollo, médula; tuétano; (fig.) fuerza, vigor; substancia, la parte esencial, el quid.

pitiful [pítịfụl], *a.* lastimoso, enternecedor; pobre, despreciable.—**pitiless** [pítịlịs], *a.* despiadado, cruel.

pittance [pítạns], *s.* pitanza, ración, porción.

pity [pịti], *s.* piedad, lástima, compasión.—*for p.'s sake*, por piedad.— *it is a p.*, es lástima, es de sentirse.— *vti.* [7] compadecer.—*vii.* apiadarse, tener piedad o compadecerse de.

pivot [pívọt], *s.* espiga, pivote, muñón. —*p. chair*, silla giratoria.—*vt.* colocar sobre un eje, o por medio de un pivote.—*vi.* girar sobre un pivote.

pixie [píksị], *s.* duendecillo.

placard [plǽkard], *s.* cartel, letrero, rótulo.—*vt.* publicar por medio de carteles; fijar (cartel o aviso).

place [pleịs], *s.* lugar, sitio; puesto; posición, empleo, colocación; grado; espacio, asiento; cubierto (en la mesa).—*in p. of*, en lugar de, en vez de.—*in that p.*, allí, allá.—*in the first p.*, en primer lugar.—*in the next p.*, luego, después.—*out of p.*, fuera de lugar; impropio, indebido. —*vt.* colocar, poner, situar; dar colocación o empleo ·a; dar salida a.— *to p. across*, atravesar.—*to p. before*, anteponer.

placid [plǽsịd], *a.* plácido, apacible, sereno.

placket [plǽkịt], *s.* abertura en la

parte superior de una saya; bolsillo o manera (de falda).

plagiarism [pléjdʒ(i)ạrizm], *s.* plagio. —**plagiarist** [pléjdʒ(i)ạrist], *a.* y *s.* plagiario.—**plagiarize** [pléjdʒ(i)ạrajz], *vt.* y *vi.* plagiar.

plague [pleig], *s.* plaga, peste; miseria, calamidad.—*vt.* importunar, fastidiar; infestar, plagar.

plaid [plæd], *s.* manta escocesa; género escocés.—*a.* a cuadros escoceses.

plain [plejn], *a.* llano, simple, sencillo; franco; corriente, ordinario; puro, sin mezcla; claro.—*in p. English*, sin rodeos, en plata.—*p.-clothes man*, detective, policía secreta.—*p. speaking*, franqueza.—*p.-spoken*, claro, franco(te).—*p. truth*, pura verdad. —*adv.* llanamente; sencillamente; claramente.—*s.* llano, llanura, planicie; vega; (Am.) pampa, sabana.

plaintiff [pléjntif], *s.* (for.) demandante, demandador.

plait [plejt], *s.* pliegue, doblez, alforza; trenza.—*vt.* plegar; tejer, trenzar.

plaintive [pléjntiv], *a.* dolorido, quejumbroso.

plan [plæn], *s.* plan, proyecto, programa; plano, dibujo.—*vti.* [1] idear, proyectar, planear, proponerse; pensar, resolver.—*vii.* hacer planes.

plane [plejn], *s.* superficie plana; plano; (carp.) cepillo, garlopa; aeroplano. —*a.* plano, llano.—*p. tree*, plátano falso.—*vt.* cepillar; desbastar; alisar. —*vi.* alisar, cepillar; (aer.) planear.

planet [plǽnit], *s.* planeta.

plank [plæŋk], *s.* tablón, tabla gruesa; tablazón; (pol.) postulados en el programa de un partido.—*vt.* entablar, enmaderar; (min.) encofrar.— —**ing** [plǽŋkiŋ], *s.* tablaje, tablazón, forro; encofrado.

plant [plænt], *s.* planta, mata; fábrica. —*vt.* plantar, sembrar; instalar; fundar, establecer.- —**ation** [-éjșọn], *s.* plantación; (Am.) ingenio; siembra, plantío; criadero de árboles.- —**er** [plǽntœ(r)], *s.* plantador, sembrador, cultivador.

plaque [plæk], *s.* placa.

plasma [plézmạ], *s.* plasma; protoplasma.

plaster [plǽstœ(r)], *s.* yeso; argamasa, mezcla; parche, emplasto.—*mustard p.*, sinapismo.—*vt.* enyesar, enlucir; (fig.) embarrar, embadurnar; cubrir (paredes, etc.) con carteles o anuncios; poner emplastos, emplastar.- —**ing** [-iŋ], *s.* enyesado, enlucido; (med.) emplastadura.

plastic [plǽstik], *s.* y *a.* plástico.—*p. surgery*, cirugía estética.

plate [plejt], *s.* plato; plancha, chapa, lámina, placa; (dent.) dentadura

postiza.—*p. armor*, blindaje.—*vt.* platear, dorar, niquelar, platinar; unir con planchas de metal; blindar.

plateau [plætóu], *s.* meseta, mesa, altiplanicie, altiplano.

plateful [pléjtful], *s.* un plato lleno; ración.

platform [plǽtfɔrm], *s.* plataforma, tablado; tarima; terraplén; andén; (pol.) programa de un partido.

platinum [plǽtinʌm], *s.* platino.

platitude [plǽtitjud], *s.* perogrullada, trivialidad, lugar común.

Platonic [platánik], *a.* platónico; (p. o P.) platónico.

platoon [platún], *s.* (mil.) pelotón.

platter [plǽtœ(r)], *s.* fuente, platón.

plausible [plózibl], *a.* plausible, razonable; verosímil.

play [plej], *vt.* jugar (algún juego); practicar (un deporte); (teat.) representar; desempeñar (un papel); (mus.) ejecutar, tocar; manipular. —*to p. a joke on*, hacer una burla a, dar una broma a.—*to p. one a (bad, dirty, mean) trick*, jugarle una mala pasada.—*to p. the fool*, hacerse el tonto, hacer el papel de bobo.—*to p. tricks*, hacer suertes; hacer travesuras.—*vi.* jugar, juguetear; entretenerse; burlarse, bromear; (mus.) tocar; (teat.) representar.—*s.* juego; jugada; recreo, diversión; (teat.) drama, comedia, pieza; representación; (teat.) ejecución, desempeño.— *at p.*, jugando.—*in p.*, chanza, de burlas.—*p. actor*, actor cómico.—*p. upon words*, equívoco, juego de palabras.- —**bill** [pléjbil], *s.* cartel, programa.- —**boy** [-bɔj], *s.* joven rico y ocioso; calavera.- —**er** [-œ(r)], *s.* jugador; actor, actriz, cómico, comediante; (mus.) ejecutante, músico.—*piano p.*, pianista.- —**ful** [-ful], *a.* jugetón, retozón, travieso.- —**ground** [-graund], *s.* campo o patio de recreo; campo de deportes.- —**house** [-haus], *s.* teatro.- —**mate** [-mejt], *s.* compañero de juego.- —**thing** [-θiŋ], *s.* juguete, niñería.- —**wright** [-rajt], *s.* dramaturgo, autor dramático, comediógrafo.

plea [pli], *s.* ruego, súplica; disculpa, pretexto; (for.) alegato, defensa.— **plead** [plid], *vti.* [4] defender (un pleito, una causa); alegar; aducir como razón, motivo o excusa.—*vii.* suplicar, implorar; abogar (por).— *to p. guilty*, confesarse culpable.—*to p. not guilty*, declararse inocente.

pleasant [plézạnt], *a.* grato, agradable, ameno; simpático, afable.—*p. journey o trip!* ¡feliz viaje!—*p. weather*, buen tiempo.- —**ry** [-ri], *s.* broma, humorada, chanza.—**please** [pliz], *vt.*

agradar; complacer, dar gusto, satisfacer, complacer.—*to be pleased to*, tener gusto en, o el gusto de; alegrarse de, complacerse en.—*to be pleased with*, estar satisfecho o contento de o con.—*vi.* querer, servirse, ser gustoso en, placerle a uno.—*if you please*, por favor, si usted tiene la bondad, si usted me hace el favor.—*to speak as one pleases*, hablar como a uno le da la gana.—**pleasing** [plízɪŋ], *a.* complaciente; agradable, ameno.—*to be p.*, gustar, dar gusto; caer bien.— **pleasure** [pléźʊ(r)], *s.* placer, gusto, deleite; complacencia.—*at one's (own) p.*, como uno quiera, como le plazca.

pleat [plit], *vt.* (cost.) plegar, hacer pliegues, plisar.—*s.* pliegue.— —**ing** [plítɪŋ], *s.* (cost.) plegado, plisado.

plebeian [plɪbíən], *a.* y *s.* plebeyo.

plebiscite [plébɪsaɪt], *s.* plebiscito.

pledge [pledź], *s.* prenda, señal; empeño, fianza; rehén; promesa.— *vt.* pignorar, empeñar, dar en prenda; dar fianza; comprometerse a, dar (la palabra).

plenary [plínərɪ], *a.* plenario; entero, completo; absoluto.

plenipotentiary [plenɪpɒténʃɪərɪ], *s.* y *a.* plenipotenciario.

plenitude [plénɪtjud], *s.* plenitud.

plentiful [pléntɪfʊl], *a.* copioso, abundante; fértil, feraz.—**plenty** [pléntɪ], *s.* abundancia, profusión, afluencia. —*the Horn of P.*, el Cuerno de la Abundancia.—*a.* (fam.) copioso, abundante.

pleurisy [plúrɪsɪ], *s.* pleuresía.

pliable [pláɪəbl], *a.* flexible; plegable; dócil.—**pliancy** [pláɪənsɪ], *s.* flexibilidad, docilidad, blandura.—**pliant** [pláɪənt], *a.* flexible, cimbreño; dócil, blando, tratable, manual.

pliers [pláɪœrz], *s. pl.* alicates, tenacillas, tenazas.

plight [plaɪt], *s.* apuro, aprieto; promesa (de matrimonio).—*vt.* empeñar o dar (palabra).

plod [plad], *vii.* [1] avanzar con lentitud; afanarse, ajetrearse, trabajar con ahinco.

plot [plat], *s.* solar, parcela; plano de un terreno; conspiración, complot; trama o argumento (de drama o novela).—*vti.* [1] tramar, urdir, fraguar; hacer el plano, la gráfica o el diagrama.—*vii.* conspirar, maquinar.

plow [plaʊ], *s.* arado.—*vt.* arar, labrar, surcar; (mar. y fig.) surcar.—**man** [pláʊmən], *s.* labrador; yuguero; patán.— **share** [-ʃɛr], *s.* reja de arado.

pluck [plʌk], *vt.* arrancar; pelar; des-

plumar; (mus.) puntear, pulsar; (fam.) robar, estafar, dejar sin un cuarto.—*to p. up*, arrancar.—*to p. up courage*, cobrar ánimo; hacer de tripas corazón, sacar fuerzas de flaqueza.—*vi.* (at) tirar de, dar un tirón.—*s.* valor, ánimo, resolución; arranque, tirón.— —**y** [plʌkɪ], *a.* animoso, resuelto.

plug [plʌg], *s.* tapón, tarugo, taco; cuña; espita; (dent.) empaste o empastadura; porción de tabaco comprimido; cala (frutas); cierre (de válvula); (elec.) enchufe, adaptador, tomacorriente; conectador; tapón o fusible; (aut.) bujía; (fam.) rocín, penco.—*vti.* [1] atarugar, obturar; (dent.) empastar, orificar; (elec.) (in) enchufar, conectar; calar (melones, etc.).

plum [plʌm], *s.* ciruela; golosina, gollería; lo mejor; la nata; puesto muy ventajoso; dividendo jugoso.— *p. pudding*, pudín inglés con pasas. —*p. tree*, ciruelo.

plumage [plúmɪdź], *s.* plumaje.

plumb [plʌm], *a.* vertical, a plomo.— *p. level*, nivel de albañil.—*s.* plomada; sonda.—*off p.*, *out of p.*, desviado de la vertical.—*adv.* a plomo, verticalmente; (fam.) completa o rematadamente.—*vt.* sondear; aplomar; emplomar, sellar con plomo; instalar cañerías.— —**er** [plʌmœ(r)], *s.* plomero.— —**ing** [-ɪŋ], *s.* plomería; oficio de plomero; sistema de cañerías interiores; instalación de cañerías; acción de sond(e)ar o aplomar.

plume [plum], *s.* pluma; plumaje, penacho.—*vt.* adornar con plumas; desplumar.

plummet [plʌmɪt], *s.* plomo, plomada; sonda.

plump [plʌmp], *a.* rollizo, regordete; gordinflón.—*adv.* de golpe; a plomo; directamente.—*vt.* soltar, dejar caer; engordar, hinchar.—*vi.* caer a plomo; hincharse, engordar, llenarse.

plunder [plʌndœ(r)], *vt.* despojar, saquear, entrar a saco; expoliar.—*s.* pillaje, saqueo, rapiña; botín.

plunge [plʌndź], *vt.* zambullir, sumergir, chapuzar; hundir; precipitar; sumir. —*vi.* sumergirse, zambullirse; precipitarse, arrojarse, lanzarse.—*s.* sumersión, zambullida; salto, arrojo, embestida; tanque para bañarse.— —**r** [plʌndźœ(r)], *s.* buzo; (mec.) émbolo; jugador o bolsista desenfrenado.

plural [plúrəl], *a.* y *s.* plural.— —**ity** [plʊrælɪtɪ], *s.* pluralidad; mayoría relativa (de votos); multitud.— —**ize** [plúrəlaɪz], *vt.* pluralizar.

plus [plʌs], *prep.* más; además de,

con, con la añadidura de.—*a.* (mat. y elec.) positivo; (fam.) y más, con algo de sobra; más otras cosas.— *to be, come out,* etc. *p.* (*something*), (fam.) salir ganando (algo).—*s.* signo más (+); cantidad positiva.

plush [plʌʃ], *s.* felpa; pana.—*a.* afelpado.

ply [plaɪ], *vti.* [7] trabajar en con ahinco; ejercer, practicar; emplear, ocupar; manejar (la aguja, el remo); importunar, acosar (con preguntas, etc.); convidar a beber varias veces; atacar tenazmente; plegar.—*vi.* ir y venir regularmente; estar constantemente ocupado o funcionando; solicitar o aguardar compradores; (mar.) hacer la travesía.—*s.* pliegue, doblez; propensión; capa (de tejido, goma, etc.).

pneumatic [njumǽtik], *a.* neumático. —*p. tire,* neumático, llanta neumática.—**pneumonia** [njumóuŋjɐ], *s.* pulmonía, neumonía.

poach [pouʧ], *vt.* escalfar; cazar o pescar en vedado; invadir.—*vi.* encenagarse; atollarse o meterse en un fangal.— **—er** [póuʧœ(r)], *s.* cazador furtivo.

pock [pak], *s.* pústula, postilla, viruela. —*p.-marked,* picado de viruelas.

pocket [pákit], *s.* bolsillo, faltriquera; cavidad, bolsón; bolsa; nasa; hoyo; hondonada, depresión; callejón sin salida; tronera.—*in p.,* con ganancia. —*out of p.,* con pérdida.—*p. clip,* sujetador (de lápiz, etc.).—*p. money,* dinero para alfileres o gastos particulares.—*p. picking,* ratería de carterista.—*p. veto,* veto presidencial tácito.—*vt.* embolsar, meter en el bolsillo; tomar, apropiarse; tragarse (una injuria).— **—book** [-buk], *s.* portamonedas, bolsa; cartera, billetera; (fig.) dinero, recursos; libro que cabe en el bolsillo.— **—knife** [-naɪf], *s.* cortaplumas.

pod [pad], *s.* vaina (de frijol, etc.); capullo (de gusano de seda).—*vi.* llenarse, hincharse; criar vainas.

poem [póuim], *s.* poema, composición poética.—*pl.* versos, rimas.—**poet** [póuit], *s.* poeta.—**poetess** [póuitis], *s.* poetisa.—**poeti(cal)** [pouétik(ɐl)], *a.* poético.—**poetics** [pouétiks], *s.* (arte) poética.—**poetry** [póuitri], *s.* poética; poesía.

poignant [póin(y)ɐnt], *a.* acerbo, punzante; conmovedor, patético.

point [point], *s.* punto; punta; fin, objeto; peculiaridad; grado (de una escala); momento crítico; instante. —*to be beside the p.,* no venir al caso.—*to get the p.,* caer en la cuenta, verle la gracia.—*to get to the p.,* venir o ir al grano.—*what's the p.?* ¿a qué viene eso? ¿de o para qué sirve?— *vt.* aguzar, afilar (lápiz, arma, etc.); (con **at, to** o **toward**) apuntar, señalar, indicar; encarar, dirigir, asestar.— *to p. out,* apuntar, señalar, mostrar. —*vi.* apuntar; propender, inclinarse a; dar, mirar hacia; (med.) madurarse (un absceso).- **—blank** [póintblǽŋk], *a.* horizontal; directo, claro, categórico.—*adv.* a quema ropa, a boca de jarro; sin ambages.- **—ed** [póintid], *a.* puntiagudo; en punta; picante, satírico; directo, acentuado, enfático. - **—er** [-œ(r)], *s.* indicador, índice; manecilla, aguja; fiel (de balanza); apuntador, puntero; buril; perro de caza; (fam.) indicación o consejo útil.- **—less** [-lis], *a.* inútil, vano; sin objeto.

poise [poiz], *s.* equilibrio; estabilidad; aplomo, serenidad; porte, talante. —*vt.* equilibrar, estabilizar.—*vi.* quedar en equilibrio.

poison [póizɐn], *s.* veneno, ponzoña.— *p.-pen letter,* (fam.) carta anónima ofensiva.—*vt.* envenenar; (fig.) corromper, inficionar.- **—er** [-œ(r)], *s.* envenenador.- **—ing** [-iŋ], *s.* envenenamiento.- **—ous** [-ʌs], *a.* venenoso, ponzoñoso.

poke [pouk], *s.* empuje, empujón; persona indolente; saquito; vejiga de aire.—*vt.* picar, aguijonear; atizar, hurgonear; asomar, sacar (la cabeza, etc.).—*to p. fun at,* mofarse de.—*to p. one's nose into,* meter las narices en; entrometerse, curiosear.—*vi.* rezagarse; andar a tientas.— **—r** [póukœ(r)], *s.* atizador; entremetido; juego de naipes.

pok(e)y [póuki], *a.* (fam.) flojo, pesado, lento; apretado, ahogado (cuarto); desaliñado (vestido).—*s.* (fam.) chirona.

polar [póulɐ(r)], *a.* polar.—*p. bear,* oso blanco.—*p. lights,* aurora boreal o austral.

polarity [polériti], *s.* polaridad.

pole [poul], *s.* (geog. y elec.) polo; pértiga, palo largo, asta, estaca; poste; jalón; (P.) polaco.—*p. vault,* salto con garrocha.

police [polís], *s.* (cuerpo de) policía.— *p. officer,* agente de policía, vigilante. —*a.* policíaco, policial.—*vt.* vigilar, mantener el orden (con la policía).- **—man** [-man], *s.* (agente de) policía, vigilante.

policy [pálisi], *s.* sagacidad; curso o plan de acción; política; regla, sistema, costumbre; póliza de seguro. —*p. holder,* asegurado, tenedor de póliza.

polish [páliʃ], *vt.* pulir, pulimentar;

lustrar; educar; civilizar.—*vi.* recibir lustre o pulimento.—*s.* pulimento, tersura, lustre; urbanidad, cultura; betún o bola para zapatos; embolada, acción de lustrar (zapatos).—**Polish** [pówliş], *a.* polaco, polonés.—*s.* polaco (idioma).

polite [poláit], *a.* cortés, bien educado, atento.- —**ness** [-nịs], *s.* cortesía, u-banidad, buena crianza, buena educación.—*for p.'sake,* por cortesía.

politic [pálitik], *a.* político; sagaz, astuto, hábil; apropiado, atinado.- —**al** [polítikạl], *a.* político; (desp.) politiquero.- —**ian** [palitíşạn], *s.* político, estadista; (desp.) politicastro, politiquero.- —**s** [pálitịks], *s.* política; asuntos, métodos o intereses políticos; (desp.) politiquería; rivalidades o maniobras de partido o facción.

poll [pouļ], *s.* lista electoral; votación; escrutinio; encuesta.—*pl.* lugar donde se vota; urnas electorales; elecciones. —*p. tax,* capitación, impuesto sobre el voto.—*vt.* dar o recibir votos; contar los votos, escrutar; someter a votación.—*vi.* votar en las elecciones.

pollen [pálẹn], *s.* polen.

pollute [polút], *vt.* contaminar; mancillar; profanar.—**pollution** [polúşọn], *s.* contaminación, corrupción; mancilla, mancha; polución.

polo [póuļou], *s.* (dep.) polo.—*water p.,* polo acuático.

poltroon [paltrún], *s.* cobarde.

polygon [páligan], *s.* polígono.

Polynesian [palinížạn], *s.* y *a.* polinesi(an)o.

pomade [poméid], *s.* pomada.

pomegranate [pámgrænịt], *s.* (bot.) granada.

pommel [pámẹl], *s.* pomo (de espada); perilla (de arzón).

pomp [pamp], *s.* pompa, fausto.- —**osity** [-ásịti], —**ousness** [pámpʌsnịs], *s.* pomposidad, fausto, ostentación; afectación, altisonancia (de estilo).- —**ous** [-ʌs], *a.* pomposo, ostentoso.

poncho [pánchou], *s.* (Am.) poncho, manta.

pond [pand], *s.* charca, laguito, estanque; vivero (de peces).

ponder [pándœ(r)], *vt.* examinar, estudiar, pesar, (fig.) rumiar.—*vi.* (con on u over) considerar, deliberar, reflexionar (acerca de).- —**ous** [-ʌs], *a.* pesado; voluminoso; tedioso.

poniard [pányạrd], *s.* puñal.

pontiff [pántịf], *s.* pontífice.—**pontifical** [pantífikạl], *a.* pontifical; papal.

pontoon [pantún], *s.* pontón; barcaza; (aer.) flotador.

pony [póunị], *s.* jaca; caballito; copa o vaso pequeño, o el licor que se sirve en ellos.

poodle [púdl], *s.* perro de lanas o de aguas.

pool [puļ], *vt.* formar una puesta (en ciertos juegos); pagar a escote; mancomunar intereses.—*vi.* formar un charco; resbalarse.—*s.* charco; alberca; estanque; piscina; puesta; fusión de intereses o de empresas; piña; combinación para especular.

poop [pup], *s.* (mar.) popa.—*to be pooped,* (fam.) estar hecho polvo.

poor [pụr], *a.* pobre, necesitado, indigente; deficiente, falto, escaso; en mal estado; de poco mérito; malo, de mala calidad; estéril (tierra); enfermizo.—*s.* (con the) los pobres.- —**house** [púrhaụs], *s.* hospicio, asilo, casa de beneficencia.- —**ly** [-lị], *a.* (fam.) indispuesto, enfermizo.—*adv.* pobremente; malamente.—*p. off,* escaso de dinero.

pop [pap], *s.* chasquido, ruido seco, detonación; pistoletazo; taponazo; bebida gaseosa; (fam.) papá; (fam.) concierto popular.—*vti.* [1] soltar, espetar, disparar; chasquear; hacer saltar un tapón.—*vii.* entrar o salir de sopetón; saltar un tapón; dar chasquidos o estallidos; detonar; reventar.—*to p. off,* (fam.) morir; dormirse.—*to p. up,* (fam.) aparecer de repente.- —**corn** [pápkorn], *s.* maíz reventón; rosetas, flores o palomitas de maíz.

Pope [poup], *s.* papa, sumo pontífice.

poplar [páplạ(r)], *s.* álamo.—*black p.,* chopo.—*p. grove,* alameda.

poplin [páplịn], *s.* popelina.

poppy [pápị], *s.* amapola.

populace [pápyụlịs], *s.* pueblo, plebe; populacho, chusma.—**popular** [pápyụlạ(r)], *a.* popular, democrático; populachero; en boga, de moda.— **popularity** [papyụlǽrịtị], *s.* popularidad, prestigio, buena acogida general.—**popularization** [papyụlǎrịzéíşọn], *s.* popularización, vulgarización. —**popularize** [pápyụlǎraịz], *vt.* popularizar, divulgar, hacer popular.—

populate [pápyụleịt], *vt.* poblar.— **population** [papyụléíşọn], *s.* población, vecindario.—**populous** [pápyụlʌs], *a.* populoso.

porcelain [pórsẹlịn], *s.* porcelana, china, loza fina.

porch [porch], *s.* pórtico, porche, entrada; corredor, galería (frontal o lateral de una casa).

porcupine [pórkyụpaịn], *s.* puerco espín.

pore [por], *s.* poro.—*vi.* (con on, upon, over) escudriñar, estudiar escrupulosamente.

pork [pork], *s.* carne de puerco.—*p. chop*, chuleta o costilla de cerdo.

porous [pórʌs], *a.* poroso, esponjoso, permeable.

porpoise [pórpʌs], *s.* delfín, marsopa.

porridge [párįdž], *s.* gachas de avena.

port [port], *s.* puerto; babor, lado izquierdo de una embarcación; porte, talante; oporto (vino).

portable [pórtʌbl], *a.* portátil.

portal [pórtạl], *s.* portal, portada; vestíbulo.

portent [pórtɛnt], *s.* portento, prodigio; presagio, augurio.—*ous* [portɛ́ntʌs], *a.* portentoso, prodigioso; de mal agüero.

porter [pórtœ(r)], *s.* mozo de cuerda, maletero; camarero, mozo de servicio (trenes, hoteles, etc.); portero.

portfolio [portfóu̯liou̯], *s.* cartera, carpeta, portapliegos; (fig.) ministerio.

porthole [pórthou̯l], *s.* (mar.) portilla, ojo de buey.

portiere [portiér], *s.* dosel, cortina de puerta.

portion [póršọn], *s.* porción, parte; cuota; dote.—*vt.* dividir, (re)partir; dotar.

portly [pórtlį], *a.* corpulento, grueso; majestuoso, serio, grave.

Porto Rican [pórto ríkạn], *a.* y *s.* puertorriqueño, portorriqueño.

portrait [pórtrịt], *s.* retrato.—*p. painter*, retratista.—*to sit for a p.*, posar para un retrato.—**portray** [portréi̯], *vt.* retratar, pintar.—**portrayal** [portréi̯ạl], *s.* representación gráfica, dibujo, pintura; descripción.

Portuguese [pórchọgiz], *a.* y *s.* portugués.—*s.* lengua portuguesa.

pose [pou̯z], *vt.* (b.a.) posar; proponer, afirmar; plantear (un problema); confundir con preguntas difíciles.—*vi.* colocarse en cierta postura; tomar posturas afectadas.—*to p. as*, pretender ser; hacerse pasar por; echárselas de.—*s.* postura, posición, actitud.

position [pọzíšọn], *s.* posición, situación, ubicación; puesto, empleo, colocación; actitud; proposición.

positive [pázịtịv], *a.* positivo; real, verdadero; categórico, rotundo; afirmativo.—*s.* realidad, certeza; (foto.) positivo; (gram.) grado positivo; (elec.) polo positivo.

posse [pásį], *s.* patrulla o fuerza civil armada.

possess [pozés], *vt.* poseer; gozar, disponer (de); señorear, dominar; posesionar.—*ion* [pozéšọn], *s.* posesión, dominio, goce; apoderamiento.—*pl.* patrimonio, propiedades, bienes.—*ive* [-iv], *s.* y *a.* posesivo.—*a.*

posesorio; posesional.—*or* [-ọ(r)], *s.* poseedor, posesor.

possibility [pasịbílịtị], *s.* posibilidad; contingencia; potencialidad; oportunidad.—**possible** [pásịbl], *a.* posible, potencial, dable.—*as far as o as much as p.*, en lo posible.—*as soon as p.*, cuanto antes.—*to render p.*, posibilitar.

post [pou̯st], *s.* poste, pilar; (mil.) puesto, plaza, guarnición, avanzada; empleo, cargo; correo, estafeta, propio.—*p.-free*, franco de porte.—*p. office*, correo, casa de correos, administración de correos, estafeta.—*p.-office box*, apartado de correos.—*vt.* pegar o fijar carteles; anunciar; poner en lista; apostar, situar; echar al correo; prohibir la entrada a (un terreno, etc.); estigmatizar; (com.) pasar los asientos al libro mayor; (fam.) informar, tener al corriente, poner al tanto de.—*p. no bills*, se prohíbe fijar carteles.—*age* [pou̯stịdž], *s.* franqueo, porte de correos.—*al* [-ạl], *a.* postal.—*box* [-baks], *s.* buzón; apartado.—*card* [-kard], *s.* tarjeta postal.—*dated* [-déịtịd], *a.* con fecha adelantada.

poster [pou̯stœ(r)], *s.* cartel, cartelón, letrero, rótulo.

posterior [pastịrịọ(r)], *a.* posterior.—*pl.* nalgas.—**posterity** [pastérịtị], *s.* posterioridad.

postman [pou̯stmạn], *s.* cartero.—**postmark** [pou̯stmark], *s.* matasellos.—**postmaster** [pou̯stmæstœ(r)], *s.* administrador de correos.

postmeridian [pou̯stmẹrídịạn], *a.* postmeridiano, de la tarde.

postpaid [pou̯stpéịd], *a.* porte pagado, franco de porte.

postpone [pou̯stpóu̯n], *vt.* diferir, aplazar; postergar; posponer.—*ment* [-mẹnt], *s.* aplazamiento; postergación; posposición.

postcript [pou̯stskrịpt], *s.* pos(t)data.

postulate [páschọleịt], *vt.* postular, pedir, solicitar.—*s.* [páschọlịt], postulado.

posture [páschọ(r)], *s.* postura, actitud.—*vt.* y *vi.* poner(se) en alguna postura.

postwar [pou̯stwór], *a.* de pos(t)guerra.—*p. period*, pos(t)guerra.

posy [póu̯zị], *s.* ramillete de flores; flor.

pot [pat], *s.* marmita, olla; pote; cacharro; tiesto (para flores); orinal; cantidad contenida en una olla; crisol; (en el juego) puesta.—*p.-bellied*, panzudo, barrigón.—*to go to p.*, (fam.) arruinarse, desbaratarse, (fig.) irse a pique.

potable [póu̯tạbl], *a.* potable.

potash [pátæš], *s.* potasa.—**potassium** [potǽsjʌm], *s.* potasio.

potato [potéitou], *s.* patata, papa.— *sweet p.*, batata, boniato, (Am.) camote.

potency [póutẹnsj], *s.* potencia; actividad (de un veneno); poder, influjo, autoridad.—**potent** [póutẹnt], *a.* potente, poderoso, eficaz.—**potentate** [póutẹnteit], *s.* potentado; potestad. —**potential** [poténšạl], *a.* potencial, posible; virtual; (fis. y gram.) potencial.—*s.* modo potencial; (fis.) potencial.—**potentiality** [potenšjǽliti], *s.* potencialidad, capacidad.

pothole [páthoul], *s.* bache.

potion [póušọn], *s.* poción, pócima.

potpourri [poupurí, patpúri], *s.* baturrillo, miscelánea, popurrí.

pottage [pátidž], *s.* potaje, menestra.

potter [pátœ(r)], *s.* alfarero.— —y [-i], *s.* alfarería; alfar (taller); cacharros (de barro).

pouch [pauch], *s.* saquito, bolsa; zurrón, morral; valija; (anat. y zool.) bolsa, saco.—*vt.* embolsar; tragar, engullir.—*vi.* formar bolsas.

poultice [póultis], *s.* cataplasma, emplasto.

poultry [póultri], *s.* aves de corral.— *p. yard*, corral, gallinero.

pounce [pauns], *s.* zarpada; salto; zarpa, garra.—*vt.* y *vi.* saltar o abalanzarse sobre; dar una zarpada; saltar, etc. de repente.

pound [paund], *s.* libra. Ver Tabla; golpazo.—*p. sterling*, libra esterlina. —*vt.* golpear; machacar, majar, aporrear; poner a buen recaudo.—*vi.* golpear; batir con violencia (el corazón); andar pesadamente; avanzar continua o enérgicamente.

pour [por], *vt.* derramar; verter, vaciar; trasegar; escanciar; gastar pródigamente.—*vi.* fluir, caer copiosa o rápidamente; llover a cántaros; salir a borbotones.

pout [paut], *s.* pucherito; berrinche. —*vi.* hacer pucheros; enfurruñarse, poner mal gesto.

poverty [pávœrti], *s.* pobreza, indigencia; falta, carencia.—*p.-stricken*, muy pobre.

powder [páudœ(r)], *s.* pólvora; polvo; polvos de tocador.—*p. magazine*, polvorín, santabárbara.—*p. puff*, borla de polvos, (Am.) mota, cisne. —*vt.* pulverizar; empolvar; polvorear; espolvorear.—*vi.* pulverizarse; ponerse polvos.— —y [-i], *a.* polvoriento; empolvado; deleznable, quebradizo.

power [páuœ(r)], *s.* fuerza, pujanza; poder, poderío, potestad; facultad, atribución; ascendiente, influjo; potencia (nación); (mat. y mec.)

potencia.—*p. of attorney*, (for.) poder. —*p. plant*, planta de fuerza motriz.— —**ful** [-ful], *a.* poderoso, potente, fuerte; influyente.— —**less** [-lis], *a.* impotente; ineficaz.

pox [paks], *s.* cualquier enfermedad que causa erupciones pustulosas.—*chicken p.*, varicela.—*small p.*, viruela.

practicable [prǽktikạbl], *a.* practicable, factible, viable; accesible, transitable. —**practical** [prǽktikạl], *a.* práctico; de hecho, real; positivo, prosaico.— *p. joke*, broma pesada.—*p. politics*, política de realidades; politiquería.—

practice [prǽktis], *s.* práctica, uso, costumbre; ejercicio; experiencia; sistema, regla, método; clientela.— *in p.*, en la práctica.—*vt.* y *vi.* practicar, ensayar(se), adiestrar(se); ejercitar(se); ejercer (una profesión).

prairie [préri], *s.* llanura, pradera, pampa, sabana.—*p. wolf*, coyote.

praise [preiz], *s.* alabanza, loa, elogio; fama, renombre.—*vt.* alabar, encomiar, ensalzar.— —**worthy** [préjzwɔ‑rði], *a.* digno de alabanza, laudable.

prance [præns], *vi.* cabriolar, corvetear, gambetear (el caballo); cabalgar o andar garbosa u orgullosamente; bailar.—*s.* cabriola, corveta.

prank [præŋk], *s.* travesura; jugarreta. —*to play pranks*, hacer diabluras.— —**ish** [prǽŋkiš], *a.* travieso, retozón, revoltoso.

prate [preit], *vi.* charlar, parlotear.—*s.* charla.—**prattle** [prǽtl], *vi.* parlotear, (fam.) chacharear; balbucear; murmurar (un arroyo).—*s.* parloteo, (fam.) cháchara.

prawn [prɔn], *s.* camarón.

pray [prei], *vt.* rogar, suplicar; implorar. —*vi.* rezar, orar; (for) hacer votos por.— —**er** [prer], *s.* oración, rezo, plegaria; súplica, ruego.—*the Lord's P.*, el Padrenuestro.—*p. beads*, rosario.—*p. book*, devocionario.—*p. desk*, reclinatorio.

preach [prich], *vt.* y *vi.* predicar; sermonear.— —**er** [prichœ(r)], *s.* predicador.— —**ing** [-iŋ], *s.* predicación; sermón.

preamble [príæmbl], *s.* preámbulo.

prearrange [priɑréindž], *vt.* arreglar de antemano, predisponer, prevenir.

precarious [prikérjʌs], *a.* precario, inseguro; peligroso, arriesgado.

precaution [prikóšọn], *s.* precaución.

precede [prisíd], *vt.* anteceder, preceder. —*vi.* preceder; ir delante; tener la primacía; sobresalir.— —**nce** [prisídẹns, présẹdẹns], *s.* prioridad, anterioridad, antelación; precedencia, superioridad.— —**nt** [présẹdẹnt], *s.*

precedente; antecedente.—*a.* precedente.

precept [prísept], *s.* precepto; ley.- —or [-ǫ(r)], *s.* preceptor.

precinct [prísiŋkt], *s.* recinto; distrito, barriada.—*police p.*, comisaría, delegación o puesto de policía.

precious [préšʌs], *a.* precioso; preciado; de gran valor; caro, querido.—*adv.* (fam.) muy.

precipice [présipis], *s.* precipicio, despeñadero.—precipitate [prisípiteit], *vt.* precipitar, despeñar, derrumbar, arrojar; acelerar, apresurar; (quím.) precipitar.—*vi.* precipitarse.—*a.* precipitado, atropellado.—*s.* (quím.) precipitado.—precipitation [prisipitéišǫn], *s.* precipitación; derrumbamiento; rocío; cantidad de lluvia; (quím.) precipitación.—precipitous [prisípitʌs], *a.* escarpado; arrojado; precipitado.

precise [prisáis], *a.* preciso, exacto; justo, ni más ni menos; estricto, escrupuloso; propio, mismísimo, idéntico.—precision [prisíẓǫn], *s.* precisión, exactitud, limitación exacta; escrupulosidad.

predatory [prédatǫri], *a.* rapaz, de presa, de rapiña.

predecessor [prédisesǫ(r)], *s.* predecesor, antecesor; antepasado.

predesignate [pridéẓigneit], *vt.* prefijar.

predestination [pridestinéišǫn], *s.* predestinación.—predestine [pridéstin], *vt.* predestinar.

predetermine [priditǿrmin], *vt.* predeterminar, prefijar.

predicament [pridíkament], *s.* dificultad, apuro, brete, compromiso; clase, categoría, situación, circunstancias; (log.) predicamento.—predicate [prédikeit], *vt.* proclamar; predicar; basar o fundar en algo; afirmar un predicado.—*vi.* afirmarse. —*s.* [prédikit], (gram. y log.) predicado, atributo.

predict [pridíkt], *vt.* predecir, pronosticar, vaticinar.— —ion [pridíkšǫn], *s.* predicción, pronóstico, profecía.

predilection [predilékšǫn], *s.* predilección.

predispose [pridispóuz], *vt.* predisponer, prevenir.—predisposition [pridispozišǫn], *s.* predisposición.

predominance [pridáminans], *s.* predominio; ascendiente, influencia.—predominant [pridáminant], *a.* predominante, prepotente.—predominate [pridámineit], *vi.* predominar, prevalecer.

prefabricate [prifébrikeit], *vt.* fabricar de antemano (casa, etc.).— —d [-id], *a.* prefabricado.

preface [préfis], *s.* prefacio, preámbulo,

prólogo.—*vt.* prologar; hacer un exordio.

prefer [prifǿr], *vti.* [1] preferir; exaltar; presentar, ofrecer; dar preferencia. —*to p. a charge*, presentar una denuncia.—*to p. a claim*, presentar una demanda.— —able [préfrabl], *a.* preferible, preferente.— —ence [préfrens], *s.* preferencia, predilección; prioridad, prelación; ventaja.

prefix [prifíks], *vt.* prefijar, anteponer. —*s.* [prifíks], prefijo.

pregnancy [prégnansi], *s.* preñez, embarazo, gravidez; gestación; (fig.) fertilidad, fecundidad.—pregnant [prégnant], *a.* encinta, grávida, preñada, embarazada; fértil, copioso, fecundo. —*p. with*, repleto, lleno de.

prejudge [pridžʌdž], *vt.* prejuzgar.

prejudice [prédžudis], *s.* prevención, prejuicio; parcialidad; daño, detrimento.—*vt.* predisponer, prevenir; perjudicar.

prelate [prélit], *s.* prelado.

preliminary [prilíminəri], *a.* preliminar; preparatorio.—*s.* preliminar.— *pl.* exámenes preliminares; pruebas eliminatorias.

prelude [préljud], *s.* preludio; presagio.

premature [primachúr], *a.* prematuro. —*p. baby*, niño sietemesino.

premeditate [priméditeit], *vt.* y *vi.* premeditar.—premeditation [primeditéišǫn], *s.* premeditación.

premier [prímjœ(r)], *s.* primer ministro, jefe de gobierno.—*a.* primero, principal.

premiere [primír], *s.* estreno (de un drama. etc.).

premise [prémis], *s.* premisa.—*pl.* (for.) aserciones anteriores; terrenos, casa, posesiones; local.

premium [prímjʌm], *s.* premio; remuneración; (com.) prima; interés. —*at a p.*, muy escaso, de gran valor, muy solicitado.

premonition [primoníšǫn], *s.* advertencia; presentimiento, corazonada.

preoccupation [priakjȳpéišǫn], *s.* preocupación.

prepaid [pripéid], *a.* porte pagado; pagado por adelantado.—*pret.* y *pp.* de TO PREPAY.

preparation [prepaÎréišǫn], *s.* preparación; preparativo; (farm.) preparado. —preparatory [pripératǫri], *a.* preparatorio; previo, preliminar.—prepare [pripér], *vt.* preparar, apercibir; disponer, prevenir; aderezar, adobar, confeccionar.—*vi.* prepararse, disponerse, hacer preparativos.—preparedness [pripéridnis], *s.* preparación, prevención, apercibimiento.

prepay [pripéi], *vti.* [10] pagar por adelantado; franquear (una carta).

preponderance [prɪpándɛɾans], *s.* preponderancia.—**preponderate** [prɪpándɛɾeɪt], *vi.* preponderar.

prepossess [prɪpɒzés], *vt.* predisponer, causar buena impresión.— **—ing** [-ɪŋ], *a.* simpático, atractivo.— **—ion** [pripozéśɒn], *s.* impresión favorable; simpatía, predisposición favorable.

preposition [prepozíśɒn], *s.* preposición.

preposterous [prɪpástɛɾas], *a.* absurdo, ridículo, descabellado.

prerequisite [prírékwɪzɪt], *a.* previamente necesario.—*s.* requisito previo.

prerogative [prɪrágatɪv], *s.* prerrogativa.

presage [présɪdź], *s.* presagio.—*vt.* presagiar.

Presbyterian [prezbɪtríɹɪan], *a.* y *s.* presbiteriano.

prescribe [prɪskráɪb], *vt.* y *vi.* prescribir; dar leyes o reglas; recetar; caducar. **—prescription** [prɪskrípśɒn], *s.* prescripción, precepto, regla; receta.

presence [prézɛns], *s.* presencia; aspecto, porte; asistencia.—*p. of mind*, presencia de ánimo, aplomo, serenidad.—**present** [prézɛnt], *a.* presente; actual, corriente (mes, semana, etc.).—*at the p. time*, hoy (por hoy), en la actualidad.—*p. company excepted*, mejorando lo presente.—*p. day*, actual, (del día) de hoy.—*p. participle*, participio activo o de presente, gerundio.—*to be p.* (at), asistir (a); presenciar; concurrir.—*s.* el presente, la actualidad; (gram.) tiempo presente; regalo, obsequio, presente.—*at p.*, al presente, actualmente, (por) ahora.—*for the p.*, por ahora, por el (o lo) presente.—*vt.* [prɪzént], presentar, introducir, dar a conocer; dar, regalar, obsequiar; manifestar, mostrar, exponer; representar, poner en escena; (for.) denunciar, acusar.—**presentation** [prezɛntéiśɒn], *s.* presentación; introducción; entrega ceremoniosa de un obsequio; (teat.) exhibición, representación.

presentiment [prɪzéntɪmɛnt], *s.* presentimiento.

presently [prézɛntlɪ], *adv.* luego, ya, dentro de poco, pronto.

preservation [prezɛrvéiśɒn], *s.* preservación, conservación.—**preservative** [prɪzɛ́rvatɪv], *a.* preservativo.— *s.* preservativo, salvaguardia.—**preserve** [prɪzɛ́rv], *vt.* preservar; proteger; reservar; conservar, mantener; salar, curar; confitar, almibarar.— *vi.* hacer conservas de fruta.—*s.* (gen. *pl.*) conserva, dulce, compota, confitura; vedado, coto.—**preserved** [prɪzɛ́rvd], *a.* conservado, en conserva.

preside [prɪzáɪd], *vi.* and *vt.* presidir.— *to p. at o over a meeting*, presidir

una reunión o asamblea.—**presidency** [prézɪdɛnsɪ], *s.* presidencia.—**president** [prézɪdɛnt], *s.* presidente.—**presidential** [prezɪdénśal], *a.* presidencial.

press [pres], *vt.* prensar; comprimir; exprimir; pisar (el acelerador, la uva, el pedal, etc.); oprimir (el botón); planchar (ropa); abrumar, oprimir; presionar, obligar, apremiar; acosar; hostigar; abrazar, dar un apretón.—*pressed for money*, apurado de dinero.—*vi.* pesar, ejercer presión; urgir, apremiar; apiñarse; ser importuno; influir en el ánimo. —*to p. forward* or *on*, avanzar, adelantarse; arremeter, embestir.— *s.* muchedumbre; apiñamiento; empujón, apretón; prisa, presión, urgencia; cúmulo de negocios; (mec.) prensa; imprenta; prensa (periódica); escaparate, armario; (mil.) leva, enganche.—*p. agent*, agente de publicidad.—*p. box*, tribuna de la prensa.—*p. clipping*, *p. cutting*, recorte de periódico.—*p. conference*, entrevista de prensa.—*p. gang*, (mil.) patrulla de reclutamiento.—*p. proof*, (impr.) prueba de prensa.— **—ing** [présɪŋ], *a.* urgente, apremiante importante; importuno.—*s.* prensado, prensadura; compresión, presión.— **—ure** [préśʊ(r)], *s.* presión; urgencia; apretón; opresión; fuerza electromotriz.

prestige [prestíź], *s.* prestigio, fama.

prestidigitator [prestɪdídźɪteɪtɒ(r)], *s.* prestidigitador.

presumable [prɪzjúmabl], *a.* presumible. —**presume** [prɪzjúm], *vt.* presumir, suponer; (con *to*) atreverse a.—*vi.* jactarse, presumir; obrar presuntuosamente; (con *on* o *upon*) abusar de.—**presumption** [prɪzʌ́mpśɒn], *s.* presunción, conjetura; suposición; engreimiento, soberbia.—**presumptuous** [prɪzʌ́mpchʊas], *a.* presuntuoso, presumido; insolente; atrevido.

presuppose [prɪsʌpóʊz], *vt.* presuponer. —**presupposition** [prɪsʌpozíśɒn], *s.* conjetura.

pretend [prɪténd], *vt.* aparentar, fingir, simular; alegar o afirmar falsamente.—*vi.* fingir; presumir, alardear.—*to p. to*, pretender, reclamar, aspirar a.—*to p. to be*, echárselas de, darse por, hacerse el.— **—er** [-œ(r)], *s.* pretendiente (a la corona o trono); el que finge.—**pretense** [prɪténs, príténs], *s.* fingimiento; pretexto, excusa; máscara, capa, velo; pretensión; ostentación; afectación, simulación.—*under false pretenses*, con falsas apariencias, con dolo.—*under p. of*, so pretexto de, a título de.—**pre-**

tentious [prǐtḗnšʌs], *a.* presuntuoso, presumido, de o con pretensiones.

preterit(e) [prḗtẹrǐt], *a.* y *s.* pretérito.

pretext [prítekst], *s.* pretexto, excusa.

prettily [prítǐlǐ], *adv.* lindamente, bonitamente.—**prettiness** [prítǐnǐs], *s.* lindeza, galanura.—**pretty** [prítǐ], *a.* lindo, bonito, (fam.) mono; bello, bueno, grande.—*a p. mess you made,* buena la hizo usted.—*a p. penny,* (fam.) una buena suma.—*adv.* algo; un poco, bastante.—*p. good,* bastante bueno.—*p. much,* bastante; casi.—*p. well,* medianamente, así así.

prevail [prǐvéǐl], *vi.* prevalecer, preponderar; ser muy frecuente; estar en boga; (con over o against) vencer a, triunfar de; sobresalir, predominar.—*to p. on, upon* o *with,* persuadir, inducir, convencer.—**prevalence** [prḗvạlẹns], *s.* predominio, preponderancia; frecuencia.—**prevalent** [prḗvạlẹnt], *a.* prevaleciente, común, muy generalizado.

prevent [prǐvént], *vt.* prevenir, precaver, evitar, impedir, desbaratar.—*vi.* obviar.—**ion** [prǐvénšọn], *s.* prevención; obstáculo, estorbo.—**ive** [prǐvéntǐv], *a.* preventivo.—*s.* preservativo, profiláctico.

previous [prívǐʌs], *a.* previo, anterior.

prey [preǐ], *s.* presa; pillaje, rapiña; víctima.—*vi.* (con on o upon), devorar (la presa); rapiñar, robar; consumir, oprimir, agobiar.

price [praǐs], *s.* precio; importe, valor.—*vt.* valuar, fijar o poner precio a.—**less** [praǐslǐs], *a.* inapreciable; sin precio.

prick [prǐk], *vt.* punzar, picar, pinchar; marcar, indicar o calcar con agujerillos; causar una punzada (dolor punzante); puntear (marcar con puntos).—*to p. on* o *forward,* aguijonear, incitar.—*to p. up one's ears,* aguzar, erguir o enderezar las orejas.—*vi.* sentir una punzada (dolor punzante); erguirse o estar erguido; picarse (el vino).—*s.* aguijón, acicate; garrocha; puntura, picadura, punzadura, pinchazo; agujerillo; (fig.) escozor, espina, remordimiento.—**le** [prǐkl], *s.* pincho, púa, espina.—*vt.* y *vi.* producir o sentir picazón.—**ly** [prǐklǐ], *a.* lleno de púas o puntas, espinoso.—*p. heat,* salpullido.—*p. pear,* higo chumbo; (Am.) tuna.

pride [praǐd], *s.* orgullo; engreimiento, vanidad; altivez, arrogancia; dignidad, amor propio; brío; persona o cosa predilecta, la flor y nata, causa de satisfacción.—*to take p. in,* ufanarse o preciarse de.—*vr.* enorgullecerse o jactarse (de).—**ful**

[práǐdfụl], *a.* orgulloso, arrogante, vanidoso.

priest [prist], *s.* sacerdote; cura, clérigo.— **hood** [prísthụd], *s.* sacerdocio; casta sacerdotal.

prig [prǐg], *s.* persona pedante, mojigata o melindrosa.— **gish** [prígǐš], *a.* pedantesco; gazmoño.

prim [prǐm], *a.* afectadamente formal o pudoroso; remilgado; etiquetero, relamido, estirado, (fam.) almidonado.

primacy [práǐmạsǐ], *s.* primacía; supremacía; precedencia.—**primal** [práǐmạl], *a.* primordial; principal.

primarily [práǐmerǐlǐ], *adv.* primariamente, en primer lugar; originalmente; principalmente.—**primary** [práǐmerǐ], *a.* primario, primero; primitivo; fundamental, principal; elemental.—*s.* (lo) primero; comicios preliminares; circuito primario; ala de un insecto.

prime [praǐm], *s.* la flor (de la vida, edad, etc.); albor, principio; alba, aurora, amanecer; la flor y nata, lo mejor; (igl.) (Hora) prima; número primo; (esgr.) primera; (impr.) virgulilla, signo (').—*a.* primero, principal; primoroso, de primera clase; selecto; original, prístino; (mat.) primo; (impr.) marcado con el signo (').—*p. mover,* fuente natural de energía o fuerza motriz; máquina generadora de energía; móvil primero; alma, palanca (de una empresa).—*vt.* informar, instruir previamente; cebar (un carburador, arma, etc.); dar la primera capa de pintura; poner el signo (').

primer [prímœ(r)], *s.* cartilla, libro primero de lectura; devocionario.

primitive [prímǐtǐv], *a.* primitivo, original; (biol.) rudimentario.—*s.* y *a.* (b.a.) primitivo (artista u obra).

primp [prǐmp], *vt.* y *vi.* vestir(se) con afectación; acicalar(se); portarse afectadamente.

primrose [prímrọuz], *s.* (bot.) primavera; color amarillo claro.—*a.* florido, gayo.—*p. path,* vida sensual.

prince [prǐns], *s.* príncipe.—*p. of the royal blood,* infante.— **ly** [prǐnslǐ], *a.* principesco, regio.—*adv.* principescamente.— **ss** [prǐnsǐs], *s.* princesa.

principal [prǐnsǐpạl], *a.* principal, esencial, capital; máximo; (arq.) maestro.—*s.* principal, jefe; director o rector (de escuela o colegio primarios o secundarios); (for.) causante, constituyente; (com.) capital o principal (puesto a interés); (arq.) jamba de fuerza.—**principle** [prǐnsǐpl], *s.* principio, origen; fundamento, motivo,

razón; principio (regla, ley); (quim.) principio activo.

print [prɪnt], *vt.* estampar, imprimir; tirar, hacer una tirada; publicar; escribir imitando letra de molde.— *s.* impresión, estampa; tipo o letra de molde; impreso, folleto, volante, periódico, etc.; grabado; estampado; molde.—*pl.* estampados.—*in p.*, impreso, publicado; en letra de molde. —*out of p.*, (edición) agotada.— —**er** [prɪntœ(r)], *s.* impresor, tipógrafo.— —**ing** [-ɪŋ], *s.* imprenta, tipografía; impresión; tirada; impreso; estampado.—*a.* de imprenta, de imprimir.

prior [prɑɪǫ(r)], *a.* anterior, precedente. —*p to*, antes de.—*s.* prior.— —**ity** [prɑɪáriti], *s.* prioridad.

prism [prɪzm], *s.* prisma; espectro solar.

prison [prɪzǫn], *s.* prisión, encierro, cárcel.—*p. term*, duración de la condena.— —**er** [-œ(r)], *s.* prisionero, recluso.

pristine [prɪstin], *a.* prístino.

privacy [prɑɪvǫsi], *s.* retiro, aislamiento, retraimiento; independencia de la vida privada; el derecho a esa independencia; reserva, secreto.— **private** [prɑɪvit], *a.* privado; particular; personal, confidencial; secreto, oculto; reservado, excusado.—*s.* soldado raso.—*pl.* partes pudendas.— **privation** [prɑɪvéɪǫn], *s.* privación; carencia; falta de bienestar, estrechez. —**privative** [prɪvǫtiv], *a.* privativo. —*s.* negación.

privilege [prɪvilidʒ], *s.* privilegio.—*vt.* privilegiar; (from) eximir.— —**d** [-d], *a.* privilegiado, exento.

privy [prɪvi], *a.* (con to) informado, enterado (en); particular, propio, personal; (ant.) privado, secreto, excusado.—*s.* retrete, letrina.

prize [prɑɪz], *s.* premio, galardón; presa, botín; adquisición, ganancia, ventaja.—*vt.* apreciar, estimar; valuar, tasar.

pro [prou], *adv.* en favor; por.—*s.* voto afirmativo; (dep. fam.) profesional. —*p. and con*, en pro y en contra.

probability [prabǫbɪliti], *s.* probabilidad.—**probable** [prábǫbl], *a.* probable, verosímil; fácil, regular.

probation [probéɪǫn], *s.* prueba, ensayo; noviciado, meritoriado.—*on p.*, a prueba.

probe [proub], *s.* (cir.) sonda, cánula; prueba, ensayo; indagación.—*vt.* (cir.) sondear, explorar; indagar.

probity [próubiti], *s.* probidad, hombría de bien.

problem [práblem], *s.* problema; cuestión.— —**atic(al)** [prablemǽtik(ǫl)], *a.* problemático.

procedure [prosídʒǫ(r)], *s.* proceder, procedimiento, conducta; (for.) procedimiento(s) judicial(es).—**proceed** [prosíd], *vi.* seguir (adelante), proseguir; marchar, adelantar, avanzar; proceder, obrar.—*to p. to business*, ir a lo que importa; poner manos a la obra; entrar en materia.—**proceeding** [prosídɪŋ], *s.* procedimiento, conducta, proceder; transacción; trámite; proceso.—*pl.* actas; (for.) actuaciones, autos.—**proceeds** [próusidz], *s.* producto, réditos; ingresos.

process [práses], *s.* procedimiento, método, sistema; proceso (conjunto o serie de fenómenos naturales); progreso, continuación; curso, serie, sucesión; (for.) causa, proceso, expediente, autos.—*vt.* someter a procedimiento especial, tratar, industrializar, elaborar; (for.) procesar.

procession [proséʃǫn], *s.* procesión; desfile; cortejo.

proclaim [prokléɪm], *vt.* proclamar; promulgar; pregonar, vocear.—**proclamation** [praklǫméɪʃǫn], *s.* proclamación; proclama, edicto, bando.

proclivity [proklíviti], *s.* propensión, tendencia, inclinación.

procrastinate [prokrǽstineit], *vt.* y *vi.* diferir, aplazar, dejar para mañana; ser moroso.

procreate [próukrieit], *vt.* procrear, engendrar.

procure [prokiúr], *vt.* procurar, obtener, conseguir; causar, ocasionar.—*vt.* y *vi.* alcahuetear.— —**r** [-œ(r)], *s.* alcahuete.— —**ss** [-is], *s.* alcahueta.

prod [prad], *vti.* [1] punzar, picar, aguijonear.—*s.* pincho; picadura, pinchazo.

prodigal [prádigǫl], *a.* pródigo.—*s.* pródigo, manirroto, derrochador.— —**ity** [pradigǽliti], *s.* prodigalidad.

prodigious [prodídʒʌs], *a.* prodigioso; ingente.—**prodigy** [prádidʒi], *s.* prodigio; portento.

produce [prodjús], *vt.* producir; causar; mostrar, presentar; (com.) rendir, rentar; (teat.) montar o poner en escena una obra; (geom.) prolongar. —*vi.* producir; fructificar.—*s.* [prádjus], producto, producción, fruto; productos agrícolas, provisiones.— —**r** [prodjúsœ(r)], *s.* productor; (teat.) empresario; generador, gasógeno.— **product** [prádʌkt], *s.* producto; resultado, efecto, fruto; (com.) rendimiento, renta; (mat.) producto.— **production** [prodʌkʃǫn], *s.* producción; presentación; (teat.) representación.—**productive** [prodʌktiv], *a.* productivo; generador; fecundo.— **productiveness** [prodʌktivnis], **pro-**

ductivity [proụdʌktívitị], *s.* productividad; fecundidad.

profanation [prafạnéiṣọn], *s.* profanación.—**profane** [proféịn], *a.* profano; secular; impío, blasfemo, irreverente. —*vt.* profanar; desacatar.

profess [profés], *vt.* profesar, creer en; declarar, manifestar; fingir, aparentar; enseñar (como profesor); ejercer una profesión.— —**ion** [proféṣọn], *s.* profesión.— —**ional** [proféṣọnạl], *a.* profesional, facultativo; de profesión. —*s.* profesional; deportista de profesión.— —**or** [-ọ(r)], *s.* profesor, catedrático.— —**orship** [-ọrṣịp], *s.* profesorado, cátedra.

proffer [práfœ(r)], *vt.* proponer, ofrecer, brindar.—*s.* oferta, propuesta, ofrecimiento.

proficiency [profíṣẹnsị], *s.* aprovechamiento, adelanto; pericia, habilidad. —**proficient** [profíṣẹnt], *a.* proficiente; experto, perito.

profile [próufaịl], *s.* contorno; perfil. —*in p.,* de perfil.—*vt.* perfilar; recortar.

profit [práfịt], *s.* provecho, beneficio, ventaja; fruto; beneficio; lucro, ganancia, utilidad.—*clear p.,* beneficio neto.—*p.-sharing system,* sistema cooperativo.—*vt.* aprovechar a, servir.—*vi.* sacar utilidad o provecho, ganar.—*to p. by,* sacar partido de, beneficiarse de.— —**able** [-ạbl], *a.* provechoso, útil, beneficioso, ventajoso; productivo, lucrativo.— —**eer** [prafịtíːr], *vi.* usurear, explotar con agio.—*s.* usurero, explotador.

profound [profáụnd], *a.* profundo; hondo; intenso; recóndito; pesado (sueño).— —**ness** [-nịs], **profundity** [profʌ́ndịtị], *s.* profundidad, hondura.

profuse [profíús], *a.* profuso; pródigo.— —**ness** [-nịs], **profusion** [profíúʒọn], *s.* profusión, abundancia, prodigalidad.

progenitor [prodʒénịtọ(r)], *s.* progenitor.

progeny [prádʒẹnị], *s.* progenie, prole, linaje.

program [próụgræm], *s.* programa, agenda; plan.

progress [prágres], *s.* progreso, adelanto; progresos, aprovechamiento; desarrollo, mejoramiento; marcha, curso.—*vt.* [progrés], adelantar, llevar adelante.—*vi.* progresar, hacer progresos.— —**ive** [progrésịv], *a.* progresivo; progresista.—*s.* progresista.

prohibit [proụhíbịt], *vt.* prohibir, vedar; impedir.— —**ion** [proụ(h)ịbíṣọn], *s.* prohibición, veda; veto.— —**ive** [proụhíbịtịv], *a.* prohibitivo.

project [prodʒékt], *vt.* proyectar; trazar, dibujar; idear; echar, arrojar, despedir.—*vi.* resaltar, sobresalir, destacarse.—*s.* [prádʒekt], proyecto; plano; empresa; (educ.) tema (en que el alumno tiene que investigar).— —**ile** [prodʒéktịl], *s.* proyectil.—*a.* proyectante, arrojadizo.- —**ion** [prodʒékṣọn], *s.* lanzamiento, echamiento; resalte; (arq.) vuelo, saliente; plan, proyecto; (geom.) proyección.— —**or** [prodʒéktọ(r)], *s.* proyectista; proyector (de cine, etc.); aparato de proyección.

proletarian [proụletérịạn], *a. y s.* proletario.—**proletariat** [proụletérịạt], *s.* proletariado.

prolific [prolífịk], *a.* prolífico, fecundo, fértil.

prologue [próụlag], *s.* prólogo.—*vt.* prologar.

prolong [prolóŋ], *vt.* prolongar, extender.— —**ation** [proloŋgéiṣọn], *s.* prolongación.

promenade [pramenád], *vi.* pasear(se). —*s.* paseo (lugar y acto); caminata, vuelta.

prominence [prámịnẹns], *s.* eminencia, altura, relieve, distinción; prominencia, protuberancia; apófisis.—**prominent** [prámịnẹnt], *a.* prominente.

promiscuous [promískyụạs], *a.* promiscuo.

promise [prámịs], *s.* promesa; cosa comprometida; esperanza.—*vt. y vi.* prometer, ofrecer; dar o hacer concebir esperanzas.—**promising** [prámịsịŋ], *a.* que promete, prometedor, halagüeño.—**promissory** [prámịsọrị], *a.* promisorio.—*p. note,* pagaré, vale.

promontory [prámọntọrị], *s.* (geog.) promontorio, punta, cabo; (anat.) promontorio, eminencia.

promote [promóụt], *vt.* promover, fomentar; provocar, suscitar; alentar, estimular; mejorar, ascender; (com.) agenciar, gestionar; capitalizar y organizar (una empresa).— —**r** [-œ(r)], *s.* promotor; gestor; agente de negocios.—**promotion** [promóụṣọn], *s.* promoción, ascenso; fomento.

prompt [prampt], *a.* pronto, listo, expedito; puntual.—*vt.* impulsar, mover, incitar; (teat.) apuntar; indicar, sugerir; (fam.) soplar, decirle a otro en voz baja lo que debe contestar.— —**er** [prámptœ(r)], *s.* (teat.) apuntador, traspunte; incitador.— —**ness** [-nịs], *s.* prontitud; puntualidad.

prone [proụn], *a.* postrado; inclinado, pendiente; dispuesto, propenso.— —**ness** [próụnịs], *s.* postración; propensión.

prong [praŋ], *s.* púa, diente, punta

(de tenedor, horquilla, etc.); pitón de asta; punta de colmillo.

pronoun [próunaun], *s.* pronombre.

pronounce [pronáuns], *vt.* pronunciar. —*vi.* pronunciar; hablar magistralmente.— —d [-t], *a.* pronunciado, marcado, fuerte, subido.— —ment [-ment], *s.* pronunciamiento, declaración.—**pronunciation** [pronʌnsiéiṣon], *s.* pronunciación.

proof [pruf], *s.* prueba; impenetrabilidad; comprobación.—*to be p. against,* ser o estar a prueba de.—*to put to the p.,* poner a prueba.—*a.* impenetrable, resistente; de prueba.—*p. sheet,* prueba de imprenta.— —read [prúfrid], *vti.* y *vii.* [9] leer y corregir pruebas.—[prúfred], *pret.* y *pp.* de TO PROOFREAD.— —reader [-ridœ(r)], *s.* corrector de pruebas.— —reading [-ridiŋ], *s.* corrección de pruebas.

prop [prap], *vti.* [1] sostener, apuntalar, afianzar; (fig.) mantener, sustentar. —*s.* apoyo, puntal; (fig.) apoyo, báculo.—*pl.* (fam.) piernas.

propaganda [prapagǽndǝ], *s.* propaganda.—**propagandist** [prapǝgǽndist], *s.* y *a.* propagandista.—**propagate** [prápǝgeit], *vti.* propagar; diseminar; propalar.—*vi.* propagarse, reproducirse; cundir.—**propagation** [prapǝgéiṣon], *s.* propagación, generalización, reproducción, diseminación, difusión.

propel [propél], *vti.* [1] propulsar, impeler, empujar.— —er [-œ(r)], *s.* impulsor, propulsor; hélice.—*p. shaft,* (aut.) eje cardán.

proper [prápœ(r)], *a.* propio, conveniente; decoroso, formal; justo, exacto; propiamente dicho; (her.) natural.— —ty [-ti], *s.* propiedad; hacienda, caudal, bienes inmuebles; posesión, dominio, pertenencia.— *personal p.,* bienes muebles.—*pl.* (teat.) guardarropía, (Am.) utilería.

prophecy [práfesi], *s.* profecía, predicción.—**prophesy** [práfesai], *vti.* y *vii.* [7] profetizar, predecir.—**prophet** [práfit], *s.* profeta.—**prophetic(al)** [profétik(ǝl)], *a.* profético.

prophylactic [proufilǽktik], *a.* y *s.* profiláctico.

propitiate [propíṣieit], *vt.* propiciar, conciliar.—**propitious** [propíṣʌs], *a.* propicio; oportuno.

proportion [propórṣon], *s.* proporción; simetría; armonía.—*pl.* tamaño, dimensiones.—*in p. as,* a medida que. —*out of p.,* desproporcionado.—*vt.* proporcionar, armonizar.— —al [-ǝl], *a.* proporcional.—*s.* (mat.) número o cantidad proporcional.

proposal [propóuzǝl], *s.* propuesta, proposición, oferta; declaración de

amor.—**propose** [propóuz], *vt.* proponer; proponerse, pensar, tener intención de.—*vi.* declararse (a una mujer).—**proposition** [prapozíṣon], *s.* proposición, propuesta; (log. y mat.) proposición; (mus.) tema; (fam.) cosa, asunto, problema, etc.

propound [propáund], *vt.* proponer; presentar.

proprietary [propráieteri], *a.* propietario; patentado (medicinas).—*s.* propietario; hacendados, propietarios; propiedad; remedio de patente.

proprietor [propráieto(r)], *s.* propietario, dueño, amo.—**propriety** [propráieti], *s.* propiedad, corrección; decoro, decencia.—*pl.* normas o cánones (del arte, sociales, etc.).

propulsion [propʌ́lṣon], *s.* propulsión; impulso, impulsión.

pro rata [prou réitǝ], a prorrata.— **prorate** [prouréit], *vt.* prorratear.

prosaic [prozéiik], *a.* prosaico; insulso, trivial.

proscribe [proskráib], *vt.* proscribir; encartar; prohibir; condenar, reprobar.

prose [prouz], *s.* prosa.—*a.* de prosa, en prosa; insulso, pesado.

prosecute [prásikiut], *vt.* continuar, (pro)seguir, llevar adelante; (for.) acusar, encausar, enjuiciar, procesar. —*vi.* querellarse ante el juez; seguir un pleito; fiscalizar.—**prosecution** [prasikiúṣon], *s.* prosecución, (pro)seguimiento; (for.) procesamiento; acusación; ministerio fiscal.—**prosecutor** [prásikiuto(r)], *s.* (for.) acusador; fiscal.

prosody [prásodi], *s.* prosodia; métrica.

prospect [práspekt], *vt.* y *vi.* (min.) explorar, buscar.—*s.* perspectiva, panorama; probabilidad; expectativa; situación, orientación; (min.) indicación o señal de veta; cata, muestra; (com.) comprador o parroquiano probable.— —ive [prospéktiv], *a.* anticipado, venidero, en perspectiva; presunto.—*s.* perspectiva, vista.— —or [práspekto(r)], *s.* explorador o buscador de minas, petróleo, etc.— —us [prospéktʌs], *s.* prospecto, programa.

prosper [práspœ(r)], *vi.* prosperar, medrar.— —ity [praspériti], *s.* prosperidad.— —ous [-ʌs], *a.* próspero, floreciente; favorable o propicio.

prostitute [prástitiut], *vt.* y *vi.* prostituir(se).—*s.* prostituta, ramera.— **prostitution** [prastitiúṣon], *s.* prostitución.

prostrate [prástreit], *a.* postrado, prosternado, humillado.—*vt.* tender, postrar; demoler, derribar; arruinar; (med.) postrar, debilitar.—*vi.*

postrarse, prosternarse.—**prostration** [prastréjŝǫn], *s.* postración, abatimiento, depresión.

protagonist [protǽgǫnist], *s.* protagonista.

protect [protékt], *vt.* proteger.— —**ion** [protékŝǫn], *s.* protección.— —**ive** [-iv], *a.* protector; (e.p.) proteccionista.— —**or** [-ǫ(r)], *s.* protector.— —**orate** [-ǫrit], *s.* protectorado.

protégé [próytǎžei], *s.* protegido, paniaguado.

protein [próyti(i)n], *s.* proteína.

protest [protést], *vt.* protestar, declarar; (com.) protestar (una letra).—*vi.* protestar.—*s.* [próytest], protesta-(ción); (com.) protesto.— —**ant** [prátiştǎnt], *a. y s.* (P.) (igl.) protestante.— —**antism** [prátiştǎntizm], *s.* (P.) protestantismo.— —**ation** [pratestéjŝǫn], *s.* protesta(ción); declaración.

protocol [próytokal], *s.* protocolo, registro.

protoplasm [próytoplæzm], *s.* protoplasma.

prototype [próytotajp], *s.* prototipo.

protract [protrǽkt], *vt.* alargar, prolongar; trazar con el transportador (en un plano).

protrude [protrúd], *vt.* empujar hacia afuera, hacer sobresalir.—*vi.* sobresalir, resaltar.

protuberance [protjúbęrǎns], *s.* protuberancia, prominencia.—**protuberant** [protjúbęrǎnt], *a.* protuberante, prominente, saliente.

proud [prayd], *a.* orgulloso; soberbio, arrogante, altanero; majestuoso; (poét.) brioso, pujante.—*to be p. of*, enorgullecerse de, ufanarse de.

prove [pruv], *vti.* [6] probar, demostrar; comprobar; acreditar, evidenciar; poner a prueba; (for.) abrir y hacer público (un testamento); (imp.) sacar prueba de.—*vii.* resultar, venir a parar, salir (bien o mal); demostrar, dar prueba de.

proverb [práværb], *s.* proverbio; adagio, refrán.— —**ial** [provérbiǎl], *a.* proverbial.

provide [provájd], *vt.* proveer, proporcionar, surtir, abastecer, suministrar; estipular.—*vi.* (con **for**) mantener, proveer lo necesario, sufragar gastos, abastecer de víveres; encargarse de; tener en cuenta; precaverse, tener cuidado; dar disposiciones para, sobre o con respecto.—*provided (that)*, con tal que, a condición de que, siempre que.

providence [právidęns], *s.* providencia; prudencia; frugalidad; (P.) la Providencia.—**providential** [pravidénŝǎl], *a.* providencial.

provider [provájdœ(r)], *s.* proveedor, abastecedor.—**providing** [provájdiŋ], *conj.* con tal que.

province [právins], *s.* provincia, región; obligación, incumbencia; esfera, competencia.—*that is not my p.*, eso no me toca, no es de mi incumbencia. —**provincial** [provínŝǎl], *a.* provincial; provinciano; rudo, grosero.—*s.* provinciano; (igl.) provincial.

provision [provížǫn], *s.* provisión, aprovisionamiento; medida, disposición, estipulación.—*pl.* provisiones, comestibles.— —**al** [-ǎl], *a.* provisional, interino.—**provisory** [provájzorį], *a.* provisional; condicional, que lleva estipulación.

provocation [pravokéjŝǫn], *s.* provocación; excitación, estímulo.—**provocative** [prováķǎtiv], *a.* provocativo, provocador.—*s.* estimulante.—**provoke** [provóyk], *vt.* provocar, irritar, encolerizar; excitar, incitar; causar, promover.—*vi.* causar enojo, excitar cólera.

prow [pray], *s.* proa.

prowess [práyįs], *s.* valentía; proeza, hazaña.

prowl [prayl], *vt. y vi.* rondar (para robar o vigilar); merodear; andar acechando; vagar.— —**er** [práyloe(r)], *s.* merodeador.

proximity [praksímiti], *s.* proximidad, inmediación.

proxy [práksi], *s.* apoderado, delegado; procuración, poder.—*by p.*, por poder.

prude [prud], *s.* mojigato, remilgado, gazmoño.

prudence [prúdęns], *s.* prudencia, cordura, circunspección.—**prudent** [prúdęnt], *a.* prudente, juicioso, circunspecto.

prudery [prúdœrį], *s.* melindre, mojigatería, remilgo, gazmoñería.—**prudish** [prúdiŝ], *a.* gazmoño, remilgado, melindroso.

prune [prun], *vt. y vi.* podar; expurgar. —*s.* ciruela pasa.

Prussian [prǽŝǎn], *a. y s.* prusiano.

pry [praj], *vti. y vii.* [7] espiar, acechar, atisbar, observar, registrar o escudriñar.—*to p. into*, fisgar, fiscalizar, curiosear, entremeterse, (fam.) husmear.—*to p. off*, despegar.—*s.* inspección, reconocimiento o registro escrupuloso; persona curiosa o entremetida; palanca, barra.— —**ing** [prájiŋ], *a.* fisgón, entremetido.

psalm [sam], *s.* salmo, himno.

pseudo [súdoy], *a.* seudo, falso.— —**nym** [súdonįm], *s.* seudónimo.

psyche [sájkį], *s.* psique; mente.— **psychiatric(al)** [sajkiǽtrįk(ǎl)], *a.* psiquiátrico.—**psychiatrist** [sajkájǎtrist], *s.* psiquiatra.—**psychiatry** [saj-

káiątri], *s.* psiquiatría.—**psychoanalysis** [saikoąnǽlįsis], *s.* psicoanálisis.—**psychoanalyst** [saikoǽnąlįst], *s.* psicoanalista.—**psychoanalyze** [saikoǽnąlaiz], *vt.* psicoanalizar.—**psychologic(al)** [saikoládźik(ąl)], *a.* psicológico.—**psychologist** [saikálodźist], *s.* psicólogo.—**psychology** [saikálodźi], *s.* psicología.—**psychopath** [sáikopæθ], *s.* psicópata.—**psychosis** [saikóuşis], *s.* psicosis.—**psychotherapy** [saikoθérapi], *s.* psicoterapia.—**psychotic** [saikátik], *s.* y *a.* psicótico, psicopático.

puberty [piúbœrti], *s.* pubertad.

public [páblik], *a.* público; común; notorio.—*p. prosecutor,* fiscal.—*s.* público.—**ation** [-éişǫn], *s.* publicación; divulgación; promulgación; proclama(ción).— —**ist** [páblişist], *s.* publicista.— **ity** [pablíşiti], *s.* publicidad.—**publish** [pábliş], *vt.* publicar; promulgar; editar.—*to p. the banns,* amonestar, correr las amonestaciones.—**publisher** [páblişœ(r)], *s.* editor.—**publishing** [páblişiŋ], *a.* editorial, de publicaciones.—*p. house,* casa editora, editorial.

puck [pak], *s.* duende travieso; disco de goma (en el hockey sobre hielo).

pucker [pákœ(r)], *vt.* (cost.) fruncir, plegar, recoger, arrugar.—*vi.* arrugarse.—*s.* (cost.) fruncido, pliegue, fuelle, arruga; (fam.) agitación.

pudding [púdiŋ], *s.* budín, pudín.—*p. dish o pan,* flanera, tortera.

puddle [pádl], *s.* charco, poza.

pudgy [pádźi], *a.* (fam.) regordete, gordinflón.

puerile [piúęril], *a.* pueril.

Puerto Rican [pwértǫ ríkąn], *a.* y *s.* = PORTO RICAN.

puff [paf], *s.* resoplido; soplo; bufido; bocanada, fumada; elogio exagerado; (cost.) bullón: especie de buñuelo.—*powder p.,* polvera, borla de polvos.—*p. adder,* víbora venenosa.—*p. box,* polvera, caja de polvos.—*p. of wind,* ráfaga, soplo, racha; ventolera.—*vt.* inflar; engreír; dar bombo; (cost.) abollonar; dar chupadas (pipa, tabaco, etc.).—*vi.* inflarse; engreírse; bufar; resoplar; jadear, hipar; echar bocanadas; fumar.—*to p. up,* hincharse, henchirse.— **y** [páfi], *a.* hinchado, inflado.

pug [pag], *s.* moño (del pelo); (alb.) torta.—*p. nose,* nariz respingada.

pugilist [piúdźilist], *s.* pugilista, púgil, boxeador.

pugnacious [pagnéişas], *a.* belicoso, peleador, discutidor.—**pugnacity** [pagnǽsiti], *s.* pugnacidad.

puke [piuk], *vt.* y *vi.* vomitar.

pull [pul], *vt.* tirar de; halar; estirar; sacar, arrancar (un diente, etc.); pelar, desplumar; bogar, remar; (fam.) sorprender, copar (un garito, etc.); prender (a uno); sacar (un arma).—*to p. a face,* hacer una mueca.—*to p. asunder o away,* arrancar o quitar con violencia.—*to p. back,* tirar hacia atrás; hacer recular o cejar.—*to p. down,* derribar, demoler; degradar; humillar, abatir.—*to p. in,* tirar hacia dentro; contener, refrenar.—*to p. in o to pieces,* hacer trizas, despedazar.—*to p. one's leg,* (fam.) tomarle el pelo a uno.—*to p. oneself together,* recobrar la calma; arreglarse, componerse.—*to p. out,* sacar, arrancar.—*to p. the trigger,* apretar el gatillo.—*to p. through,* sacar de dificultades o de un aprieto.—*to p. together,* llevarse bien; obrar de acuerdo.—*to p. up,* extirpar, desarraigar; contener, refrenar (un caballo); arrimar (una silla); subir (las persianas).—*vi.* tirar con esfuerzo; tironear, dar un tirón; ejercer tracción.—*to p. apart,* romperse por tracción.—*to p. for,* abogar por (una persona).—*to p. in,* llegar (un tren); contenerse, refrenarse.—*to p. through,* salir de un apuro.—*s.* tirón, estirón; tirador (de puerta, etc.); tracción; (fam.) influjo, influencia; (impr.) impresión con la prensa de mano; (dep.) ejercicio de remos, boga.- —**er** [púlœ(r)], *s.* el o lo que tira, saca o arranca; extractor.

pullet [púlit], *s.* polla, gallina a medio crecer.

pulley [púli], *s.* polea, trocla, garrucha; motón; (anat.) tróclea.—*p. block,* aparejo (de poleas).—*p. wheel* roldana.

pullman [púlmąn], *s.* (f.c.) coche salón; coche cama.

pullover [púlouvœ(r)], *s.* jersey, chaleco de lana.

pulmonary [pálmǫneri], *a.* pulmonar.

pulp [palp], *s.* pulpa.

pulpit [púlpit], *s.* púlpito.

pulsate [pálseit], *vi.* pulsar, latir rítmicamente.—**pulsation** [palséişǫn], *s.* pulsación, latido.—**pulse** [pals], *s.* pulso; pulsación; (bot.) legumbres colectivamente.—*to feel the p.,* tomar el pulso.

pulverize [pálvęraiz], *vt.* reducir a polvo, pulverizar.

pumice [pámis], *s.* piedra pómez.

pump [pamp], *s.* bomba (de agua, aire, etc.); zapatilla, escarpín.—*p. water,* agua de pozo.—*vt.* y *vi.* dar a la bomba, (Am.) bombear.—*to p. in,* inyectar (aire, etc.).—*to p. out,* achi-

car, sacar a bomba.—*to p. up*, inflar (un neumático, etc.).

pumpkin [pʌ́mpkin, pʌ́ŋkin], *s.* calabaza (planta y fruto).

pun [pʌn], *s.* equívoco, retruécano, juego de vocablos.—*vii.* [1] decir retruécanos o equívocos, jugar del vocablo.

punch [pʌnch], *vt.* punzar, taladrar, horadar con punzón; aguijar o conducir ganado; dar puñetazos.—*s.* punzón, sacabocado(s), máquina o aparato de taladrar; ponche (bebida); puñetazo; (fam.) energía, actividad.

punctual [pʌ́ŋkchual], *a.* puntual, exacto.—**punctuality** [pʌŋkchuǽliti], *s.* puntualidad.

punctuate [pʌ́ŋkchueit], *vt. y vi.* puntuar.—**punctuation** [pʌŋkchuéiṣǫn], *s.* (gram.) puntuación.

puncture [pʌ́ŋkchų(r)], *s.* pinchazo, perforación; puntura, punzadura, picad(ur)a; punción.—*vt.* punzar; pinchar, perforar, agujerear, picar.—*punctured wound*, herida hecha con un instrumento puntiagudo.

pungency [pʌ́ndẓensi], *s.* sabor picante; acerbidad, acrimonia, mordacidad.—**pungent** [pʌ́ndẓent], *a.* picante; punzante; acre, mordaz.

punish [pʌ́niṣ], *vt.* castigar.— **-ment** [-ment], *s.* castigo; pena, corrección.

puny [piúni], *a.* encanijado; diminuto; mezquino.

pup [pʌp], *s.* cachorro, perrillo.—*p. tent*, (fam.) tienda de campaña pequeña.

pupil [piúpil], *s.* (anat.) pupila; (for.) pupilo; discípulo, alumno.

puppet [pʌ́pit], *s.* títere, muñeco, monigote, maniquí, marioneta; (fig.) títere, que sirve de instrumento a otro.—*p. show*, función de títeres o marionetas.

puppy [pʌ́pi], *s.* cachorro, perrillo; (desp.) fatuo, petimetre.

purchase [pə́rchis], *vt.* comprar; adquirir.—*s.* compra; adquisición; (mec.) palanca, aparejo, maniobra.— **-r** [-œ(r)], *s.* comprador, marchante.

pure [piur], *a.* puro; neto; castizo.

purgative [pə́rgativ], *a.* purgativo, purgante.—*s.* (med.) purga, purgante.—**purgatory** [pə́rgatori], *s.* purgatorio.—**purge** [pœrdẓ], *vt.* purgar, purificar; depurar.—*vi.* purificarse.—*s.* (med.) purgante; purgación; depuración.

purification [piurifikéiṣǫn], *s.* purificación, depuración; expiación.—**purify** [piúrifai], *vii.* [7] purificar; purgar, limpiar, refinar; expiar; expurgar, depurar.—*vii.* purificarse.—**Puritan** [piúritan], *s. y a.* puritano.—**puritan-**

-ical [piuritǽnikal], *a.* puritano, riguroso, rígido, severo.—**purity** [piúriti], *s.* pureza; casticidad; limpieza (de sangre).

purple [pə́rpl], *a.* purpúreo, purpurino, morado; imperial, regio; brillante, vistoso.—*s.* púrpura; dignidad real o cardenalicia.

purport [pə́rport], *s.* significado; tenor, sustancia.—*vt. y vi.* [pœrpórt], significar, querer decir, implicar, dar a entender.

purpose [pə́rpǫs], *s.* propósito, fin, objeto, intención, mira; resultado, utilidad; voluntad, determinación; uso, caso.—*on p.*, de propósito, aposta.—*to come to the p.*, venir a cuento.—*to no p.*, inútilmente.—*vt. y vi.* proponer(se), intentar.— **-ful** [-ful], *a.* determinado, tenaz.

purr [pœr], *s.* ronroneo del gato; zumbido del motor.—*vi.* ronronear (el gato).

purse [pœrs], *s.* bolsa, bolso de bolsillo; portamonedas; talega, bolsa de dinero; (fig.) peculio, riqueza; colecta.—*p. bearer*, tesorero.— **-r** [pə́rsœ(r)], *s.* sobrecargo, comisario de a bordo.

pursue [pœrsiú], *vt. y vi.* perseguir, dar caza, acosar; (pro)seguir, continuar; seguir (una carrera), dedicarse a, ejercer; (for.) demandar, poner pleito, procesar.— **-r** [-œ(r)], *s.* perseguidor.—**pursuit** [pœrsiút], *s.* perseguimiento, persecución, caza; práctica, ejercicio; prosecución; busca; ocupación; pretensión; empeño.—*pl.* ocupaciones, estudios, investigaciones, actividades.

purvey [pœrvéi], *vt.* proveer, abastecer, suministrar.— **-or** [-ǫ(r)], *s.* proveedor, abastecedor.

pus [pʌs], *s.* pus, podre.

push [pųṣ], *vt.* empujar; propugnar, promover, activar; oprimir, pulsar; apremiar, obligar; importunar, molestar.—*to p. ahead o through*, pujar.—*to p. in*, encajar, hacer entrar.— *to p. off*, apartar con la mano; desalojar.—*to p. on*, incitar, aguijonear; apresurar.—*to p. out*, empujar hacia afuera; echar, expulsar.—*vi.* empujar, dar un empujón, dar empellones; apresurarse; acometer. —*to p. forward*, adelantarse dando empujones; adelantar, avanzar.— *to p. further*, seguir adelante.—*to p. in*, entremeterse.—*to p. off*, (mar.) desatracar.—*s.* impulso; empuje, empujón; arremetida; apuro, aprieto; (fam.) energía, iniciativa; (mil.) ofensiva.— **-cart** [pų́ṣkart], *s.* carretilla de mano.— **-er** [-æ(r)], *s.* persona emprendedora o agresiva.—

—ing [-iŋ], *a.* activo, emprendedor; agresivo.

pussy(cat) [púsi̱(kæt)], *s.* gatito, minino.

put [pu̱t], *vti.* poner; disponer, colocar; proponer, presentar; expresar, declarar; (dep.) lanzar (el peso).—*to p. across,* (fam.) realizar, llevar a cabo.—*to p. after,* poner detrás de (sitio); posponer a (tiempo).—*to p. a question,* hacer una pregunta.—*to p. back,* atrasar, retardar; devolver, reponer.—*to p. by,* guardar; arrinconar; desviar, apartar.—*to p. down,* poner (en el suelo, etc.); sofocar, reprimir; deprimir, abatir; depositar; anotar, apuntar; rebajar, disminuir; hacer callar.—*to p. forward,* adelantar; proponer como candidato. —*to p. in,* poner en, echar en o a, meter; poner, insertar, introducir, intercalar; presentar, hacer (reclamo, etc.); colocar (en un empleo, etc.); interponer (palabra, observación); (top., dib.) trazar (una curva, etc.); pasar o gastar (tiempo, haciendo algo).—*to p. in a word for,* interceder por, hablar en favor de.—*to p. in gear,* (aut.) hacer engranar.—*to p. in print,* imprimir.—*to p. off,* diferir, dilatar, aplazar; desechar, apartar; evadir, entretener (con promesas); quitarse, desprenderse de (ropa, etc.).—*to p. on,* poner sobre; ponerse (ropa, etc.); calzar (zapatos, etc.); echar, poner, dar, aplicar (vapor, el freno, etc.); instigar a; fingir, disimular; encender (las luces, el radio, etc.); (teat.) producir, representar, poner en escena.—*to p. out,* brotar, echar retoños; despedir, despachar, echar; apagar (la luz, el fuego); publicar; cegar; borrar, tachar; cortar, desconcertar; sacar de quicio; poner (dinero a interés), dar (a logro); extender, sacar, mostrar; enojar, irritar.—*to p. out of order,* descomponer, desordenar.—*to p. to flight,* poner en fuga, ahuyentar.—*to p. together,* juntar, acumular; (mec.) armar, montar; coordinar.—*to p. to it,* causar dificultad a, poner al parir.—*to p. to shame,* avergonzar.—*to p. up,* poner en su lugar, conservar; preparar, confeccionar; construir, erigir; (mec.) montar; presentar (como candidato); ofrecer, elevar; levantar (la mano); alojar, hospedar; enviar; ofrecer resistencia; (fam.) poner dinero en una apuesta; tramar, urdir.—*to p. up to,* incitar, instigar a; presentar o someter a; (fam.) dar instrucciones. —*to p. up with,* aguantar, soportar. —*vi.* (mar.) dirigirse, seguir rumbo.

—*pret.* y *pp.* de TO PUT.—*s.* acción del verbo TO PUT en cualquiera de sus acepciones.

putty [pᴧ́ti], *s.* masilla de aceite; cemento (esp. el de cal).—*p. knife,* espátula.—*vti.* [7] enmasillar, rellenar con masilla.

puzzle [pᴧ́zl], *s.* acertijo, adivinanza, rompecabezas; enigma, misterio, (fam.) problema arduo.—*vt.* confundir, poner perplejo; enmarañar, embrollar.—*to p. out,* resolver, descifrar, desenredar.—*vi.* estar perplejo. —*to p. over,* tratar de resolver, hincarle el diente a, devanarse los sesos sobre.

pygmy [pígmi̱], *s.* pigmeo.

pyramid [pi̱ramid], *s.* pirámide.—*vt.* y *vi.* aumentar(se), acumular(se).

pyre [pai̱r], *s.* pira, hoguera.

Q

quack [kwæk], *vi.* graznar; charlatanear; echárselas de médico; curar empíricamente o con sortilegios.—*s.* graznido del pato.—*s.* y *a.* charlatán. —*s.* curandero; medicucho, medicastro.— **—ery** [kwǽkœri̱], *s.* charlatanismo; fraude.

quadrant [kwádrᴀnt], *s.* cuadrante.

quadroon [kwadrún], *s.* cuarterón.

quadruped [kwádru̱ped], *s.* y *a.* cuadrúpedo.

quadruple [kwádrupl], *a.* cuádruple, cuádruplo.—*vt.* y *vi.* cuadruplicar(se). — **—ts** [kwádruplits], *s. pl.* gemelos cuádruples.

quagmire [kwǽgmai̱r], *s.* tremedal, cenagal; atolladero.

quail [kwei̱l], *s.* codorniz; perdiz.—*vi.* acobardarse, decorazonarse; cejar.

quaint [kwei̱nt], *a.* singular, curioso; pintoresco; original, raro.— **—ness** [kwéi̱ntni̱s], *s.* rareza, singularidad, pintorequismo.

quake [kwei̱k], *s.* temblor.—*vi.* temblar, trepidar, estremecerse.

qualification [kwali̱fi̱kéi̱şon], *s.* calificación, requisito; c(u)alidad, capacidad, idoneidad; título, habilitación; atenuación, mitigación; limitación; salvedad.—*without q.,* sin reservas o reparos.—**qualify** [kwali̱fai̱], *vti.* [7] capacitar, habilitar, hacer idóneo; calificar; modificar, limitar, restringir; templar, suavizar.—*vii.* prepararse, habilitarse; llenar los requisitos; (E.U.) prestar juramento antes de entrar en funciones.— **qualitative** [kwáli̱tei̱ti̱v], *a.* cualitativo.—**quality** [kwali̱ti̱], *s.* c(u)alidad; clase, casta, jaez; propiedad, poder o virtud; categoría, distinción, alta posición social.

quantitative [kwántįteįtįv], *a.* cuantitativo.—**quantity** [kwántįtį], *s.* cantidad, cuantía, tanto; dosis; gran cantidad, gran número; (elec.) intensidad (de una corriente).

quarantine [kwárantin], *s.* cuarentena; estación de cuarentena.—*vt.* poner en cuarentena.

quarrel [kwárẹl], *s.* reyerta, pendencia, riña, disputa.—*vii.* [2] pelear, reñir, romper la amistad.—**some** [-sʌm], *a.* pendenciero.

quarry [kwárį], *s.* cantera, pedrera; caza, presa; cuadrado, rombo (de vidrio, teja, etc.).—*vti.* [7] explotar (canteras).

quart [kwort], *s.* cuarto de galón (Ver Tabla); (mus.) cuarta.— —**er** [kwórtœ(r)], *s.* cuarto, cuarta parte; arroba (Ver Tabla); trimestre; cuarto de hora; moneda de 25 centavos; cuarto de luna, etc.; origen, procedencia; región, comarca, distrito; barrio, barriada, vecindad; (carp.) entrepaño; cuartel, merced, clemencia.—*pl.* domicilio, vivienda, morada; (mil.) cuartel; alojamiento. —*a.* cuarto.—*vt.* descuartizar, hacer cuartos; dividir en cuatro partes iguales o en cuarteles; (mil.) acuartelar, acantonar; alojar, hospedar.— —**erly** [-œrlį], *a.* trimestral.—*q. payment*, trimestre.—*s.* publicación trimestral.—*adv.* trimestralmente; en cuartos, por cuartos.— —**ermaster** [-œrmæstœ(r)], *s.* (mil.) comisario; furriel.—*q. general*, intendente del ejército.— —**et**(te) [kwortét], *s.* cuatro personas o cosas de una misma clase; (mus., poét.) cuarteto.

quartz [kworts], *s.* cuarzo, sílice.

quash [kwaš], *vt.* sofocar, reprimir; anular, invalidar.

quatrain [kwátreįn], *s.* cuarteta, redondilla.

quaver [kwéįvœ(r)], *vi.* gorjear, trinar; temblar, vibrar.—*s.* gorjeo, trino; trémolo, vibración; (mus.) corchea.— —**ing** [-įŋ], *s.* gorgorito, trino, gorjeo.

quay [ki], *s.* muelle; (des)embarcadero.

Quechuan [kéchwạn], *s.* y *a.* quechua.

queen [kwin], *s.* reina.

queer [kwįr], *a.* extraño, raro; indispuesto, desfalleciente; (fam.) chiflado, excéntrico, estrafalario; (fam.) sospechoso, misterioso; (fam.) falso; (coll.) afeminado.—*s.* (fam.) moneda falsa.—*vt.* (fam.) comprometer, poner a uno en mal lugar; echar a perder; (fam.) ridiculizar.

quell [kwel], *vt.* reprimir, sofocar, domar, sojuzgar; calmar, mitigar (un dolor).

quench [kwench], *vt.* apagar, matar

(luz, fuego); calmar, apagar (la sed); ahogar, sofocar; sosegar; extinguir; templar (hierro).

query [kwįrį], *s.* pregunta; duda; (imp.) signo interrogante (?).—*vti.* [7] marcar con signo de interrogación; preguntar, indagar, pesquisar —*vii.* expresar una duda; preguntar.

quest [kwest], *s.* pesquisa, averiguación; busca.—*vi.* y *vt.* averiguar, investigar; buscar.

question [kwéschọn], *s.* pregunta, interrogación; cuestión, caso, asunto; problema; debate, controversia; proposición a discutir; objeción, discusión.—*beside the q.*, ajeno al asunto. —*beyond* o *without q.*, fuera de duda, indiscutible.—*out of q.*, sin duda, de veras.—*q.-begging*, de carácter de círculo vicioso.—*q. mark*, signo de interrogación.—*to ask a q.*, hacer una pregunta.—*to be out of the q.*, ser indiscutible; no haber que pensar en.—*to put the q.*, interrogar; torturar; someter a votación.—*vt.* preguntar; dudar, poner en tela de juicio; desconfiar de; oponerse a, objetar; recusar.—*vi.* inquirir, preguntar, escudriñar.— —**able** [-ạbl], *a.* problemático, dudoso, discutible, sospechoso.— —**naire** [kweschọnér], *s.* cuestionario, encuesta.

quick [kwįk], *a.* rápido, veloz, ágil; ardiente; penetrante, fino; irritable, petulante; disponible, efectivo; vivo. —*s.* carne viva; lo más hondo o profundo (del alma, de la sensibilidad); lo más delicado.—*to cut* (*hurt, offend, etc.*) *to the q.*, herir en lo vivo, en el alma o profundamente.—*adv.* con presteza, prontamente, velozmente.—*q.-sighted*, de vista aguda, penetrante.—*q.-tempered*, de genio vivo, irascible.—*q.-witted*, vivo de ingenio, listo, agudo, perspicaz.— —**en** [kwíkn], *vt.* vivificar, resucitar; avivar, urgir; excitar, aguzar, animar. —*vi.* avivarse, vivificarse, revivir; moverse más aprisa; ser más sensitivo.— —**lime** [-laįm], *s.* cal viva.— —**ly** [-lį], *adv.* prontamente, pronto, aprisa.— —**ness** [-nįs], *s.* presteza, vivacidad, prontitud, celeridad; sagacidad, viveza, penetración.— —**sand** [-sænd], *s.* arena movediza.— —**silver** [-sįlvœ(r)], *s.* azogue, mercurio.

quiet [kwáįẹt], *a.* quieto, quedo; sereno, tranquilo; callado, silencioso; sencillo, modesto; apacible; (com.) inactivo (mercado, etc.).—*to be q.*, callarse; guardar silencio.—*s.* quietud; silencio; tranquilidad, calma. —*on the q.*, (fam.) a la chita callando. —*vt.* acallar, apaciguar; tranquilizar, calmar.—*vi.* aquietarse, apaciguarse.—

—ness [-nįs], *s.* quietud, sosiego, tranquilidad, paz.

quill [kwįl], *s.* pluma de ave; cañón de pluma; cañón o pluma para escribir; escritor; púa del puerco espín; devanador, canutillo; estría, pliegue de un rizado.—*vt.* desplumar; (cost.) rizar, hacer un encarrujado.

quilt [kwįlt], *s.* colcha, cobertor acolchado, edredón.—*vt.* acolchar, acojinar.

quince [kwįns], *s.* membrillo.

quinine [kwáįnaįn], *s.* quinina.

quintessence [kwįntésęns], *s.* quintaesencia.

quintuple [kwįntįupl], *a.* y *s.* quíntuplo.—*vt.* y *vi.* quintuplicarse.

quip [kwįp], *s.* pulla, escarnio, mofa.—*vii.* [1] echar pullas, mofarse.

quit [kwįt], *vti.* [3] dejar, parar, cesar o desistir de; dejarse de, soltar, dejar ir, abandonar; renunciar; evacuar, desocupar; irse, salir o marcharse de.—*vii.* desistir; parar; cejar; irse, quitarse; abandonar (una empresa, una causa, a sus amigos, etc.), zafarse.—*pret.* y *pp.* de TO QUIT.—*a.* libre, descargado.—*to be quits,* estar en paz; quedar vengado; no deberse nada.—*to call it quits,* dar (algo) por terminado.

quite [kwaįt], *adv.* completamente, enteramente, absolutamente, del todo; verdadera, efectiva o justamente; (fam.) bastante, asaz, harto, más bien.—*q. a bit,* considerable, bastante.

quitter [kwį́tœ(r)], *s.* (metal.) escorias; el que se da fácilmente por vencido; desertor (de una causa, etc.).

quiver [kwį́vœ(r)], *s.* carcaj, aljaba; estremecimiento; temblor.—*vi.* temblar; estremecerse; palpitar.

quixotic [kwįksátįk], *a.* quijotesco.

quiz [kwįz], *s.* examen o serie de preguntas; chanza, broma, guasa; zumbón, chancero, guasón.—*vti.* [1] examinar a un discípulo o clase; tomar a guasa, chancearse o mirar con aire burlón.

quota [kwóųtạ], *s.* cuota, cupo; prorrata.

quotation [kwoųtéįšǫn], *s.* citación; cita; texto citado; (com.) cotización.—*q. marks,* comillas.—**quote** [kwoųt], *vt.* y *vi.* citar; repetir un texto; (com.) cotizar.—*s.* (fam.) cita.—*pl.* (fam.) comillas.

quotient [kwóųšęnt], *s.* (mat.) cociente.

R

rabbi [rǽbaį], *s.* rabí, rabino.— **—nical** [ræbínįkạl], *a.* rabínico.

rabbit [rǽbįt], *s.* conejo.—*r. hole,* conejera.

rabble [rǽbl], *s.* canalla, chusma, populacho.

rabid [rǽbįd], *a.* (med.) rabioso; fanático, violento, feroz.—**rabies** [réįbiz], *s.* rabia, hidrofobia.

raccoon [rækún], *s.* mapache, oso lavador.

race [reįs], *s.* raza; estirpe; carrera, corrida, regata.—*r. course* o *track,* pista de carreras; hipódromo.—*vt.* hacer competir en una carrera; hacer correr deprisa.—*vi.* correr deprisa; competir en una carrera.—*r* [réįsœ(r)], *s.* corredor; caballo de carrera; auto de carrera.

racial [réįšạl], *a.* racial, étnico, de (la) raza o de (las) razas.

rack [ræk], *s.* percha, colgador; bastidor; potro del tormento; dolor, pena, angustia; (mec.) cremallera.—*r. bar,* cremallera.—*to be on the r.,* estar en angustias.—*vt.* atormentar; agobiar.—*to r. one's brains,* devanarse los sesos.

racket [rǽkįt], *s.* raqueta; confusión, baraúnda; (fam.) parranda, francachela; (fam.) negocio turbio, trapisonda.—*vi.* meter bulla.— **—eer** [rækįtįr], *s.* bandido urbano que explota la extorsión, (Am., neol.) raquetero.—*vi.* extorsionar, extraer por la intimidación y la violencia.

racy [réįsį], *a.* picante.

radar [réįda(r)], *s.* radar.

radial [réįdįạl], *a.* radial.

radiance [réįdįạns], *s.* brillo, resplandor, esplendor.—**radiant** [réįdįạnt], *a.* radiante; resplandeciente, brillante.—**radiate** [réįdįeįt], *vt.* emitir, irradiar.—*vi.* radiar, brillar.—**radiation** [reįdįéįšǫn], *s.* radiación, irradiación.—**radiator** [réįdįeįtǫ(r)], *s.* aparato de calefacción; (aut., etc.) radiador.

radical [rǽdįkạl], *a.* y *s.* radical.

radio [réįdįoų], *s.* radio; radiocomunicación.—*by r.,* por radio, radiado.—*r. amateur, fan* o *ham,* radioaficionado.—*r. announcer,* locutor, anunciador.—*r. beacon,* radiofaro.—*r. frequency,* radiofrecuencia.—*r. listener,* radioyente, radioescucha.—*r. station,* (estación) emisora o difusora.—*vt.* y *vi.* radiar, radiodifundir.- **—active** [-ǽktįv], *a.* radioactivo.—**activity** [-æktívįtį], *s.* radioactividad.- **—logist** [-álodʒįst], *s.* radiólogo.

radish [rǽdįš], *s.* rábano.

radium [réįdįʌm], *s.* (quím.) radio.

radius [réįdįʌs], *s.* (geom. y anat.) radio; alcance.

raffle [rǽfl], *vt.* (gen. con **off**) rifar, sortear.—*s.* rifa, sorteo.

raft [ræft], *s.* balsa, almadía.—*vt.*

transportar en balsa; pasar en balsa.

rafter [ráftœ(r)], *s.* viga (de techo).

rag [ræg], *s.* trapo, andrajo, harapo; persona andrajosa; (mús.) tiempo sincopado.—*r. doll,* muñeca de trapo. —*vti.* [1] rasgar; poner en música sincopada o musiquilla.—*vii.* tocar musiquilla o música sincopada.

ragamuffin [rǽgamʌfin], *s.* galopín, golfo; pelafustán, pelagatos.

rage [rejdʒ], *s.* rabia, furor, cólera; (fam.) boga, moda.—*vi.* rabiar, bramar, encolerizarse, enfurecerse.

ragged [rǽgid], *a.* roto, desharrapado, andrajoso, harapiento; mellado, áspero.

raging [réjdʒiŋ], *a.* rabioso, furioso, bramador.—*r. fever,* calentura ardiente.

raid [rejd], *vt.* invadir; (fam.) entrar o apoderarse por fuerza legal; allanar. —*vi.* hacer una irrupción.—*s.* correría, irrupción, incursión; (fam.) invasión repentina.—*air r.,* ataque aéreo.

rail [rejl], *s.* pasamano, barandilla; antepecho; (f.c.) riel, rail, carril; ferrocarril.—*by r.,* por ferrocarril.— *vt.* (a veces con **in** u **of**) poner barandilla, barrera o verja.—*vi.* (con **at** o **against**) injuriar; protestar contra.- —*ing* [réjliŋ], *s.* baranda, barandilla, pasamano; cerca, verja, enrejado; (f.c.) rieles; material para rieles.

raillery [réjlœri], *s.* zumba, chocarrería.

railroad [réjlroud], *s.* ferrocarril, vía férrea.—*a.* ferroviario, de ferrocarril, para ferrocarriles.—*r. crossing,* paso a nivel.—*r. junction,* entronque.—*vt.* (fam.) apresurar; hacer aprobar (una ley, etc.) con precipitación; hacer encarcelar falsamente.

rain [rejn], *vi.* llover.—*r. or shine,* que llueva o no; con buen o mal tiempo.— *to r. cats and dogs,* llover a cántaros.— *s.* lluvia.—*r. water,* agua lluvia.- —*bow* [réjnbou], *s.* arco iris.- —*coat* [-kout], *s.* impermeable, (Am.) capa de agua.- —*drop* [-drap], *s.* gota de agua.- —*fall* [-fol], *s.* aguacero; lluvias; cantidad de lluvia caída.- —*y* [-i], *a.* lluvioso.—*for a r. day,* por lo que pueda tronar.

raise [rejz], *vt.* levantar, alzar, poner en pie; elevar; construir, erigir; aumentar, subir; promover, ascender; criar, cultivar; hacer brotar; reclutar, alistar; reunir, recoger o juntar (dinero); levantar (en la caza); fermentar (pan).—*to r. a point,* presentar una cuestión, hacer una observación.—*to r. Cain,* o *a racket,* o *a rumpus,* (fam.) armar un escándalo, un alboroto; armar un lío.—*s.* levantamiento, alzamiento; aumento (de sueldo); ascenso.

raisin [réjzin], *s.* pasa, uva seca.

rake [rejk], *s.* rastro, rastrillo; calavera, libertino, perdido.—*vt.* rastrillar; barrer; atizar (el fuego); (mil.) enfilar, barrer.—*to r. over the coals,* (fam.) despellejar, poner como un trapo.— *vi.* pasar el rastrillo; llevar una vida disoluta.

rally [rǽli], *vti.* [7] (mil.) reunir y reanimar.—*vii.* (mil.) reunirse, rehacerse; recobrar las fuerzas, revivir.— *s.* unión o reunión (de tropas dispersas o de gente); recuperación.

ram [ræm], *s.* carnero padre, morueco; (mec.) martinete, pisón; ariete hidráulico; (mar.) espolón.—*vti.* [1] apisonar; meter por la fuerza; atestar, henchir.

ramble [rǽmbl], *vi.* vagar, callejear; divagar, ir por las ramas; discurrir.— *s.* paseo.- —*r* [rǽmblœ(r)], *s.* vagabundo, callejero; paseador.

ramp [ræmp], *s.* rampa, declive.

rampart [rǽmpart], *s.* (fort.) terraplén; muralla; baluarte.

ramrod [rǽmrad], *s.* baqueta.

ramshackle [rǽmʃækl], *a.* desvencijado, destartalado, ruinoso.

ran [ræn], *pret.* de TO RUN.

ranch [rænch], *s.* (Am.) rancho, estancia; hacienda de ganado.—*vi.* tener hacienda de ganado.- —*er* [rénchœ(r)], *s.* (Am.) ranchero; ganadero.

rancid [rénsid], *a.* rancio.

rancor [rǽŋkœ(r)], *s.* rencor, encono, inquina.- —*ous* [-ʌs], *a.* rencoroso.

random [réndɔm], *a.* fortuito, casual, impensado; sin orden ni concierto.— *at r.,* a la ventura, al azar, a troche-moche.

rang [ræŋ], *pret.* de TO RING (tocar).

range [rejndʒ], *vt.* recorrer; poner en posición; poner en fila; (a veces con **in**) alinear; arreglar, clasificar.—*vi.* vagar; estar en línea; estar a la misma altura; variar, fluctuar; (arti.) tener alcance (un proyectil).—*s.* distancia; extensión, recorrido; alcance (de un arma o proyectil); pastizal; radio de acción; fila, hilera, clase, orden; cocina económica.—*at close r.,* a quema ropa.—*r. finder,* (arti.) telémetro.—*r. of mountains,* cadena de montañas, cordillera.—*to be within the r. of,* estar a tiro, al alcance de.- —*r* [réjndʒœ(r)], *s.* guardabosque; vigilante.

rank [ræŋk], *s.* rango, posición (social, etc.); (mil.) grado, graduación, categoría; línea, hilera; (mil.) fila.—*the ranks, the r. and file,* la tropa, los soldados de fila; las masas.—*vt.* clasificar, ordenar; colocar por grados; poner en fila.—*vi.* tener tal o cual grado o

clasificación; ocupar (primero, se-gundo, etc.) lugar; (con **with**) estar al nivel (de); (con **high, low**) ocupar (alta, baja) posición.—*a.* rancio; lozano; espeso; grosero; completo; fétido.

rankle [ránkl], *vi.* enconarse, infla-marse; causar resentimiento o enojo.

ransom [ránsǫm], *s.* rescate.—*vt.* res-catar, redimir.

rap [ræp], *vti. y vii.* [1] golpear, dar un golpe seco; (fam.) criticar, zaherir.— *to r. at the door,* tocar o llamar a la puerta.—*s.* golpe seco; (fam.) crítica. —*I don't care a r.,* no me importa un bledo.—*to take the r. for,* (fam.) pagar los vidrios rotos.

rapacious [rǫpéišʌs], *a.* rapaz.

rape [reip], *s.* violación, estupro.—*vt.* violar; forzar.

rapid [rǽpid], *a.* rápido, veloz.—*s. pl.* rápidos (de un río), rabión.— **—ity** [rǫpíditi], *s.* rapidez, velocidad.

rapine [rǽpin], *s.* rapiña.

rapt [ræpt], *a.* arrebatado o extasiado. —*r. in thought,* absorto.— **—ure** [rǽpchṳ(r)], *s.* rapto, arrobamiento, embeleso, éxtasis.

rare [rer], *a.* raro; precioso; extraordi-nario; (coc.) poco pasado, a medio pasar.— **—ly** [rérli], *adv.* raramente, rara vez, por rareza; sólo de tarde en tarde; excelente o extremamente. **—rarity** [réritį], *s.* rareza; curiosidad; tenuidad.

rascal [rǽskǫl], *s.* pícaro, bribón, be-llaco, pillo.— **—ity** [ræskǽliti], *s.* bribonería, bellaquería.

rash [ræš], *a.* temerario, imprudente, precipitado.—*s.* salpullido, erupción. — **—ness** [rǽšnis], *s.* temeridad, imprudencia, precipitación.

rasp [ræsp], *s.* chirrido, sonido estri-dente; ronquera; escofina, raspador. —*vt.* chirriar; escofinar; raspar.

raspberry [rǽzberi], *s.* (bot.) fram-buesa; (fam.) trompetilla, sonido de mofa.—*r. bush,* frambueso.

rat [ræt], *s.* rata; (fam.) postizo para el pelo.—*r. trap,* ratonera.—*to smell a r.,* recelar, haber gato encerrado.

rate [reit], *s.* tarifa, precio o valor fijo; tipo (de interés, etc.); proporción, tanto (por ciento, por unidad, etc.); modo, manera; clase.—*at any r.,* de todos modos, sea como sea, en todo caso.—*at that r.,* en esa proporción; de ese modo; a ese paso.—*at the r. of,* a razón de.—*r. of exchange,* cambio, tipo del cambio.—*vt.* tasar, valuar; clasificar; considerar, justipreciar; fijar precio, tarifa, etc.—*vi.* ser con-siderado (como); estar clasificado (como).

rather [rǽǒœ(r)], *adv.* bastante, un poco, algo; más bien, mejor dicho; antes bien.—*(I) had r.* o *would r.,* preferiría, más bien quisiera.—*r. than,* más bien que, en vez de, mejor que.

ratification [rætifįkéišǫn], *s.* ratifica-ción.—**ratify** [rǽtįfai], *vti.* [7] ratifi-car, confirmar.

rating [réitin], *s.* justiprecio; clasifica-ción (de un buque, marinero, etc.); (mec.) capacidad o potencia normal; clase, rango.

ratio [réišǫu], *s.* razón, relación, pro-porción.

ration [rǽšǫn, réišǫn], *s.* (mil.) ración.— *r. book* o *card,* cartilla o tarjeta de racionamiento.—*vt.* racionar.

rational [rǽšǫnǫl], *a.* racional.- **—iza-tion** [ræšǫnǫlizéišǫn], *s.* explicación racional de acciones, creencias, etc. **—ize** [rǽšǫnǫlaiz], *vt.* interpretar racionalmente; buscar explicación racional o justificativa de.

rationing [rǽšǫniŋ, réišǫniŋ], *s.* racio-namiento.

rattan [rætǽn], *s.* bejuco.

rattle [rǽtl], *vt.* hacer sonar como una matraca; batir o sacudir con ruido; (fam.) atolondrar, aturrullar; (con **off**) decir a la carrera.—*vi.* matra-quear; parlotear.—*s.* cascabel (de crótalo); sonajero; (Am.) maruga (juguete); matraca; estertor.—*r.-brained, r.-headed,* ligero de cascos, casquivano.- **—snake** [-snejk], *s.* culebra o serpiente de cascabel.

raucous [rɔkʌs], *a.* ronco; bronco; estentóreo.

ravage [rǽvidž], *vt.* saquear, pillar, asolar, destruir.—*s.* ruina, estrago, destrucción; saqueo, pillaje.

rave [reiv], *vi.* delirar, desvariar; dis-paratar; bramar, salirse de sus casillas.—*to r. over* o *about,* entusias-marse locamente por.

raven [réivn], *s.* cuervo.—*a.* negro brillante.

ravenous [rǽvenʌs], *a.* voraz, famélico; rapaz.

ravine [rǫvín], *s.* barranca, cañada, hondonada.

ravish [rǽviš], *vt.* arrebatar, atraer, encantar; violar, estuprar.- **—ing** [-iŋ], *a.* embriagador, arrebatador.

raw [rɔ], *a.* crudo; pelado, despellejado; descarnado; desapacible; fresco; nuevo; novato, bisoño (recluta, etc.); vulgar.—*r.-boned,* huesudo.—*r. cotton (silk),* algodón (seda) en rama.—*r. flesh,* en carne viva.—*r. material,* materia prima.- **—hide** [rɔhaid], *a.* de cuero sin curtir.—*s.* cuero crudo; látigo de cuero crudo.

ray [rei], *s.* rayo (de luz, calor, etc.); (ict.) raya.

rayon [réjan], *s.* rayón

raze [rejz], *vt.* arrasar, demoler, destruir.

razor [réjzǫ(r)], *s.* navaja de afeitar.— *r. blade,* hoja o cuchilla de afeitar.

reach [rich], *vt.* llegar a o hasta; alcanzar, lograr, conseguir; penetrar.—*to r. out one's hand,* tender la mano.— *vi.* extenderse, alcanzar.—*to r. into,* penetrar en.—*s.* alcance; extensión; poder.—*beyond one's r.,* fuera del alcance de uno.—*within one's r.,* al alcance de uno; dentro del poder de uno.

react [rię́kt], *vi.* reaccionar.— **—ion** [rię́kšǫn], *s.* reacción.— **—ionary** [rię́kšǫneri], *a.* y *s.* reaccionario.

reactor [rię́ktǫ(r)], *s.* (quím.) reactivo.

read [rid], *vti.* [9] leer; marcar, indicar. —*the thermometer reads 20°,* el termómetro marca 20°.—*to r. law,* estudiar derecho.—*to r. proofs,* corregir pruebas.—*vii.* leer.—[red], *pret.* y *pp.* de TO READ.— **—able** [rídạbl], *a.* legible; ameno, entretenido.— **—er** [-œ(r)], *s.* lector; libro de lectura (de texto); corrector (de pruebas).

readily [rédịli], *adv.* fácilmente; luego; con placer, de buena gana.—**readiness** [rédịnịs], *s.* disposición, buena voluntad; prontitud; facilidad.—*in r.,* listo, preparado.

reading [rídịn], *s.* lectura; conferencia, disertación; lectura de un proyecto de ley; apertura de un testamento.— *r. matter,* material de lectura; sección de lectura (de un periódico).—*r. room,* salón de lectura.

readjust [riạdžʌst], *vt.* ajustar de nuevo; readaptar.— **—ment** [-mẹnt], *s.* readaptación; reajuste.

ready [rédị], *a.* listo, pronto, preparado; dispuesto; inclinado, propenso; al alcance; útil, disponible.—*r.-made,* ya hecho; confeccionado.—*r. money,* dinero contante; dinero al contado.

reagent [riéjdžẹnt], *s.* (quím.) reactivo.

real [ríạl], *a.* real, verdadero, auténtico, genuino, legítimo.—*r. estate,* bienes raíces o inmuebles.—*adv.* (fam.) muy, bastante.— **—ism** [-izm], *s.* realismo.— **—ist** [-ịst], *s.* realista.— **—ity** [rię́lịtị], *s.* realidad, verdad.—*in r.,* en realidad, de veras, efectivamente.— **—ization** [-izéjšǫn], *s.* realización; comprensión.— **—ize** [-ajz], *vt.* realizar, efectuar; darse cuenta, hacerse cargo de; comprender; (com.) realizar.

realm [relm], *s.* reino; región, dominio.

realtor [ríạltǫ(r)], *s.* corredor de bienes raíces.

ream [rim], *s.* resma.—*vt.* escariar, agrandar un agujero.

reanimate [riénịmejt], *vt.* reanimar, resucitar.

reap [rip], *vt.* segar; cosechar; obtener o sacar provecho de.— **—er** [rípœ(r)],

s. segador; segadora mecánica.—**—ing** [-ịn], *s.* siega, cosecha.

reappear [riạpír], *vi.* reaparecer.— **—ance** [-ạns], *s.* reaparición.

rear [rir], *a.* de atrás, trasero, posterior; último, de más atrás.—*r. admiral,* contra(a)lmirante.—*r. guard,* retaguardia.—*s.* fondo; espalda, parte de atrás o posterior; trasero; cola.—*r. view mirror,* (aut.) espejo retrovisor. —*vt.* levantar, alzar; criar, educar.— *vi.* encabritarse (el caballo).

rearm [riárm], *vt.* rearmar.— **—ament** [-ạmẹnt], *s.* rearme.

rearrange [riạréjndž], *vt.* volver a arreglar; cambiar el arreglo o el orden de; refundir.

reason [rízọn], *s.* razón; causa, motivo, porqué; argumento.—*by r. of,* con motivo de, a causa de, en virtud de.— *in (all) r.,* con justicia, con razón.—*it stands to r.,* está puesto en razón.—*r. why,* el porqué.—*to bring to r.,* meter en razón.—*within r.,* con moderación; dentro de los términos de la razón.— *vi.* razonar; discurrir.— **—able** [-ạbl], *a.* razonable, justo; equitativo, módico; prudencial.— **—ableness** [-ạblnịs], *s.* racionalidad; razón; moderación; justicia.— **—ably** [-ạblị], *adv.* razonablemente; bastante.— **—ing** [-ịn], *s.* razonamiento, raciocinio.

reassure [riạšúr], *vt.* tranquilizar.

rebate [ríbejt], *vt.* y *vi.* rebajar, descontar.—*s.* rebaja, descuento.

rebel [rébẹl], *a.* y *s.* rebelde; faccioso, insurrecto.—*vii.* [1] [ríbél], rebelarse, sublevarse.— **—lion** [ríbélyọn], *s.* rebelión, sublevación.— **—lious** [ríbélyʌs], *a.* rebelde; insubordinado.— **—liousness** [ríbélyʌsnịs], *s.* rebeldía.

rebirth [ribœ́rθ], *s.* renacimiento.

rebound [ríbáund], *vi.* (re)botar; repercutir.—*s.* [ríbaund], (re)bote; repercusión.

rebuff [ríbʌf], *s.* desaire, repulsa.—*vt.* desairar, rechazar.

rebuild [ríbíld], *vti.* [10] reedificar, reconstruir.—**rebuilt** [ríbílt], *pret.* y *pp.* de TO REBUILD.

rebuke [ríbjúk], *vt.* increpar, reprochar, reprender.—*s.* repulsa, reproche, increpación, represión, reprimenda.

recall [ríkól], *vt.* revocar, anular; recordar, acordarse de.—*to r. an ambassador,* retirar a un embajador.—*s.* recordación; revocación; (mil.) toque o aviso de llamada.

recant [ríkǽnt], *vt.* y *vi.* retractar(se); desdecirse, desmentirse.— **—ation** [ríkæntéjšǫn], *s.* retractación.

recast [rikǽst], *vti.* [9] volver a fundir; refundir, volver a escribir; volver a hacer; (teat.) volver a repartir (papeles.).—*pret.* y *pp.* de TO RECAST.

recede [risíd], *vi*. retroceder; retirarse, alejarse; desistir, volverse atrás; bajar (los precios).

receipt [risít], *s*. recibo; carta de pago; receta, fórmula.—*pl*. ingresos, entradas.—*on r. of*, al recibo de.—*to acknowledge r*., acusar recibo.—*vt*. y *vi*. firmar o extender recibo; poner el recibí.—**receive** [risív], *vt*. recibir. —*received payment*, recibí.—**receiver** [risívœ(r)], *s*. recibidor; destinatario; recipiente; (tlf.) auricular, receptor; radiorreceptor; (for.) depositario, síndico, administrador judicial.

recent [rísent], *a*. reciente.— —**ly** [-li], *adv*. recientemente.—*r. married*, recién casados.

receptacle [riséptakl], *s*. receptáculo, recipiente, vasija.—**reception** [risépşon], *s*. recepción, recibimiento, recibo; acogimiento, acogida.—*r. room*, gabinete, recibidor.—**receptionist** [risépşonist], *s*. recibidor, persona que atiende a las visitas en oficinas o empresas.

recess [risés], *s*. nicho, hueco; tregua; recreo (escolar); retiro, lugar o cosa recónditos.—*vi*. suspender temporalmente, recesar.— —**ion** [risésşon], *s*. receso, retirada; retracción; (com.) crisis o depresión temporal.

recharge [richárdž], *vt*. recargar.

recipe [résipi], *s*. receta (médica o de cocina); fórmula.

recipient [risípient], *a*. y *s*. que recibe, recipiente, recibidor.

reciprocal [risíprokal], *a*. recíproco, mutuo.—**reciprocate** [risíprokeit], *vt*. reciprocar, corresponder.—*vi*. estar a la recíproca.—**reciprocity** [resiprásiti], *s*. reciprocidad.

recital [risáital], *s*. recitación; (mus.) recital; relación, narración.—**recitation** [resitéişon], *s*. recitación, declamación.—**recite** [risáit], *vt*. y *vi*. narrar, relatar; recitar; declamar; dar o decir la lección.

reckless [réklis], *a*. imprudente, temerario; atolondrado.— —**ness** [-nis], *s*. temeridad; imprudencia; indiferencia, descuido.

reckon [rékon], *vt*. y *vi*. contar, enumerar; calcular; estimar; suponer, creer; (con **on** o **upon**) contar con, fiar en.—*to r. with*, tener en cuenta; habérselas con.— —**ing** [-iŋ], *s*. cuenta; cómputo, cálculo; ajuste de cuentas.—*day of r*., día del juicio (final).

reclaim [rikléim], *vt*. (for.) reclamar (derechos, etc.); (rei)vindicar; mejorar y utilizar (tierras); utilizar (material usado).—**reclamation** [reklaméişon], *s*. reclamación; mejoramiento.

recline [rikláin], *vt*. y *vi*. reclinar(se), recostar(se).

recognition [rekogníşon], *s*. reconocimiento.—**recognize** [rékognaiz], *vt*. reconocer; confesar, admitir.

recoil [rikóil], *s*. rechazo, reculada; (arti.) retroceso, culatazo.—*vi*. [rikóil], recular; retirarse; retroceder; culatear, patear (un arma de fuego).

recollect [rekolékt], *vt*. y *vi*. recordar; acordarse (de); [rikolékt], recoger, recolectar, reunir.— —**ion** [rekólékşon], *s*. recuerdo, recordación.

recommend [rekoménd], *vt*. recomendar.— —**ation** [-éişon], *s*. recomendación.

recompense [rékompens], *vt*. recompensar.—*s*. recompensa.

reconcile [rékonsail], *vt*. reconciliar; ajustar, conciliar.—**reconciliation** [rekonsiliéişon], *s*. reconciliación, ajuste; conformidad.

recondition [rikondíşon], *vt*. (mec.) reacondicionar; restaurar, reparar.

reconnaissance [rikánisans], *s*. reconocimiento.—**reconnoiter** [rikonóitœ(r)], *vt*. reconocer, explorar, inspeccionar.—*vi*. practicar un reconocimiento.

record [rikórd], *vt*. registrar, inscribir; protocolizar (documentos); archivar; grabar (un disco, etc.).—*recorded music*, música en discos.—*s*. [rékord], registro; partida, inscripción, anotación; acta; documento; crónica, historia; hoja de servicios, antecedentes de una persona; disco fonográfico; (for.) memorial, informe; testimonio; memoria; (dep.) marca.—*pl*. archivo, protocolo; actas, autos; memorias, datos.—*of r*., que consta (en el expediente, la escritura, etc.).—*off the r*., confidencialmente, extraoficialmente.—*on r*., registrado; de que hay o queda constancia.— —**er** [rikórdœ(r)], *s*. registrador, archivero; dulzaina, caramillo.—*r. of deeds*, registrador de la propiedad.—*tape r*., grabadora de cinta magnetofónica.

recount [rikáunt], *vt*. contar, referir, relatar; [rikáunt], recontar, hacer un recuento.—*s*. [ríkaunt], recuento.

recoup [rikúp], *vt*. resarcir, recobrar; indemnizar; desquitarse de.

recourse [ríkors], *s*. recurso, remedio, auxilio, refugio; (for.) recurso.—*to have r. to*, recurrir a, apelar a, valerse de.—*without r*., (com.) sin responsabilidad (de parte del endosante).

recover [rikávœ(r)], *vt*. recobrar, recuperar.—*vi*. recobrar la salud; reponerse, restablecerse.— —**y** [-i], *s*. recobro, recuperación; cobranza; restablecimiento; mejoría, convalecencia.

recreate [rékrieit], *vt*. y *vi*. recrear(se), divertir(se).—**recreation** [rekriéişon]

s. recreación, recreo; diversión; esparcimiento.

recruit [rįkrút], *vt.* y *vi.* (mil.) alistar, reclutar.—*s.* (mil.) recluta; novicio, novato.— —ing [-įŋ], *s.* reclutamiento.

rectangle [réktæŋgl], *s.* rectángulo.— **rectangular** [rektǽŋgyǫlǎ(r)], *a.* rectangular.

rectification [rektįfįkéįṣǫn], *s.* rectificación.—**rectify** [réktįfaį], *vti.* [7] rectificar.

rector [réktǫ(r)], *s.* rector (de universidad, orden religiosa); cura párroco.— —y [-į], *s.* casa del párroco.

rectum [réktʌm], *s.* (anat.) recto.

recuperate [rįkjúpǫreįt], *vt.* recuperar, recobrar.—*vi.* recuperar la salud, reponerse.—**recuperation** [rįkįupǫréį ṣǫn], *s.* recuperación.

recur [rįkǣr], *vii.* [1] repetirse, volver a ocurrir; (med.) recaer.

red [red], *a.* rojo, encarnado, colorado; rojo (comunista).—*r. ball*, mingo (en el billar).—*r. (blood) cell*, hematíe, glóbulo rojo.—*r.-handed*, con las manos en la masa; en flagrante.— *r.-hot*, candente, enrojecido al fuego; acérrimo; muy entusiasta o enardecido; reciente (informe, noticia, etc.). —*r. tape*, expedienteo, burocratismo; formulismo dilatorio.—*r. wine*, vino tinto.—*s.* color rojo; (pol.) rojo, comunista.—*to see r.*, (fam.) enfurecerse.— —den [rédn], *vt.* teñir de rojo.—*vi.* ponerse colorado; ruborizarse.— —dish [-įṣ], *a.* rojizo.

redeem [rįdím], *vt.* redimir; desempeñar (un objeto); rescatar; cumplir (lo prometido).— —er [-œ(r)], *s.* redentor.—*the R.*, el Redentor, el Salvador.—**redemption** [rįdémpṣǫn], *s.* redención; rescate; desempeño; amortización de una deuda.

redness [rédnįs], *s.* rojez.

redouble [rįdábl], *vt.* redoblar; repetir. —*vi.* redoblarse.

redoubt [rįdáut], *s.* (fort.) reducto.

redound [rįdáund], *vi.* redundar (en), resultar (en), contribuir (a).

redraft [rídræft], *s.* nuevo dibujo, copia o borrador; (com.) resaca.—*vt.* [rídræft], redactar, dibujar de nuevo.

redress [rįdrés], *vt.* enderezar; reparar, resarcir; remediar, compensar, desagraviar; hacer justicia.—*s.* [rídres], reparación, satisfacción, desagravio; remedio; compensación.

reduce [rįdjús], *vt.* someter.—*vt.* y *vi.* reducir(se); disminuir, aminorar, rebajar; mermar.—*vi.* adelgazar.— **reduction** [rįdákṣǫn], *s.* reducción; rebaja, disminución.

redundance [rįdándǎns], *s.* redundancia.—**redundant** [rįdándǎnt], *a.* redundante.

redwood [rédwųd], *s.* secoya, pino gigantesco de California (árbol y madera).

reed [rid], *s.* caña, junquillo, (Am.) bejuco; (mús.) lengüeta; caramillo; cualquier instrumento de boquilla.

reef [rif], *s.* arrecife, escollo.

reek [rik], *vi.* (gen. con of o with) humear, exhalar, oler a; oler mal.—*s.* tufo; vaho; hedor.

reel [ril], *s.* carrete; carretel; broca; canilla; devanadera; rollo de cinta cinematográfica.—*vt.* aspar, enrollar, devanar.—*vi.* hacer eses, tambalear, bambolear.

reëlect [rięlékt], *vt.* reelegir.- —ion [rięlékṣǫn], *s.* reelección.

reëstablish [riestǽblįṣ], *vt.* restablecer, instaurar.

refer [rįfǣr], *vti.* [1] referir, remitir; trasladar.—*vii.* referirse, remitirse, aludir; acudir; dar referencias.— *referred to*, mencionado; a que se hace referencia, a que uno se refiere.— —ee [refęrí], *s.* árbitro; juez de campo.— *vt.* y *vi.* arbitrar; servir de árbitro.— —ence [réfęręns], *s.* referencia; recomendación; alusión, mención; persona que sirve como referencia o fiador.—*in o with r. to*, respecto de, en cuanto a.—*a.* de referencia; de consulta (libro, etc.).- —endum [refęréndʌm], *s.* plebiscito, referendum.

refill [rifįl], *vt.* llenar de nuevo, rellenar, reenvasar; recambiar.—*s.* [rífįl], recambio, repuesto.

refine [rįfáįn], *vt.* y *vi.* refinar(se), purificar(se); perfeccionar(se).- —d [-d], *a.* refino, refinado; fino, cortés.— —ment [-męnt], *s.* refinamiento, cortesía; purificación, refinación.— —ry [rįfáįnœrį], *s.* refinería.—**refining** [rįfáįnįŋ], *s.* refinación, depuración.

reflect [rįflékt], *vt.* reflejar; reflexionar. —*vi.* reflexionar, meditar; reflejar.— *to r. on o upon*, desprestigiar; desdecir de.— —ion [rįfléksǫn], *s.* reflexión; reflejo; reproche, tacha.—*on o upon r.*, después de pensarlo; bien pensado. - —or [rįflέktǫ(r)], *s.* reflector.—

reflex [rífleks], *a.* reflejo.—*s.* acción refleja; reflejo, reverberación.—**reflexive** [rįfléksįv], *a.* (gram.) reflexivo, reflejo.

reform [rįfǫrm], *vt.* y *vi.* reformar(se), corregir(se); enmendar(se).—*s.* reforma, enmienda.—*r. school*, reformatorio para jóvenes.— —ation [reforméįṣǫn], *s.* reforma; (R. hist.) Reforma.- —er [rįfórmœ(r)], *s.* reformador, reformista.

refrain [rįfréįn], *vi.* refrenarse, abstenerse de, contenerse.—*s.* (poét.) estribillo; (fam.) cantinela.

refresh [rifréš], *vt.* refrescar, renovar; aliviar.—*vr.* refrescarse.— —ing [-iŋ], *a.* refrescante; alentador, placentero.— —ment [-męnt], *s.* refrigerio, tentempié; refresco.

refrigerate [rifrídžęrejt], *vt.* refrigerar, enfriar.—**refrigeration** [rifrídžęréjšǫn], *s.* refrigeración, enfriamiento.— **refrigerator** [rifrídžęreitǫ(r)], *s.* refrigerador, nevera; frigorífico; refrigerante.

refuel [rifjúęl], *vt.* y *vi.* reabastecer(se) de combustible.

refuge [réfjudž], *s.* refugio, amparo, asilo.— —e [refjudží], *s.* refugiado; asilado.

refund [rifʌnd], *s.* reembolso, restitución.—*vt.* [rifʌnd], restituir, reintegrar, reembolsar; amortizar; consolidar una deuda.— —able [rifʌndǫbl], *a.* reembolsable.

refusal [rifjúzǫl], *s.* negativa, denegación; desaire; opción, exclusiva.— **refuse** [rifjúz], *vt.* y *vi.* rehusar; rechazar; desechar; denegar; negarse a.—*s.* [réfjus], desecho, basura, desperdicio; sobra.—*r. dump*, escombrera.—*a.* desechado, de desecho.

refute [rifjút], *vt.* refutar, rebatir.

regain [rigéjn], *vt.* recobrar, recuperar.

regal [rígǫl], *a.* real, regio.

regale [rigéil], *vt.* regalar, agasajar, festejar; recrear, deleitar.—*vi.* regalarse.

regalia [rigéjliǫ], *s. pl.* regalía; insignias, distintivos; galas.—*in full r.*, (fig.) de punta en blanco; de gran gala.

regard [rigárd], *vt.* observar, mirar; considerar, reputar, juzgar; tocar a, referirse a, concernir, relacionarse con.—*as regards*, tocante a, en cuanto a, por (o en) lo que respecta a.—*s.* miramiento, consideración; estimación, respeto; relación; mirada.—*pl.* memorias, afectos, recuerdos.—*in with r. to*, (con) respecto a o de, tocante a.—*in this r.*, a este respecto.—*with (best, kind) regards*, con los mejores afectos; con saludos cariñosos.—*without (any) r. to*, sin dar miramientos por, sin hacer caso de.— —ing [-iŋ], *prep.* en cuanto a, respecto de.— —less [-lęs], *a.* descuidado, desatento.—*r. of*, sin hacer caso de, haciendo caso omiso de; a pesar de.

regatta [rigǽtǫ], *s.* regata.

regency [rídžęnsi], *s.* regencia.

regent [rídžęnt], *a.* y *s.* regente.

regime [rejžím], *s.* régimen, gobierno, administración.

regimen [rédžimen], *s.* (med., gram.) régimen.

regiment [rédžimęnt], *s.* regimiento.

region [rídžǫn], *s.* región.—*in the r. of*, en las cercanías de.— —al [-ǫl], *a.* regional.

register [rédžjstœ(r)], *s.* registro, inscripción, matrícula; lista, archivo, protocolo; padrón, nómina; registrador; indicador, contador; (mús.) registro (de la voz y del órgano).— *vt.* registrar, inscribir, matricular; protocolar; marcar (según escala o graduación); certificar (una carta).— *vi.* inscribirse; matricularse.—**registrar** [rédžjstrar], *s.* registrador, archivero.—**registration** [redžjstréjšǫn], *s.* asiento, registro; inscripción; matrícula.

regret [rigrét], *s.* pena, pesar, sentimiento; remordimiento.—*pl.* excusa (que se envía para rehusar una invitación).—*vti.* [1] sentir, deplorar, lamentar.— —table [-ǫbl], *a.* lamentable, sensible.

regular [régyǫlǫ(r)], *a.* regular, ordinario, normal, corriente; ordenado, metódico.—*s.* (mil.) soldado de línea; obrero permanente.— —ity [regyǫlǽrjtj], *s.* regularidad.—**regulate** [régyǫlejt], *vt.* regular(izar), reglamentar.—**regulation** [regyǫléjšǫn], *s.* regulación; orden, regla.—*pl.* reglamento.—*a.* reglamentario, de reglamento.—**regulator** [régyǫlejtǫ(r)], *s.* regulador (de una máquina, turbina, etc.); registro (de reloj).

rehearsal [rihársǫl], *s.* (teat.) ensayo. —**rehearse** [rihœrs], *vt.* y *vi.* (teat.) ensayar; repasar; repetir.

reheat [rihít], *vt.* recalentar; calentar de nuevo.

reign [rejn], *vi.* reinar· prevalecer, imperar, predominar.—*s.* reinado.— —ing [réjniŋ], *a.* reinante, imperante.

reimburse [rijmbœrs], *vt.* reembolsar, reintegrar.— —ment [-męnt], *s.* reembolso, reintegro.

rein [rejn], *s.* rienda; brida; (fig.) dirección; sujeción, freno.—*to give r. to*, dar rienda suelta a.—*vt.* gobernar, refrenar (un caballo); llevar las riendas de.

reindeer [réjndir], *s.* reno.

reinforce [rijnfórs], *vt.* reforzar, fortalecer.—*reinforced concrete*, hormigón armado.— —ment [-męnt], *s.* refuerzo.

reinsurance [rijnšúrǫns], *s.* reaseguro.— **reinsure** [rijnšúr], *vt.* reasegurar.

reissue [rijšu], *s.* reimpresión; nueva edición o emisión.—*vt.* volver a publicar o emitir.

reiterate [rijtęrejt], *vt.* reiterar.— **reiteration** [rijtęréjšǫn], *s.* reiteración, repetición.

reject [ridžékt], *vt.* rechazar, rehusar, repeler; arrojar; desechar; descartar.— —ion [ridžékšǫn], *s.* rechazo, desecho, exclusión, repudio.

rejoice [ridźóis], *vt.* y *vi.* regocijar(se), alegrar(se).—**rejoicing** [ridźóisiŋ], *s.* regocijo, júbilo.

rejoin [ridźóin], *vt.* reunir con, volver a la compañía de.—*vi.* [ridźóin], replicar,——der [ridźóindœ(r)], *s.* respuesta, réplica.

relapse [riláeps], *vi.* recaer; reincidir (en un error, etc.).—*s.* recaída; reincidencia.

relate [riléit], *vt.* relatar, contar, narrar; relacionar; emparentar.— —d [riléitid], *a.* relacionado; afín; emparentado, allegado.—**relation** [riléiśŋn], *s.* relación; relato, narración; parentesco; pariente.—*pl.* parentela, parientes; tratos, comunicaciones.—*in r. to*, con relación a, con respecto a.— **relationship** [riléiśŋnśip], *s.* relación; parentesco.—**relative** [rélativ], *a.* relativo.—*s.* pariente, deudo, allegado; (gram.) relativo, pronombre relativo.

relax [riláeks], *vt.* relajar, aflojar; mitigar; causar languidez.—*vi.* aflojar, ceder; descansar, esparcirse.— —**ation** [-éiśŋn], *s.* aflojamiento, flojedad; descanso, reposo; solaz, recreo, distracción, esparcimiento; mitigación; relajación, relajamiento de nervios, músculos, etc.

relay [rílei], *s.* relevo; (elec.) relevador. — *r. race*, (dep.) carrera de relevos o de equipos.—*vt.* retransmitir (un mensaje, etc.).

release [rilís], *vt.* soltar; poner en libertad; relevar; renunciar a o abandonar; aliviar; poner en circulación.—*s.* liberación; exoneración; alivio; (m.v.) escape.

relegate [rélĕgeit], *vt.* relegar.—**relegation** [relĕgéiśŋn], *s.* relegación.

relent [rilént], *vi.* aplacarse; ceder, ablandarse, enternecerse.— —**less** [-lis], *a.* implacable, inexorable.— —**lessness** [-lisnis], *s.* inexorabilidad.

relevance [rélĕvans], **relevancy** [rélĕvansi], *s.* pertinencia.—**relevant** [rélĕvant], *a.* pertinente, a propósito, apropiado; que hace o viene al caso.

reliability [riláiabíliti], **reliableness** [riláiablnis], *s.* confiabilidad; calidad de seguro o digno de confianza; formalidad; precisión; veracidad.— **reliable** [riláiabl], *a.* seguro, digno de confianza, confiable, fidedigno, formal.—**reliance** [riláians], *s.* confianza, seguridad.—**reliant** [riláiant], *a.* confiado (en sí mismo)

relic [rélik], *s.* reliquia, vestigio.

relief [rilíf], *s.* ayuda, auxilio; subsidio de paro forzoso; auxilio social; consuelo; socorro, limosna; descanso; (mil.) relevo, (b.a.) relieve, realce.— *r. agencies*, agencias de auxilio o de socorro.—*r. valve*, válvula de seguri-

dad.—*to be on r.*, recibir auxilio social.—**relieve** [rilív], *vt.* relevar, socorrer, aliviar; mitigar; realzar, hacer resaltar; (mil.) relevar.

religion [rilídźŋn], *s.* religión.—**religious** [rilídźʌs], *a.* y *s.* religioso.—**religiousness** [rilídźʌsnis], *s.* religiosidad.

relinquish [rilíŋkwiś], *vt.* abandonar, dejar, ceder.— —**ment** [-mĕnt], *s.* abandono, dejación, renuncia.

reliquary [rélikweri], *s.* relicario.

relish [réliś], *s.* buen gusto, sabor grato, dejo; sazón, condimento; entremés; goce, saboreo.—*vt.* saborear, paladear; gustar de; sazonar, condimentar.—*vi.* saber bien, ser sabroso; gustar.

reload [rilóud], *vt.* recargar; cargar de nuevo.

reluctance [rilʌ́ktans], *s.* repugnancia, renuencia, aversión, desgana, disgusto.—*with r.*, de mala gana.— **reluctant** [rilʌ́ktant], *a.* renuente, maldispuesto.—**reluctantly** [rilʌ́ktantli], *adv.* de mala gana, a regañadientes.

rely [rilái], *vii.* [7] (con **on** o **upon**) confiar o fiar en, fiarse de, contar con.

remade [riméid], *pret.* y *pp.* de TO REMAKE.

remain [riméin], *vi.* quedar(se), restar o faltar; sobrar; estarse, permanecer; continuar.— —**der** [-dœ(r)], *s.* resto, restante, residuo, sobra(nte).— —**s** [-z], *s. pl.* restos, sobras, despojos; reliquias; ruinas.

remake [riméik], *vti.* [10] rehacer.

remark [rimárk], *s.* observación, advertencia, nota.—*vt.* hacer una observación, observar, notar, reparar.— —**able** [-abl], *a.* notable, extraordinario, admirable, señalado.

remedy [rémĕdi], *s.* remedio, medicamento; cura.—*vti.* [7] curar, remediar.

remember [rimémbœ(r)], *vt.* recordar, acordarse de.—*vi.* acordarse, hacer memoria.—**remembrance** [rimémbrans], *s.* memoria; recordación; recuerdo.

remind [rimáind], *vt.* recordar.— —**er** [-œ(r)], *s.* recordatorio; advertencia.

reminiscence [riminísĕns], *s.* reminiscencia.—*pl.* memorias.—**reminiscent** [riminísĕnt], *a.* evocador, rememorativo.

remiss [rimís], *a.* remiso, descuidado. —**ion** [rimíśŋn], *s.* remisión, perdón; (com.) remesa.—**remit** [rimít], *vti.* [1] (com.) remesar; remitir; perdonar, condonar; eximir; relajar.—*vii.* (com.) hacer remesas; girar.—**remittance** [rimítans], *s.* remesa, envío, giro.

remnant [rémnant], *s.* remanente, resto,

residuo; vestigio; retazo.—*r. sale*, saldo, baratillo.

remodel [rimádẹl], *vt.* [2] modelar de nuevo; rehacer, reconstruir; renovar.

remora [rémọrặ], *s.* (ict.) rémora.

remorse [rimórs], *s.* remordimiento, cargo de conciencia.— **—ful** [-fụl], *a.* arrepentido, con remordimientos.— **—less** [-lịs], *a.* sin remordimientos, cruel, despiadado.

remote [rimóụt], *a.* remoto, apartado, lejano, distante.— **—ness** [-nịs], *s.* lejanía, gran distancia.

removable [rimúvặbl], *a.* separable; amovible; de quita y pon.—**removal** [rimúvặl], *s.* acción de quitar o levantar; remoción; deposición; eliminación; alejamiento; traslado, mudanza, cambio de domicilio.—**remove** [rimúv], *vt.* remover; quitar; eliminar; alejar, mudar, cambiar, trasladar; destituir, deponer; apartar; sacar, extirpar.—*vi.* mudarse, trasladarse, alejarse; cambiar de sitio o domicilio.—**removed** [rimúvd], *a.* apartado, alejado, distante; destituido.—**remover** [rimúvœ(r)], *s.* removedor.

remunerate [rimiúnẹreit], *vt.* remunerar.—**remuneration** [rimiụnẹréiṣọn], *s.* remuneración.

renaissance [rẹnặsáns], **renascence** [rịnésẹns], *s.* renacimiento; (R.) Renacimiento.

rend [rend], *vti.* y *vii.* [10] rasgar(se), desgarrar(se); rajar(se).

render [réndœ(r)], *vt.* hacer; dar, prestar, rendir; (mus., teat.) interpretar, ejecutar; traducir; derretir; (com.) enviar, girar (una cuenta).—*to r. assistance*, prestar auxilio, auxiliar.— **—ing** [-iṇ], *s.* traducción; interpretación.—**rendition** [rendíṣọn], *s.* versión o traducción; (mus., teat.) interpretación, ejecución; rendición; entrega.

renegade [rénigeid], *s.* renegado, desertor; apóstata.—*a.* renegado, falso, traidor.

renew [rịniú], *vt.* renovar; restaurar; reanudar; (com.) extender, prorrogar. **—al** [-ặl], *s.* renovación; reanudación; (com.) prórroga.

renounce [rịnáuns], *vt.* renunciar.— **—ment** [-mẹnt], *s.* renuncia, renunciamiento.

renovate [rénoveit], *vt.* renovar.

renown [rịnáun], *s.* renombre.

rent [rent], *vt.* alquilar, arrendar, dar o tomar en arrendamiento.—*s.* renta, alquiler; arrendamiento; rasgadura; raja, grieta.—*for r.*, se alquila o arrienda —*pret* y *pp* de TO REND —

—al [réntặl], *s.* renta; arrendamiento, alquiler.

reopen [rióupn], *vt.* y *vi.* reabrir(se), volver a abrir(se); reanudar (una discusión, etc.).— **—ing** [-iṇ], *s.* reapertura.

reorganization [riorgặnizéiṣọn], *s.* reorganización.—**reorganize** [riórgặnaiz], *vt.* reorganizar.

repaid [ripéid], *pret.* y *pp.* de TO REPAY.

repair [ripér], *vt.* reparar, restaurar, componer; remendar.—*s.* reparo, reparación, restauración; compostura, remiendo.—*out of r.*, descompuesto, en mal estado.—**reparation** [repặréiṣọn], *s.* reparación; satisfacción, desagravio.

repatriate [ripéitrịeit], *vt.* repatriar.

repay [ripéi], *vti.* [10] pagar, reembolsar; reintegrar; pagar en la misma moneda.— **—ment** [-mẹnt], *s.* pago, devolución, retorno.

repeal [ripíl], *vt.* derogar, revocar, abrogar, abolir.—*s.* revocación, derogación, abrogación.

repeat [ripít], *vt.* repetir.—*s.* repetición. **—edly** [-idli], *adv.* repetidamente, repetidas veces, a menudo.

repel [ripél], *vti.* [1] repeler, rechazar.— *vii.* ser repelente o repulsivo.— **—lent** [-ẹnt], *a.* repelente.

repent [ripént], *vt.* y *vi.* arrepentirse (de).— **—ance** [-ặns], *s.* arrepentimiento.— **—ant** [-ặnt], *a.* arrepentido, contrito.

repertory [répœrtọrị], *s.* repertorio; depósito, colección; inventario, lista; almacén.

repetition [repịtíṣọn], *s.* repetición.

replace [ripléis], *vt.* reemplazar; suplir; reponer.— **—able** [-ặbl], *a.* reemplazable; renovable.— **—ment** [-mẹnt], *s.* reemplazo, sustitución; reemplazante; pieza de repuesto; restitución, reposición.

replenish [riplénịṣ], *vt.* rellenar; llenar o surtir nuevamente.—**replete** [riplít], *a.* repleto; ahíto.

replica [réplikặ], *s.* (b.a.) réplica; copia, reproducción; (mus.) repetición.

reply [ripláị], *s.* respuesta; réplica.— *vti.* y *vii.* [7] contestar, responder; replicar.

report [ripórt], *vt.* informar acerca de, dar parte de; denunciar; comunicar; relatar; redactar un informe o dictamen; reseñar.—*it is reported*, corre la voz, se dice.—*vi.* presentar informe o dictamen; servir como reportero; comparecer, personarse.—*s.* relato, parte, noticia; comunicado; reseña; informe, dictamen; voz, rumor; reportaje, detonación.—*by r.*, según se dice.— **—er** [-œ(r)], *s.* repórter, reportero; noticiero; relator

repose [rįpóųz], *vt.* descansar, reclinar; poner (confianza o esperanza).—*vi.* reposar, descansar; tener confianza en.—*vr.* tenderse, reclinarse, recostarse.—*s.* reposo, descanso; tranquilidad, quietud.

repository [rįpázįtorį], *s.* depósito, almacén, repositorio.

represent [reprįzént], *vt.* representar; significar, exponer; [riprįzént], presentar de nuevo.— —ation [reprįzentéįşǫn], *s.* representación.— —ative [reprįzéntątįv], *a.* representativo, típico; representante.—*s.* representante; símbolo, tipo, ejemplar; (R.) diputado, representante.

repress [rįprés], *vt.* reprimir, contener.——ion [rįpréşǫn], *s.* represión.

reprieve [rįprív], *vt.* aplazar la ejecución de; suspender; aliviar (un dolor). —*s.* aplazamiento de ejecución de sentencia; tregua; suspensión; alivio.

reprimand [réprįmænd], *vt.* reprender, reconvenir, (fam.) sermonear.—*s.* reprimenda, regaño, censura.

reprint [riprínt], *vt.* reimprimir.—*s.* [ríprįnt], reimpresión; tirada aparte (de un artículo).

reprisal [rįpráįząl], *s.* represalia.

reproach [rįpróųch], *vt.* reprochar, increpar; vituperar, censurar.—*s.* reproche; vituperio; tacha, baldón.— *above r.*, sin tacha.

reprobate [réprǫbeįt], *s.* réprobo, malvado.

reproduce [rįprodjús], *vt.* reproducir; duplicar, copiar.—**reproduction** [rįprodáKşǫn], *s.* reproducción; (b.a.) copia.

reproof [rįprúf], *s.* reprobación, reproche, reprensión.—**reprove** [rįprúv], *vt.* reprobar, culpar, censurar; acusar, condenar.

reptile [réptįl], *s.* y *a.* reptil; (fig.) bajo, rastrero.

republic [rįpÁblįk], *s.* república.— —an [-ąn], *a.* y *s.* republicano.

repudiate [rįpúdįeįt], *vt.* repudiar, repeler; rechazar, renunciar; desconocer.

repugnance [rįpÁgnąns], *s.* repugnancia; aversión.—**repugnant** [rįpÁgnąnt], *a.* repugnante, repulsivo; antipático.

repulse [rįpÁls], *s.* repulsa, repulsión; denegación.—*vt.* desechar, rechazar, repeler.—**repulsive** [rįpÁlsįv], *a.* repulsivo, repugnante, repelente.

reputable [répyǫtąbl], *a.* honroso, honrado, intachable; lícito.—**reputation** [repyǫtéįşǫn], *s.* reputación; crédito, estimación, prestigio.—**repute** [rįpjút], *vt.* reputar, juzgar, tener por *s* reputación, fama, crédito.

request [rįkwést], *s.* súplica, ruego;

petición, instancia, solicitud; (com.) demanda.—*at the r. of*, o *by r.*, a petición, a solicitud o instancia de.— *on r.*, en boga, muy solicitado, pedido o buscado.—*vt.* rogar, suplicar, solicitar.

require [rįkwáįr], *vt.* requerir, demandar, exigir, necesitar.- —ment [-męnt], *s.* demanda, requerimiento, exigencia; requisito, necesidad; formalidad; estipulación.—**requisite** [rékwįzįt], *a.* necesario, forzoso, indispensable.—*s.* requisito.—**requisition** [rekwįzíşǫn], *s.* pedimento, petición, demanda; (mil.) requisa; necesidad, requisito, menester; (com.) demanda, solicitud; (for.) requisitoria.—*vt.* (mil.) requisar.

resale [ríseįl], *s.* reventa.

rescind [rįsínd], *vt.* rescindir, anular, abrogar.

rescue [réskįu], *vt.* rescatar, redimir; salvar, librar.—*s.* rescate, redención, salvación, libramiento, recobro; socorro.- —r [-œ(r)], *s.* salvador, libertador.

research [rįsœrch], *s.* investigación; búsqueda.—*vt.* investigar.

resell [rįsél], *vti.* y *vii.* [10] revender.

resemblance [rįzémbląns], *s.* parecido, semejanza.—**resemble** [rįzémbl], *vt.* (a)semejarse a, parecerse a; salir (uno) a (su padre, etc.).

resent [rįzént], *vt.* (re)sentirse de, llevar a mal, ofenderse por.- —ful [-fųl], *a.* resentido, ofendido.- —ment [-męnt], *s.* resentimiento, pique, enojo.

reservation [rezœrvéįşǫn], *s.* reservación; reserva, excepción, restricción (mental); pasaje (sitio, alojamiento, etc.) reservados de antemano.— **reserve** [rįzœrv], *vt.* reservar, guardar, retener, conservar; exceptuar, excluir.—*s.* reserva.—**reservoir** [rézœrvwar], *s.* depósito; receptáculo; cubeta; (com.) surtido de reserva; alberca; cisterna, aljibe; depósito (de gas, petróleo, etc.).

reset [rįsét], *vti.* [9] montar de nuevo.— *pret.* y *pp.* de TO RESET.

reside [rįzáįd], *vi.* residir, vivir, habitar. - —nce [rézįdęns], *s.* residencia, domicilio; casa; estancia, mansión; quedada, permanencia.- —nt [rézįdęnt], *a.* residente.—*s.* habitante, vecino; (dipl.) ministro residente.

residual [rįzídžųąl], *a.* restante, remanente.—**residue** [rézįdįu], *s.* residuo, resto, sobrante, remanente.

resign [rįzáįn], *vt* dimitir, renunciar.— *vi.* presentar la dimisión.—*vr.* resignarse, rendirse, someterse, conformarse.- —ation [rezįgnéįşǫn], *s.*

dimisión, renuncia, dejación; **resignación**, conformidad.

resilience [rizíliens], *s.* elasticidad, resorte, rebote; capacidad de recobrar la figura y el tamaño original después de deformación.—**resilient** [rizíljent], *a.* elástico; (fig.) alegre, animado.

resin [rézin], *s.* resina.

resist [rizíst], *vt.* y *vi.* resistir, rechazar; oponerse; impedir, negarse a; aguantar, soportar, hacer frente a.— **—ance** [-ans], *s.* resistencia; defensa, oposición, fuerza contraria; aguante.— **—ant** [-ant], *a.* resistente.

resold [risóuld], *pret.* y *pp.* de TO RESELL.

resole [risóul], *vt.* remontar (zapatos).

resolute [rézoljut], *a.* resuelto, determinado, firme, denodado.—**resolution** [rezolúșon], *s.* resolución; determinación; propósito; acuerdo (de una junta o asamblea); disolución de un todo.—**resolve** [rizálv], *vt.* y *vi.* resolver(se); tomar acuerdo, determinar, decidir(se), solucionar; descomponer (una fuerza, etc.); disipar, desvanecer; (con into) transformarse en o reducirse a.—*s.* resolución, determinación, propósito, acuerdo.

resonance [rézonans], *s.* resonancia.— **resonant** [rézonant], *a.* resonante, retumbante; sonoro.

resort [rizórt], *vi.* (con to) acudir, recurrir, frecuentar; pasar a, recorrer a, hacer uso de, echar mano de.—*s.* concurso, concurrencia; punto de reunión; recurso, medio, expediente; lugar de temporada o muy frecuentado.

resound [rizáund], *vt.* repetir, repercutir el sonido; cantar, celebrar.—*vi.* resonar, retumbar; formar eco; tener resonancia; tener fama, ser celebrado.

resource [risórs], *s.* recurso, medio, expediente.—*pl.* fondos, recursos; riquezas, recursos naturales.— **—ful** [-ful], *a.* listo, ingenioso, dotado de inventiva.— **—fulness** [-fulnis], *s.* inventiva, iniciativa.

respect [rispékt], *vt.* respetar, venerar, estimar; acatar, observar, guardar; corresponder, tocar, concernir, atenerse a.—*s.* respeto, estimación; reverencia, veneración, culto; acatamiento, miramiento; honra, homenaje; respecto, asunto.—*pl.* memorias, recuerdos, respetos.—*in other respects*, por lo demás.—*in r. that*, puesto que.—*in some r.*, de algún modo, hasta cierto punto.—*out of r. for o to*, en obsequio de, por consideración a.— **—ability** [rispektabíliti], *s.* respectabilidad.— **—able** [rispéktabl], *a.* respetable, formal; estimable,

honroso; acreditado, autorizado; bastante bueno; considerable.— **—ful** [-ful], *a.* respetuoso.— **—ing** [-iŋ], *prep.* con respecto a, en cuanto a, por lo que toca a, (en lo) tocante a.— **—ive** [-iv], *a.* respectivo; particular, individual; sendos.

respiration [respiréișon], *s.* respiración, respiro.—**respire** [rispáir], *vt.* y *vi.* resollar, respirar; espirar, exhalar.

respite [réspit], *s.* tregua, espera, pausa; plazo, prórroga, respiro.

respond [rispánd], *vi.* responder, contestar; reaccionar; corresponder; obedecer, acudir; venir bien, ajustarse.— **response** [rispáns], *s.* respuesta, contestación.—**responsibility** [rispansibíliti], *a.* responsabilidad; obligación, deber; solvencia.—**responsible** [rispánsibl], *a.* responsable; solvente; autorizado; de responsabilidad.—*r. for*, responsable de; causa de; autor de; origen de.

responsory [rispánsori], *s.* (igl.) responso.

rest [rest], *s.* descanso, reposo; tregua, pausa; paz, quietud; apoyo, base; resto, residuo, sobra; (poét.) cesura; (con the) los demás, los otros; el resto.—*at r.*, en paz (apl. a los muertos).—*vi.* descansar, reposar; yacer, reposar en el seno de la muerte; cesar, parar; estar en paz, vivir tranquilo; posarse o asentarse; apoyarse (en), cargar (sobre); confiar (en), contar (con); depender (de); permanecer.—*to r. assured*, perder cuidado.—*vt.* y *vi.* descansar, proporcionar descanso; apoyar o asentar; (for.) terminar la presentación de pruebas.

restaurant [réstorant], *s.* restaurante, fonda.

restful [réstful], *a.* reposado, quieto, tranquilo.

restitution [restitiúșon], *s.* restitución, restablecimiento; devolución, reintegración; reparación, indemnización; recuperación, recobro; (fís.) elasticidad.

restless [réstlis], *a.* inquieto, impaciente; bullicioso, levantisco; insomne.— **—ness** [-nis], *s.* inquietud, impaciencia, desasosiego; insomnio.

restoration [restoréișon], *s.* restauración; reintegración, instauración, rehabilitación, restablecimiento.— **restore** [ristór], *vt.* restaurar, reconstruir; reintegrar, restablecer, instaurar; restituir, reponer.

restrain [ristréin], *vt.* refrenar, reprimir, cohibir; represar; moderar, limitar, coartar; (for.) prohibir o vedar a.— **—t** [-t], *s.* moderación; sujeción, restricción, coerción, prohibición.—

restrict [ristríkt], *vt.* restringir, coartar.—**restriction** [ristríkşon], *s.* restricción, limitación, coartación.

result [rizÁlt], *vi.* resultar; inferirse; (con in) dar por resultado, venir a parar, acabar en, conducir a; causar.—*s.* resultado; conclusión, deducción.

resume [rizjúm], *vt.* reasumir; reanudar; recuperar; resumir, compendiar.—*vi.* tomar el hilo; empezar de nuevo.—**résumé** [rezųméi], *s.* resumen, sumario.—**resumption** [rizÁmpşon], *s.* reanudación; recobro.

resurrect [rezaRÉkt], *vi.* resucitar, volver a la vida.—**resurrection** [rezaRÉkşon], *s.* resurrección; renovación, restablecimiento.

resuscitate [risÁsiteit], *vt.* y *vi.* resucitar, reanimar, (hacer) revivir.

retail [ríteil], *vt.* vender al menudeo; detallar.—*s.* menudeo, venta (al) por menor; detalle.—*adv.* al por menor.—*er* [-œ(r)], *s.* comerciante al por menor, detallista, (Am.) minorista, tendero, revendedor.

retain [ritéin], *vt.* retener, guardar, conservar; represar, detener, contener; contratar.—*er* [-œ(r)], *s.* partidario; criado, dependiente; (for.) anticipo.

retake [ritéjk], *vti.* [10] volver a tomar; reasumir, recoger; (fot. y cine) volver a fotografiar o filmar.—**retaken** [ritéjkn], *pp.* de TO RETAKE.

retaliate [ritélieit], *vi.* desquitarse, vengarse; tomar represalias.—**retaliation** [ritæliéişon], *s.* talión, desquite; represalia; desagravio; pago, retorno.

retard [ritárd], *vt.* retardar, retrasar, demorar; aplazar, diferir, dilatar.—*s.* retraso, atraso, dilación, demora.

reticence [rétisens], *s.* reticencia, reserva.—**reticent** [rétisent], *a.* reticente.

retina [rétina], *s.* retina.

retinue [rétinju], *s.* tren, comitiva, séquito.

retiral [ritáiral], *s.* retiro, retirada; (com.) recogida.—**retire** [ritáir], *vi.* retirarse, irse a acostar; retirarse de la vida activa, de un empleo, etc.; jubilarse; retraerse, retroceder, recogerse, apartarse, separarse.—*vt.* (com.) recoger, retirar de la circulación; jubilar.—**retirement** [ritáirment], *s.* retiro; retraimiento; recogida, recogimiento; lugar retirado; jubilación.

retook [ritúk], *pret.* de TO RETAKE.

retort [ritórt], *vt.* redargüir; devolver (un insulto); replicar.—*s.* réplica mordaz; retorta.

retouch [ritÁch], *vt.* retocar.—*s.* retoque.

retrace [ritréjs], *vt.* desandar, volver atrás; buscar el origen de; repasar; volver a trazar.—*to r. one's steps,* volver sobre sus pasos.

retract [ritrékt], *vt.* retractar, retirar; retractarse de; retraer, encoger.—*vi.* retractarse, desdecirse; encogerse.

retreat [ritrít], *s.* retiro; soledad, retraimiento; refugio, asilo; (mil.) retirada; retreta.—*vi.* retirarse; retroceder, retraerse, refugiarse; cejar.

retribution [retribjúşon], *s.* retribución, pago; justo retorno, pena incurrida.

retrievable [ritrívabl], *a.* recuperable; reparable.—**retrieve** [ritrív], *vt.* recuperar, recobrar; restaurar, remediar; cobrar (la caza).—*vi.* cobrar la caza.—**retriever** [ritrívœ(r)], *s.* perro cobrador, perdiguero.

retroactive [retroǽktjv], *a.* retroactivo.

retrospect [rétrospekt], *s.* mirada retrospectiva.—*in r.,* en retrospectiva.—*ive* [retrospÉktjv], *a.* retrospectivo.

return [ritǿrn], *vt.* (de)volver; corresponder a, pagar, dar en cambio, recompensar; dar (gracias, fallo, respuesta, etc.); (pol.) elegir, enviar (al congreso, etc.).—*to r. a call,* pagar una visita.—*to r. a kindness,* corresponder a un favor.—*to r. a verdict,* dictar un fallo, dar un veredicto.—*vi.* volver, regresar; reaparecer; responder, replicar.—*vt.* y *vi.* volver otra vez; dar otra vuelta o doblez.—*s.* vuelta, regreso; correspondencia (a un favor, etc.), pago, recompensa; respuesta; devolución; reaparición; utilidad, rédito; cambio, trueque; informe o parte oficial; curva, vuelta; desviadero; (arq.) ala, vuelta de moldura, marco, etc.; (pol.) elección.—*pl.* resultado, cifras (de elecciones).—*by r. mail,* a vuelta de correo.—*happy returns,* felicidades en su cumpleaños.—*income tax r.,* declaración de ingresos.—*in r.,* en cambio, en pago, en recompensa.—*r. address,* señas del remitente.

reunion [rijúnyon], *s.* reunión; reconciliación; tertulia; junta.—**reunite** [rijunáit], *vt.* reunir, juntar; volver a unir; reconciliar.—*vi.* reunirse, reconciliarse.

reveal [rivíl], *vt.* revelar; dar a conocer.—*ing* [-iŋ], *a.* revelador; impúdico, sugestivo (vestido).

reveille [révęli], *s.* (mil.) toque de diana.

revel [révęl], *vii.* [2] jaranear, ir de parranda; gozarse (en).—*s.* algazara, jarana, parranda.

revelation [reveléişon], *s.* revelación; visión; (R.) Apocalipsis.

revelry [révęlri], *s.* jarana, gresca, francachela, orgía, borrachera.

revenge [rivéndž], *vt.* y *vi* vengar(se); desquitarse, satisfacerse o vengarse

de.—**s.** venganza, desquite.— **—ful**
[-fụl], **a.** vengativo.

revenue [révẹnju], **s.** rentas públicas;
(com.) renta; rédito; entrada, ingreso;
beneficio, recompensa.—**r.** officer,
aduanero; agente fiscal o del fisco.—
r. stamp, sello fiscal, sello de impuesto.

revere [rivír], **vt.** reverenciar, venerar.—
—nce [révrẹns], **s.** reverencia, veneración; reverencia (saludo); (R., igl.)
Reverencia (tratamiento).—to pay r.,
rendir homenaje.—**vt.** reverenciar,
venerar.— **—nd** [révrẹnd], **a.** reverendo, venerable; (R., igl.) Reverendo
(tratamiento).—**s.** (fam.) clérigo.-
—nt [révrẹnt], **a.** reverente.

reverie [révẹri], **s.** ensueño; embelesamiento, arrobamiento; (mus.) fanta-
sía.

reversal [rivœ́rsạl], **s.** reversión; inversión; (for.) revocación; cambio (de
opinión, etc.).—**reverse** [rivœ́rs], **vt.**
trastocar, invertir; trastornar; (for.)
revocar.—**vi.** volver a un estado
anterior, invertirse.—**a.** reverso, invertido; opuesto, contrario; (mec.) de
inversión o contramarcha.—**s.** lo
contrario, lo opuesto, respaldo, dorso,
reverso; reversión, inversión; contratiempo, revés.—**revert** [rivœ́rt], **vi.**
retroceder, volver, resurtir; (biol.)
saltar atrás; (for.) revertir.—**revertible** [rivœ́rtịbl], **a.** reversible.

review [rivjú], **vt.** rever, remirar; repasar (estudios, etc.); revisar; censurar;
reseñar, criticar o analizar (un libro,
etc.); (mil.) revistar, pasar revista a.
—**vi.** reseñar, escribir para una
revista.—**s.** repaso; examen, análisis;
reseña; censura, juicio crítico; revista;
(for.) revisión.- **—er** [-œ(r)], **s.**
crítico, revistero (literario, teatral,
etc.).

revise [riváịz], **vt.** revisar, releer,
repasar; corregir, enmendar.—**revision** [rivíẓọn], **s.** revisión, repaso;
enmienda; edición revisada.

revival [riváịvạl], **s.** renacimiento, renovación, reavivamiento; (teat.) reposición o reestreno; despertamiento
religioso.—**revive** [riváịv], **vt.** hacer
revivir, (re)avivar, resucitar; restablecer, restaurar; despertar; hacer
recordar.—**vi.** revivir; restablecerse,
reanimarse; volver en sí, renacer.

revocable [révọkạbl], **a.** revocable.—
revoke [rivóụk], **vt.** revocar, derogar.
—**vi.** (en los naipes) renunciar.

revolt [rivóụlt], **vi.** rebelarse, sublevarse; sentir repugnancia o repulsión.
—**vt.** rebelar, sublevar; causar asco o
repulsión; indignar.—**s.** sublevación,
alzamiento, rebelión.— **—ing** [-ịŋ], **a.**
odioso, repugnante, asqueroso.

revolution [revọljúṣọn], **s.** revolución,
revuelta; (mec.) giro.- **—ary** [-eri],
a. y **s.** revolucionario.- **—ist** [-ịst], **s.**
revolucionario.

revolve [riválv], **vi.** girar, dar vueltas,
rodar; moverse en ciclos, suceder
periódicamente.—**vt.** voltear, hacer
girar o rodar; revolver (en la cabeza),
considerar bajo todos los aspectos,—
—r [-œ(r)], **s.** revólver (arma).—
revolving [-ịŋ], **a.** giratorio.

reward [riwórd], **vt.** premiar, recompensar.—**s.** recompensa, premio, galardón; hallazgo; merecido; gratificación, remuneración.

rhapsody [répsọdj], **s** rapsodia.

rhetoric [rétọrịk], **s.** retórica.- **—al**
[ritárịkạl], **a.** retórico.

rheumatism [rúmạtizm], **s.** reumatismo.

rhinoceros [rajnásẹrọs], **s.** rinoceronte.

rhombus [rámbʌs], **s.** rombo.

rhubarb [rjúbarb], **s.** ruibarbo.

rhyme [rajm], **s.** rima; verso; poesía.—
without r. or reason, sin ton ni son.—
vt. rimar, versificar; emplear como
consonante.—**vi.** rimar; corresponder,
armonizarse.

rhythm [rjðm], **s.** ritmo; armonía;
(med.) periodicidad.- **—ic(al)**
[rjðmịk(ạl)], **a.** rítmico, cadencioso,
armónico.

rib [rjb], **s.** costilla; (arq.) faja, listón,
nervio, nervadura; viga de tejado;
arco; saliente; varilla (de abanico o
paraguas); tirante; (mec.) pestaña,
reborde; (cost.) vivo; (bot.) nervadura de las hojas; (fam.) costilla,
esposa.—**vti.** [1] marcar con rayas,
listones o filetes; afianzar con re-
bordes o pestañas; (cost.) poner
vivos; (fam.) embromar, burlarse de.

ribbon [rjbọn], **s.** cinta; tira, banda,
faja; galón.—**vt.** encintar.—**a.** hecho
de cinta; de forma de cinta.

rice [rajs], **s.** arroz.

rich [rjch], **a.** rico; costoso, precioso;
suntuoso, cuantioso; exquisito; vivo
(color, etc.); muy sazonado, dulce,
fuerte, etc.; fértil; (fam.) muy divertido; risible.—to get r., enriquecerse.
—**s.** pl. riqueza(s); bienes; opulencia;
sazón, dulzura, suculencia.

rickety [rjkịtj], **a.** desvencijado, destartalado; (med.) raquítico.

rid [rjd], **vti.** [3] desembarazar, quitar
de encima, zafar.—to be r. of, estar
libre o exento de.—pret. y pp. de TO
RID.- **—dance** [rjdạns], **s.** supresión,
liberación de una pejiguera o peligro.

ridden [rjdn], **pp.** de TO RIDE.

riddle [rjdl], **s.** acertijo, enigma, adivinanza, rompecabezas; (fam.) busilis,
quisicosa; misterio; criba.—**vt.** resolver, adivinar; acribillar.—**vi.** hablar
enigmáticamente.

ride [rajd], **vti.** [10] cabalgar, montar;

ir montado en o sobre; pasear o recorrer (a caballo, en automóvil, etc.).—*to r. down* u *over*, pasar por encima de, derribar y hollar; pisotear, atropellar; mandar con arrogancia.—*to r. out*, hacer frente a, resistir bien (el viento).—*vii.* cabalgar; pasear (a caballo o en un vehículo); ir en automóvil, coche, etc.; flotar; (mec.) rodar, tener juego, funcionar.—*s.* paseo (a caballo, en auto, etc.).— —r [rájdœ(r)], *s.* jinete; amazona; persona que va en automóvil, bicicleta, etc.; picador, (Am.) amansador; cosa que va montada sobre otra; pesa corrediza (de una balanza); hojuela pegada a un documento; adición a un proyecto de ley.

ridge [rid̵ʒ], *vt.* (agr.) formar camellones; acanalar, arrugar.—*vi.* tener camellones.—*s.* cerro, colina, cordillera, serranía; escollo, arrecife; arruga, costurón; camellón; caballete del tejado.—*r. roof*, tejado a dos vertientes o aguas.—*r. tile*, teja acanalada.

ridicule [rídikjul], *s.* ridículo, mofa, rechifla.—*vt.* ridiculizar, mofarse de, rechiflar.—**ridiculous** [ridíkyǫlʌs], *a.* ridículo, risible, grotesco.

riding [rájdiŋ], *s.* equitación.—*r. boots*, botas de montar.

riffraff [rífræf], *s.* canalla, gentuza.

rifle [rájfl], *s.* rifle, fusil; espiral de rifle; piedra de afilar.—*vt.* robar, arrebatar.— —man [-man], *s.* fusilero.

rig [rig], *vti.* [1] equipar, aparejar; enjarciar (un velero).—*to r. oneself up*, ataviarse, emperifollarse.—*s.* equipo, aparejo; traje, atavío; aparato.— —ging [rígiŋ], *s.* (mar.) aparejo, cordaje, jarcia; (mec.) aparejo (de poleas); equipo de arrastre (de trozas).

right [rajt], *a.* recto, justo, equitativo; propio, conveniente; correcto, exacto; cierto, real, genuino, legal, legítimo; derecho, directo; ordenado, ajustado; derecho (lado, mano); verdadero; derecho (contrario de revés).—*all r.*, bueno, conforme.—*it is r.*, está bien; es justo.—*r. and left*, a diestra y siniestra.—*r. angle*, ángulo recto.—*r. hand*, diestra; de la mano derecha.—*r.-hand man*, (fam.) hombre de confianza, brazo derecho.—*r. or wrong*, con razón o sin ella; bueno o malo.—*r. side*, lado derecho; lado de afuera, cara; haz (telas, etc.).—*to be r.*, tener razón.—*interj.* ¡bien! ¡bueno!—*adv.* rectamente, justamente; exactamente, perfectamente, precisamente; bien; correctamente; debidamente; derechamente; a la derecha.—*r. about face*, media vuelta.

—*r. now*, ahora mismo.—*r. there*, allí mismo.—*to go r. home*, ir derechito para la casa.—*s.* derecho; justicia; rectitud; propiedad, dominio, título; poder, autoridad; privilegio, prerrogativa; opción; (la) diestra, (la) derecha; (pol.) derecha(s).—*vt.* hacer justicia; enderezar.—*to r. a wrong*, enderezar un entuerto, corregir un abuso.— —eous [rájchʌs], *a.* justo, recto, equitativo; virtuoso, honrado, probo.— —eousness [rájchʌsnis], *s.* rectitud, virtud, honradez, probidad.— —ful [rájtful], *a.* legítimo.— —ist [-ist], *s.* y *a.* (pol.) derechista.

rigid [rídʒid], *a.* rígido, inflexible, yerto; austero, estricto, riguroso.— —ity [ridʒíditi], *s.* rigidez.

rigor [rígǫ(r)], *s.* rigor; inclemencia; severidad, austeridad; tesón, terquedad; exactitud; (med.) escalofrío.— —ous [-ʌs], *a.* rigoroso o riguroso; recio (tiempo); estricto, severo.

rill [ril], *s.* riachuelo, arroyuelo.

rim [rim], *s.* canto, borde, margen, orilla; llanta, aro, cerco, reborde; pestaña; ceja.

rime [rajm], *s.* escarcha; = RHYME.

rind [rajnd], *s.* corteza, pellejo, cuero, hollejo.

ring [riŋ], *s.* anillo, argolla, anilla; (joy.) anillo, sortija; circo, arena, liza; cerco; corro o corrillo; ojera; campaneo, repique; juego de campanas; campanilleo; toque de timbre; sonido metálico.—*r. finger*, dedo anular.—*r. leader*, jefe, cabecilla.—*vt.* rodear, circundar; poner una anilla a; anillar, ensortijar.—*vi.* moverse en círculo o en espiral; formar círculo.—*vti.* [10] tocar, sonar, tañer, repicar (campanas), timbre, campanilla); repetir, reiterar.—*to r. up*, llamar (a uno) por teléfono; (teat.) levantar el telón.—*vii.* sonar, tañer, campanillear; retumbar, resonar; zumbar (los oídos).—*to r. off*, terminar (una conversación telefónica); (fam.) cesar de hablar.—*to r. true*, sonar bien (una moneda, etc.); sonar a verdad.— —let [ríŋlit], *s.* anillejo, círculo; sortija, bucle, rizo; (Am.) crespo.— —worm [-wœrm], *s.* tiña.

rink [riŋk], *s.* pista de patinar.

rinse [rins], *vt.* enjuagar; lavar; aclarar (la ropa).—*s.* enjuague.

riot [rájǫt], *s.* tumulto; alboroto; motín, asonada, desorden; borrachera.— —er [-œ(r)], *s.* amotinado, alborotador.— —ous [-ʌs], *a.* amotinado, sedicioso; bullicioso, desenfrenado.

rip [rip], *vti.* y *vii.* [1] rasgar(se),

rajar(se), romper(se); descoser(se), soltar(se); arrancar(se).—*to r. off*, rasgar, arrancar; cortar.—*to r. out a seam*, descoser, desbaratar una costura.—*s.* laceración, rasgadura, rasgón; (fam.) persona, caballo o cosa que no vale nada.

ripe [raip], *a.* maduro; en sazón; hecho, acabado; preparado, a propósito; rosado, colorado; (agr.) espigado.— **—n** [ráipn], *vt.* y *vi.* madurar, sazonar(se).— **—ness** [-nis], *s.* madurez, sazón.

ripple [rípl], *vt.* rizar, ondear.—*vi.* agitarse, rizarse la superficie del agua; murmurar.—*s.* escarceo, onda, rizo (del agua); murmullo.

rise [raiz], *vii.* [10] ascender, subir, elevarse, remontarse; levantarse, ponerse en pie; levantarse (de la cama); alzarse, sublevarse; suspender una sesión; salir (el sol); nacer o brotar (las plantas o los manantiales); surgir, aparecer, presentarse; sobrevenir, suscitarse (una disputa); ascender, mejorar de posición; aumentar de volumen; subir de precio. —*to r. early*, madrugar.—*to r. to one's feet*, ponerse en pie, levantarse. —*s.* ascensión, elevación; levantamiento, insurrección; crecimiento o desarrollo; cuesta, subida; nacimiento (de un manantial); altura, eminencia; salida (de un astro); encarecimiento, alza de precios; crecimiento (de un río, etc.); origen, causa; ascenso; elevación de la voz. —*to give r. to*, dar origen a, ocasionar. —**risen** [rízn], *pp.* de TO RISE.

risk [risk], *s.* riesgo, peligro; contingencia; albur.—*vt.* arriesgar, aventurar, exponer.— **—y** [ríski], *a.* peligroso, arriesgado, aventurado; imprudente, temerario.

rite [rait], *s.* rito, ceremonia.—**ritual** [ríchual], *a.* y *s.* ritual, ceremonial.

rival [ráival], *s.* rival.—*a.* competidor, opuesto.—*vti.* [2] emular; competir con, rivalizar con.—*vii.* rivalizar.

river [rívœ(r)], *s.* río.— **—side** [-said], *s.* ladera, ribera u orilla de un río.

rivet [rívit], *s.* remache.—*vt.* remachar; (fig.) asegurar, afianzar.

rivulet [rívyülit], *s.* riachuelo, arroyuelo.

roach [rouch], *s.* cucaracha.

road [roud], *s.* camino, vía; carretera.— **—side** [róudsaid], *s.* orilla o borde del camino.— **—way** [-wei], *s.* carretera, calzada.

roam [roum], *vt.* y *vi.* vagar, andar errante.

roar [ror], *vi.* rugir, bramar.—*s.* rugido, bramido; estruendo, estrépito.

roast [roust], *vt.* asar; tostar; calcinar; (fam.) hablar mal de; ridiculizar. —*a.* asado; tostado.—*s.* asado.— **—er** [róustœ(r)], *s.* asador; tostador.

rob [rab], *vti.* y *vii.* [1] robar; saltear; saquear.—*to r. one of*, robar, hurtar o quitarle a uno (el dinero, etc.).— **—ber** [rábœ(r)], *s.* ladrón; salteador, bandido; bandolero.— **—bery** [-œri], *s.* robo, hurto, latrocinio.

robe [roub], *s.* manto; túnico o túnica; ropón, toga, traje talar; bata; corte de vestido; manta de coche.—*vt.* vestir de gala o de ceremonia; vestir, ataviar.—*vi.* vestirse; cubrirse.

robin [rábin], *s.* petirrojo.

robust [robást], *a.* robusto, vigoroso, fuerte.

rock [rak], *s.* roca, peña, peñasco; arrecife, escollo; (fig.) amparo, protección; diamante, moneda.—*on the rocks*, (bebidas) con hielo; arruinado, tronado.—*vt.* mecer, balancear; arrullar; sosegar.—*vi.* mecerse, bambolear, oscilar.— **—er** [rákœ(r)], *s.* cualquier cosa que mece o se mece; cuna; columpio; mecedora (silla); balancín.

rocket [rákit], *s.* cohete, volador.—*r. bomb*, (mil.) bomba cohete.—*r. plane*, avión cohete.—*vi.* volar o ascender verticalmente en el aire.

rocking [rákiŋ], *a.* mecedor; oscilante. —*s.* mecedura, balance, balanceo.

rocky [ráki], *a.* peñascoso, rocoso, pedregoso, duro, endurecido.

rod [rad], *s.* vara, varilla; cetro; bastón de mando; varilla de virtudes; caña de pescar; barra de cortina; vara de medir; (mec.) vástago, barra; azote; (fig.) disciplina, castigo; linaje.

rode [roud], *pret.* de TO RIDE.

rodent [róudènt], *a.* y *s.* roedor.

roe [rou], *s.* hueva, ovas de pescado. —*r. deer*, corzo.

rogue [roug], *s.* bribón, pícaro, pillo, golfo, villano; (fam.) pilluelo, perillán.—*r.'s gallery*, galería de malhechores (colección policíaca de retratos).—**roguish** [róugiš], *a.* picaresco, (fam.) tuno, travieso.

role [roul], *s.* (teat.) papel, parte.

roll [roul], *vt.* hacer rodar; girar, voltear; enrollar, abarquillar; (fund.) laminar; alisar, emparejar con rodillo; apisonar (el césped); liar; envolver, fajar; redoblar (el tambor); hacer vibrar (lengua o voz); poner (los ojos) en blanco.—*to r. up*, enrollar; (fam.) acumular; revolver. —*vi.* rodar; agitarse (las olas); ondular, fluctuar; retumbar, retemblar; bambolearse, balancearse; arrollarse, abarquillarse; dar un redoble de tambores.—*to r. about*, rodar,

divagar, andar de acá para allá.
—to r. down, bajar rodando.—to r. in
money, nadar en la abundancia.—
to r. to a stop, seguir rodando hasta
pararse.—s. rollo; rol, lista, nómina,
matrícula, registro; bollo, panecillo;
(mec.) rodillo, cilindro de emparejar
allanar o laminar; laminador; maza
de trapiche; redoble (de tambores);
retumbo del trueno; balanceo, bamboleo; oleaje; (cir.) mecha.—pl.
archivos.—r. call, lista.— —er [róul-
œ(r)], s. rodillo, tambor, cilindro;
aplanadera; alisador; ola larga; (cir.)
venda, faja.—r. coaster, montaña
rusa.—r. skate, patín de ruedas.

rolling [róulin], a. rodante; ondulante.
—s. balanceo; revuelco.

Roman [róumən], a. romano; católico
romano.—R. nose, nariz aquilina.—
s. romano.

romance [roméns], s. romance; novela,
ficción, cuento, fábula; (mús.) romanza; aventura, drama, episodio
extraño y conmovedor; (fam.) amorío, idilio.—vi. mentir; fingir fábulas;
hablar o pensar románticamente.—
a. (R.) romance; neolatino.—R.
language, lengua neolatina o romá-
nica.

Romanesque [roumənésk], a. (arq.)
románico.

romantic [romántik], a. romántico,
novelesco; sentimental; fantástico.-
—ism [romántisizm], s. romanticismo.— —ist [romántisist], s. (escritor, músico, etc.) romántico.

romp [ramp], vi. juguetear, retozar.
—s. retozo.

roof [ruf], s. tejado, techo, azotea;
bóveda, cielo; cubierta; casa, hogar,
habitación.—r. garden, jardín de la
azotea; azotea de baile y diversión.
—r. of the mouth, bóveda palatina,
paladar.—r. tile, teja.—vt. techar;
abrigar, alojar.- —ing [rúfin], s.
techado, techumbre.

room [rum], vi. vivir, hospedarse, alojarse.—s. habitación, cuarto, aposento, sala, cámara, pieza; lugar,
espacio, puesto; paraje, sitio; causa,
motivo, razón; tiempo, ocasión,
oportunidad.- —er [rúmœ(r)], s.
huésped, inquilino.- —iness [-inis],
s. espaciosidad, holgura, amplitud.-
—mate [-meit], s. compañero de
cuarto.- —y [-i], a. espacioso, capaz,
amplio, holgado.

roost [rust], s. percha de gallinero;
lugar de descanso; sueño, descanso
(de la aves domésticas).—vi. dormir
o descansar (las aves) en una percha.-
—er [rústœ(r)], s. gallo.

root [rut], s. raíz.—r. and branch, por
completo.—vi. y vt. echar o criar

raíces, arraigar(se); hozar.—to r. for,
(fam.) aplaudir, alabar, vitorear.—
to r. up o out, arrancar de raíz,
desarraigar; extirpar.—to take r.,
radicar, arraigar(se).

rope [roup], s. soga; cuerda, cordel,
cabo; driza; reata; sarta, ristra,
trenza; hilera, fila.—r. ladder, escala
de cuerdas.—r. sandal, alpargata.—
vt. atar con una cuerda; rodear con
soga; coger con lazo.—to r. in,
(fam.) atraer, embaucar, engañar.—
to r. off, cercar con cuerdas.—vi.
hacer hebras o madeja.

rosary [róuzəri], s. rosario.—rose
[rouz], s. rosa; color de rosa.—r.
tree, rosal. rosebay [róuzbei], s.
adelfa.—rosebud [róuzbʌd], s. pimpollo botón o capullo de rosa; niña
adolescente.—rosebush [róuzbuʃ], s.
rosal.

rosemary [róuzmeri], s. (bot.) romero.

rosette [rouzét], s. rosa, roseta; escarapela, moña; (arq.) rosetón, florón.

rosin [rázin], s. resina.

rostrum [rástrʌm], s. tribuna; (zool.)
rostro, pico, hocico; (mar.) espolón.

rosy [róuzi], a. róseo, rosado; sonrosado; sonrojado; (fig.) agradable,
lisonjero; optimista.—r. dream, sueño
dorado.—r.-hued, rosado.

rot [rat], vti. y vii. [1] pudrir(se),
corromper(se).—s. putrefacción, podredumbre, podre.

rotary [róutəri], a. giratorio, rotativo,
rotatorio.—rotate [róuteit], vi. girar;
alternar(se).—vt. hacer girar, dar
vuelta(s) a; alternar; (agr.) sembrar
o cultivar en rotación.—rotation
[routéiʃən], s. rotación, giro; turno;
alternativa.—by r., in r., por turnos,
alternadamente; (agr.) en rotación.

rote [rout], s. lo que se aprende de
memoria.—by r., de memoria o de
coro; mecánicamente.

rotten [rátn], a. podrido; (fam.)
malísimo; dañado, en mal estado.

rouge [ruʒ], s. colorete.—a. colorado,
encarnado.—vt. y vr. arrebolar(se),
pintar(se), dar(se) colorete.

rough [rʌf], a. áspero; tosco; fragoso,
escabroso; erizado; encrespado; desapacible; rudo, inculto; grosero,
brusco; tempestuoso, borrascoso,
agitado; chapucero; aproximativo,
general; preliminar, preparativo.—
as o at a r. guess, a ojo de buen cu-
bero.—r. diamond, diamante en
bruto; persona ruda pero de buen
fondo.—r. draft, boceto, bosquejo;
borrador.—s. matón, rufián.—in the
r., en bruto, sin pulimento.—vt.
poner áspero, tosco, escabroso; labrar
toscamente; (fam.) molestar, irritar.
—to r. it, pasar trabajos, vivir sin

comodidades.- **—en** [rʌfn], *vt.* y *vi.*
poner(se) áspero o tosco; picar,
rascar.- **—ness** [-njs], *s.* aspereza,
rudeza, tosquedad, escabrosidad;
severidad, dureza; ordinariez, brusquedad; chapucería; tempestad, tormenta.

round [raųnd], *a.* redondo, circular,
cilíndrico, esférico, orbicular; rollizo; rotundo; sonoro; cabal, grande,
cuantioso; franco, llano, ingenuo;
vivo, veloz; justo, honrado.—*r. numbers,* cifras globales.—*r. trip,* viaje
de ida y vuelta.—*r. trip ticket,*
billete de ida y vuelta.—*to go r.
and r.,* dar vuelta tras vuelta.—*s.*
círculo, esfera; círculo de personas
o cosas; redondez; vuelta, giro,
rotación; peldaño (de escala); listón
o travesaño (de silla); rodaja de
carne; (arq.) mediacaña; (mil.)
ronda; andanada, salva, disparo,
descarga; cartucho con bala; ruta,
camino, circuito; rutina, serie; (dep.)
tanda, suerte, turno; (boxeo, etc.)
asalto; (naipes) mano; (mus.) rondó;
danza.—*adv.* alrededor, en derredor,
por todos lados; a la redonda.—
all-r., completo, que sirve para todo;
cabal.—*r. about,* por el lado opuesto;
por todos lados, a la redonda.—
r.-shouldered, cargado de espaldas.
—*prep.* alrededor de; a la vuelta
de.—*vt.* redondear, dar vuelta; doblar (un cabo, una esquina); acabar,
perfeccionar.—*to r. up,* recoger, juntar, reunir; coger; recoger el ganado.
—*vi.* redondearse; desarrollarse, per-
feccionarse; dar vueltas; rondar.—
to r. out, llenarse, redondearse.-
—about [raųndạbaụt], *a.* indirecto,
vago; desviado.—*s.* chaqueta; tiovivo; rodeo. **—ness** [-njs], *s.*
redondez.— **—up** [-ʌp], *s.* rodeo de
ganado; recogida, junta; apresuramiento, aprehensión.

rouse [raųz], *vt.* despertar, animar,
excitar, suscitar; levantar (la caza);
(mar.) halar.—*vi.* despertar(se), des-
pabilarse, animarse, moverse.

route [rut, raųt], *s.* ruta, vía; rumbo,
derrotero; marcha, curso.—*vt.* encaminar, señalar ruta, pista, vía (a
trenes, aviones, etc.).

routine [rutín], *a.* rutinario.—*s.* rutina;
costumbre, hábito.

rove [roųv], *vi.* corretear, vagar,
vagabundear.—*s.* correría, paseo.—
—r [róųvœ(r)], *s.* vagabundo; persona inconstante.

row [roų], *s.* hilera, fila; paseo en lancha
o bote; remadura; [raų], camorra,
trifulca.—*vt.* [roų], conducir remando.
—*vi.* [roų], remar, bogar; [raų],
armar camorra.- **—boat** [róųboụt],

s. bote de remos.- **—dy** [raųdi], *a.*
alborotador, pendenciero.—*s.* rufián.—
—dyism [raųdịizm], *s.* rufianismo.-
—er [róųœ(r)], *s.* remero.

royal [róịạl], *a.* real, regio, magnífico.
—*to have a r. time,* divertirse en
grande, o a cuerpo de rey.- **—ist**
[-ịst], *s.* (pol.) realista.- **—ty** [-tị],
s. realeza.—*pl.* derechos de autor o
de inventor.

rub [rʌb], *vti.* [1] estregar, frotar,
friccionar; raspar, raer; incomodar,
fastidiar.—*to r. away,* quitar frotando.—*to r. down,* dar un masaje;
alisar frotando.—*to r. in,* hacer
penetrar frotando; (fam.) machacar.
—*to r. off,* quitar; limpiar frotando.
—*to r. out,* borrar.—*to r. the wrong
way,* frotar a contrapelo; irritar;
incomodar.—*to r. up,* aguijonear,
excitar; retocar, pulir.—*vii.* pasar
raspando, rozar; ser desagradable o
molesto; ir a contrapelo.—*s.* frotación, roce; tropiezo, dificultad; sarcasmo, denuesto.- **—ber** [rʌbœ(r)],
a. de caucho.—*r. band,* faja de goma,
elástico, liga.—*r. eraser,* goma de
borrar.—*r. stamp,* estampilla, sello o
cuño de goma; (fig.) el que aprueba
ciegamente.—*to r.-stamp,* estampar
con un sello de goma; (fam.) aprobar
ciegamente.—*s.* caucho, goma elás-
tica; masajista; goma de borrar;
estropajo; escofina; jugada decisiva.
—*pl.* chanclos, zapatos de goma.

rubbish [rʌbịs], *s.* basura, desperdi-
cio(s), desecho, escombro, cascajo,
ripio; (fam.) tontería.

rubble [rʌbl], *s.* piedra en bruto o sin
labrar; escombros; cascote, cascajo.

ruby [rúbị], *s.* rubí; carmín, color
rojo vivo.—*a.* rojo.

rudder [rʌdœ(r)], *s.* timón (de barco).

ruddiness [rʌdịnịs], *s.* rojez, rubicundez.—**ruddy** [rʌdị], *a.* rojo, rojizo; rubicundo.

rude [rud], *a.* rudo, brusco, descortés;
tosco, chabacano; inculto; fuerte,
vigoroso.- **—ness** [rúdnịs], *s.* grosería; descortesía; rudeza, aspereza;
rusticidad, crudeza.

rudiment [rúdịmẹnt], *s.* rudimento;
(biol.) embrión, germen.— **—ary**
[rudịméntạrị], *a.* rudimentario.

ruffian [rʌfịạn], *a.* y *s.* rufián.

ruffle [rʌfl], *vt.* (cost.) fruncir un volante, rizar; ajar, arrugar, desordenar;
encrespar; desazonar, enfadar; vejar;
redoblar (el tambor).—*vi.* rizarse,
arrugarse; desarreglarse; tremolar;
enojarse, incomodarse.—*s.* (cost.)
volante fruncido; desazón, enojo;
escarceo del agua; redoble de tambor.

rug [rʌg], *s.* alfombra.

rugged [rʌgịd], *a.* áspero, escarpado,

abrupto; tosco, basto; inculto; desapacible; descomedido; arrugado; ceñudo, regañón; desgreñado; robusto, vigoroso; tempestuoso, borrascoso.—**—ness** [-njs], *s.* escabrosidad; rudeza; robustez.

ruin [rúin], *s.* ruina, bancarrota; estrago, destrucción; degradación, perdición.—*pl.* ruinas, escombros.—*vt.* arruinar, devastar; dar al traste con, echar a perder; desbaratar; estropear; seducir, perder (a una mujer).—*vi.* arruinarse; decaer.—**—ous** [-ʌs], *a.* ruinoso, desmantelado; desastroso, funesto.

rule [rul], *s.* regla; gobierno, mando, dominio; soberanía; régimen, reinado; estatuto, precepto; regularidad, buen orden; (fig.) norma, guía, modelo; (for.) auto, fallo; (impr.) pleca, filete; raya, línea trazada.—*as a r.*, por regla general.—*r. book*, reglamento.—*r. of thumb*, regla o método empírico.—*to be the r.*, ser la regla; ser de reglamento.—*vt.* gobernar, mandar, regir; reprimir; (for.) decidir, determinar, disponer; dirigir, guiar; arreglar, ordenar; rayar (papel).—*to r. out*, excluir; descartar.—*vi.* gobernar, mandar; establecer una regla, formular una decisión; prevalecer, estar en boga; (com.) mantenerse a un tipo.—*to r. over*, mandar, gobernar, dominar.—**—r** [rúlœ(r)], *s.* soberano, príncipe; gobernador, gobernante; pauta, regla (para trazar líneas).—**ruling** [rúlin], *s.* (for.) decisión, fallo, disposición; rayadura; rayado.—*a.* gobernante, imperante.—*r. price* (com.) precio predominante.

rum [rʌm], *s.* ron.

Rumanian [ruméinian], *a.* y *s.* rumano (persona e idioma).

rumble [rʌmbl], *vi.* retumbar, rugir; avanzar con estruendo.—*vt.* hacer retumbar, etc.—*s.* rumor, ruido sordo y prolongado; estruendo.

ruminant [rúminant], *a.* y *s.* rumiante. —**ruminate** [rúmineit], *vt.* y *vi.* rumiar; considerar, reflexionar.

rumor [rúmọ(r)], *s.* rumor, runrún. —*vt.* divulgar, propalar.—*it is rumored*, se dice, corre la voz.

rump [rʌmp], *s.* rabadilla de ave; anca o grupa de caballo, etc.; nalgas; cadera de vaca; resto, retazo.

rumple [rʌmpl], *vt.* arrugar, ajar.—*s.* arruga, doblez, estrujadura.

rumpus [rʌmpʌs], *s.* (fam.) batahola, zipizape.

run [rʌn], *vti.* [10] correr, hacer correr; mover, poner en movimiento; dejar correr o salir; meter, clavar, introducir; empujar, echar; cazar, perse-

guir; tirar, trazar (una línea, en el papel o el terreno); pasar (la vista); atravesar, cruzar; derramar, manar; correr (un peligro); fundir, moldear; (cost.) bastear; tener o proponer como candidato; mandar, dominar; manejar, dirigir (una máquina, institución, empresa).—*to r. a blockade*, violar o burlar un bloqueo.—*to r. a temperature*, tener fiebre.—*to r. down*, dar caza; (mar.) echar a pique; difamar, hablar mal de; quebrantar, postrar; gastar (la salud, etc.).—*to r. for office*, aspirar a un cargo electivo.—*to r. in*, recorrer; encerrar; (fam.) prender. —*to r. into the ground*, meter en la tierra; extender hasta más abajo del suelo; (fam.) llevar al exceso.—*to r. off*, desviar; desecar, vaciar; repetir, decir de coro; imprimir.—*to r. out*, agotar; desperdiciar; (fam.) echar.—*to r. over*, atropellar, pasar encima de; hojear, repasar, revisar de prisa.—*to r. through*, ver, examinar, presentar, etc. a la ligera; atravesar, pasar de parte a parte; traspasar; hojear, leer por encima; gastar, derrochar, malbaratar.—*to r. up*, (cost.) remendar, repasar; incurrir, hacer subir (una cuenta); sumar, hacer una suma; montar o edificar de prisa; (mar.) izar.—*vii.* correr; pasar, deslizarse; marchar, andar; funcionar, moverse (un buque, reloj, máquina, etc.); derretirse, fluir, gotear o chorrear; derramarse; correrse (un color); competir, lidiar; ser candidato, presentarse como tal; (med.) supurar; (teat.) representarse consecutivamente; extenderse, ir, llegar (hasta), correr, transcurrir; tener predilección; continuar, durar; rezar, decir; tener curso, circular; salirse, dejar fugar el agua, etc.; ir, andar (en manadas, etc.).—*to r. about*, andar de lugar en lugar; corretear.—*to r. across*, atravesar corriendo; hallar; dar o tropezar con.— *to r. against*, chocar, topar, dar contra; oponerse; ser contrario a.—*to r. ahead*, correr delante; llevar ventaja. —*to r. away*, huir, escapar, zafarse; desbocarse.—*to r. away with*, arrebatar; fugarse con; (fam.) llevarse la palma, ser el protagonista en. —*a.* extraído; vaciado; derretido; (fam.) de contrabando.—*s.* corrida, carrera; curso, marcha; batida de caza; (mil.) marcha forzada; vuelta, viajecito, jornada; recorrido, trayecto; distancia; (mec.) marcha, movimiento, funcionamiento; serie, continuación; duración, vida; hilo (del discurso); (teat.) serie de repre-

sentaciones consecutivas de una pieza; lo que sale o se saca cada vez (hornada, vaciado, etc.); mando, dirección; (béisbol) carrera; arribazón (de peces); clase, tipo; aspecto, carácter.—*in the long r.*, a la larga. —*the (common) r.*, el común de las gentes; lo común, lo corriente.— *pp.* de TO RUN.— —*away* [rÁnₐwei], *a.* y *s.* fugitivo, desertor.—*s.* fuga; rapto, secuestro; desbocamiento; caballo desbocado.

rung [rᴧŋ], *pp.* de TO RING (tocar).—*s.* peldaño de escalera, escalón; travesaño.

runner [rᴧnœ(r)], *s.* corredor; andarín; pieza o parte giratoria o corrediza; mensajero; (fam.) correve(i)dile; fugitivo; contrabandista; agente, factor; alguacil; corredera; muela (de molino).

running [rᴧnįŋ], *s.* carrera, corrida; contrabando; funcionamiento.—*a.* que corre; que fluye o mana; que funciona.—*r. board*, estribo.—*r. expenses*, gastos corrientes.—*r. water*, agua corriente.

runt [rᴧnt], *s.* enano; paloma.

runway [rᴧnwei], *s.* lecho, madre, cauce; senda; rampa; (aer.) pista; vía (gen. de rieles).

rupture [rᴧpchₙ(r)], *s.* rompimiento, rotura, fractura; reventazón; ruptura, desavenencia; hernia, quebradura.—*vt.* romper, fracturar; reventar.—*vi.* abrirse, romperse, rajarse, reventar.

rural [rúrₐl], *a.* rural.

rush [rᴧš], *s.* ímpetu, embestida, acometida; prisa, precipitación; torrente, tropel, agolpamiento, asedio; lucha, rebatiña; tierra rica en oro; (bot.) junco; friolera, bagatela.— *with a r.*, de golpe; de repente.—*vi.* lanzarse, abalanzarse, precipitarse; embestir, acometer; agolparse.—*to r. forward*, lanzarse.—*to r. in*, entrar de rondón.—*to r. in upon*, sorprender. —*to r. out*, salir con precipitación.— *to r. through*, lanzarse por entre o a través de.—*vt.* empujar o arrojar con violencia; activar.—*to r. through*, ejecutar deprisa.

Russian [rᴧšₐn], *a.* y *s.* ruso (persona e idioma).

rust [rᴧst], *s.* herrumbre, orín, moho. —*vt.* y *vi.* enmohecer(se); entorpecer(se), embotar(se).

rustic [rᴧstįk], *a.* rústico, rural; agrario; agreste; campesino; sencillo; inculto. —*s.* rústico, campesino.

rustle [rᴧsl], *vt.* y *vi.* susurrar, crujir (la seda), murmurar (las hojas); (fam.) hurtar ganado.—*s.* susurro, crujido, murmullo.

rusty [rᴧstį], *a.* mohoso, herrumbroso; rojizo o amarillento; entorpecido, torpe por falta de práctica.

rut [rᴧt], *vti.* [1] hacer rodadas o surcos.—*vii.* bramar (los venados, etc.), estar en celo.—*s.* rodada, surco, bache; rutina, costumbre; sendero trillado; brama, celo de los animales; mugido, bramido; ruido, batahola.

ruthless [rúθljs], *a.* cruel, inhumano; inexorable.— —*ness* [-njs], *s.* crueldad, empedernimiento.

rye [rai], *s.* centeno; whisky de centeno.

S

saber [séjbœ(r)], *s.* sable.

sable [séjbl], *s.* (zool.) marta cibelina.

sabot [sǽbou], *s.* zueco.

sabotage [sǽbotaž], *s.* sabotaje.—*vt.* cometer sabotaje (contra, en).

saccharin [sǽkₐrįn], *s.* sacarina.— —**e** [sǽkₐrin], *a.* dulzón.

sack [sǽk], *s.* saco, costal, talega; (mil.) saqueo, saco.—*vt.* saquear.— —**cloth** [sǽkkl_θ], *s.* arpillera.

sacrament [sǽkrₐmₑnt], *s.* sacramento; eucaristía.—**sacred** [séjkrjd], *a.* (con)sagrado, sacro(santo).

sacrifice [sǽkrjfajs], *vt.* y *vi.* sacrificar, inmolar.—*s.* sacrificio, inmolación.— *at a s.*, haciendo un sacrificio; perdiendo, con pérdida.

sacrilege [sǽkrjljdž], *s.* sacrilegio.— **sacrilegious** [sækrjlídžᴧs], *a.* sacrílego.

sacristan [sǽkrjstₐn], *s.* sacristán.— **sacristy** [sǽkrjstį], *s.* sacristía.

sacrum [séjkrᴧm], *s.* (anat.) sacro.

sad [sæd], *a.* triste, pesaroso; cariacontecido; aciago, nefasto.— —**den** [sǽdn], *vt.* y *vi.* entristecer(se).

saddle [sǽdl], *s.* silla de montar, montura; silla o sillín (de bicicleta o motocicleta).—*s. horse*, caballo de silla, cabalgadura.—*vt.* ensillar; enalbardar.—*to s. with*, hacer cargar con.— —**bag** [-bæg], *s.* alforja, jaque.— —**cloth** [-klₒθ], *s.* mantilla (de silla).— —**r** [sǽdlœ(r)], *s.* talabartero.

sadism [sǽdįzm], *s.* sadismo.—**sadistic** [sædístįk], *a.* sádico, sadista.

sadness [sǽdnjs], *s.* tristeza.

safe [sejf], *a.* seguro; salvo, ileso; sin peligro; intacto; digno de confianza. —*s. and sound*, sano y salvo.—*s.-conduct*, salvoconducto, salvaguardia. —*s. deposit box*, caja de seguridad (en el banco).—*s.* caja de caudales, caja fuerte.— —**guard** [séjfgard], *s.* salvaguardia; resguardo; defensor, escolta; defensa, abrigo.—*vt.* salvaguardar, proteger; escoltar.— —**ty** [-tį], *s.* seguridad, protección; seguro (de arma de fuego).—*a.* de seguridad.—

s. pin, imperdible.—*s. razor*, maquinilla de seguridad (de afeitarse).

saffron [sǽfrǫn], *s.* (bot.) azafrán.

sag [sæg], *vti.* [1] combar, pandear.— *vii.* combarse, pandearse; aflojarse, doblegarse; hundirse.—*s.* comba, pandeo.

sage [seidź], *s.* sabio; (bot.) salvia.— *a.* sabio; sagaz; cuerdo, prudente.

said [sed], *pret.* y *pp.* de TO SAY.—*a.* (el) mencionado o citado; (for.) dicho, antedicho.—*s. and done*, dicho y hecho.

sail [seil], *s.* (mar.) vela; excursión o paseo en barco.—*pl.* velamen.—*under full s.*, a toda vela, a todo trapo.— *vi.* hacerse o darse a la vela; zarpar; salir (un buque); navegar.—*to s. before the wind*, navegar viento en popa.—*to s. close with the wind*, ceñir el viento, bolinear.—*vt.* navegar por, surcar.— **—boat** [séilbout], *s.* barco de vela, balandro, velero.- **—fish** [-fiś], *s.* aguja de mar, (Am.) pez vela, aguja de abanico.- **—ing** [-iŋ], *s.* navegación (a vela); salida o partida de un barco.—*clear o plain s.*, coser y cantar.— **—or** [-ǫ(r)], *s.* marinero; marino.

saint [seint], *s.* santo.—*s.'s day*, día del santo.—*a.* san, santo.—*vt.* canonizar. - **—hood** [séinthųd], *s.* santidad.- **—liness** [-liniș], *s.* santidad.- **—ly** [-li], *a.* santo.

sake [seik], *s.* causa, motivo, fin, objeto, razón; amor, respeto, consideración. —*for God's s.*, por Dios, por el amor de Dios.—*for mercy's s.*, por piedad, por misericordia.—*for the s. of*, en consideración a.

salad [sǽlad], *s.* ensalada.—*s. bowl*, ensaladera.—*s. dressing*, aliño, aderezo para ensalada.

salamander [sǽlamændœ(r)], *s.* salamandra.

salami [salámi], *s.* salchichón.

salary [sǽlari], *s.* sueldo, salario, pago.

sale [seil], *s.* venta; liquidación, saldo; (com.) realización.—*sales tax*, impuesto sobre las ventas.—*for s.* u *on s.*, de venta, en venta.- **—sman** [séilzman], *s.* vendedor; dependiente de tienda.- **—swoman** [-zwụman], *s.* vendedora; dependienta de tienda.

saliva [saláivȧ], *s.* saliva.

sallow [sǽlou], *a.* cetrino.

sally [sǽli], *vii.* [7] (a veces con **forth**) salir, hacer una salida.—*s.* salida.

salmon [sǽmǫn], *s.* salmón.

saloon [salún], *s.* salón; cámara de un vapor; (E.U.) taberna, cantina, tugurio.

salt [solt], *s.* sal; agudeza, ingenio chispeante.—*old s.*, lobo de mar.—*pl.* sales medicinales; sal de higuera,

---

sulfato de magnesia.—*a.* salado; salobre; curado o conservado con sal. —*s. pork*, tocino salado.—*s. shaker*, salero (de mesa).—*vt.* salar; (fig.) sazonar.—*to s. away*, ahorrar.- **—ed** [sóltjd], *a.* salado.- **—peter** [-pítœ(r)], *s.* nitro, salitre.- **—y** [-i], *a.* salado; salobre.

salutation [sælyutéişǫn], *s.* salutación, saludo; bienvenida.—**salute** [salíút], *vt.* y *vi.* saludar; cuadrarse.—*s.* saludo.

Salvadoran [sælvadóran], **Salvadorian** [sælvadórian], *s.* y *a.* salvadoreño.

salvage [sǽlvidź], *s.* salvamento; objetos salvados.—**salvation** [sælvéişǫn], *s.* salvación.

salve [sæv, sav], *s.* ungüento, pomada; remedio.—*vt.* curar (una herida) con ungüentos; salvar; remediar.

salver [sǽlvœ(r)], *s.* salva, bandeja.

same [seim], *a.* y *pron.* mismo; igual, idéntico.—*all the s.*, a pesar de eso, a pesar de todo.—*it is all the s. to me*, me es igual, lo mismo me da.— *just the s.*, del mismo modo; a pesar de eso.—*much the s. as*, casi como.— *the s.*, lo mismo; el mismo, los mismos; otro tanto.

sample [sémpl], *s.* muestra, prueba; patrón.—*s. book*, muestrario.—*vt.* sacar una muestra; probar, catar.

sanctify [sǽŋktifai], *vti.* [7] santificar, consagrar.—**sanctimonious** [sæŋktimóųniʌs], *a.* beato, mojigato.—**sanctimoniousness** [sæŋktimóųniʌsniș], *s.* beatería, mojigatería.

sanction [sǽŋkşǫn], *s.* sanción; pena; sanción, ratificación.—*vt.* sancionar; autorizar, ratificar.

sanctity [sǽŋktiti], *s.* santidad.—**sanctuary** [sǽŋkchueri], *s.* santuario.

sand [sænd], *s.* arena.—*s. bar*, barra, banco de arena.—*s. blasting*, limpiadura por chorro de arena.—*s. pit*, arenal.—*vt.* (en)arenar; (gen. con **down**) alisar con papel de lija.

sandal [sǽndal], *s.* sandalia.—*fiber s.*, *rope s.*, alpargata.

sandpaper [sǽndpeipœ(r)], *s.* papel de lija.—*vt.* lijar.—**sandstone** [sǽndstoun], *s.* piedra arenisca.—**sandstorm** [sǽndstorm], *s.* tempestad de arena.

sandwich [sǽndwich], *vt.* colocar entre dos capas; intercalar, insertar.—*s.* emparedado, bocadito, bocadillo.

sandy [sǽndi], *a.* arenoso, arenisco.

sane [sein], *a.* cuerdo; sano.

sang [sæŋ], *pret.* de TO SING.

sanguinary [sǽŋgwineri], *a.* sanguinario. —**sanguine** [sǽŋgwin], *a.* confiado, lleno de esperanza; sanguíneo.

sanitarium [sænitériʌm], *s.* enfermería, sanatorio.—**sanitary** [sǽniteri], *a.* sanitario; higiénico.—**sanitation** [sæn-

itéjȃǫn], *s.* saneamiento; sanidad.—
sanity [sǽnįtį], *s.* cordura; sensatez;
sanidad.
sank [sæŋk], *pret.* de TO SINK.
sap [sæp], *vti.* [1] zapar, minar.—*s.*
savia; (fort.) zapa; (fam.) tonto.
sapling [sǽplįŋ], *s.* renuevo, vástago.
sapphire [sǽfajr], *s.* zafiro.
Saracen [sǽrasȇn], *s.* sarraceno.
sarcasm [sárkæzm], *s.* sarcasmo.—**sarcastic** [sarkǽstįk], *a.* sarcástico.
sardine [sardín], *s.* sardina.
sash [sæȓ], *s.* (mil.) faja, banda; cinturón, ceñidor; (carp.) bastidor o marco
de ventana.—*s. window,* ventana de
guillotina.
sat [sæt], *pret.* y *pp.* de TO SIT.
satanic [sejtǽnįk], *a.* satánico.
satchel [sǽchȇl], *s.* maletín; bolsa.
sate [sejt], *vt.* hartar, saciar; hastiar.
sateen [satín], *s.* (tej.) satén, rasete.
satellite [sǽtȇlajt], *s.* satélite.
satin [sǽtįn], *s.* (tej.) raso.
satire [sǽtajr], *s.* sátira.—**satiric(al)**
[sątírįk(ȃl)], *a.* satírico.—**satirize**
[sǽtįrajz], *vt.* satirizar.
satisfaction [sætįsfǽkȓǫn], *s.* satisfacción.—**satisfactory** [sætįsfǽktǫrį], *a.*
satisfactorio; suficiente.—*a.* satisfecho, contento.—**satisfy** [sǽtįsfaj],
vti. y *vii.* [7] satisfacer.—*to s. oneself
that,* convencerse de que.
saturate [sǽchȗrejt], *vt.* saturar; empapar, impregnar.—**saturation** [sæch-
ȗréjȃǫn], *s.* saturación.
Saturday [sǽtȯȇrdį], *s.* sábado.
satyr [séjtœ(r), sǽtœ(r)], *s.* sátiro
sauce [sǫs], *s.* salsa.—*vt.* condimentar;
sazonar.— **dish** [sǫsdįȓ], *s.* salsera.—
pan [-pæn], *s.* cacerola.— **r**
[sǫscȇ(r)], *s.* platillo.—**sauciness** [sǫsį-
nįs], *s.* insolencia.—**saucy** [sǫsį], *a.*
respondón, descarado, insolente.
sauerkraut [sáȗrkraȗt], *s.* col agria.
sausage [sǫsįdž], *s.* salchicha; embutido; chorizo; longaniza; morcilla.
savage [sǽvįdž], *s.* salvaje; bárbaro;
feroz; enfurecido.—*s.* salvaje.— **ry**
[-rį], *s.* salvajismo.
savanna(h) [sȃvǽnȃ], *s.* (Am.) sabana.
save [sejv], *vt.* salvar; guardar, conservar; evitar; ahorrar, economizar.—
prep. salvo, excepto.—*conj.* sino, a
menos que, a no ser que.—**saving**
[įŋ], *a.* ahorrativo, frugal, económico;
salvador.—*s.* economía, ahorro; salvedad.—*pl.* ahorros.—*savings bank,*
caja de ahorros.—*prep.* con excepción
de, fuera de, excepto, salvo.—**savior**
[séjvyȯ(r)], *s.* salvador.—*the Saviour,*
El Salvador (Jesucristo).
saw [sǫ], *s.* (carp.) sierra.—*vti.* [6]
serrar, aserrar.—*pret.* de TO SEE.—
buck [sóbʌk], *s.* caballete de aserrar, tijera; (fam.) billete de diez

pesos.— **dust** [-dʌst], *s.* (a)serrín.—
horse [-hȯrs], *s.* = SAWBUCK.—
mill [-mįl], *s.* aserradero, aserrío.—
sawn [sǫn], *pp.* de TO SAW.—*a.* ase-
rrado.— **pit** [-pįt], *s.* aserradero.
Saxon [sǽksǫn], *a.* y *s.* sajón.
saxophone [sǽksofoȗn], *s.* saxofón.
say [sej], *vti.* y *vii.* [10] decir.—*I s.!*
¡digo!—*it is said, they s.,* se dice,
dicen.—*s.!* ¡oiga!—*so to s.,* por decirlo
así.—*to s. good-bye,* despedirse, decir
adiós.—*to s. in one's sleeve,* decir para
su capote.—*to s. nothing of,* sin mencionar.—*to s. on,* continuar hablando.
—*that is to s.,* es decir, esto es.—
you don't s. (so)! ¡calle Ud.! ¡no es
posible!—*s.* uso de la palabra; expresión de opinión; afirmación.—*s.-so,*
(fam.) opinión o juicio personal; declaración autorizada.— **ing** [séjįŋ],
s. dicho; aserto; decir, refrán.—*as the
s. goes,* como dijo el otro, como dice
el refrán.
scab [skæb], *s.* (cir.) costra, escara.
—*vii.* [1] encostrar.
scabbard [skǽbȃrd], *s.* vaina.
scabies [skéjbiz], *s.* sarna.
scaffold [skǽfoȗld], *s.* andamio, tablado; cadalso, patíbulo.— **ing** [-įŋ],
s. andamiada, andamiaje; paral.
scald [skǫld], *vt.* escaldar; (coc.) escalfar.—*s.* quemadura, escaldadura.
scale [skejl], *s.* escala; gama; platillo
de balanza; (gen. en *pl.*) balanza,
báscula; escama (de peces, reptiles);
(med.) costra; laminita, plancha, hojuela.—*to s.,* (dib.) según escala.—
vt. escamar o dos(es)camar; cubrir con
escamas; incrustar o desincrustar; escalar; (con **down**) reducir según
escala; pesar.—*vi.* (a veces con **off**)
descostrarse; desconcharse, pelarse.
scallop [skǽlǫp], *s.* (molusco) vieira;
concha de peregrino; venera; (cost.)
festón, onda.—*vt.* festonear, ondear;
(coc.) asar ostras empanadas.
scalp [skælp], *s.* cuero cabelludo.—*vt.*
arrancar el cuero cabelludo; comprar
y revender (acciones, billetes de f.c.,
teatro, etc.) a precios extraoficiales.
scaly [skéjlį], *a.* escamoso; herrumbroso.
scan [skæn], *vti.* [1] escudriñar; hojear,
repasar; medir (versos).
scandal [skǽndȃl], *s.* escándalo. **ize**
[-ajz], *vt.* escandalizar.— **ous** [-ʌs],
a. escandaloso.
Scandinavian [skændįnéjvįȃn], *a.* y *s.*
escandinavo.
scapular [skǽpyȗlȃ(r)], *s.* (igl.) escapulario; (cir.) escapulario, vendaje
para el hombro.
scar [skar], *s.* cicatriz; costurón.—*vti.*
[1] marcar con una cicatriz.
scarce [skers], *a.* raro, escaso, contado.

—scarcity [skɛ́rṣiṭi], *s.* carestía, escasez; rareza.

scare [sker], *vt.* asustar, espantar; amedrentar, intimidar.—*to s. away*, espantar, ahuyentar.—*s.* susto, sobresalto, espanto.— —crow [skɛ́rkrou], *s.* espantajo; (fam.) esperpento.

scarf [skarf], *s.* bufanda; chalina; tapete (de mesa).—*vt.* (carp.) acoplar.

scarlet [skárlit], *s.* escarlata, grana.—*a.* de color escarlata.—*s. fever*, escarlatina.

scary [skɛ́ri], *a.* (fam.) medroso, asustadizo.

scatter [skǽtœ(r)], *vt.* y *vi.* esparcir(se), diseminar(se), desparramar(se), desperdigar(se); dispersar(se).—*s.-brained*, atolondrado, ligero de cascos.

scene [sin], *s.* escena, vista; escenario; decoración.—*behind the scenes*, entre bastidores.—*to make a s.*, dar un escándalo.— —ry [sínœri], *s.* vista, paisaje; (teat.) decoraciones, decorado.—scenic [sínik], *a.* escénico; teatral; pintoresco.

scent [sent], *s.* olfato; olor, perfume, fragancia; rastro, pista.—*to throw off the s.*, despistar.—*vt.* y *vi.* oler, olfatear, husmear, ventear; rastrear.

scepter [séptœ(r)], *s.* cetro.

sceptic [sképtik], *s.* y *a.* = SKEPTIC.

schedule [skédẓul], *vt.* inventariar, catalogar; fijar el tiempo para; establecer un itinerario.—*s.* cédula; horario (de f.c., etc.); itinerario; suplemento; plan, programa; lista; tarifa.

scheme [skim], *s.* plan, proyecto, programa; planta, esquema; diseño, bosquejo; ardid, treta, artificio.—*vt.* y *vi.* proyectar, trazar; urdir, tramar.

schism [sízm], *s.* cisma; escisión.— —atic [sizmǽtik], *a.* y *s.* cismático.

scholar [skálá(r)], *s.* escolar, estudiante, colegial; becario; hombre erudito, docto.— —ly [li], *a.* erudito, ilustrado, docto.—*adv.* eruditamente, doctamente.— —ship [ṣip]. *s.* saber, erudición; beca.—scholastic [skolǽstik], *a.* escolástico; escolar.—school [skul], *s.* escuela; colegio; facultad de universidad.—*boarding s.*, colegio de internos.—*s. of fishes*, banco de peces.—*s. year*, año escolar.—*a.* escolar; de escuela; para escuela.—*s. board*, junta de educación.—*s. desk*, pupitre.—*secondary s.*, instituto de segunda enseñanza.—*vt.* instruir, enseñar, aleccionar, adiestrar.—schoolboy [skúlboj], *s.* muchacho de escuela, colegial.—schoolgirl [skúlgœrl], *s.* niña de escuela, colegiala.—schoolhouse [skúlhaus], *s.* escuela (edificio).—schooling [skúlin], *s.* instrucción elemental; educación, enseñanza.—schoolmaster [skúlmæstœ(r)], *s.* maestro de escuela.—schoolmate [skúlmejt], *s.* condiscípulo.—schoolroom [skúlrum], *s.* aula, sala de clase.—schoolteacher [skúltichœ(r)], *s.* = SCHOOLMASTER.

schooner [skúnœ(r)], *s.* goleta.

science [sájens], *s.* ciencia.—scientific [sajentífik], *a.* científico.—scientist [sájentist], *s.* científico u hombre de ciencia.

scissors [sízɔ(r)z], *s. pl.* tijeras.

scoff [skaf], *vi.* (con at) mofarse o burlarse de; befar.—*s.* mofa, escarnio, burla, befa.— —law [skáflo], *s.* el que burla el cumplimiento de la ley.

scold [skould], *vt.* y *vi.* regañar, reñir, reprender.—*s.* regañón; mujer de lenguaje soez.— —ing [skóuldin], *s.* regaño, reprensión.—*a.* regañón.

scoop [skup], *s.* pala de mano; cuchara o cucharón de draga; paletada; (fam.) hallazgo, ganancia; noticia que publica un periódico antes que los demás.—*vt.* sacar con pala o cuchara; achicar; ahuecar, cavar, excavar.

scoot [skut], *vi.* (fam.) largarse, tomar las de Villadiego.— —er [skútœ(r)], *s.* patinete, carriola; motoneta.

scope [skoup], *s.* alcance, extensión; campo, espacio o esfera de acción; (fig.) envergadura.

scorch [skɔrch], *vt.* chamuscar, rescaldar, tostar; quemar, abrasar, picar (el sol).—*vi.* quemarse, secarse; abrasarse (apl. a las plantas).—*s.* quemadura superficial, chamusquina.

score [skor], *s.* línea, raya; cuenta, tantos (en el juego); (dep.) anotación, punteo, tanteo; resultado final; (mús.) partitura; veintena.—*on that s.*, a ese respecto, en cuanto a eso.—*on the s. of*, con motivo de.—*s. keeper*, (dep.) anotador, tanteador.—*to settle a s.*, ajustar cuentas; saldar una cuenta.—*vt.* rayar; tantear, ganar tantos en un juego; (mús.) instrumentar.—*to s. a point*, (dep.) ganar un tanto; obtener un triunfo.—*vi.* marcar; llevar una cuenta; marcar los tantos en un juego; (fig.) recibir buena acogida, merecer aplausos.— —r [skórœ(r)], *s.* marcador.

scorn [skɔrn], *vt.* y *vi.* despreciar, menospreciar, desdeñar.—*s.* desdén, menosprecio, desprecio.— —ful [skórnful], *a.* desdeñoso, despreciativo.

scorpion [skórpion], *s.* escorpión, alacrán.

scot [skat], *s.* escote, tasa, gravamen, contribución; (S.) escocés.—*s. free*, libre de gravámenes; sano y salvo; impune.—Scotch [skach], *a.* escocés. —*s.* pueblo escocés; lengua escocesa; (E.U.) whisky escocés.—Scotchman

[skáchmạn], *s.* escocés.—**Scottish** [skátiš], *a.* = scotch.

scoundrel [skáundrẹl], *s.* pícaro, bribón, truhán.

scour [skaụr], *vt.* y *vi.* fregar, restregar, limpiar; pulir, alisar; quitar restregando.—*s.* recorrida; limpiador (esp. de lana).— **-er** [skáụrœ(r)], *s.* limpiador, desengrasador, asperón.

scourge [skœrdž], *s.* azote, flagelo; plaga.—*vt.* azotar, flagelar.

scout [skaụt], *s.* (mil.) explorador, batidor, escucha; niño explorador.—*vt.* y *vi.* (mil.) explorar; reconocer.—*to s. at*, burlarse de, escarnecer; rechazar con desdén.

scowl [skaụl], *vi.* fruncir el ceño o el entrecejo; enfurruñarse; tener mal cariz.—*s.* ceño, entrecejo; mal cariz.

scram [skræm], *vii.* [1] (fam.) irse de prisa.—*interj.* ¡largo! ¡fuera!

scramble [skrǽmbl], *vt.* recoger de prisa o confusamente; embrollar; (coc.) hacer un revoltillo.—*scrambled eggs*, revoltillo, huevos revueltos.—*vi.* (bot.) trepar; andar a la rebatiña, bregar.— *s.* contienda, rebatiña.

scrap [skræp], *s.* migaja, mendrugo; pedacillo, fragmento; sobras; material viejo o de desecho; (fam.) riña, camorra.—*s. iron*, hierro viejo, chatarra.—*vti.* [1] echar a la basura; descartar; desbaratar, desmantelar (un buque).—*vii.* (fam.) reñir, armar camorra.— **-book** [skrǽpbụk], *s.* álbum de recortes.

scrape [skreịp], *vt.* y *vi.* raspar, rozar; rasguñar, arañar; (a veces con up o **together**) recoger, amontonar poco a poco; tocar mal (un instrumento de cuerda); restregar los pies.—*to s. acquaintance*, trabar amistad.—*to s. along*, (fam.) ir tirando, ir escapando. —*s.* raspadura, rasguño, arañazo; enredo, lío, aprieto, apuro.— **-r** [skreịpœ(r)], *s.* raspador, rascador; (fam.) rascatripas; (mar.) rasqueta.

scratch [skræch], *vt.* y *vi.* rascar, raspar; arañar; rasguñar; rayar (el vidrio); escribir mal, garrapatear; escarbar; borrar.—*s.* rasguño, arañazo; marca o raya; (dep.) línea de arrancada en una carrera.—*s. paper* o *pad*, papel o cuadernillo de apuntes.—*to start from s.*, empezar sin nada, o de (la) nada; comenzar desde el principio.— *up to s.*, en buenas o excelentes condiciones.

scrawl [skrɔl], *vt.* garrapatear, garabatear.—*s.* garabato, garrapato.

scream [skrim], *vt.* y *vi.* chillar; gritar. —*s.* grito, alarido, chillido; (fam.) cosa o persona jocosa.

screech [skrich], *vi.* chillar, ulular.—

s. chillido, alarido.— **-y** [skríchị], *a.* chillón, agudo.

screen [skrin], *s.* biombo, mampara; pantalla; resguardo; criba, cedazo, tamiz.—*s. star*, (cine) estrella o astro de la pantalla.—*the s.*, el cine, el celuloide,. la pantalla.—*vt.* cribar, cerner, tamizar; escudar, proteger; filmar; proyectar en la pantalla.

screw [skru], *s.* tornillo.—*a.* de tornillo. —*s. bolt*, perno roscado.—*s. nut*, rosca, hembra de tornillo.—*s. plate*, terraja o tarraja.—*s. thread*, rosca (de tornillo).—*vt.* atornillar, (Am.) tornillar; torcer, retorcer.—*to s. off*, des(a)tornillar.— **-driver** [skrúdraịvœ(r)], *s.* destornillador.

scribble [skríbl], *vt.* y *vi.* escribir de prisa; garrapatear, garabatear, emborronar.—*s.* garabato, garabateo.

script [skrịpt], *s.* guión de película; (teat.) manuscrito; (rad.) libreto; letra cursiva; (for.) escritura; material escrito a máquina.—**Scripture** [skrípchụr], *s.* (Sagrada) Escritura.

scrofula [skráfyụlǝ], *s.* escrófula, (Am.) lamparón.

scroll [skroụl], *s.* rollo de papel o pergamino; rasgo, rúbrica; (arq.) cinta, voluta.—*a.* en espiral; de caracol.

scrub [skrab], *vti.* [1] fregar, estregar; restregar.—*a.* achaparrado, desmirriado; inferior.—*s.* team, (dep.) equipo de jugadores novicios o suplentes.—*s.* estropajo, escoba vieja; animal de raza mixta e inferior; persona mezquina o inferior.

scruff [skraf], *s.* nuca, pescuezo.

scruple [skrúpl], *s.* escrúpulo.—*vi.* tener escrúpulos.—**scrupulous** [skrúpyụlʌs], *a.* escrupuloso; puntilloso.— **scrupulousness** [skrúpyụljsnịs], *s.* escrupulosidad.

scrutinize [skrútịnaịz], *vt.* escudriñar, escrutar.—**scrutiny** [skrútịnị], *s.* escrutinio.

sculptor [skʌ́lptœ(r)], *s.* escultor.— **sculpture** [skʌ́lpchụ(r)], *s.* escultura. —*vt.* esculpir, cincelar.

scum [skʌm], *s.* espuma, nata; hez, escoria.—*the s. of the people*, la canalla.

scurvy [skœrvị], *s.* escorbuto.

scuttle [skʌ́tl], *s.* escotillón; trampa; barreno, agujero; carrera corta; cubo, balde (para carbón).—*vt.* barrenar, dar barreno a un barco; echar a pique.—*vi.* apretar a correr.

scythe [saịð], *s.* guadaña.

sea [si], *s.* mar.—*a.* de mar, marino, marítimo.—*beyond the s.* o *seas*, allende el mar; fuera de aguas jurisdiccionales.—*s. biscuit*, galleta de barco.—*s. breeze*, brisa de mar, virazón.—*s. chart*, carta náutica o de marear.—*s. food*, pescado y mariscos

comestibles.—*s. green*, verdemar, glauco.—*s. gull.* gaviota.—*s. lion*, foca, león marino.—*s. power*, potencia naval.— —*board* [síbɔrd], *a.* costanero, litoral.—*s.* costa; litoral.— —*coast* [-koṵst], *s.* costa, litoral.

seal [sil], *s.* sello; timbre; precinto; firma; (zool.) foca.—*under the hand and s. of,* firmado y sellado por.— *vt.* sellar, precintar; estampar; cerrar una carta o paquete (con goma o lacre).— —*ing wax* [síliŋ wæks], *s.* lacre.

seam [sim], *s.* costura, cosedura; sutura; cicatriz, marca; (min.) filón, veta; yacimiento; (mec.) junta, costura (de un tubo, una caldera, etc.).— *vt.* echar una costura, coser; marcar con cicatriz.

seaman [síman], *s.* marinero, marino.

seamless [símlis], *a.* sin costura.— **seamstress** [símstris], *s.* costurera; modistilla.—**seamy** [sími], *a.* con costuras.—*the s. side*, el lado malo.

seaplane [síplejn], *s.* hidroavión.—**seaport** [síport], *s.* puerto de mar.

sear [sir], *a.* seco, marchito.—*vt.* secar, marchitar; tostar, chamuscar; cauterizar.

search [scœrch], *vt. y vi.* buscar, explorar, escudriñar; registrar (una casa); investigar, indagar.—*to s. after,* preguntar por; indagar, inquirir.—*to s. for*, buscar; solicitar, procurar.—*to s. out*, buscar hasta descubrir.—*s.* registro, reconocimiento; pesquisa, indagación o investigación; búsqueda, busca.—*in s. of*, en busca de.—*s. for arms*, cacheo.— —*ing* [scœrchiŋ], *a.* penetrante, escrutador.— —**light** [-lajt], *s.* reflector lumínico (orientable); luz proyectada por éste.

seashore [síšɔr], *s.* playa, litoral, ribera, costa, orilla del mar.—**seasick** [sísjk], *a.* mareado.—*to get s.*, marearse.— **seasickness** [sísjknis], *s.* mareo.— **seaside** [sísajd], *s.* = SEASHORE.

season [sízɔn], *s.* estación (del año); sazón; temporada.—*in s.*, en sazón; *a su tiempo.*—*vt.* (coc.) sazonar, condimentar, aliñar; aclimatar, habituar. *vi.* sazonarse, madurarse, habituarse.— —**ing** [-iŋ], *s.* (coc.) condimento, aliño, aderezo, sazón; salsa o sal (de un cuento, etc.); desecación, cura (de la madera).

seat [sit], *s.* asiento; silla; escaño; (teat.) localidad; (sast.) fondillo de los calzones; nalga; sede (de diócesis); sitio, paraje; mansión, quinta.—*s. of war*, teatro de la guerra.—*vt.* sentar, asentar; colocar en asientos; tener asientos o cabida para; ajustar (una válvula) en su asiento; poner asiento a (una silla, etc.); echar fondillos (a

un pantalón).—*vi.* asentar, ajustar en su asiento (una válvula, etc.).

seaweed [síwid], *s.* alga marina.

secant [síkænt], *s.* (geom.) secante.

seclude [sikljúd], *vt.* apartar, recluir.— *vi.* alejarse de otros.— —**d** [sikljúdjd], *a.* alejado o apartado; retirado, solitario, recogido.—**seclusion** [sikljúžɔn], *s.* reclusión, aislamiento, soledad; retiro.

second [sékɔnd], *a.* segundo, secundario; inferior.—*every s. day*, cada dos días; un día sí y otro no.—*on s. thought*, después de repensarlo; después de pensarlo bien.—*s. hand*, segundero (de reloj).—*s. rate*, de segunda clase o categoría, de pacotilla.— —*s.* segundo; momento, instante; brazo derecho; ayudante; padrino (en un duelo); segundo (de tiempo).— *vt.* apoyar, apadrinar; secundar o apoyar (una proposición).—*adv.* en segundo lugar.— —**ary** [-eri], *a.* secundario.—*s. school*, escuela secundaria o de segunda enseñanza.— —**hand** [-hænd], *a.* de segunda mano, usado; indirecto, por conducto ajeno o de oídas.— —**ly** [-lj], *adv.* en segundo lugar.

secrecy [síkresi], *s.* secreto, reserva; sigilo.—**secret** [síkrjt], *a.* secreto; escondido, oculto, recóndito.—*s.* secreto.—**secretary** [sékrẹterj], *s.* secretario, secretaria.—**secrete** [sikrít], *vt.* esconder, ocultar, encubrir; (fisiol.) secretar.—**secretion** [sikríšɔn], *s.* (fisiol.) secreción.—**secretive** [sikrítjv], *a.* callado, reservado; secretorio.

section [sékšɔn], *s.* sección, división; porción; tajada muy delgada; departamento, negociado; (dib.) corte, sección.—*vt.* seccionar, dividir en secciones.

secular [sékyṵlǎ(r)], *a. y s.* secular.

secure [sikjúr], *a.* seguro; confiado; firme, fuerte.—*vt.* asegurar, resguardar; afianzar, fijar; garantizar; procurarse, obtener.—**security** [sikjúriti], *s.* seguridad, seguro (social); protección o defensa; fianza, garantía, prenda; fiador.—*pl.* (com.) valores, obligaciones.—*public securities*, efectos públicos.—*securities in hand*, valores en cartera.

sedate [sidéjt], *a.* sentado, sosegado, serio.—**sedative** [sédatjv], *a. y s.* (med.) sedativo, sedante, calmante.

sedge [sedž], *s.* (bot.) junco.

sediment [sédimẹnt], *s.* sedimento, borra.

sedition [sidíšɔn], *s.* sedición.—**seditious** [sidíšʌs], *a.* sedicioso.

seduce [sidjús], *vt.* seducir, deshonrar.— —**r** [-œ(r)], *s.* seductor, burlador.— —**seduction** [sidʌ́kšɔn], *s.* seducción.

see [si], *vti. y vii.* [10] ver.—*s.?* (fam.) ¿comprende? ¿sabe?—*to s. about,* pensar en; averiguar.—*to s. (a person) home,* acompañar (a una persona) a su casa.—*to s. (a person) off,* ir a despedir (a una persona).—*to s. red,* echar chispas, montar en cólera.—*to s. through (a proposition),* comprender (una proposición).—*to s. through (a person),* (fig.) leer, adivinar el pensamiento (a una persona).—*to s. (a person) through,* ayudar (a una persona) a salir del paso, o hasta lo último.—*to s. (a thing) through,* llevar (una cosa) hasta el cabo; estar (en una cosa) hasta lo último.—*to s. to,* atender a, tener cuidado de; cuidarse de.—*to s. to it that,* atender a que, ver que, hacer que.—*I see,* ¡ya! ya veo, comprendo.—*let me s.,* vamos a ver; déjeme pensar.—*s.* (igl.) silla, sede.

seed [sid], *s.* semilla, simiente; grano; pepita.—*s. plot,* semillero.—*to go o run to s.,* granar; agotarse, envejecerse.—*vt.* sembrar; despepitar.—*vi.* hacer la siembra.— **-ling** [sídliŋ], *s.* planta de semilla; planta de semillero; retoño, brote.— **-y** [-i], *a.* que tiene muchas semillas; (fam.) andrajoso, descamisado, zarrapastroso.

seeing [síiŋ], *s.* vista, visión.—*conj.—s. that,* visto que, siendo así que, puesto que, ya que.—*a.* vidente, que ve.

seek [sik], *vti. y vii.* [10] buscar; pedir, procurar, solicitar, aspirar a.—*to s. after,* buscar, tratar de obtener.—*to s. for,* buscar.

seem [sim], *vi.* parecer; parecerle a uno.—*it seems to me,* me parece.— **-ingly** [símiŋli], *adv.* aparentemente, al parecer.

seen [sin], *pp.* de TO SEE.

seep [sip], *vi.* filtrar; colarse, rezumarse, escurrirse.

seesaw [síso], *s.* vaivén, columpio.—*a.* de vaivén, de balance.—*vi.* columpiarse.

seethe [sið], *vt.* remojar, empapar.—*vi.* hervir, bullir; estar agitado; burbujear.

segment [ségmęnt], *s.* segmento; sección.

segregate [ségręgeit], *vt. y vi.* segregar(se), separar(se).—*a.* segregado, separado.— **segregation** [sęgręgéişǫn], *s.* segregación, separación.

seismic [sáizmik], *a.* sísmico.— **seismograph** [sáizmǫgræf], *s.* sismógrafo.

seize [siz], *vt.* asir, agarrar, coger; capturar, prender; apoderarse de; aprovecharse de; (for.) secuestrar, embargar, decomisar, incautarse de (bienes, etc.).—*to be seized of,* (for.) obtener posesión de.—*to be seized with,* sobrecogerse de.—*vi.* (gen con **on o upon**) agarrar, coger; apoderarse de.— **seizure** [sízü(r)], *s.* aprehensión, prisión; captura, presa; (mil.) toma; (for.) embargo, secuestro, decomiso; (med.) ataque, acceso súbito de una enfermedad.

seldom [séldǫm], *adv.* raramente, rara vez, por rareza.

select [sęlékt], *vt.* seleccionar, escoger, entresacar.—*a.* selecto, escogido.— **-ion** [sęlékşǫn], *s.* selección, elección.

self [self], *a.* uno mismo; se; sí mismo. —*s.* uno mismo, sí mismo.—*s.-conscious,* consciente de sí mismo; afectado, falto de naturalidad.—*s.-consistent,* consecuente consigo mismo.— *s.-control,* continencia; imperio sobre sí mismo.—*s.-defense,* defensa propia. —*s.-possession,* sangre fría, serenidad, aplomo.—*s.-respect,* pundonor, dignidad, decoro, respeto de sí mismo.— *s.-winding,* de cuerda automática (apl. a relojes).— **-ish** [sélfiş], *a.* egoísta, interesado.— **-ishness** [-işnjs], *s.* egoísmo.— **-same** [-séjm], *a.* idéntico, mismísimo.

sell [sel], *vti. y vii.* [10] vender(se).— *to s. on trust,* fiar, vender al fiado o al crédito.—*to s. out,* realizar, hacer venta de realización; venderlo todo.— **-er** [sélœ(r)], *s.* vendedor.— **-ing** [-iŋ], *s.* venta.

selves [selvz], *s. pl.* de SELF.

semen [símęn], *s.* semen, esperma; (bot.) simiente, semilla.

semester [sęméstœ(r)], *s.* semestre.

semicircle [sémişœrkl], *s.* semicírculo.

semicolon [sémikǫuļǫn], *s.* punto y coma (;).

seminary [séminęri], *s.* seminario.

senate [sénit], *s.* senado.—**senator** [sénątǫ(r)], *s.* senador.

send [send], *vti.* [10] enviar, despachar, expedir; lanzar, arrojar.—*to s. away,* despedir, poner en la calle.—*to s. back,* devolver; enviar de vuelta.—*to s. forth,* echar (retoños, etc.); emitir, despedir (luz, vapores); enviar, despachar.—*to s. in,* hacer entrar; introducir.—*to s. off,* despachar, expedir.— *to s. one about one's business,* enviar a paseo.—*to s. up,* mandar subir; (fam.) enviar a la cárcel.—*to s. word,* mandar recado; avisar; enviar a decir.— **-er** [séndœ(r)], *s.* remitente; (elec.) transmisor.

senile [sínail], *a.* senil, caduco, chocho. —**senility** [sęníliti], *s.* senilidad, senectud.

senior [sínyǫ(r)], *a.* mayor, de mayor edad; más antiguo.—*s.* señor mayor, anciano; socio más antiguo o principal; (E.U.) escolar del último año; (abreviado Sr.) padre.

sensation [sɛnséjṣọn], *s.* sensación.—*to be a s.*, ser un exitazo.— —**al** [-ạl], *a.* sensacional; escandaloso; emocionante.—**sense** [sɛns], *s.* sentido; razón, juicio; sensación; sentimiento; significado, interpretación.—*in a s.*, hasta cierto punto.—*to be out of one's senses,* haber perdido el juicio, no estar en sus cabales.—*vt.* percibir por los sentidos; (fam.) sentir.—**senseless** [sénslịs], *a.* insensible, privado, sin conocimiento; sin sentido, absurdo; insensato, necio.—**sensibility** [sɛnsịbịlịtị], *s.* sensibilidad.—**sensible** [sénsịbl], *a.* cuerdo, razonable; sensato; sensible; sensitivo.—**sensibly** [sénsịblị], *adv.* perceptiblemente, sensiblemente; con sensatez o sentido común. —**sensitive** [sénsịtịv], *a.* sensitivo; sensible, impresionable; susceptible; tierno; delicado; (fot.) sensibilizado. —**sensitiveness** [sénsịtịvnịs], *s.* sensibilidad; susceptibilidad; finura, delicadeza.

sensual [sénṣụạl], *a.* sensual, lascivo, lujurioso; carnal.— —**ity** [sɛnṣụélịtị], *s.* sensualidad, lascivia; lujuria.

sent [sɛnt], *pret.* y *pp.* de TO SEND.

sentence [séntɛns], *s.* (gram.) oración, cláusula; (for.) sentencia, fallo; condena (de presidio); máxima, sentencia o dicho.—*vt.* sentenciar, condenar.

sentiment [séntịmẹnt], *s.* sentimiento; afecto, simpatía; opinión, sentir; sentido, significado.— —**al** [sɛntịméntạl], *a.* sentimental.— —**ality** [sɛntịmɛntáelịtị], *s.* sentimentalismo.

sentinel [séntịnẹl], **sentry** [séntrị], *s.* (mil.) centinela.—*s. box,* garita (de centinela).

separate [sépạrẹịt], *vt.* y *vi.* separar(se); apartar(se).—*a.* [sépạrịt], separado, aparte, suelto; distinto, diferente.— **separation** [sɛpạréjṣọn], *s.* separación.

September [sɛptémbœ(r)], *s.* septiembre.

sepulcher [sépʌlkœ(r)], *s.* sepulcro, sepultura.

sequel [síkwẹl], *s.* secuela, consecuencia, efecto; continuación.—**sequence** [síkwẹns], *s.* secuencia; serie, orden de sucesión; arreglo; encadenamiento, ilación; efecto; (en los naipes) runfla de un palo.

sequin [síkwịn], *s.* lentejuela.

sequoia [sịkwójạ], *s.* abeto gigantesco de California, secoya.

serape [serápej], *s.* sarape.

Serb [sœrb], **Serbian** [sœrbịạn], *s.* y *a.* servio.

serenade [serẹnéjd], *s.* (mús.) serenata. —*vt.* dar serenata a.

serene [sẹrín], *a.* sereno, despejado; sosegado, tranquilo.—**serenity** [serén-

ịtị], *s.* serenidad; tranquilidad, calma, quietud.

serge [sœrdẑ], *s.* estameña.

sergeant [sárdẑẹnt], *s.* (mil.) sargento.

serial [sịrịạl], *a.* de o en serie; de orden (número, marca, etc.); consecutivo; formando serie; que se publica po. entregas.—*s.* obra que se publica por entregas; película por episodios.—**series** [sịrịz], *s.* serie; sucesión, cadena; ciclo.—*in s.*, (elec.) en serie.

serious [sịrịʌs], *a.* serio; formal; grave, de peso.- —**ness** [-nịs], *s.* seriedad; formalidad; gravedad.

sermon [sœrmọn], *s.* sermón.

serpent [sœrpẹnt], *s.* serpiente o sierpe.

serum [sịrʌm], *s.* suero.

servant [sœrvạnt], *s.* criado, sirviente; servidor.—*pl.* servidumbre.—*s. girl, s. maid,* criada, sirvienta, doncella, (Am.) mucama.—**serve** [sœrv], *vt.* servir; manejar, hacer funcionar (un cañón, etc.); abastecer, surtir; cumplir (una condena).—*it serves you right,* (en tono de represión) te está bien empleado; bien se lo merece Ud.—*to s. an office,* desempeñar un cargo.—*to s. a warrant,* ejecutar un auto de prisión.—*to s. one a trick,* jugar a uno una mala partida.—*to s. notice (on),* avisar o dar aviso, hacer saber, advertir, notificar.—*to s. time,* cumplir una condena en presidio. —*vi.* servir; bastar, ser suficiente o apto; (dep.) efectuar el saque, sacar. —*to s. for,* servir de; hacer oficio de. —*s.* (dep.) saque.—**server** [sœrvœ(r)], *s.* servidor.—**service** [sœrvịs], *s.* servicio; (dep.) saque; vajilla, servicio de mesa, juego (de café, etc.); entrega legal de una citación.—*at your s.*, a su disposición, a sus órdenes, servidor de Ud.—*it is of no s.*, no vale nada, de nada sirve.—*out of s.*, (mec.) que no funciona, descompuesto.—*s. station,* (aut.) estación de servicio, taller de reparaciones.—*vt.* atender a, suministrar lo necesario a o para.—**serviceable** [sœrvịsạbl], *a.* servicial, servible, útil; duradero.—**servile** [sœrvịl], *a.* servil, bajo, abyecto.—**servitude** [sœrvịtịud], *s.* servidumbre; esclavitud; vasallaje; (for.) servidumbre.

session [séṣọn], *s.* sesión; período escolar.

set [sɛt], *vti.* [9] poner; colocar, asentar; instalar, establecer; fijar, inmovilizar; señalar, engastar, montar (piedras preciosas); arreglar, regular, ajustar; establecer; componer (tipos de imprenta); poner en música; (med.) reducir (fracturas).—*to s. afire,* poner fuego a, incendiar.—*to s. ajar,* entornar, entreabrir.—*to s. an example,*

dar ejemplo.—*to s. a price on,* fijar precio a; poner precio, ofrecer premio por.—*to s. aside,* poner aparte.—*to s. a trap,* armar una trampa.—*to s. back,* hacer retroceder; atrasar, retrasar.—*to s. eyes on,* ver; mirar; clavar los ojos en.—*to s. fire to,* poner o prender fuego a, incendiar; inflamar (las pasiones).—*to s. forth,* manifestar; exponer; publicar.—*to s. in,* (joy.) montar, engastar.—*to s. off,* poner aparte, separar; poner en relieve; disparar. —*to s. up the drinks,* (fam.) convidar (a beber).—*vii.* ponerse (un astro); cuajarse, solidificarse; endurecerse; fraguar (el hormigón, etc.); correr, moverse o fluir (una corriente); empollar (las aves); (fam.) ajustar, caer bien (una prenda de vestir).—*to s. forth,* avanzar, ponerse en marcha.— *to s. in,* comenzar, aparecer, sobrevenir; cerrar (la noche).—*to set off,* salir, partir.—*to s. on o upon,* salir, partir; emprender un viaje o un negocio.—*to s. to work,* poner manos a la obra; emprender el trabajo.—*to s. up,* establecerse; principiar.—*pret.* y *pp.* de TO SET.—*a.* resuelto; fijo, invariable; establecido; arreglado, ajustado; puesto, colocado; rígido; (mec.) armado; (joy.) montado, engastado.— *to be (all) s. to,* estar listo o preparado. —*s.* juego, surtido, colección, serie, grupo, clase; equipo; aparato (de radio); (astr.) puesta; curso, dirección; (teat.) decoración; (dep.) partida; (danz.) tanda; fraguado (del cemento, etc.).—*s. of books,* colección de libros.—*s. of diamonds,* terno.— —**back** [sétbæk], *s.* retroceso, revés, contrariedad; contracorriente.

settee [setí], *s.* canapé, diván.

setter [sétœ(r)], *s.* perro perdiguero.

setting [sétiŋ], *s.* puesta de un astro, ocaso; (teat.) puesta en escena, decoraciones; (joy.) engaste, montadura; (fam.) nidada.—*s. sun,* sol poniente. —*s. up,* establecimiento; (mec.) montaje.

settle [sétl], *vt.* asentar; fijar, asegurar; arreglar; establecer, estatuir; casar; colonizar, poblar; sosegar, calmar; resolver (dudas); solucionar (un problema); señalar, fijar; saldar, finiquitar, ajustar (cuentas); componer.—*to s. on o upon,* señalar, asignar, dar en dote.—*vi.* asentarse; establecerse, radicarse; instalarse, poner casa; calmar; determinarse; saldar una cuenta. —*to s. differences,* avenirse, hacer las paces.—*to s. down,* asentarse; posarse (un hidroavión o ave).— —**ment** [-mẹnt], *s.* establecimiento; colonización; colonia; caserío, poblado; (for.) asiento, domicilio; dote; empleo, des-

tino; ajuste, arreglo; (com.) saldo, liquidación, finiquito, pago.—*s. house,* casa de beneficencia.— —r [sétlœ(r)], *s.* poblador, colono; fundador.

sever [sévœ(r)], *vt.* separar, desunir, dividir; cortar, romper.—*vi.* separarse, desunirse; partirse.

several [sévœrạl], *a.* varios, diversos; distinto(s), respectivo(s).—*s.* varios, cada uno en particular.

severe [sẹvị̣r], *a.* severo, riguroso; duro; rígido, estricto, austero; grave, serio; recio, fuerte.—**severity** [sẹvẹ́rịtị], *s.* severidad, rigor; rigidez, austeridad; seriedad, gravedad.

sew [soụ], *vti.* y *vii.* [6] coser.

sewer [sịúœ(r)], *s.* albañal, cloaca, alcantarilla.

sewing [sóụiŋ], *s.* costura.—*a.* de coser; para coser.—*s. machine,* máquina de coser.—**sewn** [soụn], *pp.* de TO SEW.

sex [seks], *s.* sexo.—*s. appeal,* atracción sexual.—*the fair s.,* el bello sexo.

sexagenarian [seksạdženérịạn], *a.* y *s.* sexagenario.

sexton [sékstọn], *s.* sacristán.

sexual [sékșụạl], *a.* sexual.—*s. intercourse,* comercio sexual.—**sexy** [séksị], *a.* sensual.

shabby [s̨ǽbị], *a.* usado, gastado, raído; andrajoso, zarrapastroso; ruin, vil.

shack [s̨æk], *s.* choza, casucha.

shackle [s̨ǽkl], *vt.* encadenar; poner esposas o grilletes a; trabar; poner obstáculos, estorbar.—*s.* grillete, grillo, esposa; traba; impedimento.—*pl.* hierros, prisiones.

shade [s̨eịd], *s.* sombra; matiz, tinte; visillo, cortina; pantalla de lámpara; visera.—*vt.* sombrear; dar sombra; resguardar de la luz; matizar.—**shading** [s̨éịdịŋ], *s.* (b.a.) sombreado.—

shadow [s̨ǽdoụ], *s.* sombra (proyectada por un objeto); oscuridad; imagen reflejada (en agua o espejo).— *vt.* oscurecer, sombrear; espiar, seguir a uno como su sombra; (b.a.) sombrear, matizar.—*vi.* oscurecerse; cambiar gradualmente de color.—**shady** [s̨éịdị], *a.* sombreado, sombrío; (fam.) suspechoso.—*to keep s.,* (fam.) guardar oculto.

shaft [s̨æft], *s.* pieza larga y estrecha o parte larga y estrecha de la misma (mango, cabo, etc. de un arma o herramienta); flecha o saeta; lanza, vara (de coche, carretón, etc.); fuste (de una columna o carruaje); (mec.) eje árbol; pozo, tiro (de mina, ascensor, etc.); cañón de chimenea.

shaggy [s̨ǽgị], *a.* peludo, velludo, hirsuto; lanudo; áspero.

shake [s̨eịk], *vti.* [10] sacudir o menear, cimbrear; hacer temblar; hacer vacilar o flaquear; agitar.—*to s. hands,*

estrecharse la mano.—to s. one's head, cabecear, mover la cabeza.—to s. up, sacudir; agitar; (fam.) regañar, sermonear.—vii. temblar; estremecerse; cimbrearse; vacilar, titubear; (fam.) dar(se) la mano.—to s. in one's shoes o boots, temblar de miedo.—to s. with cold, tiritar.—to s. with laughter, desternillarse o reventar de risa.—s. sacudida; sacudimiento; temblor; apretón de manos; instante; batido (de leche, fruta, chocolate, etc.).— shaken [šéįkn], pp. de TO SHAKE.— shaky [šéįkį], a. trémulo; vacilante, tambaleante; tembloroso; debilitado; incierto.

shall [šæl], vai. [11] (se usa para formar el futuro o para expresar obligación). —they s. not pass, no pasarán.—you s. do it, tiene Ud. que hacerlo.—(V. SHOULD).

shallow [šǽlou], a. bajo, poco profundo; superficial.—s.-brained, ligero de cascos.—s. (mar.) bajío, bajo.— —ness [-nįs], s. poca profundidad; superficialidad; frivolidad.

sham [šæm], vti. y vii. [1] simular, fingir.—s. fingimiento, ficción; (fam.) bambolla, farsa.—a. fingido, disimulado; falso, postizo.—s. battle, (mil.) simulacro.

shame [šeįm], s. vergüenza; ignominia, deshonra; bochorno.—for s.! s. on you! ¡qué vergüenza!—it is a s., es una vergüenza; es una lástima.— what a s.! ¡qué lástima!—vt. avergonzar, abochornar; deshonrar.- —ful [šéįmfuł], a. vergonzoso, escandaloso. - —less [-lįs], a. desvergonzado, sin vergüenza, descarado.

shampoo [šæmpú], s. lavado de cabeza; champú.—vt. lavar la cabeza; dar champú.

shamrock [šǽmrak], s. trébol.

shank [šǽŋk], s. caña o canilla de la pierna; zanca; (mec.) asta o astil, mango, vástago, caña.

shanty [šǽntį], s. casucha, choza.

shape [šeįp], vt. formar; dar forma a.— vi. (a veces con up) empezar a tomar, formar o mostrar progreso.—s. forma, figura, hechura (de una persona); estado, manera, modo.- —less [šéįplįs], a. informe; disforme.

share [šer], vt. repartir; compartir; (con in) participar de, tener o tomar parte en.—vi. participar o tener parte.— s. parte, porción; (com.) acción; participación.—to go shares, ir a medias.— —holder [šérhouldœ(r)], s. (com.) accionista.

shark [šark], s. tiburón, escualo; (fig.) estafador; usurero; (fam.) perito, experto.

sharp [šarp], a. agudo; puntiagudo;

cortante, afilado; sagaz; vivo, astuto; incisivo, penetrante; acre, agrio; mordaz, sarcástico; distinto, claro, bien delineado o definido; (mús.) sostenido; punzante (dolor); abrupto, pronunciado (pendiente, curva, etc.).— s. features, facciones enjutas.—s. (mús.) sostenido; estafador, fullero. —adv. V. SHARPLY.—at four o'clock s., (fam.) a las cuatro en punto.— s.-edged, afilado.—s.-pointed, puntiagudo.—s.-witted, penetrante, perspicaz.- —en [šárpn], vt. afilar; aguzar, sacar punta a, amolar.—vi. aguzarse; afilarse.- —ener [-gnœ(r)], s. afilador, aguzador.—pencil s., sacapuntas.- —er [-œ(r)], s. tahur, fullero; estafador.- —ly [-lį], adv. con filo; prontamente; brusca y mordazmente; agudamente, vivamente; sutil o ingeniosamente.- —ness [-nįs], s. agudeza, sutileza, perspicacia; mordacidad; acidez; rigor; inclemencia.- —shooter [-šutœ(r)], s. tirador certero.

shatter [šǽtœ(r)], vt. destrozar, hacer pedazos o añicos; estrellar, romper; quebrantar (la salud).—vi. hacerse pedazos, quebrarse, romperse.—s. fragmento, pedazo.

shave [šeįv], vti. [6] rasurar o afeitar; rapar; (carp.) (a)cepillar; desbastar. —vii. rasurarse, afeitarse.—s. afeitado, (Am.) afeitada.—to have a close s., salvarse en una tabla, escapar por casualidad.—shaving [šéįvįŋ]. s. afeitado, rasura(ción), (Am.) afeitada.— —pl. virutas.

shawl [šɔl], s. chal, mantón, pañolón.— Spanish s., mantón de Manila.

she [ši], pron. pers. ella; (delante de who o that) la que, aquella que.—s. -cat (-goat, -ass, etc.) gata (cabra, burra, etc.).

sheaf [šif], s. gavilla, haz; atado, manojo.—vt. agavillar.

shear [šįr], vti. [6] rapar, esquilar, trasquilar; tonsurar; cortar (gen. con tijeras o cizallas).- —er [šįrœ(r)], s. esquilador.- —s [-z], s. pl. tijeras grandes; (mec.) cizallas.

sheath [šiθ], s. vaina; funda, estuche, cubierta.- —e [šið], vt. envainar; poner vaina.

sheaves [šivz], pl. de SHEAF.

shed [šed], vti. [9] desprenderse de, largar; mudar; verter, derramar; esparcir.—vii. mudar (los cuernos, la piel, las plumas).—s. cobertizo; tejadillo.—pret. y pp. de TO SHED.

sheen [šin], s. lustre, viso.

sheep [šip], s. oveja, carnero; ovejas; ganado lanar; (fig.) rebaño, grey.— s. dog, perro de pastor.- —s. tick, garrapata.- —fold [šįpfoułd], s. redil, aprisco, majada.- —ish [-įš], a. aver-

gonzado; tímido, pusilánime.—**skin** [-skịn], *s.* badana.

sheet [šit], *s.* lámina (de metal); sábana; pliego u hoja (de papel); extensión de agua.—*s. lightning*, fucilazo(s), relampagueo.

shelf [šelf], *s.* anaquel, estante, repisa, tabla, entrepaño; saliente (de roca).

shell [šel], *s.* concha, carapacho; casco (de embarcación); cáscara (de nuez, huevo, etc.); vaina (de legumbres); cubierta, corteza; armazón (de edificio); (arti.) bomba, granada, proyectil; cápsula para cartuchos; bote o canoa para regatas.—*vt.* descascarar, desvainar, mondar, pelar; (arti.) bombardear.—*vi.* descascararse.—*to s. out*, (fam.) aflojar la mosca.

shellac [šelák], *s.* (goma) laca.—*vti.* [8] barnizar con laca.—**shellacked** [šelákt], *pret. y pp.* de TO SHELLAC.

shellfish [šélfịš], *s.* marisco(s).

shelter [šéltœr], *s.* resguardo; albergue, refugio, abrigo, asilo; protector. —*vt.* guarecer, abrigar, albergar, amparar, proteger.—*to take s.*, refugiarse, guarecerse.

shelve [šelv], *vt.* poner sobre un estante o anaquel; (fig.) poner a un lado, dar carpetazo, archivar, arrinconar.— —s [-z], *pl.* de SHELF.

shepherd [šépœrd], *s.* pastor; zagal; (fig.) párroco, cura.—*s. dog*, perro de pastor.—*s.'s hut*, tugurio.—**ess** [-ịs], *s.* pastora; zagala.

sherbet [šœ́rbịt], *s.* sorbete, helado.

sheriff [šérịf], *s.* (E.U.) oficial de justicia; alguacil mayor.

sherry [šérị], *s.* vino de Jerez.

shield [šild], *s.* escudo; broquel, rodela; resguardo, defensa; protector.—*vt.* escudar, resguardar, proteger.

shift [šịft], *vt.* cambiar; desviar; trasladar; mudar la ropa; (teat.) cambiar de decoración.—*to s. about*, revolverse, girar.—*to s. for oneself*, ingeniarse, darse maña, componérselas.—*to s. gears*, (aut.) cambiar de marcha.— *to s. into high*, (aut.) meter la directa. —*vi.* moverse; cambiar de puesto; mudarse; mudar, cambiar, variar.— *to s. for oneself*, ingeniarse, arreglárselas.—*s.* cambio; desviación; maña, subterfugio; turno o tanda de obreros.

shilling [šịlịŋ], *s.* chelín.

shin [šịn], *s.* espinilla (de la pierna).— *s. bone*, tibia, canilla, caña.—*vti. y vii.* [1] trepar.

shine [šain], *vii.* [10] (re)lucir, brillar, fulgurar, resplandecer; hacer sol o buen tiempo.—*vt.* pulir, bruñir; dar lustre (a los zapatos); limpiar (el calzado); (Méx.) embolar.—*s.* resplandor, lustre, brillo.

shingle [šịŋgl], *vt.* cubrir con ripia; techar o entejar con tejamaniles; cortar (el pelo) corto y en declive.— *s.* pelo corto rebajado gradualmente; tabla de ripia o uralita; (Am.) tejamanil; (E.U.) letrero de oficina; china, cascajo.

shining [šáinịŋ], *a.* brillante, resplandeciente; (re)luciente.

shiny [šáinị], *a.* lustroso, brillante.

ship [šịp], *s.* barco, buque, nave, navío; dirigible; avión.—*s. boy*, grumete.— *s. carpenter*, carpintero de ribera.— *s. chandler*, proveedor de buques.— *vti.* [1] embarcar; (com.) enviar, despachar, remesar.—*vii.* ir a bordo, embarcar; enrolarse como marinero.- —**board** [šípbord], *s.* (mar.) bordo.- *on s.*, a bordo.- —**builder** [-bịldœr], *s.* ingeniero naval, constructor de buques.- —**mate** [-mejt], *s.* compañero de a bordo.- —**ment** [-mẹnt], *s.* (com.) embarque; cargamento, partida; envío, despacho, consignación, remesa.- —**owner** [-ounœr], *s.* naviero, armador.- —**per** [-œr], *s.* embarcador, fletador; expedidor, remitente.- —**ping** [-ịŋ], *s.* (com.) embarque; envío, despacho.—*a.* naval, marítimo, de marina mercante.— *s. agent*, consignatario de buques.— —**wreck** [-rɛk], *s.* naufragio.—*vt.* hacer naufragar o zozobrar, echar a pique.—*shipwrecked person*, naúfrago.— —**yard** [-yard], *s.* astillero, varadero.

shirk [šœrk], *vt. y vi.* evadir(se de), eludir, evitar.

shirt [šœrt], *s.* camisa; blusa.

shiver [šívœr], *s.* temblor, (es)calofrío, estremecimiento.—*vi.* tiritar, temblar.

shoal [šoul], *s.* bajo, bajío, banco de arena; banco de peces.—*a.* poco profundo, bajo.

shock [šak], *s.* choque; sacudida, sacudimiento; golpe; susto, sobresalto, emoción; ofensa; (med.) choque, postración nerviosa.—*s. absorber*, (mec. y aut.) amortiguador.—*s. dog*, perro de lanas.—*s. troops*, tropas (escogidas) de asalto.—*vt. y vi.* sacudir, dar una sacudida; chocar, ofender, disgustar; conmover; escandalizar, horrorizar; (agr.) hacinar.- —**ing** [šákịŋ], *a.* espantoso, horrible; chocante, ofensivo.

shod [šad], *pret. y pp.* de TO SHOE.

shoe [šu], *s.* zapato; herradura.—*s. blacking*, betún para zapatos, bola.— *s. lace*, cordón, lazo (de zapatos).— *s. polish*, lustre, betún, bola.—*s. store*, zapatería.—*to be in his (their, etc.) shoes*, estar en su pellejo.—*vti.* [10] herrar (un caballo); calzar (a una persona, el ancla).- —**horn** [šúhorn], *s.* calzador.- —**maker** [-mejkœr], *s.*

zapatero.— **—string** [-striŋ], *s.* cordón, lazo (de zapato).

shone [šoun], *pret.* y *pp.* de TO SHINE.

shook [šuk], *pret.* de TO SHAKE.

shoot [šut], *vti.* [10] tirar, disparar; descargar; herir o matar con arma de fuego; fusilar, pasar por las armas; arrojar, lanzar; emitir (un rayo); rodar, filmar (una escena o película).— *to s. down*, tumbar a balazos.—*to s. off*, tirar, descargar (arma de fuego); llevarse.—*vii.* tirar, disparar armas de fuego; pasar o correr rápidamente; nacer, brotar, germinar; punzar (un dolor).—*to s. forth*, lanzarse o abalanzarse.—*to s. out*, brotar, germinar.— *to s. up*, nacer, crecer; madurar.— *s.* vástago, retoño.— **—er** [šutœ(r)], *s.* tirador.— **—ing** [-iŋ], *s.* tiroteo, tiro(s), descarga; (cine) filmación de una escena.—*s. star*, estrella fugaz.

shop [šap], *s.* tienda; taller.—*a.* de tienda; de taller.—*vii.* [1] ir de tiendas o de compras, hacer compras.— **—keeper** [šápkipœ(r)], *s.* tendero.— **—ping** [-iŋ], *s.* compras.—*to go s.*, ir de tiendas o de compras.— **—worn** [-worn], *a.* sobado, deslucido por el manoseo y trajín de la tienda.

shore [šor], *s.* costa, ribera, playa, orilla, litoral; (constr.) puntal.—*vt.* apuntalar, acodalar.

shorn [šorn], *pp.* de TO SHEAR.—*a.* mocho, chamorro.

short [šort], *a.* corto; bajo de estatura; diminuto, pequeño; falto, escaso; breve, conciso; próximo, cercano.— *in a o within a s. time o while*, en un rato; en poco tiempo; dentro de poco.—*in s. order*, prontamente.—*on s. notice*, prontamente, con poco tiempo de aviso.—*on s. term*, (com.) a corto plazo.—*s. circuit*, cortocircuito.—*s. cut*, atajo; método abreviado o corto.—*s. of this*, fuera de esto.—*s. sale*, venta de artículos que el vendedor no tiene aún.—*to be s.*, para abreviar.—*to be s. of*, estar lejos de; no responder a; estar escaso de.— *to cut s.*, interrumpir, abreviar.—*to fall s. of*, ser inferior a, no corresponder a, no alcanzar.—*to grow s.*, acortarse, disminuir.—*s.* resumen, (com.) déficit.—*for s.*, para abreviar. para mayor brevedad.—*in s.*, en resumidas cuentas.—*pl.* pantalones cortos; calzoncillos; (cine) películas cortas.—*adv.* brevemente.—*s.-handed*, escaso de personal.—*s.-tempered*, irascible.— *s.-winded*, asmático, corto de respiración.— **—age** [šórtidž], *s.* déficit; carestía, escasez, falta, merma.— **—cake** [-kɛik], *s.* (coc.) torta de frutas.— **—coming** [-kʌmiŋ], *s.* defecto; negligencia, descuido; falta.— **—en**

[-n], *vt.* y *vi.* acortar(se), abreviar(se), disminuir(se), encoger(se).— **—ening** [-ɛniŋ], *s.* acortamiento; abreviación; (coc.) manteca o grasa con que se hacen hojaldres, etc.— **—hand** [-hænd], *s.* taquigrafía, estenografía.—*a.* taquigráfico.— **—ly** [-li], *adv.* luego, al instante, dentro de poco; brevemente; en breve.—*s. after*, a poco de.—*s. afterward*, al poco rato.—*s. before*, poco antes.— **—ness** [-nis], *s.* cortedad; pequeñez; brevedad; deficiencia.— **—sighted** [-saitid], *a.* miope, cegato; falto de perspicacia.

shot [šat], *pret.* y *pp.* de TO SHOOT.— *vti.* [1] cargar con perdigones.—*s.* perdigón; munición, perdigones; bala, proyectil; tiro, disparo; escopetazo; balazo; alcance (de pistola, etc.); tirada, jugada (en el billar); inyección; (fam.) trago (de licor).—*a good s.*, un tirador certero.—*like a s.*, como un rayo; disparado.—*not by a long s.*, (fam.) ni por asomo, ni por pienso.— *to take a s. at*, hacer un tiro a; echar una púa, burla o indirecta a.— **—gun** [šátgan], *s.* escopeta.

should [šud], *vai.* [11] (se usa para formar el condicional o para expresar obligación).—*I said that I s. go*, dije que iría.—*you s. tell him*, Ud. debe (o debería) decirselo.—V. SHALL.

shoulder [šóuldœ(r)], *s.* hombro; encuentro (de un ave); pernil, cuarto delantero (de un cuadrúpedo); saliente o contenes (de carretera, camino, etc.).—*pl.* espalda(s), hombros. —*on one's shoulders*, a cuestas.—*s. blade*, omóplato u omoplato, paletilla.—*s. pad*, hombrera.—*s. to s.*, hombro con hombro; unidamente.— *to put one's s. to the wheel*, arrimar el hombro, echar una mano.—*vt.* echarse a la espalda, cargar al hombro, llevar a hombros; (fig.) cargar con, asumir. —*s. arms*, (mil.) armas al hombro.

shout [šaut], *vt.* y *vi.* vocear, gritar, vociferar; vitorear.—*s.* grito, alarido; aclamación.

shove [šʌv], *vt.* y *vi.* empujar, dar empujones o empellones.—*to s. away*, rechazar, alejar.—*to s. off*, echar afuera (una embarcación); alejarse de, dejar.—*to s. out*, empujar hacia afuera, hacer salir.—*s.* empellón, empujón, empuje.

shovel [šʌvel], *s.* pala.—*vti.* [2] traspalar, (Am.) palear.— **—ful** [-ful], *s.* palada.

show [šou], *vti.* [6] mostrar, enseñar; señalar; exhibir; indicar, probar, demostrar; poner en escena, representar (un drama); poner, proyectar (una película).—*to s. forth*, exponer, mostrar; publicar.—*to s. in*, introducir, hacer

entrar (a una persona).—*to s. off*, hacer gala de.—*to s. one's cards* o *hand*, mostrar el juego; (fig.) dejarse ver (las intenciones).—*to s. up*, hacer subir (a una persona); denunciar, descubrir, arrancar la careta a.—*vii.* aparecer, mostrarse, asomarse.—*to s. off*, alardear; pavonearse.—*to s. through*, transparentarse; entrelucir. —*to s. up*, aparecer, presentarse.—*s.* exhibición, exposición; espectáculo público; (teat.) función; ostentación; apariencia; (fam. E.U.) oportunidad. —*s. bill*, cartel, cartelón, rótulo.— *s. window*, escaparate de tienda, vidriera.— —*case* [ʃóukeis], *s.* aparador, vitrina.— —*down* [-daun], *s.* acción perentoria o definitiva; hora de la verdad.

shower [ʃáųœ(r)], *s.* chubasco, chaparrón; (baño de) ducha.—*heavy s.*, aguacero.—*vt.* llover, regar, derramar con abundancia.—*vi.* llover, caer un chubasco.

shown [ʃoųn], *pp.* de TO SHOW.—**showy** [ʃóųi], *a.* ostentoso, vistoso, suntuoso, rimbombante; chillón, charro.

shrank [ʃræŋk], *pret.* de TO SHRINK.

shrapnel [ʃrǽpneļ], *s.* (arti.) metralla; granada de metralla.

shred [ʃred], *vti.* [3] picar, desmenuzar, hacer trizas o tiras.—*s.* trizas, jirón, tira, retazo; fragmento, pizca.

shrew [ʃru], *s.* arpía, virago, mujer de mal genio; (zool.) musaraña.

shrewd [ʃrud], *a.* perspicaz, sagaz; astuto; agudo, cortante.— —*ness* [ʃrúdnis], *s.* sagacidad, astucia, sutileza.

shriek [ʃrik], *vi.* chillar, gritar.—*s.* chillido, grito agudo.

shrill [ʃriļ], *a.* chillón, estridente, agudo, penetrante.—*vt.* y *vi.* chillar.

shrimp [ʃrimp], *s.* (zool.) camarón, quisquilla; (fam.) enano.

shrine [ʃrain], *s.* santuario, capilla, templete.

shrink [ʃriŋk], *vii.* [10] encogerse, contraerse; disminuir, mermar; (con from) evadir, apartarse o huir de; retroceder.—*to s. back*, retirarse, retroceder.—*vti.* encoger, contraer.— —*age* [ʃríŋkidž], *s.* encogimiento o contracción; (com.) merma, pérdida.

shrivel [ʃríveļ], *vti.* [2] arrugar, fruncir, doblar, encoger; estrechar; marchitar. —*vii.* arrugarse, fruncirse, encogerse, deshincharse; marchitarse.

shroud [ʃraud], *s.* mortaja, sudario.— *vt.* amortajar; (fig.) cubrir, ocultar.

shrub [ʃrʌb], *s.* arbusto.— —*bery* [ʃrʌbœrį], *s.* arbustos; grupo de arbustos; maleza.

shrug [ʃrʌg], *vii.* [1] encoger de hombros.—*s.* encogimiento de hombros.

shrunk [ʃrʌŋk], *pret.* y *pp.* de TO SHRINK.—**shrunken** [ʃrʌ́ŋkẹn], *pp.* de TO SHRINK.

shudder [ʃʌ́dœ(r)], *vi.* estremecerse, temblar.—*s.* temblor, estremecimiento.

shuffle [ʃʌ́fl], *vt.* y *vi.* barajar (naipes); mezclar, revolver.—*to s. along*, arrastrar los pies, chancletear; ir tirando o pasando.—*s.* evasiva, salida; mezcla, confusión; restregamiento de los pies en el suelo, chancleteo.

shun [ʃʌn], *vti.* y *vii.* [1] huir, rehuir, esquivar, evitar.

shut [ʃʌt], *vti.* y *vii.* [9] cerrar(se).— *to s. down*, cesar en el trabajo, parar* —*to s. from*, excluir.—*to s. in*, encerrar, confinar.—*to s. off*, impedir la entrada, interceptar; cortar (el agua, etc.); interrumpir (a uno) en el teléfono, cortarle el circuito.—*to s. out*, cerrar la puerta a (uno); excluir.— *to s. up*, hacer callar; cerrar; acabar; tapar; encerrar; callarse.—*pret.* y *pp.* de TO SHUT.—*a.* cerrado.— —*down* [ʃʌ́tdaun], *s.* paro, cesación o suspensión de trabajo (en una fábrica, etc.).— —*ter* [-œ(r)], *s.* cerrador; persiana; contraventana; postigo; (foto.) obturador.

shuttle [ʃʌ́tl], *s.* (tej.) lanzadera; tren de traspaso (entre dos vías férreas); tren que va y viene entre dos lugares cercanos.—*vt.* y *vi.* mover(se) alternativamente de un lado a otro o de una parte a otra; ir y venir.

shy [ʃai], *a.* tímido; asustadizo; cauteloso; esquivo, arisco; vergonzoso; (fam.) ñoño.—*vti.* [7] (con off) hacer desviar, apartar; lanzar o arrojar.— *vii.* respingar (un caballo); asustarse.- —*ness* [ʃáinis], *s.* timidez; recato; esquivez; vergüenza, (fam.) ñoñez.

shyster [ʃáistœ(r)], *s.* (fam. E.U.) picapleitos, trapisondista, leguleyo.

Siamese [saiamíz], *s.* y *a.* siamés.

Sicilian [sisílyạn], *a.* y *s.* siciliano.

sick [sik], *a.* enfermo; malo; nauseado; (con of) cansado, disgustado, fastidiado.—*s. leave*, licencia por enfermedad.—*s. room*, enfermería.—*to be s. to one's stomach*, tener náuseas.—*vt.* azuzar, excitar o incitar (a un perro).- —*en* [síkn], *vt.* enfermar; dar asco; debilitar, extenuar.—*vi.* enfermarse; nausear, tener asco.— —*ening* [-ẹnịŋ], *a.* nauseabundo, repugnante.

sickle [síkl], *s.* hoz.

sickly [síklị], *a.* enfermizo, achacoso; enclenque; nauseabundo.—**sickness** [síknịs], *s.* enfermedad, dolencia; náusea.

side [said], *s.* lado, costado; flanco; ladera, falda; facción, partido, bando; banda (de un barco).—*by the s.*, al

lado de; cerca de.—*on all sides* u *on every s.*, por todos lados, por todas partes.—*on that s.*, a, de, en o por ese·lado.—*on the other s.*, del o al otro lado; más allá; a la otra parte.—*on this s.*, a, de en o por este lado; más acá.—*s. by s.*, lado a lado; hombro a hombro, juntos.—*a.* lateral; de lado; oblicuo; secundario, incidental. —*s. arms*, armas blancas.—*s. glance*, mirada de soslayo.—*s. issue*, cuestión secundaria.—*s. light*, luz lateral; información o detalle incidental.—*s. line*, negocio o actividad incidentales; (dep.) línea o límite del terreno de juego.—*vt.* y *vi.* (con *with*) tomar parte por, declararse por, ser de la opinión de.— —*board* [sáidbɔrd], *s.* aparador.— —*burns* [-bœrnz], *s. pl.* patillas.

sidesaddle [sáidsædl], *a.* sillón, silla de amazona.—**sideswipe** [sáidswaip], *vt.* (fam.) chocar o rozar oblicuamente. —*s.* choque o rozamiento oblicuo.— **sidetrack** [sáidtræk], *vt.* desviar; echar a un lado, arrinconar; (f.c.) meter en un desviadero.—**sidewalk** [sáidwɔk], *s.* acera, (Am.) banqueta; (Am.) vereda.—**sideways** [sáidweiz], *a.* y *adv.* de lado, lateral(mente), de soslayo, al través.—**siding** [sáidiɳ], *s.* (f.c.) apartadero, desviadero, vía muerta.

siege [sidž], *s.* sitio, asedio, cerco.— *to lay s.*, poner sitio o cerco.

sierra [siérȧ], *s.* sierra, cordillera.

siesta [siéstȧ], *s.* siesta, siestecilla.

sieve [siv], *s.* cedazo, tamiz, criba.— *vt.* = SIFT.—**sift** [sift], *vt.* cerner, cribar, tamizar.—*to s. out*, investigar.— *vi.* caer o pasar al través de un tamiz o cedazo.

sigh [sai], *vi.* suspirar.—*s.* suspiro.

sight [sait], *s.* vista; visión, perspectiva; escena, espectáculo; modo de ver; mira (de armas de fuego); agujero o abertura para mirar.—*at s.*, a la vista (letra, giro, etc.); a primera vista; al ver, cuando se vea.—*thirty days after s.*, (com.) a treinta días vista.—*to be a s.*, (fam.) parecer o estar como un adefesio; ser extraordinario o extraño.—*a.* visual; (com.) a la vista.—*vt.* alcanzar con la vista, avistar, divisar, (mar.) recalar.—*vi.* apuntar; dirigir una visual.— —*seeing* [sáitsiiɳ], *s.* visita turística a lugares de interés.

sign [sain], *s.* signo; señal, seña; rastro, indicio; muestra, letrero, rótulo.—*vt.* firmar; rubricar; suscribir (un tratado, etc.); (con *off* o *away*) firmar la cesión o traspaso de.—*vi.* firmar.— —*al* [sígnȧl], *a.* señalado, notable, memorable.—*s.* seña, señal.—*vti.* y *vii.* [2]

hacer señas, señalar, indicar.—**signatory** [sígnȧtɔri], *a.* y *s.* firmante, signatario.—**signature** [sígnȧchṷr], *s.* firma; rúbrica.— —**signer** [sáinœ(r)], *s.* firmante, signatario.

signet [sígnit], *s.* sello; timbre, estampilla.

significance [signífikȧns], *s.* significación; significado.—**significant** [signífikȧnt], *a.* significante, significativo.— **signify** [sígnifai], *vti.* y *vii.* [7] significar.

silence [sáilȧns], *s.* silencio.—*s. gives consent*, quien calla otorga.—*vt.* imponer silencio, mandar o hacer callar; sosegar, aquietar.—**silent** [sáilȧnt], *a.* silencioso; taciturno; tácito.—*s. partner*, socio comanditario.

silhouette [siluét], *vt.* hacer aparecer en silueta; perfilar.—*s.* silueta.

silk [silk], *s.* seda.—*pl.* sedería, géneros de seda.—*a.* de seda.— —*en* [sílkn], *a.* de seda; sedoso.— —*worm* [-wœrm], *s.* gusano de seda.— —*y* [-i], *a.* sedoso, sedeño; de seda.

sill [sil], *s.* umbral de puerta; solera, mesilla.—*window s.*, antepecho de ventana.

silliness [sílinis], *s.* necedad, tontería, simpleza.—**silly** [síli], *a.* necio, tonto, mentecato, bobo; simple; disparatado, ridículo.

silver [sílvœ(r)], *s.* plata; vajilla de plata o plateada.—*a.* de plata; plateado.—*vt.* platear; azogar (un espejo, etc.).— —*smith* [-smiθ], *s.* platero, orfebre.— —*ware* [-wer], *s.* vajilla de plata; artículos de plata.— —*y* [-i], *a.* plateado; argentino, argentado.

simian [símiȧn], *s.* simio, mono.

similar [símilȧ(r)], *a.* similar, semejante, análogo, parecido.— —*ity* [similériti], *s.* semejanza, analogía, parecido.— —*ly* [símilȧrli], *adv.* semejantemente, asimismo, de igual manera.—**simile** [símili], *s.* símil.— **similitude** [simílitjud], *s.* similitud, semejanza.

simmer [símœ(r)], *vi.* hervir a fuego lento.

simple [simpl], *a.* simple; sencillo; llano; ingenuo, cándido; mentecato, necio; insignificante, ordinario.— *s.-minded*, cándido, confiado, candoroso.—*s.-mindedness*, candor, sencillez.—*s.* simplón, gaznápiro, bobo; simple.— —*ton* [-tɔn], *s.* bobalicón, simplón, papanatas, gaznápiro.— **simplicity** [simplísiti], *s.* sencillez, llaneza; simplicidad; simpleza, bobería.—**simplify** [símplifai], *vti.* [7] simplificar.

simulate [símjuleit], *vt.* simular, fingir.

simultaneity [saimʌltȧníiti], *s.* simul-

taneidad.—simultaneous [saimʌltéi-niʌs], a. simultáneo.

sin [sɪn], s. pecado, culpa.—vii. [1] pecar.

since [sɪns], adv. hace; desde entonces. —four days s., hace cuatro días. —not long s., no hace mucho, hace poco.—s. when? how long s.? ¿de cuándo acá? ¿desde cuándo?—prep. desde, después de, a contar de.— conj. desde que, después que; puesto que, como, como quiera que, ya que, en vista de que.

sincere [sɪnsír], a. sincero; serio.— sincerity [sɪnsérɪtɪ], s. sinceridad.

sine [saɪn], s. (mat.) seno.

sinew [sínyu], s. tendón; fibra, nervio.

sinful [sínful], a. pecaminoso; pecador.

sing [sɪŋ], vii. y vti. [10] cantar.

singe [sɪndʒ], vt. chamuscar; quemar (las puntas del pelo).—s. chamusquina.

singer [síŋœ(r)], s. cantante, cantor(a). —singing [síŋɪŋ], a. cantante, de canto; cantor.—s. bird, ave canora.

single [síŋgl], a. único, solo; particular, individual; sencillo (no doble, etc.); soltero.—s. file, hilera; en hilera, uno tras otro.—s.-handed, solo, sin ayuda.—vt. (gen. con out) singularizar; particularizar; escoger.—s. billete de un dólar.—pl. partido de individuales (no parejas) (en el tenis, etc.).—singly [síŋglɪ], adv. individualmente, uno a uno, separadamente.

singsong [síŋsɔŋ], s. cadencia uniforme, sonsonete.

singular [síŋgiulä(r)], a. singular; extraño, extraordinario, raro; único. —s. (gram.) (número) singular.

sinister [sínɪstœ(r)], a. siniestro.

sink [sɪŋk], vti. [10] hundir, sumergir; (mar.) echar a pique o a fondo; sumir; cavar, abrir (un pozo); clavar, enterrar.—vii. hundirse, sumirse; (mar.) naufragar, zozobrar, irse a pique.—to s. on one's knees, caer de rodillas.—s. sumidero, vertedero; fregadero.— —er [síŋkœ(r)], s. plomada de pescar; el que o lo que se hunde.— —ing [-ɪŋ], s. hundimiento; abertura (de un pozo, etc.); acción de hundirse, echar a pique.—a. que (se) hunde.

sir [sœr], s. señor, caballero.—Dear S., (en cartas) Muy Señor mío (nuestro).

sinner [sínœ(r)], s. pecador(a).

sinus [sáɪnʌs], s. cavidad, abertura; (anat.) cavidad ósea.

sip [sɪp], vti. [1] sorber, libar, chupar. —s. sorbo.

siphon [sáɪfɒn], s. sifón.—vt. y vi. sacar líquidos con sifón.

sirloin [sœ́rlɔɪn], s. solomillo, lomo.

sissy [sísɪ], s. y a. (fam.) marica, afeminado.

sister [sístœ(r)], s. hermana; sor; monja.—s.-in-law, cuñada.

sit [sɪt], vti. [10] sentar; dar asiento a; tener capacidad o espacio para.—vri. sentarse.—vii. sentarse; estar sentado; posarse; empollar (las aves); reunirse, celebrar junta o sesión; formar parte de un congreso, tribunal, etc.; sentar, caer bien o mal (un vestido, etc.); descansar, apoyarse.—to s. by, sentarse o estar sentado cerca de, junto o al lado de. —to s. down, sentarse.—to s. for, servir de modelo, posar.—to s. still, estarse quieto, no moverse; no levantarse Ud.—to s. tight, (fam.) esperar sin decir nada, tenerse firme.—to s. up, incorporarse.— —e [saɪt], s. sitio, situación, local; asiento.— —ting [sítɪŋ], s. acción o modo de sentarse; sesión, junta; (a)sentada; nidada.

situate [sítʃueit], vt. situar; fijar sitio o lugar para.— —d [sítʃueitid], a. situado, sito, ubicado.—situation [sítʃuéisɒn], s. situación; ubicación; posición; colocación, plaza, empleo.

sizable [sáɪzabl], a. de tamaño razonable, adecuado; considerable.—size [saɪz], s. tamaño, medida, dimensiones; diámetro (de un tubo, alambre, etc.); apresto; cola; talla, estatura.—vt. clasificar o separar según el tamaño o estatura; valuar, justipreciar; aprestar, encolar.

sizzle [sízl], vi. chirriar (al freírse); (fam.) estar muy caliente.—s. chirrido (al freírse).

skate [skeɪt], vi. patinar.—s. patín.— —r [skéɪtœ(r)], s. patinador.—skating [skéɪtɪŋ], s. patinaje.—a. de o para patinar.—s. rink, pista o sala de patinar.

skein [skeɪn], s. madeja.

skeleton [skéletɒn], s. esqueleto; armazón.—s. key, ganzúa, llave maestra.

skeptic [sképtɪk], s. y a. escéptico.— —al [-al], a. escéptico.

sketch [skech], s. diseño, bosquejo, boceto, croquis; (teat.) pieza corta o ligera; drama o cuadro dramático de radio.—vt. diseñar, esbozar, delinear, bosquejar, hacer un croquis de.

skewer [skiúœ(r)], s. pincho.—vt. espetar.

ski [ski], s. esquí.—vi. esquiar.

skid [skɪd], vii. [1] deslizar; patinar (una rueda); (aut.) patinar o resbalar lateralmente.—s. patinazo.

skier [skíœ(r)], s. esquiador.

skiff [skɪf], s. esquife.

skill [skɪl], s. habilidad, destreza, pericia, maña.- —ed [skɪld], a.

práctico, instruido, experimentado, experto.

skillet [skílit], *s.* sartén; cacerola pequeña.

skillful [skílful], *a.* diestro, hábil, experto, ducho.

skim [skim], *vti.* [1] desnatar; espumar; examinar superficialmente, hojear (un libro).—*vii.* deslizarse o pasar rasando.—*to s. over*, resbalar, rozar.

skin [skin], *s.* piel (cutis, epidermis, tez); odre, pellejo; cuero; cáscara.—*vti.* [1] desollar, despellejar; pelar, mondar; (fam.) sacar dinero a, pelar.—*vii.* mudar la piel; (fam.) ser embaucador o engañador; (fam.) (gen. con out) escabullirse.—**flint** [skínflint], *s.* avaro.—**ny** [-i], *a.* flaco, descarnado; pellejudo.

skip [skip], *vti.* [1] saltar, omitir; saltar por encima de, pasar por alto.—*vii.* saltar, brincar.—*s.* cabriola, salto, brinco; omisión.—**per** [skípœ(r)], *s.* (mar.) patrón.

skirmish [skœrmiš], *s.* (mil.) escaramuza, refriega.—*vi.* (sos)tener una escaramuza.

skirt [skœrt], *s.* falda, faldellín, saya; orilla, margen, borde.—*pl.* (fam.) mujer, faldas.—*vt.* seguir la orilla de; costear; (cost.) orillar.—*vi.* (con along, near, etc.) ladear, (mar.) costear.

skittish [skítiš], *a.* espantadizo; tímido; retozón; caprichudo, voluble.

skull [skʌl], *s.* cráneo; calavera.—**cap** [skʌlkæp], *s.* bonete, solideo.

skunk [skʌŋk], *s.* mofeta, zorrillo; (fam.) canalla, persona ruin.

sky [skai], *s.* cielo, firmamento.—*s.-blue, s.-colored*, azul celeste, cerúleo.—*to praise to the skies*, poner en, o sobre, las nubes.—**lark** [skáilark], *s.* alondra, calandria.—**light** [-lait], *s.* claraboya, tragaluz.—**rocket** [-rakit], *s.* cohete, volador.—**scraper** [-skreipœ(r)], *s.* rascacielos.

slab [slæb], *s.* losa, baldosa; lonja, tajada gruesa; plancha, tablón; laja, lancha.

slack [slæk], *a.* flojo; poco firme, aflojado; remiso, tardo.—*s.* (mar.) seno de un cabo; flojedad; (com.) período de poca actividad; estación o tiempo muerto.—*pl.* pantalones ligeros de verano.—*s.*, **slacken** [slǽkn], *vt.* aflojar, relajar, desapretar; disminuir.—*vi.* aflojarse, relajarse; disminuir; retardarse; flojear.

slag [slæg], *s.* escoria (de metales o volcanes).

slain [slein], *pp.* de TO SLAY.

slake [sleik], *vt.* apagar (la cal, la sed); refrescar; desleir (la cal); moderar.—

slaked lime, cal muerta o apagada.—*vi.* apagarse (la cal).

slam [slæm], *vti.* [1] cerrar de golpe.—*vii.* cerrarse de golpe y con estrépito.—*s.* portazo; (fam.) crítica severa.—*s.-bang*, (fam.) de golpe y porrazo.

slander [slǽndœ(r)], *vt.* calumniar, difamar.—*s.* calumnia, difamación.—**ous** [-ʌs], *a.* calumnioso, difamatorio.

slang [slæŋ], *s.* vulgarismo; jerga, jerigonza, germanía.

slant [slænt], *vt.* y *vi.* sesgar(se), inclinar(se).—*s.* oblicuidad; inclinación; sesgo; declive; punto de vista.

slap [slæp], *vti.* [1] abofetear, acachetear.—*s.* bofetada, bofetón, manotada, manotazo.—*a s. in the face*, bofetada; insulto.—*adv.* de golpe y porrazo, de sopetón.—**dash** [slǽpdæš], *a.* y *adv.* descuidado, chapucero; de prisa, descuidadamente.

slash [slæš], *vt.* acuchillar, dar cuchilladas; cortar, hacer un corte largo en; rebajar, reducir radicalmente (sueldos, gastos, precios, etc.).—*vi.* tirar tajos y reveses.—*s.* cuchillada; corte, cortadura.

slat [slæt], *s.* tablilla (de madera o metal).

slate [sleit], *s.* pizarra; pizarra para escribir; (E.U. pol.) lista de candidatos; candidatura.

slaughter [slótœ(r)], *s.* carnicería, matanza, (fam.) degollina.—*vt.* matar, sacrificar (las reses); hacer una carnicería o matanza; destrozar.—**house** [-haus], *s.* matadero.

Slav [slav], *a.* y *s.* eslavo.

slave [sleiv], *s.* esclavo.—*vi.* trabajar como esclavo.

slaver [slǽvœ(r)], *s.* baba.—*vi.* babear.

slavery [sléivœri], *s.* esclavitud.

Slavic [slávik], *s.* lengua eslava.—*a.* eslavo.

slavish [sléiviš], *a.* servil, abyecto; esclavizado.

slay [slei], *vti.* [10] matar.—**er** [sléiœ(r)], *s.* matador; asesino.

sled [sled], *vti.* y *vii.* [1] ir o llevar en trineo.—*s.* trineo, rastra.—*s. hammer*, macho, mandarria.

sleek [slik], *a.* liso, bruñido, alisado; suave, zalamero.—*vt.* alisar, pulir, suavizar.

sleep [slip], *vti.* y *vii.* [10] dormir.—*to s. off*, curar durmiendo (un dolor de cabeza, etc.); dormirla (la borrachera, etc.).—*to s. on o upon*, descuidarse o no hacer caso de; consultar con la almohada.—*to s. out*, dormir fuera de casa; saciarse de dormir.—*to s. over*, consultar con la almohada.—*to s. soundly*,

dormir profundamente o a pierna suelta.—*s.* sueño.— **—er** [slípœ(r)], *s.* persona dormida; (f.c.) coche dormitorio, coche cama; (f.c.) traviesa, (Am.) durmiente.— **—ily** [-ịlị], *adv.* con somnolencia o soñolencia.— **—iness** [-inịs], *s.* soñolencia o somnolencia, sueño, modorra.— **—ing** [-iŋ], *a.* durmiente; dormido.— *s. car*, coche cama o coche dormitorio.— *s. partner*, socio comanditario.—*s. sickness*, encefalitis letárgica.— **—less** [-lịs], *a.* desvelado, insomne.— **—walker** [-wokœ(r)], *s.* so(m)námbulo.— **—y** [-i], *a.* soñoliento, amodorrado.—*to be s.*, tener sueño.

sleet [slit], *s.* aguanieve.—*vi.* caer aguanieve.

sleeve [sliv], *s.* (sast.) manga.— **—less** [slívlịs], *a.* sin mangas.

sleigh [slej], *s.* trineo.—*vi.* pasearse en trineo.

sleight [slajt], *s.* habilidad; ardid, estratagema.—*s. of hand*, juego de manos, prestidigitación.

slender [sléndœ(r)], *a.* delgado; esbelto; sutil; escaso; insuficiente.

slept [slept], *pret. y pp.* de TO SLEEP.

sleuth [sljuθ], *s.* detective; agente de policía secreta o investigador privado.

slew [slju], *pret.* de TO SLAY.

slice [slajs], *vt.* rebanar, cortar en tajadas; tajar, cortar.—*s.* rebanada, tajada, lonja.

slick [slịk], *vt.* alisar, pulir.—*vi.* (gen. con **up**) (fam.) componerse, acicalarse.—*a.* liso, terso, lustroso; resbaladizo, aceitoso; meloso; (fam.) diestro, mañoso; (fam.) de primera.— **—er** [slíkœ(r)], *s.* impermeable flojo; (fam.) embaucador, farsante.

slid [slịd], *pret. y pp.* de TO SLIDE.— **slidden** [slídn], *pp.* de TO SLIDE. **—slide** [slajd], *vii.* [10] resbalar(se), deslizarse, caer(se); patinar.—*vti.* hacer resbalar; (con **let**) dejar correr, no hacer caso de.—*s.* tapa corrediza; (foto.) diapositiva, transparencia; platina de microscopio; resbalón, resbaladura; resbaladero; (geol.) falla; desmoronamiento, alud; (mús.) ligado.—*a.* corredizo; de corredera.—*s. rule*, regla de cálculo.—**sliding** [slájdịŋ], *s.* deslizamiento, resbalo.—*a.* corredizo, deslizante.—*s. door*, puerta corredera.

slight [slajt], *a.* ligero, leve; pequeño, fútil, débil, delgado.—*s.* desaire, desatención, feo, desprecio.—*vt.* menospreciar, despreciar, desairar; desatender, descuidar.

slim [slịm], *a.* delgado; baladí; delicado; escaso.

slime [slajm], *s.* limo, lama, cieno, fango, babaza.—*vt. y vi.* enfangar,

enlodar.—**slimy** [slájmị], *a.* viscoso, fangoso, limoso; mucoso.

sling [slịŋ], *s.* honda; (cir.) cabestrillo; (mar.) eslinga.—*vti.* [10] tirar con honda; tirar, arrojar; eslingar, izar.— **—shot** [slíŋšat], *s.* tirador, tiragomas, tiraflechas.

slink [slịŋk], *vii.* [10] escabullirse, escaparse, escurrirse.

slip [slịp], *vti.* [1] deslizar; soltarse, zafarse, soltar, desatar; irse de (la memoria, etc.).—*to s. a cog*, equivocarse.—*to s. in*, introducir o meter (esp. secretamente).—*to s. off*, quitarse de encima, soltar.—*to s. on*, ponerse (vestido, etc.) de prisa.— *to s. one's arm around* o *through*, pasar el brazo por (la cintura, etc.). —*vii.* resbalar, deslizarse; salirse de su sitio; cometer un desliz; errar o equivocarse; olvidársele a uno. —*to s. into*, introducirse, entrometerse.—*to s. out*, salir sin ser observado; dislocarse un hueso.—*s.* resbalón; deslizamiento; tropiezo, traspié; desliz; resbaladero; declive; falta, error; descuido, lapso; (agr.) plantón; tira o pedazo (de papel); funda de almohada; combinación (de vestir); boleta, papeleta.—*s. cover*, funda (de muebles, etc.).—*s. of the tongue*, lapsus linguae.—**knot**, [slípnat], *s.* lazo o nudo corredizo.— **—per** [slípœ(r)], *s.* pantufla, chancleta, babucha; zapatilla.— **—pery** [slípœrị], *a.* resbaladizo, resbaloso; evasivo; zorro; voluble.— **—shod** [-šad], *a.* descuidado, desaliñado; tosco, mal hecho.

slit [slịt], *vti.* [9] rajar, hender; cortar en tiras; rasgar (un vestido).—*s.* cortadura larga; hendedura, tajo; ranura, abertura.—*pret. y pp.* de TO SLIT.

slogan [slóugan], *s.* consigna; lema.

sloop [slup], *s.* balandro, chalupa.

slop [slap], *vti.* [1] derramar; ensuciar, enlodar.—*vii.* derramarse; chapalear (por el fango, agua nieve, etc.).—*s.* líquido derramado en el suelo; mojadura.—*pl.* agua sucia; aguachirle, lavazas; té o café flojo.

slope [sloup], *s.* (geol. y min.) inclinación; (f.c.) talud; declive, bajada; cuesta, falda, ladera; agua, vertiente (de tejado); (fort.) rampa.—*vt. y vi.* inclinar(se).

slot [slat], *s.* (mec.) muesca, ranura, abertura, hendedura.—*s. machine*, máquina tragamonedas o traganíqueles.—*vti.* [1] acanalar, hacer una ranura en.

sloth [sloθ], *s.* pereza, haraganería; (zool.) perezoso.

slough [slaų], *s.* lodazal, cenagal,

cieno; estado de degradación; [sliu], (E.U.) charca cenagosa; [slʌf], piel o camisa que muda la serpiente; (med.) tejido muerto.—*vi.* y *vt.* echar de sí tejido muerto o la piel.

Slovak [slóuvæk], *a.* y *s.* eslovaco.

slovenliness [slʌ́venlinis], *s.* desaliño, desaseo, abandono; suciedad, porquería.—**slovenly** [slʌ́venli], *a.* desaliñado, puerco o sucio; dejado, descuidado.

slow [slou], *vt.* y *vi.* (con up o down) retardar, aflojar el paso, ir más despacio.—*a.* lento, despacioso; tardo; atrasado (el reloj); calmoso, cachazudo; lerdo, estúpido.—*s. motion*, velocidad reducida; (cine) cámara lenta.—*adv.* despacio, lentamente.- —**ly** [slóuli], *adv.* despacio, lentamente, pausadamente.- —**ness** [-nis], *s.* lentitud, retraso; cachaza; torpeza.

slug [slʌg], *s.* cualquier cosa, animal o persona de movimiento(s) lento(s); (zool.) babosa; (arti.) posta; bala; (impr.) lingote.—*vti.* [1] (arti.) cargar con posta; (fam.) aporrear.- —**gard** [slʌ́gard], *s.* haragán, holgazán, pelmazo.

sluice [slius], *s.* esclusa; compuerta; canal; (fig.) salida.—*s. gate*, compuerta.

slum [slʌm], *s.* vivienda miserable. —*pl.* arrabales, barrios bajos.—*vii.* [1] visitar los barrios bajos.—*to go slumming*, recorrer tugurios o lugares de mala vida.

slumber [slʌ́mbœ(r)], *vi.* dormitar; dormir; dormirse o descuidarse.—*s.* sueño ligero y tranquilo.

slump [slʌmp], *vi.* hundirse el pie en una materia blanda; aplastarse, rebajarse; caer, bajar.—*vt.* arrojar violentamente; hacer bajar (precios) súbitamente.—*s.* hundimiento; aplastamiento; disminución de actividad o vigor; (com.) baja repentina en los valores, bajón, desplome.

slung [slʌŋ], *pret.* y *pp.* de TO SLING.

slunk [slʌŋk], *pret.* y *pp.* de TO SLINK.

slur [slœr], *vti.* [1] menospreciar, rebajar; pasar por encima, suprimir; comerse sílabas o letras.—*s.* reparo, pulla; estigma; mancilla o mancha ligera en la reputación.

slush [slʌ̂s], *s.* lodo blando, fango; aguanieve fangosa; desperdicios de cocina; (fam.) tonterías sentimentales.

slut [slʌt], *s.* mujerzuela, ramera; mujer sucia; perra.

sly [slai], *a.* astuto, taimado, socarrón. —*on the s.*, a hurtadillas, a la chiticallando.- —**ness** [slái̯nis], *s.* socarronería, astucia, disimulo.

smack [smæk], *vt.* y *vi.* manotear, golpear; besar ruidosamente; hacer sonar o chasquear (un beso, golpe, latigazo, etc.); rechuparse, saborear; saborearse.—*vi.* (con of) saber (a), tener gusto, dejo (de); oler (a).—*s.* sabor, gusto, gustillo; beso sonado; rechupete; manotada; chasquido de látigo.

small [smɔl], *a.* pequeño, diminuto, chico; menor; bajo de estatura; corto; insignificante; despreciable, mezquino.- —**ness** [smɔ́lnis], *s.* pequeñez; bajeza, ruindad.- —**pox** [-paks], *s.* viruela(s).

smart [smart], *a.* vivo, listo, hábil; despabilado, astuto, ladino; inteligente, talentoso; agudo, sutil; punzante, mordaz; elegante, de buen tono.—*s.* escozor; dolor, aflicción. —*vi.* escocer, picar; requemar.- —**ness** [smártnis], *s.* agudeza, viveza; ingenio, talento; astucia; elegancia, buen tono.

smash [smæ̂s], *vt.* y *vi.* romper, quebrar, aplastar, destrozar.—*s.* rotura, destrozo; fracaso; ruina, quiebra.—*to go to s.*, arruinarse; hacerse añicos.

smattering [smǽterin], *s.* tintura.

smear [smir], *vt.* untar, embarrar, tiznar, manchar.—*s.* embarradura, mancha.

smell [smel], *vti.* y *vii.* [4] oler.—*to s. a rat*, haber gato encerrado.—*to s. of*, oler a.—*s.* olfato; olor (bueno o malo).—**smelt** [smelt], *vt.* fundir o derretir (metales).—**smelter** [smélt-œ(r)], *s.* fundidor; alto horno.

smile [smáil], *vi.* sonreír(se).—*s.* sonrisa.—**smiling** [smáiliŋ], *a.* risueño, sonriente.—**smilingly** [smáiliŋli], *adv.* con cara risueña.

smirch [smœrch], *vt.* ensuciar, tiznar; mancillar, deslucir.—*s.* mancilla, tizne.

smith [smiθ], *s.* forjador, herrero.- —**y** [smiθi], *s.* fragua, forja; herrería.

smitten [smitn], *pp.* de TO SMITE.—*a.* profundamente afectado; muy conmovido; muy enamorado.

smock [smak], *s.* bata corta, blusa.

smoke [smouk], *s.* humo.—*to have a s.*, dar una fumada; fumar.—*vt.* fumar; curar al humo; sahumar; (con out) ahumar, ahogar con humo; hacer salir con humo.—*vi.* fumar; humear, echar humo.- —**less** [smóuklis], *a.* sin humo.—*s. powder*, pólvora sin humo.- —**r** [smóukœ(r)], *s.* fumador; (f.c.) coche o salón de fumar; (fam.) tertulia en que se fuma.- —**stack** [-stæk], *s.* chimenea.—**smoking** [smóukiŋ], *s.* acción de fumar.—*a.* humeante.—*s. car*, (f.c.) coche fuma-

dor.—*s. jacket*, batín.—*s. room*, cuarto o salón de fumar.—**smoky** [smóukị], *a.* humeante; humoso, ahumado.

smolder [smóụldœ(r)], *vi.* arder en rescoldo; estar latente.

smooth [smuð], *a.* liso, pulido; parejo, plano, igual; uniforme; suave; tranquilo (agua, etc.); cortés, afable. —*s.-shaven*, bien afeitado.—*s.-sliding*, que se desliza con suavidad e igualdad.—*vt.* allanar, alisar, suavizar; (gen. con over) zanjar, atenuar.— **—ness** [smúðnịs], *s.* lisura, tersura, igualdad; suavidad, blandura; dulzura.

smote [smout], *pret.* de TO SMITE.

smother [smʌ́ðœ(r)], *vt.* y *vi.* ahogar(se), asfixiar(se); sofocar(se).

smoulder [smóụldœ(r)], *vi.* = SMOLDER.

smudge [smʌdž], *vt.* tiznar, ensuciar o manchar con tizne, tinta u hollín; fumigar, ahumar.—*s.* tiznajo, tiznadura, tiznón; fumigación o ahumadura.

smuggle [smʌ́gl], *vt.* pasar o meter de contrabando; hacer contrabando, contrabandear.- **—r** [smʌ́glœ(r)], *s.* contrabandista.

smut [smʌt], *s.* tiznón, tiznadura, mancha; obscenidad, indecencia; (bot., agr.) tizón.—*vti.* [1] tiznar, manchar; (fig.) mancillar.- **—ty** [-ị], *a.* tiznado; indecente, verde.

snack [snæk], *s.* bocad(ill)o, refrigerio, (fam.) tente(e)mpié, piscolabis.

snag [snæg], *s.* nudo que sobresale en la madera; tocón o tronco sumergido; obstáculo oculto ignorado.— *vti.* [1] rasgar o dañar, chocando contra algo sumergido; impedir, obstruir; arrancar troncos o tocones (de un río).

snail [snẹịl], *s.* caracol.

snake [snẹịk], *s.* serpiente, culebra. —*vi.* serpentear, culebrear.—**snaky** [snẹ́ịkị], *a.* tortuoso; solapado, astuto.

snap [snæp], *vti.* [1] chasquear, hacer estallar; dar, apretar o cerrar con golpe o estallido; romper con ruido y violencia; atrapar, arrebatar, echar la zarpa a; interrumpir; fotografiar instantáneamente.—*to s. one's fingers*, castañetear con los dedos.—*to s. up*, comprar, aceptar, etc. con avidez; cortar, interrumpir (a uno) con una réplica mordaz.—*vii.* chasquear, dar un chasquido; estallar, romperse con estallido; romperse una cosa tirante; relampaguear (los ojos); hablar fuerte; fallar un tiro.—*to s. at*, tirar mordiscos a, pegar una dentellada a; hablar mordazmente o con aspereza (a uno); aceptar una oferta con

entusiasmo y de prisa.—*to s. in two*, romperse en dos pedazos.—*to s. off*, soltarse, saltar, abrirse de golpe.—*s.* chasquido; castañeteo (con los dedos); estallido; cierre de resorte; dentellada, mordiscón; (fam.) vigor, energía; período corto (de frío); (fam.) ganga, cosa fácil.—*a.* hecho de repente, de golpe o instantáneamente.—*s. fastener*, cierre automático.- **—shot** [snǽpšat], *s.* disparo rápido, sin apuntar; fotografía instantánea.—**py** [-ị], *a.* (fam.) vivo, enérgico; elegante, garboso; mordedor; enojadizo; acre, picante; chispeante.

snare [snẹr], *s.* trampa, lazo, cepo; garlito, celada, asechanza, artimaña, red; (cir.) lazo; cuerda de tripa (para tambor).—*vt.* enredar, tender trampas o lazos.—*vi.* cazar con trampas o lazos, cepos, etc.

snarl [snarl], *vi.* gruñir, regañar; refunfuñar; hacer fu (el gato).—*vt.* enredar, enmarañar; embutir, estampar (artículos huecos de metal). —*vi.* enredarse, enmarañarse.—*s.* gruñido, regaño; (fam.) riña; maraña; hilo enredado; complicación, enredo; nudo en la madera.

snatch [snæch], *vt.* arrebatar; (fam.) raptar.—*to s. off*, arrebatar.—*vi.* (con at) tratar de agarrar o arrebatar.—*s.* arrebatamiento; arrebatiña; (fam.) rapto; pedacito; ratito.—*by snatches*, a ratos.

sneak [snik], *vi.* (con in) entrarse a hurtadillas; (con out o away) salirse a hurtadillas, escurrir el bulto; obrar solapada o bajamente; arrastrarse. —*vt.* ratear, cometer ratería, hurtar. —*s.* (fam.) persona solapada.—*s. thief*, ratero.

sneer [snịr], *vi.* hacer un gesto de desprecio; echar una mirada despectiva; mofarse de.—*vt.* expresar con un gesto de desprecio.—*s.* gesto, mirada o expresión de desprecio; mofa.

sneeze [sniz], *vi.* estornudar.—*not to be sneezed at*, no ser de despreciar, no ser un cualquiera.—*to s. at*, despreciar, menospreciar.—*s.* estornudo.

sniff [snịf], *vt.* husmear, olfatear, oliscar; inspirar o aspirar audiblemente.— *vi.* resollar, oler; sorberse los mocos; (con at) desdeñar, mostrar desprecio con resoplidos.—*s.* olfateo; olfateada.- **—le** [snịfl], *vi.* sorber por las narices; moquear; lloriquear.—*s.* moquita; lloriqueo.

snip [snịp], *vti.* [1] tijeretear; cortar con tijeras.—*to s. off*, cortar o recortar de un golpe.—*s.* tijeretada;

recorte, retazo, pedacito; parte;
(fam.) persona pequeña o insignificante.

snipe [snạip], *vt.* y *vi.* disparar o hacer
fuego desde un escondite o aposta-
dero.- **—r** [snạipœ(r)], *s.* francotirador, paco.

snivel [snívɐl], *vii.* [2] lloriquear, llorar
como una criatura.—*s.* moco.

snob [snab], *s.* esnob, persona con
pretensiones.- **—bery** [snábœri], *s.*
esnobismo, pretensiones.

snoop [snup], *s.* (fam.) entremetido;
fisgón, curioso.—*vi.* entremeterse;
husmear, fisgonear.

snooze [snuz], *vi.* (fam.) dormitar,
descabezar el sueño.—*s.* (fam.) siestecita, sueño ligero.

snore [snɔr], *vi.* roncar.—*s.* ronquido.

snot [snat], *s.* moco.

snout [snạut], *s.* hocico, morro, jeta;
trompa de elefante; cañón de un
fuelle; lanza de manguera; embocadura de un cañón.

snort [snɔrt], *vt.* y *vi.* resoplar, bufar.
—*s.* bufido, resoplido.

snow [snou], *s.* nieve; nevada.—*vi.*
nevar.—*vt.* (con **in, over, under** o **up**)
cubrir, obstruir, detener o aprisionar
con nieve.—*to s. under*, derrotar por
completo.- **—ball** [snóubɒl], *vt.*
lanzar bolas de nieve a.—*s.* pelota
de nieve.- **—drift** [-drift], *s.* ventisca,
ventisquero.- **—fall** [-fɔl], *s.* nevada.-
—flake [-fleik], *s.* copo de nieve.-
—plow [-plau], *s.* (máquina) quitanieves.- **—storm** [-stɔrm], *s.* nevada,
tormenta de nieve.- **—y** [-i], *a.*
níveo; puro, sin mancha; nevoso;
cargado de nieve.

snub [snʌb], *vti.* [1] desairar, tratar
con desprecio estudiado o afectada
arrogancia; reprender; (con **up**) parar
de repente.—*s.* desaire, repulsa;
(fam.) nariz chata.—*a.* romo, chato.

snuff [snʌf], *s.* moco, pabilo o pavesa
de candela o vela; tufo, olor; rapé.
—up *to s.*, (fam.) despabilado.—*vt.*
olfatear, oler, ventear; sorber por
la nariz; despabilar (una vela).—
vi. aspirar; tomar rapé.—*to s. it o out*,
(fam.) morirse.- **—le** [snʌfl], *vi.*
ganguear.—*s.* gangueo.—*pl.* catarro
nasal, romadizo.

snug [snʌg], *a.* cómodo, abrigado;
bien dispuesto; acomodado; apretado,
ajustado.

so [sou], *adv.* y *pron.* así; de esta manera; pues bien, conque; tan;
(fam.) muy, tan.—*how s.?* ¿cómo así?
¿cómo es eso?—*if s.*, si así es, si
lo fuere, en tal caso.—*I hope s.*, I
think s., así lo espero, lo creo.—*is
that s.?* ¿así? ¿de veras?—*just s.*,
ni más ni menos; exactamente.—*not*

s., no es así, eso no es verdad.—
S.-and-S., Fulano de tal.—*s. as to*,
para, a fin de.—*s. be it*, amén, así
sea.—*s. big*, de este tamaño, así de
grande.—*s.-called*, así llamado, llamado, según se llama.—*s. far*, hasta
aquí, hasta ahí; hasta ahora; tan
lejos.—*s. far as*, tan lejos como;
hasta, hasta donde.—*s. forth*, etcétera; y así sucesivamente.—*s. long*,
hasta luego, hasta más ver; hasta
aquí (ahí).—*s. long as*, mientras
que.—*s. many*, tantos.—*s. much*,
tanto.—*s. much a*, tanto por.—*s.
much as*, por mucho que; tanto como;
siquiera.—*s. much for*, eso en cuanto
a, eso basta en cuanto a.—*s. much
s. o that*, tanto que.—*s. much the
better*, tanto mejor.—*s. much the less*,
tanto menos.—*s. much the worse*,
tanto peor.—*s. or s.*, de un modo u
otro.—*s.-s.*, así así, tal cual, regular,
medianamente.—*s. that*, de suerte
que, de modo que; para que, a fin de
que.—*s. then*, así pues, conque, por
tanto.—*s. to say o speak*, por decirlo
así.—*conj.* con tal que; (fam.)
para que; (fam.) por lo tanto; de
modo que.

soak [souk], *vt.* empapar; remojar;
(con **in** o **up**) embeber, absorber;
(con **through**) calar, poner hecho
una sopa; (fam.) cobrar precios
exorbitantes (a uno); (fam.) beber
con exceso.—*vi.* estar en remojo;
(con **in, to** o **through**) remojarse,
esponjarse, calarse; (fam.) empinar
el codo.—*to be soaked to the skin*,
estar calado hasta los huesos.—*s.*
remojo, calada; (fam.) bebedor,
borracho; orgía.

soap [soup], *s.* jabón; (fam.) adulación;
(fam.) dinero.—*vt.* enjabonar, lavar
con jabón; (fam.) adular.- **—y**
[sóupi], *a.* jabonoso.

soar [sor], *vi.* remontarse, cernerse;
encumbrarse, aspirar; (aer.) planear
horizontalmente sin motor.—*s.* vuelo
o remonte.

sob [sab], *s.* sollozo.—*s. sister*, (fam.)
escritora de sentimentalismo cursi.
—*vii.* [1] sollozar.—*vti.* decir sollo-
zando.

sober [sóubœ(r)], *a.* cuerdo; sobrio;
sereno; templado, moderado; de
sangre fría; sombrío; de color apagado.—*in s. earnest*, de veras, con
seriedad, formalmente.—*s.-minded*,
desapasionado.—*vt.* y *vi.* desembo-
rrachar(se); poner(se) grave, serio
o pensativo; volverse sobrio, cuerdo,
moderado.—*to s. down*, serenar(se);
hacer volver o volverse cuerdo;
sosegar(se).- **—ness** [-nis], sobriety
[sobráieti], *s.* sobriedad, templanza,

moderación; cordura; seriedad; calma.

sobriquet [sóubrikei], *s.* sobrenombre, apodo.

soccer [sákœ(r)], *s.* fútbol.

sociable [sóuşabl], *a.* sociable, afable, comunicativo.—**social** [sóuşal], *a.* social; sociable; (zool.) que vive en comunidad; (bot.) que ocupa grandes áreas; de agrupación densa.—*s.* tertulia, reunión informal.—**socialism** [sóuşalizm], *s.* socialismo.—**socialist** [sóuşalist], *a.* y *s.* socialista.—**society** [sọsáięty], *s.* sociedad; comunidad; asociación, gremio; consorcio; círculos del buen tono; compañía, conversación o trato amenos.—**sociology** [sọşiálọḍẓi], *s.* sociología.

sock [sak], *s.* calcetín; escarpín; (fam.) porrazo, golpe; zapato ligero.—*vt.* (fam.) pegar, golpear con fuerza.

socket [sákịt], *s.* cuenca (del ojo); casquillo; portalámpara; enchufe; cualquier hueco donde encaja alguna cosa.

sod [sad], *vti.* [1] cubrir de césped.—*s.* césped; témpano de tierra vegetal.

soda [sóuḍạ], *s.* soda, sosa; gaseosa.

sodium [sóudịam], *s.* sodio.—*s. bicarbonate*, bicarbonato de sodio.

sodomy [sádọmị], *s.* sodomía.

sofa [sóufạ], *s.* sofá.

soft [sɔft], *a.* blando; muelle; dúctil; suave; liso; dulce, grato al oído; fofo; tierno, delicado; mimoso; afeminado; apocado; de matices delicados o apagados.—*s.-boiled eggs*, huevos pasados por agua.—*s.* —**en** [sɔfn], *vt.* ablandar; reblandecer; mitigar, suavizar; enternecer; afeminar; amortiguar o apagar (colores). —*vi.* ablandarse; reblandecerse; templarse; amansarse; enternecerse.— **-ly** [sɔftlị], *adv.* blandamente; callando; suavemente, sin ruido; lentamente.— **-ness** [-nịs], *s.* blandura; suavidad; pastosidad; maleabilidad; dulzura; ternura; morbidez.

soggy [sági], *a.* empapado, mojado; esponjoso.

soil [sɔịl], *vt.* y *vi.* manchar(se), ensuciar(se), empañar(se).—*s.* terreno, tierra vegetal; suelo; país, región; suciedad; mancha; abono; pantano en que se refugia la caza.

solace [sális], *s.* solaz.—*vt.* solazar.

solar [sóulạ(r)], *a.* solar.

sold [sould], *pret.* y *pp.* de TO SELL.—*s. out*, (com.) agotado.—*to be s. on*, (fam.) estar convencido de, o convertido a.

solder [sádœ(r)], *vt.* soldar.—*s.* soldadura.— **-ing** [-ịŋ], *s.* soldadura.— *s. iron*, soldador.

soldier [sóuldẓœ(r)], *s.* soldado, militar.

—*pl.* tropa, fuerza.— **-ly** [-lị] *a.* militar, marcial.— **-y** [-ị], *s.* soldadesca.

sole [soul], *vt.* echar suelas.—*s.* planta del pie; suela; suelo; lenguado.—*a.* único, solo; (for.) soltero; absoluto, exclusivo.—*s. agency* o *right*, (com.) exclusiva, exclusividad.—*s. agent*, agente exclusivo.

solemn [sálẹm], *a.* solemne.— **-ity** [solémnịtị], *s.* solemnidad; formalidad; pompa; rito, ceremonia.

solicit [sɔlịsịt], *vt.* solicitar.—*vi.* pretender, hacer una solicitud.— **-or** [-ǫ(r)], *s.* agente, solicitador; pretendiente.— **-ous** [-ʌs], *a.* solícito, cuidadoso.— **-ude** [-iud], *s.* solicitud, cuidado, afán.

solid [sálịd], *a.* sólido.—*a.* sólido; puro (oro, plata, etc.); macizo; cúbico; unánime; (fam.) completo, entero, verdadero.—*s. for*, unánimemente en favor de.— **-arity** [salịdǽrịtị], *s.* solidaridad.— **-solidify** [sọlịdịfai], *vti.* y *vii.* [7] solidificar(se).— **-ity** [sọlịdịtị], *s.* solidez.

soliloquy [sọlịlokwị], *s.* soliloquio, monólogo.—**solitaire** [sálịter], *s.* (joy., naipes) solitario.—**solitary** [sálịterị], *a.* solitario; retirado; solo, aislado; incomunicado.—*s.* solitario, ermitaño.—**solitude** [sálịtịud], *s.* soledad; vida solitaria.—**solo** [sóulọu], *s.* (mús.) solo.—**soloist** [sóulọuịst], *s.* (mús.) solista.

soluble [sályǫbl], *a.* soluble.—**solution** [sọlúşọn], *s.* solución.

solve [salv], *vt.* resolver; solucionar, desentrañar, desenredar, aclarar.

solvency [sálvẹnsị], *s.* solvencia.— **solvent** [sálvẹnt], *a.* solvente.—*s.* (quím.) disolvente.

somber [sámbœ(r)], *a.* sombrío, lóbrego, lúgubre, oscuro, tétrico.

some [sʌm], *a.* algo de, un poco; algún, alguno; unos pocos, varios, ciertos; algunos, unos.—*he is s. man*, (fam.) es todo un hombre.—*s. difficulty*, cierta dificultad.—*s. fine day*, el mejor día, cuando menos se piensa.—*s. house*, (fam.) gran casa.—*pron.* algunos; parte, una parte, una porción, un poco, algo (de).—*adv.* (fam.) cerca de, como, poco más o menos.— **-body** [sʌmbadị], *s.* alguien, alguno; un personaje.—*s. else*, algún otro.— **-how** [-hau], *adv.* de algún modo o manera.—*s. or other*, de un modo u otro.— **-one** [-wʌn], *pron.* alguien, alguno.

somersault [sámœrsǫlt], *s.* salto mortal, tumbo, voltereta.—*vt.* dar un salto mortal.

something [sʌmθịŋ], *s.* alguna cosa, algo.—*s. else*, otra cosa; alguna otra

cosa; algo más.—*adv.* algo, algún **tanto.**—**sometime** [sʌ́mtaim], *adv.* algún día, oportunamente, alguna vez.—*s.* last week, durante la semana pasada.—*s.* soon, un día de éstos, en breve, sin tardar mucho.—**sometimes** [sʌ́mtaimz], *adv.* algunas veces, a veces, de vez en cuando.—**somewhat** [sʌ́mhwat], *s.* alguna cosa, algo; un poco.—*adv.* algo, algún tanto, un poco.—**somewhere** [sʌ́mhwer], *adv.* en alguna parte.—*s.* else, en alguna otra parte.

somnolence [sámnoləns], *s.* somnolencia.—**somnolent** [sámnolənt], *a.* soñoliento; soporífero.

son [sʌn], *s.* hijo.—*s.-in-law,* yerno, hijo político.

song [soŋ], *s.* canción, canto, cantar, copla; balada, poema lírico; poesía, verso; bagatela, nimiedad, bicoca.—**-ster** [sóŋstœ(r)], *s.* cantor, cantante, cancionista; pájaro cantor.

sonnet [sánit], *s.* soneto.

sonorous [sonórʌs], *a.* sonoro.

soon [sun], *adv.* pronto, prontamente; de buena gana.—*as s. as,* tan pronto como; así que, no bien.—*how s.?* ¿cuándo? ¿cuándo, a más tardar?—*s. after,* poco después (de).

soot [sut], *s.* hollín, tizne.

soothe [suð], *vt.* calmar, sedar; consolar; desenfadar.—**soothing** [súðiŋ], *a.* calmante, sedante.

soothsayer [súθsejœ(r)], *s.* adivino.

sooty [súti], *a.* tiznado, holliniento.

sop [sap], *s.* sopa (cosa empapada); soborno, regalo para sobornar o apaciguar a alguien.—*vti.* [1] ensopar, empapar.—*to be sopping wet,* estar hecho una sopa, estar calado hasta los huesos.—*to s. up,* absorber.

sophism [sáfizm], *s.* sofisma.—**sophisticate** [sofístikejt], *vt.* falsificar, adulterar.—**sophisticated** [sofístikejtid], *a.* con experiencia, avezado al mundo; afectado, artificial.—**sophistication** [sofistikéjʃɔn], *s.* mundanidad, experiencia; afectación.—**sophistry** [sáfistri], *s.* sofistería.—*pl.* retóricas.

sophomore [sáfomɔr], *s.* estudiante de segundo año.

soporific [soupɔrífik], *a.* soporífero; soñoliento.

soprano [sopránou], *s.* tiple, soprano.—*a.* de soprano.

sorcerer [sórsœrœ(r)], *s.* hechicero, brujo.—**sorceress** [sórsœris], *s.* bruja, hechicera.—**sorcery** [sórsœri], *s.* sortilegio; brujería, hechicería.

sordid [sórdid], *a.* sórdido; vil, bajo; interesado, mezquino.

sore [sɔr], *s.* llaga, úlcera; lastimadura; mal, dolor; matadura (del ganado);

encono; pena, espina, memoria dolorosa; disgusto.—*a.* enconado, dolorido, sensible; apenado, apesarado; (fam.) enojado, sentido, picado; doloroso, penoso; molesto; vehemente.—*s.* throat, mal de garganta; carraspera.—*to be s. at,* estar enojado con.—*to be sorely in need of,* necesitar urgentemente.— —**ness** [sórnis], *s.* dolor, mal; calidad de dolorido, enconado o sensible; amargura de una pena.

sorrel [sárɛl], *a.* alazán, roano.—*s.* color alazán o roano; animal alazán.

sorrily [sárili], *adv.* mal, malamente, lastimosamente.—**sorrow** [sárou], *s.* pesar, dolor, pena; duelo, luto; desgracia, infortunio.—*s.-stricken,* afligido, agobiado de dolor.—*to my s.,* con gran sentimiento mío.—*vi.* afligirse, sentir pena.—**sorrowful** [sárouful], *a.* afligido, angustiado; triste, doloroso.—**sorry** [sári], *a.* apesadumbrado; arrepentido; lamentable; malo, miserable, ruin, de inferior calidad; despreciable, ridículo.—*I am s.,* lo siento, estoy apenado.

sort [sort], *s.* clase, especie, suerte; manera, modo, forma.—*after a s.* o in a s., de cierto modo, hasta cierto punto.—*all sorts of,* toda clase de.—*in like s.,* de modo análogo.—*of sorts,* de varias clases; de mala muerte.—*out of sorts,* indispuesto; malhumorado; triste.—*they are a bad s.,* son mala gente.—*vt.* (con over) separar, dividir, distribuir en grupos, clasificar; (con out) escoger, seleccionar; colocar, arreglar.—*vi.* corresponder, ajustar; estar de acuerdo; rozarse; adaptarse.

sot [sat], *s.* borrachín.

sought [sot], *pret.* y *pp.* de TO SEEK.

soul [soul], *s.* alma; psiquis; (fig.) corazón; esencia, virtud principal; inspiración; personificación; individuo, persona; vecino, habitante.—*All Souls' Day,* Día de Difuntos.—*not a s.,* nadie, ni un alma.—*on o upon my s.,* por vida mía.—**-ful** [sóulful], *a.* sentimental, espiritual.—**-less** [-lis], *a.* desalmado, vil.

sound [saund], *a.* sano, bueno; sólido, firme; ileso, incólume; puro, ortodoxo; cierto, justo; firme; cabal; (com.) solvente.—*of s. mind,* en su cabal juicio.—*safe and s.,* sano y salvo.—*s. business,* negocio seguro.—*s. sleep,* sueño profundo.—*adv.* sanamente, vigorosamente.—*s.* (geog.) estrecho; (mar. y cir.) sonda; son, sonido, tañido; ruido; vejiga natatoria (peces).—*vt.* sonar, tocar, tañer; dar el toque de; entonar; proclamar;

celebrar; probar por el sonido; son- dear; auscultar.—*to s. a note*, dar señal, avisar; formular, enunciar.— *vi.* sonar; resonar, divulgarse; dar toque de aviso o llamada.— **—ing** [sáundiŋ], *a.* sonante, resonante. **—high-s.**, retumbante.—*s.* sondeo, sondaje.— **—ly** [-liּ], *adv.* sanamente. **—to sleep s.**, dormir profundamente.— **—ness** [-nis], *s.* sanidad, salud; vigor; firmeza, solidez, estabilidad; verdad, rectitud, pureza, fuerza, validez; rectitud, justicia; pureza de la fe, ortodoxia; (com.) solvencia.

soup [sup], *s.* sopa.—*in the s.*, (fam.) en apuros.

sour [saur], *a.* agrio; ácido, fermentado, rancio; desabrido, acre, huraño, malhumorado.—*vt.* agriar, cortar (la leche, etc.); irritar, indisponer (los ánimos); desagradar; hacer fermentar.—*vi.* agriarse, cortarse; fermentar; irritarse, enojarse; corromperse.

source [sors], *s.* fuente, nacimiento, origen, causa, procedencia, germen.

sourness [sáurnis], *s.* agrura, acedía, acidez; acritud, acrimonia.

south [sauθ], *s.* sur o sud; comarca o región situada al sur.—*a.* meridional, austral.—*S. American*, sudamericano.—*adv.* hacia el sur; del sur (viento).— **—east** [-íst], *s.* y *a.* sudeste.— **—eastern** [-ístœrn], *a.* y *adv.* del sudeste.— **—ern** [sʌ́ðœrn], *a.* meridional, del sur.— **—erner** [sʌ́ðœrnœ(r)], *s.* habitante del sur.— **—ernmost** [sʌ́ðœrnmoụst], *a.* de más al sur, más meridional.— **—ward** [-wּrd], *a.* situado hacia el sur.— *adv.* hacia el mediodía.— **—west** [-wést], *s.* y *a.* sudoeste.— **—western** [-wéstœrn], *a.* en, hacia o del sudoeste.

souvenir [súvϵniּr], *s.* memoria, prenda de recuerdo.

sovereign [sávriּn], *s.* soberano, monarca.—*a.* soberano, independiente; preeminente; eficacísimo.— **—ty** [-tiּ], *s.* soberanía; estado soberano.

soviet [sóuּviet], *s.* sóviet.—*a.* soviético.

sow [sau], *s.* (zool.) puerca, cerda, marrana.—*vti.* y *vii.* [6] [sou], (agr.) sembrar; desparramar, esparcir, diseminar.

soy [soi], *s.* soja, soya; salsa de soja.— **—bean** [sóibin], *s.* soja, soya.

space [speis], *vt.* espaciar.—*s.* espacio; lugar, cabida; período, intervalo; rato; ocasión, oportunidad.— **—spacious** [spéiּʃʌs], *a.* espacioso, amplio, extenso.— **—spaciousness** [spéiּʃʌsnis], *s.* espaciosidad, extensión.

spade [speid], *s.* pala plana; (naipes) espadas; (mil.) zapa.—*to call a s. a s.*,

llamar al pan, pan y al vino, vino. —*vt.* remover o cavar con la azada.

spaghetti [spɑgéti], *s.* fideos largos; macarrones finos.

span [spæn], *s.* palmo; lapso, espacio, trecho; (arq.) luz; (aer.) envergadura, dimensión máxima transversal; ojo, apertura de puente, arco o bóveda; pareja (de caballos).—*vti.* [1] medir a palmos; atravesar; abarcar, llegar de un lado a otro de; extenderse sobre; ligar, atar.

spangle [spǽŋgl], *s.* lentejuela.

Spaniard [spǽnyּrd], *s.* español (persona española).

spaniel [spǽnyϵl], *s.* perro de aguas.

Spanish [spǽniּʃ], *s.* español (idioma). —*a.* español (de España), hispánico, hispano.—*S. shawl*, mantón de Manila.

spank [spæŋk], *vt.* zurrar, dar palmadas o nalgadas.—*s.* nalgada, palmada.

spar [spar], *s.* (mar.) mástil, palo; (min.) espato; pugilato; riña, pelea. —*vi.* boxear, pelear.

spare [sper], *vt.* ahorrar, economizar; escatimar; prescindir de, pasarse sin; conceder, dedicar (tiempo); perdonar; no abusar de, compadecer; evitar, ahorrar trabajo o molestia a; usar con moderación; eximir de.—*there's no time to s.*, no hay tiempo que perder.—*to have time to s.*, tener tiempo de sobra o libre.—*to s. oneself*, cuidarse de sí mismo, ahorrarse trabajo, molestia, etc.—*a.* disponible, sobrante; de reserva, de repuesto; enjuto; económico, mezquino; escaso; sobrio.

spark [spark], *s.* chispa; pizca; petimetre o pisaverde.—*pl.* (fam.) radiotelegrafista.—*s. plug*, bujía (de un motor).—*vt.* (fam.) galantear, enamorar.—*vi.* echar chispas, centellear.— **—le** [spárkl], *s.* centelleo, destello, chispa.—*vi.* centellear, brillar, relampaguear; ser espumoso (vinos, etc.).— **—ling** [-liּŋ], *a.* centelleante; brillante; agudo, ingenioso; espumoso.

sparrow [spǽrou], *s.* gorrión, pardal. —*s. hawk*, esparaván, gavilán, cernícalo.—*s. shot*, mostacilla.

sparse [spars], *a.* esparcido, desparramado; claro, ralo.

spasm [spǽzm], *s.* espasmo.

spat [spæt], *pret.* y *pp.* de TO SPIT (escupir).—*vti.* y *vii.* [1] (fam.) reñir, disputar ligeramente.—*s.* huevas de los mariscos; palmadita; manotada, sopapo, bofetada; riña, disputa.— *pl.* botines; polainas cortas.

spatula [spǽchּlּ], *s.* espátula.

spawn [spon], *s.* huevas; pececillos. —*vt.* y *vi.* desovar.

speak [spik], *vti.* y *vii.* [10] hablar; decir; conversar; comunicar(se); recitar.—*so to s.*, por decirlo así.—*to s. about* u *of*, hablar o tratar de.—*to s. brokenly*, chapurr(e)ar.—*to s. daggers*, decir improperios, echar chispas.—*to s. for*, hablar en favor de; hablar en nombre de; ser recomendación para; solicitar.—*to s. out*, hablar claro.—*to s. to the point*, ir al grano.—*to s. up*, hablar en alta voz; interponer; decir claridades.—**—er** [spíkœ(r)], *s.* hablante, orador; presidente de un cuerpo legislativo; locutor; altavoz.

spear [spir], *s.* lanza; venablo; arpón de pesca; brizna, brote, retoño.—*vt.* alancear, herir con lanza.—*vi.* (bot.) brotar.— **—mint** [spírmint], *s.* (bot.) hierbabuena, menta verde.

special [spéȿəl], *a.* especial; extraordinario, peculiar; diferencial; hecho especialmente.—*s. delivery*, entrega inmediata (de correo).—*s. warrant*, orden de arresto.—*s.* persona o cosa (tren, etc.) especial; carta de entrega inmediata; (fam., com.) ganga, saldo. — **—ist** [-ist], *s.* y *a.* especialista, especializado.— **—ize** [-aiz], *vt.* y *vi.* especializar(se); tener por especialidad.— **—ness** [-nis], *s.* especialidad.— **—ity** [speȿiéliti], *s.* especialidad, peculiaridad, rasgo característico.

specie [spíȿi], *s.* efectivo, numerario.

species [spíȿiz], *s.* (biol., lóg.) especie; clase, género, suerte, variedad; forma, naturaleza.—**specific** [spisífik], *a.* específico, preciso; especificativo, determinado; peculiar.—*s.* (med.) específico.—**specify** [spésifai], *vti.* [7] especificar; estipular, prescribir.—**specimen** [spésimen], *s.* espécimen, muestra; ejemplar.

speck(le) [spék(l)], *s.* manchita, mácula; motita; nube (en un ojo); lunar, señal; pizca, punto.—*vt.* manchar, motear.

spectacle [spéktəkl], *s.* espectáculo.—*pl.* espejuelos.—**spectacular** [spektékyȯlǝ(r)], *a.* espectacular; aparatoso.—**spectator** [spékteitǝ(r)], *s.* espectador, mirón.

specter [spéktœ(r)], *s.* espectro, visión.—**spectrum** [spéktrʌm], *s.* (opt.) espectro.

speculate [spékyȯleit], *vt.* y *vi.* especular.—**speculation** [spekyȯléiȿǝn], *s.* especulación.—**speculative** [spékyȯleitiv], *a.* especulativo; (com.) especulador.—**speculator** [spékyȯleitǝ(r)], *s.* especulador; (com.) especulador; (teat.) revendedor de billetes.

sped [sped], *pret.* y *pp.* de TO SPEED.

speech [spich], *s.* palabra, lenguaje, idioma; voz; discurso, arenga, perorata; disertación; (teat.) parlamento. — **—less** [spíchlis], *a.* mudo; callado.

speed [spid], *vti.* [4] ayudar, favorecer; acompañar, despedir; despachar, expedir; acelerar, apresurar, dar prisa, avivar.—*vii.* correr, apresurarse, darse prisa; andar o moverse con presteza; (aut.) exceder la velocidad permitida; adelantar, progresar.—*s.* velocidad; rapidez; presteza; progreso, buen éxito.—*s. gear*, (aut.) cambio de velocidades.—*s. limit*, velocidad máxima permitida; límite de velocidad.—*s. trap*, (aut.) aparato que registra automáticamente la velocidad de un vehículo y descubre a los infractores.— **—ily** [-ili], *adv.* rápidamente, de prisa; pronto.— **—ometer** [spidámẹtœ(r)], *s.* velocímetro, cuentaquilómetros, indicador de velocidad.— **—y** [-i], *a.* veloz, rápido, vivo.

spell [spel], *vti.* [4] deletrear; descifrar, leer con dificultad; indicar, significar; hechizar, encantar; (fam.) relevar, reemplazar.—*to s. the watch*, relevar a la guardia.—*vii.* deletrear; (fam.) descansar por un rato.—*s.* hechizo, encanto, ensalmo; fascinación; turno, tanda; (fam.) poco tiempo, rato, trecho.—*by spells*, por turnos; a ratos.—*under a s.*, fascinado.— **—bind** [spélbaind], *vti.* [10] fascinar, embelesar, hechizar.— **—bound** [spélbaund], *pret.* y *pp.* de TO SPELLBIND.—*a.* fascinado, embelesado, hechizado.— **—er** [spélœ(r)], *s.* silabario; libro de deletrear.— **—ing** [-iŋ], *s.* deletreo; ortografía, grafía.

spend [spend], *vti.* [10] gastar; consumir, agotar; pasar, emplear (tiempo, etc.).—*vii.* gastar dinero, hacer gastos; gastarse, consumirse; desovar.— **—thrift** [spéndθrift], *s.* pródigo, derrochador, manirroto.—**spent** [spent], *pret.* y *pp.* de TO SPEND.—*a.* agotado, rendido.

sperm [spœrm], *s.* esperma, semen; aceite de ballena.—*s. whale*, cachalote.

sphere [sfir], *s.* esfera; orbe; astro; esfera o círculo de acción.—**spherical** [sférikǝl], *a.* esférico.

sphinx [sfiŋks], *s.* esfinge; persona misteriosa o enigmática.

spice [spais], *s.* especia; (poét.) aroma, fragancia.—*vt.* condimentar con especias.—**spicy** [spáisi], *a.* que contiene o sabe a especias; aromático, especiado; (fig.) sabroso, picante.

spider [spáidœ(r)], *s.* araña, arácnido; sartén; cubo y rayos (de una rueda).—*s. web*, *s.'s web*, telaraña.

spigot [spígǝt], *s.* espita; tapón de espita; llave, grifo; macho, espiga (de un tubo).

spike [spaik], *s.* (bot.) espiga; alcayata, escarpia, espigón, clavo largo, perno; pico.—*vt.* clavetear; empernar, enclavijar; anular, poner fin a.

spikenard [spáiknard], *s.* (bot.) nardo.

spiky [spáiki], *a.* erizado, puntiagudo; armado de púas.

spill [spil], *s.* astilla; clavija; mecha; (fam.) vuelco, caída (del caballo o de un vehículo); derramamiento.— *vti.* [4] derramar, verter; desparramar, esparcir; (fam.) divulgar; volcar.—*vii.* derramarse, rebosar.

spin [spin], *vti.* [10] hilar; (mec.) tornear.—*to s. a yarn*, hilar; contar un cuento increíble.—*to s. out*, alargar, prolongar; retorcer, hacer bailar (un trompo).—*vii.* hilar; girar, rodar rápidamente; (aut.) girar sin avanzar (las ruedas); bailar (un trompo).—*s.* giro, vuelta; (fam.) paseo en coche o bicicleta; (aer.) barrena.

spinach [spínich], *s.* espinaca.

spinal [spáinal], *a.* (anat.) espinal.— *s. column*, columna vertebral o espina dorsal.—*s. cord*, médula espinal.

spindle [spíndl], *s.* huso; eje.

spine [spain], *s.* espinazo, espina dorsal; (bot.) espina; (zool.) púa.— **-less** [spáinljs], *a.* sin espinazo; pusilánime; servil.

spinner [spínœ(r)], *s.* hilandero; hiladera, máquina de hilar; cebo artificial para pescar.—**spinning** [spíniŋ], *s.* hilandería, arte de hilar; (aut.) rotación estacionaria de las ruedas.

spinster [spínstœ(r)], *s.* soltera, solterona; hilandera.— **-hood** [-hud], *s.* soltería.

spiral [spáiral], *s.* espiral; (aer.) vuelo en espiral.—*a.* espiral; en espiral; de caracol.—*vii.* [2] (aer.) volar en espiral; tomar forma o curso espiral.

spire [spair], *s.* (arq.) aguja; brizna de hierba; cúspide, cima, ápice; espira, espiral, caracol.—*vi.* rematar en punta; (bot.) germinar.

spirit [spírit], *s.* espíritu; aparecido, espectro; inclinación, vocación; temple; intención; ánimo, brío, valor. —*pl.* espíritus, vapores; bebidas espirituosas; estado de ánimo.—*high spirits*, alegría, animación.—*vt.* (con *away*) arrebatar, hacer desaparecer (como por ensalmo).— **-ed** [-id], *a.* vivo, brioso; animoso.— **-ual** [spír-ichual], *a.* espiritual; mental, intelectual; místico; piadoso, religioso; espiritualista.— **-ualism** [spírichu-alizm], *s.* espiritismo; espiritualismo.—**-uous** [spírichuas], *a.* espirituoso, alcohólico; embriagador.

spit [spit], *vti.* [10] escupir, esputar. —*vii.* escupir; chisporrotear.—*pret.*

y pp. de TO SPIT.—*vti.* [1] espetar, ensartar.—*s.* saliva, salivazo, escupitajo; lengua de tierra; asador, espiche.—*the s. and image* o *the spitting image*, (fam.) el vivo retrato, la imagen viva.

spite [spait], *s.* rencor, despecho, ojeriza.—*(in) s. of*, a pesar de, a despecho de, no obstante.—*vt.* mostrar resentimiento, mortificar.— **-ful** [spáitful], *a.* rencoroso; malicioso, malévolo.

spitfire [spítfair], *s.* fierabrás; mujer colérica.

spittle [spítl], *s.* saliva, escupitajo.— **spittoon** [spitún], *s.* escupidera.

splash [splæš], *vt.* salpicar, rociar, enlodar; chapotear, humedecer.—*vi.* chapotear.—*s.* salpicadura, rociada; chapoteo.— **-board** [splǽšbord], *s.* guardabarros, (Am.) guardafangos.

spleen [splin], *s.* bazo; mal humor; tristeza, esplín.

splendid [spléndid], *a.* espléndido; esplendente, brillante; ilustre, glorioso; excelente.—**splendor** [splén-do(r)], *s.* esplendor.

splice [splais], *vt.* empalmar; empotrar; (fam.) casar.—*s.* junta o empalme.

splint [splint], *vt.* (cir.) entablillar.—*s.* tira plana y delgada; astilla; (cir.) tablilla.— **-er** [splíntœ(r)], *vt.* astillar; (cir.) entablillar.—*vi.* hacerse pedazos, romperse en astillas.—*s.* astilla; esquirla (de hueso); brizna; astilla clavada en la carne.

split [split], *vti.* [9] hender, partir; rajar, cuartear, separar; dividir, repartir; (quim.) escindir, desdoblar; descomponer.—*to s. off* o *up*, desunir, desamistar.—*vii.* henderse, escindirse, rajarse, romperse a lo largo, cuartearse, resquebrajarse; estallar, reventar; dividirse; (fam.) disentir; (fam.) ser traidor, revelar secretos. —*pret. y pp.* de TO SPLIT.—*s.* hendidura, grieta, rendija, cuarteadura; división, cisma, rompimiento.—*a.* hendido, partido, rajado, cuarteado; curado (pescado).

spoil [spoil], *vti.* [4] echar a perder; estropear, desgraciar; inutilizar; viciar, corromper; malcriar, consentir; despojar, saquear.—*vii.* inutilizarse, estropearse; podrirse.—*s.* saqueo; botín.—*pl.* beneficios de un cargo público.—*spoils system*, premio de servicios políticos con empleos públicos.— **-age** [spóiljdž], *s.* desperdicio, daño, inutilización.

spoke [spouk], *s.* rayo, radio (de rueda).—*pret.* de TO SPEAK.—**spoken** [spóukn], *pp.* de TO SPEAK.— **-sman** [-sman], *s.* interlocutor; vocero, portavoz; el que lleva la palabra.

spoliation [spouļiéįâǫn], *s.* despojo, rapiña; (for.) expoliación.

sponge [spʌndʒ], *s.* esponja; (fam.) gorrón, parásito.—*s. cake*, biscocho. —*vt.* lavar o mojar con esponja; esponjar.—*to s. up*, absorber, chupar; (fam.) comer de gorra, sablear; sacar (dinero, etc.).—*vi.* embeberse; (fam.) vivir o comer a expensas de otro, darle un sablazo a uno.— —r [spʌndʒœ(r)], *s.* (fam.) gorrista, sablista, pegote.—**spongy** [spʌndʒį], *a.* esponjoso, esponjado.

sponsor [spʌnsǫ(r)], *s.* fiador; patrocinador, patrón; padrino, patrono; (rad. y T.V.) entidad que patrocina un programa; padrino o madrina; defensor, apadrinador, fomentador.— *vt.* salir fiador de, ser responsable de; apadrinar, ser padrino de; promover, fomentar, patrocinar; (rad. y T.V.) costear o presentar un programa comercial.— —**ship** [-ŝip], *s.* patrocinio.

spool [spul], *s.* carretel, bobina.—*vt.* devanar, ovillar.

spoon [spun], *s.* cuchara.—*vt.* sacar con cuchara.—*vi.* pescar con cuchara; (fam.) acariciarse, besarse.— —**ful** [spʌnfuļ], *s.* cucharada, cucharadita.

sport [spǫrt], *s.* deporte.—*pl.* deportismo.—*for* o *in s.*, de burlas, en broma.—*to be a good s.*, ser buen compañero; saber perder (en el juego).—*to make s. of*, burlarse de. —*vt.* (fam.) hacer alarde de, lucir, ostentar.—*vi.* divertirse, jugar; bromear, chancearse.—*a.* deportivo.— —**s** [-s], *a.* deportivo; de o para deportes.— —**sman** [spǫrtsmạn], *s.* deportista.

spot [spat], *s.* sitio, lugar, paraje, puesto, punto; mancha, borrón, tacha; grano; lunar.—*in spots*, (fam.) en algunos respectos; aquí y allí. —*on* o *upon the s.*, ahí mismo, allí mismo, en el acto, al punto, inmediatamente.—*to be on the s.*, (fam.) hallarse en un aprieto; estar en peligro de muerte; estar en el lugar de los hechos.—*a.* (com.) en existencia, listo para entregarse.—*s. cash*, dinero contante; pago al contado.—*vti.* [1] motear; manchar; macular; (fam.) observar, notar, distinguir.—*vii.* salir manchas; mancharse.— —**less** [spátlįs], *a.* inmaculado.— —**light** [-lajt], *s.* (teat., fot., aut., etc.) reflector (móvil).— **spotted** [spátįd], *a.* manchado.

spouse [spaǫs], *s.* esposa, esposo, cónyuge.

spout [spaǫt], *s.* chorro, surtidor; caño, conducto; espita; (arq.) gárgola; cuello de vasija; pico de cafetera

o tetera.—*to go up the s.*, (fam.) fracasar.—*vt.* y *vi.* arrojar o echar (un líquido); surgir, brotar, correr a chorro; (fam.) recitar, declamar.

sprain [sprejn], *vt.* torcer, producir un esguince.—*s.* (med.) torcedura, esguince.

sprang [spræŋ], *pret.* de TO SPRING.

sprawl [sprol], *vt.* y *vi.* tender(se); despatarrar(se); (agr.) desparramarse.

spray [sprej], *vt.* y *vi.* rociar, pulverizar un líquido.—*s.* rociada, rocío; espuma del mar; salpicadura; rociador, pulverizador; líquido de rociar; ramaje.

spread [spred], *vti.* y *vii.* [9] tender(se); extender(se), desplegar(se), desenvolver(se); desparramar(se), esparcir(se); divulgar(se); diseminar(se), propalar(se).—*to s. apart*, abrir(se), separar(se).—*to s. something (butter, etc.) on*, untar con; dar una capa de.—*to s. out the tablecloth*, extender el mantel.—*to s. with*, untar con; cubrir de.—*pret.* y *pp.* de TO SPREAD.—*a.* extendido, desparramado; (joy.) de poco brillo.—*s.* extensión, amplitud; propagación; diseminación; cobertor de cama; tapete de mesa, mantel; (fam.) festín, banquete, comilona; (com.) diferencia; anuncio con encabezamiento a través de dos páginas.

spree [spri], *s.* borrachera; juerga, parranda.—*to go on a s.*, ir (o andar) de juerga, parranda o farra.

sprig [sprig], *s.* ramita, renuevo, pimpollo.

sprightly [sprájtlį], *a.* alegre, vivo, garboso.

spring [spriŋ], *vti.* [10] soltar (un resorte o muelle); sacar o presentar de golpe; hacer volar (una mina); combar; rendir un palo o verga; (arq.) vaciar (un arco); insertar o meter doblando o forzando; saltar por encima de; pasar saltando; ojear (la caza); asegurar o montar con resortes o muelles.—*vii.* saltar, brincar, salir, brotar, manar (un líquido); dimanar, provenir; presentarse súbitamente; combarse, rendirse; nacer, crecer; levantarse, elevarse.—*to s. at*, abalanzarse sobre; saltar a.—*to s. away*, saltar a un lado; lanzarse de un salto.—*to s. forward*, abalanzarse, dispararse.— *to s. up*, nacer, brotar, desarrollarse; salir a luz; subir, engrandecerse.—*to s. upon*, abalanzarse sobre; saltar a.—*s.* muelle, resorte; elasticidad; salto, corcovo, bote; vuelta a su posición anterior; motivo, móvil; primavera; fuente, manantial; origen,

nacimiento; surtidor; combadura.—*a.* primaveral; de manantial.

sprinkle [spríŋkl], *vt.* rociar; regar; salpicar, polvorear.—*vi.* lloviznar. —*s.* rocío, rociada; llovizna; una pizca, un poquito.—*-r* [spríŋklœ(r)], *s.* rociador, regadera; (igl.) hisopo, aspersorio; carro de riego.—**sprinkling** [spríŋkliŋ], *s.* rociada, aspersión; pizca.

sprout [spraut], *vt.* hacer germinar o brotar; (agr.) desbotonar.—*vi.* retoñar, echar botones o renuevos; crecer; ramificarse.—*s.* renuevo, retoño, botón.—*Brussels sprouts,* coles de Bruselas.

spruce [sprus], *a.* garboso, apuesto, majo.—*s.* abeto.—*to s. up,* vestir(se) con esmero, emperifollar(se), poner(se) majo.

sprung [sprʌŋ], *pret.* y *pp.* de TO SPRING.

spun [spʌn], *pret.* y *pp.* de TO SPIN.

spur [spœr], *s.* espuela, acicate; incentivo, estímulo; excitación; espolón (del gallo); uña puntiaguda; pincho; (geog.) estribación; (arq.) puntal.—*on the s. of the moment,* sin pensarlo, impulsivamente.—*vti.* y *vii.* [1] espolear, acicatear, aguijonear; incitar, estimular; calzarse las espuelas; apretar el paso.—*to s. on,* espolear, estimular.

spurn [spœrn], *vt.* y *vi.* despreciar; menospreciar; rechazar a puntapiés; cocear.

spurt [spœrt], *vt.* y *vi.* arrojar o salir un chorro o chorros; brotar, surgir; hacer un esfuerzo supremo.—*s.* chorro; arrebato, esfuerzo supremo; rato, momento.

sputter [spʌtœ(r)], *vt.* y *vi.* espurrear, rociar con la boca; chisporrotear; farfullar, barbotar.—*s.* chisporroteo; chispeo de saliva; farfulla.

sputum [spjútʌm], *s.* saliva; (med.) esputo.

spy [spai], *s.* espía.—*vti.* [7] atisbar, divisar; espiar, observar; (con out) explorar, reconocer un país.—*vii.* espiar; ser espía.—*-glass* [spáiglæs], *s.* anteojo de larga vista.

squab [skwab], *s.* (orn.) pichón; persona gordiflona; cojín, otomana.

squabble [skwábl], *vt.* (imp.) empastelar.—*vi.* reñir, disputar.—*s.* pendencia, riña, disputa.

squad [skwad], *s.* (mil.) escuadra, patrulla, pelotón; partida; equipo.—*-ron* [skwádrǫn], *s.* (mar.) escuadra, armada, flota; (mil.) escuadrón; cuadro; soldados en formación; (aer.) escuadrilla.

squalid [skwálid], *a.* escuálido; miserable, sucio, asqueroso.

squall [skwɔl], *vt.* y *vi.* chillar, berrear. —*vi.* haber borrasca.—*s.* chillido, berrido; borrasca; (mar.) racha, turbonada, chubasco.

squalor [skwálǫ(r)], *s.* miseria; porquería, mugre.

squander [skwándœ(r)], *vt.* y *vi.* malgastar, despilfarrar, desparramar, disipar.—*-er* [-œ(r)], *s.* derrochador, manirroto.

square [skwer], *a.* cuadrado; en cuadro; rectangular; a escuadra; perfecto, exacto, justo, cabal; íntegro, honrado, equitativo; (fam.) completo, abundante; (com.) saldado, en paz; (mar.) en cruz; (mat.) elevado al cuadrado. —*s. dance,* baile de figuras.—*s. deal(ing),* buena fe, equidad, justicia, honradez, juego limpio.—*s.-shooter,* (fam.) persona honrada.—*to get s. with,* (fam.) desquitarse de, hacérselas pagar a.—*s.* cuadrado; cuadro; plaza, plazoleta; casilla (de tablero de damas, etc.); manzana de casas; escuadra, cartabón; proporción debida, orden, exactitud; honradez, equidad; (mil.) cuadro.—*on the s.,* (fam.) honradamente, de buena fe; a escuadra.—*out of s.,* fuera de escuadra.—*vt.* cuadrar, formar un cuadro; escuadrar; (mat.) cuadrar, elevar al cuadrado; (b.a.) cuadricular; (com.) saldar, ajustar, arreglar (cuentas); pasar balance; justificar; poner de acuerdo; medir superficies en pies, metros, etc., cuadrados.—*to s. one's self,* sincerarse, justificarse, dar satisfacción.—*vi.* estar en ángulo recto; cuadrar, encajar, convenir, estar de acuerdo.

squash [skwaʃ], *s.* (bot.) calabaza.—*vt.* aplastar, (fam.) despachurrar.

squat [skwat], *vii.* [1] agacharse, agazaparse, sentarse en cuclillas; establecerse sin derecho en un local. —*a.* agachado, puesto en cuclillas; rechoncho.—*s.* posición del que está en cuclillas.

squawk [skwɔk], *vi.* graznar; (fam.) quejarse ruidosamente.—*s.* graznido; (fam.) queja o protesta ruidosa.

squeak [skwik], *vi.* chirriar, rechinar; (fam.) delatar.—*s.* chillido, chirrido. —*to have a narrow s.,* escapar en una tabla.—**squeal** [skwil], *vi.* chillar; (fam.) delatar.—*s.* chillido.

squeamish [skwímiʃ], *a.* remilgado, delicado, escrupuloso.—*-ness* [-nis], *s.* remilgo, escrúpulo; náusea.

squeeze [skwiz], *vt.* apretar, comprimir; estrechar; estrujar, exprimir, prensar; acosar, agol.iar; rebajar (jornales).—*to s. in,* hacer entrar apretando. —*to s. through,* forzar al través de.—*vi.* pasar, entrar o salir apretando.

—s. apretadura, apretón; abrazo fuerte.

squelch [skwelch], vt. aplastar; sofocar; (fam.) hacer callar, paralizar, (fig.) desconcertar.—vi. ser vencido, desconcertado; chapotear.

squid [skwid], s. calamar.

squint [skwint], s. estrabismo; mirada bizca; mirada furtiva o de soslayo. —vt. y vi. mirar bizco, bizquear; mirar achicando los ojos; mirar de través o de soslayo.—squint-eyed, bizco, bisojo, estrábico; avieso; ambiguo.

squirm [skwœrm], vi. retorcerse, serpentear; trepar.—to s. out of a difficulty, esforzarse para vencer una dificultad o salir de un aprieto.—s. retorcimiento.

squirrel [skwœrel], s. ardilla.

squirt [skwœrt], vt. y vi. (hacer) salir a chorros; chorrear; jeringar.—s. chisguete, chorretada; (fam.) jeringazo.—s. gun, jeringa.

stab [stæb], vti. y vii. [1] herir con arma blanca, dar de puñaladas. —s. puñalada; estocada.

stability [stabíliti], s. estabilidad; firmeza, consistencia, solidez; asiento. —stabilize [stéjbilajz], vt. estabilizar. —stabilizer [stéjbilajzœ(r)], s. estabilizador.—stable [stéjbl], a. estable. —s. establo, cuadra.—vt. y vi. poner o estar en establo.

stack [stæk], s. montón, pila, rimero; hacina (de heno); cañón de chimenea; (fam.) abundancia; (mil.) pabellón de fusiles.—vt. hacinar, apilar, amontonar; poner las armas en pabellón.

stadium [stéjdiʌm], s. estadio, campo deportivo; grado de progreso o adelanto.

staff [stæf], s. báculo, bordón, cayado; apoyo, sostén; vara, bastón de mando; pértiga; vara de medir; asta (de bandera o lanza); baliza, jalón de mira; estado mayor, plana mayor; personal; facultad; junta, cuerpo. —vt. proveer de personal, funcionarios u oficiales.

stag [stæg], s. venado, ciervo; (fam.) hombre, varón, macho.—s. party, (fam.) tertulia de hombres solos.

stage [stejdž], s. (teat.) escenario, escena, tablas; (fig.) teatro (arte y profesión); escena de acción; tablado, entarimado, plataforma, estrado; andamio; etapa, jornada, grado, estado; período (de una enfermedad); platina (de microscopio); diligencia, ómnibus; (arq.) escalón, paso de escalera; (rad.) elemento, unidad; (mec.) grado.—by short stages, a pequeñas etapas, a cortas jornadas.

—s. scenery o setting, decoración, decorado.—s.-struck, fascinado por el teatro; que se muere por ser actor o actriz.—vt. preparar; ejecutar, efectuar; (teat.) poner en escena, montar, escenificar; (re)presentar.

stagecoach [stéjdžkouch], s. diligencia, ómnibus.

stagger [stægœ(r)], vi. hacer eses, tambalear, bambolear; vacilar, titubear.—vt. causar vértigos o vahídos; asustar; hacer vacilar; hacer tambalear; disponer o arreglar (plantas, etc.) al tresbolillo; alternar; espaciar (horas de trabajo, etc.).—s. tambaleo, vacilación.

stagnant [stægnant], a. estancado.— **stagnate** [stægnejt], vi. estancarse, estacionarse.—**stagnation** [stægnéjšon], s. estancamiento, paralización.

staid [stejd], pret. y pp. de TO STAY. —a. grave, serio, sosegado, formal.

stain [stejn], vt. y vi. manchar, macular; teñir; tiznar; mancillar, desdorar. —stained glass, vidrio de color.—s. mancha, mácula; tinte; solución colorante; borrón, estigma.—less [stéjnlis], a. limpio; inmaculado; que no se mancha.—s. steel, acero inoxidable.

stair [ster], s. escalón, peldaño.—pl. escalera.—case [stérkejs], —way [-wej], s. escalera; escalinata (exterior).

stake [stejk], s. estaca; (fig.) hoguera, pira; apuesta, posta o puesta; azar, riesgo; premio del vencedor; (com.) interés, ganancia o pérdida contingente.—at s., en juego, envuelto, comprometido, en peligro.—vt. jugarse, apostar; aventurar, arriesgar; (fam.) establecer a uno en los negocios, etc.; darle o prestarle dinero.

stale [stejl], a. añejo; rancio, pasado; viciado (el aire); gastado, anticuado, trillado; improductivo.—s. bread, pan duro.—s. wine, vino picado.

stalk [stok], vt. cazar al acecho.—vi. taconear, andar con paso majestuoso. —s. tallo, pedúnculo, peciolo; troncho de hortalizas; pie de copa; paso majestuoso, taconeo.

stall [stol], s. pesebre, casilla de establo; casilla, puesto (en el mercado, etc.); tabla (de carnicero); (teat.) luneta o butaca; (igl.) sitial de coro; (min.) galería; (aer.) disminución de velocidad.—vt. meter en cuadra o establo; poner puestos o casillas; atascar, atollar; poner obstáculos.—to s. off, evitar, eludir, tener a raya.—vi. estar atascado; (aut.) pararse, ahogarse (el motor); (aer.) bajar de la velocidad mínima de vuelo.—to s. for time, (fam.) dar largas; demorar para

ganar tiempo o no hacer una cosa.

stallion [stǽlyǫn], *s.* caballo semental.

stalwart [stólwặrt], *a.* fornido, membrudo; (pol.) leal, firme, fiel.

stamina [stǽmǐnặ], *s.* nervio, fibra, vigor.

stammer [stǽmœ(r)], *vt.* y *vi.* tartamudear; balbucear.—*s.* tartamudeo; balbuceo.——**er** [-œ(r)], *s.* tartamudo, gago.

stamp [stæmp], *vt.* estampar; marcar; señalar; imprimir; sellar, estampillar; timbrar (papel, cartas); poner el sello (de correo); acuñar; patear (el suelo, etc.); estigmatizar.—*to s. out*, extirpar, suprimir.—*vi.* patalear; piafar.—*s.* sello, estampilla; timbre; impresión, marca, estampa; estampador; cuño, troquel; mano de mortero; (fig.) temple, suerte, clase; laya, calaña.—*s. duties*, derechos del timbre.—*s. duty*, impuesto del timbre.

stampede [stæmpíd], *vt.* y *vi.* espantar(se); dispersar(se) en desorden.—*s.* estampida; huida en tropel; determinación repentina y unánime.

stance [stæns], *s.* postura.

stanch [stænch], *vt.* restañar; estancar. —*a.* [stanch], firme, fiel, adicto.

stand [stænd], *vti.* [10] poner derecho, colocar o poner de pie; resistir, hacer frente a; aguantar, tolerar; sostener, defender; (fam.) sufragar. —*to s. one's ground*, resistir, defender su posición o posición, mantenerse en su puesto.—*to s. treat*, (fam.) pagar la convidada.—*to s. up*, (fam.) dejar plantado a uno.—*vii.* estar, estar situado; ponerse o estar de pie; tenerse derecho; mantenerse, durar, perdurar; sostenerse; quedarse; pararse, detenerse; quedar suspenso; ponerse o estar en cierta posición; erguirse, enderezarse.—*to s. about*, rodear, cercar.—*to s. against*, hacer frente a.—*to s. aloof (from)*, retraerse (de).—*to s. aside*, apartarse. —*to s. back*, retroceder; quedarse atrás.—*to s. by*, ser o permanecer fiel a; estar listo; sostener, favorecer; atenerse a; sostenerse en; someterse a; estar de mirón; estar cerca, quedarse allí; mantenerse listo.—*to s. fast*, no cejar o ceder.—*to s. for*, estar en lugar de; significar, querer decir; tolerar; aprobar, favorecer; solicitar, pretender; presentarse como candidato u opositor; sostener, defender; apadrinar; llevar rumbo hacia.—*to s. forth*, adelantarse, avanzar; presentarse.—*to s. in good stead*, servir, ser útil.—*to s. in line*, hacer cola.—*to s. in the way*, cerrar el paso; estorbar.—*to s. in with*, juntarse o estar aliado con; estar

en gracia de.—*to s. off*, mantenerse a distancia, apartarse; negar, denegar.—*to s. on o upon*, estar colocado sobre, estar en; adherirse a; interesar, concernir, pertenecer; estimar, valuar; fijarse en; picarse de, tener su orgullo en; insistir en.—*to s. on end*, erizarse; ponerse de punta; mantenerse derecho.—*to s. on one's own feet*, valerse a sí mismo.—*to s. on tiptoe*, ponerse o estar de puntillas.—*to s. out*, mantenerse firme; apartarse; denegar; resaltar, destacarse, estar en relieve.—*to s. over*, aplazar; plantarse al lado de para vigilar o apurar. —*to s. pat*, mantenerse en sus trece. —*to s. up*, levantarse, alzarse. —*s.* puesto, sitio, lugar, posición, estación; tarima, estrado, plataforma; tribuna, grada, galería (de espectadores); mostrador, puesto en un mercado; velador, mesita, pie, estante, pedestal, sostén, soporte; actitud, opinión; parada, pausa, alto; término; inactividad, estancamiento; oposición, resistencia.—*to make a s.*, pararse y resistir.

standard [stǽndặrd], *s.* norma, tipo, pauta, patrón, modelo; (mec.) soporte, madrina, pie, montante, árbol; bandera, estandarte, pendón.—*s. of living*, nivel o norma de vida.—*a.* normal, de ley; patrón (vara, libra, etc.); clásico.—*s.-bearer*, abanderado; cacique, jefe político.—*s. book* o *work*, obra de autoridad reconocida; obra clásica.—*s. equipment*, equipo regular o de uso corriente.—*s. gauge*, marca o medida que sirve de norma. —*s. pitch*, (mús.) diapasón normal.— **—ization** [stǽndặrdizéişǫn], *s.* uniformación, normalización, reducción a un patrón común.— **—ize** [-aiz], *vt.* (Am.) estandarizar; normalizar.

standing [stǽndiŋ], *a.* derecho o en pie; levantado, de pie; erecto; con pedestal o pie; permanente, fijo, establecido; duradero, estable; parado; estancado, encharcado; (for.) vigente.—*s.* posición, reputación; categoría; puesto, sitio, paraje; duración, antigüedad; alto, parada. —*of long s.*, (que existe, dura, etc.) desde hace mucho tiempo.—**standpoint** [stǽndpǫint], *s.* punto de vista.—**standstill** [stǽndstil], *s.* parada, detención, alto; pausa.

stank [stæŋk], *pret.* de TO STINK.

stanza [stǽnzặ], *s.* estrofa.

staple [stéipl], *s.* artículo o producto principal; renglón de comercio; elemento o asunto principal; materia prima o bruta; hembra de cerrojo, grapa, aro, argolla; grapa de alambre (para sujetar papeles).—*pl.* artículos

de primera necesidad.—*a.* (com.) corriente, de consumo o uso general; principal, prominente; establecido, reconocido; vendible.—*vt.* asegurar (papeles, etc.) con grapas; coser con alambre; clasificar hebras textiles por su longitud.

star [star], *s.* estrella; cosa o persona principal; asterisco; mancha en la frente de un animal.—*shooting s.,* estrella fugaz.—*s.-spangled,* tachonado de estrellas.—*S.-Spangled Banner,* bandera estrellada (nombre dado a la bandera y el himno de E.U.A.). —*vti.* [1] adornar con estrellas; marcar con asterisco; (teat., cine) introducir como estrella.—*vii.* ser estrella (teat. cine, etc.).—*a.* sobresaliente, excelente.

starboard [stárbord], *s.* (mar.) estribor.

starch [starch], *s.* almidón, fécula; (fig.) entereza, vigor; rigidez.—*vt.* almidonar.— —*y* [stárchi], *a.* feculento; estirado, entonado.

stare [ster], *vt.* clavar o fijar la vista en o a; encararse con; mirar de hito en hito o descaradamente.—*vi.* abrir grandes ojos; mirar con fijeza, asombro o insolencia; saltar a la vista; ser muy vivo o chillón (un color); erizarse (el pelo).—*s.* mirada fija o de hito en hito; encaro.

starfish [stárfis], *s.* estrella de mar.

stark [stark], *a.* tieso, rígido; (fig.) inflexible, severo; completo, cabal; puro.

starling [stárlin], *s.* estornino.

starry [stári], *a.* estrellado; como estrellas, centelleante, rutilante.

start [start], *vt.* empezar, iniciar; poner en marcha; dar la señal de salida; levantar (la caza).—*to s. a row,* armar una gresca.—*vi.* comenzar; partir, salir; arrancar (un motor, etc.); sobresaltarse, asustarse; provenir, proceder de; aflojarse; descoyuntarse; combarse.—*to s. after,* salir tras o en busca de; seguir a.—*to s. back,* dar un respingo; emprender el viaje de regreso.—*to s. for,* ponerse en camino hacia; presentarse como candidato para.—*to s. off,* partir, ponerse en marcha.—*to s. out,* salir, partir; principiar a.—*to s. up,* levantarse precipitadamente; salir de repente; ponerse en movimiento, arrancar.—*s.* principio, comienzo; salida, partida; arranque; sobresalto, susto; respingo; ímpetu, arranque, pronto; ventaja, delantera; grieta, raja.—*at the s.,* al primer paso, al principio.—*by fits and starts,* a saltos y corcovos; a ratos.— —*er* [stártœ(r)], *s.* iniciador; el que da la señal de partida; (dep.) juez de

salida; comienzo; cosa con que se principia; (aut.) arranque, mecanismo de arranque.

startle [stártl], *vt.* y *vi.* espantar(se), dar(se) un susto; sobrecoger(se); alarmar(se).

starvation [starvéişon], *a.* que causa hambre o inanición.—*s.* hambre, inanición.—**starve** [starv], *vi.* morir de hambre; hallarse en la inopia.— *vt.* matar de hambre.

state [steit], *s.* estado; situación, condición; pompa, ceremonia.—*in a s. of nature,* desnudo; en pecado; indomado; incivilizado.—*in (great) s.,* con (gran) pompa, de (gran) ceremonia.—*in s. of o to,* en estado de. —*to lie in s.,* estar de cuerpo presente.—*a.* de estado; del estado; estatal; político, público; de lujo o gala; perteneciente a los estados o a cada estado.—*vt.* y *vi.* decir, expresar; consignar; rezar (un texto); formular (un principio, ley, etc.); enunciar, plantear.- —*liness* [stéitlinis], *s.* majestad, dignidad.- —*ly* [-li], *a.* augusto, majestuoso.- —*ment* [-ment], *s.* declaración, exposición; afirmación, aserto; manifestación; cuenta, estado de cuenta; relato, información, memoria; planteo, enunciado; proposición; (com.) balance.- —*room* [-rum], *s.* (mar.) camarote; (f.c.) salón; salón de recepción de un palacio.- —*sman* [-sman], *s.* estadista.

static [stétik], *s.* (rad.) estática.—*a.* estático.— —*s* [-s], *s.* (mec.) estática.

station [stéişon], *s.* estación (de f.c., radio, policía, vía crucis, etc.); sitio, puesto; rango o posición social; (mar.) apostadero; (mil.) puesto.— *s. master,* jefe de estación.—*vt.* estacionar, colocar, situar, apostar.— —*ary* [-eri], *a.* estacionario, fijo.— *to remain s.,* estacionarse, quedarse inmóvil.— —*er* [-œ(r)], *s.* papelero.— —*ery* [erj], *s.* papelería, objetos de escritorio; papel de cartas.

statistic(al) [statistik(al)], *a.* estadístico.—**statistics** [statistiks], *s.* estadística; datos estadísticos.

statuary [stéchueri], *s.* estatuaria; estatuario, escultor.—**statue** [stéchu], *s.* estatua.

stature [stéchu(r)], *s.* estatura, altura, tamaño; alzada; importancia.

statute [stéchut], *s.* estatuto, ley, reglamento.—*s. law,* derecho escrito.

staunch [stonch], *vt.* y *a.* = STANCH.

stave [steiv], *vti.* [4] desfondar, abrir boquete; poner duelas (a un barril). —*to s. off,* rechazar, parar; retardar, diferir.—*vii.* desfondarse, hacerse pedazos.—*s.* duela de barril; escalón,

peldaño (de escala); (mus.) penta-grama; (poét.) estrofa.

stay [stej], *vti.* [4] parar, impedir; sostener, apoyar, reforzar; aplazar; (for.) sobreseer.—*vii.* quedarse, permanecer; parar(se); tardar(se); alojarse.—*to s. away*, mantenerse alejado; no volver.—*to s. in*, quedarse en casa, no salir.—*to s. out*, quedarse fuera, no entrar.—*to s. put*, (fam.) estarse quieto o en un mismo sitio. —*to s. up*, velar, no acostarse.—*s.* estancia, residencia, permanencia; suspensión, espera, parada; (for.) sobreseimiento; impedimento, obstáculo; refuerzo; sostén, soporte; ballena de corsé; estabilidad, fijeza.

stead [sted], *s.* (con in) lugar, sitio; utilidad; ayuda.—*in his (her) s.*, en su lugar.—*in s. of*, en lugar de, en vez de, haciendo las veces de.—*to stand in (good) s.*, ser útil o de provecho.- —*fast* [stédfæst], *a.* constante, inmutable; resuelto, determinado.- —*ily* [-ili], *adv.* constantemente; de firme; regular o progresivamente.- —*iness* [-injs], *s.* estabilidad, firmeza; entereza; constancia.- —*y* [-i], *a.* firme, fijo, seguro; juicioso, formal; constante, uniforme, continuo.—*s.-going*, metódico, constante.—*vti.* [7] reforzar; impedir el movimiento de; calmar; fortalecer.

steak [stejk], *s.* biftec, bisté.

steal [stil], *vti. y vii.* [10] hurtar, robar; pasar furtivamente.—*s.* (fam.) hurto, robo.- —*th* [stel θ], *s.* cautela, reserva.—*by s.*, a hurtadillas.- —*thy* [stélθj], *a.* furtivo, escondido, clandestino.

steam [stim], *s.* vapor; vaho.—*a.* de vapor; para vapor; por vapor.—*s.* *engine*, máquina de vapor.—*s. heat(ing)*, calefacción por vapor.—*vt.* proveer de vapor; cocinar al vapor; limpiar con vapor.—*vi.* generar o emitir vapor; funcionar por vapor.- —*boat* [stímbout], —*ship* [stímʃip], *s.* buque de vapor.- —*er* [-œ(r)], *s.* buque o máquina de vapor; baño (de) María.

steed [stid], *s.* corcel.

steel [stil], *s.* acero.—*a.* de acero.—*vt.* acerar, revestir de acero; acorazar; fortalecer; hacer insensible.- —*y* [stíli], *a.* acerado, duro, inflexible.

steep [stip], *a.* empinado, pendiente, escarpado; (fam.) exorbitante.—*vt.* impregnar, remojar, macerar; poner en infusión.- —*le* [stípl], *s.* aguja, torre, campanario.- —*ness* [stípnjs], *s.* calidad de empinado o pendiente; inclinación.

steer [stjr], *s.* novillo.—*vt.* guiar, dirigir, conducir; timonear; (mar.) patronear (un barco).—*vi.* navegar, timonear; gobernarse, conducirse; obedecer al timón.- —*ing* [stjrjŋ], *s.* dirección (automóvil), gobierno (buque).—*power s.*, (aut.) dirección hidráulica o movida por motor.—*a.* de dirección o gobierno.

stem [stem], *s.* (bot.) tallo, vástago; caña, varita; estirpe, linaje; (mec. y carp.) espiga, caña; pie (de copa); (gram.) raíz; (mar.) tajamar.—*vti.* [1] ir contra, hacer frente a; embestir con la proa; represar, contener; desgranar (uvas, etc.).—*vii.* detenerse, contenerse.

stench [stench], *s.* hedor, hediondez.

stencil [sténsjl], *s.* estarcido.—*vti.* [2] estarcir.

stenographer [stenágrafœ(r)], *s.* estenógrafo, taquígrafo.—*stenography* [stenágrfji], *s.* estenografía.

step [step], *vti.* [1] plantar (el pie). —*to s. down*, reducir, disminuir; escalonar; hacer escaleras en.—*to s. off*, medir a pasos.—*to s. up*, acelerar (el paso); (elec.) elevar (la tensión de una corriente).—*vii.* dar un paso; pisar; andar, caminar.—*to s. after*, seguir o ir detrás.—*to s. aside*, apartarse, hacerse a un lado.—*to s. back*, retroceder.—*to s. down*, bajar, descender.—*to s. forth*, avanzar.— *to s. in*, entrar; intervenir; entrometerse.—*to s. on*, poner el pie sobre, pisar; andar sobre.—*to s. on the gas*, (aut.) pisar el acelerador; (fam.) menearse, darse prisa.—*to s. out*, salir; apearse (de un vehículo); apretar el paso; (fam.) andar de parranda. —*to s. over*, atravesar.—*to s. up*, subir.—*s.* paso; escalón; grada; peldaño; estribo; umbral (de la puerta de entrada); pisada, huella; comportamiento; (mús.) intervalo; diente de una llave; (rad.) elemento, unidad. —*pl.* medios, pasos, gestiones; gradería; escalinata.—*s. by s.*, paso a paso; punto por punto.- —*brother* [stépbrʌðœ(r)], *s.* medio hermano, hermanastro.- —*child* [-chajld], *s.* hijastro, hijastra.- —*daughter* [-dotœ(r)], *s.* hijastra.- —*father* [-faðœ(r)], *s.* padrastro.- —*ladder* [-lædœ(r)], *s.* escala, escalera de mano.- —*mother* [-mʌðœ(r)], *s.* madrastra.

stepsister [stépsjstœ(r)], *s.* media hermana, hermanastra.—**stepson** [stépsʌn], *s.* hijastro.

stereoscope [stérjoskoup], *s.* estereoscopio.—**stereoscopic** [sterjoskápjk], *a.* estereoscópico.

stereotype [stérjotajp], *vt.* estereotipar.

sterile [stéril], *a.* estéril.—**sterility**

[sterͅlịtị], *s.* esterilidad.—**steriliza-tion** [sterịlịzéịṣon], *s.* esterilización. —**sterilize** [stérịlaịz], *vt.* y *vi.* esterilizar.

sterling [stœrlịŋ], *a.* esterlina; genuino, de ley.

stern [stœrn], *a.* austero, severo; firme. —*s.* (mar.) popa; (fam.) rabo.— —**ness** [stœrnnịs], *s.* severidad, rigor.

stethoscope [stéθoskoụp], *s.* estetoscopio.

stevedore [stívẹdọr], *s.* estibador.

stew [stịu], *vt.* y *vi.* estofar; (fam.) inquietarse; achicharrarse.—*s.* estofado, guisado, puchero; (fam.) ansiedad; agitación mental.

steward [stịúwạrd], *s.* administrador; mayordomo; despensero; camarero (en aviones, vapores, etc.).—*s.'s* **room**, despensa.— —**ess** [-ịs], *s.* camarera (de buque o avión); aeromoza, azafata.

stick [stịk], *s.* palo, estaca; garrote, porra; vara, bastón (de mando); varilla; palillo (de tambor); barra (de lacre, tinta china, etc.); batuta; estique de escultor; (mus.) arco de contrabajo; (mar.) verga; pinchazo; adhesión; parada, demora; escrúpulo; (teat.) mal actor.—*pl.* leña menuda. —*the sticks*, (fam.) las afueras, despoblado.—*vti.* [10] pegar, adherir; clavar, hincar; prender (con alfiler); fijar (con tachuelas, etc.); meter, introducir; matar o herir de una puñalada; picar, punzar; llenar de puntas; (fam.) aturrullar.—*to s. out*, sacar, asomar, mostrar; perseverar hasta el fin.—*to s. up*, (fam.) atracar, parar para robar.—*to s. up one's hands*, poner las manos arriba en señal de entrega.—*to s. up one's nose at*, hacer ascos, despreciar, hacer un gesto despreciativo.—*vii.* estar clavado o prendido o pegado; pegarse, adherirse; permanecer fijo; ser constante; vacilar; atollarse.— *to s. at*, detenerse, sentir escrúpulos de.—*to s. at it*, (fam.) persistir.— *to s. by*, sostener, apoyar; pegarse (a alguno).—*to s. close*, mantenerse juntos.—*to s. fast*, adherirse fuertemente.—*to s. out*, salir, sobresalir, proyectarse.—*to s. to one's guns*, seguir uno en sus trece; mantenerse firme.—*to s. up for*, (fam.) volver por; salir a la defensa de.— —**y** [-ị], *a.* pegajoso, viscoso.

stiff [stịf], *a.* tieso; duro, firme; embotado; yerto, aterido; rígido, inflexible; tenso; chabacano; ceremonioso, afectado; almidonado; espeso; terco; (fam.) peliagudo; bravo (viento, etc.); fuerte, cargado (bebidas, etc.); (com.) firme (mercado, precios);

(fam.) caro.—*s.* (fam.) cadáver.— —**en** [stịfn], *vt.* atiesar; endurecer; espesar; aterir; dificultar.—*vi.* atiesarse; endurecerse; enderezarse; espesarse; obstinarse; aterirse.— —**ness** [-nịs], *s.* tiesura; rigidez; aterimiento; (med.) rigor; obstinación; dureza de estilo; espesura.

stifle [stáịfl], *vt.* sofocar, ahogar, asfixiar; apagar; suprimir, callar, ocultar.—*vi.* ahogarse, sofocarse, asfixiarse.

stigma [stịgmạ], *s.* estigma.— —**tize** [stígmạtaịz], *vt.* estigmatizar.

stiletto [stịlétoụ], *s.* estilete.

still [stịl], *vt.* acallar, hacer callar; amortiguar; aquietar; detener; destilar.—*vi.* acallarse; aquietarse.—*adv.* todavía, aún; aun; no obstante, sin embargo, a pesar de eso.—*a.* inmóvil; tranquilo, silencioso; fijo; apacible; suave, sordo (ruido); no espumoso (vino); muerto, inanimado.—*s. life*, (pint.) naturaleza muerta.—*s.* silencio, quietud; alambique.— —**ness** [stílnịs], *s.* silencio, quietud, calma.

stilt [stịlt], *s.* zanco; soporte; ave zancuda.— —**ed** [stíltịd], *a.* altisonante, pomposo.

stimulant [stímyụlant], *a.* y *s.* estimulante.—**stimulate** [stímyụleịt], *vt.* estimular.—**stimulation** [stịmyụléịṣon], *s.* estímulo, excitación; (med.) estimulación.—**stimulus** [stímyụlʌs], *s.* estímulo; incentivo; (med.) estimulante; (bot.) aguijón.

sting [stịŋ], *vti.* y *vii.* [10] picar; punzar, pinchar; estimular, aguijonear; herir, atormentar; remorder la conciencia.—*to s. to the quick*, herir en lo vivo.—*s.* aguijón; picada, picadura; picazón; (bot.) púa; remordimiento de conciencia; estímulo.

stinginess [stínḋʒịnịs], *s.* tacañería, mezquindad, avaricia.—**stingy** [stíndʒị], *a.* mezquino, tacaño, avaro; escaso, nimio.

stink [stịŋk], *vii.* [10] heder, apestar. —*s.* hedor, hediondez.— —**er** [stíŋkœ(r)], *s.* cosa o persona hedionda; (fam.) sujeto vil o despreciable.

stint [stịnt], *vt.* restringir, escatimar; asignar una tarea.—*vi.* ser económico o parco; estrecharse.—*s.* cuota, tarea; límite, restricción.

stipend [stáịpend], *s.* estipendio, sueldo.

stipple [stípl], *vt.* puntear, granear.—*s.* picado, punteado.

stipulate [stípyụleịt], *vt.* estipular, especificar.—**stipulation** [stịpyụléịṣon], *s.* estipulación, condición; convenio.

stir [stœr], *vti.* [1] agitar, menear, batir; hurgar, revolver; perturbar, excitar, incitar; conmover; ventilar, discutir.—*to s. up*, conmover, excitar;

aguijonear; poner en movimiento; revolver; suscitar (interés, etc.).— *vii.* moverse, menearse.—*s.* movimiento, conmoción, excitación, alboroto, revuelo.

stirrup [stíɾʌp], *s.* estribo.—*s. bone,* (anat.) estribo, huesecillo del oído.

stitch [stịch], *vt.* coser, hilvanar.— *to s. up,* remendar, (cir.) dar puntos. —*vi.* dar puntadas, coser.—*s.* puntada, punto; (med.) dolor punzante; (agr.) caballón, surco.

stock [stak], *s.* (bot. y hort.) tronco, cepa; patrón; injerto; linaje, estirpe; (com.) acciones, valores; capital comercial; surtido (de mercancías); mercancías almacenadas, existencias; (teat.) repertorio; enseres, muebles.—*in s.,* (com.) en existencia. —*out of s.,* (com.) agotado.—*s. company,* (com.) sociedad anónima; (teat.) compañía de repertorio.— *s. exchange,* bolsa; asociación de corredores de bolsa.—*s. in hand,* mercancías en almacén, existencias. —*to lay in a s.* (of), almacenar, proveerse (de).—*a.* perteneciente o relativo a la bolsa, la ganadería o el teatro de repertorio; normal, usual; muy usado; estereotipado; (com.) de surtido.—*vt.* poner o llevar en surtido; surtir; acumular, juntar, acopiar.— **ade** [stakéjd], *vt.* empalizar.—*s.* empalizada; vallado.— **broker** [stákbɾoṵkœ(r)], *s.* corredor de bolsa, bolsista.— **holder** [-hoṵldœ(r)], *s.* accionista, tenedor de títulos o acciones.

stocking [stákiṇ], *s.* media, calceta.

stocky [stákị], *a.* rechoncho, fornido.

stoic [stóujk], *s.* y *a.* estoico.—**stoicsim** [stóujsịzm], *s.* estoicismo; estoicidad.

stoke [stoṵk], *vt.* y *vi.* atizar (el fuego); alimentar, cargar (un horno).— **r** [stóṵkœ(r)], *s.* fogonero.

stole [stoṵl], *pret.* de TO STEAL.—*s.* estola.—**stolen** [stóṵlẹn], *pp.* de TO STEAL.

stomach [stÁmạk], *s.* estómago.—*vt.* sufrir, aguantar, tolerar.

stone [stoṵn], *s.* piedra; hueso (de las frutas).—*s.-blind,* enteramente ciego.—*s.-broke,* (fam.) tronado, arrancado.—*s.-dead,* muerto como una piedra.—*s.-deaf,* sordo como una tapia, enteramente sordo.—*s.-dumb,* enteramente mudo.—*s. mason,* albañil, cantero.—*s.'s cast, s.'s throw,* tiro de piedra, corta distancia.—*vt.* apedrear; deshuesar (frutas); (alb.) revestir de piedras.—*to s. to death,* matar a pedradas, lapidar.—**stony** [stóụnị], *a.* pedregoso; pétreo, de piedra; duro, insensible.

stood [stụd], *pret.* y *pp.* de TO STAND.

stool [stul], *s.* banquillo, taburete, escabel; banqueta; inodoro, bacín; (caza) señuelo.—*pl.* evacuación de vientre, deposiciones.—*s. pigeon,* (fam.) soplón, espía.—*vt.* atraer con añagazas o señuelos.—*vi.* echar tallos, retoños, etc.; evacuar (el vientre); atraer con señuelos; (fam.) actuar como soplón.

stoop [stup], *vi.* agacharse, doblar o inclinar el cuerpo; ir encorvado, ser cargado de espaldas; encorvarse; humillarse, rebajarse; condescender; arrojarse sobre la presa.—*vt.* rebajar, degradar.—*s.* inclinación de hombros, cargazón de espaldas; descenso, caída; abatimiento; gradería, escalinata de entrada.

stop [stap], *vti.* [1] parar; detener, atajar; suspender, paralizar; contener, reprimir; obstruir, tapar; estancar, represar.—*to s. short,* detener brusca o repentinamente.—*to s. up,* tapar, cerrar, tupir, obturar.—*vii.* parar(se); detenerse, hacer alto; demorarse; cesar; acabarse; (fam.) quedarse algún tiempo, alojarse.— *to s. (working, etc.),* cesar o dejar de (trabajar, etc.).—*s.* parada, detención; cesación; pausa, alto; interrupción; suspensión, paro (de trabajo); obstáculo, impedimento; represión; (gram.) punto; (mec.) retén; tope, lengüeta; seguro; (mús.) tecla; llave; traste (de guitarra); registro (de órgano).— **over** [stápoụvœ(r)], *s.* parada temporal en un lugar.— **page** [-ịdž], *s.* cesación, interrupción; paro (del trabajo); detención, interceptación; obstrucción, impedimento; represa; retención (sobre un pago); (med.) estrangulación.— **per** [-œ(r)], *vt.* entaponar.—*s.* tapón; taco, tarugo.

storage [stóɾịdž], *s.* (derechos de) almacenaje.—*s. battery,* (elec.) acumulador.—*to keep in s.,* almacenar.

store [stoɾ], *s.* tienda, almacén, depósito; acopio.—*pl.* pertrechos, equipos; víveres, provisiones.—*vt.* proveer o abastecer; pertrechar; acumular; tener en reserva; almacenar.— **house** [stóɾhaụs], *s.* almacén.— **keeper** [-kịpœ(r)], *s.* guardaalmacén; jefe de depósito; tendero, comerciante; (mar.) pañolero.— **room** [-rum], *s.* despensa; bodega; almacén; (mar.) pañol de víveres.

stork [stɔrk], *s.* (orn.) cigüeña.

storm [storm], *s.* tempestad, temporal, tormenta o borrasca; vendaval; arrebato, frenesí; tumulto; (mil.) ataque, asalto.—*s. troops,* tropas de asalto.—*vt.* (mil.) asaltar, tomar por asalto.—*vi.* haber tormenta; estallar

de cólera.— —y [stórmi], a. tempestuoso, borrascoso; violento, turbulento.

story [stóri], s. cuento, historia, historieta; fábula, conseja, (fam.) cuento de viejas; hablilla, rumor; enredo, trama o argumento; (fam.) mentira, embuste; (fam.) artículo (escrito); (arq.) alto, piso, planta.

stout [staut], a. fornido, forzudo; gordo, corpulento; fuerte, sólido, firme; resuelto, intrépido.—s. cerveza fuerte.

stove [stouv], s. estufa, hornillo, cocina o fogón de hierro.—pret. y pp. de TO STAVE.

stow [stou], vt. colocar, meter, alojar; esconder, ocultar; (mar.) estibar, acomodar la carga en el barco; rellenar.—to s. away on a ship, esconderse en un barco, embarcarse clandestinamente.— —away [stóu-awei], s. (mar.) polizón.

straggle [strǽgl], vi. extraviarse; rezagarse.— —r [-œ(r)], s. rezagado.

straight [streit], a. derecho, recto; directo, en línea recta; lacio (pelo); erguido; equitativo; íntegro, honrado; exacto; sin estorbos; ininterrumpido.—s. face, cara seria.—s. line, línea recta.—s.-line, en línea recta; de movimiento en línea recta. —s.-out, sincero; intransigente.— adv. directamente, en línea recta; inmediatamente, al punto.—s. ahead, todo derecho; enfrente.—s. away, en seguida, inmediatamente.—s. off, sin vacilar, sin demora.—s. runfia de cinco naipes del mismo palo.—en [stréjtn], vt. enderezar; poner en orden, arreglar.— —forward [-fórwärd], a. recto, derecho; íntegro, honrado, sincero.—adv. de frente.— —ness [-nis], s. derechura, calidad de recto o derecho; rectitud, probidad, honradez.— —way [-wei], adv. inmediatamente, en seguida.

strain [strein], vt. hacer fuerza a; poner tirante; poner, consagrar (la atención, etc.); forzar (la vista, etc.); estirar; forzar; extremar; perjudicar por esfuerzo excesivo; colar; tamizar, cribar; apretar; agarrar; (mec.) deformar —to s. a point, excederse; hacer una concesión; hacer violencia (a la lógica, la conciencia, etc.).—vi. esforzarse; estar sometido a esfuerzo; pasar o meterse por, infiltrarse.—to s. at, esforzarse por.—s. tensión, tirantez; esfuerzo violento; (med.) lesión por esfuerzo violento o excesivo; (mec.) esfuerzo; deformación; indicio; (mus.) aire, tonada; rasgo racial; parte distintiva de un poema; tono, modo de hablar; genio o dis-

posición heredada.— —er [stréjnœ(r)], s. colador, filtro, tamiz.

strait(s) [streit(s)], s. (geog.) estrecho; apuro, aprieto; estrechez.—strait jacket, camisa de fuerza.—strait-laced, estrecho, mojigato.

strand [strænd], vt. y vi. (mar.) encallar; dejar o quedarse desamparado; trenzar (un cordel).—s. costa, playa, ribera; cabo, hebra, hilo; sarta; ramal (de cable, etc.).

strange [streindž], a. extraño, singular; forastero; ajeno; desconocido; reservado, esquivo.—s. to say, lo cual es extraño; (es) cosa extraña.— —ness [stréjndžnis], s. extranjería; extrañeza, rareza; reserva, esquivez; maravilla.— —r [stréjndžœ(r)], s. extranjero, extraño, forastero; desconocido.

strangle [strǽngl], vt. estrangular; dar garrote; ahogar, sofocar.—vi. morir estrangulado, estrangularse.

strap [stræp], s. correa; tira, faja, banda; abrazadera; precinta; (mec.) cabeza de biela.—vti. [1] atar con correas; precintar; asentar (navajas de afeitar).

stratagem [strǽtadžem], s. estratagema, artimaña.—strategic(al) [stratidži-k(al)], a. estratégico.—strategy [strǽtidži], s. estrategia.

stratify [strǽtifai], vti. [7] estratificar.

straw [stro], s. paja.—not to care a s., no importarle a uno un comino.—the last s., el golpe de gracia, el acabóse.—a. de paja; pajizo.

strawberry [stróberi], s. fresa.

stray [strei], vi. descarriarse, extraviarse; desmandarse (el ganado).—a. extraviado, descarriado.—s. persona o animal descarriado o perdido.

streak [strik], s. raya, lista, línea, faja, veta; rayo de luz; vena, rasgo de ingenio; traza, pizca; antojo, capricho.—like a s., veloz como un relámpago.—s. of luck, racha.—vt. rayar, listar; abigarrar.—vi. pasar o viajar con suma rapidez.— —y [stríki], a. listado, rayado; entreverado.

stream [strim], s. corriente; arroyo, corriente de agua; flujo, chorro (de líquido, gas, luz, etc.); curso.—down s., agua abajo.—up s., agua arriba.—vt. y vi. correr, manar, fluir, brotar, salir a torrentes; derramar con abundancia; lavar en agua corriente; ondear, flotar, flamear, tremolar (una bandera); pasar dejando un rastro de luz.— —er [strímœ(r)], s. banderola, gallardete; aurora boreal, cinta (que flota en el aire); serpentina.

street [strit], s. calle.— —car [strítkar],

s. tranvía.— —**walker** [-wokœ(r)], *s.* prostituta.

strength [streŋθ], *s.* fuerza, vigor; reciedumbre; pujanza; fuerza legal; (ing.) resistencia; aguante; solidez; intensidad; vehemencia; (quim.) concentración, grado de concentración; seguridad, confianza; (mil.) efectivos. —*on* o *upon the s. of*, fundándose en, confiando en.— —**en** [stréŋθn], *vt.* fortalecer, fortificar; consolidar; corroborar; reforzar; confortar, alentar.—*vi.* fortalecerse; reforzarse; arreciar(se).—**strenuous** [strényуʌs], *a.* fuerte; activo, enérgico; acérrimo, tenaz.

stress [stres], *s.* fuerza, peso, importancia; (ing., mec.) esfuerzo; tensión; énfasis.—*vt.* someter a esfuerzo; recalcar, subrayar, poner de relieve.

stretch [strech], *vt.* extender, alargar, tender; estirar, atesar; ensanchar, dilatar; violentar, forzar; (fam.) exagerar, llevar al extremo.—*to s. a point*, excederse; ceder un poco.—*to s. forth*, alargar, extender.—*to s. oneself*, desperezarse.—*to s. out*, extender, estirar, alargar.—*vi.* alargarse, dar de sí, dilatarse; (fig.) esforzarse, exagerar.—*to s. out*, extenderse, llegar (hasta); echarse (en la cama, etc.).—*s.* alargamiento; dilatación; elasticidad; tirantez; violencia o interpretación forzada; alcance, trecho, distancia; lapso, tirada.— *at a s.*, de una vez, de un tirón.— —**er** [stréchœ(r)], *s.* estirador, dilatador, atesador; camilla, andas; ladrillo o losa (planos); (carp.) viga, madero largo, tirante; (pint.) bastidor.— *s.-bearer*, camillero.

strew [stru], *vti.* [6] regar, esparcir, derramar; rociar, salpicar.

striate [strájejt], *vt.* estriar.

stricken [strίkn], *pp.* de TO **STRIKE**.— *a.* herido (por un proyectil); atacado (por dolencias); agobiado; afligido.

strict [strίkt], *a.* estricto; exacto, riguroso, escrupuloso; estirado, tirante; (zool.) ceñido, limitado.

stridden [strídn], *pp.* de TO **STRIDE**. —**stride** [strajd], *vti.* [10] cruzar a grandes trancos; montar a horcajadas.—*vii.* andar a trancos.—*s.* paso largo, tranco, zancada.

strident [strájdent], *a.* estridente, chillón.

strife [strajf], *s.* contienda; rivalidad, porfía.

strike [strajk], *vti.* [10] golpear; percutir; batir, tocar, sonar; dar contra, chocar con; encender (un fósforo); acuñar (monedas).—*to s. off*, cortar, quitar, cercenar; cerrar (un trato). —*to s. oil*, encontrar petróleo; (fam.)

hacerse rico de pronto.—*to s. through*, traspasar, atravesar; calar.—*to s. up*, (mús.) tocar, tañer.—*to s. work*, hallar trabajo.—*vii.* golpear; dar golpes; sonar (una campana); encontrarse; ir delante, avanzar; brotar, estallar, manifestarse (una epidemia, etc.); declararse en huelga; rehusar, resistirse, plantarse; rendirse, arriar el pabellón; arraigar.—*to s. at*, acometer.—*to s. back*, dar golpe por golpe.—*to s. for*, (fam.) dirigirse hacia; acometer.—*to s. in*, meterse; juntarse, unirse; interrumpir; conformarse con.—*to s. into*, comenzar de repente; penetrar.—*to s. on*, dar contra; descubrir.—*to s. out*, tomar una resolución; arrojarse, lanzarse. —*s.* golpe; ataque rápido o inesperado; huelga, paro; (min.) descubrimiento.—*s. breaker*, obrero que reemplaza a los huelguistas.- —**r** [strájkœ(r)], *s.* huelguista; golpeador, percusor.—**striking** [strájkiŋ], *a.* sorprendente, notable; llamativo; vívido; que está en huelga; conspicuo.

string [striŋ], *s.* cuerda; cordel, bramante; ristra, sarta; hilera, fila; recua, fibra, nervio, tendón.—*pl.* (mus.) instrumentos de cuerda; (fam.) condiciones, estipulaciones.— *s. bean*, habichuela verde, judía verde, (fam.) poroto; alubia.—*to have on a s.*, (fam.) tener (a uno) en un puño.—*vti.* [10] encordar; templar (un instrumento); ensartar, enhebrar; encordelar, atar con cordel; tender (alambre, etc.); estirar, atesar; quitar las fibras.—*to s.* (*along*), (fam.) tomarle el pelo a uno; hacer esperar a uno.—*to s. out*, extender.—*to s. up*, (fam.) ahorcar.—*vii.* extenderse en línea.

strip [strip], *vti.* [1] desnudar; despojar, quitar; desguarnecer; robar; descortezar; ordeñar hasta agotar; desgarrar o cortar en tiras; desvenar, despalillar (tabaco); (mec.) desmontar.—*to s. off*, desnudar; deshojar.—*vii.* desnudarse, despojarse (de).—*s.* tira, faja, listón, lista; lonja (de carne).

stripe [strajp], *vt.* rayar.—*s.* raya, lista, banda, franja, tira; (mil.) galón, barra; cardenal (en el cuerpo); calaña, clase.- —**d** [-t], *a.* rayado, listado, a rayas.

strive [strajv], *vii.* [10] esforzarse, hacer lo posible; disputar; oponerse; contrarrestar.—**striven** [strívn], *pp.* de TO **STRIVE**.

strode [stroud], *pret.* de TO **STRIDE**.

stroke [strouk], *s.* golpe; toque; boga, remada; rasgo, trazo; (med.) ataque fulminante.—*at one s.*, de un golpe, de un tirón.—*at the s. of twelve*,

al dar las doce.—*s. of a bell*, campanada.—*s. of a pen* o *brush*, plumazo, pincelada.—*s. of the hand*, caricia.—*s. of wit*, rasgo de ingenio, chiste, gracia.—*vt.* pasar la mano por, acariciar; frotar suavemente; (cost.) alisar un plegado.

stroll [stroụl], *vi.* vagar, callejear; pasearse.—*s.* paseo, vuelta.— **—er** [stroụlœ(r)], *s.* vagabundo; paseante; cochecito de bebé; cómico de la legua.- **—ing** [stróụliṇ], *a.* ambulante.

strong [stroṇ], *a.* fuerte; firme; recio, fornido; enérgico; vivo, subido (colores); (com.) con tendencia a la alza.

strop [strap], *vti.* [1] asentar (navajas).—*s.* asentador; (mar.) estrobo.

strove [stroụv], *pret.* de TO STRIVE.

struck [strʌk], *pret.* y *pp.* de TO STRIKE.

structural [strʌ́kchụṛạl], *a.* estructural; de estructura; relativo a la estructura; (ing.) de construcción, de construcciones.—**structure** [strʌ́kchụ(r)], *s.* construcción (edificio, puente, etc.); estructura; (fig.) textura, hechura.

struggle [strʌ́gl], *vi.* luchar, pugnar, bregar; esforzarse; contender; agitarse.—*s.* esfuerzo; disputa, contienda; pugna, forcejeo; lucha, conflicto.

strung [strʌṇ], *pret.* y *pp.* de TO STRING.

strut [strʌt], *vii.* [1] contonearse; pavonearse; ensoberbecerse, inflarse.—*vti.* (ing., etc.) apuntalar.—*s.* contoneo; poste; puntal; columna.

stub [stʌb], *s.* (agr.) tocón, cepa; zoquete; fragmento, resto; colilla (de cigarro, etc.); talón.—*vti.* [1] tropezar contra una cosa baja; (agr.) desarraigar; reducir a tocón.

stubble [stʌ́bl], *s.* (agr.) rastrojo; barba cerdosa.

stubborn [stʌ́bọrn], *a.* obstinado, terco, tesonero, contumaz; reñido; inquebrantable.— **—ness** [-nịs], *s.* obstinación, testarudez, contumacia.

stucco [stʌ́koụ], *vt.* (alb.) estucar.—*s.* estuco.

stuck [stʌk], *pret.* y *pp.* de TO STICK.

stud [stʌd], *s.* (carp.) paral, montante, pie derecho; perno, pasador; tachón, clavo de adorno; botón de camisa o cuello; gemelo de puño; caballeriza; yeguada, caballada; (elec.) tornillo de contacto.—*vti.* [1] tachonar.

student [stiúdẹnt], *s.* estudiante; alumno, escolar.—*s. body*, alumnado, estudiantado.—**studio** [stiúdioụ], *s.* estudio, taller; gabinete.—**studious** [stiúdịʌs], *a.* estudioso; aplicado; estudiado.—**study** [stʌ́dị], *s.* estudio; materia que se estudia; meditación profunda; despacho, gabinete.—*vti.*

[7] estudiar; cursar (una asignatura, etc.).—*to s. up*, considerar, meditar; proyectar.—*vii.* estudiar; meditar.

stuff [stʌf], *s.* material; materia, sustancia, elemento fundamental; cosa, objeto; cachivaches, baratijas; desechos, desperdicios; cosas, ideas o sentimientos sin valor; mejunje, pócima.—*vt.* henchir, llenar; rellenar (un pavo, etc.); hartar; atestar; disecar (un animal).—*vi.* y *vr.* atracarse, hartarse, engullir, tupirse.- **—ing** [stʌ́fiṇ], *s.* relleno; (mec.) empaquetado.- **—y** [-ị], *a.* sofocante, mal ventilado; (fam.) estirado, afectado.

stumble [stʌ́mbl], *vi.* tropezar, dar un traspié.—*to s. on* o *upon*, encontrar o tropezar con.—*s.* traspié, tropezón; desliz; desatino.—*stumbling block*, obstáculo, tropiezo.

stump [stʌmp], *s.* tocón, cepa; muñón (de brazo o pierna); raigón (de una muela); poste; (b.a.) difumino; tope de cerradura; tribuna pública; arenga electoral; (fam.) desafío, reto.—*vt.* confundir, dejar patidifuso; cercenar, mutilar.—*to s. the country*, recorrer el país diciendo discursos políticos.—*vi.* renquear; (fam.) pronunciar discursos políticos.- **—y** [stʌ́mpị], *a.* lleno de tocones; rechoncho, cachigordete, (Am.) chaparro.

stun [stʌn], *vti.* [1] aturdir, atontar; pasmar, privar; atronar, ensordecer.—*s.* choque, golpe o sacudimiento (emotivos); aturdimiento.

stung [stʌṇ], *pret.* y *pp.* de TO STING.—*a.* (fam.) chasqueado, burlado, engañado.

stunk [stʌṇk], *pret.* y *pp.* de TO STINK.

stunning [stʌ́niṇ], *a.* (fam.) sorprendente; magnífico, excelente; elegante, hermoso.

stunt [stʌnt], *vt.* impedir el crecimiento o desarrollo de; no dejar medrar.—*vi.* (fam.) hacer ejercicicios malabares o gimnásticos; hacer suertes o maniobras sensacionales.—*s.* falta de crecimiento o desarrollo; animal o planta raquíticos; (fam.) suerte, ejercicio o acción de habilidad; maniobra sensacional (de aviación, etc.).—*s. flying*, vuelos acrobáticos.

stupefaction [stjupẹfǽkṣọn], *s.* estupefacción.—**stupefy** [stiúpẹfaị], *vti.* [7] atontar, atolondrar.

stupid [stiúpịd], *a.* estúpido; necio.- **—ity** [stiupídịtị], *s.* estupidez; necedad; inepcia.

stupor [stiúpọ(r)], *s.* estupor; atontamiento.

sturdy [stœ́rdị], *a.* fuerte, robusto; tenaz, porfiado.

stutter [stʌ́tœ(r)], *vi.* tartamudear.—*s.*

tartamudeo.— —er [-œ(r)], *s.* tartamudo.— —ing [-iŋ], *s.* tartamudeo. —*a.* tartamudo, balbuciente.

sty [staj], *s.* pocilga, cuchitril; lupanar; (también stye [staj]), (med.) orzuelo.

style [stajl], *s.* estilo; uso, moda; género, escuela; (cir.) estilete.—*to be in s.*, estilarse, estar de moda.—*vt.* (in)titular, nombrar, llamar.—**stylish** [stájliš], *a.* elegante; a la moda.

subconscious [sʌbkánšʌs], *a.* subconsciente.—*s.* subconsciencia.

subdivide [sʌbdjvájd], *vt.* subdividir.

subdue [sʌbdjú], *vt.* subyugar, sojuzgar, dominar; domar o amansar; mejorar (tierras); suavizar.

subject [sʌbdʒékt], *vt.* sujetar; sojuzgar, avasallar; exponer, presentar; supeditar, subordinar.—*a.* [sʌbdʒect], sujeto; propenso; supeditado.—*s. to*, sujeto a, afecto *a.*—*s.* súbdito; vasallo; materia, tópico; asignatura (de estudios); (gram.) sujeto.—*s. matter*, asunto, materia de que se trata.— —ion [sʌbdʒékšʌn], *s.* sujeción, supeditación, dependencia; sometimiento; ligadura.— —ive [sʌbdʒéktjv], *a.* subjetivo.

subjugate [sʌbdʒugejt], *vt.* subyugar, sojuzgar, someter.

subjunctive [sʌbdʒʌ́ŋktjv], *a.* y *s.* subjuntivo.

sublease [sáblis], *s.* subarriendo.—*vt.* [sáblís], subarrendar.—**sublet** [sábfét], *vti.* [9] subarrendar.—*pret.* y *pp.* de TO SUBLET.

sublimate [sáblimejt], *vt.* (quím.) sublimar; (fig.) refinar, purificar.— **sublime** [sablájm], *a.* sublime.—*s.* sublimidad, lo sublime.—*vt.* y *vi.* sublimar, exaltar; (quím.) sublimar(se).

submarine [sábmarin], *s.* y *a.* submarino.

submerge [sʌbmœ́rdʒ], *vt.* y *vi.* sumergir(se), hundir(se).—**submersible** [sʌbmœ́rsjbl], *a.* sumergible.—**submersion** [sʌbmœ́rʃʌn], *s.* sumersión.

submission [sʌbmíʃʌn], *s.* sumisión. —**submissive** [sʌbmísjv], *a.* sumiso, obediente, dócil.—**submit** [sʌbmít], *vti.* [1] someter; presentar, exponer, proponer.—*vri.* y *vii.* someterse, conformarse.

subordinate [sabórdjnjt], *a.* y *s.* subalterno, subordinado.—*vt.* [sabórdjnejt], subordinar.

suborn [sabórn], *vt.* (for.) sobornar, cohechar.— —ation [sʌbornéjšʌn], *s.* soborno, cohecho.

subscribe [sʌbskrájb], *vt.* y *vi.* suscribir(se); firmar; aprobar; abonar(se).—*to s. for*, suscribirse a.— *to s. ten dollars*, prometer una contribución de diez dólares (para una

colecta, etc.).— —r [sʌbskrájbœ(r)], *s.* suscritor, abonado; firmante, el que suscribe.—**subscription** [sabskrípšʌn], *s.* suscripción, abono; cantidad suscrita; firma.

subsequent [sábsjkwent], *a.* subsecuente, subsiguiente.—*s. to*, con posterioridad a, después de.

subside [sʌbsájd], *vi.* calmarse, atenuarse; bajar (el nivel); disminuir; irse al fondo, asentarse, (quim.) precipitarse.

subsidize [sábsjdajz], *vt.* subvencionar. —**subsidy** [sábsjdj], *s.* subvención, subsidio.

subsist [sʌbsíst], *vi.* subsistir; perdurar; sustentarse, mantenerse.—*vt.* alimentar o mantener.

substance [sábstʌns], *s.* sustancia.— **substantial** [sʌbstǽnšʌl], *a.* sólido, fuerte, resistente; importante, valioso; considerable; seguro; responsable; existente, real; duradero; esencial; corpóreo, material; sustancial, sustancioso.—*s.* realidad; parte esencial.—**substantive** [sábstʌntjv], *a.* y *s.* sustantivo.

substitute [sábstjtjut], *vt.* sustituir.—*s.* sustituto.—*a.* sustitutivo.—**substitution** [sʌbstjtjúšʌn], *s.* sustitución.

subterranean [sʌbtɛréjnjan], *a.* subterráneo.

subtle [sátl], *a.* sutil; perspicaz; apto; ingenioso.— —ty [-tj], *s.* sutileza; astucia.

subtract [sʌbtrǽkt], *vt.* y *vi.* sustraer, quitar; (mat.) restar, sustraer.— —ion [sʌbtrǽkšʌn], *s.* sustracción; resta.

suburb [sábœrb], *s.* suburbio; barrio residencial.— —an [sʌbœ́rban], *a.* y *s.* suburbano.

subversion [sʌbvœ́rʒʌn], *s.* subversión. —**subversive** [sʌbvœ́rsjv], *a.* subversivo.—*s.* persona subversiva.— **subvert** [sʌbvœ́rt], *vt.* subvertir.

subway [sábwej], *s.* subterráneo; ferrocarril subterráneo, metropolitano, (fam.) el metro, (Am.) el subte.

succeed [sʌksíd], *vt.* suceder o seguir a. —*vi.* salir bien, tener buen éxito.— *to s. in*, lograr, conseguir.—**success** [sʌksés], *s.* buen éxito, logro; prosperidad; triunfo; persona o asunto que tiene buen éxito.— **successful** [sʌksésfʉl], *a.* próspero, afortunado; productivo, satisfactorio. —**succession** [sʌkséšʌn], *s.* sucesión, serie; continuación; descendencia; herencia.—**successive** [sʌksésjv], *a.* sucesivo.—**successor** [sʌksésʌ(r)], *s.* sucesor; heredero.

succumb [sʌkÁm], *vi.* sucumbir.

such [sʌch], *a.* tal; semejante; dicho, mencionado.—*no s. (a) thing*, no

hay tal.—**s.** **a**, (fam.) tan.—*such a bad man*, un hombre tan malo.—**s. a man**, tal hombre, semejante hombre.—**s. and s.**, o **s. or s.**, tal(es) y tal(es), tal o cual.—**s. as**, (tal) como. —*there is s. a thing as*, hay algo que se llama; hay casos en que.—*pron.* tal.—**s. as**, los que, quienes.—**s. is life**, tal (o así) es la vida.

suck [sʌk], *vt.* y *vi.* chupar, libar; mamar; (mec.) aspirar.—*to s. in*, embeber, absorber, chupar.—*to s. out o up*, chupar, extraer por succión.—*s.* succión; chupada.—*to give s.*, amamantar.—**er** [sʌkœ(r)], *s.* lechón o cochinillo que todavía mama; chupador; mamador; mamón, chupón; dulce que se chupa; primo, persona fácil de engañar.—**le** [sʌkl], *vt.* amamantar, criar.—*vi.* lactar, mamar.—**ling** [-liŋ], *a.* y *s.* mamón, recental.—*a.* de teta, de cría.—**suction** [sʌkʃǝn], *s.* succión.

sudden [sʌdn], *a.* repentino, súbito; apresurado; (med.) fulminante.—**ness** [-nis], *s.* calidad de repentino, inesperado o imprevisto; brusquedad.

suds [sʌdz], *s. pl.* jabonaduras; espuma.

sue [siu], *vt.* y *vi.* (for.) demandar.—*to s. to, to s. for*, rogar, pedir, tratar de persuadir.

suet [siúit], *s.* sebo en rama; grasa, gordo.

suffer [sʌfœ(r)], *vt.* y *vi.* sufrir, padecer; soportar, tolerar.—*to s. from*, adolecer de.—**er** [-œ(r)], *s.* paciente, sufridor; víctima; perjudicado; el que tolera tácitamente.—**ing** [-iŋ], *s.* sufrimiento, padecimiento, pena, suplicio.—*a.* paciente, sufriente.

suffice [sʌfáis], *vt.* y *vi.* bastar, ser suficiente.—*s. it to say*, baste decir. —**sufficiency** [sʌfíʃęnsi], *s.* suficiencia; lo suficiente; eficacia; presunción.—**sufficient** [sʌfíʃęnt], *a.* suficiente, bastante.

suffix [sʌfíks], *vt.* añadir como sufijo. —*s.* [sʌfíks], (gram.) sufijo, afijo.

suffocate [sʌfokęit], *vt.* sofocar, asfixiar, ahogar; apagar (un fuego).—*vi.* sofocarse, asfixiarse, ahogarse.—**suffocation** [sʌfokéiʃǝn], *s.* sofocación, asfixia, ahogo.

suffrage [sʌfridʒ], *s.* sufragio, voto; aprobación, (igl.) sufragio.—**tte** [sʌfrǝdʒét], *s.* mujer sufragista.

sugar [ʃúgǝ(r)], *s.* azúcar.—*lump of s.*, terrón de azúcar.—*s. bowl*, azucarero, azucarera.—*s. cane*, caña de azúcar. —*s. making (season)*, zafra.—*vt.* azucarar, endulzar.—*to s.-coat*, confitar, garapiñar; (fig.) dorar la píldora.—*vi.* cristalizarse (el almíbar), (Am.) azucararse.— **plum**

[-plʌm], *s.* merengue, confite, dulce.

suggest [sʌgdʒést], *vt.* sugerir, insinuar; evocar.— **ion** [sʌgdʒésʧǝn], *s.* sugestión; sugerencia, insinuación.— **ive** [sʌgdʒéstiv], *a.* sugestivo; sugerente.

suicidal [siuisáidǝl], *a.* suicida.—**suicide** [siúisaid], *s.* suicidio; suicida.—*to commit s.*, suicidarse.

suit [siut], *s.* petición, súplica; galanteo; (for.) pleito, juicio; colección, serie, juego, surtido; (sast.) traje completo, (Am.) flus; (naipes) palo.—*vt.* y *vi.* convenir, acomodar, adaptar(se).—*to s. oneself*, hacer uno lo que guste. — **able** [siútǝbl], *a.* adecuado, satisfactorio, a propósito.— **case** [-kęis], *s.* maleta.— **e** [swit], *s.* serie, juego; séquito, comitiva.—*s. of rooms*, serie de departamentos o habitaciones; habitación o pieza (gen. muy lujosa).— **or** [siútǫ(r)], *s.* (for.) demandante, parte actora; pretendiente, novio; aspirante; postulante.

sulfate [sʌlfęit], *s.* sulfato.—**sulfur** [sʌlfœ(r)], *s.* azufre.

sullen [sʌlęn], *a.* hosco, arisco; lento (río); sombrío, tétrico.— **ness** [-nis], *s.* hosquedad.

sulphate [sʌlfęit], *s.* = SULFATE.—**sulphur** [sʌlfœ(r)], *s.* = SULFUR.

sultry [sʌltri], *a.* bochornoso, sofocante (verano, calor, etc.).

sum [sʌm], *s.* suma; cantidad; sustancia, esencia.—*in s.*, en esencia, suma o resumen.—*s. total*, suma total, monta o monto.—*vti.* y *vii.* [1] sumar.—*to s. up*, recapitular, resumir, compendiar; (for.) presentar su alegato.— **marize** [sʌmǝraiz], *vt.* resumir.— **mary** [-ǝri], *s.* sumario, resumen, recopilación, reseña (de un libro).

summer [sʌmœ(r)], *a.* estival, veraniego.—*s.* verano, estío; (arq.) viga maestra; dintel.—*s. boarder*, veraneante.—*vi.* veranear.

summit [sʌmit], *s.* cima, cumbre, cúspide, ápice.

summon [sʌmǫn], *vt.* (for.) citar, apercibir; llamar, convocar; mandar, requerir; (mil.) intimar.—*to s. up*, evocar; despertar, excitar (valor, fuerza, etc.).— **s** [-z], *s.* (for.) citación, apercibimiento; (mil.) intimación (de rendición).

sumptuous [sʌmpçhuʌs], *a.* suntuoso.

sun [sʌn], *s.* sol.—*vti.* [1] (a)solear. —*to s. oneself*, tomar el sol.— **burn** [sʌnbœrn], *vti.* [4] quemar(se) o tostar(se) con el sol.—*s.* quemadura de sol.— **burned** [sʌnbœrnd], **burnt** [sʌnbœrnt], *a.* quemado, tostado o bronceado por el sol.

—*pret.* y *pp.* de TO SUNBURN.
—Sunday [sándi], *s.* domingo.—
—dial [-daiəl], *s.* reloj de sol,
cuadrante solar.— —down [-daun],
s. puesta de sol.
sundries [sándriz], *s. pl.* (com.) géneros
varios.—sundry [sándri], *a.* varios,
diversos.—all and *s.*, todos y cada
uno.
sunflower [sánflayœ(r)], *s.* (bot.)
girasol.
sung [saŋ], *pret.* y *pp.* de TO SING.
sunk [saŋk], *pret.* y *pp.* de TO SINK.—
sunken [sáŋkn], *a.* sumido, hundido.
—*pp.* de TO SINK.
sunless [sánlis], *a.* sombrío; sin luz;
sin sol, nublado.—sunlight [sánlait],
s. luz del sol.—sunny [sáni], *a.*
de sol (día); asoleado; resplandeciente; alegre, risueño; halagüeño.—
s. side, lado del sol; lado bueno,
aspecto favorable.—*s. side up*, (huevos) fritos.—sunrise [sánraiz], *s.*
salida del sol, amanecer; (poét.)
Oriente.—sunset [sánset], *s.* puesta
del sol, ocaso.—sunshine [sánšain],
s. luz del sol, claridad del sol; día.
—sunstroke [sánstrouk], *s.* (med.)
insolación, (fam.) tabardillo.
sup [sap], *vti.* [1] sorber.—*vii.* cenar.
super [siúpœ(r)], *s.* (com.) cosa excelente; alta calidad; (abrev. fam.) de
SUPERINTENDENT.—*a.* (fam.) excelente.
superb [siupérb], *a.* soberbio, grandioso; (fam.) de primera.
supercargo [siupœrkárgou], *s.* (mar.)
sobrecargo.
superficial [siupœrfíšəl], *a.* superficial,
somero.
superfluous [supérfluʌs], *a.* superfluo.
superheat [siupœrhít], *vt.* recalentar.
superhuman [siupœrhiúmʌn], *a.* sobrehumano.
superimpose [siupœrimpóuz], *vt.* superponer, sobreponer.
superintend [siupœrinténd], *vt.* estar
encargado de, dirigir.— —ent [-ənt],
s. superintendente; inspector; capataz; encargado de un edificio de
apartamentos.
superior [supírio(r)], *a.* y *s.* superior.—
—ity [supiriáriti], *s.* superioridad.
superlative [siupœrlətiv], *a.* y *s.*
superlativo.
superman [siúpœrmæn], *s.* superhombre.
supernatural [siupœrnǽchʊrəl], *a.* sobrenatural.—*s.* lo sobrenatural.
superposition [siupœrpɔzíšɔn], *s.* superposición.
supersede [siupœrsíd], *vt.* reemplazar;
desalojar; invalidar; (for.) sobreseer.
superstition [siupœrstíšɔn], *s.* supersti-

ción.—superstitious [siupœrstíšʌs],
a. supersticioso.
supervise [siupœrváiz], *vt.* supervisar.
—supervision [siupœrvízɔn], *s.* supervisión.—supervisor [siupœrvái-
zɔ(r)], *s.* supervisor.
supper [sápœ(r)], *s.* cena.
supplant [saplǽnt], *vt.* suplantar.
supple [sápl], *a.* flexible; dócil, obediente; servil.
supplement [sápləmənt], *s.* suplemento;
apéndice.—*vt.* [sáplement], suple-
mentar.
suppli(c)ant [sápli(k)ənt], *s.* y *a.* supli-
cante.—**supplication** [saplikéišɔn], *s.*
súplica, ruego; (igl.) preces, rogativa.
supplier [supláiœ(r)], *s.* proveedor,
abastecedor.—supplies [sapláiz], *s.
pl.* (mil.) pertrechos; materiales,
efectos; provisiones, víveres; enseres.
—supply [sapláj], *vti.* [7] abastecer,
proveer (de); suministrar, habilitar,
suplir, reemplazar.—*s.* suministro,
provisión, abastecimiento; substituto,
suplente; (com.) abasto, oferta;
repuesto, surtido.
support [sapórt], *vt.* sostener, aguantar,
apoyar; mantener (a una persona,
etc.), proveer para; sostener (un
trato o diálogo); resistir, tolerar; abogar por, defender; probar, confirmar;
justificar.—*s.* sostén, soporte; puntal;
sustentación, sostenimiento; ayuda,
protección; sustento, manutención.—
—er [-œ(r)], *s.* mantenedor; defensor,
partidario; sostén, soporte.
suppose [sapóuz], *vt.* suponer; dar por
sentado o existente; poner por caso;
creer, imaginar.—supposition [sapo-
zíšɔn], *s.* suposición, supuesto, hipótesis.
suppository [sapázitori], *s.* supositorio.
suppress [saprés], *vt.* suprimir, acabar
con; reprimir, contener; eliminar.—
—ion [saprésɔn], *s.* supresión; (med.)
suspensión.
suppurate [sápyʊreit], *vi.* supurar.—
suppuration [sapyʊréišɔn], *s.* supuración; pus.
supremacy [siuprémasi], *s.* supremacía.
—supreme [siuprím], *a.* supremo,
sumo.—S. Being, Ser Supremo.
sure [šur], *a.* seguro, cierto, infalible;
firme; certero.—*be s. to come*, o
be s. and come, no deje(n) de venir,
venga(n) sin falta.—*for s.*, de fijo,
con seguridad.—*adv.* (fam.) ciertamente, indudablemente.—*s. enough*,
a buen seguro, con certeza; en efecto,
en realidad de verdad.— —ty [šúrti],
s. (for. y com.) fiador; fianza,
garantía; seguridad, certeza.—*of a s.*,
de seguro, como cosa cierta.—*to be* o
go s. for, ser fiador, salir garante de.

surf [sœrf], *s.* oleaje, resaca, marejada; espuma del mar.

surface [sœrfɪs], *s.* superficie.—*vt.* allanar, alisar; poner superficie a. —*vt.* y *vi.* (hacer) emerger, surgir o salir a la superficie.

surge [sœrdẑ], *s.* (mar.) oleaje; (fig.) ola, onda.—*vi.* agitarse o embravecerse (el mar); romper (las olas).— *vt.* hacer ondular; (mar.) largar.

surgeon [sœrdẑọn], *s.* cirujano.— **surgery** [sœrdẑœrj], *s.* cirugía.— **surgical** [sœrdẑjkạl], *a.* quirúrgico.

surly [sœrlj], *a.* áspero, rudo, hosco.

surmise [sœrmáiz], *vt.* conjeturar, suponer, vislumbrar.—*s.* conjetura, suposición, vislumbre.

surmount [sœrmáunt], *vt.* vencer, superar, salvar; coronar, poner (algo) sobre.

surname [sœrnejm], *s.* apellido; sobrenombre.—*vt.* apellidar, llamar.

surpass [sœrpǽs], *vt.* sobrepasar, superar, aventajar.

surplus [sœrplʌs], *s.* sobrante, excedente; (com.) superávit.—*a.* excedente, de sobra, sobrante.

surprise [sœrpráiz], *s.* sorpresa; novedad; extrañeza; asombro.—*by s.,* de sorpresa.—*vt.* sorprender.

surrender [sʌréndœ(r)], *vt.* rendir, entregar; ceder.—*vi.* rendirse, entregarse; (mil.) capitular.—*s.* rendición, entrega; (mil.) capitulación; (for.) cesión.—*s. value,* valor de rescate (de un seguro, etc.).

surround [sʌráund], *vt.* circundar, cercar, rodear, ceñir.—**-ing** [-iŋ], *a.* circunstante, circunvecino.—*s. pl.* alrededores, contornos, inmediaciones; medio, circunstancias que rodean (a una persona, hecho o lugar).

surtax [sœrtæks], *s.* recargo; impuesto adicional.

survey [sœrvéj], *vt.* inspeccionar, examinar, reconocer; medir o deslindar terrenos.—*vi.* ejecutar operaciones topográficas.—*s.* [sœrvej], examen, estudio; encuesta (de la opinión pública); medición o deslinde (de terrenos).- —**or** [sœrvéjọ(r)], *s.* topógrafo; agrimensor.

survival [sœrvájvạl], *s.* supervivencia; sobreviviente; reliquia.—*s. of the fittest,* supervivencia del más apto. —**survive** [sœrvájvt], *vt.* y *vi.* sobrevivir; salir o quedar vivo.—**survivor** [sœrvájvọ(r)], *s.* sobreviviente, superviviente.

suspect [sʌspékt], *vt.* y *vi.* sospechar (de), desconfiar (de); maliciar.—*s.* [sʌspékt], persona sospechosa.—*a.* sospechoso.

suspend [sʌspénd], *vt.* suspender.- **-ers** [-œrz], *s. pl.* tirantes del pantalón.—**suspense** [sʌspéns], *s.* suspensión; impaciencia; ansiedad; (for.) entredicho.—**suspension** [sʌspénsọn], *s.* suspensión.

suspicion [sʌspíʂọn], *s.* sospecha, recelo. —**suspicious** [sʌspíʂʌs], *a.* sospechoso; suspicaz.

sustain [sʌstéjn], *vt.* sostener, aguantar; tener, mantener; sufrir (una desgracia, pérdida, etc.); (mus.) prolongar, sostener; apoyar; confortar; alimentar; defender; establecer, probar.—**sustenance** [sástẹnạns], *s.* sustento, mantenimiento, subsistencia; alimentos.

suture [sjúchụ(r)], *vt.* (cir.) suturar.—*s.* sutura.

swagger [swǽgœ(r)], *vi.* fanfarronear; pavonearse.—*s.* jactancia, baladronada; pavoneo.

swallow [swálou], *vt.* y *vi.* tragar(se); engullir.—*to s. up,* tragar(se); absorber.—*s.* bocado, trago; deglución; (orn.) golondrina.

swam [swæm], *pret.* de TO SWIM.

swamp [swamp], *s.* pantano, ciénaga, fangal.—*vt.* empantanar, encharcar; abrumar, recargar; inundar.—*vi.* empantanarse; zozobrar.-—**y** [swámpj], *a.* pantanoso, cenagoso.

swan [swan], *s.* cisne.—*s. song,* canto del cisne; obra última.

swap [swap], *vti.* [1] cambiar, cambalachear, permutar.—*vii.* hacer trueques o cambalaches.—*s.* trueque, (fam.) cambalache.

swarm [swarm], *s.* enjambre; (fig.) hormiguero, multitud.—*vt.* y *vi.* enjambrar; pulular, bullir, hormiguear; (fam.) trepar.

swarthy [swórθj], *a.* moreno, trigueño.

swath [swaθ], *s.* ringla o ringlera de mies segada; guadañada.—*to cut a wide s.,* hacer alarde u ostentación.

sway [swej], *vt.* inclinar, ladear; influir en el ánimo de (alguno), inducir; blandir, cimbrar; gobernar, regir; (mar.) izar, guindar.—*vi.* ladearse, inclinarse; torcerse; oscilar, mecerse; ondular; flaquear, tambalear.—*s.* poder, predominio, influjo; vaivén, oscilación, ondulación, balanceo.—*to give full s. to,* dar ancho campo a.- —**backed** [swéjbækt], *a.* derrengado.

swear [swer], *vti.* y *vii.* [10] jurar.

sweat [swet], *vti.* y *vit.* [4] sudar; trasudar; hacer sudar; trabajar duro; (fam.) hacer confesar a un preso mediante interrogatorio persistente; secar en horno.—*s.* sudor, exudación, trabajo.—**er** [-œ(r)], *s.* el que suda; patrono explotador; suéter.

Swede [swid], *s.* sueco.—**Swedish** [swídjṣ], *a.* sueco.—*s.* idioma sueco.

sweep [swip], *vti.* [10] barrer; deshollinar (chimeneas); recorrer; pasar la vista por.—*to s. away*, robar sin dejar nada; arrastrar con todo.—*to s. the bottom*, dragar.—*vi.* barrer; pasar o deslizarse rápidamente; pasar arrasando; pasar con paso o ademán majestuosos.—*to s. down*, descender precipitadamente.—*s.* barredura, barrido; ojeada, vistazo; alcance, abarque, extensión—er [swipœ(r)], *s.* barrendero; basurero; barredera, barredora.——*ing* [-iŋ], *a.* que barre.—*s.* barrido.—*pl.* barreduras, basura.

sweet [swit], *a.* dulce; fragante; melodioso; bonito, lindo; agradable; amable, bondadoso; fresco; (mec.) suave y sin ruido; fértil (tierra).—*s. corn*, maíz tierno.—*s. herbs*, hierbas olorosas.—*s. pea*, guisante de olor.—*s. potato*, batata, boniato, (Am.) camote.—*s.-scented*, perfumado.—*s.-smelling*, fragante.—*s.-spoken*, melifluo.—*to have a s. tooth*, ser goloso.—*s.* dulzura; deleite; persona querida; golosina, dulce.—*pl.* dulces, golosinas.——**bread** [switbred], *s.* lechecilla o molleja de ternera.——**en** [-n], *vt.* endulzar, dulcificar; (farm.) edulcorar; mitigar; hacer salubre.—*vi.* endulzarse.——**heart** [-hart], *s.* novia, prometida; novio, prometido; persona querida, amante.—*a.* querido, cielo, vida.——**meat** [-mit], *s.* dulce, confitura, golosina.——**ness** [-njs], *s.* dulzura, melosidad, suavidad, delicadeza, bondad.

swell [swel], *vti.* y *vii.* [6] hinchar(se), inflar(se), henchir(se); engreír(se).—*to s. out*, arrojar (el árbol) sus hojas; ampollarse; bufar.—*a.* elegante, de buen tono; magnífico.—*s.* hinchazón; oleada, marejada; prominencia; ondulación del terreno.——**ing** [swéliŋ], *s.* hinchazón; tumefacción, turgencia, abotagamiento; bulto, chichón, protuberancia.

swept [swept], *pret.* y *pp.* de TO SWEEP.

swerve [swœrv], *vt.* y *vi.* desviar(se), apartar(se), extraviar(se), virar(se), torcer(se).—*s.* desviación, viraje.

swift [swift], *a.* rápido, ligero, raudo; veloz, volador; vivo, diligente; sumarísimo; (mar.) velero.——**ness** [swíftnjs], *s.* velocidad, rapidez, prontitud.

swim [swim], *vii.* [10] nadar; flotar; dejarse ir o llevar; deslizarse suavemente; tener la cabeza ida; tener mareo o vértigo; padecer vahídos.—*vti.* pasar a nado; hacer nadar o flotar.—*s.* natación; nadada; nadadera de pez; movimiento de deslizarse; mundo, corriente de las cosas; sociedad, vida social; clases influyentes.—*to be in the s.*, estar en la

corriente o marcha de las cosas.—*to take a s.*, ir a nadar.——**mer** [swímœ(r)], *s.* nadador.——**ming** [-iŋ], *a.* que nada, natatorio; para nadar.—*s. pool*, piscina, (Am.) alberca, pileta.

swindle [swíndl], *vt.* estafar, timar.—*s.* estafa, timo.——r [swíndlœ(r)], *s.* estafador, timador.

swine [swain], *s.* marrano(s), puerco(s), cerdo(s); persona soez.——**herd** [swáinhœrd], *s.* porquero, porquerizo.

swing [swiŋ], *vti.* y *vii.* [10] columpiar(se), mecer(se); balancear(se), bambolear(se); girar, hacer girar.—*vti.* blandir.—*to s. about*, dar una vuelta.—*to s. clear*, evitar un choque.—*s.* oscilación, vaivén, balanceo; columpio, mecedor; libertad de acción, libre curso; autoridad, control; (mec.) juego, recorrido, alcance.—*in full s.*, en plena operación, en su apogeo.

Swiss [swis], *a.* y *s.* suizo, helvético.

switch [swich], *s.* latiguillo, fusta; trenza postiza; fustazo; (f.c.) cambiavía, agujas; (elec.) interruptor, conmutador; acción de desviar, cambiar, conmutar (un tren, una corriente).—*s. engine*, locomotora de patio o de maniobras.—*vt.* fustigar, dar latigazos; (f.c.) desviar; (elec.) cambiar.—*to s. off*, desconectar, cortar (la corriente); apagar (las luces).—*to s. on*, conectar; encender (las luces).—*vi.* (off) desviarse, cambiarse.——**board** [swíchbord], *s.* (elec.) pizarra o cuadro de distribución; (tlf.) cuadro conmutador.

swollen [swóuln], *pp.* de TO SWELL.

swoon [swun], *vi.* desmayarse, desfallecer.—*s.* desmayo, síncope, desfallecimiento.

sword [sord], *s.* espada.

swore [swor], *pret.* de TO SWEAR.—**sworn** [sworn], *pp.* de TO SWEAR.

swum [swam], *pp.* de TO SWIM.

swung [swaŋ], *pret.* y *pp.* de TO SWING.

syllable [sílabl], *s.* sílaba.

symbol [símbol], *s.* símbolo; emblema; (teol.) credo.——**ic(al)** [simbálik(al)], *a.* simbólico.——**ism** [símbolizm], *s.* simbolismo.

symmetrical [simétrikal], *a.* simétrico.——**symmetry** [símitri], *s.* simetría.

sympathetic(al) [simpaθétik(al)], *a.* simpático; que simpatiza; afín; benévolo, compasivo.—**sympathize** [símpaθaiz], *vi.* simpatizar; compadecerse, condolerse; padecer por simpatía; congeniar.—**sympathy** [símpaθi], *s.* simpatía, afinidad; benevolencia; condolencia, lástima; pésame; (med.) simpatía.

symphony [símfoni], *s.* sinfonía.

symptom [símptǫm], *s.* síntoma.

synagogue [sínagag], *s.* sinagoga.

synchronization [siŋkronizéiṣǫn], *s.* sincronización.— **synchronize** [síŋkronaiz], *vt.* y *vi.* sincronizar.

syndicate [síndikeit], *vt.* y *vi.* (com.) sindicar(se).—*s.* [síndikit], (com.) sindicato.

synonym [sínonim], *s.* sinónimo.— **synonymous** [sinánimʌs], *a.* sinónimo.

synopsis [sinápsis], *s.* sinopsis.

syntax [síntæks], *s.* sintaxis.

synthesis [sínθesis], *s.* síntesis.—**synthetic** [sinθétik], *a.* sintético.

syphilis [sífilis], *s.* sífilis.

syringe [sírindź], *s.* (med.) jeringa.

syrup [sírʌp], *s.* jarabe; almíbar; sirope. — —**y** [-i], *a.* almibarado; meloso.

system [sístǫm], *s.* sistema.— —**atic(al)** [sistemǽtik(ǫl)], *a.* sistemático.— —**atize** [sístemǫtaiz], *vt.* sistematizar.

T

tab [tæb], *s.* lengüeta (de zapato); (fam.) cuenta.

tabernacle [tǽbœrnækl], *s.* tabernáculo.

table [téibl], *s.* mesa; tabla (matemática, de materias, etc.), cuadro; tablero; meseta.—*t. boarder*, pupilo, pensionista.—*t. cover*, tapete, cubremesa.—*t.-land*, altiplanicie, meseta. —*t. linen*, mantelería.—*t. set*, vajilla. —*vt.* y *vi.* poner sobre la mesa; formar una tabla o índice, catalogar; (carp.) ensamblar, acoplar.—*to t. a motion*, dar carpetazo a una moción, aplazar su discusión.— —**cloth** [-klɔθ], *s.* mantel; tela para manteles.— —**spoon** [-spun], *s.* cuchara.— —**spoonful** [-spunful], *s.* cucharada.— —*t.* [tǽblit], *s.* tableta, pastilla; bloc de papel; plancha, lápida; tabla.— —**ware** [-wer], *s.* servicio de mesa, artículos para la mesa.

taboo [tǎbú], *a.* proscrito, prohibido. —*s.* tabú.—*vt.* declarar tabú; (fig.) prohibir, excluir.

tabor [téibǫ(r)], *s.* tamboril.— —**et** [tæborét], *s.* taburete.

tabulate [tǽbyǔleit], *vt.* (neol.) tabular, catalogar en forma de tabla.— —**tabulator** [tǽbyǔleitǫ(r)], *s.* tabulador.

tacit [tǽsit], *a.* tácito.— —**urn** [-œrn], *a.* taciturno.

tack [tæk], *vt.* clavar con tachuelas; (mar.) cambiar de rumbo; (cost.) puntear, pegar, coser, hilvanar; unir, añadir.—*s.* tachuela, puntilla; hilván; cambio de política, nuevo plan de acción; (mar.) cambio de rumbo.

tackle [tǽkl], *vt.* agarrar, asir; atacar, abordar (un problema, etc.), luchar

con; atajar a un adversario.—*s.* aparejo; (football) atajo, agarrada; atajador—*fishing t.*, avíos de pescar.

tact [tækt], *s.* tacto; tino, tiento, ten con ten.— —**ful** [tǽktful], *a.* discreto, cauto, político.— —**ical** [-ikǫl], *a.* táctico.

tactics [tǽktiks], *s. pl.* táctica.

tactless [tǽktlis], *a.* falto de tacto o de tino, impolítico.

tadpole [tǽdpoul], *s.* (zool.) renacuajo.

taffeta [tǽfitǎ], *s.* tafetán.

tag [tæg], *s.* marbete, marca, rótulo; herrete; apéndice, rabito; pingajo; populacho, muchedumbre; cita, nota al pie.—*vti.* [1] marcar con marbete o rótulo; clavetear, poner herretes; pisar los talones, alcanzar y tocar.

tail [teil]. *s.* cola, rabo; cabo, extremidad; apéndice.—*pl.* frac.— *t. light*, farol trasero, luz de cola. —*t. spin*, (aer.) barrena.—*vt.* seguir de cerca, vigilar, espiar.

tailor [téilǫ(r)], *s.* sastre.—*t.-made suit*, traje sastre.

taint [teint], *vt.* y *vi.* manchar(se), inficionar(se), corromper(se).— *tainted food*, alimentos pasados, echados a perder.—*s.* mácula, mancha, corrupción.

take [teik], *vti.* [10] tomar; cóger, asir, agarrar; recibir, aceptar; apropiarse, apoderarse de; percibir o cobrar; llevar, conducir, acompañar; restar, deducir; usar, emplear, adoptar; considerar, tener por; admitir; adaptarse o hacerse a; coger, contraer (una enfermedad); sacar (un retrato, una copia); dar (un salto, un paso, un paseo).—*to t. aback*, desconcertar. —*to t. advantage of*, aprovecharse de. —*to t. down*, bajar; descolgar; desmontar.—*to t. for granted*, dar por sentado; no apreciar.—*to t. heart*, animarse, cobrar valor.—*to t. hold of*, asir, agarrar; tomar posesión de; encargarse de.—*to t. in*, entrar; aceptar, recibir; comprender; engañar; abarcar.—*to t. into account*, tomar en consideración.—*to t. into consideration*, tener en cuenta.—*to t. offense*, ofenderse.—*to t. on*, emprender; contratar.—*to t. out*, sacar; llevar a paseo; extraer.—*to t. over*, tomar posesión de.—*to t. pains*, esmerarse.—*to t. pity on*, apiadarse, compadecerse de.—*to t. place*, celebrarse, verificarse.—*to t. the floor*, tomar la palabra.—*to t. the trouble to*, tomarse la molestia.—*to t. to heart*, tomar a pecho.—*to t. to task*, reprender.—*to t. up*, subir; dedicarse a; recoger.—*vii.* ser poseedor, adquirir propiedad; pegar bien, tener buen éxito, (fam.) cuajar; prender

(la vacuna, el fuego, etc.); hacer su efecto, ser eficaz; (fam.) picar (el pez); sacar buen o mal retrato; pegar, adherirse; arraigar (las plantas).—*to t. after*, parecerse a, salir a; imitar a, seguir el ejemplo de; ser como.—*to t. ill*, caer enfermo.—*to t. off*, partir, salir; (aer.) despegar, hacerse al aire. —*to t. to*, aficionarse a; tomar cariño a; recurrir a; dedicarse a.—*s.* toma; cogida, redada; entrada, producto, ingresos (de una función, etc.).— *t.-in*, (fam.) fraude, engaño; estafador; entrada, ingresos.—*t.-off*, (fam.) sátira; caricatura, remedo; (aer.) despegue; (dep., gimn.) trampolín, raya de donde se salta.—taken [téikn], *pp.* de TO TAKE.—*to be t. ill*, caer enfermo.—*to be t. off o away*, morir(se).—*to be t. with*, prendarse o estar prendado de.—taking [téikiɳ], *a.* atractivo, seductor; (fam.) contagioso.—*s.* toma; (for.) embargo.—*t. for*, afición, inclinación, afecto; (fam.) arrebato, agitación.—*pl.* ingresos.

talcum [tǽlkʌm], *s.* talco.—*t. powder*, polvos de talco.

tale [teil], *s.* cuento; narración, relato; fábula, conseja; embuste, filfa; hablilla, chisme.— —bearer [téilberœ(r)], *s.* chismoso, cuentista, (fam.) correve(i)dile, enredador, soplón.

talent [tǽlent], *s.* talento, ingenio; aptitud.— —ed [-id], *a.* talentoso, de talento; hábil.

talisman [tǽlismạn], *s.* talismán.

talk [tɔk], *vt.* y *vi.* hablar; charlar, conversar.—*to t. away*, malgastar el tiempo hablando; disipar con la palabra.—*to t. into*, convencer de, inducir a.—*to t. out of*, disuadir; sonsacar.—*to t. over*, discutir, conferenciar acerca de.—*to t. to*, hablar a; reprender.—*to t. to the purpose*, hablar al alma.—*to t. up*, alabar.—*s.* conversación, plática; habla; charla; tema de una conversación; discurso; comidilla (objeto de chismes, etc.).— —ative [tókạtiv], *a.* locuaz, charlatán.— —ativeness [-ạtivnịs], *s.* locuacidad.— —er [-œ(r)], *s.* conversador; decidor, orador; charlatán.

tall [tɔl], *a.* alto; (fam.) grande.—*six feet t.*, seis pies de alto o de altura.

tallow [tǽlou], *vt.* ensebar.—*s.* sebo.

tally [tǽli], *s.* cuenta.—*t. sheet*, hoja de cuentas o apuntes.—*vti.* [7] llevar la cuenta.—*vii.* cuadrar, concordar, estar conforme.—*to t. up*, sumar, contar.

talon [tǽlon], *s.* garra.

tamale [tạmáli], *s.* (Am.) tamal.

tambourine [tæmbọrín], *s.* pandero, pandereta.

tame [teim], *a.* manso, domesticado; dócil, tratable; insustancial, insípido; (fam.) moderado.—*vt.* domar, amansar, domesticar; avasallar; suavizar; represar (un río).— —ness [téimnịs], *s.* mansedumbre, docilidad.- —r [-œ(r)], *s.* domador.

tamp [tæmp], *vt.* apisonar.

tamper [tǽmpœ(r)], *vi.* (con with) meterse en o con; falsificar, adulterar; tocar lo que no se debe; sobornar.

tampon [tǽmpan], *s.* (cir.) tapón.—*vt.* taponar.

tan [tæn], *vti.* [1] curtir; zurrar; tostar, requemar.—*a.* tostado, de color de canela.—*s.* color de canela; tostadura del sol.

tang [tæɳ], *s.* dejo, gustillo, sabor.

tangent [tǽndžẹnt], *a.* y *s.* tangente.— *to fly o go off on a t.*, salirse por la tangente.

tangerine [tǽndžẹrín], *s.* (naranja) tangerina o mandarina.

tangible [tǽndžibl], *a.* tangible, palpable.

tangle [tǽɳgl], *vt.* y *vi.* enredar(se), enmarañar(se); confundir(se).—*to t. with*, venir a las manos (con).—*s.* enredo, embrollo; confusión; alga marina.

tank [tæɳk], *s.* tanque, depósito, cuba; aljibe; (mil.) tanque.

tanner [tǽnœ(r)], *s.* curtidor.—tannery [tǽnœri], *s.* tenería, curtiduría.

tantalize [tǽntạlaiz], *vt.* torturar lentamente con lo inasequible.— tantalizing [tǽntạlaiziɳ], *a.* tentador e inasequible.

tantrum [tǽntrʌm], *s.* (fam.) berrinche, pataleta.

tap [tæp], *vti.* [1] perforar (un barril, etc. para sacar líquido) o sangrar (un árbol); unir o conectar con (para tomar agua, corriente, etc. o para interceptar o transmitir mensajes telefónicos, etc.); sacar de, tomar de; (cir.) sajar o punzar (un absceso, etc.); golpear ligeramente, dar una palmadita.—*vii.* tocar o golpear ligeramente.—*s.* espita; tapón o tarugo; (mec.) macho de terraja; toma (de agua, elec., etc.), derivación; golpecito, palmadita.—*beer on t.*, cerveza del barril o de sifón.— *t. dance*, zapateado, zapateo.—*t. room*, bar.

tape [teip], *s.* cinta, cintilla; cinta de papel o de metal.—*adhesive t.*, tela o cinta adhesiva, esparadrapo.— *red t.*, burocratismo, formulismo dilatorio.—*t. measure*, cinta para medir, cinta métrica.—*t. recorder*, grabadora (de cinta magnetofónica).

—*vt.* atar o arrollar con cinta; vendar; medir con la cinta métrica; grabar en cinta magnetofónica.

taper [téipœ(r)], *s.* velita, candela; cirio; ahusamiento de un objeto.—*vt.* afilar, adelgazar, ahusar.—*vi.* rematar en punta, tener forma ahusada; cesar poco a poco.

tapestry [tǽpįstrį], *s.* tapiz; tapicería, colgadura.

tapeworm [téįpwœrm], *s.* (lombriz) solitaria, tenia.

tapioca [tǽpióụkặ], *s.* tapioca.

tar [tar], *s.* alquitrán, brea o pez líquida; (fam.) marinero.—*vti.* [1] alquitranar, embrear, embetunar.

tardiness [tárdįnįs], *s.* tardanza, lentitud.—**tardy** [tárdį], *a.* tardío, moroso, lento.

tare [ter], *s.* (bot.) cizaña; (com.) tara.

target [tárgịt], *s.* blanco a que se tira.

tariff [tǽrįf], *s.* tarifa; arancel; impuesto.—*a.* arancelario, aduanero.—*vt.* tarifar; afectar por razón de impuestos.

tarnish [tárnįš], *vt.* deslustrar, empañar, deslucir; manchar, mancillar.—*vi.* deslustrarse; enmohecerse.—*s.* deslustre, mancha, empañadura.

tarpaulin [tarpóljn], *s.* lona embreada.

tarry [tǽrį], *vii.* [7] demorarse, tardar, entretenerse.

tart [tart], *a.* acre, ácido; agridulce; mordaz.—*s.* tarta; pastelillo de fruta.

task [tæsk], *s.* tarea, faena, labor.—*to take to t.*, amonestar, regañar.

tassel [tǽsẹl], *s.* borla.—*vti.* [2] adornar con borlas.

taste [teįst], *vt.* gustar; saborear, probar, catar.—*vi.* saber a, tener sabor o gusto.—*s.* gusto; sabor; (fig.) paladar; saboreo, paladeo; prueba, sorbo, trago, pedacito; muestra; gusto, discernimiento; afición.—*in bad t.*, de mal gusto.— *to have a t.*, *for*, gustar de.— **—ful** [téįstfụl], *a.* elegante, de buen gusto.— **—less** [-lįs], *a.* insípido; desabrido, sin gracia; de mal gusto.—**tasty** [téįstį], *a.* sabroso, gustoso.

tatter [tǽtœ(r)], *s.* andrajo, harapo, guiñapo, jirón.— **—ed** [-d], *a.* andrajoso, harapiento.

tattle [tǽtl], *vi.* chismear, comadrear; descubrir o revelar secretos indiscretamente.—*s.* charla, cháchara; chismografía.— **—r** [-œ(r)], *s.* chismoso.

tattoo [tætú], *s.* tatuaje; (mil.) retreta.—*vt.* tatuar.

taught [tɔt], *pret.* y *pp.* de TO TEACH.

taunt [tɔnt], *vt.* vilipendiar, vituperar; mofarse de; reprender.—*s.* vituperio; dicterio, sarcasmo.

taut [tɔt], *a.* tirante, tenso; listo, preparado, en regla.

tavern [tǽvœrn], *s.* taberna; mesón, posada, figón.

tax [tæks], *s.* impuesto, tributo, contribución, gabela; carga, exacción.—*vt.* imponer contribuciones a; (for.) tasar; abusar de; reprender; reprobar; (fam.) pedir como precio.—*to t. with*, acusar, tachar, imputar.— **—ation** [-éįšọn], *s.* tributación; imposición de contribuciones.

taxi(cab) [tǽksị(kæb)], *s.* auto de alquiler, taxímetro.

taxpayer [tǽkspeįœ(r)], *s.* contribuyente, tributario.

tea [ti], *s.* te; reunión en que se sirve te; infusión, cocimiento.

teach [tich], *vti.* [10] enseñar, instruir; aleccionar.—*vii.* ser maestro, enseñar. **— —er** [tíchœ(r)], *s.* maestro.— **—ing** [-įŋ], *a.* docente, enseñador, aleccionador.—*s.* enseñanza, instrucción, docencia, magisterio; doctrina.

teacup [tíkʌp], *s.* taza para te.—

teakettle [tíketl], *s.* marmita, olla de calentar agua.

team [tim], *s.* (dep.) equipo (de jugadores); conjunto de personas que trabaja coordinadamente; tronco, par, yunta (de animales de tiro).—*vt.* uncir, enganchar, enyugar.—*vi.* guiar un tronco o yunta.—*to t. up*, asociarse (con) para formar un equipo.— **—ster** [tíṃstœ(r)], *s.* tronquista; carretero; camionero.— **—work** [-wœrk], *s.* cooperación, esfuerzo coordinado de un equipo.

teapot [típat], *s.* tetera.

tear [tįr], *s.* lágrima.—*in tears*, llorando.—*t. bomb* (*gas*), bomba lacrimógena (gas lacrimógeno).—*vi.* llorar, derramar lágrimas.—*vti.* [10] [ter], desgarrar, rasgar.—*to t. asunder*, separar con violencia.—*to t. away*, arrancar, desmembrar.—*to t. down*, derribar, demoler.—*to t. one's hair*, mesarse los cabellos.—*to t. out*, arrancar, separar con violencia.—*to t. up*, arrancar, desarraigar; deshacer, desbaratar.—*vii.* rasgarse; andar precipitadamente.—*s.* rasgadura, desgarradura; precipitación; (fam.) borrachera.— **—ful** [tírfụl], *a.* lloroso, lacrimoso.

tease [tiz], *vt.* molestar, atormentar, fastidiar; embromar, torear.—*s.* broma continua; (fam.) embromador.

teaspoon [tíspun], *s.* cucharita, cucharilla.— **—ful** [-fụl], *s.* cucharadita.

teat [tit], *s.* teta; tetilla; pezón; ubre.

technical [téknịkạl], *a.* técnico, tecnológico.—**technician** [teknįšạn], *s.* técnico, experto.—**technique** [tekník], *s.* técnica, ejecución.

tedious [tídi̯ʌs], *a.* tedioso, fastidioso, pesado.- **—ness** [-nis], **tedium** [tídi̯ʌm], *s.* tedio.

teem [tim], *vi.* bullir, hormiguear.

teens [tíns], *s.* números de trece a diecinueve; edad de trece a diecinueve años.—*teen-age*, adolescencia, de trece a diecinueve años de edad.—*teen-ager*, adolescente, persona de trece a diecinueve años de edad.

teeth [tiθ], *pl.* de TOOTH.- **—ing** [tíθi̯ŋ], *s.* dentición.—*t. ring*, chupete.

teetotaler [titóu̯tᴀloe(r)], *s.* abstemio.

telegram [téle̦græm], *s.* telegrama.— **telegraph** [téle̦græf], *vt.* y *vi.* telegrafiar; enviar por telégrafo.—*s.* telégrafo.—**telegraphic** [tele̦gréfik], *a.* telegráfico.—**telegraphy** [tele̦g-ræfi], *s.* telegrafía.

telepathy [tele̦pǽθi], *s.* telepatía.

telephone [téle̦fou̯n], *vt.* y *vi.* telefonear. **—s.** teléfono.—*t. booth*, cabina o casilla de teléfonos.—*t. directory*, guía de teléfonos.—*t. exchange*, central telefónica.—*t. operator*, telefonista, operadora.

telescope [téle̦skou̯p], *s.* telescopio.— *vt.* y *vi.* encajar(se), enchufar(se) un objeto en otro.—**telescopic** [tele̦-skápik], *a.* telescópico; de enchufe.

televise [téle̦vai̯z], *vt.* trasmitir por televisión.—**television** [tele̦ví̦žo̦n], *s.* televisión.

tell [tel], *vti.* y *vii.* [10] decir; contar; expresar; explicar; revelar, descubrir; adivinar, decidir, determinar.—*to t. off*, contar, recontar; (mil.) designar. **—to t. on**, descubrir, delatar a; dejarse ver en, afectar a.—*to t. one (where to get) off*, decir a uno cuántas son cinco, cantárselas claras, soltarle cuatro frescas.—*to t. tales out of school*, revelar secretos.—*to t. volumes*, ser muy significativo.- **—er** [télœ(r)], *s.* relator, narrador; escrutador de votos; pagador o cobrador de un banco.—*t.'s window*, taquilla.- **—ing** [-iŋ], *a.* eficaz, notable.—*a t. argument*, un argumento convincente.- **—tale** [-tei̯l], *s.* soplón, chismoso.—*a.* revelador.

temerity [te̦mériti], *s.* temeridad.

temper [témpœ(r)], *vt.* moderar, mitigar, calmar; (pint.) mezclar; modificar, ajustar; (a)temperar, ablandar; (metal) templar.—*s.* mal genio; índole, humor, disposición; genio, condición; calma, ecuanimidad; temple; punto (grado de densidad). **—to lose one's t.**, perder la paciencia, enojarse.- **—ament** [témpœ̦rᴀ̦me̦nt], *s.* temperamento; complexión, naturaleza; composición; disposición; temple.- **—ance** [témpœ̦rᴀns], *s.* templanza, temperancia, sobriedad.-

—ate [témp(œ)ri̦t], *a.* sobrio, abstemio; templado, benigno; moderado.

temperature [témp(œ)rᴀchu̦(r)], *s.* temperatura.—*to have o run a t.*, tener fiebre o calentura.

tempest [témpi̦st], *s.* tempestad.—*vt.* agitar, conmover violentamente.- **—uous** [tempéschu̯ᴀs], *a.* tempestuoso, borrascoso; impetuoso.

temple [témpl], *s.* templo; (anat.) sien.

temporal [témporᴀl], *a.* temporal.—*s.* hueso temporal.

temporary [témporeri], *a.* temporal, provisional; temporero.

tempt [tempt], *vt.* tentar, incitar, provocar; seducir, atraer; poner a prueba.- **—ation** [-éi̯šo̦n], *s.* tentación; solicitación, prueba.

tenacious [te̦néi̯šᴀs], *a.* tenaz; pegajoso; porfiado, terco; firme.—**tenacity** [te̦nǽsi̦ti], *s.* tenacidad; tesón; terquedad; cohesión; adhesión.

tenant [té̦nᴀnt], *s.* arrendatario, inquilino.

tend [tend], *vt.* guardar, vigilar, cuidar; atender.—*vi.* tender, propender; dirigirse; atender.—*to tend on*, o *upon*, asistir, servir a.- **—ency** [ténde̦nsi], *s.* tendencia, propensión; dirección.

tender [té̦ndœ(r)], *a.* tierno; delicado; muelle; benigno, compasivo; sensible. **—t.-hearted**, de corazón tierno.—*t. of u over*, cuidadoso de, solícito de los sentimientos ajenos.—*s.* oferta, ofrecimiento, propuesta.—*vt.* ofrecer, presentar, proponer; enternecer, ablandar.—*vi.* hacer una oferta; enternecerse.- **—loin** [-lȯi̯n], *s.* filete.- **—ness** [-ni̦s], *s.* terneza, ternura; sensibilidad; delicadeza; benevolencia.

tendon [té̦ndo̦n], *s.* tendón.

tendril [téndri̦l], *s.* (bot.) zarcillo.

tenement [té̦ne̦me̦nt], *s.* casa de vecindad; vivienda (barata).

tenet [té̦ni̦t], *s.* dogma, principio, credo.

tennis [té̦ni̦s], *s.* tenis.

tenor [té̦no̦(r)], *s.* (mus.) tenor; tendencia; texto, contenido.—*a.* (mus.) de tenor.

tense [tens], *a.* tenso, tirante.—*s.* (gram.) tiempo.—**tension** [té̦nšo̦n], *s.* tensión, tirantez.

tent [tent], *s.* toldo; tienda de campaña, (Am.) carpa.

tentacle [té̦ntᴀkl], *s.* tentáculo.

tentative [té̦ntᴀti̦v], *a.* tentativo, de ensayo.—*s.* tentativa, ensayo, tanteo.

tenuous [té̦nyᴀs], *a.* tenue, sutil; raro.

tenure [té̦nyu̦(r)], *s.* (for.) (per)tenencia, posesión.—*t. right*, o *right of t.*, inamovilidad (de un cargo, etc.).

tepid [té̦pi̦d], *a.* tibio, templado.

term [tœrm], *s.* término, vocablo; trimestre escolar; plazo; término,

período; sesión.—*pl.* condiciones, estipulaciones; obligaciones impuestas; relaciones mutuas; precio; (com.) facilidades de pago; palabras. expresiones.—*to be on good (bad) terms with*, llevarse bien (mal) con; estar en buenas (malas) relaciones con.—*to bring to terms*, imponer condiciones a, hacer arreglos con. —*to come to terms*, arreglarse, convenirse.—*vt.* nombrar, llamar, calificar de.— —**inal** [tɑ́rminɑl], *a.* terminal.—*s.* término, final; (f.c. y elec.) terminal.- —**inate** [-ineit], *vt.* y *vi.* terminar.- —**ination** [-inéiʂɑn], *s.* terminación o fin; (gram.) desinencia.

termite [tɑ́rmait], *s.* termita, comején.

tern [tɑrn], *s.* golondrina de mar; terno.

terrace [tériʂ], *vt.* terraplenar.—*s.* terraplén; terraza; azotea; balcón, galería abierta.

terrain [teréin], *s.* terreno, campo.

terramycin [terɑmáiʂin], *s.* terramicina.

terrible [téribl], *a.* terrible; (fam.) tremendo, extremado.

terrier [tériœ(r)], *s.* perro de busca; zorrero.

terrific [terífik], *a.* terrífico, espantoso; (fam.) excelente, tremendo, formidable.—**terrify** [térifai], *vti.* [7] aterrar, aterrorizar, espantar.

territory [téritɔri], *s.* territorio, región, distrito, comarca.

terror [térɔ(r)], *s.* espanto, terror.- —**ism** [-izm], *s.* terrorismo.- —**ist** [-ist], *s.* terrorista.- —**ize** [-aiz], *vt.* aterrorizar.

test [test], *s.* prueba, ensaya, experimento; examen; comprobación; (quím.) análisis; resultado de un análisis; reacción, reactivo.—*t. flight*, (aer.) vuelo experimental o de prueba. —*t. tube*, probeta, tubo de ensayo. —*the acid t.*, la prueba suprema o decisiva.—*vt.* ensayar, comprobar, hacer la prueba de; someter a prueba; examinar (a un estudiante, etc.); (for.) atestiguar.

testament [téstɑment], *s.* testamento.

testicle [téstikl], *s.* testículo.

testify [téstifai], *vti.* y *vii.* [7] testificar, atestiguar, atestar.— —**testimonial** [testimóuniɑl], *s.* atestación; certificado; encomio; recomendación.—**testimony** [testimóuni], *s.* testimonio, declaración.—*in t. whereof*, en fe de lo cual.

tetanus [tétɑnʌs], *s.* tétano, tétanos.

text [tekst], *s.* texto.— —**book** [tɑ́kstbuk], *s.* libro de texto; libreto de ópera.

textile [tɑ́kstil], *a.* textil, tejido; de tejer, de tejidos.—*s.* tejido; material textil.—**texture** [tɑ́kschur], *s.* textura, contextura; tejido.

Thai [tái, tai], *s.* lengua siamesa.—*a.* siamés.

than [ðæn], *conj.* que; de; del que, de la que, etc.—*fewer than ten*, menos de diez.—*I am taller than he*, soy más alto que él.—*less time than they expected*, menos tiempo que el que esperaban.—*more than once*, más de una vez.

thank [θæŋk], *vt.* agradecer, dar gracias a.—*t. you*, gracias.- —**fulness** [θǽŋkfulnis], *s.* agradecimiento, gratitud.- —**less** [-lis], *a.* desagradecido; ingrato.- —**s** [-s], *s.* gracias.—*t. to*, gracias a, merced a, debido a.- —**sgiving** [θæŋksgívin], *s.* acción de gracias.—*Thanksgiving Day*, día de acción de gracias.

that [ðæt], *a.* ese, esa, aquel, aquella. —*t. way*, por aquel camino; por allí; de ese modo.—*pron.* ése, ésa, eso; aquél, aquélla, aquello; que, quien, el que, la que, lo que; el cual, la cual, lo cual.—*t. is (to say)*, es decir.—*t. is how*, así es como se hace.—*t. is t.*, eso es lo que hay, no hay más que hablar, etc.—*t. of John*, el de Juan. —*t. of yesterday*, el o lo de ayer.—*t. which*, el que, la que, etc.—*conj.* que; para que, a fin de que, con el objeto de.—*in t.*, en que, a causa de que, por cuanto.—*not but t.*, no es decir que.—*save t.*, salvo que.—*so t.*, para que, con tal que; de modo que, de suerte que.—*adv.* tan.—*not t. far*, no tan lejos.—*t. large*, así de grande, de este tamaño.—*t. many*, tantos. —*t. much*, tanto.

thatch [θæch], *s.* paja (para techos).—*vt.* techar con paja.—*thatched roof*, techumbre de paja.

thaw [θɔ], *vt.* y *vi.* deshelar(se), derretir(se).—*to t. out*, hacer(se) más tratable, menos reservado o ceremonioso, abrirse.—*s.* deshielo, derretimiento.

the [ði, ðə], *art.* el, la, lo, los, las.—*adv.* cuanto, tanto, mientras más, etc. —*t. less you say, t. better*, cuanto menos diga, tanto mejor.—*t. more he spoke, t. more we admired him*, mientras más hablaba, más lo admirábamos.

theater, theatre [θíɑtœ(r)], *s.* teatro; arte dramático.—**theatrical** [θiǽtrikɑl], *a.* teatral.—*s. pl.* funciones teatrales.

thee [ði], *pron.* (ant.) te, a ti.—*for t.* o *with t.*, para o por ti (contigo).

theft [θeft], *s.* hurto, robo, latrocinio.

their [ðer], *a.* su, sus, suyo(s), suya(s) (de ellos, de ellas).- —**s** [-z], *pron.* el suyo (de ellos), la suya (de ellas), los suyos (de ellos), las suyas (de ellas).

them [ðem], *pron.* los, las, les; ellos, ellas (precedidos de preposición).

theme [θim], *s.* tema, asunto.

themselves [ðemsélvz], *pron.* ellos mismos, ellas mismas; sí (mismos, mismas) (después de *prep.*); se (*refl.*). —*with t.,* consigo.—V. HIMSELF, HERSELF.

then [ðen], *adv.* entonces, en aquel tiempo, a la sazón; después, luego, en seguida; en otro tiempo; además; en tal caso; pues, conque; por consiguiente, por esta razón.—*but t.,* por otra parte, sin embargo, si bien es cierto que.—*by t.,* para entonces. —*now and t.,* de cuando en cuando; de vez en cuando.—*now t.,* ahora bien; tenemos pues.—*t. and there,* allí mismo, al punto.—*conj.* pues, en tal caso.

thence [ðens], *adv.* de allí, desde allí; desde entonces, desde aquel momento, de allí en adelante; de ahí, por eso, por esa razón o ese motivo.

theological [θioládʒikạl], *a.* teológico, teologal.—**theology** [θiálodʒi], *s.* teología.

theorem [θíorem], *s.* teorema.—**theoretical** [θiorétikạl], *a.* teórico, especulativo.—**theory** [θíori], *s.* teoría.

therapeutic [θerạpiútik], *a.* terapéutico. — —**s** [-s], *s.* terapéutica.—**therapy** [θérạpi], *s.* terapia.

there [ðer], *adv.* ahí, allí, allá; en eso, en cuanto a eso.—*down t.,* ahí (allí) abajo.—*over t.,* ahí.—*t. is, t. are,* hay.—*t. you are,* (fam.) eso es todo; ahí nos (me, etc.) tiene; ahí está el busilis.—*up t.,* ahí (allí) arriba.- —**abouts** [ðerạbáuts], *adv.* por ahí, por allí, cerca; acerca de eso; aproximadamente.- —**after** [ðeréeftœ(r)], *adv.* después, después de eso; conforme.- —**by** [ðerbái], *adv.* con eso, con lo cual; de tal modo, así; allí, por allí cerca; acerca de eso.- —**for** [ðerfór], *adv.* por es(t)o; para es(t)o.- —**fore** [ðérfor], *adv.* por es(to), por (lo) tanto, por ende, por consiguiente, en consecuencia, luego.- —**from** [ðerfrám], *adv.* de allí, de ahí; de eso.- —**in** [ðerín], *adv.* allí dentro; en esto, en eso.- —**of** [ðeráv], *adv.* de esto, de eso.- —**on** [ðerán], *adv.* sobre o encima de él, ella, etc.; por encima; por lo tanto; luego, al punto. - —**upon** [ðerʌpán], *adv.* sobre o encima de él, ella, etc.; por lo tanto, por consiguiente; sobre lo cual, luego, al punto.- —**with** [ðerwíð], *adv.* con eso, con esto; en eso, entonces, luego, inmediatamente.

thermometer [θœrmámetœ(r)], *s.* termómetro.—**thermos** [θœrmos], *s.*

termo(s).—**thermostat** [θœrmostæt], *s.* termóstato.

these [ðiz], *a. pl.* de THIS: estos, estas. —*pron.* éstos, éstas.

thesis [θísis], *s.* tesis.

they [ðei], *pron. pl.* de HE, SHE, IT: ellos, ellas.—*t. say,* se dice, dicen.

thick [θik], *a.* grueso; espeso; tupido, denso; atestado, lleno; estúpido; apagado (voz, etc.); impenetrable; profundo (sombra, etc.); (fam.) íntimo.—*t.-and-thin,* cabal, a toda prueba.—*s.* grueso, espesor; lo más denso, nutrido, tupido o recio.—*adv.* frecuentemente, continuadamente; densa o tupidamente.—*t.-headed,* espeso, torpe.—*t.-lipped,* bezudo, (Am.) bembón.—*t.-set,* rechoncho. —*t.-skinned,* insensible, sinvergüenza. —*to lay it on t.,* exagerar.- —**en** [θíkn], *vt. y vi.* espesar(se), condensar(se), engrosar(se); reforzar(se); enturbiar(se); complicar(se).- —**et** [-it], *s.* maleza, espesura, matorral, broza.- —**ness** [-nis], *s.* espesor; densidad; grosor; cuerpo, consistencia; capa (superpuesta); (fam.) estupidez.

thief [θif], *s.* ladrón.—**thieve** [θiv], *vt. y vi.* hurtar, robar.—**thieves** [θivz], *s. pl.* de THIEF.

thigh [θai], *s.* muslo.—*t. bone,* fémur.

thimble [θímbl], *s.* dedal.

thin [θin], *a.* delgado, fino, tenue; flaco, descarnado; ligero, transparente; aguado; (mus.) débil, poco resonante; apagado (color); escaso; pequeño. —*vti. y vii.* [1] enrarecer(se); adelgazar(se); fluidificarse.—*to t. out,* aclarar, entresacar (el monte, etc.)

thine [ðain], *pron. y a.* (ant.) tuyo, el tuyo; tu, tus.

thing [θiŋ], *s.* cosa, objeto; asunto, acontecimiento, hecho.

think [θiŋk], *vti. y vii.* [10] pensar; proponerse; creer, juzgar, conjeturar. —*as you t. fit,* como a usted le parezca mejor, como Ud. quiera.—*to t. better of,* cambiar de opinión acerca de; formar mejor opinión de.—*to t. it over,* pensarlo, meditarlo.—*to t. nothing of,* mirar con desprecio, tener en poco; creer fácil, no dar importancia a.—*to t. on o upon,* acordarse de, recordar; pensar en; reflexionar acerca de; meditar, considerar.- —**able** [θíŋkạbl], *a.* concebible.- —**er** [-œ(r)], *s.* pensador. - —**ing** [-iŋ], *s.* pensamiento, reflexión; concepto, juicio.—*to my t.,* en mi opinión.

thinness [θínnis], *s.* tenuidad, delgadez; poca consistencia; debilidad.

thirst [θœrst], *s.* sed; ansia, anhelo. —*vi.* tener o padecer sed; ansiar,

anhelar.—*to* t. *for*, tener sed de; anhelar.- —y [θɑ́ɜrstɪ], *a.* sediento. —*to be* t., tener sed.

this [ðɪs], *a.* este, esta.—*pron.* éste, ésta, esto.—*t. way*, por aquí.

thistle [θ[sl], *s.* cardo, abrojo.—*t. bird*, *t. finch*, jilguero.

tho' [ðoʊ], *conj.* = THOUGH.

thong [θaɜ], *s.* correa, tira de cuero, látigo.

thorax [θɔ́ːræks], *s.* tórax, pecho.

thorn [θɔrn], *s.* (bot.) espina, púa; espino, abrojo; (fig.) pesadumbre, zozobra.- —y [θɔ́rnɪ], *a.* espinoso; arduo.

thorough [θɑ́ːroʊ], *a.* cabal, completo, acabado, perfecto; cuidadoso, concienzudo.- —bred [-brɛd], *a.* de pura raza, casta o sangre; bien nacido. —*s.* (un) pura sangre (caballo, etc.).- —fare [-fɛr], *s.* vía pública; paso, tránsito.—*no* t., no hay paso; calle cerrada.

those [ðoʊz], *a. pl.* de THAT: aquellos, aquellas; esos, esas.—*pron.* ésos, ésas; aquéllos, aquéllas.—*t. that*, *t. which*, *t. who*, los que, aquellos que, quienes.

thou [ðaʊ], *pron.* (ant.) tú.

though [ðoʊ], *conj.* aunque, bien que, si bien, aun cuando.—*as* t., como si. —*adv.* (fam.) sin embargo; a pesar de eso.

thought [θɔt], *pret. y pp.* de TO THINK. —*s.* pensamiento; meditación, reflexión; idea; intención, propósito; recuerdo; cuidado, solicitud; poquito, pizca.—*to take t. for*, pensar en, proveer para.- —ful [θɔ́tfʊl], *a.* pensativo; considerado; precavido.- —fulness [-fʊlnɪs], *s.* calidad de meditativo, precavido o considerado; consideración; cuidado, atención; previsión.- —less [-lɪs], *a.* atolondrado, descuidado; irreflexivo; inconsiderado.- —lessness [-lɪsnɪs], *s.* descuido o inadvertencia; falta de consideración; atolondramiento; indiscreción, ligereza.

thrash [θræʃ], *vt.* zurrar, apalear; (fam.) vencer decisivamente.—*vi.* arrojarse, agitarse.—*to t. out a matter*, ventilar un asunto.- —ing [θrǽʃɪɜ], *s.* trilla; paliza.

thread [θrɛd], *s.* hilo; fibra, hebra, filamento.—*screw t.*, rosca (de un tornillo).—*t. lace*, encaje de hilo. —*vt.* enhebrar, enhilar, ensartar; colarse a través de, pasar por; (mec.) roscar, aterrajar.—*vi.* colarse en, llegar hasta.- —bare [θrɛ́dbɛr], *a.* raído, gastado.

threat [θrɛt], *s.* amenaza.- —en [θrɛ́tn], *vt. y vi.* amenazar, amagar.- —ening [θrɛ́tnɪɜ], *a.* amenazador.

threefold [θrífoʊld], *a.* trino, triple; tres veces más.—*adv.* tres veces. —threescore [θrískɔr], *s.* tres veintenas, sesenta.

thresh [θrɛʃ], *vt.* (agr.) trillar, desgranar. —*vi.* trillar el grano.- —ing [θrɛ́ʃɪɜ], *s.* trilla.—*t. floor*, era.- —er [-œ(r)], *s.* trillador; máquina trilladora.

threshold [θrɛ́ʃoʊld], *s.* umbral; entrada; (fig.) comienzo.

threw [θru], *pret.* de TO THROW.

thrice [θraɪs], *adv.* tres veces.

thrift [θrɪft], *s.* economía, frugalidad; desarrollo vigoroso (de una planta, etc.).- —y [θrɪ́ftɪ], *a.* frugal, económico.

thrill [θrɪl], *vt.* emocionar vivamente, hacer estremecer.—*vi.* emocionarse, conmoverse.—*s.* emoción, estremecimiento.- —er [θrɪ́lœ(r)], *s.* novela o película melodramática.- —ing [-ɪɜ], *a.* emocionante, conmovedor.

thrive [θraɪv], *vii.* [4] medrar, prosperar, tener buen éxito.

throat [θroʊt], *s.* garganta.

throb [θrab], *vii.* [1] latir, palpitar.—*s.* latido, pulsación, palpitación.

thrombosis [θrambóʊsɪs], *s.* trombosis.

throne [θroʊn], *s.* trono; poder o dignidad soberanos.—*vt.* entronizar. —*vi.* ocupar el trono.

throng [θraɜ], *s.* tropel de gente, muchedumbre.—*vt.* llenar de bote en bote; estrujar.—*vi.* venir en tropel, amontonarse, apiñarse.

throstle [θrásl], *s.* zorzal, tordo; (tej.) telar continuo.

throttle [θrátl], *s.* regulador, obturador, válvula reguladora.—*t. valve*, válvula de estrangulación, válvula reguladora; (aut.) acelerador.—*vt.* ahogar, estrangular.—*vi.* ahogarse, asfixiarse.

through [θru], *a.* continuo, que va hasta el fin.—*t. ticket*, (f.c., etc.) billete, boleto o boletín directo.—*adv.* de o al través, de parte a parte, de un lado a otro; desde el principio hasta el fin; enteramente, completamente.—*t. and t.*, enteramente; en todo; hasta los tuétanos.—*to be t.*, haber terminado; (fam.) no poder más.—*prep.* por; a través de; de un extremo (o lado) a otro de; por conducto o por medio de, mediante, por entre; por causa de, gracias a, por mediación de.- —out [-áʊt], *prep.* por todo, en todo; a lo largo de; durante todo.—*adv.* en todas partes; desde el principio hasta el fin; de parte a parte; en todo respecto.

throw [θroʊ], *vti. y vii.* [10] arrojar, tirar, disparar, lanzar; echar.—*to t. about*, esparcir.—*to t. aside*, desechar. —*to t. away*, arrojar; desperdiciar, malgastar; desechar, arrinconar.—

to t. **back**, rechazar, devolver.—*to t.* **out**, proferir, insinuar; expeler, excluir; esparcir, exhalar, emitir.— *to t.* **out of gear**, (mec.) desengranar, desconectar; (fig.) trastornar.—*to t.* **up**, echar al aire; elevar, levantar; renunciar a, abandonar; (fam.) vomitar.—*s.* tiro, tirada.—**thrown** [θroʊn], *pp.* de TO THROW.

thrush [θrʌʃ], *s.* tordo, zorzal; (med.) afta.

thrust [θrʌst], *vii.* [9] acometer, embestir (con espada, etc.); tirar una estocada (con); meterse, pasar abriéndose campo.—*vti.* meter; empujar; forzar; atravesar; clavar, hincar.—*to t. aside*, rechazar; empujar a un lado.—*to t. forward*, empujar, echar adelante.—*to t. in*, meter, introducir.—*to t. on*, incitar, empujar. —*to t. out*, echar fuera; sacar (la lengua, etc.).—*to t. through*, apuñalar, atravesar de parte a parte.—*to t. upon*, imponer.—*pret.* y *pp.* de TO THRUST. —*s.* empuje, empujón; estocada, cuchillada, lanzada, etc.; arremetida; derrumbe.

thud [θʌd], *s.* sonido apagado; golpe sordo.

thug [θʌg], *s.* asesino; ladrón, salteador.

thumb [θʌm], *s.* pulgar.—*under the t. of*, dominado por, bajo el talón de.—*vt.* hojear (un libro) con el pulgar; manosear con poca destreza; emporcar con los dedos.— —**tack** [vʌmtæk], *s.* chinche (de dibujo).

thump [θʌmp], *s.* golpazo, porrazo; golpe sordo.—*vt.* y *vi.* aporrear, acachetear; latir con violencia (el corazón).

thunder [θʌndœ(r)], *s.* trueno, tronido; estruendo, estampido.—*vi.* tronar; retumbar.—*vt.* (fig.) tronar; fulminar. — —**bolt** [-boʊlt], *s.* rayo, centella.— —**ing** [-iŋ], —**ous** [-ʌs], *a.* atronador; fulminante.— —**storm** [-storm], *s.* tronada.

Thursday [θœrzdi], *s.* jueves.

thus [ðʌs], *adv.* así, de este modo; por eso, por lo tanto; en estos términos; hasta ese punto, tanto, a ese grado; siendo así, en este caso.—*t. and so*, tal y tal cosa; de tal y tal modo. —*t. far*, hasta ahora; hasta aquí.

thwart [θwort], *vt.* impedir, desbaratar, frustrar.

thy [ðai], *a.* (ant.) tu, tus.

thyme [taim], *s.* (bot.) tomillo.

thyself [ðaisélf], *pron.* (ant.) tú mismo, ti mismo.

tibia [tíbiə], (anat.) tibia; (ent.) cuarta articulación.

tick [tik], *s.* tictac; garrapata; funda de colchón; (fam.) crédito, fiado.—*vt.* hacer sonar produciendo tictac.—*vi.*

hacer sonido de tictac; batir, latir; (fam.) vender o comprar al fiado. —*to t. off*, marcar.

ticket [tíkit], *s.* billete, (Am.) boleto (de tren, teatro, etc.); rótulo, marbete; marca; candidatura de un partido político; papeleta o (Am.) balota (para votar).—*t. office*, taquilla o despacho de billetes.

tickle [tíkl], *vt.* hacer cosquillas a; halagar, lisonjear; divertir; agradar. —*vi.* hacer, tener o sentir cosquillas. —**ticklish** [tíkliʃ], *a.* cosquilloso; inseguro, incierto; arduo, delicado, difícil.

tide [taid], *s.* marea; corriente; curso, marcha; flujo; tiempo, estación, sazón.—*tidal wave*, marejada, aguaje. —*vt.* llevar, conducir (la marea). —*vi.* navegar o flotar con la marea.

tidiness [táidinis], *s.* limpieza, aseo; orden.

tidings [táidiŋs], *s. pl.* nuevas, noticias.

tidy [táidi], *a.* limpio, pulcro, ordenado; (fam.) considerable.—*s.* cubierta de respaldar.—*vti.* y *vii.* [7] asear, poner en orden.

tie [tai], *vt.* atar, amarrar, liar; unir, enlazar, encadenar, vincular; restringir, limitar; (pol., dep.) empatar.— *to t. the knot*, (fam.) casarse.—*to t. tight*, apretar.—*to t. up*, atar, amarrar, asegurar; recoger; impedir, obstruir, paralizar (el tránsito, la industria, etc.); envolver; vincular (con).—*vi.* liarse; relacionarse; empatarse.—*s.* lazo, nudo, ligadura; vínculo, conexión; apego, adhesión; (dep., etc.) empate; corbata; (mus.) ligadura.—*pl.* zapatos bajos.

tier [tir], *s.* fila, hilera, ringlera; (teat.) fila de palcos.

tiger [táigœ(r)], *s.* tigre.

tight [tait], *a.* bien cerrado, hermético; tirante, tieso; apretado, estrecho; compacto; (com.) escaso, difícil de obtener; (fam.) apurado, difícil, grave; tacaño; borracho.—*t.-fitting*, muy ajustado.—*t. squeeze*, (fam.) aprieto.— —**en** [táitn], *vt.* y *vi.* estrechar(se), apretar(se); estirar(se), atesar(se).— —**ness** [-nis], *s.* tensión, tirantez; estrechez; apretadura; impermeabilidad; (fam.) tacañería.— —**s** [-s], *s.* traje de malla, calzas.

tilde [tílde], *s.* (gram.) tilde.

tile [tail], *s.* azulejo, baldosa; teja; mosaico; bloque hueco; tubo de barro cocido.—*t. roof*, tejado, techo de tejas.—*vt.* tejar; embaldosar.

till [til], *s.* gaveta o cajón para guardar dinero.—*prep.* hasta.—*conj.* hasta que.—*vt.* cultivar, labrar.— —**age** [tílidʒ], *s.* labranza, labor, cultivo.

tilt [tilt], *s.* inclinación, declive; justa,

torneo; lanzada; toldo, tendal.—*vt.* y *vi.* ladear(se), inclinar(se).—*vt.* y *vi.* (over) volcar(se).

timber [tímbœ(r)], *s.* madera o materiales de construcción; palo, fuste; maderamen, maderaje; monte, bosque, árboles de monte; viga, madero; armazón; mango de madera; (fig.) cualidades.—*t. yard*, maderería, taller de maderas.—*vt.* enmaderar.

time [tajm], *s.* tiempo; época; período, estación; hora; vez, turno; oportunidad, ocasión; (com.) prórroga; plazo; (mús.) compás.—*at a t., at the same t.*, a la vez, al mismo tiempo.—*at no t.*, nunca.—*at times*, a veces.—*behind the times*, atrasado de noticias; anticuado.—*behind t.*, atrasado, retardado.—*between times*, en los intervalos.—*for the t. being*, por ahora. —*from t. to t.*, de cuando en cuando. —*in good t.*, temprano.—*on t.*, a la hora debida; (com.) a plazos.—*to beat t.*, llevar el compás.—*to be on time*, ser puntual.—*to have a good t.*, pasar un buen rato; divertirse.—*what t. is it?* ¿qué hora es?—*vt.* adaptar al tiempo, hacer con oportunidad; regular, poner a la hora; contar o medir el tiempo de; (mús.) llevar el compás.- —**keeper** [tájmkipœ(r)], *s.* cronometrista.- —**less** [-lis], *a.* eterno.- —**liness** [-linis], *s.* oportunidad.- —**ly** [-li], *adv.* oportunamente; a tiempo.—*a.* oportuno, conveniente.- —**piece** [-pis], *s.* cronómetro, reloj.- —**table** [-tejbl], *s.* horario, itinerario.

timid [tímid], *a.* tímido.- —**ity** [timíditi], *s.* timidez.—**timorous** [tímorʌs], *a.* miedoso, timorato; tímido.

tin [tin], *s.* estaño; (hoja de) lata, hojalata; objeto de hojalatería; (fam.) dinero, moneda.—*t. can*, (recipiente de) lata.—*t. foil*, hoja de papel de estaño.—*vti.* [1] estañar, cubrir con estaño; enlatar.

tincture [tíŋkchǔ(r)], *s.* tintura; tinte. —*t. of iodine*, tintura de iodo.—*vt.* teñir; impregnar, imbuir.

tinder [tíndœ(r)], *s.* yesca; mecha.

tinge [tindž], *vi.* y *vt.* colorar, teñir, matizar.—*s.* tinte, matiz; gustillo, dejo.

tingle [tíŋgl], *vi.* y *vt.* sentir o producir hormigueo o picazón; zumbar los oídos.—*s.* picazón, hormigueo, comezón; retintín.

tinkle [tíŋkl], *vt.* y *vi.* (hacer) tintinear. —*s.* tintineo; retintín.

tinsel [tínsel], *s.* oropel, relumbrón; talco; lentejuelas.—*a.* de oropel; de relumbrón.

tint [tint], *vt.* teñir, colorar, matizar.

—*s.* tinte, color, matiz; (b.a.) media tinta.

tiny [tájni], *a.* diminuto, minúsculo.

tip [tip], *s.* punta, extremidad, cabo; casquillo, regatón; yema del dedo; puntera (zapato); propina, gratificación; aviso confidencial; palmadita, golpecito.—*vti.* [1] ladear, inclinar, voltear; dar un golpecito a; dar propina a; informar confidencialmente; guarnecer.—*to t. off*, (fam.) advertir en confianza o en secreto.— *to t. over*, volcar(se).—*vii.* ladearse, inclinarse; dar propina.

tipsy [típsi], *a.* achispado; vacilante; ladeado.

tiptoe [típtou], *s.* punta del pie.—*on t.*, de o en puntillas; ansioso.—*vi.* andar de puntillas.

tiptop [típtap], *a.* (fam.) de primera, excelente.—*s.* cima, cumbre.

tire [tájr], *s.* llanta, neumático, goma. —*vt.* cansar, fatigar; aburrir, fastidiar.—*to t. out*, rendir de cansancio. —*vi.* cansarse; aburrirse, fastidiarse.— —**d** [-d], *a.* cansado, fatigado; aburrido; provisto de llantas.- —**less** [tájrlis], *a.* infatigable, incansable; sin llanta.- —**some** [-sʌm], *a.* tedioso, cansado, aburrido.

tissue [tíšu], *s.* (biol.) tejido; gasa, tisú; (fig.) serie conexa, encadenamiento.—*t. paper*, papel de seda.—*vt.* entretejer.

tithe [tájð], *s.* diezmo; minucia; pizca.

title [tájtl], *s.* título.—*t. page*, portada.

to [tu], *adv.* hacia adelante.—*to and fro*, de un lado para otro; yendo y viniendo.—*to come to*, volver en sí. —*prep.* a, para; por; hasta; en; con; según; menos.—*five minutes to four*, las cuatro menos cinco.—*from house to house*, de casa en casa.—*he wishes to go*, desea ir.—*kind to her*, amable o bondadoso con ella.—*to a certain extent*, hasta cierto punto.—*to be or not to be*, ser o no ser.—*to my way of thinking*, según mi modo de pensar.

toad [tóud], *s.* sapo.

toast [toust], *vt.* tostar; brindar por. —*vi.* tostarse; calentarse; brindar, beber a la salud de.—*s.* tostada; brindis.- —**er** [tóustœ(r)], *s.* el que brinda; tostador; tostadera, parrilla.- —**master** [-mæstœ(r)], *s.* el que preside un banquete; maestro de ceremonias.

tobacco [tobǽkou], *s.* (bot.) tabaco.

today [tudéj], *s.* y *adv.* hoy; hoy en día.

toddle [tádl], *vi.* (del niño o viejo) titubear.- —**r** [-œ(r)], *s.* niño, niña.

toe [tou], *s.* dedo del pie; puntera, punta (del pie, de media, de zapato); pie, base (de un terraplén, etc.); (mec.) saliente, brazo.—*big t.*, dedo

gordo del pie.—*t.-in*, convergencia.
—*toes up*, muerto.—*vt.* tocar con
la punta del pie; dar un puntapié;
poner punteras.—*vi.* (con in) andar
con la punta de los pies hacia adentro;
(mec.) converger (una rueda).— —**nail**
[tóųneịl], *s.* uña (de los dedos de los
pies).

together [tugéᵭœ(r)], *adv.* juntamente;
a un tiempo; sin interrupción.—*t.
with*, a una con, juntos; junto con.
—*a.* juntos.

toil [tọịl], *vi.* afanarse, trabajar asidua-
mente; moverse con dificultad.—*vt.*
conseguir a duras penas.—*s.* faena,
trabajo; pena, afán; obra laboriosa.-
—**er** [tọịlœ(r)], *s.* trabajador, el que
se afana.

toilet [tóịlịt], *s.* vestido, tocado, atavío;
acto de vestirse; tocador; excusado,
retrete.—*t. case*, neceser.—*t. paper* o
tissue, papel higiénico.—*t. set*, juego
de tocador.

token [tóųkn], *s.* señal, muestra,
prueba; prenda, recuerdo; ficha,
disco metálico (usado en tranvías,
teléfonos, etc.).—*as a t. of*, en prenda
de.—*t. money*, moneda fragmentaria;
monedas inferiores al dólar.—*t. payment*, pago parcial (en señal de buena
fe y de adeudo).

told [tоųld], *pret.* y *pp.* de TO TELL.

tolerable [tálẹṛạbl], *a.* tolerable, sufrible; mediano, pasadero.—**tolerance**
[tálẹṛạns], *s.* tolerancia.—**tolerant**
[tálẹṛạnt], *a.* tolerante.—**tolerate**
[tálẹṛeịt], *vt.* tolerar.—**toleration**
[talẹṛéịsọn], *s.* tolerancia, indulgencia.

toll [toųl], *s.* peaje, portazgo, pontazgo;
(fig.) pérdida, número de víctimas
(en un siniestro, etc.); tañido o doble
de campanas.—*to take a heavy t.*,
(fig.) costar caro (en víctimas, etc.).
—*vt.* y *vi.* cobrar o pagar peaje o
portazgo; tañer o doblar (las campanas).—*to t. the hour*, dar la hora.

tomato [toméịtoų], *s.* tomate.

tomb [tum], *s.* tumba, sepulcro.

tomboy [támboị], *s.* muchacha traviesa.

tombstone [túmstoųn], *s.* losa, lápida
sepulcral.

tome [tóųm], *s.* tomo, volumen.

tommy-gun [támị gʌn], *s.* ametralladora ligera.

tomorrow [tumároų], *s.* y *adv.* mañana.
—*day after t.*, pasado mañana.
—*t. afternoon* (*morning, noon, night*),
mañana por la tarde (por la mañana,
al mediodía, por la noche).

ton [tʌn], *s.* tonelada.

tone [toųn], *s.* tono; sonido; metal o
timbre de la voz.—*vt.* dar o modificar
el tono, entonar; templar, afinar.
—*to t. down*, (pint.) suavizar el tono;

(mus.) amortiguar el sonido; modificar la expresión.—*to t. up*, subir de
tono; vigorizar, robustecer; (med.)
entonar, tonificar.—*vi.* corresponder
en tono o matiz.

tongs [taŋz], *s. pl.* tenazas, tenacillas;
pinzas, alicates; mordazas.

tongue [tʌŋ], *s.* lengua; lengüeta;
badajo de campana.

tonic [tánịk], *a.* y *s.* tónico.

tonight [tunáịt], *adv.* y *s.* esta noche;
durante esta noche.

tonnage [tánịdʒ], *s.* tonelaje; (com.)
derechos de tonelaje.

tonsil [tánsịl], *s.* amígdala, tonsila.-
—**itis** [-áịtịs], *s.* (med.) tonsilitis,
amigdalitis.

too [tu], *adv.* también, además,
asímismo; demasiado.—(*it is*) *too bad*,
es lástima, es de sentirse.—*t. many*,
demasiados.—*t. much*, demasiado.

took [tųk], *pret.* de TO TAKE.

tool [tul], *s.* herramienta; utensilio o
instrumento.—*pl.* útiles, bártulos,
aperos.

tooth [tuθ], *s.* diente, muela.—*to have
a sweet t.*, ser muy goloso, gustar de
los dulces.—*t. and nail*, con todo
tesón, con empeño.—*t. decay*, caries
dental.— —**ache** [túθeịk], *s.* dolor de
muelas o de diente.— —**brush** [-braš],
s. cepillo de dientes.— —**ed** [-t], *a.*
dentado, ᴄerrado, dentellado.— —**less**
[-lịs], *a.* desdentado.— —**paste** [-peịst],
s. pasta de dientes.— —**pick** [-pịk], *s.*
mondadientes, palillo.

top [tap], *s.* cima, cumbre, pico,
cúspide, vértice, cabeza, cresta (de
una montaña); ápice, punta, remate,
parte superior; superficie; cabeza
(de una página); tabla (de mesa);
coronilla (de la cabeza); copa (de
árbol); cielo (de un automóvil, etc.);
auge, apogeo; primer puesto, último
grado; tupé; trompo, peonza; (aut.)
capota, fuelle; cofa; tope.—*at o from
the t.*, por arriba.—*on t.*, con buen
éxito.—*on t. of*, encima de; además
de.—*t.-flight, t.-notch*, de primera fila,
sobresaliente.—*t. hat*, (fam.) sombrero de copa, chistera.—*vti.* [1]
desmochar (un árbol, etc.); cubrir,
coronar, rematar; llegar a la cima de,
coronar; aventajar, exceder.—*to t.
off*, rematar, terminar.—*vii.* erguirse,
ser eminente; predominar.—*to t. off
with*, terminar con.

topaz [tóųpæz], *s.* topacio.

topcoat [tápkoųt], *s.* saco; sobretodo,
gabán.

toper [tóųpœ(r)], *s.* borrachín, (fam.)
cuba.

topic [tápịk], *s.* asunto, materia, tema.

topsy-turvy [tápsị tœ́rvị], *adv.* y *a.*

trastornado, desbarajustado, patas arriba.

torch [tɔrch], *s.* antorcha.

tore [tɔr], *pret.* de TO TEAR.

torment [tɔrmént], *vt.* atormentar, torturar; afligir.—*s.* [tɔ́rment], tormento, suplicio, tortura; pena, angustia.

torn [tɔrn], *pp.* de TO TEAR.

tornado [tɔrnéjdou], *s.* tornado, huracán.

torpedo [tɔrpídou], *s.* torpedo.—*vt.* torpedear.

torpid [tɔ́rpjd], *a.* torpe; entorpecido; adormecido, aletargado.—**torpor** [tɔ́rpɔ(r)], *s.* torpeza; entorpecimiento; adormecimiento; letargo, apatía.

torrent [tárent], *s.* torrente; raudal, agolpamiento.

torrid [tárjd], *a.* tórrido; abrasador, ardiente.

tortoise [tɔ́rtjs], *s.* tortuga, galápago; .tortuga de tierra, (Am.) jicotea.

tortuous [tɔ́rchuʌs], *a.* tortuoso, sinuoso.

torture [tɔ́rchu̧(r)], *s.* tortura, tormento, suplicio.—*vt.* torturar, dar tormento; tergiversar.— **—r** [-œ(r)], *s.* atormentador, verdugo.

toss [tos], *vt.* tirar, lanzar al aire; menear, agitar, sacudir.—*to t. aside,* echar a un lado.—*to t. in a blanket,* mantear.—*to t. in o up the sponge,* darse por vencido; desistir.—*to t. off,* tragar de golpe; echar a un lado, no hacer caso de; hacer sin esfuerzo ni esmero.—*to t. out,* derrocar (un gobierno, etc.).—*vi.* corcovear; mecerse.—*to t. for, to t. up,* echar o jugar a cara o cruz.—*s.* meneo, sacudida; lanzamiento; ajetreo.

tot [tat], *s.* chiquitín, nene, nena.

total [tóu̧tal], *a.* y *s.* total.— **—itarian** [tou̧tælitérjan], *s.* y *a.* totalitario.— **—itarianism** [tou̧tælitérjạnjzm], *s.* totalitarismo.— **—ity** [tou̧tæljtj], *s.* totalidad.

totter [tátœ(r)], *vi.* tambalear, temblar, vacilar.

touch [tʌch], *vt.* tocar; tentar, palpar, manosear; alcanzar, herir; conmover, enternecer; igualar, aproximarse a; (b.a.) delinear, esbozar; tratar (un asunto); concernir, importar; aludir a, tratar por encima; afectar.—*to t. for,* (fam.) dar un sablazo, pedir prestado a; robar a.—*to t. off,* descargar (arma); hacer o acabar de prisa; bosquejar.—*to t. up,* retocar; corregir.—*vi.* tocar(se); estar en contacto.—*to t. and go,* tratar de un asunto ligeramente.—*to t. on o upon,* tocar en; tratar ligeramente de; concernir; acercarse a.—*s.* tacto (sentido); toque; dolorcito, punzada;

indirecta; prueba, examen; corazonada; pincelada; dejo; (fam.) sablazo.—*t.-and-go,* montado al pelo; precario; ligero de cascos.— **—iness** [tʌ́chjnjs], *s.* susceptibilidad, delicadeza.— **—ing** [-jŋ], *prep.* tocante a, en cuanto a, acerca de.—*a.* patético, conmovedor.—*s.* toque; tacto; contacto.— **—wood** [-wu̧d], *s.* yesca.— **—y** [-j], *a.* quisquilloso, susceptible.

tough [tʌf], *a.* correoso, duro; vigoroso, (fam.) de pelo en pecho; resistente; testarudo, tenaz; flexible y fuerte; (metal) trabajable; (fam.) difícil, penoso; rudo, vulgar.—*t. break, t. luck,* (fam.) mala pata o suerte.—*s.* villano, rufián.— **—en** [tʌ́fn], *vt.* y *vi.* hacer(se) correoso; endurecer(se).— **—ness** [-njs], *s.* tenacidad; endurecimiento; rigidez; flexibilidad; resistencia; rudeza.

toupee [tupéj], *s.* tupé, peluca.

tour [tu̧r], *s.* viaje de turismo, excursión; jira de inspección; vuelta, circuito; turno.—*vt.* viajar por, recorrer.—*vi.* viajar por distracción.— **—ist** [tú̧rjst], *a.* turístico, de turismo.—*s.* turista.— **—ism** [-jzm], *s.* turismo.

tournament [tú̧rnạment], *s.* (dep.) torneo; justa.

tourniquet [tú̧rnjket], *s.* (cir.) torniquete.

tow [tou̧], *s.* estopa; remolque; lo que va remolcado.—*vt.* remolcar.

toward(s) [tɔrd(z), tuwɔ́rd(z)], *prep.* hacia; con, para con; cosa de, alrededor de; tocante a.

towel [tau̧l], *s.* toalla.—*t. rack,* toallero.

tower [táu̧œ(r)], *s.* torre; (mil.) torreón. —*bell t.,* campanario.—*vi.* descollar, sobresalir, destacarse; remontarse.— **—ing** [-jŋ], *a.* encumbrado; sobresaliente.—*t. rage,* furia violenta.

town [tau̧n], *s.* ciudad; villa, pueblo, aldea; municipio; la ciudad, el pueblo. —*t. hall, t. house,* casa consistorial, concejo.—*t. planning,* urbanismo.

toxin [táksjn], *s.* toxina.

toy [tɔj], *s.* juguete.—*a.* de juego; diminuto.—*vi.* jugar, juguetear, retozar.

trace [trejs], *s.* rastro, huella, pisada, pista; vestigio, señal, indicio; una pizca, un ápice.—*vt.* trazar, delinear; calcar; rastrear, seguir la pista; plantear, indicar; reconstruir, determinar el origen de.

trachea [tréjkja̧], *s.* tráquea.

track [træk], *s.* vestigio, rastro, pista, huella, pisada; carril; rumbo, ruta; curso (de cometa, etc.); senda, vereda; (f.c.) vía, rieles o carriles; estera o banda (de tractor oruga); atletismo; pista (de atletismo, carreras, etc.). —*off the t.,* descarrilado; desviado,

extraviado.—*on the t.*, sobre la pista, en el rastro.—*vt.* rastrear.—*to t. down*, descubrir (el origen, escondite, etc. de).

tract [trӕkt], *s.* trecho; región, comarca, terreno; (anat.) área, canal, sistema; opúsculo, panfleto.

traction [trӕkṣǫn], *s.* tracción; acarreamiento; (fisiol.) contracción.—**tractor** [trӕktǫ(r)], *s.* tractor.

trade [treid], *s.* comercio; ramo o giro; trueque, trato, negocio; movimiento mercantil; oficio; gremio.—*t. agreement*, tratado comercial (entre naciones); pacto entre patronos y gremios obreros.—*t. mark*, marca de fábrica.—*t. name*, razón social; nombre comercial o de fábrica. —*t. school*, escuela industrial o de artes y oficios.—*t. union*, gremio, sindicato.—*t. winds*, vientos alisios. —*vt.* y *vi.* negociar, comerciar, traficar; cambiar.—*to t. in*, negociar en; entregar un objeto (auto, radio, etc.) en pago total o parcial de otro. —*to t. off*, cambalachear.—*to t. on*, aprovecharse de.— —r [tréidœ(r)], *s.* negociante, comerciante, traficante, mercader; buque mercante.— —**sman** [tréidzmạn], *s.* tendero, mercader; artesano, menestral.

tradition [trạdíṣǫn], *s.* tradición.— —**al** [-ạl], *a.* tradicional.

traffic [trӕfịk], *s.* tráfico.—*vti.* y *vii.* [8] traficar.—**trafficked** [trӕfịkt], *pret.* y *pp.* de TO TRAFFIC.

tragedy [trӕdžịdi], *s.* tragedia.— **tragic(al)** [trӕdžịk(ạl)], *a.* trágico.

trail [treil], *vt.* arrastrar; remolcar; traer, llevar (barro, etc.) en los pies, zapatos, etc.; asentar (la yerba) con el andar hasta formar vereda; rastrear, seguir la pista; (f.c.) agregar (vagones) a un tren.—*vi.* ir arrastrando; dejar rastro; rezagarse; seguir el rastro; arrastrarse, trepar (una planta).—*s.* rastro, huella; cola (de vestido, cometa, etc.); sendero, vereda; carretera; indicio.— —er [tréilœ(r)], *s.* rastreador; carro o coche remolcado; remolque.—*t. truck*, camión con remolque.

train [trein], *vt.* adiestrar, entrenar; apuntar (un arma); enfocar (un anteojo).—*vi.* adiestrarse, entrenarse. —*s.* tren; séquito, comitiva; cabalgata; recua; reguero de pólvora; serie, sucesión, curso (de las ideas, acontecimientos, etc.); cola (de ave, vestido, cometa); (mec.) juego, movimiento.— —ee [trejní], *s.* persona a quien se entrena o adiestra; (mil.) soldado recluta.— —er [tréjnœ(r)], *s.* entrenador; domador.— —**ing** [-iŋ], *s.* adiestramiento, entrenamiento, preparación.—*a.* de entrenamiento, de instrucción.

trait [treit], *s.* rasgo, característica, cualidad; golpe, toque.

traitor [tréitǫ(r)], *s.* traidor.

trajectory [trạdžéktori], *s.* trayectoria.

tram [trӕm], *s.* (min.) vagoneta.

tramp [trӕmp], *vt.* y *vi.* pisar con fuerza; caminar; vagabundear.—*s.* marcha pesada; ruido de pisadas; caminata; vagabundo.— —le [trӕmpl], *vt.* hollar, pisar, pisotear, conculcar.—*vi.* pisar fuerte.—*to t. on*, atropellar, hollar, pisotear.—*s.* pisoteo; atropello.

trance [trӕns], *s.* rapto, arrobamiento; (med.) síncope, catalepsia; estado hipnótico.

tranquil [trӕŋkwil], *a.* tranquilo, sereno. — —**lity** [trӕŋkwíljti], *s.* tranquilidad, calma, serenidad, sosiego.— —**lize** [trӕŋkwílaiz], *vt.* y *vi.* tranquilizar(se).

transact [trӕnzӕkt], *vt.* transar, negociar.— —**ion** [trӕnzӕkṣǫn], *s.* transacción, negociación.

transatlantic [trӕnzӕtlӕntịk], *a.* transatlántico.—*t. liner*, (vapor o buque) transatlántico.

transcontinental [trӕnzkantịnéntạl], *a.* transcontinental.

transcribe [trӕnskráib], *vt.* transcribir. —**transcript** [trӕnskrípt], *s.* copia, traslado.—**transcription** [trӕnskríp-ṣǫn], *s.* transcripción.

transfer [trӕnsfœr], *vti.* [1] transferir, pasar, trasladar; transbordar; (for.) traspasar, ceder.—*s.* [trӕnsfœ(r)], transferencia; traslado; transbordo; (for.) traspaso, cesión.—*t. paper*, papel de calcar.

transform [trӕnsfórm], *vt.* y *vi.* transformar(se).— —**able** [-ạbl], *a.* transformable.— —**ation** [-éiṣǫn], *s.* transformación.

transfusion [trӕnzfiúžǫn], *s.* transfusión.

transient [trӕnṣẹnt], *a.* pasajero, transitorio; que está de paso o de tránsito; transeúnte.—*s.* transeúnte. —**transit** [trӕnsịt], *s.* tránsito.—*in t.*, en tránsito.—**transition** [trӕnzíṣǫn], *s.* tránsito, paso; transición.—**transitive** [trӕnsịtịv], *a.* (gram.) transitivo. —**transitory** [trӕnsịtori], *a.* transitorio; provisional.

translate [trӕnsléit], *vt.* traducir; descifrar; transformar.—*to t. from Spanish to English*, traducir del español al inglés.—**translation** [trӕnsléiṣǫn], *s.* traducción; interpretación; traslación, remoción.—**translator** [trӕnsléitǫ(r)], *s.* traductor, intérprete.

transmission [trӕnsmíṣǫn], *s.* transmisión.—**transmit** [trӕnsmít], *vti.*

[1] transmitir.—**transmitter** [trænsmítœ(r)], *s.* remitente; transmisor.

transom [trǽnsǫm], *s.* montante, claraboya.

transparency [trænspǽrǫnsi], *s.* transparencia; (foto.) diapositiva.—

transparent [trænspǽrǫnt], *a.* transparente, diáfano, hialino; (fig.) franco, sincero.

transplant [trænsplǽnt], *vt.* trasplantar.

transport [trænspórt], *vt.* transportar, acarrear; arrebatar, conmover.—*s.* [trǽnspǫrt], transporte, transportación, acarreo; buque o avión transporte; rapto, arrobamiento; paroxismo, acceso.— **—ation** [trænsportéiʃǫn], *s.* transporte, acarreo; boleto, billete, pasaje; coste del transporte.

transpose [trænspoúz], *vt.* transponer; (mus.) transportar.

transverse [trænsvœ́rs], *a.* transversal, transverso.

trap [træp], *s.* trampa, garlito, red, lazo.—*mouse t.*, ratonera.—*t. shooting,* tiro de pichón; tiro al vuelo a un blanco movible.—*vti.* [1] coger con trampa; atrapar; hacer caer en el garlito.—*vii.* armar lazos, trampas o asechanzas.—**—door** [trǽpdǫr], *s.* escotillón, trampa; (min.) puerta de ventilación.

trapeze [trǫpíz], *s.* trapecio (de gimnasia o circo).—**trapezium** [trǫpízjʌm], *s.* (geom.) trapecio.—**trapezoid** [trǽpǫzǫid], *s.* trapezoide.

trappings [trǽpiŋz], *s. pl.* arreos, aderezos, galas.

trash [træʃ], *s.* hojarasca, paja, basura, desperdicio, escombro, desecho; bagazo; cachivache, trasto; quídam, un cualquiera.— **—y** [trǽʃi], *a.* despreciable, baladí.

traumatic [trǫmǽtik], *a.* traumático.

travel [trǽvǫl], *vti.* y *vii.* [2] viajar; recorrer.—*s.* viaje; excursión; jornada; (mec.) recorrido.—*pl.* correrías; relación de un viaje.—*t.-worn,* fatigado por el viaje.— **—er** [-œ(r)], *s.* viajero; viajante.—*traveling salesman,* viajante de comercio, agente viajero.

traverse [trǽvœrs], *a.* transversal.— *t. board,* rosa náutica o de los vientos. —*adv.* de través, en sentido transversal.—*s.* travesaño.—*vt.* atravesar, cruzar; mover transversalmente.—*vi.* atravesarse; moverse de un lado a otro.

tray [trei], *s.* bandeja; (Am.) batea; (foto.) cubeta; cualquier vasija casi plana o de bordes bajos.

treacherous [tréchœras], *a.* traidor, traicionero.—**treachery** [tréchœri], *s.* traición, perfidia, deslealtad.

tread [tred], *vti.* y *vii.* [10] pisar, hollar; andar, caminar.—*s.* paso; pisada, huella; escalón; superficie de rodadura (de rueda, neumático, etc.); banda o cadena (de tractor oruga).— **—le** [tredl], *s.* (mec.) pedal.

treason [trízǫn], *s.* traición.—*high t.,* lesa patria; lesa majestad.— **—able** [-ǫbl], *a.* pérfido, desleal, traidor.

treasure [trézy̆(r)], *s.* tesoro.—*t.-trove,* tesoro hallado.—*vt.* atesorar; acumular riquezas; guardar como un tesoro.— **—r** [trézy̆rœ(r)], *s.* tesorero. **—treasury** [trézy̆ri], *s.* tesorería; erario; (com.) caja; (T.) Ministerio de Hacienda o del Tesoro.

treat [trit], *vt.* y *vi.* tratar (bien o mal); curar; convidar, invitar.—*s.* placer; obsequio; convite.— **—ise** [trítis], *s.* tratado (libro).— **—ment** [-mǫnt], *s.* tratamiento, trato; (med.) cura, cuidado.— **—y** [-i], *s.* tratado, pacto.

treble [trebl], *a.* triple; (mus.) atiplado. —*s.* (mus.) tiple.—*vt.* triplicar.—*vi.* triplicarse.

tree [tri], *s.* árbol.—*shoe t.,* horma de zapato.—*up a tree,* puesto entre la espada y la pared.— **—less** [trílis], *a.* pelado, sin árboles.- **—top** [-tap], *s.* copa.

trellis [trélis], *s.* enrejado; emparrado.

tremble [trembl], *vi.* temblar; estremecerse; tiritar; trinar.—*s.* temblor.

tremendous [triméndʌs], *a.* tremendo.

tremolo [trémoluǫ], *s.* (mús.) trémolo.

tremor [trémǫ(r)], *s.* tremor, temblor. estremecimiento; vibración, trepidación.—**tremulous** [trémyǫlʌs], *a.* trémulo, tembloroso.

trench [trench], *vt.* y *vi.* surcar; hacer zanjas o fosos; (mil.) atrincherar.—*s.* foso, zanja; tajo; presa (de riego); trinchera.

trend [trend], *vi.* dirigirse, tender, inclinarse.—*s.* dirección, rumbo, curso, tendencia.

trespass [tréspǫs], *vi.* (con **on** o **upon**) violar, infringir; invadir, rebasar o traspasar los límites; (con **against**) pecar, faltar.—*s.* transgresión, translimitación; infracción, violación; culpa, pecado; deuda (en el padrenuestro).

tress [tres], *s.* trenza; rizo, bucle.—*pl.* cabellera.

trial [trái̯ǫl], *s.* prueba, ensayo, tanteo, tentativa; desgracia, aflicción; (for.) proceso, juicio, vista.—*a.* de prueba; experimental.—*by t.,* al tanteo.—*on t.,* (com.) a prueba; (for.) enjuiciado.

triangle [trái̯æŋgl], *s.* triángulo.— **triangular** [trai̯ǽŋgy̆lǫ(r)], *a.* triangular.

tribal [trái̯bǫl], *a.* tribal, de tribu. **—tribe** [traib], *s.* tribu.

tribulation [tr̩byɡléɪʃən], *s.* tribulación.

tribunal [tr̩biúnəl], *s.* (for.) sala, juzgado; tribunal; foro.

tributary [tr̩íbyɡteri], *a.* y *s.* tributario; subordinado, subalterno.—**tribute** [tríbjut], *s.* tributo; contribución, impuesto; homenaje.

trice [traɪs], *s.* momento, instante. —*in a t.*, en un tris; en un abrir y cerrar de ojos.

trichina [tr̩ikáɪnə], *s.* triquina.

trick [tr̩ik], *s.* treta; ardid, truco; trampa; juego de manos; chasco, burla; travesura, jugarreta; destreza, maña; marrullería; (naipes) baza; (mar.) guardia del timonel.—*to do the t.*, resolver el problema, dar en el busilis.—*vt.* engañar, embaucar.—*to t. out*, ataviar, componer, asear.—*vi.* trampear, vivir de trampas.— —**ery** [tríkœri], *s.* ardid, engaño, astucia.

trickle [tr̩íkl], *vt.* y *vi.* (hacer) gotear; escurrir.—*s.* goteo.

tricky [tríkɪ], *a.* falso, tramposo, marrullero; intrincado.

tricycle [tráɪsɪkl], *s.* triciclo.

trifle [tráɪfl], *s.* bagatela, fruslería, friolera, baratija, menudencia, chuchería.—*vt.* (con *away*) malgastar (el tiempo, etc.).—*vi.* bromear, chancearse; holgar(se).—*to t. with*, jugar con, tratar sin seriedad; burlarse de, engañar.—**trifling** [tráɪflɪŋ], *a.* frívolo, trivial.

trigger [trígœ(r)], *s.* gatillo, disparador; calzo.

trigonometry [tr̩iɡonámetr̩i], *s.* trigonometría.

trill [tr̩il], *s.* trino, gorjeo, (fam.) gorgorito; (fon.) vibración.—*vt.* vibrar (la r).—*vi.* trinar, gorjear; gotear.

trilogy [tríloʤɪ], *s.* trilogía.

trim [trɪm], *a.* ajustado, bien acondicionado; ataviado, acicalado.—*vti.* [1] componer, arreglar, pulir, ajustar, adaptar; (carp.) desbastar, acepillar; (agr.) podar; recortar (cabellos, barba); (cost.) adornar, guarnecer, ribetear; (fam.) reprender, zurrar; (fam.) derrotar; sacar ventaja a.—*to t. off*, recortar; atusar.—*to t. up*, adornar, hermosear, componer.—*vii.* vacilar, titubear; nadar entre dos aguas.—*s.* atavío, adorno, traje, vestido; estilo; condición, estado; (cost.) franja, ribete, guarnición; (arq.) molduras.— —**ming** [trímɪŋ], *s.* (cost.) guarnición, cenefa; ajuste, arreglo; (agr.) poda; recorte (del pelo, barba); (fam.) derrota.

trinity [tríniti], *s.* trinidad; (T.) Trinidad.

trinket [tríŋkit], *s.* baratija, chuchería.

trio [tríoɡ], *s.* terno; (mus.) trío.

trip [tr̩ip], *vti.* [1] hacer caer a uno (con una zancadilla), hacer tropezar; armar un lazo o zancadilla; coger a uno en falta; (mec.) disparar, soltar; desatar; (mar.) zarpar, levar anclas. —*vii.* tropezar; equivocarse, cometer un desliz o descuido; (mar.) zarpar; correr, ir aprisa.—*s.* viaje corto, excursión; tropiezo, traspiés; paso falso, desliz; zancadilla; paso o movimiento ágil.

tripe [traɪp], *s.* (coc.) callos, mondongo; (fam.) cosa sin valor, necedades.

triple [trípl], *a.* triple.—*vt.* triplicar. —**tripod** [tráɪpad], *s.* trípode.

trite [traɪt], *a.* trillado, gastado, trivial, vulgar.— —**ness** [tráɪtnɪs], *s.* vulgaridad, trivialidad.

triumph [tráɪʌmf], *s.* triunfo, victoria. —*vi.* triunfar; vencer, salir victorioso. — —**al** [traɪʌmfəl], *a.* triunfal.— —**ant** [traɪʌmfənt], *a.* triunfante, victorioso.

trivial [trívɪəl], *a.* trivial, frívolo, fútil.

trod [tr̩ad], *pret.* y *pp.* de TO TREAD. —**trodden** [tr̩ádn], *pp.* de TO TREAD.

trolley [tr̩álɪ], *s.* (elec.) polea de trole; coche o tranvía de trole.—*t. car*, (coche de) tranvía.

trombone [trámboɡn], *s.* (mus.) trombón.

troop [trup], *s.* tropa; cuadrilla, grupo; compañía (de actores); (mil.) escuadrón de caballería.—*vi.* apiñarse, ir en tropel.

trophy [tróɡfi], *s.* trofeo.

tropic [trápɪk], *s.* trópico.— —**al** [-əl], *a.* tropical.

trot [tr̩at], *vti.* [1] hacer trotar.—*t. out* (fam.) sacar a exhibir.—*vii.* trotar, ir al trote.—*s.* trote.—*at a t.*, al trote.

troubador [trúbədor], *s.* trovador.

trouble [trʌbl], *vt.* (per)turbar, disturbar; enturbiar; enfadar, hostigar; atribular, preocupar; molestar, importunar.—*to t. oneself*, tomarse la molestia; inquietarse.—*vi.* incomodarse, darse molestia, apurarse.—*s.* perturbación; disturbio, inquietud; enfermedad, mal; (mec.) avería; cuita, pena, congoja; disgusto, desavenencia; dificultad, molestia; impertinencia, engorro.—*in t.*, hallarse en dificultades.— —**maker** [-meɪkœ(r)], *s.* perturbador, agitador. — —**some** [-sʌm], *a.* penoso, pesado; importuno; dificultoso, fastidioso, molesto; pendenciero.

trough [tr̩of], *s.* artesa; comedero (para animales); abrevadero, bebedero; seno de dos olas; canal (artificial); canalón (del tejado); (meteor.) mínimo de presión.

trousers [trúzœrz], *s. pl.* pantalones.

trousseau [trúsoɡ], *s.* ajuar de novia.

trout [traɡt], *s.* trucha.

trowel [tráuel], *s.* (alb.) llana, paleta, palustre, (Am.) cuchara.

truancy [trúansi], *s.* ausencia sin permiso de la escuela o del deber. —**truant** [trúant], *s.* novillero, que se ausenta de la escuela.—*to play t.*, hacer novillos, capear la escuela.

truce [trus], *s.* (mil.) tregua; suspensión, cesación.

truck [trʌk], *vt.* y *vi.* trocar, permutar, traficar; acarrear, transportar en camión o carretón.—*s.* camión; carretón; carretilla de mano; carreta; efectos para vender o trocar; hortalizas para el mercado; (fam.) cosas sin valor, basura; trueque; (fam.) trato.

trudge [trʌdź], *vi.* andar a pie; caminar con trabajo.—*s.* (fam.) caminata, paseo largo y difícil.

true [tru], *a.* verdadero, cierto, real, efectivo; ingenuo, sincero; exacto; justo, a plomo, a nivel, alineado, bien arreglado; legítimo, genuino; fiel, leal.—*t. to life*, verosímil; al natural.

truffle [trʌfl], *s.* trufa.

truism [trúizm], *s.* perogrullada.— **truly** [trúli], *adv.* verdaderamente, en verdad; realmente, exactamente; sinceramente, de buena fe.—*yours (very) t.*, su afectísimo, su seguro servidor.

trump [trʌmp], *s.* triunfo (naipes); (fam.) real mozo, excelente persona; (poét.) trompeta; trompetazo.—*vt.* (naipes) matar con triunfo; engañar. —*to t. up*, forjar; inventar.—*vi.* (naipes) jugar un triunfo, matar.

trumpet [trʌmpit], *s.* (mus.) trompa, trompeta, clarín (instrumento y músico); bocina, megáfono.—*vi.* trompetear.—*vt.* (fig.) divulgar.

truncate [trʌɳkeit], *vt.* truncar.

truncheon [trʌnchən], *s.* porra, tranca.

trunk [trʌɳk], *s.* tronco; baúl; trompa de elefante.—*pl.* calzones cortos para deportes.—*t. line*, línea principal (f.c., elec., telf., etc.).—*a.* troncal.

trust [trʌst], *s.* confianza, fe; creencia; (com.) crédito; (for.) fideicomiso, cargo, depósito; (com.) combinación monopolista.—*vt.* y *vi.* confiar (en), contar con; tener confianza en o hacer confianza de; encargar y fiar; fiarse (de); creer, dar crédito a; vender al fiado.—**ee** [trʌstí], *s.* síndico, fideicomisario, fiduciario, depositario; miembro de un patronato.— —**ful** [trʌstful], *a.* confiado.— —**worthy** [-wœrði], *a.* fiable, confiable; fidedigno.— —**y** [-i], *a.* fiel; íntegro, confiable; firme, seguro.

truth [truθ], *s.* verdad, realidad; veracidad; exactitud.— —**ful** [trúθful],

a. verídico; verdadero, exacto.— —**fulness** [-fulns], *s.* veracidad; exactitud; realismo.

try [trai], *vti.* [7] probar, ensayar; procurar, tratar de, intentar; exasperar, cansar; comprobar, (for.) procesar; ver (una causa); (metal.) purificar, refinar.—*to t. on*, probarse (ropa).—*to t. one's hand*, hacer uno la prueba.—*to t. out*, probar, someter a prueba.—*vii.* probar, ensayar; procurar, hacer lo posible; (mar.) capear.—*s.* prueba, ensayo.— —**ing** [tráiiɳ], *a.* de prueba; molesto, exasperador, irritante; angustioso, penoso.

tub [tʌb], *s.* cuba; batea; tina; cubeta; bañera; (fam.) acto de bañarse.

tube [tjub], *s.* tubo; cámara de llanta o neumático; (rad.) válvula, bombillo, tubo.

tuber [tjúbœ(r)], *s.* (bot.) tubérculo; (anat.) tubérculo, hinchazón, prominencia.— —**cle** [-kl], *s.* tubérculo.— —**cular** [tjubœrkyulā(r)], *a.* tuberculoso, tísico.— —**culosis** [tjubœrkyulóusis], *s.* tuberculosis.

tubing [tjúbiɳ], *s.* tubería.—**tubular** [tjúbyulā(r)], *a.* tubular.

tuck [tʌk], *s.* (cost.) alforza.—*vt.* alforzar; arropar; doblar, aprestar. —*to t. up*, arremangar.— —**er** [tʌkœ(r)], *s.* (cost.) escote.—*vt.* (E.U., fam.) (a menudo con **out**) cansar, fatigar.

Tuesday [tjúzdi], *s.* martes.

tuft [tʌft], *s.* penacho, cresta; borla; manojo, ramillete; tupé, moño; macizo (de plantas).

tug [tʌg], *vti.* [1] tirar de, arrastrar; remolcar.—*vii.* esforzarse, tirar con fuerza.—*s.* tirón, estirón; (mar.) remolcador.

tuition [tjuíʃən], *s.* instrucción o enseñanza; precio de la enseñanza, matrícula (mensual, anual, etc.) que se paga por ella.

tulip [tjúlip], *s.* tulipán.

tulle [tul], *s.* tul.

tumble [tʌmbl], *vi.* caer, dar en tierra. —*to t. down*, desplomarse; voltear, rodar; dar saltos, brincar; revolcarse; (fam.) comprender, caer en ello.—*to t. out*, (fam.) levantarse.—*vt.* revolver; tirar, arrojar.—*to t. over o about*, tumbar, derribar; volcar; desarreglar, trastornar; ajar o arrugar (la ropa); cazar al vuelo; pulir por fricción.—*s.* caída, tumbo; vuelco, voltereta; desorden, confusión.— —**r** [tʌmblœ(r)], *s.* vaso (de mesa); cubilete; acróbata, saltimbanqui, titiritero.

tumor [tjúmǫ(r)], *s.* tumor.

tumult [tjúmʌlt], *s.* tumulto, escándalo;

agitación.— —uous [tjumʌlchↄʌs], a. tumultuoso, alborotado.

tun [tʌn], s. tonel, cuba.

tuna [túnậ], s. (ict.) atún; (bot.) tuna; nopal.—t. fish, atún.

tune [tjun], s. (mús.) aire, tonada, son, melodía; afinación, concordancia, armonía.—in t., templado, afinado. —out of t., destemplado, desafinado, desentonado.—to the t. of, al son de, tocando o entonando.—vt. templar, afinar, entonar; ajustar, adaptar; (rad.) sintonizar.—to t. up, (mec.) poner a punto el motor.—vi. armonizar, modular.—to t. in, (rad.) sintonizar.— —r [tjúnœ(r)], s. afinador, templador; (rad.) sintonizador.

tungsten [tʌ́ŋstẹn], s. (quím.) tungsteno.

tunic [tjúnịk], s. túnica; (mil.) casaca, guerrera.

tuning [tjúnịŋ], s. (mús.) acto de templar, afinación; (rad.) sintonización.—t. fork, (mús.) diapasón.

tunnel [tʌ́nẹl], s. túnel; (min.) socavón. —vti. y vii. [2] horadar; construir o abrir un túnel.

tunny [tʌ́nị], s. atún.—striped t., bonito.

turban [tœ́rbạn], s. turbante.

turbid [tœ́rbịd], a. turbio, espeso; turbulento.

turbine [tœ́rbịn], s. turbina.

tureen [tyrín], s. sopera, salsera.

turf [tœrf], s. césped; terrón (con césped); carreras de caballos, hipódromo.

Turk [tœrk], s. turco.

turkey [tœ́rkị], s. pavo.

Turkish [tœ́rkịṣ], a. turco.—s. idioma turco.

turmoil [tœ́rmọjl], s. disturbio, tumulto, alboroto.

turn [tœrn], vt. voltear, hacer girar; transformar; (mec.) tornear; invertir (posición); revolver (en la mente); doblar (una esquina, etc.).—to t. against, predisponer en contra de; causar aversión a o contra.—to t. around, voltear, dar vuelta a.—to t. aside, desviar, hacer a un lado.— to t. away, despedir, echar; desviar. —to t. back, devolver, restituir; volver atrás.—to t. down, plegar, doblar; poner boca abajo; bajar, disminuir (intensidad de una llama, etc.); (fam.) abandonar; rechazar, rehusar.—to t. from, desviar o alejar de.—to t. in, replegar; doblar hacia adentro; entregar.—to t. into, convertir en, cambiar en.—to t. off, cortar (el agua, el vapor, etc.); cerrar (la llave del agua, etc.); desconectar o apagar (la luz, el radio, etc.); (mec.) tornear.—to t. on, abrir (la llave del

agua, etc.); dar (vapor, etc.); conectar o encender (la luz, el radio, etc.); establecer el servicio (de electricidad, etc.).—to t. out, echar, expeler, arrojar; sacar hacia afuera; apagar (la luz, etc.); producir; volver al revés; doblar, torcer; echar al campo (los animales).—to t. over, transferir, pasar, trasladar; invertir, volcar; revolver.—to t. up, voltear; levantar; cavar (el suelo); arremangar; subir (el cuello).—vi. girar, rodar, voltear, torcer, seguir otra dirección; voltearse; convertirse en; ponerse (pálido, colorado, etc.); mudar (de posición, opinión, etc.). —my head turns (round), se me va la cabeza.—to t. about o around, volverse; voltearse.—to t. against, volverse contra.—to t. aside, desviarse.—to t. back, retroceder; volverse.—to t. down a street, torcer por una calle.—to t. in, guarecerse; entrar; llegar a casa; (fam.) irse a la cama.—to t. into, entrar en; transformarse en.—to t. off, torcer, desviarse.—to t. on, depender de; volverse contra; acometer a.—to t. out, resultar; asistir, acudir; estar vuelto hacia afuera; (fam.) salir de casa; levantarse.—to t. over, revolverse, dar vueltas; volcarse (un auto, etc.).—to t. short, dar media vuelta. —to t. to, recurrir o acudir a; dirigirse hacia o a; convertirse en; redundar en.—to t. up, acontecer; aparecer; tirar hacia arriba (la nariz).—to t. upon, estribar, depender de; recaer sobre.—s. vuelta, giro; rodeo; recodo; turno, tanda; lance; ocasión; cambio, mudanza; torcedura; curso, dirección; fase, aspecto, cariz; proceder, procedimiento; partida o pasada (buena o mala) hecha a alguno; inclinación, propensión; giro de frase; vuelta, paseo corto; (teat.) pieza corta; (dep.) contienda, partido; (com.) transacción.—a friendly t., un favor. —at every t., a cada instante.— to take another t., cambiar de aspecto, tomar otro sesgo o cariz.—to take turns, turnarse, alternar.

turnbuckle [tœ́rnbʌkl], s. (mec.) torniquete.—turncoat [tœ́rnkọut], s. desertor, renegado, tránsfuga.— turner [tœ́rnœ(r)], s. (mec.) tornero.

turnip [tœ́rnịp], s. nabo.

turnover [tœ́rnọuvœ(r)], a. doblado o vuelto hacia abajo.—s. vuelco, voltereta; (com.) movimiento de mercancías; ciclo de compra y venta; cambio (de personal); reorganización; empleo parcial turnado.

turnpike [tœ́rnpajk], s. camino o barrera de portazgo.

turnstile [tœ́rnstaįl], *s.* torniquete (en una entrada, etc.).—**turntable** [tœ́rn- teįbl], *s.* placa giratoria; platillo del gramófono.

turpentine [tœ́rpentaįn], *s.* trementina; aguarrás.—*oil of t.,* aguarrás.

turquoise [tœ́rkwoįz], *s.* (min.) turquesa.

turret [tœ́rįt], *s.* torre(cilla); (fort.) roqueta; (mar. y aer.) torre blindada.

turtle [tœ́rtl], *s.* tortuga de mar, carey.— —**dove** [-dʌv], *s.* tórtola.

tusk [tʌsk], *s.* colmillo (de elefante, jabalí, etc.).

tussle [tʌ́sl], *s.* lucha, agarrada.—*vi.* forcejear, tener una agarrada.

tutor [tįútǫ(r)], *s.* tutor, ayo, preceptor; (for.) curador.—*vt.* enseñar, instruir.— —**ing** [-įŋ], *s.* instrucción.

tuxedo [taksídou], *s.* "smoking", traje de media etiqueta.

tweed [twid], *s.* paño de lana de dos colores.—*a.* hecho de este paño.

tweezers [twízœrz], *s. pl.* tenacillas, pinzas.

Twelfth-night [twélfθ náįt], *s.* pascua, víspera del día de los Reyes.

twice [twaįs], *adv.* dos veces; al doble.

twig [twįg], *s.* (bot.) ramita, vástago; varilla.

twilight [twáįlaįt], *s.* crepúsculo.—*by t.,* entre dos luces.—*a.* oscuro, sombrío.

twin [twįn], *s. y a.* gemelo, mellizo.

twine [twaįn], *vt.* retorcer; enroscar. —*vi.* enroscarse; ensortijarse; caracolear.—*to t. about,* abrazar.—*s.* cuerda, cordel.

twinge [twįndż], *vt. y vi.* causar o sentir un dolor agudo; atormentar; sufrir. —*s.* dolor agudo, punzada; remordimiento.

twinkle [twíŋkl], *vt. y vi.* destellar, (hacer) centellear, rutilar, titilar; (hacer) parpadear, pestañear.—*s.* destello, centelleo; pestañeo; guiño, guiñada; momento, instante.

twirl [twœrl], *vt. y vi.* (hacer) girar.—*s.* rotación, vuelta; rasgueo.

twist [twįst], *vt.* (re)torcer, enroscar, entretejer, enrollar; doblar, doblegar; trenzar; ceñir.—*vi.* enroscarse, torcerse, envolverse; virar; ensortijarse; serpentear, caracolear.—*s.* torsión, torcedura; tirón, sacudida; cordoncillo; peculiaridad; contorsión, quiebro; rosca de pan, pan retorcido; efecto dado a la pelota (en baseball).

twitch [twįch], *vt.* tirar o sacudir bruscamente.—*vi.* crisparse.—*s.* tirón, sacudida; contracción espasmódica.— —**ing** [twįchįŋ], *s.* tic nervioso.

twitter [twįtœ(r)], *vi.* gorjear (pájaros); temblar de agitación.—*s.* gorjeo; inquietud.

twofold [tufóųld], *a.* doble; duplicado:

de dos clases o aspectos.—*adv.* duplicadamente, al doble.

tycoon [taįkún], *s.* (E.U., fam.) magnate industrial.

type [taįp], *s.* tipo.—*vt. y vi.* mecanografiar.— —**write** [-raįt], *vti. y vii.* [10] mecanografiar.- —**writer** [táįp- raįtœ(r)], *s.* máquina de escribir.— —**writing** [-raįtįŋ], *s.* mecanografía; trabajo de mecanógrafo.- —**written** [táįprįtn], *pp.* de TO TYPEWRITE.—*a.* mecanografiado.— —**wrote** [táįprouṭ], *pret.* de TO TYPEWRITE.

typhoid [táįfoįd], *a.* (med.) tifoideo. —*s.* fiebre tifoidea.

typhoon [taįfún], *s.* tifón.

typhus [táįfʌs], *s.* (med.) tifus, (Am.) tifo.

typical [típįkąl], *a.* típico.—**typify** [típįfaį], *vti.* [7] representar, ejemplificar, simbolizar.

typist [táįpįst], *s.* mecanógrafo.

tyrannical [tįrǽnįkąl], *a.* tiránico, tirano.—**tyranny** [tírąnį], *s.* tiranía. —**tyrant** [táįrąnt], *s.* tirano.

U

udder [ʌ́dœ(r)], *s.* ubre.

ugliness [ʌ́glįnįs], *s.* fealdad; fiereza. —**ugly** [ʌ́glį], *a.* feo; repugnante; perverso; fiero; insolente, rudo; peligroso.

ulcer [ʌ́lsœ(r)], *s.* úlcera, llaga.- —**ate** [-eįt], *vt. y vi.* ulcerar(se).

ulterior [ʌltírįǫ(r)], *a.* ulterior.— **ultimate** [ʌ́ltįmįt], *a.* último, final; fundamental; primario.

ultrasonic [ʌltrasánįk], *a.* ultrasónico. —**ultraviolet** [ʌltrąvájolįt], *a.* ultravioleta.

umbilical [ʌmbílįkąl], *a.* umbilical; central.

umbrella [ʌmbrélą], *s.* paraguas; sombrilla.

umpire [ʌ́mpaįr], *s.* árbitro; arbitrador. —*vt. y vi.* arbitrar.

unable [ʌnéįbl], *a.* inhábil, incapaz, impotente; imposibilitado.—*to be u.,* no poder, serle a uno imposible.

unabridged [ʌnąbrídżd], *a.* íntegro, completo, sin abreviar.

unadulterated [ʌnądʌ́ltœreįtįd], *a.* genuino, puro, sin mezcla.

unaffected [ʌnąféktįd], *a.* inafectado; franco, natural; impasible.

unanimity [yunąnímįtį], *s.* unanimidad. —**unanimous** [yųnǽnįmʌs], *a.* unánime.

unanswerable [ʌnǽnsœrąbl], *a.* incontestable, incontrovertible.

unarmed [ʌnármd], *a.* desarmado, indefenso, inerme.

unassuming [ʌnąsiúmįŋ], *a.* modesto.

unattainable [ʌnətéinəbl], a. inasequible, irrealizable.

unattractive [ʌnətréktiv], a. desagradable, poco atractivo.

unauthorized [ʌnɔ́θəraizd], a. sin autorización.

unavailable [ʌnəvéiləbl], a. inasequible.
—unavailing [ʌnəvéiliŋ], a. inútil, vano, infructuoso.

unavoidable [ʌnəvɔ́idəbl], a. inevitable, ineludible.

unaware [ʌnəwér], a. ignorante o inconsciente de, ajeno a.

unbalanced [ʌnbǽlənst], a. desequilibrado; (fam.) chiflado; (com.) no balanceado.

unbearable [ʌnbérəbl], a. intolerable, insufrible.

unbecoming [ʌnbikʌ́miŋ], a. indecoroso; impropio, indigno; que sienta mal (vestido, etc.).

unbending [ʌnbéndiŋ], a. inflexible.

unbias(s)ed [ʌnbáiəst], a. imparcial.

unbound [ʌnbáund], a. no encuadernado, en rústica; suelto, desatado.

unbreakable [ʌnbréikəbl], a. irrompible; impenetrable.—unbroken [ʌnbróukn], a. intacto, entero; inviolado; continuo; invicto; indómito.

unbutton [ʌnbʌ́tn], vt. desabotonar, desabrochar.

uncanny [ʌnkǽni], a. misterioso, pavoroso.

unceasing [ʌnsísiŋ], a. incesante.— —ly [-li], adv. sin cesar.

uncertain [ʌnsɜ́rtən], a. incierto; perplejo, indeciso.— —ty [-ti], s. incertidumbre; (lo) incierto; irresolución; inseguridad.

unchangeable [ʌnchéindʒəbl], a. inalterable, inmutable; igual.—unchanged [ʌnchéindʒd], a. inalterado.

uncharitable [ʌnchǽritəbl], a. no caritativo, duro.

unchastity [ʌnchǽstiti], s. incontinencia, impureza.

unchecked [ʌnchékt], a. desenfrenado, sin control.

uncivil [ʌnsívil], a. incivil, descortés, grosero.— —ized [-aizd], a. bárbaro, salvaje.

unclassifiable [ʌnklǽsifaiəbl], a. inclasificable.

uncle [ʌ́ŋkl], s. tío.

unclean [ʌnklín], a. sucio, desaseado, impuro; obsceno.

unclothe [ʌnklóuð], vti. [4] desnudar, quitar la ropa a.

uncoil [ʌnkɔ́il], vt. desenrollar.

uncollectable [ʌnkəléktəbl], a. incobrable.

uncombed [ʌnkóumd], a. despeinado.

uncomfortable [ʌnkʌ́mfərtəbl], a. incómodo, molesto; intranquilo; indispuesto, con malestar.

uncommon [ʌnkámən], a. poco común, raro, infrecuente.

unconcern [ʌnkənsɜ́rn], s. indiferencia, frialdad.

unconditional [ʌnkəndíʃənəl], a. absoluto, incondicional; a discreción.

uncongenial [ʌnkəndʒíniəl], a. antipático, incompatible.

unconnected [ʌnkənéktid], a. inconexo.

unconquerable [ʌnkáŋkœrəbl], a. invencible, insuperable, inconquistable.

unconscious [ʌnkánʃʌs], a. inconsciente; privado, sin conocimiento; que ignora; desconocido, involuntario.— *the u.*, (psic.) lo inconsciente.— —ness [-nis], s. insensibilidad; inconsciencia.

unconstitutional [ʌnkanstitjúʃənəl], a. inconstitucional.— —ity [ʌnkanstitiuʃənǽliti], s. inconstitucionalidad.

unconventional [ʌnkənvénʃənəl], a. despreocupado, informal, libre.

uncork [ʌnkɔ́rk], vt. descorchar, destapar.

uncouth [ʌnkúθ], a. tosco, zafio, grosero.

uncover [ʌnkʌ́vœ(r)], vt. destapar, descubrir; desabrigar; poner al descubierto.—vi. descubrirse, desabrigarse.

unction [ʌ́ŋkʃən], s. unción, ungimiento; untura, untamiento; ungüento; (igl.) extremaunción; fervor; divina gracia.—unctuous [ʌ́ŋkchuʌs], a. untuoso, craso; zalamero.

uncultivated [ʌnkʌ́ltiveitid], a. yermo, inculto; rústico, grosero.

uncultured [ʌnkʌ́lchɜrd], a. inculto, ignorante.

uncut [ʌnkʌ́t], a. sin cortar; sin tallar, en bruto (gemas).

undamaged [ʌndǽmidʒd], a. ileso, indemne.

undaunted [ʌndɔ́ntid], a. denodado, impávido, intrépido.

undecided [ʌndisáidid], a. indeciso; irresoluto.

undecipherable [ʌndisáifœrəbl], a. indescifrable.

undefinable [ʌndifáinəbl], a. indefinible.

undeniable [ʌndináiəbl], a. innegable.

under [ʌ́ndœ(r)], a. inferior, de abajo. —*u.-secretary*, subsecretario.—*adv.* debajo; más abajo; menos.—*prep.* debajo de, bajo; so; menos de o que; a; en; en tiempo de, en la época de; conforme a, según.—*to be u. an obligation*, deber favores, estar obligado.—*u. a cloud*, en aprietos. —*u. arms*, bajo las armas.—*u. color of*, so color de.—*u. consideration*, en consideración.—*u. contract*, bajo contrato; conforme al contrato.—*u.*

cover, al abrigo, a cubierto.—*u. fire*, en combate; bajo el fuego del enemigo; (fig.) atacado, criticado, en aprietos.—*u. steam*, al vapor.— *u. way*, en camino, en marcha; andando; principiando.— —*brush* [-brʌš], *s.* maleza, broza.— —*clothes* [-klouðz], —*clothing* [-klouðiŋ], *s.* ropa interior.— —*dog* [-dog], *s.* el que pierde; el más débil.—*the underdogs*, los de abajo.— —*estimate* [-éstimeit], *vt.* menospreciar, subestimar.— —*fed* [-féd], *a.* malnutrido.— —*go* [-góu], *vti.* [10] sufrir, padecer; aguantar, sobrellevar; pasar por, ser sometido a; arrostrar.— —*gone* [-gon], *pp.* de TO UNDERGO.— —*graduate* [-grédžuit], *s.* estudiante universitario no graduado (E.U.); estudiante preuniversitario o de bachillerato.— —*ground* [-graund], *a.* subterráneo; secreto.—*u. movement*, organización clandestina de resistencia política o patriótica.—*adv.* bajo tierra; ocultamente.— —*grown* [-groun], *a.* de pequeña estatura, de desarrollo incompleto.— —*handed* [-hǽnded], *a.* disimulado, clandestino.— —*line* [-láin], *vt.* subrayar.— —*lying* [-láiiŋ], *a.* subyacente; fundamental.— —*mine* [-máin], *vt.* socavar, minar, zapar; debilitar, arruinar subrepticiamente.— —*neath* [-níθ], *adv.* debajo.—*prep.* debajo de, bajo.— —*paid* [-péid], *pret.* y *pp.* de TO UNDERPAY.— —*underpay* [Andœrpéi], *vti.* [10] pagar insuficientemente.— —*rate* [-réit], *vt.* menospreciar, desestimar, rebajar.— —*undersell* [-sél], *vti.* [10] malbaratar; vender a menor precio que.— —*shirt* [-šœrt], *s.* camiseta.— —*sign* [-sáin], *vt.* su(b)scribir.—*the undersigned*, el que firma, el infrascrito, el suscrito, el abajo firmado.— —*sized* [-sáizd], *a.* de tamaño o estatura menor que lo normal.— —*skirt* [-skœrt], *s.* enagua(s); refajo, sayuela.— —*sold* [-sóuld], *pret.* y *pp.* de TO UNDERSELL.

understand [Andœrstǽnd], *vti.* y *vii.* [10] entender, comprender; saber, ser sabedor, hacerse cargo, tener conocimiento de, tener entendido (que); sobrentender.— —*able* [-ǽbl], *a.* comprensible.— —*ing* [-iŋ], *s.* entendimiento, inteligencia; modo de ver o entender; comprensión; acuerdo, arreglo, armonía, mutua comprensión. —*a.* entendedor, inteligente, comprensivo.—**understood** [Andœrstúd], *pret.* y *pp.* de TO UNDERSTAND.

understudy [Andœrstádi], *s.* (teat.) actor suplente.

undertake [Andœrtéik], *vti.* y *vii.* [10] emprender, acometer, intentar;

comprometerse a, responder de, encargarse de.—**undertaken** [Andœrtéikn], *pp.* de TO UNDERTAKE.— —*r* [Andœrtéikœ(r)], *s.* empresario de pompas fúnebres; contratista.— **undertaking** [Andœrtéikiŋ], *s.* empresa; contratación; empresa funeraria; (for.) compromiso, promesa; empeño o garantía.—**undertook** [Andœrtúk], *pret.* de TO UNDERTAKE.

undertow [Andœrtou], *s.* resaca.

undervalue [Andœrvélyu], *vt.* desestimar, menospreciar, despreciar; tasar en menos del valor real.

underwear [Andœrwer], *s.* ropa interior.

underwent [Andœrwént], *pret.* de TO UNDERGO.

underworld [Andœrwœrld], *s.* hampa, vida del vicio, bajos fondos de la sociedad; el mundo terrenal; antípodas; averno, infierno.

undeserved [Andizœrvd], *a.* inmerecido.— —*undeserving* [Andizœrviŋ], *a.* indigno.

undesirable [Andizáirabl], *a.* indeseable; inconveniente, desventajoso; pernicioso.

undetermined [Anditœrmind], *a.* indeterminado.

undeveloped [Andivélopt], *a.* no desarrollado, rudimentario; inexplotado.

undid [Andíd], *pret.* de TO UNDO.

undignified [Andígnifaid], *a.* indecoroso, falto de dignidad.

undisciplined [Andísiplind], *a.* indisciplinado; falto de corrección; sin instrucción.

undisturbed [Andistœrbd], *a.* imperturbable, impasible; intacto, sin cambio.

undo [Andú], *vti.* [10] anular, desvirtuar, contrarrestar; reparar (un daño); arruinar, perder; causar pesadumbre a; deshacer; desatar; (mec.) desmontar.—**undone** [Andán], *pp.* de TO UNDO.—*a.* sin hacer; sin terminar; deshecho.—*to be u.*, estar perdido o arruinado.—*to come u.*, deshacerse, desatarse.—*to leave nothing u.*, no dejar nada por hacer.

undoubtedly [Andáutidli], *adv.* indudablemente.

undress [Andrés], *vt.* desnudar, desvestir; (cir.) desvendar.—*vi.* desnudarse.—*s.* paños menores; ropa de casa.

undue [Andú], *a.* indebido, desmedido; ilícito, injusto; (com.) por vencer.

undulate [Andjuleit], *vi.* ondular, ondear, fluctuar.—*vt.* hacer ondear. —*a.* [Andjulit], ondeado, ondulado.

unduly [Andjúli], *adv.* indebidamente; irregularmente, ilícitamente.

undying [Andáiiŋ], *a.* imperecedero.

unearth [ʌnɛ́rθ], *vt.* desenterrar.

uneasily [ʌnízịlị], *adv.* inquietamente; incómodamente, penosamente.—

uneasiness [ʌnízịnịs], *s.* inquietud, desasosiego, ansiedad; incomodidad, disgusto, malestar.—**uneasy** [unízị], *a.* inquieto, ansioso; molesto, incómodo; desgarbado; difícil, pesado. —*to be u.*, no tenerlas todas consigo.

uneducated [ʌnɛ́dʒukejtịd], *a.* falto de educación, indocto, ignorante.

unemployed [ʌnịmplóịd], *a.* sin empleo, desocupado, cesante; ocioso.—**unemployment** [ʌnịmplóịmẹnt], *s.* desempleo, desocupación, cesantía, paro forzoso, ociosidad.

unequal [ʌníkwạl], *a.* desigual, dispar; ineficaz, insuficiente, inferior; desproporcionado; injusto, parcial; falto de uniformidad.—*to be u. to*, no tener fuerzas para, ser incapaz de.

unerring [ʌnɛ́rịŋ], *a.* infalible.

uneven [ʌnívẹn], *a.* desigual; escabroso; irregular, poco uniforme; non, impar (número).— —**ness** [-nịs], *s.* desigualdad; escabrosidad, aspereza; abolladura; desnivel; irregularidad.

unexpected [ʌnịkspéktịd], *a.* inesperado, impensado; repentino.

unfailing [ʌnféịlịŋ], *a.* inagotable; indefectible; seguro, infalible.

unfair [ʌnfɛ́r], *a.* doble, falso, desleal; injusto; (for.) leonino.

unfaithful [ʌnféịθfụl], *a.* infiel; desleal; inexacto.— —**ness** [-nịs], *s.* infidelidad, deslealtad; inexactitud.

unfamiliar [ʌnfạmíljạ(r)], *a.* poco familiar, poco común; no conocido; poco conocedor.

unfashionable [ʌnfǽʃọnạbl], *a.* pasado de moda.

unfasten [ʌnfǽsn], *vt.* desatar, desabrochar, desenganchar, desprender, soltar, aflojar, zafar.

unfathomable [ʌnfǽðọmạbl], *a.* insondable; sin fondo; impenetrable.

unfavorable [ʌnféịvọrạbl], *a.* desfavorable, contrario, adverso.

unfeeling [ʌnfílịŋ], *a.* insensible, impasible, empedernido.

unfit [ʌnfít], *a.* inepto, incapaz, incompetente; impropio, inoportuno; inadaptable, inadecuado, inservible.

unfold [ʌnfóụld], *vt.* desplegar, desdoblar, desenvolver, desarrollar, abrir; extender; descifrar, poner en claro; manifestar, explicar.—*vi.* abrirse, desenvolverse, desarrollarse.

unforeseen [ʌnfɔrsín], *a.* imprevisto, impensado, inesperado.

unforgettable [ʌnforgétạbl], *a.* inolvidable.

unforgivable [ʌnforgívạbl], *a.* imperdonable.

unfortunate [ʌnfɔ́rchụnịt], *a.* desafortunado, infeliz, desventurado; infausto, aciago.—*s.* desventurado, desgraciado.— —**ly** [-lị], *adv.* por desgracia.

unfounded [ʌnfáụndịd], *a.* infundado; (for.) improcedente.

unfriendly [ʌnfréndlị], *a.* poco amistoso; hostil, enemigo; desfavorable, perjudicial.—*an u. act*, un acto hostil.

unfurl [ʌnfɛ́rl], *vt.* desplegar, desarrollar, desdoblar, extender.

unfurnished [ʌnfɛ́rnịʃt], *a.* desamueblado; desprovisto.

ungrateful [ʌngréịtfụl], *a.* desagradecido, ingrato; desagradable.

unguent [ʌ́ŋgwẹnt], *s.* ungüento.

unhappiness [ʌnhǽpịnịs], *s.* infelicidad, desgracia, desdicha.—**unhappy** [ʌnhǽpị], *a.* infeliz, desgraciado, desdichado; infausto, aciago.

unharmed [ʌnhármd], *a.* ileso, incólume, sano y salvo; a salvo, sin daño.

unharness [ʌnhárnịs], *vt.* desguarnecer, desenganchar.

unhealthy [ʌnhélθị], *a.* enfermizo, achacoso; insalubre, malsano.

unheard [ʌnhɛ́rd], *a.* que no se ha oído. —*u. of*, inaudito, desconocido.

unhinge [ʌnhíndʒ], *vt.* desquiciar, sacar de quicio; desequilibrar, trastornar (el juicio).

unhitch [ʌnhích], *vt.* descolgar, desatar; desenganchar, desaparejar (bestias).

unhook [ʌnhúk], *vt.* desenganchar, desabrochar; descolgar.

unhurt [ʌnhɛ́rt], *a.* ileso, indemne.

uniform [yúnịfɔrm], *a.* uniforme; semejante; acorde; constante.—*s.* uniforme.—*in full u.*, de gran uniforme, de gala.—*vt.* uniformar; hacer uniforme; vestir de uniforme.— —**ity** [yunịfɔ́rmịtị], *s.* uniformidad, uniformación.—**unify** [yúnịfaị], *vti.* [7] unificar, unir.

unilateral [yunịlǽtẹrạl], *a.* unilateral.

unimaginable [ʌnịmǽdʒịnạbl], *a.* inimaginable.

unimportant [ʌnịmpɔ́rtạnt], *a.* de poca o ninguna importancia, insignificante.

uninhabitable [ʌnịnhǽbịtạbl], *a.* inhabitable.—**uninhabited** [ʌnịnhǽbịtịd], *a.* deshabitado.

uninjured [ʌníndʒụrd], *a.* ileso, incólume; sin daño.

unintelligible [ʌnịntélịdʒịbl], *a.* ininteligible.

unintentional [ʌnịnténsọnạl], *a.* involuntario; no intencional.

union [yúnjọn], *s.* unión; conformidad, concordia; mancomunidad, fusión; (E.U.) las estrellas de la bandera nacional; sindicato, gremio.

unique [yụník], *a.* único en su género, original.

unison [yúnịsọn], *s.* unisonancia; (fig.)

concordancia, armonía.—*in u.*, todos juntos, a una.

unit [yúnįt], *s.* unidad.—*a.* individual; unitario.

Unitarian [yunįtérįan], *a.* y *s.* (igl.) unitario.

unite [yųnáįt], *vt.* unir, reunir; avenir; concordar.—*vi.* unirse; concertarse. —**unity** [yúnįtį], *s.* unidad; unión, concordia; (mat.) la unidad.

universal [yunįvérsal], *a.* universal. —**universe** [yúnįvərs], *s.* universo. —**university** [yunįvérsįtį], *s.* universidad.—*a.* universitario.

unjust [Andžást], *a.* injusto.— —**ifiable** [Andžástįfáįabl], *a.* injustificable.

unkempt [Ankémpt], *a.* desgreñado; desaseado; tosco.

unkind [Ankáįnd], *a.* duro, brutal, intratable.— —**ness** [-nįs], *s.* dureza, brutalidad, falta de amabilidad.

unknown [Annóųn], *a.* desconocido, ignoto.—*u. quantity*, (mat.) incógnita. —*u. to one*, sin saberlo uno.—*s.* cosa o persona desconocida; (mat.) incógnita.

unless [Anlés], *conj.* a menos que, a no ser que, como no sea, no siendo; salvo, con excepción de que, excepto, si no, si no es que.

unlike [Anláįk], *a.* diferente, dispar. —*adv.* de otro modo; a diferencia de.— —**ly** [-lį], *adv.* improbablemente.—*a.* inverosímil, improbable, difícil.

unlimited [Anlímįtįd], *a.* ilimitado; sin restricción.

unload [Anlóųd], *vt.* descargar; exonerar, aligerar; (fam., com.) deshacerse de una mercancía.—*vi.* descargar.

unlock [Anlák], *vt.* abrir (una cerradura, cerrojo, etc.); dar libre acceso; revelar (secretos).

unlucky [Anlákį], *a.* de mala suerte; desgraciado; infausto; de mal agüero.

unmanageable [Anmǽnįdžabl], *a.* inmanejable.

unmarried [Anmǽrįd], *a.* soltero.

unmerciful [Anmǽrsįfųl], *a.* inclemente, despiadado; cruel.

unmerited [Anmérįtįd], *a.* inmerecido.

unmistakable [Anmįstéįkabl], *a.* inequívoco, inconfundible, evidente.

unmoved [Anmúvd], *a.* inmovible, fijo; inmutable; inflexible, inexorable.

unnatural [Annǽchųral], *a.* forzado, artificial o afectado; contranatural, monstruoso; desnaturalizado.

unnecessary [Annéseserį], *a.* innecesario, inútil, superfluo.

unnoticed [Annóųtįst], *a.* inadvertido.

unoccupied [Anákįųpaįd], *a.* desocupado o vacante.

unofficial [Anǫfíśal], *a.* oficioso, extraoficial.

unorthodox [Anórθǫdaks], *a.* heterodoxo.

unpack [Anpǽk], *vt.* desempaquetar, desembalar.

unpaid [Anpéįd], *a.* no pagado o por pagar.

unparalleled [Anpǽraleld], *a.* único, sin igual, sin paralelo.

unpardonable [Anpárdǫnabl], *a.* imperdonable; (mat.) la unidad.

unpatriotic [Anpeįtrįátįk], *a.* antipatriótico.

unpaved [Anpéįvd], *a.* sin pavimentar, desempedrado.

unpleasant [Anplézant], *a.* desagradable.— —**ness** [-nįs], *s.* calidad de desagradable; desagrado o desazón; (fam.) riña, desavenencia.

unpopular [Anpápyǫlǫ(r)], *a.* impopular.— —**ity** [Anpapyǫlérįtį], *s.* impopularidad.

unprecedented [Anprésędentįd], *a.* sin precedente, inaudito, nunca visto.

unprepared [Anprįpérd], *a.* desprevenido, desapercibido.

unprincipled [Anprínsįpld], *a.* sin principios, sin conciencia.

unprofitable [Anpráfįtabl], *a.* no lucrativo; inútil, vano.

unprotected [Anprǫtéktįd], *a.* sin protección, sin defensa.

unpublished [Anpáblįšt], *a.* inédito, no publicado.

unqualified [Ankwálįfaįd], *a.* inepto; incompetente; sin títulos; sin reservas, incondicional; entero, completo.

unquestionable [Ankwéschǫnabl], *a.* incuestionable, indiscutible.

unravel [Anrǽvl], *vti.* [2] desenredar, desenmarañar; aclarar; descifrar. —*vii.* desenredarse; desenlazarse.

unreal [Anríal], *a.* irreal, quimérico, ilusorio; inmaterial, incorpóreo; insincero.— —**ity** [Anríélįtį], *s.* irrealidad.

unreasonable [Anrízǫnabl], *a.* fuera de razón, irrazonable; irracional; exorbitante.—**unreasoning** [Anrízǫnįŋ], *a.* irracional.

unrecognizable [Anrékǫgnaįzabl], *a.* irreconocible; desconocido.

unrefined [Anrįfáįnd], *a.* no refinado, impuro, en bruto; inculto, grosero, ordinario.

unreliable [Anrįláįabl], *a.* indigno de confianza, informal.

unrepentant [Anrįpéntant], *a.* impenitente.

unrest [Anrést], *s.* inquietud, desasosiego.

unripe [Anráįp], *a.* verde, agraz; prematuro.

unrivaled [Anráįvald], *a.* sin rival, sin par.

unroll [ʌnróul], *vt.* desarrollar, desenrollar, desenvolver, desplegar.—*vi.* abrirse, desarrollarse.

unruly [ʌnrúli], *a.* indócil, inmanejable, ingobernable, indómito; revoltoso, levantisco; intratable; desarreglado.

unsafe [ʌnséif], *a.* peligroso, inseguro.

unsalable [ʌnséilạbl], *a.* invendible.

unsanitary [ʌnsǽniteri], *a.* antihigiénico; insalubre.

unsatisfactory [ʌnsætisfǽktori], *a.* insatisfactorio; malo, inaceptable.

unscrew [ʌnskrú], *vt.* des(a)tornillar, desenroscar.

unscrupulous [ʌnskrúpiulʌs], *a.* sin escrúpulos, desaprensivo.

unseasonable [ʌnsízọnạbl], *a.* intempestivo; prematuro; indebido, inconveniente.—*at u. hours,* a deshora. —**unseasoned** [ʌnsízọnd], *a.* sin sazonar, insípido; verde (madera).

unseat [ʌnsit], *vt.* desarzonar; echar abajo (de un puesto).

unselfish [ʌnsélfiʃ], *a.* desinteresado, generoso, abnegado.——**ness** [-nis], *s.* desinterés, generosidad, abnegación.

unserviceable [ʌnsǿrvisạbl], *a.* inútil, inservible.

unsettle [ʌnsétl], *vt.* perturbar, trastornar.——**d** [-d], *a.* inestable, variable, inconstante; desarreglado, descompuesto; no establecido, no instalado, sin residencia fija; indeciso; incierto; (com.) por pagar, no liquidado, pendiente; turbio, revuelto; inhabitado, despoblado; lunático.

unshaken [ʌnʃéikn], *a.* firme, inmovible.

unsheltered [ʌnséltœrd], *a.* desamparado, desvalido.—**unsheltering** [ʌnséltœriŋ], *a.* inhospitalario.

unsightly [ʌnsáitli], *a.* feo, repugnante.

unskilled [ʌnskíld], *a.* inexperto.— **unskillful** [ʌnskílful], *a.* inhábil, desmañado.

unsociable [ʌnsóuʃạbl], *a.* insociable, huraño.

unsophisticated [ʌnsọfístikeitid], *a.* sencillo, ingenuo.

unsound [ʌnsáund], *a.* defectuoso, erróneo, falso; poco firme, falto de fuerza.

unspeakable [ʌnspíkạbl], *a.* indecible; inefable; atroz.

unstable [ʌnstéibl], *a.* inestable.

unsteady [ʌnstédi], *a.* inestable, inseguro, no firme; vacilante, tambaleante; inconstante, veleidoso.

unsuccessful [ʌnsʌksésful], *a.* infructuoso, sin éxito; desafortunado.

unsuitable [ʌnsiútạbl], *a.* inapropiado, inadaptable; incompetente.

unsuspected [ʌnsʌspéktid], *a.* insospechado.—**unsuspecting** [ʌnsʌspéktiŋ], *a.* cándido, confiado.

untamed [ʌntéimd], *a.* indómito, bravío, cerrero.

untaught [ʌntót], *a.* indocto; no enseñado, sin instrucción, ignorante.

unthinkable [ʌnθíŋkạbl], *a.* inimaginable.—**unthinking** [ʌnθíŋkiŋ], *a.* descuidado, irreflexivo.

untidy [ʌntáidi], *a.* desaliñado, desarreglado, falto de pulcritud.

untie [ʌntái], *vt.* desatar, desligar; deshacer (un nudo); aflojar, soltar, zafar.

until [ʌntíl], *prep.* hasta.—*conj.* hasta que.—*not u.,* no antes que.

untimely [ʌntáimli], *a.* intempestivo, inoportuno, prematuro.—*adv.* intempestivamente; a destiempo, prematuramente.

untiring [ʌntáiriŋ], *a.* infatigable.

untold [ʌntóuld], *a.* nunca dicho; indecible, incalculable.

untouchable [ʌntʌ́chạbl], *a.* intocable, intangible.—**untouched** [ʌntʌ́cht], *a.* intacto, ileso; insensible, impasible.

untoward [ʌntórd], *a.* adverso, desfavorable.

untrained [ʌntréind], *a.* indisciplinado; inexperto, imperito.

untranslatable [ʌntrænsléitạbl], *a.* intraducible.

untried [ʌntráid], *a.* no probado o ensayado; no experimentado; novel.

untroubled [ʌntrʌ́bld], *a.* no molestado o perturbado; tranquilo; claro, transparente.

untrue [ʌntrú], *a.* falso; mendaz; engañoso.

untruth [ʌntrúθ], *s.* falsedad, mentira; infidelidad.——**ful** [-ful], *a.* falso, mentiroso.

unused [ʌniúzd], *a.* inusitado, insólito; no usado, nuevo; desacostumbrado. —**unusual** [ʌniúʒuạl], *a.* raro, extraordinario, extraño; excepcional; insólito, inusitado; desacostumbrado.

unveil [ʌnvéil], *vt.* quitar el velo a, revelar, descubrir; inaugurar (un monumento).—*vi.* quitarse el velo, descubrirse.

unwary [ʌnwéri], *a.* incauto, imprudente, irreflexivo.

unwelcome [ʌnwélkʌm], *a.* mal recibido o acogido; desagradable, incómodo, importuno.

unwholesome [ʌnhóulsʌm], *a.* dañino, nocivo, malsano, insalubre.

unwieldy [ʌnwíldi], *a.* pesado, difícil de manejar.

unwilling [ʌnwíliŋ], *a.* renuente.——**ly** [-li], *adv.* de mala gana.——**ness** [-nis], *s.* mala gana, repugnancia, renuencia.

unwise [ʌnwáiz], *a.* imprudente; ignorante.

unwittingly [ʌnwítiŋli], *adv.* sin saber, inconscientemente.

unworthiness [ʌnwɚ́ðiɲis], *s.* indignidad, falta de mérito.—**unworthy** [ʌnwɚ́ði], *a.* indigno, desmerecedor.

unwrap [ʌnrǽp], *vti.* [1] desenvolver.

unwritten [ʌnrítn], *a.* no escrito; en blanco; tradicional.—*u. law,* derecho consuetudinario; derecho natural.

unyielding [ʌnyíldiŋ], *a.* inflexible, inexorable, inconmovible, firme; reacio, terco.

up [ʌp], *a.* que va hacia arriba; levantado (de la cama); empinado; erecto; ascendente (tren, etc.).—*adv.* arriba, hacia arriba, para arriba; en pie, derecho; de pie, levantado; (fam.) bien enterado, competente, a la altura de; llegado, acabado, concluido; enteramente, totalmente, completamente.—*it is all u.,* todo se acabó.—*time is u.,* se ha cumplido el tiempo; ha expirado el plazo; ha llegado la hora.—*to be u.* in u on, estar al corriente de, al día de o versado en.—*to be u. to,* ser suficiente o competente para; estar a la altura de; estar haciendo o urdiendo, andar (en travesuras, intrigas, etc.).—*to be u. to one,* depender de, ser asunto de, o tocarle a uno.—*u. above,* arriba, más arriba.—*u.-and-doing,* emprendedor, activo.—*u.-and-down,* vertical, de vaivén; (fam.) franco, claro.—*u. to,* hasta; capaz de; tramando; al corriente de, sabedor de.—*u. to date,* hasta la fecha.— *u.-to-date,* moderno, al día.—*what's u.?* ¿qué hay? ¿de qué se trata?— *prep.* hacia arriba de; a lo largo de; en lo alto de.—*u. one's sleeve,* en secreto, para sí.—*vti.* [1] subir, elevar; aumentar (precios, etc.).—*s.* prosperidad.—*ups and downs,* vaivenes, altibajos, vicisitudes.—*interj.* ¡arriba! ¡aúpa!

upbringing [ʌ́pbriŋiŋ], *s.* crianza, educación.

upheaval [ʌphíval], *s.* solevantamiento; trastorno, cataclismo.

upheld [ʌphéld], *pret.* y *pp.* de TO UPHOLD.

uphill [ʌphíl], *adv.* cuesta arriba.—*a.* ascendente; penoso, dificultoso.

uphold [ʌphóuld], *vti.* [10] sostener, apoyar, defender.

upholster [ʌphóulstœ(r)], *vt.* rellenar y cubrir muebles; tapizar; poner colgaduras, cortinas, etc.—**y** [-i], *s.* tapicería.

upkeep [ʌ́pkip], *s.* conservación, mantenimiento.

uplift [ʌplíft], *vt.* elevar, levantar, alzar.—*s.* [ʌ́plift], levantamiento, elevación.

upon [ʌpán], *prep.* en, sobre, encima de.

upper [ʌ́pœ(r)], *a.* superior, de encima o de arriba; (más) alto.—*s.* (fam.) litera alta.—*pl.* botines.—*on one's uppers,* (fam.) en aprietos, tronado, sin dinero.

upright [ʌ́prait], *a.* derecho, vertical, recto; probo, honrado.—*s.* montante, pieza vertical; soporte, apoyo.— **-ness** [-ɲis], *s.* calidad de vertical; rectitud, probidad.

uprising [ʌpráiziŋ], *s.* levantamiento (acto de levantar algo); levantamiento, insurrección; cuesta, pendiente.

uproar [ʌ́pror], *s.* grita, bulla, bullicio, conmoción; (fig.) rugido.— **-ious** [ʌprórias], *a.* ruidoso, tumultuoso; bullanguero.

uproot [ʌprút], *vt.* desarraigar.

upset [ʌpsét], *vti.* [9] trastornar, desbaratar; volcar, derribar; desconcertar, turbar; (mar.) zozobrar. —*vi.* volcarse; (mar.) zozobrar. —*pret.* y *pp.* de TO UPSET.—*a.* trastornado; volcado; turbado; erigido; fijo, determinado.—*u. price,* precio mínimo fijado en una subasta. —*s.* [ʌ́pset], vuelco; trastorno.

upside [ʌ́psaid], *s.* parte superior, lo de arriba.—*u. down,* lo de arriba abajo; al revés, invertido; (fam.) patas arriba; en confusión, trastornado.

upstairs [ʌ́pstɚz], *adv.* arriba, en el piso de arriba.—*a.* alto (piso, etc.); de arriba (de las escaleras).

upstart [ʌ́pstart], *a.* y *s.* advenedizo; encumbrado, presuntuoso.

upturn [ʌ́ptœrn], *s.* vuelta hacia arriba; alza.—*vt.* [ʌptɚrn], volver hacia arriba; trastornar; volcar.— **-ed** [ʌptɚ́rnd], *a.* respingada (nariz).

upward [ʌ́pwɚd], *a.* vuelto hacia arriba; ascendente.— **-(s)** [-(z)], *adv.* hacia arriba; más.—*from ten cents u.,* de diez centavos en adelante.

uranium [yuréɲiʌm], *s.* uranio.

urban [ɚ́ban], *a.* urbano.— **-e** [œrbéin], *a.* fino, cortés.— **-ity** [œrbǽɲiti], *s.* urbanidad.

urchin [œ́rchin], *s.* rapaz, granuja, pilluelo, golfillo; (zool.) erizo.

urge [œrdʒ], *vt.* urgir, apresurar, apremiar; incitar; acosar; solicitar; recomendar con ahinco.—*vi.* apresurarse; estimular; presentar argumentos o pretensiones.—*s.* impulso, estímulo; ganas.— **-ncy** [œ́rdʒensi], *s.* urgencia.— **-nt** [œ́rdʒent], *a.* urgente, apremiante.

urinal [yúriɲal], *s.* urinario.—**urinate** [yúriɲeit], *vt.* y *vi.* orinar.—**urine** [yúrin], *s.* orina, orines.

urn [œrn], *s.* urna; jarrón.

Uruguayan [yụṛọgwéi̯an, yụṛọgwái̯an], *a.* y *s.* uruguayo.

us [ʌs], *pron.* nos; nosotros.

usage [yúsi̯dʒ], *s.* trato, tratamiento; uso, usanza.—**use** [yus], *s.* uso; aprovechamiento; aplicación; servicio, utilidad, provecho; necesidad; ocasión de usar; costumbre, uso. —*no u.* (*of*) *talking*, es inútil discutirlo, eso no tiene discusión; sin duda, es claro que.—*to have no u. for*, no necesitar o no servirse de; (fam.) no tener muy buena opinión de, tener en poco.—*vt.* [yuz], usar, utilizar; hacer uso, servirse de; acostumbrar, soler.—*to u. up*, gastar, consumir, agotar; (fam.) rendir (de cansancio). —*vi.* soler, acostumbrar.—*he used to come every day*, el venía todos los días o acostumbraba venir todos los días.—*the city used to be smaller*, antes la ciudad era más pequeña. —**useful** [yúsfụl], *a.* útil, provechoso. —**usefulness** [yúsfụlni̯s], *s.* utilidad. —**useless** [yúsli̯s], *a.* inútil; ocioso; inservible; inepto.—**uselessness** [yúslịsni̯s], *s.* inutilidad.—**user** [yúzœ(r)], *s.* el que usa o utiliza; consumidor; comprador.

usher [ʌ́ʃœ(r)], *s.* (teat., etc.) acomodador; ujier.—*vt.* introducir, acomodar, acompañar; anunciar.

usual [yúʒụạl], *a.* usual, acostumbrado, común.—*as u.*, como de costumbre, como siempre.

usufruct [yúzụfrʌkt], *s.* usufructo.

usurer [yúʒọrœ(r)], *s.* usurero.— **usurious** [yuʒúri̯ʌs], *a.* usurario.

usurp [yuzœ́rp], *vt.* usurpar; arrogarse.— **er** [-œ(r)], *s.* usurpador.

usury [yúʒọri̯], *s.* usura.

utensil [yuténsịl], *s.* utensilio.—*pl.* útiles.

uterus [yútœrʌs], *s.* útero.

utilitarian [yutịlịtéri̯an], *a.* utilitario. —**utility** [yutʃlịti], *s.* utilidad; servicio.—**utilize** [yútịlai̯z], *vt.* utilizar, hacer uso de, aprovechar.

utmost [ʌ́tmoụst], *a.* extremo, sumo; mayor, más grande; más posible; más distante; último, postrero.—*s.* lo sumo, lo mayor, lo más.—*to the u.*, hasta no más.

utter [ʌ́tœ(r)], *a.* total, entero, cabal, completo; absoluto; terminante.—*vt.* proferir, pronunciar; decir, expresar; dar (un grito, etc.); descubrir, publicar, revelar; engañar, defraudar con (moneda falsa); hacer pasar fraudulentamente; emitir, poner en circulación.— **ance** [-ạns], *s.* pronunciación; expresión, lenguaje; aserción, declaración.— **ly** [-lị], *adv.* completamente, de remate.

uvula [yúvyọlạ], *s.* (anat.) campanilla, úvula, galillo.

V

vacancy [véi̯kạnsị], *s.* vacío; vacante; empleo vacante; local o cuarto desocupado.—**vacant** [véi̯kạnt], *a.* vacío, vacante; desocupado; libre. —**vacate** [véi̯kei̯t], *vt.* evacuar, dejar vacío; desocupar; abandonar; dejar vacante; (for.) anular, rescindir, revocar.—*vi.* salir, irse, marcharse; desalojar; vacar; desocupar.—**vacation** [vei̯kéi̯ʃọn], *s.* vacación, asueto; (for.) anulación, revocación.

vaccinate [vǽksi̯nei̯t], *vt.* vacunar.— **vaccination** [vǽksi̯néi̯ʃọn], *s.* vacunación, inoculación.—**vaccine** [vǽksin], *s.* vacuna.

vacillate [vǽsịlei̯t], *vi.* vacilar.—**vacillation** [vǽsịléi̯ʃọn], *s.* vacilación.

vacuum [vǽkyụạm], *s.* vacío.—*a.* de vacío; (mec.) aspirante.—*in a v.*, en el vacío.—*v. cleaner*, aspirador (de polvo), limpiador al vacío.

vagabond [vǽgạband], *a.* vagabundo, errante; fluctuante.—*s.* vago, (fam.) pelafustán.—**vagrancy** [véi̯grạnsi̯], *s.* vagancia.—**vagrant** [véi̯grạnt], *s.* y *a.* vago, vagabundo.

vague [vei̯g], *a.* vago, indefinido, impreciso; incierto; dudoso.- **ness** [véi̯gni̯s], *s.* vaguedad.

vain [vei̯n], *a.* vano, vanidoso; inútil; fútil, insustancial.—*in v.*, en vano.

valance [vǽlạns], *s.* cenefa, doselera.

Valencian [vạlénʃi̯ạn], *s.* y *a.* valenciano.

valentine [vǽlẹntai̯n], *s.* misiva o regalo del día 14 de Feb. (San Valentín); misiva anónima, jocosa o satírica.

valiant [vǽlyạnt], *a.* valiente, valeroso, bravo; (fam.) de puños.

valid [vǽli̯d], *a.* válido; valedero.— **ate** [-ei̯t], *vt.* validar.- **ity** [vạlídịtị], *s.* validez; fuerza legal.

valise [vạlís], *s.* maleta, valija, saco de viaje.

valley [vǽli̯], *s.* valle.

valor [vǽlọ(r)], *s.* valor, valentía, ánimo, fortaleza.- **ous** [-ʌs], *a.* valeroso, valiente, intrépido.

valuable [vǽlyụạbl], *a.* valioso; precioso, apreciable, preciado.—*s. pl.* joyas u otros objetos de valor.— **valuation** [vǽlyụéi̯ʃọn], *s.* justiprecio, tasación, valoración.—**value** [vǽlyụ], *s.* mérito, valor; precio, valuación; aprecio, estimación; (mus.) valor de una nota.—*vt.* tasar, valorar; hacer caso de, tener en mucho; considerar.

valve [vǽlv], *s.* válvula; ventalla; valva.

vamp [vǽmp], *s.* (fam.) sirena, mujer peligrosa.- **ire** [vǽmpai̯r], *s.*

vampiro; estafador; aventurero (apl. esp. a mujeres).

van [væn], *s.* vehículo (camión, etc.) cubierto para transportar muebles, etc.

vane [vein], *s.* veleta; aspa (de molino); paleta (de hélice).

vanguard [vǽngard], *s.* vanguardia.

vanilla [vǽnila], *s.* vainilla.

vanish [vǽnis], *vi.* desvanecerse, desaparecer, esfumarse.

vanity [vǽniti], *s.* vanidad.—*v. box, v. case,* neceser para polvos, etc.

vanquish [vǽnkwis], *vt.* y *vi.* vencer.

vapor [véipo(r)], *s.* vapor; vaho; hálito.— **—ize** [-ais], *vt.* y *vi.* evaporar(se).— **—izer** [-aisœ(r)], *s.* vaporizador.

variable [vériabl], *s.* y *a.* variable.— **variance** [vérians], *s.* variación, cambio; desavenencia, discrepancia. —*to be at v.,* estar en desacuerdo (con).— **variation** [vériéison], *s.* variación; variedad; (gram.) flexión.

varicose [vérikous], *a.* varicoso.—*v. vein,* varice, várice.

varied [vérid], *a.* variado, vario; alterado, (zool., orn.) abigarrado, multicolor.— **variegated** [vérigeitid], *a.* abigarrado, jaspeado, veteado; diverso, diversificado.— **variety** [varáieti], *s.* variedad, diversidad; surtido; tipo, clase, especie.—*v. show* (teat.) función de variedades.— **various** [vérias], *a.* varios, algunos, unos cuantos; desemejante, diferente; inconstante; veteado, abigarrado.

varnish [várnis], *s.* barniz.—*vt.* barnizar.

vary [véri], *vti.* y *vii.* [7] variar, cambiar; diversificar(se); desviar(se).

vase [veis], *s.* jarrón, vaso; florero, búcaro.

vaseline [vǽselin], *s.* vaselina.

vast [væst], *a.* vasto; inmenso.

vat [væt], *s.* tina, tanque, cuba.

vaudeville [vóudvil], *s.* función de variedades.

vault [volt], *s.* (arq.) bóveda, cúpula; cueva, bodega, subterráneo; tumba; (igl.) cripta; (fig.) cielo, firmamento; (dep.) voltereta, salto con garrocha. —*vt.* (arq.) abovedar, voltear.—*vt.* y *vi.* (dep.) voltear, saltar (con garrocha o apoyando las manos).

veal [vil], *s.* (carne de) ternera.— *v. cutlet,* chuleta de ternera.

veer [vir], *vi.* desviarse; cambiar (el viento, etc.).—*vt.* y *vi.* (mar.) virar.

vegetable [védatabl], *s.* vegetal, planta. —*pl.* verduras, hortalizas, legumbres. —*a.* vegetal; de hortalizas.— **vegetarian** [ved3etérian], *a.* y *s.* vegetariano.— **vegetate** [véd3eteit],

vi. vegetar.—**vegetation** [vedáetéison], *s.* vegetación.

vehemence [víhimens], *s.* vehemencia. —**vehement** [víhiment], *a.* vehemente, impetuoso, extremoso.

vehicle [víhikl], *s.* vehículo; medio; (farm.) excipiente.

veil [veil], *vt.* velar, cubrir con velo; encubrir, disimular, tapar.—*s.* velo.

vein [vein], *s.* vena; veta; (fig.) humor, genio.— **—ed** [-d], *a.* venoso; veteado, jaspeado.

vellum [vélʌm], *s.* vitela, pergamino.

velocity [vilásiti], *s.* velocidad.

velum [vílʌm], *s.* cubierta membranosa; velo del paladar.

velvet [vélvit], *s.* terciopelo.—*a.* de terciopelo.— **—y** [-i], *a.* aterciopelado.

vender [véndœ(r)], *s.* vendedor ambulante.— **vendor** [véndo(r)], *s.* (for.) vendedor, cedente.

veneer [venír], *vt.* enchapar; revestir; ocultar, disfrazar.—*s.* material para enchapar, chapa; capa exterior, apariencia.

venerable [vénerabl], *a.* venerable; sagrado; antiguo.— **venerate** [vénereit], *vt.* venerar, reverenciar.— **veneration** [veneréison], *s.* veneración.

venereal [venírial], *a.* venéreo.

Venezuelan [venezwéilan], *a.* y *s.* venezolano.

vengeance [vénd3ans], *s.* venganza. —*with a v.,* con violencia, con toda su alma; con creces, extremadamente. —**vengeful** [vénd3ful], *a.* vengativo.

venial [vínial], *a.* venial; perdonable.

venom [vénom], *s.* veneno; rencor, malignidad.— **—ous** [-ʌs], *a.* venenoso; dañoso; maligno.

venous [vínʌs], *a.* venoso; veteado.

vent [vent], *s.* respiradero, abertura, lumbrera; salida; paso; fogón de arma de fuego; (zool.) ano; emisión; desahogo.—*vt.* expresar, desahogar, (fam.) desembuchar.—*to v. one's spleen,* descargar uno la bilis.— **—ilate** [véntileit], *vt.* ventilar.— **—ilation** [-iléison], *s.* ventilación.— **—ilator** [-ileito(r)], *s.* ventilador.

ventriloquist [ventrílokwist], *s.* ventrílocuo.

venture [vénchu(r)], *s.* riesgo, ventura, albur; (com.) pacotilla; operación o empresa arriesgada; especulación. —*vt.* arriesgar, aventurar.—*vi.* osar, atreverse; aventurarse, arriesgarse.

veranda [virǽnda], *s.* pórtico, soportal, porche, mirador.

verb [vœrb], *s.* verbo.— **—al** [vœrbal], *a.* verbal; oral; literal.

verbena [vœrbína], *s.* (bot.) verbena.

verdant [vœrdant], *a.* verde, verdoso; inocente, sencillo.

verdict [vค่rdikt], *s.* veredicto, fallo; opinión, dictamen.

verdigris [vค่rdigris], *s.* verdín.— verdure [vค่rḋฺur], *s.* verde, verdor; frondas.

verge [vค่rḋฺ], *s.* borde, margen; confín; (arq.) fuste; vara, báculo.—*on o upon the v. of,* al borde de; a punto de, al, a dos dedos de.—*vi.* acercarse a, tender.

verify [vค่rifai], *vti.* [7] verificar, justificar, constatar, demostrar; cerciorarse de; cumplir (una promesa); (for.) afirmar bajo juramento; acreditar.

veritable [vค่ritabl], *a.* verdadero.— verity [vค่riti], *s.* verdad, realidad.

vermin [vค่rmin], *s.* miseria, musaraña; bichos, piojos, chinches, etc.

vernacular [vคrnákyolä(r)], *a.* vernáculo, nativo; (med.) local.—*s.* idioma vernáculo.

versatile [vค่rsatil], *a.* versátil, de variados talentos o aptitudes; adaptable; voluble.—versatility [vคrsatิ́liti], *s.* versatilidad, adaptabilidad, variedad de talentos; veleidad.

verse [vคrs], *s.* verso; (igl.) versículo.— —d [-t], *a.* versado, perito.—versicle [vค่rsikl], *s.* versículo.—versification [vคrsifikéฺ̇șฺ̇n], *s.* versificación.— version [vค่ṙฺn], *s.* versión; interpretación; (cir.) versión.

versus [vค่rsʌs], *prep.* contra.

vertebra [vค่rtebṙฺ], *s.* (*pl.* vertebrae [vค่rtibri]) vértebra.— —te [vค่rtibreit], *s.* y *a.* vertebrado.

vertex [vค่rteks], *s.* (*pl.* vertices [vค่rtisiz]) vértice; cima, cumbre, cúspide, ápice.

vertical [vค่rtikal], *a.* vertical.— —ity [vคrtikéliti], *s.* verticalidad.

vertigo [vค่rtigou], *s.* (med.) vértigo, vahído.

vervain [vค่rvein], *s.* (bot.) verbena.

very [vค่ri], *a.* mismo, propio, idéntico; verdadero, real; mismísimo.—*for that v. reason,* por lo mismo.—*the v. idea of doing it,* sólo la idea, o la mera idea de hacerlo.—*this v. day,* hoy mismo.—*adv.* muy, mucho, muchísimo.—*v. many,* muchísimos. —*v. much,* mucho, muchísimo; sumamente, muy.—*v. much so,* muy mucho, muchísimo, en sumo grado.

vesicle [vésikl], *s.* vesícula.

vespers [véspœrz], *s.* vísperas.

vessel [véṡฺl], *s.* embarcación, barco, buque; vasija, vaso.

vest [vest], *s.* chaleco.—*vt.* investir (de autoridad), conferir; (for.) hacer entrega, dar posesión.—*to v. in,* revestir de, investir de. poner en posesión de.—*to v. with,* (re)vestir de. —*vi.* vestirse; ser válido.

vestibule [véstibiul], *s.* vestíbulo; zaguán.

vestige [véstiḋฺ], *s.* vestigio, huella, señal; reliquia; rudimento.

vestment [véstment], *s.* prenda de vestir; ropa, vestidura; (igl.) vestimenta; sabanilla (de altar).

vestry [véstri], *s.* vestuario, sacristía; junta que administra los asuntos de una iglesia episcopal protestante.

veteran [véteran], *s.* y *a.* veterano.

veterinarian [veterinérian], *a.* y *s.* veterinario.

veto [vítou], *vt.* poner el veto; vedar, prohibir; rehusar la aprobación de, vetar.—*s.* veto.

vex [veks], *vt.* disgustar, irritar, enfadar. — —ation [vekséฺ̇șฺ̇n], *s.* disgusto, irritación, enfado.

via [váiฺ̇], *prep.* por (la vía de).—*s.* vía.— —duct [váiadʌkt], *s.* viaducto.

vial [váial], *s.* redoma, frasco, ampolleta, pomo.

viand [váiand], *s.* vianda.—*pl.* comida, alimentos, provisiones.

vibrate [váibreit], *vt.* y *vi.* vibrar.— vibration [vaibréฺ̇șฺ̇n], *s.* vibración.

vice [vais], *s.* vicio, inmoralidad; defecto, falta; resabio (caballo, etc.). —*prefijo* vice.—*v.-admiral,* vicealmirante.—*v.-president,* vicepresidente.— —roy [váisrɔi], *s.* virrey.

vicinity [visiniti], *s.* vecindad, cercanía, inmediaciones, alrededores.

vicious [víฺ̇ʌs], *a.* vicioso. depravado; defectuoso, imperfecto; (fam.) maligno, rencoroso; dañino.—*v. dog,* perro bravo, que muerde.— —ness [-nis], *s.* malignidad, depravación.

vicissitude [visisitiud], *s.* vicisitud.

victim [víktim], *s.* víctima; (for.) interfecto.

victor [víktɔ(r)], *s.* vencedor, triunfador.— —ious [viktɔ́riʌs], *a.* victorioso. — —y [víktori], *s.* victoria, triunfo.

victuals [vítalz], *s. pl.* (fam. o dial.) víveres, provisiones, comestibles.

vie [vai], *vi.* competir, rivalizar, disputar(se).

view [viu], *vt.* mirar, ver; contemplar; examinar, inspeccionar, reconocer; considerar, especular.—*s.* vista, mirada; inspección; contemplación; visión; escena, panorama, paisaje, perspectiva; alcance de la vista; modo de ver, criterio; opinión, parecer; fase, aspecto; mira, intento, propósito.—*v. finder,* (foto.) visor.— —point [viúpɔint], *s.* punto de vista.

vigil [víḋฺil], *s.* vela, velación, vigilia, desvelo; vigilancia; (igl.) vigilia.— —ance [-ans], *s.* desvelo; vigilancia.— —ant [-ant], *a.* vigilante.

vignette [vinyét], *s.* (impr., foto.) viñeta; corto bosquejo literario.

vigor [vígɒ(r)], *s.* vigor; fuerza, fortaleza; verdor, lozanía.— —ous [-ʌs], *a.* vigoroso, fuerte.

vile [vail], *a.* vil, bajo.— —ness [váilnịs], *s.* vileza, bajeza.

villa [vílặ], *s.* villa, quinta.— —ge [vílidặ], *s.* aldea, pueblo, caserío.— —ger [vílidặœ(r)], *s.* aldeano.

villain [vílặn], *s.* villano, malvado.— —ous [-ʌs], *a.* villano, malvado; asqueroso, repugnante.— —y [-i], *s.* villanía, vileza, infamia.

vim [vịm], *s.* fuerza, vigor; energía, brío.

vindicate [víndịkeịt], *vt.* vindicar.— **vindictive** [vịndíktịv], *a.* vengativo.

vine [vain], *s.* (bot.) enredadera; vid, parra.— —gar [vínịgặ(r)], *s.* vinagre.— —yard [vínyàrd], *s.* viña, viñedo.— —vintage [víntịdặ], *s.* vendimia.— *v.* wine, vino añejo.—**vintner** [víntnœ(r)], *s.* vinatero.

violate [váịoleịt], *vt.* violar.—**violation** [vaịoléịṣɒn], *s.* violación.—**violence** [váịolęns], *s.* violencia.—**violent** [váịolęnt], *a.* violento.

violet [váịolịt], *s.* (bot.) violeta; color violado.—*a.* violado, violáceo.

violin [vaịolín], *s.* violín; violinista.— —ist [-ịst], *s.* violinista.—**violoncello** [violanchéloụ], *s.* violoncelo.

viper [váịpœ(r)], *s.* víbora.— —ish [-ịṣ], *a.* viperino.

virgin [vœ́rdặịn], *s.* virgen.— —al [-ặl], *a.* virginal.— —ity [vœrdặínịtị], *s.* virginidad.

virile [vírịl], *a.* viril.—**virility** [vịrílịtị], *s.* virilidad.

virtual [vœ́rchụạl], *a.* virtual.

virtue [vœ́rchụ], *s.* virtud.—**virtuoso** [vœrchụóụsoụ], *s.* (mús.) virtuoso.— **virtuous** [vœ́rchụạs], *a.* virtuoso.

virulence [vírụlęns], *s.* virulencia; malignidad, acrimonia.—**virulent** [vírụlęnt], *a.* virulento, ponzoñoso; maligno, cáustico.—**virus** [váịrʌs], *s.* virus; virulencia, influencia maligna.

visa [vízặ], *s.* visa, visado.

viscera [vísęrặ], *s. pl.* vísceras, entrañas.— —l [vísęrạl], *a.* visceral.

viscosity [vịskásịtị], *s.* viscosidad.

viscount [váịkaụnt], *s.* vizconde.— —ess [-ịs], *s.* vizcondesa.

viscous [vískʌs], *a.* viscoso, pegajoso.

visibility [vịzịbílịtị], *s.* visibilidad.— **visible** [vízịbl], *a.* visible.—**vision** [vízɒn], *s.* visión, vista; clarividencia, perspicacia, previsión; fantasma; fantasía; revelación profética; (cine) representación de los pensamientos o sueños de un actor.—**visionary** [vízɒnerị], *a.* y *s.* visionario.

visit [vízịt], *vt.* visitar; hacer un reconocimiento o registro de.—*vi.*

visitarse; hacer visitas, ir de visita.— —*s.* visita, visitación; reconocimiento, registro, inspección.— —ation [-éịṣɒn], *s.* visitación, visita; inspección, registro, reconocimiento; gracia o castigo del cielo.— —or [-ɒ(r)], *s.* visitante, visitador.

visor [váịzɒ(r)], *s.* visera.

vista [vístặ], *s.* vista, perspectiva.

visual [vízụạl], *a.* visual.— —ization [vịzụạlịzéịṣɒn], *s.* visualización (representación mental).

vital [váịtặl], *a.* vital, fundamental; fatal, mortal.— —ity [vaịtǽlịtị], *s.* vitalidad, energía vital.— —ize [váịtặlaịz], *vt.* vitalizar.

vitamin [váịtặmịn], *s.* vitamina.

vitiate [víṣịeịt], *vt.* viciar; inficionar, infectar, corromper; (for.) viciar, invalidar.

vitreous [vítrịʌs], *a.* vítreo, vidrioso.

vitriol [vítrịɒl], *s.* vitriolo.— —ic [vịtrịálịk], *a.* ferozmente mordaz.

vivacious [vịvéịṣʌs], *a.* vivo, vivaracho, vivaz.—**vivacity** [vịvǽsịtị], *s.* vivacidad, viveza.—**vivid** [vívịd], *a.* vivo, vívido, gráfico; intenso; subido, brillante (color); animado, enérgico, activo.

vocabulary [vokǽbyụlerị], *s.* vocabulario, léxico.

vocal [vóụkặl], *a.* vocal (rel. a la voz); oral; vocinglero, voceador.— —ist [-ịst], *s.* cantante.— —ize [-aịz], *vt.* y *vi.* vocalizar.

vocation [vokéịṣɒn], *s.* oficio, profesión; vocación.— —al [-ạl], *a.* vocacional; práctico; de artes y oficios.

vogue [voụg], *s.* moda, boga.

voice [voịs], *s.* voz; habla, palabra; el que habla en nombre de otro; opinión.— —with one v., por unanimidad.—*vt.* decir, expresar; interpretar; hacerse eco de; (mus.) escribir la parte vocal de; hacer sonoro.— —less [vóịslịs], *a.* mudo; que no tiene voz ni voto; sordo, no sonoro.

void [voịd], *a.* vacío, desocupado, hueco; vacante; vano, ilusorio; (for.) nulo, inválido.—*v. of,* falto, privado, desprovisto de.—*s.* vacío; claro, laguna.—*vt.* (for.) anular, invalidar; vaciar, evacuar.—*vi.* vaciarse, evacuarse.

volatile [válặtịl], *a.* volátil; sutil, fugaz; voluble, pasajero.—**volatilize** [válặtịlaịz], *vt.* y *vi.* volatilizar(se).

volcanic [valkǽnịk], *a.* volcánico.— **volcano** [valkéịnoụ], *s.* volcán.

volition [volíṣɒn], *s.* voluntad; volición.

volley [válị], *s.* (mil.) descarga cerrada, andanada; salva; (dep.) voleo de la pelota.—*vt.* y *vi.* lanzar una descarga; (dep.) volear.

volt [voụlt], *s.* (elec.) volt, voltio;

(equit.) vuelta.— —age [vóųltįdź], s. voltaje, tensión.

volume [vályǫm], s. tomo, volumen, obra; volumen, bulto; caudal de río; importe, suma, gran cantidad; (mat. y mus.) volumen; (fís.) masa.— **voluminous** [voljúmįnʌs], a. voluminoso, abultado; prolijo, copioso.

voluntary [válʌnteɾį], a. voluntario.— s. voluntario; cualquier acción voluntaria.—**volunteer** [valʌntíɾ], s. voluntario.—vt. contribuir u ofrecer voluntariamente.—vi. ofrecerse o hacer algo; servir como voluntaria.

volute [volįút], s. (arq.) voluta.

vomit [vámįt], vt. y vi. vomitar, arrojar. —s. vómito; vomitivo, emético.

voracious [voréįšʌs], a. voraz, devorador; rapaz o de rapiña.

vortex [vórteks], s. (pl. **vortices** [vórtįsįz]) vórtice, vorágine; remolino, torbellino.

vote [voųt], s. voto; votación; sufragio. —vt. votar por; (fam.) dominar el voto de.—to v. down, rechazar por votación.—vi. votar, dar voto.— —r [vóųtœ(r)], s. votante, elector.— **voting** [vóųtįŋ], s. votación.

vouch [vaųch], vt. atestiguar, certificar, atestar, testificar; garantizar, responder de o por.—vi. salir fiador.—to v. for, avalar, responder por.— —er [váųchœ(r)], s. comprobante, recibo, documento justificativo; fiador.—vt. atestar, confirmar, certificar.

vow [vaų], s. voto, promesa solemne. —vt. hacer promesa solemne de, hacer voto de, jurar.—vi. hacer un voto.

vowel [váųęl], s. (gram.) vocal.—a. vocal, vocálico.

voyage [vóįįdź], s. viaje marítimo, travesía.—vi. viajar por mar.— —r [vóįįdźœ(r)], s. viajero.

vulcanization [valkạnįzéįšǫn], s. vulcanización.—**vulcanize** [válkạnaįz], vt. vulcanizar.

vulgar [válgạ(r)], a. vulgar, grosero; común; público, generalmente sabido; vernáculo.— —ity [vʌlgǽɾįtį], s. vulgaridad, grosería.

vulnerable [válnęɾạbl], a. vulnerable.

vulture [válchų(r)], s. buitre.

W

wad [wad], s. taco; bolita, pelotilla, rollo (de papeles, billetes de banco, etc.); material para rellenar muebles (guata, etc.); (fam.) dinero, dineral, ahorros.—vti. [1] (cost.) acolchar, enguatar; rellenar (muebles, colchones, etc.); (arti.) atacar.

waddle [wádl], vi. anadear, contonearse al andar.—s. anadeo, contoneo, meneo.

wade [weįd], vt. y vi. vadear; meterse en agua baja y andar en ella.—to w. in o through, andar con dificultad (en el lodo, etc.); terminar con dificultad o con tedio.—to w. into, (fam.) atacar resueltamente.

wafer [wéįfœ(r)], s. oblea; (igl.) hostia; (coc.) barquillo; (farm.) sello.

wag [wæg], vti. [1] sacudir, mover o menear ligeramente.—to w. the tail, mover la cola o rabo.—vii. oscilar, balancearse; ir pasando, deslizarse; (fam.) irse.—s. meneo; coleo; movimiento de cabeza; bromista, burlador.

wage [weįdź], vt. emprender, sostener; hacer (guerra), dar (batalla).—s. (gen. **wages**) salario, paga, jornal.— w. earner, jornalero, trabajador; asalariado.

wager [wéįdźœ(r)], vt. y vi. apostar. —s. apuesta.—to lay a w., hacer una apuesta.

wagon [wǽgǫn], s. vagón, carro, carretón, carreta, carromato; furgón.

waif [weįf], s. niño, animalito u objeto extraviado o abandonado.

wail [weįl], vt. y vi. deplorar, llorar, lamentar(se).—s. lamentación, gemido.

waist [weįst], s. (anat.) cintura; talle; cinto, corpiño.— —coat [wéįstkoųt, wéskǫt], s. chaleco.— —line [-laįn], s. cintura.

wait [weįt], vt. esperar, aguardar.—vi. estar aguardando; atender; estar listo; servir; ser criado, sirviente o mozo (de fonda).—to w. at table, servir a la mesa.—to w. for, esperar. —to w. on o upon, ir a ver o presentar sus respetos a; servir a; atender a, despachar (en una tienda); (fam.) acompañar.—s. espera; (fam.) plantón; demora.—in w., al o en acecho.— —er [wéįtœ(r)], s. mozo de café o restaurante, camarero.— —ress [-ɾįs], s. criada, moza, camarera.

waive [weįv], vt. renunciar a; desistir de; diferir, posponer; repudiar.— —r [wéįvœ(r)], s. renuncia (de un derecho, etc.); repudio.

wake [weįk], vti. y vii. [5] despertar(se). —to w. up, despertar(se), animar(se). —s. vel(at)orio; (mar.) estela.—in the w. of, tras; inmediatamente después de; a raíz de.— —ful [wéįkfųl], a. vigilante, en vela; desvelado.— —n [-n], vt. y vi. despertar(se).

wale [weįl], s. cardenal, verdugo, verdugón; (tej.) relieve.

walk [wɔk], vi. andar, caminar, ir a pie; pasear(se); (equit.) ir al paso; conducirse, portarse.—to w. away, irse, marcharse.—to w. back, regresar. —to w. out, salir, irse; declararse en huelga.—to w. over, ir al paso

(caballo); (fam.) ganar fácilmente; abusar de.—*to w. up*, subir (a pie); acercarse.—*to w. up and down*, pasearse, ir y venir.—*vt.* hacer andar, (sacar a) pasear; recorrer, andar o pasar de una parte a otra de; andar por; hollar; llevar (un caballo) al paso.—*s.* paseo, caminata; modo de andar; paso del caballo; paseo, alameda; acera; carrera, oficio, empleo, estado, condición; método de vida, conducta, porte.

wall [wɔl], *s.* pared; tabique; muro o tapia; muralla.—*low mud w.*, tapia. —*to drive, push o thrust to the w.*, poner entre la espada y la pared; acosar.—*to go to the w.*, hallarse acosado; verse obligado a ceder; (com.) quebrar.—*vt.* emparedar, tapiar, murar.

wallet [wɔ́lit], *s.* cartera; bolsa de cuero; mochila; alforja.

wallflower [wɔ́lflaɥœ(r)], *s.* (bot.) al(h)elí; (fam.) mujer que en un baile "come pavo" o "plancha el asiento".

wallop [wɔ́lɔp], *vt.* (fam.) zurrar; vencer decisivamente.—*s.* (fam.) golpe rudo, bofetón; tunda; fuerza.

wallow [wɔ́loɥ], *vi.* revolcarse; chapotear (en el lodo); estar encenagado o sumido en el vicio.—*s.* revolcadura; revolcadero.

walnut [wɔ́lnʌt], *s.* (bot.) nuez; nogal.

walrus [wɔ́lrʌs], *s.* morsa.

waltz [wɔlts], *vi.* valsar.—*s.* vals.

wan [wan], *a.* pálido, descolorido.

wand [wand], *s.* vara; varilla de virtudes; batuta.

wander [wándœ(r)], *vi.* errar, vagar; delirar; perderse, extraviarse; desviarse, apartarse.—*vt.* recorrer, andar por.— **—er** [-œ(r)], *s.* vagabundo; transgresor.

wane [weɪn], *vi.* menguar, disminuir; decaer.—*s.* disminución; decadencia; menguante (de la luna); (carp.) bisel.

want [want], *vt.* necesitar, querer, desear; pedir con urgencia, exigir. —*vi.* estar necesitado, pasar necesidades; faltar.—*s.* necesidad, carencia; privación, indigencia; exigencia; solicitud, demanda.—*for w. of*, a o por falta de.—*to be in w.*, estar necesitado.— **—ing** [wántin], *a.* falto, defectuoso, deficiente; menguado; necesitado, escaso.—*to be w.*, faltar.

wanton [wántɔn], *a.* desenfrenado; protervo; (poét.) retozón, travieso; extravagante; libre; lascivo; desconsiderado; imperdonable; injustificable. —*s.* libertino; ramera; persona frívola.—*vt.* malgastar; echar a perder.—*vi.* retozar; hacer picardías; pasar el tiempo en liviandades.-

—ness [-nɪs], *s.* desenfreno, licencia; retozo.

war [wor], *s.* guerra; arte militar.—*a.* de o relativo a la guerra; bélico, marcial.—*vii.* [1] guerrear, estar en guerra.—*to w. on*, hacer la guerra a.

warble [wɔ́rbl], *vi.* trinar, gorjear; murmurar (un arroyo).—*s.* gorjeo, trino.— **—r** [-œ(r)], *s.* ave cantora.

ward [wɔrd], *vt.* (off) resguardarse de; evitar, parar o desviar (un golpe). —*s.* pupilo o menor en tutela; barriada, barrio o distrito de ciudad; sala, división de hospital, etc.; tutela; protección; defensa, posición defensiva.— **—en** [wɔ́rdɛn], *s.* custodio, celador, capataz; alcaide, carcelero; conserje; bedel.

wardrobe [wɔ́rdroʊb], *s.* guardarropa, ropero, armario; vestuario; ropa.

warehouse [wérhaɥs], *s.* almacén, depósito.—*vt.* almacenar. **wares** [werz], *s. pl.* mercancías, efectos, géneros de comercio.

warfare [wɔ́rfer], *s.* guerra; arte militar; operaciones militares; lucha, combate.—**warlike** [wɔ́rlaɪk], *a.* bélico(so), marcial.

warm [worm], *a.* caluroso, caliente, cálido; templado, tibio; acalorado; fogoso, violento; conmovido, apasionado; expresivo; afectuoso; (pint.) que tira a rojo o amarillo; reciente, fresco; (fam.) cercano al objeto buscado; molesto; peligroso.—*to be w.*, tener calor; estar o ser caliente (una cosa); (con it por sujeto) hacer calor.—*vt.* calentar; caldear, abrigar; entusiasmar; (fam.) zurrar.—*to w. over o up*, calentar (comida fría). —*vi.* (con up) entusiasmarse; acalorarse; tomar bríos.—*to w. to(ward)*, simpatizar con; cobrar cariño o afición a.— **—th** [-θ], *s.* calor (moderado); celo, entusiasmo; cordialidad; enojo.

warn [worn], *vt.* avisar, prevenir, advertir, poner sobre aviso; aconsejar, amonestar; (for.) apercibir.—*vi.* servir de escarmiento.— **—ing** [wɔ́rnin], *s.* aviso, advertencia; escarmiento.—*a.* de alarma.

warp [worp], *s.* torcedura, comba; (tej.) urdimbre; (mar.) remolque, calabrote. —*w. and woof*, (tej.) trama y urdimbre.—*vt.* (re)torcer; encorvar, combar, alabear; prevenir el ánimo; (tej.) urdir; (mar.) remolcar.—*vi.* torcerse; combarse; desviarse, alejarse; (tej.) urdir; (mar.) ir a remolque.

warrant [wárɑnt], *vt.* garantizar; responder por; aseverar, certificar; justificar; autorizar.—*s.* (for.) auto, mandamiento, orden, cédula; autorización, poder; documento justifica-

tivo; testimonio; sanción; motivo,
razón.— **—y** [-į], *s.* garantía;
seguridad; autorización.

warrior [wórįǫ(r)], *s.* guerrero.—
warship [wórṣįp], *s.* navío o buque
de guerra.

wart [wǫrt], *s.* verruga.

wartime [wórtajm], *s.* período o tiempo
de guerra.—*a.* relativo a dicho
período; de guerra.—**warworn** [wór-
worn], *a.* agotado por el servicio
militar.

wary [wérį], *a.* cauto, cauteloso,
prudente, precavido, prevenido.—*to*
be w. of, desconfiar de.

was [waz, wʌz], (*1a. y 3a. pers. sing.*)
pret. de TO BE.

wash [waṣ], *vt.* lavar; fregar.—*to w.*
away, off o out, lavar, borrar, hacer
desaparecer; quitar lavando; llevarse
(el agua o un golpe de mar).—*vi.*
lavarse; lavar ropa; no perder el color
o no estropearse cuando se lava.—*s.*
lavado, lavadura; ropa lavada o para
lavar; lavatorio, lavazas, agua sucia.
—*w. basin,* palangana.—*w. stand,*
lavabo.—*w. tub,* tina.—*a.* de o para
lavar; lavable.— **—able** [wáṣabl], *a.*
lavable.— **—er** [-œ(r)], *s.* máquina de
lavar; lavador; (mec.) arandela.—
w. woman, lavandera.— **—ing** [-įŋ],
s. lavado, lavamiento; ropa lavada;
ropa sucia.—*w. machine,* lavadora,
máquina de lavar.

wasp [wasp], *s.* avispa.—*wasp's nest,*
avispero.

waste [wejst], *vt.* malgastar, derrochar,
desperdiciar; gastar, consumir; desolar, talar.—*vi.* gastarse, consumirse;
desgastarse, dañarse.—*to w. away,*
demacrarse, consumirse; ir a menos,
menguar.—*a.* desechado, inútil;
yermo; desolado; arruinado;
sobrante.—*to lay w.,* devastar, asolar.
—*s.* despilfarro; decadencia; merma,
pérdida; despojos, desperdicios; erial;
extensión, inmensidad; devastación;
escombros.— **—ful** [wéjstfųl], *a.*
manirroto, pródigo; ruinoso, antiecon-
nómico; destructivo.— **—fulness**
[-fųlnįs], *s.* prodigalidad, derroche.

watch [wach], *s.* reloj (de bolsillo);
vela, desvelo o vigilia; velorio;
vigilancia, cuidado, observación;
centinela, vigilante; cuarto, guardia,
turno de servicio.—*to be on the w.,*
estar alerta.—*to keep w. over,* vigilar a.
—*w. charm,* dije.—*wrist w.,* reloj de
pulsera.—*vt.* vigilar, observar; ver,
oír (T.V., radio, etc.); atisbar, espiar;
cuidar, guardar.—*to w. one's step,*
tener cuidado, andarse con tiento.
—*vi.* estar alerta; hacer guardia;
velar.—*to w. for,* esperar; buscar.
—*to w. out for,* tener cuidado con.—

to w. over, guardar, vigilar; velar por,
cuidar de; inspeccionar; estar a cargo
de.—*w. out!* ¡cuidado!— **—ful** [wách-
fųl], *a.* despierto, vigilante, observador, que está alerta; desvelado.—
—man [-mąn], *s.* sereno, guardián.—
—tower [-tąųœ(r)], *s.* atalaya;
mirador.— **—word** [-wœrd], *s.* santo
y seña; lema.

water [wótœ(r)], *s.* agua; extensión de
agua (lago, río, etc.); marea; líquido
semejante al agua (lágrimas, etc.).
—*like w.,* en abundancia.—*w. closet,*
inodoro, excusado, retrete.—*w. color,*
acuarela; color para acuarela.—
w.-cooled, enfriado por agua.—
w. front, barrio de los muelles.—
w. main, cañería maestra (de agua).
—*vt.* regar; humedecer, mojar; aguar,
diluir, echar agua a; abrevar; dar
agua a (un barco, locomotora, etc.).
—*vi.* chorrear agua o humedad;
tomar agua (un barco, etc.); beber
agua (los animales).—*my eyes w.,*
me lloran los ojos.—*my mouth waters,*
se me hace la boca agua.— **—cress**
[-kres], *s.* berros.— **—fall** [-fǫl], *s.*
cascada, catarata, salto de agua.—
—melon [-melǫn], *s.* sandía, melón de
agua.— **—proof** [-pruf], *a.* a prueba
de agua, impermeable.—*vt.* imperme-
abilizar.— **—spout** [-spąųt], *s.* tromba;
remolino.— **—tight** [-tajt], *a.* hermético.— **—way** [-wej], *s.* vía acuática
o fluvial; canal o río navegable.—
—y [-į], *a.* acuoso, aguado; insípido,
soso; lloroso.

watt [wat], *s.* vatio.

wave [wejv], *s.* ola; onda, ondulación;
movimiento de la mano, ademán;
(tej. y joy.) aguas, visos.—*vt. y vi.*
(hacer) ondear o flamear, blandir(se);
ondular (el pelo, etc.); hacer señas *o*
señales.—*to w. good-bye,* agitar la
mano, el pañuelo, etc. en señal de
despedida.— **—r** [wéjvœ(r)], *vi.*
ondear, oscilar; tambalear, balancearse; vacilar, titubear, fluctuar.
—wavy [wéjvį], *a.* ondeado, rizado;
ondulante.

wax [wæks], *s.* cera; cerumen; parafina.
—*a.* de cera, ceroso; encerado.—*vt.*
encerar; encerotar (hilo).—*vi.* crecer
(la luna); hacerse, ponerse.

way [wej], *s.* vía; camino, senda;
conducto, paso; espacio recorrido;
rumbo, dirección; marcha, andar,
velocidad (de un buque, etc.); modo,
medio, manera; uso, costumbre.—
all the w., en todo el camino; del todo;
hasta el fin.—*a long w. off,* muy lejos.
—*by the w.,* a propósito, ya que viene
al caso; de paso.—*by w. of,* que viene
de, pasando por; por vía de, a modo
de; a título de.—*every w.,* por todas

partes, de todos lados; de todos modos.—*no w.*, de ningún modo, de ninguna manera.—*on the w.*, de camino, de paso.—*on the w. to*, rumbo a, camino de.—*that w.*, por ahí, por allí; de ese modo, así.—*the other w. around*, al contrario, al revés. —*this w.*, por aquí; así, de este modo. —*to be in the w. of*, impedir, estorbar. —*to give w.*, ceder.—*to have one's (own) w.*, hacer uno lo que quiera; salirse con la suya.—*to make w.*, abrir paso.—*under w.*, en camino, en marcha; empezado, haciéndose. —*w. in*, entrada.—*w. out*, salida.— *w. through*, pasaje.—waylaid [wejléjd], *pret. y pp.* de TO WAYLAY.— waylay [wejléj], *vti.* [10] estar en acecho para asaltar o robar; asaltar; detener a alguien en su camino.- —side [wéjsajd], *s.* orilla o borde del camino.—*a.* que está junto al camino.- —ward [wéjwɑrd], *a.* descarriado; díscolo, voluntarioso; vacilante.

we [wi], *pron.* nosotros, nosotras.

weak [wik], *a.* débil, enclenque, endeble, flaco; (com.) flojo (precio o mercado). - —en [wíkn], *vt.* debilitar; quebrantar; atenuar.—*vi.* debilitarse, flaquear, desfallecer, resentirse.- —ly [-li], *adv.* débilmente.—*a.* enfermizo, achacoso, enclenque.- —ness [-njs], *s.* debilidad, debilitamiento; decaimiento; inconsistencia; fragilidad; flaqueza, desliz; (fam.) el flaco, el lado de montar.

wealth [welθ], *s.* riqueza, opulencia; lujo; caudal, abundancia.- —y [wélθj], *a.* rico, adinerado, acaudalado.

wean [win], *vt.* destetar; apartar poco a poco (de un hábito, de una amistad, etc.); enajenar el afecto de.

weapon [wépɒn], *s.* arma.—*pl.* medios de defensa (de animales y vegetales); armas.

wear [wer], *vti.* [10] llevar o traer puesto (un traje, etc.), usar, gastar (bigote, sombrero, etc. habitualmente); desgastar, deteriorar.—*to w. away*, gastar o consumir.—*to w. down*, (des)gastar (por rozamiento).—*vii.* gastarse, consumirse; durar, perdurar; pasar, correr (el tiempo).— *to w. away*, decaer; gastarse, consumirse.—*to w. off*, usarse, gastarse; borrarse; desaparecer.—*to w. well*, durar largo tiempo, ser duradero.—*s.* uso, gasto, deterioro; moda, boga; prendas de vestir; durabilidad.—*w. and tear*, uso; desgaste o deterioro natural (debido al uso).- —iness [wírjnjs], *s.* lasitud, cansancio; aburrimiento, fastidio.- —ing [wérju], *s.* uso; desgaste,

deterioro; pérdida, decaimiento.— *a.* de uso; desgastador; agotador, fatigoso.—*w. apparel*, ropa, prendas de vestir. —isome [wírjsɒm], *a.* fatigoso; tedioso, pesado.—weary [wíri], *vti.* [7] cansar, fatigar; hastiar, aburrir, molestar.—*to w. of*, agotar la paciencia.—*vii.* fatigarse, cansarse, aburrirse.—*a.* cansado; aburrido, hastiado; tedioso, fastidioso.

weasel [wízɛl], *s.* comadreja.

weather [wéðœ(r)], *s.* tiempo (estado atmosférico).—*pl.* vicisitudes de la suerte.—*it is good (bad) weather*, hace buen (mal) tiempo.—*a.* del tiempo, relativo al tiempo.—*w.-beaten*, curtido por la intemperie.—*w.-bound*, detenido por el mal tiempo.—*w. bureau*, observatorio, oficina metereológica. —*w. forecast(ing)*, predicción o pronóstico del tiempo.—*w.-worn*, deteriorado por la intemperie o por los agentes atmosféricos.—*vt.* aguantar (el temporal); resistir a, sobrevivir (a la adversidad); orear, secar al aire; (mar.) doblar o montar (un cabo). —*to w. out*, vencer (obstáculos).—*vi.* curtirse en la intemperie.

weave [wiv], *vti.* [6] tejer, tramar; entrelazar, entretejer, trenzar; urdir, forjar (cuentos).—*vii.* tejer, trabajar en telar.—*s.* tejido; textura.- —r [wívœ(r)], *s.* tejedor; araña tejedora.

web [web], *s.* tela, tejido; bobina o rollo de papel; (orn.) membrana interdigital.—*spider's w.*, tela de araña.- —bed [-d], *a.* unido por una telilla o membrana; (orn.) palmípedo.

wed [wed], *vti.* [3] casarse con; casar. —*vii.* casarse.—*pp.* de TO WED.— wedded [wédjd], *a.* casado; conyugal. —*w. to*, (fig.) empeñado en, declarado por, aferrado en.- —ding [wédju], *s.* boda, nupcias.—*pl.* casamiento; unión, enlace.—*a.* de boda, nupcial; de novia.

wedge [wedʒ], *s.* cuña, calzo; prisma triangular.—*entering w.*, cuña, entrada, medio de entrar; para abrir brecha.—*vt.* acuñar, meter cuñas, calzar.

wedlock [wédlak], *s.* matrimonio, vínculo matrimonial.

Wednesday [wénzdj], *s.* miércoles.

weed [wid], *s.* maleza, cizaña.—*vt.* desyerbar, arrancar las malas hierbas.

week [wik], *s.* semana.—*to w.-end*, pasar el fin de semana, ir a descansar durante el fin de semana.—*w.-end*, fin de semana.—*w.-ender*, el que sale de vacación durante el fin de semana. —*w. in w. out*, semana tras semana. —ly [wíklj], *a.* semanal.—*adv.* semanalmente, por semana.—*s.* semanario.

weep [wip], *vti.* y *vii.* [10] llorar; lamentar, condolerse de.— —**er** [wípœ(r)], *s.* plañidera, lloraduelos; llorón; señal de luto.—*pl.* velo de viuda; festón musgoso pendiente de algunos árboles.— —**ing** [-iŋ], *s.* llanto, lloro.—*a.* plañidero, llorón.— *w. willow*, sauce llorón.

weevil [wívil], *s.* gorgojo, gusano del trigo.

weft [weft], *s.* (tej.) trama.

weigh [wei], *vt.* pesar; considerar, reflexionar acerca de.—*to w. anchor*, levar anclas.—*to w. down*, exceder en peso; sobrepujar; sobrecargar, agobiar, oprimir.—*to w. out*, pesar, clasificar por peso.—*vi.* pesar, ser pesado; ser importante.—*to w. down*, hundirse por su propio peso.—*to w. on*, gravar, ser gravoso; levar anclas, hacerse a la vela.— —**t** [-t], *vt.* cargar, gravar; aumentar el peso de; poner un peso a.—*s.* peso; pesa; carga; gravamen; lastre; importancia, autoridad.— —**ty** [wéjti], *a.* de peso, pesado; grave, serio, importante.

weird [wird], *a.* misterioso, horripilante, sobrenatural, raro, fantástico.

welcome [wélkʌm], *a.* bienvenido; grato, agradable.—*you are w.*, (respuesta a "muchas gracias", etc.) de nada, no hay de que; sea usted bienvenido.—*you are w. to it*, está a su disposición; se lo doy y presto con gusto; (irónico) buen provecho le haga.—*s.* bienvenida, buena acogida. —*vt.* dar la bienvenida a, recibir con agrado.

weld [weld], *vt.* soldar; unir; unificar. —*vi.* ser soldable, soldarse.—*s.* soldadura.— —**er** [wéldœ(r)], *s.* soldador.— —**ing** [-iŋ], *s.* soldadura.

welfare [wélfer], *s.* bienestar, felicidad, prosperidad; beneficencia.

well [wel], *vi.* manar, brotar, fluir.—*s.* pozo; manantial, ojo de agua; aljibe, cisterna; origen; tintero.—*a.* bueno, en buena salud; salvo, sano; satisfactorio, conveniente; agradable; provechoso, ventajoso.—*it is just as w.*, menos mal.—*w. and good*, bien está, santo y muy bueno.—*w.-being*, bienandanza, felicidad, bienestar.— *w.-doer*, bienhechor.—*w.-doing*, benéfico; beneficencia.—*adv.* bien; muy; favorablemente; suficientemente; convenientemente; con propiedad, razonablemente; en sumo grado. —*as w.*, también.—*as w. as*, tanto como; además de.—*she is w. over forty*, anda por encima de los cuarenta años.—*w.-appointed*, bien provisto; bien equipado.— *w.-bred*, bien criado o educado.— *w.-thought of*, bien mirado.—*w.-timed*,

oportuno.—*w.-to-do*, acomodado.— *w.-worn*, usado, trillado, gastado.— *interj.* ¡vaya, vaya! ¡qué cosa!

Welsh [welš], *a.* galés.—*s.* idioma galés. — —**man** [wélšman], *s.* galés.

welt [welt], *s.* roncha, verdugón; (cost.) ribete, vivo; (carp.) refuerzo; (fam.) costurón; azotaina, tunda.—*vt.* ribetear; (fam.) azotar levantando ronchas.

wen [wen], *s.* lobanillo.

went [went], *pret.* de TO GO.

wept [wept], *pret.* y *pp.* de TO WEEP.

were [wœr], *pret. sing.* de *2a* pers. y *pl.* de *indic.* y *sing.* y *pl.* de *subj.* de TO BE.—*as it w.*, por decirlo así; como si fuese.—*if I w. you*, yo en su caso, si yo fuera usted.—*there w.*, había, hubo.

west [west], *s.* oeste, poniente, occidente, ocaso.—*a.* occidental, del oeste.—*W. Indian*, natural de las Antillas inglesas.—*adv.* a o hacia el poniente; hacia el occidente.— —**ern** [wéstœrn], *a.* occidental.—*s.* novela o película del oeste o de vaqueros.- —**erner** [-œrnœ(r)], *s.* natural o habitante del oeste.— —**ward** [-wȧrd], *a.* que tiende o está al oeste.—*adv.* hacia el oeste.

wet [wet], *a.* mojado; húmedo; lluvioso. —*w. blanket*, aguafiestas.—*w. nurse*, nodriza.—*w. through*, empapado, hecho una sopa.—*s.* humedad; lluvia; antiprohibicionista (enemigo de la Ley Seca en E.U.).—*vti.* [3] mojar, humedecer.—*pret.* y *pp.* de TO WET.- —**ness** [wétnis], *s.* humedad.—

whack [hwæk], *vt.* (fam.) pegar, golpear. —*vi.* dar una tunda; ajustar cuentas; participar de.—*s.* (fam.) golpe; participación; porción; tentativa.

whale [hwejl], *s.* ballena; cachalote; algo enorme, descomunal o de magnífica calidad.—*vi.* dedicarse a la pesca de la ballena.—*vt.* vapulear, dar una tunda.

wharf [hworf], *s.* muelle, (des)embarcadero, descargadero.

what [hwat], *pron., a.* y *adv.* qué; lo que; cuál; cómo; cualquiera.— *he knows w.'s w.*, sabe lo que se trae, sabe cuántas son cinco.—*w. a boy!* ¡qué muchacho!—*w. else?* ¿qué más? —*w. for?* ¿para qué? ¿por qué?—*w. of it?* ¿y qué? ¿y eso qué importa? —*w. people may say*, el qué dirán.- —**(so)ever** [hwat(so)évœ(r)], *pron.* cuanto, cualquier cosa que, todo lo que; sea lo que fuere, que sea.—*a.* cualquier(a).—*w. you say*, diga Ud. lo que diga.

wheat [hwit], *s.* trigo.—*w. field*, trigal.

wheedle [hwídl], *vt.* y *vi.* engatusar, hacer zalamerías, halagar.

wheel [hwil], *s.* rueda; rodaja; torno; polea.—*steering w.*, volante (de automóvil); rueda del timón.—*vt.* (hacer) rodar; transportar sobre ruedas; (hacer) girar; poner ruedas. —*vi.* rodar, girar; (fam.) ir en bicicleta.—*to w. about o around,* cambiar de rumbo o de opinión.—**—barrow** [hwílbærou], *s.* carretilla.

whelp [hwelp], *s.* (zool.) cachorro; osezno (de oso).—*vi.* parir (la hembra de animal carnívoro).

when [hwen], *adv. y conj.* cuando, al tiempo que, mientras que; que, en que; en cuanto, así que, tan pronto como; y entonces.—*since w.?* ¿desde cuándo? ¿de cuándo acá?— **—ce** [-s], *adv.* de donde o desde donde, de que o quien; de qué causa; de ahí que, por eso es por lo que; por consiguiente. — **—(so)ever** [-(so)évœ(r)], *adv.* cuando quiera que, siempre que, en cualquier tiempo que sea, todas las veces que.

where [hwer], *adv.* donde, dónde; en donde, por donde; en dónde, por dónde; adonde, adónde.— **—abouts** [hwérabauts], *s.* paradero.—*adv.* donde, dónde, en qué lugar.— **—as** [hweréz], *conj.* considerando, por cuanto, visto que, en vista de que, puesto que, siendo así que; mientras que, al paso que.— **—by** [hwerbái], *adv.* por lo cual, con lo cual, por donde, de que; por medio del cual; ¿por qué? ¿cómo?— **—fore** [hwérfor], *adv.* por lo cual; por eso.—*s.* porqué, causa, motivo.— **—in** [hwerín], *adv.* donde, en donde, en lo cual; en qué, (en) dónde.— **—of** [hweráv], *adv.* de lo cual, de (lo) que; cuyo; de qué, de quién.— **—on** [hwerán], *adv.* en que, sobre lo cual, sobre que; en qué.— **—upon** [hwerʌpán], *adv.* sobre lo cual, después de lo cual, con lo cual; entonces; en qué, sobre qué.— **—ver** [hwervœ(r)], *adv.* dondequiera que o por dondequiera que, adondequiera que.— **—withal** [hwerwiðól], *adv.* con que, con lo cual, ¿con qué?—*s.* [hwérwiðol], dinero necesario.

whet [hwet], *vti.* [1] afilar, amolar; estimular, incitar; aguzar o abrir el apetito.

whether [hwéðœ(r)], *conj.* si; sea, sea que, ora, ya.—*w. you will or not,* que quieras que no quieras, tanto si quieres como si no quieres.

whetstone [hwétstoun], *s.* piedra de afilar, piedra de amolar.

whey [hwei], *s.* suero.

which [hwich], *pron. y a.* qué, cuál; el cual, la cual, lo cual, los cuales, las cuales; que; el que, la que, lo que, los que, las que.—*all of w., all w.,* todo

lo cual.—*w. of them?* ¿cuál de ellos? —*w. way?* ¿por dónde? ¿por qué camino?— **—ever** [hwichévœ(r)], *pron. y s.* cualquiera (que); el que.

while [hwail], *s.* rato; lapso o espacio de tiempo.—*a (little) w. ago,* hace poco rato, no hace mucho.—*all this w.,* en todo este tiempo.—*for a w.,* por algún tiempo.—*to be worth w.,* valer la pena.—*conj.* mientras (que), en tanto que, al mismo tiempo que; aun cuando, si bien.—*to w. away,* pasar, entretener el tiempo.

whim [hwim], *s.* antojo, capricho; fantasía.

whimper [hwímpœ(r)], *vi.* sollozar; lloriquear, gimotear.—*vt.* decir lloriqueando.—*s.* quejido, lloriqueo, gimoteo.

whimsical [hwímzikal], *a.* caprichoso, fantástico.

whine [hwain], *vi.* gemir, quejarse, lamentarse; lloriquear, gimotear.—*s.* quejido, lamento; lloriqueo, gimoteo.

whip [hwip], *vti.* [3] azotar, fustigar, flagelar; zurrar; (fam.) vencer, ganar a; batir (leche, huevos, etc.); sobrecoser; envolver (una soga, etc.) con cuerdecilla.—*to w. away,* arrebatar, llevarse.—*to w. in,* meter con violencia; reunir, hacer juntar; mantener juntos.—*to w. off,* ahuyentar a latigazos; quitar de repente; despachar prontamente.— *to w. on,* ponerse rápidamente.— *to w. out,* arrebatar; sacar prontamente.—*to w. up,* coger de repente; preparar en el momento; batir.—*s.* azote; látigo; latigazo; movimiento circular de vaivén.

whir [hwœr], *vti. y vii.* [1] zumbar.—*s.* zumbido; aleteo.— **—l** [-l], *vt. y vi.* girar, rodar, voltejear, remolin(e)ar. —*s.* giro, vuelta, volteo, remolino.— **whirlpool** [hwœrlpul], *s.* vórtice, vorágine, remolino.—**whirlwind** [-wind], *s.* torbellino, remolino de viento.

whisk [hwisk], *s.* escobilla, cepillo; movimiento rápido.—*vt.* cepillar, barrer.—*vi.* menear la cola; marcharse deprisa.

whisker [hwískœ(r)], *s.* pelo de la barba.—*pl.* patillas; barba; bigotes del gato, de la rata, etc.

whiskey [hwíski], *s.* whiskey (bebida alcohólica).

whisper [hwíspœ(r)], *vt. y vi.* cuchichear, secretear; murmurar, susurrar; apuntar, soplar, sugerir.—*s.* cuchicheo, susurro, murmullo.

whistle [hwísl], *vt. y vi.* silbar; chiflar.— *to w. for,* llamar silbando; (fam.) buscar en vano.—*s.* silbo, silbido; silbato, pito; (fam.) gaznate.

whit [hwit], *s.* ápice, pizca, jota, etc.
white [hwait], *a.* blanco; puro, inmaculado.—*w. feather,* (fig.) cobardía o señal de cobardía.—*w. lead,* albayalde.—*w. lie,* mentirilla, mentira blanca o venial.—*w. lily,* azucena.—*w.-livered,* pálido, débil; cobarde.—*w. slavery,* trata de blancas.—*s.* blanco (color); persona blanca; clara del huevo; esclerótica; (impr.) espacio en blanco.- —*n* [hwáitn], *vt. y vi.* blanquear(se), emblanquecer(se).- —*ness* [-nis], *s.* blancura, albura, albor; palidez; pureza, candor.- —*wash* [-waś], *s.* lechada, blanqueo.—*vt.* (alb.) blanquear, enlucir, encalar, dar lechada a; encubrir (las faltas de alguno).
whitish [hwáitiś], *a.* blanquecino.
whittle [hwítl], *vt.* mondar; sacar pedazos (a un trozo de madera); aguzar, sacar punta.—*to w. away* o *down,* cortar o reducir poco a poco.
whiz [hwiz], *vii.* [1] zumbar (por la gran velocidad); (fig.) pasar o ir muy deprisa.—*s.* zumbido (debido a la velocidad); (fam.) fenómeno, persona muy destacada, cosa muy buena.
who [hu], *pron.* quién, quiénes; quien, quienes; que; el, la, los, las que; el, la cual, los, las cuales.—*w. goes there?* ¿quién vive?- —*ever* [huévœ(r)], *pron.* quienquiera que, cualquiera que; quien, el que, la que, etc.
whole [houl], *a.* todo, entero, completo, total; íntegro, intacto; enterizo, continuo; sano; ileso.—*w.-hearted,* sincero, enérgico, activo.—*w.-heartedly,* de todo corazón; con tesón. —*s.* totalidad, todo, conjunto.—*as a w.,* en conjunto.—*on* o *upon the w.,* en conjunto, en general.- —*sale* [hóulseil], *a. y adv.* (com.) (al) por mayor; en grande.—*s.* venta o comercio (al) por mayor.—*vt. y vi.* vender (al) por mayor.- —*some* [-sam], *a.* sano, saludable, salutífero; edificante.—*wholly* [hóuli], *adv.* totalmente, del todo, por completo.
whom [hum], *pron.* (a) quién. (a) quiénes; (a) quien, (a) quienes; que; al (a la, a los, a las) que; al (a la) cual, a los (a las) cuales.
whoop [hup], *s.* grito; alarido; estertor de la tosferina; chillido del buho. —*vt. y vi.* gritar, vocear.—*vi.* respirar ruidosamente (después de un paroxismo de tos).—*to w. it up,* armar una gritería.—*whooping cough,* tosferina, coqueluche.
whore [hor], *s.* prostituta, ramera, puta.
whose [huz], *pron.* cuyo, cuya, cuyos, cuyas; de quien, de quienes; de quién, de quiénes.
why [hwai], *adv.* ¿por qué? ¿para qué?

¿a qué? por qué, por el cual, etc.— *the reason w.,* la razón por la cual. —*we don't know w.,* no sabemos por qué.—*s.* porqué, causa, razón, motivo.—*interj.* ¡cómo . . .! ¡pero . . .! ¡si . . .!—*w., I just saw her!* pero si la acabo de ver!
wick [wik], *s.* mecha, pabilo, torcida.
wicked [wíkid], *a.* malo, malvado, inicuo; travieso, picaresco.- —*ness* [-nis], *s.* maldad, iniquidad.
wicker [wíkœ(r)], *a.* de mimbre, tejido de mimbres.—*s.* mimbre.
wicket [wíkit], *s.* portillo, postigo, portezuela.
wide [waid], *a.* ancho, anchuroso; holgado; vasto.—*five inches w.,* cinco pulgadas de ancho.—*adv.* lejos, a gran distancia; anchamente; extensamente; descaminadamente; fuera de lugar o del caso.—*far and w.,* por todas partes.—*w.-open,* abierto de par en par.- —*ly* [wáidli], *adv.* lejos, a gran distancia; extensivamente; muy, mucho; ancha u holgadamente. - —*n* [-n], *vt.* ensanchar, extender, ampliar, dilatar.—*vi.* ensancharse, dilatarse.- —*spread* [-spred], *a.* esparcido, diseminado; general, extenso.
widow [wídou], *s.* viuda.- —*ed* [-d], *a.* viudo; enviudado.- —*er* [-œ(r)], *s.* viudo.
width [widθ], *s.* anchura, ancho.
wield [wild], *vt.* esgrimir; manejar; (fig.) empuñar (el cetro); mandar, gobernar.
wife [waif], *s.* esposa, señora, mujer.
wig [wig], *s.* peluca.
wiggle [wígl], *vt. y vi.* menear(se) rápidamente; culebrear.—*s.* culebreo; meneo.
wild [waild], *a.* salvaje, silvestre; selvático, montés; fiero, feroz, bravo; inculto, desierto, despoblado; turbulento, borrascoso; alocado, descabellado; desenfrenado; insensato; impetuoso, violento.—*w. boar,* jabalí. —*w.-goose chase,* empresa quimérica. —*w. oats,* excesos de la juventud.- —*cat* [wáildkæt], *s.* gato montés; negocio arriesgado; pozo (de petróleo) de exploración; (fam.) locomotora sin vehículos.—*a.* atolondrado, sin fundamento; ilícito, no autorizado. —*w. strike,* huelga repentina, no autorizada por el sindicato.- —*erness* [wíldœrnis], *s.* desierto, yermo; despoblado, soledad.- —*ness* [wáildnis], *s.* escabrosidad, fragosidad; tosquedad; rudeza, ferocidad; travesura; desvarío, locura.
wile [wail], *vt.* engañar, sonsacar; (fam.) engatusar.—*to w. away,* pasar (el

rato).—*s.* ardid, red, superchería, treta, fraude, engaño; astucia.

will [wil], *s.* voluntad; albedrío; decisión; intención; gana, inclinación; precepto, mandato; (for.) testamento. —*vt.* querer; legar.—*vai.* y *v. defect.* [11] (como auxiliar forma el futuro): *he w. speak,* él hablará; (como defectivo se traduce en el presente por 'querer'): *w. you sit¹ down?* ¿quiere Ud. sentarse?

willful [wílful], *a.* voluntarioso, testarudo; premeditado, voluntario.— **—ness** [-nis], *s.* testarudez; premeditación.—**willing** [wílin], *a.* gustoso; complaciente; espontáneo. —**willingness** [wílinnis], *s.* buena voluntad, gusto, complacencia.

will-o'-the-wisp [wil o ðȩ wísp], *s.* fuego fatuo.

willow [wílou], *s.* sauce.- **—y** [-i], *a.* esbelto, cimbreante.

wilt [wilt], *vt.* marchitar, ajar.—*vi.* agostarse, marchitarse, secarse; (fam.) amansarse; irse con el rabo entre las piernas.

wily [wáili], *a.* astuto, marrullero.

wimple [wímpl], *s.* toca.

win [win], *vti.* y *vii.* [10] ganar, vencer; lograr, conquistar; persuadir, atraer; prevalecer.—*to w. out,* triunfar, salir bien, lograr buen éxito.—*s.* (fam.) victoria.

wince [wins], *vi.* retroceder, recular; respingar.—*s.* respingo.

winch [winch], *s.* montacargas, malacate, cabria, cabrestante; manubrio, cigüeña.

wind [wind], *s.* viento, aire; aliento; flatulencia; palabrería.—*pl.* (mús.) instrumentos de viento; los músicos que los tocan.—*between w. and water,* a flor de agua.—*to catch o get one's w.,* recobrar el aliento.—*to get w. of,* husmear, descubrir.—*w. aft,* viento en popa.—*vti.* [10] [wajnd], quitar el resuello; olfatear; devanar, ovillar; enrollar; tejer; (re)torcer; dar cuerda a; manejar, dirigir, gobernar; perseguir, seguir las vueltas o los rodeos de.— *to w. off,* desenrollar.—*to w. out,* desenmarañar, desenredar, salir de un enredo.—*to w. up,* concluir; devanar, ovillar; dar cuerda (a un reloj).—*vii.* enrollar, arrollarse; (con **up**) enroscarse; culebrear; ir con rodeos; insinuarse; (re)torcerse, ensortijarse.—*to w. about,* enrollarse. —*to w. along,* serpentear, culebrear.- **—bag** [wíndbæg], *s.* (fam.) charlatán; palabreo vano.- **—fall** [wíndfol], *s.* fruta caída del árbol; ganga, ganancia inesperada, (fam.) chiripa.- **—ing** [wájndin], *s.* vuelta, revuelta, giro, rodeo; recodo, recoveco, tortuosidad;

combadura; (elec., etc.) arrollamiento; (min.) extracción del mineral.—*w. up,* acto de dar cuerda (a un reloj); liquidación; conclusión, desenlace.—*a.* sinuoso; enrollado; en espiral.- **—lass** [wíndlas], *s.* torno.- **—mill** [wíndmil], *s.* molino de viento; (aer.) turbina de aire.

window [wíndou], *s.* ventana; ventanilla; vidriera, escaparate (de tienda). —*w. blind,* persiana, celosía (en el interior); postigo, contraventana, puertaventana (en el exterior).— *w. sill,* antepecho de ventana.- **—pane** [-pein], *s.* cristal o vidrio de ventana.—**windpipe** [wíndpajp], *s.* tráquea; gaznate.—**windshield** [wíndšild], *s.* (aut.) parabrisa(s).—*w. wiper,* limpiavidrios del parabrisas.—**windy** [wíndi], *a.* ventoso; ventiscoso; borrascoso; expuesto al viento; pomposo; flatulento.—*it is w.,* hace viento.

wine [wajn], *s.* vino; color de vino, rojo oscuro.—*w. cellar,* bodega.—*w. skin,* bota o pellejo de vino.

wing [win], *s.* ala; flanco; lado; aspa (de molino); (teat.) bastidor; bambalina.

wink [wink], *vi.* pestañear, parpadear; guiñar; centellear, dar luz trémula. —*to w. at,* hacer la vista gorda.—*s.* pestañeo, parpadeo; un abrir y cerrar de ojos; guiño, guiñada; siestecita.

winner [wínœ(r)], *s.* ganador, vencedor. —**winning** [wínin], *s.* triunfo.—*pl.* ganancias.—*a.* victorioso, triunfante; ganancioso; atractivo; persuasivo.— *w. back,* desquite.—*w. manners,* don de gente.

winsome [wínsʌm], *a.* atractivo, simpático.

winter [wíntœ(r)], *s.* invierno.—*a.* hibernal, invernal.—*vi.* invernar.— **wintry** [wíntri], *a.* invernal; como de invierno.

wipe [wajp], *vt.* limpiar frotando; enjugar; frotar, restregar.—*to w. away,* secar (frotando).—*to w. off,* borrar, cancelar; limpiar, lavar.— *to w. out,* borrar, cancelar, suprimir; destruir, extirpar, aniquilar, exterminar; agotar.

wire [wajr], *s.* alambre; (fam.) telegrama.—*barbed w.,* alambre de púas. —*w. gauze, w. screening,* tela metálica. —*w. tapping,* interceptación de mensajes telefónicos o telegráficos.— *vt.* poner alambres; atar con alambre; instalar conductores eléctricos.—*vt.* y *vi.* telegrafiar.- **—less** [wájrlis], *s.* radiocomunicación; telégrafo o teléfono sin hilos.—*a.* inalámbrico, sin hilos o alambres; de o por radiocomunicación.—**wiry** [-i], *a.* de

alambre; como un alambre; tieso,
tenso; flaco pero fuerte.

wisdom [wízdǫm], *s.* sabiduría, sapiencia; discernimiento, juicio, cordura;
prudencia, sentido común; máxima,
apotegma.—*w. tooth,* muela del
juicio.—**wise** [waįz], *a.* sabio, docto,
erudito; cuerdo, sensato, discreto;
atinado; (fam.) vivo, listo.—*the three
W. Men,* los tres Reyes Magos.—*s.*
modo, manera.—*in any w.,* de cualquier modo.—*in no w.,* de ningún
modo, absolutamente.- —**crack**
[wájzkræk], *s.* (fam.) agudeza, chiste,
dicho u observación agudos.—*vi.*
(fam.) decir agudezas.

wish [wįš], *vt.* y *vi.* desear, querer;
hacer votos por; pedir.—*to w. for,*
apetecer, ansiar, anhelar, querer,
hacer votos por.—*s.* deseo, anhelo;
cosa deseada; voto; súplica.—*to make
a w.,* pensar en algo que se desea.-
—**bone** [wíšboųn], *s.* espoleta de la
pechuga de las aves, (fam.) hueso de
la suerte.- —**ful** [-fų̣l], *a.* deseoso;
ávido, ansioso.

wistful [wístfų̣l], *a.* anhelante, ansioso,
ávido; pensativo, triste.

wit [wįt], *s.* rasgo de ingenio, agudeza;
ingenio; hombre de ingenio.—*pl.*
juicio, sentido, razón; industria.—
to be at one's wits' end, no saber uno
qué hacer o decir; (fam.) perder la
chaveta.—*to live by one's wits,* vivir
de gorra, ser caballero de industria.

witch [wįch], *s.* bruja; (fam.) mujer
encantadora o fascinante; niña
traviesa.- —**craft** [wíchkræft], *s.*
brujería; sortilegio; fascinación.

with [wįð], *prep.* con; para con; en
compañía de.—*a man w. good sense,*
un hombre de juicio.—*that country
abounds w. oil,* ese país abunda en
petróleo.—*the lady w. the camellias,*
la dama de las camelias.—*to part w.,*
separarse de.—*to struggle w.,* luchar
contra.—*w. all speed,* a toda prisa,
a toda velocidad.

withdraw [wįðdró], *vti.* [10] retirar;
apartar, quitar, sacar, retirar de;
desdecirse de, retractar o retractarse
de.—*vii.* retirarse, separarse; irse,
salir.- —**al** [-ḷ], *s.* retiro, retirada;
recogida.—**withdrawn** [wįðdrón], *pp.*
de TO WITHDRAW.—**withdrew** [wįð-
drú], *pret.* de TO WITHDRAW.

wither [wíðœ(r)], *vt.* marchitar; ajar,
deslucir; debilitar; avergonzar, sonrojar.—*vi.* marchitarse, secarse.

withheld [wįðhéld], *pret.* y *pp.* de
TO WITHHOLD.—**withhold** [wįðhóųld],
vti. [10] retener; negar, rehusar;
apartar; detener, impedir.—*vii.*
reprimirse, contenerse.—*to w. one's*

consent, negar la aprobación, **no dar**
el consentimiento.

within [wįðín], *prep.* dentro de, en lo
interior de, en el espacio de; a la
distancia de; al alcance de; a poco de;
casi a, cerca de.—*w. an inch,* pulgada
más o menos; (fig.) a dos dedos (de).
—*w. bounds,* a raya.—*w. hearing,*
al alcance de la voz.—*adv.* dentro,
adentro; dentro de uno; en casa, en
la habitación.

without [wįðáųt], *prep.* sin; falto de;
fuera de, más allá de.—*to do w.,*
pasarse sin, prescindir de.—*adv.*
fuera, afuera, por fuera, hacia afuera,
de la parte de afuera; exteriormente.
—*conj.* (fam.) si no, a menos que.

witness [wítnįs], *s.* testigo; espectador;
testimonio.—*in w. whereof,* en fe de
lo cual.—*vt.* presenciar; dar fe.

witty [wíti], *a.* satírico, sarcástico;
ingenioso, agudo; gracioso, ocurrente.

wives [waįvz], *s. pl.* de WIFE.

wizard [wízǝrd], *a.* hechicero, mágico.
—*s.* hechicero, mago, brujo.- —**ry**
[-ri], *s.* hechicería, magia.

wobble [wábl], *vi.* balancearse, tamba-
learse; (fam.) vacilar.—*vt.* hacer
tambalear(se) o vacilar.—*s.* bamboleo, tambaleo.

woe [woų], *s.* infortunio, miseria, pesar,
calamidad.—*w. is me!* ¡desgraciado
de mí!

woke [woųk], *pret.* de TO WAKE.

wolf [wulf], *s.* lobo; (fam.) mujeriego,
libertino.—*to cry w.,* dar falsa alarma.
—*w. cub,* lobezno, lobato.—*vt.* (fam.)
engullir, devorar.—**wolves** [wulvz],
s. pl. de WOLF.

woman [wúmǝn], *s.* mujer.—*w. hater,*
misógino.—*w. voter,* electora.—*w.
writer,* escritora.- —**hood** [-hụd], *s.*
estado o condición de mujer adulta;
sexo femenino, las mujeres.- —**kind**
[-kaįnd], *s.* las mujeres; el sexo
femenino.- —**ly** [-lį], *a.* mujeril,
de mujer, femenino.—*adv.* mujeril-
mente; femeninamente.

womb [wum], *s.* útero, matriz; (fig.)
madre; caverna; seno, entrañas.

women [wímįn], *s. pl.* de WOMAN.

won [wʌn], *pret.* y *pp.* de TO WIN.

wonder [wʌ́ndœ(r)], *vt.* desear saber;
sorprenderse, maravillarse de; pre-
guntarse.—*I w. what he means,*
¿qué querrá decir?—*vi.* admirarse.
—*to w. at,* extrañar, maravillarse de.
—*s.* admiración; maravilla, portento,
milagro; enigma, cosa extraña o
inexplicable.—*no w.,* no es extraño,
no es mucho.- —**ful** [-fų̣l], *a.* maravilloso, asombroso; admirable,
excelente.

wont [wʌnt], *a.* acostumbrado.—*to*

be w., soler, tener la costumbre.—s. uso, costumbre, hábito.

won't [wount], contr. de WILL NOT.

woo [wu], vt. y vi. cortejar, galantear, enamorar; pretender a una mujer; solicitar, importunar; esforzarse por obtener (fama, etc.).

wood [wud], s. madera; leña; madero. —pl. bosque, selva, monte.—a. de o para madera o para almacenarla, transportarla o labrarla; de monte, que vive o crece en la selva.—to be out of the woods, haber puesto una pica en Flandes; estar a salvo.— w. carving, talla en madera.—w. engraving, grabado en madera.— w. screw, tornillo tirafondo.- —cut [wúdkʌt], s. grabado en madera.- —cutter [-kʌtœ(r)], s. leñador; grabador en madera.- —ed [-jd], a. provisto de madera; arbolado; boscoso.- —en [-n], a. de palo o madera; grosero, rudo; estúpido, inexpresivo.- —land [-lænd], s. arbolado, monte, bosque, selva.—a. [-land], de bosque, selvático.- —(s)man [-(z)man], s. leñador, hachero.- —pecker [-pekœ(r)], s. pájaro carpintero, picaposte, picamaderos.- —work [-wœrk], s. enmaderamiento, maderaje, maderamen; obra de carpintería; ebanistería.

woof [wuf], s. (tej.) trama, textura.

wool [wul], s. lana; pasa (cabello rizado en el negro).—a. lanar; de lana.— w.-bearing, lanar.- —(l)en [wúljn], a. de lana; lanudo; lanero.—w. yarn, estambre.—s. paño o tejido de lana. —pl. ropa o prendas de lana.- —ly [-j], a. lanudo; lanar; de lana; crespo, pasudo (cabello); (b.a.) falto de detalles; aborregado (cielo).

word [wœrd], s. palabra; vocablo, voz; aviso, recado, mensaje; noticia(s); santo y seña; voz de mando, orden, mandato.—pl. contienda verbal; (mús.) letra (de una canción, etc.).— by w. of mouth, de palabra.—in so many words, en esas mismas palabras, textualmente; claramente, sin ambages.—in the words of, según las palabras de, como dice.—on my w., bajo mi palabra, a fe mía.—to have a w. with, hablar con.—to have words, (fam.) tener unas palabras, disputar. —to leave w., dejar dicho.—vt. expresar; redactar.- —iness [wœrdjnjs], s. verbosidad.- —ing [-jŋ], s. redacción, fraseología; expresión, términos.

wore [wor], pret. de TO WEAR.

work [wœrk], vti. [4] trabajar; laborar; explotar (una mina, etc.); fabricar, elaborar; obrar sobre, influir en; hacer trabajar o funcionar; manipular; surtir efecto; resolver (un problema).—to w. one's way through, abrirse camino por o en; pagar uno con su trabajo los gastos de.—to w. through, penetrar; atravesar a fuerza de trabajo.—vii. trabajar o funcionar; tener buen éxito, ser eficaz; ir (bien o mal); obrar u operar (un remedio). —to w. at, trabajar en; ocuparse en o de.—to w. down, bajarse.—to w. free, aflojarse o soltarse con el movimiento o el uso.—to w. loose, aflojarse, soltarse con el uso.—to w. out, tener buen éxito; surtir efecto; resultar.—s. trabajo; tarea, empresa; labor; obra; (cost.) labor.—out of w., sin trabajo, cesante.—(to be) at w., (estar) ocupado, trabajando o funcionando.—to be hard at w., estar muy atareado.- —er [wœrkœ(r)], s. trabajador, obrero, operario; abeja u hormiga obrera.- —ing [jŋ], s. obra, trabajo; funcionamiento; laboreo, explotación; maniobra.—a. que trabaja, trabajador; de trabajo; fundamental.—w. class, clase obrera.—w. day, día de trabajo o laborable; jornada.—w. theory, postulado.- —ingman [-jŋman], s. obrero, jornalero, operario.- —man [-man], s. trabajador, obrero, operario.- —manship [-mansjip], s. hechura, mano de obra; artificio; primor o destreza del artífice.- —shop [-sap], s. taller, obrador.

world [wœrld], s. mundo.—W. War, guerra mundial.—w.-wide, mundial, global, de alcance mundial.—w. without end, para siempre jamás; por los siglos de los siglos.- —ly [wœrldlj], a. mundano, mundanal, carnal, terreno, terrenal, terrestre; seglar, profano.—adv. mundanalmente, profanamente.

worm [wœrm], s. gusano; lombriz; oruga; polilla, carcoma; gorgojo.— w.-eaten, carcomido, apolillado, picado o comido de gusanos.—vt. y vi. insinuarse, introducirse o arrastrarse (como un gusano).—to w. from o out of, arrancar un secreto; quitar gusanos o lombrices.—vi. trabajar u obrar lentamente y por bajo mano.

worn [worn], pp. de TO WEAR.—w.-out, gastado, raído; estropeado; cansado; agotado.

worry [wœrj], vti. y vii. [7] preocupar(se), inquietar(se); apurar(se), afligir(se).—s. preocupación, inquietud, cuidado, apuro.

worse [wœrs], a. peor, más malo; inferior; en peor situación.—to be w. off, estar en peores circunstancias, o quedar peor.—to get w., empeorar(se). —to make o render w., empeorar.—

w. and w., de mal en peor; peor que nunca; cada vez peor.—*adv.* peor; menos.—*s.* menoscabo, detrimento; (lo) peor.—*to change for the w.*, empeorar(se).

worship [wœ́rȿip], *s.* culto, adoración; reverencia, respeto.—*your w.*, usía; vuestra merced.—*vti.* [2] adorar; reverenciar, honrar.—*vii.* adorar; profesar culto o religión.— —(p)per [-œ(r)], *s.* adorador, devoto.

worst [wœrst], *a.* pésimo, malísimo.— *the w.*, el, o la, o lo peor.—*adv.* del peor modo posible; pésimamente.—*vt.* vencer, rendir o derrotar a; triunfar de.

worsted [wústịd], *s.* estambre.

worth [wœrþ], *s.* mérito; consideración, importancia; valor, valía; monta, precio; nobleza, excelencia, dignidad. —*a.* que vale o posee; equivalente a; de precio o valor de; digno de, que vale la pena de.—*to be w.*, valer, costar; merecer; tener.—*to be w. -while*, valer la pena.— —less [wœ́r- lịs], *a.* inútil, inservible; sin valor; indigno, despreciable.— —y [wœ́rðị], *a.* digno; apreciable, benemérito; merecedor.

would [wụd], *vai.*, *pret.* de WILL (forma el modo condicional): *she said she w. come*, dijo que vendría.—*v. defect.*, *pret.* de WILL.—*w. you sit down?* ¿querría Ud. sentarse?

wound [waụnd], *pret.* y *pp.* de TO WIND (devanar).—*s.* [wund], herida; llaga, lesión; ofensa, golpe, daño.—*vt.* y *vi.* herir, lesionar, llagar, lastimar; ofender, agraviar.

wove [woụv], *pret.* y *pp.* de TO WEAVE. —**woven** [wóụvn], *pp.* de TO WEAVE.

wrangle [ræŋgl], *vi.* reñir; disputar.—*s.* pendencia, riña; disputa, altercado.

wrap [ræp], *vti.* [3] arrollar o enrollar; envolver.—*to w. up*, arrollar; envolver; arropar; embozar; cubrir, ocultar.—*vii.* arrollarse; envolverse. —*to w. up (in)*, envolverse (en).—*s.* bata; abrigo.—*pl.* abrigos y mantas (de viaje, etc.).— —per [ræpœ(r)], *s.* envoltura, cubierta; faja de periódico; bata, peinador; pañal de niño.— —ping [ræpịŋ], *a.* de envolver, de estraza (papel).—*s.* envoltura, cubierta.

wrath [ræþ], *s.* ira, cólera.— —ful [rǽþful], *a.* airado, colérico.

wreath [riþ], *s.* corona, guirnalda; festón; trenza; espiral.— —e [rið], *vt.* enroscar, entrelazar, tejer (coronas o guirnaldas); ceñir, rodear.—*vi.* enroscarse, ensortijarse.

wreck [rek], *s.* naufragio; destrozo, destrucción; buque naufragado, barco perdido; restos de un naufragio.—*vt.*

hacer naufragar; arruinar, echar a pique; demoler, desbaratar.—*vi.* naufragar, zozobrar, irse a pique; fracasar.

wrench [rench], *vt.* arrancar, arrebatar; (re)torcer; dislocar, sacar de quicio. —*to w. one's foot*, torcerse el pie.—*s.* arranque, tirón; torcedura; (mec.) llave de tuercas.—*monkey w.*, llave inglesa.

wrestle [resl], *vt.* luchar con; forcejear contra.—*vi.* luchar a brazo partido; esforzarse; disputar.— —r [réslœ(r)], *s.* luchador.—**wrestling** [résliŋ], *s.* (dep.) lucha grecorromana; lucha a brazo partido.

wretch [rech], *s.* infeliz, desventurado, miserable; ente vil, despreciable.— —ed [réchịd], *a.* infeliz, miserable; calamitoso; vil, despreciable; perverso; mezquino; malísimo, detestable.—**wretchedness** [réchịdnịs], *s.* miseria; desgracia; vileza.

wriggle [rigl], *vt.* menear, retorcer, hacer colear.—*vi.* colear, culebrear, undular; retorcerse.

wring [riŋ], *vti.* [10] torcer, retorcer; arrancar; estrujar, exprimir, escurrir; forzar; atormentar, aquejar.—*to w. out*, exprimir.

wrinkle [ríŋkl], *s.* arruga; surco, buche; (fam.) capricho, maña; artificio; idea, ocurrencia; indicio, insinuación.—*vt.* arrugar, fruncir.—*to w. up*, arrugar, plegar.—*vi.* arrugarse; encarrujarse.

wrist [rist], *s.* (anat.) muñeca; (mec.) muñón.—*w. watch*, reloj de pulsera.

writ [rit], *s.* (for.) escrito, orden, auto, mandamiento, decreto judicial.— *Holy W.*, Sagrada Escritura.

write [rait], *vti.* [10] escribir; describir. —*to w. after*, copiar de.—*to w. a good hand*, hacer o tener buena letra.— *to w. off*, (com.) cancelar, saldar. —*to w. out*, redactar; copiar, transcribir; escribir completo (sin abreviar).—*to w. up*, narrar, relatar; describir; (fam.) ensalzar por escrito; (com.) poner al día (el libro mayor); valorar en demasía una partida del activo.—*vii.* escribir, tener correspondencia; ser escritor o autor. —*to w. back*, contestar a una carta. —*to w. on*, continuar escribiendo; escribir acerca de.— —r [ráitœ(r)], *s.* escritor; literato; hombre de letras, autor.

writhe [raið], *vt.* (re)torcer.—*vi.* retorcerse; contorcerse (por algún dolor).—**writhing** [ráiðiŋ], *s.* retorcimiento, contorsión.

writing [ráitiŋ], *s.* escritura; letra; escrito; (el arte de) escribir.—*a.* de o para escribir.—*at the present w.* o *at this w.*, al tiempo que esto se escribe,

ahora mismo.—*(to put) in w.*, (poner) por escrito.—*w. desk*, escritorio.—*w. pad*, block de papel.—**written** [rítn], *pp.* de TO WRITE.

wrong [roŋ], *s.* injusticia, sinrazón, agravio; mal, daño, perjuicio; culpa; error; falsedad.—*to be in the w.*, no tener razón.—*to do w.*, obrar o hacer mal; hacer daño, perjudicar.—*a.* erróneo, desacertado; injusto; censurable; falso; irregular; equivocado; inconveniente; mal hecho, mal escrito, etc.—*he took the w. book*, cogió el libro que no era, o se equivocó de libro.—*adv.* mal, sin razón o causa; injustamente; al revés.—*vt.* causar perjuicio a; hacer mal a; ofender; agraviar; ser injusto con.

wrote [rout], *pret.* de TO WRITE.

wrought [rot], *pret. y pp.* de TO WORK.—*a.* forjado, labrado, trabajado.—*w. iron*, hierro forjado.—*w.-up*, (sobre)excitado, perturbado.

wrung [rʌŋ], *pret. y pp.* de TO WRING.

wry [raj], *a.* torcido, doblado, sesg(ad)o; pervertido, tergiversado.—*w. face*, gesto, visaje, mueca, mohín.

X

Xmas [krísmas], *s.* = CHRISTMAS.

X-rays [éks rejz], *s. pl.* rayos X, catódicos o Roentgen.

xylophone [zájlofoun], *s.* xilófono; (Am.) especie de marimba.

Y

yacht [yat], *s.* yate.

Yankee [yǽŋki], *a. y s.* (fam.) yanqui (natural del Norte de los EE.UU.).

yard [yard], *s.* corral; patio; cercado; yarda (medida). Ver Tabla.—**—stick** [yárdstik], *s.* yarda graduada de medir; patrón, modelo; criterio.

yarn [yarn], *s.* hilaza; hilo, hilado; estambre; (fam.) cuento chino, historia inverosímil.

yaw [yo], *vi. y vt.* (mar.) guiñar.—*s.* guiñada.

yawn [yon], *vi.* bostezar; quedarse con la boca abierta; anhelar; abrirse.—*s.* bostezo; abrimiento; abertura.

yea [yej], *adv.* sí, ciertamente; y aún, más aún, no solamente.—*y. or nay*, sí o no.—*s.* sí, voto afirmativo.—*the yeas and nays*, los votos en pro y en contra.

year [yir], *s.* año.—*pl.* años, edad; vejez.—**—book** [yírbuk], *s.* anuario.—**—ly** [-li], *a.* anual.—*adv.* anualmente; una vez al año; al año.

yearn [yœrn], *vi.* anhelar.—*to y. for*, suspirar por.—**—ing** [yœrniŋ], *s.* anhelo.

yeast [yist], *s.* levadura, fermento.

yell [yel], *vt. y vi.* dar alaridos, vociferar; decir a gritos.—*s.* alarido, grito, aullido; grito salvaje o de guerra.

yellow [yélou], *a.* amarillo; sensacional, escandaloso (periódico, etc.); (fam.) cobarde, gallina.—*y. fever*, fiebre amarilla.—*s.* amarillo (color).—*vi.* ponerse amarillo, amarillear.—**—ish** [-iš], *a.* amarillento.

yelp [yelp], *vi.* (re)gañir (el perro).—*s.* gañido.

yeoman [yóuman], *s.* (*pl.* yeomen [yóumen]), (mar.) pañolero; (E.U.) subalterno de marina.—*y. service*, servicio leal o notable.

yes [yes], *adv.* sí.—*y. indeed*, sí por cierto, ya lo creo.—*s.* respuesta afirmativa o favorable.—*y. man*, hombre servil, que obedece ciegamente.

yesterday [yéstœrdi], *s. y adv.* ayer.—**yesteryear** [yéstœryir], *adv.* antaño.

yet [yet], *conj.* con todo, sin embargo, no obstante; mas, pero, empero; aun así.—*adv.* aún, todavía, hasta ahora; a lo menos; más, además, más que.—*as y.*, hasta ahora, hasta aquí, todavía.—*not y.*, todavía no, aún no.

yield [yild], *vt.* producir; redituar, rentar, dar, dejar; dar de sí, ceder; condescender; devolver, restituir; admitir, pasar por, conceder; otorgar.—*to y. up*, ceder, entregar; devolver; abandonar.—*vi.* producir; dar utilidad; ceder, someterse; consentir; flaquear.

yoke [youk], *s.* yugo.—*pl.* yunta de bueyes; pareja de animales de tiro.—*vt.* uncir; acoplar, unir.

yolk [youk], *s.* yema (de huevo).

yonder [yándœ(r)], *adv.* allí, allá, acullá.—*a.* aquel, aquella, aquellos, aquellas.

yore [yor], *s.*—*in days of y.*, de otro tiempo; de antaño.

you [yu], *pron.* tú, usted, vosotros, ustedes; te, a ti, le, la, a usted, os, a vosotros, les, a ustedes; se, uno.

young [yʌŋ], *a.* joven; nuevo; tierno; fresco, reciente.—*y. fellow*, joven, mozo.—*y. lady*, muchacha, señorita, jovencita (joven).—*y. man*, muchacho, joven.—*s.* hijuelos, la cría de los animales.—**—ster** [yʌ́ŋstœ(r)], *s.* jovencito, mozalbete; niño, chiquillo, pequeñuelo.

your [yur], *a.* tu(s), vuestro(s), vuestra(s); su(s), de usted(es).—**—s** [-z], *pron.* el tuyo, la tuya, los tuyos, las tuyas; el vuestro, etc.; el, la, lo, los o las de usted(es); el suyo, etc.—*y. affectionately*, su afectísimo.—**—self** [-sélf], *pron.* tú mismo, tú misma; usted mismo, usted misma.—**—selves**

[-sélvz], *s. pl.* vosotros, vosotras o ustedes mismos (mismas).

youth [yuθ], *s.* juventud. mocedad; mozalbete, joven; la juventud. los jóvenes.- **—ful** [yúθful]. *a.* juvenil; joven, mozo; fresco, vigoroso; juguetón.—*y. exploits,* mocedades.

Yugoslav [yúgosláv], *s.* yugoeslavo.- **—ian** [-ian],- **—ic** [-ik], *a.* yugoeslavo.

Yuletide [yúltajd], *s.* Pascua de Navidad, natividad.

Z

zany [zéjnj], *a.* y *s.* cómico, bufo.

zeal [zil], *s.* celo, fervor, ahinco.- **—ot** [zélot], *s.* entusiasta, fanático.- **—ous** [zélʌs], *a.* entusiasta, fervoroso.

zebra [zíbrą], *s.* cebra.

zebu [zíbiu]. *s.* cebú.

zenith [zínjθ], *s.* cenit; (fig.) apogeo.

zephyr [zéfœ(r)], *s.* céfiro.

zero [zírou]. *s.* cero.

zest [zɛst], *s.* deleite, gusto; gusto, sabor.—*vt.* dar gusto o sabor.

zinc [ziŋk], *s.* cinc o zinc.

zipper [zípœ(r)], *s.* cierre de cremallera, automático o relámpago.

zodiac [zóudjæk], *s.* zodíaco.

zone [zoun], *s.* zona; distrito, sección; territorio; banda circular, faja.—*vt.* dividir en zonas o secciones.

zoo [zu], *s.* jardín o parque zoológico.- **—logic(al)** [zouoládźik(al)], *a.* zoológico.- **—logist** [zouálodźist], *s.* zoólogo.- **—logy** [zouálodźj], *s.* zoología.

NOMBRES GEOGRAFICOS QUE DIFIEREN EN ESPAÑOL Y EN INGLES

A

Abyssinia [æbjsʃnjǎ], Abisinia.
Adriatic [ejdrjǽtɪk], Adriático.
Ægean [idʒían], Egeo.
Afghanistan [æfgǽnɪstæn], Afganistán.
Africa [ǽfrɪkǎ], Africa.
Alexandria [ælegzǽndrjǎ], Alejandría.
Algeria [ældʒírjǎ], Argelia.
Algiers [ældʒírz], Argel.
Alps [ælps], Alpes.
Alsace-Lorraine [ælséʃs o ælsǽs / loréʃn], Alsacia Y Lorena.
Amazon [ǽmazan], (Río de las) Amazonas.
America [amérɪkǎ], América.
Andalusia [ændǎlúʒǎ], Andalucía.
Antilles [æntʃliz], Antillas.
Antwerp [ǽntwœrp], Amberes.
Apennines [ǽpenajnz], Apeninos.
Appalachians [æpalǽchjanz], (Montañas) Apalaches.
Asia Minor [éjʒǎ / májnɔ(r)], Asia Menor.
Assyria [asʃrjǎ], Asiria.
Athens [ǽθjnz], Atenas.
Atlantic [ætlǽntɪk], Atlántico.

B

Babylon [bǽbjlan], Babilonia.
Balearic Islands [bæljǽrjk, Islas Baleares.
Balkans [bólkanz], Balcanes.
Baltic [bóltjk], Báltico.
Barbary [bárbarɪ], Berbería.
Basel [bázęl], Basilea.
Bavaria [bavérjǎ], Baviera.
Belgium [béldʒ(i)ʌm], Bélgica.
Belgrade [belgréjd], Belgrado.
Belize [belíz], Belice, Beliza.
Berlin [bœrlʃn], Berlín.
Bern [bœrn], Berna.
Bethlehem [béθlj(h)em], Belén.
Biscay [bʃskej], Vizcaya.
Black Sea, Mar Negro.
Bologna [boulóunyǎ], Bolonia.
Bonn [ban], Bona.
Bordeaux [bordóu], Burdeos.
Bosporus [básporas], Bósforo.
Brazil [brazʃl], Brasil.
Bretagne [bretány], **Brittany** [brʃtanɪ], Bretaña.
British Columbia [brʃtjʃ kolʌmbjǎ], Columbia Británica.
British Honduras [handúras], Belice, Honduras Británicas.
British Isles, Islas Británicas.
Brussels [brʌsęlz], Bruselas.
Bucharest [búkarést], Bucarest.
Burgundy [bœrgʌndɪ], Borgoña.
Burma [bœrmǎ], Birmania.
Byzantium [bjzænʃjʌm], Bizancio.

C

Calcutta [kælkʌtǎ], Calcuta.
Cameroons [kæmęrúnz], Camerún, Kamerún.

Canada

Canada [kǽnadǎ], Canadá.
Canary Islands, Canarias.
Cape Horn, Cabo de Hornos.
Cape of Good Hope, Cabo de Buena Esperanza.
Caribbean [kærɪbʃan, karʃbjan], Caribe.
Carthage [kárθjdʒ], Cartago.
Caspian [kǽspjan], Caspio.
Castile [kæstʃl], Castilla.
Catalonia [kætalóunjǎ], Cataluña.
Caucasus [kókasʌs], Cáucaso.
Cayenne [kajén, kején], Cayena.
Ceylon [sjlán], Ceilán.
Chaldea [kældʃǎ], Caldea.
Champagne [ʃæmpéjn], Champaña.
Cologne [kʌlóun], Colonia.
Constantinople [kanstæntjnóupl], Constantinopla.
Copenhagen [koupęnhéjgęn], Copen(h)ague.
Corinth [korʃnθ], Corinto.
Corsica [kórsjkǎ], Córcega.
Crete [krit], Creta.
Croatia [kroéjǎ], Croacia.
Curaçao [kyuraaóu], Curazao.
Cyprus [sájprʌs], Chipre.
Czechoslovakia [chekoslovǽkjǎ], Checoslovaquia.

D

Dalmatia [dælméjǎ], Dalmacia.
Damascus [damǽskʌs], Damasco.
Danube [dǽnjub], Danubio.
Dardanelles [dardanélz], Dardanelos.
Dead Sea, Mar Muerto.
Delphi [délfaj], Delfos.
Denmark [dénmark], Dinamarca.
Douro River [dóury], Duero (Río).
Dover [dóuvœ (r)], Duvres.
Dresden [drézdęn], Dresde.
Dunkirk [dʌnkœrk], Dunquerque.

E

East Indies [ʃndiz], Indias Orientales.
Edinburgh [édjnbœrou], Edimburgo.
Egypt [ʃdʒjpt], Egipto.
Elbe [élbǎ], Elba.
England [ʃŋglænd], Inglaterra.
English Channel, Canal de la Mancha, Paso de Calais.
Escurial [eskyúrjal], Escorial.
Ethiopia [iθjóupjǎ], Etiopía, Abisinia.
Euphrates [yufréjtiz], Eufrates.
Europe [yúrɔp], Europa.

F

Finland [fʃnland], Finlandia.
Flanders [flǽndœrz], Flandes.
Florence [flórɛns], Florencia.
France [fræns], Francia.
Frankfort-on-the-Main [frǽŋkfɔrt], Francfort del Mein.

G

Galilee [gǽljlɪ], Galilea.
Gascony [gǽskonɪ], Gascuña.

297

Gaul [gɔl], Galia.
Geneva [dženívə], Ginebra.
Genoa [dženowə], Génova.
Germany [džœrmǝni], Alemania.
Ghent [gent], Gante.
Gold Coast [gould koust],
Costa de Oro.
Great Britain [grejt brítn],
Gran Bretaña.
Greece [gris], Grecia.
Greenland [grínlǝnd], Groenlandia.
Guadeloupe [gwadǝlúp], Guadalupe.
Guam [gwam], Guaján, Guam.
Guiana [giǽnǝ, giánǝ], Guayana.

H

Hague [heig], (La) Haya.
Haiti [héjti], Haití, Isla Española.
Hamburg [hǽmbœrg], Hamburgo.
Havana [hǝvǽnǝ], La Habana.
Hawaii [hǝwáji], Hawaí, Hauaí.
Hebrides [hébridiz], Hébridas.
Hindustan [hindustǽn], Indostán.
Hispaniola [hjspanyóulǝ],
La Española.
Holland [hálǝnd], Holanda.
Holy Land, Tierra Santa.
Hungary [hʌ́ŋgǝri], Hungría.

I

Iceland [ájslǝnd], Islandia.
India [índjǝ], India, Indostán.
Indian Ocean, (Mar de las) Indias,
(Océano) Índico.
Ionia [ajóunjǝ], Jonia.
Ireland [ájrlǝnd], Irlanda.
Istanbul [istǽnbúl], Estambul.
Italy [ítǝli], Italia.
Ivory Coast, Costa del Marfil.
Izmir [ízmir], Esmirna.

J

Japan [džapǽn], Japón.
Jericho [džérikou], Jericó.
Jerusalem [džjrúsalem], Jerusalén.
Jugoslavia [yugouslávjǝ], = YUGOSLA-
VIA.
Jutland [džʌ́tlǝnd], Jutlandia.

K

Kashmir [kǽšmjr], Cachemira.
Khartoum [kartúm], Kartum.
Key West, Cayo Hueso.
Korea [kourjǝ], Corea.
Kurdistan [kœ́rdjstǽn], Kurdistán.

L

Labrador [lǽbrǝdor], Tierra del
Labrador.
Lapland [lǽplǝnd], Laponia.
Lausanne [louzǽn], Lausana.
Lebanon [lébanǝn], Líbano.
Leghorn [léghorn], Liorno.
Leningrad [léningrǽd], Leningrado.
Lesser Antilles [lésœ(r) æntíliz],
Las Pequeñas Antillas.
Lhasa [lásǝ], Lasa.
Libya [líbjǝ], Libia.
Liége [ljéž, ljéjž], Lieja.
Lisbon [lízbǝn], Lisboa.
Lithuania [ljθuéjnjǝ], Lituania.
Lombardy [lámbǝrdi], Lombardia.
London [lándǝn], Londres.
Lorraine [lorějn], Lorena.
Louisiana [luizjǽnǝ], Luisiana.

Low Countries, Países Bajos,
Holanda.
Lower California [lóuœ(r)
kælifórnyǝ], Baja California.
Lucerne [lusœ́rn], Lucerna.
Luxemburg [lʌ́ksembœrg],
Luxemburgo.

M

Madeira [mǝdírǝ], Madera.
Majorca [mǝdžórkǝ], Mallorca.
Malay [méjlej, mǝléj], Malaca.
Marseilles [marséj(lz)], Marsella.
Martinique [martjník], Martinica.
Mecca [mékǝ], Meca.
Mediterranean [medjtǝréjnjǝn],
Mediterráneo.
Memphis [mémfjs], Menfis.
Mexico [méksjkou], México, Méjico.
Minorca [mjnórkǝ], Menorca.
Mississippi [mjsjsípj], Misisipí.
Missouri [mjzúrj], Misurí.
Mobile [moubíl], Mobila.
Montpellier [monpelyé], Mompellier.
Morocco [mǝrákou], Marruecos.
Moscow [máskau], Moscú.
Moselle [mouzél], Mosela.
Musqat [mʌskǽt], Omán.

N

Naples [néjplz], Nápoles.
Navarre [navár], Navarra.
Nazareth [nǽzareθ, nǽzrjθ], Nazaret.
Netherlands [néðœrlǝndz], Países
Bajos, Holanda.
New Castile, Castilla la Nueva.
New England, Nueva Inglaterra.
Newfoundland [njúfʌndlǽnd],
Terranova.
New Mexico, Nuevo México
(o Méjico).
New Orleans [órljǝnz, orlínz],
Nueva Orleáns.
New South Wales, Nueva Gales
del Sur.
New York [yórk], Nueva York.
New Zealand [zílǝnd], Nueva
Zelandia.
Nice [nis], Niza.
Nile [najl], Nilo.
Normandy [nórmǝndj], Normandía.
North America, América del Norte.
North Carolina [kærolájnǝ], Carolina
del Norte.
North Dakota [dǝkóutǝ], Dakota del
Norte.
Norway [nórwej], Noruega.
Nova Scotia [nóuvǝ skóušǝ],
Nueva Escocia.
Nyasaland [nyásalænd], Niaslandia.

O

Oceania [oušjǽnjǝ], Oceanica
[oušjǽnjkǝ], Oceanía.
Old Castile, Castilla la Vieja.
Olympus [oulímpʌs], Olimpo.
Ostend [asténd], Ostende.

P

Pacific [pasífjk], Pacífico.
Palestine [pǽlestajn], Palestina.
Panama [pǽnǝmǝ], Panamá.
Paris [pǽrjs], París.
Parnassus [parnǽsʌs], Parnaso.
Peking [pjkíŋ], Pekín.

298

Peloponnesus [pelopanísʌs], Peloponeso.

Pennsylvania [pensilvéiniǎ], Pensilvania.

Persian Gulf [pə́rʒən], Golfo Pérsico.

Peru [perú], Perú.

Philadelphia [filadélfiǎ], Filadelfia.

Philippines [fílipinz], Filipinas.

Phoenicia [finíšǎ], Fenicia.

Poland [póuland], Polonia.

Polynesia [paliníšǎ], Polinesia.

Pompeii [pampéji], Pompeya.

Port-au-Prince [port o prins], Puerto Príncipe.

Porto Rico [pórtou ríkou], Puerto Rico.

Prague [prag], Praga.

Provence [provʌ́ns], Provenza.

Providence [právidens], Providencia.

Prussia [prʌ́šǎ], Prusia.

Pyrenees [pírɛ́niz], Pireneos.

R

Red Sea, Mar Rojo.

Rhine [rajn], Rin o Rhin.

Rhineland [rájnlænd], Renania.

Rhodes [roudz], Rodas.

Rhodesia [roudíʒǎ], Rodesia.

Rhone [roun], Ródano.

Rocky Mountains, Montañas Rocosas o Rocallosas.

Rome [roum], Roma.

Rouen [ruán], Ruán.

Russia [rʌ́šǎ], Rusia.

S

Saragossa [sǽragásǎ], Zaragoza.

Sardinia [sardíniǎ], Cerdeña.

Saudi Arabia [saúdi ǎréibiǎ], Arabia Saudita.

Saxony [sǽksoni], Sajonia.

Scandinavia [skændinéiviǎ], Escandinavia.

Scotland [skátland], Escocia.

Seine [sejn, sɛn], Sena.

Seoul [sau̯l], Seúl.

Serbia [sɛ́rbiǎ], Servia.

Seville [sevíl], Sevilla.

Sicily [sísili], Sicilia.

Sierra Leone [siɛ́rǎ lióun(i)], Sierra Leona.

Slavonia [slavóuniǎ], Eslavonia.

Slovakia [slovákiǎ], Eslovaquia.

Slovenia [slovíniǎ], Eslovenia.

South Africa, Sud-África.

South America, América del Sur, Sud-América, Sur-América.

South Carolina [kærolái̯nǎ], Carolina del Sur.

South Dakota [dǎkóutǎ], Dakota del Sur.

Soviet Union [sóuvjet], Unión Soviética.

Spain [spejn], España.

Spanish America, Hispano-América, América Española.

Sparta [spártǎ], Esparta.

Spoleto [spoléitou], Espoleto.

Stockholm [stákhou(l)m], Estocolmo.

Strait of Magellan [mǎdʒélǎn], Estrecho de Magallanes.

Sudan [sudǽn], Sudán.

Sweden [swídɛn], Suecia.

Switzerland [swítsœrland], Suiza.

Syracuse [sírakjus], Siracusa.

Syria [síriǎ], Siria.

T

Tagus [téigʌs], Tajo.

Tahiti [tahíti], Tahití.

Tanganyika [tænganyíkǎ], Tanganica.

Tangier [tændʒír], Tánger.

Texas [téksas], Tejas.

Thailand [tájland], Thailandia.

Thames [temz], Támesis.

Thebes [θibz], Tebas.

Thrace [θrejs], Tracia.

Tobago [toubéigou], Tabago.

Tokyo [tóukjou], Tokio.

Toulouse [tulúz], Tolosa.

Trent [trent], Trento.

Troy [troj], Troya.

Tunis(ia) [t(i)únis; t(i)uníšǎ], Túnez (ciudad, país).

Turkey [tœ́rki], Turquía.

Tuscany [táskani], Toscana.

Tyrol [tíral, tiróu̯l], Tirol.

U

Ukraine [yúkrein, yukréin], Ucrania.

Union of South Africa, Unión Sudafricana.

United Kingdom, Reino Unido.

United States of America, Estados Unidos de América.

Upper Volta [vóu̯ltǎ], Alto Volta.

USSR [yu ɛs ɛs ar], URSS.

V

Venice [vénis], Venecia.

Versailles [vœrséilz, versáy], Versalles.

Vesuvius [vɛsúvjʌs], Vesubio.

Vienna [viénǎ], Viena.

Virgin Islands, Islas Vírgenes.

W

Wales [wejlz], Gales.

Warsaw [wórso], Varsovia.

Watling Island [wátliŋ], Isla de San Salvador.

West Indies [índiz], Antillas.

West Virginia [vœrdʒínyǎ], Virginia Occidental.

Y

Yugoslavia [yugou̯sláviǎ], Yugoeslavia.

Z

Zanzibar [zǽnzibar], Zanzíbar.

Zealand [ziland], Zelandia.

Zion [zái̯on], Sion.

Zululand [zúlulænd], Zululandia.

NOMBRES PROPIOS DE PERSONAS Y DE PERSONAJES HISTORICOS, LITERARIOS Y MITOLOGICOS

(Sólo se incluyen los que difieren en ambas lenguas. Se excluyen los diminutivos y afectivos que se forman añadiendo "ito," "illo," etc., v.gr. Agustinito, Juanillo, Juanico, etc.)

A

Abelard [ǽbẹlard], Abelardo.
Abraham [éịbrạhæm], Abrahán.
Achilles [ạkíliz], Aquiles.
Adam [ǽdạm], Adán.
Æneas [ịníạs], Eneas.
Æschylus [éskịlʌs], Esquilo.
Æsop [ísọp, ísap], Esopo.
Agatha [ǽgạθạ̈], Agueda, Ágata.
Agnes [ǽgnịs], Inés.
Alan [ǽlạn], Alano.
Albert [ǽlbœrt], Alberto.
Alexander [ælịgzǽndœ(r)], Alejandro.
Alfred [ǽlfrịd], Alfredo.
Alice [ǽlịs], Alicia.
Allan [ǽlạn], **Allen** [ǽlẹn], Alano.
Alphonso [ælfánsoụ], Alfonso, Alonso, Ildefonso.
Andrew [ǽndru], Andrés.
Angel [éịndžẹl], Ángel.
Anne [æn], **Anna** [ǽnạ̈], Ana.
Anthony [ǽnθonị], Antonio.
Archimedes [arkịmídiz], Arquímedes.
Aristophanes [ærịstáfạniz], Aristófanes.
Aristotle [ǽrịstatl], Aristóteles.
Arnold [árnọld], Arnaldo, Arnoldo.
Arthur [árθœ(r)], Arturo.
Attila [ǽtịlạ̈], Atila.
Augustine [ógʌstin, ɔgʌ́stịn], Agustín.
Augustus [ɔgʌ́stʌs], Augusto.

B

Bacchus [bǽkʌs], Baco.
Bartholomew [barθálomịu], Bartolomé.
Basil [bǽzịl], Basilio.
Beatrice [bíạtrịs], Beatriz.
Benedict [bénẹ̈dịkt], Benito.
Benedicta [benẹ̈díktạ̈], Benita.
Benjamin [béndžạmịn], Benjamín.
Bernard [bǿernạrd, bernárd], Bernardo.
Bertha [bǿerθạ̈], Berta.
Bonaventura [bánạvɛnchṻrạ̈], Buenaventura, Ventura.
Brutus [brútʌs], Bruto.
Buddha [búdạ̈], Buda.

C

Caesar [sízạ̈(r)], César.
Calvin [kǽlvịn], Calvino.
Camille [kạmíl], Camila.
Camillus [kạmílʌs], Camilo.
Caroline [kǽrolaịn], Carolina.
Cassandra [kạsǽndrạ̈], Casandra.
Catharine [kǽθạrịn], **Catherine** [kǽθẹrịn], Catalina.
Cato [kéịtoụ], Catón.
Catullus [kạtʌ́lʌs], Catulo.
Cecile [sịsíl], Cecilia.
Charlemagne [šárlẹmeịn], Carlomagno.
Charles [charlz], Carlos.
Charlotte [šárlọt], Carlota.
Christ [kraịst], Cristo.
Christine [krịstín], Cristina.
Christopher [krístofœ(r)], Cristóbal.
Cicero [sísẹroụ], Cicerón.
Claire, Clare [kler], Clara.
Claude [klɔd], Claudio.
Clement [klémẹnt], Clemente.
Clovis [klóụvịs], Clodoveo.
Columbus [kolʌ́mbʌs], Colón.
Confucius [kọnfịúšʌs], Confucio.
Constance [kánstạns], Constanza, Constancia.
Constantine [kánstạntaịn], Constantino.
Cyrus [sáịrʌs], Ciro.

D

Daisy [déịzị], Margarita.
Delilah [dịláịlạ̈], Dalila.
Demosthenes [dịmásθẹniz], Demóstenes.
Dennis [dénịs], Dionisio.
Diogenes [daịádžẹniz], Diógenes.
Dionysius [daịonísịʌs], Dionisio.
Dominic [dámịnịk], Domingo.
Dorothy [dóroθị, dároθị], Dorotea.

E

Edith [ídịθ], Edita.
Edmund [édmʌnd], Edmundo.
Edward [édwạ̈rd], Eduardo.
Eleanor, Elinor [élịnọ(r)], Leonor.
Eliza [ịláịzạ̈], Elisa.
Elizabeth [ịlízạbẹθ], Isabel.
Ellen [élẹn], Elena.
Eloise [éloiz], Eloísa.
Em(m)anuel [ịmǽnyụel], Manuel.
Emil [éịmịl], Emilio.
Emily [émịlị], Emilia.
Emma [émạ̈], Ema, Manuela.
Epicurus [ɛpịkyúrʌs], Epicuro.
Erasmus [ịrǽzmʌs], Erasmo.
Ernest [ǿernịst], Ernesto.
Ernestine [ǿernɛstin], Ernestina.
Esther [éstœ(r)], Ester.
Euclid [yúklịd], Euclides.
Eugene [yudžín], Eugenio.
Eugénie [œžɛní], Eugenia.
Eve [iv], Eva.

F

Felicia [fịlíšịạ̈], Felisa, Felicia.
Ferdinand [fǿerdịnænd], Fernando.
Florence [flórẹns], Florencia.
Frances [frǽnsịs], Francisca.
Francis [frǽnsịs], **Frank** [fræŋk], Francisco.

Frederica [frederíkà], Federica.
Frederick [frédęrịk], Federico.

G

Galen [géịlęn], Galeno.
George [dźordź], Jorge.
Geraldine [dźéraldin], Gerarda.
Gerard [dźịrárd], Gerardo.
Gertrude [gœrtrud], Gertrudis.
Gilbert [gílbœrt], Gilberto.
Godfrey [gádfrị], Godofredo.
Gracchus [grǽkʌs], Graco.
Grace [greịs], Engracia.
Gregory [grégorị], Gregorio.
Gustave [gʌ́stav], Gustavus
   [gʌstéịvʌs], Gustavo.

H

Hadrian [héịdrịạn], Adriano.
Hannah [hǽnạ], Ana.
Hannibal [hǽnịbạl], Aníbal.
Harold [hǽrọld], Haroldo.
Helen [héljn], Elena.
Henrietta [hęnrịétạ], Enriqueta.
Henry [hénrị], Enrique.
Herbert [hœrbœrt], Heriberto.
Herman [hœrmạn], Arminio.
Herod [hérọd], Herodes.
Herodotus [hịrádọtʌs], Herodoto.
Hezekiah [hezękáịạ], Ezequías.
Hippocrates [hịpákrạtiz], Hipócrates.
Homer [hóụmœ(r)], Homero.
Horace [hórịs], Horacio.
Hortense [horténs], Hortensia.
Hubert [hịúbœrt], Huberto.
Humbert [hʌ́mbœrt], Humberto.
Humphrey [hʌ́mfrị], Hunfredo.

I

Ignatius [ịgnéịs̆ʌs], Ignacio.
Inez [áịnez, ínez], Inés.
Innocent [ínosęnt], Inocencio.
Isabella [izạbélạ], Isabel.
Isidore [ízịdor], Isidro, Isidoro.

J

James [dźeịmz], Jaime, Jacobo,
   Santiago.
Jane [dźeịn], Juana.
Jasper [dźǽspœ(r)], Gaspar.
Jeffrey [dźéfrị], Geofredo.
Jehovah [dźịhóụvạ], Jehová.
Jeremiah [dźerémáịạ], Jeremías.
Jerome [dzịróụm, dźérọm],
   Jerónimo, Gerónimo.
Jesus Christ [dźízʌs], Jesucristo.
Joachim [yóụạkịm], Joaquín.
Joan [dźoụn], Juana.
Joan of Arc [ark], Juana de Arco.
John [dźạn], Juan.
Jonathan [dźánạθạn], Jonatán,
   Jonatás.
Joseph [dźóụzęf], José.
Josephine [dźóụzęfin], Josefina.
Joshua [dźás̆ụạ], Josué.
Judith [dźúdịθ], Judit.
Julian [dźúlyạn], Julián, Juliano
   (emperador).
Juliet [dźúlyęt, dźulịét], Julia,
   Julieta.
Julius [dźúlyʌs], Julio.
Justinian [dźʌstínịạn], Justiniano.

K

Katharine [kǽθạrịn], Katherine
   [kǽθạrịn], Catalina.

L

Laurence, Lawrence [lóręns],
   Lorenzo.
Lazarus [lǽzạrʌs], Lásaro.
Lenore [lịnór], Lenora.
Leo [líoụ], León.
Leonard [lénạrd], Leonardo.
Leonora [lionórạ], Lenora.
Leopold [líọpoụld], Leopoldo.
Lewis [lúịs], Luis.
Livy [lívị], Livio.
Louis [lúịs, lúị], Luis.
Louise [luíz], Luisa.
Lucan [lúkạn], Lucano.
Lucian [lús̆ạn], Luciano.
Lucretia [lukrís̆ạ], Lucrecia.
Lucretius [lukrís̆ạs], Lucrecio.
Lucy [lúsị], Lucía.
Luke [luk], Lucas.
Luther [lúθœ(r)], Lutero.

M

Magdalen [mǽgdạlęn], Magdalena.
Magellan [mạdźélạn], Magallanes.
Margaret [márgạrịt], Margarita.
Marian [mérịạn], Marion [mérịọn],
   Mariana.
Marjorie [márdźọrị], Margarita.
Mark [mark], Marco, Marcos.
Martha [márθạ], Marta.
Mary [mérị], María.
Matthew [mǽθịu], Mateo.
Maurice [mórịs], Mauricio.
Messiah [mesáịạ], Mesías.
Michael [máịkęl], Miguel.
Michelangelo [maịkęlǽndźeloụ],
   Miguel Angel.
Miriam [mírịạm], María.
Mohammed [moụhǽmid], Mahoma.
Moses [móụzịz], Moisés.

N

Nathan [néịθạn], Natán.
Nathaniel [nạθǽnyęl], Nataniel.
Nebuchadnezzar [nebyụkạdnézạ(r)],
   Nabucodonosor.
Nero [níroụ], Nerón.
Nicholas [níkolạs], Nicolás.
Noah [nóụạ], Noé.

O

Octavius [aktéịvịʌs], Octavio.
Oliver [álịvœ(r)], Oliverio.
Otto [átoụ], Otón.
Ovid [ávịd], Ovidio.

P

Patrick [pǽtrịk], Patricio.
Paul [pọl], Pablo.
Pauline [polín], Paula, Paulina.
Perseus [pœrsus], Perseo.
Peter [pitœ(r)], Pedro.
Philip [fílịp], Felipe, Felipo
   (de Macedonia).
Philippa [fịlípạ], Felipa.
Pilate [páịlạt], Pilatos.
Pindar [píndạ(r)], Píndaro.
Pius [páịʌs], Pío.
Plato [pl(eị)toụ], Platón.
Plautus [plótʌs], Plauto.
Pliny [plínị], Plinio.
Plutarch [plútark], Plutarco.
Prometheus [promíθụs], Prometeo.
Ptolemy [tálęmị], Tolomeo,
   Ptolomeo.

301

Pythagoras [piθǽgǝrǝs], Pitágoras.

ABREVIATURAS MAS USUALES EN INGLES

A

a., acre(s).
A.B., Bachelor of Arts.
abbr., abbreviation.
abr., abridgment, abridged.
A.C., alternating current; Air Corps.
acct., account.
Adm., admiral(ty).
Afr., Africa(n).
aft., afternoon
agcy., agency
agr(ic)., agriculture, agricultural.
agt., agent.
Ala., Alabama.
Alas., Alaska.
a.m., ante meridiem (before noon).
A.M., Master of Arts, before noon; amplitude modulation

amp., ampere; amperage.
amt., amount.
anat., anatomy
anon., anonymous.
ans., answer.
A.P., Associated Press.
app., appendix; appointed.
Apr., April.
apt., apartment.
Ar., Arabic; Aramaic.
arith., arithmetic(al).
Ariz., Arizona.
Ark., Arkansas.
assn., association.
assoc., association; associate.
asst., assistant.
att., attorney.
Att.Gen., Attorney General.
atty., attorney

Aug., August.
ave., avenue.

B

b., base; book, born, brother.
B., British.
B.A., Bachelor of Arts.
bal., balance.
B.B.A., Bachelor of Business Administration.
B.C., before Christ.
bd., board; bond; bound.
b.e., B/E, bill of exchange.
bet., between.
Bibl., Biblical, bibliographical
biog., biographical; biography

302

biol., biological; biology.
bk., book.
b.l., **B/L**, bill of lading.
bldg., building.
blvd., boulevard.
b.p., bills payable; boiling point.
Br., British; Britain.
Bro(s)., brother(s).
b.s., balance sheet; bill of sale.
B.S(c)., Bachelor of Science.
bus., business.
bx., box.

C

c., cent; chapter; cubic; current; center.
C., Cape; Catholic; centigrade.
C.A., Central America; Chartered Accountant.
cal., calorie; caliber.
Cal(if)., California.
Can., Canada; Canadian.
cap., capital; capitalize(d); Chapter.
Capt., Captain.
Cath., Catholic.
cent., centigrade; central; century.
cert., certificate; certify.
cf., confer; compare.
C.F.I., cost, freight, and insurance.
C.G., Coast Guard.
Ch., Church.
chap., chapter.
chem., chemical, chemistry
C.I.F., cost, insurance, and freight (c.i.f., *o* c.s.f. costo, seguro y flete)
c.o., **c/o.**, care of, carried over.
C.O., Commanding Officer.
Co., company, county.
C.O.D., collect (*o* cash) on delivery (cóbrese a la entrega)
Col., Colonel; Colorado.
Colo., Colorado.
com., commerce.
Com., Commander, Commission(er); Committee; Commodore.
comp., comparative; compare; compound
con., conclusion; contra (against, opposing).
Cong., Congress(ional).
Conn., Connecticut.
cont., containing, contents; continent, continue(d)
cor., corrected, correction, corresponding corner.

Corp., Corporal; corporation.
cp., compare.
C.P.A., Certified Public Accountant.
Cpl., Corporal.
cr., credit(or).
C.S.A., Confederate States of America.
C.S.T., Central Standard Time.
ct., cent.
Ct., Connecticut.
cts., cents; certificates.
c.w.o., cash with order.

D

d., died; dime; dollar.
D.A., District Attorney.
Dan., Danish.
D.C., District of Columbia; direct current.
D.D., Doctor of Divinity.
D.D.S., Doctor of Dental Surgery.
Dec., December.
deg., degree(s).
Del., Delaware.
Dem., Democrat(ic).
dep., department; deputy.
dept., department.
der(iv)., derivation; derivative.
D.H.C., Doctor Honoris Causa.
dial., dialect(al).
diam., diameter.
diff., difference; different.
disc., discount; discovered.
dist., distance; district.
div., divided, dividend, division.
D.Lit., Doctor of Literature.
D.Litt., Doctor of Letters.
doz., dozen(s).
Dr., Doctor.
dup., duplicate.
D.V., Deo volente (God willing).
dz., dozen(s).

E

E., east(ern), English.
ea., each.
econ., economic(s), economy
ed., edition, editor
educ., education(al).
e.g., exempligratia (for example), v.g.
elec(t)., electric(al), electricity.
Eng., England, English
esp(ec)., especially
est., established.
E.S.T., Eastern Standard Time
etc., et cetera (and so forth)

Eur., Europe(an).
ex., example; exception; executive.
exc., except(ed); exception.
exch., exchange.
exp., export(ed); express; expenses.

F

F., Fahrenheit; Father; French; Friday.
Fahr., Fahrenheit.
FBI, Federal Bureau of Investigation.
Feb., February.
Fed., Federal.
ff., following.
fin., financial.
Fla., Florida.
F.M., frequency modulation.
f.o.b., free on board (libre a bordo).
fol(l)., following.
fr., francs; from.
Fr., France; French.
Fri., Friday.
ft., foot, feet.
Ft., fort.

G

G., German.
Ga., Georgia.
gal(l)., (*pl.*, **gals.**), gallon(s).
G.B., Great Britain.
Gen., General.
geog., geographic(al); geography.
Ger., German(y).
Gov., government; Governor.
Govt., government.
G.P.O., General Post Office.
Gt.Br(it)., Great Britain.

H

hdqrs., headquarters.
H.E., His Eminence; His Excellency.
H.H., His (*o* Her) Highness; His Holiness.
H.I., Hawaiian Islands.
H.M., His (*o* Her) Majesty.
H.M.S., His (*o* Her) Majesty's service, ship *o* steamer.
Hon., Honorable.
h.p., horse power; high pressure.
H.Q., headquarters.
H.R., House of Representatives.
hr(s)., hour(s)
ht., height; heat.

I

I., Island.
Ia., Iowa.
Ice(l)., Iceland(ic).
Id(a)., Idaho
Ill., Illinois

303

inc., incorporated; including; increase.
Ind., Indiana; India; Indian; Indies.
ins., insurance.
inst., instant; institute.
int., interest; international.
inv., invented; inventor; invoice.
I.O.U., I owe you.
I.Q., intelligence quotient.
Is(l)., Island(s); Isle(s).
It(al)., Italian; Italy.
ital., italic.

J

Jam., Jamaica.
Jan., January.
Jap., Japan(ese).
J.C., Jesus Christ; Julius Caesar.
J.P., Justice of the Peace.
Jr., Junior.
Jul., July.
Jun., June; Junior.

K

K., King; Knight(s).
Kan(s)., Kansas.
Ken., Kentucky.
Knt., Knight.
k.o., knockout.
kt., carat.
Kt., Knight.
Ky., Kentucky.

L

l., latitude; length; line.
L., lake; Latin.
La., Louisiana.
lat., latitude.
Lat., Latin.
Leg(is)., legislature; legislative.
Lieut., Lieutenant.
liq., liquid; liquor.
lon(g)., longitude.
Lt., Lieutenant.
Ltd., Limited.

M

M., Monday, member.
M.A., Master of Arts.
mag., magazine; magnetism.
Maj., Major
Mar., March.
Mass., Massachusetts.
M.C., Master of Ceremonies; Member of Congress.
M.D., Medical Doctor
Md., Maryland.
mdse., merchandise
Me., Maine.
Mex., Mexican; Mexico.
mfg., manufacturing.
Mgr., manager
Mich., Michigan.
Minn., Minnesota.
misc., miscellaneous; miscellany.
Miss., Mississippi

Mo., Missouri; Monday.
mo(s)., month(s).
Mon., Monday.
Mont., Montana.
M.P., Member of Parliament; Military Police.
m.p.h., miles per hour.
Mr., Mister, Master.
Mrs., Mistress.
M.S(c)., Master of Science.
Mt(s)., Mount, Mountain(s).

N

N., North(ern).
N.A(m)., North America(n).
nat(l)., national.
NATO, North Atlantic Treaty Organization.
N.B., New Brunswick; nota bene (note well).
N.C., North Carolina.
N.Dak., North Dakota.
Neb(r)., Nebraska.
N.Eng., New England.
Neth., Netherlands.
Nev., Nevada.
n.g., (fam.) no good.
N.G., National Guard.
N.H., New Hampshire.
N.J., New Jersey.
N.M(ex)., New Mexico.
No. (*pl.,* **nos.**), number.
noncom., noncommissioned officer.
Norw., Norwegian; Norway.
Nov., November.
nt.wt., net weight.
N.Y., New York.
N.Y.C., New York City.
N.Z(eal)., New Zealand.

O

O., Ohio; Ontario; Ocean.
O.A.S., Organization of American States.
obs., observation; observatory; obsolete.
Oct., October.
O.K., all right, correct.
Okla., Oklahoma.
Ont., Ontario.
ord., order; ordinance.
Ore(g)., Oregon.

P

p., page, part, pint
Pa., Pennsylvania.
Pac., Pacific
payt., payment
p.c., per cent; post card
pd., paid.
Penn., Pennsylvania
Ph.D., Doctor of Philosophy.
photog., photographic, photography
phys., physician, physics.
P I., Philippine Islands

pkg(s)., package(s).
pl., place; plate; plural.
P.M., Postmaster; paymaster; post meridiem (after noon).
P.O.D., Post Office Department; pay on delivery.
pop., population.
pos., positive.
pp., pages.
P.R., Porto Rico *o* Puerto Rico.
pr., pair; price.
pres., present; presidency.
Pres., President.
prin., principal.
Prof., Professor.
Prot., Protestant.
pro tem., pro tempore (temporarily).
prov., province; provincial.
P.S., postscript.
pt., part; payment; point; pint; port.
pub., public; published; publisher.
P.X., (military) post exchange.

Q

Q., Quebec; Queen.
qt., quantity; quart.
qu., quart(er); queen; query; question.
Que., Quebec.
ques., question.
quot., quotation.
q.v., quod vide (which see).
qy., query

R

R., Republican, river, Royal.
R.A., Rear Admiral; Royal Academy.
R.C., Roman Catholic, Red Cross.
Rd., Road.
rec., receipt.
rec'd., recd., received.
ref., reference; referred, reformed.
reg., registry, regular
Reg(t)., regiment.
Rep., Representative; Republic(an)
Rev., Reverend
R.I., Rhode Island.
R.I.P., rest in peace.
R.N., registered nurse.
r.p.m., revolutions per minute.
R.R., railroad.
R.S.V.P., Répondez, s'il vous plait (please answer)
Ry., railway, railroad.

S

S., Saturday, Sunday, South(ern)
S.A., South America(n); South Africa

304

South Australia; Salvation Army.
Sab., Sabbath.
S.Am., South America.
Sat., Saturday.
S.C., South Carolina; Supreme Court.
Scot., Scotch, Scottish; Scotland.
S.Dak., South Dakota.
SEATO, Southeast Asia Treaty Organization.
sec., second(ary); secretary; section.
Sen., Senate; Senator.
Sep(t)., September; Septuagint.
seq., sequel; the following.
Serg(t)., Sergeant.
serv(t)., servant.
Sgt., Sergeant.
S.I., Staten Island.
Soc., Society.
Sp., Spain; Spanish.
spt., seaport.
Sr., senior; sir.
S.S., steamship; Sunday School.
St., Saint; Street.
str., steamer.
sub., substitute; suburban.
Sun(d)., Sunday.
sup., superior.
Supp., Supplement.
Supt., superintendent.

T

tbs., tablespoon(s).
tel., telegram; telegraph; telephone.
teleg., telegram; telegraph.
Tenn., Tennessee.
Ter(r)., Territory.
Tex., Texas.
Th., Thur(s)., Thursday.
tp., township.

trans., translation; translated; transaction.
treas., treasurer; treasury.
tsp., teaspoon(s).
Tu(es)., Tuesday.

U

U., University.
U.K., United Kingdom
ult., ultimate.
ult(o)., ultimo (the past month) (el mes pasado).
Univ., University.
U.P.I., United Press International.
U.S., United States.
U.S.A., United States of America; United States Army; Union of South Africa.
U.S.A.F., United States Air Force.
U.S.C.G., United States Coast Guard.
U.S.M., United States Mail.
U.S.M.C., United States Marine Corps.
U.S.N., United States Navy.
U.S.S., United States Ship; United States Senate.
U.S.S.R., USSR, Union of Soviet Socialist Republics.
usu., usual(ly).
Ut., Utah.

V

v., verse; versus; volume.
Va., Virginia.
V.A., Veterans' Administration.
var., variant; variation; variety; various.

vet., veteran; veterinary.
Vice Pres., Vice President.
vid., vide (see).
viz., videlicet (namely).
vocab., vocabulary.
vol., volume; volunteer.
V.P., Vice President.
vs., versus.
Vt., Vermont.

W

w., week; weight; with.
W., Wednesday; Welsh; west(ern).
Wash., Washington (estado).
Wed., Wednesday.
W.I., West Indian; West Indies.
Wis(c)., Wisconsin.
wk., week; work.
wt., weight.
W.Va., West Virginia.
Wy(o)., Wyoming.
wk., week; work.
wt., weight.
W.Va., West Virginia.
Wy(o)., Wyoming.

X

Xn., Xtian., Christian.

Y

Y., Young Men's Christian o Hebrew Association.
y., yard; year.
Y.M.C.A., Young Men's Christian Association.
Y.M.H.A., Young Men's Hebrew Association.
yr., year; your.

Z

Z., Zone.

TABLAS DE PESOS Y MEDIDAS
(TABLES OF WEIGHTS AND MEASURES)

Avoirdupois Weights
(Unidades comunes de peso)
1 ounce (oz.) = 28.35 gramos (g.)
1 pound (lb.) = 16 ounces = 435,59 gramos
1 hundredweight (cwt.) = 112 pounds = 50,8 kilogramos

Troy and Apothecaries' Weights
(Unidades de peso usadas en joyería y farmacia)
1 ounce = 31,10 gramos
1 pound = 12 ounces = 373,24 gramos

Liquid and Dry Measures
(Medidas de capacidad para líquidos y áridos)

Liquid (Líquidos)
1 pint (pt.) = 0,47 litros (l.)
1 quart (qt.) = 2 pints = 0,94 litros
1 gallon (gal.) = 4 quarts = 3,78 litros
1 barrel (b.) = 31.5 gallons = 119,07 litros

Dry (Áridos)
1 pint (pt.) = 0,55 litros
1 quart (qt.) = 2 pints = 1,1 litros
1 gallon (gal.) = 4 quarts = 4,40 litros
1 peck (pk.) = 2 gallons = 8.80 litros
1 bushel = 4 pecks = 35 litros

Linear Measures
(Medidas de longitud)
1 inch (in.) o 1″ = 2,54 centímetros (cm.)
1 foot (ft.) o 1′ = 12 inches = 30,48 centímetros
1 yard (yd.) = 3 feet = 91,44 centímetros
1 mile (m.) = 1,760 yards = 1,609 kilómetros (km.)

Square Measures
(Medidas de superficie)
1 square inch (sq.in.) = 6,45 centímetros cuadrados (cm.²)
1 square foot (sq.ft.) = 144 square inches = 0,93 metros cuadrados
1 square yard (sq.yd.) = 9 square feet = 0.836 metros cuadrados (m.²)
1 acre = 4,830 square yards = 40,468 hectáreas
1 square mile (sq.m.) = 640 acres = 2,59 kilómetros cuadrados (km.²)

TERMOMETRO
32° Fahrenheit (punto de congelación) = 0° centígrados
212° Fahrenheit (punto de ebullición) = 100° centígrados
Para reducir grados Fahrenheit a grados centígrados multiplíquese por 5/9 e réstense 32°.